Tolley's Corporation Tax 2000–01

by
Glyn Saunders MA
Gina Antczak FCA ATII

Tolley Publishing

Published by Tolley
2 Addiscombe Road
Croydon CR9 5AF
England
020-8686 9141

Typeset in Great Britain by
Interactive Sciences
Gloucester

Printed in Great Britain by
The Bath Press,
Bath

ISBN 0 75450 837–4

About This Book

Corporation tax commenced in 1964 as the tax to be levied on the income, profits and gains of companies. Much of the law and practice relating to income tax and capital gains continued to apply to companies but a separate body of legislation was superimposed and has been added to during the subsequent years. It is this additional legislation and practice currently applying to companies which is contained in this work together with some additional information of interest to users.

In this 36th edition are contained all the current provisions relevant to corporation tax, including those of the Finance Act 2000, Revenue Statements of Practice and Extra-Statutory Concessions, other Revenue Statements and information, case law and further important information up to 1 July 2000.

The enactments relating to income tax and corporation tax (other than on chargeable gains) were consolidated in the Income and Corporation Taxes Act 1988, those relating to chargeable gains in the Taxation of Chargeable Gains Act 1992, and those relating to capital allowances in the Capital Allowances Act 1990. A summary of the approach adopted to consolidated statutory references is given overleaf.

Comments and suggestions for improvements are always welcomed.

TOLLEY PUBLISHING

Consolidation of Tax Enactments

With effect generally for 1988/89 and subsequent years of assessment and for companies' accounting periods ending after 5 April 1988, the *Taxes Acts* provisions relating to income tax and corporation tax were consolidated in the *Income and Corporation Taxes Act 1988* (*ICTA 1988*), although this does not apply to those corporation tax provisions dealing with chargeable gains. The consolidation does not affect the application of the provisions concerned, but references to provisions which ceased to have effect before consolidation are omitted, as is the commencement date of the consolidated provisions (unless still relevant to application of the current provisions).

Tolley's Corporation Tax 2000/01 continues, as in previous years, to set out the position for the previous six years, but occasional references are still required to earlier years. In strictness, the legislation applicable to accounting periods before those to which the consolidation applies is that in force prior to the consolidation, and the Revenue (while acknowledging that 'on previous consolidation, inspectors, Commissioners and taxpayers alike got used to the new references in dealing with previous periods'), have indicated that claims etc. for those periods should refer to the statute then applicable.

Accordingly, the approach which has been adopted to statutory references in this edition is as follows:

(i) Remaining references to the previous consolidation *Act* are in the form '*ICTA 1970, s XXX*' or '*ICTA 1970, Sch XX*'. Where there has been no change in the legislation in the last six years, only the currently applicable reference is quoted.

(ii) Where the legislation has changed during the last six years, the earlier provisions continue to be described in the text, and the appropriate earlier statutory reference is quoted. Legislation current during that six years but now repealed is similarly dealt with. Where any part of the current legislation was introduced during that six years, the commencement date is quoted, but the statutory reference for that date is generally omitted.

(iii) In any case where a claim or election for an accounting period ending before 6 April 1988 may be involved, the appropriate earlier statutory reference is quoted. The earlier reference is also given in certain cases where the reference may have achieved a particular familiarity, e.g. in the case of *sections 233* or *460* of *ICTA 1970*.

(iv) Where a full pre-consolidated statutory reference is required, this may be obtained from Tolley's Corporation Tax 1987/88 or an appropriate earlier edition.

(v) The Table of Statutes in this issue includes all references to earlier legislation appearing in the text (as above).

A similar approach has been adopted on the consolidation of the enactments relating to capital allowances in the *Capital Allowances Act 1990*, which took effect generally for chargeable periods ending after 5 April 1990, and on those relating to corporation tax on capital gains in the *Taxation of Chargeable Gains Act 1992*, which took effect generally for chargeable periods beginning after 5 April 1992.

Contents

The following subjects are in the same alphabetical order in this Book. A detailed index and tables of cases and statutes are at the end of the Book.

PAGE
iii About This Book
iv Consolidation of Tax Enactments
vii Notes
ix Abbreviations and References

CHAPTER
1 Introduction and Rates of Tax

2 Accounting Periods
3 Advance Corporation Tax
4 Anti-Avoidance
5 Assessments and Appeals

6 Banks
7 Building Societies

8 Capital Allowances
9 Capital Gains
10 Certificates of Tax Deposit
11 Charities
12 Claims
13 Close Companies
14 Clubs and Societies
15 Compensation, Damages Etc.
16 Connected Persons
17 Construction Industry Tax Scheme
18 Controlled Foreign Companies
19 Corporate Venturing Scheme

20 Distributions
21 Double Tax Relief

22 European Community Legislation
23 Exchange Gains and Losses
24 Exempt Organisations

25 Financial Instruments
26 Foreign Income Dividends
27 Franked Investment Income
28 Friendly Societies

29 Groups of Companies

30 Housing Associations Etc.
31 Income Tax in relation to a Company

Contents

32 Industrial and Provident Societies
33 Inland Revenue: Administration
34 Inland Revenue Explanatory Pamphlets
35 Inland Revenue Extra-Statutory Concessions
36 Inland Revenue Press Releases
37 Inland Revenue Statements of Practice
38 Interest on Overpaid Tax
39 Interest on Unpaid Tax
40 Investment Companies

41 Life Insurance Companies
42 Liquidation Etc.
43 Loan Relationships
44 Losses

45 Mutual Companies

46 Oil Companies

47 Partnerships
48 Payment of Tax
49 Penalties
50 Profit Computations
51 Purchase by a Company of its Own Shares

52 Regional Development Grants
53 Residence
54 Returns

55 Self-Assessment
56 Small Companies—Reduced Rates
57 Statutory Bodies

58 Temporary Employment Subsidy
59 Time Limits

60 Unit and Investment Trusts

61 Value Added Tax
62 Venture Capital Trusts

63 Finance Act 2000

64 Table of Cases

65 Table of Statutes

66 Index

Notes

Financial Years run from 1 April. The 'financial year 2000' means the year from 1 April 2000 to 31 March 2001.

Years of Assessment run from 6 April. Thus '2000/01' or 'the year 2000/01' means the year from 6 April 2000 to 5 April 2001.

Inland Revenue explanatory pamphlets may be obtained from the local inspector of taxes (except where otherwise stated, see list in Chapter 33) and are free.

Inland Revenue Press Releases and Statements of Practice are obtainable individually from Inland Revenue Information Centre, SW Wing, Bush House, Strand, London WC2B 4RD (tel. 020–7438 6420/5), and are published on the Revenue's website (http:/www.inlandrevenue.gov.uk/news/press.htm)

Retention of Tolley's. Subscribers should preserve each year's issue of 'Tolley's' because the necessity to include each year considerable new material involves the omission of some of the outdated matter.

Tolley's Income Tax 2000/01 is the companion publication of Tolley's Corporation Tax and is a comprehensive detailed guide to income tax with relevant statute and case law etc. up to and including the 2000 Finance Act. Much of its material is of relevance to companies, especially as computations of income amounts forming part of taxable profit for corporation tax purposes are based on income tax law. £59.95.

Tolley's Capital Gains Tax 2000/01 is a detailed guide to the statutes and case law up to and including the 2000 Finance Act. In the same alphabetical format as Tolley's Income Tax and Tolley's Corporation Tax. £59.95.

Tolley's Inheritance Tax 2000/01 is a detailed guide to the inheritance tax provisions up to and including the 2000 Finance Act. £59.95.

Tolley's Value Added Tax 2000/01 is a comprehensive guide to value added tax, covering legislation, Customs & Excise notices and leaflets and all other relevant information. It is published in two editions, up to March 2000 and up to and including the 2000 Finance Act. £85.00 (includes both editions).

Tolley's Tax Cases 2000 contains over 2,500 summaries of cases up to 1 January 2000 relevant to current legislation. Arranged alphabetically by subject, it includes sections on Close Companies and Corporation Tax. £54.95.

Tolley's Tax Computations 2000/01 contains copious worked examples covering income tax, corporation tax, capital gains tax, inheritance tax and value added tax. £54.95.

Tolley's Practical Tax is an eight-page fortnightly, containing news, articles and other items of practical use to all involved with UK tax. By subscription only.

Abbreviations and References

ABBREVIATIONS

ACT	=	Advance Corporation Tax.
APRT	=	Advance Petroleum Revenue Tax.
APRTA 1986	=	Advance Petroleum Revenue Tax Act 1986.
art	=	Article.
CAA	=	Capital Allowances Act.
CA	=	Court of Appeal.
CCA	=	Court of Criminal Appeal.
CCAB	=	Consultative Committee of Accountancy Bodies.
Ch D	=	Chancery Division.
CES	=	Court of Exchequer (Scotland).
Cf.	=	compare.
CFC	=	Controlled Foreign Company.
CGT	=	Capital Gains Tax.
CGTA 1979	=	Capital Gains Tax Act 1979.
CIR	=	Commissioners of Inland Revenue ('the Board').
CJEC	=	Court of Justice of the European Communities.
CT	=	Corporation Tax.
CTT	=	Capital Transfer Tax.
CTTA 1984	=	Capital Transfer Act 1984.
EC	=	European Communities.
EEC	=	European Economic Community.
EU	=	European Union.
Ex D	=	Exchequer Division.
FA	=	Finance Act.
FII	=	Franked Investment Income.
FY	=	Financial Year.
HC(I)	=	High Court (Ireland).
HL	=	House of Lords.
ICAEW	=	Institute of Chartered Accountants in England and Wales.
ICTA	=	Income and Corporation Taxes Act.
IHTA 1984	=	Inheritance Tax Act 1984.
IR	=	Inland Revenue.
KB	=	King's Bench Division.
NI	=	Northern Ireland.
OTA	=	Oil Taxation Act.
PC	=	Privy Council.
PDA	=	Probate, Divorce and Admiralty Division (now Family Division).
QB	=	Queen's Bench Division.
RI	=	Republic of Ireland (Eire).
s	=	Section.
SCS	=	Scottish Court of Session.
Sch	=	Schedule
SI	=	Statutory Instrument.
SP	=	Revenue Statement of Practice.
Sp C	=	Special Commissioners.
SR&O	=	Statutory Rules and Orders.

Abbreviations and References

TCGA 1992	=	Taxation of Chargeable Gains Act 1992.
TMA 1970	=	Taxes Management Act 1970.
VAT	=	Value Added Tax.
VATA 1994	=	Value Added Tax Act 1994.

REFERENCES (*denotes a series accredited for citation in court).

All E R	=	*All England Law Reports, (Butterworths, Halsbury House, 35 Chancery Lane, London WC2A 1EL).
AC or App Cas	=	*Law Reports, Appeal Cases, (Incorporated Council of Law Reporting for England and Wales, 3 Stone Buildings, Lincoln's Inn, London WC2A 3XN).
Ch	=	*Law Reports, Chancery Division.
Ex D	=	*Law Reports, Exchequer Division (see also below).
IR	=	*Irish Reports, (Law Reporting Council, Law Library, Four Courts, Dublin).
LR Ex	=	*Law Reports, Exchequer Division.
SSCD	=	Simon's Tax Cases Special Commissioners' Decisions, (Butterworths as above).
STC	=	*Simon's Tax Cases, (Butterworths as above).
STI	=	Simon's Tax Intelligence, (Butterworths as above).
TC	=	*Official Reports of Tax Cases, (H.M. Stationery Office, PO Box 276, London, SW8 5DT.
WLR	=	*Weekly Law Reports, (Incorporated Council of Law Reporting, as above).

The first number in the citation refers to the volume, and the second to the page, so that [1999] 1 All ER 15 means that the report is to be found on page fifteen of the first volume of the All England Law Reports for 1999. Where no volume number is given, only one volume was produced in that year. Some series have continuous volume numbers.

Where legal decisions are very recent and in the lower courts, it must be remembered that they may be reversed on appeal. But references to the official Tax Cases (TC) and to the Appeal Cases (AC) may generally be taken as final.

In English cases, Scottish and Northern Irish decisions (unless there is a difference of law between the countries) are generally followed but are not binding, and Republic of Ireland Decisions are considered (and vice versa).

Acts of Parliament, Command Papers, 'Hansard' Parliamentary Reports and Statutory Instruments (SI) (formerly Statutory Rules and Orders (SR & O)) are obtainable from H.M. Stationery Office, (bookshop at 49 High Holborn, WC1V 6HG; mail orders to P.O. Box 276, London SW8 5DT; telephone orders to 020-7873 9090). **Hansard** references are to daily issues and do not always correspond to the columns in the bound editions. **N.B.** Statements in the House, while useful as indicating the intention of enactments, have no legal authority and the Courts may interpret the wording of an Act differently, although they may in limited circumstances be prepared to consider evidence of parliamentary intent.

1 Introduction and Rates of Tax

Simon's Direct Tax Service D2.

1.1 GENERAL

Since 1 April 1964, companies have been liable to corporation tax on their 'profits' (i.e. income and chargeable gains).

A company making qualifying DISTRIBUTIONS (20) had, before 6 April 1999, to pay ADVANCE CORPORATION TAX (3). Such tax (ACT) was then set off against the company's 'mainstream' corporation tax liability on its income for the ACCOUNTING PERIODS (2) in which the distributions were made. The ACT paid was generally treated as a tax credit in the hands of the recipient of the distributions. Such distributions received by a company were called FRANKED INVESTMENT INCOME (27) and the credit is generally available for set-off against its own liability to ACT. This is known as the 'imputation system'. See, however, 3.1 ADVANCE CORPORATION TAX as regards the abolition of ACT from 6 April 1999.

1.2 THE CHARGE TO TAX

Any company which is resident in the UK is chargeable to corporation tax in respect of all its 'profits' *wherever arising*. A non-resident company which carries on a trade in the UK through a branch or agency is liable to corporation tax on the income and gains of the branch or agency (see 53.4 RESIDENCE). [*ICTA 1988, ss 6(1), 8(1), 11; TCGA 1992, s 10(3)*]. See 18 CONTROLLED FOREIGN COMPANIES for treatment of interests in certain non-resident companies.

Members of a group of companies are each dealt with independently, but there are a number of special provisions relating to the taxation of such members. Similar rules apply to the members of a consortium. See 29 GROUPS OF COMPANIES.

'*Profits*' are defined as income and chargeable gains. [*ICTA 1988, s 6(4)(a)*]. See 50 PROFIT COMPUTATIONS and 9 CAPITAL GAINS.

Corporation tax is charged on the profits of '*financial years*', which run from 1 April, e.g. the 'financial year 1995' means the year from 1 April 1995 to 31 March 1996. [*ICTA 1988, ss 6(1), 834(1)*].

The profits of a company are calculated (and assessments are made) by reference to its ACCOUNTING PERIODS (2) and are then, when necessary, apportioned on a time basis between the financial years in which the accounting period falls, according to the number of days falling in each year. [*ICTA 1988, ss 8(3), 72*].

Advance corporation tax (prior to its abolition from 6 April 1999) was payable without assessment by reference to 'return periods' (see 3.4 ADVANCE CORPORATION TAX).

'*Company*' for corporation tax purposes means 'any body corporate or unincorporated association' (including an authorised unit trust as defined in *ICTA 1988, s 468(6)*). It does not include a partnership, a local authority or a local authority association. [*ICTA 1988, s 832(1)(2)*]. See *Conservative and Unionist Central Office v Burrell CA 1981, 55 TC 671* (in which the Conservative Party was held not to be an unincorporated association) and *Blackpool Marton Rotary Club v Martin Ch D 1988, 62 TC 686* (Rotary Club an unincorporated association and not a partnership). For the treatment of income arising to certain unit trusts for the benefit of individuals, see 60.2 UNIT AND INVESTMENT TRUSTS.

Anything to be done by a company under the *Taxes Acts* must be done by the 'proper officer of the company' (usually the company secretary, except where a liquidator has been appointed) or by any person having express, implied or apparent authority to act on its behalf (again, unless a liquidator has been appointed). [*TMA 1970, s 108(1)(3); FA 1993, 14 Sch 7*]. See also 48.5 PAYMENT OF TAX.

Reduced rates of corporation tax apply to 'small' companies. These are defined by reference to their profits in an accounting period. See 56 SMALL COMPANIES—REDUCED RATES.

1.3 **RATES OF TAX**

(*a*) **Corporation tax on income**

The **full and small companies rates** of corporation tax for each financial year are as set out in the following table.

	Full rate	Small companies rate	Starting rate
Financial years 1973 to 1978	52%	42%	—
Financial years 1979 to 1981	52%	40%	—
Financial year 1982	52%	38%	—
Financial year 1983	50%	30%	—
Financial year 1984	45%	30%	—
Financial year 1985	40%	30%	—
Financial year 1986	35%	29%	—
Financial year 1987	35%	27%	—
Financial years 1988 and 1989	35%	25%	—
Financial year 1990	34%	25%	—
Financial years 1991 to 1995	33%	25%	—
Financial year 1996	33%	24%	—
Financial year 1997	31%	21%	—
Financial year 1998	31%	21%	—
Financial year 1999	30%	20%	—
Financial year 2000	30%	20%	10%

For financial year 2001, the full rate is set at 30%. The starting and small companies rates for financial year 2001 will be set in the 2001 Budget.

[*FA 1974, ss 9, 10(2); F(No 2)A 1975, ss 26, 27(2); FA 1976, ss 25, 27(2); FA 1977, ss 18, 20; FA 1978, ss 15, 17(2); FA 1979, s 2; FA 1980, ss 19, 21; FA 1981, ss 20, 22; FA 1982, ss 21, 23; FA 1983, ss 11, 13; FA 1984, ss 18, 20; FA 1986, s 18; FA 1987, ss 21, 22(1); FA 1988, ss 26, 27(1); FA 1989, ss 34, 35; FA 1990, ss 19, 20; FA 1991, ss 23(1), 24, 25; F(No 2)A 1992, ss 21, 22; FA 1993, ss 53, 54; FA 1994, ss 85, 86; FA 1995, ss 37, 38; FA 1996, ss 77, 78; F(No 2)A 1997, s 18; FA 1998, ss 28, 29; FA 1999, ss 27, 29; FA 2000, ss 35, 36*].

See 56 SMALL COMPANIES—REDUCED RATES for profit limits for the starting rate or small companies rate to apply and for marginal relief limits.

(*b*) **Corporation tax on chargeable gains**

For accounting periods beginning **after 16 March 1987**, the whole of the chargeable gains (less allowable losses) is included in the profits chargeable to corporation tax. [*TCGA 1992, s 8*]. The rate of corporation tax applicable will either be the full rate as in (*a*) above or the starting or small companies rate (with marginal relief as appropriate). See 56 SMALL COMPANIES—REDUCED RATES.

For accounting periods beginning before 17 March 1987 and ending after 16 March 1987, there are transitional provisions whereby, broadly, the accounting period is split into two notional accounting periods. The first period is deemed to end immediately before 17 March 1987 and is treated as below for accounting periods ending before 17 March 1987. The second period is deemed to commence on 17 March 1987 and is treated as above for accounting periods beginning after 16 March 1987. [*FA 1972, s 93(2)(3); F(No 2)A 1987, s 74(1)(3)(4)(6), Sch 5 paras 1, 2*].

For accounting periods ending before 17 March 1987, corporation tax on chargeable gains is levied at the full rate of corporation tax, but those gains are reduced for tax purposes by such fractions as Parliament may from time to time determine giving an effective rate of tax of 30% in most cases. The fractions determined are as follows.

Financial years 1973 to 1982	$\frac{11}{26}$	[*FA 1974, s 10(1)(a)*].
Financial year 1983	$\frac{2}{5}$	[*FA 1984, s 18*].
Financial year 1984	$\frac{1}{3}$	[*FA 1984, s 18*].
Financial year 1985	$\frac{1}{4}$	[*FA 1984, s 18*].
Financial year 1986	$\frac{1}{7}$	[*FA 1984, s 18*].

Where an accounting period straddles financial years in which different fractions apply, the chargeable gains for that period are apportioned and reduced accordingly. [*FA 1972, s 93*].

See 41 LIFE INSURANCE COMPANIES for the corporation tax treatment of chargeable gains of such companies.

(*c*) **Resolutions to reduce corporation tax**

Until the introduction of self-assessment for companies (see 55 SELF-ASSESSMENT), where a Budget Resolution was passed during the year imposing a lower rate of corporation tax than that previously enacted for the year, any assessment made in the six months following the passing of the Resolution was at the rate set by the Resolution. Unless an *Act* was passed within that six-month period setting that rate for the year, any such assessment was adjusted accordingly. Similar provisions applied where a lower small companies' rate or different marginal relief fraction (or both) were set by a Budget Resolution passed in the financial year. [*ICTA 1988, s 8A; FA 1993, s 206; FA 1996, Sch 24 para 10*].

See 42.5 LIQUIDATIONS for treatment in the financial year in which a company's affairs are wound up.

(*d*) **Advance corporation tax**

Date of dividend etc.	*Rate of ACT*	
6 April 1973 — 31 March 1974	$\frac{3}{7}$ths	(i.e. 30% of dividend etc. plus ACT)
1 April 1974 — 31 March 1975	$\frac{33}{67}$ths	(i.e. 33% of dividend etc. plus ACT)
1 April 1975 — 31 March 1977	$\frac{35}{65}$ths	(i.e. 35% of dividend etc. plus ACT)
1 April 1977 — 31 March 1978	$\frac{34}{66}$ths	(i.e. 34% of dividend etc. plus ACT)
1 April 1978 — 31 March 1979	$\frac{33}{67}$ths	(i.e. 33% of dividend etc. plus ACT)
1 April 1979 — 31 March 1986	$\frac{3}{7}$ths	(i.e. 30% of dividend etc. plus ACT)
1 April 1986 — 31 March 1987	$\frac{29}{71}$sts	(i.e. 29% of dividend etc. plus ACT)
1 April 1987 — 31 March 1988	$\frac{27}{73}$rds	(i.e. 27% of dividend etc. plus ACT)
1 April 1988 — 31 March 1993	$\frac{1}{3}$rd	(i.e. 25% of dividend etc. plus ACT)
1 April 1993 — 31 March 1994	$\frac{9}{31}$sts	(i.e. 22.5% of dividend etc. plus ACT)
1 April 1994 — 5 April 1999	**$\frac{1}{4}$th**	(i.e. 20% of dividend etc. plus ACT)

[*FA 1972, s 84(1)(2); FA 1974, s 12; F(No 2)A 1975, s 28; FA 1976, s 26; FA 1977, s 19; FA 1978, s 16; F(No 2)A 1979, s 5; FA 1980, s 20; FA 1981, s 21; FA 1982, s 22; FA 1983, s 12; FA 1984, s 19; FA 1985, s 35; FA 1986, s 17(1); FA 1987,*

1.3 Introduction and Rates of Tax

s 20(1); FA 1988, s 23; FA 1989, s 30; FA 1990, s 17; FA 1991, s 21; FA 1992, s 10(1); FA 1993, s 78(1)].

Any ACT payable in respect of a distribution made *before 6 April* in a financial year in which the rate was changed was calculated at the rate fixed for the preceding financial year. [*ICTA 1988, s 246(6)*]. The rate was therefore effectively fixed from 6 April to 5 April (a 'year of assessment') notwithstanding the continuing reference to a 'financial year'.

ACT is **abolished** after 5 April 1999 (see 3.1 ADVANCE CORPORATION TAX).

2 Accounting Periods

Simon's Direct Tax Service D2.107.

2.1 Assessments to corporation tax are made on the basis of accounting periods but, for calculating the corporation tax payable thereon, the profit of each accounting period is, if necessary, apportioned, on a time basis, between the financial years (see 1.2 INTRODUCTION) which overlap the accounting period. Corporation tax is then charged on each proportion so computed at the rate fixed for the financial year concerned. [*ICTA 1988, s 8(3)*].

2.2 *Example*

For the year ended 30 June 1999, the following information is relevant to A Ltd, a company with no associated companies.

	£	
Schedule D, Case I	1,560,600	
Schedule A	35,000	
Schedule D, Case III	30,000	
Charges paid (gross)	1,000—	on 31.7.98
	9,000—	on 31.3.99

The rate of corporation tax for the financial year 1998 is 31% and the rate for the financial year 1999 is 30%.

The corporation tax computation of A Ltd for the 12-month accounting period ended on 30.6.99 is as follows.

		£	
Schedule D, Case I		1,560,600	
Schedule A		35,000	
Schedule D, Case III		30,000	
		1,625,600	
Charges		10,000	
		£1,615,600	
Total profits apportioned			
1.7.98 — 31.3.99	$\frac{9}{12}$ ×	£1,615,600	£1,211,700
1.4.99 — 30.6.99	$\frac{3}{12}$ ×	£1,615,600	£403,900
Tax chargeable			
31% × £1,211,700			375,627
30% × £403,900			121,170
Total tax charge			£496,797

2.3 An accounting period of a company **begins** whenever

(*a*) 'the company, not then being within the charge to corporation tax, comes within it, whether by the company becoming resident in the UK or acquiring a source of income, or otherwise', or

(*b*) a previous 'accounting period of the company ends without the company then ceasing to be within the charge to corporation tax'. [*ICTA 1988, s 12(2)*].

A company resident in the UK, if not otherwise within the charge to corporation tax, is treated as coming within the charge when it commences business. [*ICTA 1988, s 12(4)*]. If a chargeable gain or allowable loss accrues to a company not otherwise in an accounting period, an accounting period then begins and the gain or loss accrues in that period. [*ICTA 1988, s 12(6)*]. As regards whether a company is 'within the charge to corporation tax' in the absence of income or gains, see *Walker v Centaur Clothes Group Ltd HL, [2000] STC 324.*

2.4 An accounting period of a company **ends** on the first occurrence of any of the following

(*a*) the expiration of twelve months from the beginning of the accounting period;

(*b*) an accounting date of the company or, if there is a period for which the company does not make up accounts, the end of that period;

(*c*) the company's beginning or ceasing to trade or to be, in respect of the trade or (if more than one) of all the trades carried on by it, within the charge to corporation tax;

(*d*) the company's beginning or ceasing to be resident in the UK;

(*e*) the company's ceasing to be within the charge to corporation tax. [*ICTA 1988, s 12(3)*].

Where *more than one trade* is carried on and accounting dates differ, and each of the accounting dates is on or after 1 July 1999, the day appointed for the commencement of self-assessment for companies (see 55 SELF-ASSESSMENT), the company determines which date is to prevail under (*b*). The Board may, however, select such different one of those dates as appears to them appropriate where they are of the opinion, on reasonable grounds, that the date selected by the company is inappropriate. Previously, the Board determined which of those dates was to prevail. [*ICTA 1988, s 12(5)(5A); FA 1996, Sch 24 para 11*].

Where the *beginning or end of an accounting period is uncertain*, the inspector may choose such period (not exceeding twelve months) as appears to him appropriate and, on further facts coming to his knowledge, he may revise that period, but the company has rights of appeal. [*ICTA 1988, s 12(8)*]. See *R v Ward, R v Special Commr (ex p Stipplechoice Ltd) (No 3) QB 1988, 61 TC 391*, where determination of an appeal was quashed because the company did not receive notification that the inspector intended to seek confirmation of the assessment under appeal after revision of the terminal date. The validity of extended time limit assessments made by virtue of the predecessor to *section 12(8)*, and subsequently varied by the inspector, was challenged in *Kelsall v Stipplechoice Ltd CA 1995, 67 TC 349*. It was held that the question of whether there was doubt as to the beginning or end of an accounting period at the time the assessment was made (so that the dates could subsequently be revised by the inspector) is to be determined subjectively by reference to the state of mind of the inspector at that time. This reversed the decision in the High Court (*[1992] STC 681*), where it was also held that no further leave of the General or Special Commissioners was required for the revision of an extended time limit assessment made by virtue of *section 12(8)* where the original leave to assess was given on the footing that it would be open to the company to contend for a different accounting date on appeal. The Court of Appeal expressed no view on this aspect of the decision.

Where *accounts are made up for a period in excess of twelve months*, apportionments of profits or gains to different periods are, except where otherwise provided, made on a time basis [*ICTA 1988, s 834(4)*], and in the case of profits or gains chargeable under Schedule D, Case I, II or VI it is specifically provided that apportionment is to be made on the basis of the number of days falling in each period. [*ICTA 1988, s 72; FA 1995, s 121*]. Where, however, a more satisfactory basis of arriving at the profit of each accounting period is available, the inspector may apply that basis instead (*Marshall Hus & Partners Ltd v Bolton Ch D 1980, 55 TC 539*). Other Schedule D income is apportioned on an arising basis [*ICTA*

1988, ss 9(1), 64, 65], except that, from 1 April 1998, income from an overseas property business (see 50.27 PROFIT COMPUTATIONS) chargeable under Schedule D, Case V is computed as if it were a Schedule A business (so that Schedule D, Case I principles apply). [*ICTA 1988, s 70A(5); FA 1998, Sch 5 para 25*]. Also, for accounting periods ending on or after 1 April 1996, the Schedule D, Case III charge in respect of a non-trading credit on loan relationships is in any event calculated by reference to accounting periods (see 43.3, 43.5 LOAN RELATIONSHIPS). Chargeable gains are apportioned on an arising basis. [*TCGA 1992, s 8(1)*]. Charges are included in the period in which they are paid. [*ICTA 1988, s 338 (1)*].

Where *accounts are made up to slightly varying dates* (e.g. the last Saturday in a specified month), provided the variation is not more than four days from a mean date, the Revenue will (if the taxpayer agrees in writing) normally accept treatment of each period of account as if it were a twelve month accounting period ending on the mean date. (Revenue Company Taxation Manual, CT 56).

See Revenue Pamphlet IR 1, C12 for concessional yearly accounting periods where a retail co-operative society prepares half-yearly or quarterly accounts.

See also 3.10 ADVANCE CORPORATION TAX.

2.5 *Example*

B Ltd prepares accounts for 16 months ending on 31 March 2000. The following information is relevant.

	£
Profit for 16 months	800,000
Schedule D, Case III income (not in respect of loan relationships) received on 1 March and 1 September each year	50,000
Charges paid on 1 January each year (gross)	70,000
Capital gain (after indexation) arising on 1.6.99	100,000
Tax written down value of plant pool at 1.12.98	40,000
Plant purchased 1.2.99	200,000
Plant purchased 1.2.00	246,000
Proceeds of plant sold 31.12.99 (less than cost)	4,000

B Ltd will be chargeable to corporation tax as follows.

	Accounting period 12 months to 30.11.99	Accounting period 4 months to 31.3.00
	£	£
Adjusted profits (apportioned 12:4)	600,000	200,000
Capital allowances (see note)	(90,000)	(110,567)
Schedule D, Case I	510,000	89,433
Schedule D, Case III	100,000	50,000
Chargeable gain	100,000	—
	710,000	139,433
Charges on income	(70,000)	(70,000)
Chargeable profits	£640,000	£69,433

Note

Capital allowances are calculated as follows.

12 months to 30.11.99

	FYAs	Pool	Allowances
	£	£	£
WDV b/f		40,000	
Additions	200,000		
FYA at 40%	(80,000)		80,000
	120,000		
WDA at 25%		(10,000)	10,000
Transfer to pool	(120,000)	120,000	
Total allowances			£90,000
WDV c/f		£150,000	

4 months to 31.3.00

	FYAs	Pool	Allowances
	£	£	£
WDV b/f		150,000	
Additions	246,000		
FYA at 40%	(98,400)		98,400
	147,600		
Disposals		(4,000)	
		146,000	
WDA at 25% × 4/12		(12,167)	12,167
Transfer to pool	(147,600)	147,600	
Total allowances			£110,567
WDV c/f		£281,433	

It is assumed that the conditions for first-year allowances are met. Writing-down allowances, but not first-year allowances, are a proportionately reduced percentage of 25% if the accounting period is only part of a year. [*CAA 1990, s 24*(*2*)].

2.6 For accounting periods in relation to *liquidations* and other insolvency aspects, see 42.6 LIQUIDATION ETC.

3 Advance Corporation Tax

General note. See 3.1 below as regards the **abolition of ACT** from 6 April 1999.

Simon's Direct Tax Service D1.3.

The headings in this chapter are as follows.

3.1 Liability to pay ACT
3.2 Rate of ACT
3.3 Reduction in amount of ACT payable by reference to franked investment income (FII) received
3.4 Dates when ACT is payable
3.5 — example
3.6 Set-off of ACT against corporation tax
3.7 — example
3.8 Surplus ACT — how it can be used
3.9 — example
3.10 Effects of certain changes in ownership of a company
3.11 Companies in partnership
3.12 Preference dividends
3.13 Dividends paid to non-resident shareholders

3.1 LIABILITY TO PAY ACT

A company resident in the UK which, before 6 April 1999, makes a qualifying distribution (which includes the payment of a dividend — see 20 DISTRIBUTIONS) becomes liable to pay advance corporation tax (ACT) [*ICTA 1988, s 14(1); FA 1998, Sch 3 para 8*] (subject to relief for FRANKED INVESTMENT INCOME (27) received — see 3.3 below).

Intra-group dividends are exempt if an election is made as described under 29.2 GROUPS OF COMPANIES.

As regards *ultra vires* dividends, see Revenue Company Taxation Manual, CT 2007a *et seq.*.

ACT is abolished from 6 April 1999 [*FA 1998, s 31*], subject to a continuing 'shadow' system for relief of surplus ACT at that date (see 3.8 below).

3.2 RATE OF ACT

The rate of ACT is expressed as a fraction of the amount or value of the dividend or other distributions, as follows (the rates in effect applying in a year of change from 5 April, see below).

Date of dividend etc.	*Rate of ACT*	
6 April 1988 — 5 April 1993	$\frac{1}{3}$rd	(i.e. 25% of dividend etc. plus ACT)
6 April 1993 — 5 April 1994	$\frac{9}{31}$sts	(i.e. 22.5% of dividend etc. plus ACT)
6 April 1994 — 5 April 1999	**$\frac{1}{4}$th**	(i.e. 20% of dividend etc. plus ACT)

(For earlier years, and for enacting provisions, see 1.3(*d*) INTRODUCTION AND RATES OF TAX.)

Thus a dividend during the year to 5 April 1999 of £160 results in a liability to ACT of £40.

The rate is fixed by the formula

$$\frac{I}{100 - I}$$

where I is the lower rate of income tax for the year of assessment beginning in the financial year. [*ICTA 1988, s 14(3); FA 1993, s 78(1)(2); FA 1998, Sch 3 para 8*].

If the rate for a financial year differs from that fixed for the previous year, the rate previously in force continues to apply up to 5 April in the financial year. [*ICTA 1988, s 246(6); FA 1998, Sch 3 para 18*].

For ACT on preference dividends etc. at a rate fixed before 6 April 1973, see 3.12 below.

3.3 **REDUCTION IN AMOUNT OF ACT PAYABLE BY REFERENCE TO FRANKED INVESTMENT INCOME RECEIVED**

If a company receives 'franked investment income', attributable to a distribution made before 6 April 1999, in an accounting period, its liability to ACT on its 'franked payments' is reduced.

The liability is calculated on an amount which, when the ACT is added to it, is equal to the excess of its 'franked payments' made over such 'franked investment income' received in that accounting period. Thus with an ACT rate of one-quarter, the liability is 20% of that excess.

[*ICTA 1988, s 241(1)(2); FA 1998, s 31(3), Sch 3 para 14*].

'*Franked payments*' are the sum of the amount or value of dividends or other qualifying distributions (see 20.8 DISTRIBUTIONS) made by the company before 6 April 1999 and such proportion of each such distribution as corresponds to the rate of ACT in force when the distribution is made. [*ICTA 1988, s 238(1); FA 1998, s 31(2), Sch 3 para 11*].

The rate of ACT from 6 April 1994 to 5 April 1999 is one-quarter, so that a distribution of £360 represents a franked payment of £450.

'*Franked investment income*' ('FII') is the sum of the amount or value of dividends and other qualifying distributions (see 20.8 DISTRIBUTIONS) received by a UK resident company from another UK resident company and such proportion of each distribution as corresponds to:

(i) before 6 April 1999, the rate of ACT in force when the distribution is made; or

(ii) after 5 April 1999, the 'tax credit fraction' in force when the distribution is made.

[*ICTA 1988, ss 231(1), 238(1), 832(1); F(No 2)A 1997, s 30(2); FA 1998, Sch 3 paras 11, 39*].

The tax credit fraction is initially set at one-ninth from 6 April 1999. [*F(No 2)A 1997, s 30(3)*]. The rate of ACT from 6 April 1994 to 5 April 1999 is one-quarter, so that a dividend of £360 amounts to FII in the hands of a UK recipient company of £450 for distributions before 6 April 1999, and to £400 for distributions on or after that date. [*FA 1993, s 78(4)*].)

The following are **not** included in the definition of franked payments or FII:

(*a*) (before 6 April 1999) group income, being dividends within certain groups of companies or between members of a consortium which, under an election, are paid without incurring ACT liability (see 29 GROUPS OF COMPANIES);

(*b*) dividends or interest received from BUILDING SOCIETIES (7). [*ICTA 1988, s 476(3), s 477A(3)(b); FA 1990, Sch 5 para 4*].

Example

X plc's accounting period runs from 1 July to 30 June. On 8 April 1998, it pays a dividend of £540, which gives rise to an ACT liability of £135. On 3 May 1998, it receives from Y

Ltd a dividend of £360, which carries a tax credit of £90. It neither makes nor receives any other dividends in the accounting period. Its overall ACT liability is calculated as follows.

	£		£	£	
Dividend paid	540	+	135	= 675	(Franked payment)
Dividend received	360	+	90	= 450	(FII)
Excess of franked payments over FII				£225	
ACT payable @ 20%				£45	

See 3.4 below where the FII is received in one return period and the franked payment made in another.

Surplus FII. If, during an accounting period of a company beginning **before 6 April 1999**, its FII exceeds its franked payments, the excess is described as a 'surplus of franked investment income' and is carried forward into, and treated as FII of, the next accounting period. [*ICTA 1988, s 238(1)(1A), s 241(3); FA 1995, Sch 8 para 18; FA 1998, Sch 3 paras 11, 14*]. For the alternative use of surplus FII against losses etc. (which ceases from 2 July 1997), see 27.3 FRANKED INVESTMENT INCOME.

Restrictions by reference to a date when the rate of ACT changes. If the rate of ACT changed (as on 6 April 1994), the periods before and from the date of change were, where relevant, regarded as *separate accounting periods* for the above purposes. Thus, if a dividend was paid in March 1994, ACT thereon was not reduced by reference to FII received after 5 April 1994 even if in the same accounting period of the company concerned. [*ICTA 1988, s 246(5); FA 1998, Sch 3 para 18*]. Where ACT was paid at the wrong rate, the difference was either adjusted on the next payment or paid to, or reclaimed from, the Collector of Taxes.

3.4 DATES WHEN ACT IS PAYABLE

ACT is payable by a company to the Revenue within 14 days of the end of the 'return period' during which the qualifying distribution was made. [*ICTA 1988, Sch 13 paras 1, 3*]. *Schedule 13* **ceases to apply** in relation to return periods and accounting periods beginning **on or after 6 April 1999**. [*FA 1998, Sch 3 para 41*].

A '*return period*' ends on 31 March, 30 June, 30 September, 31 December and at the end of the ACCOUNTING PERIODS (2) of the company. [*ICTA 1988, Sch 13 para 1*]. If the rate of ACT changes (as on 6 April 1993 and 6 April 1994), the periods before and from the date of change are, where relevant, treated as separate accounting periods for this purpose. [*ICTA 1988, s 246(6)(b); FA 1998, Sch 3 para 18*]. Similarly where franked payments are made or FII received in the period beginning with 1 April 1999 and ending with 5 April 1999, that period is treated as a separate return period. [*F(No 2)A 1997, Sch 4 para 23(6)*].

A return (form CT 61(Z)), showing details of franked payments, franked investment income (FII) (see 3.3 above) and ACT payable, must be made within 14 days of the end of a return period. [*ICTA 1988, Sch 13 paras 1, 2, 4(2)*].

ACT (calculated as described in 3.3 above in relation to accounting periods) is payable in respect of the excess of franked payments made in the return period over FII. For this purpose, FII comprises:

(*a*) that received in the return period;

(*b*) surplus FII carried forward to the accounting period in which the return period falls (insofar as it has not been utilised in an earlier return period);

(*c*) surplus FII carried forward from earlier return periods in the same accounting period.

[*ICTA 1988, Sch 13 paras 2, 3; F(No 2)A 1997, Sch 4 para 23*].

FII received in a return period later than that in which a franked payment is made cannot be carried back, and ACT must be paid for the earlier period. A claim for repayment may, however, be made for the later period, provided that the return period in which the franked payment was made and that in which the FII is received are in the same accounting period. The maximum repayment is the tax credit comprised in the FII received, or in the excess of the FII received over franked payments made in the same return period. [*ICTA 1988, Sch 13 para 4*].

See 39 INTEREST ON UNPAID TAX for interest payable if ACT is not paid by the due date. See also 26.11 FOREIGN INCOME DIVIDENDS.

Qualifying distributions made on a date not falling within an accounting period of the company. A return must be made, and ACT paid, within 14 days of the date of the payment. [*ICTA 1988, Sch 13 para 9*].

Qualifying distributions which are not payments and payments of uncertain nature must be shown separately in returns. ACT thereon is not payable until assessed [*ICTA 1988, Sch 13 para 7*] and is then payable within 14 days after the issue of the notice of assessment. [*ICTA 1988, Sch 13 para 10(2)*].

See 3.10 below for effect of certain changes of ownership of a company.

3.5 *Example*

C Ltd prepares accounts to 31 March each year. During the two years ended 31 March 1999, it pays and receives the following dividends.

		£
20.6.97	Paid	8,000
3.3.98	Received	11,200
25.6.98	Paid	8,000
30.11.98	Received	5,600
25.3.99	Paid	4,800

The ACT movements are summarised by the following table.

Return period	Franked payment	FII	Cumulative franked payments less FII	ACT paid/ (repaid)
	£	£	£	£
Year ended 31.3.98				
30.6.97	10,000		10,000	2,000
30.9.97 No return			10,000	
31.12.97 No return			10,000	
31.3.98		14,000	(4,000)	(2,000)*
Surplus FII carried forward			£(4,000)	

Return period	Franked payment	FII	Cumulative franked payments less FII	ACT paid/ (repaid)
	£	£	£	£
Year ended 31.3.99				
Surplus FII brought forward			(4,000)	
30.6.98	10,000		6,000	1,200
30.9.98 No return			6,000	
31.12.98		7,000	(1,000)	(1,200)*
31.3.99	6,000		5,000	1,000
Net ACT paid in year				£1,000

* The ACT repayment is restricted to the ACT previously paid in the accounting period. [*ICTA 1988, Sch 13 para 4*].

3.6 **SET-OFF OF ACT AGAINST CORPORATION TAX**

ACT paid by a company (and not repaid) in respect of a distribution made in the accounting period is set against its liability to 'mainstream' corporation tax on its 'profits' for that accounting period. For cases turning on whether there was an accounting period (in relation to surplus ACT, see 3.8 below), see *Walker v Centaur Clothes Group Ltd HL, [2000] STC 324* and *Aproline Ltd v Littlejohn (Sp C 36), [1995] SSCD 201.*

'*Profits*' for this purpose are profits on which corporation tax falls finally to be borne.

The *maximum* set-off is the amount of ACT that would have been payable in respect of a franked payment equal to the profits and made at the end of the accounting period. An accounting period straddling 5 April 1999 (for distributions after which date ACT is abolished) is for this purpose treated as ending on 5 April 1999, a proportionate part of the company's profits of the actual accounting period being apportioned to that period. Any ACT not so relieved is described as 'surplus ACT' (for which see 3.8 below).

[*ICTA 1988, s 239(1)–(3)(6); FA 1998, Sch 3 para 12*].

Where different rates of ACT are in force for different parts of an accounting period, the *maximum* set-off of ACT against the corporation tax liability is determined by apportioning the profits on a *time* basis between the different parts of the accounting period, calculating the maximum for each part as if it were a separate accounting period and aggregating the results. [*ICTA 1988, s 246(5); FA 1998, Sch 3 para 18*].

Correction of excessive ACT. Any necessary assessment may be made to recover tax which ought to have been paid as a result of an excessive set-off of ACT, and to restore the tax position of those concerned. [*ICTA 1988, s 252; FA 1998, Sch 3 para 21*].

Where an assessment for an accounting period ending on or before 30 September 1993 is made as a result of a surrender of ACT (see 29.8 GROUPS OF COMPANIES), interest under *TMA 1970, s 86* (see 39.3 INTEREST ON UNPAID TAX) runs from the normal reckonable date. Where an assessment for such a period could have been made under *ICTA 1988, s 252(1)* but for a claim to carry back surplus ACT (see 3.8 below), interest runs as if the claim had not been made, and the *section 252* assessment had been raised, until nine months after the end of the accounting period in which the surplus ACT arose. Similarly, where such a claim is made to carry back surplus ACT against unpaid corporation tax of an earlier period, interest is payable from the reckonable date on the unpaid tax of the earlier period without reduction for the surplus ACT carried back, except so far as concerns interest for any time after the day following the expiry of nine months from the end of the accounting period in which the surplus ACT arose. [*FA 1989, s 157*]. See now 39.1 INTEREST ON UNPAID TAX.

See 3.10 below for the effect of certain changes in the ownership of a company.

See 21.7 DOUBLE TAX RELIEF for allocations of ACT set-off.

See 46.3, 46.4 OIL COMPANIES regarding special provisions relating to oil companies.

For restrictions regarding company partners, see 44.16 LOSSES.

Simon's Direct Tax Service. See D1.310.

3.7 *Example*

E Ltd, a company with no associated companies, has the following profits for the year ending 31 March 1999.

	£
Schedule D, Case I	1,600,400
Schedule A	6,000
Building society interest	15,000
Chargeable gains	3,600

Annual charges of £75,000 (gross) are paid.

During the year, E Ltd pays a final dividend of £800,000 in respect of the year ended 31.3.98, and an interim dividend of £520,000 in respect of the year ending 31.3.99. ACT on dividends amounts to £200,000 and £130,000 respectively. The dividends are paid on 30.6.98 and 31.1.99.

The CT liability will be as follows.

	£	£
Schedule D, Case I		1,600,400
Schedule A		6,000
Schedule D, Case III		15,000
		1,621,400
Chargeable gains		3,600
		1,625,000
Annual charges		(75,000)
Chargeable profits		£1,550,000
CT at 31%		480,500
Deduct lesser of		
ACT paid	330,000	
Maximum set-off 20% × £1,550,000	310,000	310,000
Surplus ACT	£20,000	
'Mainstream' CT liability		£170,500

3.8 SURPLUS ACT—HOW IT CAN BE USED

Surplus ACT (see 3.6 above) can be **carried back** to accounting periods beginning in the six years preceding the accounting period in which the surplus ACT arose. It must be applied for a more recent period before a more remote period. Claims to carry back ACT of different periods may be given effect in the order in which they were made (*Carr v Armpledge Ltd CA, [2000] STC 410*). The company must claim the relief within two years of the end of the accounting period in which the surplus ACT arose. [*ICTA 1988, s 239(3); FA 1998, Sch 3 para 12*]. Alternatively, it may be **carried forward** and treated as ACT payable in respect of the next accounting period or, if it cannot then be used, of the following accounting period and so on. It cannot, however, be carried forward to an accounting period beginning after 5 April 1999 (and since for the purposes of ACT set-off an accounting period straddling that date is treated as ending on that date (see 3.6 above), the surplus ACT as at that date is in effect dealt with under the 'shadow ACT' rules referred to below from 6 April 1999). [*ICTA 1988, s 239(4); FA 1998, Sch 3 para 12*]. Surplus ACT may only be set against corporation tax liabilities of other periods, it may not be repaid by set-off against franked investment income of those periods.

See 38.1, 38.3 INTEREST ON OVERPAID TAX, 39.1 INTEREST ON UNPAID TAX as regards interest where surplus ACT is set against corporation tax for accounting periods ending after 30 September 1993.

In a case in which subsequent losses carried back to a year for which a claim had been made under the predecessor to *section 239(3)* resulted in an additional surplus of ACT for that year, it was held that the original claim only applied to the surplus ascertainable by reference to events which have happened at the time of the claim (*Procter & Gamble Ltd v Taylerson CA 1990, 63 TC 481* and see Revenue Tax Bulletin August 1993 p 86). See also *Savacentre Ltd v CIR CA 1995, 67 TC 381* as regards informal requirements for claims.

For a case in which a Revenue contention that relief for surplus ACT should be denied on the grounds that, at the time it was paid, the company had no source of income within the charge to corporation tax, and hence no accounting period, was rejected, see *Walker v Centaur Clothes Group Ltd HL, [2000] STC 324* (and see *Aproline Ltd v Littlejohn (Sp C 36), [1995] SSCD 201*).

See also *Pigott v Staines Investment Co Ltd Ch D 1995, 68 TC 342*, in which a scheme to set surplus ACT against earlier years' profits of a company brought into a group was successful.

The maximum set-off is calculated as under 3.6 above by reference to 'profits'. See also 3.10 below.

Surplus ACT in an accounting period can generally be surrendered to a subsidiary. See 29.8 GROUPS OF COMPANIES. See also 46.3 OIL COMPANIES for special provisions applying to such companies.

See also 26 FOREIGN INCOME DIVIDENDS as regards relief for surplus ACT under special scheme.

Privatisation. Surplus ACT arising to the successor company on privatisation may not be carried back to a period before the transfer (*CIR v Aberdeen Milk Co Ltd CS, [1999] STC 787*).

'Shadow ACT' from 6 April 1999. Following the abolition of ACT for distributions made after 5 April 1999, a system of 'shadow ACT' is introduced to enable surplus ACT as at that date to be relieved broadly in accordance with companies' expectations prior to abolition.

The *Corporation Tax (Treatment of Surplus Advance Corporation Tax) Regulations 1999* (*SI 1999 No 358*), introduced under the enabling provisions of *FA 1998, s 32*, broadly have effect as follows.

(*a*) An accounting period straddling 5 April 1999 is treated as two separate accounting periods, ending on and commencing immediately after that date, with profits being time-apportioned between those accounting periods.

(*b*) The pre-6 April 1999 limit on the amount which may be set against corporation tax liabilities (i.e. 20% of corporation tax profits) is retained.

(*c*) The offset capacity thus available is allocated first to 'shadow ACT' for the accounting period, computed on a similar basis and at the same rate as applied before

6 April 1999, although no actual corporation tax relief is given for amounts so allocated. If the shadow ACT exceeds the offset capacity for the period, it is treated as 'surplus shadow ACT', to be carried back and treated as shadow ACT in respect of distributions made in accounting periods beginning in the previous six years (but not before 6 April 1999), with any unused balance being carried forward to the next accounting period. Surplus shadow ACT is, however, not carried back so as to displace actual surplus ACT relieved in an earlier period (see (*d*) below) except in the period beginning 24 months before the *end* of the accounting period in which the surplus shadow ACT arose and ending the day before the commencement of that period.

(*d*) The distributions in respect of which the shadow ACT computation is made include all distributions within *ICTA 1988, Pt VI* (see 20.1–20.16 DISTRIBUTIONS), including both qualifying and non-qualifying distributions (see 20.18 DISTRIBUTIONS), and also certain deemed distributions arising in respect of benefits provided to participators in close companies (see 20.20 DISTRIBUTIONS), but *excluding* manufactured dividends within *ICTA 1988, Sch 23A* (see Tolley's Income Tax under Anti-Avoidance) and most intra-group distributions (see *SI 1999 No 358, reg 11(2)*).

(*e*) Where FRANKED INVESTMENT INCOME (27) ('FII') is received in an accounting period, or surplus FII is brought forward (including a surplus arising before 6 April 1999), shadow ACT is *not* treated as having been paid in that period except to the extent that franked distributions (i.e. distributions plus the shadow ACT thereon) exceed the sum of nine-eighths of the FII received and the amount of any surplus FII brought forward. The definition of FII is, however, subject to a number of restrictions in relation to replacement of interest income by income consisting of distributions, arrangements to pass on the value of FII, distributions received by dealers and intra-group distributions (see *SI 1999 No 358, regs 7–10*).

(*f*) Any balance of the offset capacity available for an accounting period is allocated to surplus ACT brought forward at 6 April 1999, for which actual corporation tax relief is then given.

(*g*) A company may opt out of the shadow ACT system by notifying the inspector that it will not seek, or will cease to seek, recovery of unrelieved surplus ACT. Where such notice is given in the accounting period beginning on 6 April 1999 (as in (*a*) above) and relates to that period, the company is thereby excluded from the shadow ACT arrangements *ab initio*. Where it is given in any accounting period and indicates that the company wishes that accounting period to be the last for which it will seek recovery of unrelieved surplus ACT (the 'final accounting period'), then no further recovery will be possible after that period. In those circumstances, and also in relation to the accounting period in which all surplus ACT is exhausted, the shadow ACT computation continues to be made for (normally) the following accounting period, with any surplus shadow ACT arising in that period being carried back to displace surplus ACT relieved as under (*c*) above in the final accounting period (and in that case the accounting period from which the surplus shadow ACT is carried back becomes the final accounting period, i.e. the last period for which surplus ACT relief may be obtained). (These displacement provisions are more complex where accounting periods are not of twelve months' duration.) The latter prevents excessive relief being obtained by the restriction of dividends, and consequent ability to reclaim unrelieved surplus ACT, in the final period within the arrangements, followed by the payment of exceptional dividends in (normally) the following accounting period. There are special rules in relation to determination of the final accounting period for these purposes in the case of groups of companies (see generally (*j*) below).

(*h*) The provisions of *ICTA 1988, ss 245–245B* relating to changes in ownership of companies (see 3.10 below) are imported *mutatis mutandis* into the shadow ACT rules.

(*i*) The profits against which unrelieved surplus ACT may be set include amounts chargeable on the company in respect of CONTROLLED FOREIGN COMPANIES (18) (see *SI 1999 No 358, regs 3(3), 20*).

(*j*) Special rules determine when and how shadow ACT generated within a group of companies is to be allocated, and the allocation of group surplus shadow ACT. Broadly, no company in a group gets relief for surplus ACT until all group shadow ACT has been offset. Where a group member generates shadow ACT in excess of its maximum capacity to utilise it in the period in which it is generated, the excess is to be allocated by the parent company to another or other group member(s), but not so as to displace their own shadow ACT or to exceed their maximum capacity for using shadow ACT in the same period. Where the total group shadow ACT exceeds the group capacity to use it, the balance remaining after the allocation to other group companies is to remain in the company in which it arose and to be carried forward. Where the total group shadow ACT does not exceed the group capacity, the parent company determines which other group members are to receive the allocation and the amounts to be allocated to them, in accordance with their capacity to use that amount. The Board may allocate the excess in accordance with the regulations where the company fails to do so, but such allocation can subsequently be overridden by an allocation made by the parent company.

There are also provisions dealing with a company joining or leaving a group, or being a member of more than one group. 'Group' for these purposes is broadly a company and its 51% subsidiaries, but is specially defined to take into account certain special rights (see *SI 1999 No 358, reg 6*).

(*k*) There are also special provisions relating to foreign tax credit relief (*SI 1999 No 358, reg 12(4)*), to recovery of surplus ACT wrongly set off (*SI 1999 No 358, reg 19*) and to life assurance companies (*SI 1999 No 358, reg 22*).

Simon's Direct Tax Service. See D1.311, D1.312.

3.9 *Examples*

(A)

H Ltd is a trading company with no associated companies. The following tables summarise the company's chargeable profits and its distributions.

	Year ended 30.9.93	6 months to 31.3.94	Year ended 31.3.95	Year ended 31.3.96
	£	£	£	£
Chargeable profits	42,000	22,000	15,000	7,000
Dividends paid	—	—	—	51,800
ACT on dividends	—	—	—	12,950
The appropriate rates of ACT and CT are				
ACT	$\frac{25}{75}$ $\frac{9}{31}$	$\frac{9}{31}$	$\frac{20}{80}$	$\frac{20}{80}$
CT	25%	25%	25%	25%

3.9 Advance Corporation Tax

The following table shows how the ACT can be used.

	£	£	£	£
CT liability	10,500	5,500	3,750	1,750
ACT set-off				
1996 dividend	(3,600)	(4,950)	(3,000)	(1,400)
1999 dividend (see below)	(6,375)	—	—	—
'Mainstream' liability	£525	£550	£750	£350

The maximum ACT set-off for the year ended 30.9.93 (during which the ACT rate changed) is calculated by reference to the rate applicable during each part of the period, profits being time-apportioned for this purpose (i.e. $\frac{1}{4} \times £21{,}000 + \frac{9}{40} \times £21{,}000 = £9{,}975$).

	Year ended 31.3.97	Year ended 31.3.98	Year ended 31.3.99	Year ended 31.3.00
	£	£	£	£
Chargeable profits	30,000	30,000	1,000	24,000
Dividends paid	—	—	93,600	12,000
ACT on dividends	—	—	23,400	—
Shadow ACT	—	—	—	3,000
The appropriate rates of ACT and CT are				
ACT	$\frac{20}{80}$	$\frac{20}{80}$	$\frac{20}{80}$	—
Shadow ACT	—	—	—	$\frac{20}{80}$
CT	24%	21%	21%	20%

The following table shows how the ACT can be used.

	£	£	£	£
CT liability	7,200	6,300	210	4,800
ACT set-off				
1999 dividend	(6,000)	(6,000)	(200)	—
Surplus ACT relief (see below)	—	—	—	(1,800)
'Mainstream' liability	£1,200	£300	£10	£3,000
Surplus ACT carried forward at period end	—	—	£4,825	£3,025

The 'shadow ACT' computation for the year ended 31.3.00 is as follows (assuming the dividend is paid after 5.4.99).

	Year ended 31.3.00
	£
Chargeable profits	24,000
ACT set-off capacity	4,800
Shadow ACT	3,000
Surplus ACT relieved	£1,800

Strictly the profits should be apportioned to two notional accounting periods ending on

5.4.99 and commencing on 6.4.99, but where no dividends are paid in the first such period this is of no computational significance where a shadow ACT system is operated.

(B)

J Ltd (which has no associated companies) pays a dividend of £1,000 on 30 June 2000 and receives a dividend of £800 on the same date.

J Ltd will have made a franked payment as follows.

	£
Distribution	1,000
Shadow ACT (@$\frac{20}{80}$)	250
Franked payment	£1,250

J Ltd will have received franked investment income:

	£
Distribution	800
Tax credit (@$\frac{100}{90}$)	89
Franked investment income	£889
Amount available to set against franked payments (FII × $\frac{9}{8}$)	£1,000
Shadow ACT treated as paid ((1,250 – 1,000) ×20%)	£50

3.10 **EFFECTS OF CERTAIN CHANGES IN OWNERSHIP OF A COMPANY** [*ICTA 1988, ss 245, 245A, 245B; FA 1989, s 98; FA 1998, Sch 3 paras 15–17*]

Major change in business. If a 'major change in the nature or conduct of a trade or business' takes place within three years of (or at the same time as) a change in ownership of a company (see 44.13 LOSSES) occurring **before 6 April 1999**, a new accounting period is deemed to commence at the time of the change in ownership for the purposes of

(*a*) calculating the relief against ACT payable by reference to FII (see 3.3 above),

(*b*) determining return periods (see 3.4 above), and

(*c*) setting off ACT against 'mainstream' liability. 'Income' or 'profits' as the case may be (see 3.6 above) of the company is apportioned to the revised accounting periods on a time basis.

Furthermore, surplus ACT paid in respect of distributions made by the company may neither be carried forward (see 3.8 above) from the accounting period ending with the change in ownership (whether deemed as above or actual) (such surplus ACT accordingly being lost), nor be carried back (under *ICTA 1988, s 239(3)*, see 3.8 above) from the accounting period beginning with the change in ownership (again whether deemed or actual) or a subsequent accounting period to a period ending before or with the change. [*ICTA 1988, s 245(1)–(3A); FA 1993, s 81; FA 1998, Sch 3 para 15*]. The prohibition on the carry forward of surplus ACT also applies to ACT surrendered to the company (see 29.8 GROUPS OF COMPANIES). [*ICTA 1988, s 245(6); FA 1998, Sch 3 para 15*]. (Surrendered ACT cannot in any event be carried back, see 29.11 GROUPS OF COMPANIES.)

See, however, 29.58 GROUPS OF COMPANIES for the interaction of *section 245* and the demerger provisions of *ICTA 1988, ss 213–218.*

These provisions cease to apply to changes in ownership occurring **on or after 6 April 1999** following the abolition of ACT.

'*Major change in the nature or conduct of a trade or business*' includes

(i) a major change in the type of property dealt in or services or facilities provided;

(ii) a major change in customers, outlets or markets;

(iii) the company's ceasing to be a 'trading company' and becoming an 'investment company' (or vice versa);

(iv) where the company is an investment company, a major change in the nature of its investments.

The change may be the result of a gradual process which began outside the relevant period. [*ICTA 1988, s 245(4); FA 1998, Sch 3 para 15*]. See 44.13 LOSSES for the Revenue practice as regards what constitutes a major change in the nature or conduct of a trade or business.

'*Trading company*' means a company the business of which consists wholly or mainly of the carrying on of a trade or trades.

'*Investment company*' means a company (other than a 'holding company'), the business of which consists wholly or mainly of making investments whence the principal part of its income is derived.

'*Holding company*' means a company the business of which consists wholly or mainly in the holding of shares or securities of companies which are its 90% subsidiaries and which are trading companies. [*ICTA 1988, s 245(5); FA 1998, Sch 3 para 15*].

Revival of business. Similar consequences ensue if, once the scale of the activities in its trade or business has become small or negligible, there is a change in the ownership of the company before any considerable revival of that trade or business. [*ICTA 1988, s 245(1)(b); FA 1998, Sch 3 para 15*].

Surrendered ACT. Where there is a change in the ownership of a company (see 44.13 LOSSES) to which ACT has been surrendered (see 29.8 GROUPS OF COMPANIES) in respect of a distribution made before the change, and in the period from three years before to three years after the change there is 'a major change in the nature or conduct of a trade or business' (see above) of the surrendering company, the surrendered ACT may not be carried forward to an accounting period ending after the change (the accounting period in which the change occurred being treated as two separate accounting periods, up to and after the change, for this purpose). [*ICTA 1988, s 245A; FA 1989, s 98; FA 1998, Sch 3 para 16*].

Assets acquired after change. Where there is a change in the ownership of a company (see 44.13 LOSSES) which carries forward surplus ACT of an accounting period beginning before the change to an accounting period ending after the change (the accounting period in which the change occurs being treated as two separate accounting periods, up to and after the change, for this purpose), and

(A) after the change the company acquires an asset from a fellow group member under the no gain, no loss provisions of *TCGA 1992, s 171* (see 9.19 CAPITAL GAINS), and

(B) within three years of the change in ownership, a chargeable gain accrues to the company on its disposal, before 6 April 1999, of that asset (or of an asset deriving its value in whole or part from that asset),

the ACT set-off limit (see 3.6 above) for the period in which the chargeable gain arises is reduced by the lesser of

(1) the ACT payable (ignoring any franked investment income set-off) in respect of a distribution at the end of the period which, together with the ACT, is equal in amount to the chargeable gain, and

(2) the surplus ACT of the deemed accounting period ending with the date of the change in ownership.

[*ICTA 1988, s 245B; FA 1989, s 98; FA 1998, Sch 3 para 17*].

Application of losses provisions. Certain provisions in *ICTA 1988, s 768*, and the rules in *ICTA 1988, s 769* for ascertaining change in ownership of a company, are applied to *ICTA 1988, ss 245–245B*. For *sections 768* and *769*, see 44.13 LOSSES.

Simon's Direct Tax Service. See D1.313.

3.11 COMPANIES IN PARTNERSHIP

There are anti-avoidance provisions in *ICTA 1988, s 116* which restrict the set-off of ACT in the circumstances set out in 44.16 LOSSES.

3.12 PREFERENCE DIVIDENDS

A preference or other dividend, the rate of which was fixed before 6 April 1973, is to be paid after that date and before 6 April 1999 at such amount as, when added to ACT at the rate in force at that date (i.e. three-sevenths) totals the former gross rate. Thus a preference share issued before 6 April 1973 at a gross rate of 10% will, notwithstanding subsequent changes in the rate of ACT, thenceforth carry a right to a cash dividend of 7%. Only the tax credit will vary with the rate of ACT. [*ICTA 1988, s 255; FA 1998, Sch 3 para 23*].

3.13 DIVIDENDS PAID TO NON-RESIDENT SHAREHOLDERS

See 21.9 DOUBLE TAX RELIEF.

4 Anti-Avoidance

4.1 The **anti-avoidance legislation** contained in *ICTA 1988, ss 125, 127A, 235–237, 399, 703–709, 729–739, 741–746, 775–786, Sch 5AA* and *TCGA 1992, ss 137, 138* can apply to both companies and individuals. See full details in Tolley's Income Tax and Tolley's Capital Gains Tax (under Anti-Avoidance). See also 4.8 below.

Those aspects of the legislation relating purely to companies are covered at 4.2–4.6 below and at 9.13–9.17 CAPITAL GAINS. See also 8.3 CAPITAL ALLOWANCES, 13.18 CLOSE COMPANIES, 18 CONTROLLED FOREIGN COMPANIES, 29.9, 29.31, 29.36, 29.50 GROUPS OF COMPANIES, 44.10, 44.14, 44.15, 44.18 LOSSES, 46.5 OIL COMPANIES.

For a detailed work on this subject, see Tolley's Anti-Avoidance Provisions.

For the **general approach of the Courts** to transactions entered into solely to avoid or reduce tax liability, leading cases are *Duke of Westminster v CIR HL 1935, 19 TC 490; W T Ramsay Ltd v CIR, Eilbeck v Rawling HL 1981, 54 TC 101; CIR v Burmah Oil Co Ltd HL 1981, 54 TC 200; Furniss v Dawson (and related appeals) HL 1984, 55 TC 324; Countess Fitzwilliam v CIR HL, [1993] STC 502;* and *CIR v McGuckian HL 1997, 69 TC 1.* See also *Cairns v MacDiarmid CA 1983, 56 TC 556; Ingram v CIR Ch D, [1985] STC 835; Craven v White, CIR v Bowater Property Developments Ltd,* and *Baylis v Gregory HL 1988, 62 TC 1,* heard together in the HL; *Shepherd v Lyntress Ltd Ch D 1989, 62 TC 495; Moodie v CIR and Sinnett HL 1993, 65 TC 610; Hatton v CIR Ch D, [1992] STC 140; Ensign Tankers (Leasing) Ltd v Stokes HL 1992, 64 TC 617;* and *Pigott v Staines Investment Co Ltd Ch D 1995, 68 TC 342.*

The classical interpretation of the constraints upon the Courts in deciding cases involving tax avoidance schemes is summed up in Lord Tomlin's statement in the *Duke of Westminster* case that '. . . every man is entitled if he can to order his affairs so that the tax attaching . . . is less than it otherwise would be.' The case concerned annual payments made under covenant by a taxpayer to his domestic employees, which were in substance, but not in form, remuneration. The judgment was thus concerned with the tax consequences of a single transaction, but in *Ramsay*, and subsequently in *Furniss v Dawson*, the Courts have set bounds to the ambit within which this principle can be applied in relation to modern sophisticated and increasingly artificial arrangements to avoid tax. *Ramsay* concerned a complex 'circular' avoidance scheme at the end of which the financial position of the parties was little changed, but it was claimed that a large capital gains tax loss had been created. It was held that where a preconceived series of transactions is entered into to avoid tax, and with the clear intention to proceed through all stages to completion once set in motion, the *Duke of Westminster* principle does not compel a consideration of the individual transactions and of the fiscal consequences of such transactions taken in isolation.

The HL opinions in *Furniss v Dawson* are of outstanding importance, and establish, inter alia, that the *Ramsay* principle is not confined to 'circular' devices, and that if a series of transactions is 'preordained', a particular transaction within the series, accepted as genuine, may nevertheless be ignored if it was entered into solely for fiscal reasons and without any commercial purpose other than tax avoidance, even if the series of transactions as a whole has a legitimate commercial purpose.

However, in *Craven v White* the House of Lords indicated that for the *Ramsay* principle to apply all the transactions in a series have to be preordained with such a degree of certainty that, at the time of the earlier transactions, there is no practical likelihood that the transactions would not take place. It is not sufficient that the ultimate transaction is simply of a kind that was envisaged at the time of the earlier transactions.

The inheritance tax case *Fitzwilliam v CIR* appears to further restrict the application of the *Ramsay* principle, in that the HL found for the taxpayer in a case in which all their

Lordships agreed that, once the scheme was embarked upon, there was no real possibility that the later transactions would not be proceeded with. There is, however, some suggestion that a decisive factor was that the first step in the transactions took place before the rest of the scheme had been formulated.

See ICAEW Guidance Note TR 588 'Furniss v Dawson' for guidance on the Revenue approach to the application of the principles outlined above.

Simon's Direct Tax Service. See **A1.316, A1.317.**

4.2 'DIVIDEND STRIPPING' [*ICTA 1988, s 736*]

This section applies where a **share dealing company holds shares or securities amounting to 10% of all the shares etc. of that class** issued by a company resident in the UK and, as a result of one or more distributions made in respect of that holding, the value at any accounting date (but see below) of any share or security comprised therein is materially reduced below its value at the time when it was acquired. So much of that reduction as is attributable to the distribution or distributions (the '*relevant reduction*'), is treated as a trading receipt of the dealing company when the holding is realised (or appropriated so that it is no longer dealing stock). Until such realisation or appropriation, the relevant reduction is treated as an addition to the value of the holding for valuation purposes.

Where only part of the holding is realised or appropriated, a proportionate part of the relevant reduction is brought into account as a trading receipt.

A reduction in value immediately before realisation or appropriation (as well as at an accounting date) is within this section.

Securities, shares, etc. having different entitlements or obligations are treated as being of different classes, and a company's holdings of different classes are treated as separate holdings. Subject to this, however, a company has a 10% holding in a particular class if the aggregate of its own holdings and those of persons connected with it (see 16 CONNECTED PERSONS) amounts to 10%.

A company is a *dealing company* in relation to a holding if a profit on its sale would be taken into account in computing the company's trading profits.

Where *section 736* applies in relation to a distribution to which *ICTA 1988, s 732* (reduction in price of shares purchased by dealers) also applies, any reduction, under that section, in the purchase price of the shares is to be adjusted 'as seems appropriate to the Board'. [*ICTA 1988, s 736(5)*].

Simon's Direct Tax Service. See **B3.730.**

4.3 TREASURY CONSENTS — TRANSFER ETC. OF SECURITIES TO NON-RESIDENTS [*ICTA 1988, ss 765–767; FA 1988, s 105(6); FA 1990, s 68*]

Consent must be obtained from the Treasury for a body corporate resident in the UK

(*a*) to cause or permit a non-resident body corporate over which it has 'control' to create or issue any share or debenture; or

(*b*) to transfer, or cause or permit to be transferred, to any person any share or debenture of a non-resident body corporate over which it has 'control' (or a beneficial interest in such share or debenture), if the resident body has an interest in such share or debenture. [*ICTA 1988, s 765(1)(c)(d)*].

'*Control*' is the power to secure that the affairs of a body corporate are conducted in accordance with the wishes of the resident body, whether by shareholding, voting power or powers given by Articles of Association etc., and whether directly or through another body corporate. If the non-resident body would be a partnership if resident in the UK, the resident body has control if it is entitled to more than half of the income or assets of the non-resident body. [*ICTA 1988, ss 767(5), 840*].

Exemptions apply as follows.

(i) The giving by a non-resident body corporate to its bankers of any security for moneys due or to become due from one to the other by reason of a transaction entered into between them in the normal course of the latter's business as bankers (see (*a*) above). [*ICTA 1988, s 765(2)*].

(ii) The giving by a non-resident body corporate to an 'insurance company' of any security for moneys due or to become due from one to the other by reason of a transaction entered into between them in the ordinary course of the latter's business by way of investment of its 'funds' (see (*a*) above). [*ICTA 1988, s 765(3)*].

For this purpose '*insurance company*' means a body corporate lawfully carrying on business as an insurer, and '*funds*' means the funds held by it in connection with that business. [*ICTA 1988, s 767(5)*].

(iii) The transfer of shares to qualify a person to act as a director (exempted from (*b*) above). [*ICTA 1988, s 765(1)(d)*].

(iv) Neither (*a*) nor (*b*) above applies to a transaction which is a movement of capital within *Directive No 88/361/EEC, Article 1* (which, from 1 January 1994, is extended to such movements within the European Economic Area). Where but for this exemption a transaction would be unlawful (in particular, where it is not within the general consents), the UK resident company must

(A) within six months of the transaction give to the Board such information relating to the transaction or to persons connected with it as the Board may by regulation require (see *SI 1990 No 1671*), and

(B) give to the Board such further particulars as the Board may by notice require, within 60 days.

Penalties of up to £3,000 (and £600 per day for continued failure) may be imposed under *TMA 1970, s 98* for failure to comply with the above requirements. [*ICTA 1988, s 765A; FA 1990, s 68; SI 1990 No 1671*].

Revenue Pamphlet IR 131, SP 2/92, 28 February 1992, sets out the views of the Treasury and the Inland Revenue where there may be doubt as to whether a transaction is a movement of capital to which *Article 1* relates, and gives guidance on the procedure for making a report as required under (A) above. See also Revenue Tax Bulletin April 2000 p 746.

Granting of consent. The Treasury may give a general consent or confine it to specified transactions of, or relating to, a specified body corporate ('special' consent). Conditions may be imposed in either case and a general consent may be revoked. The consent 'shall be published in such a way as to give any person entitled to the benefit of it an adequate opportunity of getting to know of it, unless in the opinion of the Treasury publication is not necessary for that purpose'. [*ICTA 1988, s 765(4)*].

A list of the General Consents is available from the Inland Revenue Information Centre, SW Wing, Bush House, Strand, London WC2B 4RD (and see Revenue Tax Bulletin April 2000 p 746 as regards the application in practice of their requirements). Notes for guidance on applications for Special Treasury Consent may be obtained from the same address.

Applications (including three copies of all letters) are normally sent to The Secretary, HM Treasury (AP), Parliament Street, London SW1P 3AG (tel. 020–7270 3000), but in urgent cases two copies of all letters (with all the accounts and supporting documents) may be sent to Inland Revenue International Division, Room 311, Melbourne House, Aldwych, London WC2B 4LL (in which case the one letter sent to the Treasury should indicate clearly that copies have been sent to the Revenue).

Penalties. Any person who knowingly and actively participates in an offence under this section is liable to imprisonment for two years or to a fine of £10,000 or to both. If the offender is a body corporate, the maximum fine is £10,000 or three times the amount of tax attributable to the income, profits or gains (including chargeable gains) arising in the three years immediately preceding the commission of the offence, whichever is the greater. [*ICTA 1988, s 766(1)(3)*].

Proceedings under this section may not be instituted in England or Wales without the consent of the Attorney-General, or in Northern Ireland without the consent of the Attorney-General for Northern Ireland. In any proceedings against a director (or purported director) of the resident body corporate, he is assumed to be a party to any act of that body, unless he proves that it was done without his consent or connivance, and to have known that such an act would result in an offence under this section, unless he proves the contrary. [*ICTA 1988, s 766(2)(4)*].

See 49 PENALTIES.

Company becoming non-resident. See 53.6, 53.7 RESIDENCE.

Simon's Direct Tax Service. See **D4.113** *et seq.*.

4.4 TRANSFER PRICING

Accounting periods ending before 1 July 1999. Where either the buyer or the seller (each being a 'body of persons' or a partnership) is controlled by the other party to the contract, or both are controlled by the same person(s), any sale (including letting and hiring of property, grant or transfer of rights or licences, or giving of business facilities) at a price other than market price at the time of completion (or, if earlier, of giving possession) may (if the Board so directs) be adjusted by the Revenue as follows

(*a*) if the price is **below** market price, the latter is substituted in computing the *seller's* profits unless the buyer, being a UK resident trader, is entitled to deduct the price paid in computing his own profits;

(*b*) if the price is **above** market price, the latter is substituted in computing the *buyer's* profits unless the seller, being a UK resident trader, would have to bring in, as a trade receipt, the price received.

The extension of these provisions to the 'giving of business facilities' is capable of bringing the making of interest-free loans within their scope (*Ametalco UK v CIR; Ametalco Ltd v CIR (Sp C 94), [1996] SSCD 399*).

'*Control*', for this purpose, means the power of a person by shareholding or voting power (whether direct or through another company) or under Articles of Association, to secure that the company's affairs are conducted according to that person's wishes. For this purpose, there may be attributed to a person the powers of

(i) his nominees;

(ii) his spouse;

(iii) the brother, sister, ancestor or lineal descendant of himself or of his spouse;

(iv) the spouse of a person within (iii);

(v) any person with whom he is in partnership;

(vi) the spouse, brother, sister, ancestor or lineal descendant of any person within (v);

(vii) the nominees of any person within (ii) to (vi).

If the person is the trustee of a settlement, he is deemed to have the powers of any settlor, and of any individual or body corporate connected with that settlor. See 16 CONNECTED PERSONS. As to trustee holdings, see *Lithgows CS 1960, 39 TC 270.*

In the case of partnerships, 'control' includes the right to a share of more than one-half of the firm's assets or profits. [*ICTA 1988, s 773, s 839(1)–(4)(8), s 840; FA 1995, Sch 17 para 20*].

The Board may, by notice in writing given to any body corporate, require it to supply, within such time (not being less than 30 days) as may be specified in the notice, such particulars as may be so specified of any 'related transaction' which appears to the Board

(A) to be, or to be connected with, a transaction which might fall within the section;

(B) to be relevant in determining whether a direction under the section could or should be given;

(C) to be relevant in determining the market price of any property sold.

A '*related transaction*' is one to which the body corporate to which notice is given (or a body corporate 'associated' with it) was a party. Bodies corporate are '*associated*' if one is controlled by the other or both are controlled by the same person or persons.

Where the Board feels that a direction might be given in respect of a transaction each party to which is a 51% subsidiary of the same UK parent, one being non-resident, notice may be served on the parent requiring access to the books, accounts etc. of the parent or of its subsidiaries which relate to that transaction. The parent has a right of appeal first to the Board and then, within 30 days of the Board's rejection, to the Special Commissioners.

An inspector may in certain circumstances and with the Board's authority enter premises to examine books, etc. [*ICTA 1988, s 772(1)–(7)*].

Where a direction is given, all necessary adjustments are made, by assessment, repayment or otherwise, to give effect to it. [*ICTA 1988, s 770(3)*]. This applies equally to adjustment of open assessments (*Glaxo Group Ltd and others v CIR CA 1995, 68 TC 166*). Appeals involving questions arising from directions are to that extent to be referred to and determined by the Special Commissioners. [*ICTA 1988, s 772(8)*].

Nothing in *section 770* is to affect the operation of any provision of *CAA 1990*. [*ICTA 1988, s 773(1)*].

In 1995 and 1996, the OECD published its report 'Transfer Pricing Guidelines for Multinational Enterprises and Tax Administrations' and supplementary material, containing guidelines on the general principles to be applied in determining transfer prices for tax purposes. These can be purchased from HMSO outlets. An article in the Revenue Tax Bulletin October 1996 pp 345–349 sets out the Revenue's position on those guidelines and also provides some practical guidance on the operation of the Mutual Agreement Procedure contained in UK double taxation conventions.

An Inland Revenue leaflet 'The Transfer Pricing of Multinational Enterprises' is also available from the Board, drawing attention to the UK provisions and to the Board's powers.

See 23.17 EXCHANGE GAINS AND LOSSES as regards interaction with these provisions.

Accounting periods ending on or after 1 July 1999. For accounting periods ending **on or after 1 July 1999**, for which corporate self-assessment applies, and subject to transitional arrangements (see below), *ICTA 1988, ss 770–773* are replaced by a new *ICTA 1988, s 770A, Sch 28AA*. [*FA 1998, s 108(1)(2)(5), Sch 16 ; SI 1998 No 3173*]. *Schedule 28AA* is to be construed so as best to secure consistency between the effect given to the basic rules of the *Schedule* (under *paragraph 1*, see below) and the principles of the OECD model tax convention and transfer pricing guidelines. [*ICTA 1988, Sch 28AA para 2*]. The guidelines are currently published by the OECD as 'Transfer Pricing Guidelines for Multinational Enterprises and Tax Administrations', and can be purchased from HMSO outlets. An article in the Revenue Tax Bulletin October 1996 pp 345–349 sets out the Revenue's views on those guidelines and provides practical guidance on the operation of the mutual agreement procedure contained in UK double taxation conventions. See also the Revenue leaflet 'The Transfer Pricing of Multinational Enterprises'.

Schedule 28AA applies where provision (the '*actual provision*') has been made or imposed as between two persons (the '*affected persons*') by means of a transaction or series of transactions, and at the time the provision was made or imposed either

(I) one of the affected persons was directly or indirectly participating in the management, control or capital of the other, or

(II) there was a person or persons who was or were directly or indirectly participating in the management, control or capital of each of the affected persons.

Except as below, if the actual provision differs from the provision which would have been made at arm's length as between independent enterprises (or if no provision would have been so made) and confers a 'potential advantage' in relation to UK taxation on one of the affected persons or (whether or not the same advantage) on each of them, the profits and losses (and certain items treated as losses) of the potentially advantaged person, or of each of them, are computed for tax purposes as if the arm's length provision had been made or imposed (or, as the case may be, no provision made) instead of the actual provision.

A 'transaction' for these purposes includes schemes or arrangements of any kind, understandings and mutual practices (whether or not legally enforceable), and a 'series' of transactions includes a number of transactions entered into in pursuance of, or in relation to, the same scheme or arrangement. A series of transactions is not prevented from being regarded as the means by which provision has been made or imposed between two persons by reason only that there is no transaction in the series to which both those persons are parties, or one or more transactions to which neither of them is a party, or that the parties to any scheme or arrangement in pursuance of which the transactions are entered into do not include one or both of them.

A person is for these purposes treated as directly participating in the management, control or capital of another person at a particular time if and only if, at that time, the other person is a body corporate or partnership which that person controls (within *ICTA 1988, s 840*, see 51.4(2)(vii) PURCHASE BY A COMPANY OF ITS OWN SHARES). Similarly indirect participation requires that the person (the '*potential participant*') either would be taken to be participating directly if certain rights and powers (see *ICTA 1988, Sch 28AA para 4(3)–(6)(10)–(12)*), including future rights and powers, were attributed to him, or is one of a number of 'major participants' in the other person's enterprise. A person is a '*major participant*' in another person's enterprise when the other person is a body corporate or partnership, and he is one of two persons who control (as above) the other person, each of whom has at least 40% of the holdings, etc. giving that control (again after attribution of certain rights and powers as above).

The actual provision confers a '*potential advantage*' on a person in relation to UK taxation where its effect, compared to that of the corresponding arm's length provision, would be a reduction in chargeable profits or increase in losses (or conversion of profits into losses) of that person for any chargeable period. Where, however, the following conditions are satisfied in relation to each of the persons as between whom an actual provision was made, no such potential advantage is conferred on either of them (except in the case of 'ring-fenced trades', see below):

(*aa*) they are within the charge to income or corporation tax in respect of profits arising from the activities in relation to which the actual provision was made or imposed (and not exempt in respect of all or any part of the income or profits from those activities), and where it is an income tax charge which applies, they are UK-resident for all chargeable periods for which it so applies;

(*bb*) they neither have an entitlement to a foreign tax credit in any chargeable period in relation to profits from such activities, nor would have any such entitlement if there were any such profits or if they exceeded a certain amount;

(*cc*) the amounts taken into account in computing profits or losses from such activities for any chargeable period in relation to which (*aa*) above is satisfied do not include any income from which a deduction is made for foreign tax (where no credit is allowable); and

(*dd*) (in the case of a person who is an insurance company within *ICTA 1988, s 431*) the profits from such activities in respect of which the company is within the charge to corporation tax do not include any in the computation of which acquisition expenses have been brought into account under *FA 1989, s 86* (see 41.2 LIFE INSURANCE COMPANIES) or in relation to which a lower rate of tax is fixed by *FA 1989, s 88* or *s 88A* (see 41.7 LIFE INSURANCE COMPANIES).

[*ICTA 1988, Sch 28AA paras 1–5, 14*].

Elimination of double counting. Where a potential advantage is conferred (as above) on only one of the affected persons (the '*advantaged person*'), and the other person (the '*disadvantaged person*') is within (*aa*) above (or would be if any exemption from tax were disregarded), then (except as below) the disadvantaged person may claim application of the arm's length provision rather than the actual provision (over-riding any applicable time limits for the necessary adjustments). Such a claim may only be made if the arm's length provision has similarly been applied in the case of the advantaged person (in his return or following a determination, see below), and the computations in the case of each of them on that basis must be consistent. The claim must be made within two years of the making of the return or the giving of the notice taking account of the determination, as the case may be, and a claim based on a return which is subsequently the subject of such a notice may be amended within two years of the giving of the notice. (These time limits may be extended in certain cases where the Board fails to give proper notice to disadvantaged persons, see below.)

Where such a claim is made, it is assumed, as respects any foreign tax credit which has been or may be given to the disadvantaged person, that that foreign tax does not include tax which would not be or have become payable if the arm's length provision had also been substituted for the purposes of that tax, and that the profits from the activities in relation to which the actual provision was made or imposed and in respect of which the tax credit relief arises are reduced to the same extent as they are treated as reduced by virtue of the claim.

Where the application of the arm's length provision in a computation following such a claim involves a reduction in the amount of any income, and that income also falls to be treated as reduced under *ICTA 1988, s 811(1)* by an amount of foreign tax (where credit relief is not available), the former reduction is treated as made before the latter, and the deductible foreign tax excludes that paid on so much of the income as is represented by the amount of the former reduction.

Any adjustment to double tax reliefs as above may be given effect by set-off against any relief or repayment arising from the claim, and may be made without regard to any time limit on assessments or amendments.

[*ICTA 1988, Sch 28AA paras 6, 7*].

Capital allowances and capital gains. These provisions do not affect the computation of capital allowances or balancing charges under *CAA 1990*, or of capital gains or allowable losses under *TCGA 1992*, and do not require any income or losses to be treated as on capital rather than revenue account. [*ICTA 1988, Sch 28AA para 13*].

Determinations requiring the sanction of the Board. A determination of an amount falling to be brought into account under these provisions, other than in certain cases where an agreement has been reached between the Board and the person concerned (see *FA 1998, s 110(5)–(7)*), requires the Board's sanction. Where such a determination is made for the purpose of giving a closure notice, giving a notice amending a partnership assessment or making a discovery assessment, and the notice of the closure, amendment or discovery assessment is given to any person without the determination, so far as taken into account in the notice or assessment, having been approved by the Board, or without a copy of the Board's approval having been served on that person at or before the time the notice was given, the closure or amendment notice or discovery assessment is deemed to have been given or made (and in the case of an assessment notified) as if the determination had not been taken into account. The approval must apply specifically to the case in question and the amount determined, but may otherwise be given (either before or after the making of the determination) in any such form or manner as the Board may determine. An appeal relating to a determination approved by the Board may not question the Board's approval except to the extent that the grounds for questioning the approval are the same as the grounds for questioning the determination itself. [*FA 1998, s 110*]. For the requirement that the Revenue give notice of determinations to persons who it appears to them may be 'disadvantaged persons' (as above) by reference to the subject-matter of the determination, see *FA 1998, s 111*.

Appeals. An appeal against an amendment of a return, the refusal of a claim or a discovery assessment or determination involving the application of *Schedule 28AA* lies to the Special Commissioners. Where the appeal relates to any provision as between two persons each within (*aa*) above, each person is entitled to appear before and be heard by the Special Commissioners, or to make written representations to them, and the Commissioners must determine that aspect of the appeal separately from any other, that separate determination being treated as made in an appeal to which each of those persons was a party. [*ICTA 1988, Sch 28AA para 12*].

Miscellaneous. Amounts brought into account in respect of EXCHANGE GAINS AND LOSSES (23) and FINANCIAL INSTRUMENTS (25) adjustments are not subject to application of an arm's length provision as above, but this does not affect the application of *Schedule 28AA* for the purposes of *FA 1993, ss 136, 136A* in the case of certain loan interest (see 23.17 EXCHANGE GAINS AND LOSSES). [*ICTA 1988, Sch 28AA para 8*]. There are also special provisions relating to transactions involving oil and gas [*ICTA 1988, Sch 28AA paras 9, 10*] and to 'ring-fenced' oil and gas exploration activities (see 46.3 OIL COMPANIES). [*ICTA 1988, Sch 28AA para 11*].

The provisions apply to unit trust schemes (see 60.1 UNIT AND INVESTMENT TRUSTS) as if they were bodies corporate, with appropriate modification. [*ICTA 1988, Sch 28AA para 14(5)*].

Transitional provisions. Schedule 28AA does not apply in the case of any potentially disadvantaged person as respects the consequences, at any time before 17 March 2001, of the difference between an actual and an arm's length provision if:

(1) the actual provision is made or imposed under contractual arrangements entered into by that person before 17 March 1998;

(2) the control requirement in (I) or (II) above (as the case may be) is satisfied in the case of the actual provision and that person only by his indirect participation as a major participant in the other person's enterprise (see above);

(3) that person's rights and obligations under the actual provision have not been varied or continued by a transaction entered into after 17 March 1998 and before that time; and

(4) that person is not, and has not been, a party to any transaction by virtue of which he could, in the period between 17 March 1998 and that time, have secured the variation or termination of those rights and obligations.

[*FA 1998, s 108(6)*].

The Revenue International Division, Room 311, Melbourne House, Aldwych, London WC2B 4LL may be approached for pre-transaction guidance on the likely tax treatment in particular cases when financial arrangements are in the process of being put in place. See Revenue Tax Bulletin October 1998 pp 579–582, 587, 588 for general guidance on the record-keeping required for self-assessment under the above provisions and on the application of the provisions to financial transactions and arrangements; December 1998 pp 603–605 for guidance on penalties under those provisions; and April 2000 pp 740–742 for the practical implications of the new regime for non-UK resident landlords.

Advance pricing agreements. A taxpayer may apply to the Board for an agreement, on a prospective basis, on the resolution of complex transfer pricing issues relating to any one or more of the following matters which fall, or might fall, to be determined.

(*a*) The attribution of income to a branch or agency through which the taxpayer has been carrying on, or is proposing to carry on, a trade in the UK.

(*b*) The attribution of income to any permanent establishment of the taxpayer (wherever situated) through which he has been carrying on, or is proposing to carry on, any business.

(*c*) The extent to which income which has arisen or which may arise to the taxpayer is to be taken for any purpose to be income arising outside the UK.

(*d*) The treatment for tax purposes of any provision operating between the taxpayer and any 'associate' of his. Persons are '*associates*' for this purpose if (as in (I) and (II) above in relation to *Schedule 28AA*) one directly or indirectly participates, at the time of the making or imposition of the provision, in the management, control or capital of the other, or the same person or persons so participate in the management, control or capital of each of them (with further special provision in relation to sales of oil).

(*e*) The treatment for tax purposes of any provision operating between a 'ring fence trade' carried on by the taxpayer and any other activities the taxpayer carries on. A '*ring fence trade*' for this purpose is a trade which is treated as a separate trade under *ICTA 1988, s 492(1)* (oil extraction activities, see 46.3 OIL COMPANIES), or would be so treated if a different trade were also carried on.

The application must set out the taxpayer's understanding of what would, in his case, be the effect, in the absence of any agreement, of the provisions in relation to which clarification is sought, and in what respects clarification is required. He must also propose how the clarification might be effected in a manner consistent with that understanding.

Where the Board and the taxpayer have entered into such an agreement (an 'advance pricing agreement' or 'APA') in relation to a chargeable period, then (except as below) any questions relating to those matters are, to the extent provided for in the APA, to be determined in accordance with the APA rather than by reference to the legislative provisions which would otherwise have applied. However, where the relevant matter falls within (*d*) or (*e*) above and not within (*a*), (*b*) or (*c*) above, the only legislative provisions which can be displaced are those contained in *Schedule 28AA* (as above). Where an APA relating to a chargeable period beginning or ending before the date of the APA provides for the manner in which consequent adjustments are to be made, those adjustments are to be made in the manner provided for in the APA.

An APA does not, however, have effect in relation to the determination of any question which relates to:

(i) a time after that from which an officer of the Board has revoked the APA in accordance with its terms; or

(ii) a time after or in relation to which any provision of the APA has not been complied with, where the APA was conditional upon compliance with that provision; or

(iii) any matter as respects which any other essential conditions have not been, or are no longer, satisfied.

The APA must contain a declaration that it is made for the purposes of *FA 1999, s 85*. It may be made on or after 27 July 1999 and may apply in relation to any chargeable period ending on or after that date (and this may include periods ending before the date of the APA). It is for the Board to ensure that the APA is modified so as to be consistent with any double taxation arrangements.

Where the APA makes provision for its modification or revocation by the Board, this may take effect from such time (including a time before the modification or revocation) as the Board may determine.

Any party to an APA must provide the Board with all such reports and other information as he may be required to provide under the APA or by virtue of any request made by an officer of the Board in accordance with its terms.

An APA is deemed never to have been made where, before it was made, the taxpayer fraudulently or negligently provided the Board with false or misleading information in relation to the application for the APA or in connection with its preparation, and the Board notifies the taxpayer that the APA is nullified by reason of the misrepresentation. A penalty not exceeding £10,000 may apply for so giving such false or misleading information.

[*FA 1999, ss 85, 86*].

Effect of APA on third parties. Where an APA has effect in relation to any provision between the taxpayer and another person, then in applying the 'double counting' rules (see above) of *Schedule 28AA* to the other person, the arrangements set out in the APA similarly apply in determining any question as to

(A) whether the taxpayer is a person on whom a potential advantage in relation to UK taxation is conferred by the actual provision, or

(B) what constitutes the arm's length provision in relation to the actual provision.

This is subject to any APA made between the Board and the other person. The notice requirements of *FA 1998, s 111* are correspondingly amended.

[*FA 1999, s 87*].

For a detailed explanation of how APAs are administered, see Revenue Pamphlet IR 131, SP 3/99, 31 August 1999. The contact address for APA applications and other information is Andrew Hickman, Business Tax Group (APA), Inland Revenue, International Division, Victory House, 30–34 Kingsway, London WC2B 6ES (tel. 020–7438 6916; fax 020–7438

7629) or, where oil taxation is involved, Janice Cross, Deputy Director (APAs), Inland Revenue, Oil Taxation Office, Melbourne House, Aldwych, London WC2B 4LL (tel. 020–7438 7579; fax 020–7438 6910). See also Revenue Tax Bulletin October 1999 pp 697, 698 for a note on the scope of agreements, and for procedural guidance relating to bilateral agreements in the light of the Revenue's experiences and observations in concluding agreements with treaty partners under double tax treaty mutual agreement procedures.

Arbitration Convention. The Convention (*90/463/EEC*) on the elimination of double taxation in connection with the adjustment of profits of associated enterprises requires Member States to adopt certain procedures and to follow the opinion of an advisory commission in certain cases of dispute relating to transfer pricing adjustments. The Convention came into force on 1 January 1995 and will continue in force until 31 December 2004, with automatic five-year extensions thereafter unless the signatory States decide otherwise (see Revenue Tax Bulletin August 1998 pp 575, 576). *ICTA 1988, s 815B* makes provision for domestic legislation and agreements to be over-ridden where necessary under the Convention, and *ICTA 1988, s 816(2A)* and *FA 1989, s 182A* provide the necessary information powers and confidentiality requirements in relation to disclosures of information to an advisory commission. [*F(No 2)A 1992, s 51*]. See Revenue Tax Bulletin October 1997 pp 465–467 for guidance on Arbitration Convention procedures. Enquiries about the application of the Convention may be made to Andrew Hickman, Inland Revenue, International Division, Victory House, 30–34 Kingsway, London WC2B 6ES (tel. 020–7438 6916, fax. 020–7438 7629) or, in relation to sales of oil, etc., to Janice Cross, Oil Taxation Office, Melbourne House, Aldwych, London WC2B 4LL (tel. 020–7438 7579, fax. 020–7438 6910).

Simon's Direct Tax Service. See B3.927.

4.5 TRANSACTIONS OF CERTAIN DEALING AND NON-DEALING COMPANIES [*ICTA 1988, s 774*]

This section applies if a company dealing in securities, land or buildings is entitled to a deduction in computing its profits for a payment made to, or for depreciation of a right against, an associated company which does not deal in shares etc. Where the amount of the payment or depreciation is not brought into account in computing the profits or gains of the non-dealing company, the non-dealing company is charged to tax under Schedule D, Case VI. If the non-dealing company carries on a trade, the amount may be charged as part of its normal trading income, if the company so elects. If it carries on a number of trades, the amount may be allotted to whichever trade the non-dealing company chooses.

A payment made in respect of abortive expenditure of a non-dealing company carrying on (or formed to carry on) a trade is excluded.

The amount is deemed to have been received on the last day of the dealing company's accounting period.

The Board has powers to require information of any person who may have incurred liability under this section.

Simon's Direct Tax Service. See D2.512.

4.6 PAYMENTS OF INTEREST ETC. BETWEEN RELATED COMPANIES [*ICTA 1988, s 341*]

For accounting periods ending before 1 April 1996, where a company makes a payment to a 'related' company, and the payment is a charge on income of the paying company and chargeable to tax under Schedule D, Case III in the hands of the receiving company, the payment is to be treated for corporation tax purposes as received by the recipient company on the same day as that on which it is for those purposes treated as paid by the paying company. Two companies are 'related' for this purpose if

(*a*) one company controls the other (within *ICTA 1988, s 840*, see 51.4(2)(vii) PURCHASE BY A COMPANY OF ITS OWN SHARES) or another person controls both of them, or

(*b*) one company is a '51% subsidiary' (see 29.3 GROUPS OF COMPANIES) of the other or both are 51% subsidiaries of a third company.

See also 31.4 INCOME TAX IN RELATION TO A COMPANY as regards return and set-off of such payments.

Section 341 is repealed for accounting periods ending after 31 March 1996. [*FA 1996, Sch 14 para 17*]. See now 43 LOAN RELATIONSHIPS.

Simon's Direct Tax Service. See D2.613.

4.7 **OWN SHARE PURCHASES ETC. AND OTHER SPECIAL DIVIDENDS** [*FA 1997, s 69, Sch 7; F(No 2)A 1997, s 25(5)–(7), Sch 6 para 21*]

The special treatment described below applies to 'qualifying distributions' (see 20.18 DISTRIBUTIONS), made after 7 October 1996 by UK-resident companies, which fall within either or both of the following.

(*a*) Payments made on the redemption, repayment or purchase by the company of its own shares, or on the purchase of rights to acquire its own shares (see 51 PURCHASE BY A COMPANY OF ITS OWN SHARES).

(*b*) Distributions in relation to which there are any kind of arrangements by virtue of which one or more of the 'specified matters' is or was to any extent made in any way referable to, or to the carrying out of, a transaction in securities (within *ICTA 1988, s 703*, see Tolley's Income Tax under Anti-Avoidance). This does not apply where that transaction was completed before 8 October 1996 unless some or all of the arrangements were made on or after that date. The '*specified matters*' are whether the distribution is made, the time it is made, its form and its amount.

Subject to the exceptions and modifications referred to below, such distributions made **before 6 April 1999** are treated as FOREIGN INCOME DIVIDENDS (26) ('FIDs') with effect from 8 October 1996, over-riding the election for such treatment under *ICTA 1988, s 246A* (see 26.2 FOREIGN INCOME DIVIDENDS). The dividend certificate must state that the distribution is a FID by virtue of these provisions. See 29.2 GROUPS OF COMPANIES for the circumstances in which a group income election may apply to a distribution within these provisions.

Distributions treated as income of trustees. Where a distribution within (*a*) above is or has been made to trustees (other than trustees of a unit trust scheme within *ICTA 1988, s 469* (see 60.2 UNIT AND INVESTMENT TRUSTS)), the 'relevant part' (and a corresponding part of the deemed FID) is treated as income within *ICTA 1988, s 686* to which the 34% discretionary trust rate accordingly applies. This has effect from 1997/98, and is deemed to have had effect for 1996/97, but only for distributions made on or after 5 December 1996. The '*relevant part*' of the distribution is so much (if any) as does not fall to be treated as income of the settlor and is not income either.

(i) within *section 686(2)(a)* (i.e. income to be accumulated or which is payable at the trustees' or any other person's discretion), or

(ii) arising under a trust established for charitable purposes only, or

(iii) from investments or deposits or other property held for pension purposes (as under *section 686(2)(c)*).

There are consequential changes to *section 686* to ensure that appropriate relief is given for trust management expenses. For these and generally, see Tolley's Income Tax under Settlements.

Exceptions. The following distributions are excluded from the application of these provisions in the circumstances described.

(1) *Stock options.* A distribution is not within (*b*) above solely because it is made in consequence of an election in respect of a stock dividend option (see Tolley's Income Tax under Stock Dividends).

(2) *Fixed rate preference share dividends.* A dividend on a fixed rate preference share (as defined) is not within (*b*) above by reason only that a specified matter is made referable to the issue terms.

(3) *Pre-sale distributions.* An 'excepted pre-sale distribution' is not within (*b*) above if the only transactions in securities to which any of the specified matters are referable are 'relevant transactions'.

A distribution is an '*excepted pre-sale distribution*' if, on or within 14 days of the making of the distribution, there is a '*major change in the ownership*' of the distributing company, i.e. if a single person acquires a holding of, or two or more persons between them acquire holdings together amounting to, 75% or more of its ordinary share capital. A '*relevant transaction*' is any transaction in securities by which any such holding is acquired. In comparing a person's holdings at any two dates, he is to be treated at the later date as having acquired whatever he did not hold at the earlier date, irrespective of intervening acquisitions and disposals. It is beneficial ownership which is considered, and comparisons are made in percentage terms throughout. Acquisitions of shares on death are left out of account, as is any gift which was unsolicited and made without regard to these provisions. Where the existence of extraordinary rights or powers renders ownership of the ordinary share capital an inappropriate test of change of ownership, holdings of all kinds, or of any particular kind, of share capital, voting power or any other special kind of power may be taken into account instead.

(4) *Manufactured dividends.* Payment of an amount consisting of a manufactured dividend (within *ICTA 1988, Sch 23A*, see Tolley's Income Tax under Anti-Avoidance) is generally excluded from the operation of these provisions. However, where that amount is representative of a distribution to which these provisions apply, the payment is deemed to be such a distribution, except insofar as *Schedule 23A* makes different provision in relation to the payment. Where the distribution of which that amount is representative is within (*a*) above, the payment is treated for the purposes of *Schedule 23A* as representative of a dividend on the shares concerned in the redemption, etc..

See also 29.2 GROUPS OF COMPANIES as regards exclusion from these provisions of certain distributions subject to a group income election.

Dealers in securities. For the treatment of distributions within these provisions received by dealers in securities, see 51.7 PURCHASE BY A COMPANY OF ITS OWN SHARES.

Authorised unit trusts. For the treatment of distributions within these provisions in the distribution accounts of authorised unit trusts, see 60.1 UNIT AND INVESTMENT TRUSTS.

For the Revenue's views on the scope of these provisions, with a number of illustrative examples, see Revenue Tax Bulletin June 1997 pp 429–434.

These provisions are repealed for distributions made after 5 April 1999.

Simon's Direct Tax Service. See **D1.110A**.

4.8 CHANGE IN OWNERSHIP OF A COMPANY

There are a number of anti-avoidance provisions relating to the change in ownership of a company which are dealt with as indicated below.

3.10	ADVANCE CORPORATION TAX [*ICTA 1988, s 245*].
9.6, 9.23, 9.35, 9.47–9.52	CAPITAL GAINS (reconstructions, amalgamations, pre–entry losses and group transactions) [*TCGA 1992, ss 176–179*].
29.20, 29.22, 29.23	GROUPS OF COMPANIES [*ICTA 1988, ss 403A–403C, 409, 410*].
40.5	INVESTMENT COMPANIES [*ICTA 1988, ss 768B, 768C, Sch 28A*].
44.13	LOSSES (restrictions on losses carried forward) [*ICTA 1988, ss 768–769*].
48.4	PAYMENT OF TAX (change in ownership of company) [*ICTA 1988, ss 767A, 767B*].

5 Assessments and Appeals

Simon's Direct Tax Service D2.7.

5.1 Assessments to tax for accounting periods **prior to the introduction of self-assessment** (see below) are made by inspectors and notices of assessment are served which must also state the date of issue and the time limit for making appeals (see below). [*TMA 1970, s 29(1)(2)(5); F(No 2)A 1975, s 44(5); FA 1998, Sch 19 para 12*]. For basis of assessment, see 2.1 ACCOUNTING PERIODS.

Following the introduction of the 'Pay and File' system of corporation tax returns and payments (see 54.1 RETURNS) for accounting periods ending after 30 September 1993, assessments are in general issued in agreed figures, although they are still needed to finalise the position unless no liability arises.

Estimated assessments are still on occasion appropriate or necessary. The main occasions envisaged by the Revenue are:

(*a*) when a return has been filed and either side wishes a contentious matter to proceed to appeal, or it is apparent that significant further tax is due which the company neither pays nor reflects in an amended return;

(*b*) when a company has failed to file a return (assessment generally being considered about 18 months after the end of the accounting period);

(*c*) when it seems unlikely that the liability will be agreed before the expiry of the normal time limit for raising assessments. (Revenue Tax Bulletin February 1993 p 53).

Self-assessment. For accounting periods ending **on or after 1 July 1999**, a system of self-assessment is introduced. See 55 SELF-ASSESSMENT. *FA 1998, Sch 18 paras 41–49* (see 55.8 SELF-ASSESSMENT) provide the necessary powers and procedures where a loss of tax is discovered.

5.2 Notice of appeal against a corporation tax assessment (or Revenue amendment to a self-assessment) must be given, within 30 days after the date of issue of the assessment (or amendment) notice, to the inspector who issued it (or on whose behalf it was issued), and must specify the grounds of appeal. [*TMA 1970, s 31; FA 1994, Sch 19 para 7; FA 1996, Sch 19 para 6, Sch 22 para 4*].

5.3 Appeals may be settled by agreement between the taxpayer and the inspector under *TMA 1970, s 54*. If a formal hearing is necessary the appeal will come before the General Commissioners for the division in which the company carries on its trade or business, or in which its head office or principal place of business is situated, or where it resides (or, if the taxpayer agrees, such other division as the Board may direct), unless the taxpayer elects that the appeal shall be dealt with by the Special Commissioners (and the General Commissioners do not direct otherwise), or the General Commissioners transfer the appeal to the Special Commissioners. [*TMA 1970, s 31(4), s 44(1)(3), s 46(1), Schs 2, 3; FA 1984, s 127, Sch 22 paras 3, 5; FA 1988, s 133(1); FA 1996, Sch 22 paras 6, 10*]. The Lord Chancellor has wide powers to make regulations governing the jurisdiction of the Commissioners and the practice and procedure of appeals before them, including regulations enabling the Special Commissioners to order costs of hearings before them and to publish reports of their decisions. See *SI 1994 Nos 1811–1813* and Tolley's Income Tax under Appeals. [*F(No 2)A 1992, Sch 16 paras 3, 4*].

For accounting periods ending **on or after 1 July 1999**, appeals under the self-assessment provisions of *FA 1998, Sch 18* must specify the grounds of appeal, although on the hearing of the appeal the Commissioners may consider new grounds if they are satisfied that their omission was not wilful or unreasonable. An appeal against

(*a*) a Revenue amendment of a self-assessment during an enquiry to prevent a loss of tax, or of a company tax return on completion of the enquiry where the company fails to amend the return within 30 days, or

(*b*) a Revenue determination, where a return incorrectly states an amount affecting a tax liability of another period or another company, of the amount which ought to have been stated in the return, or

(*c*) an assessment other than a self-assessment

is to the Special Commissioners. Otherwise, subject to *TMA 1970, ss 44–59*, an appeal is to the General Commissioners unless the company elects for it to be heard by the Special Commissioners. The Revenue may, however, refer any such election to the General Commissioners, who must direct that the election be disregarded unless satisfied that the company has arguments to present or evidence to adduce on the merits of the appeal.

[*FA 1998, Sch 18 paras 92–94; FA 1999, Sch 11 para 9; SI 1998 No 3173*].

See generally 55 SELF-ASSESSMENT.

5.4 An appeal against a corporation tax assessment relates to the total profits chargeable, and sources of profit not specified in the assessment may be taken into account in determining the appeal. An estimated assessment was raised on a company showing chargeable profits consisting of building society interest and dividends less charges. The Commissioners' decision on appeal, to increase the assessment to an amount comprising agreed figures for Schedule A income and capital gains less management expenses and charges, was upheld (*Owton Fens Properties Ltd v Redden Ch D 1984, 58 TC 218*).

5.5 For further details see Tolley's Income Tax (under Assessments and under Appeals). For the powers of the Revenue in relation to unpaid tax, see Tolley's Income Tax under Back Duty and Payment of Tax.

6 Banks

Cross-reference. 21.11 DOUBLE TAX RELIEF.

Simon's Direct Tax Service D4.11.

6.1 **Banking businesses** are assessable on their profits under normal taxation provisions with interest on advances to customers included under Schedule D, Case I. For the Schedule D, Case VI charge on certain net receipts arising during compulsory liquidation, see *F(No 2)A 1992, Sch 12.*

See *Pattison v Marine Midland Ltd HL 1983, 57 TC 219*, 23.2 EXCHANGE GAINS AND LOSSES, as regards matching of foreign currency assets and liabilities, and that chapter generally as regards special legislation.

In general, the term 'bank' is defined by reference to the carrying on of a *bona fide* banking business, but for certain purposes it is specially defined as:

(*a*) the Bank of England;

(*b*) an institution authorised under the *Banking Act 1987*;

(*c*) a European authorised institution (within the *Banking Co-ordination (Second Council Directive) Regulations 1992*) in relation to the establishment of a branch of which the requirements of *Sch 2 para 1* of those regulations have been complied with; or

(*d*) an international organisation of which the UK is a member and which is designated as a bank for the particular purpose by Treasury order (e.g. the European Investment Bank, see *SI 1996 No 1179*).

See 6.2 below, 11.9(F), 11.9(3) CHARITIES, 20.18 DISTRIBUTIONS, 31.3(*b*) INCOME TAX IN RELATION TO A COMPANY, 54.10, 54.11 RETURNS. [*ICTA 1988, s 840A; FA 1996, Sch 37 para 1(1)*].

6.2 The normal rules for deduction of tax from payments of **yearly interest** (see 31.3(*b*) INCOME TAX IN RELATION TO A COMPANY) do not apply, for advances made on or after 29 April 1996, to interest payable on an advance from a bank (within *ICTA 1988, s 840A*, see 6.1 above) where the person beneficially entitled to the interest is within the charge to corporation tax in respect of it, or to interest paid by such a bank in the ordinary course of its business. Previously, the exclusion applied to yearly interest payable in the UK on an advance from a bank carrying on a *bona fide* banking business in the UK or paid by such a bank in the ordinary course of such a business. There are transitional provisions preserving relief as regards interest payable or paid on or after 29 April 1996 on an advance made before that day. [*ICTA 1988, s 349(3)(a)(b)(3AA)(3AB); FA 1996, Sch 37 Pt II*]. For what constitutes a *bona fide* banking business, see *Hafton Properties Ltd v McHugh Ch D 1986, 59 TC 420*. See below as regards payments 'in the ordinary course' of business. The bank may be required by an inspector to make a return of interest paid. [*TMA 1970, s 17; FA 1990, s 92*]. See 54.10 RETURNS.

Payments by individuals to certain banks of 'relevant loan interest' are, however, paid under deduction of tax [*ICTA 1988, s 369*] (see 31.5 INCOME TAX IN RELATION TO A COMPANY), and see 6.9 below as regards payment of 'relevant interest' by banks. Where relevant (as above), interest which is a trading receipt of the bank's UK business is treated as payable in the UK, even if the loan agreement permits payment to be made both within and outside the UK. (Revenue Pamphlet IR 131, SP 1/95, 30 January 1995). (This replaces an earlier Statement (C5), and where a taxpayer has taken advantage of the original Statement, it will continue to apply to existing transactions as at the date of the new Statement, where this is to the taxpayer's benefit.) By concession, where a UK bank enters into such a loan agreement after 29 January 1995, the interest is treated as payable in the UK even where it is required under the loan agreement to be paid outside the UK. (Revenue Pamphlet IR 1, C26). Tax relief for interest paid by UK resident branch banks on loans from their non-resident parent banks is restricted by reference to a formula the percentage rates used in which are agreed quarterly with H.M. Inspector of Taxes, City 4 District, City Gate House, Finsbury Square, London EC2A 1RB.

Interest paid by a bank after 28 April 1996 is accepted by the Revenue as being paid 'in the ordinary course of its business' unless either (i) the characteristics of the transaction giving rise to the interest are primarily attributable to an intention to avoid UK tax, or (ii) the borrowing relates to the capital structure of the bank (and this includes borrowings conforming to any of the definitions of tier 1, tier 2 or (subject to transitional provisions) tier 3 capital, whether or not they count towards such capital). Banks not recognised as such by the Revenue before 29 April 1996 continue to have to deduct tax in certain cases. (Revenue Pamphlet IR 131, SP 4/96, 13 May 1996). SP 4/96 replaces an earlier Statement of Practice SP 12/91, issued on 9 October 1991, which had broadly similar effect.

6.3 **Debts of overseas governments, etc.**. Detailed provisions for tax relief for sovereign debt were introduced for accounting periods ending after 19 March 1990, the regulations thereunder being in *SI 1990 No 2529* (as amended by *SI 1993 No 1623*). The overall effect is to restrict the percentage of a debt which may be allowed for any period of account, and to spread the relief for debts sold by allowing losses in annual instalments. [*ICTA 1988, ss 88A, 88B, 88C; FA 1990, s 74*]. These provisions are, however, **abolished** for accounting periods ending **after 31 March 1996**. [*FA 1996, Sch 41 Pt V(3)*]. See now 43 LOAN RELATIONSHIPS.

There is a concessional relief for certain receipts and debts the proceeds of which cannot be remitted to the UK but which form part of profits within Case I or Case II of Schedule D (for which see Tolley's Income Tax under Schedule D, Cases I and II). This concession applies to unremittable interest accrued on a loan made in the normal course of trade by a bank or other financial institution. It does not apply to the principal, or to a loan made in a currency other than the local currency of the country imposing currency restrictions where the interest is paid in the local currency and is available to be re-lent in that currency. (Revenue Pamphlet IR 1, B38).

6.4 Where a banking business is carried on in the UK **by a person not resident** or not ordinarily resident in the UK, the provisions of *ICTA 1988, ss 474, 475* apply. See 53.8 RESIDENCE.

6.5 **Non-resident central banks** as specified by Order in Council are exempt from tax on interest, public annuities and dividends paid out of UK public revenue (but may be taxable thereon if carrying on business in the UK) and also on chargeable gains. [*ICTA 1988, s 516; FA 1996, Sch 7 para 21*]. Profits, income and chargeable gains of the issue departments of the Reserve Bank of **India** and the State Bank of **Pakistan** are exempt. [*ICTA 1988, s 517; TCGA 1992, s 271(8)*].

6.6 **Savings banks** are treated as INVESTMENT COMPANIES (40). For accounting periods ending before 1 April 1996, they are exempt from tax on so much of the income from their funds as is applied in the payment of interest to any depositor (and see now 43 LOAN RELATIONSHIPS). [*ICTA 1988, ss 130, 484(1); FA 1996, Sch 14 para 29*].

6.7 Banks

6.7 For security given in certain circumstances by a non-resident company to its bankers, see 4.3(i) ANTI-AVOIDANCE.

6.8 Contributions to the Deposit Protection Fund are deductible as expenses in computing trading profits, and any repayment of such contribution is treated as a trading receipt. [*Banking Act 1979, s 33*].

6.9 **DEDUCTION OF TAX FROM INTEREST** [*ICTA 1988, ss 480A–482A; FA 1990, Sch 5 paras 7–12; FA 1991, s 75; SI 1990 No 2232; SI 1992 Nos 12–15; F(No 2)A 1992, Sch 8 para 4; SI 1992 No 3234; FA 1993, s 59; SI 1994 No 295; FA 1995, s 86; SI 1995 No 1370; FA 2000, s 111(3)(6), s 145(10)(11)*]

Any 'deposit-taker' paying or crediting interest on a 'relevant deposit' must deduct therefrom a sum representing income tax thereon (at the lower rate (before 1996/97, the basic rate) for the year of assessment in which the payment is made), unless the conditions for gross payment contained in *The Income Tax (Deposit-takers) (Interest Payments) Regulations 1990 (SI 1990 No 2232)* (see below) are met. Income tax chargeable under Schedule D, Case III on such interest is computed on the full amount of the interest arising in the year. *ICTA 1988, s 349* does not apply to such payments.

The deposit-taker must treat all deposits as relevant deposits unless satisfied to the contrary, but if so satisfied may treat a deposit as not being a relevant deposit until he comes into possession of information reasonably indicative that the deposit is, or may be, a relevant deposit.

For these purposes '*deposit-taker*' means the Bank of England, any institution authorised under the *Banking Act 1987* (or municipal bank within that *Act*), the Post Office, any local authority and any other deposit-taker prescribed by Treasury order. From 1 January 1993 a 'European deposit-taker' within *SI 1992 No 3218, reg 82(3)* is included (see *SI 1992 No 3234*). A '*relevant deposit*' (subject to the exclusions below) is a deposit where either:

(*a*) the person beneficially entitled to any interest is an individual (or the persons so entitled are all individuals), or is a Scottish partnership all the partners of which are individuals; or

(*b*) the person entitled to the interest receives it as the personal representative of a deceased individual (but note particularly the ordinary residence requirement at (xii) below); or

(*c*) (from 6 April 1996) the interest arises to the trustees of a discretionary or accumulation trust (as under *ICTA 1988, s 686*, see Tolley's Income Tax under Settlements). This does not apply to deposits made before 6 April 1995 unless the deposit-taker has, since that date but before the making of the payment, been notified by the Board or the trustees that the interest is income of such a trust (and the Board has wide information powers in relation to such notices). The form of notification by the trustees is laid down by *SI 1995 No 1370*, under which payments may continue to be made gross for up to 30 days after receipt of notice (whether by the trustees or by the Revenue) where deduction within that period has not become reasonably practicable. Notification may be cancelled by the Revenue where appropriate. There are transitional provisions treating the source as ceasing where a payment on a deposit made before 6 April 1996 is brought within the scheme before 6 April 1998.

Excluded are:

(i) deposits in respect of which a certificate of deposit (as defined in *ICTA 1988, s 56(5)*) has been issued for £50,000 or more (or foreign equivalent at the time the deposit is made) and which are repayable within five years;

(ii) non-transferable deposits of £50,000 or more (or foreign equivalent at the time the deposit is made) repayable at the end of a specified period of not more than five years;

(iii) a '*qualifying deposit right*', i.e. a right to receive an amount in pursuance of a deposit of money under an arrangement under which no certificate of deposit has been issued, although the person entitled to the right could call for the issue of such a certificate, which otherwise meets the conditions in (i) above.

(iv) debentures (as defined in *Companies Act 1985, s 744*);

(v) loans made by a deposit-taker in the ordinary course of his business;

(vi) debts on securities listed on a recognised stock exchange;

(vii) deposits in a '*general client account deposit*', i.e. a client account, other than an account for specific clients, if the depositor is required by law to make payments representing interest to any of the clients whose money it contains;

(viii) Lloyd's underwriters' premiums trust funds;

(ix) deposits by Stock Exchange money brokers (recognised by the Bank of England) in the course of business as such a broker;

(x) deposits held at non-UK branches of UK resident deposit-takers;

(xi) deposits with non-UK resident deposit-takers held other than in UK branches; and

(xii) deposits in respect of which the 'appropriate person' has declared in writing to the deposit-taker that:

  (1) where (*a*) above applies, the individual (or all of the individuals) concerned is (are), at the time of the declaration, not ordinarily resident in the UK; or

  (2) where (*b*) above applies, the deceased, at the time of his death, was not ordinarily resident in the UK; or

  (3) where (*c*) above applies, at the time of the declaration the trustees are not UK resident and do not have any reasonable grounds for believing that any of the beneficiaries (as defined for this purpose) is a UK ordinarily resident individual or a UK resident company.

The '*appropriate person*' is any person beneficially entitled to the interest, or entitled to receive it in his capacity as a personal representative or trustee, or to whom it is payable. The declaration must be in such form, and contain such information, as is required by the Board, and must include an undertaking to notify the deposit-taker should any individual concerned become ordinarily resident in the UK, or the trustees or any company concerned become resident in the UK, or any UK ordinarily resident individual or UK-resident company become a beneficiary of the trust to which the declaration relates. The Revenue have powers to review all declarations received by a deposit-taker. For payments before 6 April 2001, a certificate by the deposit-taker is required in cases where a declaration of non-ordinary residence does not include the depositor's permanent address, but from that date the address must be included in any such declaration. Declarations in similar terms made to a building society which converts to company status (see 7.6 BUILDING SOCIETIES) are, by concession, treated as having been made to the successor company. (Revenue Pamphlet IR 1, A69).

The deposit-taker has to treat all deposits as relevant deposits unless satisfied to the contrary, but if so satisfied can treat a deposit as not being a relevant deposit until he comes into possession of information reasonably indicative that the deposit is, or might be, a relevant deposit.

The Treasury and the Board are given wide powers to alter the legislation by statutory instrument, in particular in relation to the declaration required at (xii) above.

In the case of depositors who make the appropriate declaration for their deposit to be excluded from being a relevant deposit (see (xii) above) to a deposit-taker other than a bank, the normal deduction rules under *ICTA 1988, s 349(2)* are disapplied by *section 349(3)(h)* (introduced by *FA 1993, s 59*) as they are disapplied in the case of banks by *section 349(3)(a)*.

The collection procedure of *ICTA 1988, Sch 16* (see 31.4 INCOME TAX IN RELATION TO A COMPANY) applies, *mutatis mutandis*, to such payments whether or not the deposit-taker is UK-resident. In outline, returns are required at quarterly intervals, and tax is due without assessment within 14 days of the date for making the return. Income tax suffered by deduction in a return period may be set against liability of the period under these provisions.

The Board has wide regulatory powers for giving effect to these provisions.

The Inland Revenue Financial Intermediaries and Claims Office may be contacted for technical advice in relation to the tax deduction scheme on 0151–472 6156.

Gross payment may be made on relevant deposits where the person beneficially entitled to the interest is UK ordinarily resident and has supplied the appropriate certificate to the deposit-taker to the effect that he is unlikely to be liable to income tax for the year of assessment in which the payment is made or credited (taking into account for this purpose all interest arising in the year of assessment concerned which would, in the absence of such a certificate, be received under deduction of tax). The certificate must be in prescribed form and must contain the name, permanent address, date of birth and (where applicable) national insurance number of the person beneficially entitled to the interest, and the name (and if necessary branch) of the deposit-taker and account number. It must also contain an undertaking to notify the deposit-taker if the person beneficially entitled to the payment becomes liable to income tax for the year in which the payment is made or credited. Revenue Explanatory Leaflet IR 110 outlines the conditions for certification (which are described in detail below) and contains the appropriate Form R85(1990) on which application may be made (and of which further copies may be obtained from banks, building societies, post offices and tax offices).

Such a certificate may only be given by:

(i) a depositor aged 16 or over at the beginning of the year of assessment in which the payment is made or credited, or who attains age 16 during that year, who is beneficially entitled to the payment; or

(ii) the parent or guardian of a person beneficially entitled to the payment who is under 16 at the beginning of that year; or

(iii) a person authorised by power of attorney to administer the financial affairs of the person beneficially entitled to the payment; or

(iv) the parent, guardian, spouse, son or daughter of a mentally handicapped person, or any person appointed by a court to manage the affairs of a mentally handicapped person; or

(v) a person appointed by the Secretary of State to receive benefits on behalf of a person who is for the time being unable to act.

A certificate may not be given where the payment is treated as income of a parent of the person beneficially entitled to the payment, or where the Board has issued a notice in relation to the account concerned requiring deduction of tax (see below).

The certificate must be supplied before the end of the year of assessment in which the payment is made or credited, or, in the case of a certificate given by a person who will attain 16 years of age during a year of assessment, before the end of that year.

A person who gives such a certificate fraudulently or negligently, or fails to comply with any undertaking contained in the certificate, is liable under *TMA 1970, s 99A* (introduced by *FA 1991, s 82*) to a penalty up to £3,000.

Tax deducted from payments in a year prior to receipt of a certificate relating to that year may be refunded, and a like amount recovered by the deposit-taker from the Board, provided that a certificate of deduction of tax has not been furnished to the depositor prior to receipt of the gross payment certificate.

In Revenue Press Release 13 August 1992, the Revenue position as regards incorrect certification for gross payment was explained. In asking those who had registered to reconsider their position (and, if appropriate, to ask for their registration with the bank or building society to be cancelled), the Revenue made clear that where, as a result of their audited sample, cases of incorrect registration were identified, gross payment would cease and tax (and possibly interest and penalties) would be imposed in respect of any interest already received. No interest and penalties would be applied in cases of simple misunderstanding of the position, and a penalty would be considered only where false or fraudulent declarations had knowingly been made on the registration form (or there had been a deliberate failure to cancel the registration).

A certificate ceases to be valid:

(*a*) where the deposit-taker is notified (as above) that the person beneficially entitled to the payment is liable to income tax for the year in which the payment is made;

(*b*) where it was given by a parent or guardian, at the end of the year of assessment in which the person beneficially entitled to the payment attains 16 years of age;

(*c*) where it was given by a person who attained 16 years of age during the year of assessment in which a payment was made or credited, but who was not the holder of the account to which the certificate relates, and that person fails to become the holder before the first payment is made or credited after the end of that year of assessment;

(*d*) where the deposit-taker is notified that the person by or on whose behalf the certificate was given has died; and

(*e*) where the Board, having reason to believe that a person beneficially entitled to a payment of interest has become liable to income tax, give notice requiring the deposit-taker to deduct tax from payments of interest made, more than 30 days after the issue of the notice (or from earlier payments, if practicable), to or for the benefit of that person on a specified account held by or on behalf of that person.

A notice under (*e*) above must be copied to the person to whom it refers, and a further certificate in respect of the account referred to in the notice may not be given by or on behalf of that person (unless the notice is subsequently cancelled, see below).

A notice under (*e*) above may be cancelled (and the deposit-taker and person referred to in the notice so informed) if the Board are satisfied that the person referred to in the notice was not at the date of the notice, and has not since become, liable to income tax, or is no longer so liable.

Certificates of non-liability given to a building society which converts to company status (see 7.6 BUILDING SOCIETIES) are, by concession, treated as having been given to the successor company. (Revenue Pamphlet IR 1, A69).

Tax position of recipient company. The tax deduction scheme described above does not apply to interest on deposits by companies. Such payments by banks are made gross, although payments by other deposit-takers may fall to be made under deduction of tax under *ICTA 1988, s 349(2)*.

Joint accounts. The position as regards certification by each of joint holders of an account is considered separately. Payments are apportioned equally to each joint holder, and tax deducted in respect of that part of a payment to which certification does not apply. The deposit-taker may, however, deduct tax from the whole of payments in respect of joint accounts where certification does not apply to all the joint holders, after giving notice to the Board of its intention to do so (which notice the deposit-taker may subsequently cancel).

Information. The Board may by notice require any deposit-taker (within not less than 14 days) to furnish them with such information (including books, records etc.) as they require, in particular

(I) for verification of payments made without deduction of tax and of the validity of certification for gross payment, and

(II) for verification of the amount of tax deducted from payments of interest (but this does not include copies of books, records etc. from which the depositor can be ascertained).

Copies of the deposit-taker's books, records etc. must be made available when required by the Board. Certificates for gross payment must be retained for at least two years after they expire.

Subject to *FA 1989, s 182(5)*, information obtained under these provisions may not be used other than for the purposes of the provisions or for the ascertainment of the tax liability of the deposit-taker or of the person beneficially entitled to interest paid without deduction of tax to whom the information relates.

The Board may also make regulations providing for the exclusion from its information powers of accounts held by non-UK ordinary residents.

For Revenue audit powers and further information powers, see *SI 1992 Nos 12, 15*.

The Revenue have published a Code of Practice (No 4) setting out their standards for the carrying out of inspections of tax deduction schemes operated by financial intermediaries.

Simon's Direct Tax Service. See D4.1101 *et seq.*.

7 Building Societies

7.1 For years up to and including 1985/86, a building society normally entered into special arrangements with the Revenue. For 1986/87 to 1990/91 inclusive, this system was replaced by regulations made by statutory instrument by the Board, the main such regulations being *The Income Tax (Building Societies) Regulations 1986 (SI 1986 No 482)*. [*ICTA 1988, ss 476–478*].

For 1991/92 and subsequent years, building societies deduct lower rate tax (before 1996/97, basic rate tax) from interest payments unless a certificate is supplied to the effect that the recipient is unlikely to be liable to income tax for the year. [*ICTA 1988, s 477A; FA 1990, s 30, Sch 5*]. Regulations provide for the detailed implementation of the scheme (see *The Income Tax (Building Societies) (Dividends and Interest) Regulations 1990 (SI 1990 No 2231)*).

7.2 For these purposes, a building society is one within the meaning of the Building Societies Act 1986. [*ICTA 1988, s 832(1); Building Societies Act 1986, s 120, Sch 18*].

7.3 **TAX LIABILITY OF A BUILDING SOCIETY ITSELF**

(*a*) A building society deducts lower rate (before 1996/97, basic rate) income tax from certain payments to investors, others being made gross (see 7.4 below). For accounting periods ending after 31 March 1996, liability for interest and dividends is treated as arising under a loan relationship, and so relievable under the LOAN RELATIONSHIPS (43) provisions. Previously, the sum of interest and dividend payments, together with the income tax deducted and accounted for, was allowed as a deduction in computing the society's trading income, but in the case of 'marketable securities' (e.g. permanent interest bearing shares, see 7.4 below), no deduction was allowed for any excess over a reasonable commercial rate on the principal. Terminal bonuses under contractual savings schemes within *ICTA 1988, s 326* are treated in the same way as dividends, and dividends and interest are not treated as distributions of the society or as FRANKED INVESTMENT INCOME (27) of any UK-resident company. [*ICTA 1988, s 477A(3)–(4); FA 1990, Sch 5 paras 2, 4; FA 1991, s 52; FA 1996, Sch 14 para 28*].

The collection procedure of *ICTA 1988, Sch 16* (see 31.4 INCOME TAX IN RELATION TO A COMPANY) applies in the normal way in relation to the income tax deducted by the building society from payments to investors (whether under regulations under *section 477A* or, in the case of 'marketable securities' (see 7.4 below), under *ICTA 1988, s 349(3A)*), except that returns are required for each complete payment quarter (i.e. a quarter ending on the last day of February, May, August and November in an accounting period, and for each part of an accounting period which is not a complete payment quarter. [*SI 1990 No 2231; FA 1991, Sch 11 para 3*]. Relief under *ICTA 1988, Sch 16 para 5* (see 31.4 INCOME TAX IN RELATION TO A COMPANY) for tax borne by deduction may not be claimed more than once in respect of the same deduction. [*FA 1991, Sch 11 para 4*].

These provisions apply also to annuities and other annual payments from which income tax is deductible under *ICTA 1988, s 349(1)*. [*SI 1991 No 512*].

(*b*) See 7.7 below as regards costs of issue of permanent interest bearing shares.

(*c*) For the purpose of corporation tax on chargeable gains, assets disposed of by one society to another on an amalgamation or transfer of engagements are treated as disposed of for a consideration of such amount as would secure that no gain or loss accrues on the disposal. [*TCGA 1992, s 215*].

(*d*) For accounting periods ending before 1 April 1996, the Revenue treat as trading transactions all realisations of gilt-edged stocks and similar securities by building societies. Profits from such realisations are accordingly treated as liable to tax at the full rate of corporation tax or at the small companies rate (see 56 SMALL COMPANIES—REDUCED RATES) rather than being exempt. (Revenue Press Release 23 February 1984). See now 43 LOAN RELATIONSHIPS.

Simon's Direct Tax Service. See **D4.731** *et seq.*.

7.4 **INTEREST AND DIVIDENDS PAID TO INVESTORS** [*ICTA 1988, s 477A; FA 1990, Sch 5 para 4; SI 1990 No 2231; FA 1991, s 52, Sch 11; SI 1992 Nos 10, 11, 2915; FA 1996, Sch 38 para 6; FA 2000, s 111(4)(6)*]

Tax position of recipient company. Interest and dividends paid or credited by building societies to companies (including all bodies corporate and unincorporated associations other than partnerships and local authority associations) in respect of shares in, deposits with or loans to the society are paid without deduction of tax by virtue of the regulations contained in *SI 1990 No 2231* (as amended by *SI 1992 No 2915*). Such interest etc. is chargeable under Schedule D, Case III.

The Inland Revenue Financial Intermediaries and Claims Office may be contacted for technical advice in relation to the tax deduction scheme on 0151–472 6156.

Marketable securities. Dividends or interest paid in respect of shares or securities (other than 'qualifying certificates of deposit' or a 'qualifying deposit right') listed, or capable of being listed, on a recognised stock exchange when the dividend, etc. became payable are not within the regulations under *section 477A* referred to above, but are subject to deduction of tax under *ICTA 1988, s 349* unless the securities are within the 'quoted Eurobonds' exemption (see 31.3(*b*) INCOME TAX IN RELATION TO A COMPANY). 'Permanent interest bearing shares' (see 7.7 below) issued by a society are within these provisions.

A '*qualifying certificate of deposit*' is a certificate of deposit for £50,000 or more, exclusive of interest, (or foreign equivalent at the time of the deposit) repayable within five years. A '*qualifying deposit right*' is a right to receive an amount in pursuance of a deposit of money under an arrangement under which no certificate of deposit has been issued, although the person entitled to the right could call for the issue of such a certificate, which otherwise meets the same conditions as a qualifying certificate of deposit. [*ICTA 1988, s 349(3A)(3B)(4), s 477A(1A); FA 1991, Sch 11 paras 1, 2; F(No 2)A 1992, Sch 8 para 3*].

Information powers apply broadly as under 6.9 BANKS.

Code of Practice. The Revenue have published a Code of Practice (No 4) setting out their standards for the carrying out of inspections of tax deduction schemes operated by financial intermediaries.

See also 31.4 INCOME TAX IN RELATION TO A COMPANY.

For the tax position of recipient individuals etc., see Tolley's Income Tax under Building Societies.

Simon's Direct Tax Service. See **D4.727** *et seq.*.

7.5 **INTEREST PAID BY BORROWERS**

Payments of 'relevant loan interest' by certain borrowers are made under deduction of tax. See 31.5 INCOME TAX IN RELATION TO A COMPANY.

7.6 TRANSFER OF BUSINESS TO COMPANY

FA 1988, s 145, Sch 12 introduced various provisions, as below, where there is a transfer of the whole of a building society's business to a successor company in accordance with the *Building Societies Act 1986* and *The Building Societies (Transfer of Business) Regulations 1988* (*SI 1988 No 1153*).

Trading stock. For the purposes of valuation of trading stock on discontinuance of a trade under *ICTA 1988, s 100*, '*financial trading stock*', i.e. assets constituting trading stock under that *section* which are held by the society by virtue of the regulations under *Building Societies Act 1986*, is valued at cost, and is brought into the successor company's trade at the same amount. [*FA 1988, Sch 12 para 2*].

Capital allowances. For capital allowance purposes, the society's trade is not treated as ceasing and the successor company is not treated as commencing a new trade. Allowances are computed on a continuing basis. [*FA 1988, Sch 12 para 3*].

Capital gains: assets transferred. If the society and the successor company are not members of the same group of companies (within *TCGA 1992, s 170*, see 9.18 CAPITAL GAINS) at the time of transfer of the business, then

(*a*) they are treated for capital gains purposes as if any transfer of an asset was made at such an amount as would produce neither a gain nor a loss to the society, and

(*b*) if the transfer of the business causes a company to cease to belong to the same group as the society, the notional sale and reacquisition under *TCGA 1992, s 179* (see 9.47 CAPITAL GAINS) does not apply.

If the society and the successor company cease to belong to the same group at some time after the transfer of the business, *TCGA 1992, s 179* similarly does not apply to any asset acquired from the society or another group member either

(i) by the successor company on or before the transfer, or

(ii) by any other company which, at the time of the transfer, is a member of the same group.

If a company which is a member of the same group as the society at the time of the transfer ceases to be a member of that group, and becomes a member of the same group as the successor company, and subsequently leaves the latter group, *TCGA 1992, s 179* applies on the latter event to any 'relevant asset' acquired by it otherwise than from the successor company as if the acquisition had been from the successor company. This does not, however, apply where the company which acquired the asset and the company from which it was acquired cease simultaneously to be members of the successor company's group but continue to be members of the same group as one another, and one of those companies is a 75% subsidiary of the other. '*Relevant asset*' means an asset acquired by the company from the society, or from another company which belongs to the same group at the time of the transfer, when the company, the society and (if applicable) the other company were members of the same group.

From 1 April 2000, the change in the residence requirement as regards groups of companies introduced by *FA 2000* (see 9.18 below) is applied for the purposes of these provisions. [*TCGA 1992, s 216; FA 2000, Sch 29 para 31, Sch 40 Pt II(12)*].

Shares and rights to shares in successor company. If, in connection with a transfer, members of a society are given rights to acquire free shares in a successor company, or to acquire such shares in priority to other subscribers, or at a discount, any such right is treated for capital gains tax purposes as an option (within *TCGA 1992, s 144*) granted for no consideration and having no value at the time of grant. Otherwise, shares issued to members by the successor company, or disposed of to members by the society, are regarded as acquired for any new consideration given and as having at the time of acquisition a value equal to such new consideration (if any). Where shares are so issued or disposed of to trustees on terms providing for their transfer to members for no new consideration, and they constitute settled property in the trustees' hands, then

(*a*) they are regarded as acquired by the trustees for no consideration,

(*b*) a member's interest in the settled property is regarded as acquired for no consideration and as having no value at the time of acquisition,

(*c*) on the member's becoming absolutely entitled to any of the settled property, or where such entitlement would arise but for the member's being an infant or otherwise under disability, the shares are treated as disposed of and re-acquired by the trustees at no gain/no loss, and

(*d*) on the member's disposing of his interest in the settled property, any gain is a chargeable gain (notwithstanding *TCGA 1992, s 76(1)*).

Any gain on the disposal by the society of shares in the successor company in connection with the transfer is not a chargeable gain. [*TCGA 1992, s 217*].

The conferral of any benefit as above on a member of a society in connection with a transfer, or any payment in lieu of such a benefit, or any distribution in pursuance of *Building Societies Act 1986, s 100(2)(b)*, is not regarded as either the making of a distribution (see 20 DISTRIBUTIONS) or the payment of a dividend by the society (see 7.4 above). [*FA 1988, Sch 12 para 6*].

Contractual savings schemes. The disregarding for income tax and capital gains tax purposes of certain sums payable under SAYE schemes within *ICTA 1988, s 326* continues to apply to payments after the transfer under a scheme which was within that *section* in relation to the society immediately before the transfer, notwithstanding that it ceased to be so by reason of the transfer. [*FA 1988, Sch 12 para 7*].

Stamp duty. Transfers under *Building Societies Act 1986, s 97(6)(7)* are exempt from stamp duty. [*FA 1988, Sch 12 para 8*].

Declarations, etc. given to a society prior to incorporation. Declarations made as to the ordinary residence of depositors, and certificates of non-liability given to societies, in order that interest may be paid gross are treated as having been made or given to the successor company (see 6.9 BANKS). (Revenue Pamphlet IR 1, A69).

Simon's Direct Tax Service. See **D4.771–D4.773.**

7.7 PERMANENT INTEREST BEARING SHARES

Since 1991, under the *Building Societies (Designated Capital Resources) (Permanent Interest Bearing Shares) Order 1991* (*SI 1991 No 702*), made under *Building Societies Act 1986*, building societies have been able to issue a type of perpetual share known as a 'permanent interest bearing share' ('PIBS'). *FA 1991, s 51, Sch 10* introduced taxation provisions in relation to 'qualifying shares'. A share in a building society is a '*qualifying share*' if it is either a PIBS or a similar freely transferable security of a description specified for the purpose in Treasury regulations. Following changes to the building society legislation, including the repeal of *SI 1991 No 702*, provision is made for the definition of 'PIBS' in those regulations to be retained for tax purposes (subject to minor modifications) by the *Capital Gains Tax (Definition of Permanent Interest Bearing Share) Regulations 1999* (*SI 1999 No 1953*).

PIBS do not constitute loan relationships (see 43.2 LOAN RELATIONSHIPS), although interest arising on them is within the loan relationship rules (see 43.10 LOAN RELATIONSHIPS).

Capital gains exemption. Other than in relation to relief for losses on loans to traders under *TCGA 1992, s 254* (which is repealed in relation to loans made on or after 17 March 1998), building society shares which are qualifying shares expressed in sterling (and which are not convertible into, or redeemable in, a currency other than sterling) are *for purposes other than those of corporation tax* (and subject to *TCGA 1992, s 117(2)*) 'qualifying corporate bonds' within *TCGA 1992, s 117*, and hence exempt from capital gains tax. As regards corporate holders, however, they are *not* qualifying corporate bonds and hence chargeable gains (or allowable losses) arise on disposal in the normal way. [*TCGA 1992, s 117(A1)(4)–(6)(11)–(13)*].

Accrued income scheme. 'Securities' for the purposes of *ICTA 1988, ss 711–728* (accrued income scheme) includes building society shares which are qualifying shares. [*ICTA 1988, s 710(2A); FA 1991, Sch 10 para 2*].

Incidental costs of issue. A deduction is allowed, in computing the trading income of a building society for corporation tax purposes, for the incidental costs of obtaining finance by the issue of qualifying shares, provided that the amount of any dividend or interest on the shares is an allowable deduction. The incidental costs allowed are expenditure (including abortive expenditure) on fees, commissions, advertising, printing and other incidental matters (but not stamp duty) wholly and exclusively for the purpose of obtaining the finance or of providing security for it or repaying it. Costs in consequence of, or for protection against, exchange rate losses, or of repayment of the shares so far as attributable to their issue at a discount or repayment at a premium, are excluded. [*ICTA 1988, s 477B; FA 1991, Sch 10 para 3*].

Preferential rights of acquisition. Where a building society confers on members or former members priority rights to acquire shares in the society which are qualifying shares, the rights are regarded, for capital gains tax purposes, as options acquired for no consideration and having no value when acquired. [*TCGA 1992, s 149*].

Simon's Direct Tax Service. See **D4.705.**

8 Capital Allowances

Simon's Direct Tax Service B2.

Other sources. See Tolley's Capital Allowances.

8.1 Capital allowances are described in detail, including many worked examples, in Tolley's Income Tax under that heading. Those provisions which are peculiar to corporation tax, or have special relevance to companies, are set out below.

8.2 In the case of companies, which are assessed to corporation tax on a current year basis, capital allowances and balancing charges arise by reference to actual accounting periods, instead of by reference to 'basis periods'. In this respect, the legislation refers to '**chargeable periods**' which are the accounting periods of companies (and years of assessment in the case of individuals etc.). [*ICTA 1988, s 832(1)*].

Where an accounting period is less than twelve months, writing-down allowances are proportionately reduced.

With effect from 6 April 1994, certain allowances for a trade started part way through an accounting period are proportionately restricted (although this does not apply to trades set up and commenced after 5 April 1994 and before 6 April 1995). [*ICTA 1988, s 520(4)(a)(ii), s 530(2)(a)(ii); CAA 1990, s 24(2)(a)(ii), s 98(6); FA 1994, s 213(4)(8), s 214(4)(6), s 218(1A); FA 1995, s 102*].

(Similar treatment applies for income tax purposes generally from 1997/98, and in certain cases from 1994/95.)

For corporation tax purposes, capital allowances (or balancing charges) in respect of a trade are treated as **trading expenses** (or receipts) of the accounting period to which they relate. [*CAA 1990, s 144*]. (Similar treatment applies for income tax purposes generally from 1997/98, and in certain cases from 1994/95.) Trading losses which are attributable to capital allowances qualify for loss relief in the ordinary way. See 44 LOSSES, particularly 44.6 for the special extension of carry-back relief for losses attributable to first-year allowances on machinery and plant.

For capital allowances for investment companies and life assurance companies, see 40.2 INVESTMENT COMPANIES and 41.2 LIFE INSURANCE COMPANIES.

Capital allowances due to other companies in respect of non-trading activities are normally deducted primarily from the specified source of income. Any excess may be

(*a*) carried forward against such income in succeeding accounting periods, [*CAA 1990, s 145(2)*], or

(*b*) deducted from profits generally, [*CAA 1990, s 145(3)*], or

(c) set off under *ICTA 1988, s 242* (until its repeal) against a surplus of FRANKED INVESTMENT INCOME (27).

Notes. (1) A claim for relief under (*b*) above may, if the allowances exceed the profit of the accounting period, require the excess to be relieved (as far as possible) against the profits of an immediately preceding period of equal length. [*CAA 1990, s 145(4)*]. (2) Neither (*b*) nor (*c*) is available to a lessor company not carrying on a *trade* of leasing where the lessee does not use the assets concerned for the purposes of a trade, and group relief is similarly restricted in such circumstances (see 29.18 GROUPS OF COMPANIES). [*CAA 1990, s 61(5)(7)*].

Accounting periods ending on or after 1 July 1999. [*FA 1998, Sch 18 Pt IX*]. A capital allowance claim under self-assessment must be included in the company tax return (or amended return) (see 55.3 SELF-ASSESSMENT) for the accounting period for which the claim is made. It must specify the amount claimed, which must be expressed in figures at the time the claim is made. It must be made (and may be amended or withdrawn) at any time up to the latest of

(i) the first anniversary of the filing date for the company tax return,

(ii) 30 days after closure of any enquiry into that return (unless the enquiry, being otherwise out of time, was limited, as referred to in 55.7 SELF-ASSESSMENT, to matters to which a previous amendment making or withdrawing a capital allowance claim relates, or which are affected by the amendment),

(iii) 30 days after notice of any amendment of that return by the Revenue following such an enquiry, and

(iv) 30 days after determination of any appeal against an amendment within (iii),

or at a later time if the Revenue allow it. See below (in relation to earlier accounting periods ending after 30 September 1993) for Revenue Statement of Practice SP 11/93 setting out the Revenue approach to the admission of late claims. SP 11/93 is, however, to be amended or replaced for claims under self-assessment.

These time limits override the normal time limits for amendment of a company tax return. Amendments or withdrawals of claims must be made by amending the return.

If the effect of a claim is to reduce the available capital allowances for another accounting period for which a return has already been made, the company has 30 days to make the necessary amendments of that return. If it fails to do so, the Revenue may, by written notice and subject to a right of appeal within 30 days of the issue of the notice, amend the return to correct the position (notwithstanding any time limit otherwise applicable).

Accounting periods ending before 1 July 1999. [*CAA 1990, Sch A1; FA 1990, s 102*]. Claims (and withdrawals of claims) for capital allowances for such an accounting period may not (except as below) be made more than six years after the end of the period and may in all cases be made at any time within the two years following the end of the period. Subject to that, they may be made up to the later of:

(i) the date on which a corporation tax assessment for the period becomes final and conclusive; and

(ii) the date on which a determination under *TMA 1970, s 41A* (see 44.9 LOSSES) for the period of an amount which is affected by the claim (or withdrawal) has become final.

The Board have power to extend any of these time limits, and may admit late claims where, for reasons beyond the company's control, a timeous claim could not have been made. This would exclude for example cases of oversight or negligence of the claimant company; or of failure, without good reason, to compute the necessary figure; or of the wish to avoid commitment pending clarification of the effects of a claim; or of the illness or absence of an adviser to the company; or of the illness or absence of an officer of the company unless it arose at a critical time preventing a timeous claim, there was good reason why the claim could not be made before the absence or illness arose, there was no other person who could have made the claim timeously, and (in the case of absence) there was good reason for the officer's unavailability. An application for admission of a late claim should explain why the claim could not have been made within the statutory time limit, and must be made within three months of the event giving rise to the late claim. (Revenue Pamphlet IR 131, 11/93, 8 October 1993).

Where an assessment is under appeal when the six-year time limit referred to above expires, conditional claims may be made within the following three months. Such claims must be conditional, but only as to the amount claimed, on matter(s) specified in the claim which are relevant to determination of the assessment.

Claims (and withdrawals) are to be included in the return (or amended return) under *TMA 1970, s 11* (see 54.2 RETURNS) for the period and, except in the case of conditional claims (as above), the amount of the claim must be quantified when the claim is made. Claims may be made for less than the full amount available.

Assessments (or amendments) to give effect to the above are not out of time if made up to one year after the date on which the determination of the amount affected by the claim (where relevant) becomes final or (in any other case) the assessment for the period to which the claim relates becomes final and conclusive, or, in the case of withdrawal of a claim, within one year from the date of the withdrawal. Final determinations are adjusted in accordance with valid claims and withdrawals.

8.3 **'CONTROL' AND 'MAIN BENEFIT' TRANSACTIONS** [*CAA 1990, ss 157, 158*]

Sales of any property (other than machinery or plant, see 8.4 below) are within the anti-avoidance provisions of *CAA 1990, ss 157, 158* if

(*a*) the buyer is a body of persons over which the seller has control, or

(*b*) the seller is a body of persons over which the buyer has control, or

(*c*) both buyer and seller are bodies of persons under the control of a third person, or

(*d*) the sole or main benefit apparently arising from the sale (or from a series of transactions of which the sale is one) is the obtaining of an allowance or deduction under the Act.

'Body of persons' includes a partnership. [*CAA 1990, s 157(2)*].

(*a*), (*b*) and (*c*) also include cases where the buyer and seller are CONNECTED PERSONS (16), or where the relevant interest in an industrial building or structure is transferred other than by way of sale, and (*d*) includes cases where the only or main benefit is the obtaining of an *increased* allowance or deduction or the avoidance or reduction of a charge.

The normal effect of these provisions is to substitute market value for the purchase price (if different) of property to which they apply. However, where the transaction is within (*a*), (*b*) or (*c*) above, and not within (*d*), the parties to the sale may elect, by notice in writing to the inspector, that the asset change hands at its written-down value for capital allowances purposes (if this value is lower than market value), and any subsequent balancing charge on the buyer is computed by reference to allowances made to both buyer and seller. Such an election is not available if either

(i) the circumstances are such that an allowance or charge which could otherwise fall to be made on any of the parties in consequence of the sale will not be capable of so falling, or

(ii) the buyer is a 'dual resident investing company' (see 29.31 GROUPS OF COMPANIES), or

(iii) (in the case of a 'qualifying dwelling-house') unless both buyer and seller are at the time of the sale, or were previously, 'approved bodies' (within *Housing Act 1980, s 56(4)*).

The election must be made within two years after the sale.

[*CAA 1990, s 158; FA 1993, s 117; FA 1994, s 119*].

Simon's Direct Tax Service. See **B2.108.**

8.4 TRANSACTIONS BETWEEN CONNECTED PERSONS ETC.

Where a trader purchases machinery or plant from a connected person (see 16 CONNECTED PERSONS), he is entitled to a first-year allowance only where the machinery etc. has not previously been used for trade purposes by the seller or any other connected person. If that condition is met, the allowance will be given on the smallest of

(i) the purchaser's capital expenditure,

(ii) the capital expenditure incurred by the seller (or any person connected with the seller), and

(iii) the open market value when acquired by the purchaser.

Writing-down allowances available to the purchaser will also be restricted to those available on a sum equal to the disposal value brought into account on the seller. For disposals resulting from a transaction or transactions between connected persons, the limit on this disposal value is the greater or greatest cost incurred by any of those connected persons. If no disposal value is brought into account on the seller, writing-down allowances are calculated on the smallest of (i) to (iii) above.

These provisions apply equally where the machinery, etc. is transferred by contract or assignment, and similarly to transactions either involving sale and lease-back or having as the sole or main benefit expected to accrue the obtaining of an allowance. In the case of a 'sole or main benefit' transaction, first-year allowances are not given in any circumstances. [*CAA 1990, ss 26(3), 75, 76*].

These provisions are subject to the special finance lease provisions in *ICTA 1988, s 76A* (introduced by *F(No 2)A 1997, s 46*), and, in the case of certain sale and leaseback type transactions, to a joint election under *CAA 1990, s 76B* (introduced by *FA 2000, s 77*) for allowances to be given to the lessor, rather than the seller (or assignor), disregarding the open market value at (iii) above (and, in the case of finance leases, the notional written-down value for the seller). See Tolley's Income Tax under Capital Allowances. See also 8.3 above as regards certain transfers of industrial buildings, and 29.31 GROUPS OF COMPANIES as regards certain transactions involving 'dual resident investing companies'.

Simon's Direct Tax Service. See **B2.365.**

9 Capital Gains

Cross-reference. See also 23.29 EXCHANGE GAINS AND LOSSES, 24 EXEMPT ORGANISATIONS.

Simon's Direct Tax Service C3.1.

Other sources. See Tolley's Capital Gains Tax.

The headings in this chapter are as follows.

9.1	Liability of companies to corporation tax on their capital gains
9.2	Rate of corporation tax in respect of capital gains
9.3	Capital losses
9.4	Liquidation
9.5	Recovery from shareholders
9.6	Reconstructions and amalgamations
9.7	Transfer of assets to non-resident company
9.8	Transfer of UK trade between companies in different EC Member States
9.9	Transfer of non-UK trade between companies in different EC Member States
9.10	Interest charged to capital
9.11	Government securities etc. and qualifying corporate bonds
9.12	Shares — acquisitions and disposals within short period
9.13	Value-shifting
9.14	—certain disposals of shares by companies
9.15	—interpretation of 9.13 and 9.14 above
9.16	—transactions treated as a reorganisation of share capital
9.17	Close company transferring asset at undervalue
9.18	Groups of companies
9.19	—disposals of capital assets by one member of a group to another treated as if made at a 'no gain, no loss' price — exceptions
9.20	—disposal outside group treated as having been preceded by intra-group transfer
9.21	—intra-group transfers of assets under scheme for transfer by non-resident of UK branch or agency
9.22	—intra-group transfers of assets which are trading stock of one company but not of the other
9.23–9.36	—restriction on set-off of pre-entry losses where a company joins a group
9.37–9.42	—restriction on set-off of losses against pre-entry gains where a company joins a group
9.43	—disposal or acquisition outside a group — miscellaneous
9.44	— rollover relief
9.45	— assets held on 31 March 1982
9.46	—collection of unpaid tax from other members of the group
9.47, 9.48	—company ceasing to be a member of a group
9.49	—company becoming an investment trust after acquiring asset intra-group
9.50	—company becoming a venture capital trust after acquiring asset intra-group
9.51	—intra-group disposal which materially reduces the value of the shares or securities of one party
9.52	—restriction on capital losses because of 'depreciatory transactions'
9.53	Dual resident companies
9.54	Privatisation
9.55	Indexation allowance

9.1 LIABILITY OF COMPANIES TO CORPORATION TAX ON THEIR CAPITAL GAINS

Companies resident in the UK (and non-resident companies in respect of UK branch or agency assets — see 53.4 RESIDENCE) are liable to corporation tax on their chargeable gains (i.e. capital gains chargeable to tax). These gains are included in their profits subject to corporation tax as described in 9.2 below. [*ICTA 1988, s 6(3); TCGA 1992, s 10(3)*].

Companies accordingly do not pay 'capital gains tax' as such but their chargeable gains less allowable losses are computed *in accordance with the provisions relating to capital gains tax* (for which see Tolley's Capital Gains Tax) **except**

(i) computations are made by reference to accounting periods instead of years of assessment [*TCGA 1992, s 8(3)*],

(ii) provisions in the legislation confined solely to individuals do not apply to companies [*TCGA 1992, s 8(4)(5)*],

(iii) the indexation allowance rules applied (subject to transitional provisions) to disposals after 31 March 1982, and not 5 April 1982 as for individuals, and the *FA 1985* rules operated similarly after 31 March 1985 instead of 5 April 1985 [*FA 1982, s 86(1)(a); FA 1985, s 68, Sch 19*],

(iv) taper relief, applicable to individuals, trustees etc. after 5 April 1998, does not apply to companies, for which, however, indexation is not frozen at its April 1998 level [*FA 1998, ss 121, 122*],

(v) identification rules for shares and securities acquired after 5 April 1998 are different for companies [*FA 1998, ss 123, 124*], and

(vi) as further indicated below.

See *TCGA 1992, ss 284A, 284B* (introduced by *FA 1999, s 76*) for anti-avoidance legislation bringing into charge certain gains deferred under extra-statutory concessions.

European single currency (the 'euro'). Under *FA 1998, s 163*, the Treasury has power to make regulations to implement tax changes needed as a result of the introduction of the single currency. See *SI 1998 No 3177*, in particular *regs 36–39*.

9.2 RATE OF CORPORATION TAX IN RESPECT OF CAPITAL GAINS

The whole of the chargeable gains (less allowable losses under 9.3 below) of a company is included in the profits chargeable to corporation tax. The rate of corporation tax applicable will either be the full rate as in 1.3 INTRODUCTION AND RATES OF TAX or the starting rate or small companies rate (see SMALL COMPANIES—REDUCED RATES (56)) (with marginal relief as appropriate) but the rate so determined applies to both income and chargeable gains included in the chargeable profits. If the company's accounting period straddles different financial years, chargeable profits are apportioned on a time basis between the years. [*ICTA 1988, ss 8(3), 13, 13AA*].

For a summary of the provisions applicable for accounting periods ending before 17 March 1987, or straddling that date, see 1.3(*b*) INTRODUCTION AND RATES OF TAX.

See 7 BUILDING SOCIETIES, 41 LIFE INSURANCE COMPANIES and 60 UNIT AND INVESTMENT TRUSTS for special provisions in relation to these organisations.

9.3 CAPITAL LOSSES

The amount of chargeable gains assessable for an accounting period is the total chargeable gains accruing to the company in that period less allowable losses in that period and allowable losses brought forward from any previous period. The resulting net figure is treated as in 9.2 above. Allowable losses include short-term losses accruing under Schedule D, Case VII for years before 1971/72 which remain unrelieved. [*TCGA 1992, s 8(1), Sch 11 para 12*]. This is the only instance where losses incurred before 6 April 1965 can be carried forward. It is expressly provided in *TCGA 1992, s 8(2)* that an allowable loss does not include any loss which, if it had been a gain, would have been exempt from corporation tax in the hands of the company. Capital losses *cannot* normally be offset against trading profits or other income (but see 44.19 LOSSES). However, trading losses can be offset against chargeable gains within the same accounting period and, if unexhausted, against chargeable gains arising in earlier periods (44.2, 44.6 LOSSES). Management expenses of an investment company may be offset against chargeable gains within the same or a succeeding accounting period. [*ICTA 1988, s 75(3)*].

Capital losses are generally computed in the same way as capital gains. With the introduction of self-assessment for accounting periods ending on or after 1 July 1999 (see 55 SELF-ASSESSMENT), a capital loss is not an allowable loss unless it is claimed in a quantified amount. The time limit for such claims is six years after the end of the accounting period in which the loss was incurred. Where unused losses are brought forward and set against chargeable gains in a later accounting period, losses incurred after the start of self-assessment are used before earlier ones. [*TCGA 1992, s 16; FA 1995, s 113*].

9.4 LIQUIDATION

The vesting of a company's assets in a liquidator is disregarded. All the acts of the liquidator in relation to such assets are treated as acts of the company. [*TCGA 1992, s 8(6)*].

See also 42 LIQUIDATION ETC..

9.5 RECOVERY FROM SHAREHOLDERS [*TCGA 1992, s 189*]

Where a person connected with a UK resident company (see 16 CONNECTED PERSONS) receives, or becomes entitled to receive, in respect of shares in that company, a *capital distribution* which is not a reduction of capital but which constitutes, or is derived from, a disposal of assets from which a chargeable gain accrues to the company, and the company does not pay, within a specified time (see below), the corporation tax due from it for the accounting period in which the gain accrues, the recipient of the distribution may, by assessment within two years of the due date, be required to pay so much of that corporation tax as relates to chargeable gains but not exceeding the lesser of

(i) a part of that tax, at the rate in force when the gain accrued, proportionate to his share of the total distribution made by the company, and

(ii) the value of the distribution he received or became entitled to receive.

The person then has a right of recovery against the company, including any interest charged on him under *TMA 1970, s 87A* (see 39.1 INTEREST ON UNPAID TAX).

The time specified (as above) is the date the tax became payable by the company or, if later, the date the assessment was made on the company.

See also 48.4 PAYMENT OF TAX as regards recovery of tax from third parties generally.

9.6 RECONSTRUCTIONS AND AMALGAMATIONS [*TCGA 1992, s 139*]

Subject to the following, where a scheme of company reconstruction or amalgamation involves the transfer of a company's business to another company for no consideration (other than the assumption of liabilities of the business), capital assets (not used as trading stock by either company) are regarded as being transferred at a 'no gain, no loss' price, and the acquiring company takes over the disposing company's acquisition date.

For disposals before 1 April 2000, the above is conditional on both companies being UK resident at the time of the transfer. For disposals on or after that date, the conditions are:

(i) that either the transferee company is UK resident at the time of acquisition or the assets are 'chargeable assets' in relation to that company immediately after that time; and

(ii) that either the transferor company is UK resident at that time or the assets are 'chargeable assets' in relation to that company immediately before that time.

For these purposes, an asset is a '*chargeable asset*' in relation to a company at a particular time if, on a disposal by the company at that time, any gain would be a chargeable gain and within the charge to corporation tax by virtue of *TCGA 1992, s 10* (non-UK resident company trading through UK branch or agency, see 53.4 RESIDENCE).

[*TCGA 1992, s 139(1)(1A)(2)(9); FA 2000, Sch 29 para 5*].

Strictly, the second company should carry on substantially the same business and have substantially the same members as the first, but in practice the identity of shareholdings is not insisted upon where the scheme is for *bona fide* commercial reasons or where there is segregation of trades or businesses into identifiable parts which are capable of being carried on in their own right. (Revenue Pamphlet IR 131, D14). This applies equally to a demerger within *ICTA 1988, ss 213–218* (see 29.35 GROUPS OF COMPANIES) involving the transfer of shares in a 75% subsidiary to a newly formed company. (Revenue Pamphlet IR 131, SP 5/85, 21 May 1985).

Anti-avoidance. *TCGA 1992, s 139* does not apply unless the scheme is for *bona fide* commercial reasons and not to avoid corporation tax, capital gains tax or income tax, or where the Board, on written application by the acquiring company, has notified its satisfaction with the scheme before the transfer is made. Such application for clearance should be made (by either company) to Inland Revenue, Capital Gains Clearance Section, Sapphire House, 550, Streetsbrook Road, Solihull, West Midlands B91 1QU (tel. 0121–713 4600). It should give full details of the transactions and of all the companies directly involved, their tax districts and references. Copies of accounts for the last two years for which accounts have been prepared should accompany the application. Applications for clearance under both *TCGA 1992, s 138* and *s 139* may be made in a single letter. Where application is made in a single letter both under the capital gains provisions and under other provisions (e.g. *ICTA 1988, s 215, s 225* or *s 707*), a copy of the letter should in all cases be sent direct to Solihull. If the application is not acknowledged within ten days, the Clearance Section in Solihull should be telephoned to check the position. (Revenue Press Release 9 August 1989). The Board may, within 30 days of receipt, call for further particulars (to be supplied within 30 days, or longer if the Board allows; if the information is not supplied, the application lapses). Subject to this, the Board must notify its decision within a further 30 days. If not so notified, or if dissatisfied with the decision, the applicant may within a further 30 days require the Board to refer the application to the Special Commissioners for their decision. All material facts and considerations must be disclosed, otherwise any decision is void. If any tax arising on the transfer is not paid by the disposing company within six months of a specified date, then, within two years of that date, the tax may be assessed on any person who

(*a*) holds all or any of the assets to which the tax relates, and

(*b*) is either the acquiring company or any other group member to which the assets have been subsequently transferred.

The date specified (as above) is the date the tax became payable by the company or, if later, the date the assessment was made on the company.

The tax charge will be proportionate to the assets held and the paying company has the right of recovery against the original disposing company of the tax charged and any interest thereon under *TMA 1970, s 87A* (see 39.1 INTEREST ON UNPAID TAX). Where the disposing company has been wound up, any tax due from it may be recovered from the acquiring company. [*TCGA 1992, s 139(5)–(8)*].

The provisions of *TCGA 1992, s 139* do not apply to the transfer of the whole or part of a company's business to a unit trust scheme (where it is either within *TCGA 1992, s 100(2)* or an authorised unit trust, see 60.1 UNIT AND INVESTMENT TRUSTS), to an investment trust (see 60.4 UNIT AND INVESTMENT TRUSTS) or, for transfers after 16 March 1998, to a venture capital trust (see 62.2 VENTURE CAPITAL TRUSTS). [*TCGA 1992, s 139(4); FA 1998, s 134(1)(4)*].

Where *section 139* has applied in relation to a transfer to a company which was not then an investment trust but which subsequently becomes one for an accounting period, then any assets of the business transferred which are still owned by the company at the beginning of that accounting period are deemed to have been sold and immediately reacquired by the transferee company, immediately after the transfer, at their market value at that time. For accounting periods ending on or after 1 July 1999, the resulting chargeable gain or allowable loss is deemed to accrue to the transferee company immediately before the end of the accounting period preceding that in which the company becomes an investment trust. Notwithstanding normal time limits, a corporation tax assessment in respect of any resulting liability can be made within six years after the end of the accounting period in which the company becomes an investment trust.

Similar provisions apply where, after a transfer to which *section 139* applied and after 16 March 1998, the transferee company becomes a venture capital trust (within *ICTA 1988, s 842AA*, see 62.2 VENTURE CAPITAL TRUSTS). They apply by reference to the time at which the Board's approval for the purposes of *section 842AA* comes into effect, and the resulting gain or loss is deemed to accrue immediately before that time rather than at the time of the deemed disposal. In a case in which the Board's approval has effect as from the beginning of an accounting period, any consequential corporation tax assessment can be made, notwithstanding normal time limits, within six years after the end of that accounting period. These provisions do not apply if those above relating to investment trusts have already applied (in relation to the same transfer of assets) and *vice versa*.

[*TCGA 1992, ss 101, 101B; FA 1996, s 140; FA 1998, s 134(2)(3)(5); SI 1998 No 3173*].

See 9.53 below as regards disapplication of *section 139* in relation to certain dual resident companies.

See Simon's Direct Tax Service D2.303.

Exchange of securities on or before 31 July 1998 by share dealers in connection with conversion operations, nationalisation etc. by Government. The securities received together with any additional consideration will take the place of the securities given up without involving any disposal until the new securities are realised. Election may be made within two years of the end of the accounting period in which the exchange takes place for these provisions *not* to apply. These provisions are **repealed** for exchanges made after 31 July 1998. [*ICTA 1988, s 471; FA 1996, Sch 21 para 12; FA 1998, s 101(1)(3)*].

Life insurance companies. See 41.16 LIFE INSURANCE COMPANIES.

9.7 **TRANSFER OF ASSETS TO NON-RESIDENT COMPANY** [*TCGA 1992, s 140*]

Where a UK resident company carrying on a trade outside the UK through a branch or agency transfers the whole or part of that trade together with its assets, or its assets other than cash, to a company not resident in the UK in exchange, wholly or partly, for shares (or shares and loan stock) in that company, so that thereafter it holds one-quarter or more of the transferee company's ordinary share capital, and the chargeable gains on the transfer exceed the allowable losses, the proportion of the resulting net chargeable gains relating to the shares (in proportion that the market value of the shares at the time of the transfer bears to the market value of the whole consideration received) may be claimed by the transferor company as being deferred and not treated as arising until the happening of one of the following events:

(i) the *transferor company disposes* of all or any of the shares received. The appropriate proportion of the deferred gain (insofar as not already charged under this specific provision or under (ii) below) is then added to the consideration received on the disposal. The '*appropriate proportion*' is the proportion which the market value of the shares disposed of bears to the market value of the shares held immediately before the disposal. However, deferred gains relating to events occurring before 1 April 1982 are disregarded for this purpose;

(ii) the *transferee company disposes*, within six years of the transfer, of the whole or part of the assets on which chargeable gains were deferred. The gain chargeable (insofar as it has not already been charged under this provision or under (i) above) is the proportion which the deferred gain on the assets disposed of bears to the total deferred gains on assets held immediately before the disposal.

For purposes of (i) or (ii) above, intra-group transfers (see 9.18 *et seq.* below) are disregarded (including for (ii), disposals which would qualify under *TCGA 1992, s 171* but for the residence or chargeability requirements) and a charge will arise when a subsequent owner makes a disposal outside the group.

No claim may be made under these provisions as regards a transfer in relation to which a claim is made under *TCGA 1992, s 140C* (see 9.9 below).

[*TCGA 1992, s 140, Sch 4 para 4; F(No 2)A 1992, s 46(4); FA 2000, Sch 29 para 23*].

See also 41 LIFE INSURANCE COMPANIES.

Simon's Direct Tax Service. See **D2.305**.

9.8 **TRANSFER OF UK TRADE BETWEEN COMPANIES IN DIFFERENT EC MEMBER STATES**

A special relief may be claimed where a 'qualifying company' resident in one EC Member State transfers the whole or part of a trade carried on by it in the UK to a 'qualifying company' resident in another Member State in exchange for securities (including shares) in the latter company, provided that certain conditions (see below) are met. On such a claim, any assets included in the transfer are treated for the purposes of corporation tax on chargeable gains as transferred for a no gain/no loss consideration, and *TCGA 1992, s 25(3)* (deemed disposal by non-resident on ceasing to trade in the UK through a branch or agency, see Tolley's Capital Gains Tax under Overseas Matters) does not apply to the assets by reason of the transfer.

A '*qualifying company*' is a body incorporated under the law of a Member State.

A company is regarded for the above purposes as resident in a Member State under the laws of which it is chargeable to tax because it is regarded as so resident (unless it is regarded under a double tax relief arrangement entered into by the Member State as resident in a territory not within any of the Member States).

The conditions referred to above are:

(*a*) (i) if the transferee company is non-UK resident immediately after the transfer, any chargeable gain accruing to it on a disposal of the assets included in the

(i) transfer would form part of its corporation tax profits under *TCGA 1992, s 10(3)* (see 53.4 RESIDENCE), or

(ii) if it is UK resident at that time, none of the assets included in the transfer is exempt from UK tax on disposal under double tax relief arrangements; and

(*b*) the transfer is effected for *bona fide* commercial reasons and not as part of a scheme or arrangement a main purpose of which is avoidance of income tax, corporation tax or capital gains tax.

Advance clearance in relation to (*b*) above may be obtained from the Board on the application of the companies, subject to the same conditions and appeal procedures as apply to clearances under *TCGA 1992, s 138* (see Tolley's Capital Gains Tax under Anti-Avoidance). Applications for clearance (preferably with three copies in the case of lengthy applications) should be sent to Inland Revenue, Capital Gains Clearance Section, Sapphire House, 550 Streetsbrook Road, Solihull, West Midlands B91 1QU (tel. 0121–713 4600).

[*TCGA 1992, ss 140A, 140B; F(No 2)A 1992, s 44*].

Capital allowances. Where the above provisions apply (and, if immediately after the transfer the transferee company is non-UK resident, where at that time it carries on in the UK through a branch or agency a trade consisting of or including the trade (or part) transferred), the transferee company takes over the capital allowance position of the transferor company in relation to the assets transferred, so that no allowances or charges arise from the transfer. Any necessary apportionments are made on a just and reasonable basis (with appropriate appeals procedures). *ICTA 1988, s 343(2)* (see 44.10 LOSSES) does not apply where a claim is made under these provisions. [*CAA 1990, s 152B; F(No 2)A 1992, s 67*].

Simon's Direct Tax Service. See D2.304A.

9.9 TRANSFER OF NON-UK TRADE BETWEEN COMPANIES IN DIFFERENT EC MEMBER STATES

Where

(*a*) a 'qualifying company' resident in the UK transfers to a 'qualifying company' resident in another Member State the whole or part of a trade carried on by the UK company immediately before the transfer through a branch or agency in a Member State other than the UK,

(*b*) the transfer includes all the UK company assets used in that trade or part (with the possible exception of cash),

(*c*) the transfer is wholly or partly in exchange for securities (including shares) in the non-UK company,

(*d*) the aggregate of the chargeable gains accruing to the UK company on the transfer exceeds the aggregate of the allowable losses so accruing, and

(*e*) the transfer is effected for *bona fide* commercial reasons and not as part of a scheme or arrangement a main purpose of which is avoidance of income tax, corporation tax or capital gains tax,

the UK company may claim that the transfer be treated as giving rise to a single chargeable gain of the excess at (*d*) above. No claim may, however, be made where a claim is made under *TCGA 1992, s 140*, see 9.7 above, in relation to the same transfer.

A '*qualifying company*' is a body incorporated under the law of a Member State.

For the purposes of (*a*) above, a company is not regarded as resident in the UK if it is regarded under any double tax relief arrangements to which the UK is a party as resident in a territory not within any of the Member States. A company is regarded as resident in another Member State under the laws of which it is chargeable to tax because it is regarded as so resident (unless it is regarded under a double tax relief arrangement entered into by the Member State as resident in a territory not within any of the Member States).

Advance clearance in relation to (*e*) above may be obtained from the Board on the application of the UK company, subject to the same conditions and appeal procedures as apply to clearances under *TCGA 1992, s 138* (see Tolley's Capital Gains Tax under Anti-Avoidance). Applications for clearance (preferably with three copies in the case of lengthy applications) should be sent to Inland Revenue, Capital Gains Clearance Section, Sapphire House, 550 Streetsbrook Road, Solihull, West Midlands B91 1QU (tel. 0121–713 4600).

ICTA 1988, s 442(3) (see 41.11 LIFE INSURANCE COMPANIES) is ignored in arriving at the chargeable gains and allowable losses accruing on the transfer.

[*TCGA 1992, ss 140C, 140D; F(No 2)A 1992, s 45*].

Double tax relief. Where the above provisions apply, and the UK company produces to the inspector an 'appropriate certificate' from the tax authorities of the Member State in which the company carried on the trade immediately before the transfer, the amount stated in the certificate is treated for double tax relief purposes as tax paid in that other Member State.

An '*appropriate certificate*' is one which states that gains accruing to the UK company on the transfer would, but for the Mergers Directive (*90/434/EEC*), have been chargeable to tax in the other Member State, and which states the amount of tax which would, but for that Directive, have been payable in respect of the gains. The tax must be calculated after any permissible set-off of losses arising on the transfer and on the assumption that any available reliefs are claimed. There are provisions to deal with cases where a certificate cannot be obtained from the relevant tax authority.

For accounting periods ending on or after 1 July 1999 (to which company self-assessment applies, see 55 SELF-ASSESSMENT), the requirement for an 'appropriate certificate' is replaced by a requirement that the gains accruing to the UK company on the transfer would, but for the Mergers Directive, have been chargeable to tax in the other Member State, and the onus is on the company to calculate the amount of notional foreign tax in support of a relief claim (see Revenue Capital Gains Manual, CG 45734).

[*ICTA 1988, s 815A; F(No 2)A 1992, s 50; FA 1996, Sch 20 para 39*].

Foreign tax on balancing charges may be allowed for credit as above, *provided that* there is a capital gain (however small) within the above rules. (Revenue Capital Allowances Manual, CA 595).

Simon's Direct Tax Service. See D2.304B.

9.10 INTEREST CHARGED TO CAPITAL [*TCGA 1992, s 40*]

Interest on money borrowed by a company for the construction of any building, structure or works, and referable to a period before disposal, may be added to the expenditure allowable as a deduction under *TCGA 1992, s 38* in computing the gain on the disposal by the company of the building etc., provided that the expenditure on the construction itself was allowable, and that the interest is neither allowable as a deduction in computing any profits or gains for corporation tax purposes (nor would be so but for an insufficiency of profits or gains) nor a charge on income (see 50.3 PROFIT COMPUTATIONS).

9.11 **GOVERNMENT SECURITIES ETC. AND QUALIFYING CORPORATE BONDS**

See Tolley's Capital Gains Tax for the exemption of government and public corporation securities and qualifying corporate bonds, for the restriction of losses arising from acquisitions and disposals within a short period (when not within 9.12 below), and for acquisitions and disposals within the same stock exchange period. For accounting periods ending after 31 March 1996, however, see the general taxation provisions relating to LOAN RELATIONSHIPS (43).

If government and public corporation securities or qualifying corporate bonds are appropriated by a company *from* dealing stock in such circumstances that any gain accruing on their disposal would be exempt from corporation tax on chargeable gains, there is a deemed disposal and reacquisition immediately before the appropriation. Where the securities, etc. are appropriated *to* dealing stock, any loss arising on a subsequent disposal cannot exceed the loss which would have arisen if the securities, etc. had been acquired at their market value at the date of the appropriation. [*ICTA 1988, s 126A; TCGA 1992, Sch 10 para 14(6)*]. *Section 126A* is repealed following the introduction of the LOAN RELATIONSHIPS (43) provisions referred to above. [*FA 1996, Sch 41 Pt V(3)*].

Simon's Direct Tax Service. See D2.307, D2.308.

9.12 **SHARES — ACQUISITIONS AND DISPOSALS WITHIN SHORT PERIOD**

The ordinary rules (see Tolley's Capital Gains Tax) for matching disposals with 'acquisitions' are modified for disposals by a company of shares (including securities) if:

(*a*) the company acquired shares ('*available shares*') of the same class within one month before or after the disposal where the disposal was through a stock exchange or Automated Real-Time Investments Exchange Ltd, or otherwise within six months before or after the disposal; and

(*b*) the number of that class of shares held by the company during the period prescribed under (*a*) before the disposal was not less than 2% of the number issued.

Where the company making the disposal ('company X') is a member of a group and the period prescribed under (*a*) above begins on or after 1 April 2000, the following apply.

(i) Where shares of the same class are held by another group member, and at any time in that prescribed period before the disposal either

(A) the other group member is UK resident, or

(B) the shares are 'chargeable shares' in relation to that other group member,

those shares are treated for the purposes of (*b*) above as held by company X.

(ii) Where shares of the same class are acquired by another group member, and either (i)(A) or (i)(B) applies at the time of acquisition, those shares are treated for the purposes of (*a*) above as acquired by company X.

(iii) Where shares of the same class are acquired by company X from a company which was a member of the group throughout that prescribed period before and after the disposal, and either (i)(A) or (i)(B) applies throughout that part of that period during which the other group member held the shares, those shares are disregarded for the purposes of (*a*) above.

Shares are '*chargeable shares*' in relation to a company at a particular time if, on a disposal by the company at that time, any gain would be a chargeable gain and within the charge to corporation tax by virtue of *TCGA 1992, s 10* (non-UK resident company trading through

UK branch or agency, see 53.4 RESIDENCE). Membership of a group is determined as in 9.18 below, taking into account the change in the residence requirement from (broadly) 1 April 2000.

Where the company making the disposal is a member of a group and the period prescribed under (*a*) above begins before 1 April 2000, similar provisions apply but taking into account the fact that under 9.18 below, as it applied before the change in the residence requirement, a group is restricted to UK-resident companies.

Disposals are matched with available shares before other shares and with available shares acquired by the disposing company before those acquired by a fellow group member, and then with acquisitions before the disposal (latest ones first) rather than after (when earliest ones are taken first).

Where disposals are identified with acquisitions of another group member, the cost to that member will be allowed to the disposing company plus the usual incidental costs of disposal. Shares identified with a disposal are precluded from further identification with a later disposal.

'*Acquisitions*' above do not include shares acquired as trading stock or from another group member.

The above identification rules have priority over those generally applicable (see Tolley's Capital Gains Tax under Shares and Securities—Identification Rules) and, additionally, shares acquired and disposed of on the same day are matched under *TCGA 1992, s 105.*

[*TCGA 1992, ss 106, 108(8); FA 2000, Sch 29 para 18*].

Simon's Direct Tax Service. See **D2.309.**

9.13 **VALUE-SHIFTING** [*TCGA 1992, ss 29–34*]

For the provisions of general application to individuals, etc. as well as companies, see Tolley's Capital Gains Tax under Anti-Avoidance. *FA 1989, ss 135–137* introduced various extensions to the scope of *CGTA 1979, s 26*, with effect from 14 March 1989, which apply to companies disposing of assets, and these, now contained in *TCGA 1992, ss 30–34*, are described below.

TCGA 1992, s 30 applies to the disposal of an asset if a scheme has been effected or arrangements made (whether before or after the disposal) whereby the value of the asset, or of a 'relevant asset', has been materially reduced and a 'tax-free benefit' is conferred at any time on

(*a*) the person making the disposal or a person connected with him (see 16 CONNECTED PERSONS), or

(*b*) any other person unless tax avoidance was not a main purpose of the scheme or arrangements.

Where the disposal of the asset precedes its acquisition, references to a reduction include references to an increase.

The consideration for the disposal in the capital gains computation is increased by a just and reasonable amount having regard to the scheme or arrangements and the 'tax-free benefit'. Where the consideration for the disposal of one asset has been so increased and the 'tax-free benefit' was an increase in the value of another asset, the consideration for the first subsequent disposal of that other asset is reduced by a just and reasonable amount. (There is no provision for the acquirer's cost to be correspondingly adjusted.)

These provisions do not apply to, *inter alia*, disposals between companies in a group (see 9.18 below). [*TCGA 1992, s 30(1)(4)–(7)(9); FA 1996, Sch 20 paras 46, 47*].

An asset ('the second asset') is a '*relevant asset*' if

(1) the disposal of an asset (here called 'the first asset') is made by a company ('the disposing company'),

(2) the first asset comprises shares in, or securities (within *TCGA 1992, s 132*) of, a company, and

(3) the second asset is owned at the time of disposal of the first asset by a company 'associated' (see 9.15 below) with the disposing company.

A reduction in value of a relevant asset is not taken into account except in a case where

(A) during the period from the reduction in value to the time immediately before the disposal of the first asset there is no disposal of it other than one within *TCGA 1992, s 171(1)* (see 9.19 below),

(B) no disposal of that asset is treated as occurring during that period under *TCGA 1992, s 179* (see 9.47 below), and

(C) if the reduction had not occurred, but any consideration given for the relevant asset and any other material circumstances (including any consideration given before the disposal for the first asset disposed of) were unchanged, the value of the first asset would have been materially greater at the time of its disposal.

[*TCGA 1992, s 30(2); FA 2000, Sch 40 Pt II(12)*].

A '*tax-free benefit*' arises to a person if he becomes entitled to money or money's worth, or his interest in the value of any asset is increased, or he is wholly or partly relieved of any liability to which he is subject, *and* none of the foregoing benefits, when conferred, is otherwise liable to income tax, capital gains tax or corporation tax. [*TCGA 1992, s 30(3)*].

It is understood that the Revenue do not regard ordinary group relief transactions (e.g. the purchase of group relief) as falling within *TCGA 1992, s 30*.

Where a disposal within *TCGA 1992, s 30* forms the basis of a claim for relief under *ICTA 1988, ss 573, 574* (see 44.19 LOSSES), *section 30* applies if *any* benefit is conferred, whether tax-free or not. [*ICTA 1988, s 576(2)*].

Simon's Direct Tax Service. See D2.635.

9.14 **Certain disposals of shares by companies.** The following provisions apply where a disposal within 9.13 above ('the *section 30* disposal') is of shares ('the principal asset') which are owned by a company ('the first company') in another company ('the second company'). [*TCGA 1992, s 30(8)*].

Distributions within a group followed by a disposal of shares. If a reduction in the value of an asset is attributable to the payment of a dividend by the second company while the two companies are 'associated' (see 9.15 below), it is not treated as a reduction for the purposes of 9.13 above except to the extent (if any) that the dividend is attributable (see below) to 'chargeable profits' of the second company; and, in such a case, the tax-free benefit is ascertained without regard to any part of the dividend that is not attributable to such profits.

'*Chargeable profits*' are

(*a*) the 'distributable profits' of a company, to the extent that they arise from a 'transaction caught by this *section*', and

(*b*) the 'distributable profits' of a company, to the extent that they represent so much of a distribution received from another company as was attributable to chargeable profits of that company (including ones similarly representing a distribution).

'*Distributable profits*' are such profits computed on a commercial basis as, after allowance for any provision properly made for tax, the company is empowered, assuming sufficient funds, to distribute to persons entitled to participate in its profits. So far as possible, in ascertaining distributable profits, losses and other amounts to be set against profits must be set against profits other than ones which could be chargeable profits.

Profits arising on a '*transaction caught by this section*' are profits of a company ('company X') where the following three conditions are met but the three exceptions to them (see below) do not apply.

(1) The transaction is

  (i) a no gain/no loss disposal by company X to another group company within *TCGA 1992, s 171(1)* (see 9.19 below), or

  (ii) an exchange, or a transaction treated as an exchange for *TCGA 1992, s 135(2)(3)*, of shares in or debentures of a company held by company X for shares in or debentures of another company which immediately after the transaction is 'associated' (see 9.15 below) with company X, and which is treated as a reorganisation by *TCGA 1992, s 135(3)*, or

  (iii) a revaluation of an asset in the accounting records of company X.

(2) No disposal of the 'asset with enhanced value'

  (i) occurs, other than one within *TCGA 1992, s 171(1)*, during the period beginning with the transaction within (1) above and ending immediately before the *section 30* disposal, or

  (ii) is treated as having occurred during that period by virtue of *TCGA 1992, s 179* (see 9.47 below).

(3) Immediately after the *section 30* disposal the asset with enhanced value is owned by a person other than the disposing company or a company 'associated' with it (see 9.15 below).

'*Asset with enhanced value*' is defined as follows, according to which transaction within (1)(i), (1)(ii) or (1)(iii) above occurs, respectively: the asset acquired from company X; the shares or debentures acquired by company X as a result of the exchange; and the revalued asset.

The three exceptions to the foregoing three conditions are as follows.

(A) At the time of the transaction within (1) above, company X carries on a trade, and a profit on a disposal of the asset with enhanced value would form part of the trading profits.

(B) By reason of the nature of the asset with enhanced value, there could be no chargeable gain or allowable loss on its disposal.

(C) Immediately before the *section 30* disposal, the company owning the asset with enhanced value carries on a trade, and a profit on disposal would form part of the trading profits.

Attribution of profits to a distribution is made by determining the total distributable profits and chargeable profits which remain at the time of distribution, after allowing for all earlier distributions and distributions to be made then or subsequently in respect of other classes of shares, etc., and so far as possible attributing distributable profits other than chargeable profits.

Chargeable profits are treated as arising to shareholders, etc. proportionately to their holdings of shares, etc..

[*TCGA 1992, s 31; FA 2000, Sch 40 Pt II(12)*].

In practice, a dividend paid by a consortium-owned company to a member of the consortium and not attributable to chargeable profits is similarly not treated as giving rise to a value-shifting adjustment under 9.13 above. (ICAEW Technical Release TAX 20/94, 30 November 1994).

Asset-holding company leaving the group. Where the *section 30* disposal occurred before 9 March 1999, the above provisions were not triggered if that disposal was to a non-resident subsidiary in such a way that the asset with enhanced value continues to be owned within the capital gains group of which the company making the disposal is a member. This is because the condition at (3) above is not then satisfied. That asset could subsequently be sold by the non-resident subsidiary to a third party unaffected by the value-shifting provisions. The following counteracting provisions were accordingly introduced as regards any disposal of an asset on or after 9 March 1999. They apply wherever profits of a company would be profits on a transaction caught by *TCGA 1992, s 31* (see above) but for the fact that condition (3) above is not satisfied. In those circumstances, the profits are treated as arising on a transaction caught by *section 31* (with the result that *TCGA 1992, s 30* (see 9.13 above) has effect) if, at any time during the period of six years beginning with the date of the *section 30* disposal, either:

(*aa*) an event occurs which consists of the 'asset-holding company' ceasing to be a member of the 'disposal group' (otherwise than by virtue of the principal company of the group becoming a member of another group, i.e. the group being taken over); or

(*bb*) the 'asset-holding company' ceases to be a member of the 'disposal group' by virtue only of the principal company of the group becoming a member of another group *and* an event occurs as a result of which either

- (i) there is no member of the 'disposal group' of which the 'asset-holding company' is a 75% subsidiary, or
- (ii) there is no member of the 'disposal group' of which the 'asset-holding company' is an effective 51% subsidiary (see 9.18 below).

These provisions do not, however, apply (and there is thus no double charge), if, during that six-year period but prior to the occurrence of an event within (*aa*) or (*bb*) above, a disposal of the asset with enhanced value has been treated as having occurred by virtue of *TCGA 1992, s 179* (company leaving a group after acquiring an asset intra-group, see 9.47 below).

The '*asset-holding company*' at any time is the company holding the asset with enhanced value at that time. The '*disposal group*' is the group of which the company which made the *section 30* disposal was a member at the time of that disposal (or a group regarded as being the same as that group under *TCGA 1992, s 170(10)*, see 9.18 below).

Where *TCGA 1992, s 30* has effect as above, the consideration for the *section 30* disposal is not adjusted, but a chargeable gain is treated as accruing to the 'chargeable company' immediately before the event within (*aa*) or (*bb*) above. The '*chargeable company*' is normally the company which made the disposal. If, however, that company is, immediately before the event within (*aa*) or (*bb*) above, no longer a member of the disposal group, the chargeable company is the principal company of that group where the disposal was before 1 April 2000, or, for later disposals, any other member of the group immediately before the event which is so designated for the purpose by the Board by notice served on the company. The amount of the imputed gain is the shortfall between the allowable loss or chargeable gain which accrued on the *section 30* disposal and the allowable loss or chargeable gain which would have accrued on that disposal if the consideration had been treated as increased as in 9.13 above.

If an allowable loss arose on the *section 30* disposal and has not been otherwise utilised, it may be set against the imputed gain arising as above, notwithstanding the connected persons rule in *TCGA 1992, s 18(3)*.

[*TCGA 1992, s 31A; FA 1999, s 74, Sch 9 paras 2, 5; FA 2000, Sch 29 para 17*].

Disposals within a group followed by a disposal of shares. A reduction in the value of an asset is not treated as a reduction for the purposes of 9.13 above if it is attributable to the disposal of any asset ('the underlying asset') by the second company while the two companies are 'associated' (see 9.15 below), and the disposal is within *TCGA 1992, s 171(1)*, unless

(I) the actual consideration for the disposal of the underlying asset is less than both its market value and its 'cost',

(II) the disposal is not effected for *bona fide* commercial reasons and forms part of a scheme or arrangements of which a main purpose is the avoidance of a corporation tax liability, and

(III) the first company is not treated as disposing of an interest in the principal asset by virtue of a distribution in a dissolution or winding-up of the second company.

For the purpose of (I) above, the '*cost*' of an asset is the aggregate of any capital expenditure incurred by the company in acquiring or providing it, or in respect of it while owned after its acquisition.

In the case of a part disposal of an underlying asset,

(AA) the market value in (I) above is the market value of the asset acquired by the transferee, and

(BB) the amounts attributed to the cost of the underlying asset are reduced to the '*appropriate proportion*' thereof, i.e.

  (i) the proportion of capital expenditure properly attributed in the company's accounting records to the asset acquired by the transferee; or

  (ii) if (i) does not apply, such proportion as is just and reasonable.

[*TCGA 1992, s 32; FA 1996, Sch 20 para 47*].

9.15 **Interpretation of** 9.13 **and** 9.14 **above.** The following interpretational provisions apply.

As regards any asset ('the original asset'), the provisions in (1)–(5) below apply in relation to the enactments mentioned in (*a*) and (*b*) below.

(*a*) The enactments concerning relevant assets in *TCGA 1992, s 30(2)*: namely, in 9.13 above, (1)–(3) and (A)–(C).

(*b*) The enactments concerning distributions within a group followed by a disposal of shares in *TCGA 1992, s 31(7)–(9)*: namely, in 9.14 above, the second and third conditions ((2) and (3)) and the three exceptions ((A)–(C)) to the three conditions.

The provisions in (1)–(5) below also apply in connection with *TCGA 1992, s 31A* (see 9.14 above) for the purpose of determining any question in relation to the asset with enhanced value.

(1) In (A) and (B) in 9.13 above and in condition (2) in 9.14 above, references to the disposal of an asset do not include a part disposal. The same applies as regards the reference in relation to 9.14(*aa*) and (*bb*) above to a disposal occurring by virtue of *TCGA 1992, s 179*.

(2) For the purposes of the enactments referred to in (*a*) and (*b*) above, references to an asset are to the original asset, except that if subsequently one or more assets are treated under (4) or (5) below as the same as the original asset,

(i) if there has been no disposal falling within (A) or (B) in 9.13 above or (2) in 9.14 above, the references are to the asset(s) so treated; and

(ii) in any other case, the references are to the asset(s) representing that part of the value of the original asset remaining after allowing for earlier disposals within the relevant provision.

For the above purposes a disposal includes a part disposal which would have been within (A) or (B) in 9.13 above or (2) in 9.14 above if it had not been excluded by (1) above.

For the purposes of *TCGA 1992, s 31A* at 9.14 above, the following apply where one or more assets is treated under (4) or (5) below as the same as the asset with enhanced value.

(I) If, in the period beginning with the transaction in 9.14(1) above and ending immediately before the event in 9.14(*aa*) or (*bb*) above, there is no disposal of the asset with enhanced value to any person other than on a no gain/no loss intra-group disposal within *TCGA 1992, s 171(1)* (see 9.19 below), and no disposal of that asset is treated as having occurred by virtue of *TCGA 1992, s 179* (see 9.47 below), then references to the asset with enhanced value are to the asset(s) treated under (4) or (5) below as the same as that asset.

(II) In any other case, references to the asset with enhanced value are to the asset(s) representing that part of the value of the asset with enhanced value remaining after allowing for disposals of either kind referred to in (I) above.

(3) If, by virtue of (2) above, a reference to an asset is treated as a reference to two or more assets,

(i) the assets are treated as a single asset,

(ii) a disposal of any of them is a part disposal, and

(iii) the reference to the second asset in (3) in 9.13 above, to the asset in condition (3) in 9.14 above and to the asset in the definition of 'asset-holding company' in 9.14 above is in each case a reference to all or any of those two or more assets.

(4) If there is a part disposal of an asset, that asset and the asset acquired by the transferee are treated as the same.

(5) Where

(i) the value of an asset is derived from another asset owned by the same or an 'associated' company (see below), and

(ii) assets have been merged or divided or have changed their nature, or rights or interests in or over assets have been created or extinguished,

the two assets are treated as the same.

Where a reduction in the value of a relevant asset is to be taken into account under *TCGA 1992, s 30(2)* (see (1)–(3) and (A)–(C) in 9.13 above) and at the time of the disposal of the first asset in 9.13(1) by the disposing company

(A) references to the relevant asset are treated under (1)–(5) above as references to two or more assets treated as a single asset, and

(B) one or more, but not all, of those assets is owned by a company 'associated' (see below) with the disposing company,

the amount of the reduction in the value of the relevant asset to be taken into account is reduced to such an amount as is just and reasonable.

For the purposes of the provisions in TCGA 1992, s 31 concerning distributions within a group followed by a disposal of shares (see 9.14 above), the reduction in value of the principal asset (see 9.14 above) is to be reduced to such amount as is just and reasonable if

(*aa*) a dividend paid by the second company is attributable to that company's chargeable profits, and

(*bb*) the criterion in (2), (3) or (C) in 9.14 above is satisfied by reference to an asset, or assets treated as a single asset, treated under (2)(ii) above as the same as the asset with enhanced value.

Where *TCGA 1992, s 31A* (see 9.14 above) treats profits as arising on a transaction caught by *TCGA 1992, s 31* (see 9.14 above) and either condition (2) or condition (*aa*) or (*bb*) in 9.14 above is satisfied by reference to an asset (or assets treated as a single asset) treated by virtue of (2)(II) above as the same as the asset with enhanced value, the reduction in value of the principal asset (see 9.14 above) is to be reduced to such amount as is just and reasonable.

The definitions relating to groups of companies in TCGA 1992, s 170(2)–(11) apply as in 9.18 below; and companies are '*associated*' if they are members of the same group.

[*TCGA 1992, s 33; FA 1996, Sch 20 para 47; FA 1999, s 74, Sch 9 paras 3, 5*].

9.16 **Transactions treated as a reorganisation of share capital.** If the following conditions apply, a 'disposing company' is treated as receiving the amount specified in (*b*) below on a part disposal within *TCGA 1992, s 128(3)* of the 'original holding'.

(*a*) But for the rules whereby shares, etc. held after a reorganisation, reconstruction, etc. are treated as the same as those held beforehand, *TCGA 1992, s 30* in 9.13 above would apply on an exchange by a company (the 'disposing company') of shares, etc. in another company (the 'original holding') for shares, etc. in a further company which immediately afterwards is not in the same group (as defined in *TCGA 1992, s 170(2)–(11)*, see 9.18 below) as the disposing company.

(*b*) If *TCGA 1992, s 30* had applied, any allowable loss or chargeable gain on the disposal would have been calculated as if the consideration had been increased by an amount.

Similarly if, but for the rules referred to in (*a*) above, *section 30* would have applied by virtue of *TCGA 1992, s 31A* (see 9.14 above) on an exchange of the kind referred to in (*a*) above, *section 31A* is applied (with appropriate modification) as if the said rules did not apply. In the computation of the shortfall under that *section*, an allowable loss is in this case regarded as a chargeable gain of nil.

These provisions are interpreted as if *TCGA 1992, s 136* had effect generally for the capital gains tax legislation.

[*TCGA 1992, s 34; FA 1999, s 74, Sch 9 paras 4, 5*].

9.17 **CLOSE COMPANY TRANSFERRING ASSET AT UNDERVALUE**

Where, after 5 April 1965 (31 March 1982 where, on the ultimate disposal after 5 April 1988, market value at that date is substituted for cost), a close company transfers an asset to any person otherwise than at arm's length for a consideration less than market value, the difference is apportioned among the issued shares of the company so as to reduce the deductible cost in the capital gains tax computation on disposal of those shares; but this does not apply to transfers within a group. [*TCGA 1992, s 125*]. By concession, *section 125* is not applied where the transferee is a participator (or associate) and the transfer is treated as an income distribution under *ICTA 1988, s 209(2)(b)* or *(4)* (see 20.3, 20.8 DISTRIBUTIONS) or as a capital distribution under *TCGA 1992, s 122* (see Tolley's Capital Gains Tax under Shares and Securities), or where the transferee is an employee and is assessed under Schedule E on the excess of the market value of the asset over any amount paid for it. (Revenue Pamphlet IR 1, D51).

Where the transfer is to a trust for the benefit of the employees of the transferring company, the difference that is apportioned is limited (where it would otherwise be greater) to any excess of allowable expenditure over the transfer consideration. [*TCGA 1992, s 239*].

Simon's Direct Tax Service. See C3.131.

9.18 **GROUPS OF COMPANIES**

For the purposes of the following sections (9.18–9.52), the following apply.

Definition of company. '*Company*' (except in the case of 9.21 below) means one within the meaning of the *Companies Act 1985* or the corresponding enactment in Northern Ireland or which is constituted under any other Act, Royal Charter, or letters patent or under the law of a country outside the UK. It also includes a registered INDUSTRIAL AND PROVIDENT SOCIETY (32), a building society (see 7.2 BUILDING SOCIETIES) and (from 17 March 1998) an incorporated friendly society (see 28.2 FRIENDLY SOCIETIES).

Residence requirement. Before (broadly) April 2000, and in all cases except those dealt with under 9.21 and 9.51 below, the company had to be resident in the UK. *FA 2000* removes this condition and thus enables any company, whatever its country of residence, to be a member of a group, and to be taken into account in establishing the existence of a group, for the purposes of corporation tax on chargeable gains. See 29.14 GROUPS OF COMPANIES for the corresponding group relief provisions. The change is generally effective from 1 April 2000, although consequential changes to pre-existing anti-avoidance legislation took effect on 21 March 2000. The consequences, and effective dates, of the change in the residence requirement are dealt with elsewhere as appropriate. Transitional measures ensure continuity of treatment as regards a pre-existing group of companies (and see (iii) below).

[*TCGA 1992, s 170(2)(a)(9); FA 1998, s 136(1)(4); FA 2000, s 102, Sch 29 paras 1, 46(1)–(3)*].

Definition of group. A '*group*' comprises

(*a*) a company ('*the principal company of the group*') and

(*b*) that company's '75 per cent subsidiaries' (i.e. where not less than 75% of the 'ordinary share capital' is beneficially owned directly or indirectly by the principal company), and those subsidiaries' 75 per cent subsidiaries (and so on), except that any 75 per cent subsidiary which is not 'an effective 51 per cent subsidiary' of the principal company is excluded. Beneficial ownership is not affected by the existence of an option which may require disposal of shares at a future date (see *J Sainsbury plc v O'Connor CA 1991, 64 TC 208*).

This definition is subject to the following rules.

(i) A company ('the subsidiary') which is a 75 per cent subsidiary of another company cannot be a principal company of a group, unless

(A) because of the exclusion in (*b*) above, the two companies are not in the same group,

(B) the requirements of the definition of a group in (*a*) and (*b*) are otherwise satisfied, and

(C) no further company could, under this provision, be the principal company of a group of which the subsidiary would be a member.

(ii) If a company would otherwise belong to more than one group (the principal company of each of which is below called the '*head of a group*'), it belongs only to the group which can first be determined under the following tests.

(I) The group to which it would belong if the exclusion of a company which is not an 'effective 51 per cent subsidiary' in (*b*) above were applied without the inclusion of any amount to which the head of a group

(*a*) is entitled of any profits available for distribution to equity holders of a head of another group, or

(*b*) would be entitled of any assets of a head of another group available for distribution to its equity holders on a winding-up.

(II) The group the head of which is entitled to a greater percentage than any other head of a group of its profits available for distribution to equity holders.

(III) The group the head of which would be entitled to a greater percentage than any other head of a group of its assets available for distribution to equity holders on a winding-up.

(IV) The group the head of which owns (as in *ICTA 1988, s 838(1)(a)*) directly or indirectly more of its ordinary share capital than any other head of a group.

(iii) *Transitional.* If a group is reconstituted purely because of the amendment made by *FA 2000* to the residence requirement (see above), such that the principal company of the 'old' group is not the principal company of the 'new' group, a subsidiary which is not an 'effective 51 per cent subsidiary' of the 'new' principal company remains part of the group for so long as it remains such a subsidiary of the 'old' principal company.

A company ('the subsidiary') is '*an effective 51 per cent subsidiary*' of another company ('the parent') at any time if and only if

(A) the parent is entitled to more than 50 per cent of any profits available for distribution to equity holders of the subsidiary, and

(B) the parent would be entitled to more than 50 per cent of any assets available for distribution to the equity holders on a winding-up.

ICTA 1988, Sch 18 (group relief: equity holders and profits or assets available for distribution, see 29.16, 29.17 GROUPS OF COMPANIES) applies with minor modification for (ii) and (A) and (B) above. One modification to *Schedule 18* for these purposes disapplies the requirement that certain arrangements for changes in profit or asset shares are assumed to take place in applying the 50% test. The anti-avoidance measures of *paras 5B–5E* of *Schedule 18* (introduced by *F(No 2)A 1992, Sch 6*, see 29.17 GROUPS OF COMPANIES, with effect from 15 November 1991) do not apply for these purposes.

[*TCGA 1992, s 170(2)–(8); ICTA 1988, s 838; FA 1990, s 86; F(No 2)A 1992, Sch 6 para 5; FA 2000, Sch 29 para 46(4)–(6)*].

A group remains the same group so long as the same company remains the principal company of the group, and if at any time the principal company of a group becomes a member of another group, the first group and the other group are regarded as the same, and the question whether or not a company has ceased to be a member of a group is determined accordingly. [*TCGA 1992, s 170(10)*].

The passing of a resolution, or the making of an order, or any other act for the winding-up of a member of a group is not treated as an occasion on which any company ceases to be a member of the group. [*TCGA 1992, s 170(11)*].

Simon's Direct Tax Service. See **D2.622**.

General. '*Ordinary share capital*' means all issued share capital of a company except that carrying a fixed rate of dividend only. [*ICTA 1988, s 832(1)*]. Any share capital of a registered industrial and provident society is treated as ordinary share capital. 'Issued share capital' does not include founder members' deposits in a company limited by guarantee (*South Shore Mutual Insurance Co Ltd v Blair (Sp C 215), [1999] SSCD 296*).

As regards nationalised industries, etc. see *TCGA 1992, s 170(12)–(14)* as amended.

Where it is assumed, for any purpose, that a group member has acquired or sold an asset, it is also assumed that it was not a sale to, or acquisition from, a group member. [*TCGA 1992, s 171(1) as originally enacted; TCGA 1992, s 171(6) as introduced by FA 2000, Sch 29 para 2(5)*].

9.19 **Disposals of capital assets by one member of a group to another are treated as if made at a 'no gain, no loss' price** except for:

(i) *assumed* (as opposed to actual) transfers;

(ii) a disposal of a *debt* due from a group member effected by satisfying it (or part of it);

(iii) a disposal on redemption of *redeemable shares*;

(iv) a disposal of an interest in shares in consideration of a *capital distribution*;

(v) the receipt of *compensation* for destruction etc. of assets (in that the disposal is treated as being to the insurer or other person who ultimately bears the burden of furnishing the compensation);

(vi) a disposal by or to an investment trust (and see 9.49 below);

(vii) a disposal to a 'dual resident investing company' (see 29.31 GROUPS OF COMPANIES);

(viii) a disposal on or after 17 March 1998 by or to an incorporated friendly society entitled to tax exemptions under *ICTA 1988, s 461B* (see 28.2 *et seq.* FRIENDLY SOCIETIES);

(ix) a disposal on or after 17 March 1998 by or to a venture capital trust (and see 9.50 below).

The change in the residence requirement referred to in 9.18 above has effect for these purposes in relation to disposals on or after 1 April 2000. The conditions for intra-group transfers of assets on or after that date to be treated as no gain, no loss disposals are:

(*a*) that either the transferor company is UK resident at the time of disposal or the asset is a 'chargeable asset' in relation to that company immediately before that time; and

(*b*) that either the transferee company is UK resident at that time or the asset is a 'chargeable asset' in relation to that company immediately after that time.

For these purposes, an asset is a '*chargeable asset*' in relation to a company at a particular time if, on a disposal by the company at that time, any gain would be a chargeable gain and within the charge to corporation tax by virtue of *TCGA 1992, s 10* (non-UK resident company trading through UK branch or agency, see 53.4 RESIDENCE).

For disposals before 1 April 2000, the effect of the residence requirement was that both transferor and transferee had to be UK resident and members of the same group of UK-resident companies.

[*TCGA 1992, s 171; FA 1994, s 251(7)(b); FA 1998, s 135(1)(4), s 136(2)(5); FA 2000, Sch 29 para 2*].

As regards (iv), the assets acquired in the capital distribution are nevertheless treated as transferred at a 'no gain, no loss' price (see *Innocent v Whaddon Estates Ltd Ch D 1981, 55 TC 476*). Where an exchange of securities for those in another company is, under *TCGA 1992, ss 127, 135*, not treated as involving a disposal of the original shares or the acquisition of a new holding, it is not treated as a 'no gain, no loss' transfer as above. [*TCGA 1992, s 171(3)*]. Where the consideration given for shares consists of qualifying corporate bonds, see Revenue Tax Bulletin December 1996 p 372 for an analysis of the consequences.

Where a disposal is to be dealt with on a 'no gain, no loss' basis, indexation allowance will be taken into account (see Tolley's Capital Gains Tax under Indexation).

The Revenue have indicated that they will not seek to apply the '*Ramsay* principle' (see 4.1 ANTI-AVOIDANCE) where straightforward transfers of assets between members of the same group enable asset sales to be routed through group members with allowable capital losses. Where the effect of a series of transactions is to transfer the benefit of capital losses from one group to another, the *Ramsay* principle may be applicable, depending on the relationship between the amounts of the loss involved, the period for which the company with the loss has been within the group and on the circumstances in which the losses have arisen. (ICAEW Guidance Note TR 588, 25 September 1985).

Simon's Direct Tax Service. See **D2.623**.

9.20 **Disposal outside group treated as having been preceded by intra-group transfer.** Where two companies ('X' and 'Y') are members of a group, and X disposes of an asset after 31 March 2000 to a person outside the group (the 'actual disposal'), X and Y may jointly elect to the effect that, for the purposes of corporation tax on chargeable gains:

(*a*) the asset (or a specified part of it) is deemed to have been transferred by X to Y immediately before the actual disposal;

(*b*) that transfer is deemed to be a no gain, no loss disposal within *TCGA 1992, s 171* (see 9.18 above); and

(*c*) the actual disposal (or the part of it to which the election relates) is deemed to have been made by Y.

The election must be made in writing to an officer of the Board within two years after the end of the accounting period of X in which the actual disposal was made, and can only be made if an actual transfer of the asset (or part) from X to Y would have been a no gain, no loss disposal within *section 171*.

Any payment agreed between X and Y in connection with the election is ignored in computing profits or losses for corporation tax purposes, and is not regarded as a distribution or a charge on income, provided that it does not exceed the amount of the chargeable gain or allowable loss treated, as a result of the disposal, as accruing to Y.

This provision is intended to facilitate the bringing together of chargeable gains and allowable losses within one group company.

[*TCGA 1992, s 171A; FA 2000, s 101*].

9.21 **Intra-group transfers of assets under scheme for transfer by non-resident of UK branch or agency.** For disposals before 1 April 2000, where

(*a*) there is a scheme for the transfer by a non-UK resident company ('company A') which carries on a trade in the UK through a branch or agency of the whole or part of the trade to a UK resident company ('company B'),

(*b*) company A disposes of an asset to company B in accordance with the scheme at a time when both companies are members of the same group, and

(*c*) a claim relating to the asset is made by both companies within two years after the end of the accounting period of company B during which the disposal is made,

the asset is treated as disposed of by company A and acquired by company B for a no gain, no loss consideration, and *TCGA 1992, s 25(3)* (deemed disposal by non-resident on ceasing to trade in the UK through a branch or agency, see Tolley's Capital Gains Tax under Overseas Matters) does not apply to the asset by reason of the transfer.

The definitions of 'company' and 'group' in 9.18 above are for these purposes extended to include non-UK resident companies.

The relief does not apply where company B is a dual resident investing company (see 29.31 GROUPS OF COMPANIES) or an investment trust (see 60.4 UNIT AND INVESTMENT TRUSTS). No relief is given unless any gain accruing to company A on the disposal of the asset in accordance with the scheme, or, where that disposal occurs after the transfer has taken place, on a disposal of the asset immediately before the transfer, would be a chargeable gain and would, under *TCGA 1992, s 10(3)*, form part of its profits for corporation tax purposes.

See also 53.1 RESIDENCE as regards *FA 1994, s 249.*

These provisions are **abolished** for disposals **on or after 1 April 2000**, following the extension of groups to include non-resident companies (see 9.18 above).

[*TCGA 1992, s 172; FA 1994, s 251(7)(c); FA 2000, Sch 29 para 3*].

Simon's Direct Tax Service. See D4.127.

9.22 **Intra-group transfers of assets which are trading stock of one company but not of the other.** Where a company ('company A') acquires an asset as trading stock of a trade from another member of the group ('company B'), and the asset did not form part of the trading stock of a trade carried on by company B, company A is treated for the purposes of *TCGA 1992, s 161* as acquiring the asset otherwise than as trading stock and immediately appropriating it as trading stock. The effect is that, subject to an election being made under *section 161(3)*, a chargeable gain or allowable loss accrues to company A based on the difference between market value and the no gain, no loss transfer value (see 9.19 above).

Where a company ('company C') disposes of an asset forming part of the trading stock of a trade to another member of the group ('company D'), and the asset is acquired by company D otherwise than as trading stock of a trade carried on by it, company C is treated for the purposes of *TCGA 1992, s 161* as appropriating the asset immediately before the disposal for a purpose other than use as trading stock. The effect is that company C is deemed to have acquired the asset at that time at the amount brought into the accounts of the trade for tax purposes on the deemed appropriation.

As regards acquisitions and disposals on or after 1 April 2000, the change in the residence requirements relating to groups of companies (see 9.18 above) applies in determining whether a company is a member of a group for the above purposes, but references above to a trade do not include a trade carried on by a non-UK resident company unless it is carried on in the UK through a branch or agency.

[*TCGA 1992, s 173; FA 2000, Sch 29 para 11*].

Acquisition 'as trading stock' implies a commercial justification for the acquisition, see *Coates v Arndale Properties Ltd HL 1984, 59 TC 516, Reed v Nova Securities Ltd HL 1985, 59 TC 516* and *N Ltd v Inspector of Taxes (Sp C 90), [1996] SSCD 346.*

Simon's Direct Tax Service. See **D4.624.**

9.23 Restriction on set-off of pre-entry losses where a company joins a group.

General outline and commencement. TCGA 1992, Sch 7A restricts losses accruing to a company before the time it becomes a member of a group of companies and losses accruing on assets held by any company at such a time.

The restrictions apply for the calculation of the amount to be included in respect of chargeable gains in a company's total profits for any accounting period ending after 15 March 1993. However, the restrictions apply only in relation to the deduction from chargeable gains accruing after 15 March 1993 of amounts in respect of, or of amounts carried forward in respect of,

(*a*) 'pre-entry losses' accruing, before it became a member of a UK capital gains group, to a company whose membership of that group began or begins after 31 March 1987, and

(*b*) losses accruing on the disposal of any assets so far as it is by reference to such a company that the assets fall to be treated as being or having been 'pre-entry assets' or assets incorporating a part referable to pre-entry assets.

[*TCGA 1992, s 177A, Sch 7A; FA 1993, s 88, Sch 8*].

The restriction is widely drawn, and whilst its stated principal intention is to prevent the fiscal effectiveness of an acquisition of a 'capital loss' company (i.e. a company that has a *realised* allowable loss as its only commercial feature) it may also impinge on an acquisition of a company solely for commercial reasons where it becomes a member of a group whilst holding an asset which is later disposed of (whether by the company itself, or by another group member to whom the asset has been transferred) outside the group at a loss. Further restrictions are imposed by *FA 1994, s 94* in relation to the deduction of a loss from a chargeable gain where either the gain or the loss accrues after 10 March 1994. After 20 March 2000, the change in the residence requirement as regards groups of companies (see 9.18 above) is applied for the purposes of these provisions.

See Revenue Capital Gains Manual CG 47500 *et seq.*.

Simon's Direct Tax Service. See **D2.638A** *et seq.*.

9.24 *Application and construction of TCGA 1992, Sch 7A. Schedule 7A* has effect, in the case of a company which is or has been a member of a group of companies (within *TCGA 1992, s 170*, see 9.18 above, and referred to as '*the relevant group*'), in relation to any 'pre-entry losses'. A '*pre-entry loss*', in relation to a company, means any allowable loss that accrued to it at a time before it became a member of the relevant group or the 'pre-entry proportion' (see 9.25–9.28 below) of any allowable loss accruing to it on the disposal of any 'pre-entry asset'. [*TCGA 1992, Sch 7A para 1(1)(2)*].

A '*pre-entry asset*', in relation to any disposal, means any asset that was held, at the time immediately before the 'relevant event' occurred in relation to it, by any company (whether or not the one which makes the disposal) which is or has at any time been a member of the relevant group. Originally, the '*relevant event*' occurred in relation to a company when it became a member of the relevant group. This now applies only if the company is UK resident at that time or the asset is then a 'chargeable asset' (defined as in 9.19 above) in relation to it, and if neither of those is the case a relevant event subsequently occurs when the company becomes UK resident or the asset become a chargeable asset in relation to it. This amendment is in consequence of the change in the residence requirement for groups of companies (see 9.18 above) and has effect in computing chargeable gains for accounting periods ending after 20 March 2000. The question of whether a company is a member of a group at any time on or before that date is, however, to be determined by reference to the residence requirement as it applied before that change. If a company becomes a member of a group on 21 March 2000 purely as a result of the change in the residence requirement, *Schedule 7A* is not thereby brought into effect. [*TCGA 1992, Sch 7A para 1(3)(3A); FA 2000, Sch 29 para 7(2)(3)(6)–(9)*].

Subject to 9.26 below, an asset is not, however, a pre-entry asset if the company which held the asset at the time the relevant event occurred in relation to it is not the company which makes the disposal and since that time the asset has been disposed of otherwise than on the no gain, no loss basis of *TCGA 1992, s 171* (see 9.19 above), except where the company making the disposal retains an interest in or over the asset (when the interest is treated as a pre-entry asset). [*TCGA 1992, Sch 7A para 1(4); FA 2000, Sch 29 para 7(4)(6)–(8)*].

Subject to 9.26 below, an asset ('*the second asset*'), which derives its value wholly or partly from another asset ('*the first asset*') acquired or held by a company at any time, is treated as the same asset if it is held subsequently by the same company, or by any company which is or has been a member of the same group of companies as that company (e.g. a freehold derived from a leasehold where the lessee acquires the reversion). Where this treatment applies, whether under this provision or otherwise (e.g. under *TCGA 1992, s 43*, for which see Tolley's Capital Gains Tax), the second asset is treated as a pre-entry asset in relation to a company if the first asset would have been. [*TCGA 1992, Sch 7A para 1(8)*].

In relation to a pre-entry asset, references in *Schedule 7A* to '*the relevant time*' are references to the time when the relevant event occurred in relation to the company by reference to which that asset is a pre-entry asset. Where a relevant event has occurred in relation to a company more than once, an asset is a pre-entry asset in relation to that company if it would be a pre-entry asset in relation to that company in respect of any of those occasions, but in these circumstances any reference to the time when a relevant event occurred in relation to the company is a reference to the last such occasion. [*TCGA 1992, Sch 7A para 1(5); FA 2000, Sch 29 para 7(5)–(8)*].

Subject to so much of *para 9(6)* (see 9.32 below) as requires groups of companies to be treated as separate groups for the purposes of *TCGA 1992, Sch 7A para 9*, if

(*a*) the principal company of a group (the '*first group*') has at any time become a member of another group (the '*second group*') so that the two groups are treated as the same under *TCGA 1992, s 170(10)* (see 9.18 above), and

(*b*) the second group, together (in pursuance of *TCGA 1992, s 170(10)*) with the first group, is the relevant group,

then except where the circumstances are as in *TCGA 1992, Sch 7A para 1(7)* (below), the members of the first group are treated for the purposes of *Schedule 7A* as having become members of the relevant group at that time, and not (by virtue of *TCGA 1992, s 170(10)*) at the times when they became members of the first group. [*TCGA 1992, Sch 7A para 1(6)*].

The circumstances mentioned in *para 1(6)* are where:

(1) the persons who immediately before the time when the principal company of the first group became a member of the second group owned the shares comprised in the issued share capital of the principal company of the first group are the same as the persons who, immediately after that time, owned the shares comprised in the issued share capital of the principal company of the relevant group; and

(2) the company which is the principal company of the relevant group immediately after that time

  (i) was not the principal company of any group immediately before that time, and

  (ii) immediately after that time had assets consisting entirely, or almost entirely, of shares comprised in the issued share capital of the principal company of the first group.

[*TCGA 1992, Sch 7A para 1(7)*].

Where an allowable loss accrues to a company under *TCGA 1992, s 116(10)(b)* (crystallisation of gain or loss on shares exchanged on reorganisation, etc. for qualifying corporate bonds, see Tolley's Capital Gains Tax and 9.30 below), that loss is deemed to accrue at the time of the reorganisation etc. for the purposes of deciding whether a loss accrues before a company becomes a member of the relevant group. [*TCGA 1992, Sch 7A para 1(9)*]. Likewise, the annual deemed disposals of unit trust etc. holdings of a life assurance company's long-term business fund under *TCGA 1992, s 212* (see 41.17 LIFE INSURANCE COMPANIES) are deemed to occur for this purpose without regard to the 'spreading' provisions of *TCGA 1992, s 213*. [*TCGA 1992, Sch 7A para 1(10)*].

9.25 *Pre-entry proportion of losses on pre-entry assets.* Subject to 9.26–9.28 below, the '*pre-entry proportion*' of an allowable loss accruing on the disposal of a pre-entry asset is the allowable loss that would accrue on that disposal if that loss were the sum of the amounts determined, for every item of '*relevant allowable expenditure*' (i.e. expenditure within *TCGA 1992, s 38(1)(a)* or *(b)*), according to the following formula:

$$A \times \frac{B}{C} \times \frac{D}{E} \text{ where}$$

A is the total amount of the allowable loss;

B is the sum of the amount of the item of relevant allowable expenditure concerned and, for disposals before 30 November 1993, the '*indexed rise*' in that item (as in *TCGA 1992, s 54* (see Tolley's Capital Gains Tax) but ignoring the effect of *TCGA 1992, s 110* where the above formula is applied for the purposes of 9.26 below);

C is the sum of the total amount of all such expenditure and, for disposals before 30 November 1993, the indexed rises in each of the items comprised in that expenditure;

D is the length of the period beginning with 'the relevant pre-entry date' and ending with the relevant time or, if that date is after that time, nil (i.e. there is no pre-entry proportion if the relevant time precedes the relevant pre-entry date); and

E is the length of the period beginning with the relevant pre-entry date and ending with the day of disposal.

[*TCGA 1992, Sch 7A para 2(1)(2)(9); FA 1994, s 93(8)(a)*].

'*The relevant pre-entry date*', in relation to any item referred to above, is the later of 1 April 1982 and the date the asset was acquired or provided or, as the case may be, improvement expenditure became due and payable (such date being subject to the assumptions of *TCGA 1992, Sch 7A para 2(4)(5)* (below) and additionally, in relation to the deduction of a loss from a chargeable gain where either the gain or the loss accrues after 10 March 1994, to those of *para 2(6A)(6B)*). [*TCGA 1992, Sch 7A para 2(3); FA 1994, s 94(1)(2)(4)*].

Where any 'original shares' are treated as the same asset as a 'new holding' (within *TCGA 1992, s 127*), the above formula and (where applicable) the provisions in 9.26 below are applied (except, for disposals before 30 November 1993, in relation to the calculation of any indexed rise):

(*a*) as if any item referred to above consisting in consideration given for the acquisition of the new holding had been incurred at the time the original shares were acquired; and

(*b*) where there is more than one such time, as if that item were incurred at those different times in the same proportions as the consideration for the acquisition of the original shares.

[*TCGA 1992, Sch 7A para 2(4); FA 1994, s 93(8)(b)*].

Without prejudice to (*a*) and (*b*) above, the formula is applied to any asset which

(i) was held by a company at the time when it became a member of the relevant group, and

(ii) is treated as having been acquired by that company on *any* no gain/no loss corresponding disposal,

as if the company and every person who acquired that asset or 'the equivalent asset' at a 'material time' had been the same person and, accordingly, as if the asset had been acquired by the company when it or the equivalent asset was acquired by the first of those persons to have acquired it at a material time, and the time at which any expenditure had been incurred were to be determined accordingly. [*TCGA 1992, Sch 7A para 2(5)*].

A '*material time*' is any time before an acquisition of an asset in circumstances as in (ii) above and is, or is after, the last occasion before the occasion on which any person acquired that asset or the equivalent asset otherwise than on an acquisition which is within (ii) above, or is an acquisition by virtue of which any asset is treated as the equivalent asset; and the formula is applied in relation to any asset within (i) and (ii) above without regard to *TCGA 1992, s 56(2)* (consideration on no gain/no loss disposal deemed to include indexation allowance). [*TCGA 1992, Sch 7A para 2(6)*].

In relation to the deduction of a loss from a chargeable gain where either the gain or the loss accrues after 10 March 1994, and notwithstanding anything in *TCGA 1992, s 56(2)* (see above), where in the case of the disposal of any pre-entry asset any company has, between the relevant time and the time of the disposal, acquired that asset or 'the equivalent asset', and the acquisition was either an acquisition in pursuance of a no gain/no loss disposal under *TCGA 1992, s 171* (see 9.19 above) or an acquisition by virtue of which an asset is treated as 'the equivalent asset', the items of relevant allowable expenditure in the above formula, and the times they are treated as having been incurred, are determined on the assumption that the company by reference to which the asset in question is a pre-entry asset, and the company which acquired the asset or the equivalent asset as above (and every other company which has made such an acquisition), were the same person and, accordingly, that the pre-entry asset had been acquired by the company disposing of it at the time when it or the equivalent asset would have been treated as acquired by the company by reference to which the asset is a pre-entry asset. [*TCGA 1992, Sch 7A para 2(6A)(6B); FA 1994, s 94(1)(2)(4)*].

In relation to the deduction of a loss from a chargeable gain where either the gain or the loss accrues after 10 March 1994, for the purposes of the provisions in *TCGA 1992, Sch 7A para 2(5)(6)(6A)(6B)* (above), '*the equivalent asset*', in relation to another asset acquired or disposed of by any company, is any asset which falls in relation to that company to be treated (whether under *TCGA 1992, Sch 7A para 1(8)* (see 9.24 above) or otherwise) as the same as the other asset or which would fall to be so treated after applying, as respects other assets, the assumptions for which those provisions provide. In relation to the deduction of a loss from a chargeable gain where both the gain and the loss accrue before

11 March 1994, for the purposes of the provisions in *para 2(5)(6)* (above), '*the equivalent asset*', in relation to the acquisition of any asset by any company, is any asset which (whether under *para 1(8)* or otherwise) would be treated in relation to that company as the same as the asset in question. [*TCGA 1992, Sch 7A para 2(7); FA 1994, s 94(1)(2)(4)*].

The above provisions and (where applicable) those in 9.26 below have effect where a loss accrues to a company under *TCGA 1992, s 116(10)(b)* (crystallisation of gain or loss on shares exchanged on reorganisation, etc. for qualifying corporate bonds; see 9.24 above), and the shares are treated under 9.26 below as including pre-entry assets, as if the disposal on which the loss accrues were the disposal of the shares assumed to be made by *section 116(10)(a)* at the time of reorganisation etc. [*TCGA 1992, Sch 7A para 2(8)*].

In relation to disposals on or after 30 November 1993, where, by virtue of *TCGA 1992, s 55(8)* (introduced by *FA 1994, s 93(4)*), the allowable loss (or part) accruing on the disposal of a pre-entry asset is attributable to an amount of rolled-up indexation, the total relevant allowable expenditure is treated for the purposes of *TCGA 1992, Sch 7A para 2* as increased by that rolled-up amount, each item of expenditure being treated as increased by the attributable proportion of the total. [*TCGA 1992, Sch 7A para 2(8A); FA 1994, s 93(8)(c)*].

Also in relation to disposals on or after 30 November 1993, where *TCGA 1992, s 56(3)* (introduced by *FA 1994, s 93(5)*) applies to reduce the total allowable expenditure on the disposal of a pre-entry asset on which an allowable loss accrues, the amount of each item of relevant allowable expenditure is treated for the purposes of *para 2* as reduced by so much of that reduction as is attributable to it. [*TCGA 1992, Sch 7A para 2(8B); FA 1994, s 93(8)(c)*].

9.26 *Disposals of pooled assets.* Subject to 9.27 and 9.28 below, the provisions below apply where any assets acquired by any company fall to be treated with other assets as indistinguishable parts of the same asset ('*a pooled asset*') and the whole or part of that asset is referable to pre-entry assets.

For the purposes of *Schedule 7A*, where a pooled asset has at any time contained a pre-entry asset, the pooled asset is treated, until on the assumptions below all the pre-entry assets included in the asset have been disposed of, as incorporating a part which is referable to pre-entry assets, the size of that part being determined as below. [*TCGA 1992, Sch 7A para 3(1)(2)*].

Where there is a disposal of any part of a pooled asset and the proportion of the asset which is disposed of does not exceed the proportion of that asset which is represented by any part of it which is not, at the time of disposal, referable to pre-entry assets, that disposal is treated for the purposes of *Schedule 7A* as confined to assets which are not pre-entry assets. Consequently, no part of any loss accruing on that disposal is treated as a pre-entry loss (except where *para 4(2)*, see 9.27 below, applies), and the part of the pooled asset which after the disposal is treated as referable to pre-entry assets is correspondingly increased (without prejudice to the effect of any subsequent acquisition of assets to be added to the pool in determining whether, and to what extent, any part of the pooled asset is to be treated as referable to pre-entry assets). [*TCGA 1992, Sch 7A para 3(3)(11)*].

Where such a disposal does give rise to such an excess, the disposal is treated for the purposes of *Schedule 7A* as relating to pre-entry assets only so far as required for the purposes of the excess. Consequently

(*a*) any loss accruing on that disposal is treated for the purposes of *Schedule 7A* as an allowable loss on a pre-entry asset,

(*b*) the pre-entry proportion of that loss is deemed (except where *para 4(3)*, see 9.27 below, applies) to be the amount (insofar as it does not exceed the amount of the loss actually accruing) which would have been the pre-entry proportion under 9.25 above of any loss accruing on the disposal of the excess if the excess were a separate asset, and

(*c*) the pooled asset is treated after the disposal as referable entirely to pre-entry assets (without prejudice to the effect of any subsequent acquisition of assets to be added to the pool in determining whether, and to what extent, any part of the pooled asset is to be treated as referable to pre-entry assets).

[*TCGA 1992, Sch 7A para 3(4)(11)*].

Where there is a disposal of the whole or part of a pooled asset at a time when the asset is referable entirely to pre-entry assets, (*a*) and (*b*) above apply to the disposal of the asset or the part as they apply in relation to the assumed disposal of the excess mentioned in the preamble to (*a*) and (*b*) but, where the whole of an asset only part of which is referable to pre-entry assets is disposed of, the reference in (*b*) above to the excess is taken as a reference to that part. [*TCGA 1992, Sch 7A para 3(5)*].

In applying (*b*) above, for the purposes of determining what would have been the pre-entry proportion of any loss accruing on the disposal of any assets as the separate asset mentioned in (*b*) above, it is assumed that none of the assets treated as comprised in that separate asset has ever been comprised in a pooled asset with any assets other than those which are taken to constitute that separate asset. [*TCGA 1992, Sch 7A para 3(6)*].

Assets comprised in any asset which is treated as separate are identified on the following assumptions:

(i) that assets are disposed of in the order of the relevant pre-entry dates in relation to the acquisition consideration as under 9.25 above;

(ii) subject to (i), that assets with earlier relevant times are disposed of before those with later ones;

(iii) that disposals made when a company was not a member of the relevant group are made in accordance with *para 3(1)–(6)* and (i) and (ii) above, as they have effect in relation to the group of companies of which the company was a member at the time of disposal or, as the case may be, of which it had most recently been a member before that time; and

(iv) subject to (i)–(iii) above, that a company disposes of assets in the order in which it acquired them.

[*TCGA 1992, Sch 7A para 3(7)*].

Where there is more than one relevant pre-entry date in relation to the consideration for any acquisition, the date in (i) above is the earlier or earliest of those dates if any such date relating to an option to acquire the asset is disregarded. [*TCGA 1992, Sch 7A para 3(8)*].

Where a second asset falls to be treated as acquired at the same time as a first asset which was acquired earlier (whether under *para 1(8)*, see 9.24 above, or otherwise), and the second asset is either comprised in a pooled asset partly referable to pre-entry assets, or is or includes an asset which is to be treated as so comprised, (i)–(iv) above apply not only in relation to the second asset as if it were the first asset but also, in the first place, for identifying the asset which is to be treated as the first asset under the above provisions. [*TCGA 1992, Sch 7A para 3(10)*].

Where the formula in 9.25 above is applied to an asset treated as above as a separate asset, the amount or value of the asset's acquisition or disposal consideration and any related incidental costs are determined, not under *TCGA 1992, s 129* or s *130*, but by apportioning the consideration or costs relating both to that asset and to other assets acquired or disposed of at the same time according to the proportion that is borne by that asset to all the assets to which the consideration or costs related. [*TCGA 1992, Sch 7A para 3(9)*].

9.27 *Rules to prevent pre-entry losses on pooled assets being treated as post-entry losses ('anti-flooding')*. The provisions below apply if:

(*a*) there is a disposal of any part of a pooled asset which under 9.26 above is treated as including a part referable to pre-entry assets;

(*b*) the assets disposed of are or include assets ('*the post-entry element of the disposal*') which for the purposes of 9.26 above are treated as having been included in the part of the pooled asset which is not referable to pre-entry assets;

(*c*) an allowable loss ('*the actual loss*') accrues on the disposal; and

(*d*) the amount which in computing the allowable loss is allowed as a deduction of relevant allowable expenditure ('*the expenditure actually allowed*') exceeds such expenditure attributable to the post-entry element of the disposal.

[*TCGA 1992, Sch 7A para 4(1)*].

Subject to *para 4(6)* below, where the post-entry element of the disposal comprises all of the assets disposed of, the actual loss is treated for the purposes of *Schedule 7A* as a loss accruing on the disposal of a pre-entry asset; and the pre-entry proportion of that loss is treated as being the amount (insofar as it does not exceed the amount of the actual loss) of the excess referred to in (*d*) above. [*TCGA 1992, Sch 7A para 4(2)*].

Also subject to *para 4(6)* below, where the actual loss is treated under 9.26 above as a loss accruing on the disposal of a pre-entry asset, and the expenditure actually allowed exceeds the actual cost of the assets to which the disposal is treated as relating, the pre-entry proportion of the loss is treated as being the amount which (insofar as it does not exceed the amount of the actual loss) is equal to the sum of that excess and what would, apart from these provisions and those in 9.28 below, be the pre-entry proportion of the loss accruing on the disposal.

For this purpose, the actual cost of the assets to which the disposal is treated as relating is taken to be the sum of

(i) the relevant allowable expenditure attributable to the post-entry element of the disposal, and

(ii) the amount which, in computing the pre-entry proportion of the loss under *para 3(4)(b)* and *para 3(6)*, for which see 9.26 above, would be treated for the purposes of C in the formula in 9.23 above as the total amount allowable as a deduction of relevant allowable expenditure in respect of such of the assets disposed of as are treated as having been incorporated in the part of the pooled asset referable to pre-entry assets.

[*TCGA 1992, Sch 7A para 4(3)(4)*].

Without prejudice to *para 4(6)* below, where *para 4(2)* or *(3)* above applies for the purpose of determining the pre-entry proportion of any loss, no election can be made under 9.28 below for the purpose of enabling a different amount to be taken as the pre-entry proportion of that loss. [*TCGA 1992, Sch 7A para 4(5)*].

Where

(A) the pre-entry proportion of the loss accruing to any company on the disposal of any part of a pooled asset falls to be determined under *para 4(2)* or *(3)* above,

(B) the amount determined thereunder exceeds the amount determined under *para 4(7)* below ('the alternative pre-entry loss'), and

(C) the company makes an election for the purpose,

the pre-entry proportion of the loss determined as specified in (A) above is reduced to the amount of the alternative pre-entry loss. [*TCGA 1992, Sch 7A para 4(6)*]. For this purpose '*the alternative pre-entry loss*' is whatever, apart from these provisions, would have been the pre-entry proportion of the loss on the disposal in question, if the identification of the assets disposed of for the purposes of *Schedule 7A* were to be made disregarding the part of the pooled asset which was not referable to pre-entry assets, except to the extent (if any) by which the part referable to pre-entry assets fell short of what was disposed of. [*TCGA 1992, Sch 7A para 4(7)*].

An election for the purposes of (C) above with respect to any loss must be made by the company incurring the loss by notice to the inspector given within the period of two years beginning with the end of the accounting period of that company in which the disposal giving rise to the loss is made, or within such longer period as the Board may by notice allow (although elections made by 27 July 1995 will in any event be accepted, see Revenue Tax Bulletin May 1994 p 129). The provisions in 9.28 below may be taken into account under *para 4(7)* in determining the amount of the alternative pre-entry loss as if an election had been made under 9.28, but only if the election under (C) above contains an election corresponding to the election that, apart from this provision, might have been made under 9.28 below. [*TCGA 1992, Sch 7A para 4(8)*].

For the purposes of the above, the relevant allowable expenditure attributable to the post-entry element of the disposal is the amount which, in computing any allowable loss accruing on a disposal of that element as a separate asset, would have been allowed as a deduction of relevant allowable expenditure if none of the assets comprised in that element had ever been comprised in a pooled asset with any assets other than those which are taken to constitute that separate asset for the purposes of this provision. [*TCGA 1992, Sch 7A para 4(9)*]. To identify the assets which are to be treated for this purpose as comprised in the post-entry element of the disposal, a company is taken to dispose of assets in the order in which it acquired them. [*TCGA 1992, Sch 7A para 4(10)*].

TCGA 1992, Sch 7A para 3(9), for which see 9.26 above, is applied *mutatis mutandis* for the purposes of *para 4(9)* above, as is *para 3(10)*, for which see 9.26 above, for the purposes of this provision in relation to *para 4(10)* above. [*TCGA 1992, Sch 7A para 4(11)*].

In the above provisions, references to an amount allowed as a deduction of relevant allowable expenditure are references to the amount falling to be so allowed in accordance with *TCGA 1992, 38(1)(a)* and *(b)* and (so far as applicable) *s 42*, together (for disposals before 30 November 1993) with the indexed rises in the items comprised in that expenditure or, as the case may be, in the appropriate portions of those items. Nothing in the above provisions affects the operation of the rules contained in 9.26 above for determining, for any purposes other than those of *para 4(7)* above, how much of any pooled asset at any time consists of a part which is referable to pre-entry assets. [*TCGA 1992, Sch 7A para 4(12)–(14); FA 1994, s 93(9)*].

9.28 *Alternative calculation by reference to market value.* Subject to *TCGA 1992, Sch 7A para 4(5)*, see 9.27 above, and the following provisions, if an otherwise allowable loss accrues on the disposal by any company of any pre-entry asset, and that company makes an election accordingly, the pre-entry proportion of that loss (instead of being the amount determined under the preceding provisions of *Schedule 7A*) is to be whichever is the smaller of

(*a*) the amount of any loss which would have accrued if that asset had been disposed of at the relevant time at its market value at that time, and

(*b*) the amount of the otherwise allowable loss accruing on the actual disposal of that asset.

[*TCGA 1992, Sch 7A para 5(1)(2)*].

In relation to disposals on or after 30 November 1993, in determining the amount of any notional loss under (*a*) above, it is assumed that the prohibition on indexation allowance enhancing an allowable loss under *FA 1994, s 93* has effect for disposals on or after the day on which the relevant time falls. [*TCGA 1992, Sch 7A para 5(2A); FA 1994, s 93(10)*].

Where no loss would have accrued on the deemed disposal assumed in (*a*) above, the loss accruing on the disposal mentioned in (*b*) above is deemed not to have a pre-entry proportion. [*TCGA 1992, Sch 7A para 5(3)*]. The election mentioned above must be made by the company incurring the loss by notice to the inspector given within the period of two years beginning with the end of its accounting period in which the disposal giving rise to the loss is made, or within such longer period as the Board may by notice allow. [*TCGA 1992, Sch 7A para 5(8)*]. Elections made by 27 July 1995 will in any event be accepted. (Revenue Tax Bulletin May 1994 p 129).

The provisions in *para 5(5)* below apply where an election is made in relation to any loss accruing on the disposal ('*the real disposal*') of the whole or any part of a pooled asset, and the case is one in which (but for the election) the provisions in 9.26 above would apply for determining the pre-entry proportion of a loss accruing on the real disposal. [*TCGA 1992, Sch 7A para 5(4)*]. In these circumstances, these provisions have effect as if the amount specified in (*a*) above were to be calculated:

(i) on the basis that the disposal which is assumed to have taken place was a disposal of all the assets falling within (*aa*)–(*cc*) below; and

(ii) by apportioning any loss that would have accrued on that disposal between

  (A) such of the assets falling within (*aa*)–(*cc*) below as are assets to which the real disposal is treated as relating, and

  (B) the remainder of the assets so falling,

  according to the proportions of any pooled asset whose disposal is assumed which would have been, respectively, represented by assets mentioned in (A) above and by assets mentioned in (B) above.

Where assets falling within (*aa*)–(*cc*) below have different relevant times there is assumed to have been a different disposal at each of those times. [*TCGA 1992, Sch 7A para 5(5)*].

Assets fall to be included within (A) and (B) above if:

(*aa*) immediately before the time which is the relevant time in relation to those assets, they were comprised in a pooled asset which consisted of or included assets which fall to be treated for the purposes of 9.26 above as

  (i) comprised in the part of the pooled asset referable to pre-entry assets, and

  (ii) disposed of on the real disposal;

(*bb*) they were also comprised in such a pooled asset immediately after that time; and

(*cc*) the pooled asset in which they were so comprised immediately after that time was held by a member of the relevant group.

[*TCGA 1992, Sch 7A para 5(6)*].

Where

(AA) an election is made under *para 4(6)*, see 9.27 above, requiring the determination by reference to these provisions of the alternative pre-entry loss accruing on the disposal of any assets comprised in a pooled asset, and

(BB) under that election any amount of the loss that would have accrued on an assumed disposal is apportioned in accordance with (i) and (ii) above to assets ('*the relevant assets*') which

  (I) are treated for the purposes of that determination as assets to which the disposal related, but

  (II) otherwise continue after the disposal to be treated as incorporated in the part of that pooled asset which is referable to pre-entry assets,

then, on any further application of these provisions for the purpose of determining the pre-entry proportion of the loss accruing on a subsequent disposal of assets comprised in that pooled asset, that amount (without being apportioned elsewhere) is deducted from so much of the loss accruing on the same assumed disposal as, apart from the deduction, would be apportioned to the relevant assets on that further application of these provisions. [*TCGA 1992, Sch 7A para 5(7)*].

9.29 *Restrictions on the deduction of pre-entry losses.* In the calculation of the amount to be included in respect of chargeable gains in any company's total profits for any accounting period:

(*a*) if in that period there is any chargeable gain from which the whole or any part of any pre-entry loss accruing in that period is deductible in accordance with the provisions in 9.30 below, the loss or, as the case may be, that part of it is deducted from that gain;

(*b*) if, after all the deductions in (*a*) above have been made, there is in that period any chargeable gain from which the whole or any part of any pre-entry loss carried forward from a previous accounting period is deductible in accordance with the provisions in 9.30 below, the loss or, as the case may be, that part of it is deducted from that gain;

(*c*) the total chargeable gains (if any) remaining after all the deductions in (*a*) or (*b*) above is subject to deductions in accordance with *TCGA 1992, s 8(1)* (chargeable gains less allowable losses of company to be included in chargeable profits) in respect of any allowable losses that are not pre-entry losses; and

(*d*) any pre-entry loss which has not been the subject of a deduction under (*a*) or (*b*) above (as well as any other losses falling to be carried forward under *section 8(1)*) are carried forward to the following accounting period of that company.

[*TCGA 1992, Sch 7A para 6(1)*].

Subject to (*a*)–(*d*) above, any question as to which or what part of any pre-entry loss has been deducted from any particular chargeable gain is decided:

(i) where it falls to be decided in respect of the setting of losses against gains in any accounting period ending before 16 March 1993 as if:

  (A) pre-entry losses accruing in any such period had been set against chargeable gains before any other allowable losses accruing in that period were set against those gains;

  (B) pre-entry losses carried forward to any such period had been set against chargeable gains before any other allowable losses carried forward to that period were set against those gains; and

  (C) subject to (A) and (B) above, the pre-entry losses carried forward to any accounting period ending after 15 March 1993 were identified with such losses as may be determined in accordance with such elections as may be made by the company to which they accrued;

and

(ii) in any other case, in accordance with such elections as may be made by the company to which the loss accrued;

and any question as to which or what part of any pre-entry loss has been carried forward from one accounting period to another shall be decided accordingly. [*TCGA 1992, Sch 7A para 6(2)*].

An election under (i)(C) above must be made by the company by notice to the inspector within two years of the end of its accounting period which was current on 16 March 1993. An election under (ii) above must similarly be made within two years of the end of the company's accounting period in which the gain in question accrued. [*TCGA 1992, Sch 7A para 6(3)*].

For the purposes of *Schedule 7A*, where any matter falls to be determined under these provisions by reference to an election, but no election is made, it shall be assumed, so far as consistent with any elections that have been made, that losses are set against gains in the order in which the losses accrued; and that the gains against which they are set are also determined according to the order in which they accrued with losses being set against earlier gains before they are set against later ones. [*TCGA 1992, Sch 7A para 6(4)*].

9.30 *Gains from which pre-entry losses are to be deductible.* A pre-entry loss that accrued to a company before it became a member of the relevant group is deductible from a chargeable gain accruing to that company if the gain is one accruing:

(*a*) on a disposal made by that company before the date on which it became a member of the relevant group ('*the entry date*');

(*b*) on the disposal of an asset which was held by that company immediately before the entry date; or

(*c*) on the disposal of any asset which:

  (i) was acquired by that company on or after the entry date from a person who was not a member of the relevant group at the time of the acquisition; and

  (ii) since its acquisition from that person has not been used or held for any purposes other than those of a trade which was being carried on by that company at the time immediately before the entry date and which continued to be carried on by that company until the disposal.

[*TCGA 1992, Sch 7A para 7(1)*].

The pre-entry proportion of an allowable loss accruing to any company on the disposal of a pre-entry asset is deductible from a chargeable gain accruing to that company if:

(A) the gain is one accruing on a disposal made, before the date on which it became a member of the relevant group, by that company and that company is the one ('*the initial company*') by reference to which the asset on the disposal of which the loss accrues is a pre-entry asset;

(B) the pre-entry asset and the asset on the disposal of which the gain accrues were each held by the same company at a time immediately before it became a member of the relevant group; or

(C) the gain is one accruing on the disposal of an asset which

  (i) was acquired by the initial company (whether before or after it became a member of the relevant group) from a person who, at the time of the acquisition, was not a member of that group; and

(ii) since its acquisition from that person has not been used or held for any purposes other than those of a trade which was being carried on, immediately before it became a member of the relevant group, by the initial company and which continued to be carried on by the initial company until the disposal.

[*TCGA 1992, Sch 7A para 7(2)*].

Where two or more companies become members of the relevant group at the same time and those companies were all members of the same group of companies immediately before they became members of the relevant group, then, without prejudice to the provisions in 9.32 below:

(*aa*) an asset is treated for the purposes of (*b*) above as held, immediately before it became a member of the relevant group, by the company to which the pre-entry loss in question accrued if that company is one of those companies and the asset was in fact so held by another of those companies;

(*bb*) two or more assets are treated for the purposes of (B) above as assets held by the same company immediately before it became a member of the relevant group wherever they would be so treated if all those companies were treated as a single company; and

(*cc*) the acquisition of an asset is treated for the purposes of (*c*) and (C) above as an acquisition by the company to which the pre-entry loss in question accrued if that company is one of those companies and the asset was in fact acquired (whether before or after they became members of the relevant group) by another of those companies.

[*TCGA 1992, Sch 7A para 7(3)*].

TCGA 1992, Sch 7A para 1(4) (see 9.24 above) is applied *mutatis mutandis* for determining, for the purposes of the above provisions, whether an asset on the disposal of which a chargeable gain accrues was held at the time when a company became a member of the relevant group. [*TCGA 1992, Sch 7A para 7(4)*].

Subject to *para 7(6)* (below), where a gain accrues on a disposal of the whole or any part of

(1) any asset treated as a single asset but comprising assets only some of which were held at the time mentioned in (*b*) or (B) above, or

(2) an asset which is treated as held at that time by virtue of a provision requiring an asset which was not held at that time to be treated as the same as an asset which was so held (see 9.24 above),

a pre-entry loss is deductible under (*b*) or (B) above from the amount of that gain to the extent only of such proportion of that gain as is attributable to assets held at that time or, as the case may be, represents the gain that would have accrued on the asset so held. [*TCGA 1992, Sch 7A para 7(5)*].

Where

(AA) a chargeable gain accrues under *TCGA 1992, s 116(10)* on the disposal of a qualifying corporate bond which has been exchanged for shares etc. (see Tolley's Capital Gains Tax under Qualifying Corporate Bonds and 9.24 above),

(BB) that bond was not held as required by (*b*) or (B) above at the time mentioned respectively in (*b*) or (B), and

(CC) the whole or any part of the asset which is the 'old asset' for the purposes of *TCGA 1992, s 116* was so held, the question as to whether that gain is one accruing on the disposal of an asset the whole or any part of which was held by a particular company at that time is determined for the purposes of *para 7* as if the bond were deemed to have been so held to the same extent as the old asset. [*TCGA 1992, Sch 7A para 7(6)*].

9.31 *Change of a company's nature.* If

(*a*) within any period of three years, a company becomes a member of a group of companies and there is (either earlier or later in that period, or at the same time) a major change in the nature or conduct of a trade carried on by that company, or

(*b*) at any time after the scale of the activities in a trade carried on by a company has become small or negligible, and before any considerable revival of the trade, that company becomes a member of a group of companies,

the trade carried on before that change, or which has become small or negligible, is disregarded for the purposes of 9.30(*c*) and (C) above in relation to any time before the company became a member of the group in question.

A '*major change in the conduct of a trade*' includes a reference to a major change in services or facilities provided in the trade or a major change in customers of the trade or a change in the nature of investments held. Regard will also be had to appropriate changes in other factors such as the location of the company's business premises, the identity of the company's suppliers, management or staff, the company's methods of manufacture, or the company's pricing or purchasing policies to the extent that these factors indicate that a major change has occurred. Efficiency changes and technological advancements would not in themselves indicate that a major change in the nature or conduct of a trade has occurred. The Revenue will compare any two points in three years which include the date of change of ownership of the company. This applies even if the change is the result of a gradual process which began outside the period of three years mentioned in (*a*) above. They take note of both qualitative and quantitative issues, as discussed in the cases of *Willis v Peeters Picture Frames Ltd CA(NI) 1982, 56 TC 436* and *Purchase v Tesco Stores Ltd Ch D 1984, 58 TC 46* respectively. (Revenue Pamphlet IR 131, SP 10/91). See also 44.13 LOSSES.

Where the operation of the above provisions depends on circumstances or events at a time after the company becomes a member of any group of companies (but not more than three years after), an assessment to give effect to the provisions may be made within six years from that time or the latest such time. [*TCGA 1992, Sch 7A para 8*].

The above provisions are similar to those in *ICTA 1988, s 768* regarding the disallowance of trading losses on a change in ownership of a company. See 44.13 LOSSES for coverage of these provisions.

9.32 *Identification of the 'relevant group' and application of TCGA 1992, Sch 7A to every connected group.* The provisions below apply where there is more than one group of companies which would be the relevant group in relation to any company.

Where any loss has accrued on the disposal by any company of any asset, *Schedule 7A* does not apply by reference to any group of companies in relation to any loss accruing on that disposal unless:

(*a*) that group is a group in relation to which that loss is a pre-entry loss because it is an allowable loss that accrued to that company at a time before it became a member of the group or, if there is more than one such group, the one of which that company most recently became a member;

(*b*) that group, in a case where there is no group falling within (*a*) above, is either

(i) the group of which that company is a member at the time of the disposal, or

(ii) if it is not a member of a group of companies at that time, the group of which that company was last a member before that time;

(*c*) that group, in a case where there is a group falling within (*a*) above or, in relation to the deduction of a loss from a chargeable gain where either the gain or the loss accrues after 10 March 1994, (*b*) above, is a group of which that company was a member at any time in the accounting period of that company in which it became a member of the group falling within (*a*);

(*d*) that group is a group the principal company (see 9.18 above) of which is or has been, or has been under the control (within *ICTA 1988, s 416*) of,

(i) the company by which the disposal is made, or

(ii) another company which is or has been a member of a group by reference to which *Schedule 7A* applies in relation to the loss in question under (*a*), (*b*) or (*c*) above; or

(*e*) that group is a group of which either

(i) the principal company of a group by reference to which *Schedule 7A* applies, or

(ii) a company which has had that principal company under its control,

is or has been a member.

In the case of a loss accruing on the disposal of any asset where, under (*a*)–(*e*) above, there are two or more groups ('*connected groups*') by reference to which *Schedule 7A* applies, the further provisions in *para 9(3)–(5)* below apply. [*TCGA 1992, Sch 7A para 9(1)(2); FA 1994, s 94(1)(3)(4)*].

Schedule 7A is applied separately in relation to each of the connected groups (so far as they are not groups in relation to which the loss is a pre-entry loss because it is a loss that accrued to a company at a time before it became a member of the group) for the purpose of determining whether the loss on the disposal of any asset is a loss on the disposal of a pre-entry asset, and calculating the pre-entry proportion of that loss. [*TCGA 1992, Sch 7A para 9(3)*].

Subject to *para 9(5)* below, the provisions in 9.29 above have effect:

(A) as if the pre-entry proportion of any loss accruing on the disposal of an asset which is a pre-entry asset in the case of more than one of the connected groups were the largest pre-entry proportion of that loss as calculated under *para 9(3)* above; and

(B) so that, where the loss accruing on the disposal of any asset is a pre-entry loss because it is an allowable loss that accrued to a company at a time before it became a member of a group in the case of any of the connected groups, the pre-entry loss for the purposes of 9.29 above is that loss, and not any amount which is the pre-entry proportion of that loss in relation to any of the other groups.

[*TCGA 1992, Sch 7A para 9(4)*].

Where, on the separate application of *Schedule 7A* in the case of each of the groups by reference to which *Schedule 7A* applies, there is, in the case of the disposal of any asset, a pre-entry loss by reference to each of two or more of the connected groups, no amount in respect of the loss accruing on the disposal is to be deductible under 9.30 above from any chargeable gain if any of the connected groups is a group in the case of which, on separate applications of the provisions in 9.30 in relation to each group, the amount deductible from that gain in respect of that loss is nil. [*TCGA 1992, Sch 7A para 9(5)*].

Notwithstanding that the principal company of one group (‘*the first group*’) has become a member of another (‘*the second group*’), those two groups are not treated for the purposes of the above provisions as the same group by virtue of *TCGA 1992, s 170(10)* (see Tolley's Capital Gains Tax) if the principal company of the first group was under the control, immediately before it became a member of the second group, of a company which at that time was already a member of the second group. In addition, in relation to accounting periods ending after 16 March 1998, again where the principal company of the first group has become a member of the second group, the two groups are not for those purposes treated, in relation to any company that is (or has become) a member of the second group, as the same group if the time at which that company became a member of the first group falls in the same accounting period as that in which the principal company of the first group became a member of the second group. [*TCGA 1992, Sch 7A para 9(6); FA 1998, s 138*]. For an example, see Revenue Capital Gains Manual, CG 47944.

Where, in the case of the disposal of any asset:

(*aa*) two or more groups which but for *para 9(6)* above would be treated as the same group are treated as separate groups because of the treatment therein; and

(*bb*) one of those groups is a group of which either

- (i) the principle company of a group by reference to which *Schedule 7A* applies by virtue of (*a*), (*b*) or (*c*) above in relation to any loss accruing on the disposal, or
- (ii) a company which has had that principal company under its control,

is or has been a member,

the above provisions have effect as if that principal company had been a member of each of the groups mentioned in (*aa*) above.

[*TCGA 1992, Sch 7A para 9(7)*].

9.33 *Appropriations to stock in trade.* Where, but for an election under *TCGA 1992, s 161(3)*, there would be deemed to have been a disposal at any time by any company of any asset, the amount by which the market value of the asset may be treated as increased in pursuance of that election does not include the amount of any pre-entry loss that would have accrued on that disposal; and *Schedule 7A* has effect as if the pre-entry loss of the last mentioned amount had accrued to that company at that time. [*TCGA 1992, Sch 7A para 10*].

9.34 *Continuity provisions.* The provisions below apply where provision has been made by or under any enactment (‘*the transfer legislation*’) for the transfer of property, rights and liabilities to any person from:

(*a*) a body established by or under any enactment (as defined) for the purpose, in the exercise or statutory functions (as defined), of carrying on any undertaking or industrial or other activity in the public sector or of exercising any other statutory functions;

(*b*) a subsidiary of such a body; or

(*c*) a company wholly owned by the Crown (as defined).

A loss is not a pre-entry loss for the purposes of *Schedule 7A* in relation to any company to whom a transfer has been made by or under the transfer legislation if that loss:

(i) accrued to the person from whom the transfer has been made; and

(ii) falls to be treated, in accordance with any enactment made in relation to transfers by or under that legislation, as a loss accruing to that company.

For the purposes of *Schedule 7A*, where a company became a member of the relevant group by virtue of the transfer by or under the transfer legislation of any shares in or other securities of that company or any other company;

(A) a loss that accrued to that company before it so became a member of that group is not a pre-entry loss in relation to that group; and

(B) no asset held by that company when it so became a member of that group shall by virtue of that fact be a pre-entry asset.

[*TCGA 1992, Sch 7A para 11*].

9.35 *Companies changing groups on certain transfers of shares.* For the purposes of *Schedule 7A*, and without prejudice to the provisions in 9.34 above, where

(*a*) a company which is a member of a group of companies becomes at any time a member of another group of companies as the result of a disposal of shares in or other securities of that company or any other company, and

(*b*) that disposal is one of the no gain/no loss disposals mentioned in *TCGA 1992, s 35(3)(d)* (assets held on 31 March 1982, see Tolley's Capital Gains Tax),

Schedule 7A has effect in relation to the losses that accrued to that company before that time and the assets held by that company at that time as if any time when it was a member of the first group were included in the period during which it is treated as having been a member of the second group.

[*TCGA 1992, Sch 7A para 12*].

9.36 *Example*

C Ltd has a 100% subsidiary, D Ltd. D Ltd acquired a 100% subsidiary, E Ltd, on 1 April 1996 and a 75% subsidiary, F Ltd, on 1 April 1998. All the companies prepare their accounts to 31 March. The following information is relevant (neither E Ltd nor F Ltd having realised any gains or losses except as stated).

(i) At 1 April 1996, E Ltd had unrelieved capital losses of £12,000 and its assets included a freehold property which it had acquired on 1 July 1992 for £70,000 and on which it had incurred enhancement expenditure of £10,000 on 1 October 1993. The property was valued at £70,000 at 1 April 1996. During the year ended 31 March 1999, E Ltd realised chargeable gains of £3,000 on assets held at 1 April 1996 and it also realised an allowable loss of £1,000 on an asset purchased on 31 May 1996. On 1 October 1999, the company sold the above-mentioned freehold property for £55,000.

(ii) F Ltd had no capital losses brought forward at 1 April 1998. At that date, it held 10,000 ordinary shares in XYZ plc, a quoted company. It had acquired 6,000 of these on 1 May 1992 for £10,000 and 4,000 on 1 June 1996 for £7,000. The shares had an indexed pool value of £21,862 at 1 April 1998, and their market value at that date was £11,000. On 1 November 1998, F Ltd acquired a further 5,000 XYZ ordinary shares for £3,000 and on 31 August 1999 it sold 12,000 such shares for £6,000.

F Ltd also made two disposals other than of XYZ shares during the year to 31 March 2000, realising chargeable gains on each. The first disposal, on which the gain was £5,500, was of an asset acquired by transfer from C Ltd (at no gain/no loss by virtue of *TCGA 1992, s 171*). The second, on which the gain was £3,500, was acquired from outside the group in December 1998 and used since that time in F Ltd's trade, which has continued unchanged since 31 March 1998.

The provisions restricting set-off of pre-entry losses have the following effects.

(i) *E Ltd*

For the year to 31.3.99, E Ltd can elect (before 1 April 2001) for the whole of the £3,000 gain to be regarded as covered by pre-entry losses. The £10,000 losses carried forward at 31.3.99 then comprise pre-entry losses of £9,000 and other losses of £1,000. In the absence of an election, losses are set against gains on a first in/first out basis for these purposes, so the same result would accrue in this case. See 9.29 above.

The £9,000 pre-entry losses are carried forward and may be set only against gains on other assets held by E Ltd immediately before 1.4.96 or gains on assets acquired by it on or after that date from outside the group and not used or held for any purposes other than those of the trade carried on by E Ltd immediately before that date and which continued to be carried on by it up to the date of disposal. See 9.30 above.

The overall loss on the disposal of the freehold property is as follows.

	£	£
Proceeds (1.10.99)		55,000
Cost (1.7.92)	70,000	
Enhancement expenditure (1.10.93)	10,000	80,000
Allowable loss		£25,000

The pre-entry proportion of the allowable loss is calculated as follows.

	£
$£25{,}000 \times \dfrac{70{,}000}{80{,}000} \times \dfrac{3y\ 9m\ (1.7.92 - 1.4.96)}{7y\ 3m\ (1.7.92 - 1.10.99)} =$	11,315
$£25{,}000 \times \dfrac{10{,}000}{80{,}000} \times \dfrac{2y\ 6m\ (1.10.93 - 1.4.96)}{6y\ 0m\ (1.10.93 - 1.10.99)} =$	1,302
Pre-entry proportion	£12,617
Balance of allowable loss	£12,383

See 9.25 above.

E Ltd may elect (before 1 April 2002) to use an alternative method of computing the pre-entry proportion of the allowable loss, as follows.

	£	£
Market value (1.4.96)		70,000
Cost (1.7.92)	70,000	
Enhancement expenditure (1.10.93)	10,000	80,000
Pre-entry proportion of allowable loss		£10,000
Balance of allowable loss (£25,000 – £10,000)		£15,000

See 9.28 above.

The whole of the loss of £25,000 is available for carry-forward but the pre-entry proportion of the allowable loss (£10,000 on the assumption that the election referred to above is made) can be set only against the same types of gain against which the pre-entry losses of £9,000 can be set (see above).

(ii) *F Ltd*

Allowable loss on XYZ plc ordinary shares

	Number of shares	Qualifying expenditure £	Indexed pool £
Acquisition 1.5.92	6,000	10,000	
Acquisition 1.6.96	4,000	7,000	
At 1.4.98	10,000	17,000	21,862
Indexed rise to 1.11.98:			
£21,862 × 0.011			240
Acquisition 1.11.98	5,000	3,000	3,000
	15,000	20,000	25,102
Indexed rise to 31.8.99:			
£25,102 × 0.007			176
			25,278
Disposal 31.8.99	(12,000)	(16,000)	(20,222)
Pool carried forward	3,000	£4,000	£5,056

	£
Proceeds 31.8.99	6,000
Cost	16,000
Allowable loss	£10,000

Indexation allowance would be £4,222 (£20,222 – £16,000), but indexation allowance cannot increase an allowable loss.

Pre-entry proportion of allowable loss

Stage 1 (see 9.26 above)

The proportion of the pool disposed of (12,000 shares) exceeds the proportion *not* referable to pre-entry assets (5,000 shares). The excess of 7,000 shares is regarded as a separate asset made up as follows.

		Cost £
6,000 shares acquired 1.5.92		10,000
1,000 shares acquired 1.6.96	(£7,000 × $\frac{1}{4}$)	1,750
		£11,750

	£
Proceeds of 7,000 shares £6,000 × $\frac{7}{12}$	3,500
Cost as above	11,750
Notional allowable loss on pre-entry assets	£8,250

The pre-entry proportion of the allowable loss is calculated as follows.

		£
$£8{,}250 \times \dfrac{10{,}000}{11{,}750} \times \dfrac{5y\ 11m\ (1.5.92 - 1.4.98)}{7y\ 4m\ (1.5.92 - 31.8.99)}$	=	5,665
$£8{,}250 \times \dfrac{1{,}750}{11{,}750} \times \dfrac{1y\ 10m\ (1.6.96 - 1.4.98)}{3y\ 3m\ (1.6.96 - 31.8.99)}$	=	693
Pre-entry proportion of allowable loss (subject to below)		£6,358

Stage 2 (see 9.27 above)

		£
The amount deductible in computing the allowable loss is	(I)	16,000
The amount deductible which is attributable to the post-entry element of the disposal (5,000 shares acquired on 1.11.98) is	(II)	3,000

As (I) exceeds (II), an adjustment is required to the figure calculated at *Stage 1* above, as follows.

	£	£
Expenditure actually allowed		16,000
Deduct Actual cost of assets disposed of:		
pre-entry element (see *Stage 1* above)	11,750	
post-entry element (see (II) above)	3,000	14,750
Excess		£1,250

The excess is added to the pre-entry proportion as calculated at *Stage 1* above. The pre-entry proportion of the allowable loss is thus

£6,358 + £1,250 = £7,608

(Because an adjustment is required under *Stage 2*, the election for the alternative method (see 9.28 above) is *not* available. If the election *had been* available, the calculation would have been as follows.

	£
Market value of 10,000 shares held at 1.4.98	11,000
Unindexed pool value at 1.4.98	17,000
Notional loss on 10,000 shares	£6,000

As only 7,000 of the 10,000 shares held at 1.4.98 are regarded as included in the disposal on 31.8.99 (see *Stage 1* above), the pre-entry proportion of the allowable loss would have been £6,000 × $\frac{7}{10}$ = £4,200.)

Stage 3 (see 9.27 above)

As the adjustment at *Stage 2* applies, F Ltd may elect (before 1 April 2002) that the pre-entry proportion of the loss calculated at *Stage 2* (£7,608) be reduced to the amount of the 'alternative pre-entry loss', if lower. In calculating the alternative pre-entry loss, *Stage 1* is recomputed as if the disposal was primarily of pre-entry assets, as follows.

	Cost
	£
6,000 shares acquired 1.5.92	10,000
4,000 shares acquired 1.6.96	7,000
	£17,000

	£
Proceeds of 10,000 shares £6,000 × $\frac{10}{12}$	5,000
Cost as above	17,000
Notional allowable loss on pre-entry assets	£12,000

The pre-entry proportion of the allowable loss is calculated as follows.

$$£12{,}000 \times \frac{10{,}000}{17{,}000} \times \frac{5y\ 11m\ (1.5.92 - 1.4.98)}{7y\ 4m\ (1.5.92 - 31.8.99)} = 5{,}695$$

$$£12{,}000 \times \frac{7{,}000}{17{,}000} \times \frac{1y\ 10m\ (1.6.96 - 1.4.98)}{3y\ 3m\ (1.6.96 - 31.8.99)} = 2{,}787$$

	£
Alternative pre-entry loss (subject to below)	£8,482

In fact, the alternative loss is higher than the pre-entry proportion of the allowable loss calculated at *Stage 2* (£7,608), so, subject to *Stage 4* (below), the election would not be made.

Stage 4 (see 9.27, 9.28 above)

In making an election under *Stage 3*, F Ltd may specify that the alternative method (see 9.28 above) be used, as follows.

	£
Market value of 10,000 shares held at 1.4.98	11,000
Unindexed pool value at 1.4.98	17,000
Notional loss on 10,000 shares	£6,000

As all the 10,000 shares held at 1.4.98 are regarded as included in the disposal on 31.8.99 (see *Stage 3*), the alternative pre-entry loss is £6,000. It is therefore beneficial for F Ltd to make the election mentioned at *Stage 3*, imputing an election as under 9.28 above.

The pre-entry proportion of the allowable loss is then reduced from £7,608 (*Stage 2*) to	£6,000
Balance of allowable loss is £10,000 – £6,000 =	£4,000

Utilisation of losses (see 9.29, 9.30 above)

The pre-entry loss may be set against the gain of £3,500. It may not be set against the gain of £5,500. The balance of the allowable loss can be set against the gain of £5,500. F Ltd's chargeable gains for the year ended 31.3.00 are therefore as follows.

	£	£
Total gains		9,000
Deduct Pre-entry losses	3,500	
Other allowable losses	4,000	7,500
Chargeable gains		£1,500
Losses carried forward (all pre-entry losses) £(6,000 – 3,500)		£2,500

9.37 **Restriction on set-off of losses against pre-entry gains where a company joins a group**

General outline and commencement. TCGA 1992, Sch 7AA restricts the losses that a company (the '*relevant company*') may set against capital gains which arose before it joined a group of companies, or before it was transferred from one group to another. It applies to accounting periods ending after 17 March 1998 where the company joined the group after that date. The only losses which are allowed against such earlier gains are those arising in the company before it joined the new group and those arising after that time on assets it held when it entered the new group. [*TCGA 1992, s 177B, Sch 7AA; FA 1998, s 137, Sch 24*].

Whilst the stated intention of these provisions is to prevent tax avoidance by groups of companies using 'gain buying' in order to set losses against gains which have arisen on assets held in different economic ownership, they may also impinge on an acquisition of a company solely for commercial reasons where it becomes a group member whilst holding an asset which is later disposed of (whether by the company itself or by another group member to whom the asset has been transferred) outside the group at a gain.

Insurance companies. A chargeable gain or allowable loss treated as accruing at the end of an accounting period under *TCGA 1992, s 213(1)c)* or *s 214A(2)(b)* (see 41.17 LIFE INSURANCE COMPANIES) is for these purposes treated as having accrued before the time (or the earliest time) at which the relevant company joined a group of companies. [*TCGA 1992, Sch 7AA para 7; FA 1998, s 137, Sch 24*].

Simon's Direct Tax Service. See **D2.685** *et seq.*.

9.38 *Company joining a group of companies.* For the purposes of *Schedule 7AA*, a company joins a group of companies when, at any time on or after 17 March 1998, it becomes a member of any group of which it was not a member immediately before becoming a member. When the 'principal company' (see 9.18 above) of one group becomes a member of another group, all the other members of the first group are for these purposes treated as joining the other group. [*TCGA 1992, Sch 7AA para 1(3)(4); FA 1998, s 137, Sch 24*]. The change in the residence requirement brought in by *FA 2000* (see 9.18 above) is taken into account in determining for the purposes of these provisions whether a company is a member of a group at any time after 20 March 2000. [*FA 2000, Sch 29 para 8*].

9.39 *Pre-entry gains.* A '*pre-entry gain*' is a chargeable gain accruing to a relevant company in an accounting period (the '*gain period*') in which the company joins a group of companies but after the gain has accrued to it. The chargeable gains to be included in the relevant company's total profits for that period (notwithstanding anything in *TCGA 1992, Sch 7A* (pre-entry losses, see 9.23 *et seq.* above)) are the sum of the 'adjusted amounts' of the pre-entry gains of the period and other net chargeable gains (disregarding certain losses applied in reducing pre-entry gains, see below).

The '*adjusted amount*' of a pre-entry gain for a gain period is the amount of that gain after deducting 'qualifying losses' of the period (so far as not set against other pre-entry gains), but excluding 'pre-entry losses' unless deductible from the gain under *TCGA 1992, Sch 7A para 7* (see 9.30 above) and certain losses on disposals to CONNECTED PERSONS (16). Losses so set against pre-entry gains are not available for carry-forward.

The following are '*qualifying losses*' of a period:

(*a*) a loss brought forward to that period;

(*b*) a loss of the gain period which accrued before or at the same time as the pre-entry gain;

(*c*) a loss of the gain period which accrued after the pre-entry gain but before the relevant company joined any group; and

(*d*) a loss of the gain period which accrued after the pre-entry gain and at the same time as or after the relevant company joined any group provided that immediately before the time when it joined the group the asset on which the loss arose was held either by the company itself or by another company which was a member of the same group and which joined the new group at the same time.

As regards (*d*) above, see 9.40, 9.41 below in relation to certain assets acquired at different times but treated as the same asset.

[*TCGA 1992, Sch 7AA paras 1(2), 2–4; FA 1998, s 137, Sch 24*].

9.40 *Pooled assets.* Where an allowable loss arises on a disposal of 'securities' (as widely defined) which are pooled for capital gains purposes, special rules apply to determine the extent to which the securities were held at a time when the relevant company (or a member of its group) joined a new group (the '*entry time*') (see 9.39 above). The rules apply in respect of any such disposal made in the gain period and at or after the '*relevant entry time*' (i.e. the entry time or, if there is more than one such time in the gain period, the earliest entry time).

Actual losses on the disposals referred to above are matched with the 'notional net pre-entry loss' in the order in which the actual losses accrued. The actual aggregate loss is regarded as a loss on disposal of securities held at the entry time to the extent that there is (or, in the case of a second or subsequent entry time, that there remains) an amount with which it can be so matched.

For the purposes of determining the '*notional net pre-entry loss*', securities acquired at or after the relevant entry time ('*post-entry securities*') are not added to the pool existing immediately before the relevant entry time, which thus continues to consist only of securities acquired (and not disposed of) before that time ('*pre-entry securities*'). Disposals within these provisions (see above) are matched with the pool of pre-entry securities in preference to post-entry securities. Gains and losses on those disposals matched with pre-entry securities are computed and aggregated. If the net result of that aggregation is a loss, the amount of that loss is the notional net pre-entry loss. If the net result is a gain, there is no notional net pre-entry loss. For an example, see Revenue Capital Gains Manual, CG 48214.

For the purposes of determining whether securities are pre-entry or post-entry securities, *TCGA 1992, s 127* (reorganisation of share capital) is to be disregarded in as much as it would treat a new holding as having been acquired at the same time as an original holding.

There are provisions to ensure that securities held by the relevant company or by any 'associated company' at the relevant entry time are taken to be pre-entry securities if, since the relevant entry time but prior to the disposal in question, they have been disposed of by way of intra-group disposal. An '*associated company*' is one which was a member of the same group as the relevant company immediately before the relevant entry time and which joined the new group, along with the relevant company, at that time.

[*TCGA 1992, Sch 7AA para 5; FA 1998, s 137, Sch 24*].

9.41 *Assets acquired at different times.* Special rules apply to the following.

(*a*) An asset which is treated as a single asset but comprises assets only some of which were held at the 'entry time' (see 9.40 above) by the relevant company or an 'associated company' (see 9.40 above).

(*b*) An asset which is treated as held at the entry time by the relevant company (or by another company which was a member of the same group immediately before the entry time and which joined the new group at the same time) by virtue of any provision which treats an asset not held at that time as one which was so held.

An apportionment is necessary if an asset within (*a*) or (*b*) above (other than a pooled asset as in 9.40 above) is disposed of (or part disposed of) by the relevant company (at a loss) in the gain period (see 9.38 above) and at or after the entry time.

The proportion of the allowable loss treated as relating to a pre-entry asset (which is thus a qualifying loss, see 9.39 above) is made up of:

(i) the proportion of the loss which, on a just and reasonable apportionment, is properly attributable to assets in fact held at the entry time; and

(ii) such proportion of the loss not within (i) above as represents the loss that would have accrued if the asset disposed of had been the asset in fact held at that time.

[*TCGA 1992, Sch 7AA para 6; FA 1998, s 137, Sch 24*].

9.42 *Example*

G Ltd has a 100% subsidiary, H Ltd. On 1 May 2000, G Ltd acquired from A Ltd all the shares in its two wholly-owned subsidiaries, B Ltd and C Ltd. Before that date, on 1 March 2000, C Ltd had sold an asset realising a gain of £120,000. All companies make up accounts to the year ending 31 December.

On 1 June 2000, B Ltd transferred machinery to C Ltd for its net book value of £150,000, and, on the same date, H Ltd transferred a freehold property and a leasehold property to C Ltd for their net book values of £400,000 and £350,000 respectively. All these assets were transferred intra-group under *TCGA 1992, s 171*, so that neither a chargeable gain nor an allowable loss arises.

On 10 June 2000 C Ltd sold the freehold property realising a loss of £95,000.

On 12 July 2000 C Ltd sold the leasehold property realising a gain of £75,000.

On 1 September 2000 C Ltd sold the machinery realising a loss of £65,000.

The provisions restricting set-off the losses against pre-entry gains have the following effects.

Only qualifying losses may be set against pre-entry gains. The loss on the disposal of the machinery of £65,000 is a qualifying loss because the asset on which it is incurred was owned at the entry date by a company in the same group (the A Ltd group) as C Ltd. The loss of £95,000 is not a qualifying loss as it does not satisfy any of the conditions for a qualifying loss:

(*a*) it is not a pre-entry loss brought forward by C Ltd;

(*b*) it is not a pre-entry loss accruing to C Ltd in the gain period prior to the entry date of 1 May 2000 (either before, at the same time or after the gain accrued); and

(*c*) it is not a loss occurring after 1 May 2000 but on an asset held by C Ltd or B Ltd at the entry date.

The adjusted amount of the pre-entry gain is as follows.

Pre-entry gain £120,000 less qualifying loss £65,000 = £55,000

The chargeable gain to be included in C Ltd's profits is calculated as follows.

	£	£	£
Adjusted pre-entry gains			55,000
Total gains (£120,000 + £75,000)		195,000	
Less: pre-entry gain		(120,000)	
		75,000	
Total losses (£95,000 + £65,000)	160,000		
Less: loss allowed in adjusted pre-entry gain	(65,000)	(95,000)	nil
Chargeable gain			£55,000
Loss carried forward		£20,000	

Without the pre-entry gains provisions, the net gain assessable would have been £35,000 (£195,000 – £160,000) with no losses to carry forward.

9.43 **Disposal or acquisition outside a group—miscellaneous**

(*a*) Where there is a disposal of an asset acquired in circumstances in which *TCGA 1992, s 171* applied, or would have applied but for certain exceptions (see 9.19 above and the exceptions at 9.19 (ii)–(iv)(vi)–(x)), or *TCGA 1992, s 140A* (see 9.8 above) or (before 1 April 2000) *TCGA 1992, s 172* (see 9.21 above) applied, restriction of allowable losses by reference to capital allowances (see *TCGA 1992, s 41* and Tolley's Capital Gains Tax under Disposal) applies in relation to capital allowances made to the person from whom it was acquired (so far as not taken into account in relation to a disposal by that person) and so on as respects previous such acquisitions. This does not affect the 'no gain, no loss' consideration for which the asset is deemed under the above-mentioned provisions to have been acquired. [*TCGA 1992, s 41(8), s 174(1)–(3); F(No 2)A 1992, s 46(1)(5); FA 2000, Sch 29 para 12, Sch 40 Pt II(12)*].

Where a company which is or has been a group member disposes of an asset which it acquired from another group member as a result of a no gain, no loss disposal within *TCGA 1992, s 171(1)* (see 9.19 above), the provisions relating to the valuation of assets held on 6 April 1965 apply as if all group members were one person (see Tolley's Capital Gains Tax under Assets held on 6 April 1965). As regards acquisitions before 1 April 2000, this provision was dependent on the asset having been acquired at a time when both parties to the transaction were members of a group, regardless of whether or not the transfer was within 9.19 above, except that it did not apply if the transfer was within 9.19(vi) (transfer by or to an investment trust). The change in the residence requirement for groups of companies brought in by *FA 2000* (see 9.18 above) applies in determining whether a company is a member of a group for these purposes at any time on or after 1 April 2000. [*TCGA 1992, s 174(4)(5); FA 2000, Sch 29 para 13*].

See Simon's Direct Tax Service D2.625.

(*b*) Where a company disposes of an asset acquired after 5 April 1988 from a fellow group member, and the no gain/no loss provisions of *TCGA 1992, s 171* (see 9.19 above) applied on the acquisition, an election under *TCGA 1992, s 35(5)* (see 9.45 below and Tolley's Capital Gains Tax under Assets held at 31 March 1982) by the transferee company does not apply on the subsequent disposal, but such an election made by the transferor company applies on that subsequent disposal whether or not the transferee company has made such an election. Where, however, the acquisition by the transferor company was also within *section 171* and took place after 5 April 1988, an election by the transferor company does not have effect on the ultimate disposal, but an election made by the last company by which the asset was acquired after 5 April 1988 otherwise than within *section 171* (or, if there is no such company, by the company which held the asset on 5 April 1988) does have effect on the ultimate disposal. [*TCGA 1992, Sch 3 para 2*].

9.44 **Rollover relief** on the *replacement of business assets* is granted under *TCGA 1992, ss 152–158* (see Tolley's Capital Gains Tax under Rollover Relief) and in relation to groups

(i) all the trades carried on by group members are treated as a single trade (except as regards intra-group transfers);

(ii) *TCGA 1992, s 154* (special rules for depreciating assets) applies as if all group members were the same person.

A disposal by a company when it is a member of a group, and an acquisition by another company when it is a member of the same group, are treated as made by the same person. Claims to relief made after 28 November 1994 must be made by both companies concerned. It is not necessary for the companies making the disposal and acquisition to be members of the group throughout the period between the transactions, as long as each is a member at the time of its own transaction.

Where a non-trading group member disposes of or acquires assets used only for the trades within (i) above, relief is given as if it were carrying on a trade. This treatment is statutory where the disposal or the acquisition is after 28 November 1994, but was previously applied by concession. (Revenue Pamphlet IR 1, D30).

The relief is not available in respect of consideration applied in the acquisition of new assets by a 'dual resident investing company' (see 29.31 GROUPS OF COMPANIES). See also 9.53 below as regards other dual resident companies.

Relief is also denied where the acquisition of the new asset is after 28 November 1994, and is one to which any of the no gain/no loss provisions in *TCGA 1992, s 35(3)(d)* (see Tolley's Capital Gains Tax under Assets held on 31 March 1982) applies.

Compulsory acquisitions of land. For the purposes of the rollover relief under *TCGA 1992, s 247* (see Tolley's Capital Gains Tax under Land), a disposal by a company when it is a member of a group, and an acquisition by another company when it is a member of the same group, are treated as made by the same person, provided that either the disposal or the acquisition is after 28 November 1994 and that, for claims after 28 November 1994, relief is claimed by both companies. Relief is, however, denied where the acquisition of the new land is after 28 November 1994, and is one to which any of the no gain/no loss provisions in *TCGA 1992, s 35(3)(d)* (see Tolley's Capital Gains Tax under Assets held on 31 March 1982) applies.

Disposal or acquisition on or after 1 April 2000. Where either the acquisition or the disposal (or both) is on or after 1 April 2000, the change in the residence requirements relating to groups of companies (see 9.18 above) applies in determining whether a company is a member of a group for the above purposes, and where either the acquisition or the disposal (but not both) was before that date, this applies also to that acquisition or disposal. There is also an additional condition where the disposal and acquisition are by different group companies that:

(i) either the company making the disposal is UK resident at the time of the disposal or the assets are 'chargeable assets' (see 9.19 above) in relation to that company immediately before that time; and

(ii) either the company making the acquisition is UK resident at the time of the acquisition or the assets are chargeable assets in relation to that company immediately after that time.

Also from 1 April 2000, 'trade' for the above purposes does not include a trade carried on by a non-UK resident company unless it is carried on in the UK through a branch or agency.

[*TCGA 1992, ss 175, 247(5A); FA 1995, s 48(1)(3)(4); FA 2000, Sch 29 para 10*].

Where (i) above applies in a case where one member of a group makes the disposal and a second the acquisition, it may happen that the disposal takes place after the first company has ceased to trade, or the acquisition takes place before the second company commences trading. Relief will then be restricted in respect of the period during which the assets disposed of were not used for business purposes, and will be conditional on the replacement assets not being used or leased for any purpose prior to the second company's commencing trading, and being taken into use for the purposes of the trade on its commencement. (Revenue Pamphlet IR 131, SP 8/81, 18 September 1981).

Simon's Direct Tax Service. See D2.626.

9.45 **Assets held on 31 March 1982.** See Tolley's Capital Gains Tax under Assets held on 31 March 1982 for details of these provisions generally, and in particular for the election under *TCGA 1992, s 35(5)* for all disposals by a person after 5 April 1988 of assets held on 31 March 1982 to be subject to the general re-basing rule of *TCGA 1992, s 35(1)(2)*. This election is subject to the following special provisions in relation to groups of companies.

Election by principal company. No group member other than the 'principal company' of a group (for which see *TCGA 1992, s 170* as in 9.18 above) may make an election under *TCGA 1992, s 35(5)* unless the company did not become a group member until after the 'relevant time'. An election by the principal company does, however, have effect as an election by any other company which is a group member at the 'relevant time', except that this does not apply to a company which, in some period after 5 April 1988 and before the 'relevant time', makes a disposal, at a time when it is not a group member, of an asset held on 31 March 1982, and does not itself make the election within the prescribed time limit. The time limit for the making of the election by the principal company is two years (or such longer time as the Board may allow) from the end of the accounting period in which occurs the first disposal after 5 April 1988 of an asset held on 31 March 1982 by a company which is a group member (other than an 'outgoing company' in relation to the group) or which is an 'incoming company' in relation to the group. See, however, Revenue Pamphlet IR 131, SP 4/92, 14 May 1992, as regards certain disposals which are ignored for this purpose. See Revenue Capital Gains Manual, CG 46374 for the circumstances in which a late election may be accepted.

An election by the principal company of a group continues to apply to a company leaving the group after the 'relevant time', unless it is an 'outgoing company' in relation to the group and the principal company election is made after it ceases to be a group member.

The '*relevant time*' is the earliest of:

(i) the first time when a group member (other than an 'outgoing company' in relation to the group) makes a disposal after 5 April 1988 of an asset held on 31 March 1982;

(ii) the time immediately after the first occasion on which an 'incoming company' in relation to the group becomes a group member; and

(iii) the time when the principal company makes the election.

An '*outgoing company*', in relation to a group, is a company which ceases to be a group member before the end of the period during which an election could be made which would apply to it, and at a time when no such election has been made.

An '*incoming company*', in relation to a group, is a company which makes its first disposal after 5 April 1988 of an asset held on 31 March 1982 at a time when it is not a group member, and which becomes a group member before the expiry of the time limit for making an election which would apply to it without that election having been made.

In relation to any determination, after 31 March 2000, whether a company is a member, or the principal member, of a group, the change in the residence requirement introduced by *FA 2000* (see 9.18 above) applies.

[*TCGA 1992, s 35(5), Sch 3 paras 8, 9; FA 1996, Sch 21 para 35; FA 2000, Sch 29 para 38*].

Simon's Direct Tax Service. See D2.628.

9.46 Collection of unpaid tax from other members of the group and controlling directors

Gains accruing on or after 1 April 2000. Where a chargeable gain accrues to a company (the 'taxpayer company') on or after 1 April 2000 and either

(i) that company is UK resident at the time the gain accrues, or

(ii) the gain is within the charge to corporation tax by virtue of *TCGA 1992, s 10(3)* (non-UK resident company trading in the UK through a branch or agency, see 53.4 RESIDENCE),

the following rules apply where all or part of the corporation tax assessed on the taxpayer company for the accounting period in which the gain accrues remains unpaid six months after it became payable.

The Board may serve on any of the following persons a notice requiring that person to pay, within 30 days, the unpaid tax or, if less, an amount equal to corporation tax on the chargeable gain at the rate in force when the gain accrued:

(*a*) if the taxpayer company was a member of a 'group' at the time when the gain accrued, the 'principal company' of the 'group' at that time and any other company which was, at any time in the twelve months before the gain accrued, a member of the same 'group' and owned the asset disposed of, or any part of it, or where that asset is an interest or right in or over another asset, owned either asset or any part of either asset;

(*b*) if the gain forms part of the chargeable profits of the taxpayer company for corporation tax purposes by virtue of *TCGA 1992, s 10(3)* (see (ii) above), any person who is, or during the twelve months before the gain accrued was, a 'controlling director' of the taxpayer company or of a company which has, or within that twelve-month period had, 'control' over the taxpayer company.

For the purpose of (*a*) above, '*group*' and '*principal company*' are as defined as in 9.18 above but as if references there to 75 per cent subsidiaries were to 51 per cent subsidiaries. The change in the residence requirement introduced by *FA 2000* applies in determining whether a company is a member of a group at any time in the twelve-month period referred to in (*a*) and (*b*) above. As regards (*b*) above, '*control*' is as under *ICTA 1988, s 416* (see 13.2 CLOSE COMPANIES), and a '*controlling director*' is a 'director' (within the extended meaning under *ICTA 1988, s 168(8)(9), s 417(5)(6)*) with such control.

The notice must state the amount of tax assessed, the original due date and the amount required from the person on whom it is served. It has effect, as regards collection, interest and appeals, as if it were a notice of assessment on that person. The notice must be served within three years beginning with the date on which the liability of the taxpayer company for the accounting period in question was finally determined (including a determination under *FA 1998, Sch 18 para 36* or *37* in the absence of a full return, see 55.10 SELF-ASSESSMENT). In the case of a self-assessed liability, including one superseding a determination, the date of determination of the liability is taken as the last date on which notice of an enquiry into the return may be given (see 55.7 SELF-ASSESSMENT), or, if such notice is given, 30 days after the action which concludes the enquiry process. In the case of a discovery assessment (see 55.8 SELF-ASSESSMENT), it is the due and payable date or (if there is an appeal against the assessment) the date the appeal is finally determined.

A person paying an amount under these provisions may recover it from the taxpayer company, but such an amount is not deductible for any tax purpose.

[*TCGA 1992, s 190; FA 2000, Sch 29 para 9*].

Gains accruing before 1 April 2000. If corporation tax on a chargeable gain of a group member is not paid within six months of a 'specified date', then, within two years of that date, the tax may be assessed on (*a*) the principal company of the group at the time when the gain accrued or (*b*) any other company which, in any part of the two years preceding that time, was a group member and owned the asset disposed of (or a right, interest, etc. therein). The company paying the tax then has rights of recovery of the tax and of any interest thereon under *TMA 1970, s 87A* (see 39.1 INTEREST ON UNPAID TAX) from the company to which the chargeable gain accrued, or from the principal company of the group when the gain accrued, if different. In the latter case, that principal company has the right of recovery from the company to which the chargeable gain accrued and, insofar as tax, etc. is not so recovered, of a just proportion from any present member of the group which has previously owned, while still a group member, the asset disposed of. The '*specified date*' is the date the tax became payable by the company or, if later, the date of the assessment on the company. [*TCGA 1992, s 190 as originally enacted; FA 2000, Sch 29 para 9(1)(3)*].

See also 53.4 RESIDENCE as regards tax unpaid by non-resident companies.

Simon's Direct Tax Service. See D2.627.

9.47 Where **a company ceasing to be a member of a group** owns a capital asset which has been transferred to it by another group member within the preceding six years, that company is treated as if, immediately after its acquisition of the asset, it had sold, and immediately reacquired, the asset at its then market value. There will thus be a liability on the market value less the sum of the 'no gain, no loss' transfer price and any indexation allowance due under 9.19 above or, conversely, an allowable loss. Any chargeable gain or allowable loss arising is treated as accruing immediately after the beginning of the company's accounting period in which (or at the end of which) the company ceases to be a member of the group, or (if later) the time when the company actually acquires the asset from a fellow group member. Where the asset is acquired by an intra-group transfer on or after 1 April 2000, these provisions apply only if the transfer satisfied the conditions for no gain, no loss treatment (see 9.19 above). [*TCGA 1992, s 179(1)(1A)(3)(4); FA 2000, Sch 29 para 4(2)(6)*]. The time limit for electing for 6 April 1965 value (normally two years from the end of the accounting period in which the disposal took place) is concessionally extended. (Revenue Pamphlet IR 131, D21).

These provisions do not apply if, before the chargeable company leaves the group (or leaves a second group, see below), it has already been deemed to have sold and reacquired the asset in question at the time mentioned above by virtue of its having since become an investment trust or a venture capital trust (see, respectively, 9.49 and 9.50 below). [*TCGA 1992, s 179(2C)(2D); FA 1998, s 133(2)(3), s 135(3)(5)*].

ICTA 1988, ss 403A, 403B (limits on group relief by reference to overlapping periods, see 29.20 GROUPS OF COMPANIES) have effect subject to the above (and prior to the commencement of those provisions, an apportionment under *ICTA 1988, s 409(2)* (see 29.22 GROUPS OF COMPANIES) similarly took the above into account). [*TCGA 1992, s 179(4); F(No 2)A 1997, Sch 7 para 8*].

The provisions also apply to a company leaving a group which acquired an asset as described above where it or an 'associated company' also leaving the group at the same time owns (otherwise than as trading stock)

(i) the asset, or

(ii) property to which a gain on the disposal of the original asset has been carried forward under rollover relief, or

(iii) an asset the value of which is wholly or partly derived from the original asset.

[*TCGA 1992, s 179(3)(10)(b)(c)*].

The provisions do not apply in relation to transfers of assets between associated companies leaving the group at the same time. [*TCGA 1992, s 179(2)*]. This does not exclude cases where the association ceases at the time the companies leave the group (*Dunlop International AG v Pardoe CA 1999, 72 TC 71*). Where, however, the company which acquired the asset subsequently, after 28 November 1994, leaves another group which has a 'connection' with the first, the provisions apply as if it was the second group of which both companies were members at the time of the acquisition. There is a '*connection*' between the two groups if, when the company leaves the second group, the 'principal company' (see 9.18 above) of that group is under the 'control' of the principal company of the first group (or, if the first group no longer exists, of the principal company at the time the company left the first group), or of certain other companies exercising higher levels of 'control'. '*Control*' in this context is as under *ICTA 1988, s 416* (see 13.2 CLOSE COMPANIES) but disregarding control by banks deriving from loan capital or debt issued or incurred in the normal course of the banking business. Where the recipient company's departure from the second group takes place after 16 March 1998, the definition of 'connected' groups is widened so that this provision will apply where common control of the two groups is exercised by any person or persons (which thus includes natural persons as well as companies). [*TCGA 1992, s 179(2A)(2B)(9A); FA 1995, s 49; FA 1998, s 139; FA 2000, Sch 29 para 4(3)(4)(6)*].

The above provisions also do not apply where a company ceases to be a member of a group in consequence of another group member ceasing to exist. [*TCGA 1992, s 179(1); F(No 2)A 1992, s 25*]. The Revenue take the view that this 'liquidation let out' only applies to the case of a parent company ceasing to be a member of a group on the occasion of its only subsidiary ceasing to exist on dissolution (or all its subsidiaries ceasing to exist simultaneously on dissolution). (Revenue Capital Gains Manual, CG 45441–45445).

In relation to events at any time, the Revenue has confirmed it does not apply the deemed sale and reacquisition where the company receiving the asset ceases to be a group member as a result of its only subsidiary leaving the group except where the parent company emigrates, thereby causing the group to break up. (Revenue Capital Gains Manual, CG 45450).

If

(*a*) a company ceases to be a member of a group only through the principal company becoming a member of another group (e.g. see 9.18 above), and

(*b*) under the provisions described above, it would be treated as selling an asset at any time,

the following provisions apply.

(A) The company in question is not treated as selling the asset at that time.

(B) If

(i) within six years of that time the company in question ceases at any time ('*the relevant time*') to satisfy the following conditions, namely that it is

(*aa*) a 75 per cent subsidiary of one or more members of the other group mentioned in (*a*) above, and

(*bb*) an 'effective 51 per cent subsidiary' (as defined in 9.18 above) of one or more of those members; and

(ii) at the relevant time the company in question or a company in the same group, owns (otherwise than as trading stock) the asset, or property to which a chargeable gain has been rolled over from the asset,

the company in question is treated as if, immediately after acquiring the asset, it had sold and reacquired it at its market value at the time of acquisition.

(C) Any gain or loss on the deemed sale is treated as arising at the relevant time.

[*TCGA 1992, s 179(5)–(8)*].

Companies are '*associated*' if they would form a group by themselves. [*TCGA 1992, s 179(10)(a)*].

If, under any of the foregoing provisions, a deemed sale arises, and on an actual sale at market value at that time any loss or gain would, under the value shifting provisions of *TCGA 1992, s 30* (see 9.13 above), have been calculated as if the consideration were increased by an amount, the market value at the time of the deemed sale is treated as having been greater by that amount. [*TCGA 1992, s 179(9)*].

In relation to gains accruing before 1 April 2000, if the tax is not paid within six months of a specified date, then, within two years of that date, it may be assessed on (*a*) the principal company of the group or (*b*) a company which owned the asset on that date or when the chargeable company left the group. There is then a right of recovery of the tax and of any interest thereon under *TMA 1970, s 87A* (see 39.1 INTEREST ON UNPAID TAX) from the chargeable company. The date specified as above is the date the tax became payable by the company or, if later, the date the assessment was made on the chargeable company. For gains accruing on or after 1 April 2000, see the general recovery provisions at 9.46 above. [*TCGA 1992, s 179(11)(12); FA 2000, Sch 29 para 4(5)(7)*].

Certain mergers are exempt from this provision if the merger was carried out for '*bona fide* commercial reasons' and that the avoidance of liability to tax was not a main purpose of the merger. [*TCGA 1992, s 181; FA 1996, Sch 20 para 58; FA 2000, Sch 29 para 28*].

See 7.6 BUILDING SOCIETIES as regards application of these provisions where a building society's business is transferred to a company.

Simon's Direct Tax Service. See D2.630, D2.631.

9.48 *Example*

A Ltd had the following transactions.

1.3.80	Purchased a freehold property £10,000.
31.3.82	Market value £25,000.
1.12.94	Sold the freehold to B Ltd (a wholly-owned subsidiary) for £20,000 (market value £50,000).
31.7.00	Sold its interest in B Ltd (at which time B Ltd continued to own the freehold property).

Both companies prepare accounts to 30 April.

Relevant values of the RPI are: March 1982: 79.44, December 1994: 146.0.

(i) A Ltd's disposal of the property to B Ltd is to be treated as one on which, after taking account of the indexation allowance, neither gain nor loss arises.

Indexation factor

$$\frac{146.0 - 79.44}{79.44} = 0.838$$

	£
Cost to A Ltd	10,000
Indexation allowance £25,000 × 0.838 (see note (*a*))	20,950
Deemed cost to B Ltd	£30,950

(ii) Following the sale of A Ltd's shares in B Ltd on 31.7.00 (i.e. within six years after the transaction in (i) above), B Ltd will have a deemed disposal as follows.

Deemed disposal on 1.12.94

	£	£	£
Market value at 1.12.94		50,000	50,000
Cost (as above)	30,950		
Less indexation to date	20,950		
		10,000	
Market value at 31.3.82			25,000
Unindexed gain		40,000	25,000
Indexation allowance £25,000 × 0.838		20,950	20,950
Indexed gain		£19,050	£4,050
Chargeable gain subject to CT			£4,050
B Ltd's new base cost for future gains			£50,000

Although the deemed disposal occurs on 1 December 1994, i.e. immediately after B Ltd's acquisition, the gain is treated as accruing on 1 May 2000, i.e. the beginning of the accounting period in which B Ltd left the group, being later than the date of the deemed disposal. The gain thus forms part of B Ltd's profits for the year ended 30 April 2001.

Notes

(*a*) The indexation allowance on the no gain/no loss transfer is calculated by reference to the market value at 31 March 1982 as this is higher than the original cost. [*TCGA 1992, s 55*(*1*)(*2*)].

(*b*) For re-basing purposes, B Ltd is deemed to have held the asset at 31 March 1982. [*TCGA 1992, Sch 3 para 1*]. *TCGA 1992, s 55*(*5*)(*6*) apply in the computation of B Ltd's chargeable gain.

9.49 **Company becoming an investment trust after acquiring asset intra-group.** Similar treatment as in 9.47 above (company leaving group) applies where a company (the '*acquiring company*') becomes an investment trust (within *ICTA 1988, s 842*, see 60.4 UNIT AND INVESTMENT TRUSTS) for an accounting period beginning after 16 March 1998 and, within six years before the commencement of that period, it had acquired an asset from another company in its group, the corresponding disposal having been treated by virtue of *TCGA 1992, s 171* (intra-group transfers, see 9.19 above) as a no gain/no loss disposal. The provisions apply where, at the beginning of the accounting period in which it became an investment trust, the acquiring company owns, otherwise than as trading stock, either the asset itself or replacement property (i.e. property into which a chargeable gain on disposal of the asset has been rolled over, see 9.44 below). An asset acquired is deemed for these purposes to be the same as an asset owned subsequently if the value of the latter asset is derived, wholly or partly, from the original asset (in particular where the original was a leasehold and the lessee has acquired the freehold reversion). The provisions do not apply if the acquiring company was an investment trust at the time of the corresponding disposal (in which case the no gain/no loss treatment would not have applied, see 9.19(vi) above) nor if it has been an investment trust for any intervening accounting period.

The acquiring company is treated as if, immediately after the corresponding disposal, it had sold and immediately reacquired the asset at its market value at that time. The resulting chargeable gain or allowable loss is treated as accruing immediately before the end of the acquiring company's accounting period which immediately preceded that in which it became an investment trust. Notwithstanding normal time limits, any consequential corporation tax assessment may be made at any time within six years after the end of the accounting period in which the company became an investment trust. These provisions are disapplied if, prior to the company becoming an investment trust, the above treatment has already applied to the asset by virtue either of 9.47 above or 9.50 below (company becoming a venture capital trust).

[*TCGA 1992, s 101A; FA 1998, s 133(1)(3)*].

Simon's Direct Tax Service. See D2.653.

9.50 **Company becoming a venture capital trust after acquiring asset intra-group.** The same treatment as in 9.49 above (company becoming an investment trust) applies where the acquiring company was granted approval as a venture capital trust (VCT) (within *ICTA 1988, s 842AA*, see 62.2 VENTURE CAPITAL TRUSTS) with effect from a time after 16 March 1998, and within six years before that time it had acquired an asset intra-group by means of a no gain/no loss disposal under *TCGA 1992, s 171* (see 9.19 above). The provisions apply where, at the time the approval became effective, the acquiring company owned, otherwise than as trading stock, either the asset itself (with the same rules as in 9.49 above as to derivation of assets) or replacement property (as in 9.49 above). The provisions do not apply if the acquiring company was a VCT at the time of the intra-group disposal (in which case the no gain/no loss treatment would have applied only if that disposal occurred before 17 March 1998, see 9.19(vii) above) nor if it has been a VCT at any time in the intervening period. Nor do they apply if, prior to the company becoming a VCT, the said treatment has already applied to the asset by virtue either of 9.49 above or 9.47 above (company leaving group).

The chargeable gain or allowable loss resulting from the deemed disposal at market value immediately after the intra-group transfer is treated as accruing to the acquiring company immediately before the time approval as a VCT became effective. Notwithstanding normal time limits, any consequential corporation tax assessment may, in a case in which the Board's approval has effect as from the beginning of an accounting period, be made at any time within six years after the end of that accounting period.

[*TCGA 1992, s 101C; FA 1998, s 135(2)(5)*].

Simon's Direct Tax Service. See **D2.655**.

9.51 **Depreciatory transactions.** Where two or more group companies are parties to a disposal of assets after 6 April 1965 (31 March 1982 where, on the ultimate disposal after 5 April 1988, market value at that date is substituted for cost), at other than market value, **which materially reduces the value of the shares or securities of one of those companies** (a '*depreciatory transaction*'), any loss arising on the ultimate disposal of those shares by a member or former member of the group (having been a member when the transaction took place) is to be allowable only so far as is 'just and reasonable'. Account may be taken of any other transaction which may have

(i) enhanced the value of the assets of the company the shares in which are being disposed of, *and*

(ii) depreciated the value of the assets of any other member of the group.

The restriction is applied to the allowable loss after indexation, rather than to the unindexed loss before indexation (*Tesco plc v Crimmin Ch D 1997, 69 TC 510*). See, however, 9.55 below as regards prohibition on indexation allowance creating or enhancing a loss.

Where such a reduction is made, any chargeable gain accruing on the disposal within six years of the transaction of the shares etc. in any other party thereto is to be reduced as is 'just and reasonable' (but not so as to exceed the reduction in the allowable loss). Regard may also be had to the effect of the depreciatory transaction on the value of the shares at the date of disposal.

A 'depreciatory transaction' also includes any other transaction where

(*a*) the company, the shares or securities in which are the subject of the ultimate disposal, or any 75% subsidiary of that company, was party to that transaction; and

(*b*) the parties to the transaction were, or included, two or more companies which, when the transaction occurred, were in the same group.

A transaction is not depreciatory to the extent that it is a payment which is brought into account in computing a chargeable gain or allowable loss of the company making the ultimate disposal. Cancellation within *Companies Act 1985, s 135* of shares or securities of one group member which are owned by another is deemed to be a depreciatory transaction unless it falls within this exemption.

Claims under *TCGA 1992, s 24(2)* that shares or securities have become of negligible value also come within this section.

References to the disposal of assets include appropriation by one member of a group of the goodwill of another.

'*Securities*' includes loan stock or similar securities, whether secured or unsecured.

'*Group of companies*' includes non-resident companies (i.e. before the general inclusion of such companies from 1 April 2000, see 9.18 above).

[*TCGA 1992, s 176; FA 1996, Sch 20 para 57; FA 2000, Sch 29 para 24*].

As regards distributions out of post-acquisition profits, see Revenue Capital Gains Manual, CG 46580 *et seq.*.

Simon's Direct Tax Service. See **D2.632**.

9.52 **The restriction on capital losses because of 'depreciatory transactions'** (see 9.51 above) also applies where a 'first company' has a holding in a 'second company' which amounts (with or without the addition of holdings by CONNECTED PERSONS (16)) to 10% of all the holdings of the same class in the second company (and the first company is not a dealing company in relation to the holding) and a distribution is, or has been, made in respect of the holding which materially reduces the value of the holding. Distributions brought into account in computing a chargeable gain or allowable loss accruing to the ultimate disponor are ignored. [*TCGA 1992, s 177; FA 2000, Sch 29 para 25*].

Simon's Direct Tax Service. See **D2.634**.

9.53 DUAL RESIDENT COMPANIES

Special provisions applied **before 30 November 1993** to '*dual-resident companies*', i.e. companies resident both in the UK and, under any double taxation relief arrangements, in a territory outside the UK. From that date, they are replaced by *FA 1994, s 249*, which has effect to treat companies otherwise regarded as UK-resident as non-resident where they are so treated under such arrangements. See 53.1 RESIDENCE.

9.54 PRIVATISATION

British Telecommunications plc ('British Telecom') is treated for all purposes of corporation tax as being the same person as British Telecommunications, to whose business it succeeded on privatisation, except that it is not regarded as a nationalised undertaking within *TCGA 1992, s 170(12)*. [*Telecommunications Act 1984, s 72*]. Similar provisions apply in relation to the successor companies to the British Airways Board and the National Freight Corporation [*ICTA 1988, s 513*], the British Airports Authority [*British Airports Act 1986, s 77*], the British Gas Corporation [*Gas Act 1986, s 60*], the British Steel Corporation [*British Steel Act 1988, s 11*], the General Practice Finance Corporation [*Health and Medicines Act 1988, s 6*], statutory port undertakings [*Ports Act 1991, s 35*], the National Research Development Council and National Enterprise Board [*British Technology Group Act 1991, s 12*], milk marketing boards [*Agriculture Act 1993, Sch 2 Pt I; FA 1996, s 203*], Northern Ireland Airports Ltd [*FA 1994, s 253, Sch 25*] and the Atomic Energy Authority [*Atomic Energy Authority Act 1995, Sch 3*]. See also *Water Act 1989, s 95, Electricity Act 1989, s 90, Sch 11, Environmental Protection Act 1990, ss 6–9, Coal Industry Act 1994, Sch 4* and *Broadcasting Act 1996, Sch 7*, and, as regards the *Railways Act 1993, FA 1994, s 252, Sch 24*.

Surplus ACT arising to the successor company on privatisation may not be carried back to a period before the transfer (*CIR v Aberdeen Milk Co Ltd CS, [1999] STC 787*).

9.55 INDEXATION ALLOWANCE

The basic indexation provisions applicable to individuals up to 5 April 1998 continue to apply to companies. For companies, however, they applied initially to disposals after

31 March 1982 instead of 5 April 1982, and the revised rules introduced by *FA 1985* applied to disposals after 31 March 1985 instead of 5 April 1985. The rules introduced by *FA 1988* apply only to disposals after 5 April 1988. See Tolley's Capital Gains Tax for full details.

10 Certificates of Tax Deposit

10.1 Companies may make deposits, evidenced by Certificates of Tax Deposit, with the Inland Revenue for the subsequent payment of tax, and any liability met by the tendering of such a deposit (and accrued interest) is treated as paid on the normal due date, or on the date of the deposit if later. Petroleum royalties may also be paid in this way. The minimum initial deposit is £2,000 with minimum additions of £500 subject to a continuing minimum of £2,000. Certificates are obtainable from the office of any Collector of Taxes. Deposits of £100,000 or over must be made by direct remittance to the Bank of England.

Series 7 Certificates may, however, not be purchased for use against corporation tax liabilities, income tax liabilities under PAYE or the construction industry tax deduction scheme, or VAT liabilities.

Interest, which is payable gross but taxable, will accrue for a maximum of six years from the date of deposit to the date of payment of tax (or, if earlier, the normal due date for payment of tax, i.e. disregarding the fact that the payment date may be later due to late issue of the assessment in question or to an appeal having been made against the assessment). A deposit may be withdrawn for cash at any time but will then receive a reduced rate of interest. Where a certificate is used in settlement of a tax liability, interest at the higher rate up to the normal due date may be less than interest at the encashment rate up to the reckonable date. In such circumstances the taxpayer may instruct the Collector to calculate interest on the latter basis. (ICAEW Technical Release TAX 13/93, 30 June 1993). The rates of interest, published by the Treasury, and calculated by reference to the rate on comparable investment with the Government, vary with the size and period of the deposit, and the rate payable on a deposit is adjusted to the current rate on each anniversary of the deposit.

Deposits are not transferable except in settlement of tax payable by the depositor's holding company, subsidiary company, or fellow-subsidiary.

For rates of interest, see Tolley's Income Tax. Information on current rates may be obtained from the Reuters Monitor Service, Page Index TREG and TREH, from any Collector of Taxes, or from Inland Revenue Financial Accounts Office on Worthing (01903) 700222 ext 2064/5.

Simon's Direct Tax Service. See A3.1327 *et seq.*.

11 Charities

(See also Revenue Pamphlets IR 64, IR 75 and IR 113, all of which are due to be updated following *FA 2000*.)

Cross-references. See also 24 EXEMPT ORGANISATIONS and 50.6 PROFIT COMPUTATIONS.

Simon's Direct Tax Service C4.5.

Other sources. See Tolley's Charities Manual.

11.1 **'Charity'** means any body of persons or trust resident in the UK and established for charitable purposes only. [*ICTA 1988, s 506(1)*]. See *Dreyfus Foundation Inc v CIR HL 1955, 36 TC 126* as to requirement for UK residence. Charities which are registered under *Charities Act 1993* are eligible for relief (see 11.2 below), and must submit periodic accounts as required by the Charity Commissioners. Relief, however, is not conditional on registration.

'Charitable purposes' comprise the relief of poverty, the advancement of education and of religion, and other purposes 'beneficial to the community' (per Lord MacNaghten in *Special Commrs v Pemsel HL 1891, 3 TC 53*). There is an overriding requirement of 'public benefit' (which is not satisfied if the beneficiaries are confined to a company's workforce and/or their dependants (*Oppenheim v Tobacco Securities Trust Co Ltd HL, [1951] AC 297*)) unless the trust is for the relief of poverty (*Dingle v Turner HL, [1972] AC 601*). For examples of purposes held to be charitable, see Tolley's Income Tax under Charities.

Under *Recreational Charities Act 1958, s 1*, the provision, in the interests of social welfare, of facilities for recreation or other leisure time occupation is deemed to be charitable (subject to the 'public benefit' criterion).

By concession, where land given for educational and certain other charitable purposes ceases to be used for such purposes and, under the *Reverter of Sites Act 1987*, is held by the trustees on a trust for sale for the benefit of the revertee, then unless the revertee is known to be a charity, there is a deemed disposal and reacquisition for capital gains purposes, which may give rise to a chargeable gain. Any income arising from the property will be liable to income tax, and a chargeable gain may also arise on a subsequent sale of the land. By concession, where the revertee is subsequently identified as a charity or disclaims all entitlement to the property (or where certain orders are made by the Charity Commissioners or the Secretary of State), provided that charitable status is re-established within six years of the date on which the land ceased to be held on the original charitable trust, any capital gains tax paid as above in the interim period will be discharged or repaid (with repayment supplement where appropriate) as will any income tax (provided that the income charged was used for charitable purposes). Partial relief will be given where the above conditions are only satisfied in respect of part of the property concerned. A request by the trustees for postponement of the tax payable will be accepted by the Revenue where the revertee has not been identified and this concession may apply. (Revenue Pamphlet IR 1, D47).

In respect of covenanted donations by companies, the Trustees of the National Heritage Memorial Fund are treated as established for charitable purposes only. [*ICTA 1988, s 339(9)*].

As regards the time at which charitable purposes arise, see *Guild and Others (as Trustees of the William Muir (Bond 9) Ltd Employees' Share Scheme) v CIR CS 1993, 66 TC 1* (trustees of share scheme required to repay loans out of proceeds of distribution and to apply balance to charitable purposes; held not to apply proceeds of distribution for charitable purposes).

Charitable Trusts (Validation) Act 1954 validates as charitable a trust set up before 1953, notwithstanding that it embraced non-charitable purposes, if its income and property were applied for charitable purposes only. All non-charitable powers are removed by the Act.

See, however, 11.9 below as regards restrictions on relief.

The Revenue have issued a booklet 'Guidelines on the Tax Treatment of Disaster Funds' (obtainable free of charge from Customer Services Manager, Financial Intermediaries and Claims Office, St John's House, Merton Road, Bootle, Merseyside L69 9BB (tel. 0151–472 6043) or FICO (Scotland), Trinity Park House, South Trinity Road, Edinburgh EH5 3SD (tel. 0131–551 8127)) to help people organising disaster appeal funds to decide what form their fund should take and to deal with any tax implications. See generally Revenue publication 'Fund-raising for Charity'.

A leaflet 'Setting up a Charity in Scotland' is also available free of charge from FICO (Scotland), who may be contacted for enquiries on whether a body is charitable.

A 'Charity Fund-raising Pack' is available free of charge from Customer Services Manager, FICO, St John's House, Merton Road, Bootle, Merseyside L69 9BB (tel. 0151–472 6043) or FICO (Scotland) (as above). It contains the following booklets: 'Trading by Charities' (an Inland Revenue booklet); 'VAT — Charities' (Customs and Excise); and (except in Scotland) 'Charities and Fund-raising: A Summary' (Charity Commissioners). The Charity Commissioners for England and Wales have also published more comprehensive advice for charity trustees in 'Charities and Fund-raising' (CC20), available from any of their offices, including St Alban's House, 57–60 Haymarket, London SW1Y 4QX. Detailed guidance on the use of professional fund-raisers and commercial participation is available in the Home Office publication 'Charitable Fund-raising: Professional and Commercial Involvement' (ISBN 0 11 341133 2, £5.50 from HMSO, tel. 0207–873 9090). See also Tolley's Fundraising for Charity.

The Revenue have published a Code of Practice (No 5) setting out their standards for the carrying out of inspections of charities' records.

Simon's Direct Tax Service. See **C4.505**.

11.2 SPECIFIC EXEMPTIONS AND RELIEFS FROM TAX

Apart from the exemptions at 11.3–11.8 below, charities are subject to tax on investment and rental income and gains and on profits from trades carried on in order to raise funds. The Schedule D exemptions at 11.3, 11.4 and 11.6 below are not general exemptions and hence do not extend to trades not falling within 11.6 below or to Case VI income generally (cf. *Grove v Young Men's Christian Association KB 1903, 4 TC 613* and *Rotunda Hospital, Dublin v Coman HL 1920, 7 TC 517*).

The exemptions are subject to the restrictions at 11.9 below.

Claims can be made, generally within six years of the end of the accounting period to which they relate, to Inland Revenue, FICO (Trusts and Charities), St John's House, Merton Road, Bootle, Merseyside L69 9BB or, in Scotland, FICO (Scotland), Trinity Park House, South Trinity Road, Edinburgh EH5 3SD. [*ICTA 1988, s 505(1)*]. The Board have powers to require the production of books, documents etc. relevant to any claim for exemption under *ICTA 1988, s 505(1), s 507* or *s 508* (see 24.3, 24.8, 24.11, 24.12, 24.17 EXEMPT ORGANISATIONS) leading to the repayment of income tax or the payment of tax credits. [*F(No 2)A 1992, s 28*].

Simon's Direct Tax Service. See **C4.518** *et seq.*.

11.3 **Rents — Schedules A and D.** Profits or gains in respect of rents or other receipts from an estate, interest or right in or over any land (whether in the UK or elsewhere) vested in any person for charitable purposes are exempt to the extent they are applied to charitable purposes only. [*ICTA 1988, s 505(1)(a); FA 1996, s 146(2)(5)*]. For accounting periods ended on or before 31 March 1996, the exemption did not strictly apply to rents etc. from land outside the UK, but such rents were exempt by concession. (Revenue Pamphlet IR 1, B9). Also, the legislation specifically referred to 'lands . . . belonging to a hospital, public school or almshouse, or vested in trustees for charitable purposes'. The special relief to hospitals etc. could often be covered by the relief to trusts for charitable purposes (cf. *Scottish Woollen Technical College v CIR CS 1926, 11 TC 139*) and was in any case of reduced importance since the abolition by *FA 1963* of the Schedule A charge on owner-occupied property.

11.4 **Interest and distributions.** Income of a charity, or applicable for charitable purposes under an Act of Parliament, charter, decree, deed of trust or will, is exempt so far as applied to charitable purposes and consisting of **Schedule C** income (see below), **Schedule D, Case III** income (or equivalent overseas income within **Schedule D, Case IV or V**), **Schedule D, Case V** income consisting of distributions which would be within Schedule F if the paying company were UK resident or distributions within **Schedule F**.

For accounting periods ended on or before 31 March 1996, the Schedule D exemption strictly applied only to yearly interest and annual payments but was extended by concession to bank interest whether yearly or not, to gross building society interest and dividends, to profits on discounting transactions within Schedule D, Case III and to overseas income not strictly exempt (Revenue Pamphlet IR 1, B9 — superseded by *FA 1996, s 146*).

Where under a will, a business was bequeathed to trustees to carry it on and pay the net profits to a charity, the amounts so paid were held to be annual payments (*R v Special Commrs (ex p Shaftesbury Homes) CA 1922, 8 TC 367*). In *Lawrence v CIR KB 1940, 23 TC 333* copyright royalties were held to be annual payments.

Schedule C income of trustees which is applicable towards repairs of any cathedral, college, church, chapel etc., is also exempt so far as applied to those purposes only. For accounting periods ending after 31 March 1996, the charge (and corresponding exemptions) under Schedule C is transferred to Schedule D. [*ICTA 1988, s 505(1)(c)(d); FA 1996, s 146(3)(5), Sch 7 para 19*].

For restrictions to the exemption in the case of certain distributions made before 6 April 1999, see Tolley's Income Tax under Anti-Avoidance.

See also 25.21(*b*) FINANCIAL INSTRUMENTS as regards exemption of certain net non-trading gains on foreign exchange and financial instruments.

11.5 **Dividend tax credits.** Before 6 April 1993, the tax credit attached to a qualifying distribution was at the basic rate of income tax (i.e. 25% of the gross amount of the distribution, which is equivalent to one-third of the actual amount of the distribution). [*ICTA 1988, s 231(1)*]. From 6 April 1993 to 5 April 1999, the tax credit is at the lower rate of income tax (i.e. 20% of the gross amount of the distribution, equivalent to 25% of the actual amount of the distribution). [*FA 1993, s 78(1)(3)*]. From 6 April 1999, it is further reduced to 10% of the gross amount of the distribution, i.e. one-ninth of the actual amount of the distribution. Also from 6 April 1999, however, the tax credit attached to a qualifying distribution ceases to be repayable to exempt bodies, including charities. [*F(No 2)A 1997, s 30*]. For the compensatory transitional reliefs following each of these changes, see below. For restrictions on the recovery of tax credits in the case of certain distributions made before 6 April 1999, see Tolley's Income Tax under Anti-Avoidance.

Transitional relief following reduction in rate of tax credit from 6 April 1993. As a transitional relief for charities, and for other bodies similarly treated under *ICTA 1988, s 507* or *s 508* (see 24.3, 24.8, 24.11, 24.12, 24.17 EXEMPT ORGANISATIONS), a compensatory payment may be claimed by the charity etc. in respect of qualifying distributions received from UK companies between 6 April 1993 and 5 April 1997 inclusive, and in respect of which the charity etc. is entitled to payment of the attached tax credit. The payment is in addition to payment of the tax credit itself, and is treated for the purposes of *ICTA 1988, s 252* (see 3.8 ADVANCE CORPORATION TAX) as if it were a payment of tax credit.

The claim must be made within two years after the end of the chargeable period in which the distribution is made. Where (and to the extent that) the claim is accepted, the charity etc. will be entitled to be paid by the Board, out of money provided by Parliament, a proportion of the amount or value of the distribution as follows:

(*a*) one-fifteenth for a distribution made in 1993/94;

(*b*) one-twentieth for a distribution made in 1994/95;

(*c*) one-thirtieth for a distribution made in 1995/96;

(*d*) one-sixtieth for a distribution made in 1996/97.

Any entitlement to a payment under these provisions is subject to a power of the Board to determine, whether before or after the payment is made, and having regard to *ICTA 1988, s 235* (distributions of exempt funds), *ICTA 1988, s 237* (bonus issues) and *ICTA 1988, s 703* (anti-avoidance provisions) (for which see Tolley's Income Tax under Anti-Avoidance), that the charity etc. is to be treated as not entitled to the payment or to a part of it. An appeal may be made against any such decision by written notice to the Board within 30 days of receipt of written notification of the decision, the appeal being to the Special Commissioners.

[*FA 1993, s 80*].

Claims for payments under these transitional arrangements should be made on a special claim form R68 (TR), to be completed in addition to the usual form (R68) claiming payment of tax credits on dividends.

Transitional relief following abolition of repayment of tax credits from 6 April 1999. As a transitional relief for charities, and for other bodies similarly treated under *ICTA 1988, s 507* or *s 508* (see 24.3, 24.8, 24.11, 24.12, 24.17 EXEMPT ORGANISATIONS), a compensatory payment may be claimed by the charity etc. in respect of qualifying distributions received from UK companies between 6 April 1999 and 5 April 2004 inclusive, provided that the charity is entitled to exemption from tax in respect of the distribution. The payment is treated for the purposes of *ICTA 1988, s 252* (see 3.6 ADVANCE CORPORATION TAX) as if it were a payment of tax credit.

The claim must be made within two years after the end of the chargeable period in which the distribution is made. Where (and to the extent that) the claim is accepted, the charity etc. will be entitled to be paid by the Board, out of money provided by Parliament, a proportion of the amount or value of the distribution as follows:

(*a*) 21% for a distribution made in 1999/2000;

(*b*) 17% for a distribution made in 2000/01;

(*c*) 13% for a distribution made in 2001/02;

(*d*) 8% for a distribution made in 2002/03;

(*e*) 4% for a distribution made in 2003/04.

Any entitlement to a payment under these provisions is subject to a power of the Board to determine, whether before or after the payment is made, and having regard to *ICTA 1988, s 703* (anti-avoidance provisions, see Tolley's Income Tax under Anti-Avoidance), that the charity etc. is to be treated as not entitled to the payment or to a part of it. An appeal may be made against any such decision by written notice to the Board within 30 days of receipt of written notification of the decision, the appeal being to the Special Commissioners. For the purposes of *section 703 et seq.*, the payment is treated as repayment of tax. *F(No 2)A 1997, Sch 5* similarly removes or restricts the right to payments under these provisions where anti-avoidance provisions in *ICTA 1988, ss 235–237* (distributions of exempt funds, bonus issues, see Tolley's Income Tax under Anti-Avoidance) would have applied before 6 April 1999 to deny repayment of tax credits.

[*F(No 2)A 1997, s 35, Sch 5*].

Claims for payments under the transitional relief arrangements should be made on form R68 (introduced from April 1999), accompanied by Schedule R68(TCTR).

11.6 **Trading profits — Schedule D.** Profits of trades carried on (in the UK or elsewhere) by, and applied solely for the purposes of, charities are exempted if either

(*a*) the trade is exercised in the course of carrying out a primary purpose of the charity; or

(*b*) the work is mainly carried on by its beneficiaries.

[*ICTA 1988, s 505(1)(e); FA 1996, s 146(4)(5)*].

See also the specific exemptions at (i)–(iv) below.

For accounting periods ending before 1 April 1996, the extension of the exemption to overseas trades applied only by concession. (Revenue Pamphlet IR 1, B9). For trades held to fall within the exemption, see *Glasgow Musical Festival Assn CS 1926, 11 TC 154*; *Royal Choral Society v CIR CA 1943, 25 TC 263* and *Dean Leigh Temperance Canteen Trustees v CIR Ch D 1958, 38 TC 315*. For regular trading within Case I see *British Legion, Peterhead Branch v CIR CS 1953, 35 TC 509*. (In practice, the Revenue may in such cases allow a reasonable deduction for services etc. provided free.) For annual shows of agricultural societies, see 24.1 EXEMPT ORGANISATIONS.

A 'Charity Fund-raising Pack' is available from the Financial Intermediaries and Claims Office (see 11.1 above for details), which includes a Revenue publication 'Trading by Charities' (available separately) giving advice on the tax treatment of particular types of trade commonly carried on by charities. This incorporates the guidance given in the earlier Revenue booklet 'Fund-Raising for Charity'. It includes guidance as to the type of fund-raising activities originally covered by extra-statutory concession C4 (see (ii) below) and the conditions the activities must satisfy, the kind of profits covered by the concession and the consequences if an event is not covered by it, and offers a telephone helpline which charities may call for further advice.

(i) **Exemption for small trades.** For accounting periods of charity companies beginning on or after 1 April 2000, a tax exemption applies, on a claim made to the Board, to profits and other income which is chargeable to tax under Schedule D, Case I or Case VI and is not otherwise exempted from tax, provided the income is applied solely for the purposes of the charity and either

(*a*) the gross income (potentially within this exemption and before deducting expenses) for the chargeable period, i.e. the tax year or company accounting period, does not exceed the 'requisite limit'; or

(*b*) the charity had, at the beginning of the chargeable period, a reasonable expectation that its gross income (as above) would not exceed that limit.

The '*requisite limit*' is the greater of

(1) £5,000, and

(2) the lesser of £50,000 and 25% of the charity's total incoming resources for the chargeable period.

Both the above monetary limits are proportionately reduced for chargeable periods of less than twelve months.

The extension of the exemption to Schedule D, Case VI income is intended to cover miscellaneous fund-raising activities not within Case I. Certain specified tax charges under Case VI are excluded.

[*FA 2000, s 46*].

The Revenue's interim guidance is that they will consider any evidence to satisfy the reasonable expectation test in (*b*) above. Such evidence may include minutes of meetings at which the expectations were discussed, copies of cash-flow forecasts and business plans prepared for these meetings and copies of the previous year's accounts.

(ii) **Small-scale fund-raising events.** Before 1 April 2000, profits from events such as bazaars, jumble sales, gymkhanas, carnivals etc., arranged by voluntary organisations or charities, held for, and promoted as being held for, the purpose of raising funds for charity, are not taxed if

(*a*) the organisation or charity is not regularly carrying on these trading activities,

(*b*) it is not competing with other traders, and

(*c*) the profits are transferred to charities or otherwise applied for charitable purposes.

After 31 March 2000, the exemption is extended to cover up to 15 of each type of event in any one location in any financial year of the charity etc. and includes events accessed electronically. Small events, e.g. jumble sales or coffee mornings, do not count toward the limit to the extent that the gross takings therefrom do not exceed £1,000 in any week. The limit of 15 is increased or reduced proportionately for financial years of more or less than 12 months.

The extended exemption brings the definition of a qualifying event in line with the corresponding VAT exemption for fund-raising events, for which see the corresponding chapter of Tolley's Value Added Tax. Any event meeting the criteria for the VAT exemption will automatically qualify for the income tax exemption if the condition at (*c*) above is satisfied.

(Revenue Pamphlet IR 1, C4 revised by Revenue Press Release 31 March 2000).

(iii) **Lotteries.** For accounting periods beginning after 31 March 1995, lottery profits applied solely to the charity's purposes are exempt, provided that the lottery is promoted and conducted in accordance with *Lotteries and Amusements Act 1976, s 3* or *s 5* (or NI equivalent). [*ICTA 1988, s 505(1)(f); FA 1995, s 138*]. Similar relief for earlier periods is given on a concessional basis. (Revenue Press Release 11 July 1994).

(iv) **Underwriting commissions** are taxable, whether chargeable under Schedule D, Case I (as trading income) or Case VI (although see (i) above for exemption for small trades). Where, however, a charity was granted exemption from tax on commissions chargeable under Case VI for accounting periods beginning before 1 April 1996, such treatment was not disturbed. From 1 April 1996, all such exemption ceased. See Revenue Tax Bulletin December 1995 p 265.

11.7 **Capital Gains.** Charities are exempt from capital gains tax on gains applicable, and applied, for charitable purposes. [*TCGA 1992, s 256(1)*]. Where property held on charitable trusts ceases to be subject to those trusts without actually having been disposed of, the trustees are nevertheless deemed to have disposed of, and immediately reacquired, the property at its market value at that time, and the notional gain arising is liable to tax. Furthermore, insofar as that property represents, directly or indirectly, gains which have accrued to the trustees from disposals made during the currency of the charity, tax is chargeable as if the exemption had never applied. Tax on such gains may be assessed within three years after the year of assessment or accounting period in which the cessation occurs. [*TCGA 1992, s 256*]. For payments made after 9 August 1998 (and for earlier payments in cases where the tax liability remains open), the exemption applies to liability under *TCGA 1992, s 87* in respect of capital payments received from offshore trusts. (Revenue Tax Bulletin August 1998 pp 573, 574).

See also *TCGA 1992, s 257* as regards gifts to charities treated as made for a 'no gain, no loss' consideration.

11.8 **Miscellaneous.** Charities are exempt from tax on offshore income gains — see Tolley's Income Tax under Offshore Funds.

Charitable unit trust schemes are excluded from the normal income tax treatment of unauthorised unit trusts, and are thus able to pass on their income to participating charities without deducting tax. [*SI 1988 No 267; SI 1994 No 1479*].

Employee secondment. For deduction under Schedule D, Case I etc. for employees seconded by companies to charities, see 50.6 PROFIT COMPUTATIONS.

11.9 **Restrictions on exemptions.** A restriction of the exemptions in 11.2 *et seq.* above applies in any chargeable period in which a charity

(*a*) has 'relevant income and gains' of £10,000 or more (but see below) which exceed the amount of its 'qualifying expenditure', and

(*b*) incurs, or is treated as incurring, 'non-qualifying expenditure'.

Where (*a*) and (*b*) above apply, exemption under *ICTA 1988, s 505(1)* and *TCGA 1992, s 256* is not available for so much of the excess at (*a*) as does not exceed the 'non-qualifying expenditure' incurred in that period. Where the exemption is not so available, the charity may, by notice in writing, specify which items of its 'relevant income and gains' are wholly or partly to be attributed to the amount concerned (covenanted payments to the charity within *ICTA 1988, s 347A(7)* being treated as a single item where due from individuals before 6 April 2000 or from companies before 1 April 2000). If, within 30 days of a request to do so, the charity does not give such notice, the Board determines the attribution.

The £10,000 *de minimis* limit in (*a*) above is proportionately reduced where a chargeable period is less than twelve months, and does not apply where two or more charities acting in concert are engaged in transactions aimed at tax avoidance and where the Board, by notice in writing, so direct. An appeal, as against a decision on a claim, may be made against such a notice.

'*Relevant income and gains*' means the aggregate of

(i) income which, apart from *section 505(1)*, would not be exempt from tax, together with any income which is taxable notwithstanding *section 505(1)*, and

(ii) gains which, apart from *TCGA 1992, s 256*, would be chargeable gains, together with any gains which are chargeable gains notwithstanding *section 256*.

'*Non-qualifying expenditure*' is expenditure other than 'qualifying expenditure'. If the charity invests any funds in an investment which is not a 'qualifying investment', or makes a loan (not as an investment) which is not a 'qualifying loan', the amount invested or lent is treated as non-qualifying expenditure. Where the investment or loan is realised or repaid in whole or in part in the chargeable period in which it was made, any further investment or lending of the sum realised or repaid in that period is, to the extent that it does not exceed the sum originally invested or lent, ignored in arriving at non-qualifying expenditure of the period.

Where the aggregate of the qualifying and non-qualifying expenditure incurred in a chargeable period (the '*primary period*') exceeds the relevant income and gains of that period, so much of the excess as does not exceed the non-qualifying expenditure constitutes '*unapplied non-qualifying expenditure*'. Except to the extent (if any) that it represents the expenditure of 'non-taxable sums' received in the primary period, the unapplied non-qualifying expenditure may be treated as non-qualifying expenditure of a chargeable period ending not more than six years before the end of the primary period.

'*Non-taxable sums*' are donations, legacies and other sums of a similar nature which, apart from *ICTA 1988, s 505(1)* and *TCGA 1992, s 256*, are not within the charge to tax.

Where an amount of unapplied non-qualifying expenditure (the '*excess expenditure*') falls to be treated as non-qualifying expenditure of earlier periods, it is attributed only to those periods in which, apart from the attribution in question but taking account of any previous attribution, the relevant income and gains exceed the aggregate of the qualifying and non-qualifying expenditure in that period; and such attribution is not to be greater than the excess. Attributions are made to later periods in priority to earlier periods. Any excess expenditure which cannot be attributed to an earlier period is ignored altogether for attribution purposes. Adjustments by way of further assessments, etc. are made in consequence of an attribution to an earlier period.

'*Qualifying expenditure*' is expenditure incurred for charitable purposes only. A payment made (or to be made) to a body situated outside the UK is not qualifying expenditure unless the charity concerned has taken all reasonable steps to ensure that the payment will be applied for charitable purposes. Expenditure incurred in a particular period may be treated as incurred in another period if it is properly chargeable against income of that other period and is referable to commitments (contractual or otherwise) entered into before or during that other period.

'*Qualifying investments*' are the following.

(A) Investments within *Trustee Investments Act 1961, Pts I, II (para 13 (mortgages, etc.) excepted) and III*.

(B) Investments in a common investment fund established under *Charities Act 1960, s 22* (or NI equivalent) or *Charities Act 1993, s 24*, or a common deposit fund established under *Charities Act 1960, s 22A* or *Charities Act 1993, s 25*, or similar funds under other enactments.

(C) Any interest in land other than a mortgage, etc.

(D) Shares or securities of a company listed on a recognised stock exchange (within *ICTA 1988, s 841*) or dealt in on the Unlisted Securities Market.

(E) Units in unit trusts (as defined).

(F) Deposits with a recognised bank or licensed institution (but see below) in respect of which interest is payable at a commercial rate, but excluding a deposit made as part of an arrangement whereby the bank, etc. makes a loan to a third party.

(G) Certificates of deposit within *ICTA 1988, s 56(5)*.

(H) Loans or other investments as to which the Board are satisfied, on a claim, that the loans or other investments are made for the benefit of the charity and not for the avoidance of tax (whether by the charity or by a third party). Loans secured by mortgage, etc. over land are eligible.

Deposits within (F) above (and money placed within (3) below) on or after 29 April 1996 must be with a bank within *ICTA 1988, s 840A* (see 6.1 BANKS) rather than with a recognised bank or licensed institution.

'*Qualifying loans*'. A loan which is not made by way of investment is a qualifying loan if it is one of the following.

(1) A loan made to another charity for charitable purposes only.

(2) A loan to a beneficiary of the charity which is made in the course of carrying out the purposes of the charity.

(3) Money placed on a current account with a recognised bank or licensed institution (as in (F) above) otherwise than under arrangements as in (F) above.

(4) A loan, not within (1) to (3) above, as to which the Board are satisfied, on a claim, that the loan is made for the benefit of the charity and not for the avoidance of tax (whether by the charity or by a third party).

[*ICTA 1988, s 505(3)–(8), s 506, Sch 20; Charities Act 1992, Sch 6 para 17; SI 1992 No 1900; FA 1995, Sch 17 para 7; FA 1996, Sch 37 paras 2, 5, 10, Sch 38 para 6; FA 2000, s 41(5)(9)*].

Payments between charities. Any payment received by one charity from another, other than in return for full consideration, which would otherwise not be chargeable to tax (and which is not of a description within any of the relieving provisions of *ICTA 1988, s 505*, see 11.2 *et seq.* above), is chargeable to tax under Schedule D, Case III, but is eligible for relief under *section 505(1)(c)* (see 11.4 above) as if it were an annual payment. [*ICTA 1988, s 505(2)*].

Simon's Direct Tax Service. See C4.527.

11.10 GIFT AID DONATIONS BY COMPANIES

Donations made on or after 1 April 2000 [*ICTA 1988, s 339; FA 1990, s 26; FA 1997, s 64; FA 2000, s 40*]

A company may claim relief as a charge on income (see 50.3 PROFIT COMPUTATIONS) for a 'qualifying donation' to a charity, provided that the company is not itself a charity. The provisions for relief of payments under deeds of covenant (see 11.11 below) are now subsumed within these provisions. See further below for the exclusion of certain payments by CLOSE COMPANIES (13).

A '*qualifying donation*' is a single payment of a sum of money made by the company to a charity, excluding

(*a*) a payment which is to be regarded as a distribution (see 20 DISTRIBUTIONS) under any provisions of the *Taxes Acts* other than *ICTA 1988, s 209(4)* (transfer of assets or liabilities by a company to its members at undervalue, see 20.9 DISTRIBUTIONS); and

(*b*) a payment deductible in computing profits for corporation tax purposes (see 50.6 PROFIT COMPUTATIONS).

The payment is treated as an annual payment in the hands of the recipient.

'*Charity*' for this purpose includes the British Museum, the British Museum (Natural History), the National Heritage Memorial Fund, the Historic Buildings and Monuments Commission for England, and any scientific research association within *ICTA 1988, s 508*.

A payment by a close company (see 13 CLOSE COMPANIES) is not a qualifying donation if:

(i) it is made subject to a condition as to repayment; or

(ii) the company or a connected person (see 16 CONNECTED PERSONS), or a person connected with such a person, receives a benefit in consequence of the gift, and either:

 (A) the aggregate value of the benefits received in relation to the gift exceeds

  (1) 25% of a donation of up to £100,

  (2) £25 where the donation is more than £100 but not more than £1,000, or

  (3) $2\frac{1}{2}$% of a donation of more than £1,000; or

 (B) the aggregate of the value of the benefits received in relation to the gift and the value of any other benefits received in relation to qualifying donations made by the company to the charity earlier in the accounting period exceeds £250; or

(iii) it is conditional on, associated with, or part of an arrangement involving the acquisition of property by the charity from the company or a connected person (see 16 CONNECTED PERSONS), otherwise than by way of a gift.

Where a benefit:

(1) consists of the right to receive benefits at intervals over a period of less than twelve months;

(2) relates to a period of less than twelve months; or

(3) is one of a series of benefits received at intervals in consequence of making a series of gifts at intervals of less than twelve months,

the value of the benefit and the amount of the gift are 'annualised' for the purposes of (ii) above. Where a one-off benefit is received in consequence of making a gift which is one of a series of gifts made at intervals of less than twelve months, the amount of the gift is likewise 'annualised' for the purposes of (ii)(A) above (but not in this case the value of the benefit). For these purposes a gift or benefit is '*annualised*' by multiplying the amount or value by 365 and dividing the result by the number of days in the period of less than twelve months or the average number of days in the intervals of less than twelve months as appropriate.

For the purpose of calculating the donor benefits, where an accounting period straddles 1 April 2000, the accounting period is treated as two separate accounting periods, the first ending on 31 March 2000 and the second beginning on 1 April 2000.

Charity trading subsidiaries. Where a qualifying donation is made by a company that is wholly owned by a charity, the company can claim that the donation, or any part of it, is to be treated as made in an earlier accounting period falling wholly or partly within the nine months prior to the date of the donation. A claim to have the payment treated as paid in an earlier accounting period must be made within two years from the end of the accounting period in which the payment is made, or such longer period as the Board may allow. A company is treated as wholly owned by a charity if all its ordinary share capital is directly or indirectly owned by one or more charities, or if it is limited by guarantee and every person beneficially entitled to participate in its divisible profits, or to share in the net assets available for distribution in a winding-up, is or must be a charity or a company wholly owned by a charity.

For a similar relief for donations by individuals, see Tolley's Income Tax under Charities. See generally Revenue Pamphlet IR 113.

Donations made before 1 April 2000 [*ICTA 1988, s 339; FA 1989, s 60(2); FA 1990, s 26; FA 1993, s 67*]

A UK resident company, not (except as below) being a close company (see 13 CLOSE COMPANIES), may claim relief as a charge on income (see 50.3 PROFIT COMPUTATIONS) for a 'qualifying donation' to a charity.

A '*qualifying donation*' is a single payment of a sum of money made by the company to a charity, excluding

(*a*) a covenanted donation (see 11.11 below), and

(*b*) a payment deductible in computing profits for corporation tax purposes (see 50.6 PROFIT COMPUTATIONS).

The company must deduct basic rate income tax from any payment it wishes to claim as a qualifying deduction, and account for the tax so deducted under *ICTA 1988, Sch 16* (see 31.4 INCOME TAX IN RELATION TO A COMPANY), and the payment is treated as an annual payment in the hands of the recipient, whether or not it ultimately proves to be a qualifying donation.

'*Charity*' for this purpose includes the British Museum, the British Museum (Natural History), the National Heritage Memorial Fund, the Historic Buildings and Monuments Commission for England, and any scientific research association within *ICTA 1988, s 508*.

The requirement that the donor not be a close company does not apply if

(i) the payment (after deduction of basic rate tax) is at least £250,

(ii) it is not made subject to a condition as to repayment,

(iii) either

  (*a*) neither the company, nor a person connected with it (see 16 CONNECTED PERSONS), nor a person connected with such a person, receives a benefit in consequence of the payment, or

  (*b*) the aggregate value of all such benefits so received in consequence of the payment does not exceed one-fortieth of the amount of the payment after deduction of tax, and the total value of such benefits so received in respect of that payment and any other qualifying donations made by the company to the charity earlier in the accounting period does not exceed £250, and

(iv) it is not conditional on, associated with, or part of an arrangement involving, the acquisition of property by the charity from the company or a connected person (as in (iii) above), otherwise than by way of gift.

The donor company must give to the charity a certificate in prescribed form (i.e. Form R240(SD)) to the effect that tax has been deducted from the payment and, in the case of a payment by a close company, that the conditions at (i) to (iv) above are satisfied.

Payments made by charities may not be qualifying donations.

For a similar relief for donations by individuals, see Tolley's Income Tax under Charities. See generally Revenue Pamphlet IR 113.

Simon's Direct Tax Service. See **D2.212**.

11.11 COVENANTED PAYMENTS

The separate tax relief for payments to a charity made under deed of covenant is **withdrawn** for payments made by companies **on or after 1 April 2000**. Payments on or after that date are relieved under the Gift Aid scheme (see 11.10 above). [*FA 2000, s 41*].

For payments made **before 1 April 2000**, if a company bound itself by a deed of covenant (otherwise than for consideration in money or money's worth) to pay a regular sum to a charity, the charity is able to gross up the sum received and reclaim the basic rate tax deducted in the circumstances outlined below. [*ICTA 1988, s 660 prior to repeal; ICTA 1988, s 660A(9); FA 1995, Sch 17 para 1*]. Such a payment is not deductible in computing income, is not a distribution, and is normally treated as a charge on income provided that basic rate income tax is deducted and accounted for under *ICTA 1988, Sch 16* (see 31.4 INCOME TAX IN RELATION TO A COMPANY). [*ICTA 1988, ss 337(2), 338, 339, 505(6)*]. To minimise any delay in making repayments of tax to charities, the Revenue could, in appropriate circumstances, provisionally repay tax apparently suffered by deduction before the full verification procedure had been completed. (Revenue Pamphlet IR 131, SP 3/87, 26 March 1987).

(*a*) The covenant had to be for a period capable of exceeding three years, i.e. there could be nothing in the deed itself which permitted its termination within that period. However, where a period was mentioned which was capable of exceeding three years at the time the covenant was made, the fact that it proved to be shorter did not affect the tax advantages (*Black CA 1940, 23 TC 715*). The covenant could not be revocable (except with the consent of the payee), though a power to vary the payments which was outside, and independent of, the covenant was not necessarily fatal (*Wolfson HL 1949, 31 TC 141*). See also (*e*) below. Covenants could not be backdated (*St Luke's Hostel Trustees CA 1930, 15 TC 682*). For an unsuccessful attempt retrospectively to amend a deed to achieve the intended effect for tax purposes, see *Racal Group Services Ltd v Ashmore CA 1995, 68 TC 86*. See also (*d*) below. See also 11.10 above as regards certain donations similarly treated as charges on income, and generally Tolley's Income Tax under Settlements.

(*b*) For claims relating to deeds of covenant by individuals, a charity could, for periods before 6 April 1999, provide a composite certificate covering all payments, accompanied by completed forms R185 (Covenant) for all first-year payments. For covenants by companies, forms R185(AP) were required for all payments, as were the deeds of covenant for first claims. From 6 April 1999, payments received under deed of covenant should be recorded on Schedule R68(A) accompanying the claim form R68, using the new forms introduced from 6 April 1999. Certificates R185 (Covenant) and R185(AP) are no longer required from covenantors, but the deeds must be available for inspection at any FICO audit. Proper records must be kept in support of claims, and should be retained for up to six years after the expiry of covenants. (Revenue Press Release 7 May 1992). See generally the Charity Tax Pack obtainable from Inland Revenue, FICO (Trusts and Charities), St John's House, Merton Road, Bootle, Merseyside L69 9BB.

(*c*) The payment had to be 'pure income profit' in the hands of the charity and not in return for goods and services etc. See Tolley's Income Tax under Deduction of Tax at Source. Certain rights of admission to view preserved property or to observe conserved wildlife granted in consideration of a covenant were disregarded for this purpose. [*FA 1989, s 59*].

(*d*) The insertion of escape clauses in a deed which enable the covenantor of his own volition to terminate the covenant without the consent of the charity concerned could invalidate the covenant for tax purposes. Covenants which were accepted by the Revenue as valid, and on which repayments of tax were made, but which were invalid as a result of escape clauses, continued to be treated as effective until they expired. (Revenue Pamphlet IR 131, SP 4/90, 20 March 1990).

(*e*) Where a covenanted donation to a charity was made by a company wholly owned by a charity (see below) after (but within nine months of the end of) the accounting period in which it was required under the terms of the covenant to be made, it could be treated as a charge on income paid in the latter period. This applied where

(i) the donation was made in an accounting period beginning after 31 March 1997, and

(ii) it met the general conditions (as above) for treatment as a charge on income.

A company was treated as wholly owned by a charity if all its ordinary share capital was directly or indirectly owned by one or more charities, or if it was limited by guarantee and every person beneficially entitled to participate in its divisible profits, or to share in the net assets available for distribution in a winding-up, was or had to be a charity or a company wholly owned by a charity.

[*ICTA 1988, s 339(7AA)–(7AC); FA 1997, s 64*].

For a general overview of these provisions, with examples, see Revenue Tax Bulletin June 1997 pp 438–440.

A Revenue leaflet 'Deeds of Covenant — Guidance for Charities' is available free of charge from Customer Services Manager, Financial Intermediaries and Claims Office, St John's House, Merton Road, Bootle, Merseyside L69 9BB (tel. 0151–472 6043) to help charities to get their arrangements right for tax purposes. It includes simple forms of covenant for individual donors which charities can use if they wish. See also Revenue Tax Bulletin October 1998 pp 597, 598 for additional commentary on the validity of covenants.

Claims for repayment must be made within six years after the end of the accounting period in which the payment fell due. A claim for repayment of tax deducted from covenanted donations was refused where the claim was made more than six years after the end of the chargeable periods within which the payments were due, although the payments had in fact been made within the six years preceding the date of claim. (*CIR v Crawley Ch D 1986, 59 TC 728*).

The Trustees of the National Heritage Memorial Fund, the Historic Buildings and Monuments Commission for England, and the Trustees of the British Museum and of the British Museum (Natural History) were treated as charities in respect of covenanted donations. [*ICTA 1988, s 660(4) prior to repeal; ICTA 1988, s 347A(8); FA 1995, Sch 17 para 4*].

11.12 GIFTS IN KIND TO CHARITIES [*ICTA 1988, s 83A; FA 1999, s 55*]

With effect **from 27 July 1999**, relief is available to persons (including companies) carrying on a trade, profession or vocation who give certain articles to charities within *ICTA 1988, s 506* (see 11.1 above) or to bodies treated as such under *ICTA 1988, s 507(1)* (see 24.3, 24.8, 24.11, 24.17 EXEMPT ORGANISATIONS). The gift must consist of either:

(*a*) articles manufactured, or of a type sold, in the course of the donor's trade; or

(*b*) machinery or plant used in the donor's trade, profession or vocation.

Where the donor is eligible for relief, no amount is required to be brought into account for tax purposes in respect of the donated article either as a trading receipt or (for capital allowance purposes) as a disposal value. However, if the donor or any connected person (see 16 CONNECTED PERSONS) receives any benefit in any way attributable to the gift, the donor is chargeable on an amount equal to the value of that benefit, for the chargeable period in which it is received, under either Schedule D, Case I or II or, if he is not chargeable to tax under either of those Cases for that period, under Schedule D, Case VI.

See 11.14 below for the earlier, more limited relief for gifts for third world health or education.

11.13 GIFTS ETC. OF SHARES AND SECURITIES [*ICTA 1988, s 587B*; *FA 2000, s 43*]

With effect **from 1 April 2000**, relief is available to companies other than charities which dispose of the whole of the beneficial interest in the '*qualifying investments*' listed below, otherwise than by way of a bargain at arm's length, to charities within *ICTA 1988, s 506* or to bodies treated as such under *ICTA 1988, s 507(1)*:

(*a*) shares and securities listed or dealt in on a recognised stock exchange;

(*b*) units in authorised unit trusts (see 60.1 UNIT AND INVESTMENT TRUSTS);

(*c*) shares in open-ended investment companies (see 40.6 INVESTMENT COMPANIES); and

(*d*) interests in offshore funds (i.e. collective investment schemes, within the meaning of the *Financial Services Act 1986*, falling within *ICTA 1988, s 759(1)(a)*, *(b)* or *(c)*, see Tolley's Income Tax under Offshore Funds).

The donor can claim relief for the 'relevant amount' as a charge on income for the accounting period in which the disposal is made. Where relief is claimed under *ICTA 1988, s 587B*, no relief can be claimed under *ICTA 1988, s 83A* (see 11.12 above) or any other provision for the same disposal.

The '*relevant amount*' is the market value of the shares at the time of the disposal less the amount or value of any consideration for the disposal. This is to be reduced by the amount of any benefits received by the donor company or any connected person (see 16 CONNECTED PERSONS). The relevant amount is to be increased by the incidental costs of disposal, in full if there is no consideration, otherwise to the extent that the consideration received is less than that which is treated as received under *TCGA 1992, s 257(2)(a)* (disposal at no gain/ no loss).

The above relief is in addition to existing capital gains tax relief (see Tolley's Capital Gains Tax). Where the asset is subsequently disposed of by the charity, its base cost for capital gains tax purposes as determined by *TCGA 1992, s 257(2)(a)* (disposal at no gain, no loss), is to be reduced by the relevant amount, or, if less than the relevant amount, to nil.

Special provisions apply to companies carrying on a life assurance business (see 41 LIFE INSURANCE COMPANIES).

11.14 GIFTS FOR RELIEF IN POOR COUNTRIES [*FA 1998, s 47; FA 1999, s 55(2)(3)*]

A relief was introduced for a limited period for certain gifts to charities of articles to be used, either for medical purposes (including medical research and health promotion) or by educational establishments, in some 80 of the world's poorest countries. The countries or territories concerned were designated by the Treasury by order (or were of a description specified in such an order). See *SI 1998 No 1868* and Revenue Press Release 31 July 1998. Gifts must have been made in the period beginning on 31 July 1998 and ending on **26 July**

1999, the relief being replaced after that date by the wider relief described at 11.12 above.

The relief is available to companies (and to other persons) carrying on a trade, profession or vocation. The gift must consist of either:

(*a*) articles manufactured, or of a type sold, in the course of the donor's trade; or

(*b*) machinery or plant used in the donor's trade, profession or vocation.

Where the donor claims the relief, no amount is required to be brought into account for tax purposes in respect of the donated article either as a trading receipt or (for capital allowance purposes) as a disposal value. However, if the donor or any connected person (see 16 CONNECTED PERSONS) receives any benefit in any way attributable to the gift, the donor is chargeable on an amount equal to the value of that benefit, for the chargeable period in which it is received, under either Schedule D, Case I or II or, if not chargeable to tax under either of those Cases for that period, under Schedule D, Case VI.

A claim must be made within two years of the end of the accounting period in which the gift was made. It must specify the article given and the charity to which it was given.

12 Claims

Simon's Direct Tax Service. See **D2.737.**

12.1 **Pre-self-assessment.** Claims may be made to the inspector dealing with the company's affairs (certain claims required in law to be made to the Board are in practice made to the inspector) whenever the Taxes Acts provide for a claim to be made. An error or mistake in a claim may be rectified by a supplementary claim. [*TMA 1970, s 42(1)(2)(8)*]. Group relief and capital allowance claims are not made under *TMA 1970, s 42*. See 8.2 CAPITAL ALLOWANCES, 29.23 GROUPS OF COMPANIES. Such claims are made in the return required under *TMA 1970, s 11* (see 54.2 RETURNS), as are claims for repayment of tax deducted at source and (where still available) for payment of tax credit. [*FA 1990, ss 97–103, Schs 15–17*].

Accounting periods ending on or after 1 July 1999. Following the introduction of self-assessment (see 55 SELF-ASSESSMENT), and subject to any express provision to the contrary, claims and elections made after notice has been given requiring the delivery of a company tax return must be made in the return, or by amendment of the return, if they can be so made and must be expressed in figures. A claim etc. made by a company which could have been made by amending the return is treated for this purpose as an amendment of the return. Otherwise, *TMA 1970, Sch 1A* (as amended by *FA 1998, Sch 19 para 42*) provides the procedure for claims etc.. See 55.4 SELF-ASSESSMENT.

For consequential claims, elections etc. arising out of Revenue assessments or amendments to self-assessments (which may generally be made within one year from the end of the accounting period in which the assessment was made or the enquiry into the relevant return closed), or where an assessment is made in a case involving fraud or negligence, see 55.9 SELF-ASSESSMENT.

12.2 **TIME LIMITS**

Unless otherwise specified, claims for relief from corporation tax must be made within six years of the end of the accounting period to which they relate. [*TMA 1970, s 43(1); FA 1998, Sch 18 para 55, Sch 19 para 21*]. See 59 TIME LIMITS and Tolley's Income Tax under Time Limits—Fixed Dates and Time Limits—Miscellaneous.

12.3 **APPEALS**

Pre-self-assessment. An appeal in writing must be lodged within 30 days after notification of the decision to which it relates. This period is extended to three months where the appeal relates to a non-resident's claim on a question of residence, ordinary residence or domicile or of the exemption of pension funds for overseas employees. [*TMA 1970, s 42*]. Appeals from decisions of the inspector normally lie to the General Commissioners or (at the taxpayer's option) the Special Commissioners, and those from decisions of the Board to the Special Commissioners. [*TMA 1970, Sch 2*].

Accounting periods ending on or after 1 July 1999 (see *SI 1998 No 3173*). Appeals continue to have to be made in writing within 30 days of the issue of a notice of amendment to a self-assessment or of a notice of an assessment which is not a self-assessment or of a notice disallowing a claim or election. [*TMA 1970, s 31; FA 1994, Sch 19 para 7; FA 1996, Sch 19 para 6, Sch 22 para 4*]. As regards claims etc. to which *TMA 1970, Sch 1A* applies (see below), appeals against amendments to claims etc. must be made within 30 days of the amendment being made, again extended to three months where the appeal relates to certain residence etc. claims or to pension funds for overseas employees. [*TMA 1970, Sch 1A para*

9; FA 1994, Sch 19 para 35]. *TMA 1970, Sch 1A* (as amended by *FA 1998, Sch 19 para 42*) deals with all aspects of claims not within *FA 1998, Sch 18 paras 57, 58* (mainly those not included in the company tax return (or amended return), see 55.4 SELF-ASSESSMENT). [*FA 1998, Sch 18 para 59*]. *TMA 1970, ss 46B–46D* (as amended) have effect as respects the Tribunal to which an appeal under that *Schedule* lies.

12.4 **ERROR OR MISTAKE RELIEF** [*TMA 1970, s 33; FA 1994, Sch 19 para 8; FA 1998, Sch 18 para 51, Sch 19 para 15*]

Relief may be claimed within the six year time limit (see 12.2 above) against any over-assessment due to an error or mistake in, or an omission from, any return. No relief is due where the return did not form the basis of the assessment or was made in accordance with the practice generally prevailing at the time, or (in relation to accounting periods ending on or after 1 July 1999, to which self-assessment applies) in respect of an error or mistake in a claim or election included in the return (see 55.13 SELF-ASSESSMENT). Such relief is to be given as may be 'reasonable and just' in the circumstances.

Claims should be made to the Board, from whom an appeal lies to the Special Commissioners and (on a point of law arising in connection with the computation of profits) to the High Court.

See also Tolley's Income Tax under Claims.

Simon's Direct Tax Service. See A3.10.

13 Close Companies

Simon's Direct Tax Service D3.

The headings in this chapter are as follows.

13.1	Close company — definition	13.11	— excluded loans
13.2	— 'control'	13.12	— procedure
13.3	— 'participator'	13.13	— loans written off or released
13.4	— 'director'	13.14	— example
13.5	— 'associate'	13.15	Additional items treated as distributions
13.6	Exceptions	13.16	Close company transferring asset at undervalue
13.7	— example	13.17	Demergers
13.8	Apportionment of undistributed income etc.	13.18	Close investment-holding companies
13.9	Loans to participators		
13.10	— loans or advances		

13.1 **CLOSE COMPANY — DEFINITION**

A company is close if

(*a*) it is under the 'control' of five or fewer 'participators' [*ICTA 1988, s 414(1)*], or

(*b*) it is under the control of participators who are 'directors' [*ICTA 1988, s 414(1)*], or

(*c*) five or fewer participators, or participators who are directors, together possess or are entitled to acquire such rights as would, in the event of a winding-up, entitle them to receive the greater part of the assets available for distribution among participators (assuming assets distributed to company participators are similarly distributed on). The test is applied with and without taking rights as a loan creditor into account. Participators in and directors of companies entitled to receive assets in such a notional winding-up are treated as participators in or directors of the company under consideration, but company participators are disregarded (except as above) unless acting in a fiduciary or representative capacity. [*ICTA 1988, s 414(2)–(2D); FA 1989, s 104(1)*].

For exceptions, see 13.6 below.

Simon's Direct Tax Service. See D3.102–D3.112, D3.121.

13.2 **'Control'** means the ability to exercise, or to acquire, control, whether direct or indirect, over the company's affairs. It includes the possession of, or right to acquire,

(i) the greater part of the share capital or issued share capital, or

(ii) the greater part of the voting power, or

(iii) so much of the issued share capital as would give the right to receive the greater part of the company's income, were all that income distributed; or

(iv) rights to the greater part of the company's assets in a distribution on a winding-up or in any other circumstances. [*ICTA 1988, s 416(2)*].

Future rights and rights of nominees are included. [*ICTA 1988, s 416(4)(5)*]. The first-mentioned holder of shares in joint ownership is treated as able alone to exercise the rights attaching thereto. (*Harton Coal Co Ltd Ch D 1960, 39 TC 174*).

Two or more persons have control of a company if their aggregated rights satisfy the above conditions. [*ICTA 1988, s 416(3)*]. There may be attributed to any person the rights and powers of any 'associate' or associates of his, or of any company or companies controlled by him (with or without his associates), together with those of any nominee of such company or associate. However the rights and powers of associates' associates and of companies controlled only by associates, are disregarded. [*ICTA 1988, s 416(6)*]. See 13.5 below. For circumstances in which the Revenue are bound so to attribute such rights and powers, see *R v CIR (ex p Newfields Developments Ltd) CA, [2000] STC 52.*

See also Revenue Pamphlet IR 131, C4 and 56.7 SMALL COMPANIES—REDUCED RATES.

13.3 **'Participator'** means a person having a share or interest in the capital or income of the company and includes

(i) any person possessing, or entitled to acquire, share capital or voting rights;

(ii) any 'loan creditor' (see below);

(iii) any person possessing, or entitled to acquire, a right to receive, or to participate in, distributions or any amount payable by the company (in cash or in kind) to loan creditors (see below) by way of premium on redemption ('distribution' is not to be given the extended meaning explained in 20.20 DISTRIBUTIONS); and

(iv) any person entitled to ensure that present or future income or assets of the company will be applied directly or indirectly for his benefit.

Future rights are included. [*ICTA 1988, s 417(1)*].

A '*loan creditor*' is a person to whom money is owed by the company in respect of

(A) any money borrowed by the company, or

(B) any capital asset acquired by the company, or

(C) any right to receive income created in the company's favour, or

(D) any redeemable loan capital issued by the company, or

(E) any debt the value of which (to the company) at the time the debt was incurred (including any premium thereon) substantially exceeded the consideration therefor.

[*ICTA 1988, s 417(7)*].

The definition includes persons other than the actual creditor who have a beneficial interest in the debt or loan capital. [*ICTA 1988, s 417(8)*].

A person carrying on a banking business is not deemed to be a loan creditor in respect of any loan capital issued or debt incurred by the company for money lent by him to the company in the ordinary course of that business. [*ICTA 1988, s 417(9)*]. As to what constitutes a *bona fide* banking business, see *Hafton Properties Ltd v McHugh Ch D 1986, 59 TC 420.*

Similarly, a recognised money broker is not treated as a participator in a stock-jobbing company solely by reason of short-term loans or advances arising in the ordinary course of their respective trades. (Revenue Pamphlet IR 1, C8).

13.4 **'Director'** includes any person

(i) who occupies the position of director (by whatever name called); or

(ii) in accordance with whose directions or instructions the directors are accustomed to act (although it is thought that the Revenue will not seek to bring professional advisers, acting purely in their capacity as such, within this head); or

(iii) who is a manager of the company (or otherwise concerned in the management of the company's trade or business) and who is the beneficial owner of, or able directly or indirectly to control, at least 20% of the ordinary share capital (i.e. all issued share capital other than that entitled only to a fixed rate of dividend) of the company. For this purpose, the holdings and powers of his associates may be attributed to him. For the meaning of 'associates', see 13.5 below.

[*ICTA 1988, s 417(5)(6)*].

13.5 An **'associate'** of a person who is a participator is

(i) any relative of that person, i.e. that person's husband or wife, parent or remoter forebear, child or remoter issue, or brother or sister,

(ii) any partner of that person,

(iii) the trustee(s) of any settlement of which that person, or any relative of his (living or dead), is or was a settlor, (see 16.7 CONNECTED PERSONS for the definitions of 'settlement' and of 'settlor'),

(iv) where that person is interested in any shares or obligations of the company which are subject to a trust or which are part of the estate of a deceased person, the trustee(s) or personal representatives concerned and, if the participator is a company, any other company interested in those shares or obligations.

[*ICTA 1988, s 417(3)(4)*].

Trustees are interested in shares comprised in the settlement (*J Bibby & Sons Ltd v CIR HL 1945, 29 TC 167*). Holders of units in a unit trust are not 'associates' merely by reason of their common membership of the unit trust. (CCAB Memorandum, June 1968).

'*Wife*' does not include 'widow', see *Vestey's Executors v CIR HL 1949, 31 TC 1*. Note that the definition of 'associate' (unlike that of 'connected person' in *ICTA 1988, s 839*) does not include the husband or wife of a relative. See 16 CONNECTED PERSONS.

13.6 EXCEPTIONS

The following are not close companies:

(*a*) a **non-resident** company (see 53 RESIDENCE);

(*b*) a registered **industrial and provident society** (see 32 INDUSTRIAL AND PROVIDENT SOCIETIES);

(*c*) a **building society** or similar entity (see 7.2 BUILDING SOCIETIES);

(*d*) a company **controlled by the Crown** or by persons acting on behalf of the Crown and independently of any other person (provided that it could not also be treated as under the control of five or fewer persons acting independently of the Crown);

(*e*) a company **controlled by another company which is not close** (other than by reason of non-residence) or by more than one such company, provided that such a non-close company is one of the necessary five or fewer participators without which the original company could not be treated as close;

(*f*) a company which can only be close by **taking as a participator,** entitled to receive assets on a winding-up (see 13.1 and 13.2(iv) above), **a loan creditor which is a non-close company** (other than by reason of non-residence);

(*g*) certain companies with **listed shares** (see further below).

[*ICTA 1988, s 414(1)(4)–(6), s 415; FA 1989, s 104(3)*].

The conditions for exception under (*g*) above are as follows.

(A) Shares or stock (exclusive of shares etc. entitled to a fixed rate of dividend, whether also participating in profits or not) must, within the twelve months before the date at which the company's status is to be determined, have been dealt in on, and listed in the official list of, a 'recognised stock exchange'.

(B) Such shares carrying at least 35% of the total 'voting power' in the company must be 'beneficially held' by 'the public'.

(C) The voting power (including that attributable to shares etc. entitled to a fixed rate of dividend) possessed by 'principal members' of the company must not exceed 85% of the total voting power in the company. [*ICTA 1988, s 415(1)(2); FA 1996, Sch 38 para 6*].

'*Recognised stock exchange*' means The Stock Exchange (or such other recognised investment exchange as may be prescribed by the Board for this purpose) and any non-UK stock exchange designated by the Board. [*ICTA 1988, s 841*]. See Revenue Company Taxation Manual, CT 6211 and Revenue Tax Bulletin April 1999 p 657. The position may be affected by a double taxation agreement (see 21 DOUBLE TAX RELIEF).

'*Voting power*' includes the power exercisable by any associate or associates of the shareholder, or of any company or companies controlled by him (with or without his associates), together with that of any nominee of his or of such company or associate. [*ICTA 1988, ss 415(7), 416(5)(6)*]. See also 13.2 above.

Shares '*beneficially held*' by a person include those allotted unconditionally to, or acquired unconditionally by, him but not yet registered in his name. [*ICTA 1988, s 416(1)*].

'*The public*' for this purpose does not include

(i) a director of the company (see 13.4 above);

(ii) an associate of such director (see 13.5 above);

(iii) any company controlled by such director or associate, or by two or more directors and/or associates;

(iv) a company associated with the quoted company (i.e. where one company controls the other or both are under common control [*ICTA 1988, s 416(1)*]) either at the time the question arises for determination or within the preceding twelve months (as to the interpretation of 'associated company', see Revenue Pamphlet IR 131, C4 and 56.7 SMALL COMPANIES—REDUCED RATES);

(v) any fund wholly or mainly for the benefit of the directors or employees, present or past, of the company or of any company within (iii) or (iv) above, or their dependants;

(vi) a 'principal member' of the company (but see below);

(vii) the nominees of (i)–(vi) above.

[*ICTA 1988, s 415(3)–(5)*].

(vi) above does not exclude from '*the public*' a 'principal member' which is a non-close company (other than by reason of non-residence) or is an exempt approved occupational pension scheme. [*ICTA 1988, s 415(4)(a)(b)*].

A '*principal member*' of a company is a person possessing more than five per cent of the voting power of that company or, where there are more than five such persons, one of the five persons possessing the greatest percentages. Where there are equal percentage holdings (so that the greatest percentages are held by more than five persons), a principal member is any one of that number (provided he holds more than five per cent). [*ICTA 1988, s 415(6)*].

Example

A holds 10% of the voting power of X Ltd. B and C hold 8% each, D and E hold 7% each and F holds 6%. No other member holds more than 5%. A, B, C, D and E each hold more than 5% and are principal members of the company, as they are the five persons holding the greatest percentages. F is not a principal member, as he does not meet the latter requirement. If, with the facts as above, G acquires a 10% holding, he will also become a principal member of the company. Since D and E have equal shareholdings, both will remain principal members, making six in total.

Where, for a short period straddling the end of one accounting period and the beginning of another, less than 35% of the voting rights in a company are held by the public, so that the company is close for that period, 'sympathetic consideration' will be given to the situation by the Revenue. (Revenue Pamphlet IR 131, C4).

Simon's Direct Tax Service. See **D3.113, D3.114**.

13.7 *Example*

A plc is a quoted company whose ordinary share capital is owned as follows.

		%
B	a director	10
C	wife of B	5
D	father of B	4
E		17
F	business partner of E	2
G	a director	10
H		8
I Ltd	a non–close company	30
J		7
100	other shareholders	7
		100

It can be shown that A plc is a close company by considering the following three steps.

(i) Is A plc controlled by five or fewer participators or by its directors?

		%	%
I Ltd			30
B	own shares	10	
	C's shares	5	
	D's shares	4	
			19
E	own shares	17	
	F's shares	2	
			19
			68

As A plc is controlled by three participators, the initial conclusion is that the company is close.

(ii) Is A plc a quoted company, with at least 35% of the voting power owned by the public?

	%
I Ltd	30
J	7
100 other shareholders	7
	44

As at least 35% of the share capital is owned by the public it appears that A plc is exempt from close company status, subject to step (iii).

(iii) Is more than 85% of the voting power in A plc owned by its principal members?

	%
I Ltd	30
B	19
E	19
G	10
H	8
	86

Although J owns more than 5% of the share capital, he is not a principal member because five other persons each hold more than J's 7% and so themselves constitute the principal members.

Because the principal members own more than 85% of the share capital A plc is a close company.

13.8 **APPORTIONMENT OF UNDISTRIBUTED INCOME ETC.** [*ICTA 1988, ss 423–430, Sch 19; FA 1989, s 103, Sch 17 Pt V*]

These provisions are repealed in relation to accounting periods beginning **after 31 March 1989**. Previously, the excess of a close company's 'relevant income' over its distributions (or in certain cases the whole 'relevant income') was liable to apportionment amongst its participators, subject to a number of exceptions and relieving measures. For detailed coverage, see Tolley's Corporation Tax 1996/97 or earlier.

Simon's Direct Tax Service. See D3.3.

13.9 **LOANS TO PARTICIPATORS** [*ICTA 1988, ss 419, 420*]

Where a close company, otherwise than in the ordinary course of a business carried on by it which includes the lending of money, makes any loan or advances any money to an individual who is a 'participator' in the company or is an 'associate of a participator', an amount equal to 25% of the amount of the loan or advance (before the abolition of ACT, defined by reference to the rate of ACT for the financial year in which the loan etc. was made) is assessed on and recoverable from the company as if it were corporation tax chargeable for the accounting period in which the loan, etc. was made. For accounting periods ending after 30 September 1993, such an amount is due from the company without assessment. [*ICTA 1988, s 419(1); FA 1998, Sch 3 para 24*]. The Revenue do not accept that separate accounts with the same participator may be aggregated or 'netted off' for these purposes. (Revenue Company Taxation Manual, CT 6652).

For a case in which a loan by an investment company to its chairman was held to have been made in the ordinary course of its business, so that *section 419* did not apply, see *The Deanby Investment Co Ltd v Brennan (Sp C 234), [2000] SSCD 172.*

'*Participator*' and '*associate of a participator*' are as defined in 13.3 and 13.5 above, save that a participator in a company which controls the lending company is specifically included. [*ICTA 1988, s 419(1)(7)*].

These provisions also apply to a loan etc. made to a company receiving it in a fiduciary or representative capacity (or, in relation to a loan etc. made in an accounting period ending before 31 March 1996, to a non-resident company) as if the company was an individual. [*ICTA 1988, s 419(6); FA 1996, s 173(4)(6)*]. Such a company must also be a participator or an associate of a participator.

The inspector has appropriate information powers. [*FA 1989, Sch 12 Pt I*].

See further ICAEW Technical Release TAX 11/93, 'Tax implications of certain payments to directors' (25 June 1993) for guidance as to application of these provisions in practice.

Simon's Direct Tax Service. See **D3.4**.

13.10 **Loans or advances** which are within these provisions include

(*a*) a debt incurred to the close company (unless for goods or services supplied by it in the ordinary course of its trade or business and on credit no longer than normally allowed to customers, with a maximum of six months);

(*b*) the assignment to the close company of a debt due to a third party;

(*c*) a loan or advance not otherwise within *section 419(1)* where, under arrangements made by any person otherwise than in the ordinary course of a business carried on by him, some person other than the close company making the loan etc. makes a payment or transfers property to, or releases or satisfies (in whole or in part) a liability of, an individual who is a participator, or the associate of a participator, in the lending company. '*Individual*' here includes fiduciary, representative and non-resident companies as mentioned in 13.9 above. Loans etc. which would be included for tax purposes in the total income of the participator or associate are excluded;

(*d*) loans etc. by a company controlled by the close company and not otherwise within *section 419(1)* (but see below);

(*e*) loans etc. not within *section 419(1)* made by a company of which a close company subsequently acquires control (such loans being treated as made at the date of acquisition of control) (but see below).

[*ICTA 1988, s 419(2)(5)(6), s 420(1), s 422*].

As regards (*a*) above, in *Andrew Grant Services Ltd v Watton and cross-appeal Ch D 1999, 71 TC 333*, the company supplied services to a partnership in which it was a limited partner, and of which its controlling director was the general partner, under an agreement for reimbursement of the amounts charged in the company's accounts (plus a mark up), but with no formal or implied agreement as to the time payment would be made. It was held that the debt was incurred for the purposes of *section 419* when the debtor became legally committed to expenditure in relation to the services supplied to the partnership.

The provisions in (*d*) and (*e*) above apply equally where two or more close companies control, or acquire control of, the lending company. The loan is apportioned between them in proportion to the nature and amount of their respective interests in the lending company. *Sections 419* and *422* are to be interpreted in relation to the company which actually made the loan. These provisions *do not apply* if it is shown that there is no arrangement (otherwise than in the ordinary course of business) connecting the making of the loan with

(i) the acquisition of control, or

(ii) the making of any payment or the transfer of any property (whether directly or indirectly) by the close company to the lending company, or

(iii) the releasing or satisfying by the close company (in whole or in part) of any liability of the lending company.

[*ICTA 1988, s 422*].

The misappropriation of the company's money by a participator may give rise to a debt within (*a*) above. (*Stephens v Pittas Ltd Ch D 1983, 56 TC 722*).

13.11 **Excluded loans.** Loans etc. are excluded from *section 419* if they are made to a director or employee of a close company (or of its associated company) *and*

(*a*) the total loans outstanding from the close company and any associated company to the borrower (or, for loans made before 6 April 1990, to the wife or husband of the borrower) made *after* 30 March 1971, together with any such loans made *before* 31 March 1971 for the purpose of purchasing an only or main residence, do not exceed £15,000 (and the total of pre-31 March 1971 'housing' loans outstanding does not exceed £10,000); *and*

(*b*) the borrower works full-time for the close company or any of its associated companies; *and*

(*c*) the borrower does not have a 'material interest' in the close company or any of its associated companies.

[*ICTA 1988, s 420(2)*; *FA 1988, Sch 3 para 16*].

A company is an '*associated company*' if it controls, or is under the control of, the close company or both are under common control. [*ICTA 1988, s 416(1)*].

'*Director*' is as defined in 13.4 above. [*ICTA 1988, s 417(5)*].

'*Wife*' does not include a widow, see *Vestey's Exors v CIR HL 1949, 31 TC 1*.

A director or employee is generally treated as working *full-time* if his hours are at least three-quarters of the company's normal working hours subject, it is understood, to a minimum of 28 hours per week.

A person has a '*material interest*' in a company if he (alone or with associates) or any associate (see 13.5 above) of his

(i) is the beneficial owner of, or otherwise able directly or indirectly to control, more than five per cent of the ordinary share capital of the company, or

(ii) in the case of a close company, is entitled to more than five per cent of the company's assets available for distribution to participators. [*ICTA 1988, ss 168(11), 420(2); FA 1989, Sch 12 para 8*].

If the borrower acquires such a material interest whilst any part of a post-30 March 1971 loan remains outstanding, the company is to be regarded as making to him at that time a loan equal to the amount outstanding. [*ICTA 1988, s 420(2)*].

13.12 **Procedure.** Assessments under *section 419* are subject to the general administrative provisions relating to corporation tax, except as below. If the loan, etc. is repaid or (after 5 April 1999) released or written off, the tax is repaid or discharged (or, under self-assessment, set off in the company tax return), with proportional treatment if only part of the loan is repaid, released or written off. For a loan etc. made in an accounting period ending after 30 March 1996, where the repayment, release or writing off of the loan etc. (or part) occurs after the tax under these provisions has become due and payable, the repayment or discharge of that tax is not made before nine months after the end of the accounting period in which the loan, etc. was repaid, released or written off. A claim for repayment must be made within six years of the end of the financial year in which the loan is repaid, released or written off. If, however, the tax was paid late, and a charge to INTEREST ON UNPAID TAX (39) incurred, the interest is not refunded. [*ICTA 1988, s 419(4)–(4B); TMA 1970, s 109(1)(4); FA 1996, s 173(3)(6); FA 1998, Sch 3 para 24, Sch 19 para 47(3)(4)*].

In *Earlspring Properties Ltd v Guest CA 1995, 67 TC 259*, it was held that a failure to notify liability under *section 419* constituted neglect and gave rise to a liability to interest under *TMA 1970, s 88* and to penalties. See also *Joint v Bracken Developments Ltd Ch D 1994, 66 TC 560*. See below and generally Tolley's Income Tax above under Back Duty.

Tax under *section 419* is due and payable nine months after the end of the accounting period, and INTEREST ON UNPAID TAX (39) arises accordingly. For loans, etc. made in accounting periods ending before 31 March 1996, it was due and payable within 14 days after the end of the accounting period. If the loan, etc. is repaid, released or written off, interest ceases from the date of the repayment, etc.. [*ICTA 1988, s 419(3); TMA 1970, s 109(3)(3A); FA 1996, s 173(2)(6); FA 1998, Sch 3 para 6*]. Payslips will not be issued routinely in advance of assessment, and companies paying in advance of assessment should do so under cover of a letter identifying the liability and the accounting period to which it relates. Interest charges will not be raised, or demand notes for tax or interest issued, until the liability has been assessed. (Revenue Tax Bulletin August 1993 p 85).

13.13 **Loans written off or released.** Where a loan or advance charged under *section 419* is wholly or partly written-off or released, the borrower is treated as receiving as part of his total income an amount equal to the amount so written off or released, grossed up at the lower rate of income tax or, from 6 April 1999, the Schedule F ordinary rate of income tax (currently 10%). The notional lower or Schedule F ordinary rate tax is not repayable, and there is no liability to pay it. However, tax at the higher rate of 40% or, from 6 April 1999, the Schedule F upper rate, currently 32.5%, may be payable on the gross amount of the notional income (broadly to the extent that the total income exceeds the basic rate income tax limit). The grossed-up amount of the income is treated as not brought into charge to income tax for the purposes of *ICTA 1988, ss 348, 349(1)* (so that it may not be used to cover charges). [*ICTA 1988, s 421(1); F(No 2)A 1992, s 19(6); FA 1993, s 77(4)(5); FA 1996, s 122(6), Sch 6 para 9; F(No 2)A 1997, Sch 4 para 11*]. Where, under the terms of a deed, a company accepted the replacement of the participator by a third party as its debtor, this amounted to the release of the debt (*Collins v Addies; Greenfield v Bains CA 1992, 65 TC 190*).

See 13.12 above as regards repayment to the company where a loan etc. is released or written off after 5 April 1999.

Where the borrower is dead, or the loan was made to a trust which has come to an end, these provisions apply, with necessary modifications, to the person from whom the debt was due at the time of release or writing-off. [*ICTA 1988, s 421(2)*].

Where any part of a loan or advance written-off or released is treated as the income of the borrower under *ICTA 1988, s 677* (sums paid to settlor otherwise than as income), liability does not arise under *ICTA 1988, s 421* in respect of that part. [*ICTA 1988, s 421(3)*].

Where the borrower is both a participator in and an employee of the lending company, and the waiver of a loan is subject to charge under *section 421* (as above), it is understood that the Revenue would not seek to treat the amount written off or released as a distribution under *ICTA 1988, s 209* or *s 410* (see 20 DISTRIBUTIONS) or to raise an assessment under the beneficial loan provisions of *ICTA 1988, s 160(2)* (see Tolley's Income Tax under Schedule E). (Tolley's Practical Tax 1993 p 144).

13.14 *Examples*

(A)

P is a participator in Q Ltd, a close company. Q Ltd loaned P £75,000 on 29 August 1992. On 24 May 1998 P repaid £37,500 and on 30 September 1998 Q Ltd agreed to waive the balance of the loan.

The effect of these transactions on Q Ltd and P is as follows.

Q Ltd

On 29.8.92 The company became liable to pay, within 14 days of it being assessed, 'notional ACT' of £75,000 × $\frac{25}{75}$

£25,000

On 24.5.98 The company is entitled to repayment of 'notional ACT' to the extent of £37,500 × $\frac{25}{75}$

£12,500*

On 30.9.98 No more 'notional ACT' can be recovered

P

On 30.9.98 P's 1998/99 taxable income is increased by (£75,000 – £37,500) × $\frac{100}{80}$

£46,875

and he is credited with lower rate income tax paid of £46,875 at 20%

£9,375.00

* The repayment of 'notional ACT' is at the same rate as that paid on the advance, regardless of any change in the rate of ACT in the meantime.

(B)

S is a participator in R Ltd, a close company which makes up its accounts to 30 September. R Ltd loaned S £80,000 on 29 August 1997. On 24 May 1999 S repays the loan.

The effect of these transactions on R Ltd is as follows.

On 30.6.98 The company is liable to pay 'notional ACT' of £80,000 × $\frac{20}{80}$

£20,000

On 31.3.2000 The company is entitled to make a claim for repayment of the ACT paid.

On 30.6.2000 Following a claim, the company is entitled to a repayment of the 'notional ACT' paid

£20,000

(C)

T is a participator in V Ltd, a close company. V Ltd loaned T £100,000 on 10 May 1999. On 2 March 2000, T repays £73,000 and on 30 September 2000, V Ltd agrees to waive the balance of the loan. V Ltd has a year end of 31 March and is not a large company for instalment payment purposes.

The effect of these transactions is as follows.

V Ltd

On 1.1.01	The company becomes liable to pay corporation tax of (£100,000 – £73,000 =) £27,000 × 25%	£6,750
On 31.12.01	The company is due a repayment of £27,000 × 25%	£6,750

T

On 30.9.2000	T's 2000/01 taxable income is increased by £27,000 × $\frac{10}{9}$	£30,000
	and he is credited with Schedule F ordinary rate tax paid of £30,000 at 10%	£3,000.00
	If T pays tax at the higher rate, the deemed income will be subject to tax at the Schedule F upper rate of 32.5% on £30,000	9,750.00
	Less: tax credit (as above)	3,000.00
	T's tax liability	£6,750.00

13.15 **ADDITIONAL ITEMS TREATED AS DISTRIBUTIONS**

As regards certain benefits provided by close companies to participators and/or directors, which are classed as distributions, see 20.9, 20.11, 20.19 DISTRIBUTIONS. See also 20.16(*h*)(*j*) DISTRIBUTIONS for items *not* treated as distributions.

13.16 **CLOSE COMPANY TRANSFERRING ASSET AT UNDERVALUE**

See 9.17 CAPITAL GAINS.

13.17 **DEMERGERS**

For treatment of certain 'chargeable payments' made following an 'exempt distribution', see 29.51 GROUPS OF COMPANIES.

13.18 **CLOSE INVESTMENT-HOLDING COMPANIES**

The SMALL COMPANIES—REDUCED RATES (56) provisions do not apply to a company for any accounting period at the end of which the company is a 'close investment-holding company'.

A close company is a '*close investment-holding company*' for an accounting period unless throughout the period it exists wholly or mainly for one or more of the following purposes.

(*a*) The carrying on of trade(s) on a commercial basis.

(*b*) The making of investments in land, or estates or interests in land, let, or intended to be let, other than to CONNECTED PERSONS (16) of the company or to certain individuals related to such connected persons.

(*c*) The holding of shares in and securities of, or making loans to, a company or companies which, or each of which, is either

  (i) a 'qualifying company', or

  (ii) a company under its 'control', or under the 'control' of the same company as it, which itself exists wholly or mainly for the purpose of holding shares in or securities of, or making loans to, one or more 'qualifying companies'.

(*d*) The co-ordination of the administration of two or more 'qualifying companies'.

(*e*) The purposes of trade(s) carried on on a commercial basis by one or more 'qualifying companies', or by a company which has 'control' of the company in question.

(*f*) The making, by one or more 'qualifying companies' or by a parent company, of investments within (*b*) above.

A '*qualifying company*' in relation to the company in question is a company which is under its 'control', or under the 'control' of the same company as it, and which exists wholly or mainly for either or both of the purposes in (*a*) or (*b*) above.

'*Control*' for all these purposes is as under *ICTA 1988, s 416* (see 13.2 above).

A company is not treated as failing to comply with the above conditions in the accounting period beginning at the commencement of its winding-up (see 42.6 LIQUIDATION ETC.) if it complied with them in the immediately preceding period. If, however, there is an interval between cessation of trading and commencement of winding-up, this will obviate the relief (see *Taxation* 1 February 1990, p 496).

[*ICTA 1988, s 13(1)(a), s 13AA(8)(b), s 13A; FA 1989, s 104; FA 1999, s 28(1)*].

Tax credits. In relation to distributions made before 6 April 1999 by close investment-holding companies, restrictions are placed on the availability of tax credits. These apply where arrangements of any kind, whether in writing or not, relating to the distribution of profits exist, or have existed, a main purpose of which is to enable repayments, or greater repayments, of tax credit to be made to one or more individuals, and by virtue of those arrangements any UK resident individual otherwise entitled to such repayment receives a qualifying distribution being either

(i) a payment on the redemption, etc. by a company of its own shares (see PURCHASE BY A COMPANY OF ITS OWN SHARES (51)), or

(ii) any other distribution in respect of company shares or securities whose value is greater than might have been expected but for the arrangements.

In those circumstances, repayments to such individuals are restricted to such extent as appears just and reasonable. This does not, however, apply to a dividend paid in respect of ordinary share capital in an accounting period throughout which there was only one class of ordinary share capital, provided that no person waived entitlement to any dividend payable in the period or failed to receive any such dividend.

For these purposes, tax credits are set against income tax in the order that results in the greatest repayment.

These provisions **cease to apply** to distributions made after 5 April 1999, following the general abolition of tax credit repayments. They are also subject to the provisions applicable to pension funds in relation to distributions made after 1 July 1997 (see 27.1 FRANKED INVESTMENT INCOME).

[*ICTA 1988, s 231(3)–(3D); FA 1989, s 105; FA 1996, Sch 20 para 12; F(No 2)A 1997, ss 19(1), 30(7), Sch 8 Pt II(9)*].

The inspector has appropriate information powers. [*FA 1989, Sch 12 Pt I*].

Simon's Direct Tax Service. See **D3.2.**

14 Clubs and Societies

See 55.3 SELF-ASSESSMENT as regards tax returns by members' clubs and similar organisations.

See generally Revenue Pamphlet IR 46.

14.1 A club or society, being either an incorporated body or an unincorporated association, is liable to corporation tax on its income and capital gains, which includes interest received and profits from non-members (see 14.2 below). For the special treatment of certain societies, see 7 BUILDING SOCIETIES, 11 CHARITIES, 24 EXEMPT ORGANISATIONS, 28 FRIENDLY SOCIETIES, 30 HOUSING ASSOCIATIONS, 32 INDUSTRIAL AND PROVIDENT SOCIETIES and 45 MUTUAL COMPANIES. Generally, see Revenue explanatory pamphlet IR 46 'Clubs, Societies and Associations'. See *CIR v Worthing Rugby Football Club Trustees CA 1987, 60 TC 482* and *Blackpool Marton Rotary Club v Martin Ch D 1988, 62 TC 686*. See also Revenue Tax Bulletin October 1998 p 600 for the Revenue approach to such bodies with trivial liabilities.

14.2 MUTUAL TRADING

A members' club does not carry on a trade and is not liable on its surplus from the provision of facilities for members, even though the membership fluctuates. Any surplus arising from the supply of goods or services to non-members is taxable. See 45.1 MUTUAL COMPANIES. See also 14.8 below as regards members' sports clubs.

14.3 LOAN AND MONEY SOCIETIES

Dividends and interest paid to members are subject to deduction of income tax at an average rate based on the reduced rates which would be applicable to members. The grossed-up amounts are then deductible in computing the societies' corporation tax liability. (Revenue Pamphlet IR 1, C2). The concession is withdrawn from April 2001. See Revenue Press Release 3 March 2000.

14.4 HOLIDAY CLUBS AND THRIFT FUNDS

Such funds and clubs formed annually for the purpose of saving for holidays are regarded as being outside the scope of corporation tax. Where income not subjected to composite rate tax is received, liability in respect of such income paid to members or expended for their benefit is restricted to the total amount which would have been charged had the members received the income directly. (Revenue Pamphlet IR 1, C3). The concession is withdrawn from April 2001. See Revenue Press Release 3 March 2000.

14.5 INVESTMENT CLUBS

Chargeable gains and allowable losses made by investment clubs are apportioned among the members, each individual being assessed to capital gains tax on his share of the whole. If the club has not more than 20 members with an *average* investment of not more than £5,000, then if the annual subscription to the club does not exceed £1,000, and its total annual gains are less than £5,000, the secretary may apply (on Form 185-1) for the gains and losses to be agreed by the inspector of the district in which he lives. Each member's share can then be accepted by his own local inspector without further argument. Otherwise, the total gains and the member's share must be separately agreed.

14.6 **LOTTERIES ETC.**

Where a football pool or small lottery is to be run by a supporters' club or other society on the basis that a stated percentage or fraction of the cost of each ticket will be given to a club or body conducted and established wholly or mainly for one or more of the purposes specified in *Lotteries and Amusements Act 1976*, the donation element as stated in the cost of each ticket may be excluded in computing for tax purposes the profits of the trade of promoting the pool or lottery. (Revenue Pamphlet IR 131, C1).

14.7 **DISSOLUTION**

An unincorporated association which sells its only fixed asset and closes down is liable to corporation tax on any chargeable gain arising by virtue of *ICTA 1988, s 832(1)*. However, the distribution of the surplus on a winding-up is subject to ACT. In view of this anomaly, such cases will be referred to the Board for consideration. (CCAB Memorandum 6 March 1974).

14.8 **MEMBERS' SPORTS CLUBS**

For the Revenue's views on the circumstances in which a members' sports club's commercial activities can give rise to taxable trading profits (or to allowable trading losses), see Revenue Tax Bulletin December 1997 pp 488–490.

VAT repayments. Repayments under *SI 1994 No 687* which are returned to members *pro rata* to the VAT originally paid by them do not give rise to a distribution for tax purposes. Interest on the repayments is chargeable to corporation tax, but other supplemental payments are not chargeable. See Revenue Tax Bulletin April 1995 p 209.

15 Compensation, Damages Etc.

15.1 For capital sums received as compensation for damage or injury to, or the destruction or depreciation of, assets, see Tolley's Capital Gains Tax under Disposal. For compensation for loss of office, etc., see Tolley's Income Tax under Compensation for Loss of Employment. Other types of compensation received or paid are dealt with below.

15.2 COMPENSATION FOR COMPULSORY ACQUISITION

Following *Stoke-on-Trent City Council v Wood Mitchell & Co Ltd CA 1978, [1979] STC 197*, any element of compensation, paid by an authority possessing compulsory purchase powers for the acquisition of property used for a trade or profession, representing temporary loss of profits, will be treated as a trading receipt. Compensation for losses on trading stock and to reimburse revenue expenditure, such as removal expenses and interest, will be similarly treated. (Revenue Pamphlet IR 131, SP 8/79, 18 June 1979).

15.3 CANCELLATION OR VARIATION OF TRADING AGREEMENTS

Compensation etc. received on the cancellation or variation of contracts which, if completed, would have given rise to trading receipts, is normally also treated as a trading receipt of the accounting period in which the cancellation or variation took place. See *Short Bros Ltd v CIR CA 1927, 12 TC 955* (cancellation of shipbuilding contract); *Northfleet Coal & Ballast Co Ltd KB 1927, 12 TC 1102* (cancellation of contract for minerals extraction); *J Robinson & Sons v CIR KB 1929, 12 TC 1241* and *Creed v H & M Levinson Ltd Ch D 1981, 54 TC 477* (cancellation of contract for sale of goods); *Greyhound Racing Association (Liverpool) Ltd v Cooper KB 1936, 20 TC 373* (surrender of hiring agreement); *Bush, Beach & Gent Ltd v Road KB 1939, 22 TC 519* (cancellation of merchanting franchise); *Shove v Dura Manufacturing Co Ltd KB 1941, 23 TC 779* (cancellation of commission agreement); *Shadbolt v Salmon Estate (Kingsbury) Ltd KB 1943, 25 TC 52* (withdrawal of building rights); *Sommerfelds Ltd v Freeman Ch D 1966, 44 TC 43* (breach of contract for sale of goods — rights assigned). For further cases on this point, see Tolley's Tax Cases. See also 15.6 below.

15.4 TERMINATION OF AGENCIES

Compensation received on the termination of agencies is a trading receipt (unless the agency, by reason of its relative size, etc., is part of the 'whole structure of the recipient's profit-making apparatus', see 15.7 below). See *Kelsall Parsons & Co v CIR CS 1938, 21 TC 608* (manufacturers' agency); *Fleming v Bellow Machine Co Ltd Ch D 1965, 42 TC 308* (distributors' sub-agency); *Anglo-French Exploration Co Ltd v Clayson CA 1956, 36 TC 545* and *Blackburn v Close Bros Ltd Ch D 1960, 39 TC 164* (provision of agency, managerial and secretarial services). In all these cases, compensation was held to be a trading receipt, but compare *Ellis v Lucas Ch D 1966, 43 TC 276* where a certified accountant, who was auditor to a number of companies and carried out related accountancy work, was paid compensation on his agreeing to relinquish his post as auditor. In the absence of a finding by the Commissioners that the auditorship did not constitute an asset of the taxpayer's profession, except insofar as it included general accountancy work, so much of the payment as did not relate to general accountancy work was compensation for loss of office and therefore within the charge to tax under Schedule E (although exempt under what is now *ICTA 1988, s 188*) (see Tolley's Income Tax under Compensation for Loss of Employment and Damages) and only the balance constituted a trading receipt. For further cases on this point, see Tolley's Tax Cases. See also 15.5 below.

For payments received on termination of building society agencies, see Revenue Capital Gains Tax Manual, CG 13050 *et seq.*.

15.5 **EX GRATIA PAYMENTS**

In *Walker v Carnaby, Harrower, Barham & Pykett Ch D 1969, 46 TC 561*, a sum equivalent to the audit fee was paid to a firm of accountants as a solatium on their agreeing not to seek re-election as auditors to a group of companies. It was held that, but for being voluntary, the payment would have been taken into account as part of the firm's profits, but that 'ordinary commercial principles' did not require the bringing into account of a voluntary payment not made as consideration for past services, but in recognition of such services or by way of consolation for the termination of a contract. Voluntary payments were also held not to be assessable under Schedule D in *Brander & Cruickshank HL 1970, 46 TC 574* (loss of company secretaryships by firm of advocates); *Chibbett v Joseph Robinson & Sons KB 1924, 9 TC 48* (loss of office as ship-managers on liquidation); *Simpson v John Reynolds & Co (Insurances) Ltd CA 1975, 49 TC 693* (loss of client by insurance brokers) and *Murray v Goodhews CA 1977, 52 TC 86* (termination of caterers' tenancies). However, ex gratia payments to an estate agent who, contrary to local custom, had not been given an agency which he expected were held to be assessable as additional remuneration for work already carried out (*McGowan v Brown & Cousins Ch D 1977, 52 TC 8*), and a non-contractual payment to a diamond broker by a fellow-broker, as compensation for transfer of a client's business after substantial work had been done on the client's behalf but before any corresponding benefit had been gained from purchases by the client, was held to be a trading receipt (*Rolfe v Nagel CA 1981, 55 TC 585*). See also *Falkirk Ice Rink Ltd CS 1975, 51 TC 42* where the payment related to future services, and for further cases on this point, see Tolley's Tax Cases.

15.6 **OTHER RECEIPTS ASSESSABLE AS INCOME**

Damages awarded to producers for breach of a sole licence to perform a play were held assessable in *Vaughan v Parnell & Zeitlin Ltd KB 1940, 23 TC 505* as was statutory compensation for the restriction of development rights (*Johnson v W S Try Ltd CA 1946, 27 TC 167*). Retrospective compensation for requisitioned trading stock was held to be a trading receipt of the year of requisition in *Newcastle Breweries Ltd HL 1927, 12 TC 927*, as were compensation to a shipping company for delay in the overhaul of a ship (*Burmah Steam Ship Co v CIR CS 1930, 16 TC 67*) and to a jetty owner for loss of use (*London & Thames Haven Oil Wharves Ltd v Attwooll CA 1966, 43 TC 491*). For further cases on this point, see Tolley's Tax Cases. See also 15.7 below.

15.7 **COMPENSATION RELATING TO CAPITAL ASSETS**

An agreed sum received on the termination of 'pooling agreements' between two companies was held to be a capital receipt on the ground that the agreements '*related to the whole structure of the appellants' profit-making apparatus*' in *Van Den Berghs v Clark HL 1935, 19 TC 390*. This was followed in *Barr, Crombie & Co Ltd v CIR CS 1945, 26 TC 406* (terminating ship-managers' agreement) and *Sabine v Lookers Ltd CA 1958, 38 TC 120* (variation of car distributor's agreement). See also *British-Borneo Petroleum Syndicate Ltd v Cropper Ch D 1968, 45 TC 201* (cancellation of royalty agreement).

Compensation paid to a company making fireclay goods for refraining from working a fireclay bed was held to be capital in *Glenboig Union Fireclay Co Ltd v CIR HL 1922, 12 TC 427* but cf. *Waterloo Main Colliery Co Ltd v CIR (No 1) KB 1947, 29 TC 235* where compensation for the requisition of part of a mining area was held to be a trading receipt.

Reimbursement for restoration expenditure on a ship which had deteriorated whilst requisitioned was held to be a capital receipt in *Francis West CS 1950, 31 TC 402*, but compensation for loss of use of a requisitioned ship was assessable as a trading receipt in *Ensign Shipping Co Ltd v CIR CA 1928, 12 TC 1169*. For further relevant cases, see Tolley's Tax Cases. See also 15.6 above.

15.8 **PAYMENT OF COMPENSATION**

(*a*) **Deductible as revenue expenditure.** A substantial payment by a principal for the cancellation of an expensive agency agreement was held deductible in *Anglo-Persian Oil Co Ltd v Dale CA 1931, 16 TC 253*, on the grounds that it was made not only to commute revenue expenditure but also to rationalise the principal's working arrangements. The decision was applied in *Croydon Hotel & Leisure Co Ltd v Bowen (Sp C 101), [1996] SSCD 466*, in which a payment for the termination of a hotel management agreement was held to be allowable. Contrast *Mallett v Staveley Coal & Iron Co Ltd CA 1928, 13 TC 772* where a payment to surrender certain onerous mining leases was held to secure an advantage for the enduring benefit of the trade and therefore to be capital expenditure. For other items held to be revenue expenditure, see *Commr of Taxes v Nchanga Consolidated Copper Mines Ltd PC 1964, [1964] AC 948* and *United Steel Companies* (below), *Mitchell v B W Noble Ltd CA 1927, 11 TC 372* (payment to get rid of director) and *O'Keeffe v Southport Printers Ltd Ch D 1984, 58 TC 88* (payments on cessation in lieu of notice). See also *G Scammell & Nephew v Rowles CA 1939, 22 TC 479.*

(*b*) **Capital expenditure.** A payment by the operator of a single ship for cancelling an order for a second was held to be on capital account (*'Countess Warwick' Steamship Co Ltd v Ogg KB 1924, 8 TC 652*) as were payments by a steel company to secure the closure of railways steelworks (*United Steel Companies Ltd v Cullington (No 1) CA 1939, 23 TC 71*, which also involved payments by sub-contractors on revenue account); for cessation of mining to prevent subsidence (*Bradbury v The United Glass Bottle Manufacturers Ltd CA 1959, 38 TC 369*); for the cancellation of an electricity agreement on the closure of a quarry (*William Sharp & Son CS 1959, 38 TC 341*) and as compensation on the termination of tied tenancies by a brewery company (*Watneys London Ltd v Pike Ch D 1982, 57 TC 372*).

(*c*) **Other expenditure not deductible.** Damages paid by a brewery to a hotel guest injured by a falling chimney were held to have been incurred as a property owner and not as a trader (*Strong & Co of Romsey Ltd v Woodifield HL 1906, 5 TC 215*). Penalties for the breach of war-time regulations (and associated costs) were disallowed in *Alexander von Glehn & Co Ltd CA 1920, 12 TC 232* and damages for breach of American anti-trust law (but **not** the associated legal expenses) in *Cattermole v Borax & Chemicals Ltd KB 1949, 31 TC 202*. See also *Fairrie v Hall KB 1947, 28 TC 200* (damages for libel) and *Knight v Parry Ch D 1972, 48 TC 580* (damages for breach of contract of employment).

(*d*) **Date of payment.** Where damages awarded by a court against a solicitor were later compounded, the compounded amount (accepted as allowable) was held to be an expense of the year in which the court award was made (*Simpson v Jones Ch D 1968, 44 TC 599*). See also *Hugh T Barrie Ltd CA (NI) 1928, 12 TC 1223.*

For further relevant cases, see Tolley's Tax Cases.

16 Connected Persons

[*ICTA 1988, s 839 as amended*]

Simon's Direct Tax Service C2.110.

16.1 **An individual** is connected with his spouse, any 'relative' (see 16.7 below) of himself or of his spouse, and with the spouse of any such relative. It appears that a widow or widower is no longer a spouse (*Vestey's Exors and Vestey v CIR HL 1949, 31 TC 1*). Spouses divorced by decree nisi remain connected persons until the divorce is made absolute (*Aspden v Hildesley Ch D 1981, 55 TC 609*).

16.2 **A trustee of a 'settlement'**, in his capacity as such, is connected with

(*a*) the 'settlor' (if an individual) (see 16.7 below), and

(*b*) any person connected with the settlor (if within (*a*)), and

(*c*) a 'body corporate connected with the settlement' (see 16.7 below).

16.3 **Partners** are connected with each other and with each other's spouses (see 16.1 above) and relatives (see 16.7 below) except in connection with acquisitions and disposals of partnership assets made 'pursuant to *bona fide* commercial arrangements'.

16.4 **A 'company' (see 16.7 below) is connected with another company if**

(*a*) the same person 'controls' both, or

(*b*) one is controlled by a person who has control of the other in conjunction with persons connected with him, or

(*c*) a person controls one company and persons connected with him control the other, or

(*d*) the same group of persons controls both, or

(*e*) the companies are controlled by separate groups which can be regarded as the same by interchanging connected persons.

16.5 **A company is connected with a person who** (either alone or with persons connected with him) has control of it. It is understood that the Revenue will accept that a **partnership and a company under common control** are connected (see Tolley's Practical Tax 1981 p 142) in relation to the treatment for capital allowances of assets transferred on a succession.

16.6 **Persons acting together to secure or exercise control of a company** are treated in relation to that company as connected with each other and with any other person acting on the direction of any of them to secure or exercise such control. For the meaning of 'acting together to secure or exercise control', see *Steele v EVC International NV (formerly European Vinyls Corp (Holdings) BV) CA 1996, 69 TC 88*. Control may be 'exercised' passively. (See *Floor v Davis HL 1979, 52 TC 609*).

16.7 '*Company*' includes any body corporate, unincorporated association or unit trust scheme. It does not include a partnership.

'*Control*' is as defined in *ICTA 1988, s 416* (see 13.2 CLOSE COMPANIES).

'*Relative*' means brother, sister, ancestor or lineal descendant.

'*Settlement*' includes any disposition, trust, covenant, agreement, arrangement or, for 1995/96 onwards, transfer of assets. [*ICTA 1988, s 681(4) (repealed); ICTA 1988, s 660G(1); FA 1995, Sch 17 para 1*].

'*A body corporate connected with the settlement*' is a close company (or one which would be close if resident in the UK) the participators in which include the trustees of the settlement, or a company of which such a close company etc. has control (as defined by *ICTA 1988, s 840* — see 4.4 ANTI-AVOIDANCE). [*ICTA 1988, s 681(5) (repealed); ICTA 1988, ss 682A(2), 839(3A); FA 1995, Sch 17 paras 11, 20*].

'*Settlor*' is any person by whom the settlement was made or who has directly or indirectly (or by a reciprocal arrangement) provided, or undertaken to provide, funds for the settlement. [*ICTA 1988, s 681(4) (repealed); ICTA 1988, s 660G(1)(2); FA 1995, Sch 17 para 1*].

16.8 The same definitions are applied for the purposes of corporation tax on chargeable gains by *TCGA 1992, s 286.*

16.9 **VARIATIONS**

Specific variations are made in the rules given above for the particular purposes of *TCGA 1992, s 177* (see 9.52 CAPITAL GAINS) and *ICTA 1988, s 736* (see 4.2 ANTI-AVOIDANCE). For the purposes of these sections, persons acting together to secure or exercise control of, or to acquire a holding in, a company are connected with each other and with any other person acting on the direction of any of them to secure or exercise such control or to acquire such a holding.

17 Construction Industry Tax Scheme

See also Revenue Pamphlets IR 14/15(CIS), IR 40(CIS), IR 109, IR 116(CIS), IR 117(CIS), IR 148, IR 157 and IR 164(CIS).

Simon's Direct Tax Service E5.5.

17.1 SCHEME APPLICABLE FROM 1 AUGUST 1999

With effect for payments made **on or after 1 August 1999**, the scheme for deduction of tax from payments to construction sub-contractors who do not have a tax certificate entitling them to gross payment, and the arrangements and conditions for the issue of such certificates, are substantially revised. The revised scheme is described at 17.2 *et seq.* below. It is intended that, under the revised scheme, most sub-contractors will *not* hold tax certificates, but will hold registration cards (see 17.3 below) and receive payments after deduction on account of tax. The main changes from the scheme as it applied before 1 August 1999 (see 17.8 below) are as follows.

(*a*) The 23% deduction is replaced by a deduction of a percentage determined by the Treasury by order, which may not exceed the basic rate (and is set at 18% for 2000/01).

(*b*) A minimum anticipated annual turnover (prescribed by regulation and, in the case of firms or companies, broadly geared to the number of individuals who are partners or directors) is a precondition for the issue of a tax certificate.

(*c*) The limited certificates for school leavers and where a bank guarantee is in force are withdrawn.

(*d*) A general exemption from deduction is provided where conditions to be prescribed are met in relation to a payment under any contract and to the person making the payment.

(*e*) All public offices and departments of the Crown, and such statutory bodies as are designated in regulations, are normally to be treated as contractors for the purposes of the deduction scheme. However, for these and the other public bodies treated as contractors, an exemption based on the average annual construction expenditure test already used for businesses is introduced. Government departments treated as contractors will be subject to the same obligations, sanctions and Revenue powers of enforcement as other contractors.

(*f*) The average annual expenditure on construction operations which renders the person incurring the expenditure a contractor for the purposes of the deduction scheme is increased from £250,000 to £1,000,000.

(*g*) The conditions for a tax certificate for an individual partner in a firm are generally aligned with those for sole traders, insofar as they relate to the circumstances of the individual. The individual conditions relating to the length of time the business has been carried on are removed.

(*h*) The fine (maximum £5,000) on summary conviction for certain fraudulent attempts to obtain or misuse a tax certificate is replaced by a penalty up to £3,000.

Exemption certificates covering periods beginning before and ending after 31 July 1999 cease to have effect after that date.

Registration cards. As referred to above, in conjunction with the revised deduction scheme, a mandatory registration card system is introduced for sub-contractors not holding a tax certificate. See 17.2, 17.3 below. In outline, the registration card system is as follows.

(i) The card carries the sub-contractor's name and photograph, the tax reference and the national insurance number.

(ii) Contractors are required to check cards before making payments under deduction.

(iii) The cards are available on request to anyone working, or intending to work, in the construction industry.

(iv) A penalty of up to £3,000 applies for failure by a contractor to take the necessary steps to require the production of registration cards and to check their validity, or to make accurate returns in relation to registration card payments (unless there were reasonable grounds for accepting the validity of a card and all reasonable steps were taken to ensure the correctness of the return).

Transitional arrangements. For the period 1 August 1999 to 5 September 1999, arrangements were made for the issue by tax offices of temporary Tax Payment Cards (forms CIS65) which enabled contractors to make payments under deduction of tax in certain cases where the sub-contractor had not applied for a registration card or certificate in time for the scheme commencement or, exceptionally, had applied for but not received it. Additionally, up to 5 November 1999, contractors were able to accept registration card, temporary tax payment card or certificate details where the document was photocopied onto the sub-contractor's original headed paper, and where contractors still believed they would be unable to pay their workers and/or complete the appropriate vouchers, they could apply for a dispensation. Payments after 5 November 1999 can only be made where the full new scheme conditions are complied with. (Revenue Press Releases 7 July 1999, 15 July 1999).

Scheme review. A joint working group, comprising officials from the Revenue and the Department of the Environment, Transport and the Regions and construction industry representatives, has been set up to review the new construction industry scheme. Individual representations, which the group will take into account, may be made to Philip Hogan, Construction Industry Scheme Review, Compliance Division, Inland Revenue, 22 Kingsway, London WC2B 6NR (e-mail: philip.hogan@ir.gsi.gov.uk).

17.2 **Payments from which tax must be deducted.** Where a 'contractor' carrying on a business which includes 'construction operations' makes any payment (except as below) to, or to the nominee of, a 'sub-contractor' under a contract relating to 'construction operations' in the UK or on offshore installations within UK territorial waters, then, unless the recipient meets the conditions for gross payment (see 17.4 below), the payer must deduct, and pay over to the Revenue, a specified percentage of so much of the payment (excluding any VAT and CITB levy) as does not represent the cost of materials. Before making any such payment, the contractor must ensure that the sub-contractor produces a valid registration card (see 17.3 below), and must satisfy himself that the person producing it is the person to whom it was issued (or an authorised user of a company card, being a director or secretary of the company), unless he has done so on a previous occasion and has no reason to doubt that it remains valid for the person who produced it. Possession of a registration card by a sub-contractor does not, however, relieve the contractor of the responsibility to establish whether the sub-contractor is employed or self-employed (see 17.7 below). A penalty not exceeding £3,000 may apply for failure by a contractor to carry out these checks. These provisions do not apply to payments under a contract of employment, payments chargeable under Schedule E by virtue of *ICTA 1988, s 134* (workers supplied by agencies — see Tolley's Income Tax under Schedule E), or payments excluded by regulations. The percentage deduction rate is determined by the Treasury by order, and may not exceed the basic rate of income tax. [*ICTA 1988, s 559(1)–(4A), s 560(1), s 561(1), s 566(2B), s 567(1)(b); FA 1995, s 139, Sch 27 para 1; FA 1996,* *s 178(1); FA 1998, s 55(2)(3); SI 1993 No 743, reg 7F; SI 1998 Nos 2620, 2622, reg 8; SI 2000 No 922*].

The specified rate of deduction is reduced from 23% to 18% with effect from 6 April 2000. [*SI 2000 No 921*].

It is understood that the 'cost of materials' which may be excluded in determining the amount subject to deduction may include a reasonable commercial charge for plant supplied by the sub-contractor for the period of the contract. Where a sub-contractor does not supply evidence of the cost to him of materials, the contractor should make a fair estimate of the actual cost. See Revenue Pamphlet IR 14/15(CIS), paras 3.3, 3.4.

A '*sub-contractor*' is a party to a contract relating to 'construction operations' who is under a duty to carry out, or to furnish his own, or others', labour in the carrying out of, such operations, or otherwise answerable to the contractor for the carrying out of such operations by others. See generally Revenue Pamphlet IR 14/15(CIS), paras 2.8–2.11.

A '*contractor*' is:

(*a*) any person carrying on a business which includes 'construction operations';

(*b*) any person carrying on a business at any time if his average annual expenditure on construction operations in the three years up to the end of his last period of account exceeded £1,000,000 or, where the business was not being carried on at the beginning of that three-year period, if his total expenditure on such operations up to the end of that last period of account exceeded £3,000,000. A person who is a contractor under this provision will continue within that definition until he satisfies the Board that his expenditure on construction operations has been below £1,000,000 in each of three successive years beginning in or after that period of account. For the purposes of these expenditure limits, where a trade is transferred from one company to another and *ICTA 1988, s 343* (no change of ownership) applies, the transferor's expenditure will be treated as the transferee's, with apportionment by the Board (subject to appeal) when only part of the trade is transferred; and

(*c*) any public office or department of the Crown; any local authority; any development corporation or new town commission; the Commission for the New Towns; the Housing Corporation; the Secretary of State for Wales (in relation to a contract made under *Housing Associations Act 1985, s 89*); any housing association or trust; Scottish Homes; the Northern Ireland Housing Executive; any NHS trust (or NI equivalent); and the Corporate Officers of the Houses of Parliament. Apart from the Secretary of State for Wales, such offices, departments and bodies are, however, defined as contractors only at a time when their average annual expenditure on 'construction operations' in the three-year period to 31 March immediately preceding that time exceeded £1,000,000, but once so included they continue to be so until expenditure on 'construction operations' has been below £1,000,000 in each of three successive years after the end of the three-year period.

The definition includes a person who is himself a sub-contractor in relation to construction operations, e.g. a gang-leader.

[*ICTA 1988, s 559(1), s 560(2)–(5); FA 1995, Sch 27 para 2; FA 1998, Sch 8 para 2(2)–(4); Government of Wales Act 1998, Sch 16 para 58; SI 1993 No 743, reg 3A, Sch A1; SI 1998 No 2622, regs 4, 37; SI 1999 No 2159, reg 9*].

Where payments by any of the bodies, etc. which are contractors by virtue of (*b*) or (*c*) above are made under a contract in respect of which the total contract payments (excluding materials) do not exceed (and are not likely to exceed) £1,000, and the body, etc. is approved by the inspector for the purpose, the payments are excluded from the application of these provisions. [*SI 1993 No 743, reg 20B; SI 1998 No 2622, reg 13*].

Private householders having work done on their own premises are *not* contractors for these purposes. See generally Revenue Pamphlet IR 14/15(CIS), paras 2.3–2.7.

'*Construction operations*' are widely defined to cover installing heating, lighting, drainage, etc. systems, internal cleaning of buildings in the course of their construction, alteration or repair, and internal or external painting, as well as constructing, altering, repairing or demolishing buildings, walls, roadworks, etc., but to *exclude* drilling for oil or gas, mining operations, the professional work of architects, surveyors, etc., the installation, etc. of sculptures, murals, and other artistic works, signwriting, advertisements, seating, blinds, shutters, security and public address systems, computer or telecommunications wiring through pre-existing ducts and the manufacture of components for heating, lighting, drainage, etc. systems. The Treasury may add to these categories by order made by statutory instrument. [*ICTA 1988, s 567*]. Carpet fitting is outside the scope of the scheme. (Revenue Pamphlet IR 131, SP 12/81, 20 November 1981). For detailed guidance on the scope of 'construction operations', see Appendix B to Revenue Pamphlet IR 14/15(CIS).

A signed *tax payment voucher* (form CIS25) must be given by the contractor to the sub-contractor within 14 days of the end of a tax month in respect of all payments made under deduction of tax as above during the month. The contractor must also within 14 days of the end of each tax month either send the top copies of all forms CIS25 to the Inland Revenue (where three-part forms CIS25(I) or (M) have been used) or transmit specified particulars to them electronically (where single-part forms CIS25(E) have been used). [*SI 1993 No 743, reg 7; SI 1998 No 2622, reg 7*].

See generally Revenue Pamphlets IR 14/15(CIS), chapter 3 and IR 164(CIS) 'Advice to sub-contractors going onto deduction'. As regards disputes about, or corrections to, deductions, see IR 14/15(CIS), paras 7.3–7.5.

17.3 **Registration cards** (see 17.2 above) are issued or replaced by an inspector or other person nominated by the Board. An inspector may require their surrender or cancel them. They must be produced for inspection, or surrendered, when required by any authorised officer of the Board. A refusal to issue or replace a registration card, or its cancellation, is subject to the normal right of appeal, although it is expected that cards will be available on request to anyone intending to commence work, or working, within the construction industry. They need only complete a form, supply a photograph and attend an identity check (see Revenue Pamphlet IR 14/15(CIS), para 1.6).

Cards (form CIS4(P)) other than temporary cards carry the sub-contractor's name, photograph and signature, the national insurance number (or, exceptionally, a 'system identifier'), and a distinctive reference number assigned to the card. They may also include a name under which the business is carried on. They have no expiry date. In the case of a partner in a firm, they must include the name of the firm for which the partner is acting. Company cards issued to a director or secretary of the company authorised to use the card must similarly include the name of the company for whom the director or secretary is acting. If a business name is included on a partner's or company card, it must be the same for all partners or directors and secretaries. Temporary registration cards (form CIS4(T)), which carry a date of expiry instead of the national insurance number, may be issued with a maximum validity of three months.

[*ICTA 1988, s 566(2A); FA 1996, s 178; SI 1993 No 743, regs 7A–7E, Sch 1; SI 1998 No 2622, regs 8, 38*].

See 17.7 below as regards penalties relating to registration card failures.

17.4 **Sub-contractors' tax certificates.** Where a tax certificate (form CIS5 or CIS6) has been issued to a sub-contractor and is in force when a payment is made, and the various regulatory requirements as regards production and validation, etc. of the certificate (see below) are complied with, the deduction requirements under 17.2 above do not apply. Possession of a tax certificate by a sub-contractor does not, however, relieve the contractor of the responsibility to establish whether the sub-contractor is employed or self-employed (see 17.7 below). Certificates form CIS5, which do not have to be produced to contractors (see alternative verification procedure described below) and which obviate the requirement to supply gross payment vouchers to contractors (see below), may only be issued when the inspector considers that a form CIS6 certificate would be inappropriate in all the circumstances. The Inland Revenue have indicated that a CIS5 certificate will only be issued to a company which either

(*a*) is a plc or a subsidiary of a plc, or

(*b*) has a turnover of at least £3 million, or has taken over and will continue an established concern with such a turnover which was previously owned by a director or directors of the company and which met certain other conditions as to previous compliance, or

(*c*) is a subsidiary or associate of an established company holding a CIS5 (or predecessor 714C) certificate (and which would still qualify for a CIS 5 certificate), or

(*d*) shows that operating with a CIS6 certificate would cause substantial difficulties.

As regards (*d*), evidence would have to be produced either of an administrative need, i.e. that using CIS6 certificates would involve either a high volume of vouchers – normally 300 or more per year but 150 or more per year may suffice in certain cases – or an excessive amount of time spent travelling specifically to present a certificate – at least 200 hours over a three-year period or 100 hours in any one of those years, or of a commercial need, i.e. where the applicant's trade is largely based on, or potentially involves, work for contractors who give work only to CIS5 certificate holders. (Revenue Tax Bulletin April 1999 pp 635, 636).

For more detailed guidance on the issue of CIS5 certificates, see Revenue Subcontractors in the Construction Industry Manual.

Verification. Before a gross payment can be made, and subject to the alternative verification procedure described below for CIS5 certificate holders, the sub-contractor must produce the certificate to the contractor, who must satisfy himself by inspecting the certificate that the sub-contractor is the user of the certificate (or authorised to produce it on behalf of a company which is the user). Where the user receives the payment as a nominee, the person nominating the user must also produce his certificate for validation. Further inspections of the certificate are not required for so long as the contractor has no reason to doubt that it is still valid.

There is an alternative verification procedure where the user of a CIS5 certificate (not being a nominee) has notified the inspector of particulars of the company bank account into which payments, which must be under a written contract between the company and the contractor, are to be made. The user may produce to the contractor a 'certification document' signed by the secretary or a director of the company, and provided that the contractor has no reason to doubt that the information shown on the document is correct (and the payment date falls within the period of validity of the certificate referred to in the document), he may make payments gross. The certification document must certify that the company is the user of a valid company tax certificate form CIS5. It must specify the name, address (of the registered office) and registration number of the user, the distinctive number, expiry date (and, if any, commencement date) of the certificate, and details of the nominated bank account. It may also include the user's business name. To allay any doubt concerning the certification document, the contractor may, within 14 days of receipt of the document, apply to the inspector for confirmation that a valid certificate has been issued to the company and that the information on the certification document agrees with the inspector's records.

[*SI 1993 No 743, regs 33, 34; SI 1998 No 2622, reg 25*].

Payments. Payments to a holder of certificate form CIS5 should only be made by cheque or credit transfer, and *never* by cash (see Revenue Pamphlet IR 14/15(CIS), paras 5.12, 5.13).

Completion of vouchers. A sub-contractor with a certificate form CIS6 must, within 14 days after the end of each income tax month, give two signed copies of a gross payment voucher (form CIS24) containing specified particulars to the contractor in respect of all contract payments received gross in the month (or, if the contractor so requests, for each such payment). The contractor must complete the form with his distinctive reference number and deliver the appropriate copy to the sub-contractor. Where vouchers are not supplied, or are incorrectly completed, by the sub-contractor, and further payments are due, the contractor should reconsider the validity of the certificate. Duplicates should be requested of vouchers claimed to have been lost in the post. If a proper voucher is not supplied despite the contractor taking reasonable steps to obtain one, he should report the matter to the Revenue.

Where a sub-contractor has a certificate form CIS5, the contractor must complete a construction gross payment voucher (form CIS23(M) or CIS23(I)) containing specified particulars in respect of all gross payments in any income tax month (or transmit the specified particulars to the Inland Revenue electronically). Within 14 days after the end of each income tax month the contractor must forward to the Inland Revenue all forms CIS24, CIS23(M) or CIS23(I) given to or obtained or completed by him in the month. [*SI 1993 No 743, regs 35, 37A, 38, 39; SI 1998 No 2622, regs 26, 29–31*].

Issue of a certificate. Application for a tax certificate is made on form CIS2 or CIS3 as appropriate, and at least one month should be allowed for the application to be approved. Ten working days should be allowed after notification of approval for issue of the certificate.

For a tax certificate to be issued, the Revenue must be satisfied that the sub-contractor is carrying on a business in the UK consisting of or including the carrying out of construction operations (see 17.2 above), or the furnishing (or arranging for the furnishing) of labour for such operations, with proper premises, equipment, stock and other facilities. There must be a bank account through which the business is substantially conducted and proper records must be kept, and the applicant must also satisfy the 'turnover test' described at 17.5 below. Certificates are normally valid for either three years or one year, depending on the basis on which the turnover test is satisfied (see 17.5 below), although the initial issue of certificates under the new scheme will adjust the three-year period by up to six months to achieve an even rate of expiry of certificates. Certificates issued to partners in a firm or to a company at different times will have a common expiry date. The Board has wide powers to cancel certificates and require their surrender (and see 17.7 below).

An *individual applicant* (whether or not a partner in a firm) must have complied timeously with all tax and national insurance obligations (including supplying accounts and other information relating to any business of the applicant to the inspector on request) in respect of periods ending within the three years preceding the date of application (the '*qualifying period*'). There must be reason to expect that future such obligations will be complied with, and provided that this expectation is not rendered open to doubt, 'minor and technical failings' in relation to past obligations may be disregarded at the Board's discretion (but see *T & C Hill (Haulage) v Gleig (Sp C 227), [2000] SSCD 64* for a case in which refusal of a certificate was upheld on the grounds of late submission of returns and payment of tax liabilities after the due date). See Revenue Pamphlet IR 40(CIS), Appendix 2 for the Revenue interpretation of 'minor and technical failings'. Where the applicant claims not to have been subject to an obligation for these purposes, he must satisfy the Board of that fact by evidence prescribed by regulation, and where he claims to have been non-resident, he must also satisfy the Board by such evidence that any comparable foreign obligations have been met (see *SI 1993 No 743, regs 22–23B; SI 1998 No 2622, regs 15–17*). Any company of which the individual had control (within *ICTA 1988, s 416(2)–(6)*) during the qualifying period must also satisfy those conditions in respect of any accounting period ending within the qualifying period at a time when the applicant had such control.

A *company applicant* (whether or not a partner in a firm) must have a similarly satisfactory record of past and prospective compliance with all its taxation and National Insurance and certain Companies Act obligations. In *Gorge Fabrications Ltd v Wilson (Sp C 214), [1999] SSCD 293*, the Special Commissioner upheld an inspector's refusal of a certificate to a company which had, within the three year period in question, entered into a voluntary arrangement with its creditors resulting in 75% of its outstanding corporation tax liabilities (amounting to £2,927) remaining unpaid (its PAYE/NIC liabilities of over £30,000 having been treated as preferential and met in full). The Board may also, in certain cases where there is a limited history of construction operations, or where there has been a change of control, issue a direction under *ICTA 1988, s 561(6)* that the directors (and, if the company is close, the beneficial shareholders) must satisfy any or all of the conditions imposed on individual applicants (see above). Where the introduction of a new shareholder into a close private company results in a change of control, the company must notify the inspector of the new shareholder within 30 days (see *SI 1993 No 743, reg 42*).

Each of the *partners in a firm* (applying as such), in addition to meeting the requirements for individual or company applicants (as above), as appropriate, must also satisfy the requirements as to the meeting of tax obligations (and requests by the inspector) in relation to the firm's business.

[*ICTA 1988, ss 561, 562, 564, 565; FA 1995, Sch 27 paras 3–7; SI 1993 No 743, regs 25, 26; SI 1998 No 2622, regs 19, 20; SI 1999 No 2156*].

Changes in a business. Where an individual or firm incorporates, or a partnership becomes a sole trader, the new business will require a new certificate. However, if the business is essentially the same, the new business may apply immediately on the basis of the three-year test (applied in the light of the particular circumstances of the case), rather than having to wait six months to apply on the basis of the six-month test. Changes in the number of partners in a firm or directors/shareholders in a company, without any change in the business, do not require the turnover test to be re-applied before the certificate falls to be renewed, unless the inspector suspects manipulation of the threshold provisions. New partners/directors can apply for additional certificates. (Revenue Pamphlet IR 40(CIS) p 6).

Old scheme certificates. Certificates issued under the scheme applicable before 1 August 1999 cease to have effect after 31 July 1999 regardless of the expiry date shown on the certificate. [*SI 1998 No 2620, reg 4*].

Simon's Direct Tax Service. See **E5.525** *et seq.*.

17.5 **Turnover test**. *Individuals (other than in relation to applications as partners in firms).* The turnover test requires the applicant to satisfy the Board that, during the period of validity of the certificate, the aggregate annual amount of 'relevant payments' received is likely to be not less than the 'individual turnover threshold' of £30,000. (It should, however, be noted that Revenue Pamphlet IR 40(CIS) states: 'If you are using the six month test, you should show the actual amount you received in the period. Where you are using a three year test on the basis of accounts, we would not expect you to adjust figures for gross construction turnover and materials for debtors or creditors to arrive at the net "payments received" in the three years. Just use the figures earned, as shown in your accounts.'.) '*Relevant payments*' are all payments, net of the cost of materials, under contracts relating to, or to the work of individuals participating in the carrying out of, construction operations (see 17.2 above), whether or not within the scheme (i.e. including work for private householders, etc.).

To satisfy the Board, either a six-month test or a three-year test must be satisfied (and depending on which test is satisfied, the certificate will generally be valid for one year or three years (subject to variation on the initial issue, see 17.4 above) respectively). The six-month test is not available where the applicant has been a sub-contractor for a continuous period of four years up to the date of application and three successive one-year certificates have been issued to him.

The six-month test requires the production of evidence (i.e. tax payment vouchers and gross payment vouchers and documentary evidence of relevant payments and of the direct cost of materials) that relevant payments (i.e. turnover) during a consecutive period of up to six tax months in the year preceding the date of application amounted to at least 70% of the individual turnover threshold (i.e. currently £21,000).

The three-year test requires the production of such evidence that relevant payments (i.e. turnover) in a consecutive period of three years in the four years preceding the date of application averaged at least 90% of the average of the individual turnover thresholds for those three years (i.e. currently £27,000) and were at least equal to that threshold in two of the three years. Accounts will also generally be required.

Companies. The turnover test requires a company applicant to satisfy the Board that either

(i) the annual receipts test is satisfied, or

(ii) all the company's shareholders are themselves companies limited by shares with current valid certificates.

The annual receipts test requires that, during the period of validity of the certificate, the aggregate annual amount of 'relevant payments' (as above) received is likely to be not less than the smaller of

(*a*) the individual turnover threshold (currently £30,000), as above, multiplied by the number of 'relevant persons' in relation to the company, and

(*b*) a specified amount (currently £200,000).

A person is a '*relevant person*' in relation to a company if he is a director of the company or (where the company is a close company) a beneficial owner of shares in the company. To satisfy the Board as regards (*a*) above, the six-month or three-year tests described above in relation to individual applicants are applied, but by reference to the '*multiple company turnover threshold*', i.e. (subject to special rules where a business is transferred by an individual or firm to a company as a going concern) the individual turnover threshold multiplied by the number of relevant persons. For the six-month test, the number of relevant persons is the maximum number at any time in the six-month (or shorter) period concerned. For the three-year test it is the maximum number at any time in the relevant year, except that for applications before 1 August 2001, by concession, the maximum number at any point during the last six months of the three-year period may be substituted for each of the three years if this will assist the sub-contractor to meet the test. (Revenue Pamphlet IR 1, B52). As regards (*b*) above (the '*alternative company turnover threshold*'), the three-year test is applied, but by reference to the £200,000 annual limit.

Individuals applying as partners in firms. The turnover test requires the partners in the firm to satisfy the Board that, during the period of validity of the certificate, the aggregate annual amount of 'relevant payments' (as above) received is likely to be not less than the smaller of

(A) the sum of the individual turnover threshold (as above) multiplied by the number of individual partners and, for each corporate partner (other than a company within (ii) above), the turnover threshold which would have applied if the company had itself applied for a certificate (as above), and

(B) a specified amount (currently £200,000).

To satisfy the Board as regards (A) above, the six-month or three-year tests described above in relation to individual applicants are applied, but by reference to the '*multiple partnership turnover threshold*', i.e. the individual turnover threshold multiplied by the sum of the number of individual partners and the number of relevant persons which would have been taken into account under (*a*) above in relation to company partners. For the six-month test, the number of partners is the maximum number at any time in the six-month (or shorter) period concerned. For the three-year test it is the maximum number at any time in the relevant year, except that for applications before 1 August 2001, by concession, the maximum number at any point during the last six months of the three-year period may be substituted for each of the three years if this will assist the subcontractor to meet the test. (Revenue Pamphlet IR 1, B52). As regards (B) above (the '*alternative partnership turnover threshold*'), the three-year test is applied, but by reference to the £200,000 annual limit. [*ICTA 1988, s 562(2A)(2B), s 564(2A)–(2C), s 565(2A)–(2D); FA 1995, Sch 27 paras 4, 6, 7; FA 1998, Sch 8 paras 3–5; FA 1999, s 53; SI 1993 No 743, regs 21A–21E; SI 1998 No 2622, reg 14; SI 1999 No 2159, regs 4–6*].

See generally Revenue Tax Bulletin December 1998 pp 615–617 and, as regards how the test is applied where the applicant's business changes (e.g. where a partnership becomes a sole trader or *vice versa* or a sole trader or partnership becomes a company, or where sole traders or partnerships merge to form a new partnership), June 1999 pp 667, 668.

Simon's Direct Tax Service. See **E5.513** *et seq.*.

17.6 **Renewal of certificates.** Applications for renewal of a certificate may be made at any time within six months before the date of expiry. The conditions are exactly the same as for the initial issue. [*SI 1993 No 743, reg 27*].

17.7 **Administration.** Detailed administrative arrangements for the operation of the scheme are contained in *The Income Tax (Sub-contractors in the Construction Industry) Regulations 1993* (*SI 1993 No 743*) as amended by the *(Amendment) Regulations 1998* (*SI 1998 No 2622*) and *1999* (*SI 1999 No 825*). The arrangements for accounting for deductions and for interest on unpaid or overpaid tax (see *SI 1993 No 743, regs 8–19; SI 1998 No 2622, regs 9, 10; SI 1999 No 825, reg 2; SI 2000 No 1151*) broadly follow those for PAYE (see Tolley's Income Tax under Pay As You Earn and Revenue Pamphlet IR 14/15(CIS), chapter 6), and there are detailed provisions governing the form and use of sub-contractor's tax certificates (see *SI 1993 No 743, reg 24, Sch 1; SI 1998 No 2622, regs 18, 38; SI 1999 No 2159, reg 10*) and the requirements for contractors' end of year returns of all payments to sub-contractors (see *SI 1993 No 743, reg 40A; SI 1998 No 2622, reg 33*). See also below under *Failure to deduct and under-deduction*. The Inland Revenue have powers to inspect records of contractors and sub-contractors (see *SI 1993 No 743, reg 41; SI 1998 No 2622, reg 34; SI 1999 No 2159, reg 8*). Further regulations may be made by statutory instrument. [*ICTA 1988, s 566; FA 1995, Sch 27 para 9; FA 1998, Sch 8 para 6*]. See Revenue Pamphlet IR 109 as regards negotiation of settlements. The Revenue have published a Code of Practice (No 3, available from local tax offices) setting out their standards for the way in which inspections of contractors' records are conducted and the rights and responsibilities of taxpayers.

Contractors are able to submit some of the vouchers information using electronic data interchange ('EDI'). [*SI 1993 No 743, reg 7(4)(b), reg 37A(2)(b), reg 40A(9)(b), reg 44A;*

SI 1998 No 2622, regs 7(4)(5), 29, 33, 35]. Full details should have been sent to all known contractors and sub-contractors by the end of 1998. For an outline of how EDI may be used, see Revenue Press Release 1 September 1998.

Multiple contractors. There are provisions allowing a contractor to elect to be treated as a different contractor for each of any specified groups of sub-contractors. [*SI 1993 No 743, reg 4*].

Appeals. There is a right of appeal (to the Commissioners, within 30 days) against the refusal or cancellation of a sub-contractor's tax certificate, and the Commissioners have the jurisdiction to review the exercise of any discretionary powers by the Board. [*ICTA 1988, s 561(9)*]. See also below under *Failure to deduct and under-deduction* and *Assessment*.

Cancellation. A certificate may at any time be cancelled by the Board, and its surrender demanded, if it was issued on false information, or has been misused by the holder, or if the holder no longer meets the requirements for the issue of a certificate or if, in the case of a company, there has been a change of control (within *ICTA 1988, s 840*) and the information required concerning that change has not been furnished. [*ICTA 1988, s 561(8)*].

Employment status. Where a worker in the construction industry is recategorised as an employee, the Revenue adopt a practical approach to the year of change. The liability for the year is calculated as if there was a Schedule D cessation, but with no prior year adjustments, and a Schedule E commencement on the date of the change. Schedule D profits of the year of cessation are generally taken either as those actually arising in the year or as the appropriate proportion of the profits from the end of the previous year's basis period to cessation, but any basis giving a reasonable result may be accepted. A due proportion of a full year's capital allowances is given for the final year, with no disposal value being brought in. See Taxation Vol 138, No 3596 p 643, 6 March 1997 for this and other aspects.

Possession of a registration card (see 17.3 above) or tax certificate (see 17.4 above) by a sub-contractor does not relieve the contractor of the responsibility to establish whether the sub-contractor is employed or self-employed. A telephone helpline (0345–335588) is available for contractors and workers needing general assistance in determining whether workers are employed or self-employed.

See generally Revenue Pamphlets IR 56 and IR 148 and Revenue Tax Bulletin April 1997 pp 405–413.

Penalties. For fraudulent attempts to obtain or misuse a certificate, penalties of up to £3,000 may be exacted. [*ICTA 1988, s 561(10)(11); FA 1995, Sch 27 para 3*]. A maximum penalty of £3,000 similarly applies for failure to comply with obligations in relation to registration cards (see 17.2 above). [*ICTA 1988, s 566(2B)–(2F); FA 1996, s 178*]. Penalties under *TMA 1970, s 98A* apply in cases of failure to make required end-of-year returns. [*SI 1993 No 743, reg 40A(16); SI 1998 No 2622, reg 33*].

Deduction of tax. If exemption is not obtained, but a registration card is produced, the sub-contractor will receive payments under deduction of tax as under 17.2 above, and will receive from the contractor(s) form(s) CIS25 vouching the tax deducted (see 17.2 above). He will be treated for tax purposes as having received the full amount, the tax deducted and vouched on forms CIS25 being treated as a payment in respect of his income or corporation tax liability on the profits of the trade in the year of assessment or accounting period in which the deduction was made. In the case of an individual, any excess is treated as a payment on account of his Class 4 contributions under the *Social Security Acts*. [*ICTA 1988, s 559(4)–(5A); FA 1995, s 139(1); FA 1998, Sch 8 para 2(1)*]. To the extent that any liability for a year of assessment is met by tax deducted in that year, no interest charge will arise in e.g. a case of failure to notify liability.

Provisional repayments to individuals (or partners in firms) of tax vouched on forms CIS25 may, on application to the inspector, be made before the end of the tax year to which they relate. They may not be made after the end of the tax year. All earlier year income tax and Class 4 national insurance liabilities of the business must have been paid, and repayment is restricted to the excess of the deductions over the sum of the liability to income tax and Class 4 national insurance for the year on profits or gains of the business and on any income arising during the year up to the date of application from which tax has not been deducted (in either case whether or not yet due and payable) and any other sums due and payable from the applicant, including sums he has himself deducted as a contractor. A claim, accompanied by all the forms CIS25 relevant to the claim, is required on form CIS40 (obtainable from local tax offices), or form CIS41 in the case of a partner. In the case of a claim by a partner, the form must be signed by all individual partners and by the secretary or a director of all corporate partners. [*SI 1993 No 743, reg 20A; SI 1998 No 2622, reg 12*].

Failure to deduct and under-deduction. If the contractor fails to deduct the tax, he is nevertheless liable for the tax which should have been deducted (see *Ladkarn Ltd v McIntosh Ch D 1982, 56 TC 616*). However, where the Collector is satisfied that the contractor took reasonable care, and that the failure was due to an error made in good faith or to a genuine belief that the payment was not subject to deduction, the Collector may waive the liability. An appeal may be made (within 30 days) against a decision not so to waive liability. Liability in respect of such failure may also be waived at the contractor's request where the inspector is satisfied that the sub-contractor to whom the payment was made either was not chargeable to tax thereon or has made the appropriate return and paid the tax and any Class 4 contributions. [*SI 1993 No 743, reg 10*].

See Revenue Pamphlet IR 109 as regards negotiation of settlements.

Assessment. If the inspector considers it necessary to do so in all the circumstances, he may raise an assessment on the contractor in any amount which, to the best of his judgement, the contractor is liable to pay under the scheme regulations. The assessment is treated in the same way as an income tax assessment for assessment, appeal and recovery purposes. Tax is due and payable 14 days after the date of the assessment. [*SI 1993 No 743, reg 14*]. As regards interest on tax unpaid or overpaid on such assessments, similar provisions apply as for PAYE (see Tolley's Income Tax under Pay As You Earn). [*SI 1993 No 743, regs 16–18*].

17.8 SCHEME APPLICABLE BEFORE 1 AUGUST 1999

For detailed coverage of the scheme applicable before 1 August 1999, see the 1998/99 or earlier editions of this work. For a summary of the main changes on introduction of the new scheme from 1 August 1999, see 17.1 above. The provisions under the earlier scheme which are more likely to be of continuing relevance (e.g. in relation to failure to deduct, recovery of amounts deducted, assessments on contractors and penalties) are similar to those applicable under the new scheme (see 17.7 above), except that a maximum penalty of £3,000 for fraudulent attempts to obtain or misuse a certificate replaces the maximum fine of £5,000 under the old scheme.

Certificates issued under the old scheme cease to have effect after 31 July 1999 regardless of the expiry date shown on the certificate. [*SI 1998 No 2620, reg 4*].

18 Controlled Foreign Companies

Cross-reference. See also 23 EXCHANGE GAINS AND LOSSES.

Simon's Direct Tax Service D4.131 *et seq.*.

The headings in this chapter are as follows.

18.1 Introduction
18.2 Controlled foreign company
18.3 — 'residence'
18.4 — territories with a 'lower level of taxation'
18.5 — example
18.6 Companies chargeable in respect of CFC
18.7 Basis of charge
18.8 — example
18.9 — 'chargeable profits'
18.10 — 'creditable tax'
18.11 Exceptions
18.12 — 'acceptable distribution policy'
18.13 — example
18.14 — 'exempt activities'
18.15 — 'public quotation condition'
18.16 Notices and appeals
18.17 Assessment, recovery and postponement of tax
18.18 Miscellaneous

18.1 INTRODUCTION

The provisions described in this chapter apply in relation to an accounting period (see 18.7 below) of a company which was, in that accounting period, a 'controlled foreign company' (a 'CFC') (see 18.2 below). Prior to the commencement of self-assessment (see below), they apply only where the Board of Inland Revenue have reason to believe that the requirements are met and so direct. [*ICTA 1988, s 747(1)(2), s 751(4); FA 1998, Sch 17 para 1(2)*]. A charge (see 18.7 below) may then arise on certain companies having an 'interest' (see 18.6 below) in the CFC. For limitations on direction-making powers and clearances, see 18.11 below.

The Revenue have issued **Guidance Notes** on the provisions described in this chapter, which are available from Inland Revenue Reference Library, Room 28, New Wing, Somerset House, London WC2R 1LB (price £10.00) or on the Revenue's website (see 33.1 INLAND REVENUE: ADMINISTRATION). These are referred to below where Revenue interpretation or practice is explained in the Notes. Guidance on particular cases may be sought (provided that it is not with a view to facilitating tax avoidance) from International Division Registry, Inland Revenue, 3rd Floor, Victory House, 30–34 Kingsway, London WC2B 6ES. Clearances may be sought from the same source (and see section 2.6 of the Revenue Notes referred to above).

There are also a number of useful flowcharts in Revenue Company Taxation Manual, CT 8899.

See also Revenue Tax Bulletin August 1994 pp 138–141 for the Revenue response to various questions on the controlled foreign company provisions, particularly in relation to interest paid to a non-resident out of income from the UK.

Self-assessment. Substantial changes are made to the CFC rules to bring them within self-assessment. These changes thus apply for accounting periods of UK-resident companies ending **on or after 1 July 1999**, for which self-assessment applies. [*FA 1998, s 113, Sch 17; SI 1998 No 3173*]. The legislation then applies automatically where all the necessary conditions are met, rather than only following a Board's direction. UK companies will thus be required to include details of significant interests in CFCs in their tax returns and to self-assess any CFC tax due. A number of the conditions are eased to minimise compliance costs. In particular, the minimum share in a CFC which will trigger the provisions is raised from 10% to 25% (see 18.7 below), and the minimum CFC profit limit for the provisions to apply is increased from £20,000 to £50,000 (see 18.11 below). The detailed changes are described below in relation to each relevant section.

Special provision is made for cases where a liability arises under the CFC provisions in respect of an accounting period of a CFC, in the case of at least one UK-resident company for an accounting period which is within the self-assessment rules and in the case of at least one other such company for an accounting period which is not within those rules. Broadly, separate determinations and computations are made, in the case of UK-resident companies which are within self-assessment as if all other relevant companies were also within self-assessment, and in the case of UK-resident companies not within self-assessment as if all other relevant companies were also not within self-assessment. [*FA 1998, Sch 17 para 37*].

See generally Part 2 of the Revenue Notes referred to above, and in particular section 2.1 as regards completion of the self-assessment return.

18.2 CONTROLLED FOREIGN COMPANY

A company which is:

(*a*) resident outside the UK (see 53.2 RESIDENCE),

(*b*) 'controlled' by persons resident in the UK, and

(*c*) subject to a 'lower level of taxation' (see 18.4 below) in the territory in which it is 'resident' (see 18.3 below)

is a '*controlled foreign company*'. [*ICTA 1988, s 747(1)(2)*]. Any company which is resident both in the UK and, under double taxation relief arrangements, in a territory outside the UK is treated as resident outside the UK (and as not resident in the UK). The original specific provision to this effect is now superseded by the general provision of *FA 1994, s 249* (see 53.1 RESIDENCE). [*ICTA 1988, s 749(4A); FA 1990, s 67(1)(4); FA 1994, s 251(4)*].

With effect from 21 March 2000, '*control*' of a company is defined for these purposes as the power of a person to secure that the affairs of the company are conducted in accordance with his wishes, either by means of shareholding or voting power in or in relation to the company or any other company, or by virtue of any powers conferred by the articles of association or other document regulating the company or any other company. Two or more persons together having such power are taken as controlling the company. In determining whether a person or persons have such control, a wide range of rights and powers is attributed to them, insofar as not already so attributed (see *ICTA 1988, s 755D(5)–(11)*). These include future rights and powers and rights and powers of certain connected and other persons. [*ICTA 1988, s 755D; FA 2000, Sch 31 para 4(1)*]. Where a company would not otherwise be treated as controlled by UK-resident persons, it is so treated if there are two persons, one of whom is UK resident, who together control the company, and a '40% test' is satisfied in relation to each of them. This requires that each of them has interests, rights and powers representing at least 40% of the holdings, rights and powers in respect of which they fall to be taken as together controlling the company (after a similar attribution of rights and powers as applies in determining that control), and that in the case of the non-UK resident such holdings etc. do **not** exceed 55%. [*ICTA 1988, ss 747(1A), 755D(3)–(11); FA 2000, Sch 31 paras 2, 4(1)*]. Before 21 March 2000, '*control*' was as defined by *ICTA 1988, s 416* (see 13.2 CLOSE COMPANIES), with appropriate minor modification. [*ICTA 1988, s 756(3); FA 2000, Sch 31 para 4(2)*].

The advice of Revenue International Division may be sought (see 18.1 above) where there is doubt as to whether an overseas entity is a company.

18.3 **'Residence'**. For the purposes of these provisions, a company is regarded, in any accounting period in which it is resident outside the UK (see 53.2 RESIDENCE), as '*resident*' in the territory in which, throughout that period, it is liable to tax by reason of domicile, residence or place of management. 'Territory' includes jurisdictions which do not have full independent status, such as the Channel Islands, but not individual states of a federal state (e.g. in the USA), and 'tax' in this context means a tax similar in nature to UK income tax or corporation tax, and not e.g. turnover or payroll taxes or flat-rate levies. (For these and for the interpretation of 'domicile, residence or place of management', see paras 4.4.7–4.4.11 of the Revenue Notes referred to at 18.1 above). If there are two or more such territories, the company is regarded as resident in only one of them, namely:

(i) the company's place of effective management (for which see para 4.4.14 of the Revenue Notes referred to at 18.1 above) throughout the period or, if two or more territories would still be the territory of residence under this definition, the one from those territories in which the greater amount of the company's assets is situated immediately before the end of the period, determined by reference to their market value at that time;

(ii) if (i) does not apply, the territory in which the greater amount of the company's assets is situated immediately before the end of the period (determined as in (i));

(iii) if (i) and (ii) do not apply to determine a single territory of residence, the territory which may be specified by the Board in its direction (see 18.1 above).

If there are no such territories, the company is conclusively treated as resident in that accounting period in a territory subject to a 'lower level of taxation', and thus as within 18.2(*c*) above. [*ICTA 1988, s 749(1)–(4) as originally enacted*].

See generally section 4.4 of the Revenue Notes referred to at 18.1 above.

Self-assessment. For accounting periods to which self-assessment applies (see 18.1 above), and subject to the continuing application of an earlier election as described below, where there is more than one territory in which the company is liable to tax by reason of domicile, residence or place of management and (i) and (ii) above do not apply, an election may be made, by any one or more persons who together have a 'majority assessable interest' in the CFC in the accounting period, specifying in which of those territories the CFC is to be regarded as resident for these purposes. One or more persons have such a '*majority assessable interest*' in a CFC in an accounting period if it is likely that, were an apportionment of chargeable profits to be made for the period, more than 50% of the aggregate amounts so chargeable would be chargeable on him or on them together. If no timeous election (see below) is made, the Board may designate in which of those territories the CFC is to be regarded as resident on a just and reasonable basis. Where such an election or Board's designation has effect for an accounting period, the CFC continues to be regarded as resident in the same territory for subsequent accounting periods up to (but not including) the next one in which the territories in which the CFC is liable to tax by reason of domicile, residence or place of management are different. An election under this provision, which is irrevocable, must be made to the Board within twelve months after the end of the CFC accounting period in relation to which it is made, must be signed by the persons making it, and must state, as regards each of those persons, the percentage of chargeable profits and creditable tax (if any) of the CFC for that period which would be likely to be apportioned to them in the event of an apportionment being made. A designation by the Board as above is irrevocable, and must be notified to every UK-resident company which it appears to the Board would be chargeable under these provisions were an apportionment of chargeable profits of the accounting period in question to be made. [*ICTA 1988, ss 749, 749A; FA 1998, Sch 17 para 4*].

18.4 **Territories with a 'lower level of taxation'.** A company regarded as resident in a particular territory outside the UK (see 18.3 above) is considered to be subject to a '*lower level of taxation*' (see 18.2 above) for an accounting period if the tax paid under the law of that territory in respect of profits (other than capital profits) from that period (the 'local tax') is less than three-quarters of the 'corresponding UK tax' on those profits.

The '*corresponding UK tax*' on the profits of an accounting period is the corporation tax (at the small companies rate where appropriate) which would be chargeable, on the assumptions set out in *ICTA 1988, Sch 24* (see 18.9 below), on the CFC's 'chargeable profits' (see 18.9 below) for that period. For this purpose:

(i) it is assumed that an apportionment of chargeable profits falls to be made under these provisions (see 18.6 below). (For accounting periods prior to the introduction of self-assessment (see 18.1 above), the assumption is that a direction has been given by the Board under these provisions (see 18.1 above) in respect of that period and that, as regards capital allowances, the Board have made any declaration they could have made (see 18.9(x) below) and of which they have given the appropriate written notice.);

(ii) double taxation relief in respect of the local tax is disregarded; and

(iii) a deduction is made from the corporation tax calculated as above in respect of

(*a*) any amount which would be set off under *ICTA 1988, s 7(2)* (sums received under deduction of income tax, see 31.5 INCOME TAX IN RELATION TO A COMPANY) on the assumptions set out in *ICTA 1988, Sch 24* (see 18.9 below), and

(*b*) any income or corporation tax actually charged in respect of the chargeable profits,

provided that such amounts have not been, and do not fall to be, repaid to the company.

Tax paid in third countries is relieved against both local tax and corresponding UK tax, according to the rules applicable in each jurisdiction (see para 4.2.10 of the Revenue Notes referred to at 18.1 above).

[*ICTA 1988, s 750(1)–(4); FA 1993, s 119; FA 1998, Sch 17 para 5*].

See generally section 4.2 of the Revenue Notes referred to at 18.1 above.

See 18.11 below as regards countries in which a company will be excluded from charge under these provisions.

Designer rate regimes. Where a company would be treated under the above rules as subject to a lower level of taxation in a territory in an accounting period but for the local tax not being less than three-quarters of the corresponding UK tax, but that local tax is determined under 'designer rate tax provisions', the company is treated as being subject to a lower level of taxation in that territory in that period. '*Designer rate tax provisions*' are provisions which appear to the Board to be designed to enable companies to exercise significant control over the amount of tax they pay, and which are specified in regulations (which may make different provision for different cases or with respect to different territories, and may contain supplementary, incidental, consequential or transitional provisions). The first such regulations may take effect for accounting periods beginning up to 15 months before the date the regulations are made. [*ICTA 1988, s 750A; FA 2000, Sch 31 para 3*].

It is intended that the first regulations will apply for accounting periods beginning after 5 October 1999 to the following.

(*a*) Guernsey — bodies with international tax status;

(*b*) Jersey — international business companies;

(*c*) Isle of Man — international companies;

(*d*) Gibraltar — income tax qualifying companies; and

(*e*) Ireland — companies taxed in accordance with *Taxes Consolidation Act 1997, s 448(7)*.

Further regimes may in future be added to this list.

(Revenue Press Release 6 October 1999).

Simon's Direct Tax Service. See **D4.136.**

18.5 *Example*

CC Co, an unquoted company, is incorporated and resident in Blueland and carries on business there as a wholesaler. It obtains the majority of its goods from associated companies although 10% is obtained from local suppliers. The goods are exported to UK customers — the major one of which is ADE Co Ltd. CC Co has a share capital of 1,000 ordinary shares which are owned as follows:

SS Co Ltd (non-UK resident company)	50
ADE Co Ltd (UK incorporated and resident company)	150
John James (UK domiciled and resident individual)	300
Mrs James (wife of John James)	300
Caroline James (daughter of Mr & Mrs James) living in France	200
	1,000

The shareholders of SS Co Ltd are all non-UK residents. The shareholders of ADE Co Ltd are Mr & Mrs Andrew James (parents of John James).

The following figures (converted into sterling) have been obtained for CC Co for the year to 30 April 2001.

	£
Profit before tax	7,000,000
Depreciation	1,000,000
Dividend proposed for year	500,000
Blueland tax paid on profits of year	1,200,000
Market value of plant and machinery at 1.5.00	2,500,000
Additions to plant and machinery in year	1,800,000
Original cost of industrial buildings (acquired prior to 1.5.00)	1,500,000

There were no disposals of fixed assets during the year.

The Revenue have not given any direction under *ICTA 1988, s 747(1)* with respect to any earlier accounting period of CC Co.

CC is a controlled foreign company because

(i) it is resident outside the UK

(ii) it is controlled by persons resident in the UK, as follows

18.5 Controlled Foreign Companies

	UK residents Ordinary shares	Non-UK residents Ordinary shares
ADE Co Ltd	150	
John James	300	
Mrs James	300	
SS Co Ltd		50
Caroline James		200
	750	250
Percentage holding	75%	25%

(iii) it is subject to a lower level of taxation in the country where it is resident, as follows

Notional UK chargeable profits

Year ended 30 April 2001	£
Profit before tax	7,000,000
Add Depreciation	1,000,000
	8,000,000
Capital allowances (see note below)	1,135,000
	£6,865,000
£6,865,000 @ 30%	£2,059,500
75% thereof	£1,544, 625
Overseas tax paid	£1,200,000

The overseas tax paid is less than three-quarters of the 'corresponding UK tax' so the company is regarded as being subject to a lower level of taxation.

Note

Capital allowances

Plant and machinery	Pool	Allowances
	£	£
Market value at 1.5.00	2,500,000	
Additions	1,800,000	
	4,300,000	
WDA (25%)	(1,075,000)	c/f 1,075,000
WDV c/f	£3,225,000	

	£
	b/f 1,075,000
Industrial buildings allowance	
Original cost of building = £1,500,000	
WDA £1,500,000 at 4%	60,000
Total allowances	£1,135,000

It is assumed that the company is not small or medium-sized for the purposes of plant and machinery first-year allowances.

18.6 COMPANIES CHARGEABLE IN RESPECT OF CFC

Where these provisions apply in respect of an accounting period of a CFC (see 18.1 above), the 'chargeable profits' (see 18.9 below) and 'creditable tax' (see 18.10 below) are apportioned amongst all the persons (whether UK resident or not) having an 'interest' (see below) in the CFC at any time in the accounting period. Any UK resident company to which those sums are apportioned is then chargeable on a sum as if it were corporation tax (see 18.7 below). [*ICTA 1988, s 747(3)(4); FA 1998, Sch 17 para 1(3)(4)*].

The following have an '*interest*' in a CFC:

(*a*) any person possessing, or entitled to acquire, share capital or voting rights in the CFC;

(*b*) any person possessing, or entitled to acquire, a right to receive or participate in distributions of the CFC ('distribution' not being limited by reference to UK resident companies, see 20 DISTRIBUTIONS) or (except as below) any amounts payable (in cash or kind) by the CFC to loan creditors (as defined in *ICTA 1988, s 417*, see 13.3 CLOSE COMPANIES) by way of premium on redemption;

(*c*) any person entitled to secure (other than on a default of the CFC or any other person, which has not occurred, under an agreement) that income or assets, present or future, of the CFC will be applied directly or indirectly for his benefit;

(*d*) any other person who, with or without others, has control (see 18.2(*b*) above) of the CFC;

(*e*) (except as below) if the Board consider it appropriate, a loan creditor (as in (*b*) above) of the CFC.

In (*a*), (*b*) and (*c*), the entitlement to do anything includes present entitlement to do it at a future date and future entitlement. [*ICTA 1988, s 749(5)–(7)*]. See paras 6.2.4–6.2.7 of the Revenue Notes referred to at 18.1 above. As regards (*e*), the Board would not normally treat an arm's length loan creditor as having an interest in a CFC where either

(i) the creditor was acting in the ordinary course of his business, or

(ii) neither he, nor persons connected or associated with him, had any interest in the company other than the loan in question.

Self-assessment. For accounting periods to which self-assessment applies (see 18.1 above), rights as a loan creditor do not constitute an interest for these purposes. Also, there is provision for looking through intermediate interests in companies, so that a person or persons having an interest in a company which has an interest in a CFC are treated as having a corresponding interest in the CFC. Joint interests (other than in a fiduciary or representative capacity) are treated as being in equal shares. [*ICTA 1988, s 749B; FA 1998, Sch 17 para 4*].

Any determination by the Revenue of the amounts of chargeable profits and creditable tax for a CFC accounting period which fall to be apportioned under these provisions requires the sanction of the Board. There is, however, an exception, in relation to a notice of closure of an enquiry into a company tax return or a discovery assessment, where those amounts are the subject of an agreement with the Board (for the requirements for which see *ICTA 1988, s 754B(6)–(9)* introduced by *FA 1998, Sch 17 para 11*). Where a determination thus requiring the sanction of the Board is made for the purpose of giving a closure notice or making a discovery assessment, and the notice of the closure or discovery assessment is given without the determination, so far as taken into account in the notice or assessment, having been approved by the Board, or without notification of such approval having been served at or before the time the notice was given, the closure notice or discovery assessment is deemed to have been given or made as if the determination had not been taken into account. Notification of the Board's approval must be in writing, and must state that the Board have given approval on the basis that stated amounts of chargeable profits and creditable tax (which may be nil) fall to be apportioned under these provisions for the accounting period in question. The approval must apply specifically to the case in question and the amount determined, but may otherwise be given (either before or after the making of the determination) in any such form or manner as the Board may determine. An appeal relating to a determination approved by the Board may not question the Board's approval except to the extent that the grounds for questioning the approval are the same as the grounds for questioning the determination itself. [*ICTA 1988, s 754B; FA 1998, Sch 17 para 11*]. See generally section 2.3 of the Revenue Notes referred to at 18.1 above as regards Revenue enquiries into CFC returns.

18.7 **BASIS OF CHARGE**

Where a part of a CFC's 'chargeable profits' (see 18.9 below) is apportioned (as below) to a UK resident company (see 18.6 above), a sum equal to corporation tax at the 'appropriate rate' on those profits, less the part of the CFC's 'creditable tax' (see 18.10 below) (if any) so apportioned, is chargeable on the company as if it were corporation tax. No charge arises, however, unless at least 25% of the CFC's 'chargeable profits' for the period in question (10% for periods prior to the commencement of self-assessment, see 18.1 above) is apportioned either to the UK resident company or to persons 'connected' (see 16 CONNECTED PERSONS) or 'associated' (as defined in *ICTA 1988, s 783(10)*) with it.

The '*appropriate rate*' is the full corporation tax rate (or average rate) applicable to the accounting period in which ends the CFC's 'accounting period' (see below) whose 'chargeable profits' are the subject of the apportionment. [*ICTA 1988, s 747(4)(5); FA 1998, Sch 17 para 1(4)(5)*].

Apportionment. Prior to the commencement of self-assessment (see 18.1 above), an apportionment of chargeable profits and creditable tax is made according to the respective interests of those with an interest (see 18.6 above) in the CFC at any time during the 'accounting period' in question. The Board may attribute to each such person an interest corresponding to his interest in the CFC's assets available for distribution in a winding-up, etc..

If the CFC is not a 'trading company' (i.e. a company whose business consists wholly or mainly of the carrying on of a trade or trades) the Board may treat a loan creditor (see 18.6(*b*) above) as having an interest to the extent to which the CFC's income has been, or is available to be, applied against his loan capital or debt.

Where the same interest is held directly by one person and indirectly by another, the Board may treat that interest as held solely by the person(s) holding that interest indirectly, so that in particular if that person (or one of these persons) is UK resident, it may be treated as held by that person (or by all of these persons whether UK resident or not), except that

(1) where the interest is held directly by a UK resident company, it is treated as held solely by that company;

(2) where the interest is held directly by a non-UK resident and indirectly by only one UK resident company, it is treated as held solely by the UK resident company; and

(3) where the interest is held directly by a non-UK resident and indirectly by two or more UK resident companies, it is treated as held solely by whichever of those UK resident companies holds the interest by virtue of holding directly an interest in a non-UK resident company holding the interest in the CFC (whether directly or indirectly).

Interests held in a fiduciary or representative capacity may be apportioned amongst identifiable beneficiaries.

Subject to this, apportionment is in proportion to shareholdings of the same class, or other interests of the same description, which remain unchanged throughout the period in question.

The Board has a general power, subject to these specific provisions, to make the necessary apportionment on a just and reasonable basis. [*ICTA 1988, s 752 as originally enacted*].

An '*accounting period*' of a CFC begins whenever

(*a*) the company comes under the control (see 18.2(*b*) above) of persons resident in the UK, or

(*b*) the CFC, not having previously been subject to an apportionment under these provisions (see 18.6 above), commences business, or

(*c*) an accounting period ends without the CFC ceasing either to carry on business or to have any source of income at all,

and ends when

(i) it ceases to be under the control (as above) of persons resident in the UK, or

(ii) it becomes, or ceases to be, liable to tax by reason of domicile, residence or place of management in a territory, or

(iii) it ceases to have any source of income at all.

In addition, the normal rules of *ICTA 1988, s 12(3)(5)(7)* relating to the end of accounting periods, and to the winding-up, of UK resident companies (see 2.4 ACCOUNTING PERIODS and 42.6 LIQUIDATION ETC.) apply, with the omission of the provisions relating to a company's coming or ceasing to be within the charge to corporation tax. Also, where it appears to the Board that the beginning or end of an accounting period is uncertain, they may specify an appropriate period not exceeding twelve months as an accounting period, and the period specified may subsequently be amended in the light of further facts. [*ICTA 1988, s 751(1)–(5); FA 1990, s 67(2); FA 1994, s 251(4); FA 1998, Sch 17 para 6*]. See also 23.31 EXCHANGE GAINS AND LOSSES.

Self-assessment. For accounting periods to which self-assessment applies (see 18.1 above), an apportionment of chargeable profits and creditable tax for an accounting period is to be made as follows. Where:

(A) the persons with 'relevant interests' in the CFC at any time in the period have those interests by virtue only of direct or indirect holdings of ordinary shares in the CFC;

(B) each of those persons is either UK-resident throughout the period or not UK-resident at any time in the period; and

(C) no company has an 'intermediate interest' in the CFC at any time in the period other than by virtue of a direct or indirect holding of ordinary shares in the CFC, the apportionment is made amongst the persons within (A) above in direct proportion to the percentage holding of the CFC's issued ordinary shares which their relevant interests represent (see below). Otherwise, the apportionment is made on a just and reasonable basis amongst the persons who have a 'relevant interest' in the CFC at any time in the period (and see 18.17 below for the Board's right to determine a basis different from that selected by the company in certain cases).

A UK-resident company with a direct interest in a CFC has a '*relevant interest*' in the CFC by virtue of that interest. This applies similarly to an indirect interest in the CFC unless it arises by virtue of a direct or indirect interest in another UK-resident company. A '*related person*' (i.e. a person, other than a UK-resident company, who is connected or associated (as above) with a UK-resident company which has a relevant interest in the CFC) with a direct or indirect interest in a CFC has a '*relevant interest*' in the CFC by virtue of that interest except

(I) to the extent that a UK-resident company has the whole or any part of the same interest indirectly (by virtue of a direct or indirect interest in the related person), and itself has a relevant interest in the CFC by virtue of that indirect interest, and

(II) in the case of an indirect interest, if it is held by virtue of a direct or indirect interest in a UK-resident company or another related person.

A direct interest in a CFC which does not give rise to a relevant interest under the above rules is nonetheless a '*relevant interest*' except to the extent that another person has the whole or a part of the same interest indirectly and itself has a relevant interest in the CFC by virtue of that indirect interest.

No '*relevant interest*' arises in a CFC except as above. The percentage of the issued ordinary shares of a CFC which a relevant interest by virtue of a holding of those shares represents for an accounting period is determined under *ICTA 1988, s 752B* (introduced by *FA 1998, Sch 17 para 7*), broadly by taking successive proportions in the case of indirect holdings and by averaging where holdings vary over the period.

See *ICTA 1988, s 752C* (introduced by *FA 1998, Sch 17 para 7*) as regards nominee or bare trustee holdings and other holdings in a fiduciary or representative capacity, and as regards interpretation generally.

[*ICTA 1988, ss 752–752C; FA 1998, Sch 17 para 7*].

See generally sections 6.3–6.5 of the Revenue Notes referred to at 18.1 above.

Simon's Direct Tax Service. See D4.146.

18.8 *Example*

Following the example at 18.5 above, CC Co's notional UK chargeable profits and creditable tax are apportioned among the persons who had an interest in the company during its accounting period.

Shareholder	% shareholding	Attributable profits	Creditable tax
		£	£
SS Co Ltd	5	343,250	60,000
ADE Co Ltd	15	1,029,750	180,000
John James	30	2,059,500	360,000
Mrs James	30	2,059,500	360,000
Caroline James	20	1,373,000	240,000
	100%	£6,865,000	£1,200,000

ADE Co Ltd is the only UK resident company to which chargeable profits and creditable tax are apportioned. ADE Co Ltd is chargeable to corporation tax on a sum equal to the profits of CC Co which are apportioned to it, and this corporation tax charge is then reduced by the apportioned amount of creditable tax. The corporation tax rate applicable is the rate (or average rate) applicable to ADE Co Ltd's own profits for the accounting period in which CC Co's accounting period ends. ADE Co Ltd has a 30 April year end.

ADE Co Ltd

Tax computations — before apportionment

Year to 30 April 2001

	£
Schedule D, Case I	8,000,000
Losses brought forward	—
	8,000,000
Schedule D, Case III	50,000
Schedule D, Case V	1,250,000
Chargeable gains	250,000
	£9,550,000
UK tax at 30%	2,865,000
DTR on Schedule D, Case V income	(412,500)
Mainstream CT liability	£2,452,500

Tax computations — after apportionment

Schedule D, Case I	8,000,000
Losses brought forward	—
	8,000,000
Schedule D, Case III	50,000
Schedule D, Case V	1,250,000
Chargeable gains	250,000
CFC apportionment	1,029,750
	£10,579,750
UK tax at 30%	3,173,925
DTR on Schedule D, Case V income	(412,500)
CFC creditable tax	(180,000)
Mainstream CT liability	£2,581,425
Additional tax	£128,925

18.9 **'Chargeable profits'** of a CFC for an accounting period are the total profits (but excluding chargeable gains), as defined for corporation tax purposes, on which, on the assumptions set out in *ICTA 1988, Sch 24* (see below) and after allowing for any available deductions from those profits, it would be chargeable to corporation tax for the period. The *Schedule 24* assumptions do not, however, affect the corporation tax liability of any non-UK resident company in respect of any trade carried on in the UK through a branch or agency. [*ICTA 1988, s 747, Sch 24 para 1(5)*].

Where (under (ii) below) a company is deemed to become, or cease to be, resident during a period of account, profits will generally be time-apportioned, but if the true profit of the period of deemed residence can be established by reference to transactions, etc. of that period at reasonable cost, then it should be used instead (see para 5.2.6 of the Revenue Notes referred to at 18.1 above).

Except as otherwise provided in *Schedule 24*, it is assumed that, for the purpose of calculating chargeable profits or corresponding UK tax under that *Schedule* for any accounting period, such a calculation has been made for all previous accounting periods which did not precede the first such period for which an apportionment has been made under these provisions (see 18.6 above), or is treated as having been made (see (i) below). [*ICTA 1988, Sch 24 para 2(2)*].

Double tax treaty exemptions which may have applied to income of the CFC are of no application in relation to the computation of chargeable profits (*Bricom Holdings Ltd v CIR CA 1997, 70 TC 272*).

The assumptions set out in *Schedule 24* are as follows.

(i) For the purpose of determining the chargeable profits of an accounting period at a time when no apportionment has been made under these provisions (see 18.6 above) for that or any earlier accounting period, it is assumed, for the purposes of any provision of *Schedule 24* which refers to the first accounting period for which an apportionment has been made, that an apportionment has been made for that period. Similarly where neither has an apportionment been made for that or any earlier accounting period nor has it been established that that or any earlier accounting period is an 'ADP exempt period', that accounting period is treated, for the purposes of any provision of *Schedule 24* which refers to the first accounting period for which an apportionment has been made or which is an ADP exempt period, as one for which an apportionment has been made or which is an ADP exempt period. An '*ADP exempt period*' is an accounting period beginning after 27 November 1995 in respect of which the company pursued an acceptable distribution policy (see 18.12 below).

(ii) The CFC is UK resident with effect from the beginning of the first accounting period in respect of which an apportionment has been made under these provisions or which is an ADP exempt period (as above), and remains UK resident until it ceases to be controlled by UK residents. This assumption does not, however, require any assumption to be made of a change in the place(s) at which the CFC's activities are carried on.

(iii) The CFC is not a close company (see 13 CLOSE COMPANIES).

(iv) The CFC has made all relevant claims and elections so as to obtain maximum relief, subject, for accounting periods in respect of which an apportionment has been made under these provisions or which are ADP exempt periods (as above), to a right of the UK resident company which has (or such companies which together have) a 'majority interest' in the CFC, by notice to the Board, to modify or cancel such claims or elections. See Revenue Company Taxation Manual, CT 8622 as regards form of notice of disclaimer. Such notice must be given within 20 months of the end of the accounting period (for periods prior to the commencement of self-assessment (see 18.1 above), within the normal time limit for making appeals under these provisions (see 18.16 below) for an accounting period for which a direction is given, or within 20 months of the end of the accounting period if it is an ADP exempt period). In either case, the Board may allow a longer period (and see para 5.3.8 of the Revenue Notes referred to at 18.1 above). '*Majority interest*' for this purpose is by reference to chargeable profits of the CFC (for the period, or first period, for which the relief in question is available) apportioned to a company or companies as a proportion of such profits apportioned to *all* UK resident companies and giving rise to any liability on such companies (see 18.7 above) (in the case of an ADP exempt period, on the assumption that an apportionment has been made for the period). As regards disclaimers and variations, see paras 5.3.4–5.3.7 of the Revenue Notes referred to at 18.1 above.

(v) The CFC is not a member of a group or consortium (see 29 GROUPS OF COMPANIES). Notwithstanding this assumption, for accounting periods ending on or after 1 April 2000, where there is in fact a surrender by the CFC by way of group relief (see 29.14 GROUPS OF COMPANIES), the CFC's chargeable profits are to be increased to the extent of the relief surrendered and allowed.

(vi) The conditions for an election by the CFC under *ICTA 1988, s 247* (group income, see 29.2 GROUPS OF COMPANIES) are not fulfilled.

(vii) (For accounting periods beginning before 6 April 1999) no ACT may be surrendered to the CFC (see 29.8 GROUPS OF COMPANIES).

(viii) Except insofar as the CFC may carry on a trade in the UK through a branch or agency, it can never be the 'successor' to another company within *ICTA 1988, s 343* (company reconstructions, see 44.10 LOSSES).

(ix) Where trading losses have been incurred by the CFC in an accounting period during which it was non-UK resident (and which is not an ADP exempt period for which it is assumed to be UK resident under (ii) above) and which ended less than six years before the start of the first accounting period for which an apportionment has been made under these provisions, the UK resident company or companies having a majority interest (see (iv) above) in the CFC may claim to have chargeable profits of the CFC computed for any such period as is specified in the claim (and for subsequent accounting periods) on the assumption that an apportionment has been made in respect of the period specified in the claim. The claim must be made in writing to the Board within 20 months after the end of the first accounting period for which an apportionment has been made (for periods prior to the commencement of self-assessment (see 18.1 above), within 60 days of the notice being given to the company of the Board's direction or amended direction relating to that period (see 18.16 below)), or within such longer time as the Board may in any particular case allow. For accounting periods prior to the commencement of self-assessment (see 18.1 above), no claim may be made where the earliest loss period for which a claim could otherwise be made, or any earlier accounting period, is specified in a declaration by the Board under (x) below, since a direction is anyway deemed to have been given for the period so specified.

(x) Writing-down allowances and balancing adjustments are given or charged as if machinery or plant on which expenditure was incurred before the 'starting period' (i.e. the first accounting period for which an apportionment has been made under these provisions or which is an ADP exempt period) was not brought into use for trade purposes before the starting period, and is thus brought in at market value at the beginning of that period.

For accounting periods prior to the commencement of self-assessment (see 18.1 above), if the Board so declare, the computation may also assume that capital allowances on industrial buildings and machinery and plant were granted in periods before the starting period if it was the availability of such allowances which prevented a direction being given in relation to the earliest such period.

Where the chargeable profits for an accounting period are to be computed and expressed in a currency other than sterling (see below), any amount relevant to the computation of capital allowances for the period which was arrived at in relation to accounting periods before the first one beginning on or after 23 March 1995 is converted into the relevant foreign currency at the London closing rate on the first day of the period. The amounts referred to in *CAA 1990, ss 34, 35* (relating to expensive motor cars) and *CAA 1990, s 96* (relating to dwelling-houses) are, for such a period, converted into the relevant foreign currency at the London closing rate for the day the expenditure in question was incurred.

It is not possible to disclaim or postpone plant and machinery allowances under (iv) above for periods for which an apportionment under these provisions has not been made and which are not ADP exempt periods, since the right to disclaim applies only to such periods. Capital allowances other than plant and machinery allowances are given according to the normal rules (see paras 5.3.13–5.3.16 of the Revenue Notes referred to at 18.1 above).

(xi) Relief for unremittable overseas income is extended to include inability to remit to the territory of residence, and notice of desire for such relief may be given by the UK resident company or companies having a majority interest in the CFC (see (iv) above).

(xii) Where the chargeable profits for an accounting period are computed and expressed in a currency other than sterling (see below), the EXCHANGE GAINS AND LOSSES (23) provisions are revised to apply by reference to that currency rather than by conversion to sterling (for which see in particular 23.8, 23.18, 23.21, 23.23, 23.24 EXCHANGE GAINS AND LOSSES). Exchange gains and losses of accrual periods constituting or falling within accounting periods before the 'first relevant accounting period' (see below) are disregarded as regards later accounting periods.

(xiii) For accounting periods to which self-assessment applies (see 18.1 above), the application of the transfer pricing provisions (see 4.4 ANTI-AVOIDANCE) to the computation of CFC chargeable profits is modified (see *ICTA 1988, Sch 24 para 20* introduced by *FA 1998, Sch 17 para 24*). Broadly, a compensatory adjustment is made to CFC profits where, as a result of transactions between the CFC and a UK company, the latter's profits have been increased under the transfer pricing rules. Also, subject to certain conditions, those rules (and the related provision at *ICTA 1988, s 209(2)(da)*, see 20.6 DISTRIBUTIONS) do not apply to transactions between CFCs. (See below as regards pre-self-assessment periods.)

[*ICTA 1988, Sch 24; FA 1995, Sch 25 para 6; FA 1996, Sch 36 para 3; FA 1998, Sch 3 para 43, Sch 17 paras 17–24; FA 2000, Sch 27 para 10*].

Prior to the commencement of corporate self-assessment (see (xiii) above), *ICTA 1988, s 770* (see 4.4 ANTI-AVOIDANCE) may apply to increase chargeable profits of the CFC in respect of transactions with 'connected persons' other than UK traders. Where *section 770* has been applied to increase a UK company's profits in respect of transactions with the CFC, the Revenue will in practice ensure that double taxation does not result.

Computation of chargeable profits in a currency other than sterling. Where a company's chargeable profits fall to be determined for the 'first relevant accounting period' of the company or any subsequent accounting period, then notwithstanding any other rule (statutory or otherwise), they are computed and expressed for any such period in the currency used in the accounts for the 'first relevant accounting period'. Where, as a result of the adoption of the euro by a State, the currency used for the 'first relevant accounting period' is to be replaced by the euro, there is provision for the euro to be substituted for accounting periods ending on or after 1 January 1999 (although, unless the ecu was the currency previously used, the local currency may continue to be used for accounting periods during any part of which it continues to be a legal sub-unit of the euro).

The '*first relevant accounting period*' is determined as follows.

(*a*) Where an apportionment has been made under these provisions as regards an accounting period beginning before 23 March 1995 (i.e. the day appointed for the commencement of the exchange gains and losses provisions, see 23.32 EXCHANGE GAINS AND LOSSES), it is the accounting period beginning on that day.

(*b*) Where there is no accounting period within (*a*) above, it is the first subsequent accounting period for which an apportionment has been made, or, except in the case of accounting periods of trading companies which began before 28 November 1995, for which it can reasonably be assumed that an apportionment would have been made but for its pursuing an 'acceptable distribution policy' (see 18.12 below).

Similarly, where a company's chargeable profits fall to be determined for any accounting period beginning on or after 23 March 1995 and falling before its first relevant accounting period, they are computed and expressed for any such period in the currency used in the accounts for the accounting period concerned.

In either case, the 'accounts' concerned are those the company is required to keep by the law of the country or territory under whose law it is incorporated or formed, or if it is not required under that law to keep accounts, those which most closely correspond to those required under UK law.

The chargeable profits computed and expressed in a currency other than sterling (as above) for an accounting period are converted into sterling by reference to the London closing rate for the last day of the accounting period for the purposes of:

(1) determining the apportioned amount thereof under *ICTA 1988, s 747(4)* (see 18.6 above);

(2) the exception under *ICTA 1988, s 748(1)(d)* (see 18.11(iv) below); and

(3) the calculation of corresponding UK tax under *ICTA 1988, s 750(2)(3)* (see 18.4 above).

[*ICTA 1988, s 747(4A)(4B), s 747A, s 748(4)(5), s 750(5)–(8); FA 1995, Sch 25 paras 2–5; FA 1996, Sch 36 para 1; FA 1998, Sch 17 para 2; SI 1998 No 3177, reg 40*].

See generally sections 5.1–5.4 of the Revenue Notes referred to at 18.1 above.

Simon's Direct Tax Service. See **D4.144.**

18.10 **'Creditable tax'** of a CFC's accounting period is the aggregate of

(i) the double taxation relief, in respect of tax on income brought into account in determining chargeable profits of the period (see 18.9 above), which would be available on the assumptions set out in *ICTA 1988, Sch 24* (see 18.9 above and 21.2 DOUBLE TAX RELIEF) and assuming the company to be liable to corporation tax on those chargeable profits;

(ii) the set-off available under *ICTA 1988, s 7(2)* (sums received under deduction of income tax, see 31.5 INCOME TAX IN RELATION TO A COMPANY) against those chargeable profits on the assumptions in (i) above; and

(iii) the amount of any income or corporation tax actually charged in respect of those chargeable profits, less any such tax which has been or falls to be repaid to the CFC.

[*ICTA 1988, s 751(6); FA 1998, Sch 17 para 6(6)*].

Tax spared in the overseas territory, and for which provision is made in the relevant double tax agreement, may be included in creditable tax up to the limit specified in the agreement (see para 5.5.5 of the Revenue Notes referred to at 18.1 above). Foreign taxes are converted into sterling for these purposes at the exchange rate prevailing at the time the taxes become payable (see para 5.5.6 of those Notes).

18.11 EXCEPTIONS

A CFC is excepted from an apportionment under these provisions (see 18.6 above) for an accounting period if

(i) it pursues an 'acceptable distribution policy' (see 18.12 below) in respect of the period, or

(ii) throughout the period it is engaged in 'exempt activities' (see 18.14 below), or

(iii) it meets the 'public quotation' condition (see 18.15 below), or

(iv) its chargeable profits for the period do not exceed £50,000 (£20,000 for periods prior to the commencement of self-assessment, see 18.1 above) or pro rata for periods of less than twelve months, or

(v) (for accounting periods to which self-assessment applies, see 18.1 above) it is, as respects the period, resident (within the meaning of regulations made for these purposes) in a territory specified in those regulations, and meets such conditions with respect to its income or gains, and any other conditions, as may be specified in those regulations, or

(vi) in that period

(*a*) insofar as any transaction(s) reflected in the profits of the period achieved a 'reduction in UK tax', either it was minimal or that reduction was not a main purpose of the CFC, or of any person having an interest (see 18.6 above) in it in that period, in carrying out the transaction(s), and

(*b*) it was not a main reason for the CFC's existence to achieve a 'reduction in UK tax' by a 'diversion of profits' from the UK.

[*ICTA 1988, s 748(1)(3), Sch 25 para 18; FA 1996, Sch 36 para 2; FA 1998, Sch 17 para 3*].

As regards (v) above, see *The Controlled Foreign Companies (Excluded Countries) Regulations 1998* (*SI 1998 No 3081*). These exclude territories on a basis similar to that previously applicable through application of the list of excluded countries in which the motive test was automatically treated as satisfied (see below), subject to more detailed definition of the various requirements. The main difference is that a *de minimis* limit of £50,000 (on an annual basis) is introduced (if greater than the previous limit of 10% of commercially quantified income) for the non-local source income a company may have and still be treated as carrying on business in a single territory. See generally section 3.1 of the Revenue Notes referred to at 18.1 above.

Clearances. For accounting periods of non-trading CFCs ending after 29 November 1993 and of trading CFCs beginning after 27 November 1995, the Revenue will be prepared to confirm, on the facts provided, whether the CFC meets either the 'exempt activities' test (see 18.14 below) or the 'motive' test (see below), and will thus not be subject to these provisions. It should in most cases be possible for the Revenue to give an advance ruling covering a number of years, provided that all the relevant facts have been accurately disclosed and there is no change in the nature and conduct of the CFC's business. Details of how to make a clearance application and guidance on the information which will be required can be obtained from International Division (Controlled Foreign Companies), Room 311, Melbourne House, Aldwych, London WC2B 4LL (tel. 0207–438 6945). (Revenue Press Release 9 November 1994; Revenue Tax Bulletin June 1996 p 317). See section 2.6 of the Revenue Notes referred to at 18.1 above for clearance procedures.

Motive test. For the Revenue view of the 'motive test' in (vi) above, see (A)–(H) below. As regards that test, a transaction (or two or more transactions taken together) achieves a '*reduction in UK tax*' if, had it not been effected, any person would have been liable for, or for more, UK tax, or would have been entitled to a smaller (or no) relief from or repayment of UK tax. For these purposes, UK tax means income, corporation and capital gains taxes. There is a reduction in UK tax by a '*diversion of profits*' from the UK in an accounting period resulting from a CFC's existence if it is reasonable to suppose that (1) and (2) below would have applied had it not been for the CFC's existence (or for the existence of a company resident outside the UK, 'connected' (see 16 CONNECTED PERSONS) or 'associated' (as defined in *ICTA 1988, s 783(10)*) with the CFC, which fulfils or could fulfil, directly or indirectly, substantially the same function as the CFC in relation to any UK resident company or companies).

(1) The whole or substantial part of the CFC's receipts in the period would have been received by a UK resident individual or company, or by such a company it is reasonable to suppose would have been established in those circumstances; and

(2) that company or individual (or any other person resident in the UK) would have been liable for (or for more) UK tax or entitled to a lesser (or no) relief from or repayment of UK tax.

[*ICTA 1988, Sch 25 paras 16, 17, 19; FA 1996, Sch 36 para 4(6)*].

The Revenue Notes referred to at 18.1 above contain several guidelines on the application of the 'motive test' at (vi) above.

(A) The motive test is entirely separate from the tests at (i) to (v) above, and failure to satisfy those other tests will not prejudice consideration of the motive test, except that where there is a marginal and isolated failure to satisfy those other tests this is regarded as an indication that the CFC is not being used to reduce tax liabilities (paras 3.6.24, 3.6.25).

(B) In determining what the tax position would have been had a transaction not been carried out, hypothetical transactions which might have taken place instead are not taken into account (paras 3.6.8, 3.6.9).

(C) Tax consequences remote from the transaction are not regarded as resulting from it (e.g. a fee received for giving tax planning advice to an unconnected UK resident would not lead to failure of the motive test merely because that person achieved a tax reduction by acting on that advice) (para 3.6.10).

(D) A reduction in tax which is substantial in absolute terms will not be regarded as 'minimal' merely because it represents a relatively small proportion of the total liability of the company concerned (para 3.6.11).

(E) In some circumstances it may be reasonable to suppose that, if a CFC had not been established, its business would have been done by competitors or not at all, e.g. where a locally incorporated company is an essential requirement for doing business in a territory (para 3.6.28).

(F) The motives of a CFC's customers have no relevance to the motive test (para 3.6.13).

(G) The transfer of the activities of an overseas branch to a non-resident subsidiary will often be made for predominantly commercial reasons, e.g. as a necessary preliminary to expanding the overseas business or attracting local capital, and in such cases the motive test will often be satisfied as tax considerations will normally be only a subsidiary reason for the transfer. Where significant profits are taken out of corporation tax, however, the Revenue will wish to consider in depth the reasons for incorporation (paras 3.6.30, 3.6.31).

(H) A holding company will satisfy the motive test where its main purpose is

(i) receiving dividends and interest from its overseas subsidiaries as a mere staging post in the course of the process of reinvestment of the profits concerned in the trading operations of the overseas subsidiaries concerned, or

(ii) holding of funds outside the source country for the purpose of reinvestment in that country because of rigorous exchange controls, inflation, exchange fluctuations or political instability and the risk of expropriation (para 3.6.34).

(I) Where a company falls within the 'control' requirement for a CFC (see 18.2(*b*) above) *solely* as a result of the attribution rules for associates in *ICTA 1988, s 416(6)*, and those associates are limited partners in a limited partnership (within *Limited Partnership Act 1907*) which complies with the 1987 statement approved by the Revenue with the British Venture Capital Association on the use of unlimited partnerships as venture capital investment funds, then the motive test will apply to that company (provided that the partners are not otherwise associates within *ICTA 1988, s 417(3)*) (para 3.6.32).

(J) Where a UK interest holder in a CFC has a loan relationship as a creditor with the CFC, and the increase in value for the loan relationships legislation reflects the chargeable profits arising for an accounting period, the motive test will be accepted as applying for that period (para 3.6.33).

For periods prior to the commencement of corporate self-assessment, the Revenue have published a list of excluded countries, residence in which will automatically ensure that a company is treated as satisfying the conditions at (v) above (subject, in the case of countries in Part II of the list, to certain qualifications). Clearance may informally be sought in relation to groups operating in countries not on the list, including advance clearance where shares in a CFC are sold. (Revenue Press Release 5 October 1993). Revisions to the list were made for accounting periods beginning after 8 July 1998. (Revenue Press Release 9 July 1998). See (v) above for the regulations which replace this non-statutory procedure under self-assessment.

For detailed coverage of the Revenue approach to the motive test, see Revenue Company Taxation Manual, CT 8520 to CT 8564.

Simon's Direct Tax Service. See D1.141, D1.142.

18.12 **'Acceptable distribution policy'. Accounting periods of trading CFCs (see 18.7 above) beginning after 27 November 1995 and of non-trading CFCs ending after 29 November 1993.** As regards 18.11(i) above, a CFC pursues an '*acceptable distribution policy*' in respect of such an accounting period if, and only if, the amount of all dividends paid for the accounting period during, or within 18 months (later, exceptionally, at the Board's discretion — see para 3.2.10 of the Revenue Notes referred to at 18.1 above) of the end of, that period, other than out of specified profits, which is paid to UK residents is not less than 90% of the CFC's 'net chargeable profits' for that period. A dividend which is not paid for the period(s) the profits of which are, in relation to the dividend, 'relevant profits' for the purposes of *ICTA 1988, s 799* (see 21.6 DOUBLE TAX RELIEF) is treated as so paid, and where a dividend is paid for a period which is not an accounting period but which falls wholly within an accounting period, it is treated as paid for that accounting period. A dividend paid for a period falling within two or more accounting periods is apportioned and treated as separate dividends paid for each accounting period.

A dividend paid by a CFC after 8 March 1999 for an accounting period ending after that date is disregarded for these purposes to the extent that the relevant profits in relation to the dividend (see *ICTA 1988, s 799(3)(4)*) derive from dividends or other distributions paid to the CFC at any time to which *ICTA 1988, s 208* (UK company distributions, see 20.17 DISTRIBUTIONS) applied, or would have applied had the CFC then been UK-resident. Dividends paid by a CFC *to* a company are also disregarded for these purposes unless they are taken into account in computing the recipient company's income for corporation tax.

Where the CFC accounts are drawn up in a foreign currency, they do not have to be translated into sterling for these purposes. A dividend equalling 90% of the appropriate foreign currency profits will meet the test. (See para 3.2.35 of the Revenue Notes referred to at 18.1 above.)

'*Net chargeable profits*' of an accounting period are the chargeable profits for that period (see 18.9 above) less the amount of any creditable tax (see 18.10 above) which would arise for the period were an apportionment to be made (see 18.6 above) if the restriction of *ICTA 1988, s 797* did not apply to limit relief to the attributable corporation tax (see 21.5 DOUBLE TAX RELIEF). Where the CFC pays a dividend out of specified profits representing dividends received, directly or indirectly, from another CFC, so much of those profits as is equal to the dividend paid out of them is left out of account in determining chargeable profits.

The gross amount of the dividend (i.e. the amount before deduction of any tax withheld on payment to the UK recipient) is taken into account for the purposes of the acceptable distribution test (see paras 3.2.37, 3.2.38 of the Revenue Notes referred to at 18.1 above).

The above 90% test is applied by reference to a part only of the net chargeable profits where, throughout the accounting period, the CFC has either

(*a*) only one class of shares in issue, or

(*b*) only two classes of shares in issue, being either fixed rate preference shares (as defined in *ICTA 1988, Sch 18 para 1*, see 29.16 GROUPS OF COMPANIES) carrying no voting rights (or only carrying such a right, contingent upon non-payment of a dividend on the shares, which has not become exerciseable prior to payment of a dividend for the period in question) (the 'non-voting shares') or shares carrying the right to vote at general meetings (the 'voting shares')

and

(i) at the end of the period, some of the issued shares are held by persons resident outside the UK, and

(ii) no person has an interest in the CFC (see 18.6 above) other than one derived from issued shares.

Where (*a*) above applies, the fraction of net chargeable profits considered is that fraction of the issued shares at the end of the period which gives rise to interests in the CFC at that time by persons resident in the UK. If such persons hold both immediate and indirect interests in the CFC, and the immediate interests do not reflect the proportion of issued shares by virtue of which they have those interests (e.g. where they hold shares in a company having a direct or indirect interest in the CFC), the number of shares held by them is treated for this purpose as reduced to such number as is appropriate having regard to the immediate interests held by persons resident in the UK and any intermediate shareholdings between those interests and the shares in the CFC. Where (*b*) above applies, the amount of net chargeable profits considered is

$$\frac{P \times Q}{R} + \frac{(X - P) \times Y}{Z}$$

where

P is the amount of dividends (as above) paid in respect of non-voting shares,

Q is the number of non-voting shares by virtue of which UK residents have interests in the CFC at the end of the period,

R is the number of non-voting shares in issue at that time,

X is the net chargeable profits for the period,

Y is the number of voting shares by virtue of which UK residents have interests in the CFC at the end of the period, and

Z is the number of voting shares in issue at that time.

The number of shares under Q and Y may be reduced in the same way as where (*a*) above applies (see above) where UK resident persons hold both immediate and indirect interests in the CFC.

See paras 3.2.27–3.2.33 of the Revenue Notes referred to at 18.1 above.

Dividends taken into account. Where the main condition detailed below is satisfied in relation to a particular accounting period (the '*relevant accounting period*'), dividends to be taken into account, in addition to those paid for that period, are any paid (other than out of specified profits) for the immediately preceding accounting period and (if the condition is satisfied for that period) for the accounting period before that and so on. There is an additional condition in each case, that the dividend is not an '*excluded dividend*', i.e. it is not paid, in whole or part, out of total profits from which are derived the chargeable profits for an '*excluded period*', i.e. a period in respect of which an apportionment under these provisions falls to be made. (For accounting periods prior to the commencement of self-assessment (see 18.1 above) this additional condition was that, in each case, the accounting period was not an '*excluded period*', i.e. a period for which a direction was given (see 18.1 above).) The main condition in relation to any such accounting period is that either there were no 'relevant profits' for the period or

(A) a dividend or dividends is (are) paid for the period to UK residents,

(B) the amount or aggregate amount of such dividends is not less than the relevant profits for the period (or, where only a part of the net chargeable profits is taken into account, a corresponding part of those relevant profits), and

(C) any dividends to be taken into account are paid not later than the time by which dividends paid for the relevant accounting period are required to be paid.

'*Relevant profits*' are the profits which would be the relevant profits for the purposes of *ICTA 1988, s 799* (see 21.6 DOUBLE TAX RELIEF) if a dividend were actually paid for the period. See also para 3.2.17 of the Revenue Notes referred to at 18.1 above for the calculation of relevant profits.

Where no apportionment could be made under these provisions for an earlier period because the company pursued an acceptable distribution policy for that period, dividends are excluded from treatment as above to the extent that they are required to be taken into account for that purpose.

A dividend paid by a CFC to a non-UK resident company is regarded as paid to a UK resident to the extent that it is represented by a subsequent dividend paid to that UK resident by that other company (or by a 'related' company) out of profits derived, directly or indirectly, from the whole or part of the initial dividend paid by the CFC. The subsequent dividend must be taken into account in computing the recipient company's income for corporation tax. A company is '*related*' to another if at least 10% of its voting power is 'controlled' (see 18.2(*b*) above) by that other company or its parent company, or where there is a chain of such relationships.

See generally section 3.2 of the Revenue Notes referred to at 18.1 above.

Trading CFC accounting periods beginning before 28 November 1995. For such accounting periods, the above provisions apply with the following differences:

(I) the acceptable distribution policy is by reference to 50% of 'available profits' rather than 90% of net chargeable profits. '*Available profits*' are so much of the relevant profits of an accounting period (if a dividend were paid for the period) for the purposes of *ICTA 1988, s 799* as does not consist of an excess of capital profits over capital losses, except that

(*a*) for an accounting period of less than twelve months duration, the chargeable profits (see 18.9 above, but with the additional assumption set out in 18.4(i) above) will be substituted if greater and if the Board so declare, and

(*b*) where the CFC pays a dividend out of specified profits representing dividends received, directly or indirectly, from another CFC, so much of those profits as is equal to the dividend paid out of them is left out of account in determining available profits.

Capital profits and losses for this purpose are those which accrue on the disposal of assets and which would not be revenue items under normal corporation tax principles.

Where a company has no available profits in an accounting period, it cannot pursue an acceptable distribution policy. Where, exceptionally, chargeable profits in such a case exceed the £20,000 *de minimis* limit (see 18.11(iv) above), no direction is sought where it can be shown that there has been no manipulation of profits arising in the ordinary course of the company's commercial activities in order to reduce the amount available for distribution;

(II) the amount X in the formula referred to above is the available profits rather than the net chargeable profits;

(III) the provisions for taking into account dividends paid for earlier accounting periods do not apply; and

(IV) for accounting periods ending before 30 November 1993, the requirement was that the proportion of all dividends paid (as above) for the period, or for another period falling wholly or partly within the period, 'represent' at least 50% of the available profits. A dividend '*represents*' those profits which were relevant profits in relation to the dividend, any necessary apportionment between periods being made, and treating a dividend not paid for a specific period as paid for the period(s) whose profits were relevant profits in relation to the dividend.

Non-trading CFC accounting periods ending before 30 November 1993. For such accounting periods, the above provisions apply as they do for trading companies for accounting periods beginning before 28 November 1995, except that the test is by reference to 90% rather than 50% of available profits.

Revenue practice. Revenue Tax Bulletin August 1994, pp 138–141 contains various Revenue interpretations. In particular, the following may be noted.

(*aa*) Subject to the general anti-avoidance provision described at (I)(*a*) above, an accounting period may be split at 30 November 1993, so that the new rules apply only to the part period from that date. This presumably applies equally at 28 November 1995.

(*bb*) Interest (including short interest) paid to a non-resident out of UK income can be deducted from chargeable profits, with an adjustment where the UK income was received net of tax. Interest treated as a distribution under *ICTA 1988, s 209(2)(e)(iv)* or *(v)* may similarly be deducted, unless paid as part of arrangements for the indirect payment from the UK to a person outside the UK of an amount which would be treated as a distribution were it paid directly.

(*cc*) *ICTA 1988, s 770* (transfer pricing, see 4.4 ANTI-AVOIDANCE) can apply to an accounting period for which the acceptable distribution policy test has been applied, and although the Revenue will ensure by whatever means are appropriate that this will not result in double taxation in the UK, it is for the CFC so to arrange its affairs as to avoid international double taxation.

(*dd*) Additional distributions may be made to satisfy the acceptable distribution policy if the computation of the net chargeable profits is revised by the Revenue, and the normal time limit of 18 months from the end of the accounting period will generally be extended in such cases.

Directions. For accounting periods prior to the commencement of self-assessment (see 18.1 above), the Board may, subject to appeal (see 18.16 below), give a direction in respect of an accounting period after the end of the period before it is possible to establish whether an acceptable distribution policy has been pursued in respect of the period.

[*ICTA 1988, s 748(1)(a)(2), Sch 25 Pt I; FA 1990, s 67(3)(4); FA 1994, s 134; FA 1996, Sch 36 para 4(1)–(4); FA 1998, Sch 17 paras 3(6), 26–28; FA 1999, s 88*].

Self-assessment returns where it is not established whether an acceptable distribution policy applies. For accounting periods to which self-assessment applies (see 18.1 above), where a UK-resident company has an interest in a CFC at any time during an accounting period of the CFC, and at the time when the company delivers its company tax return it is not established whether or not the CFC has pursued an acceptable distribution policy in relation to that period, then:

(i) if the company considers that the CFC is likely to do so, it must make the return on the basis that it does so;

(ii) otherwise, it must make the return on the basis that it does not do so.

The Revenue do not object to a company erring on the side of caution by acting as under (ii) above even though it thinks it likely that an acceptable distribution policy will be pursued (see para 2.2.1 of the Revenue Notes referred to at 18.1 above).

If (i) above applies but in the event the CFC does not do so, or if (ii) above applies but in the event the CFC does do so, the company must amend the return accordingly. Any such amendment must be made within 30 days after the end of the period allowed for establishing an acceptable distribution policy in relation to the CFC accounting period, i.e. the period ending 18 months after the end of the accounting period or at such later time as the Board allows for payment of a dividend (see above). Otherwise, the normal return amendment provisions apply. If it has not been established by the end of the period allowed that the CFC pursued an acceptable distribution policy in relation to an accounting period, it is for these purposes assumed that it did not do so. Failure to make a timeous amendment where (i) above applies but the CFC did not in the event pursue an acceptable distribution policy in relation to the period renders the company liable to a penalty not exceeding the amount of tax understated. [*ICTA 1988, s 754A; FA 1998, Sch 17 para 10*].

Simon's Direct Tax Service. See **D4.138** *et seq.*

See 21.6 DOUBLE TAX RELIEF for the separate streaming for double tax relief purposes of certain dividends paid in pursuit of an acceptable distribution policy.

18.13 *Example*

DEF Co Ltd, a UK incorporated and resident company with two associated companies, holds 35% of the shares of LNB Co, an unquoted non-trading controlled foreign company resident in Pinkland, where tax is levied at only 10%.

LNB Co has chargeable profits (see 18.9 above) for the year ended 31 March 2000 of £500,000. No withholding tax is applicable in Pinkland.

The following information is available in respect of DEF.

Year to 31 March	2000	2001
	£	£
Schedule D, Case I profit	600,000	780,000
Schedule D, Case III income	10,000	10,000
Chargeable gains	90,000	—
Schedule D, Case V income (gross) (tax suffered £30,000)	100,000	—

LNB Co

Calculation of profits apportioned to DEF Co Ltd and dividend required to avoid apportionment.

	£
Chargeable profits for the year ended 31 March 2000	500,000
Deduct Creditable tax	50,000
Net chargeable profits	£450,000
Amount of distribution required to avoid apportionment 90% × £450,000	£405,000

	Apportionment of profit	Dividend
DEF share	£	£
35% × £500,000: 35% × £405,000	175,000	141,750
Creditable/underlying tax	17,500	15,750
		157,500

DEF Co Ltd

With apportionment

Year to 31 March		2000	2001
		£	£
Schedule D, Case I		600,000	780,000
Schedule D, Case III		10,000	10,000
Chargeable gains		90,000	—
Schedule D, Case V income		100,000	—
CFC apportionment		175,000	—
		£975,000	£790,000
UK tax thereon at 30%		292,500	237,000
Less			
DTR on Case V income	(30,000)		
CFC creditable tax	(17,500)	(47,500)	
Mainstream tax payable		£245,000	£237,000

If dividend paid in y/e 31.3.2001

Year to 31 March	2000	2001
	£	£
Schedule D, Case I	600,000	780,000
Schedule D, Case III	10,000	10,000
Chargeable gains	90,000	—
Schedule D, Case V income	100,000	157,500
	£800,000	£947,500
UK tax thereon at 30%	240,000	284,250
Less		
DTR	(30,000)	(15,750)
Mainstream tax payable	£210,000	£268,500
Tax saving (cost)	£35,000	£(31,500)

DEF Co Ltd will make a net tax saving of £3,500 in tax if LBN Co pays the required dividend for the year ended 31 March 2000 by 31 March 2001.

18.14 **'Exempt activities'.** As regards 18.11(ii) above, a CFC is engaged in '*exempt activities*' in an accounting period if, and only if, throughout that accounting period, it has a 'business establishment' in the territory in which it is 'resident' (see below), its business affairs in that territory are 'effectively managed' there, and either (1), (2), (3) or (4) below is satisfied.

(1) (*a*) At no time in the accounting period does the company's main business (for which see paras 3.3.25, 3.3.26 of the Revenue Notes referred to at 18.1 above) consist of either investment business (see paras 3.3.27–3.3.32 of those Notes), including the holding of intellectual property (see *ICTA 1988, Sch 25 para*

9 as amended by Copyright, Designs and Patent Act 1988, Sch 7 para 36(9); FA 1998, s 112(2)(5)) or of dealing in goods (i.e. buying and selling goods in unchanged form, see para 3.3.34 of those Notes) for delivery to or from the UK or to or from connected or associated persons (see 18.11 above) which are not actually delivered to the territory in which it is resident, and

(*b*) in the case of a company mainly engaged in the period in wholesale, distributive or financial business (as exemplified in *ICTA 1988, Sch 25 para 11(1) as amended by FA 1998, s 112(3)–(5)*), less than 50% of its gross trading receipts from that business (net of the cost of any description of property or rights, sale proceeds of which are included therein) is derived, directly or indirectly, from connected or associated persons (see 18.11 above) or, for accounting periods beginning after 27 November 1995, persons with an 'interest' in the company. In the case of accounting periods to which self-assessment applies (see 18.1 above), a person has an '*interest*' for this purpose if, on an apportionment under these provisions, at least 25% of the CFC's chargeable profits of the period would be apportioned to that person. (Previously, such an '*interest*' arose where at any time in the accounting period the person had an 'interest' in the CFC within 18.6 above, although in practice only an interest of at least 10% was taken into account (see Revenue Tax Bulletin June 1996 p 317).) For accounting periods beginning after 20 March 2000, this requirement is extended to all companies mainly engaged in service provision, and in the case of a company which is a CFC only by virtue of joint control by two persons within *ICTA 1988, s 747(1A)* (see 18.2 above), the connected or associated persons to be considered also include persons connected or associated with either of those two persons. Special provisions apply as regards application of the requirement to banking or similar concerns and to insurance business of any kind (see *ICTA 1988, Sch 25 para 11(3)–(9)* and paras 3.3.39–3.3.57 of the Revenue Notes referred to at 18.1 above).

(2) The company is a 'local holding company', i.e. a 'holding company' 90% of whose gross income in the accounting period is derived directly from companies it controls (see 18.2(*b*) above) and which, throughout that period, are resident in the territory in which the holding company is 'resident' (see below) and either

(*a*) (for accounting periods to which self-assessment applies (see 18.1 above)) are not themselves holding companies or 'superior holding companies' but either are engaged in exempt activities or are 'exempt trading companies', or

(*b*) (for earlier accounting periods) are engaged in exempt activities otherwise than as 'holding companies'.

For accounting periods beginning after 20 March 2000, the income must in addition be received by the 'holding company' in its territory of residence.

(3) The company is a 'holding company' other than a local holding company (see (2) above) 90% of whose gross income during the accounting period is derived directly from companies it controls (see 18.2(*b*) above) and which are themselves throughout the period either local holding companies or

(*a*) (for accounting periods to which self-assessment applies (see 18.1 above)) not themselves 'holding companies' or 'superior holding companies' but either engaged in exempt activities or 'exempt trading companies', or

(*b*) (for earlier accounting periods) are engaged in exempt activities otherwise than as 'holding companies'.

For accounting periods beginning after 20 March 2000, there is an additional condition that either 90% of the gross income of the 'holding company' must consist of 'qualifying dividends', or the company from which the 'holding company' directly derives 90% of its gross income must, throughout the accounting period in question, be resident in the territory in which the 'holding company' is resident and in which it must receive that income. A '*qualifying dividend*' is any dividend other than one for which the paying company is entitled to a deduction against its profits for tax purposes under the law of the territory in which it is resident.

(4) The company is a 'superior holding company' 90% of whose gross income during the accounting period represents 'qualifying exempt activity income of its subsidiaries' and is derived directly from companies it controls (see 18.2(*b*) above) and each of which, throughout that accounting period, either

(*a*) not itself being a 'superior holding company', is otherwise either engaged in exempt activities or an 'exempt trading company', or

(*b*) is itself a 'superior holding company' 90% of whose gross income during the accounting period represents 'qualifying exempt activity income of its subsidiaries' and is derived directly from companies which it controls (see 18.2(*b*) above) and which themselves fall within this subparagraph or within (*a*) above.

For accounting periods beginning after 20 March 2000, there is an additional condition that either 90% of the gross income of the 'superior holding company' (under either leg of the test) must consist of 'qualifying dividends' (as in (3) above), or the company from which the 'superior holding company' directly derives 90% of its gross income must, throughout the accounting period in question, be resident in the territory in which the 'superior holding company' is resident and in which it must receive that income.

In (2), (3) and (4) above, a 'holding company' or 'superior holding company' is treated as controlling any trading company in which it holds the maximum amount of ordinary share capital permitted under the law of the territory in which that trading company is resident, and from whose laws it derives its status as a company. For accounting periods beginning after 20 March 2000, this deemed control is extended to any trading company which is a CFC under the 40% joint control test (see 18.2 above) where the non-UK resident joint owner also controls the 'holding company' or 'superior holding company'. For the 90% of gross income test, see *ICTA 1988, Sch 25 para 12(4)–(6)* and paras 3.3.77–3.3.81, 3.3.84 of the Revenue Notes referred to at 18.1 above. See Revenue Tax Bulletin October 1995 pp 249, 250 for the circumstances in which a holding company may be deemed to pass the motive test where its subsidiaries carry on broadly commercial activities along the lines of the exempt activities test, or where it controls a holding company which is not a local holding company.

As regards (4) above, see *ICTA 1988, Sch 25 para 12A(3)(4)* (introduced by *FA 1998, Sch 17 para 33*) as regards the profits out of which dividends are regarded as paid, and see also para 3.3.75 of the Revenue Notes referred to at 18.1 above.

A '*business establishment*' means 'premises' from which the company's business in the territory in which it is 'resident' (see below) is wholly or mainly carried on, and which are, or are intended to be, occupied and used with a reasonable degree of permanence. The Revenue interpretation of this requirement is set out at paras 3.3.8–3.3.13 of the Revenue Notes referred to at 18.1 above. An office building, or even a single office, shared by a number of companies can be the 'business establishment' of each company. The requirement that the premises be 'occupied and used with a reasonable degree of permanence' depends on the nature of the company's business. Thus a holding company's business might need only occasional attendance of its staff at the premises, and the use of an office on such occasions would suffice, provided that it was retained by the company for its use for a considerable period of time. Continuous occupation of the office during normal working hours would not be required. The occasional hiring of, say, a hotel room for meetings would not qualify as having a 'business establishment'.

Again, a company (e.g. a bank) purporting to do business with the general public would be expected to have an office, shop, etc. actually occupied by its staff for at least a substantial part of each working day.

'*Premises*' includes an office, shop, factory or other building (or part); a mine, oil well, gas well or quarry or other place of extraction of natural resources; or a building, construction or installation site where the project has a duration of at least twelve months. A company whose business in the territory of residence is carried on from a number of sites in the territory will be treated as having a business establishment there even if no one site can be identified as the main place of business in the territory (see para 3.3.10 of Revenue Notes referred to at 18.1 above).

'*Resident*' in this context is as defined in 18.3 above, except that in the case of a non-UK resident company which is not liable to tax in any territory by reason of domicile, residence or place of management, but whose affairs are 'effectively managed' in a territory outside the UK in which companies are not liable to tax by reason of domicile, residence or place of management, it is treated for this purpose as resident in the latter territory or, if there is more than one, to such a territory as is notified to the Board for this purpose by the UK resident company or companies having a majority interest in the CFC (see 18.9(iv) above).

The requirement that the CFC's business affairs be '*effectively managed*' in the territory of residence is not regarded as satisfied unless the number of employees in the territory is adequate to deal with the volume of the company's business, and unless any services provided for persons resident outside the territory (other than through a branch or agency liable to UK tax on its profits or gains, or for arm's length consideration through any other person so liable) are not in fact performed in the UK (or are merely incidental to services performed outside the UK). Employees in the territory include persons engaged in the company's business but paid by a person connected (see 16 CONNECTED PERSONS) with, and resident in the same territory as, the CFC, provided that they are engaged in the CFC's business (wholly or mainly so engaged in the case of a company other than a 'holding company' or 'superior holding company'). The requirement as to the number of employees does not mean that every person involved in the company's business must be located in the territory of residence, but the staff employed there must be sufficient, in numbers and in qualifications and experience, to supervise and control profit-making activities of the company (see para 3.3.16 of Revenue Notes referred to at 18.1 above).

A '*holding company*' is a company whose business consists wholly or mainly in holding shares or securities in companies which are either its 90% subsidiaries and local holding companies (see (2) above) or its 51% subsidiaries and trading companies or companies in which it holds the maximum permitted amount of ordinary share capital (see below); or a company which would satisfy that condition if so much of its business were disregarded as consists in holding property or rights wholly or mainly for use by fellow resident companies controlled by it (see 18.2(*b*) above). However, in determining whether a company is a local holding company for this purpose, the reference in the definition of holding company to companies which are 90% subsidiaries and local holding companies is omitted. Determination of 51% or 90% subsidiary status is by reference to direct ownership, of more than 50% or not less than 90% respectively, of ordinary share capital.

For the purposes of (2) and (3) above, income of a holding company is treated as *not* being derived directly from a company it controls where the controlled company from which it derives (*a*) (for accounting periods to which self-assessment applies (see 18.1 above)) is not itself a holding company or 'superior holding company' but either is engaged in exempt activities or is an 'exempt trading company', or

(*b*) (for earlier accounting periods) is engaged in exempt activities otherwise than as a holding company,

and the income was, or could have been, paid out of any non-trading income (i.e. income which would not be chargeable on a UK resident company under Schedule D, Case I on normal corporation tax principles) of the controlled company derived, directly or indirectly, from a third company connected or associated with it (see 18.11 above).

For the purpose of (2), (3) and (4) above, in the case of a holding company or 'superior holding company' part of whose business consists of activities other than holding shares, securities, property or rights, gross income of an accounting period is determined by

(i) leaving out of account any part derived from any activity which, of itself, would satisfy (1) above; and

(ii) to the extent that the company's receipts from any other activities included proceeds of sale of any description of property or rights, deducting the cost of the property or rights (up to the amount of the receipts therefrom), and making no other deduction in respect of that activity.

A '*superior holding company*' is a company whose business consists wholly or mainly in holding shares or securities in holding companies or local holding companies or other superior holding companies, or which would satisfy that condition if so much of its business were disregarded as consists in holding property or rights wholly or mainly for use by fellow resident companies controlled by it (see 18.2(*b*) above).

A company is an '*exempt trading company*' throughout a period if it is a trading company throughout each of its accounting periods falling wholly or partly within the period, and in each of those accounting periods:

(A) it is not subject to a lower level of taxation (see 18.4 above) in the territory in which it is resident;

(B) it is within 18.11(v) above; and

(C) it satisfies the conditions in 18.11(vi) above,

and income of a company during a period represents '*qualifying exempt activity income of its subsidiaries*' if it is derived directly or indirectly from companies which it controls (see 18.2(*b*) above) and which, throughout that period, fall within (4)(*a*) above, but which are not holding companies other than local holding companies.

[*ICTA 1988, s 748(1)(b), Sch 25 Pt II; FA 1996, Sch 36 para 4(5); FA 1998, s 112, Sch 17 paras 29–33; FA 2000, Sch 31 paras 5–9*].

See generally section 3.3 of the Revenue Notes referred to at 18.1 above.

Simon's Direct Tax Service. See D4.139.

18.15 The **'public quotation condition'** is met by a CFC in an accounting period if

(i) shares or stock (other than that entitled to a fixed rate of dividend, whether also participating in profits or not) have, within the twelve months to the end of the accounting period, been dealt in on, and listed in the official list of, a recognised stock exchange (i.e. one designated as such by the Board, see paras 3.4.9–3.4.11 of the Revenue Notes referred to at 18.1 above) in its territory of residence, and

(ii) such shares, etc. carrying at least 35% of the total voting power in the company have been 'beneficially held by the public' throughout the accounting period, and have been acquired unconditionally by the public, and

(iii) the voting power possessed by 'principal members' of the company (including that attributed to shares entitled to a fixed rate of dividend) has not at any time in the accounting period exceeded 85% of the total voting power in the company.

Shares etc. are '*beneficially held by the public*' if held by any person other than a person connected or associated with the CFC (see 18.7 above) or a 'principal member' of the company.

A '*principal member*' of a company is a person possessing more than 5% of the voting power in the company or, where there are more than five such persons, those five persons holding the highest percentages. Where more than one person possesses a percentage which would, if held by only one person, be the fifth largest percentage holding, each of those persons is a principal member in addition to the four persons possessing higher percentage holdings.

Any person's holding of shares for these purposes includes all nominee holdings for him, and a person's voting power includes that of his associates (see 13.5 CLOSE COMPANIES), of any company which he controls (see 18.2(*b*) above) with or without his associates, and of any nominees for him, his associates or such companies. Voting power of associates' associates and of companies controlled only by associates is disregarded.

[*ICTA 1988, Sch 25 paras 13–15; FA 1996, Sch 38 para 6*].

See generally section 3.4 of the Revenue Notes referred to at 18.1 above.

Simon's Direct Tax Service. See D4.140.

18.16 **NOTICES AND APPEALS** [*ICTA 1988, ss 753, 754(3) as originally enacted*]

The following provisions **cease to apply** for accounting periods to which self-assessment applies (see 18.1 above). [*FA 1998, Sch 17 para 8*].

A direction under these provisions (see 18.1 above) must be notified to all UK resident companies which it appears to the Board had an interest in the CFC (see 18.6 above) in the accounting period to which the direction relates. The contents of the required notice are specified (see *ICTA 1988, s 753(2)*). Notice must similarly be given of any amendment to the accounting period specified in a direction (see 18.7 above).

Any company to which such notice is given may appeal to the Special Commissioners in writing to the Board within 60 days of the date of the notice on the grounds that

(*a*) the direction should not have been given (or amended), or

(*b*) the amount of chargeable profits or creditable tax specified in the notice is incorrect, or

(*c*) the recipient of the notice did not have an interest in the CFC at any time during the period in question, or

(*d*) the conditions for a declaration as to periods for which certain allowances are to be deemed to have been given (see 18.9(xi) above) are not fulfilled, or

(*e*) the conditions for a declaration that chargeable profits be substituted for available profits for an accounting period of less than twelve months (see 18.12 above) are not fulfilled.

The grounds of appeal must be specified, but the Commissioners may allow the appellant to put forward any other ground, and take it into consideration, if satisfied that the omission was neither wilful nor unreasonable.

If such a declaration as is mentioned in (*d*) or (*e*) above is made in circumstances such that a notice as above is not required, notice must be given specifying the declaration(s) to every company previously given notice of the direction, and appeal rights as above apply in relation to such a declaration specified in such a notice.

If the inspector considers the chargeable profits or creditable tax specified in a notice to be incorrect, he must notify the revised amounts to all those originally notified of the direction, subject to the same appeal rights as the original notice unless the revision itself resulted from an appeal or from certain notices given to the Board by UK resident companies (see 18.9(iv) and (xii) above).

On any appeal, the Special Commissioners may review any decision of the Board or inspector relevant to a ground of the appeal.

The Board may make regulations concerning appeals procedures by statutory instrument (although no such regulations have in fact been made).

18.17 ASSESSMENT, RECOVERY AND POSTPONEMENT OF TAX

Accounting periods prior to the commencement of self-assessment (see 18.1 above)

The normal corporation tax provisions apply to *assessment* and *collection* of a sum charged as under 18.7 above, including those relating to appeals, administration, penalties, interest, and priority in insolvency. The sum is treated as corporation tax falling to be assessed for the accounting period in which ends the CFC's accounting period in which the chargeable profits giving rise to the sum assessed arose. The assessment must specify the total of chargeable profits and creditable tax apportioned to persons having each of the interests specified at 18.6(*a*) to (*e*) above, and to shareholders of each class where more than one class of shares is in issue. No particular person may, however, be identified as having any such interest.

Appeals may not be brought on grounds on which appeal was, or could have been, made against a direction notice or amended notice (see 18.16 above).

The *postponement* provisions of *TMA 1970, s 55* (see 48.3 PAYMENT OF TAX) apply to an appeal against a notice under these provisions (see 18.16 above) where, before the appeal is determined, the appellant is assessed (as above) by reference to the chargeable profits specified in that notice. They also apply, suitably modified, where an appeal is also made against the assessment itself.

The *reliefs* which may be claimed against a liability under an assessment under these provisions are as follows.

(*a*) *Trading losses, etc.* Where a trading loss, Schedule A loss, charge on income, management expense, excess capital allowance, group relief claim or non-trading loan relationship deficit exceeds any other profits of an accounting period for which a company is regarded as liable to corporation tax in respect of chargeable profits apportioned to it (as above), the company may claim to set against its liability a sum equal to corporation tax, at the rate (or average rate) applicable to profits of the accounting period, on all or part of the loss, etc. (which is then treated as having been set off against profits of the company). Group relief claims may be made up to the end of the accounting period after that for which relief is to be claimed (if otherwise out of time), and the normal time limits apply for claims under this relief (see 12.2 CLAIMS).

(*b*) *Advance corporation tax.* For accounting periods beginning before 6 April 1999, surplus ACT (see 3.8 ADVANCE CORPORATION TAX) of an accounting period for which a company is regarded as liable to corporation tax in respect of chargeable profits apportioned to it (as above) may, on a claim, be set against that liability (so far as it is not relieved, and could not be relieved, under (*a*) above), and is then treated as having been set against a corporation tax liability of the period. The maximum set-off allowed is the ACT for which the company would have had to account on a distribution made at the end of the accounting period, where the amount of the distribution plus the ACT in respect of it is equal to the apportioned chargeable profits in respect of which the company is chargeable for the period less any deduction under (*a*) above. Accounting periods which straddle 5 April 1999 are for this purpose treated as ending on that date, with proportionate apportionment to that period of the chargeable profits and deductions.

Similar provision is made from 6 April 1999 under the 'shadow ACT' regulations (see 3.8 ADVANCE CORPORATION TAX).

(*c*) *Dividends from the CFC.* The total of assessments on UK resident companies under these provisions in respect of a CFC's chargeable profits (the '*gross attributed tax*') is treated as underlying tax for double taxation relief purposes (see 21.6 DOUBLE TAX RELIEF) where a dividend is paid by the CFC wholly or partly out of profits from which those chargeable profits derive. The gross attributed tax is *not*, however, treated as increasing the amount of the dividend income in determining liability on that income.

If *ICTA 1988, s 796* or *s 797* (see 21.5 DOUBLE TAX RELIEF) act to limit the foreign tax credit by reference to the UK tax on the dividends concerned, the amount so debarred from relief, insofar as it does not exceed the foreign tax *other than* underlying tax attributable to the dividend, is set against the gross attributed tax assessed on UK resident companies. On a claim by any of those companies, the tax so assessed on it is reduced and, if appropriate, repaid.

Any condition for double tax relief under *ICTA 1988, s 788* (by agreement with other countries) or *s 790* (unilateral relief) (see 21.2, 21.3 DOUBLE TAX RELIEF) requiring a particular degree of control of the company paying the dividend is treated as satisfied for these purposes.

Where the CFC dividend is paid out of unspecified profits, and any part of its chargeable profits is apportioned other than to UK resident companies, the gross attributed tax is attributed to the proportion of the chargeable profits apportioned to UK resident companies (the '*taxed profits*'). So much of the dividend as is received by, or by a 'successor in title' of, any such company is regarded as paid primarily out of the taxed profits. '*Successor in title*' for this purpose refers to a successor in respect of the whole or part of the interest in the CFC (see 18.6 above) giving rise to a charge under these provisions.

If

(i) relief has been allowed for the purposes of corporation tax on chargeable gains, on a disposal of shares, in respect of a sum assessed under these provisions (see 18.18 below), and

(ii) that sum forms part of the gross attributed tax in relation to a dividend, as above, and

(iii) a person receiving the dividend in respect of the shares referred to in (i) above (the '*primary dividend*') or any other dividend in respect of shares in a company resident outside the UK representing profits consisting directly or indirectly of or including the primary dividend, is entitled to relief by way of underlying tax (as above) by reference to the whole or part of the gross attributed tax,

then the relief available as in (iii) above is reduced or extinguished by deducting therefrom the amount allowed by way of relief as in (i) above.

Special recovery powers. Where the same interest in a CFC is held directly by one person and indirectly by another, and the company to be treated as holding the interest is defined by 18.7(1) to (3) above, special recovery powers apply to any overdue tax chargeable on that company. The Board may serve notice of liability to that overdue tax on another UK resident company (the '*responsible company*') which holds or has held, directly or indirectly, the same interest in the CFC as the chargeable company. Interest both up to the date of the notice and thereafter is then payable by the responsible company. If tax and interest is not paid by the responsible company within three months of the date of the Board's notice, it may be recovered from either the responsible company or the company originally chargeable.

[*ICTA 1988, s 754, Sch 26 as originally enacted; FA 1998, Sch 3 para 44, Sch 5 para 46*].

Accounting periods to which self-assessment applies (see 18.1 above)

The normal corporation tax provisions apply to the charge to tax of a sum under these provisions as under 18.7 above, including those relating to company tax returns, to the assessment, collection and receipt of corporation tax, and to appeals, administration, penalties, interest and priority in insolvency. The provisions of *TMA 1970* thus apply as if references to corporation tax referred also to amounts charged under these provisions, and as if references to company profits referred also to chargeable profits apportioned to a company under these provisions. A sum chargeable under these provisions is chargeable for the accounting period in which ends the CFC accounting period whose chargeable profits were apportioned.

Just and reasonable apportionments. Where an apportionment of chargeable profits for an accounting period of a CFC falls to be made on a just and reasonable basis (see 18.7 above), and a company uses a particular basis in its tax return, the Board may determine that a different basis is to be used, and require the company to provide such documents and information as are reasonably required for this purpose. A basis so determined is then treated as if it were the only basis permissible. A determination may be questioned (in an appeal against an amendment to the company's tax return) only on the ground that the basis determined is not just and reasonable.

Appeals against amendments to company tax returns (or against discovery assessments or determinations) relating to charges under these provisions are to the Special Commissioners. Where their determination of a particular question is likely to affect the liability of more than one person under these provisions in relation to the CFC concerned, every such person is entitled to appear and be heard by the Special Commissioners, or to make written representations to them, and their determination of that question is treated as separate from any other determination on the appeal and as if each of those persons were a party to the appeal on that question.

As regards the *reliefs* which may be claimed against a liability under these provisions, these are the same as those which applied prior to the commencement of self-assessment (see (*a*)–(*c*) above), except that as regards (*a*) above (trading losses, etc.) the amounts which may be relieved in terms of tax thereon against tax on apportioned chargeable profits are not restricted to the excess over other profits of the accounting period in question (and the specific time limits referred to no longer apply).

Where the same interest in a CFC is held directly by one person and indirectly by another, the *special recovery powers* which applied before the commencement of self-assessment (see above) also continue to apply.

[*ICTA 1988, s 754, Sch 26; FA 1998, Sch 3 para 44, Sch 5 para 46, Sch 17 paras 9, 34, 36*].

See generally Part 7 of the Revenue Notes referred to at 18.1 above.

Simon's Direct Tax Service. See **D1.147–D1.150**.

18.18 **MISCELLANEOUS**

Corporation tax on chargeable gains on disposal of shares: relief may be claimed where:

(i) an apportionment is made under these provisions (see 18.6 above) in respect of a CFC's accounting period;

(ii) a UK resident company (the '*claimant company*') disposes of shares, acquired before the end of that accounting period, in either the CFC or another company whose shares give rise to the claimant company's interest in the CFC (see 18.6 above); and

(iii) chargeable profits (see 18.7 above) of the CFC are apportioned to the claimant company, and a sum accordingly becomes chargeable on it as if it were corporation tax (see 18.6 above).

Where a claim is made, in the computation of the chargeable gain accruing on the disposal in (ii) above, a deduction is allowed of the sum chargeable to tax as in (iii) above, reduced to the proportion thereof that the average market value, in the period for which the apportionment was made, of the interest in the CFC in respect of which the charge as in (iii) above arose bears to the average market value in that period of the shares disposed of. A sum chargeable to tax as at (iii) above may only be relieved once in this way.

Relief may, however, be restricted where, before the disposal, a dividend is paid by the CFC out of profits from which the chargeable profits in (iii) above derived. If either

(*a*) the effect of the payment of the dividend is to reduce the value of the shares disposed of as in (ii) above, or

(*b*) the claimant company obtains relief as under 18.17(*c*) above in respect of a dividend paid on the shares disposed of as in (ii) above, by reference to sums including that referred to in (iii) above,

then relief is denied in respect of so much of the sum chargeable to tax as corresponds to the part of the chargeable profits in (iii) above corresponds to the profits which the dividend represents.

Claims for relief must be made within three months of the later of the end of the accounting period in which the disposal occurs and the date the charge to tax in (iii) above becomes final and conclusive.

Identification of shares disposed of for this purpose is with those acquired earlier before those acquired later.

[*ICTA 1988, Sch 26 para 3; FA 1998, Sch 17 para 35*].

See Simon's Direct Tax Service D4.149.

See generally section 7.3 of the Revenue Notes referred to at 18.1 above.

See 18.17(*c*) above as regards restriction of dividend relief following relief under this provision.

Information relating to CFCs. For accounting periods prior to the commencement of self-assessment (see 18.1 above), the Board has substantial powers to require by written notice within a specified time (not less than 30 days) details from UK resident companies of suspected CFCs. The notice may require any 'relevant' (as defined) books, accounts, or other records or documents of the company on which it is served, or of any other company which it appears it may control (with or without other UK residents), to be made available for inspection. On application by the company, the requirement as to the books, etc. of any other company specified in the notice may be waived by the Board (and refusal by the Board to agree to such a waiver is subject to a right of appeal to the Special Commissioners within 30 days of the refusal). [*ICTA 1988, s 755; FA 1998, Sch 17 para 12*]. See Simon's Direct Tax Service D4.152.

ICTA 1988, s 739 (transfer of assets abroad). Where a sum forming part of a CFC's chargeable profits (see 18.9 above) would otherwise be deemed income of an individual under *section 739* (see Tolley's Income Tax under Anti-Avoidance) that deemed income is reduced by the proportion of those chargeable profits which gives rise to a liability to tax on UK resident companies by virtue of an apportionment under these provisions (see 18.7 above). [*ICTA 1988, s 747(4)(b)*].

Insurance companies: self-assessment. For the treatment of chargeable profits and creditable tax apportioned to companies carrying on life assurance business for accounting periods to which self-assessment applies (see 18.1 above), see *ICTA 1988, s 755A* introduced by *FA 1998, Sch 17 para 13*. Broadly, they are treated as if they represented a dividend paid by the CFC. See also *ICTA 1988, s 755B* (introduced by *FA 1998, Sch 17 para 14* for such accounting periods), which extends certain time limits in respect of any amendment of or enquiry into an insurance company's tax return which has regard to accounts of a CFC prepared on a non-annual basis, and *ICTA 1988, s 755C* (introduced by *FA 1998, Sch 17 para 15* for such accounting periods) which provides regulation-making powers relating to cases where a CFC carrying on general insurance business prepares accounts on a non-annual basis (and see now *SI 1999 No 1408* which *inter alia* introduces a new *ICTA 1988, s 754AA* dealing with returns where it is not established whether a non-resident company carrying on such business is a CFC).

See generally Part 8 of the Revenue Notes referred to at 18.1 above.

19 Corporate Venturing Scheme

19.1 **INTRODUCTION**

For shares issued on or after 1 April 2000 but before 1 April 2010, a scheme is introduced whereby most trading companies are able to obtain corporation tax relief at 20% ('*investment relief*') on corporate venturing investments, i.e. acquisitions (by cash subscription) of minority shareholdings in 'small higher risk' trading companies. In addition, investing companies are able to postpone chargeable gains ('*deferral relief*') on disposals of corporate venturing investments where they reinvest in other shares attracting investment relief. Also, an allowable capital loss on the disposal of a corporate venturing investment, computed net of investment relief, can be relieved against *income* of the accounting period in which the loss arises and accounting periods ending in the previous 12 months (but may alternatively be relieved against chargeable gains in the normal way). [*FA 2000, s 63(1)(4), Sch 15 para 1*].

Investee companies are limited to those with gross assets not exceeding £15 million immediately before the investment and £16 million immediately afterwards. Such companies must exist for the purpose of carrying on trading activities other than the kind of 'lower risk' activity excluded under the Enterprise Investment Scheme (see Tolley's Income Tax) or the provisions for venture capital trusts (62). Potential investee companies may request advance clearance from the Revenue. The maximum investment qualifying for relief is 30% of the issued ordinary share capital of the investee company, and no minimum investment is stipulated. It is a further condition that at least 20% of the ordinary share capital of the investee company be held by individuals (other than directors and employees of the investing company). To qualify for the relief, the investing company must retain the shares acquired for at least three years. Investing companies carrying on financial trades (e.g. banking, share dealing etc.) are not eligible.

The remainder of this chapter is set out under the following headings.

19.2 Investment relief
19.3 — Form of relief
19.4 — Claims for relief
19.5 Qualifying investing company
19.6 Qualifying issuing company
19.7 — Qualifying trades
19.8 General requirements
19.9 Advance clearance
19.10 Withdrawal or reduction of investment relief
19.11 — Disposal
19.12–19.14 — Value received by investing company
19.15 — Value received by other persons
19.16 — Put options and call options
19.17 Identification rules
19.18 Chargeable gains and allowable losses
19.19 — Computation of allowable loss
19.20 — Set-off of allowable loss against income
19.21 — Deferral relief
19.22 Company restructuring
19.23 — Company reconstructions and amalgamations
19.24 — Issuing company becoming wholly-owned subsidiary of new holding company

19.2 **INVESTMENT RELIEF**

Eligibility. An investing company is eligible for investment relief (see 19.3 below) in respect of an amount subscribed by it for shares in an investee company (the '*issuing company*') if:

(*a*) the shares (the '*relevant shares*') are issued to the investing company;

(*b*) the investing company is a 'qualifying investing company' (see 19.5 below);

(*c*) the issuing company is a 'qualifying issuing company' (see 19.6 below) in relation to the relevant shares; and

(*d*) the general requirements at 19.8 below are met.

For advance clearance as regards (*c*) and (*d*) above, see 19.9 below.

Qualification period. In these provisions, the '*qualification period*' is normally the three-year period beginning with the date of issue of the relevant shares. If, however, the money raised by the issue is employed wholly or mainly for the purposes of a qualifying trade (or trades) (see 19.7 below) which, on the date of issue, was not being carried on by the issuing company or a qualifying subsidiary (see 19.6 below), the qualification period begins on the date of issue and ends immediately before the third anniversary of the date of commencement of the trade (or the latest such date where there is more than one such trade).

[*FA 2000, Sch 15 paras 2, 3*].

19.3 **Form of relief.** Where an investing company is eligible for investment relief (see 19.2 above) in respect of amounts subscribed by it for shares, its corporation tax liability for the accounting period in which the shares are issued is reduced, on a claim (see 19.4 below), by the lesser of:

(*a*) 20% of the amount (or aggregate amount) subscribed; and

(*b*) the amount which reduces the liability to nil.

[*FA 2000, Sch 15 para 39*].

Investment relief is said to be 'attributable to shares' if relief as above has been obtained in respect of those shares and has not been withdrawn — see 19.10 below. Where for any one accounting period relief has been obtained by reason of more than one issue of shares, the relief is attributed to those issues in proportion to the amounts subscribed. Relief attributable to any one issue of shares is attributed *pro rata* to each share in that issue, and any reduction of relief (see 19.10 below) is similarly apportioned between the shares in question. For these purposes, any bonus shares, issued in respect of the original shares and being shares in the same company, of the same class and carrying the same rights, are treated as if comprised in the original issue, and relief is apportioned to them accordingly. This applies only if the original shares have been held continuously since issue (as in 19.20(*a*) below), and, where it does apply, the bonus shares are themselves treated as having been held continuously since the time of the original issue. [*FA 2000, Sch 15 para 45*].

19.4 **Claims for relief.** No deadline is specified for making a claim, so the general six-year time limit applies as in 12.2 claims. A claim for relief cannot be made in respect of any investment until the 'funded trade' has been carried on by the issuing company or a subsidiary for at least four months (disregarding time spent *preparing* to carry on the trade) and the investing company has received from the issuing company a 'compliance certificate' (see below). No postponement of tax pending appeal (see 48.3 payment of tax) can be made on the grounds of eligibility for investment relief until a claim for that relief can be and has been made. The '*funded trade*' is the trade or trades by reference to which the requirement at 19.8 below as to 'use of money raised' is met (or, where applicable, the notional trade of research and development therein mentioned). A claim *can* be made if the funded trade ceases within less than four months by reason of the winding-up or dissolution of the company or subsidiary concerned or its going into administration or receivership (both as defined), provided that this is for commercial reasons and not part of tax avoidance arrangements.

A '*compliance certificate*' is a certificate issued, with the authority of the Revenue and in such form as they may direct, by the issuing company in respect of the relevant shares and confirming that, from the issuing company's point of view, the requirements for investment relief are for the time being met in relation to the shares. To obtain authority for the issue of a certificate, the issuing company must provide the Revenue with a 'compliance statement' in respect of the issue of shares which includes the relevant shares. Where notice of an event giving rise to withdrawal etc. is given to the Revenue by or in relation to the issuing company (see 19.10 below), any authority already given is invalid unless renewed.

A '*compliance statement*' is a statement, in respect of an issue of shares, to the effect that, from the issuing company's point of view, the requirements for investment relief are for the time being met in relation to the shares and have been met at all times since the shares were issued. The statement must be in required form and must contain any additional information the Revenue reasonably require, a declaration that it is correct to the best of the company's knowledge and belief, and such other declarations as the Revenue reasonably require. A compliance statement cannot be made until such time as the funded trade has been carried on for at least four months (or such shorter time as is specified above). It *must* be made within two years after the end of the accounting period in which the shares were issued or, if later, two years after the minimum period of trading condition is satisfied.

The issuing company may give notice of appeal, within 30 days, against a Revenue refusal to authorise a compliance certificate (as if that refusal were the disallowance of a claim other than for discharge or repayment of tax — see 12.3 claims).

The issuing company is liable to a penalty of up to £3,000 for issuing a compliance certificate which is made fraudulently or negligently or without Revenue authority, or for making a compliance statement fraudulently or negligently.

[*FA 2000, Sch 15 paras 40–44, 102(4)*].

19.5 QUALIFYING INVESTING COMPANY

The investing company is a '*qualifying investing company*' (see 19.2(*b*) above) in relation to the relevant shares if it meets all the requirements below as to absence of material interest, reciprocal arrangements, control and tax avoidance, the nature of its activities, and the relevant shares being a chargeable asset. [*FA 2000, Sch 15 para 4*].

No material interest requirement. At no time in the qualification period (see 19.2 above) must the investing company have a material interest in the issuing company. For this purpose, a person has a material interest in a company if he (alone or together with any person connected with him (within *ICTA 1988, s 839*, see 16 connected persons)) directly or indirectly possesses, or is entitled (or will in future be entitled) to acquire (at present or at a future date), more than **30%** of

(*a*) the 'ordinary share capital' of, or

(*b*) the voting power in,

the company or any 51% subsidiary. In applying the test, there must be attributed to a person any rights or powers of any associate of his (as defined by *FA 2000, Sch 15 para 99*). For these purposes, a company's '*ordinary share capital*' comprises

(i) all of its issued share capital other than 'relevant preference shares', and

(ii) all of its loan capital (as widely defined but excluding a bank overdraft or an ordinary business debt) that carries a right to convert into, or to acquire, shares which would fall within (i) above.

'*Relevant preference shares*' are, broadly, non-voting, non-convertible shares issued for new consideration and carrying no right to dividends other than dividends which

(A) are of a fixed amount or at a rate which is fixed or which varies according to a standard published interest rate, a tax rate, a retail price index or an official share price index, and

(B) which are not dependent on the company's business results or asset values and do not represent more than a reasonable commercial return on the investment.

[*FA 2000, Sch 15 paras 5, 7, 9, 102(3)*].

No reciprocal arrangements requirement. The investing company's subscription for the relevant shares must not be part of any arrangements which provide for any other person to subscribe for shares in a 'related company'. A '*related company*' is a company in which the investing company, or any other person who is party to the arrangements, has a 'material interest' (as defined immediately above). Arrangements are disregarded to the extent that they provide for the issuing company to subscribe for shares in any qualifying subsidiary (see 19.6 below). [*FA 2000, Sch 15 para 6*].

No control requirement. At no time in the qualification period (see 19.2 above) must the investing company 'control' the issuing company. '*Control*' is determined in accordance with *ICTA 1988, s 416(2)–(6)* (see 13.2 close companies) as modified for this purpose. [*FA 2000, Sch 15 para 8*].

No tax avoidance requirement. The relevant shares must be subscribed for by the investing company for commercial reasons and not as part of a tax avoidance scheme or arrangement. [*FA 2000, Sch 15 para 14*].

Non-financial activities requirement. Throughout the qualification period (see 19.2 above), the investing company:

(*a*) if a '*single company*' (i.e. a company which is not a parent company or a 51% subsidiary), must exist wholly for the purpose of carrying on one or more 'non-financial trades'; and

(*b*) if a '*group company*' (i.e. a parent company and any of its subsidiaries), must be part of a 'non-financial trading group' and must either exist wholly for the purpose of carrying on one or more 'non-financial trades' or businesses other than trades or be the parent company of the group.

In determining the purpose for which a company exists, purposes having no significant effect (other than in relation to incidental matters) on the extent of the company's activities are disregarded. Purposes for which a company exists are also disregarded to the extent that they consist of:

(i) (as regards a single company) the holding and managing of property used by the company for one or more 'non-financial trades' carried on by it;

(ii) (as regards a group company) any activities within (I) or (II) below; or

(iii) (as regards any company) holding shares to which investment relief is attributable (see 19.3 above) unless the holding of such shares is a substantial part of the company's business.

A trade is a '*non-financial trade*' if

(A) it is conducted on a commercial basis and with a view to profit, and

(B) it does not consist, wholly or as to a substantial part, in the carrying on of 'financial activities'.

'*Financial activities*' include for this purpose:

(1) banking, or money-lending, carried on by a bank, building society or other person;

(2) debt factoring, finance-leasing or hire-purchase financing;

(3) insurance;

(4) dealing in shares, securities, currency, debts or other assets of a financial nature; and

(5) dealing in commodity or financial futures or options.

A group is a '*non-financial trading group*' unless the business of the group (treating the activities of the group companies, taken together, as a single business) consists, wholly or as to a substantial part, in the carrying on of trades other than non-financial trades (as above) and/or businesses other than trades. Activities of a group company are disregarded to the extent that they consist of:

(I) holding shares in or securities of, or making loans to, another group company;

(II) holding and managing property used by a group company for the purposes of one or more non-financial trades carried on by a group company; or

(III) holding shares to which investment relief is attributable (see 19.3 above), unless the holding of such shares is a substantial part of the company's business.

Amendments to the non-financial activities requirement may be made in the future by Treasury Order.

[*FA 2000, Sch 15 paras 10–12, 101, 102(1)*].

Requirement as to shares being a chargeable asset. The relevant shares must be a 'chargeable asset' of the investing company immediately after they are issued to it. For this purpose, an asset is a '*chargeable asset*' at a particular time if, on a disposal at that time, a gain would be a chargeable gain. [*FA 2000, Sch 15 para 13*].

19.6 QUALIFYING ISSUING COMPANY

The issuing company is a '*qualifying issuing company*' (see 19.2(*c*) above) in relation to the relevant shares if it meets all the requirements below as to unquoted status, independence, individual-owners, partnerships and joint ventures, qualifying subsidiaries, gross assets, and trading activities. [*FA 2000, Sch 15 para 15*].

Unquoted status requirement. At the time of issue of the relevant shares, none of the issuing company's shares, debentures or other securities must be listed on a recognised stock exchange or a 'designated' exchange outside the UK or be dealt in outside the UK by 'designated' means, and there must be no arrangements in existence for such a listing or such dealing. This applies whether or not the company is UK-resident. '*Designated*' means designated by order of the Board for the purposes of *ICTA 1988, s 312(1B)* (enterprise investment schemes, see Tolley's Income Tax). The company does not fail to meet the requirement simply because a designation order is made, or a stock exchange obtains recognition, after the time of issue of the shares.

If, at the time of issue of the relevant shares, arrangements are in existence for the issuing company to become a wholly-owned subsidiary of a new holding company by means of a share exchange within 19.24 below, there must be no arrangements made for any of the new company's shares, debentures or other securities to be listed or dealt in as above.

[*FA 2000, Sch 15 para 16*].

Independence requirement. At no time in the qualification period (see 19.2 above) must the issuing company be a 51% subsidiary of another company or otherwise under the control (within *ICTA 1988, s 840*) of another company or of another company and persons connected with it (within *ICTA 1988, s 839*, see 16 CONNECTED PERSONS). No arrangements must exist at any time during the qualification period whereby the company could become such a subsidiary or fall under such control (whether during that period or otherwise). Arrangements with a view to a company reconstruction within 19.24 below are disregarded for this purpose. [*FA 2000, Sch 15 paras 17, 102(3)*].

Individual-owners requirement. Throughout the qualification period (see 19.2 above), at least **20%** of the issued ordinary share capital of the issuing company must be beneficially owned by one or more 'independent individuals'. An '*independent individual*' is one who is not, at any time during the qualification period when he holds ordinary shares in the issuing company, a director or employee of the investing company or of any company connected with it (within *ICTA 1988, s 839*, see 16 CONNECTED PERSONS), or a relative (i.e. husband, wife, forebear or issue) of such a director or employee. Where an independent individual owned shares immediately prior to his death, they are treated for these purposes as continuing to be owned by an independent individual until they cease to form part of the deceased's estate. [*FA 2000, Sch 15 paras 18, 102(3)*].

Partnerships and joint ventures requirement. At no time in the qualification period (see 19.2 above) must the issuing company or any qualifying subsidiary (see below) be a member of a partnership or a party to a joint venture where:

(*a*) a trade by reference to which the trading activities requirement (see below) is met by the issuing company is being carried on, or is to be carried on, by the partners in partnership or, as the case may be, by the company or a qualifying subsidiary (see below) as a party to the joint venture;

(*b*) the other partners or parties to the joint venture include at least one other company; and

(*c*) the same person(s) is/are the beneficial owner(s) of more than 75% of the issued share capital or the ordinary share capital of both the issuing company and at least one of the other partners/parties.

For these purposes, there must be attributed to any person any share capital held by an associate of his (within *FA 2000, Sch 15 para 99*).

[*FA 2000, Sch 15 para 19*].

Qualifying subsidiaries requirement. At no time in the qualification period (see 19.2 above) must the issuing company have a 'subsidiary' other than a 'qualifying subsidiary'. For this purpose, a '*subsidiary*' of a company is any company which it controls (within *ICTA 1988, s 416(2)–(6)*, see 13.2 CLOSE COMPANIES), with or without the aid of CONNECTED PERSONS (16). A subsidiary is a '*qualifying subsidiary*' of another company (the '*relevant company*') if the following conditions are met:

(i) the relevant company, or another of its subsidiaries, possesses at least 75% of the issued share capital of, and the voting power in, the subsidiary, and is beneficially entitled to at least 75% of the assets available for distribution to shareholders on a winding-up etc. and of the profits available for distribution to shareholders;

(ii) no other person has control (within *ICTA 1988, s 840*) of the subsidiary; and

(iii) no arrangements exist whereby (i) or (ii) could cease to be satisfied (though see also below).

The fact that a subsidiary or another company is wound up or otherwise dissolved or goes into administration or receivership (both as defined) does not mean the subsidiary ceases to be a qualifying subsidiary, provided that the winding-up etc., and anything done as a consequence of administration or receivership, is for genuine commercial reasons and not part of a tax avoidance scheme or arrangements. Similarly, the fact that arrangements may exist to dispose of the entire interest held in the subsidiary does not prevent the subsidiary from being a qualifying subsidiary if the disposal is to be for commercial reasons and not part of a tax avoidance scheme or arrangements.

[*FA 2000, Sch 15 paras 20, 21, 102(3)(4)*].

Gross assets requirement. The value of the company's gross assets must not exceed £15 million immediately before the issue of the relevant shares or £16 million immediately afterwards. If the company is the parent company of a group, those limits apply by reference to the aggregate value of the gross assets of the group (disregarding certain assets held by any member of the group which correspond to liabilities of another member). The limits may be amended in the future by Treasury Order. [*FA 2000, Sch 15 paras 22, 101*].

See Revenue Pamphlet IR 131, SP 5/98 (referred to at 62.3(*e*) VENTURE CAPITAL TRUSTS) for the Revenue's approach to the gross assets requirement (in relation, at present, to other legislation but expected to be extended to the corporate venturing scheme).

Trading activities requirement. Throughout the qualification period (see 19.2 above), the issuing company must meet the trading activities requirement, which is as follows. If the company is a single company (i.e. neither the parent company of a group nor a 51% subsidiary), it must exist wholly for the purpose of carrying on one or more 'qualifying trades' (see 19.7 below) and must actually be carrying on such a trade or preparing to do so. Purposes having no significant effect (other than in relation to incidental matters) on the extent of the company's activities are disregarded.

If the company is a parent company, the business of the group (treating the activities of the group companies, taken together, as a single business) must not consist wholly or as to a substantial part in any 'non-qualifying activities', and at least one company in the group must satisfy the above trading activity requirement for a single company. '*Non-qualifying activities*' means 'excluded activities' (as in 19.7 below, and with similar exceptions in relation to the letting of ships and the receiving of royalties or licence fees) and non-trading activities.

Where the trading activities requirement would otherwise be met by reason of the issuing company or a subsidiary *preparing* to carry on a qualifying trade, the requirement is treated as not having been met at any time if that trade does not commence within two years after the issue of the relevant shares.

Purposes for which a company exists are disregarded to the extent that they consist of:

(A) (as regards a single company) the holding and managing of property used by the company for one or more qualifying trades carried on by it;

(B) (as regards a group company) any activities within (1), (2) or (4) below; or

(C) (as regards any company) holding shares to which investment relief is attributable (see 19.3 above), unless the holding of such shares is a substantial part of the company's business.

For the purposes of determining the business of a group, activities of a group company are disregarded to the extent that they consist of:

(1) holding shares in or securities of, or making loans to, another group company;

(2) holding and managing property used by a group company for the purposes of one or more qualifying trades carried on by a group company;

(3) holding shares to which investment relief is attributable (see 19.3 above), unless the holding of such shares is a substantial part of the company's business; or

(4) incidental activities of a company which meets the above trading activities requirement for a single company.

A company does not cease to meet the trading activities requirement purely by reason of it or a qualifying subsidiary (see above) being wound up or otherwise dissolved, provided that the winding-up or dissolution is for commercial reasons and not part of a tax avoidance scheme or arrangements. A similar let-out applies in relation to a company or its qualifying subsidiary going into administration or receivership (both as defined) and to anything done as a consequence thereof.

Amendments to the trading activities requirement (including the provisions at 19.7 below) may be made in the future by Treasury Order.
[*FA 2000, Sch 15 paras 23, 24, 101, 102(1)(4)*].

19.7 **Qualifying trades.** A trade is a '*qualifying trade*' (see the trading activities requirement at 19.6 above) if:

(i) it is carried on wholly or mainly in the UK;

(ii) it is conducted on a commercial basis and with a view to profit; and

(iii) it does not consist wholly or as to a substantial part in the carrying on of any 'excluded activities' (see below).

See Revenue Pamphlet IR 131, SP 7/98 (at 62.3(*b*) VENTURE CAPITAL TRUSTS) for the Revenue's approach to the requirement at (i) above (in relation, at present, to other legislation but expected to be extended to cover the corporate venturing scheme). 'Substantial' in (iii) above is not defined, but in its application to similar legislation is taken by the Revenue to mean 20% or more of total activities.

Activities of research and development (within *ICTA 1988, s 837A*, see 50.25 PROFIT COMPUTATIONS) from which it is intended that a 'connected qualifying trade' will be derived or will benefit are treated as a notional qualifying trade, but preparing to carry on such activities is not treated as preparing to carry on a qualifying trade. A '*connected qualifying trade*' is a qualifying trade carried on either by the company carrying out the research and development or, where applicable, by another member of the group.

'*Excluded activities*' are as follows:

(*a*) dealing in land, commodities or futures, or in shares, securities or other financial instruments;

(*b*) dealing in goods otherwise than in an ordinary trade of wholesale or retail distribution (for more detail, see the similar exclusion at 62.3(*b*) VENTURE CAPITAL TRUSTS);

(*c*) banking, insurance, money-lending, debt-factoring, hire-purchase financing or other financial activities;

(*d*) leasing or receiving royalties or licence fees (see further below);

(*e*) providing legal or accountancy services;

(*f*) property development (as defined);

(*g*) farming or market gardening;

(*h*) holding, managing or occupying woodlands, any other forestry activities or timber production;

(*j*) operating or managing hotels or comparable establishments (including guest houses, hostels and other establishments whose main purpose is to offer overnight accommodation with or without catering) or property used as such (see further below);

(*k*) operating or managing nursing homes or residential care homes (both as defined) or property used as such (see further below);

(*l*) providing services or facilities for any business consisting to a substantial extent of activities within (*a*)–(*k*) above and carried on by another person, where a person has a controlling interest (see below) in both that business and the business of the provider company.

The term 'leasing' in (*d*) above includes the letting of ships on charter or other assets on hire. A trade will be not be excluded by reason only of its consisting of letting ships, other than oil rigs or pleasure craft (both as defined), on charter, provided certain conditions are satisfied.

As regards the receiving of royalties or licence fees (see (*d*) above), a trade is not excluded from being a qualifying trade solely because at some time in the qualification period (see 19.2 above) it consists to a substantial extent in the receiving of royalties or licence fees substantially attributable (in terms of value) to the exploitation of intangible assets, such as intellectual property, which have been created by the company carrying on the trade or by a fellow group company — for more details, see the similar let-out at 62.3(*b*) VENTURE CAPITAL TRUSTS.

The exclusions at (*j*) and (*k*) above apply only if the person carrying on the activity has an estate or interest (e.g. a lease) in the property concerned or occupies that property.

As regards (*l*) above, see the comparable exclusion at 62.3(*b*) VENTURE CAPITAL TRUSTS as regards the meaning of 'controlling interest', which applies similarly here, though without the modifications there mentioned to *ICTA 1988, s 416*.

[*FA 2000, Sch 15 paras 25–33, 102(1)*].

19.8 **GENERAL REQUIREMENTS**

For investment relief to be available in respect of the relevant shares (see 19.2 above), the following requirements (see 19.2(*d*) above) must be met as to the shares, the use of money raised by the issue, the absence of pre-arranged exits and the absence of a tax avoidance motive. [*FA 2000, Sch 15 para 34*].

The shares. The relevant shares must be ordinary, fully paid up, shares and must be subscribed for wholly in cash. Shares are not fully paid up for this purpose if there is any undertaking to pay cash to the issuing company at a future date. At no time in the qualification period (see 19.2 above) must the shares carry any present or future preferential right to dividends or to assets on a winding-up, or any present or future right to be redeemed. [*FA 2000, Sch 15 para 35*].

Use of money raised. The money raised by the 'relevant issue of shares' must be employed wholly (disregarding any insignificant amount) for the purposes of a 'relevant trade' not later than:

(*a*) the end of the 12 months beginning with the date of issue; or

(*b*) if later, the end of the 12 months beginning when the issuing company or a subsidiary begins to carry on the relevant trade.

For these purposes, employing money for the purposes of *preparing* to carry on a trade (other than a notional trade of research and development — see 19.7 above) is equivalent to employing it for the purposes of a trade.

The '*relevant issue of shares*' means the issue of shares which includes the relevant shares. A '*relevant trade*' is a trade by reference to which the issuing company meets the trading activities requirement in 19.6 above. Where the trade by reference to which the trading activities requirement is met is a notional trade of research and development (see 19.7 above), the term 'relevant trade' also refers to any qualifying trade which is derived or benefits from that notional trade and is carried on by the issuing company or a qualifying subsidiary (see 19.6 above); in this case, the money raised by the issue must be employed for the purposes of that trade before the third anniversary of the date of issue of the shares, notwithstanding that a later date may be given by (*b*) above.

[*FA 2000, Sch 15 para 36*].

No pre-arranged exits. The arrangements (as very broadly defined) under which the relevant shares are issued to the investing company (including arrangements preceding the issue but relating to it and, in certain cases, arrangements made on or after the issue and within the qualification period) must not:

- (i) provide for the eventual disposal by the investing company of the relevant shares or other shares or securities of the issuing company;
- (ii) provide for the eventual cessation of a trade of the issuing company or a person connected with it;
- (iii) provide for the eventual disposal of all, or a substantial part of, the assets of the issuing company or of a person connected with it; or
- (iv) provide (by means of any insurance, indemnity, guarantee or otherwise) partial or complete protection for investors against the normal risks attaching to the investment (but excluding commercial arrangements which merely protect the issuing company and/or its subsidiaries against normal business risks).

Arrangements with a view to a company reconstruction within 19.24 below are excluded from (i) above. Arrangements applicable only on an unanticipated winding-up of the issuing company for commercial reasons are excluded from (ii) and (iii) above.

[*FA 2000, Sch 15 paras 37, 102(1)*].

No tax avoidance motive. The relevant shares must be issued for commercial reasons and not as part of a tax avoidance scheme or arrangement. [*FA 2000, Sch 15 para 38*].

19.9 ADVANCE CLEARANCE

A *potential* qualifying issuing company (see 19.6 above) may apply to the Board for an advance clearance notice in respect of an issue of shares. An application must contain particulars, declarations and undertakings as required and must disclose all material facts and circumstances. An advance clearance notice states that, on the basis of the particulars etc. provided by the applicant, the Revenue are satisfied that, at the time the shares are issued, the requirements of 19.6–19.8 above will be met (or, in the case of a requirement that can only be met in the future, will for the time being be met).

Within 30 days after receiving an application (or within 30 days after an 'information notice' is complied with), the Board must either issue an information notice (or further information notice), issue an advance clearance notice, or refuse the application. An '*information notice*' is a notice requiring further particulars to be provided within such time, not being less than 30 days, as is stated therein. If the applicant fails to comply timeously with an information notice, the Board need not proceed further with the application. If the shares in question are issued before the advance clearance notice is given or the application refused, then again the Board need not proceed further.

Within 30 days after a refusal of an application, or a failure to give a decision, the applicant can require the Board to transmit the application, together with any information notices given and further particulars provided, to the Special Commissioners, whose approval, if given, has effect as if it were an advance clearance notice given by the Revenue.

An advance clearance notice is rendered void if it transpires that any particulars provided did not fully and accurately disclose all facts and circumstances material for the decision, or if the applicant or any subsidiary (including any new subsidiary) fails to act in accordance with any declaration or undertaking given as part of the application.

[*FA 2000, Sch 15 paras 89–92*].

19.10 WITHDRAWAL OR REDUCTION OF INVESTMENT RELIEF

Investment relief falls to be withdrawn or reduced on a disposal of the relevant shares (see 19.11 below), if value is received in respect of the shares (see 19.12–19.15 below), or on the grant of certain options relating to the shares (see 19.16 below).

Where investment relief given falls to be withdrawn or reduced, and also where it is found not to have been due, the withdrawal etc. is achieved by means of an assessment under Schedule D, Case VI for the accounting period of the investing company *in which the relief was given*. For relief to be withdrawn on the grounds that the issuing company is not a qualifying issuing company (see 19.6 above), or that the general requirements at 19.8 above are not met, or by virtue of value received by the investing company (see 19.12 below) or other persons (see 19.15 below), certain statutory notice procedures must be followed. The investing company may give notice of appeal, within 30 days, against a Revenue notice pending withdrawal of relief on such grounds (as if the giving of that notice were the disallowance of a claim other than for discharge or repayment of tax — see 12.3 CLAIMS).

The Revenue cannot make an assessment to withdraw (or reduce) investment relief, or give statutory notice pending withdrawal of relief on the above-mentioned grounds, more than six years after the end of whichever is the later of the following accounting periods:

(*a*) the accounting period in which falls the deadline for employing money raised by the issue of the shares (see 19.8 above); and

(*b*) the accounting period in which occurs the event giving rise to withdrawal (or reduction) of relief.

The above is subject to the extended time limit for assessments in cases of fraud or negligence (see 55.8 SELF-ASSESSMENT).

In most cases, interest on overdue tax runs from the date of the event giving rise to withdrawal (or reduction) of relief, if this is later than the normal due date, or the latest such date, for payment of corporation tax for the accounting period for which the assessment is made (see 48.1 PAYMENT OF TAX).

[*FA 2000, Sch 15 paras 60–63*].

Information. Certain events giving rise to withdrawal or reduction of investment relief must be notified to the Revenue, generally within 60 days, by the investing company or the issuing company (or any person connected with the issuing company and having knowledge of the matter), as the case may be. The Revenue have power to require information from such persons where they have reason to believe that such notice should have been given or from a person whom they believe to have given or received value which would have triggered a requirement to give such notice but for the amount of value being insignificant (see 19.12 below). The penalty provisions of *TMA 1970, s 98* apply in the event of non-compliance with these information provisions. [*FA 2000, Sch 15 paras 64–66, Sch 16 para 1*].

19.11 **Disposal.** Where, during the qualification period (see 19.2 above), the investing company disposes of any shares to which relief is attributable (see 19.3 above) and which it has held continuously since their issue (see 19.20(*a*) below), relief is withdrawn or reduced as set out below. See 19.10 above re consequences of withdrawal etc..

If the disposal is either

(*a*) by way of bargain at arm's length for full consideration, or

(*b*) by way of a distribution on a dissolution or winding-up of the issuing company, or

(c) a disposal within *TCGA 1992, s 24(1)* (entire loss, destruction etc. of asset), or

(d) a deemed disposal under *TCGA 1992, s 24(2)* (assets of negligible value),

the relief attributable to the shares disposed of is withdrawn, or is reduced by 20% of the disposal consideration (if such reduction would not amount to full withdrawal). If the relief initially obtained was less than 20% of the amount subscribed for those shares (i.e. because the company's corporation tax liability was insufficient to fully absorb the available relief), the reduction is correspondingly restricted.

In the case of any other disposal, for example a transaction not at arm's length, the relief attributable to the shares disposed of is withdrawn.

[*FA 2000, Sch 15 para 46*].

For the above purposes, shares are regarded as being disposed of if they are so regarded for the purposes of corporation tax on chargeable gains, and see also 19.23 below (certain company reconstructions and amalgamations treated as disposals). [*FA 2000, Sch 15 para 96*]. In the case of a part disposal, see 19.17 below for the rules for identifying shares disposed of.

19.12 **Value received by investing company.** Subject to 19.14 below (replacement value), where during the 'period of restriction' the investing company 'receives value' (see 19.13 below), other than an 'amount of insignificant value', from the issuing company, investment relief attributable to the relevant shares is withdrawn, or is reduced by 20% of the amount of value received (if such reduction would not amount to full withdrawal). If the relief initially obtained was less than 20% of the amount subscribed for those shares (i.e. because the company's corporation tax liability was insufficient to fully absorb the available relief), the reduction is correspondingly restricted. These provisions apply equally to receipts of value by and from persons connected (within *ICTA 1988, s 839*, see 16 CONNECTED PERSONS), at any time in the period of restriction, with the investing company or, as the case may be, the issuing company. See 19.13 below for the meaning of 'value received' and the determination of the amount of value received. See 19.10 above re consequences of withdrawal etc..

The '*period of restriction*' in relation to the relevant shares is the period beginning one year before their issue and ending at the end of the qualification period in 19.2 above.

Where two or more issues of shares have been made by the same issuing company to the same investing company, in relation to each of which investment relief is claimed, and value is received during a period of restriction relating to more than one such issue, the value received is apportioned between them by reference to the amounts subscribed for each of those issues.

An '*amount of insignificant value*' is an amount of value which:

(*a*) does not exceed £1,000; or

(*b*) is insignificant in relation to the amount subscribed by the investing company for the relevant shares.

If at any time in the period beginning one year before the date of issue of the relevant shares and ending with the date of issue, there are in existence arrangements (as very broadly defined) providing for the investing company to receive, or become entitled to receive, any value from the issuing company at any time in the period of restriction (see above), no amount of value received by the investing company is treated as an amount of insignificant value.

There are provisions to aggregate a receipt of value, whether insignificant or not, with amounts of insignificant value received previously, and treating that aggregate, if it is not itself an amount of insignificant value, as an amount of value received at the time of the latest actual receipt.

Where relief is withdrawn or reduced by reason of a disposal (see 19.11 above), the investing company is not treated as receiving value from the issuing company in respect of the disposal.

[*FA 2000, Sch 15 paras 47, 48, 51–53, 102(1)*].

19.13 *Meaning of, and amount of, value received.* The investing company '*receives value*' from the issuing company if the latter (and see 19.12 above re connected persons):

(*a*) repays, redeems or repurchases any part of the investing company's holding of the issuing company's share capital or securities, or makes any payment to the investing company in respect of the cancellation of any of the issuing company's share capital or any security;

(*b*) repays, in pursuance of any arrangements for or in connection with the acquisition of the relevant shares, any debt owed to the investing company other than one incurred by the issuing company on or after the date of issue of the shares and otherwise than in consideration of the extinguishment of a debt incurred before that date;

(*c*) makes any payment to the investing company in respect of the cancellation of any debt owed to it;

(*d*) releases or waives any liability of the investing company to the issuing company (which it is deemed to have done if discharge of the liability is twelve months or more overdue) or discharges, or undertakes to discharge, any liability of the investing company to a third person;

(*e*) makes a loan or advance to the investing company which has not been repaid in full before the issue of the relevant shares; for this purpose a loan includes any debt incurred, other than an ordinary trade debt (as defined), and any debt due to a third person which is assigned to the issuing company;

(*f*) provides a benefit or facility for the directors or employees of the investing company or any of their associates (as defined), except in circumstances such that, if a *payment* had been made of equal value, it would have been a 'qualifying payment';

(*g*) disposes of an asset to the investing company for no consideration or for consideration less than market value (as defined), or acquires an asset from the investing company for consideration exceeding market value; or

(*h*) makes a payment to the investing company other than a 'qualifying payment'.

References above to a debt or liability do not include one which would be discharged by making a 'qualifying payment'. References to a payment or disposal include one made indirectly to, or to the order of, or for the benefit of, the person in question.

Each of the following is a '*qualifying payment*':

(i) a reasonable (in relation to their market value) payment for any goods, services or facilities provided by the investing company in the course of trade or otherwise;

(ii) the payment of interest at no more than a reasonable commercial rate on money lent;

(iii) the payment of a dividend or other distribution which represents no more than a normal return on investment;

(iv) a payment to acquire an asset at no more than its market value;

(v) a payment not exceeding a reasonable and commercial rent for property occupied; and

(vi) a payment discharging an ordinary trade debt.

The *amount of value received* is:

(A) in a case within (*a*), (*b*) or (*c*) above, the amount received or, if greater, the market value of the shares, securities or debt in question;

(B) in a case within (*d*) above, the amount of the liability;

(C) in a case within (*e*) above, the amount of the loan etc. less any amount repaid before the issue of the relevant shares;

(D) in a case within (*f*) above, the cost (net of any consideration given for it by the recipient or his associate) of providing the benefit etc.;

(E) in a case within (*g*) above, the difference between market value and the consideration received (if any); and

(F) in a case within (*h*) above, the amount of the payment.

[*FA 2000, Sch 15 paras 49, 50, 99, 102(5)*].

19.14 *Replacement value.* The provisions at 19.12 above are disapplied if the person from whom the value was received (the '*original supplier*') receives, by way of a 'qualifying receipt' and whether before or after the original receipt of value, at least equivalent replacement value from the original recipient. A receipt is a '*qualifying receipt*' if it arises by reason of:

(*a*) a payment by the original recipient to the original supplier other than a qualifying payment as in 19.13 above or a payment for any shares or securities in any company in circumstances not within (*c*) below;

(*b*) (where the original receipt of value falls within 19.13(*d*) above) an event having the effect of reversing the original event; or

(*c*) (where the original receipt of value falls within 19.13(*g*) above) the acquisition of an asset by the original recipient from the original supplier for consideration exceeding market value (as defined), or the disposal of an asset by the original recipient to the original supplier for no consideration or for consideration less than market value.

The amount of replacement value is:

(i) in a case within (*a*) above, the amount of the payment;

(ii) in a case within (*b*) above, the same as the amount of the original value; and

(iii) in a case within (*c*) above, the difference between market value and the consideration received (if any).

The receipt of replacement value is disregarded if:

(A) it occurs before the start of the period of restriction (see 19.12 above);

(B) there was an unreasonable delay in its occurrence; or

(C) it occurs more than 60 days after the relief falling to be withdrawn (or reduced) has been determined on appeal.

Where

(1) the receipt of replacement value is a qualifying receipt (as above), and

(2) the event giving rise to the receipt is (or includes) a subscription for shares by the investing company or a person connected (within *ICTA 1988, s 839*, see 16 CONNECTED PERSONS) with it at any time in the period of restriction,

the subscriber is not eligible for investment relief, enterprise investment scheme income tax relief (see Tolley's Income Tax) or enterprise investment scheme capital gains deferral relief (see Tolley's Capital Gains Tax) in relation to those shares or any other shares in the same issue.

[*FA 2000, Sch 15 paras 54, 55, 102(3)(5)*].

19.15 **Value received by other persons.** Investment relief is withdrawn (or reduced) in certain cases of value received by persons other than the investing company (see 19.10 above re consequences of withdrawal etc.). This applies where, during the period of restriction (as in 19.12 above), the issuing company or a 'subsidiary':

(*a*) repays, redeems or repurchases any part of its share capital from a member (other than the investing company) who does not thereby suffer a withdrawal or reduction of any investment relief, enterprise investment scheme income tax relief (see Tolley's Income Tax) or enterprise investment scheme capital gains deferral relief (see Tolley's Capital Gains Tax) attributable to his shares; or

(*b*) makes any payment to any such member in respect of the cancellation or extinguishment of any of the share capital of the issuing company or subsidiary.

The investment relief attributable to the relevant shares held by the investing company is withdrawn, or is reduced by 20% of the amount received by the member (if such reduction would not amount to full withdrawal). If the relief initially obtained was less than 20% of the amount subscribed for those shares (i.e. because the company's corporation tax liability was insufficient to fully absorb the available relief), the reduction is correspondingly restricted. The amount received is also apportioned between investing companies (by reference to amounts subscribed) where the receipt of value causes a withdrawal or reduction of more than one such company's investment relief. Where the receipt of value falls into overlapping periods of restriction in relation to more than one issue of shares which includes shares to which investment relief is attributable, the value received is similarly apportioned between issues.

If the amount received by the member in question is insignificant in relation to the remaining share capital of the issuing company or, as the case may be, subsidiary, it is disregarded. In applying this test, the market value, immediately before the event concerned, of the shares to which the event relates is substituted for the amount received if this would give a greater amount. The assumption is made that the shares in question are cancelled at the time of the event. This let-out does not apply if at any time in the period beginning one year before the date of issue of the relevant shares and ending with the date of issue, there are in existence arrangements (as very broadly defined) providing for a payment within these provisions to be made, or entitlement to such a payment to come into being, at any time in the period of restriction.

For the above purposes, a '*subsidiary*' is a company which is a 51% subsidiary of the issuing company at any time in the period of restriction, whether or not at the time of receipt of value.

The above provisions do not apply to the redemption, within twelve months of issue, of any share capital of nominal value equal to the authorised minimum issued to comply with *Companies Act 1985, s 117* (or NI equivalent).

[*FA 2000, Sch 15 paras 56–58, 102(1)*].

19.16 **Put options and call options.** Where there is granted during the qualification period (see 19.2 above)

(*a*) an option, the exercise of which would bind the grantor to purchase any of the relevant shares from the investing company, or

(*b*) an option, the exercise of which would bind the grantor, in this case the investing company, to sell any of the relevant shares,

investment relief attributable (see 19.3 above) to those of the relevant shares which would (on given assumptions) be treated as disposed of on exercise of the option is withdrawn. See 19.10 above re consequences of withdrawal.

[*FA 2000, Sch 15 para 59*].

19.17 IDENTIFICATION RULES

The rules below apply, for the purpose of identifying shares disposed of, where a company makes a part disposal of a holding of shares of the same class in the same company, and the holding includes shares to which investment relief is attributable (see 19.3 above) and which have been held continuously (see 19.20(*a*) below) since the time of issue. The rules apply for the purposes of the corporate venturing scheme and for the purposes of corporation tax on chargeable gains generally. As regards the latter, the normal rules (see Tolley's Capital Gains Tax under Shares and Securities) are disapplied.

Where shares comprised in the holding have been acquired on different days, a disposal is identified with acquisitions on a first in/first out basis. In matching the shares disposed of with shares acquired on a particular day, shares to which investment relief is attributable and which have been held continuously are treated as being disposed of *after* any other shares acquired on that day.

If, on a reorganisation of share capital (e.g. a scrip issue), a new holding falls, by virtue of *TCGA 1992, s 127*, to be equated with the original shares (see Tolley's Capital Gains Tax under Shares and Securities, and see also 19.22 below), shares comprised in the new holding are deemed for the above purposes to have been acquired when the original shares were acquired.

[*FA 2000, Sch 15 para 93*].

19.18 CHARGEABLE GAINS AND ALLOWABLE LOSSES

A gain on the disposal at any time by the investing company of shares to which investment relief is attributable (see 19.3 above) is a chargeable gain, though see 19.21 below as regards possibility of deferral relief. A loss on such a disposal is an allowable loss — see 19.19 below as to the computation of the loss and 19.20 below as regards possibility of setting the loss against income rather than gains. For the rules for identifying disposals with acquisitions, see 19.17 above.

19.19 **Computation of allowable loss.** If a loss would otherwise accrue on a disposal by the investing company of shares to which investment relief is attributable, and the investment relief does not fall to be withdrawn (as opposed to reduced) as a result of the disposal (see 19.10 above), the company's acquisition cost for the purposes of corporation tax on chargeable gains is reduced by the amount of investment relief attributable to the shares immediately after the disposal, but not so as to convert the loss into a chargeable gain. This applies only if the condition at 19.20(*a*) below (shares held continuously) is met from issue to disposal. [*FA 2000, Sch 15 para 94*].

19.20 **Set-off of allowable loss against income.** Subject to all the conditions at (*a*)–(*c*) below being satisfied and a claim being made, an allowable loss, on a disposal by the investing company of shares to which investment relief is attributable (see 19.3 above), may be set against *income* (as an alternative to setting it against chargeable gains in the normal way — see 9.3 CAPITAL GAINS). The loss is as computed after applying the reduction at 19.19 above. The conditions are as follows.

(*a*) The shares must have been held continuously by the company from time of issue to time of disposal. If, during any period,

  (i) the company was deemed under any provision of *TCGA 1992* to have disposed of and immediately reacquired the shares, or

  (ii) following a scheme of reconstruction or amalgamation within *TCGA 1992, s 136* (or which would have been within that *section* but for the provisions of *TCGA 1992, s 137(1)*, which excludes schemes effected other than for *bona fide* commercial reasons or for tax avoidance), the company was deemed by virtue of 19.23 below to have made a disposal of shares which it retained under the scheme,

  it is not treated for the purposes of the corporate venturing scheme provisions as having held the shares continuously throughout that period.

(*b*) The investment relief must not fall to be withdrawn in full as a result of the disposal.

(*c*) The disposal must be either:

  (i) by way of bargain at arm's length for full consideration; or

  (ii) by way of a distribution on a dissolution or winding-up of the issuing company; or

  (iii) a disposal within *TCGA 1992, s 24(1)* (entire loss, destruction etc. of asset); or

  (iv) a deemed disposal under *TCGA 1992, s 24(2)* (assets of negligible value).

The set-off is against income of the accounting period in which the loss is incurred. As regards any unrelieved balance, the claim may be extended to income of accounting periods ending within the 12 months immediately preceding the accounting period in which the loss is incurred. Income of an accounting period beginning before, and ending within, that 12 months is apportioned on a time basis so as to exclude income thereby deemed to have accrued prior to that 12-month period. The income of each accounting period included in the claim is treated as reduced by the loss, or by so much of it as cannot be relieved in a later accounting period. Losses of earlier accounting periods are relieved in priority to those of later periods. Relief is given before any relief claimed under *ICTA 1988, s 573* (loss incurred by investment company on disposal of unlisted shares — see 44.19 LOSSES) and before any deduction for charges on income or other amounts which may be deducted from or set against or treated as reducing profits of any description. Once relief has been obtained under these provisions for an amount of loss, that amount cannot be relieved under *section 573(2)* or against chargeable gains.

Claims must be made within two years after the end of the accounting period in which the loss is incurred.

Where a claim is made under these provisions, *TCGA 1992, s 30* (value shifting to give tax-free benefit, see 9.13 CAPITAL GAINS) has effect in relation to the disposal if *any* benefit is conferred, whether tax-free or not. No loss relief against income is available if the disposal is the result of a company reconstruction or amalgamation effected for tax avoidance rather than commercial reasons.

[*FA 2000, Sch 15 paras 67–72, 97*].

19.21 **Deferral relief** is available where a chargeable gain would otherwise accrue to the investing company

(*a*) on a disposal of shares to which investment relief was attributable (see 19.3 above) immediately before the disposal and which satisfy the condition at 19.20(*a*) above (shares held continuously) from issue to disposal, or

(*b*) on the occurrence of a chargeable event under these provisions (see below),

and the company makes a 'qualifying investment'. A '*qualifying investment*' is a subscription for shares ('*qualifying shares*') on which investment relief is obtained under the corporate venturing scheme, other than shares issued by a 'prohibited company'. The qualifying shares must be issued to the investing company within the one year immediately preceding or the three years immediately following the time the chargeable gain in question accrues. If the qualifying shares are issued *before* the gain accrues, they must have been held continuously (see 19.20(*a*) above) by the investing company from issue until the time the gain accrues, and investment relief must still be attributable to them. A '*prohibited company*' means either:

(i) the company whose shares are disposed of (as in (*a*) above) or, or as the case may be, in relation to whose shares the chargeable event occurred (as in (*b*) above); or

(ii) a company which, when the gain accrues or when the qualifying shares are issued, is a member of the same group as the company in (i) above.

Deferral relief is said to be 'attributable to shares' if expenditure on those shares has been used to defer the whole or part of a chargeable gain and no chargeable event has occurred resulting in the deferred gain being brought back into charge.

The following themselves become qualifying shares:

(A) any bonus shares, issued in respect of the qualifying shares and being shares in the same company, of the same class and carrying the same rights;

(B) any shares issued on a company reconstruction within 19.24 below in exchange for qualifying shares.

Postponement of the original gain. On a claim by the investing company, the whole or part of the chargeable gain can be deferred. The amount to be deferred is the lower of :

(I) the amount of the gain (or the amount remaining in charge after any previous deferral relief claim);

(II) the amount subscribed for the qualifying shares (to the extent that it has not been used in previous deferral relief claims); and

(III) the amount specified by the company in the claim.

No time limit is specified for making a claim, so the general six-year time limit applies as in 12.2 CLAIMS.

Deferred gain becoming chargeable. The deferred gain will become chargeable on the occurrence of, *and at the time of*, one of the following chargeable events:

(1) a disposal of qualifying shares by the investing company; or

(2) any other event giving rise to a withdrawal of, or reduction in, the investment relief attributable to qualifying shares (see 19.10 above).

If the qualifying investment is made before the gain accrues, there is disregarded for the purposes of (2) above any reduction made by reason of an event occurring before the gain accrues.

The chargeable gain accruing to the investing company at the time of the chargeable event is equal to so much of the deferred gain as is attributable to the shares in relation to which the chargeable event occurs. For these purposes, a proportionate part of the net deferred gain (i.e. the deferred gain less any amount brought into charge on an earlier chargeable event, e.g. a part disposal) is attributed to each of the qualifying shares held immediately before the chargeable event. Thus, a part disposal of qualifying shares brings into charge a proportionate part of the deferred gain.

Provision is made to ensure that a previously deferred gain accruing as above is brought into charge under *TCGA 1992, s 10* (see 53.4 RESIDENCE) in the case of a non-UK resident company carrying on a trade or vocation through a UK branch or agency.

[*FA 2000, Sch 15 paras 73–79*].

19.22 COMPANY RESTRUCTURING

Reorganisations of share capital. The following applies where a company holds shares in another company, being shares of the same class, held in the same capacity and forming part of the ordinary share capital of that other company, and there is a reorganisation within the meaning of *TCGA 1992, s 126*. If the shares fall within two or more of the categories below, *TCGA 1992, s 127*, or, where appropriate, *TCGA 1992, s 116*, applies separately to each category. (This is subject to the disapplication of those provisions in the circumstances set out below.) The categories are:

(*a*) shares to which deferral relief is attributable (see 19.21 above);

(*b*) shares to which investment relief, but not deferral relief, is attributable (see 19.3 above) and which have been held continuously (see 19.20(*a*) above) by the company since they were issued; and

(*c*) shares in neither of the categories above.

[*FA 2000, Sch 15 para 80*].

Rights issues etc.. Where

(i) a reorganisation (within *TCGA 1992, s 126*) involves an allotment of shares or debentures in respect of and in proportion to an existing holding,

(ii) investment relief is attributable (see 19.3 above) to the shares in the existing holding or to the allotted shares, and

(iii) if investment relief is attributable to the shares in the existing holding, those shares have been held continuously (see 19.20(*a*) above) by the company since they were issued,

the share reorganisation rules of *TCGA 1992, ss 127–130* are disapplied. The effect is that the allotted shares are treated as a separate holding acquired at the time of the reorganisation. This does not apply in the case of bonus shares where these are issued in respect of shares comprised in the existing holding and are of the same class and carry the same rights as those shares.

If, in a case otherwise within *TCGA 1992, s 116(10)* (see Tolley's Capital Gains Tax under Qualifying Corporate Bonds),

(A) the old asset consists of shares to which investment relief is attributable and which have been held continuously (see 19.20(*a*) above) by the company since they were issued, and

(B) the new asset consists of a qualifying corporate bond,

the usual treatment is disapplied. The effect is that the investing company is deemed to have disposed of the shares at the time of the relevant transaction, and the resulting chargeable gain or allowable loss crystallises *at that time.*

[*FA 2000, Sch 15 para 81*].

19.23 **Company reconstructions and amalgamations.** Subject to 19.24 below, *TCGA 1992, s 135* (exchange of securities for those in another company) and *s 136* (schemes of reconstruction or amalgamation involving issue of securities), which equate the new holding with the original shares, are disapplied in the following circumstances:

(a) a company holds shares in another company (Company A);

(*b*) investment relief is attributable (see 19.3 above) to those shares;

(*c*) those shares have been held continuously (see 19.20(*a*) above) by the investing company since they were issued; and

(*d*) there is a reconstruction or amalgamation whereby a third company issues shares or debentures in exchange for, or in respect of, Company A shares or debentures.

The result is that the transaction is treated, both for the purposes of the corporate venturing scheme provisions and for the purposes of corporation tax on chargeable gains generally, as a disposal of the original shares (and an acquisition of a new holding).

[*FA 2000, Sch 15 paras 82, 96*].

19.24 **Issuing company becoming wholly-owned subsidiary of new holding company.** Notwithstanding 19.23 above, *TCGA 1992, s 135* is not disapplied (and there is thus no disposal and acquisition) where, by means entirely of an exchange of shares, all the shares in one company (the '*old shares*') are acquired by another company, and the conditions below are satisfied. Following such a share exchange, the shares thereby issued by the acquiring company (the '*new shares*') stand in place of the old shares, so that:

(i) any investment relief or deferral relief attributable to the old shares (see, respectively, 19.3, 19.21 above) is attributed to the new shares for which they were exchanged;

(ii) the new shares are treated as having been issued at the time the old shares were issued and as having been held continuously (see 19.20(*a*) above) by the investing company since that time (provided the old shares had been so held);

(iii) generally speaking, anything done, or required to be done, by or in relation to the acquired company is treated as having been done etc. by or in relation to the acquiring company; and

(iv) certain of the requirements of 19.5, 19.6 above which were met to any extent in relation to the old shares are deemed to be met to the same extent in relation to the new shares.

The conditions to be satisfied are as follows.

(*a*) The consideration for the old shares consists entirely of the issue of the new shares.

(*b*) New shares are issued only at a time when the issued shares in the acquiring company consist entirely of subscriber shares (and any new shares already issued in consideration of old shares).

(*c*) The consideration for new shares of each description consists entirely of old shares of the 'corresponding description'.

(*d*) New shares of each description are issued to holders of old shares of the 'corresponding description' in respect of, and in proportion to, their holdings.

(*e*) Before any exchange of shares takes place, the Revenue have given an 'approval notification'.

For the purposes of (*c*) and (*d*) above, old and new shares are of a '*corresponding description*' if, assuming they were shares in the same company, they would be of the same class and carry the same rights. All references above to 'shares' (other than to 'subscriber shares') include references to 'securities'. An '*approval notification*' (see (*e*) above) is given by the Revenue, on an application by either company involved, if they are satisfied that the share exchange will be effected for commercial reasons and does not form part of a scheme or arrangements to avoid liability to corporation tax or capital gains tax.

The provisions of *FA 2000, Sch 15 para 80* (see 19.22 above) are applied to a reconstruction within the above provisions where a company's holding of 'old shares' falls within more than one of the categories there mentioned.

[*FA 2000, Sch 15 paras 83–87*].

20 Distributions

Cross-references. See 7.6 BUILDING SOCIETIES, 26 FOREIGN INCOME DIVIDENDS, 29 GROUPS OF COMPANIES and 51 PURCHASE BY A COMPANY OF ITS OWN SHARES.

Simon's Direct Tax Service D1.1.

The headings in this chapter are as follows.

20.1 Scope of distributions
20.2 — dividends
20.3 — any distribution in respect of shares
20.4 — issue of redeemable share capital or any security
20.5 — interest or other distribution exceeding a reasonable commercial return
20.6 — interest or other distribution paid by 75% subsidiary
20.7 — interest in respect of certain securities
20.9 — transfer of assets or liabilities
20.10 — repayment of share capital followed by bonus issue
20.11 — repayment of share capital
20.12 — 'new consideration'
20.13 — 'shares'
20.14 — 'security'
20.15 — 'in respect of' shares
20.16 Items not treated as distributions
20.17 Effect of distribution
20.18 Qualifying and non-qualifying distributions
20.19 Close companies — additional distributions
20.20 — benefits to participators and their associates
20.21 — example
20.22 Mutual and non-trading companies
20.23 Friendly societies

20.1 **SCOPE OF DISTRIBUTIONS**

The term 'distribution' is widely defined in *ICTA 1988, ss 209–211*. Subject to the exceptions listed at 20.16 below, it includes any of the items listed at 20.2 to 20.11 below. See also the additional items at 20.19, 20.20 below.

Simon's Direct Tax Service. See **D1.103–D1.108**.

20.2 **Dividends** (including capital dividends). [*ICTA 1988, s 209(2)(a)*].

20.3 **Any distribution** (whether in cash or otherwise) **in respect of shares in the company** the cost of which is borne by the company, except insofar as

(i) it represents a repayment of share capital (but see 20.11 below), or

(ii) it is equal to any 'new consideration' (see 20.12 below) received by the company for the distribution.

[*ICTA 1988, s 209(2)(b), s 254(9)*].

However, a transfer of assets (other than cash) or of liabilities made between companies resident in the UK is not to be treated as a distribution provided that neither company is the '51% subsidiary' of a non-resident company and that the companies are not under the control of the same person or persons either at the time of, or as a result of, the transfer. [*ICTA 1988, s 209(6)*].

A company is a '*51% subsidiary*' if more than 50% of its ordinary share capital is owned directly or indirectly by another. [*ICTA 1988, s 838(1)(a)*].

See also, however, 20.9 below and 51 PURCHASE BY A COMPANY OF ITS OWN SHARES.

20.4 **The issue** in respect of shares or securities in the company **of redeemable share capital** or any security (insofar as it is not referable to 'new consideration', see 20.12 below). [*ICTA 1988, s 209(2)(c)*]. The value of any redeemable share capital (or security) is the amount of the share capital (or principal) together with any premium payable on redemption (or maturity), or in a winding-up, or in any other circumstances. [*ICTA 1988, s 209(8)*]. The paying-up of issued share capital by the company also falls under this head. [*ICTA 1988, s 254(10)*]. See also 20.18 below.

20.5 Any **interest or other distribution** in respect of securities (except any part representing principal), the cost of which is borne by the company, to the extent that it **exceeds a reasonable commercial return**. [*ICTA 1988, s 209(2)(d)*].

20.6 (After 28 November 1994) any **interest or other distribution** (except any part representing principal or within 20.5 above), the cost of which is borne by the company, **in respect of securities held by a company of which the issuing company is a '75% subsidiary'** (or where both companies are 75% subsidiaries of a third company), to the extent that it would not have fallen to be paid if there had been no formal or informal relationship, arrangements or other connection between the companies (other than the securities themselves). The determination of whether such a relationship, etc. exists must take account of all factors, including whether, in the absence of the relationship, etc., the loan would have been made at all, or in a different amount, or at a different rate of interest or on other agreed terms. The taxpayer is required either to show that no relationship, etc. exists or to show the amount of interest which would have been paid in the absence of the relationship, etc.. Where there is a relationship, etc., and it is not part of the lending company's business to make loans generally, the latter is disregarded. However, in determining

(i) the appropriate level or extent of the issuing company's overall indebtedness,

(ii) whether it might be expected that the issuing company and a particular person would have become parties to a transaction involving the issue of a security by the issuing company or the making of a loan, or a loan of a particular amount, to that company, and

(iii) the rate of interest and other terms that might be expected to be applicable in any particular case to such a transaction,

no account is to be taken of (or of any inference capable of being drawn from) any other formal or informal relationship, etc. between the issuing company and any other person, unless that person has no 'relevant connection' with the issuing company, or is a member of the same 'UK grouping'. A person has a '*relevant connection*' with the issuing company if they are CONNECTED PERSONS (16) within *ICTA 1988, s 839* or if that person is an 'effective 51% subsidiary' of the issuing company or the issuing company is such a subsidiary of that person. '*UK grouping*' is defined by reference to 'effective 51% subsidiary' relationships. '*Effective 51% subsidiary*' is as under *TCGA 1992, s 170(7)* (see 9.18 CAPITAL GAINS) but applied as if the question of whether the effective 51% subsidiaries of a company (the '*putative holding company*') resident in the UK and not dual resident (see 29.31 GROUPS OF COMPANIES) include either the issuing company or a company of which the issuing company is an effective 51% subsidiary were to be determined without regard to any beneficial entitlement of the putative holding company to any profits or assets of any company resident outside the UK.

This does *not*, however, apply to any interest, etc. paid to a charity (including any of the bodies treated as charities, see 24.3, 24.8, 24.11, 24.17 EXEMPT ORGANISATIONS). See also 20.7 below as regards certain other exceptions from distribution treatment.

[*ICTA 1988, s 209(2)(da)(8A)–(8F), s 212(4); FA 1995, s 87(1)–(4)*].

See Revenue Tax Bulletin June 1995 pp 218–220 for the Revenue's approach to the question of what would have happened in the absence of a relationship, etc. as above, and for a detailed discussion of the relevance of debt/equity and income cover ratios. In particular, it is stressed that the provisions are capable of applying to treat the whole of the interest on a loan as a distribution even though a loan on identical terms could have been obtained from a third party (the instance being quoted of a company replacing a fixed interest third party loan with a loan at a higher (though currently commercial) rate of interest for the same remaining term from a related company). Advances from companies in Austria, Barbados, the Faroe Islands, Fiji, Germany, Israel, Japan, Kenya, Luxembourg, South Africa, the Sudan and Zambia are identified as those most likely to be affected by the new provisions. Guidance may be obtained from Inland Revenue International Division 5/2, Melbourne House, Aldwych, London WC2B 4LL, to whom correspondents should identify the parties concerned and supply as much information as possible about the existing financial structures and/or proposals. See also Revenue Tax Bulletin June 1998 pp 554–556 for the Revenue response to various questions put to them by representative bodies on the application of *section 209(2)(da)*.

20.7 Any **interest** (or other distribution not representing principal or within 20.5 or 20.6 above), the cost of which is borne by the company, in respect of:

(i) bonus securities issued under 20.4 above in respect of shares (after 5 April 1965) or securities (after 5 April 1972) of the company; or

(ii) securities convertible directly or indirectly into shares in the company which are neither listed on a recognised stock exchange nor issued on terms reasonably comparable to those on which securities so listed were issued; or

(iii) securities issued after 5 April 1972 carrying a right to receive shares in, or securities of, the company (being neither quoted nor issued on comparable terms, see (ii) above); or

(iv) securities the interest on which varies with the results of the company's business. For payments made after 20 March 2000, this does not apply by reason only of the terms of a security providing for the interest to be reduced if the results improve or increased if they deteriorate (commonly known as 'ratchet loans'); or

(v) (before 29 November 1994) securities held by a non-resident company where

- (*a*) the issuing company is its '75% subsidiary', or
- (*b*) both are '75% subsidiaries' of a non-resident company (and see now 20.6 above); or

(vi) (before 29 November 1994) securities held by a non-resident company where both are '75% subsidiaries' of a company resident in the UK (unless 90% or more of the issuing company's share capital is directly owned by a company so resident) (and see now 20.6 above); or

(vii) securities carrying rights such that it is 'necessary or advantageous' for the holder, disposer, or acquirer of those securities to hold, dispose of, or acquire, a proportionate holding of shares. Such securities are '*connected with*' the shares; or

(viii) 'equity notes' held by a company which either is '*associated with*' the issuing company (i.e. one is a '75% subsidiary' of the other or both are such subsidiaries of a third company) or is a '*funded company*' (i.e. there are arrangements involving the company being put in funds (directly or indirectly) by the issuing company or by a company associated with the issuing company).

[*ICTA 1988, s 209(2)(e)(10)(11), s 254(2); F(No 2)A 1992, s 31; FA 1995, s 87(2)(4); FA 1996, Sch 38 para 6; FA 2000, s 86(1)*].

A company is a '*75% subsidiary*' if not less than 75% of its ordinary share capital is owned directly or indirectly by another. [*ICTA 1988, s 838*].

Interest within (i)–(iv), (vii) or (viii) above or, after 28 November 1994, 20.6 above on securities issued by a company to another company within the charge to corporation tax is *not* treated as a distribution *provided that* the recipient company is neither exempt from tax in respect of the interest, etc. (other than under the general corporation tax exemption of UK company distributions) nor (where 20.6 above applies) otherwise outside the matters in respect of which that company is within the charge to corporation tax, *unless* the securities are within (iv) above and

(*a*) the principal does not exceed £100,000,

(*b*) the principal and interest must be repaid within five years of the principal being paid to the borrower, and

(*c*) the obligation was entered into before 9 March 1982, or was entered into before 1 July 1982 pursuant to negotiations in progress on 9 March 1982, the borrower having before that date applied for the loan and supplied any documents required in support of his application.

Where the repayment period of either principal or interest is extended after 8 March 1982 (but is still within (*b*) above), (i)–(iv), (vii) and (viii) above and 20.6 above do not apply to any interest etc. paid after the repayment period in force at that date.

[*ICTA 1988, s 212; F(No 2) A 1992, s 31(3); FA 1995, s 87(4)*].

By concession, (v) above does not apply to interest paid by a bank (or other deposit-taker under *Banking Act 1987*) 'in the ordinary course' of business (for which see 6.2 BANKS) to the extent that it does not exceed that which would have been paid on arm's length terms. Interest on a loan subordinated to claims of depositors or otherwise forming part of the capital of the business is not considered to be paid in the ordinary course of business. (Revenue Pamphlet IR 1, C18).

As regards (viii) above, a security is an '*equity note*' if, as regards the whole or any part of the principal, any of the following apply:

(1) under the terms of issue, either there is no particular redemption date, or the latest (or only) redemption date falls more than 50 years after the date of issue; or

(2) under the terms of issue, redemption is to occur more than 50 years after the date of issue if a particular event occurs, and (judged at the time of issue) that event is certain or likely to occur; or

(3) the issuing company can secure that there is no particular redemption date or that the redemption date falls more than 50 years after the date of issue.

[*ICTA 1988, s 209(9); F(No 2)A 1992, s 31(2)*].

The Revenue have confirmed that ownership of shares in the company holding the security will not of itself be treated as bringing the issuing company within (3) above, and that a demand loan is not regarded as an equity note. The word 'arrangements' in relation to the definition of a funded company implies a purposive connection, and would not for example apply were a bank group to loan money to a company which, as a separate matter, happened to acquire equity notes issued by the group. (Law Society Press Release 15 February 1993; ICAEW Technical Release TAX 5/93, 17 February 1993).

See generally Revenue Tax Bulletin May 1993 p 68 as regards the definition of an equity note.

20.8 As regards 20.5, 20.6 and 20.7 above:

(i) no amount is regarded as representing principal secured by a security insofar as it exceeds 'new consideration' (see 20.12 below) received by the company for its issue [*ICTA 1988, s 209(3)*]; and

(ii) (for distributions made after 31 March 1996) where a security is issued at a premium consisting of 'new consideration', references to the principal represented by a distribution are taken as referring to the aggregate of the principal and the premium represented by the distribution (and a similar rule applies as regards 20.5 above in relation to the reasonable commercial return for the use of principal represented by a distribution). [*ICTA 1988, s 209(3A); FA 1996, Sch 14 para 11*].

20.9 **The transfer of assets or liabilities** between a company and its members insofar as the market value of any benefit received by a member exceeds that of any 'new consideration' (see 20.12 below) given by him. Such a transfer is not, however, to be treated as a distribution if it is made between companies resident in the UK and *either*

(i) the transferor company is a 51% subsidiary (see below) of the transferee company, *or*

(ii) both are 51% subsidiaries of a company resident in the UK.

[*ICTA 1988, s 209(4)(5)*].

Such a transfer will not be treated as a distribution under any of the other provisions of *section 209*. (CCAB Memorandum, June 1970).

In determining whether a company is a 51% subsidiary of another, that other's holding (whether direct or indirect) of shares in a non-resident company or of shares any profit on the sale of which would be a trading receipt, are disregarded. [*ICTA 1988, s 209(7)*].

Transfers of assets (other than cash) or of liabilities are excluded if they fall within *section 209(6)*, see 20.3 above, where '51% subsidiary' is defined without the restriction on shareholdings to which regard is to be had.

For the 'unwinding' of distributions inadvertently caught by *section 209(4)*, see Revenue Corporation Tax Manual, CT 1529a.

20.10 **Repayment of share capital followed by a bonus issue.** Where a company repays share capital (and see 20.11 below), or has done so at any time after 6 April 1965, and at the same time or later issues any share capital as paid up (otherwise than by the receipt of 'new consideration', see 20.12 below), the amount so paid up is treated as a distribution. Such a distribution is treated as made in respect of the bonus shares and is limited to the total amount of share capital repaid less any amount previously treated as a distribution under this provision. [*ICTA 1988, s 210(1)*]. Where the bonus share capital is issued after 5 April 1973, this provision only applies if the issue is made within ten years of the repayment or is of redeemable share capital. [*ICTA 1988, s 210(3)*]. The original rules apply unaltered, however, if the company is under the control of not more than five persons or is unquoted (disregarding debentures and preference shares), unless it is under the control of a company (or companies) which is (or are) neither controlled by five or fewer persons nor unquoted. [*ICTA 1988, ss 210(3), 704D*]. 'Control' is as defined in 13.2 CLOSE COMPANIES.

Example

In 1991 X Ltd, a close company, redeemed £50,000-worth of variable-rate preference shares. In 1994 it made a bonus issue of one ordinary share of £1 for every ten held, which amounted to £20,000. In 1996 it made a further bonus issue of ordinary shares on a 1:11 basis, which also amounted to £20,000. X Ltd is treated as having made a distribution of

£20,000 in each of the financial years 1994 and 1996 If X Ltd makes a similar bonus issue of 1:12 in 2000, the amount treated as a distribution (assuming that there has been no further repayment of share capital) will be limited to £10,000, being the balance of the £50,000 repaid in 1991.

These provisions do not apply to the repayment of fully-paid 'preference shares' which

(i) existed as such on 6 April 1965, or

(ii) were issued as such after 6 April 1965 wholly for 'new consideration not derived from ordinary shares'

and in either case remained fully-paid preference shares until the date of repayment. [*ICTA 1988, s 210(2)*].

'*Preference shares*' are defined for this purpose as shares carrying the right to a dividend at a fixed percentage of the nominal value only and such other rights in respect of dividends and capital as are comparable with those general for fixed-dividend shares listed in the Official List of the Stock Exchange. Thus variable-rate preference shares (as in the example above) are outside this definition.

'*New consideration not derived from ordinary shares*' means 'new consideration' (see 20.12 below) except insofar as it consists of

(*a*) the surrender, transfer or cancellation of 'ordinary shares' in the company or any other company, or

(*b*) the variation of rights in such shares, or

(*c*) consideration derived from a repayment made in respect of such shares.

'*Ordinary shares*' are all shares except preference shares as defined above.

[*ICTA 1988, s 210(4); FA 1996, Sch 38 para 7*].

20.11 **Repayment of share capital.** Where a company issues (or has issued at any time after 6 April 1965) any 'share capital' as paid up (the amount so paid up not constituting 'new consideration' (see 20.12 below) or a qualifying distribution), any subsequent distribution in respect of that share capital is not treated as a repayment of share capital (so that the exclusion from distribution treatment in 20.3(i) does not apply), except insofar as the repayment exceeds the amount so paid up. (The excess is generally a distribution as under 20.3 above.). [*ICTA 1988, s 211(1)(3)*].

'Share capital' for this purpose includes

(*a*) all the shares of the same class;

(*b*) shares issued in respect of any shares under (*a*) above;

(*c*) shares exchanged for any shares under (*a*) above (whether directly or indirectly);

(*d*) shares into which any shares under (*a*) above have directly or indirectly been converted. [*ICTA 1988, s 211(4)*].

Where shares have been issued at a premium representing new consideration, the premium (less any amount that has been applied in paying up share capital) is treated as part of the share capital in determining whether any repayment is to be treated as a distribution. [*ICTA 1988, s 211(5)(6)*]. Subject to this, premiums paid on the redemption of share capital are not to be treated as repayments of share capital. [*ICTA 1988, s 211(7)*].

A distribution is outside *section 211(1)* if it is made

(i) more than ten years after an issue of shares within that subsection, and

(ii) otherwise than in respect of redeemable share capital, and

(iii) by a company which is neither under the control of five or fewer persons nor unquoted (disregarding debentures and preference shares), or which is controlled by a company (or companies) which is or are neither controlled by five or fewer persons nor unquoted.

[*ICTA 1988, ss 211(2), 704D*].

20.12 '*New consideration*' means consideration provided otherwise than out of the assets of the company (i.e. where the cost does not fall on the company). Amounts retained by the company by way of capitalising a distribution do not constitute new consideration, but a premium paid on the issue of shares which is later applied in paying up further share capital may be treated as new consideration (except insofar as it has been taken into account to enable a distribution to be treated as a repayment of share capital (see 20.11 above)). [*ICTA 1988, s 254(1)(5)*].

Consideration derived from the value of any share capital or security of, or from voting or other rights in, a company is new consideration only if it represents

(i) money or value received from the company as a qualifying distribution (see 20.17 below); or

(ii) money received from the company which, for the purposes of *Part VI* of *ICTA 1988*, constitute a repayment of share capital (see 20.11 above) or of the principal of the security; or

(iii) the giving up of the right to the share capital or security on its cancellation, extinguishment or acquisition by the company.

But insofar as any amount under (ii) or (iii) exceeds any payment made to the company for the issue of the share capital or security or, in the case of share capital which constituted a qualifying distribution (see 20.18 below), exceeds the nominal value of that share capital, it is not to be treated as new consideration. [*ICTA 1988, s 254(6)(7)*].

20.13 '*Shares*' includes stock and any other interest of a member in a company. [*ICTA 1988, s 254(1)*].

20.14 '*Security*' includes securities not creating or evidencing a charge on assets. Interest paid, or other consideration given, by a company for money advanced without the issue of a security is nevertheless treated as if paid or given in respect of a security issued for that advance by the company. Where securities are issued at a discount, and are not listed on a recognised stock exchange, the principal secured is to be taken as not exceeding the issue price, unless the terms of issue are reasonably comparable with those of securities so listed. [*ICTA 1988, s 254(1)(11); FA 1996, Sch 38 para 6*].

20.15 A thing is to be regarded as done '*in respect of*' shares or securities if it is done to the holder or former holder thereof (as such), or in pursuance of a right granted or offer made in respect of a share. Anything so done by reference to shareholdings at a particular time is regarded as done to the then holder or his personal representatives. [*ICTA 1988, s 254(12)*]. If reciprocal arrangements are entered into among companies to make distributions to each other's members, the acts of one may be attributed to another. [*ICTA 1988, s 254(8)*].

20.16 **ITEMS NOT TREATED AS DISTRIBUTIONS**

(*a*) Distributions made in respect of share capital on LIQUIDATION ETC. (42) [*ICTA 1988, s 209(1)*], or (in most circumstances) on *dissolution under Companies Act 1985, s 652 or s 652A*. (Revenue Pamphlet IR 1, C16).

(*b*) Small distributions to members on *dissolution of an unincorporated association* which is of a social or recreational nature and has not carried on a trade or investment business. (Revenue Pamphlet IR 1, C15).

(*c*) *Covenanted donations to charity* paid before 1 April 2000 (see 11.11 CHARITIES), provided that the covenant is for annual payments and over a period which may exceed three years and is not capable of earlier termination without the consent of the payee. [*ICTA 1988, s 339(6)(8); FA 2000, Sch 40 Pt II(1)*].

(*d*) Payments for *group relief* or for the *surrender of ACT* (see 29.13, 29.24 GROUPS OF COMPANIES) [*ICTA 1988, ss 240(8), 402(6); FA 1998, Sch 3 para 13*], except insofar as they exceed the amount surrendered.

(*e*) *Share or loan interest* paid by registered INDUSTRIAL AND PROVIDENT SOCIETIES (32) or certain co-operative associations. [*ICTA 1988, s 486(1)(8)(9)*].

(*f*) *Dividends or bonuses* deductible in computing the income of REGISTERED INDUSTRIAL AND PROVIDENT SOCIETIES (32) or MUTUAL COMPANIES (45). [*ICTA 1988, s 486(10)–(12)*].

(*g*) *Dividends or interest* payable in respect of shares in, deposits with, or loans to, BUILDING SOCIETIES (7). [*ICTA 1988, s 476(3)(c), s 477A(3)(b); FA 1990, Sch 5 para 4*].

(*h*) *Stock dividends* (see Tolley's Income Tax under Stock Dividends). [*ICTA 1988, s 230*].

(*i*) *Interest on securities* not within 20.5–20.7 above.

(*j*) Money provided by a close company for the *purchase of its shares by trustees of its profit sharing scheme*. (CCAB Memorandum TR 308, June 1978).

(*k*) Certain *purchases by a company of its own shares* (see PURCHASE BY A COMPANY OF ITS OWN SHARES (51)). [*ICTA 1988, ss 219–229*].

The Revenue will give 'sympathetic consideration' to cases where a terminal payment is made by a continuing company to an arm's length director or employee, where the sum is both reasonable in amount (having regard to past services and length of service), and an admissible deduction for corporation tax purposes. (CCAB Memorandum TR 127, 19 February 1974).

A bonus issue of *non-redeemable share capital* does not constitute a distribution unless it follows a repayment of share capital (see 20.11 above).

20.17 EFFECT OF DISTRIBUTION

A distribution is not chargeable to corporation tax in the hands of the recipient company, nor taken into account in computing the income of the paying company for corporation tax purposes. [*ICTA 1988, s 208*]. But see 20.18 below.

Where the special rules in *ICTA 1988, ss 219–229* do *not* apply on the occasion of a PURCHASE BY A COMPANY OF ITS OWN SHARES (51), so that the purchase is treated as a distribution, and the shareholder is itself a company, the distribution is included in the consideration which, for the purposes of corporation tax on chargeable gains, the shareholder company is treated as receiving for disposal of the shares.

20.18 QUALIFYING AND NON-QUALIFYING DISTRIBUTIONS

A company resident in the UK was, until 6 April 1999, liable to ADVANCE CORPORATION TAX (3) in respect of its qualifying distributions (but not its non-qualifying distributions) made before 6 April 1999. [*ICTA 1988, s 14(1); FA 1998, Sch 3 para 8*]. A UK-resident recipient of such a distribution is entitled to a tax credit (see 3.3 ADVANCE CORPORATION TAX), and the distribution, together with the tax credit, is FRANKED INVESTMENT INCOME (27) in the hands of a UK-resident recipient company. [*ICTA 1988, s 238(1); FA 1998, Sch 3 para 11*].

Non-qualifying distributions are

(*a*) bonus redeemable share capital and bonus securities within *ICTA 1988, s 209(2)(c)* (see 20.4 above) which are not distributions within *ICTA 1988, s 210* (see 20.9 above), and

(*b*) share capital or securities which the distributing company has directly or indirectly received from the issuing company as a distribution under (*a*) above.

Qualifying distributions are all other distributions. [*ICTA 1988, s 14(2)*].

Returns of non-qualifying distributions must be made under *ICTA 1988, s 234(5)–(9)*. See 54.8 RETURNS.

Any company making a payment of dividend or interest to any person must, within a reasonable period, send a written statement giving details of the payment to that person or, if the payment is made direct to a bank (within *ICTA 1988, s 840A*, see 6.1 BANKS) or building society, either to the bank or building society or to the account holder. Nominee recipients are similarly obliged to provide a statement when passing on the payment. The statement must include:

(i) in the case of interest (not being a qualifying distribution or part), the gross amount, the rate and amount of income tax deducted from the gross amount, the net amount actually paid and the date of payment;

(ii) in the case of a dividend or interest which is a qualifying distribution or part, the amount paid, the date of payment and the related tax credit.

For the continued application of the requirement under (ii) above following the abolition of ACT and, in most cases, of tax credit repayments, see Revenue Tax Bulletin April 1999 p 655.

The Board have powers by regulation to provide alternative rules for compliance. [*ICTA 1988, s 234A; F(No 2)A 1992, s 32; FA 1996, Sch 37 paras 2, 7*].

For dividends payable to non-residents, see 21.9 DOUBLE TAX RELIEF.

Simon's Direct Tax Service. See D1.111.

20.19 **CLOSE COMPANIES—ADDITIONAL DISTRIBUTIONS**

Certain payments made and benefits given to participators and their associates by close companies are treated as distributions, see 20.20 below. Unless otherwise stated, terms have the same meaning as in 13.1–13.5 CLOSE COMPANIES. The exceptions listed in 20.16 above apply. [*ICTA 1988, s 418*].

20.20 **Benefits to participators and their associates**. Where a close company incurs expense in, or in connection with, the provision for any 'participator' (or an associate of his) of living or other accommodation, entertainment, domestic or other services, or of other benefits or facilities of whatever nature, so much of that expense as is not made good by the participator is treated as a distribution. [*ICTA 1988, s 418(2)(8)*]. Amounts already treated as a benefit to a director or to an employee with emoluments at a rate of £8,500 p.a. or more for income tax purposes (see Tolley's Income Tax under Schedule E) are excluded, as is the provision of living accommodation taxable as a benefit on any employee, and the provision of retirement pensions, terminal payments etc. [*ICTA 1988, s 418(3)*].

'*Participator*' includes a participator in a company which controls the company providing the benefit. [*ICTA 1988, s 418(8)*].

Reciprocal arrangements whereby each of a number of companies makes a payment etc. to a participator in another are included. [*ICTA 1988, s 418(7)*].

The measure of the distribution is the cash equivalent of the benefit or expense as defined in the Schedule E benefits legislation (see Tolley's Income Tax under Schedule E) less any amount made good to the company. [*ICTA 1988, s 418(4)*].

These provisions do not apply where the company and the participator are resident in the UK and

(*a*) one is a '51% subsidiary' of the other or both are 51% subsidiaries of a third company so resident, and

(*b*) the benefit arises on or in connection with the transfer of assets or liabilities between the company and the participator. [*ICTA 1988, s 418(5)*].

'*51% subsidiary*' is as defined in 20.8 above. [*ICTA 1988, s 418(6)*].

Simon's Direct Tax Service. See **D3.117**.

20.21 *Example*

R is a participator in S Ltd, a close company, but he is neither a director nor an employee earning £8,500 a year or more. For the whole of 1998/99, S Ltd provided R with a new car of which the 'price' for tax purposes (i.e. under *ICTA 1988, ss 168A–168G*) was £21,200, and in which R made no journeys on the company's business. R was required to, and did, pay S Ltd £500 a year for the use of the car. The cost of providing the car, charged in S Ltd's accounts for its year ended 31 March 1999, was £5,000.

Deemed distribution

If the benefit of the car were assessable under Schedule E, the cash equivalent would be:

	£
£21,200 @ 35% (no business use)	7,420
Less contribution	500
	£6,920

S Ltd is treated as making a distribution of £6,920 to R.

ACT payable £6,920 × 20/80	£1,730
Income of R for 1998/99 £6,920 × 100/80	£8,650
Tax credit for R for 1998/99 £8,650 @ 20%	£1,730

The income is Schedule F income and thus taxable at 20% except to the extent that it falls within R's higher rate band, in which case it would be taxable at 40%.

S Ltd's taxable profits

In computing S Ltd's profits chargeable to corporation tax, the actual expenditure charged (£5,000) must be added back.

Note. For 1999/2000 and subsequent years, no ACT liability arises on the company providing the benefit (although the deemed distribution may be taken into account under the 'shadow ACT' provisions, see 3.8 ADVANCE CORPORATION TAX). As regards the recipient of the benefit, the deemed distribution is grossed up by the addition of a tax credit of 10%. The tax credit is non-repayable but satisfies the liability to Schedule F ordinary rate tax on the grossed-up amount or, to the extent that the liability arises at the Schedule F upper rate of 32.5%, may be set against such liability.

20.22 MUTUAL AND NON-TRADING COMPANIES

Payments made to members of

(*a*) MUTUAL COMPANIES (45) (other than those carrying on life assurance business), or

(*b*) companies which were not formed to carry on, and which have never carried on, a trade or the business of holding investments,

are within the above provisions only if made out of income chargeable to corporation tax or out of FRANKED INVESTMENT INCOME (27) (including group income (see 29.2 GROUPS OF COMPANIES) before 6 April 1999) or (before 6 April 1999) FOREIGN INCOME DIVIDENDS (26). [*ICTA 1988, s 490; FA 1994, Sch 16 para 14; F(No 2)A 1997, Sch 6 para 9; FA 1998, Sch 3 para 28*].

20.23 FRIENDLY SOCIETIES

Payments made by certain FRIENDLY SOCIETIES (28) are qualifying distributions. [*ICTA 1988, s 461(3)*].

21 Double Tax Relief

Cross-references. See 4.4 ANTI-AVOIDANCE; 9.53 CAPITAL GAINS; 18 CONTROLLED FOREIGN COMPANIES; 29.31 GROUPS OF COMPANIES; 53 RESIDENCE.

Simon's Direct Tax Service. See Binder 9 International.

Other sources. See Tolley's Double Taxation Relief.

The headings in this chapter are as follows.

21.2	Unilateral relief	21.8	— example
21.3	Relief by agreement	21.9	Dividends, interest, etc. paid to non-residents
21.4	— example	21.10	Agreements in force
21.5	Method of giving relief	21.11	Banks
21.6	Measure of relief	21.12	Oil companies
21.7	Allocation of charges etc. and advance corporation tax		

21.1 Double Tax Relief is dealt with generally under that heading in Tolley's Income Tax. Additional matters particularly relevant to companies are set out below. See also Revenue Pamphlet IR 6.

21.2 **UNILATERAL RELIEF**

Unilateral relief under *ICTA 1988, s 790* is available on dividends received from overseas companies

(*a*) for overseas tax directly charged on the dividend which would not have been charged if the dividend had not been paid, and

(*b*) where the dividend is paid by a company resident overseas to a company resident in the UK, and the payee (or a company of which it is a 'subsidiary') controls at least ten per cent of the voting power in the overseas company, for tax in respect of the overseas company's profits paid under the law of the country in which it is resident, and

(*c*) (for accounting periods beginning before 1 April 2000) where the claimant company is assessable under Schedule D, Case I in respect of insurance business carried on, wholly or in part, through an overseas branch or agency, for any UK tax and any overseas tax on profits payable by companies resident in the overseas territory. The dividend must be referable to the claimant company's insurance business.

For accounting periods ending on or after 21 March 2000, this is extended to dividends paid to a company resident outside the UK but forming part of the profits of a UK branch or agency of the company. Relief is, however, limited in such cases to the amount which could be claimed in the same circumstances by a UK-resident company. For insurance companies for accounting periods beginning on or after 1 April 2000, see *FA 2000, Sch 30 paras 16–19* (and see 41.14 LIFE INSURANCE COMPANIES).

'*Subsidiary*' means a company of which 50% or more of the voting power is controlled, directly or indirectly, by the other.

[*ICTA 1988, s 790(4)–(6A), s 794(2)(bb), ss 800–802; FA 2000, Sch 30 paras 4, 14*].

Matching credit for tax spared below immediate overseas subsidiary. Where:

(i) an amount of tax would, but for a relief, have been payable by a company ('company A'), in respect of any of its profits, under the law of its territory of residence;

(ii) company A pays a dividend out of those profits to another company ('company B') resident in the same territory;

(iii) company B, out of profits consisting of or including all or part of that dividend, pays a dividend after 20 March 2000 to a UK-resident company ('company C'); and

(iv) had company B been UK resident, it would have been entitled under a double tax agreement with its actual territory of residence to relief for the spared tax,

then the spared tax is taken into account for the purposes of unilateral relief for underlying tax as if it had been payable and paid. If these conditions are not fulfilled, unilateral relief is not available for spared tax in respect of any dividend paid by a non-UK resident company to a UK-resident company, notwithstanding any double tax agreement with the territory concerned providing any relief for spared tax. Without prejudice to the above specific relief, for dividends paid after 20 March 2000, treaty relief for underlying tax which is spared below the level of the immediate non-resident subsidiary is denied unless it is specifically provided for in a double tax agreement. [*ICTA 1988, s 788(5), s 790(10A)–(10C); FA 2000, Sch 30 paras 2, 3*].

For the scope of 'dividends', see *Memec plc v CIR CA 1998, 71 TC 77* (in which receipts under a silent partnership agreement were held not to attract relief), and see also Revenue Tax Bulletin February 1999 p 627 for an article on the classification of foreign entities for UK tax purposes.

To be eligible for relief, the taxes must be charged on income and correspond to income tax or corporation tax in the UK but, subject to this, provincial, state and municipal taxes are included. [*ICTA 1988, s 790(12)*]. See *Yates v GCA International Ltd and cross-appeal Ch D 1991, 64 TC 37* where a tax imposed on gross receipts less a fixed 10% deduction was held to correspond to UK income tax or corporation tax. Following that decision, the Revenue amended their practice. (Revenue Pamphlet IR 131, SP 7/91, 26 July 1991). For claims made on or after 13 February 1991, and earlier claims unsettled at that date, foreign taxes will be examined to determine whether, in their own legislative context, they serve the same function as UK income and corporation taxes in relation to business profits, and are thus eligible for unilateral relief. As regards those overseas taxes which the Inland Revenue considers admissible (or inadmissible) for relief, these are listed by country in the Revenue Double Taxation Relief Manual, which is available for inspection at Tax Enquiry Centres, at D2100 *et seq.*. See also Revenue Inspector's Manual, IM 1121, and Revenue Tax Bulletin August 1995 p 244 and October 1996 p 358 as regards recent re-classification of certain South African, Algerian, Argentinian, Brazilian and Peruvian taxes. Current information may be obtained on 0207–438 6643.

Special provision is made for the relief of foreign tax relating to accrued interest in relation to which a non-trading credit (or, if the Treasury so provides by order, a trading credit) is brought into account (see 43.3 LOAN RELATIONSHIPS), and for foreign tax to be disregarded where it is attributable to interest accruing under a loan relationship (see 43.2 LOAN RELATIONSHIPS) at a time when the company concerned was not a party to the relationship (unless it ceased to be a party under certain repo or stock-lending arrangements). For accounting periods ending after 20 March 2000, the latter provision is extended to require foreign tax attributable to 'qualifying payments' within *FA 1994, s 153(a)* or *(b)* (see 25.6(*a*)(*b*) FINANCIAL INSTRUMENTS) to be disregarded where it is attributable to a time when the company was not a party to the interest rate or currency contract concerned. [*ICTA 1988, s 807A; FA 1996, Sch 14 para 46; FA 1997, s 91; FA 2000, Sch 30 para 24*].

Foreign tax levied by reference to the value of assets employed to produce income chargeable to UK tax may, in practice, be allowed as a business expense under normal Schedule D, Case I rules. (Revenue International Tax Handbook, ITH 602).

Prevention of double relief. For claims made after 20 March 2000, credit may not be given for foreign tax for which relief is available in the territory in which it would otherwise be payable, either under double tax arrangements or under the law of that territory in consequence of any such arrangements. It is also made clear that unilateral relief will not be allowed where credit could be claimed under a double tax agreement under 21.3 below, or in cases or circumstances in which such an agreement made after 20 March 2000 specifically prohibits relief. [*ICTA 1988, s 793A; FA 2000, Sch 30 para 5*].

Simon's Direct Tax Service. See **F1.145** *et seq.*.

21.3 RELIEF BY AGREEMENT

Subject to the following general provisions, the extent of such relief depends on the terms of the relevant double tax agreement, which should be carefully studied.

Arrangements under such an agreement may provide for

(i) relief from income or corporation tax in respect of income,

(ii) charging UK income to non-UK residents,

(iii) determining income to be attributed to non-UK residents or their agencies, etc., or to UK residents who have special relationships with non-UK residents,

(iv) granting non-UK residents the right to set-off or repayment of the tax credit in respect of distributions made to them by UK resident companies, or

(v) exchange of information concerning taxes covered by the agreement, particularly in relation to the prevention of fiscal evasion.

[*ICTA 1988, s 788(2)(3)*].

See 21.2 above for the disregarding for these purposes (by virtue of *ICTA 1988, s 807A*) of tax attributable to certain payments under loan relationships or interest rate or currency contracts at a time when the company concerned is not a party to the relationship or contract.

As regards (iv) above, the general abolition of the repayment of tax credits after 5 April 1999 does not affect the entitlement of a non-UK resident to payment in respect of a tax credit under such arrangements (although it should be noted that in practice, with the reduction after that date to one-ninth in the rate of tax credit, such repayments will be very limited). [*F(No 2)A 1997, s 30(9)(10)*]. Similarly, the tax credit payment restrictions applicable to pension funds in relation to distributions made after 1 July 1997 do not apply to non-residents' entitlements under such arrangements. [*ICTA 1988, s 231A(6)(b); F(No 2)A 1997, s 19(2), Sch 8 Pt II(9)*].

As regards the concept of 'permanent establishment' on which taxation rights are based under most treaties, the Revenue take the view that a website, or a server on which e-commerce is conducted through a website, is not of itself a permanent establishment. (Revenue Press Release 11 April 2000).

Mutual agreement procedure. Double tax agreements normally contain a 'mutual agreement procedure' provision enabling a taxpayer who considers that the action of a tax authority has resulted, or will result, in taxation not in accordance with the agreement to present his case to the competent authority in his state of residence. The UK competent authority is the Inland Revenue, and the address to which all relevant facts and contentions should be sent is International Division, Melbourne House, Aldwych, London WC2B 4LL. For the presentation of such cases, and for giving effect to solutions and agreements reached under such procedures, see *ICTA 1988, s 815AA* introduced by *FA 2000, Sch 30 para 28.*

In *R v CIR (ex p. Commerzbank AG) QB 1991, 68 TC 252*, interest on unpaid tax was thus held not to fall within the scope of double tax agreements, but on a reference to the European Court of Justice (see *68 TC 264*), the Court upheld the view that, in the case of EC Member States, such discrimination against non-UK resident companies was prevented by the relevant Articles of the Treaty of Rome. For claims to such interest following that judgment, see 38.3 INTEREST ON OVERPAID TAX. See Revenue Double Taxation Relief Manual, DT 1950 *et seq.* for Revenue approach to non-discrimination claims generally.

See, however, Revenue Pamphlet IR 131, SP 2/95, 7 February 1995 (27.3 FRANKED INVESTMENT INCOME) for the Revenue view of the restricted operation of non-discrimination clauses in double tax treaties.

Special relationships: interest. Agreements under *section 788* making provision in relation to interest may also have a provision dealing with cases where, owing to a special relationship, the amount of interest paid exceeds the amount which would have been paid in the absence of that relationship, and requiring the interest provision to be applied only to that lower amount. Any such special relationship provision has to be construed:

(*a*) as requiring account to be taken of all factors, including whether, in the absence of the relationship, the loan would have been made at all, or would have been in a different amount, or a different rate of interest and other terms would have been agreed. This does not apply, however, where the special relationship provision expressly requires regard to be had to the debt on which the interest is paid in determining the excess interest, and accordingly expressly limits the factors to be taken into account, and in the case of a loan by one company to another, the fact that it is not part of the lending company's business to make loans generally is disregarded; and

(*b*) as requiring the taxpayer either to show that no special relationship exists or to show the amount of interest which would have been paid in the absence of that relationship.

[*ICTA 1988, s 808A; F(No 2)A 1992, s 52*].

For the purposes of (*a*) above, the absence of cross-default and cross-guarantee provisions in the case of an intra-group loan will not of itself be taken into account in determining whether the amount of interest exceeds that which would have been paid in the absence of a special relationship, or whether the loan would have been made at all. (Law Society Press Release 15 February 1993).

Special relationships: royalties. Agreements may make similar provision in relation to royalties. Where royalties are payable on or after 28 July 2000, any special relationship provision, unless it expressly requires regard to be had to the use, right or information for which royalties are paid in determining the excess royalties, has to be construed as requiring account to be taken of all factors. These include:

(A) in the absence of the relationship, whether the royalty agreement would have been made at all, or the rate or amount of royalties and other terms which would have been agreed; and

(B) if the asset in respect of which the royalties are paid (or any asset which it represents or from which it is derived) had previously been in the beneficial ownership of

   (i) the person liable to pay the royalties,

   (ii) a person who has at any time carried on a business which, when the royalties fall due, is carried on in whole or part by the person liable to pay the royalties, or

(iii) a person who is or has been an 'associate', as specially defined, of a person within (i) or (ii),

the amounts paid under the transaction(s) which resulted in the asset falling into its present beneficial ownership, the amounts which would have been so paid in the absence of the special relationship, and the question as to whether the transaction(s) would have taken place at all in the absence of that relationship.

The taxpayer must also show either that no special relationship exists, or the amount of royalties which would have been paid in the absence of the relationship, and if he cannot show that (B) above does not apply, he must show that the transaction(s) mentioned therein would have taken place in the absence of a special relationship, and the amounts which would then have been paid under those transaction(s).

[*ICTA 1988, s 808B; FA 2000, Sch 30 para 25*].

Dividends. Where a dividend is paid to a UK resident company (or, for accounting periods ending on or after 21 March 2000, to a non-resident company but forming part of the profits of a UK branch or agency) by a 'related company' in the circumstances set out in 21.2(*b*) above, relief is given for the following taxes payable by the overseas company in respect of its profits

(*a*) any UK income or corporation tax; and

(*b*) any tax imposed by the law of any other territory.

Where the overseas company has received a dividend from a third company similarly related to the overseas company, relief may similarly be claimed (subject to certain restrictions on the taxes to be taken into account) for underlying tax payable by the third company, to the extent that it would have been taken into account had it been paid direct to a UK-resident company entitled to relief. Dividends payable through a chain of related companies may similarly be relieved. See, however, below as regards a general restriction on the amount of relief applicable where dividends are paid through so-called 'mixer' companies. [*ICTA 1988, s 801; FA 2000, Sch 30 para 4(7)–(9)(14)*]. Where an 'avoidance scheme' is involved, underlying tax relating to a dividend paid after 25 November 1996 includes an amount in respect of tax payable (by reference to the profits which bear that tax) at a rate in excess of the full corporation tax rate in force at the time the dividend was paid, relief is restricted as if tax had been payable at the corporation tax rate. An '*avoidance scheme*' for this purpose is a scheme or arrangement of any kind, a main purpose of which is to claim relief for an amount of underlying tax, and the parties to which include the company claiming the relief (or a related company or a connected person within *ICTA 1988, s 839*) and a person not under the control (as specially defined) of that company at any time before anything is done in relation to the scheme etc.. [*ICTA 1988, s 801A; FA 1997, s 90; FA 2000, Sch 30 para 4(10)–(12)(14)*]. See Example at 21.4 below. For an indication of Revenue practice as to the circumstances in which *section 801A* may be applied, see Revenue Tax Bulletin June 1997 p 441.

In relation to dividends received by a UK-resident company after 20 March 2000 from an overseas company, relief for underlying tax is extended to include cases where profits of an overseas company ('company A'), which have borne foreign tax, become profits of another overseas company ('company B') other than by payment of a dividend (e.g. following a merger), and company B then pays a dividend to another company out of those profits. For the purposes of underlying tax relief, company B is treated as having paid the tax paid by company A in respect of those of its profits which have become profits of company B. However, the amount of relief accordingly available to a UK-resident company is limited to that which would have been available had the profits been transferred from company A to company B by way of dividend. [*ICTA 1988, s 801B; FA 2000, Sch 30 para 12*].

There are also provisions enabling two or more overseas companies which are taxed as a single entity in the country or territory in which they are resident to be treated as a single company for underlying tax relief purposes in relation to the payment of a dividend to another company on or after 21 March 2000 by any one of the overseas companies. [*ICTA 1988, s 803A; FA 2000, Sch 30 para 15*].

For the scope of 'dividends' attracting treaty relief, see *Memec plc v CIR CA 1998, 71 TC 77* (in which receipts under a silent partnership agreement were held not to attract relief), and see also Revenue Tax Bulletin February 1999 p 627 for an article on the classification of foreign entities for UK tax purposes.

Credit for underlying tax (i.e. any tax not chargeable directly on, or by deduction from, the dividend) along a chain of shareholdings is concessionally given to

(i) portfolio shareholders (where relief is given under the relevant double tax agreement for underlying tax); or

(ii) resident insurance companies carrying on part of their business through an overseas branch or agency; or

(iii) resident companies controlling at least ten per cent of the voting power of an overseas company carrying on insurance business. Credit under this last head is subject to apportionment.

(Revenue Pamphlet IR 1, C1).

For underlying tax generally see *Barnes v Hely-Hutchinson HL 1939, 22 TC 655; Canadian Eagle Oil Co Ltd v R HL 1945, 27 TC 205; Brooke Bond & Co Ltd v Butter Ch D 1962, 40 TC 342.*

Restriction of relief — 'mixer' companies. Provisions which effectively eliminate the tax advantage of routing overseas dividends through 'mixer' companies in favourable foreign jurisdictions (such as the Netherlands) apply to claims for credit relief made on or after 31 March 2001, unless the dividend concerned was paid to the UK-resident company before that date. (For the purposes of such claims made on or after that date, however, all payments of dividends to the 'mixer' company or at more remote levels are deemed to have been subject to the new provisions.) In relation to such claims, the relievable underlying tax in respect of any dividend paid up through an overseas subsidiary is restricted to the corporation tax rate in force at the time the dividend was paid, applied to the amount of the dividend grossed-up at that rate. The restriction does **not**, however, apply where the overseas companies paying and receiving the dividend are 'related' (see above) and are both resident in the same overseas territory (subject to Treasury regulations which may prescribe cases where this exclusion will not apply). [*ICTA 1988, s 799(1)(b)(1A), s 801(2A); FA 2000, Sch 30 paras 8, 11*]. See also 21.6 below for provisions which permit a degree of 'onshore pooling' of dividend income against the tax on which relief at a rate of up to 45% may be obtained for underlying tax so capped in certain cases.

Simon's Direct Tax Service. See F1.111 *et seq.*.

21.4 *Example*

T Ltd, a UK-resident company liable to corporation tax at the full 30% rate for the year ended 31 March 2001, receives a dividend on 1 January 2001 of £18,500 (tax withheld £925) from X inc, a non-UK resident company in which it holds 20% of the voting power. It claims relief for underlying tax of £6,500 as follows.

£1,500 tax at 10% on profits of £15,000 out of which £13,500 dividend paid

£5,000 tax at 50% on profits of Y pty (a subsidiary of X inc) from whom dividend received out of which £5,000 dividend paid.

T Ltd computes relief as follows.

	£	£
Gross dividend received		18,500
plus underlying tax		6,500
		£25,000
Tax thereon at 30%		7,500
less underlying tax	6,500	
tax withheld	925	7,425
Corporation tax payable		£ 75

It transpires, however, that the dividend from Y pty was bought in as part of a tax avoidance scheme, so that the provisions of *ICTA 1988, s 801A* apply. The computation is therefore revised as follows.

	£	£
Gross dividend received		18,500
plus underlying tax (see below)		3,643
		22,143
Tax thereon at 30%		6,643
less underlying tax	3,643	
tax withheld	925	4,568
Corporation tax payable		£2,075

Underlying tax

The relief for underlying tax in respect of the dividend from Y pty is recalculated as if the tax rate on the underlying profits had been the corporation tax rate of 30% applicable at the time of receipt of the dividend from X inc by T Ltd.

£5,000 × $\frac{100}{70}$ = £7,143 on which 30% tax is £2,143.

The total underlying tax is thus (£2,143 + £1,500=) £3,643

21.5 METHOD OF GIVING RELIEF

Relief is to be allowed by way of credit against attributable corporation tax (i.e. UK tax otherwise chargeable) on that income, up to the amount of that tax. [*ICTA 1988, s 797(1)*]. This applies both to unilateral relief [*ICTA 1988, s 790(1)–(3)*] and to relief by agreement, though it is confined in the latter case to those UK taxes which are covered by the agreement. [*ICTA 1988, s 793*]. Relief is only available against UK tax chargeable under the same Schedule and Case as that under which the foreign income on which the foreign tax was borne is chargeable (*George Wimpey International Ltd v Rolfe Ch D 1989, 62 TC 597*). Relief must be claimed within six years after the end of the accounting period for which the income is chargeable or, after 20 March 2000, within one year after the end of the accounting period in which the foreign tax is paid, if later. Where, on or after 17 March 1998, the amount of foreign tax payable is adjusted subsequent to a claim for relief, with the result that the tax credit becomes excessive, the taxpayer must give written notice to the Revenue of this fact within one year of the date on which the adjustment is made, subject to a penalty for failure to comply which may not exceed the excess relief. For the Revenue view of what constitutes an 'adjustment', and when an adjustment is made, see Revenue Tax Bulletin June 1999 p 673. Certain cases where the adjustment is taken into account under regulations relating to Lloyd's underwriters are excluded from this requirement. [*ICTA 1988, s 806; FA 1996, Sch 21 para 23; FA 1998, s 107; FA 2000, Sch 30 para 20*].

For claims made after 20 March 2000, it is in addition provided that relief under an agreement is limited to that which would be allowed if all reasonable steps had been taken, including all relevant claims, elections, etc., under the law of the territory concerned or under double tax arrangements with that territory, to minimise the foreign tax payable. Guidance is to be published on what the Revenue considers taxpayers can and cannot reasonably be expected to do, but the former is likely to include appeals against excessive assessments, claims for reliefs generally known to be available, and selection of any option which produces a lower tax liability, and the latter is likely to include claims to reliefs whose availability is uncertain, and where disproportionate expenditure would be required to pursue a claim, substituting carry-forward claims for carry-back claims and *vice versa*, and attempting to exercise influence the taxpayer does not have on the underlying tax paid by a subsidiary. [*ICTA 1988, s 795A; FA 2000, Sch 30 para 6*].

Both reliefs apply, *mutatis mutandis*, to corporation tax on chargeable gains. [*ICTA 1988, ss 788(1), 790(1)*]. Relief for overseas tax paid is available against UK tax on chargeable gains provided that both liabilities relate to the same source, i.e. notwithstanding that they may arise at different times or be charged on different persons. (Revenue Pamphlet IR 131, SP 6/88, 4 November 1988).

Utilisation of unrelieved foreign tax. These provisions apply, in the case of foreign branch or agency profits, to 'unrelieved foreign tax' arising in any accounting period ending after 1 April 2000 (but not so as to permit carry back to an accounting period ending before that date). '*Unrelieved foreign tax*' on any income is the excess of the amount of the credit for foreign tax which would (disregarding the limitation to corporation tax on that income, see 21.5 below) be available under any double tax arrangements against corporation tax in respect of the income over the amount which is actually so allowed. (There are no comparable provisions for unilateral relief (see 21.2 above).)

Where an amount of unrelieved foreign tax arises in respect of any UK-resident company 'qualifying income', the unrelieved foreign tax may, on a claim, be treated as if it were paid in respect of, and computed by reference to, income of the same description and from the same source in either

(*a*) the next accounting period (and successive accounting periods), whether or not there is any income from that source in that accounting period, or

(*b*) such one or more preceding accounting periods, beginning not more than three years before that in which the unrelieved foreign tax arises, as results from applying the rules described below,

or partly in one way and partly in the other. The rules referred to in (*b*) above require that the unrelieved foreign tax must be so treated that:

(1) credit for it (or for any remaining balance) is allowed against corporation tax in respect of income of a later period before an earlier one; and

(2) before allowing credit for it against corporation tax in respect of any income of an accounting period, credit for foreign tax must be allowed first for foreign tax in respect of the income of that period (other than unrelieved foreign tax of another period), and then for unrelieved foreign tax arising in an earlier accounting period before a later one.

Where unrelieved foreign tax of an accounting period is treated as paid in respect of income of another accounting period, no further application of these provisions may be made in relation to that tax.

'*Qualifying income*' of a branch or agency is profits of the branch or agency which are chargeable under Schedule D, Case I (or certain other such profits of LIFE INSURANCE COMPANIES (41)).

If a particular branch or agency ceases in an accounting period, unrelieved foreign tax relating to it may not be carried forward from that period. If the company subsequently in the same period has a branch or agency in the same territory, it is treated as a new and different source. However, two or more overseas branches or agencies in the same territory which are taxed as one under the law of that territory are treated for the purposes of these provisions as a single branch or agency.

Claims to relief under (*a*) or (*b*) above must be made within six years of the end of the accounting period in which the unrelieved foreign tax arose (or, if later, within one year of the end of the accounting period in which the foreign tax in question is paid) and must specify the amounts to be dealt with under each of (*a*) and (*b*) above.

[*ICTA 1988, ss 806L, 806M; FA 2000, Sch 30 para 23*].

There are similar provisions relating to underlying tax relief on dividend income (see 21.6 below). See *ICTA 1988, ss 806D–806G* introduced by *FA 2000, Sch 30 para 21.*

21.6 MEASURE OF UNDERLYING TAX RELIEF

The underlying tax is calculated in accordance with *ICTA 1988, s 799* (as amended), by reference to the paying company's 'relevant profits' (i.e. its profits available for distribution) as shown by the accounts and not as computed for foreign tax purposes (*Bowater Paper Corporation Ltd v Murgatroyd HL 1969, 46 TC 37*). This is added to any tax chargeable directly on, or deducted from, the dividend, and the total is deducted from the UK tax as under 21.5 above. The Revenue have indicated that they follow the spirit and letter of the *Bowater* case in determining 'relevant profits', though they regard these as including capital profits credited to capital reserves. Unrealised gains on currency re-alignments are not regarded as available for distribution unless actually distributed or included in the accounts as distributable. (Revenue Company Taxation Manual, CT 8411). In relation to dividends paid after 20 March 2000, *FA 2000, Sch 30 para 9* introduces new *ICTA 1988, s 799(5)–(7)*, under which 'profits available for distribution' are specifically defined as those shown in accounts drawn up in accordance with the law of the country or territory in which the distributing company is incorporated or formed, with no provision for reserves, bad debts or contingencies except as required under that law.

Rates of underlying tax are calculated by the FICO (International), Double Taxation (Rates) Section, Fitz Roy House, P.O. Box 46, Nottingham NG2 1BN (tel. 0115–974 2033) in accordance with the following formula.

$$\frac{\text{actual tax paid} \times 100}{\text{actual tax paid} + \text{relevant profit}}$$

This formula automatically takes into account any deferred taxation charged plus under- and over-provisions for tax in previous years. (CCAB Memorandum 19 October 1979).

Example

A Ltd, a company resident in the UK, receives a dividend of £1,000 gross from B Ltd, an overseas company in which it controls ten per cent of the voting power. Overseas tax of £100 is deducted. The *underlying tax rate* for the dividend is agreed at 18%.

21.6 Double Tax Relief

Gross dividend			£1,000.00
Underlying tax @ 18%			219.51
Underlying assessable income			£1,219.51
Corporation tax thereon @ say 30%			£365.85
Overseas tax suffered:	Direct tax	£100.00	
	Underlying tax	219.51	
Tax credit relief due			319.51
Corporation tax payable			£46.34

If the corporation tax liability were at 20% (£243.90), the relief would be restricted to this amount.

The underlying tax for which relief is given is limited in certain cases to the amount of the tax actually paid by the overseas company on the particular profits out of which the dividend is paid. This applies in particular to dividends declared by and from a company resident in Belize, the Gambia, Malaysia, Malta or Singapore (where relief is given under an agreement) or Guernsey or Jersey (where the relief is unilateral), each of which operates a 'company tax deducted' system whereby tax is deducted from the dividend at the standard corporate rate and accounted for to the tax authorities, but subject to subsequent adjustment. Insofar as that tax is refunded or found not to be due, double tax relief is denied. (Revenue Pamphlet IR 131, SP 12/93, 27 July 1993).

Where companies merge, relief may in certain circumstances be obtained for tax paid in respect of pre-merger profits by the company resulting from the merger. See Revenue Tax Bulletin October 1997 pp 473, 474.

For the calculation of relief for Californian corporate franchise tax, see Revenue Tax Bulletin February 1995 p 194.

A series of leaflets, giving general guidance on computing an underlying rate and information about underlying tax in more than 75 countries, is available from FICO (International), address as above.

Onshore pooling and utilisation of unrelieved foreign tax. In relation, broadly, to dividends paid on or after 31 March 2001, relief for underlying tax on dividends paid up through overseas subsidiaries is generally restricted to the full corporation tax rate in force when the dividend is paid (the 'cap' aimed at avoidance through the use of so-called 'mixer' companies, see 21.3 above). However, a partial relief from this capping restriction is provided by the concurrent introduction of a system of 'onshore pooling' of certain foreign dividends, against the tax on which may be set the excess tax over the cap, allowing relief up to a maximum of 45% in total. Relief may similarly be obtained up to the same overall 45% limit for unrelieved withholding and underlying tax on dividends received directly from overseas subsidiaries. The two main exclusions from the onshore pool are dividends paid by controlled foreign companies to satisfy the acceptable distribution policy test (see below), or dividends representing such dividends, and dividends for which relief is itself restricted (as above). Other exclusions, both from pooling and from the categories of dividend on which unrelieved tax may be treated as eligible for relief under these provisions, are dividends treated (or which could be treated) as trading income under *ICTA 1988, s 393* (see 44.4 LOSSES), dividends the underlying tax on which is subject to restriction under *ICTA 1988, s 801A* (see 21.3 above) or *ICTA 1988, s 803* (see 21.11 below), and dividends treated under *ICTA 1988, s 811* as reduced by foreign tax paid for which no credit is allowable (see Tolley's Income Tax under Double Tax Relief). Provision is made for relief to be given in the same accounting period or in accounting periods beginning not more than three years before that in which the relievable tax arises, or to be carried forward, broadly in the same way as applies in relation to foreign tax on income other than dividend income (see 21.5 above). Repayment supplement is restricted where relief is carried back to an earlier accounting period, in the same way as applies in relation to the carry back of losses, loan relationship deficits, etc. (see 38.1 INTEREST ON OVERPAID TAX). Regulations are to be introduced allowing the surrender of foreign tax relievable as above between members of GROUPS OF COMPANIES (29). [*ICTA 1988, ss 806A–806J, 826(7BB)(7BC); FA 2000, Sch 30 paras 21, 29*]. These provisions are applied *mutatis mutandis* to UK branches or agencies of non-UK residents. [*ICTA 1988, s 806K; FA 2000, Sch 30 para 22*].

Controlled foreign company dividends. Where a controlled foreign company ('CFC') is exempt from a profit apportionment under *ICTA 1988, s 747* solely by virtue of the payment of a dividend or dividends satisfying the 'acceptable distribution policy' test (see 18.12 CONTROLLED FOREIGN COMPANIES), and any dividend by virtue of which that test is met is a dividend paid by the CFC to another non-UK resident company and subsequently paid on to a UK resident, there are provisions for the separate streaming of the dividend for all credit relief purposes, thus in effect preventing the avoidance of tax on dividends paid in order to gain exemption from CFC apportionment. These provisions have effect as above, broadly for dividends paid on or after 31 March 2001. [*ICTA 1988, s 801C; FA 2000, Sch 30 para 13*].

Simon's Direct Tax Service. See **F1.131** *et seq.*.

21.7 ALLOCATION OF CHARGES ETC. AND (BEFORE 6 APRIL 1999) ADVANCE CORPORATION TAX

In arriving at corporation tax attributable to the relevant income or gain for a relevant accounting period, the following is to be taken into account.

(i) Charges on income, expenses of management or other amounts which can be deducted from or set against or treated as reducing profits of more than one description may be allocated as the company thinks fit. [*ICTA 1988, s 797(3)*]. Charges so allocated may not, however, exceed the income against which they are set (*Commercial Union Assurance Co plc v Shaw CA, [1999] STC 109*).

(ii) For accounting periods beginning before 6 April 1999, the foreign tax credit is deducted from the attributable corporation tax (see 21.5 above) before ADVANCE CORPORATION TAX (3) is deducted. The maximum amount of ACT which may be set against corporation tax relating to a particular item of income or gain is the lower of

   (*a*) the limit which would apply under *ICTA 1988, s 239(2)* (see 3.6 ADVANCE CORPORATION TAX) if the relevant income or gain were the company's only income or gain, and

   (*b*) the corporation tax liability in respect of that income or gain as reduced by the foreign tax credit. [*ICTA 1988, s 797(4)(5); FA 1998, Sch 3 para 35*].

(iii) Where a non-trading credit relating to interest (or, for accounting periods ending after 20 March 2000, to non-interest items) is brought into account as regards a loan relationship (see 43.3 LOAN RELATIONSHIPS), special provision is made for the attribution of corporation tax to such credits for the purposes of relief of any foreign tax on the item. [*ICTA 1988, s 797A; FA 1996, Sch 14 para 43; FA 1998, s 82(2); FA 2000, Sch 30 para 7*]. Where this does not apply, and there is a non-trading deficit (see 43.3 LOAN RELATIONSHIPS) on the company's loan relationships, the deficit is allocated for foreign tax relief purposes in the same way as relief is claimed under *FA*

1996, s 83. [*ICTA 1988, s 797(3A)(3B); FA 1996, Sch 14 para 42; FA 1998, s 82(2)*].

Simon's Direct Tax Service. See **F2.103.**

21.8 *Example*

The following information about A Ltd (which owns 20% of the voting power of B Ltd, a non-resident company) for the year ended 31 March 1999 is relevant.

	£
UK income	1,200,000
UK chargeable gains	300,000
Overseas income (tax rate 40%) from B Ltd (gross)	300,000
Charges paid (gross)	150,000
ACT paid	300,000

A Ltd may allocate charges and ACT as it wishes in order to obtain maximum double tax relief. The following calculation shows how this is best done.

	UK income and gains	Overseas income	Total
	£	£	£
Income and gains	1,500,000	300,000	1,800,000
Deduct Charges	150,000	—	150,000
	£1,350,000	£300,000	£1,650,000
CT at 31%	418,500	93,000	511,500
Deduct Double tax relief	—	(93,000)	(93,000)
	418,500	—	418,500
Deduct ACT	(270,000)	—	(270,000)
'Mainstream' liability	£148,500	—	£148,500

If charges were set off against overseas income first, the following tax would be payable.

	UK income and gains	Overseas income	Total
	£	£	£
Income and gains	1,500,000	300,000	1,800,000
Deduct Charges	—	150,000	150,000
	£1,500,000	£150,000	£1,650,000
CT at 31%	465,000	46,500	511,500
Deduct Double tax relief	—	(46,500)	(46,500)
Deduct ACT	(300,000)	—	(300,000)
'Mainstream' liability	£165,000	—	£165,000

This gives a maximum double tax relief of £46,500, with no ACT carried forward. Compared with the recommended allocation, £46,500 of double tax relief (£93,000 – £46,500) is lost, representing an increase in the mainstream liability of £16,500 (£165,000 – £148,500) and a decrease of £30,000 in the surplus ACT carried forward.

Note

If the same figures applied for the year ended 31 March 2000, but with no payment of ACT and a CT rate of 30%, the saving would be £45,000, i.e. additional relief for the overseas tax at 30% on the amount of the charges, £150,000, relieved instead against UK income.

21.9 DIVIDENDS, INTEREST, ETC. PAID TO NON-RESIDENTS

Dividends. The Revenue could previously make arrangements with a UK resident company whereby it could pay to a non-resident shareholder that part of the tax credit relating to a dividend to which he was entitled under the terms of a double tax agreement (see 21.3 above). Such payment by the company discharged a corresponding amount of its liability to ACT. [*SI 1973 No 317*]. All such arrangements cease, however, on 6 April 1999. [*SI 1999 No 1927*]. See generally Revenue Tax Bulletin February 1999 pp 626, 627.

Under most agreements, half of the tax credit attached to a dividend, less a deduction by reference to a percentage of the sum of the dividend and the tax credit (see below), may be paid to the non-resident or set off against UK liabilities. See *Steele v EVC International NV (formerly European Vinyls Corp (Holdings) BV) CA 1996, 69 TC 88* for refusal of tax credit in the case of certain 'connected' companies. See also *Océ van Grinten NV v CIR (Sp C 231), [2000] SSCD 127* for a challenge to the deduction from the payment of the half tax credit.

Where a treaty provides for an overseas recipient of distributions from a UK resident company to receive a tax credit determined by reference to the credit a UK resident individual would receive, subject to a deduction calculated by reference to the sum of the distribution and the tax credit paid, the deduction is to be calculated without any allowance for the deduction itself. [*FA 1989, s 115*].

Where set-off or repayment of a sum in respect of a tax credit would be available under an agreement, it may nevertheless be denied where the non-resident recipient is, or is an 'associated company' of, a company with a 'qualifying presence' in a 'unitary state'. A company has such a '*qualifying presence*' if it is a member of a 'group' $7\frac{1}{2}$% of whose property, payroll or sales in the territory of which the state is a part are in that state. The Treasury may instead provide by order either that a company has a qualifying presence in a 'unitary state' if it is liable to tax on income or profits in that state, or alternatively that it has such a presence if its principal place of business is in that state, including the place(s) where central management and control and immediate day-to-day management are exercised. A '*unitary state*' is broadly a state, etc. which reserves the right to tax companies with sources of income within the state by taking into account the company's activities outside the territory of which the state is a part. The Treasury has powers to prescribe states, etc. as unitary states. A fine may be imposed where a tax credit is repaid despite its being within these provisions, and there are provisions for claiming tax credits following remedial legislation effective before 1 January 1987 in the unitary state, and to prevent avoidance by the payment of interest or the allowing of a discount in substitution for a distribution. Other terms are specifically defined in *ICTA 1988, s 812(5)*. These provisions, if applied, will take effect for distributions on or after a date to be appointed by the Treasury by statutory instrument, although implementation has now been indefinitely deferred, see Revenue Press Release 15 September 1993. [*ICTA 1988, ss 812–815; FA 1996, Sch 20 para 38; FA 1998, Sch 3 para 37*].

Interest etc.. Where payments required or authorised to be made under deduction of UK income tax are made to non-UK residents, the payer may be authorised by the Financial Intermediaries and Claims Office ('FICO'), by a notice under *SI 1970 No 488*, to make payments without deduction of tax, or under deduction of tax at a specified or maximum rate. Payments may normally only be so made once the notice has been given by FICO following application by the overseas recipient, and there may be a substantial delay in FICO being in a position to issue a notice in response to such an application. Accordingly, from 1 September 1999, a Provisional Treaty Relief scheme is introduced for two types of loan, the one-to-one company loan (provided that there is no common shareholding or ownership) and the syndicated loan, where there is a syndicate manager. This allows the UK borrower to apply for immediate authority to make payments incorporating the treaty relief, pending FICO's decision on the issue of a formal notice. It is a condition of the scheme that the recipient's application for relief (certified by the overseas tax authority) is received by FICO within three months of the provisional authority, and if that condition is not met, or the relief is found not to be due, FICO will look to the payer for the tax that should have been deducted (and any interest thereon). In the case of a syndicated loan, a composite application for relief (which does not need overseas tax authority certification) must be made by the syndicate manager within three months of the provisional authority. Application for provisional relief is made on form PTRPAY1 (in the case of one-to-one loans) or form PTRSM1 (in the case of syndicated loans), which may be obtained from Complex Claims Group (Provisional Treaty Relief Scheme), FICO, Fitz Roy House, PO Box 46, Nottingham NG2 1BD (tel. 0115–974 1904, fax. 0115–974 1918). Explanatory 'Guidelines' may be obtained from the same address. For a summary of the scheme, see Revenue Tax Bulletin June 1999 pp 668–670.

Simon's Direct Tax Service. See F1.302–F1.304.

21.10 AGREEMENTS IN FORCE

Agreements with the following countries came into force from the date specified in each agreement and remain so until further notice. *SI* dates and numbers are given in round brackets. For the agreement relating to Eire, see Tolley's Income Tax. For details of agreements, see Simon's Direct Tax Service F4. Representations on points interested parties would like to see addressed in negotiating particular treaties, or on other matters relating to the treaty negotiation programme or the treaty network, should be addressed to Mrs Jas Sahni, Inland Revenue, International Division, 2nd Floor, Victory House, 30–34 Kingsway, London WC2B 6ES.

Antigua and Barbuda (1947/2865, 1968/1096); **Argentina** (1997/1777) from 1 April 1998 (UK) and 1 January 1998 (Argentina); **Australia** (1968/305, 1980/707); **Austria** (1970/1947, 1979/117, 1994/768); **Azerbaijan** (1995/762) from 1 April 1996 (UK) and 1 January 1996 (Azerbaijan);

Bangladesh (1980/708); **Barbados** (1970/952, 1973/2096); **Belarus** (1995/2706) (and see note below); **Belgium** (1987/2053); **Belize** (1947/2866; 1968/573; 1973/2097); **Bolivia** (1995/2707) from 1 April 1996 (UK) and 1 January 1996 (Bolivia); **Bosnia-Hercegovina** (see note below); **Botswana** (1978/183); **British Honduras** (see Belize); **Brunei** (1950/1977, 1968/306, 1973/2098); **Bulgaria** (1987/2054); **Burma** (see Myanmar);

Canada (1980/709, 1980/780, 1980/1528, 1985/1996, 1987/2071, 1996/1782); **China** (1981/1119, 1984/1826, 1996/3164) (and see note below); **Croatia** (see note below); **Cyprus** (1975/425, 1980/1529); **Czech Republic** (see note below);

Denmark (1980/1960, 1991/2877, 1996/3165);

Egypt (1980/1091); **Eire** (1976/2151, 1976/2152, 1995/764, 1998/3151); **Estonia** (1994/3207) from 1 April 1995 (UK) and 1 January 1995 (Estonia);

Falkland Islands (1997/2985) from 1 April 1997 (UK) and 1 January 1997 (Falkland Islands); **Faroe Islands** (1961/579, 1971/717, 1975/2190) until 31 March 1997; **Fiji**

(1976/1342); **Finland** (1970/153, 1980/710, 1985/1997, 1991/2878, 1996/3166); **France** (1968/1869, 1973/1328, 1987/466, 1987/2055);

Gambia (1980/1963); **Germany** (1967/25, 1971/874); **Ghana** (1993/1800, and see note below) from 1 April 1995 (UK) and 1 January 1995 (Ghana); **Greece** (1954/142); **Grenada** (1949/361, 1968/1867); **Guernsey** (1952/1215, 1994/3209); **Guyana** (1992/3207);

Hungary (1978/1056);

Iceland (1991/2879); **India** (1981/1120, 1993/1801); **Indonesia** (1994/769) from 1 April 1995 (UK) and 1 January 1995 (Indonesia); **Isle of Man** (1955/1205, 1991/ 2880, 1994/3208); **Israel** (1963/616, 1971/391); **Italy** (1990/2590); **Ivory Coast** (1987/169);

Jamaica (1973/1329); **Japan** (1970/1948, 1980/1530); **Jersey** (1952/1216, 1994/3210);

Kazakhstan (1994/3211, 1998/2567); **Kenya** (1977/1299); **Kiribati and Tuvalu** (1950/750, 1968/309, 1974/1271); **Korea (South)** (1978/786, 1996/3168) (new treaty applies from 1 April 1997 (UK) and 1 January 1997 (Korea));

Latvia (1996/3167) from 1 April 1997 (UK) and 1 January 1997 (Latvia); **Lesotho** (1997/2986) from 1 April 1998; **Luxembourg** (1968/1100, 1980/567, 1984/364);

Macedonia (see note below); **Malawi** (1956/619, 1964/1401, 1968/1101, 1979/302); **Malaysia** (1973/1330, 1987/2056, 1997/2987) (new treaty applies from 1 April 1999 (UK) and 1 January 1999 and 1 January 2000 (Malaysia)); **Malta** (1962/69, 1975/426, 1995/763) (new treaty applies from 1 April 1996 (UK) and 1 January 1996 (Malta)); **Mauritius** (1981/1121, 1987/467); **Mexico** (1994/3212); **Mongolia** (1996/2598) from 1 April 1997 (UK) and 1 January 1997 (Mongolia); **Montserrat** (1947/2869, 1968/576); **Morocco** (1991/2881); **Myanmar** (1952/751);

Namibia (1962/2352, 1967/1490); **Netherlands** (1967/1063, 1980/1961, 1983/1902); **New Zealand** (1984/365); **Nigeria** (1987/2057); **Norway** (1985/1998);

Oman (1998/2568) from 1 April 1996 (UK) and 1 January 1996 (Oman);

Pakistan (1987/2058); **Papua New Guinea** (1991/2882); **Philippines** (1978/184); **Poland** (1978/282); **Portugal** (1969/599);

Romania (1977/57); **Russia** (1994/3213) from 1 April 1998 (UK) and 1 January 1998 (Russia) (and see note below);

St. Christopher (St. Kitts) and Nevis (1947/2872); **Sierra Leone** (1947/2873, 1968/1104); **Singapore** (1997/2988) from 1 April 1998 (UK) and 1 January 1999 (Singapore); **Slovak Republic** (see note below); **Slovenia** (see note below); **Solomon Islands** (1950/748, 1968/574, 1974/1270); **South Africa** (1969/864); **South West Africa** (see Namibia); **Spain** (1976/1919, 1995/765); **Sri Lanka** (1980/713); **Sudan** (1977/1719); **Swaziland** (1969/380); **Sweden** (1961/619, 1984/366); **Switzerland** (1978/1408, 1982/714, 1994/3215);

Thailand (1981/1546); **Trinidad and Tobago** (1983/1903); **Tunisia** (1984/133); **Turkey** (1988/932);

Uganda (1993/1802); **Ukraine** (1993/1803)(see note below); **USA** (1946/1331, 1955/499, 1961/985, 1980/568, 1980/779, 1994/1418, 1996/1781); **USSR** (see note below); **Uzbekistan** (1994/770) from 1 April 1995 (UK) and 1 January 1995 (Uzbekistan) (and see note below);

Venezuela (1996/2599) from 1 April 1997 (UK) and 1 January 1997 (Venezuela); **Vietnam** (1994/3216) from 1 April 1995 (UK) and various dates (Vietnam);

Yugoslavia (see note below);

Zambia (1972/1721, 1981/1816); **Zimbabwe** (1982/1842).

Shipping & Air Transport only—Algeria (Air Transport only) (1984/362), Argentina (but see now above), Belarus (but see now above), Brazil (1968/572), Cameroon (Air Transport only) (1982/1841), China (Air Transport only) (1981/1119), Ethiopia (Air Transport only) (1977/1297), Hong Kong (Air Transport only) (1998/2566) from 1 April 1998, Iran (Air Transport only) (1960/2419), Jordan (1979/300), Kuwait (Air Transport only) (1984/1825), Lebanon (1964/278), Russia (but see now above), Saudi Arabia (Air Transport only) (1994/767) from 3 October 1994, Venezuela (but see now above), U.S.S.R. (but see now above), Ukraine (but see now above), Uzbekistan (but see now above), Zaire (1977/1298).

(*Notes. China*. The Convention published as *SI 1984 No 1826* does not apply to the Hong Kong Special Administrative Region which comes into existence on 1 July 1997. (Revenue Tax Bulletin October 1996 p 357). See above as regards Air Transport agreement.

Czechoslovakia. The Convention published as *SI 1991 No 2876*, which took effect from 1 April 1992 (UK) and 1 January 1992 (Czechoslovakia), is treated as remaining in force between the UK and, respectively, the Czech Republic and the Slovak Republic. (Revenue Pamphlet IR 131, SP 5/93, 19 March 1993).

Ghana. The Convention published as *SI 1978 No 785* was subsequently found never to have been ratified in Ghana and consequently never to have had effect. The Arrangement published as *SR&O 1947 No 2868* with the Gold Coast accordingly continued in effect, and was reapplied from 1 April 1991 until such time as the new Convention (*SI 1993 No 1800*) came into effect. For the period from 1 April 1977 to 31 March 1991, whichever is more favourable to the taxpayer may be applied, out-of-date claims under the 1947 Arrangement being accepted for this purpose. (Revenue Press Release 31 January 1991).

U.S.S.R. The Convention published as *SI 1986 No 224* (which also continued in force the air transport agreement published as *SI 1974 No 1269*) is to be regarded as having been in force between the UK and Uzbekistan and the Russian Federation, and as continuing in force with Belarus, until the coming into force of, respectively, *SI 1994 No 770*, *SI 1994 No 3213* and *SI 1995 No 2706*. As regards the other former Soviet Republics, the UK will continue to apply the provisions of that Convention on the basis that it is still in force until such time as new agreements take effect with particular countries. (Revenue Tax Bulletin June 1998 p 559).

Yugoslavia. The Convention published as *SI 1981 No 1815* is treated as remaining in force between the UK and, respectively, Croatia, Slovenia, Macedonia and the Former Republic of Yugoslavia. The position as regards the remainder of former Yugoslavia remains to be established. (Revenue Tax Bulletin June 1998 p 559).)

21.11 BANKS

There are special provisions intended to prevent excessive double taxation relief being obtained in respect of interest on loans to non-residents, and on dividends where underlying tax relates to such loans. These are extended from 17 March 1998 (deferred, in the case of payments under arrangements entered into before that day, to 1 January 1999) to cover certain foreign dividends where the foreign tax includes underlying tax, and interest and dividend income of associates (within *ICTA 1988, s 783(10)*), or CONNECTED PERSONS (16), of banks and other financial traders. [*ICTA 1988, ss 798–798B, 803; FA 1996, Sch 14 para 44; FA 1998, ss 103–106; SI 1988 No 88; SI 1999 No 3330*]. See Revenue Tax Bulletin April 1996 p 306.

A foreign bank trading in the UK through a branch or agency may claim tax credit relief for tax withheld by a third country from interest on a loan to a resident of that country. [*ICTA 1988, s 794(2)(c)*]. For accounting periods ending after 20 March 2000, this is replaced by a wider relief available on similar terms to all non-UK resident persons (whether companies or individuals) with UK branches or agencies. [*ICTA 1988, s 794(2)(bb); FA 2000, Sch 30 para 4(4)–(6)(14)*].

See *CIR v Commerzbank AG; CIR v Banco Do Brasil SA Ch D 1990, 63 TC 218* for a case on interest exemption under the UK/USA Agreement.

See also 44.25 LOSSES.

Simon's Direct Tax Service. See **F1.123**.

21.12 **OIL COMPANIES**

There are special provisions relating to oil fields which straddle international boundaries. [*FA 1980, s 107*].

22 European Community Legislation

22.1 Statements of the European Council and European Commission are graded under the *EC Treaty* as follows.

(*a*) **Regulations** are binding in their entirety and have general effect in all Member States. They are directly applicable in the legal systems of Member States and do not have to be implemented by national legislation.

(*b*) **Directives** are binding as to result and their general effect is specific to named Member States. The form and methods of compliance are left to individual Member States, which are normally given a specific period in which to implement the necessary legislation.

(*c*) **Decisions** are binding in their entirety and are specific to a Member State, commercial enterprise or private individual. They take effect on notification to the addressee.

(*d*) **Recommendations and opinions** are not binding and are directed to specific subjects on which the Council's or Commission's advice has been sought.

22.2 European Community law is effective in the UK by virtue of *European Communities Act 1972, s 2*, and the European Court of Justice has held that 'wherever the provisions of a Directive appear . . . to be unconditional and sufficiently precise, those provisions may . . . be relied upon as against any national provision which is incompatible with the Directive insofar as the provisions define rights which individuals are able to assert against the State' (*Becker v Finanzamt Munster-Innenstadt [1982] 1 CMLR 499*). Judgments in the European Court of Justice also have supremacy over domestic decisions, even if the proceedings commenced in another Member State.

22.3 In contrast to the extensive application of EU legislation in the VAT sphere, direct taxes are currently subject to only the following three specific measures.

(*a*) *Council Regulation 2137/85* (25 July 1985) concerning European Economic Interest Groupings.

(*b*) *Directive 90/434/EEC* (23 July 1990) concerning mergers, divisions, transfers of assets and exchanges of shares concerning companies of different Member States.

(*c*) *Directive 90/435/EEC* (23 July 1990) concerning distributions of profits to parent companies.

As regards (*a*), see the related UK legislation at 50.12 PROFIT COMPUTATIONS, and as regards (*b*), 9.8, 9.9 CAPITAL GAINS. As regards (*c*), see Tolley's Income Tax under Deduction of Tax at Source. The Revenue Consultative Document on EC Direct Tax Measures published in December 1991 sets out the manner in which (*b*) and (*c*) are considered to be implemented through these changes.

For a case on the application of *Directive 90/434/EEC*, see *Leur-Bloem v Inspecteur der Belastingdienst/Ondernemingen Amsterdam 2 (Case C–28/95) ECJ, [1997] STC 1205.*

In addition to the above, *Convention 90/436/EEC* (23 July 1990), concerning arbitration in double taxation disputes, came into force on 1 January 1995. See 4.4 ANTI-AVOIDANCE.

22.4 Three further *Directives* have been proposed, concerning interest and royalty payments between parent and subsidiary companies, relief for losses of branches or subsidiaries in other Member States, and carry-over of losses of undertakings. The first has now been withdrawn, and there is currently little prospect of progress on adoption of the other two.

23 Exchange Gains and Losses

Simon's Direct Tax Service B3.17.

Other Sources. See Tolley's Taxation of Foreign Exchange Gains and Losses.

The headings in this chapter are as follows.

23.1	Introduction
23.2	General case law and practice
23.3, 23.4	— Revenue practice
23.5, 23.6	Special provisions for qualifying companies
23.7–23.10	— accrual of gains and losses
23.11	— trading gains and losses
23.12	— example
23.13, 23.14	— non-trading gains and losses
23.15	— alternative method of calculation
23.16	— main benefit test — loss relief restriction
23.17	— arm's length test — loss relief restriction
23.18	— deferral of unrealised gains
23.19	— example
23.20	— irrecoverable debts
23.21	— early termination of currency contracts
23.22	— reciprocal currency contracts
23.23	— excess gains or losses
23.24	— local currency
23.25	— exchange rate to be used
23.26	— entitlement to, and identification of, an asset
23.27	— subjection to, and identification of, a liability
23.28	— assets and liabilities — general
23.29	— chargeable gains
23.30	— partnerships which include qualifying companies
23.31	— miscellaneous
23.32	— commencement and transitional provisions
23.33	Corporation tax currency provisions
23.34	— certain interest not allowed as a deduction
23.35	— post–FA 2000: the basic corporation tax rule: sterling to be used
23.36	— post–FA 2000: use of currency other than sterling
23.37	— post–FA 2000: currency equivalents
23.38	— pre–FA 2000: the basic corporation tax rule: sterling to be used
23.39	— pre–FA 2000: currency other than sterling for trades
23.40, 23.41	— pre–FA 2000: parts of trades

23.1 INTRODUCTION

For accounting periods beginning on or after 23 March 1995, a new regime applies to the determination, and charge or relief, of exchange gains and losses of companies (other than certain charitable companies, investment trusts and deemed companies in relation to authorised unit trusts, see 23.6 below). See 23.5 *et seq.* below for details of these provisions. For earlier accounting periods (and for companies to which the provisions do not apply), the position continues to be as described at 23.2 *et seq.* below (which also applies to taxpayers other than companies).

23.2 GENERAL CASE LAW AND PRACTICE

Under general case law, exchange differences are taken into account in computing trading profits if they relate to the circulating capital of the business but not otherwise. In *Overseas Containers (Finance) Ltd v Stoker CA 1989, 61 TC 473*, exchange losses arising on loans transferred to a finance subsidiary set up to convert the losses to trading account were held not to arise from trading transactions.

In *Davies v The Shell Co of China Ltd CA 1951, 32 TC 133*, a petrol marketing company operating in China required agents to deposit Chinese dollars with it, repayable on the ending of the agency. Exchange profits it made on repaying the deposits were held to be capital. In *Firestone Tyre & Rubber Co Ltd v Evans Ch D 1976, 51 TC 615*, a company repaid in 1965 a dollar balance due to its US parent, the greater part of the balance representing advances in 1922–1931 to finance the company when it started. The Commissioners' finding that 90% of the substantial resultant exchange loss was capital, and not allowable, was upheld. A profit by an agent on advances to the principal to finance purchases by the agent on behalf of the principal was held to be a trading receipt (*Landes Bros v Simpson KB 1934, 19 TC 62*), as was a profit by a tobacco company on dollars accumulated to finance its future purchases (*Imperial Tobacco Co Ltd v Kelly CA 1943, 25 TC 292*). See also *McKinlay v H T Jenkins & Son Ltd KB 1926, 10 TC 372*; *Ward v Anglo-American Oil Ltd KB 1934, 19 TC 94*; *Beauchamp v F W Woolworth plc HL 1989, 61 TC 542*; and contrast *Radio Pictures Ltd v CIR CA 1938, 22 TC 106*. Where a bank operated in foreign currencies and aimed at, and generally succeeded in, matching its monetary assets and liabilities in each currency, it was held that there could be no profit or loss from matched transactions where there were no relevant currency conversions (*Pattison v Marine Midland Ltd HL 1983, 57 TC 219*). In *Whittles v Uniholdings Ltd (No 3) CA 1996, 68 TC 528*, it was held that a dollar loan and a simultaneous forward contract with the same bank for dollars sufficient to repay the loan had to be treated, for tax purposes, as separate transactions, each giving rise to its own consequences.

Simon's Direct Tax Service. See B3.1706, B3.1707.

23.3 **Revenue practice.** Following the decision in the *Marine Midland* case (see 23.2 above), the Revenue issued a Statement of Practice (see now Revenue Pamphlet IR 131, SP 1/87, 17 February 1987) setting out their views on the general treatment of exchange differences for tax purposes. These are summarised at 23.4 below. Subject to the special provisions described at 23.5 *et seq.* below, which apply to 'qualifying companies' for accounting periods beginning after 22 March 1995, SP 1/87 continues to apply to non-qualifying companies and to individuals and partnerships.

Simon's Direct Tax Service. See B3.1708.

23.4 Where currency assets are matched by currency liabilities in a particular currency, so that a translation adjustment on one would be cancelled out by a translation adjustment on the other, no adjustment is required for tax purposes.

Where currency assets are not matched, or are incompletely matched, with currency liabilities in a particular currency, the adjustment required to the net exchange difference debited or credited in the profit and loss account is determined along the following lines.

(i) The aggregate exchange differences, positive and negative, on capital assets and liabilities in the profit and loss account figure are ascertained;

(ii) if there are no differences as at (i), no adjustment is required;

(iii) if the net exchange difference as at (i) is a loss, and the net exchange difference in the profit and loss account is also a loss, the smaller of the two losses is the amount disallowed for tax purposes;

(iv) if the net exchange difference as at (i) is a profit, and the net exchange difference in the profit and loss account is also a profit, the smaller of the two profits is allowed as a deduction for tax purposes;

(v) if the net exchange difference as at (i) is a loss, and the net exchange difference in the profit and loss account is a profit, or vice versa, no adjustment is required for tax purposes.

Where net exchange differences are taken to reserve rather than to the profit and loss account, the nature of the assets and liabilities will need to be considered to determine whether or not a tax adjustment is required, applying the principles as above.

In considering whether a trader is matched in a particular foreign currency, *forward exchange contracts* and *currency futures* entered into for hedging purposes may be taken into account, provided the hedging is reflected in the accounts on a consistent basis from year to year and in accordance with accepted accountancy practice. *Currency swap agreements* are treated as converting the liability in the original currency into a liability in the swap currency for the duration of the swap. Hedging through *currency options* does not result in any matching.

The Statement of Practice also indicates that the accounts treatment of financial assets of financial concerns held on the 'realisation' basis (i.e. where profits for tax purposes are assessable only on their disposal) will be acceptable for tax purposes where the profits or losses on realisation are in effect recognised for accounts purposes net of exchange differences.

Where an *overseas trade*, or an *overseas branch* of a trade, is carried on primarily in a non-sterling economic environment, the Revenue will accept computations based on

(*a*) local currency accounts, with the adjusted profit (before capital allowances) translated into sterling at either average or closing rate, or

(*b*) the sterling equivalent of local currency accounts, translated using the 'net investment/closing rate' method (see Statement of Standard Accounting Practice SSAP 20 paras 25, 46), or

(*c*) sterling accounts produced by the 'temporal' method (see SSAP 20 paras 4–12),

provided the same method is applied consistently from year to year. The principles outlined in the Statement of Practice should be applied in considering any adjustment necessary in respect of exchange differences in the foreign currency accounts.

Where *roundabout loan arrangements* are employed in unmatched or partly matched situations, the Revenue consider that, applying the *Ramsay* principle (see 4.1 ANTI-AVOIDANCE), such arrangements may fall to be treated for tax purposes by reference to their composite effect, depending on the facts of the particular case.

Groups of companies and non-trading companies. The principles outlined in the Statement of Practice apply only to individual trading companies and are inapplicable to a group of companies as a whole, or in a way which recognises 'matching' between assets and liabilities of different companies in a group. The Statement of Practice has no application to non-trading companies.

It will generally be for the trader to justify the adoption of any basis other than that outlined above in the particular circumstances of his case.

23.5 SPECIAL PROVISIONS FOR QUALIFYING COMPANIES

The main elements of the provisions in *FA 1993, ss 60, 92–96, 125–170, Schs 15–18*, which are described in detail in 23.6 *et seq.* below, are as follows.

(*a*) Exchange gains and losses in respect of qualifying assets and liabilities and forward currency contracts are recognised as they accrue between set translation times.

(*b*) Trading exchange gains and losses are treated as trading items, net non-trading exchange gains are assessed under Schedule D, Case VI, and there are special provisions for the relief of net non-trading exchange losses.

(*c*) Certain unrealised exchange gains on long-term capital items may be deferred.

(*d*) Exchange differences are generally calculated in sterling, although trading profits or losses (excluding capital allowances) may in certain circumstances be calculated in non-sterling currencies.

(*e*) Regulations may provide for the matching of borrowings with certain non-qualifying assets.

(*f*) Capital gains tax will cease to apply to qualifying assets.

(*g*) Anti-avoidance provisions are designed to prevent abuse of these provisions.

There are a number of exclusions from the operation of the provisions, and special rules in relation to insurance companies.

For the commencement of these provisions, see 23.32 below.

The Revenue have published an Explanatory Statement on Exchange Gains and Losses and Financial Instruments, containing guidance on these provisions and those relating to FINANCIAL INSTRUMENTS (25), to which reference is made in the text as appropriate. The Statement is available (price £4) from Reference Library, New Wing, Somerset House, London WC2R 1LB. Section 2.1 of the Explanatory Statement indicates that the new rules mirror normal accountancy practice, so that it should not generally be necessary to compute exchange gains and losses separately for each individual transaction. Section 2.5 indicates that the new rules will not apply to non-resident companies unless they carry on a trade in the UK (subject to special rules concerning CONTROLLED FOREIGN COMPANIES (18) (see 23.15(A), 23.31 below)).

Simon's Direct Tax Service. See B3.1711 *et seq.*.

23.6 A company is a '*qualifying company*' unless it is:

(*a*) for any accounting period ending before 1 April 1996, a company established for charitable purposes only;

(*b*) the trustees of a unit trust scheme (who may by virtue of *ICTA 1988, s 468(1)* be treated as a company, see 60.1 UNIT AND INVESTMENT TRUSTS), for any accounting period as respects which it is an authorised unit trust; or

(*c*) a company for any accounting period for which it is approved for the purposes of *ICTA 1988, s 842* (investment trusts, see 60.4 UNIT AND INVESTMENT TRUSTS).

[*FA 1993, s 152; FA 1996, Sch 41 Pt V(3)*].

Simon's Direct Tax Service. See B3.1712.

23.7 **Accrual of gains and losses.** Where a qualifying company

(i) holds a 'qualifying asset' or owes a 'qualifying liability', or

(ii) enters into a 'currency contract', or

(iii) holds an asset or owes a liability consisting of a right to settlement or a duty to settle under a 'qualifying debt',

an 'initial exchange gain' or 'initial exchange loss' falls to be calculated in the circumstances described at 23.8–23.10 below respectively, and to be treated as described at 23.10 *et seq.* below. [*FA 1993, ss 125–127*].

A company holds an asset at any time when it is entitled to it (see 23.26 below) and owes a liability at any time when it is subject to it (see 23.27 below). [*FA 1993, ss 154(14), 155(13)*].

Simon's Direct Tax Service. See **B3.1716** *et seq.*.

23.8 *Accrual on qualifying assets and liabilities.* Where a qualifying company holds a 'qualifying asset' or owes a 'qualifying liability', an '*exchange difference*' arises for an 'accrual period' as regards the asset or liability where there is a difference between the 'local currency equivalent' of the 'basic valuation' of the asset or liability at the 'translation times' which begin and end the accrual period. If the exchange difference represents an increase over the accrual period in the case of an asset, or a decrease in the case of a liability, an '*initial exchange gain*' equal to the difference accrues to the company for the period as regards the asset or liability. If it represents a decrease in the case of an asset or an increase in the case of a liability, an '*initial exchange loss*' similarly accrues. [*FA 1993, s 125*].

The following are '*qualifying assets*' as regards a qualifying company.

(*a*) A right to settlement under a 'qualifying debt' (whether or not it is a debt on a security).

(*b*) A unit of currency.

(*c*) A share (in any company) held in 'qualifying circumstances'.

Excluded from (*a*), however, are a right under a 'currency contract' (see 23.9 below), and (for accounting periods ending before 1 April 1996) a right to settlement under a debt on a security which did not represent a 'normal commercial loan' when it was created (unless it is a deep gain security (within *FA 1989, Sch 11*) or the right is held in 'qualifying circumstances'). For accounting periods ending after 31 March 1996, the latter exclusion is replaced by an exclusion where the company having the right holds an asset representing the debt which is either a convertible security within *FA 1996, s 92* (see 43.9 LOAN RELATIONSHIPS) or represents a loan relationship linked to the value of chargeable assets within *FA 1996, s 93* (see 43.9 LOAN RELATIONSHIPS). A '*normal commercial loan*' for this purpose is a loan of or including new consideration which carries no right either to conversion into other shares or securities (except corporate bonds within *TCGA 1992, s 117*) or to the acquisition of additional shares or securities. [*FA 1993, s 153(1)(3)(4); FA 1995, Sch 24 para 4; FA 1996, Sch 14 para 70(1)*].

A duty to settle under a 'qualifying debt' (whether or not it is a debt on a security) is a '*qualifying liability*' as regards a qualifying company, provided that it is not

(i) a duty under a currency contract, or

(ii) (for accounting periods ending before 1 April 1996) a duty to settle under a debt on a security which did not represent a 'normal commercial loan' (as above) when it was created (unless it is a deep gain security).

A provision made by a qualifying company in respect of a duty to which it may become subject and which would be within the above definition is also a '*qualifying liability*', provided that the duty to settle would be owed for trade purposes, and the provision falls to be taken into account (apart from these provisions) in computing corporation tax profits or losses of the trade.

The following are also '*qualifying liabilities*':

(A) a duty to transfer a right to settlement under a 'qualifying debt' which is a debt on a security, where the duty subsists under a contract and the company is not entitled to the right, provided that the right would be a qualifying asset if the company were entitled to it; and

(B) a duty to transfer a share or shares, where the duty subsists under a contract and the company is not entitled to the share(s), provided that the share (or each of the shares) would be a qualifying asset if the company were entitled to it.

[*FA 1993, s 153(2)(5)–(9); FA 1995, Sch 24 para 4; FA 1996, Sch 14 para 70(2)*].

A '*qualifying debt*' is a debt falling to be settled by the payment of money (an ecu being regarded as money), or by the transfer of a right to settlement under another debt falling to be settled by the payment of money. [*FA 1993, s 153(10)*].

For these purposes, interest accrued in respect of a debt is not treated as part of the debt. [*FA 1993, s 153(12)*].

'*Qualifying circumstances*', in relation to an asset consisting of a share or a right to settlement, are circumstances where

(I) the qualifying company carries on a trade,

(II) a transfer of the asset would fall to be taken into account (apart from these provisions) in computing corporation tax profits or losses of the trade, and

(III) if the asset were held at the end of an accounting period, the valuation to be shown in the accounts for that time would fall to be found by taking the 'local currency equivalent' at that time of the valuation put on the asset by the company (whether at that time or earlier) expressed in the nominal currency of the asset (the 'local currency' concerned being that of the trade for the accounting period).

[*FA 1993, s 153(11)*].

As regards a qualifying asset or liability or a currency contract (see 23.9 below), an '*accrual period*' is a period which begins with a 'translation time' (other than the last), and ends with the next 'translation time', as regards the asset, liability or contract. [*FA 1993, s 158(4)*].

A '*translation time*' as regards as asset, liability or contract is any one of the following.

(*aa*) The time immediately after the company becomes entitled to the asset, subject to the liability, or entitled to rights and subject to duties under the contract.

(*bb*) The time immediately before the company ceases to be entitled to the asset, subject to the liability, or entitled to rights and subject to duties under the contract.

(*cc*) Any time when an accounting period of the company ends, provided that it is later than the time in (*aa*) and earlier than the time in (*bb*).

[*FA 1993, s 158(1)–(3)*].

The '*local currency equivalent*' of a valuation of an asset or liability, or of an amount, is that valuation or amount expressed in terms of the 'local currency' (sometimes known as 'translation'). The 'local currency' is generally sterling, but see 23.24 below. [*FA 1993, ss 163(1), 164(5)*].

The '*basic valuation*' of an asset or liability is generally such valuation as the company puts on it with regard to the time immediately after the company becomes entitled or subject to it or, if different, that which it would put on it with regard to that time under normal accountancy practice. Where that valuation would otherwise be in a currency other than the 'nominal currency', it is converted to the nominal currency equivalent by reference to the London closing exchange rate for the day.

As regards a liability falling within (A) or (B) above, the '*basic valuation*' is the consideration for the company becoming subject to the liability (including the open market value, at the time when the company becomes subject to the liability, of any non-pecuniary consideration). Where the consideration is part pecuniary, the non-pecuniary part is expressed in the same currency as the part which is pecuniary. Where, however, the basic valuation would accordingly be in a currency other than the nominal currency, it is converted to the nominal currency, calculated by reference to the London closing exchange rate for the day on which the company becomes subject to the liability.

For accounting periods ending after 31 March 1996, and in relation to transfers after that date, where a company becomes entitled to a right of settlement under a qualifying debt on a security on any transfer by virtue of which it becomes a party to a loan relationship, and that transfer is with accrued interest, the basic valuation of that right is the consideration for its becoming entitled to that right less the accrued interest transferred. For transfers before 1 April 1996, where the company becomes entitled to a right to settlement under a qualifying debt on a security in circumstances such that *ICTA 1988, s 713(2)(b)* or *s 713(3)(b)* (accrued income scheme) applies, the '*basic valuation*' of the right is the consideration for the company becoming entitled to the right, adjusted for any sums charged or relieved under those provisions (any necessary apportionments being made on a just and reasonable basis). For this purpose, any pecuniary consideration is expressed in sterling, and any non-pecuniary consideration is taken as equal to its open market value, at the time when the company becomes entitled to the right, expressed in sterling. Where the nominal currency of the right is not sterling, the valuation found in sterling as above is converted to the nominal currency, by reference to the London closing exchange rate for the day on which the company becomes entitled to the right.

[*FA 1993, s 159(1)–(9); FA 1996, Sch 14 para 73*].

As regards a qualifying asset consisting of a right to settlement under a qualifying debt, or a qualifying liability other than one within (A) above, the '*nominal currency*' is the 'settlement currency' of the debt. As regards a qualifying asset consisting of a unit of currency, the '*nominal currency*' is the currency concerned. As regards a qualifying asset consisting of a share held in qualifying circumstances or a qualifying liability within (A) above, the '*nominal currency*' is the currency in which the share is (or shares are) denominated. [*FA 1993, s 160*]. The '*settlement currency*' of a debt is the currency in which ultimate settlement of the debt falls (or would fall) to be made, except that where the amount of that currency falls (or would fall) to be determined by reference to the value at any time of an asset consisting of or denominated in another currency, the '*settlement currency*' is that other currency. Where the settlement currency cannot be determined under these provisions, it is the currency that can reasonably be regarded as the most appropriate having regard to these provisions and deeming the state of affairs at settlement to be the same as the state of affairs immediately after the company becomes entitled or subject to the asset or liability in question. For these purposes the ecu is regarded as a currency. [*FA 1993, s 161*].

Simon's Direct Tax Service. See B3.1720.

23.9 *Accrual on currency contracts.* Where a qualifying company enters into a 'currency contract', there is an '*exchange difference*' for an accrual period (see 23.8 above) as regards the contract where, as regards either of the currencies involved, there is a difference between the local currency equivalent (see 23.8 above) of the amount of the currency at the translation times (see 23.8 above) which begin and end the accrual period.

A '*currency contract*' is a contract under which a company becomes entitled to a right, and subject to a duty, to receive payment at a specified time of a specified amount of a currency (the '*first currency*'), and simultaneously to pay in exchange a specified amount of another currency (the '*second currency*'). It is immaterial whether those rights and duties may be exercised and discharged by the making or receiving of a net payment of an amount representing any difference in value between the payments at the specified time, and a contract requiring a payment of such an amount at a specified time is treated as a currency contract. Where, as a result of the adoption of the euro by a State, the conversion of the amounts of one or both of the currencies in a currency contract results in the contract being rescinded and replaced by a new contract which, but for the adoption of the euro, would have been a currency contract, the new contract is in effect treated as if it were the original currency contract. [*SI 1998 No 3177, reg 10*].

In relation to the first currency, if the exchange difference represents an increase over the accrual period, an '*initial exchange gain*' equal to the difference accrues to the company for the period as regards the contract. If it represents a decrease, an '*initial exchange loss*' similarly accrues. In relation to the second currency, a decease gives rise to an '*initial exchange gain*', an increase to an '*initial exchange loss*'.

[*FA 1993, s 126; FA 1994, s 115(1); SI 1994 No 3233, reg 3*].

For general guidance on the treatment of currency contracts, see section 7 of the Explanatory Statement referred to at 23.5 above, and Annexes 1 and 2 thereto.

A company becomes entitled to a right, and subject to a duty, under a contract when it enters into the contract. It holds a currency contract at a particular time if it is then entitled to rights and subject to duties under the contract, regardless of when the rights and duties fall to be exercised and performed. [*FA 1993, s 157*].

Simon's Direct Tax Service. See B3.1721.

23.10 *Accrual on debts whose amounts vary.* Where a qualifying company holds an asset consisting of a right to settlement under a qualifying debt (see 23.8 above) or owes a liability consisting of a duty to settle under such a debt, and the nominal amount of the debt outstanding varies during an accrual period, 23.8 above does not apply. Instead, two amounts (the 'first amount' and the 'second amount') are determined, and the difference between those amounts represents either an '*initial exchange gain*' or an '*initial exchange loss*' for the accrual period.

For these purposes, where an amount in respect of any discount or premium relating to a debt accrues at any time under the LOAN RELATIONSHIPS (43) provisions (or would do so were an accruals basis of accounting used), then there is deemed to be a variation at that time in the nominal amount of the debt outstanding. The variation is an increase by the amount accruing (or which would accrue) in the case of a discount, a decrease by that amount in the case of a premium.

Where the company holds a right to settlement under the debt, and the second amount exceeds the first, an '*initial exchange gain*' accrues to the company in respect of the right. Where the first amount exceeds the second, an '*initial exchange loss*' accrues. Where the company has a duty to settle under the debt, the second amount exceeding the first gives rise to an '*initial exchange loss*', the first exceeding the second to an '*initial exchange gain*'. In all cases, a negative first amount is less than the second amount.

The '*first amount*' is the net amount of the local currency equivalents of

(*a*) the nominal amount of the debt outstanding at the translation time which begins the accrual period, and

(*b*) any increases or decreases in that nominal amount during the accrual period at the times they occur.

The '*second amount*' is the local currency equivalent of the nominal amount of the debt outstanding at the translation time which ends the accrual period.

The nominal amount of a debt outstanding at any time is the outstanding amount at that time expressed in terms of the settlement currency of the debt (see 23.8 above). Where a payment or repayment is made at any time in a currency other than the settlement currency of the debt, and it falls to be decided whether there is in consequence an increase or decrease in the nominal amount of the debt outstanding, the amount of the payment or repayment is taken to be its equivalent expressed in terms of the settlement currency of the debt (any translation being by reference to the London closing exchange rate for the day in which the time concerned falls).

Where there is a difference between the 'basic valuation' of the asset or liability and the nominal amount of the debt outstanding at the translation time with which the accrual period begins,

(i) in arriving at the first amount, the nominal amount taken into account at the beginning of the accrual period is replaced by the basic valuation, and decreases in the nominal amount are replaced by proportionate decreases of the basic valuation, and

(ii) in arriving at the second amount, the nominal amount taken into account at the end of the accrual period is replaced by the basic valuation, increased by any increases in the nominal amount during the accrual period and decreased by any proportionate decreases taken into account under (i) above.

[*FA 1993, ss 127, 162; FA 1996, Sch 14 para 67*].

For '*basic valuation*', see 23.8 above. However, where this provision and either *FA 1993, s 125* (see 23.8 above) or this provision apply respectively to two consecutive accrual periods as regards an asset or liability, then the basic valuation of the asset or liability as regards the later period is taken to be either

(A) the nominal amount of the debt outstanding immediately before the beginning of the later period, or

(B) if this provision, modified as above where the basic valuation differs from the initial nominal amount of the debt, applies as regards the earlier period, the second amount as determined under (ii) above.

The same basic valuation applies as regards subsequent accrual periods, subject to any further application of this provision.

[*FA 1993, s 159(10)–(12)*].

Simon's Direct Tax Service. See **B3.1722**.

23.11 **Trading gains and losses.** Where an initial exchange gain accrues to a qualifying company for an accrual period (see 23.8–23.10 above) as regards an asset, liability or contract which, at any time in the period, was held or owed for the purposes of a trade (or part of a trade), the gain (or that part justly and reasonably attributed to the trade (or part)) is an '*exchange gain*' of the trade (or part) for the period. The amount of the exchange gain is treated as a receipt of the trade (or part) for the accounting period in which the accrual period falls (or with which it coincides). An initial exchange loss may similarly give rise to a loss in the trade (or part).

For these purposes, a part of a trade is any part which is treated as a separate business for the purposes of *FA 1993, s 93* (use of non-sterling currency for corporation tax purposes, see 23.36 below) for the accounting period which constitutes or contains the accrual period in question. For accounting periods beginning before 1 January 2000 or ending before 21 March 2000, a similar rule applied by reference to the earlier corporation tax provisions (see 23.40 below).

It is irrelevant whether the asset, contract or liability is held or owed on capital or revenue account, and the general prohibitions on trading deductions under *ICTA 1988, s 74* do not prevent the deduction of an exchange loss.

Where an exchange gain or loss of a trade (or part) would otherwise accrue as regards a liability consisting of a duty to settle under a qualifying debt (see 23.8 above), but a charge is allowed under *ICTA 1988, s 338* (see 50.3 PROFIT COMPUTATIONS) in respect of the debt, the exchange gain or loss is treated as not accruing. A charge is for this purpose treated as allowed if it would be allowed if the duty were settled by payment out of the company's chargeable profits, or if the company's profits were sufficient, or both.

Where a qualifying company accounting period begins on or after its 'commencement day' (see 23.32 below), and a gain or loss attributable to currency fluctuations (whether or not realised) accrues to the company as regards a qualifying asset or a qualifying liability or a currency contract otherwise than by virtue of these provisions, the gain or loss is not taken into account in calculating the company's trading profits or losses for corporation tax purposes for the period.

[*FA 1993, s 128; FA 1995, Sch 24 para 2; FA 2000, s 106(6)(17)*].

An exchange gain or loss under *FA 1993, s 128* may be taken into account as an adjustment under *FA 1994, s 162* (see 25.12 FINANCIAL INSTRUMENTS).

Simon's Direct Tax Service. See B3.1726.

23.12 *Example*

Tinman plc, a UK trading company, prepares its annual accounts to 31 March. On 4 December 2000 it sells goods to a customer in the land of Oz for Oz$540,000. The customer pays Oz$140,000 on account on 1 February 2001, and the balance of Oz$400,000 remains outstanding on 31 March 2001. The exchange rates on the relevant dates are as follows.

4 December 2000	£1 = Oz$3
1 February 2001	£1 = Oz$2.9
31 March 2001	£1 = Oz$2.75

The account can be summarised over the accrual period (4 December 2000 to 31 March 2001) as follows.

Date	*Amount (Oz$)*	*Exchange rate (Oz$/£)*	*(Decrease)*	*£ equivalent*
4 December 2000	540,000	3.0	—	180,000
1 February 2001	400,000	2.9	(140,000)	(48,276)
31 March 2001	400,000	2.75	—	145,455

The exchange gain is calculated as follows.

	£	£
Sterling equivalent 31 March 2001		145,455
Less sterling equivalent 4 December 2000	180,000	
adjusted for decrease	(48,276)	131,724
Exchange gain		£13,731

The exchange gain falls to be included in Tinman plc's profits chargeable to corporation tax for the year ended 31 March 2001.

23.13 **Non-trading gains and losses.** Where an initial exchange gain accrues to a qualifying company for an accrual period (see 23.8–23.10 above) as regards an asset, liability or contract, any part of the gain which is not an exchange gain of a trade (or part) (see 23.11 above) is a '*non-trading exchange gain*' for the period. An initial exchange loss may similarly give rise to a '*non-trading exchange loss*'.

However, a non-trading exchange gain or loss is treated as not accruing (if it would otherwise do so) where the asset or liability concerned consists of a right to settlement, or duty to settle, under a qualifying debt, and:

(*a*) in the case of a right to settlement, the right is a right to receive income (and, for accounting periods ending after 31 March 1996, not interest falling to be brought into account under the LOAN RELATIONSHIPS (43) provisions);

(*b*) in the case of a duty to settle, a charge is allowed under *ICTA 1988, s 338* in respect of the debt (or would be so allowed were the duty settled by payment out of the company's chargeable profits, or were the company's profits sufficient).

The amount of the non-trading exchange gain or loss is treated as a receipt or loss in respect of the asset, liability or contract in the accounting period in which the accrual period falls (or with which it coincides), and the provisions at 23.14 below apply. Where, however, in relation to an accounting period ending before 1 April 1996, the amount or aggregate amount the company is treated as receiving under this provision ('*amount A*') equals the amount or aggregate amount of the losses it is so treated as having incurred ('*amount B*'), 23.14 below does not apply.

ICTA 1988, s 396 (relief for Case VI corporation tax losses, see 44.24 LOSSES) does not apply to losses a company is treated as incurring under this provision, nor may Case VI losses be set against amounts a company is treated as receiving under this provision.

[*FA 1993, s 129; FA 1995, Sch 24 para 3; FA 1996, Sch 14 para 68*].

For accounting periods ending before 1 April 1996, non-trading gains and losses under *FA 1993, s 129* are amalgamated with any non-trading gains and losses under *FA 1994, s 160* (see 25.10 FINANCIAL INSTRUMENTS) and the net amount charged or relieved under 23.14 below. [*FA 1994, s 160(2); FA 1996, Sch 14 para 75*]. See now 43.3 LOAN RELATIONSHIPS.

Simon's Direct Tax Service. See B3.1727.

23.14 **Charge and relief of non-trading gains and losses.** Receipts and losses under 23.13 above are dealt with as follows.

Accounting periods ending after 31 March 1996

An amount which a company is treated as receiving under 23.13 above is brought into account as if it were a non-trading credit in respect of a loan relationship (see 43.3 LOAN RELATIONSHIPS). A loss is similarly treated as a non-trading debit. [*FA 1993, s 130; FA 1996, Sch 14 para 69*].

Accounting periods ending before 1 April 1996

Where a company is treated as receiving an amount, and is not treated as incurring a loss, under 23.13 above, it is treated as receiving annual profits or gains, chargeable to tax under Schedule D, Case VI, equal in amount to amount A (see 23.13 above). Where the company is treated as both receiving an amount and incurring a loss, and amount A exceeds amount B, the amount chargeable under Schedule D, Case VI is that excess. [*FA 1993, s 130 as originally enacted*].

In an accounting period in which a company is treated as incurring a loss, and is not treated as receiving an amount, under 23.13 above, a '*relievable amount*' arises equal to amount B (see 23.13 above). Where the company is treated as both incurring a loss and receiving an amount, and amount B exceeds amount A, a '*relievable amount*' arises equal to that excess. The company may claim relief as follows within two years of the end of the accounting period (or within such further period as the Board may allow).

(*a*) The whole or part of the relievable amount may be treated as a loss available for surrender as group relief (see 29.18 GROUPS OF COMPANIES).

(*b*) The whole or part of the relievable amount may be set off against any profits of the accounting period (after relief of brought-forward losses).

(*c*) Any part of the relievable amount not relieved under (*a*) or (*b*) above, but limited to the amount of the 'relevant exchange profits', may for corporation tax purposes be set against the 'exchange profits' of preceding accounting periods falling wholly or partly within the 'permitted period' (later accounting periods being relieved before earlier). For an accounting period beginning before the start of the 'permitted period', only that part of the exchange profits which may be attributed to the permitted period by time apportionment may be relieved.

Any part of the relievable amount not relieved under (*a*)–(*c*) above is treated as a loss incurred under 23.13 above in the next accounting period (amount B for that period being determined accordingly). There are provisions preventing double relief being given for a relievable amount.

'*Exchange profits*' of an accounting period are the annual profits or gains the company is treated as receiving in that accounting period as above.

'*Relevant exchange profits*' means the total of exchange profits of accounting periods (or parts) falling within the 'permitted period' unrelieved by earlier losses (i.e. losses of accounting periods before that in which the relievable amount arose) or by relief under *ICTA 1988, s 338* for trade charges (see 50.3 PROFIT COMPUTATIONS) or, in the case of an investment company, for charges wholly and exclusively incurred for business purposes. (The net exchange profits are time-apportioned for an accounting period beginning before the start of the permitted period.)

The '*permitted period*' is the period of three years immediately preceding the accounting period in which the relievable amount arose.

A loss carried forward to the next accounting period as above may only be relieved against net non-trading exchange gains of that period. Relief under (*a*)–(*c*) above is only available for that period to the extent that losses other than losses brought forward exceed any gains brought in under 23.13 above for the period. Any balance of losses unrelieved is carried forward to the following accounting period.

[*FA 1993, ss 131, 132*].

The relief under these provisions by set-off against other profits of the accounting period applies before relief for losses generally under *ICTA 1988, s 393A(1)* (see 44.2 LOSSES), but may not be given against 'ring-fenced' profits from petroleum extraction activities (see 46.3 OIL COMPANIES). However, relief under these provisions by set off against exchange profits of earlier accounting periods applies after relief under *section 393A(1)*, and is not given so as to interfere with relief of trade charges under *ICTA 1988, s 338* (see 50.3 PROFIT COMPUTATIONS) (or of business charges of investment companies under that *section*).

[*FA 1993, s 133*].

Simon's Direct Tax Service. See B3.1727, B3.1728.

23.15 **Alternative method of calculation.** Regulations (see *SI 1994 No 3227* as amended) provide for an alternative method of calculation of the amount of an initial exchange gain or loss in certain cases. In such cases 23.8–23.10 above do not apply as regards determination of those amounts, which are instead found by adding together the accrued amounts for each day in the accrual period. Subject to those regulations, the accrued amount for a day in an accrual period is found by dividing the amount determined under 23.8–23.10 above by the number of days in the accrual period. Where an accrual period does not begin at the beginning or end at the end of a day, such a day is for this purpose treated as a complete day. [*FA 1993, Sch 15 para 1*].

Exempt circumstances. Regulations (see *SI 1994 No 3227, regs 2, 12*) provide for the alternative method of calculation to apply where (apart from the regulations) an initial exchange gain or loss (other than a gain treated as a non-trading exchange gain under *FA 1993, s 140(9)*, see 23.18 below) accrues under 23.8–23.10 above in an accrual period as regards an asset, liability or contract which at any time in a day in the accrual period was held or owed in 'exempt circumstances'. The regulations also provide that, as regards any such day, the accrued amount is to be ascertained in accordance with prescribed rules, and are framed so that the accrued amount as regards a day depends on the extent to which the exempt circumstances apply. The regulations are, however, disapplied in relation to an exchange gain within *FA 1993, s 136(11)(d)* or *s 136A(9)(d)* (see 23.17 below).

'*Exempt circumstances*' are when an asset or contract is held, or a liability owed, either:

(*a*) for the purposes of long term insurance business;

(*b*) for the purposes of mutual insurance business;

(*c*) for the purposes of the occupation of commercial woodlands;

(*d*) by an approved housing association; or

(*e*) by an approved self-build society.

[*FA 1993, Sch 15 paras 2, 6*].

Unremittable income. Regulations (see *SI 1994 No 3227, reg 3*) provide that, where prescribed conditions are fulfilled, and (apart from the regulations) an initial exchange gain or loss accrues under 23.8 or 23.10 above in an accrual period as regards an asset consisting of either a right to settlement under a qualifying debt or a unit of currency, and at any time on a day in the accrual period income represented by the asset was unremittable, the alternative method of calculation is to apply. The regulations also prescribe rules for ascertainment of the accrued amount as regards any such day, and are so framed that the accrued amount as regards a day depends on the extent to which the income it represents is unremittable.

Income is unremittable for this purpose if, in relation to the income, the appropriate claim under *ICTA 1988, s 584* (see 53.3 RESIDENCE) has been made, the conditions for the claim were satisfied, and those conditions have not ceased to be satisfied.

[*FA 1993, Sch 15 para 3; FA 1996, Sch 20 para 70*].

Matched liabilities. Regulations (see *SI 1994 No 3227, regs 4–12* as amended) provide that where, apart from the regulations, an initial exchange gain or loss accrues for an accrual period as regards a liability which consists of a duty to settle under a qualifying debt, and which is eligible to be matched on any day in the accrual period with an asset held by the company (and where other prescribed conditions are fulfilled), an election may be made to match the liability with the asset on any such day. The alternative method of calculation will then apply in determining the amount of the gain or loss. The regulations also prescribe rules for ascertainment of the accrued amount as regards any day for which an election has effect. The regulations are, however, disapplied in relation to an exchange gain within *FA 1993, s 136(11)(d)* or *s 136A(9)(d)* (see 23.17 below).

Eligibility of a liability to be matched with an asset is determined in accordance with rules which prescribe the descriptions of liabilities and assets which may be matched.

The regulations also provide broadly as follows.

(A) The conditions attaching to matching elections are set out. An election, which is irrevocable, must be made by the company owing the liability to be matched (except in the case of CONTROLLED FOREIGN COMPANIES (18), see (B) below). Partial matching is permitted, and an election for partial matching may be varied to increase the amount or percentage matched. An election may be treated as relating to another liability meeting the necessary conditions where the original liability ceases to match the asset concerned. Similarly, following a reorganisation within *TCGA 1992, s 126*, it may continue to have effect in relation to the new holding if the new holding meets the necessary conditions. In certain circumstances an election may have retrospective effect.

(B) Where the company owing the liability is a controlled foreign company, an election may be made by a UK resident company which has (or such companies which together have) a majority interest in the CFC (within *ICTA 1988, Sch 24 para 4(3)(4)*) in computing chargeable profits under *ICTA 1988, Sch 24* (see 18.9 CONTROLLED FOREIGN COMPANIES).

(C) Exchange differences are to be brought into account when an asset the subject of matching arrangements is disposed of (subject to deferral in the case of certain no gain, no loss disposals under *TCGA 1992*). There are special rules where a transfer to a non-resident company within *TCGA 1992, s 140* is involved.

(D) Gains and losses are computed and deferred where shares are replaced by a new holding within *TCGA 1992, s 127*, and that section or *TCGA 1992, s 116* applies.

For the Revenue view of the application of certain of these regulations, see sections 2.22, 2.23 of the Explanatory Statement referred to at 23.5 above. See also Revenue Tax Bulletin August 1996 p 338.

[*FA 1993, Sch 15 paras 4, 6*].

For the availability of a matching election where a local currency election (see 23.39 below) has been made in respect of a trade carried on through an overseas branch, see sections 2.20, 2.21 of the Explanatory Statement referred to at 23.5 above. For intra-group transactions to facilitate matching, see section 2.24 of that Statement.

Currency contracts: matching. Where

(I) as regards a currency contract, an initial exchange gain or loss accrues (or would apart from the regulations accrue) to a company for an accrual period in relation to the second currency (see 23.9 above),

(II) the relevant duty (i.e. the company's duty under the contract as regards the second currency) is eligible to be matched on any day in the accrual period with an asset held by the company (and other prescribed conditions are fulfilled), and

(III) an election is made and has effect under the regulations to match the duty with the asset on any such day,

the alternative method of calculation will apply in determining the amount of the gain or loss. The regulations described above in relation to matched liabilities apply for these purposes with appropriate modification.

[*FA 1993, Sch 15 paras 4A, 6; FA 1994, s 116(2); SI 1994 No 3227, regs 4–12; SI 1996 No 1347*].

Combination of circumstances. Where regulations as above relating to exempt circumstances, to unremittable income and to matched liabilities (or to any two of these three) apply as regards the same liability and for the same accrual period, there is provision for further regulations which may instead provide for ascertainment of the accrued amount as regards any day falling within the period and identified in accordance with prescribed rules. [*FA 1993, Sch 15 para 5*]. Further regulations may similarly make such provision where regulations as above relating to exempt circumstances and matching of currency contracts apply as regards the same contract and for the same accrual period. [*FA 1993, Sch 15 para 5A; FA 1994, s 116(3)*].

Local currency. Where regulations as above relate to exempt circumstances, to unremittable income, to matched liabilities, to matching of currency contracts or to combinations of circumstances, 23.24 below has effect as if references to 23.8–23.10 above included references to the alternative calculation schedule (*FA 1993, Sch 15*) and to the provisions of those regulations. [*FA 1993, Sch 15 para 7*].

General. Regulations (as above) are so framed that the accrued amount as regards a day is nil (so that an initial exchange gain or loss may be extinguished), and may make different provision about exchange gains and exchange losses. [*FA 1993, Sch 15 paras 8, 9*].

Simon's Direct Tax Service. See **B3.1736** *et seq.*.

23.16 **Main benefit test.** *Loss relief restriction.* Where an exchange loss (whether trading or non-trading) would otherwise accrue to a company for an accrual period as regards an asset which is a right to settlement, or a liability which is a duty to settle, under a qualifying debt, that loss is not treated as so accruing if the nominal currency of the asset or liability is such that a main benefit expected to arise from holding the asset or owing the liability is the accrual of the loss (and, prior to the commencement of corporate self-assessment, if the Board so direct). [*FA 1993, s 135; FA 1998, s 109(1)(4)*]. For the circumstances in which, where required, a direction will be made, see section 3.6 of the Explanatory Statement referred to at 23.5 above. See Simon's Direct Tax Service B3.1756.

Use of non-sterling currency. For accounting periods beginning on or after 1 January 2000 and ending on or after 21 March 2000, where a non-sterling currency would otherwise be used for the purposes of calculating the exchange gain or loss on a qualifying asset or liability (see 23.8–23.13 above and 23.24 below), then if:

(*a*) the main benefit that might be expected to accrue from use of that currency for those purposes is that no net initial exchange gain would accrue to the company, and

(*b*) a net initial exchange gain would accrue to the company if sterling were used for those purposes,

then sterling must be used to calculate the exchange gain on the asset or liability concerned. [*FA 1993, s 135A; FA 2000, s 106(7)(17)*].

Determination of adjustment. See 23.17 below as regards determinations of adjustments under these provisions which require the sanction of the Board.

23.17 **Arm's length test — loss relief restriction.** Where

(*a*) a qualifying company acquires an asset consisting of a right to settlement, or incurs a liability consisting of a duty to settle, under a qualifying debt in a transaction which it would not have entered into, or whose terms would have been different, if the parties to the transaction had been dealing at arm's length, and

(*b*) an exchange loss (whether trading or non-trading) would otherwise accrue to the company for an accrual period as regards that asset or liability,

that loss is treated as not accruing to the company for that period (but, prior to the commencement of corporate self-assessment, only if the Board so direct). Where the accrual period is not the last to occur as regards the asset or liability while it is held or owed by the company, any loss so treated may be carried forward and set against exchange gains (of the same trade or part-trade or non-trading, as the case may be) for subsequent accrual periods as regards the same asset or liability (for earlier periods before later ones).

Where the only feature of the transaction which would have been different had it been at arm's length is that the amount of the debt would have been less (but not nil), the loss is not denied relief as above, but is treated as reduced to the amount it would have been had the amount of the debt been that which would have been incurred at arm's length (but, prior to the commencement of corporate self-assessment, only if the Board so direct). The amount by which the loss is so reduced may be carried forward as above.

Where

(i) the asset concerned is a right arising under a loan made by the company,

(ii) the only feature of the transaction which would have been different had it been at arm's length is that interest would have been charged, or charged at a higher rate, and

(iii) for the accounting period which constitutes or includes the accrual period, the whole of the loan has been treated under *ICTA 1988, s 770* or, as the case may be, falls to be treated under *ICTA 1988, Sch 28AA* (transfer pricing, see 4.4 ANTI-AVOIDANCE) as if interest had been charged (or charged at a higher rate),

the loss is not denied relief as above. If part of the loan has been, or falls to be, treated as in (iii) above, a corresponding part only of the loss is not denied relief, and the balance may be carried forward as above (but, prior to the commencement of corporate self-assessment, only if the Board so direct).
[*FA 1993, s 136(1)–(10); FA 1998, s 108(3)(5), s 109(1)(4)*].

Where an inward loan has been, or falls to be, adjusted under *ICTA 1988, s 770* or *Sch 28AA*, the terms to be considered under *section 136* are the terms as so adjusted for tax purposes (see section 3.9 of the Explanatory Statement referred to at 23.5 above).

Groups of companies. None of the above restrictions apply where the companies concerned are members of the same group (under *TCGA 1992, s 170*, see 9.18 CAPITAL GAINS) when the transaction is entered into and throughout the accounting period which constitutes or includes the accrual period in which the loss accrues, provided that:

(A) the counterparty to the qualifying company incurring the loss concerned incurs a corresponding liability, or acquires a corresponding asset, under a qualifying debt as a result of the transaction, and an exchange gain in the same currency as the loss accrues to the counterparty as regards that liability or asset for an accrual period ending at the same time as that for which the loss accrues;

(B) throughout the accrual period concerned, each company holds or owes the asset or liability either for the purposes of one trade or for non-trading purposes; and

(C) 'amount X' and 'amount Y' are the same, where '*amount X*' is the amount of the loss concerned, and '*amount Y*' is the amount of the gain accruing to the counterparty as regards the corresponding liability or asset disregarding 23.18 below.

The changes to the residence requirements for groups introduced by *FA 2000* (see 9.18 CAPITAL GAINS) have effect for these purposes for accrual periods beginning on or after 1 April 2000.

[*FA 1993, s 136(11)(12); FA 2000, Sch 29 para 41*].

Initial exchange losses. Where the loss concerned represents the whole or part of an initial exchange loss in respect of a debt whose amount may vary (see 23.10 above), the reliefs from the non-arm's length prohibition on loss relief (other than carry-forward of the loss against future exchange gains on the same asset or liability) are disapplied. [*FA 1993, s 136(13)*]. Similar provisions, with appropriate modifications, are, however, applied to such losses by *FA 1993, s 136A*, introduced in *SI 1994 No 3232* by virtue of *FA 1993, s 136(14)*.

'Arm's length' considerations. In considering what transactions would have been entered into at arm's length, all factors are to be taken into account, including any interest or other sums that would have been payable, any currency that would have been involved, and the amount that any loan would have been. [*FA 1993, s 136(14)*].

Currency contracts. Where a qualifying company enters into a currency contract which would not have been entered into at all, or whose terms would have been different, if the parties thereto had been dealing at arm's length, and an exchange loss (whether trading or non-trading) would otherwise accrue to the company for an accrual period as regards that contract, that loss is treated as not accruing to the company for that period (but, prior to the commencement of corporate self-assessment, only if the Board so direct). Where the accrual period is not the last to occur as regards the contract while it is held by the company, any loss so treated may be carried forward and set against exchange gains (of the same trade or part-trade or non-trading, as the case may be) for subsequent accrual periods as regards the same contract (for earlier periods before later ones).

In considering for this purpose what transactions would have been entered into at arm's length, all factors are to be taken into account, including any currency and any amounts that would have been involved.

[*FA 1993, s 137; FA 1998, s 109(1)(4)*].

Determinations requiring the sanction of the Board. A determination of the amount of an adjustment under *FA 1993, s 136, s 136A* or s *137* (or under *FA 1993, s 135* or *s 135A*, see 23.16 above), in respect of the disregarding or reduction of any exchange loss, requires the Board's sanction, other than in certain cases where an agreement has been reached between the Board and the person concerned (see *FA 1998, s 110(5)–(7)*). Where such a determination is made for the purpose of giving a closure notice, giving a notice amending a partnership assessment or making a discovery assessment, and the notice of the closure, amendment or discovery assessment is given to any person without the determination, so far as taken into account in the notice or assessment, having been approved by the Board, or without a copy of the Board's approval having been served on that person at or before the time the notice was given, the closure or amendment notice or discovery assessment is deemed to have been given or made (and in the case of an assessment notified) as if the determination had not been taken into account. The approval must apply specifically to the case in question and the amount determined, but may otherwise be given (either before or after the making of the determination) in any such form or manner as the Board may determine. An appeal relating to a determination approved by the Board may not question the Board's approval except to the extent that the grounds for questioning the approval are the same as the grounds for questioning the determination itself. [*FA 1998, s 110; FA 2000, s 106(16)*].

Non-sterling trades. Where an exchange loss is carried forward for set-off against future exchange gains as above, and the loss and the gain are in different currencies, the loss is translated into the currency in which the gain is expressed for the purpose of the set-off. The translation is by reference to the London closing exchange rates for the first day of the accounting period coinciding with, or containing, the accrual period for which the set-off takes place. [*FA 1993, s 138*].

For guidance on the circumstances in which a direction will be given under the above provisions, see sections 3.7 to 3.16 of the Explanatory Statement referred to at 23.5 above.

Simon's Direct Tax Service. See **B3.1757** *et seq.*.

23.18 **Deferral of unrealised gains.** Where (apart from this provision) an 'unrealised' exchange gain (whether trading or non-trading) would accrue to a company as regards a 'long-term capital asset or liability' for an accrual period constituting or falling within an accounting period, the company may make a claim in relation to that gain (or part of it). Where such a claim is made as regards an asset or liability, the gain (or part) stipulated in the claim is treated as not accruing for the accrual period for which it would (apart from the claim) have accrued. For the next accrual period throughout which the asset is held or owed by the company, an exchange gain equal in amount to the gain deferred is treated as accruing to the company as regards the asset or liability. If the asset or liability is held or owed solely for the purposes of a trade (or part of a trade), the gain is an exchange gain of the trade (or part), and is within 23.11 above. If it is held or owed for non-trading purposes, it is a non-trading exchange gain, and is within 23.13 above. If it is held partly for trade and partly for non-trade purposes, the amount stipulated in the claim is apportioned on a just and reasonable basis, each apportioned part being dealt with accordingly as above. The application of this provision is subject to any further deferral claim as above.

Where an exchange gain of a trade (or part) is carried forward as above to a period in which the asset or liability in question is to any extent held or owed in 'exempt circumstances' (see 23.15 above), the gain is to that extent treated as a non-trading exchange gain to which 23.13 above applies. Any necessary apportionment is made on a just and reasonable basis.

For these purposes, a part of a trade is any part which is treated as a separate business for the purposes of *FA 1993, s 93* (use of non-sterling currency for corporation tax purposes, see 23.36 below) for the accounting period which constitutes or contains the accrual period to which the gain is deferred. For accounting periods beginning before 1 January 2000 or ending before 21 March 2000, a similar rule applied by reference to the earlier corporation tax provisions (see 23.40 below).

A claim as regards an accounting period may not be made or withdrawn more than two years after the end of the period if an assessment to corporation tax for the period has become final and conclusive, or more than six years after the end of the period in any other case, subject to any extension determined by the Board. It must stipulate the amount to be deferred and identify the asset or liability concerned. No claim may be made unless an amount is available for relief for the accounting period (see below), and the gains subject to the claim must not exceed that amount. Only one claim may be made as regards an accounting period, but a claim may be made in relation to more than one gain where two or more gains fall within the provisions. The amount to be deferred must correspond to, and be in the same currency as, the amount to be brought in in the following period.

An exchange gain or loss is '*unrealised*' for these purposes if the accrual period concerned is one which ends solely by virtue of an accounting period of the company coming to an end.

An asset or liability is a '*long-term capital asset or liability*' if it is a right to settlement or duty to settle under a qualifying debt and represents capital throughout the accounting period concerned, and the earliest time at which the creditor can require settlement of the debt, under the original terms, is not less than one year from its creation.
[*FA 1993, ss 139, 140, 143(1)(4); FA 2000, s 106(8)(17)*].

Amount available for relief. An amount is available for relief for an accounting period as above if 'amount A' is exceeded by the lower of 'amount B' or 'amount C', and the amount available is the excess, where:

(*a*) '*Amount A*' is one-tenth of the company's profits for the accounting period on which corporation tax would fall finally to be borne (within *ICTA 1988, s 238(4)*) apart from any claim under this provision and any group relief claim;

(*b*) '*Amount B*' is the total unrealised exchange gains which accrue or would (apart from a claim under this provision) accrue to the company as regards long-term capital assets or liabilities (or both) in an accrual period or periods falling in or coinciding with the accounting period, less the total unrealised exchange losses which would so accrue as regards such assets or liabilities; and

(*c*) '*Amount C*' is the total exchange gains which accrue or would (apart from a claim under this provision) accrue to the company as regards 'relevant items' in an accrual period or periods falling in or coinciding with the accounting period, less the total exchange losses which would so accrue as regards such items.

[*FA 1993, s 141(1)–(5)*].

'*Relevant items*' are currency contracts and rights to settlement or duties to settle under a qualifying debt.

As regards Amounts B and C, exchange gains and losses may be of a trade or part-trade or non-trading.

[*FA 1993, s 141(6)(7)*].

Non-sterling trades. A gain or loss falling within the above deferral provisions which is expressed in a currency other than sterling is treated for these purposes as of an amount equal to the sterling equivalent.

For accounting periods beginning on or after 1 January 2000 and ending on or after 21 March 2000, the sterling equivalent is calculated by reference to the exchange rate applicable under *FA 1993, s 94* (conversion of non-sterling currency used for corporation tax purposes, see 23.37 below) in the case of the profits or losses for the accounting period concerned of the business (or part) to which the gain or loss relates (or would do so apart from a claim to deferral under these provisions). Where part of an exchange gain of a business (or part) is treated under *FA 1993, s 140(3)* (as above) as not accruing to a company for an accrual period, and the local currency of the business (or part) for the accounting period in which the accrual period falls (or with which it coincides) is a currency other than sterling (see 23.36 below), the amount the company is treated as receiving under 23.11 or 23.13 above in respect of the accounting period and by virtue of the gain (as reduced) is the amount computed and expressed in that currency.

Also for such accounting periods, where an exchange gain of a business (or part) is treated as above as accruing to a company for an accrual period, and the local currency of the business (or part) for the accounting period in which the accrual period falls (or with which it coincides) is a currency other than sterling, the amount of the gain is treated as the 'local currency equivalent' (see 23.8 above) expressed in sterling. The translation is made by reference to the London closing exchange rate for the last day of the accrual period.

For earlier accounting periods, these provisions apply by reference to the provisions previously applicable to the use of non-sterling currencies for corporation tax purposes (see 23.39 below) and only by references to trades and trading profits and gains etc..

[*FA 1993, s 142; FA 2000, s 106(9)–(11)(17)*].

General. Where an unrealised exchange gain representing the whole or part of an initial exchange gain accruing under 23.10 above would accrue as required for a deferral claim as above, and the whole or part of the unrealised exchange gain (apportioned on a just and reasonable basis) is attributable to any part by which the nominal amount of the debt has decreased, the company may not make a deferral claim as regards the part (or whole) so attributable. [*FA 1993, s 143*].

Regulations make special provision in certain cases, broadly as follows.

(i) Where a long-term capital debt is repaid and replaced by a similar debt within 30 days before or after the repayment, exchange gains and losses on the original debt are treated as unrealised, and gains may be deferred and treated as accruing on the replacement debt, subject to conditions as above.

(ii) The company's profits, for the purposes of calculating Amount A under (*a*) above, exclude overseas income and gains.

(iii) The calculation of the amount available for relief as above is modified where the claimant is a member of a group (and see sections 2.25 and 2.26 of the Explanatory Statement referred to at 23.5 above).

[*FA 1993, s 143(7); SI 1994 No 3228; SI 1996 No 1348*].

Euroconversion. The conversion of long-term capital assets and liabilities from the currency of a State which has adopted the euro into euros (a 'euroconversion', see *SI 1998 No 3177, reg 3*) is in effect disregarded for these purposes. [*SI 1998 No 3177, reg 7*].

Simon's Direct Tax Service. See B3.1746 *et seq.*.

23.19 *Example*

On 1 October 1999, Tinkerbell plc, a UK trading company which prepares its accounts to 30 September, obtains a three year loan of NNL$750,000 from its Neverneverland parent, to buy plant. For the years ending 30 September 2000 and 30 September 2001, the following information relating to Tinkerbell plc is relevant.

	1 October 1999	30 September 2000	30 September 2001
Exchange rate NNL$/£	1.5	1.6	1.69
Loan from parent (in £)	500,000	468,750	443,787

	Y/e 30 September 2000	Y/e 30 September 2001
	£	£
Net exchange gains on qualifying advances, borrowings and currency contracts	36,000	18,000
Profits chargeable to corporation tax (inclusive of net exchange gains)	150,000	275,000

The exchange gains available for deferral for the years ending 30 September 2000 and 30 September 2001 are calculated as follows.

Y/e 30 September 2000

	£
Lower of unrealised exchange gains on long-term capital assets and liabilities (£500,000 – £468,750 =) £31,250 and net exchange gains £36,000	31,250
Less 10% of £150,000	15,000
Maximum deferral claim possible	£16,250
Profits chargeable to corporation tax if maximum deferral claim made (£150,000 – £16,250 =)	£133,750

Y/e 30 September 2001
(assuming maximum deferral claim is made for y/e 30 September 2000)

	£
Lower of unrealised exchange gains on long–term capital assets and liabilities (£468,750 – £443,787 + £16,250 =) £41,213 and net exchange gains (£18,000 + £16,250 =) £34,250	34,250
Less 10% of (£275,000 + £16,250 =) £291,250	29,125
Maximum deferral claim possible	£5,125
Profits chargeable to corporation tax if maximum deferral claim made (£275,000 + £16,250 – £5,125 =)	£286,125

23.20 **Irrecoverable debts.** Where

(*a*) a qualifying company holds an asset or owes a liability consisting of a right to settlement, or duty to settle, under a qualifying debt, and

(*b*) as regards an accounting period of the company, all of the debt outstanding immediately before the end of the period could at that time reasonably have been regarded as irrecoverable,

the company is treated as if at the end of that accounting period it ceased to be entitled to the asset or subject to the liability. Where these conditions are satisfied as regards part of the debt, the nominal amount of the debt is treated as correspondingly reduced immediately after the beginning of the next accounting period. [*FA 1993, s 144; FA 1996, Sch 20 para 68*].

Irrecoverable debts that become recoverable. Where

(i) a debt has been treated as extinguished in an accounting period as above,

(ii) at a time falling after the end of the accounting period all or part of the debt is actually outstanding, and

(iii) at that time all or part of the debt actually then outstanding could reasonably have been regarded as recoverable,

then the company is treated as if, immediately after that time, the debt were reinstated in the amount so regarded as recoverable. Where a debt has been reduced rather than extinguished, or reinstated as above, further subsequent reinstatements may be made. [*FA 1993, s 145; FA 1996, Sch 20 para 69*].

Simon's Direct Tax Service. See B3.1720.

23.21 **Early termination of currency contract.** Where a qualifying company ceases to be entitled to rights and subject to duties under a currency contract, and either

(i) at the time it so ceases it has neither received nor made payments of any currency under the contract, or

(ii) it so ceases by virtue of the making or receiving of a net payment (in any currency) representing any difference in value between the reciprocal payments required under the contract,

the company is treated as follows:

(*a*) if it has a 'net contractual gain of a trade', it is treated as incurring a trading loss of the same amount in respect of the 'last relevant accounting period';

(*b*) if it has a 'net contractual loss of a trade', it is treated as receiving a trading gain of the same amount in respect of the 'last relevant accounting period';

(*c*) if it has a 'net contractual non-trading gain', it is treated as incurring under 23.13 above a loss equal in amount to that gain in the 'last relevant accounting period', and amount B is construed accordingly;

(*d*) if it has a 'net contractual non-trading loss', it is treated as receiving under 23.13 above an amount equal to that loss in the 'last relevant accounting period', and amount A is construed accordingly.

The '*last relevant accounting period*' is the accounting period in which the contract ceased.

The '*net contractual gain of the trade*' is the excess (if any) of the amounts the company is treated as receiving under 23.11 above over those it is treated as incurring under 23.11 above in respect of the trade (or part) and the contract and the last relevant accounting period and the company's earlier accounting periods (disregarding amounts brought in under this provision). The '*net contractual loss of the trade*' is the excess of those it so treated as incurring over those it is so treated as receiving. The '*net contractual non-trading gain or loss*' is similarly determined by reference to amounts the company is treated as receiving and incurring under 23.13 above. Where the amounts brought in under 23.11 above are in a currency other than the 'local currency of the trade' (see 23.18 above) for the last relevant accounting period, they are treated for these purposes as being in that local currency, calculated by reference to the London closing exchange rate for the day on which the contract ceased.

Where the company would otherwise have a net contractual gain or loss of a trade and either the trade ceased before the contract ceased or the company carries on 'exempt activities' immediately before that time, the company is treated for these purposes as not having that net contractual gain or loss, but as having a net contractual non-trading gain or loss of the same amount (converted, if necessary, to its sterling equivalent by reference to the London closing exchange rate for the day on which the contract ceased).

'*Exempt activities*' are defined in the same terms as 'exempt circumstances' under 23.15 above.

[*FA 1993, s 146; FA 1994, s 115(2)*].

Simon's Direct Tax Service. See B3.1731.

23.22 **Reciprocal currency contracts.** Where a qualifying company enters into a currency contract which it closes out by entering into a second currency contract with reciprocal rights and duties, the company is treated as ceasing, at the time it enters into the second contract, to be entitled to rights and subject to duties under the first contract without having received or made any payment in pursuance of that contract, and the second contract is disregarded for the purposes of these provisions. [*FA 1993, s 147*]. See **Simon's Direct Tax Service B3.1732.**

23.23 **Excess gains or losses.** Regulations prescribe conditions under which relief from tax is to be afforded in respect of an asset or liability, where

(*a*) an unrelieved loss other than an exchange loss has accrued to a qualifying company as regards the asset or liability on the company's ceasing to be entitled or subject to it by virtue of an arm's length transaction, and

(*b*) exchange gains (whether trading or non-trading) have previously accrued to the company as regards the asset or liability in excess of any exchange losses which have so accrued.

On a claim being made by the company, an initial exchange loss (see 23.8 above) is treated as arising in respect of the asset or liability, equal in amount to the lesser of the amount in (*a*) (net of any non-taxable compensation, etc. received in respect of the loss) and the amount of the net exchange gains in (*b*). The claim must be made within two years of the end of the accounting period in which the non-exchange loss accrued.

Similar provisions apply to bring into charge an initial exchange gain where a non-chargeable gain accrues on the company's ceasing to be entitled to an asset or liability in respect of which net exchange losses have previously arisen.

Where a non-exchange loss for which relief has been obtained as above is subsequently recovered, there are provisions for cancellation of the relief.

A non-sterling exchange gain or loss is for these purposes converted into sterling at the London closing exchange rate for the last day of the accrual period for which the gain or loss accrues.

[*FA 1993, s 148; SI 1994 No 3229*].

Simon's Direct Tax Service. See **B3.1766.**

23.24 **Local currency.** For accounting periods beginning on or after 1 January 2000 and ending on or after 21 March 2000, for the purposes of 23.8–23.10 above, the '*local currency*' is sterling, except where, at any time in the accrual period, an asset or contract was held, or a liability owed, by a qualifying company for the purposes of a business, or part of a business, and the currency in which the profits and gains of the business (or part) are computed for the accounting period in which the accrual period falls (or with which it coincides) is a non-sterling currency (see 23.36, 23.37 below). In these circumstances, that non-sterling currency is treated as the local currency. If, throughout the accrual period, only one local currency is involved, 23.8–23.13 above are applied by reference to that currency. If two or more are involved, they are applied separately by reference to each, and any exchange gain or loss of a business (or part) is ignored unless found in the currency which is the local currency of the business (or part) for the accounting period. In any other case, 23.8–23.13 above are applied by reference to sterling and are then applied separately by reference to each local currency involved (other than sterling), any exchange gains or loss of a business (or part) being ignored unless found in the local currency of that business (or part) for the accounting period (whether sterling or otherwise). For these purposes, a part of a business is any part of a business which is treated as a separate business for the accounting period for the purposes of *FA 1993, s 93* (see 23.36 below).

For earlier accounting periods, these provisions apply by reference to the provisions previously applicable to the use of non-sterling currencies for corporation tax purposes (see 23.39 below) and only by references to trades and trading profits and gains etc..

[*FA 1993, ss 149, 163; FA 2000, s 106(1)–(5)(12)(13)(17)*].

For the application of *FA 1993, s 149* where a local currency election (see 23.35 below) has been made in respect of a trade carried on through an overseas branch, see sections 2.17–2.19 of the Explanatory Statement referred to at 23.5 above.

Simon's Direct Tax Service. See **B3.1717.**

23.25 **Exchange rate to be used.** *Translation times.* Provision is made for determination of the exchange rate to be used in finding the local currency equivalent at a translation time of the basic valuation of an asset or liability, the nominal amount of a debt outstanding, or an amount of currency.

(*a*) Where the translation time results solely from the ending of an accounting period:

(i) any arm's length exchange rate used in the accounts as regards the asset etc. concerned for the last day of the accounting period for the two currencies concerned is used for that purpose;

(ii) in the case of a currency contract (see 23.9 above), where, in conformity with normal accountancy practice, an exchange rate for the two currencies concerned is *not* used in the accounts as regards the contract for the last day of the accounting period, any arm's length exchange rate implied in the contract is used for that purpose;

(iii) where neither (i) nor (ii) applies, the London closing exchange rate for the two currencies concerned for the last day of the accounting period is used for that purpose.

(*b*) Where (*a*) does not apply:

(i) where the exchange rate used in the accounts as regards the asset etc. concerned at the translation time represents the average of arm's length rates for all the days falling within a period, and there is no significant difference between the rates for any two consecutive such days, that is the exchange rate used for that purpose;

(ii) where (i) does not apply but an arm's length exchange rate is used in the accounts at the translation time, that is the exchange rate used for that purpose;

(iii) in the case of a currency contract (see 23.9 above), where, in conformity with normal accountancy practice, an exchange rate for the two currencies concerned is *not* used in the accounts as regards the contract at the translation time, any arm's length exchange rate implied in the contract is used for that purpose;

(iv) where none of (i)–(iii) applies, but it is the company's normal practice to use an average exchange rate over a period, and the London closing exchange rate for the two currencies concerned for any day (other than the first) falling within the 'relevant period' does not differ significantly from that for the preceding day, then the exchange rate used for that purpose is the average of the London closing exchange rates for all the days falling within the relevant period;

(v) where none of (i)–(iv) applies, the exchange rate used for that purpose is the London closing exchange rate for the two currencies concerned for the day in which the translation time falls.

'*Relevant period*' in (*b*)(iv) above means the period beginning at the same time as the accounting period in which the translation time falls and ending at the end of the day in which the translation time falls.
[*FA 1993, s 150*].

Debts whose amounts vary. (*b*)(i)–(v) (other than (iii)) above apply in determining the exchange rate to be used in finding the local currency equivalent of any amount, at a time immediately after the nominal amount of a debt outstanding decreases or increases, with references to the translation time replaced by references to the time immediately after the increase or decrease. [*FA 1993, s 151*].

Simon's Direct Tax Service. See **B3.1717.**

23.26 **Entitlement to, and identification of, an asset.** A company becomes entitled to an asset when its entitlement becomes unconditional, and in determining whether or not a company is unconditionally entitled to an asset, any transfer of the asset, or of any interest in or right over it, by way of security is ignored, except that:

(*a*) where it agrees (other than by way of a currency contract) to acquire an asset by transfer, it becomes entitled to it when the contract is made and not on a later transfer made pursuant to the contract;

(*b*) where it agrees to dispose of an asset by transfer, it ceases to be entitled to it when the contract is made and not on a later transfer made pursuant to the contract;

(*c*) if a contract is conditional, for the purposes of (*a*) and (*b*) above it is made when the condition is satisfied;

(*d*) if it ceases to be entitled to an asset and at a later time becomes entitled to the same asset, the asset is treated, with effect from the later time, as if it were a different asset.

The question whether a company becomes unconditionally entitled at a particular time to an asset falling within 23.8(*a*) above is determined without reference to whether or not there is a later time at or before which the whole or any part of the debt is required to be paid. This does not apply where the asset consists of a right to interest, in which case the company becomes unconditionally entitled to the asset at the time at or before which the interest is required to be paid.

Rights of the same kind to settlement under debts on securities, to which a company becomes entitled at different times, are treated as different assets, and the question of whether a transaction involves one or a number of such assets is determined according to the facts of the case concerned.

In deciding whether rights to settlement under debts on securities of a particular kind are held by a company, those acquired earlier are treated as disposed of before those acquired later (references to acquisition and disposal being to becoming and ceasing to be entitled). A similar identification rule applies in relation to shares held by a company. In either case, however, a different rule used in the company's accounts in accordance with normal accountancy practice is to be used for this purpose instead of the statutory identification rule.

Where a company would otherwise become or cease to be entitled to an asset at a particular time by virtue of the above provisions and, in drawing up its accounts in accordance with normal accountancy practice, it regards itself as becoming or ceasing to be entitled to the asset at a different time, the following further provisions apply.

(i) Where the asset falls within 23.8(*a*) above, and the time at which the company regards itself as becoming entitled to it is earlier than the time which would otherwise apply, the company is taken to become entitled to it at the earlier time. As regards any time beginning with the earlier time and ending immediately before the time which would otherwise have applied, the nominal amount of the debt is taken to be such amount as the company treats as the nominal amount in its accounts or, if different, that which it would so treat in accordance with normal accountancy practice.

(ii) Where the asset falls within 23.8(*a*) above and the debt concerned is a debt on a security, or where the asset is a share, and the time at which the company regards itself as becoming entitled to it is later than the time which would otherwise apply, the company is taken to become entitled to it at the later time.

(iii) Where the asset falls within 23.8(*a*) above and the debt concerned is a debt on a security, or where the asset is a share, and the time at which the company regards itself as ceasing to be entitled to it is later than the time which would otherwise apply, the company is taken to cease to be entitled to it at the later time.

For accounting periods ending after 31 March 1996, a company is treated as becoming entitled to so much of any asset as consists in a right to receive interest brought into account under the LOAN RELATIONSHIPS (43) provisions at the following time (rather than that provided for under (i) above):

(A) where an accruals basis was used, the time the interest is treated as accruing;

(B) where a mark to market basis was used, the time the interest is treated as having become due and payable.

[*FA 1993, s 154; FA 1994, s 114(1)(2); FA 1996, Sch 14 para 71*].

See also 23.28 below.

Simon's Direct Tax Service. See **B3.1719**.

23.27 **Subjection to, and identification of, a liability.** A company becomes subject to a liability which is a qualifying liability consisting of a duty to settle under a qualifying debt when it becomes unconditionally subject to it, except that:

(*a*) where it agrees to acquire such a liability by transfer, it becomes subject to it when the contract is made and not on a later transfer made pursuant to the contract;

(*b*) where it agrees to dispose of a liability by transfer, it ceases to be subject to it when the contract is made and not on a later transfer made pursuant to the contract;

(*c*) if a contract is conditional, for the purposes of (*a*) and (*b*) above it is made when the condition is satisfied;

(*d*) if it ceases to be subject to such a liability and at a later time becomes subject to the same liability, the liability is treated, with effect from the later time, as if it were a different liability.

The question whether a company becomes unconditionally subject at a particular time to a qualifying liability consisting of a duty to settle under a qualifying debt (see 23.8 above) is determined without reference to whether or not there is a later time at or before which the whole or any part of the debt is required to be paid. This does not apply where the liability consists of a duty to pay interest, in which case the company becomes unconditionally subject to the liability at the time at or before which the interest is required to be paid.

Where a company would otherwise become subject to such a liability at a particular time by virtue of the above and, in drawing up its accounts in accordance with normal accountancy practice, it regards itself as becoming subject to the liability at an earlier time, it is taken to have become subject to the liability at that earlier time. As regards any time beginning with that earlier time and ending immediately before the time which would otherwise have applied, the nominal amount of the debt is taken to be such amount as the company treats as the nominal amount in its accounts, or, if different, that which it would so treat in accordance with normal accountancy practice. For accounting periods ending after 31 March 1996, however, a company is treated as becoming subject to so much of any liability as consists in a liability to pay interest brought into account under the LOAN RELATIONSHIPS (43) provisions at the time the interest is treated as accruing (where an accruals basis was used) or having become due and payable (where a mark-to-market basis was used).

As regards a qualifying liability consisting of a provision by the company, the company becomes subject to such a liability at the time with effect from which it makes the provision, and ceases to be subject to such a liability at the time with effect from which it deletes the provision or (if different) the time with effect from which it would delete it under normal accountancy practice. Where it changes the amount of such a provision, it is treated with effect from the time the change becomes effective as deleting the earlier provision and as making a new provision in the revised amount.

As regards a qualifying liability within 23.8(A) or (B) above, a company ceases to be subject to such a liability, if this has not otherwise occurred earlier, when it becomes entitled to the right or share(s) concerned.

[*FA 1993, s 155; FA 1994, s 114(3); FA 1996, Sch 14 para 72*].

See also 23.28 below.

Simon's Direct Tax Service. See **B3.1719**.

23.28 **Assets and liabilities — general.** The following questions are to be determined according to the facts of the case concerned.

(*a*) Whether a transaction (or series of transactions) involves the creation of one asset consisting of a right to settlement under a debt or a number of assets consisting of a number of such rights.

(*b*) Whether a transaction (or series of transactions) involves the creation of one liability consisting of a duty to settle under a debt or a number of liabilities consisting of a number of such duties.

(*c*) Whether a transaction (or series of transactions) involves the creation of both an asset (or assets) held and a liability (or liabilities) owed by the same company.

Where a company, in drawing up its accounts in accordance with normal accountancy practice, regards itself as becoming entitled or subject to an asset or liability at a particular time, and as ceasing to be entitled or subject to the asset or liability at a later time, it is taken to become and cease to be so entitled or subject at those times provided that

(i) at the earlier time it could reasonably be expected that it would become so entitled or subject, and

(ii) the asset or liability does not in fact come into existence before the later time but, if it did, would be a right to settlement, or duty to settle, under a qualifying debt.

In the period between the earlier and later times, the nominal amount of the debt is taken to be such amount as the company treats as the nominal amount in its accounts or, if different, that which it would so treat in accordance with normal accountancy practice.

[*FA 1993, s 156*].

Shares and rights to settlement of the same kind. Shares are of the same kind, and rights to settlement under debts on securities are of the same kind, if they are so treated by the practice of a recognised stock exchange, or would be so treated if dealt with on such an exchange. [*FA 1993, s 164(9)(10)*].

Security in the expression 'debt on a security' has the meaning given by *TCGA 1992, s 132*. [*FA 1993, s 164(11)*].

Simon's Direct Tax Service. See **B3.1719**.

23.29 **Chargeable gains.** The following provisions apply in relation to chargeable gains.

Currency. No chargeable gain or allowable loss accrues on the disposal (within *TCGA 1992*) by a qualifying company, on or after its 'commencement day' (see 23.32 below), of currency other than sterling, provided that immediately before the disposal the company did not hold the currency in '*exempt circumstances*' (defined in the same terms as under 23.15 above). [*FA 1993, Sch 17 paras 2, 3*].

Debts other than securities. For accounting periods ending before 1 April 1996, no chargeable gain or allowable loss accrues on the disposal (within *TCGA 1992*) by a qualifying company, on or after its commencement day, of a debt the right to settlement under which is a qualifying asset, and the settlement currency of which is a currency other than sterling, provided that immediately before the disposal the company did not hold the debt in exempt circumstances (as above), and that the debt is not a debt on a security (including a debenture deemed to be a security under *TCGA 1992, s 251(6)*). [*FA 1993, Sch 17 para 4; FA 1995, Sch 24 para 5*]. This provision is repealed by *FA 1996, Sch 41 Pt V(3)* for later accounting periods. See now 43 LOAN RELATIONSHIPS.

Debts on securities: disposals. For accounting periods ending before 1 April 1996, this provision applies where a qualifying asset consists of a right to settlement under a debt on a security, and on or after its commencement day there occurs an event giving rise to a disposal (within *TCGA 1992*) of the security, or which would give rise to such a disposal but for *TCGA 1992, s 127* (reorganisations), and immediately before that event the company did not hold the security in exempt circumstances (as above). In these circumstances, in applying *TCGA 1992, s 117* (meaning of 'qualifying corporate bond') in relation to the event,

(*a*) in the definition of 'corporate bond', the requirement that the bond be in sterling is ignored, and

(*b*) where the settlement currency of the debt is a currency other than sterling:

  (i) the definition of 'normal commercial loan' has effect as if *ICTA 1988, Sch 18 para 1(5)(b)(c)* (see generally 9.18 CAPITAL GAINS) were omitted; and

  (ii) *TCGA 1992, s 117(10)* (relating to securities issued within a group) is ignored.

Where (*a*) and (*b*) have effect in applying *TCGA 1992, s 117* in relation to an event as above, they similarly have effect in relation to any earlier transaction (but not one before the company's commencement day) to which *TCGA 1992, ss 127–130* apply (or would apply but for *TCGA 1992, s 116*), and under which the company became entitled to the right, where the company then held the right at all times until the occurrence of the event. *TCGA 1992, ss 127–130* deal broadly with reorganisations under which a new holding is equated with the original shares, and *TCGA 1992, s 116* excludes certain cases where either the original shares or the new holding (but not both) consist of or include qualifying corporate bonds within *TCGA 1992, s 117*.

[*FA 1993, Sch 17 para 5; FA 1995, Sch 24 para 6*].

This provision is repealed by *FA 1996, Sch 41 Pt V(3)* for later accounting periods. See now 43 LOAN RELATIONSHIPS.

Debts on securities: relief. For accounting periods ending before 1 April 1996, this provision applies where a qualifying company has made a loan under which the debt is a debt on a security, and the right to settlement under the debt is a qualifying asset. In these circumstances the following apply in relation to relief claims made on or after the company's commencement day.

(i) In applying *TCGA 1992, s 117* (meaning of 'qualifying corporate bond') for the purposes of *TCGA 1992, s 254* (relief for debts on qualifying corporate bonds), the requirement that the bond be in sterling is ignored.

(ii) Where the settlement currency of the debt is a currency other than sterling, then in applying *TCGA 1992, s 117* for the purposes of *TCGA 1992, s 254*:

(*a*) the definition of 'normal commercial loan' has effect as if *ICTA 1988, Sch 18 para 1(5)(b)(c)* (see generally 9.18 CAPITAL GAINS) were omitted; and

(*b*) *TCGA 1992, s 117(10)* (relating to securities issued within a group) is ignored.

(iii) In applying *TCGA 1992, s 254(6)* in a case where a security would not be a qualifying corporate bond but for (i) or (ii) above, the 'allowable amount' under that *subsection* is found by deducting from what the amount would otherwise be the amount of any net exchange loss or losses (whether trading or non-trading) accruing to the company as regards the asset for a period or periods ending on or before the '*relevant date*', i.e. the date when the security's value became negligible or the outstanding amount of the principal of the loan was or proved to be irrecoverable. The amount of an exchange loss expressed in a currency other than the basic currency (i.e. the currency in which the allowable amount is expressed) is for these purposes treated as the basic currency equivalent on the day the related claim is made, calculated by reference to the London closing exchange rate for that day.

[*FA 1993, Sch 17 para 6*].

This provision is repealed by *FA 1996, Sch 41 Pt V(3)* for later accounting periods. See now 43 LOAN RELATIONSHIPS.

Reconstructions, groups etc. This provision applies where there is a disposal or acquisition (within *TCGA 1992*) of

(A) currency,

(B) a qualifying asset consisting of the right to settlement under a debt which is not a debt on a security,

(C) a qualifying asset consisting of the right to settlement under a debt on a security (within *TCGA 1992, s 132*), or

(D) an obligation which by virtue of *TCGA 1992, s 143* is regarded as an asset to the disposal of which that Act applies and which is a duty under a currency contract.

Where

(I) the disposal or acquisition is by a qualifying company and is made on or after the company's commencement day, and immediately before the disposal or after the acquisition, as the case may be, the asset is held wholly for 'qualifying purposes', and

(II) *TCGA 1992, s 139, s 171* or (before 1 April 2000) *s 172* would otherwise apply,

the *section* concerned does not apply as regards the disposal or acquisition and the corresponding acquisition or disposal. '*Qualifying purposes*' are purposes of long term or mutual insurance business.

[*FA 1993, Sch 17 para 7; FA 2000, Sch 29 para 43*].

Indexation allowance: non-chargeable assets. For disposals before 30 November 1993, the provisions above relating to currency and to debts other than securities are ignored in construing *TCGA 1992, s 103(7)* (meaning of 'non-chargeable asset' for the purpose of restriction on availability of indexation allowance). [*FA 1993, Sch 17 para 8; FA 1994, s 93(7)*].

Simon's Direct Tax Service. See B3.1768.

23.30 **Partnerships which include qualifying companies.** With effect for accounting periods ending after 31 March 1996, Revenue Pamphlet IR 131, SP 4/98, 16 November 1998 replaces an earlier Statement of Practice (SP 9/94, which was included in the Explanatory Statement referred to at 23.5 above). These deal with the application of foreign exchange, FINANCIAL INSTRUMENTS (25) and LOAN RELATIONSHIPS (43) legislation to partnerships which include companies within those provisions. Where the current provisions are in point in relation to an accounting period of such a partnership, the approach of *FA 1994, s 172* as regards financial instruments (see 25.19 FINANCIAL INSTRUMENTS) will be adopted. Thus where the partnership consists wholly of qualifying companies (within 23.6 above), the current provisions will be applied to the partnership as if it were a qualifying company.

For partnerships with one or more members which are not qualifying companies, the general rules, which require profits and losses to be computed as if the partnership were a company, ensure that corporation tax is applied to corporate members and income tax to individual members (see 47.2 PARTNERSHIPS). In such cases, partnership profits and losses will be computed both on the basis that the partnership is a qualifying company and on the basis that it is not, the appropriate computation being employed in relation to partners which are qualifying companies and those which are not (including in the latter case a separate corporation tax computation in the unusual case of a corporate partner which is not a qualifying company).

For these purposes, the partnership will be treated as itself entitled and subject to the assets and liabilities in question.

The main elements of the Statements of Practice are as follows.

Valuations of assets and liabilities (see 23.8 above) should be made in accordance with the accounting methods used by the partnership.

Anti-avoidance. The main benefit and arm's length rules at 23.16, 23.17 above will apply to the partnership (including any individual partners).

Capital gains tax. TCGA 1992, s 59 (disposal of partnership assets) will continue to apply to the disposal of shares in partnership assets to which members who are not qualifying companies are entitled, regardless of the operation of the current (or the financial instruments or loan relationships) provisions.

Losses. A qualifying company's share of partnership trading exchange losses (or financial instrument losses or loan relationship deficits) will be relievable in the normal way. Its share of net partnership non-trading exchange gains or losses (and net non-trading gains or losses on financial instruments or loan relationship credits or debits) will in practice be merged with any other non-trading exchange gains or losses (or non-trading gains or losses on financial instruments or loan relationship credits or debits) accruing to it in its own right, for charge or relief in the normal way.

Differing accounting periods. Where partnership and company accounting periods differ, profits and losses will be allocated between the relevant company accounting periods, usually on a time basis.

Commencement day (see 23.32 below) where no partnership accounts are drawn up will be the first day of any period beginning after 22 March 1995 for which any financial statements are drawn up, or the earliest of the commencement days of qualifying company members.

Local currency elections (see 23.39 below). The Revenue previously considered that such elections could only be made by partnerships consisting wholly of qualifying companies. With effect for accounting periods ending after 31 March 1996, their revised view is that an election may be made where at least one of the partners is a qualifying company, subject to the conditions of *SI 1994 No 3230* being applied to the partnership as if it were a company. All partners subject to corporation tax must sign the election, which will be irrevocable and will not cease to be valid on subsequent partnership changes. See 23.35 *et seq.* below for provisions replacing such elections.

Deferral of unrealised exchange gains (see 23.18 above). Claims may be made by partnerships which include qualifying companies. The whole of the profits, etc. of the partnership, as computed for corporation tax purposes, will be taken into account in computing the amount which may be deferred, but the deferral, and subsequent recovery, will be by reference to the proportion appropriate to qualifying company members. The special rules for groups of companies do not, however, apply to partnerships. Deferral claims in respect of any gains arising to a qualifying company other than through the partnership are dealt with separately.

Matching elections (see 23.15 above). The Revenue previously considered that such elections were available to partnerships including qualifying companies only in relation to ships, aircraft and assets subject to capital gains tax held by a branch outside the UK. With effect for accounting periods ending after 31 March 1996, their revised view is that an election may be made for the full range of eligible assets. All partners subject to corporation tax must sign the election, and must also undertake to return any gain triggered by the disposal of a matched asset if they have left the partnership or reduced their asset share ratio. No election may be made to match a liability of a qualifying company which is not a share of a partnership liability with a partnership asset.

Anti-avoidance provisions (see 23.16 above) apply to the partnership (including any individual members) as if it were a qualifying company.

(Revenue Pamphlet IR 131, SP 9/94, 20 December 1994).

Simon's Direct Tax Service. See **B3.1711**.

23.31 **Miscellaneous.** *Anti-avoidance: change of accounting period.* Anti-avoidance provisions apply where a company changes the date on which an accounting period is to begin, and but for the change an exchange gain or gains would have accrued to the company or been bigger, or an exchange loss or losses would not have accrued to the company or would have been smaller (in each case whether trading or non-trading), and a purpose of the change was to secure those effects. In such a case the inspector (or on appeal the Commissioners) may arrive at the exchange gains and losses as if there had been no change of accounting date, and adjust the corporation tax liability for the accounting period as is just and reasonable. [*FA 1993, s 166*].

Controlled foreign companies. Where, for the purposes of the controlled foreign company legislation, a non-UK resident company accounting period begins by virtue of *ICTA 1988, s 751* (see 18.7 CONTROLLED FOREIGN COMPANIES), and an exchange gain or loss accrues for an accrual period constituting or falling within that accounting period, then if the company subsequently becomes UK resident, that exchange gain or loss is disregarded for any accounting period beginning on or after the date the company became UK resident. [*FA 1993, s 168A; FA 1995, Sch 25 para 7*].

Insurance companies. There are regulations (see *SI 1994 No 3231; SI 1996 No 673; SI 1996 No 1485; SI 1997 No 1155*) making special provision about the treatment for corporation tax purposes of exchange differences arising as regards assets and liabilities held or owed by insurance companies. [*FA 1993, s 168; FA 1995, s 52(2)*]. See Simon's Direct Tax Service B3.1767.

Orders and regulations. The various requisite order- and regulation-making powers are provided. [*FA 1993, s 167; FA 1996, Sch 14 para 74; FA 2000, s 106(15)*].

Amendments to other enactments. Amendments are made to other enactments as follows.

(*a*) *TMA 1970, s 87A* (see 39.1 INTEREST ON UNPAID TAX) is amended to ensure that interest on unpaid corporation tax is not affected by the carry back of non-trading losses under 23.14 above.

(*b*) *ICTA 1988, s 56* (transactions in deposits or debts) is amended to deal with the interaction of these provisions with the charge under that *section*. (*Section 56* ceases to apply for corporation tax purposes for accounting periods ending after 31 March 1996 except in relation to rights in existence on or before that date.)

(*c*) *ICTA 1988, s 242* (set-off of losses etc. against surplus of franked investment income, see 27.3 FRANKED INVESTMENT INCOME) is amended to enable relievable amounts under 23.14 above to be set against franked investment income. (Repealed for accounting periods ending after 31 March 1996.)

(*d*) *ICTA 1988, s 407* (see 29.26 GROUPS OF COMPANIES) is amended to give group relief for an accounting period in priority to relief for non-trading losses carried back under 23.14 above.

(*e*) *ICTA 1988, s 826* (see 38.1 INTEREST ON OVERPAID TAX) is amended to ensure that interest on overpaid tax (repayment supplement) does not arise as a result of the carry back of non-trading losses under 23.14 above.

(*f*) In determining UK equivalent profits under the offshore funds legislation in *ICTA 1988, Sch 27 para 5* (see Tolley's Income Tax under Overseas Matters), these provisions are ignored.

(*g*) *FA 1989, Sch 11* (deep gain securities, see Tolley's Income Tax under Interest Receivable) is amended to deal with the interaction of these provisions with the deep gain securities legislation. (Repealed for accounting periods ending after 31 March 1996.)

[*FA 1993, Sch 18; FA 1995, Sch 24 paras 7–12; FA 1996, Sch 14 paras 1, 6, 22, 48, Sch 41 Pt V(3)*].

23.32 **Commencement and transitional provisions.** Except in relation to chargeable gains (to which *FA 1993, Sch 17*, see 23.29 above, applies instead), these provisions apply where a qualifying asset or liability is one to which the company becomes entitled or subject on or after its 'commencement day', or the rights and duties under a currency contract are ones to which it becomes entitled and subject after that day.

The company is treated as becoming entitled or subject to a qualifying asset or liability at the beginning of its 'commencement day' where it is held or owed both immediately before and at the beginning of that day, and currency contracts are similarly treated. As regards assets and liabilities of a prescribed description, regulations may instead prescribe a later time at which the company is treated as becoming entitled or subject to the asset or liability, and may also provide for an election by the company overriding such a deferment of the commencement (and see now *SI 1994 No 3226*).

The '*commencement day*' for a company is the first day of its first accounting period to begin after 22 March 1995.

Where these provisions apply to an asset, liability or contract by virtue of the above, the transitional arrangements of *FA 1993, Sch 16* apply. Under these, regulations may make such provisions as the Treasury think fit, for which see *SI 1994 No 3226* (as amended), broadly providing as follows.

(*a*) As regards certain fluctuating debts, the commencement day may be deferred for up to six years where earlier exchange differences were not recognised for tax purposes.

(*b*) Exchange differences on a debt irrecoverable at the commencement day are excluded from these provisions.

(*c*) *FA 1993, s 150* (see 23.25 above) is modified in determining the exchange rate for the first translation time for an existing asset, liability or currency contract.

(*d*) The basic valuation (see 23.8 above) of an existing asset or liability is, subject to exceptions, its value immediately before the commencement day.

(*e*) Provision is made in relation to the computation, attribution and set-off, relief or charge of pre-commencement gains and losses.

(*f*) Provision is similarly made in relation to pre-commencement gains and losses on debts of fixed amount and term.

[*FA 1993, s 165; SI 1994 Nos 3224, 3226; SI 1995 No 408; SI 1996 No 1349*].

See Revenue Tax Bulletin February 1996 p 282 for an explanation of the application of *SI 1994 No 3226* to a deep discount or qualifying indexed security held at commencement.

Disapplication of certain no gain, no loss provisions. Where a qualifying asset is disposed of after 31 December 1994 by one qualifying company to another, and the disposal takes place before the commencement day of the disposing company and on or after that of the acquiring company, the following provisions, insofar as they require a disposal to be treated as giving rise to neither a gain nor a loss for capital gains purposes, do not apply to the transaction:

(*a*) *TCGA 1992, ss 139, 140A, 171, 172* (see 9.6, 9.8, 9.19, 9.21 CAPITAL GAINS);

(*b*) *TCGA 1992, ss 215, 216* (see 7.3(*c*), 7.6 BUILDING SOCIETIES);

(*c*) *TCGA 1992, s 217A* (see 28.2 FRIENDLY SOCIETIES); and

(*d*) *ICTA 1988, s 486(8)* (see 32.3 INDUSTRIAL AND PROVIDENT SOCIETIES).

[*FA 1995, s 131*].

Simon's Direct Tax Service. See **B3.1771** *et seq.*.

23.33 **CORPORATION TAX CURRENCY PROVISIONS**

In tandem with the provisions dealt with at 23.5–23.32 above, corporation tax provisions of general application were introduced with effect for accounting periods beginning on or after 23 March 1995 (except in the case of *FA 1993, s 60*, see 23.34 below). Except as follows, the provisions relating to the use of non-sterling currencies (see 23.38–23.41 below) are replaced by the *Finance Act 2000* provisions described at 23.35–23.37 below for accounting periods beginning on or after 1 January 2000 and ending on or after 21 March 2000. Where, however, for the accounting period immediately preceding the first accounting period to which the replacement provisions would otherwise apply, a company did *not* make a local currency election (see 23.39 below) in respect of a trade (or part), the company may elect, by notice given to an officer of the Board before 1 September 2000, for the replacement provisions not to apply in relation to that trade (or part) until the first accounting period beginning on or after 1 July 2000. [*FA 1993, s 95(6); SI 1994 No 3224; FA 2000, s 105(4)(5)*].

Simon's Direct Tax Service. See **B3.1716, B3.1717, B3.1748**.

23.34 **Certain interest not allowed as a deduction.** Where a qualifying company becomes subject to a qualifying debt (see 23.8 above) on or after its commencement day (see 23.32 above) and the interest payable exceeds a commercial return on the capital repayable (expressed in the 'settlement currency' (see 23.8 above)), then in computing the corporation tax chargeable for an accounting period, the excess interest paid in the period is disallowed as a deduction from total profits (if otherwise allowable). [*FA 1993, s 60*].

23.35 **Post–FA 2000: the basic corporation tax rule: sterling to be used.** Subject to 23.36, 23.37 below, a business's profits or losses, including management expenses and non-trading capital allowances and balancing charges, are computed and expressed in sterling. [*FA 1993, s 92; FA 2000, s 105(1)*].

23.36 **Post–FA 2000: use of currency other than sterling.** These provisions apply where, in any accounting period, a company carries on a business, and one of the two following conditions is fulfilled.

(*a*) The accounts of the company as a whole are prepared in a non-sterling currency in accordance with normal accounting practice and, if the company is non-UK resident, it makes a return of UK branch accounts prepared in a non-sterling currency in accordance with such practice. 'Branch' includes any collection of assets and liabilities.

(*b*) Either

(i) the accounts of the company as a whole are prepared in sterling but, so far as relating to the business, from financial statements prepared in a non-sterling currency using the closing rate/net investment method (as in Statement of Standard Accounting Practice SSAP 20), or

(ii) if the company is non-UK resident, it makes a return of UK branch accounts prepared in sterling but, so far as relating to the business, prepared from financial statements prepared in a currency other than sterling using that method.

In these circumstances, the profits or losses of the business for corporation tax purposes (other than chargeable gains or allowable losses under *TCGA 1992*) for that accounting period are determined as follows.

(1) Take the amount of all the profits and losses of the business computed and expressed in the '*relevant foreign currency*' (i.e. the non-sterling currency referred to in (*a*) or (*b*) above or, where (*a*) above applies and two non-sterling currencies are involved, that in which the return of accounts is prepared).

(2) Take account of any brought-forward management expenses, trading losses or non-trading loan relationship deficits so computed and expressed.

(3) Take the sterling equivalent (see 23.37 below) of the amount found by applying (1) and (2).

For these purposes, sterling amounts in the capital allowances provisions are taken as the foreign currency equivalent (see 23.37 below), and different parts of a business carried on through different branches which would be dealt with differently under the above rules are treated as separate businesses.

For these purposes 'accounts' are the annual accounts required for *Companies Act 1985* purposes (or NI equivalent). If no such accounts are required, they are those the company is required to keep under the law of the country or territory in which it is incorporated or, if it is not required to keep any such accounts, those most closely corresponding to *Companies Act* accounts. 'Return of accounts' of a UK branch means return of such accounts as the Revenue may require under *FA 1998, Sch 18 para 3* (see 55.3 SELF-ASSESSMENT).

[*FA 1993, s 93; FA 2000, s 105(1)*].

23.37 **Post–FA 2000: currency equivalents.** Translation into sterling of a receipt or expense for an accounting period is either:

(*a*) by reference to the rate used in the preparation of the company accounts as a whole for the period; or (*b*) by reference to the London closing exchange rate for the '*relevant day*', i.e. the day on which the company becomes entitled to the receipt or incurs (or is treated as incurring) the expense.

(*a*) above applies only if the rate is either an arm's length exchange rate for the relevant day, or an appropriate average of arm's length exchange rates for a period ending with that day (or a period not exceeding three months including that day) during which there was no significant day-to-day variation.

The translations required by 23.36(3) above are by reference to the London closing exchange rate for the last day of the accounting period in question, except that:

(1) where 23.36(*a*) above applies, the company may elect, as regards the business (or part), by written notice to an officer of the Board, to use an appropriate average of arm's length exchange rates for the period instead. The election applies from the first day of the accounting period in which the notice is given. The election may similarly be withdrawn from the first day of the first accounting period beginning on or after the date of the notice of withdrawal, and no further election may then be made to have effect before the third anniversary of the day the withdrawal takes effect; and

(2) where 23.36(*b*) above applies, and the company's accounts, so far as relating to the business (or part), are prepared by reference to an appropriate average of arm's length exchange rates for the accounting period, that exchange rate is to be used instead.

Any receipt or expense taken into account in making a calculation under 23.36(1) or (2) above which is denominated in a currency other than the non-sterling currency referred to in 23.36(*a*) or (*b*) above is translated into that currency by reference to the London closing exchange rate for the relevant day. The translation into that currency of sterling amounts in the capital allowances provisions is similarly by reference to the London closing exchange rate for the day on which the capital expenditure is incurred.

These provisions do **not** affect the operation of the provisions dealt with at 23.5–23.32 above or the CONTROLLED FOREIGN COMPANIES (19) provisions.

[*FA 1993, s 94; FA 2000, s 105(1)*].

For the first accounting period to which these provisions apply to a company, the brought-forward amounts referred to at 23.36(2) above are translated into the relevant currency by reference to the London closing exchange rate for the last day of the immediately preceding accounting period, and that rate is also applied to any balance of expenditure brought forward for machinery and plant capital allowance purposes. [*FA 2000, s 105(2)(3)*].

23.38 **Pre–FA 2000: the basic corporation tax rule: sterling to be used.** A company's trading profits or losses are computed and expressed in sterling for corporation tax purposes, subject to any regulations made under 23.39 or 23.40 below. [*FA 1993, s 92*].

23.39 **Pre–FA 2000: currency other than sterling for trades.** Where a company so elects, the 'basic profits or losses' of a trade for an accounting period are to be computed and expressed for corporation tax purposes in a local currency specified in the election (a 'local currency election'), provided that the currency meets certain conditions prescribed by regulations. Broadly, the currency must be that of the primary economic environment in which the trade is carried on, and the relevant accounts or other financial statements, etc. must be prepared in that currency. For guidance on these requirements, see respectively section 4 and section 2.16 of the Explanatory Statement referred to at 23.5 above. The election may have limited retrospective effect, and must include specified particulars of the trade and the place it is carried on and a statement as to why the company believes the prescribed conditions will be met. It will cease to have effect at the end of any accounting period in which the currency ceases to meet the prescribed conditions.

Special provision is made (by amendment to the relevant regulations) for the introduction of the euro with effect from 1 January 1999.

For this purpose, the '*basic profits or losses*' of a trade for an accounting period are all the profits or losses of the trade for the period except

(*a*) any trading receipt or expense of the trade arising under *CAA 1990, s 144(2)* (allowances and charges to be treated as trading expenses and receipts), and

(*b*) any such amount as is mentioned in 23.18 above in relation to non-sterling trades and is treated as received in respect of the trade.

Where the basic profits or losses of a trade for an accounting period are to be computed and expressed in a currency other than sterling for corporation tax purposes, the amount of those basic profits or losses is treated for those purposes as their sterling equivalent, calculated by reference to an average arm's length exchange rate for the accounting period concerned if the company so elects, otherwise by reference to the London closing exchange rate for the last day of the accounting period. The profits or losses of the trade for the period for corporation tax purposes are then found by adjusting the basic profits or losses in sterling to take account of the amounts excluded under (*a*) and (*b*) above.

[*FA 1993, ss 93, 95; SI 1994 No 3230; SI 1998 No 3177, Pt X*].

23.40 **Pre–FA 2000: parts of trades.** The regulations described at 23.39 above, modified as necessary, apply as regards an accounting period in which a company carries on part of a trade in the UK and a different part or parts through a branch or branches outside the UK, or carries on different parts of a trade through different branches outside the UK. They provide for the 'basic profits and losses' of the different parts to be computed and expressed for corporation tax purposes in such different currencies as may be found under the regulations, where the company so elects in accordance with the regulations. The regulations require that one currency is used for each part trade, at least two currencies are used (although the same currency may be used for more than one part and must be used for different branches in the same country), and sterling is used for any part for which no election is made.

For this purpose, the '*basic profits or losses*' of part of a trade for an accounting period are all the profits or losses of that part for the period, except

(*a*) any trading receipt or expense of the trade arising under *CAA 1990, s 144(2)* (allowances and charges to be treated as trading expenses and receipts), and

(*b*) where the basic profits or losses of the part of the trade are to be computed and expressed in a currency other than sterling, any such amount as is mentioned in 23.18 above in relation to non-sterling trades and is treated as received in respect of the part of the trade.

Where the basic profits or losses of different parts of a trade for an accounting period are to be computed and expressed in two or more different currencies, the profits or losses of the trade for the period for corporation tax purposes are found as follows:

(i) for each part whose basic profits and losses are computed and expressed in a currency other than sterling, the sterling equivalent is determined (by reference to an average arm's length exchange rate for the accounting period concerned if the company so elects, otherwise by reference to the London closing exchange rate for the last day of the accounting period concerned), and account is taken of any such amount as is mentioned in 23.18 above in relation to non-sterling trades and is treated as received in the period in respect of the part;

(ii) to the sum of the amount(s) found under (i) is added the sum of the basic profits or losses of each part whose basic profits or losses are computed and expressed in sterling;

(iii) the total sum found under (ii) is adjusted for any trading receipt or expense of the trade arising under *CAA 1990, s 144(2)* in the period.

[*FA 1993, ss 94, 95; SI 1994 No 3230*].

There are special provisions for elections relating to parts of trades in relation to petroleum extraction activities. [*FA 1993, s 94A; FA 1994, s 136; SI 1994 No 3230, reg 4(2)*].

23.41 For the purposes of 23.39 and 23.40 above, the ecu is regarded as a currency other than sterling. [*FA 1993, s 95(5)*].

24 Exempt Organisations

Any income tax provision conferring an exemption from income tax also applies to corporation tax. [*ICTA 1988, s 9(4)*].

24.1 **Agricultural societies** established to promote 'the interests of agriculture, horticulture, livestock breeding or forestry' are exempt from tax on profits or gains 'from any exhibition or show held for the purposes of the society . . . if applied solely to the purposes of the society'. [*ICTA 1988, s 510*]. See *Peterborough Royal Foxhound Show Society v CIR KB 1936, 20 TC 249; Glasgow Ornithological Association CS 1938, 21 TC 445*. An agricultural society may also qualify for relief as a charity.

24.2 **Non-resident central banks** as specified by Order in Council are exempt from tax on certain classes of income [*ICTA 1988, s 516; FA 1996, Sch 7 para 21*]; the issue departments of the Reserve Bank of India and the State Bank of Pakistan are exempt from all taxes. [*ICTA 1988, s 517; TCGA 1992, s 271(8)*]. See 6.5 BANKS.

24.3 **The British Museum** and **The Natural History Museum** are, on a claim, exempt from tax as CHARITIES (11). [*ICTA 1988, s 507; TCGA 1992, s 271(6); FA 1989, s 60; Museums and Galleries Act 1992, Sch 8 para 1(8)(9)*].

24.4 CHARITIES (11) are generally exempt.

24.5 **The Crown** is not within the taxing Acts; see *ICTA 1988, s 49(2)* and *s 829(2)*, *Bank voor Handel v Administrator of Hungarian Property HL 1954, 35 TC 311*, and *Boarland v Madras Electric Supply Corpn Ltd HL 1955, 35 TC 612*. But see *ICTA 1988, s 829(1)* as to assessment, deduction and payment of tax by public offices and departments of the Crown.

24.6 **International organisations** (e.g. the United Nations (*SI 1974 No 1261*)) may be specified by Order in Council as exempt from certain taxes (*International Organisations Act 1968*), as may certain financial bodies under the *Bretton Woods Agreement Act 1945* (e.g. the International Monetary Fund (*SI 1946 No 36*)) and other bodies under the *European Communities Act 1972* (e.g. the North Atlantic Salmon Conservation Organisation (*SI 1985 No 1773*)). The International Development Association is exempt [*International Development Association Act 1960, s 3* and *SI 1960 No 1383*] as are the International Finance Corporation [*International Finance Corporation Act 1955, s 3* and *SI 1955 No 1954*] and the International Maritime Satellite Organisation. [*ICTA 1988, s 515; TCGA 1992, s 271(5)*]. The Treasury may also designate any of the international organisations of which the UK is a member (e.g. The European Bank for Reconstruction and Development (*SI 1991 No 1694*)) for the purpose of exemption from various requirements for the deduction of tax from payments made in the UK. [*ICTA 1988, s 582A; FA 1991, s 118; FA 1996, Sch 7 para 22*].

24.7 FRIENDLY SOCIETIES (28) within *ICTA 1988, ss 460–463* are generally exempt.

24.8 **The Historic Buildings and Monuments Commission for England** is exempt from tax, on a claim, as if it is a charity the whole of whose income is applied only for charitable purposes, and from tax on chargeable gains without claim. [*ICTA 1988, ss 339(9), 507(1), 577(9); TCGA 1992, s 271(7)*].

24.9 **Housing Associations and self-build societies** have certain exemptions. See 30 HOUSING ASSOCIATIONS ETC..

24.10 **Local authorities, local authority associations and health service bodies** (as defined by, respectively, *ICTA 1988, s 842A, s 519(3)* and *s 519A*). The income and gains of such bodies are exempt from corporation tax. [*ICTA 1988, s 519; TCGA 1992, s 271(3); FA 1990, s 127; National Health Service and Community Care Act 1990, s 61(1); FA 1995, s 144*].

For payments of interest by local authorities, see 31.8 INCOME TAX IN RELATION TO A COMPANY.

24.11 The **National Heritage Memorial Fund** has the same exemptions as CHARITIES (11). A claim must be made, except in relation to chargeable gains. [*ICTA 1988, s 507(1); TCGA 1992, s 271(7)*].

24.12 A **scientific research association** is granted the same exemptions from tax as a charity (see 11 CHARITIES) and is exempted from corporation tax on capital gains if

(*a*) its object is research which may lead to an extension of trade and it is approved by the Secretary of State, and

(*b*) it is prohibited by its Memorandum or similar instrument from distribution of its income or property, in any form, to its members (other than as reasonable payments for supplies, labour, power, services, interest and rent).

[*ICTA 1988, s 508; TCGA 1992, s 271(6)*].

The Department of Trade and Industry (which is primarily responsible for determining whether a body is a scientific research association) issued new guidance on 4 September 1998 on the criteria they will apply, with effect from that date, in making such determinations. By concession, tax exemptions will continue to be granted on the previous basis for accounting periods beginning before 1 September 1999, provided that exemption would have continued to apply under the previous practice and the association continues to satisfy (*b*) above. This applies also to bodies established before 4 September 1998 which would have obtained approval under the previous practice. (Revenue Pamphlet IR 1, C31).

Simon's Direct Tax Service. See C4.535.

24.13 Some STATUTORY BODIES (57) receive a measure of exemption.

24.14 **Approved occupational pension, retirement benefit and personal pension schemes**, parliamentary pension schemes, National Insurance supplementary benefit schemes and certain overseas pension funds are exempt from tax on investment income and on chargeable gains arising on investments forming part of the fund. A contract entered into in the course of dealing in financial futures or traded options is regarded as an investment, and this treatment is extended to all futures and options contracts, and exemption applies to all income derived from transactions relating to such contracts (the fact that a contract may be capable of closure by payment of a sum rather than by delivery not being relevant for these purposes). [*ICTA 1988, s 592, ss 613–615, s 620(6); FA 1990, s 81; TCGA 1992, s 271(1)*].

Exemption of pension funds does not extend to repayment of tax credits attached to qualifying distributions made after 1 July 1997. [*F(No 2)A 1997, ss 19, 30, Sch 8 Pt II(9)*].

For the special provisions applicable to certain international pooled pension funds, see 60.2 UNIT AND INVESTMENT TRUSTS.

Scheme surpluses. A 40% charge may arise on any payment made to an employer out of funds of an exempt scheme approved under *section 592(1)*. Although regulations provide for the charge to be treated as a charge to corporation tax for the purposes of assessment and collection, the payment is not treated as income of the employer, and the amount charged is not available for any exemption, relief or set-off. [*ICTA 1988, s 601; SI 1987 No 352*]. Where those provisions do not apply, any such repayment is taxable as a trading receipt, or under Schedule D, Case VI if the scheme did not relate to a trade. [*ICTA 1988, s 601(5)*]. See Tolley's Income Tax under Retirement Schemes for details of these charges and of the Board's powers to require scheme surpluses to be reduced under *ICTA 1988, Sch 22*. Under the latter provision, a proportion of the income and gains of an exempt approved scheme may cease to attract exemption as above if the requirements as to the reduction of a surplus are not met.

Approved superannuation funds which, immediately before 6 April 1980, enjoyed a similar exemption under *ICTA 1970, s 208* (repealed from that date by *FA 1971, Sch 3 para 1*) may claim exemption for chargeable gains arising from the disposal of investments held for the purposes of the fund, and for income derived from investments or deposits, underwriting commissions, and interest payable on certificates of deposit, insofar as such income, etc. is applied for those purposes. [*ICTA 1988, s 608*]. Annuities paid out of such a fund are taxable under Schedule E, and PAYE applies accordingly. These provisions apply if the following conditions are satisfied.

(*a*) The fund has not been approved, and is not being considered for approval, under *FA 1970, Pt II, Ch II* or *ICTA 1988, Pt XIV, Ch I*.

(*b*) No contribution has been made to it since 5 April 1980.

Exemption may be claimed only if the terms on which benefits are payable from the fund have remained unaltered since 5 April 1980 (apart from certain minor rule amendments, see Revenue Pamphlet IR 1, B43).

Simon's Direct Tax Service. See E7.2.

24.15 **Trade Unions.** Registered trade unions, provided that they are precluded from assuring more than £4,000 by way of gross sum or £825 p.a. by way of annuity (excluding annuities approved under *ICTA 1988, s 620(9)*) in respect of any one person, are exempt. The exemption is granted in respect of non-trading income and chargeable gains which are applicable and applied for the purpose of 'providing benefits', i.e. sickness, injury and superannuation payments, payments for loss of tools, etc.. The limits may be increased by Treasury order. [*ICTA 1988, s 467; FA 1991, s 74*]. This includes legal expenses incurred in representing members at Industrial Tribunal hearings of cases alleging unfair dismissal, or in connection with a member's claim in respect of an accident or injury he has suffered, and general administrative expenses of providing such benefits. (Revenue Pamphlet IR 131, SP 1/84, 17 February 1984). The exemption also applies to employers' associations registered as trade unions [*ICTA 1988, s 467(4)(b)*] and to the Police Federations for England and Wales, Scotland, and Northern Ireland, and other police organisations with similar functions. [*ICTA 1988, s 467(4)(c)*].

24.16 UNIT AND INVESTMENT TRUSTS (60) and VENTURE CAPITAL TRUSTS (62) are exempt from corporation tax on their capital gains. [*TCGA 1992, s 100(1); FA 1995, s 72(2)*].

24.17 The **United Kingdom Ecolabelling Board** may claim exemption as if it were a charity (see 11 CHARITIES). [*ICTA 1988, s 507(1)(e); SI 1992 No 2383, reg 2*].

24.18 For the concessionary exemption of certain clubs and societies, see 14 CLUBS AND SOCIETIES, and for the principle that a person cannot derive a taxable profit from trading with itself, see 45 MUTUAL COMPANIES.

25 Financial Instruments

See also 23 EXCHANGE GAINS AND LOSSES and 43 LOAN RELATIONSHIPS and, for provisions on the use of derivatives, Tolley's Income Tax under Anti-Avoidance.

Simon's Direct Tax Service B3.18.

Other sources. See Tolley's Taxation of Corporate Debt and Financial Instruments.

The headings in this chapter are as follows.

25.1 Introduction
25.2 Special provisions for qualifying companies
25.3 — accrual of profits and losses
25.4 — qualifying companies
25.5 — qualifying contracts
25.6 — qualifying payments
25.7 — basis of accounting
25.8 — basis of accounting: linked currency options
25.9 — basis of accounting: adjustments for changes
25.10 — treatment of profits and losses
25.11 — termination etc. of qualifying contract
25.12 — exchange gains and losses on currency contracts
25.13 — irrecoverable payments
25.14 — released payments
25.15 — anti-avoidance: transfers of value by qualifying companies
25.16 — anti-avoidance: transfers of value to associated companies
25.17 — anti-avoidance: transactions not at arm's length
25.18 — anti-avoidance: qualifying contracts with non-residents
25.19 — partnerships which include qualifying companies
25.20 — transitional provisions
25.21 — miscellaneous

25.1 INTRODUCTION

For accounting periods beginning on or after 23 March 1995, a new regime applies to the determination, and charge or relief, of profits and losses associated with financial instruments used by companies for managing interest rate and currency risk. The provisions are contained in *FA 1994, ss 147–177, Sch 18*, and are described at 25.2 *et seq.* below. They are, however, subject to the provisions of *FA 1996, ss 80–105, Schs 8–15* which came into effect on 1 April 1996 (see 43 LOAN RELATIONSHIPS).

The Revenue have published an Explanatory Statement on Exchange Gains and Losses and Financial Instruments, containing guidance on these provisions and those relating to EXCHANGE GAINS AND LOSSES (23), to which reference is made in the text as appropriate. The Statement is available (price £4) from Reference Library, New Wing, Somerset House, London WC2R 1LB. Section 6.19 indicates that the new rules will not apply to non-resident companies unless they carry on a trade in the UK (subject to special rules concerning CONTROLLED FOREIGN COMPANIES (18)).

For earlier accounting periods (and where the new provisions do not apply), the tax treatment of such instruments is determined on general principles, resulting in a high degree of uncertainty as to the correct treatment to be applied in many instances. Some assistance may be obtained, however, from the body of case law and practice relating to exchange gains and losses (prior to the enactment of the detailed provision in *FA 1993*), for which see 23.2–23.4 EXCHANGE GAINS AND LOSSES. See also 50.28 PROFIT COMPUTATIONS.

See Revenue Tax Bulletin December 1998 pp 617, 618 for an article giving preliminary guidance on the Revenue approach to the taxation of global trading in the financial sector, in particular in relation to the means of rewarding capital provision and the assumption of risk within a highly integrated business.

25.2 **SPECIAL PROVISIONS FOR QUALIFYING COMPANIES**

The main elements of the provisions in *FA 1994, ss 147–177, Sch 18*, which are described in detail in 25.3 *et seq.* below, are as follows.

(*a*) Profits and losses on qualifying instruments held by qualifying companies follow acceptable accounting treatment by reference to the qualifying payments they make and receive.

(*b*) Profits or losses are taxed as income.

(*c*) Profits or losses on contracts held for trade purposes are taken into account in measuring trading income in the normal way.

(*d*) Non-trading profits or losses are treated in the same way as non-trading exchange gains and losses (see 23.14 EXCHANGE GAINS AND LOSSES).

(*e*) Anti-avoidance provisions apply to protect the Exchequer.

(*f*) Special rules apply to particular classes of company.

(*g*) The provisions do not apply where an amount representing the same profit or loss is brought into account under the LOAN RELATIONSHIPS (43) provisions of *FA 1996, Ch II, Pt IV*.

25.3 **Accrual of profits and losses.** Where, as regards a 'qualifying contract' held by a 'qualifying company', 'amount A' exceeds 'amount B' for an accounting period, the excess is a profit on the contract accruing to the company for the period. Where 'amount B' exceeds 'amount A', a loss similarly accrues. Subject to the various adjustments referred to at 25.9, 25.11, 25.17 below (each of which is applied after any adjustments made under an earlier *section* or *sections*), those amounts are defined as follows, depending on whether the company's profit or loss on the contract for the accounting period falls to be computed on a mark to market basis incorporating a particular method of valuation, or on a particular accruals basis.

Mark to market basis. 'Amount A' is the aggregate of the amount (or aggregate amount) of 'qualifying payment(s)' becoming due and payable to the company in the period and any increase for the period (or part for which contract held) in the value of the contract on the mark to market basis. '*Amount B*' is the aggregate of the amount (or aggregate amount) of 'qualifying payment(s)' becoming due and payable by the company in the period and any decrease for the period (or part for which contract held) in the value of the contract on the mark to market basis. See sections 6.20 and 6.21 of the Explanatory Statement referred to at 25.1 above for guidance on these calculations.

Particular accruals basis. 'Amount A' is so much of the 'qualifying payment(s)' received (or falling to be received) by the company as is allocated to the period on the particular accruals basis, and '*Amount B*' is so much of such payment(s) made or falling to be made by the company as is so allocated.

Where a contract is a 'qualifying contract' as a result of a transfer or transfers of money's worth being disregarded under *FA 1994, s 152* (see 25.5 below), so much of any 'qualifying payment', and (where the mark to market basis applies) of any increase or reduction in the value of the contract, as relates to such transfer(s) is ignored in determining Amounts A and B.

Where the mark to market basis applies and a 'qualifying contract' becomes held by the company during an accounting period, it is assumed in determining Amounts A and B that the value of the contract is nil immediately after it becomes so held. Similarly where a 'qualifying contract' ceases to be held during an accounting period, the value is assumed to be nil immediately before it ceases to be so held, unless the contract is discharged by the making of payments none of which is a 'qualifying payment'.

[*FA 1994, s 155*].

Simon's Direct Tax Service. See B3.1815.

25.4 **Qualifying companies.** A '*qualifying company*' is any company within the charge to corporation tax. This does not, however, include the trustees of a unit trust scheme which is an authorised unit trust as respects an accounting period (who are deemed for other purposes to be a company by *ICTA 1988, s 468(1)*, see 60.1 UNIT AND INVESTMENT TRUSTS)), or, in relation to 'currency contracts and options', an investment trust approved under *ICTA 1988, s 842* (see 60.4 UNIT AND INVESTMENT TRUSTS). [*FA 1994, s 154*].

Simon's Direct Tax Service. See B3.1803.

25.5 **Qualifying contracts.** A '*qualifying contract*' as regards a qualifying company is an 'interest rate contract or option', a 'currency contract or option' or a 'debt contract or option', to the rights or duties under which the company becomes entitled or subject on or after the company's 'commencement day'. [*FA 1994, ss 147(1), 147A(1); FA 1996, s 101(2); SI 1994 No 3225*]. For interest rate and currency contracts and options, the '*commencement day*' is the first day of its first accounting period beginning on or after 23 March 1995. For debt contracts or option, it is 1 April 1996, subject to transitional provisions as below. [*FA 1994, ss 147(4), 147A(1), 177(1); FA 1996, s 101(2), Sch 14 para 78(1)(a)*].

A company becomes entitled and subject to any such rights and duties when it becomes party to the contract or option. It holds the contract or option at any time at which it is entitled and subject to rights and duties under it, regardless of when the rights and duties fall to be exercised and performed. [*FA 1994, s 177(2); FA 1996, Sch 14 para 78(2)*].

As regards currency contracts or options held both immediately before and at the beginning of the commencement day, the company is treated as becoming entitled and subject to rights and duties thereunder at the latter time, and the same applies as regards interest rate contracts or options if the company's commencement day falls more than twelve months after the appointed day (see above). [*FA 1994, s 147(2)(3)*]. Where the company's commencement day falls within twelve months from the appointed day, the company may (except as below) elect for similar treatment to apply as regards interest rate contracts or options. If no election is made, then as regards interest rate contracts or options held six years after the commencement day, the company is treated as becoming entitled and subject to rights and duties thereunder on the first day of its first accounting period beginning after the end of that six years. [*FA 1994, s 148(1)–(3)*]. The election, which is irrevocable, must be made by notice served on the inspector within three months of the commencement day. No election may, however, be made by a company which is a member of a group of companies unless it is the principal company of the group, or it became a member of the group after the principal company's commencement day. An election by the principal company of a group has effect as regards companies whose commencement day falls within twelve months from the appointed day and which were members of the group on the principal company's commencement day. It continues to apply to companies leaving the group after that day, unless the election is made after the company leaves the group and it leaves the group before the expiry of the period during which the company could make an election (disregarding the group restriction) and before such an election has been made. The provisions of *TCGA 1992, s 170* (see 9.18 CAPITAL GAINS) apply as regards the meaning of 'group of companies' and 'principal company of a group'. [*FA 1994, s 148(4)–(9)*].

As regards debt contracts or options held both immediately before and on the commencement day, the company is treated as becoming entitled or subject to rights or duties thereunder on that date. A special transitional provision applies where, on a disposal on 31 March 1996, and apart from the LOAN RELATIONSHIPS (43) provisions applicable from that date, either:

(*a*) the gain accruing on disposal would have been treated as a chargeable gain; or

(*b*) amounts with respect to the disposal would have been brought into account for an accounting period beginning before 1 April 1996 in computing trading profits or gains.

In those circumstances, the commencement day is the first day of the first accounting period ending after 31 March 1996. See also 43.10 LOAN RELATIONSHIPS. [*FA 1994, s 147A(2)(3); FA 1996, ss 101(2), Sch 15 para 25*].

An '*interest rate contract*' is a contract under which (whether or not subject to conditions) a company becomes entitled to a right to receive, or subject to a duty to make, a 'variable rate' payment at a specified time, and under which the only transfers of money or money's worth provided for are such payments, payments falling within *FA 1994, s 149(3)(4)* (see below) or payments falling within *FA 1994, s 151* (see below). [*FA 1994, s 149(1)(2)*]. The contract may include provision for a reciprocal 'fixed' or 'fixed rate' payment, and the contract terms may be satisfied by the making of a single net payment where two counter-payments fall to be made at the same time. [*FA 1994, s 149(3)(4)*]. A '*fixed*' payment is a payment of an amount specified in the contract. A '*fixed rate*' payment is a payment the amount of which falls to be determined (wholly or mainly) by applying to a notional principal amount specified in the contract, for a period so specified, a rate the value of which is at all times the same as that of a fixed rate of interest so specified, and a '*variable rate*' payment is similarly defined by reference to a variable rate of interest so specified. [*FA 1994, s 149(6)*]. For the Revenue view of the interpretation of these definitions, see section 6.12 of the Explanatory Statement referred to at 25.1 above. Where, as a result of the adoption of the euro by a State, a change in a variable rate of interest results in a change in the variable rate payment under a contract and hence to the rescission of the original contract and the making of a new contract, the new contract is in effect treated as if it were the original contract. [*SI 1998 No 3177, reg 8*].

An '*interest rate option*' is an option to enter into an interest rate contract (or an option to enter into such an option) if the only transfers of money or money's worth for which the option provides are payments falling within *FA 1994, s 151* (see below). [*FA 1994, s 149(5)*].

A '*currency contract*' is a contract under which the company becomes entitled to a right and subject to a duty to receive payment at a specified time of a specified amount of one currency (the '*first currency*') and to pay in exchange at the same time a specified amount of another currency (the '*second currency*'), and under which the only transfers of money or money's worth provided for are such payments, payments falling within *FA 1994, s 150(3)(4)* or *(9)* (see below) or payments falling within *FA 1994, s 151* (see below). [*FA 1994, s 150(1)(2)*]. For general guidance on the treatment of currency contracts, see section 7 of the Explanatory Statement referred to at 25.1 above, and Annexes 1 and 2 thereto.

The contract may include provision for the company to become entitled to receive, or to become subject to a duty to make, at a specified time, a payment the amount of which falls to be determined wholly or mainly by applying a specified rate of interest to a specified amount of the first currency (in relation to entitlements) or the second currency (in relation to duties). It may also include provision for the company to become entitled to a right and subject to a duty to receive payment at a specified time of a specified amount of the second currency and to pay in exchange at the same time a specified amount of the first currency. [*FA 1994, s 150(3)(4)*]. In both of these permissible additional provisions, the specified time must be earlier than that specified in the essential provision of the contract (as in the preceding paragraph) and a specified rate of interest must be a rate the value of which at any time is the same as that of the specified rate of interest. [*FA 1994, s 150(5)*]. Where, as a result of the adoption of the euro by a State, a change in the rate of interest specified in a currency contract results in the rescission of the original contract and the making of a new contract, the new contract is in effect treated as if it were the original contract. [*SI 1998 No 3177, reg 9*]. Similarly where the conversion of the amounts of one or both of the currencies in a currency contract results in the contract being rescinded and replaced by a new contract which, but for the adoption of the euro, would have been a currency contract, the new contract is in effect treated as if it were the original currency contract. [*SI 1998 No 3177, reg 10*].

A '*currency option*' is

(*a*) an option to enter into a currency contract (or an option to enter into such an option), provided that the only transfers of money or money's worth for which the option provides are payments falling within *FA 1994, s 151* (see below), or

(*b*) an option the exercise of which at any time would result in the company becoming entitled to a right and subject to a duty to receive payment at that time of a specified amount of one currency and at the same time to pay in exchange a specified amount of another currency, provided that the only transfers of money or money's worth for which the option provides are such payments or payments falling within *FA 1994, s 151* (see below).

[*FA 1994, s 150(6)(7)*].

Where a contract is subject to a condition precedent the fulfilment of which at any time would result in the company becoming entitled and subject as under (*b*) above, the contract before fulfilment of the condition is treated as an option within (*b*) above, the fulfilment of the condition being treated as the exercise of that option, and the contract after fulfilment being treated as the contract resulting from that exercise. [*FA 1994, s 150(8)*].

It is immaterial that the rights and duties referred to above, in relation to payments of currency or (with appropriate modification) by reference to interest, may be satisfied by the making of a net payment of an amount determined by reference to the local currency equivalents at the relevant time of counter-payments required to be made at the same time, and a contract requiring a payment of such an amount at a specified time is treated as a currency contract. [*FA 1994, s 150(9)–(12); SI 1994 No 3233, reg 2*].

A '*debt contract*' is a contract (other than an interest rate or currency contract or option), other than one to which *FA 1996, s 92* or *s 93* (convertible securities or securities indexed to chargeable assets, see 43.9 LOAN RELATIONSHIPS) applies, where either:

(i) (whether or not subject to conditions) a company is entitled, or subject to a duty, under the contract to become a party to a loan relationship (see 43.2 LOAN RELATIONSHIPS), and the only transfers of money or money's worth for which the contract provides (apart from those under the loan relationship) fall within the following:

  (*a*) a payment representing the price for becoming a party;

  (*b*) a payment determined by reference to the value at any time of the money debt by reference to which the loan relationship subsists;

  (*c*) a settlement payment determined by reference to the difference at specified times between the price for becoming a party and the value of the money debt by reference to which the relationship subsists (or would, if the relationship existed, subsist); and

  (*d*) payments falling within *FA 1994, s 151* (see below); or

(ii) (where (i) above does not apply, and whether or not subject to conditions) a company is entitled, or subject to a duty, under the contract to become treated as a person with rights and liabilities corresponding to those of a party to a loan relationship, and the only transfers of money or money's worth for which the contract provides are payments falling within *FA 1994, s 151* (see below) and settlement payments determined by reference to the difference at specified times between the price for becoming treated as a person with rights and liabilities corresponding to those of a party to a relationship and the value of the money debt by reference to which the relationship subsists (or would, if the relationship existed, subsist).

This applies equally where the entitlement or duty is to become a party to a relationship equivalent to a specified loan relationship, or relates to the making of payments within (i)(*a*), (*b*) or (*c*) above in relation to a specified loan relationship (and similarly in relation to an entitlement or duty to become treated as a person with rights and liabilities corresponding to those of a party to a loan relationship). The transfer of money's worth having a value of a particular amount is treated as a payment of that amount for these purposes.

Where a contract contains both provisions under which, whether or not subject to conditions, a company is entitled, or subject to a duty, to become a party to a loan relationship, and provisions having effect other than for the purposes of or in relation to such provisions, the first-mentioned provisions, together with the other contents of the contract attributable on a just and reasonable basis to those provisions, are treated as a separate contract. Where the contents of a contract are attributed between those two categories of provision, and the contract provides for a payment in money or money's worth which cannot be attributed only to one such category, the payment is apportioned between those categories on a just and reasonable basis.

Where, as a result of the adoption of the euro by a State, there is a euroconversion (see *SI 1998 No 3177, reg 3*) of a loan relationship, or of corresponding rights and liabilities, which results in the rescission of the original debt contract and the making of a new debt contract, the new contract is in effect treated as if it were the original contract. [*SI 1998 No 3177, reg 11*].

A '*debt option*' is an option to enter into a debt contract, or into an option for such an option, if the only transfers of money or money's worth for which the option provides are payments falling within *FA 1994, s 151* (see below).

[*FA 1994, s 150A; FA 1996, Sch 12*].

Provisions which may be included. A qualifying contract may include provision under which the company becomes entitled to a right to receive a payment in consideration of its entering into the contract or option, or becomes subject to a duty to make a payment in consideration of another person's entering into the contract or option. It may also include provision for all or any of the following payments in respect of the contract or option.

(i) A reasonable arrangement fee.

(ii) Reasonable costs incurred.

(iii) A payment for securing, or in consequence of, its variation or termination.

(iv) A compensation payment for, or in consequence of, failure to comply with it.

[*FA 1994, s 151; FA 1996, s 101(4)*].

Provisions which may be disregarded. Where

(A) but for the inclusion in a contract or option of provisions for one or more transfers of money or money's worth, it would be a qualifying contract, and

(B) the present value of the transfer, or the aggregate of such values, is small (i.e. generally less than 5%, see Revenue Company Taxation Manual, CT 13494)

compared with the aggregate of the present values of all 'relevant payments' as regards the later of the time the contract or option was entered into and the time the provisions were included in the contract or option,

the contract or option is treated for the purposes of *FA 1994, s 149* or *s 150* or *150A* (as appropriate) as if those provisions were not included in it.

'*Relevant payments*' are, in relation to a contract, 'qualifying payments' thereunder, or, in relation to an option, 'qualifying payments' thereunder and payments which, if it were exercised, would be 'qualifying payments' under the contract arising by virtue of its exercise.

[*FA 1994, s 152*].

For guidance on several issues relating to the above, see sections 6.11 to 6.18 of the Explanatory Statement referred to at 25.1 above.

Simon's Direct Tax Service. See B3.1804 *et seq.*.

25.6 **Qualifying payments.** A '*qualifying payment*' is:

(*a*) in relation to a qualifying contract which is an interest rate contract, a payment falling within *FA 1994, s 149(2)–(4)* (see 25.5 above);

(*b*) in relation to a qualifying contract which is a currency contract, a payment falling within *FA 1994, s 150(3)* or *(9)* (see 25.5 above);

(*c*) in relation to a qualifying contract which is a currency option, a payment falling within *FA 1994, s 150(9)* (see 25.5 above);

(*d*) in relation to a qualifying contract which is a debt contract, a payment falling within *FA 1994, s 150A(5)(6)* (see 25.5 above);

(*e*) in relation to any qualifying contract, a payment falling within *FA 1994, s 151* (see 25.5 above).

The following are also '*qualifying payments*' in relation to a qualifying contract.

(i) A payment which, if it were a payment under the contract, would be within *FA 1994, s 151* (see 25.5 above), and a payment for securing the acquisition or disposal of the contract.

(ii) Where the qualifying contract is an interest rate or currency contract, and the company closes it out by entering into another contract with reciprocal obligations, any payment received by the company in consideration of its entering into the reciprocal contract, or paid by it in consideration of another person's entering into that contract. All other payments under the reciprocal contract, and all subsequent payments under the qualifying contract, are ignored for all tax purposes.

(iii) Where the qualifying contract is a currency contract, and there is a difference between the local currency equivalents of the amounts of the first and second currencies (see 25.5 above) at the time immediately after the company becomes entitled to rights and subject to duties under the contract, the amount of the difference is (except for the purposes of certain transitional provisions, see 25.20 below) treated as a '*qualifying payment*' received (where the first currency equivalent exceeds the second currency equivalent) or made (where the second currency equivalent exceeds the first) by the company at the time specified in the contract for the purposes of *FA 1994, s 150(2)* (see 25.5 above).

[*FA 1994, s 153; FA 1996, s 101(6)*].

Simon's Direct Tax Service. See B3.1810.

25.7 **Basis of accounting.** Where, for the purposes of the accounts (i.e. those required by the *Companies Act 1985* or equivalent) of a qualifying company for an accounting period, profits and losses on a qualifying contract held by the company are computed either on a mark to market basis, or on an accruals basis, satisfying the following requirements, the profits and losses for the period on the contract are computed on the same basis for the purposes of the charge under these provisions (see 25.10 below). In any other case, profits and losses on the contract are computed on a basis which does satisfy those requirements and which is specified in an agreement with the inspector or, failing such agreement, in a notice served on the company by the inspector.

Requirements: mark to market basis. As regards a qualifying contract held by the company:

(*a*) computing profits or losses on the contract on that basis must accord with normal accountancy practice;

(*b*) all '*relevant payments*' (i.e. qualifying payments made or received, or falling to be made or received, by the company) must be allocated to the accounting period in which they become due and payable; and

(*c*) the method of valuation adopted must secure the contract is brought into account at a fair value (i.e. on an arm's length basis).

Requirements: accruals basis. As regards a qualifying contract held by the company:

(i) computing profits or losses on the contract on that basis must accord with normal accountancy practice;

(ii) all 'relevant payments' (as above) must be allocated to the accounting periods to which they relate (disregarding those in which they are made or received or become due and payable); and

(iii) where necessary, such payments must be apportioned on a just and reasonable basis between two or more accounting periods to which they relate.

In determining whether this requirement is satisfied, regard is to be had to the corresponding treatment of any reciprocal payment(s) (i.e. payments being consideration (or part) for the relevant payment), but not to that of any other payment(s).

[*FA 1994, s 156*].

Simon's Direct Tax Service. See **B3.1815**.

25.8 **Basis of accounting: linked currency options.** The profit or loss on a qualifying contract which is a 'linked currency option' is computed on a mark to market basis of accounting. If the profit or loss would otherwise be computed on an accruals basis, the mark to market basis to be applied is such as satisfies the requirements of *FA 1994, s 156* (see 25.7 above), or would satisfy them but for the 'normal accountancy practice' requirement, and is specified in an agreement with the inspector or, failing such agreement, in a notice served on the company by the inspector.

A currency option is a '*linked currency option*' if the following conditions are fulfilled.

(*a*) If the option is exercisable by the company against the other party, another currency option is exercisable by that party against the company, or *vice versa*. Options exercisable by or against associated companies (within *ICTA 1988, s 416*, see 56.7 SMALL COMPANIES—REDUCED RATES) of either party are taken into account for this purpose. Where the currency option falls within *FA 1994, s 150(8)* (see 25.5 above), references to an option being exercisable are to be taken as referring to the contract being subject to fulfilment of a condition precedent resulting in a transfer of value (as defined).

(*b*) The terms of the two options in (*a*) must be such that they must be exercised (if at all) at the same (or substantially the same) time, and that the rights and duties under the contract which would arise if the one option were exercised are the same (or substantially the same) as those under the contract which would arise if the other option were exercised.

[*FA 1994, s 157*].

Simon's Direct Tax Service. See B3.1815.

25.9 **Basis of accounting: adjustments for changes.** The following apply where the profit or loss of a qualifying company for an accounting period is computed on a new accounting basis differing from that adopted for the immediately preceding accounting period.

(*a*) Amount A (see 25.3 above) is increased by any amount(s) not included in it for a preceding accounting period but which would have been so included had the new basis been adopted for that period, and a similar rule applies to Amount B (see 25.3 above).

(*b*) Amount A is decreased or, as the case may require, Amount B increased (see 25.21(*a*) below) by any amount(s) included in Amount A for a preceding accounting period but which would not have been so included had the new basis been adopted for that period, and a similar rule applies in relation to Amount B.

(*c*) (*a*) and (*b*) above also apply, with appropriate modification, where a contract or option becomes a qualifying contract by virtue of *FA 1994, s 147(2)* or *s 148(2)(3)* (see 25.5 above) at the start of an accounting period.

[*FA 1994, s 158*].

Simon's Direct Tax Service. See B3.1815.

25.10 **Treatment of profits and losses.** The treatment of a profit or loss accruing to a qualifying company as regards a qualifying contract for an accounting period (see 25.3 above) depends on whether the contract was at any time in the period held for trade purposes.

Trading profits and losses. Where throughout the period the contract was held solely for trade purposes, the whole of the profit or loss is treated as a trading profit or loss of the period (notwithstanding the provisions of *ICTA 1988, s 74*). Otherwise, the profit or loss is apportioned on a just and reasonable basis, so much as is attributable to trade purposes being so treated.

Non-trading profits or losses. Any part of the profit or loss not so treated as a trading profit or loss (or the whole of the profit or loss where appropriate) is treated as a non-trading profit or loss of the period. For accounting periods ending after 31 March 1996, a non-trading profit is brought into account as if it were a non-trading credit in respect of a loan relationship (see 43.3 LOAN RELATIONSHIPS), and a non-trading loss is similarly treated as a non-trading debit. For earlier accounting periods, the provisions of *FA 1993, s 129(5)(6)(9), ss 130–133* relating to exchange gains and losses (see 23.13, 23.14 EXCHANGE GAINS AND LOSSES) have effect, with appropriate modification, for the charge or relief of such profits or losses, so that a net amount is charged or relieved under both regimes.

[*FA 1994, ss 159, 160; FA 1996, Sch 14 para 75*].

Simon's Direct Tax Service. See B3.1813, B3.1814.

25.11 **Termination etc. of qualifying contract.** Where at any time in an accounting period a qualifying contract held by a qualifying company is terminated, or disposed of, or so varied as to cease to be a qualifying contract, and as regards the contract Amounts A and B fall to be determined for the period on a particular accruals basis under *FA 1994, s 155(5)* (see 25.3 above), Amounts A and/or B are adjusted in respect of so much of any qualifying payment as has previously been included in Amount A or Amount B but has not become due and payable to or by the company before the termination etc. of the contract. [*FA 1994, s 161*].

25.12 **Exchange gains and losses on currency contracts.** Where, as regards a currency contract, Amounts A and B fall to be determined for an accounting period on a mark to market basis under *FA 1994, s 155(4)* (see 25.3 above), Amounts A and/or B are adjusted for any 'exchange gain' or 'exchange loss' (see 23.11 EXCHANGE GAINS AND LOSSES) accruing to the company for the period as regards the contract. [*FA 1994, s 162*].

25.13 **Irrecoverable payments.** Where, on a claim within two years of the end of an accounting period, the whole or part of a qualifying payment to which a company is entitled at the end of the period could reasonably be regarded at that time as having become irrecoverable in the period, an appropriate adjustment, depending on whether the mark to market or a particular accruals basis has been adopted under *FA 1994, s 155* (see 25.3 above), is made to Amount A or, as the case may require, Amount B (see 25.21(*a*) below). A corresponding adjustment is made in any later accounting period in which an amount so treated as irrecoverable is in fact recovered. [*FA 1994, s 163; FA 1996, Sch 20 para 71*].

25.14 **Released payments.** Where, at any time in an accounting period, a company is released from a duty to make the whole or part of a qualifying payment, then as regards the qualifying contract and period, a corresponding adjustment is made to Amount B or, as the case may require, Amount A (see 25.21(*a*) below). [*FA 1994, s 164*].

25.15 **Anti-avoidance: transfers of value by qualifying companies.** Special provisions apply where, as a result of a qualifying company entering into a 'relevant transaction' on or after its commencement day (see 25.5 above), or as a result of the expiry on or after that day of an option held by it which, until its expiry, was a qualifying contract, there is a transfer of value by the company to an 'associated company' or an 'associated third party'. For the accounting period in which the transaction was entered into or the option expired, a corresponding adjustment is made to Amount B or, as the case may require, Amount A (see 25.21(*a*) below). There is such a transfer of value where the company's net assets are reduced, and those of the associated company or third party increased, as a result of the transaction or expiry, and the adjustment is equal to that reduction. Reasonable arrangement fees and costs within *FA 1994, s 151(2)(a)(b)* (see 25.5(i)(ii) above) are not taken into account for this purpose.

A '*relevant transaction*' is a transaction through which either the company becomes party to a qualifying contract, or the terms of a qualifying contract to which it is a party are varied. An '*associated company*' is as under *ICTA 1988, s 416* (see 56.7 SMALL COMPANIES—REDUCED RATES). A third party other than an associated company is an '*associated third party*' at the time when the relevant transaction is entered into or the option expires if the transaction is entered into, or the option allowed to expire, in pursuance of arrangements made with the third party, and, in pursuance of those arrangements, a transfer of value (as above) has been or will be made directly or indirectly to an associated company of the qualifying company by the third party or by a company which, when the arrangements were made, was an associated company of the third party. The inspector has appropriate information powers in relation to determination of the status of third parties.

[*FA 1994, s 165*].

See sections 6.27 and 6.28 of the Explanatory Statement referred to at 25.1 above as regards non-exercise of options and transfers of value through third parties.

Simon's Direct Tax Service. See B3.1816.

25.16 **Anti-avoidance: transfers of value to associated companies.** Special provisions apply where an adjustment is made under *FA 1994, s 165* (see 25.15 above), and either the transfer of value was to an associated company which was itself a qualifying company, or the transfer of value was to an associated third party and the related transfer of value is to an associated company which is itself a qualifying company and results from that company entering into a relevant transaction. An adjustment in the same amount is made for the 'corresponding accounting period or periods' of the associated company to Amount A or, as the case may require, Amount B (see 25.21(*a*) below).

The '*corresponding accounting period or periods*' means the accounting period or periods which comprise or together comprise the accounting period of the qualifying company in which the transaction was entered into or the option expired, with any necessary apportionment where there is more than one corresponding accounting period.

[*FA 1994, s 166*].

Simon's Direct Tax Service. See B3.1816.

25.17 **Anti-avoidance: transactions not at arm's length.** Special provisions apply where the parties to a 'relevant transaction' would not have entered into it had they been dealing at arm's length (and, prior to the commencement of corporate self-assessment, where the Board so direct).

For each 'relevant accounting period' throughout which the other party is a qualifying company, a deduction is made from each of Amount A and Amount B to reduce it to nil.

For each 'relevant accounting period' for any part of which the other party is *not* a qualifying company, a deduction is made from Amount B so as to reduce it to nil, and the same amount is deducted from Amount A (but not so as to reduce Amount A to less than nil), and for each such 'relevant accounting period' other than the first, there is also deducted from Amount A or, as the case may require, added to Amount B such an amount as will secure that 'Amount C' does not exceed 'Amount D', where:

(*a*) '*Amount C*' is any amount by which the aggregate of Amounts A (adjusted as above) for the period and all previous relevant accounting periods exceeds such aggregate of Amounts B; and

(*b*) '*Amount D*' is any amount by which the aggregate of Amounts A (prior to adjustment as above) for the period and all previous relevant accounting periods exceeds such aggregate of Amounts B.

Similar adjustments are made where the parties would have entered into the transaction but on different terms (and, prior to the commencement of corporate self-assessment, the Board so direct), but by reference to the '*relevant proportion*' of the respective amounts, i.e. such proportion as may be just and reasonable having regard to the differences between the actual terms and those which would have applied at arm's length.

For all these purposes, any transfer of value the subject of an adjustment under *FA 1994, s 165* or *s 166* (see 25.15, 25.16 above) is disregarded. Otherwise, all factors are taken into account, including (in the case of an interest rate contract or option) any notional principal amounts and rates of interest that would have been involved, (in the case of a currency contract or option) any currencies and amounts that would have been involved, (in the case of a debt contract or option) the amount of the debt by reference to which any loan relationship that would have been involved would have subsisted, and any terms as to repayment, redemption or interest that, in the case of that debt or any asset representing it, would have been involved, and (in any such case) any transactions related to the relevant transaction.

A '*relevant transaction*' is a transaction entered into on or after the qualifying company's commencement day (see 25.5 above) as a result of which the company becomes party to a qualifying contract, or the terms of such a contract to which it is a party are varied. A '*relevant accounting period*' is the accounting period in which the transaction was entered into and each subsequent accounting period for all or part of which the company is party to the contract.

Determinations requiring the sanction of the Board. A determination of the amount of an adjustment under these provisions requires the Board's sanction, other than in certain cases where an agreement has been reached between the Board and the person concerned (see *FA 1998, s 110(5)–(7)*). Where such a determination is made for the purpose of giving a closure notice, giving a notice amending a partnership assessment or making a discovery assessment, and the notice of the closure, amendment or discovery assessment is given to any person without the determination, so far as taken into account in the notice or assessment, having been approved by the Board, or without a copy of the Board's approval having been served on that person at or before the time the notice was given, the closure or amendment notice or discovery assessment is deemed to have been given or made (and in the case of an assessment notified) as if the determination had not been taken into account. The approval must apply specifically to the case in question and the amount determined, but may otherwise be given (either before or after the making of the determination) in any such form or manner as the Board may determine. An appeal relating to a determination approved by the Board may not question the Board's approval except to the extent that the grounds for questioning the approval are the same as the grounds for questioning the determination itself.

[*FA 1994, s 167; FA 1996, Sch 14 para 76; FA 1998, s 109(3)(4), s 110*].

Simon's Direct Tax Service. See B3.1816.

25.18 **Anti-avoidance: qualifying contracts with non-residents.** Special provisions apply (except as below) where, as a result of any transaction entered into on or after its commencement day (see 25.5 above), either:

(*a*) a qualifying company and a non-resident both become party to a qualifying contract; or

(*b*) the company becomes party to a qualifying contract to which a non-resident is party; or

(*c*) a non-resident becomes party to a qualifying contract to which the company is party.

For each 'relevant accounting period' for any part of which the other party is not a qualifying company, a deduction is made from Amount B so as to reduce it to nil, and the same amount is deducted from Amount A (but not so as to reduce Amount A to less than nil), and for each such 'relevant accounting period' other than the first, there is also deducted from Amount A or, as the case may require, added to Amount B such an amount as will secure that 'Amount C' does not exceed 'Amount D', those amounts being defined as under *FA 1994, s 167* (see 25.17 above).

A '*relevant accounting period*' is the accounting period in which the transaction was entered into and each subsequent accounting period for all or part of which the company and the non-resident are party to the contract.

These special provisions do not apply:

(i) to a qualifying company which is a bank, building society or financial trader (as defined, and see below) and which holds the contract (otherwise than as agent or nominee) solely for UK trade purposes;

(ii) where the non-resident holds the contract (otherwise than as agent or nominee) solely for the purposes of a UK trade (or part) carried on through a branch or agency; or

(iii) where arrangements made under *ICTA 1988, s 788* with the government of the territory in which the non-resident is resident (or, if the non-resident is party to the contract as agent or nominee of another person, with the government of the territory in which that other person is resident) make provision, whether for relief or otherwise, in relation to interest.

[*FA 1994, ss 168, 177(1)*].

As regards (i) above, for the guidelines used by the Revenue in deciding whether a company should be approved as a financial trader, see Revenue Pamphlet IR 131, SP 3/95, 21 March 1995.

Simon's Direct Tax Service. See B3.1816.

25.19 **Partnerships which include qualifying companies.** A partnership of which one or more members is a qualifying company (see 25.4 above) is treated as a qualifying company under the current provisions. Where one or more members of such a partnership is *not* a qualifying company, then for any accounting period for which profit or loss accrues to the partnership as regards one or more qualifying contracts, partnership profits and losses are computed both on the basis that the partnership is a qualifying company and on the basis that it is not, and the appropriate computation is employed in relation to partners which are qualifying companies and those which are not (in addition to any separate income tax computation which may be required). [*FA 1994, s 172*]. The partnership will accordingly be treated as itself entitled and subject to the assets and liabilities in question.

With effect for accounting periods ending after 31 March 1996, Revenue Pamphlet IR 131, SP 4/98, 16 November 1998 replaces an earlier Statement of Practice (SP 9/94, which was included in the Explanatory Statement referred to at 25.1 above). These deal with the application to such partnerships of the current provisions and those dealing with EXCHANGE GAINS AND LOSSES (23) and LOAN RELATIONSHIPS (43), in particular applying the approach of *FA 1994, s 172* (as above) to the former (see 23.30 EXCHANGE GAINS AND LOSSES). Further subjects are covered by the Statements of Practice as follows.

Valuations of assets and liabilities (see 25.7, 25.8 above) should be made in accordance with the accounting methods used by the partnership.

Anti-avoidance. The provisions at 25.15–25.18 above will apply to the partnership (including any individual partners).

Capital gains tax. TCGA 1992, s 59 (disposal of partnership assets) will continue to apply to the disposal of shares in partnership assets to which members who are not qualifying companies are entitled, regardless of the operation of the current (or the exchange gains and losses or loan relationships) provisions.

Losses. A qualifying company's share of partnership trading losses on financial instruments (or trading exchange losses or loan relationship deficits) will be relievable in the normal way. Its share of net partnership non-trading gains or losses on financial instruments (and net non-trading exchange gains or losses and loan relationship credits or debits) will in practice be merged with any other non-trading gains or losses on financial instruments (or non-trading exchange gains or losses or loan relationship credits or debits) accruing to it in its own right, for charge or relief in the normal way.

Differing accounting periods. Where partnership and company accounting periods differ, profits and losses will be allocated between the relevant company accounting periods, usually on a time basis.

Commencement day (see 25.5 above) where no partnership accounts are drawn up will be the first day of any period beginning after 22 March 1995 for which any financial statements are drawn up, or the earliest of the commencement days of qualifying company members.

(Revenue Pamphlet IR 131, SP 9/94, 20 December 1994).

25.20 **Transitional provisions.** Where, at any time, a currency contract held by a qualifying company becomes a qualifying contract under *FA 1994, s 147(2)* (i.e. at the beginning of the company's commencement day, see 25.5 above), two transitional provisions apply.

(*a*) Where the contract is, at that time, held for the purposes of a trade (or part of a trade), in circumstances such that any profit or loss as regards the contract for an accounting period beginning before that time would be a profit or loss of that trade (or part), *FA 1994, s 153(4)* (definition of qualifying payment, see 25.6(iii) above) has effect as if *section 147(2)* did not apply (i.e. *section 153(4)* does not apply on the contract becoming a qualifying contract).

(*b*) Where the circumstances are such that any profit or loss as regards the contract for the accounting period beginning with that time would *not* be a profit or loss of a trade (or part of a trade) carried on by the company, *FA 1994, s 158(2)(4)* (adjustments for changes in basis of accounting, see 25.9(*a*) above) have effect in relation to the contract and the period as if *FA 1994, s 153(4)(5)* were omitted (i.e. as if 25.6(iii) above did not apply to extend the definition of a qualifying payment).

[*FA 1994, s 175; FA 1995, s 132*].

Under (*b*) above, the transitional rules may operate to impute a deemed receipt in respect of pre-commencement exchange gains. In the case of a company which was not subject to a direction under the CONTROLLED FOREIGN COMPANIES (18) legislation for its pre-commencement accounting period (without having to make an acceptable distribution to preclude such a direction), but which could become subject to such a direction for the following accounting period solely because of the deemed receipt, the Board will take this into account in considering whether a direction should be made. (Revenue Tax Bulletin June 1995 p 222).

25.21 **Miscellaneous.**

(*a*) *Amounts to be deducted from Amount A or, as the case may require, Amount B and vice versa.* Any of the current provisions (other than *FA 1994, s 167*, see 25.17 above) which requires any amount to be deducted from Amount A or, as the case may require, added to Amount B requires the deduction to be made from Amount A unless it exceeds Amount A, in which case Amount A is to be reduced to nil and the excess added to Amount B. If Amount A is nil, the whole amount is added to Amount B. The same applies, with requisite modifications, to amounts to be deducted from Amount B or, as the case may require, added to Amount A. [*FA 1994, s 177(3)(4)*].

(*b*) *Charities.* For accounting periods ending before 1 April 1996, where a qualifying company is established for charitable purposes only, the exemption from tax of interest and other annual payments (see 11.4 CHARITIES) applies also to any annual profits or gains charged to tax under *FA 1993, s 130* (see 23.14 EXCHANGE GAINS AND

LOSSES). This relates to non-trading exchange gains, but is extended to apply to the aggregate of non-trading exchange gains and losses and non-trading profits or losses under the current provisions by *FA 1994, s 160* (see 25.10 above). However, no part of a net loss for any period under *FA 1993, s 131* (again as extended by *FA 1994, s 160*) may be set off against any income which, had it been applied for charitable purposes only, would have been exempt under *ICTA 1988, s 505* (see 11.2 *et seq.* CHARITIES). [*FA 1994, s 171; FA 1996, Sch 41 Pt V(3)*].

(*c*) *Insurance and mutual trading companies.* Special provisions in *FA 1994, Sch 18* apply to life assurance business (including annuity business) and to any other mutual trading or insurance or other mutual business. Otherwise, the provisions described at 25.3 to 25.20 above apply to insurance and mutual trading companies as they do to other qualifying companies. The Treasury has regulation-making powers. [*FA 1994, s 169*].

(*d*) *Investment trusts.* In applying the income retention test for approval of an investment trust under *ICTA 1988, s 842* (see 60.4(*g*) UNIT AND INVESTMENT TRUSTS), non-trading profits under *FA 1994, s 160* (see 25.10 above) for a period are treated as income derived from shares or securities. [*FA 1994, s 170*].

(*e*) *Prevention of deduction of tax.* A qualifying company is not required to deduct income tax from qualifying payments. [*FA 1994, s 174*].

(*f*) *Prevention of double charge.* Any amount charged on a qualifying company, or brought in in computing profits or losses of such a company, under the current provisions is not otherwise chargeable to corporation tax or brought in in computing profits or losses or chargeable gains. A corresponding restriction applies to any amount relieved or relievable under the current provisions. [*FA 1994, s 173; FA 1996, Sch 14 para 77*].

(*g*) *Amendments to other enactments.* (i) *ICTA 1988, s 434A(1)* (see 41.7 LIFE INSURANCE COMPANIES) is amended to exclude non-trading losses under these provisions. (ii) In determining UK equivalent profits under the offshore funds legislation in *ICTA 1988, Sch 27 para 5* (see Tolley's Income Tax under Overseas Matters), the current provisions are ignored. [*FA 1994, s 176; FA 1995, Sch 8 para 20; FA 1996, Sch 14 para 23*].

(*h*) *Regulations.* The Treasury may by order amend any of *FA 1994, ss 149–153* (see 25.5, 25.6 above), including corresponding amendments to *FA 1993, s 126* and consequential amendments relating to currency contracts, and such an order may include such supplementary, incidental, consequential or transitional provisions as it considers necessary or expedient. [*FA 1994, s 177(6)*]. See now *SI 1994 No 3233.*

26 Foreign Income Dividends

Simon's Direct Tax Service D1.7.

General note. The foreign income dividend provisions are **repealed** from 6 April 1999. See 26.1 below.

The headings in this chapter are as follows.

26.1	Introduction	26.7	— example
26.2	Election for treatment as a FID	26.8	International headquarters companies
26.3	Receipt of FID		
26.4	Payment of FID	26.9	— payment of a FID by an IHC
26.5	Matching of FID with distributable foreign profits	26.10	Adjustments where profits or foreign tax altered
26.6	Repayment or set-off of ACT	26.11	Returns and collection

26.1 INTRODUCTION

A company paying a dividend **on or after 1 July 1994 and before 6 April 1999** may elect for it to be treated as a 'foreign income dividend' ('FID'). For dividends paid after 28 November 1995, the company must be UK resident. [*ICTA 1988, ss 246A(1), 246Y; FA 1994, Sch 16 para 1; FA 1996, Sch 27 para 1; F(No 2)A 1997, s 36(1)*]. An election may apply to part of a dividend (see Revenue Tax Bulletin June 1995 p 226). The consequences of such treatment are described in detail at 26.2 *et seq.* below, but in general terms they are as follows.

(*a*) ACT is payable when a FID is paid.

(*b*) If the FID was paid out of foreign source profits, any surplus ACT in respect of the FID is repayable by the Revenue.

(*c*) The foreign source profits out of which a FID may be paid are those of the current or immediately preceding accounting periods or, if those profits were insufficient, those of any subsequent accounting period. It may also be paid out of the foreign source profits of a 51% subsidiary.

(*d*) Shareholders are treated as receiving income of the FID grossed up at the lower rate of income tax (currently 20%). Lower and basic rate taxpayers have no further liability, but there is no tax credit. Higher rate taxpayers are liable at the difference between the higher and lower rates of income tax.

(*e*) An international headquarters company (as defined) may pay a FID without paying ACT.

See Revenue Tax Bulletin August 1994 pp 141–146 for a Revenue summary, with examples, of how the foreign income dividend provisions work in practice.

Distributions on or after 8 October 1996 consisting of the redemption, repayment, or PURCHASE BY A COMPANY OF ITS OWN SHARES (51) and certain other special dividends are treated as if they were foreign income dividends. See 4.7 ANTI-AVOIDANCE.

These provisions are repealed (and consequential changes made) by *F(No 2)A 1997, Sch 6, Sch 8 Pt II(11)*. **No election may be made for FID treatment in respect of any distribution made on or after 6 April 1999.** [*F(No 2)A 1997, s 36*]. Exceptionally, where a FID (other than one to which *ICTA 1988, s 246D* (receipt by individuals, etc., see 26.3 below) applies) is paid before 6 April 1999 but is received on or after that date, the recipient is treated as receiving a qualifying distribution (see 20.8

DISTRIBUTIONS) made by a UK resident company equal in amount to nine-tenths of the FID. [*F(No 2)A 1997, Sch 6 para 23*].

26.2 **ELECTION FOR TREATMENT AS A FID**

An election may **not** be made in the following circumstances.

(*a*) Where a dividend is paid, or to be paid, other than in cash.

(*b*) Where there are arrangements for the shareholder to choose whether, or in what form, dividends are to be paid, which may include a choice for payment by a company other than the one which issued the share. The existence of an article permitting the directors to offer e.g. a scrip alternative does not prevent the company from electing for a particular dividend to be a FID, as long as such an alternative is not offered to that particular dividend. Similarly the general right of a shareholder to waive a dividend, which does not arise in respect of the specific shareholding, does not affect the FID status of the dividend. (Revenue Tax Bulletin August 1994 p 143; ICAEW Technical Release TAX 9/94, 7 June 1994). See also Revenue Tax Bulletin June 1998 p 554 as regards shares held by employee benefit trusts.

(*c*) Where at a given time a company pays one dividend on the same terms in respect of each of two or more shares of the same class, an election may not be made as regards any of the dividends unless it is made as regards each of them.

(*d*) Where at a given time a company pays two or more dividends on the same terms in respect of each of two or more shares of the same class, an election may not be made as regards any of the dividends in respect of a particular share unless it is made as regards the corresponding dividend in respect of each of the other shares.

(*e*) A company with more than one class of share capital may not make an election as regards any dividend, unless at a given time it pays a dividend on the same terms in respect of each share of each class, in which case it may make an election as regards each such dividend. For this purpose a dividend is paid on the same terms as another if in each case the amount of the dividend bears the same proportion to the nominal value of the share in respect of which it is paid. 'Fixed rate preference shares' (within *ICTA 1988, Sch 28B para 13(6)* (before 2 July 1997, *ICTA 1988, s 95(5)*) are for this purpose not treated as constituting a class of share capital.

(*f*) An election cannot be made as regards a distribution which already falls to be treated as a FID under *FA 1997, Sch 7* (see 4.7 ANTI-AVOIDANCE).

Arrangements for payment of a dividend declared in sterling to be made in a foreign currency on some shares, by reference to the exchange rate on, for example, the date of declaration of the dividend, would not contravene the requirement at (*b*) above, and would not involve payment of the dividend on different terms even where there was a movement in the exchange rate between the time the dividend was declared and the time it was paid. (Revenue Tax Bulletin April 1996 p 304).

An election as regards a dividend in respect of which a group income election is in force (see 29.2 GROUPS OF COMPANIES) is treated as comprising a notification to the collector that the group income election shall not apply to the dividend. A revocation of the election is similarly treated as a revocation of such deemed notice (which may not otherwise be revoked), which is accordingly treated as never having been made.

[*ICTA 1988, s 246A; FA 1994, Sch 16 para 1; FA 1997, Sch 7 para 2(2); F(No 2)A 1997, s 25(1)*]

An election in respect of a particular dividend must be made (and may be revoked) by notice in prescribed form (i.e. by letter — see Revenue Tax Bulletin August 1994 p 142) to the inspector not later than the time the dividend is paid. Another election may be made within that time limit following a revocation. Where (*c*), (*d*) or (*e*) above applies, the same notice must be used to elect as regards all the dividends concerned, which may be identified by means of a general description. [*ICTA 1988, s 246B; FA 1994, Sch 16 para 1*].

Simon's Direct Tax Service. See **D1.702**.

26.3 **RECEIPT OF FID**

No tax credit entitlement arises under *ICTA 1988, s 231(1)* (see 3.3 ADVANCE CORPORATION TAX) in respect of receipt of a FID. [*ICTA 1988, s 246C; FA 1994, Sch 16 para 1*].

Individuals. Individual recipients are treated as receiving income of the amount of the FID grossed up at the lower rate of income tax for the year of assessment of the payment (currently 20%). Tax at the lower rate is treated as having been paid on that income or (if there are deductions from total income) on so much of it as is part of total income. Liability at the difference between the higher and lower rates of income tax may therefore arise. No repayment may be made of the lower rate tax so treated as paid, and the income is treated as not brought into charge for the purposes of *ICTA 1988, ss 348, 349(1)* (so that it may not be used to cover charges).

ICTA 1988, s 233(1)(1A) (concerning certain persons, other than UK resident companies, who are not entitled to tax credits, see Tolley's Income Tax under Allowances and Tax Rates) do not apply to FIDs where either:

(*a*) the person beneficially entitled to it is an individual; or

(*b*) it is paid to personal representatives; or

(*c*) it is income within *ICTA 1988, s 686* (discretionary trust income) paid to trustees; or

(*d*) (after 25 November 1996) it is paid to trustees of a unit trust scheme within *ICTA 1988, s 469* (unauthorised unit trusts, see 60.2 UNIT AND INVESTMENT TRUSTS).

[*ICTA 1988, s 246D(1)(2)(5); FA 1994, Sch 16 para 1; FA 1996, Sch 27 para 2; FA 1997, s 72*].

There are special provisions relating to FIDs paid to personal representatives and trustees. [*ICTA 1988, s 246D(3)(4); FA 1994, Sch 16 para 1*].

Companies. A FID is not franked investment income. Where a company both pays and receives FIDs in an accounting period, it is liable to pay ACT only on the excess of FIDs paid over those received. An excess in a period of FIDs received over those paid is carried forward and treated for this purpose as FIDs received in the next following accounting period (and so on for subsequent periods), although no such excess is carried forward from an accounting period beginning on or before 5 April 1999 and ending on or after that date. [*ICTA 1988, ss 246C, 246F(1)–(3)(5); FA 1994, Sch 16 para 1; FA 1996, s 122(5); F(No 2)A 1997, Sch 6 para 22(1)*].

Simon's Direct Tax Service. See **D1.707**.

26.4 **PAYMENT OF FID**

Although payment of a FID gives rise to a liability to pay ACT in the normal way, it does not give rise to a franked payment being made by the company for ACT purposes. The normal collection provisions of *ICTA 1988, Sch 13* (see 3.4 ADVANCE CORPORATION TAX) are, however, applied to ACT paid in respect of FIDs (see 26.11 below). See 26.3 above as regards the set-off for this purpose of FIDs paid against FIDs received. There are special provisions in relation to international headquarters companies (see 26.8 below) and certain payments classified as 'manufactured dividends' (see Tolley's Income Tax under Anti-Avoidance). [*ICTA 1988, ss 246E, 246F; FA 1994, Sch 16 para 1; FA 1997, Sch 10 para 10(2); F(No 2)A 1997, Sch 6 para 22(1)*]. See Simon's Direct Tax Service D1.706.

The information to be supplied to the recipient of a FID under *ICTA 1988, s 234A* (see 20.18 DISTRIBUTIONS) has to be in prescribed form and to state that it carries no tax credit. Failure to comply with this requirement prevents the company from electing for matching of the FID with foreign source profits (see 26.5 below), so that no repayment of surplus ACT can be made. [*ICTA 1988, s 246G; FA 1994, Sch 16 para 1*]. No specific form of voucher is specified, but the Revenue Tax Bulletin August 1994 p 142 gives the following guidance.

(*a*) A heading 'Foreign Income Dividend Certificate' should appear at the top of the certificate.

(*b*) The usual 'tax credit' box should be replaced by a box headed 'Income tax treated as paid which is not repayable'.

(*c*) The tax position for the recipient can be given by the following text: 'For income tax purposes the FID is treated as having suffered income tax at the lower rate. Your taxable income is the sum of the dividend and the income tax treated as paid. Lower and basic rate taxpayers will have no more tax to pay. Higher rate taxpayers will have further tax to pay. Where all or part of the FID is taxable at higher rate, relief will be given for the income tax treated as paid on that income. This income tax treated as paid is not repayable.'

Two dividends, of which only one is a FID, may be included on the same voucher, as long as it clearly identifies the two separate elements and makes plain that the tax credit relates only to the ordinary dividend. (Revenue Tax Bulletin June 1995 p 226).

The inspector has powers to require the provision by the company of such information in relation to FIDs as may reasonably be required for the purposes of these provisions. Penalties under *TMA 1970, s 98* (see 49.5 PENALTIES) apply for failure to comply. [*ICTA 1988, s 246H; FA 1994, Sch 16 paras 1, 10*].

26.5 MATCHING OF FID WITH DISTRIBUTABLE FOREIGN PROFITS

A company paying a FID in an accounting period may elect that the FID (or part) be matched with (or with part of) a 'distributable foreign profit' of the company. Different parts of a FID may be matched with different distributable foreign profits (or parts), and different FIDs (or parts) may be matched with different parts of the same foreign distributable profits. A FID (or part) may, however, only be matched with a distributable foreign profit (or part) of equal amount. A distributable foreign profit (or part) may only be matched with a FID (or part) once.

An entry in the company's computation showing the required matching will be accepted as an election. (Revenue Tax Bulletin August 1994 p 142).

Where a company pays a FID in a given accounting period, the FID (or part) may be matched with (or with part of) a distributable foreign profit for that period or the accounting period immediately preceding it (although matching may apply to both those accounting periods without the distributable foreign profits of either having to be exhausted). If there is no unmatched distributable foreign profit for an accounting period or the preceding accounting period, a FID (or part) paid in the period may be matched with (or with part of) a distributable foreign profit for the next accounting period and for subsequent accounting periods not later than the first accounting period beginning after 5 April 1999.

A '*distributable foreign profit*' for an accounting period is so much of the company's 'foreign source profit' for the period as exceeds the 'relevant amount of tax'.

A company's '*foreign source profit*' for an accounting period is so much of its income or gains in respect of which double taxation relief is afforded as forms part of its chargeable profits for the period (i.e. the profits on which corporation tax falls finally to be borne, see *ICTA 1988, s 238(4)*). Any deduction for charges on income, management expenses or other amounts which can be deducted from, set against or treated as reducing profits of more than one description may be allocated for this purpose as the company thinks fit.

The '*relevant amount of tax*' is:

(*a*) where the foreign tax payable in respect of the foreign source profit exceeds the corporation tax payable (before double taxation relief) in respect of that profit, the amount of the foreign tax payable in respect of that profit;

(*b*) where (*a*) does not apply, the corporation tax payable, before double taxation relief, in respect of the foreign source profit (for accounting periods ending before 29 November 1995, an amount equal to the aggregate of the foreign tax payable in respect of the foreign source profit and the amount of corporation tax payable in respect of that profit after double taxation relief).

'Foreign tax' for these purposes refers to tax imposed by the laws of a territory outside the UK for which double taxation relief is afforded (and certain foreign taxes the subject of special reliefs in the foreign territory, see *ICTA 1988, s 788(5)*), and 'double taxation relief' may be under an agreement under *ICTA 1988, s 788* or unilateral relief under *ICTA 1988, s 790(1)* (see 21.3, 21.2 DOUBLE TAX RELIEF).

[*ICTA 1988, ss 246I, 246J; FA 1994, Sch 16 para 1; FA 1996, Sch 27 para 3; F(No 2)A 1997, Sch 6 para 22(2)*].

Subsidiaries. A parent company paying a FID in an accounting period may elect (with the written consent of the subsidiary) that the dividend (or part) be matched with (or with part of) an 'eligible profit' of a '51% subsidiary'. An entry in the company's computation showing the required matching will be accepted as an election, and the written consent of the subsidiary must be signed by the company secretary or an authorised person. (Revenue Tax Bulletin August 1994 p 142). The rules described above as regards partial matching etc. and as regards the period(s) for which a distributable foreign profit may be matched apply equally to the matching of eligible profits. An eligible profit which is the subject of such an election is then treated as a separate distributable foreign profit for the parent company's accounting period and as matched, and the subsidiary's foreign distributable profits are accordingly reduced or extinguished. The underlying foreign source profits are treated as correspondingly divided between parent and subsidiary.

The subsidiary must be a '*51% subsidiary*' (i.e. a company more than 50% of whose ordinary share capital it owns directly or indirectly, but ignoring for this purpose any shares held as trading stock by their direct owner) throughout the '*relevant period*' (i.e. the accounting period in which the FID is paid and any part of the subsidiary's accounting period(s) falling outside that period for which there is a distributable foreign profit which is to be matched with the FID under the election).

A distributable foreign profit of a subsidiary is an '*eligible profit*' for the parent company's accounting period if the subsidiary's accounting period for which it arises coincides with, or with part of, the parent company's accounting period. Where only part of the subsidiary's accounting period so coincides, then a corresponding proportion of the subsidiary's distributable foreign profit for that period is an '*eligible profit*' for the parent company's accounting period.

[*ICTA 1988, ss 246K, 246L, 246M; FA 1994, Sch 16 para 1; F(No 2)A 1997, Sch 6 para 22(2)*].

Simon's Direct Tax Service. See **D1.704, D1.705**.

26.6 **REPAYMENT OR SET-OFF OF ACT**

Where a company (other than an international headquarters company, see 26.8 below) pays a FID in an accounting period (the '*relevant period*'), and it also pays an amount of ACT in respect of qualifying distributions actually made by it in the period (the '*relevant ACT*'), it may make a claim for an amount of that ACT to be repaid or set off, or partly repaid and partly set off, as below. The amount which may be so treated is so much of the relevant ACT as is 'available to be dealt with under this *section*' and as does not exceed the 'notional foreign source ACT' for the relevant period.

The relevant ACT '*available to be dealt with under this section*' is so much as remains after deducting any part of it which has been:

(*a*) repaid;

(*b*) set off against the corporation tax liability for the relevant period (or which would have been so set off but for brought forward, carried back or surrendered ACT);

(*c*) dealt with as surplus ACT under *ICTA 1988, s 239(3)* (see 3.8 ADVANCE CORPORATION TAX);

(*d*) surrendered under *ICTA 1988, s 240* (see 29.8 GROUPS OF COMPANIES); or

(*e*) previously applied under the current provisions.

'*Notional foreign source ACT*' for the relevant period is the amount of ACT which the company would have paid in respect of distributions made by it in the period, and which would not have been set against the company's corporation tax liability for the period, on the following assumptions.

(i) The 'qualifying FIDs' were the only distributions made in the relevant period.

(ii) No distributions were received (or treated under *ICTA 1988, s 246F* (see 26.4 above) as received) in the relevant period.

(iii) No brought forward, carried back or surrendered ACT was treated as having been paid in respect of distributions made in the relevant period.

(iv) No ACT paid in respect of distributions made in the relevant period was surrendered.

(v) The profits of the relevant period on which corporation tax fell finally to be borne (see *ICTA 1988, s 238(4)*) consisted only of the matched foreign source profits (see 26.5 above).

(vi) (For accounting periods ending after 28 November 1995) where any of the 'matched foreign source profits' were arrived at after deducting charges on income etc. (see 26.5 above), the double taxation relief to be taken, in determining the corporation tax finally to be borne, to have been available to have been allowed by reference to the foreign source profits is determined as if no such reduction had been made.

(vii) The amount of corporation tax charged in respect of a 'matched foreign source profit' actually arising in an accounting period other than the relevant period was found by reference to the rate of foreign tax actually chargeable in respect of the profit, and the rate of corporation tax which would have applied had the profit arisen in the relevant period.

A FID is a '*qualifying FID*' if it is a 'matched FID' paid in the relevant period and the paying company so elects. A FID is a '*matched FID*' if, at the time of the claim, the whole of it is matched with the whole or part of a distributable foreign profit, and any part of a FID which is so matched is treated as a separate dividend and accordingly as a '*matched FID*'. The company may, however, elect that matched FIDs paid in the relevant period are qualifying FIDs only if the total amount of FIDs paid in the relevant period (other than FIDs incapable of being matched because of a failure to give proper notice to the recipient, see 26.4 above) exceeds the total amount of FIDs received or treated as received (see 26.3 above) in the period. The election may then only be made as regards matched FIDs up to the amount of that excess.

A '*matched foreign source profit*' is a foreign source profit of which a 'matched foreign distributable profit' forms part, and a '*matched foreign distributable profit*' is a distributable foreign profit the whole or part of which is, at the time of the claim, matched with a qualifying FID or part, or with different qualifying FIDs or parts. There are provisions for dealing with partial matching on a proportional basis.

[*ICTA 1988, ss 246N, 246P; FA 1994, Sch 16 para 1; FA 1996, Sch 27 para 3*].

Repayment or set-off. Surplus ACT to be relieved under these provisions is so far as possible set against any remaining corporation tax liability, any excess being repaid (but not earlier than nine months after the end of the relevant accounting period). Where ACT repaid or set off under *ICTA 1988, s 246N* (above) has already been carried forward and set off in a later accounting period (and the relief for that period could not be attributed to any other source of ACT), the set off for that later period is treated under *ICTA 1988, s 252* (see 3.6 ADVANCE CORPORATION TAX) as if it ought not to have been made. [*ICTA 1988, s 246Q(1)–(5)(8)–(10); FA 1994, Sch 16 para 1*].

Claims. The company tax return or amended return (see 54.2 RETURNS) for the relevant accounting period is treated as a claim for relief under these provisions if it contains such particulars as the inspector may require. Otherwise, a separate claim must be made supported by such particulars. There are provisions for supplementary claims where, after a claim for relief for an accounting period has been made, an election is made matching FID(s) paid in the period with distributable foreign profits of later periods. [*ICTA 1988, ss 246Q(6)(7), 246R; FA 1994, Sch 16 para 1; FA 1998, Sch 19 para 44*].

A **provisional repayment** may be made (but not before nine months has elapsed from the end of the accounting period) if the inspector is satisfied on the basis of provisional corporation tax computations that an amount will ultimately be repayable under the FID provisions (and the submission of such provisional computations in support of the repayment claim will be treated as an election for the appropriate matching). (Revenue Tax Bulletin August 1994 p 143).

Simon's Direct Tax Service. See **D1.711** *et seq.*.

26.7 *Example*

Q Ltd is a UK-resident company with an interest in LH Co, a company resident in Shangri-La. Q Ltd prepares accounts to 31 March, and the following details are relevant for the year to 31 March 1999 (all figures in this example are in thousands of pounds).

26.7 Foreign Income Dividends

Trading profits		2,000
Dividends from LH Co (net)		375
Foreign tax suffered thereon		125
Charges paid (gross)		200
Dividends paid (net):		
1.6.98	1,000	
1.12.98	400	
15.1.99	300	
		1,700
ACT paid		425

There was surplus ACT of 200 brought forward at 1 April 1998. Q Ltd has no capacity for recovering surplus ACT by carrying it back to previous years.

Q Ltd is *not* an international headquarters company.

Without any elections to treat dividends paid as foreign income dividends, Q Ltd's tax position is as follows.

	UK income	Overseas income	Total
Income	2,000	500	2,500
Deduct Charges	200	—	200
Profits chargeable to CT	1,800	500	2,300
CT @ 31%	558	155	713
Deduct Double tax relief	—	125	125
	558	30	588
Deduct ACT*	360	30	390
'Mainstream' liability	198	—	198

* ACT set-off is the lower of 20% of profit and the amount of UK corporation tax otherwise payable.

Surplus ACT	
B/f at 1.4.98	200
ACT paid — y/e 31.3.99	425
	625
ACT set-off — y/e 31.3.99	390
C/f at 31.3.99	235

If Q Ltd wishes to elect under *section 246A* for the 15.1.99 dividend of 300 to be treated as a foreign income dividend (FID), and thus obtain further set-off or repayment of ACT, the necessary steps are as follows.

(1) Elect not later than the time the dividend is paid for it to be treated as a FID.

(2) Elect (see 26.5 above) to match the FID of 300 with part of distributable foreign profit of 345 (500 – 125 – 30), and for the matched FID of 300 to be a qualifying FID (see 26.6 above).

(3) Identify available surplus ACT (see 26.6 above):

ACT paid — y/e 31.3.99	425
Deduct Set-off against CT	390*
Available surplus ACT	35

* For this purpose, current year ACT is deemed to have been set off in priority to surplus ACT brought forward.

(4) Identify notional foreign source ACT (see 26.6 above):

Matched foreign source profit	500
Notional CT @ 31%	155
Deduct Double taxation relief	125
	30
Deduct ACT on FID (75 maximum)	30
Notional foreign source ACT (75 – 30)	45

(5) Claim repayment or further set-off of the lower of the amounts identified at (3) and (4) above (i.e. 35).

Q Ltd's tax position is then as follows.

	UK income	Overseas income	Total
Income	2,000	500	2,500
Deduct Charges	200	—	200
Profits chargeable to CT	1,800	500	2,300
CT @ 31%	558	155	713
Deduct Double tax relief	—	125	125
	558	30	588
Deduct ACT on non-FIDs	350	—	350
	208	30	238
Deduct ACT on FIDs	10	30	40
'Mainstream' liability	198	—	198
ACT repayable		35	
Net CT liability		163	

Surplus ACT	
B/f at 1.4.98	200
ACT paid on non-FIDs	350
ACT paid on FIDs	75
	625
ACT set-off — y/e 31.3.99	390
	235
ACT repayable	35
C/f at 31.3.99	200

26.8 INTERNATIONAL HEADQUARTERS COMPANIES

A company is an '*international headquarters company*' ('IHC') in an accounting period if either of the following conditions (*a*) or (*b*) is fulfilled.

(*a*) At each given time in the accounting period, not more than 20% of the company's ordinary share capital is ultimately beneficially owned by persons who are not companies and who are UK-resident (tracing ownership of shares not directly owned by a person who is not a company through any corporate holders to persons who are not companies on such basis as is reasonable); and either

(i) the company is wholly owned throughout the accounting period by a company which is a 'foreign held company' in the accounting period, or

(ii) at each given time in the accounting period, each shareholder owns at least 5% of the company's share capital, and at least 80% is owned either by persons who are not companies and who are not UK-resident at any time in the accounting period, or by companies which are 'foreign held companies' in the accounting period.

A company is a '*foreign held company*' in an accounting period if either

(A) at each given time in the period at least 80% of its share capital is owned by persons not UK-resident at any time in the period, or

(B) throughout the accounting period the company is wholly owned by another company within (A).

(*b*) (i) The company is a '100% subsidiary' throughout the accounting period of a company which is not UK-resident at any time in the accounting period; and

(ii) shares in the parent company are listed on a non-UK stock exchange (and have *not* been listed on a UK stock exchange or, if so listed, the issuer is not subject in relation to the shares to the full requirements applicable by virtue of 'listing rules' (see *Financial Services Act 1986, s 142(6)*) to the listing of shares on that exchange) throughout the accounting period and the preceding twelve months, and have been the subject of dealings on such an exchange during that period.

A company is a '*100% subsidiary*' of another if all of its share capital is directly or indirectly owned by the other (as for the purposes of *ICTA 1988, s 838*, but based on voting rights in general meeting by virtue of beneficial ownership).

For accounting periods ending before 29 November 1995, the reference in (*b*)(i) above to a '100% subsidiary' was instead to a 'wholly-owned subsidiary', and an alternative condition ((*c*) below) applied by virtue of which a company could be an IHC.

(*c*) Either:

(i) the company is throughout the accounting period wholly owned by another company which is itself throughout that accounting period wholly owned by a company which is not UK resident at any time in that accounting period and which satisfies the conditions at (*b*)(ii) above; or

(ii) all the company's share capital is throughout the accounting period beneficially owned between them by two or more intermediary companies all of which are wholly owned by a company which is not UK resident at any time in that accounting period and which satisfies the conditions at (*b*)(ii) above; or

(iii) all the company's share capital is throughout the accounting period beneficially owned between them by two or more companies (the 'relevant companies'), and one of the relevant companies is a company which is not UK resident at any time in that accounting period, which throughout that period wholly owns all the other relevant companies, and which satisfies the conditions at (*b*)(ii) above.

A company for these purposes wholly owns another if it is the beneficial owner of all its share capital. Percentage ownership of a company's share capital (other than in the case of the 20% ownership referred to in (*a*) above) is based on voting rights by virtue of beneficial ownership in general meeting.

A company paying a FID in an accounting period may treat itself as an IHC if it considers at the time of the payment that it is likely to be an IHC in that period, provided that if the accounting period is the company's second or a subsequent accounting period, it was an IHC for the preceding accounting period. Where the FID was paid in the first accounting period ending after 28 November 1995, the question of whether the company was an IHC for the immediately preceding accounting period is determined by reference to the rules applicable to the later accounting period.

[*ICTA 1988, s 246S; FA 1994, Sch 16 para 1; FA 1996, Sch 27 para 4, Sch 38 para 6*].

Simon's Direct Tax Service. See **D1.721** *et seq.*.

26.9 **Payment of a FID by an IHC.** Where, during an accounting period, a company treats itself (see 26.8 above) as an IHC at the time it pays a FID, it is not liable to pay ACT in respect of the FID. If, however, it is not an IHC in that accounting period, it is treated as always having been liable to pay ACT on the FID, and the normal relief provisions described at 26.6 above apply. [*ICTA 1988, ss 246T, 246V; FA 1994, Sch 16 para 1*].

Where, having treated itself as an IHC in relation to payment of a FID in an accounting period, the company is an IHC for the period, then if the ACT it has thereby been relieved from liability to pay (and has not paid) exceeds the ACT which would have been repaid or set off if it had not been an IHC and had made the appropriate claim (see 26.6 above), it is required to account for an amount equal to the excess as if it were ACT payable in respect of a distribution in the last ACT return period in the accounting period. If the ACT which would have been repaid etc. exceeds that for which liability to pay was relieved, the excess is repaid on a claim by the company as if it were a repayment of ACT paid in respect of distributions made in the accounting period and falling to be repaid as under 26.6 above. [*ICTA 1988, s 246U; FA 1994, Sch 16 para 1; FA 1998, Sch 19 para 45*]. There are provisions for payments and repayments where a FID is subsequently matched with a distributable foreign profit of a subsequent accounting period. [*ICTA 1988, s 246W; FA 1994, Sch 16 para 1*].

26.10 ADJUSTMENTS WHERE PROFITS OR FOREIGN TAX ALTERED

Where any amount is paid or repaid or set off under the above provisions, and there is an alteration to the profits of a company or of an amount of foreign tax payable which renders such payment or repayment or the amount set off excessive or insufficient, then the relevant elections and computations may be revised on a just and reasonable basis. [*ICTA 1988, s 246X; FA 1994, Sch 16 para 1*].

26.11 RETURNS AND COLLECTION

The provisions of *ICTA 1988, Sch 13* (see 3.4 ADVANCE CORPORATION TAX) are amended to require the inclusion in the normal return (form CT61(Z)) of details of FIDs paid and received, and the payment of the appropriate amount of ACT in respect of FIDs, and dealing with the receipt of FIDs after payment of ACT. Special arrangements apply as regards IHCs (see *ICTA 1988, Sch 13 paras 3A, 3B* inserted by *FA 1994, Sch 16 para 3(7)*), in particular dealing with assessments where an officer of the Board considers that there was not a reasonable basis for a company treating itself as an IHC. Special returns are required of certain manufactured dividends which, being representative of FIDs, are treated as FIDs (see Tolley's Income Tax under Anti-Avoidance). [*ICTA 1988, Sch 13; FA 1994, Sch 16 para 3; FA 1996, Sch 23 Pt I*].

27 Franked Investment Income

27.1 DEFINITION OF FRANKED INVESTMENT INCOME

Franked investment income ('FII') is the sum of the amount or value of dividends and other qualifying DISTRIBUTIONS (20) received by a UK resident company from another UK resident company and such proportion of each distribution as corresponds to:

(*a*) before 6 April 1999, the rate of ADVANCE CORPORATION TAX (3) ('ACT') in force when the distribution is made; or

(*b*) after 5 April 1999, the 'tax credit fraction' in force when the distribution is made.

[*ICTA 1988, ss 231(1), 238(1), 832(1); F(No 2)A 1997, s 30(2); FA 1998, Sch 3 paras 11, 39*].

The tax credit fraction is initially set at one-ninth from 6 April 1999. [*F(No 2)A 1997, s 30(3)*]. The rate of ACT from 6 April 1994 to 5 April 1999 is one-quarter (and see 1.3(*d*) INTRODUCTION AND RATES OF TAX for earlier rates). Thus a dividend of £360 amounts to FII in the hands of a UK recipient company of £450 for distributions before 6 April 1999, or of £400 for distributions thereafter.

Exceptions. The following are **not** FII.

(i) (Before 6 April 1999) group income, being dividends within certain groups of companies and consortia which, under an election, are paid without paying ACT. See 29.2 GROUPS OF COMPANIES.

(ii) Dividends or interest received from BUILDING SOCIETIES (7). [*ICTA 1988, s 476(3)(c), s 477A(3)(b); FA 1990, Sch 5 para 4*].

(iii) (Before 6 April 1999) FOREIGN INCOME DIVIDENDS (26) [*ICTA 1988, s 246C*] and certain other distributions treated in the same way as foreign income dividends (see 4.7 ANTI-AVOIDANCE).

Simon's Direct Tax Service. See D1.301.

27.2 EFFECT WHEN A COMPANY RECEIVES FII

The recipient UK company can (subject to below) claim to have the tax credit paid to it only if it is wholly exempt from corporation tax (or exempt on all but trading income), or the distribution is expressly exempt under any provision of the *Tax Acts* (other than the general provision exempting distributions from corporation tax in *ICTA 1988, s 208*). [*ICTA 1988, s 231(2)*]. For distributions made after 1 July 1997, tax credit repayments may not be made, *inter alia*, to pension funds (as widely defined) or to insurance companies in respect of pension business income (see 41 LIFE INSURANCE COMPANIES), although this does not apply to FRIENDLY SOCIETIES (28). From 6 April 1999, entitlement to tax credit repayments is generally abolished, except in relation to certain double taxation arrangements (see 21.3 DOUBLE TAX RELIEF). [*F(No 2)A 1997, ss 19, 23, 30, Sch 3, Sch 8 Pt II(9)*].

Otherwise, before 6 April 1999, the company is given relief by setting off the FII received against 'franked payments' made by it, so that ACT is payable by reference to the balance only. See 3.3 ADVANCE CORPORATION TAX. This relief is normally temporary in that less ACT paid means less ACT credit available against the mainstream corporation tax liability.

'*Franked payments*' are the sum of the amount or value of dividends or other qualifying distributions (see 20.18 DISTRIBUTIONS) made by the company and such proportion of each such distribution as corresponds to the rate of ACT in force when the distribution is made.

[*ICTA 1988, s 238(1); F(No 2)A 1997, Sch 4 para 8; FA 1998, Sch 3 para 11*].

27.3 **SURPLUS FII**

If, during an accounting period of a company beginning **before 6 April 1999**, its FII exceeds its franked payments, the excess, except insofar as it cannot be used to frank distributions, is described as a 'surplus of franked investment income' and is carried forward into, and treated as, FII of the next accounting period. [*ICTA 1988, s 238(1)(1A), s 241(3); FA 1995, Sch 8 para 18; FA 1998, Sch 3 paras 11, 14*].

Relief for trading losses etc.: general provisions. For accounting periods beginning **before 2 July 1997,** a company may claim that any surplus of FII (as above) for an accounting period be treated as profits chargeable to corporation tax for the purpose of obtaining relief against total profits for

(*a*) trading losses under *ICTA 1988, s 393(2)* or *s 393A(1)* (see 44.2 and 44.6 LOSSES),

(*b*) charges paid under *ICTA 1988, s 338,*

(*c*) management expenses under *ICTA 1988, ss 75, 76,*

(*d*) capital allowances (to be given by discharge or repayment and available primarily against income of a specified class, see 8.2 CAPITAL ALLOWANCES) under *CAA 1990, s 145(3),*

(*e*) losses of investment companies, on disposal of unlisted shares subscribed for in certain trading companies, under *ICTA 1988, s 573* (see 44.19 LOSSES),

(*f*) non-trading deficits on loan relationships (see 43.3 LOAN RELATIONSHIPS).

The amount of surplus FII which may be so treated is restricted, for accounting periods which straddle 1 July 1997, to the surplus FII the company would have had for the accounting period had it ended on 1 July 1997.

For accounting periods ending before 1 April 1996, (*f*) above referred to certain 'relievable amounts' in respect of exchange losses under *FA 1993, s 131(4)* (see 23.31 EXCHANGE GAINS AND LOSSES).

Effect is given to the claim by the Revenue paying to the company the amount of the tax credit relating to the surplus FII so set off, which is then not available to frank subsequent distributions. [*ICTA 1988, s 242(1)(2); FA 1993, Sch 18 para 3; FA 1996, Sch 14 para 12(1); F(No 2)A 1997, s 20*].

Relief must be given against profits chargeable to corporation tax before being given against FII under these provisions, and the surplus of FII must be calculated without reference to any amount brought forward from the preceding accounting period. [*ICTA 1988, s 242(3)(9)*].

Where relief is claimed for trading losses, capital allowances or losses on unquoted shares in trading companies against surplus FII of an earlier accounting period, relief is restricted to that proportion of the surplus FII corresponding to the part of that earlier accounting period whose profits may be relieved under the appropriate carry-back provision. [*ICTA 1988, s 242(4)*].

Time limit. Claims must be made:

(i) in the case of claims within (*a*), (*d*) or (*e*) above, within two years of the end of the period in which the loss was incurred or for which the capital allowances are due (or, as regards (*a*), such longer period as the Board may allow);

(ii) in the case of claims within (*b*) or (*c*) above, within six years of the end of the period in which the charges were paid or the management expenses incurred (or treated as incurred under *ICTA 1988, s 75(3)*);

(iii) in the case of claims within (*f*) above, within two years of the end of the period to which the amount for which relief is to be obtained relates (or such longer period as the Board may allow).

[*ICTA 1988, s 242(8); FA 1991, Sch 15 para 5; FA 1993, Sch 18 para 3; FA 1996, Sch 14 para 12(2)*].

Non-resident companies. The Revenue consider that a non-UK resident company cannot claim repayment of tax credits under *section 242*, notwithstanding the existence of a non-discrimination clause in a double taxation convention between the UK and the country in which the company is resident. (Revenue Pamphlet IR 131, SP 2/95, 7 February 1995).

Relief for trading losses: special provisions for financial concerns. For accounting periods beginning **before 2 July 1997**, banks, share dealing companies and other companies for which FII would fall to be included in trading income but for the fact that it is taxed under other provisions, may claim that a surplus of FII (calculated as for the general provisions described above, including the restriction on the amount available for accounting periods straddling 1 July 1997) be treated as trading income for the purpose of obtaining relief for trading losses by carry-forward or under the terminal loss provisions (see 44.4 and 44.8 LOSSES). Such a claim may be made instead of, or in addition to, a claim under *section 242*. [*ICTA 1988, s 243(1)(2)(7); FA 1991, Sch 15 para 6(1); F(No 2)A 1997, s 20*].

Relief is given against trading income chargeable to corporation tax before being given against FII under these provisions. [*ICTA 1988, s 243(3)*].

Time limit. Claims must be made within six years after the end of the accounting period to which they relate. [*ICTA 1988, s 243(6); FA 1991, Sch 15 para 6(3)*].

Later year's adjustment. Where relief has been given under *section 242* for a trading loss, or for a charge on income paid wholly and exclusively for the purposes of the trade, or where relief has been given under *section 243* for a loss brought forward, and in a later accounting period beginning **before 2 July 1997** the franked payments made by the company exceed its FII, the company is treated as having, in the immediately preceding accounting period, incurred a trading loss equal to the smallest of

(i) the excess,

(ii) the amount on which relief as above was given, and

(iii) the balance of any amount under (ii) remaining after previous applications of this provision,

which loss is accordingly brought forward to the later accounting period.

The provision does not apply if the company has ceased to carry on the trade, or to be within the charge to corporation tax in respect of it. It does, however, apply (with necessary adaptations) when relief under *section 242* has been given under any of (*c*)–(*f*) above (including relievable amounts for accounting periods ending before 1 April 1996), and where so extended it applies as long as the company remains within the charge to corporation tax at all. Capital allowances of a trading company are, however, treated as trading losses for this purpose unless the company otherwise elects. In the case of losses on unquoted shares in trading companies, the loss treated as brought forward from the preceding accounting period is a loss for the purposes of corporation tax on chargeable gains, and is not available against income. [*ICTA 1988, s 242(5)–(7)(9), s 243(4); FA 1997, s 71; F(No 2)A 1997, s 20(2)*].

Regardless of whether a loss is restored as above, any ACT paid in respect of the excess of franked payments over FII in a later accounting period beginning **before 2 July 1997** is reduced by the amount of the tax credit previously repaid, and only the reduced amount (if any) may be set against the company's corporation tax liabilities. This restriction continues to apply for such accounting periods until the tax credit has been exhausted. [*ICTA 1988, s 244(2); F(No 2)A 1997, s 20(3)*].

Simon's Direct Tax Service. See **D2.413, D2.414.**

27.4 *Examples*

(A) *Relief*

The following information is relevant to B Ltd, a company with two associated companies.

	12 months ended 31.3.94	12 months ended 31.3.95	6 months ended 30.9.95	12 months ended 30.9.96	12 months ended 30.9.97
	£	£	£	£	£
Trading profit/ (loss)	200,000	400,000	160,000	200,000	(1,200,000)
Chargeable gains	—	40,000	—	—	100,000
Franked investment income	70,000	40,000	30,000	36,000	80,000
Franked payments	30,000	—	20,000	20,000	—

There was no surplus FII carried forward at 1.4.93. The surplus FII at 30.9.97 did not exceed that which the company would have had at 1.7.97 had an accounting period ended on that date.

The company claims relief under *section 393A(1)(a)(b)* for its loss for the year ended 30.9.97, and also makes claims under *section 242* for all the above accounting periods.

The loss is relieved as follows.

		£
Loss incurred		1,200,000
Set-off against profits	— y/e 30.9.97	(100,000)
Set-off against surplus FII	— y/e 30.9.97	(80,000)
		1,020,000
Set-off against profits	— y/e 30.9.96	(200,000)
Set-off against surplus FII	— y/e 30.9.96	(16,000)
		804,000
Set-off against profits	— p/e 30.9.95	(160,000)
Set-off against surplus FII	— p/e 30.9.95	(10,000)
		634,000
Set-off against profits	— y/e 31.3.95	(440,000)
Set-off against surplus FII	— y/e 31.3.95	(40,000)
		c/f 154,000

		£
		b/f 154,000
Set-off against profits	— y/e 31.3.94	(100,000)
Set-off against surplus FII	— y/e 31.3.94 (note (*b*))	(19,375)
Loss unrelieved		£34,625

B Ltd's only remaining corporation tax liability for the five accounting periods under review is for the year ended 31.3.94, on profits of £100,000.

Following the above claims, franked receipts and payments can be summarised as follows.

	Y/e 31.3.94	Y/e 31.3.95	P/e 30.9.95	Y/e 30.9.96	Y/e 30.9.97
	£	£	£	£	£
Surplus FII b/f	—	20,000	20,000	20,000	20,000
FII	70,000	40,000	30,000	36,000	80,000
Franked payments	(30,000)	—	(20,000)	(20,000)	—
Section 242 reduction	(20,000)	(40,000)	(10,000)	(16,000)	(80,000)
Surplus FII c/f	£20,000	£20,000	£20,000	£20,000	£20,000
Tax credit repayable	£3,875	£8,000	£2,000	£3,200	£16,000

The total tax credit repayable is £33,075. See note (*b*) as regards the *section 242* reduction for y/e 31.3.94.

Notes

(*a*) There is no obligation to make a *section 242* claim for *each* accounting period to which the loss may be carried back. It could be made for only one or for some of those periods.

(*b*) The FII for the year ended 31 March 1994 (£70,000) will have been calculated by reference to an ACT rate of 22.5%. For the purposes of the *section 242* claim, however, the FII comprised in the surplus FII for that year (£40,000) is recalculated by reference to a notional 20% ACT rate. £40,000 – (£40,000 @ 22.5%) = £31,000. £31,000 × $\frac{100}{80}$ = £38,750, of which one-half may be the subject of a *section 242* claim. The tax credit repayable is £3,875 (£19,375 @ 20%). However, in computing the surplus FII available for carry-forward after the *section 242* claim, the full £20,000 is regarded as having been relieved.

(*c*) Of the £1,200,000 loss of the year ended 30 September 1997, the time-apportioned part arising before 2 July 1997 (i.e. $\frac{274}{365}$ths, or £900,822) is available to be carried back up to three years. [*ICTA 1988, s 393A(2)–(2B); F(No 2)A 1997, s 39*]. As £396,000 is relieved against current and preceding year profits, no restriction arises in this respect.

(B) *Later year adjustments*

In the example at (A) above, because the loss for which relief was obtained arose in the accounting period straddling 1 July 1997, no adjustments may be made in later periods where franked payments exceed franked investment income. Had the events described in (A) all occurred two years earlier (disregarding, for simplicity, any difference this would have made to the amount of surplus FII set off or tax credit payable), and the following further information been applicable to the two succeeding years, the position would have been as detailed below.

27.4 Franked Investment Income

	Y/e 30.9.96	Y/e 30.9.97
	£	£
Trading profit	500,000	806,000
Chargeable gains	194,000	—
Franked investment income	10,000	10,000
Franked payments	90,000	210,000

Franked receipts and payments can be summarised as follows.

	Y/e 30.9.96	Y/e 30.9.97
	£	£
Surplus FII b/f	20,000	—
FII	10,000	10,000
	30,000	10,000
Franked payments	(90,000)	(210,000)
Excess franked payments	£(60,000)	£(200,000)

For each of the above periods, the loss for the year to 30.9.95 previously relieved under *section 242* is reinstated (and becomes available under *section 393(1)*) to the extent of the lower of excess franked payments and loss relief previously given under *section 242* and not previously reinstated.

For the year to 30.9.96

Section 242 relief previously given	£165,375
Excess franked payments	£60,000
Loss reinstated	£60,000

For the year to 30.9.97

Section 242 relief previously given	£165,375
Deduct loss previously reinstated	60,000
	£105,375
Excess franked payments	£200,000
Loss reinstated	£105,375

The company's corporation tax position for the two above accounting periods is as follows.

		Y/e 30.9.96		Y/e 30.9.97
		£		£
Schedule D, Case I		500,000		806,000
Section 393(1) relief:				
Actual (see *Example* (A) above)		(34,625)		—
Loss reinstated		(60,000)		(105,375)
		405,375		700,625
Chargeable gains		194,000		—
		£599,375		£700,625
	£		£	
Corporation tax @ 33%/31%		197,793		224,200
ACT paid: £60,000 @ 20%	12,000			
£200,000 @ 20%			40,000	
Less amount not available for set-off (i.e. amount of tax credit previously repaid, see (A) above)	12,000	—	21,075	18,925
Mainstream liability		£197,793		£205,275

28 Friendly Societies

[*ICTA 1988, ss 459–466*]

Simon's Direct Tax Service D4.601 *et seq.*.

28.1 **UNREGISTERED SOCIETIES**

On making a claim, those with incomes not exceeding £160 p.a. are wholly exempt from income tax and corporation tax (on both income and chargeable gains). [*ICTA 1988, s 459; F(No 2)A 1992, Sch 9 para 4*].

28.2 **REGISTERED AND INCORPORATED SOCIETIES**

On making a claim, these are exempt from income and corporation tax (on both income and chargeable gains) on profits from 'life or endowment business' (see 28.4 below), subject to exceptions and conditions as below. [*ICTA 1988, ss 460(1), 461(1), 461B(1); F(No 2)A 1992, Sch 9 paras 5, 7*]. These exceptions and conditions do not, however, affect exemptions for profits arising under contracts made before 4 May 1966. [*ICTA 1988, s 462(2)*]. In relation to accounting periods beginning after 31 December 1993, Treasury regulations (see *SI 1999 No 622*, which, for accounting periods ending on or after 1 July 1999, replaces *SI 1993 No 3112* as amended) apply *ICTA 1988, Sch 19AB* (pension business — payments on account of tax credits and deducted tax, see 41.6 LIFE INSURANCE COMPANIES) *mutatis mutandis* to tax exempt business of friendly societies, provided that not all the business of the society is tax-exempt. This is without prejudice to *ICTA 1988, s 463(1)*, see 28.7 below. [*FA 1993, s 121*]. However, the amendments to *Schedule 19AB* which prohibit the payment of tax credits to insurance companies in respect of pension business income do not apply to friendly societies until 6 April 1999. [*F(No 2)A 1997, Sch 3 para 12*]. Also, although tax credit payments are generally abolished from that date, they are temporarily reinstated in relation to distributions to friendly societies in respect of tax exempt business until 5 April 2004 [*FA 1998, s 90*], and this applies similarly to non-exempt individual savings account business (see 28.7 below and 41.1 LIFE INSURANCE COMPANIES).

See 28.7 below for amendments to certain corporation tax provisions in their application to friendly societies' life and endowment business. In particular, relief for expenses attributable to exempt business against profits and gains from non-exempt business is prohibited, overturning the decision in *Homeowners Friendly Society Ltd v Barrett (Sp C 31), [1995] SSCD 90* with retrospective effect (except in certain cases where appeals were in progress at 21 April 1995).

Incorporated societies. The *Friendly Societies Act 1992* enables friendly societies to incorporate and take on new powers, and to provide a wider range of financial services through subsidiaries. *F(No 2)A 1992, s 56, Sch 9* introduced a large number of amendments and additional provisions to ensure that registered societies which incorporate, and societies newly established as incorporated societies, receive the same treatment as regards tax exemption as existing registered societies [*F(No 2)A 1992, Sch 9 paras 1–19*], and that the incorporation of a registered society neither affects those exemptions nor results in any tax charges as a result of the incorporation, either on the society or on its members. [*F(No 2)A 1992, Sch 9 paras 20, 21*].

28.3 **Policy limits.** The exemption in 28.2 above does not apply to profits from pension or individual savings account business, or from other life or endowment business consisting of the granting of annuities exceeding £156 p.a., or of the assurance of gross sums under contracts under which the total premiums payable in any twelve-month period exceed a maximum figure as follows:

for contracts made after 30 April 1995	£270
for contracts made after 24 July 1991 and before 1 May 1995	£200
for contracts made after 31 August 1990 and before 25 July 1991	£150
for contracts made after 31 August 1987 and before 1 September 1990	£100

Where the premium under a contract made after 31 August 1987 and before 1 May 1995 is increased by a variation after 24 July 1991 and before 1 August 1992, or after 30 April 1995 and before 1 April 1996, the contract is treated for these purposes as having been made at the time of the variation. In determining these limits, no account is taken of any bonus or addition declared upon an assurance or accruing thereon by reference to an increase in the value of any investments, and, in relation to premium limits, so much of any premium as relates to exceptional risk of death is disregarded, as is 10% of premiums payable more frequently than annually. [*ICTA 1988, s 460(2)–(12); FA 1990, s 49(1)(2); FA 1991, Sch 9 para 1; F(No 2)A 1992, Sch 9 para 5; FA 1995, Sch 10 para 1*].

28.4 **Policy conditions.** The exemption in 28.2 above of a society's 'life or endowment business' only applies to so much of that business as is attributable to policies which are 'qualifying policies', or which would be 'qualifying policies' but for members' holdings of policies with other societies causing them to exceed the limits on the contracts an individual may hold. [*ICTA 1988, s 462(1)*]. The following conditions must be satisfied in respect of all policies issued by a society under contracts made after 3 May 1966.

(*a*) The interval (the 'term' of the policy) between the making of the insurance (or, if the term started within the previous three months, the commencement of the term) and payment of the sum assured (or of the first instalment of the annuity) is at least ten years, with a saving for sums payable on the death or retirement due to ill health of the life insured or the person liable to pay the premiums. This requirement is reduced to five years from the beginning of the term if the payment is made to an infant and the premium payable in any year does not exceed £13, or if the payment is one of a series payable at intervals of five years or more, each of which (other than the final payment) does not exceed four-fifths of the premiums paid since the preceding payment.

(*b*) The premiums are of equal or rateable amounts, payable at intervals not exceeding one year over the whole term of the policy (or, in the case of certain premium increases under variations made after 30 April 1995 and before 1 April 1996 (see 28.3 above), over the remainder of the policy). For this purpose, the term of the policy excludes any period after the life insured or person liable to pay the premiums attains a specified age, provided that at least ten years of the term has then elapsed. A policy providing for commutation of future premiums after the expiration of ten years or of half the term (whichever occurs earlier), or when the person liable to pay the premiums becomes non-resident, is nevertheless deemed to satisfy these conditions. Premiums may also be paid by surrendering a sum which has become payable on the maturity of any other policy issued by the same society (or by a predecessor of it), in the course of its tax-exempt 'life or endowment business', to the person liable to pay the premiums or to his parent, and they may be waived by reason of disability.

(*c*) (Before 1 May 1995), the surrender value of the policy for the first ten years, or three-quarters of the term, whichever is the shorter, must not exceed the premiums paid or, if greater, the value (if any) prescribed by *Industrial Assurance Act 1923, s 24* or *Industrial Assurance and Friendly Societies Act 1929, s 3*.

[*ICTA 1988, Sch 15 para 3(2)–(4); F(No 2)A 1992, Sch 9 para 19; FA 1995, Sch 10 paras 3, 4*].

The exemption in 28.2 above does not in any event apply in relation to profits attributable to contracts expressed at the outset not to be made in the course of tax-exempt 'life or endowment business', and either

(i) made on or after 20 March 1991 for the assurance of gross sums, or

(ii) made before that date, where the society so elects.

An election under (ii) above has effect for accounting periods ending after 24 July 1991, and had to be made before 1 August 1992.

A society could also elect for the exemption not to apply to profits attributable to contracts where, at the outset of the contract, it is assumed by the society not to be made in the course of tax-exempt life or endowment business (without being expressed either to be or not to be so), and the policy issued in pursuance of it is in the required form of a 'qualifying policy'. Such an election has effect for accounting periods ending after 24 July 1991. It had to be made before 1 August 1992, and the inspector (or the Commissioners on appeal) had to be satisfied that it was possible to identify all the contracts to which it relates. [*ICTA 1988, s 460(2)(ca), s 462A; FA 1991, Sch 9 para 2*].

A friendly society includes all its branches. A society formed on the amalgamation of others is treated as being different from those others. However, if each of those others was within the exemption, and at least one was not a 'new society', the society resulting from the amalgamation is treated as having been registered before 4 May 1966. [*ICTA 1988, s 466*].

'*Life or endowment business*' means any business within *Friendly Societies Act 1992, Sch 2 Head A, Classes I–IV*; any pension business; and the issue of, or undertaking of liability under, policies of insurance on human life and the granting of annuities on human life ('life assurance business'), but excluding sickness benefit policies unless at least 60% of the premiums is attributable to the sickness provision and the policy also assures a gross sum, independent of sickness, on which no bonus or addition may be declared. Also excluded is the granting of annuities bought with the proceeds of maturity or surrender of any other policy issued by the same society in the course of its tax exempt life or endowment business. With effect from 1 September 1996, business within *Friendly Societies Act, Sch 2 Head A, Class IV* is included only if also within *Class I, II* or *III*, and the restriction on sickness benefit policies ceases to apply. [*ICTA 1988, s 466(1)(2); F(No 2)A 1992, Sch 9 para 14; FA 1996, s 171(1)*].

A policy issued by a friendly society is a '*qualifying policy*' only if it meets the conditions at (*a*), (*b*) and (*c*) above, and if in addition the minimum sum assured is at least 75% of the total premiums payable and (in relation to contracts with a 'new society' made before 25 July 1991) it is with a member over the age of 18 years. [*ICTA 1988, Sch 15 para 3(1); FA 1991, Sch 9 para 4; F(No 2)A 1992, Sch 9 para 19*]. A health insurance policy ceases to be a qualifying policy if the rights conferred by it are surrendered in whole or part. For the detailed application of the 75% test, see *ICTA 1988, Sch 15 para 3(5)–(11), para 4*. In the case of a society which is not a 'new society', a policy can be a qualifying policy even if it was made with a person under 18 years of age or the rights have been wholly or partly surrendered. Where a society which is not a 'new society' begins carrying on tax exempt life or endowment business, or carrying on such business on an enlarged scale or of a new character, the Board may direct that it be treated, in respect of new business, as if it were a 'new society'. [*ICTA 1988, s 465; F(No 2)A 1992, Sch 9 para 12*].

Policy includes an instrument evidencing a contract to pay an annuity on human life. [*ICTA 1988, s 466(2)*].

A '*new society*' is a society registered after 3 May 1966, or one registered in the previous three months which did not carry on any life or endowment business during that period, or an incorporated society, provided that it was not, before incorporation, excluded from being a new society. [*ICTA 1988, s 466(2); F(No 2)A 1992, Sch 9 para 14(5)*].

Before 19 March 1985, broadly similar conditions applied, except for the requirement that policies be 'qualifying policies' (which was not necessary as all friendly society policies were qualifying policies) and absence of provision for a waiver of the requirement as to regular rateable premiums in cases of disability.

There are transitional provisions under which profits arising from certain policies issued in respect of insurances made after 31 May 1984 and before 19 March 1985, which either do not meet the 75% test under *ICTA 1988, Sch 15 para 3(5)–(11)* (see above) or fail to satisfy the conditions in *para 3(2)* (see above), are excluded from the exemption. The conditions in *section 460(1)* (see above) do not apply in respect of such policies. [*ICTA 1988, s 462(1)*].

Simon's Direct Tax Service. See **D4.604**.

28.5 **Conditions imposed on society's business.** Profits arising from 'life or endowment business' (see 28.4 above) are not within the exemption if the society was registered after 31 December 1957 and issued a single premium policy during the three months to 3 May 1966, or is an incorporated successor to such a society. [*ICTA 1988, s 460(2)(a)(aa); F(No 2)A 1992, Sch 9 para 5(3)*].

For such business carried on before 1 June 1984, the exemption also did not apply if the society was one which was registered after 3 February 1966, did not carry on life or endowment business before 3 May 1966, and by its rules could carry on life or endowment business other than

(i) industrial assurance business as defined in *Industrial Insurance Act 1923, s 1(2)*,

(ii) certain sickness assurance, and

(iii) contracts exclusively for the assurance of a gross sum or annuity payable on death to or for the benefit of the deceased's widow (or widower, see Revenue Press Release 15 April 1981) or dependent child.

[*ICTA 1970, s 333(2)*].

If a society registered before 4 May 1966 commenced life or endowment business, or enlarged the scale or changed the character of such business, the Registrar had power to serve notice that it be treated as not being within the exemption. [*ICTA 1970, s 335(2)–(5), as amended*].

Where the rules are altered or there are amalgamations or acquisitions of societies, the exemption or non-exemption of previous contracts is unaffected. [*ICTA 1988, s 460(7)–(10)*].

As regards (iii) above, the Revenue were advised in 1984 that, contrary to what was generally believed, the promotion of contracts as investment or endowment contracts, on the basis of their surrender value after ten years,

(A) rendered their issue *ultra vires* and therefore the contracts not fully enforceable, and

(B) required that a lump sum intended to be payable on the surrender of an annuity be taken into account in the application of the monetary limits (see 28.3 above).

Under this new interpretation of the law, many policies would have been *ultra vires* or in excess of the tax exempt limits. For contracts made before 1 June 1984, therefore, *Friendly Societies Act 1984, s 1* altered the law to what it was previously thought to be.

Advice was also given that, in the application of the monetary limits, any increase in the value of an investment-linked policy over the basic gross sum assured must be taken into account. *Friendly Societies Act 1984, s 2* now provides for such an increase to be ignored, irrespective of when the policy was made.

28.6 **Societies registered after 31 May 1973.** For societies registered after 31 May 1973, the exemption outlined in 28.2–28.5 above is, after 26 March 1974, restricted to life or endowment business, and a payment made to a member after that date otherwise than in the course of such business is treated as a qualifying distribution (see 20.18 DISTRIBUTIONS) insofar as it exceeds any sum paid or repaid by him to the society, less any payment made by the society to him after 26 March 1974. [*ICTA 1988, s 461(1)(3)*]. Similar provisions apply in relation to non-life or endowment business of incorporated successors to registered societies subject to the restriction, the denial of exemption being extended to include profits from subsidiaries. [*ICTA 1988, s 461B(1)–(3); F(No 2)A 1992, Sch 9 para 7*].

A society is outside the above provision if

(*a*) its business is limited to the provision, in accordance with the rules of the society, of benefits for or in respect of employees of a particular employer or of a group of persons approved by the Registrar, or

(*b*) it was registered before 27 March 1974 and its rules limit the aggregate amount payable in contributions and deposits to £1 per month, or such greater amount as may be authorised by the Registrar. [*ICTA 1988, s 461(2)*].

If a society registered before 1 June 1973 begins life or endowment business (see 28.4 above), or enlarges the scale or changes the character of such business, the Registrar may direct that it is to be treated as registered after 31 May 1973. [*ICTA 1988, s 461(6)–(10)*]. Incorporated societies may be the subject of directions with similar effect. [*ICTA 1988, s 461C; F(No 2)A 1992, Sch 9 para 7*].

28.7 **Life and endowment business** which is **not exempt** is treated in the same way as mutual insurance business (or, for accounting periods ending after 31 August 1996, other long term business) carried on by insurance companies, subject to regulations made by the Treasury. Transfers (in whole or part) of the business of a friendly society to another society or to a company which is not a friendly society, and amalgamations of friendly societies and their conversion into companies which are not friendly societies, and transfers of long term business of insurance companies to friendly societies, are treated in the same ways as transfers of long term business between insurance companies, again subject to Treasury regulations. [*ICTA 1988, s 463; FA 1990, s 50; FA 1996, s 171(5)(6)*]. The Treasury regulations both for modifications of the Corporation Tax Acts and for transfers of business are consolidated in *SI 1997 No 473* (as amended by *SI 1997 No 2877*, *SI 1998 No 1871, reg 25* and *SI 1999 No 2636*), with transitional amendment regulations in *SI 1997 Nos 471, 472*. See also *SI 1997 No 481* (amending *SI 1995 No 3237*, see 41.14 LIFE INSURANCE COMPANIES). See 45 MUTUAL COMPANIES and 41.16 LIFE INSURANCE COMPANIES.

28.8 **Societies ceasing to be registered.** Where a society ceases to be registered under *Friendly Societies Act 1974, s 84* or *Friendly Societies Act 1992, s 91*, its existing tax exempt life and endowment business and any other exempt business, insofar in each case as it relates to contracts already entered into, remains exempt and each is treated as a separate business. In the latter case, the exemption is lost if the benefits are increased. [*ICTA 1988, s 460(11)(12), s 461(4), s 461B(5)–(7); F(No 2)A 1992, Sch 9 para 7*].

29 Groups of Companies

Cross-references. See 4.6 ANTI-AVOIDANCE; 9.18–9.52 CAPITAL GAINS; 18 CONTROLLED FOREIGN COMPANIES; 23.17, 23.29 EXCHANGE GAINS AND LOSSES; 42.1 LIQUIDATION ETC.; 48.1 PAYMENT OF TAX; 50.16 PROFIT COMPUTATIONS.

Simon's Direct Tax Service D2.6.

The headings in this chapter are as follows.

29.1 Introduction
29.2 Intra-group dividends, charges and interest
29.3 — companies eligible
29.4 — invalid election
29.5 — elections made before 6 April 1973
29.6 — retrospective elections
29.7 — multiple elections
29.8 Surrender of ACT
29.9 — '51% subsidiary'
29.10 — restriction on surrender
29.11 — effect on subsidiary
29.12 — example
29.13 — payments for surrendered ACT
29.14 Group relief
29.15 — 'members of a group of companies'
29.16 — 'equity holder'
29.17 — profits available for distribution
29.18 — kinds of group relief
29.19 — 'corresponding accounting period'
29.20 — limits on group relief
29.21 — example
29.22 — companies joining or leaving a group
29.23 — claims
29.24 — payment for group relief
29.25 — other limitations on relief
29.26 — relationship to other reliefs
29.27 — consortia
29.28 — examples
29.29 — group/consortium relief interaction
29.30 — example
29.31 — dual resident investing companies
29.32 Arrangements for payment of tax
29.33 Surrender of tax refund, etc. within group
29.34 — example
29.35 Demergers
29.36 — exempt distributions
29.37 — 'distributing company'
29.38 — 'member'
29.39 — 'shares'
29.40 — '75% subsidiary'
29.41 — 'ordinary share capital'
29.42 — 'trade'
29.43 — 'group'
29.44 — 'unquoted company'
29.45 — 'control'
29.46 — 'relevant company'
29.47 — 'trading company'
29.48 — 'holding company'
29.49 — relief from tax on capital gains
29.50 — anti-avoidance
29.51 — 'chargeable payment'
29.52 — 'payment'
29.53 — 'company concerned in an exempt distribution'
29.54 — winding-up etc.
29.55 — returns
29.56 — power to obtain information
29.57 — clearance
29.58 — consequences of demerger

29.1 INTRODUCTION

Membership of a group may affect the tax treatment of dividends and charges paid between companies (see 29.2–29.7 below). It may also enable certain losses etc. of one company to be relieved against the profits of another (29.14–29.16 below) and unused ACT (prior to its abolition) to be surrendered from one company to another (see 29.8–29.13 below). See also 44.21 LOSSES as regards restriction of losses where a fellow group member is the subject of a write-off of Government investment.

Note. For these reliefs, which may also apply to consortia (see 29.27 below), the definition of 'group' varies as indicated below. See also 9.18 CAPITAL GAINS.

29.2 **INTRA-GROUP DIVIDENDS, CHARGES AND INTEREST**

An election may be made jointly by the paying company and the receiving company, provided that each is resident in the UK and that the conditions set out in 29.3 below are satisfied, that *ICTA 1988, s 247* shall apply to intra-group charges or (where they are paid before 6 April 1999) dividends, or to both. For accounting periods ending after 31 March 1996, an election in relation to charges applies equally to interest payments in relation to which a debit falls to be brought into account on the paying company under the LOAN RELATIONSHIPS (43) provisions. The effect of such an election is:

(*a*) that income tax is not deductible from payments representing charges on the paying company's income or deductible interest (but see 29.3 below) and *ICTA 1988, ss 349, 350* (see Tolley's Income Tax under Deduction of Tax at Source) do not apply; and

(*b*) that ACT is not payable in respect of dividends passing between them, which do not, therefore, constitute franked payments of one or FRANKED INVESTMENT INCOME (27) of the other, but are referred to as 'group income'.

These provisions **cease to apply to dividends paid after 5 April 1999**, following the abolition of ACT.

[*ICTA 1988, s 247(1)(2)(4)(4A); FA 1996, Sch 14 para 13; FA 1998, Sch 3 para 19*].

An election must be made by notice to the inspector, specifying the grounds of entitlement. The inspector may then accept the election, or reject it within three months, in which latter case the electors have the same rights of appeal as the paying company would have against an assessment. See Tolley's Income Tax under Appeals. If accepted, the election is effective from the date of notification of acceptance (or three months from the giving of the notice, whichever is the earlier) in relation to dividends or charges paid after that date (but see 29.6 below). Either company may revoke an election from the date of giving notice in writing to that effect to the inspector. Where an election in respect of *dividends* is in force, the paying company may give written notice to the Collector that it is not to apply to such dividends (or parts of dividends) as are specified in the notice. Form CT61Z (return under *ICTA 1988, Sch 13*) contains a space for entry of such dividends; suitable completion of that form is accepted as satisfying the requirement for written notice. An election ceases to be in force on the companies' ceasing to fulfil the necessary conditions, and each company must at once notify the inspector of such cessation. [*ICTA 1988, ss 247(3), 248; FA 1998, Sch 3 paras 19, 20*].

The election applies in respect of dividends or payments received in trust *for* the electing company, but not in respect of dividends or payments received by that company in a fiduciary capacity. Neither does it apply to dividends etc. on investments held as trading stock nor where the recipient company is entitled by virtue of any exemption to reclaim payment of the tax credit otherwise arising, or would be so entitled but for *ICTA 1988, s 235* (distribution to exempt funds) or *s 237* (disallowance of reliefs in respect of bonus issues) (see Tolley's Income Tax under Anti-Avoidance). [*ICTA 1988, s 247(5)(10); FA 1998, Sch 3 para 19*].

Except as below, an election under *section 247* does not apply to FOREIGN INCOME DIVIDENDS (26), and an election for a dividend to be treated as a foreign income dividend (see 26.1, 26.2 FOREIGN INCOME DIVIDENDS) is treated as a notice that any *section 247* election is not to apply in the case of such a dividend. [*ICTA 1988, ss 246A(10), 247(5A); FA 1994, Sch 16 paras 1, 13*]. However where, on or after 26 November 1996, a UK-resident company receives a distribution from a wholly-owned or fellow subsidiary (see below), and *FA 1997, Sch 7* would otherwise apply to the distribution (so that it would be treated as a foreign income dividend, see 4.7 ANTI-AVOIDANCE), a *section 247* election may apply to the distribution, and if it does so the distribution is treated as one to which *FA 1997, Sch 7* does not apply. The paying company is treated for this purpose as a wholly-owned or fellow subsidiary if the recipient company directly or indirectly owns all its ordinary share capital, or if a third (UK-resident) company owns all the ordinary share capital of both companies. *ICTA 1988, s 838* applies in determining direct or indirect ownership of share capital. [*ICTA 1988, s 247(5B)–(5D); FA 1997, Sch 7 para 10*].

An election which refers only to charges will be treated as extending to payments of interest in relation to which a debit falls to be brought into account under the LOAN RELATIONSHIPS (43) provisions. (Revenue Tax Bulletin April 1996 p 310).

See also 4.6 ANTI-AVOIDANCE as regards certain payments between related companies.

Simon's Direct Tax Service. See D2.611 *et seq.*.

29.3 **Companies eligible.** The election is available only where the companies are resident in the UK and

(*a*) the paying company is a '51% subsidiary' of the other, or of a company resident in the UK of which the recipient company is also a 51% subsidiary (but see (*c*) below), or

(*b*) the paying company is a 'trading' or 'holding company' owned by a 'consortium' of which the recipient company is a member and not itself a '75% subsidiary' of any other company and not capable of becoming so by virtue of any existing 'arrangements' (see 29.23 below), or

(*c*) (in the case of payments other than dividends) the recipient company is a 51% subsidiary of the paying company.

[*ICTA 1988, s 247(1)(1A)(4); FA 1989, s 99(2)(3)(7); FA 1998, Sch 3 para 19*].

A '*51% (75%) subsidiary*' is a body corporate more than 50% (not less than 75%) of the 'ordinary share capital' of which is beneficially owned directly or indirectly by another. [*ICTA 1988, s 838*]. Share capital owned directly or indirectly in a non-resident body corporate, or owned indirectly through a company which holds it as trading stock, is disregarded in determining 51% subsidiary status, and a company is not treated as a 51% subsidiary unless the parent company would be beneficially entitled to more than 50% of any profits available for distribution to equity holders and of any assets so available on a winding-up (see 29.17 below). [*ICTA 1988, s 247(8)(8A); FA 1989, s 99(4)(6)(7)*]. '*Ordinary share capital*' means all the issued share capital of the company except non-participating shares carrying a fixed-rate dividend. [*ICTA 1988, s 832(1)*]. 'Issued share capital' does not include founder members' deposits in a company limited by guarantee (*South Shore Mutual Insurance Co Ltd v Blair (Sp C 215), [1999] SSCD 296*).

A '*holding company*' means a company the business of which consists wholly or mainly in holding shares or securities of trading companies which are its *90% subsidiaries* (i.e. in which it holds directly not less than 90% of the ordinary share capital). [*ICTA 1988, s 247(9)(a)*].

A '*trading company*' is a company the business of which consists wholly or mainly of the carrying on of a trade or trades. [*ICTA 1988, s 247(9)(b)*].

A company is owned by a '*consortium*' if three-quarters or more of its ordinary share capital is beneficially owned amongst them by companies resident in the UK, each owning at least one-twentieth and beneficially entitled to at least one-twentieth of any profits available for distribution to equity holders and of any assets so available on a winding-up (see 29.17 below). Such companies are the *'members of the consortium'*. [*ICTA 1988, s 247(9)(c); FA 1989, s 99(5)(6)(7)*].

29.4 **Invalid election.** The effect of an election invalidly made or which has become invalid (see 29.2 above) is that the inspector may make such assessments, adjustments or set-offs as may be necessary to restore the electors to the position in which they would have been had ACT been paid on, or income tax deducted from, payments made under the invalid election. Any tax consequently assessed on the paying company and not paid within three months of the payable date may be assessed on the recipient company (without prejudice to the liability of the former). [*ICTA 1988, s 247(6)(7); FA 1998, Sch 3 para 19*]. This also applies to a payment made in anticipation of an election. (See also 29.6 below.)

29.5 **Elections made before 6 April 1973** are treated as elections made under 29.2–29.4 above from 6 April 1973 onwards. [*FA 1972, s 91(4); Interpretation Act 1978, s 17(2)(b)*].

29.6 **Retrospective elections.** The Revenue will normally accede to a request that an election be treated as applying to charges, etc. paid before the election became effective, provided that there is no disturbance to assessments which have become final and conclusive or to claims already given effect, and that:

(*a*) a timeous election would have remained valid at the date of payment;

(*b*) the omission to make a timeous election was due to illness, genuine oversight or some similar cause; and

(*c*) the recipient company agrees to this treatment.

(Revenue Company Taxation Manual, CT 2635).

29.7 **Multiple elections.** It is understood that the following principles are applied.

(*a*) Where only two companies are involved a single election is acceptable provided it is signed by the person duly authorised to act on behalf of each company (which may be the same person).

(*b*) The Revenue will accept a single election covering three or more companies in a group provided that all the necessary facts, and the application of the election between any two of those companies, are shown, and that the election is signed on behalf of each company concerned.

(*c*) The Revenue will accept that any group member may, by board resolution, authorise a named person to make a joint election on its behalf for the purposes of *section 247*. If the same person is appointed by every group member, one signature would suffice on the notice of election, but the Revenue would require each member to send in a certified copy of the resolution, and another certified copy when the appropriate officer is changed. The Revenue will accept an appointment by the secretary of a group member under proper delegation of authority from the board.

The Revenue are satisfied with the form of election set out below (to be sent to the Inspector of Taxes for each Tax District concerned).

Dear Sir
XYZ Limited and Subsidiaries
Election under ICTA 1988, s 247
We the companies listed below ('the group') elect under *ICTA 1988, s 247* that:

(i) payments of dividends referred to in subsection (1) of that section may be made within the group without giving rise to payments of advance corporation tax; and

(ii) payments of interest and other annual payments referred to in subsection (4) of that section may be made within the group without deduction of income tax.

Company	*Tax District and Reference*	*Percentage Shareholding*	*Signed Director/Secretary*
Parent			
(XYZ Ltd)			
Subsidiaries			
(X Ltd)			
(Y Ltd)			
(Z Ltd)			

(CCAB Memorandum TR 340, 16 May 1979).

It is advisable, where the matter may be in doubt, to insert, 'all of which are resident in the UK', after ('the group') in the first line of the recommended form of election.

See generally Revenue Company Taxation Manual, CT 2630 *et seq.*.

29.8 **SURRENDER OF ACT**

The benefit of any ACT paid by, and not repaid to, a company resident in the UK (the 'surrendering company') in respect of **dividends** may be surrendered in whole or in part to any *51% subsidiary* of that company which is also resident in the UK. A similar surrender may be made of ACT in respect of distributions consisting of the redemption, repayment or purchase by a company of its own shares (see 51 PURCHASE BY A COMPANY OF ITS OWN SHARES), but not in respect of other non-dividend distributions. A surrender may be made to more than one subsidiary in such proportion as may be determined by the company. Each subsidiary must have qualified as such throughout the accounting period in which the dividend was paid. [*ICTA 1988, s 240(1)(10)*]. For a company's liability to pay ACT and the benefits attaching to ACT paid, see 3 ADVANCE CORPORATION TAX.

These provisions **cease to apply to surrendering company accounting periods beginning on or after 6 April 1999**, following the abolition of ACT. [*FA 1998, Sch 3 para 13*].

A claim to surrender ACT must be made within six years after the end of the accounting period in which the ACT is paid and requires the consent of the subsidiary or subsidiaries concerned. Such consent is to be 'notified to the inspector in such form as the Board may require', but in the absence of such prescribed form, a letter is usually sufficient. [*ICTA 1988, s 240(6)*]. ACT may be surrendered regardless of whether it has already been set against the tax payable on an assessment which has become final. (Revenue Pamphlet IR 131, SP 7/89, 12 October 1989).

A claim in terms of a formula will be accepted, but the claim cannot take account of any event occurring after the date of the claim (although the outcome of such events need not be known at that date). It may, however, take account of any other claim (e.g. a claim to group relief for losses not at that time surrendered elsewhere) which could have been made at the date of claim. Otherwise, a claim can (as above) be withdrawn and a new claim submitted within the normal time limit. Although a subsidiary to which ACT is surrendered under a formula claim cannot strictly take the benefit of the surrender until the claim is determined, in practice where relief is claimed which does not exceed the expected benefit, the Revenue will not seek to collect tax so covered. (Revenue Tax Bulletin February 1995 p 196, August 1995 p 244).

See 3.6 ADVANCE CORPORATION TAX as regards correction of excessive ACT and interest charge following surrender. See 3.10 ADVANCE CORPORATION TAX for restrictions on surrendered ACT following a change in ownership of the claimant company.

See 46.3 OIL COMPANIES for special provisions relating to such companies.

Self-assessment. For surrendering company accounting periods **beginning before 6 April 1999 and ending on or after 1 July 1999**, the day appointed for the commencement of self-assessment for companies (see 55 SELF-ASSESSMENT), *ICTA 1988, s 240* is revised and a new *ICTA 1988, Sch 13A* introduced to facilitate the surrender of ACT within groups. In particular, explicit provision is made for the withdrawal of claims (with the consent of the subsidiary concerned) and for their replacement by alternative claims (amendment of claims being prohibited); for self-assessment of any liability arising from the making or withdrawal of claims or from claims to amounts subsequently found not to have been available for surrender; and for enquiries into such self-assessments (on terms similar to those applicable under *FA 1998, Sch 18 Pt IV*, see 55.7 SELF-ASSESSMENT). Multiple claims (as regards either subsidiary or period) are treated as separate claims, and the amount surrendered must be quantified at the time of a claim. The time limit for claims continues to be six years after the end of the surrendering company accounting period concerned, and withdrawals of claims must be made by the end of that six-year period or, if earlier (and except in certain cases involving further assessments by the Board), by the time the assessment becomes final for the accounting period of the subsidiary in which the surrender was effective. Claims must be included in a company tax return (or amended return) (see 55.3 SELF-ASSESSMENT) where possible. Otherwise, claims (and withdrawals of claims) must be in such form as the Board may determine. A claim is treated as withdrawn before a simultaneous claim is made. [*ICTA 1988, s 240, Sch 13A; FA 1996, Sch 25; FA 1998, Sch 3 paras 13, 42, Sch 19 para 50*].

Simon's Direct Tax Service. See D2.655.

29.9 **'51% subsidiary'** (cf. 29.3 above). A body corporate is the 51% subsidiary of another if and so long as more than 50% of its ordinary share capital (see 29.3 above) is owned directly or indirectly by that other. [*ICTA 1988, s 838*]. For the purposes of 29.8 above, the parent company is to be treated as not owning

(*a*) any share capital held as trading stock, or

(*b*) any share capital which it owns indirectly, and which is directly held by another body corporate as trading stock, or

(*c*) any share capital held directly or indirectly in a non-resident body corporate.

[*ICTA 1988, s 240(10); FA 1998, Sch 3 para 13*].

A company which would otherwise qualify as a 51% subsidiary is nevertheless not to be so treated if arrangements exist whereby any person has or could obtain, or any persons together have, or could obtain, 'control' of the subsidiary but not of the parent, or if the parent company fails to show that

(i) it is beneficially entitled to more than 50% of 'profits available for distribution' to 'equity holders', as such, of the subsidiary, and

(ii) it would be beneficially entitled to more than 50% of assets of the subsidiary available for distribution to its equity holders as such on a winding-up.

For a case in which such arrangements were held to preclude surrender of ACT to a subsidiary, see *Cricket plc v Inspector (Sp C 157), [1998] SSCD 101.*

The power of a Minister to direct a statutory body as to disposals of its (or any subsidiary's) assets does not constitute such 'arrangements'.

[*ICTA 1988, s 240(11)(12); FA 1998, Sch 3 para 13*].

For the Revenue's interpretation of 'arrangements', see 29.23 below.

'*Control*' is as defined in *ICTA 1988, s 840* (see 51.4(2)(vii) PURCHASE BY A COMPANY OF ITS OWN SHARES).

For '*equity holder*' and '*profits available for distribution*' see *ICTA 1988, Sch 18* (dealt with in 29.16–29.18 below). [*ICTA 1988, s 240(11)(13); FA 1998, Sch 3 para 13*].

The Revenue will not deny group relief between a parent and a sub-subsidiary solely on the ground that the intermediate company has control of the latter but not of the former. (Revenue Pamphlet IR 131, SP 5/80, 26 March 1980).

29.10 **Restriction on surrender.** ACT which a company has set against its earlier years' liabilities (see 3.8 ADVANCE CORPORATION TAX) cannot be surrendered under these provisions, and ACT which a company has so surrendered cannot be either set against earlier years' liabilities or carried forward as surplus ACT. [*ICTA 1988, s 240(7); FA 1998, Sch 3 para 13*].

29.11 **Effect on subsidiary.** The subsidiary is treated as having paid the ACT surrendered in respect of a distribution made by it on the same date as that on which the dividend to which it relates was paid by the surrendering company. If the ACT surrendered relates to dividends paid on different dates, it is apportioned among them, the amount relating to each notional distribution by the subsidiary being 'the appropriate part of the surrendered amount'. [*ICTA 1988, s 240(2)(3); FA 1998, Sch 3 para 13*].

The ACT surrendered is then available to be set off against the subsidiary's mainstream corporation tax liability for that accounting period, or carried forward to a subsequent accounting period (see 3.6, 3.8 ADVANCE CORPORATION TAX). It **cannot** be carried back under *ICTA 1988, s 239(3)*, but in determining the amount of surplus ACT to be carried forward or back, surrendered ACT is to be set against the subsidiary's mainstream liability before ACT paid by the subsidiary itself. [*ICTA 1988, s 240(4); FA 1998, Sch 3 para 13*].

No ACT surrendered may be set off against the subsidiary's corporation tax liability for any accounting period unless it was a 51% subsidiary of the surrendering company for the whole of that period, or both companies were 51% subsidiaries of a third company. [*ICTA 1988, s 240(5); FA 1989, s 97; FA 1998, Sch 3 para 13*].

29.12 *Example*

A Ltd pays £7,200 in dividends in its accounting period ended 31 December 1998. Due to losses brought forward, A Ltd has no mainstream corporation tax liability for that year. A Ltd's 60%-owned subsidiary, B Ltd, has a mainstream corporation tax liability in each relevant year, and consents to the surrender by A Ltd of the ACT paid. On these facts, the following situations might arise, depending on the accounting periods of A Ltd and B Ltd and the dates of dividend payments.

(*a*) A Ltd paid a single dividend on 1 June 1998, with an associated ACT payment of £1,800, and the accounting periods of the companies are coterminous. The entire £1,800 is therefore available to be set against B Ltd's mainstream liability subject to the maximum laid down in *section 239(2)* (see 3.6 ADVANCE CORPORATION TAX).

(*b*) A Ltd paid an interim dividend of £1,800 (ACT £450) on 31 March 1998 and pays a final dividend of £5,400 (ACT £1,350) on 31 December 1998. The 'appropriate part of the surrendered amount' is calculated as below.

Surrendered amount	£1,800
The part of the surrendered amount appropriate to the interim dividend is	
$\frac{\text{Interim dividend (31 March 1998)}}{\text{Total dividend for year}} = \frac{1,800}{7,200} \times £1,800$	450
The part of the surrendered amount appropriate to the final dividend is	£1,350

Note that it is not correct to take the ACT actually paid on the interim dividend. If the rate of ACT had changed between the dividend payments, apportionment would produce a different figure.

B Ltd's accounting period runs from 1 April to 31 March, so that, of the ACT surrendered, £450 will fall into the accounting period ended 31 March 1998 and the balance into that ended 31 March 1999. It is assumed that B Ltd's mainstream corporation tax liability for the first accounting period was £2,500 and for the second is £5,000.

Accounting period to 31 March 1998

Mainstream liability	£2,500
Deduct: Appropriate part of surrendered amount	450
Corporation tax payable	£2,050

Accounting period to 31 March 1999

Mainstream liability	£5,000
Deduct: Appropriate part of surrendered amount	1,350
Corporation tax payable	£3,650

(*c*) The situation is as in (*a*) above, and B Ltd has the full amount of ACT surrendered (£1,800) available for its accounting period ended 31 December 1998, for which it has mainstream liability of £1,344 on profits of £6,400. It had mainstream liability for the accounting period ended 31 December 1997 of £4,350 on profits of £20,000; it paid no ACT for that accounting period, but pays ACT of £6,000 for the accounting period ended 31 December 1998.

The ACT surrendered to it cannot be carried back against the mainstream liability for the accounting period ended 31 December 1997, but, in calculating its surplus ACT for the accounting period ended 31 December 1998, surrendered ACT is treated as relieved in priority to its own ACT. The calculations are as below.

Mainstream liability for accounting period ended 31 December 1998	£1,344
Deduct: Surrendered ACT (maximum)	1,280
Corporation tax payable	£64

Its own ACT is 'surplus' (see 3.6 ADVANCE CORPORATION TAX) and can be carried back to the accounting period ended 31 December 1997, as below.

Mainstream liability	£4,350
Deduct: Surplus ACT carried back (maximum)	4,000
Corporation tax payable	£350

Surplus ACT available to be carried forward (assuming no carry–back to earlier periods is possible)

Surrendered to B Ltd (£1,800 – £1,280)	=	£ 520
Paid by B Ltd (£6,000 – £4,000)	=	2,000
Total surplus ACT		£2,520

29.13 **Payments for surrendered ACT.** A payment not exceeding the ACT surrendered which is paid in respect thereof under an agreement between the subsidiary and the surrendering company is ignored in computing the profits or losses of either company, and constitutes neither a distribution nor a charge on income. [*ICTA 1988, s 240(8); FA 1998, Sch 3 para 13*].

29.14 **GROUP RELIEF**

Relief from corporation tax for the items specified in 29.18 below may be surrendered (in whole or in part) by one 'member of a group of companies' (the 'surrendering company') and claimed by another such member (the 'claimant company') against its own corporation tax liability by way of 'group relief'. The relief is also available to and from certain consortium companies, see 29.27 below. Both companies must be resident in the UK or, from 1 April 2000, either resident in the UK or carrying on a UK trade through a branch or agency. [*ICTA 1988, s 402(1)–(3B), s 413(5) (as originally enacted); FA 2000, Sch 27 paras 1, 2, 6*]. See 29.23 below as regards anti-avoidance provisions restricting relief.

Simon's Direct Tax Service. See **D2.641** *et seq.*.

29.15 Companies are **'members of a group of companies'** if one is the **'75% subsidiary'** of the other or both are 75% subsidiaries of a third company. [*ICTA 1988, s 413(3)(a)*]. For accounting periods ending before 1 April 2000, all the companies must be UK-resident [*ICTA 1988, s 413(5) as originally enacted*] or resident elsewhere in the European Union or European Economic Area (following the ECJ decision in *ICI plc v Colmer*, see 29.27 below). For accounting periods ending on or after 1 April 2000, the residence of the companies constituting the group is not relevant (although only UK-resident companies and companies carrying on a UK trade through a branch or agency may claim group relief, see 29.14 above). See, however, 29.20 below as regards limitation of the application of this extended definition of 'group' to parts of accounting periods falling after 31 March 2000. [*FA 2000, Sch 27 paras 2, 6(1)*].

'*75% subsidiary*' means a body corporate not less than 75% of the ordinary share capital (see 29.3 above) of which is beneficially owned directly or indirectly by another body corporate. [*ICTA 1988, s 838*]. Beneficial ownership is not affected by the existence of an option which may require disposal of shares at a future date (*J Sainsbury plc v O'Connor CA 1991, 64 TC 208*). For the purposes of group relief, however, a company is treated as not owning

(*a*) any share capital held as trading stock, or

(*b*) any share capital which it owns indirectly and which is directly held by another body corporate as trading stock, or (*c*) (before 1 April 2000) any share capital held directly or indirectly in a non-resident body corporate.

[*ICTA 1988, s 413(5); FA 2000, Sch 27 para 2*].

Any share capital of registered INDUSTRIAL AND PROVIDENT SOCIETIES (32) is treated as ordinary share capital. [*ICTA 1988, s 413(4)*].

The company owning the shares must also be beneficially entitled to **at least 75%** of profits available for distribution to equity holders as such of the subsidiary **and** of assets similarly available in a winding-up. [*ICTA 1988, s 413(7)*].

Simon's Direct Tax Service. See **D2.642, D2.646A**.

29.16 An **'equity holder'** of a company is a holder of its 'ordinary shares' or a 'loan creditor' in respect of a loan other than a 'normal commercial loan'. [*ICTA 1988, Sch 18 para 1(1)*].

'*Ordinary shares*' means, for this purpose, all shares other than '*fixed-rate preference shares*', which are defined as shares

(*a*) issued for consideration which is or includes new consideration (as defined in *ICTA 1988, s 254*, see 20.12 DISTRIBUTIONS), and

(*b*) carrying no rights to conversion into other shares or securities or acquisition of additional shares or securities, and

(*c*) on which any dividends are limited to a fixed amount, or to a fixed percentage of the nominal value, and represent no more than a reasonable commercial return on the new consideration received by the company for the issue of the shares, and

(*d*) on which any repayment right is limited to such consideration or is reasonably comparable with rights generally attached to listed fixed-dividend shares.

As regards (*b*) above, rights of conversion into shares or securities of the company's 'quoted parent company' are disregarded, as are rights of conversion into shares satisfying (*a*), (*c*) and (*d*) above, or securities satisfying (ii) and (iii) below, not themselves carrying conversion (other than into shares or securities in the 'quoted parent company') or acquisition rights.

[*ICTA 1988, Sch 18 para 1(2)(3)(5A)(5B)(8); FA 1989, s 101(2)(4)*].

A company is another company's '*quoted parent company*' for these purposes if and only if

(A) the other company is its 75% subsidiary (see 29.15 above), for which purpose it is assumed that the company *is* the 'quoted parent company' of the other,

(B) the parent is not itself a 75% subsidiary, and

(C) the parent's ordinary shares (or each class thereof) are listed on a recognised stock exchange or dealt in on the Unlisted Securities Market.

[*ICTA 1988, Sch 18 para 1(5C)(5D); FA 1989, s 101(4); FA 1996, Sch 38 para 6*].

'*Loan creditor*' is as defined in *ICTA 1988, s 417(7)* (see 13.3 CLOSE COMPANIES) except that banks are specifically included. [*ICTA 1988, Sch 18 para 1(4)*].

'*Normal commercial loan*' is one representing (in whole or in part) new consideration (as defined in *ICTA 1988, s 254*) and

(i) which carries no right of conversion into other shares or securities or acquisition of additional shares or securities, and

(ii) the interest on which is dependent neither on the results of the company's business (or part thereof) nor on the value of its assets, and represents no more than a reasonable commercial return on the new consideration lent, and

(iii) on which any repayment right is limited to such consideration or is reasonably comparable with the amount generally repayable (in respect of an equal amount of new consideration) under the terms of issue of listed securities.

As regards (i) above, rights of conversion into shares or securities of the company's quoted parent company (as above) are disregarded, as are rights of conversion into shares satisfying (*a*), (*c*) and (*d*) above, or securities satisfying (ii) and (iii) above, not themselves carrying conversion (other than into shares or securities in the quoted parent company) or acquisition rights.

A loan is not within (ii) above by reason only of the fact that:

(I) the terms of the loan provide for a reduction in the rate of interest in the event of an improvement in that business (or part) or an increase in the value of any of those assets, or (from 21 March 2000) for an increase in the rate of interest in the event of a deterioration in the business (or part) or a diminution in the value of any of those assets; or

(II) where the loan was to be applied in the acquisition of land other than with a view to resale at a profit (or to incidental loan costs), and was secured only on that land, the terms of the loan are such that the only way the loan creditor can enforce payment is by exercising rights granted as security over that land.

[*ICTA 1988, Sch 18 para 1(5)(5A)(5B)(8); FA 1989, s 101(3)(4); FA 1991, s 77; FA 2000, s 86(2)*].

The criterion at (ii) above is not of itself regarded as requiring a non-recourse loan to be treated as other than a 'normal commercial loan'. (Tolley's Practical Tax 1985 p 23).

Where any person has, directly or indirectly, provided new consideration for shares or securities in the company and that person (or any person connected with him, see 16 CONNECTED PERSONS) uses in his trade assets belonging to the company which have been the subject of certain capital allowances, that person and no other is treated as an equity holder in respect of those shares or securities and as beneficially entitled to any distribution of profits or assets attributable to those shares or securities. [*ICTA 1988, Sch 18 para 1(6); FA 2000, Sch 19 para 6*].

Where this provision applies to a bank which has provided new consideration solely by way of a normal commercial loan in the normal course of its banking business, and the cost of the assets so used is less than such new consideration, the bank is treated as a loan creditor for an amount equal to that cost and therefore as an equity holder in respect of that amount. [*ICTA 1988, Sch 18 para 1(7)*].

29.17 **Profits available for distribution** represent the total profits of the subsidiary for the 'accounting period' or, if there is no such profit, £100 (the 'profit distribution'). All payments not otherwise treated as DISTRIBUTIONS (20) are included. In the case of a non-resident company trading through a UK branch or agency (see 29.14 above), the total profits are determined as if it were UK-resident. [*ICTA 1988, Sch 18 para 2; FA 2000, Sch 27 para 5(3)*]. It is understood that the profits referred to are the distributable profits having regard to company law requirements, rather than those computed for tax purposes. (Tolley's Practical Tax 1993 p 63).

The **assets available for distribution in a winding-up** comprise any excess of assets over liabilities as shown in the subsidiary's balance sheet at the end of the accounting period, or (if there is no such excess or the balance sheet is prepared to a different date) £100. Any such asset received by the equity holder on a winding-up is treated as a distribution to him, notwithstanding that it would not otherwise be so treated.

Any new consideration provided by an equity holder for its shares which is then loaned to, or used to acquire shares in, that equity holder or any person connected with it (see 16 CONNECTED PERSONS) is to be deducted from the total distributable assets and from those distributable to that equity holder. [*ICTA 1988, Sch 18 para 3*].

The percentage of the profits or assets to which an equity-holding company is, or would be, beneficially entitled includes any indirect entitlement through another body corporate. [*ICTA 1988, Sch 18 para 6*].

'*Accounting period*' means any which is current at a time relevant to the group relief claim. [*ICTA 1988, Sch 18 para 7*].

There are detailed anti-avoidance provisions relating to the calculation of the relevant percentages in relation to equity holders of shares or securities with restricted or terminable rights. [*ICTA 1988, Sch 18 paras 4, 5; FA 2000, Sch 27 para 5(4)*]. These also require comparisons to be made between the results of various bases of calculation, in particular in relation to option arrangements (the latter in effect reversing the decision in *J Sainsbury plc v O'Connor CA 1991, 64 TC 208*). [*ICTA 1988, Sch 18 paras 5A–5F; F(No 2)A 1992, Sch 6; FA 2000, Sch 27 para 5(5)*]. See 29.23 below for the Revenue interpretation of 'option arrangements'.

29.18 **Kinds of group relief.** Group relief is available on the amounts listed below in the manner specified.

(*a*) **Trading losses** computed as under *ICTA 1988, s 393(2)* or *s 393A(1)* (see 44.2 LOSSES) except losses

(i) from trades falling within Schedule D, Case V, and

(ii) from trades not carried on on a commercial basis and with a view to the realisation of gain (with an exception for statutory functions)(see 44.9 LOSSES), and

(iii) which are denied relief by *ICTA 1988, s 397* (see 44.14 LOSSES).

The available losses include certain 'relievable amounts' in respect of exchange losses (see 23.14 EXCHANGE GAINS AND LOSSES). 'Non-trading deficits' on loan relationships are also in effect treated as trading losses for these purposes (see 43.3 LOAN RELATIONSHIPS).

(*b*) **Capital allowances** to be given by discharge or repayment of tax and available primarily against a specified class of income may be surrendered insofar as they exceed such income for an accounting period (before deduction of losses or capital allowances brought forward) and do not arise to a non-trading lessor (see Note (2) under 8.2 CAPITAL ALLOWANCES). See 44.2 LOSSES.

(*c*) **Management expenses** of investment companies (not brought forward from an earlier accounting period). See 40 INVESTMENT COMPANIES. This relief does not apply to LIFE INSURANCE COMPANIES (41).

(*d*) **Charges on income.**

(*e*) (From 1 April 1998) **Schedule A losses,** excluding losses brought forward from earlier periods and losses incurred in a Schedule A business which was not carried on either on a commercial basis or in the exercise of statutory functions (see 50.27 PROFIT COMPUTATIONS).

In computing amounts available for an accounting period straddling 1 April 1998, separate computations are made for the periods before and from that date.

Amounts within (*a*) and (*b*) above are eligible for surrender regardless of whether the surrendering company has other profits of the same accounting period against which they could be set. Amounts within (*c*), (*d*) and (*e*) above are available for surrender only to the extent that, in aggregate, they exceed the surrendering company's 'gross profits' of the accounting period, any excess being taken to consist first of charges on income, then of Schedule A losses and finally of management expenses. '*Gross profits*' for this purpose are profits without any deduction in respect of amounts within (*a*)–(*e*) above or of any losses etc. of other periods.

The availability of group relief as above is subject to restriction in the case of dual resident investing companies (see 29.31 below) and certain ring-fenced activities (see 46.3 OIL COMPANIES).

[*ICTA 1988, ss 403–403ZE; CAA 1990, s 61(7); FA 1998, Sch 5 paras 29, 55, 75*].

Accounting periods ending after 30 September 1993 and before 1 July 1999 — amount available for group relief. See 44.9 LOSSES as regards determination of the amount(s) available for group relief prior to the introduction of self-assessment (see 55 SELF-ASSESSMENT). [*TMA 1970, ss 41A–41C; FA 1990, s 95; FA 1998, Sch 19 para 19*]. Where, as a result of such a determination (or a direction relating to it) becoming final, a company has surrendered by way of group relief more relief of a particular description than is available to it for the accounting period (net of any relieved in a final and conclusive assessment on the company itself), the company must, within 30 days of the determination (or direction) becoming final, reduce or withdraw its consent to surrender(s) to give effect to the determination. If it fails to do so, the necessary adjustment will be made by the inspector by written notice to the surrendering company and to any other company affected by the adjustment. However, the surrendering company has 30 days from the giving of such notice to give written notice to the inspector specifying the manner in which the adjustment is to be made.

The amounts taken into account for these purposes for an accounting period include amounts surrendered for a deemed accounting period under *ICTA 1988, s 409* (prior to its repeal, see 29.22 below) comprised in the accounting period.

The inspector's power to make an assessment to recover excessive group relief (see 29.25 below) applies equally where the excess arises from an adjustment under these provisions, and such an assessment is not out of time provided that it is made within one year of the determination (or direction) to which the adjustment relates becoming final.

Any tax charged by assessment following an adjustment as above which is unpaid at a time six months after the assessment becomes final and conclusive may, within two years of that time, be assessed on any other company which benefited from relief surrendered by the same company for the same accounting period, subject to a limitation to the amount of tax it saved by virtue of the surrender. The company may then recover the tax, together with any interest it has paid thereon under *TMA 1970, s 87A* (see 39.1 INTEREST ON UNPAID TAX), from the company on which the liability originally arose.

[*FA 1990, s 96; F(No 2)A 1997, Sch 8 Pt II (14); FA 1999, s 92(6)*].

Interaction with carry-forward relief. Group relief may be given for a loss notwithstanding that the surrendering company has already obtained relief for the loss by carry-forward under *ICTA 1988, s 393(1)* (see 44.4 LOSSES). The necessary adjustments may be made to withdraw the relief previously given, relief being treated as given for losses of earlier accounting periods before later ones. Assessments for this purpose are not out of time if made within one year of the date of the surrendering company's giving to the inspector notice of its consent to the surrender. [*ICTA 1988, s 411A; FA 1990, s 101; FA 1999, Sch 11 para 1*].

For the position under self-assessment, see 29.23 below.

Simon's Direct Tax Service. See **D2.643** *et seq.*.

29.19 A '*corresponding accounting period*' is any accounting period of the claimant company which falls wholly or partly within the accounting period of the surrendering company in which the amount for which group relief is claimed arose. [*ICTA 1988, s 413(2A); F(No 2)A 1997, Sch 7 para 7*]. **Prior to commencement of the provisions described at 29.20 below** (which apply broadly for accounting periods ending after 1 July 1997) this definition was contained in *ICTA 1988, s 408*, which also provided that if the accounting periods did not exactly coincide, the group relief available to the claimant company is reduced by the fraction A/B, and that company's total profits against which the relief may be set is reduced by the fraction A/C, where

A is the length of the period common to both accounting periods,

B is the length of the surrendering company's accounting period, and

C is the length of the corresponding period of the claimant company.

[*ICTA 1988, s 408; F(No 2)A 1997, Sch 7 para 6*].

Example 1

A Ltd owns 80% of the ordinary shares of B Ltd. A Ltd's accounting periods run from 1 July to 30 June and B Ltd's from 1 January to 31 December. In its accounting period to 30 June 1996, A Ltd makes trading losses of £5,000 which it surrenders to B Ltd.

The corresponding accounting periods of B Ltd are the calendar years 1995 and 1996, in which it has profits of £6,000 and £3,000 respectively. For each of these accounting periods

A = 6 months (1 July to 31 December and 1 January to 30 June)

B = 12 months

C = 12 months

Accounting period to 31 December 1995

Maximum amount obtainable from A Ltd is $\frac{6}{12} \times$ £5,000 = £2,500

Maximum amount allowable to B Ltd is $\frac{6}{12} \times$ £6,000 = £3,000

The relief is therefore restricted to £2,500. B Ltd's corporation tax computation is

Profits	£6,000
Deduct: Group relief	2,500
Profits chargeable	£3,500

Accounting period to 31 December 1996

Maximum amount obtainable from A Ltd is $\frac{6}{12} \times$ £5,000 = £2,500

Maximum amount allowable to B Ltd is $\frac{6}{12} \times$ £3,000 = £1,500

The relief is therefore restricted to £1,500 and B Ltd's corporation tax computation is

Profits	£3,000
Deduct: Group relief	1,500
Profits chargeable	£1,500

The balance of A Ltd's losses which cannot be relieved against B Ltd's profits (£1,000) is available for surrender to another group company or for relief under other provisions.

Example 2

Assume the same facts as in *Example 1*, except that B Ltd's accounting periods after 31 December 1995 run to 31 March 1996 and 31 March 1997, for which its profits are £1,000 and £2,500 respectively.

The corresponding accounting periods of B Ltd are now

(i) the calendar year 1995,

(ii) the three months to 31 March 1996 and

(iii) the year to 31 March 1997.

The relief allowable for each is as follows.

(i)	As in *Example 1* above	£2,500
(ii)	Maximum amount obtainable from A Ltd is $\frac{3}{12} \times$ £5,000	= £1,250
	Maximum amount allowable to B Ltd is $\frac{3}{3} \times$ £1,000	= £1,000
	The relief allowable is therefore	£1,000
(iii)	Maximum amount obtainable from A Ltd is $\frac{3}{12} \times$ £5,000	= £1,250
	Maximum amount allowable to B Ltd is $\frac{3}{12} \times$ £2,500	= £ 625
	The relief allowable is therefore	£ 625

In practice, therefore, the relief available is restricted to the smaller of

(*a*) the proportion (on a time basis) of the surrendering company's loss, etc. appropriate to the common period, and

(*b*) the proportion (on a time basis) of the claimant company's profits appropriate to the common period.

These provisions are **repealed** by *F(No 2)A 1997, Sch 8 Pt II(14)* following the introduction of the wider anti-avoidance provisions in *ICTA 1988, ss 403A–403C* by *F(No 2)A 1997, Sch 7*, for which see 29.20 below.

29.20 **Limits on group relief.** Where the accounting period of either the claimant or the surrendering company in relation to a claim ends **after 1 July 1997** (subject to the detailed commencement provisions described below), the amount for which group relief may be claimed against total profits may not exceed the lesser of

(*a*) the 'unused part of the surrenderable amount for the overlapping period', and

(*b*) the 'unrelieved part of the claimant company's total profits for the overlapping period'.

The amount referred to in (*a*) above is so much of the total amount available for surrender for the accounting period of the surrendering company as is attributable (see below) to the 'overlapping period' and has not been the subject of any prior surrenders attributable to the 'overlapping period'.

The amount referred to in (*b*) above is so much of the total profits of the claimant company for the accounting period of the claim as is attributable (see below) to the 'overlapping period', reduced by any previously claimed group relief attributable to the 'overlapping period'.

The '*overlapping period*' is the period common to the accounting periods of both the claimant company and the surrendering company to which the claim relates, but excluding any part of the common period when those companies are not both members of the same group and (from 1 April 2000), in the case of a non-UK resident company, carrying on a UK trade through a branch or agency.

The amount of prior surrenders attributed to the overlapping period is determined by attributing each earlier effective surrender in respect of the accounting period in question to the overlapping period in relation to that surrender, then further attributing a part (see below) of each such amount to any period common to the overlapping periods of the earlier surrender and the surrender in question and aggregating all the amounts so attributed. The amount of previously claimed group relief attributable to the overlapping period is similarly determined.

For the above purposes the group relief allowable on any claim is determined as at the time when it becomes final (i.e. when it can no longer be withdrawn) as if every claim which had previously become final were a prior claim and every claim which has not become final were a subsequent claim. Claims which would otherwise be treated as having been made at the same time are deemed to have been made in such order as the company or companies making them elect or jointly elect, or in the absence of such an election in such order as the Revenue may direct.

[*ICTA 1988, s 403A; F(No 2)A 1997, Sch 7 para 2; FA 2000, Sch 27 para 3*]

Attribution to overlapping periods. Where an apportionment falls to be made under *section 403A* to determine how much of an amount for a period falls to be attributed to a part of the period, the apportionment is generally made on a time basis according to how much of the whole period coincides with the part. However, where as regards some or all of the apportionments to be made in any particular case this would lead to an unjust or unreasonable result in relation to any person, the apportionments are, to the extent necessary to avoid injustice and unreasonableness, made in such other manner as may be just and reasonable. [*ICTA 1988, s 403B; F(No 2)A 1997, Sch 7 para 2*]. For 'just and reasonable' apportionment, see Revenue Company Taxation Manual, CT 2700a, 2700b.

De-grouping charge. See 9.47 CAPITAL GAINS for the effect on *ICTA 1988, ss 403A, 403B* of the application of the de-grouping provisions of *TCGA 1992, s 179*.

Consortia. The above rules apply *mutatis mutandis* to consortium group relief claims (see 29.27 below). Additionally the following limitations apply.

(i) Where the claimant company is a member of a consortium, the amount which may be set off against its total profits for the overlapping period is the lowest in that period of the following percentages of the surrenderable amount:

(A) the percentage (or average percentage) of the surrendering company's ordinary share capital which is beneficially owned by the claimant company;

(B) the percentage (or average percentage) of any profits available for distribution to the surrendering company's equity holders to which the claimant company is beneficially entitled; and

(C) the percentage (or average percentage) of any assets of the surrendering company available for distribution to its equity holders on a winding-up to which the claimant company would be beneficially entitled.

(ii) Where the surrendering company is a member of a consortium, the amount which may be set off against the total profits of the claimant company for the overlapping period is the lowest in that period of the following percentages of those total profits:

(A) the percentage (or average percentage) of the claimant company's ordinary share capital which is beneficially owned by the surrendering company;

(B) the percentage (or average percentage) of any profits available for distribution to the claimant company's equity holders to which the surrendering company is beneficially entitled; and

(C) the percentage (or average percentage) of any assets of the claimant company available for distribution to its equity holders on a winding-up to which the surrendering company would be beneficially entitled.

(iii) Where the claimant (or surrendering) company is a subsidiary of a holding company owned by a consortium, (i) (or (ii)) above applies by reference to the holding company rather than the claimant (or surrendering) company.

Terms used in (i)–(iii) are defined as above and as in 29.15–29.17 above and 29.27 below.

In determining the average percentage of a member's interest in a consortium, a weighted average taking into account the length of time involved will be used. (Revenue Pamphlet IR 131, C6).

[*ICTA 1988, s 403C; F(No 2)A 1997, Sch 7 para 2; FA 2000, s 100(1)(5)*].

Commencement. The above provisions generally apply where the accounting period of either the claimant or the surrendering company in relation to a claim ends **on or after 2 July 1997**. However, they do not apply where the overlapping period in relation to the claim would fall entirely before that date, and where the overlapping period begins before but ends on or after that date, the restriction applies only by reference to the part of the claimant company's accounting period beginning on that date (on the assumptions set out in *F(No 2)A 1997, Sch 7 para 9(4)(5)*). [*F(No 2)A 1997, Sch 7 para 9*].

Relief for or in respect of non-resident companies. Following the extension (from 1 April 2000) of group relief to non-resident companies carrying on a UK trade through a branch or agency (see 29.14 above), provisions are introduced effective from that date broadly restricting relief to profits and losses attributable to the UK branch or agency.

Losses, etc. available for surrender by the non-resident company for an accounting period are those attributable to activities which

(i) are not attributable to activities which are exempt under any double taxation relief arrangements (see 21.10 DOUBLE TAX RELIEF), disregarding any claim requirement, and

(ii) are attributable to activities the income or gains from which for that period are or (if there were any) would be brought into account in computing chargeable profits for corporation tax purposes.

There is also an exclusion for any amount corresponding to, or represented by, an amount which is allowable for foreign tax purposes against any 'non-UK profits', although this does not apply to amounts which are, or are an element in computing, profits exempted from that foreign tax. 'Foreign tax' for this purpose means any tax corresponding to income or corporation tax (including local and regional taxes), and any foreign tax provision by virtue of which the deductibility of an amount is dependent on whether or not it is deductible for UK tax purposes is disregarded. '*Non-UK profits*' are amounts (or elements in computing amounts) charged to foreign tax and not included in corporation tax total profits of any person for any accounting period.

Similarly the total profits for an accounting period against which relief may be claimed by a non-resident company are restricted to amounts comprised in the company's corporation tax chargeable profits for the period and not arising from activities exempt from corporation tax under any double taxation relief arrangements (and this restriction on the scope of total profits applies also for the purposes of the definition of 'non-UK profits' as above).

For these purposes, amounts are exempt under double tax relief arrangements if their effect is to cause any income or gains arising from the activities to be disregarded in computing chargeable profits.

[*ICTA 1988, s 403D; FA 2000, Sch 27 paras 4, 6*].

Relief for overseas losses of UK-resident companies. A loss, etc. of a UK-resident company is *not* available for surrender by way of group relief if it is 'attributable' to a branch or agency through which the company carries on a trade outside the UK, and all or any part of it is, or represents, an amount allowable against 'non-UK profits' (as above) of any other person for the purposes of foreign tax under the law of the territory where the branch or agency is situated. This restriction does *not* apply to amounts referable to life assurance business. 'Foreign tax' for this purpose means any tax corresponding to income or corporation tax (including local and regional taxes), and where, under a foreign tax provision, the deductibility of an amount is dependent on whether or not it is deductible for UK tax purposes, it is treated as deductible for the foreign tax purposes if, and only if, the UK-resident company is treated for the purposes of that tax as also resident in the territory in which the foreign tax is charged.

This provision applies for accounting periods commencing on or after 1 April 2000, and to losses, etc. of accounting periods straddling that date to the extent that they are attributable to the part of the period beginning on that date. Any necessary apportionments for this purpose are made on a time basis, or on a just and reasonable basis if time apportionment would not produce such a result.

A loss, etc. is 'attributable' to a branch or agency for this purpose if it would be available for surrender by way of group relief if it were computed only by reference to that branch or agency and by the application of the same principles as apply to a branch or agency through which a non-UK resident company carries on a trade in the UK (as above).

[*ICTA 1988, s 403E; FA 2000, Sch 27 paras 4, 6*].

29.21 *Example*

X Ltd incurs a trading loss in the year ending 31 December 2000 of £120,000. Throughout that period, it has two wholly-owned subsidiaries Y Ltd and Z Ltd. Y Ltd prepares accounts to 31 March, and has profits of £100,000 in the year ending 31 March 2000. Z Ltd prepares accounts to 30 September and has profits of £400,000 in the year ending 30 September 2000. No group relief claims or surrenders have been made other than those referred to below.

Y Ltd claims the maximum relief for the year ending 31 March 2000 by surrender from X Ltd.

Overlapping period three months to 31 March 2000.

Maximum loss available for surrender

$\frac{3}{12}$ × £120,000 = £30,000

Maximum profits against which loss surrendered may be set

$\frac{3}{12}$ × £100,000 = £25,000

Thus X Ltd surrenders losses of £25,000 to Y Ltd.

Z Ltd then claims the maximum relief for the year ending 30 September 2000 by surrender from X Ltd.

Overlapping period nine months to 30 September 2000.
Maximum loss available for surrender

	£
$\frac{9}{12}$ × £120,000 =	90,000
less amount previously surrendered (note (*a*))	25,000
	£65,000

Maximum profits against which loss surrendered may be set

$\frac{9}{12}$ × £400,000 = £300,000

Thus X Ltd surrenders losses of £65,000 to Z Ltd.

The balance of X Ltd's loss (£30,000) may be surrendered against losses of subsequent periods of Y Ltd and Z Ltd.

Notes

(*a*) As the overlapping period in relation to the surrender to Y Ltd falls entirely within the overlapping period in relation to the surrender to Z Ltd, the whole of the loss surrendered in relation to the earlier period is deducted from that available for the later period.

(*b*) Prior to enactment of these provisions, no deduction would have been made as under (*a*) above, so that the whole of X Ltd's loss would have been relieved under the claims and surrenders described above.

29.22 **Companies joining or leaving a group.** Prior to the commencement of the provisions described at 29.20 above (which apply broadly for accounting periods ending after 1 July 1997), the following special provisions applied to companies joining or leaving a group. The claimant and surrendering companies had to have been members of the same group at some time during the accounting period of the surrendering company and a corresponding accounting period of the claimant company. Where a company began or ceased to be a member of the group during its accounting period then, for group relief purposes, that accounting period is deemed to end and a new one to begin, any profit or loss being apportioned to those periods. [*ICTA 1988, s 409; F(No 2)A 1997, Sch 7 para 6*]. See also 9.47 CAPITAL GAINS. Apportionment is normally on a time basis, but it may be on a 'just and reasonable' basis where time apportionment would work unreasonably or unjustly (for which see Revenue Company Taxation Manual, CT 2700a, 2700b). [*ICTA 1988, s 409(2)*]. In its application to consortia (see 29.27 below) where two or more members claim or surrender relief, the basis of apportionment must be the same on each claim. [*ICTA 1988, s 409(4)*]. It should be noted that the anti-avoidance provisions relating to 'relevant arrangements' (see 29.23 below) are of wide scope, and may impinge upon normal commercial transactions.

Example

Assume the same facts as in *Example 2* in 29.19 above, except that A Ltd does not become a member of the group until 1 March 1996.

For group relief purposes, an accounting period of A Ltd is deemed to end on 28 February 1996 and another one to begin on 1 March 1996. A Ltd cannot surrender to B Ltd any loss attributable to the 'accounting period' to 28 February 1996, and to find the corresponding accounting periods of B Ltd one must look only at A Ltd's 'accounting period' from 1 March to 30 June 1996. B Ltd's corresponding accounting periods are therefore

(i) the three months ended 31 March 1996 and

(ii) the year ended 31 March 1997.

Assuming the time apportionment basis is applied (see above), the relief obtainable for these periods is

(i)	Total group relief available to B Ltd $\frac{4}{12}$ × £5,000	= £1,667
	Maximum relief for the corresponding accounting period $\frac{1}{4}$ × £1,667	= £ 417
	Total profits of B Ltd £1,000	
	Profits available for group relief $\frac{1}{3}$ × £1,000	= £ 333
	The relief available is therefore	£ 333
(ii)	Total group relief available to B Ltd $\frac{4}{12}$ × £5,000	= £1,667
	Maximum relief for the corresponding accounting period $\frac{3}{4}$ × £1,667	= £1,250
	Total profits of B Ltd £2,500	
	Profits available for group relief $\frac{3}{12}$ × £2,500	= £ 625
	The relief available is therefore	£ 625

Where **two or more claimant companies** became or ceased to be members of the same group as the surrendering company in its accounting period to which the claims relate, and the claimant companies were themselves members of a group, and during any part of that accounting period *none* of the claimant companies was a member of the same group as the surrendering company, then the maximum loss available for surrender is restricted to the proportion arising in the part of the surrendering company's accounting period during which at least one claimant company was a member of the same group as the surrendering company. However, (*a*) the restriction is applied separately in relation to each group if claimant companies are members of different groups, and (*b*) claims are not taken into account if claimant and surrendering company join or leave a group at the same time and one is a 75% subsidiary of the other, or both are 75% subsidiaries of another company, before and after that time. [*ICTA 1988, s 411(3)–(5)*].

Similarly, where a claimant company became or ceased to be a member of the same group(s) as **two or more surrendering companies** in its accounting period for which the claim is made, and the surrendering companies were themselves members of a group, and during any part of that accounting period *none* of the surrendering companies was a member of the same group as the claimant company, then the maximum of the profits which may be relieved under the group relief claim is the proportion arising in that part of the claimant company's accounting period during which at least one surrendering company was a member of the same group. (*a*) and (*b*) above apply equally in these circumstances, in relation to surrendering rather than claimant companies. [*ICTA 1988, s 411(6)–(8)*].

Example

G Ltd has a wholly-owned subsidiary F Ltd, and on 30 June 1996 acquires another such subsidiary, H Ltd. The figures for the year to 31 December 1996 are as follows.

G Ltd	Profit	£50,000
F Ltd	Profit	£12,000
H Ltd	Loss	£36,000

G Ltd and F Ltd can between them claim only the £18,000 of H Ltd's loss arising after it joined the group (the profits of the corresponding periods for G Ltd and F Ltd, £25,000 and £6,000 respectively, being sufficient to absorb the whole £18,000).

It should however be noted that these restrictions do not apply where one of the surrendering or claimant companies was a group member throughout the relevant accounting period (and the claim is not excluded from consideration by *section 411(5)*, see above). Where such a continuing group member existed, the overall limitation on relief did not apply. See now, however, 29.20 above.

These provisions are repealed by *F(No 2)A 1997, Sch 8 Pt II(14)* following the introduction of the wider anti-avoidance provisions in *ICTA 1988, ss 403A–403C* by *F(No 2)A 1997, Sch 7*, for which see 29.20 above.

Simon's Direct Tax Service. See **D2.645**.

29.23 Claims

Accounting periods ending on or after 1 July 1999 (self-assessment) [FA 1998, Sch 18 Pt VIII; FA 1999, s 92; FA 2000, Sch 27 para 11]

A claim to group relief under self-assessment must be included in the company tax return (or amended return) (see 55.3 SELF-ASSESSMENT) for the accounting period for which the claim is made. It must specify the amount claimed (which must be expressed in money at the time the claim is made) and the surrendering company. For accounting periods ending on or after 1 April 2000, it must also state whether any of the following:

(*a*) the claimant company;

(*b*) the surrendering company; or

(*c*) any other company by reference to which either those companies are members of the same group or the conditions for consortium relief are satisfied,

was not UK resident in either or both of the surrendering company's accounting period to which the surrender relates or the corresponding accounting period of the claimant company.

The claim must be made (and may be withdrawn) at any time up to the latest of

(i) the first anniversary of the filing date for the company tax return,

(ii) 30 days after closure of any enquiry into that return (unless the enquiry, being otherwise out of time, was limited (see 55.7 SELF-ASSESSMENT) to matters to which a previous amendment making or withdrawing a group relief claim relates, or which are affected by the amendment),

(iii) 30 days after notice of any amendment of that return by the Revenue following such an enquiry, and

(iv) 30 days after determination of any appeal against an amendment within (iii),

or at a later time if the Revenue allow it. See below (in relation to earlier accounting periods ending after 30 September 1993) for Revenue Statement of Practice SP 11/93 setting out the Revenue approach to the admission of late claims. SP 11/93 is, however, to be replaced by a new Statement of Practice before the earliest date on which a group relief claim under self-assessment can be late.

These time limits override the normal time limits for amendment of a company tax return. Withdrawals of claims must be made by amending the return, and a claim can only be amended by withdrawal and replacement by another claim.

A claim may be made after the surrendering company has left the group (*A W Chapman Ltd v Hennessey Ch D 1981, 55 TC 516*).

A claim may be made for less than the full amount available for surrender at the time of the claim, but is ineffective if it is for more than that amount. The amount available for surrender at any time is the total amount available under *ICTA 1988, s 403* (see 29.18 above) on the basis of the surrendering company's tax return, disregarding any amendment whose effect is deferred pending completion of an enquiry (see 55.7 SELF-ASSESSMENT), *less* all amounts for which notices of consent (see below) have been given and not withdrawn. Withdrawals are given effect before any claims made on the same day. Where claims are made on the same day for an aggregate amount in excess of the amount available for surrender, the Revenue determines which of the claims is to be ineffective to prevent an excess arising. In practice, they will treat as ineffective the claim(s) in the lowest amount(s) consistent with achieving this objective (see Revenue Booklet 'A Guide to Corporation Tax Self Assessment', para 8.4.5).

Claims may be made by more than one company in respect of the same surrendering company accounting period. [*ICTA 1988, s 402(5)*].

A claim requires the written consent of the surrendering company (and a consortium claim also that of each member of the consortium), which must be given to the officer of the Board to whom the company makes its tax returns at or before the time the claim is made, and a copy of which must accompany the claim. The consent notice must give the names and tax district references of the surrendering company and the company to which relief is being surrendered, the amount of the relief, and the surrendering company accounting period to which the surrender relates. It may not be amended, but may be withdrawn (by notice to the officer to whom the consent was notified) and replaced within the normal time limits (as above). Notice of withdrawal must be accompanied by the written consent of the claimant company, unless the withdrawal is the result of a reduction in the amount available for surrender (for which see below), and the claimant company must, so far as it may do so, amend its return accordingly.

See, however, below as regards simplified claim and surrender procedures.

Where the surrendering company has already made its return for the period to which the surrender relates, it must, at the same time as giving its consent, amend its return to reflect that consent. Where the consent relates to a trading loss for which relief has already been obtained by carry-forward, the surrendering company must (notwithstanding any time limits otherwise applicable) amend its return(s) for the subsequent period(s) in which relief was given for the loss to reflect the consent (relief for such periods being treated as given for carry-forward losses of earlier accounting periods before later ones).

Where there is a reduction in the total amount available for surrender (as above) below the amount for which consent to surrender has already been given, the company must, within 30 days, withdraw its consent (and may issue new notices of consent) so as bring the total of amounts for which consent is given within the total amount available. Copies of the withdrawal notices and any new consents must be sent to the companies affected and to the Revenue. If the company fails to take such corrective action, the Revenue may by written notice to the company give directions as to which consents are to be treated as reduced or eliminated to the extent necessary to achieve that objective (subject to appeal in writing by the company within 30 days of the notice to the officer by whom it was given), and must copy the notice to any claimant company affected by those directions. A claimant company notified of any withdrawal or new consent or Revenue direction must, so far as it may do so, amend its return for the period in question accordingly.

Where a claimant company becomes liable to tax in consequence of receiving a notice of withdrawal or new consent or Revenue direction (as above), and any of the tax is unpaid six months after the company's 'time limit for claims' (see below), the Revenue may, up to two years after that time limit, make an assessment in the name of the claimant company on any other company which has obtained group relief as a result of the surrender. The amount of the assessment is limited to the lesser of the amount of the unpaid tax and the amount of tax the other company saves by virtue of the surrender. The other company may recover the tax (and any interest thereon) from the claimant company. The company's 'time limit for claims' for this purpose is the latest of the dates in (i)–(iv) above on which the company could make or withdraw a group relief claim for the accounting period for which the claim in question was made.

An assessment may be made to recover group relief which in the opinion of the Revenue is or has become excessive. This is without prejudice to the making of a discovery assessment (see 55.8 SELF-ASSESSMENT) or to the making of adjustments by way of discharge or repayment of tax. As regards notices of assessment, time limits and appeals, the same conditions apply as in relation to discovery assessments. Where a claimant company fails, or is unable, to amend its return following receipt of a notice of withdrawal or new consent or Revenue direction (as above), an assessment may be made (if otherwise out of time) up to one year after the date of the notice (the date of the new notice if a new notice of consent follows a withdrawal notice).

The Corporation Tax (Simplified Arrangements for Group Relief) Regulations 1999 (*SI 1999 No 2975*) provide for a group of companies all, or substantially all, of whose tax returns are made to the same tax office to enter into special arrangements enabling an authorised company within the group to act for the group in relation to group relief claims. The authorised company may then, in a form provided or authorised by the Board, provide a written statement containing the information necessary for the amendment of company tax returns of the companies covered by the arrangements for the purpose of making or withdrawing group relief claims and surrenders. Group companies remain liable for any incorrect claim or return arising from the authorised company's statement. Consortium companies which can claim or surrender group relief may be included in the arrangements (and the authorised company may be a consortium company). For the detailed requirements as to the making of an application by an authorised company, and the consequences of entering into such arrangements, see *SI 1999 No 2975*. These arrangements replace and extend those available for pre-self-assessment accounting periods under Revenue Statement of Practice SP 10/93, 8 October 1993 (see 54.2 RETURNS). In particular, it is no longer necessary for all the companies included in the arrangements to have identical accounting periods.

See Simon's Direct Tax Service D2.630.

Accounting periods ending before 1 July 1999 [ICTA 1988, Sch 17A; FA 1990, Sch 15]

Claims to group relief can be made (and may be withdrawn) up to the later of

(*a*) two years from the end of the accounting period for which relief is claimed, and

(*b*) the date that an assessment for that accounting period becomes final and conclusive,

but not (except as below) beyond six years after the end of the accounting period. The Board have powers to extend those time limits and may admit late claims where, for reasons beyond the company's control, a timeous claim could not have been made. This would exclude for example cases of oversight or negligence of the claimant company; or of failure, without good reason, to compute the necessary figure; or of the wish to avoid commitment pending clarification of the effects of a claim; or of the illness or absence of an adviser to the company; or of the illness or absence of an officer of the company unless it arose at a critical time preventing a timeous claim, there was good reason why the claim could not be made before the absence or illness arose, there was no other person who could have made the claim timeously, and (in the case of absence) there was good reason for the officer's unavailability. An application for admission of a late claim should explain why the claim could not have been made within the statutory time limit, and must be made within three months of the event giving rise to the late claim. (Revenue Pamphlet IR 131, SP 11/93, 8 October 1993).

Where an assessment is under appeal when the six-year time limit expires, conditional claims may be made within the following three months. Such claims must be conditional, but only as to the amount claimed, on matter(s) specified in the claim which are relevant to determination of the assessment.

A claim may be made after the surrendering company has left the group (*A W Chapman Ltd v Hennessey Ch D 1981, 55 TC 516*).

Claims (and withdrawals) are to be included in the return (or amended return) under *TMA 1970, s 11* (see 54.2 RETURNS) for the period, and may be for less than the full amount available. Except in the case of conditional claims (as above), the amount of the claim must be quantified when the claim is made.

A claim requires the consent of the surrendering company, notice of which must be given by that company to its inspector no later than the time the claim is made. A copy of the notice (i.e. of the relevant section of form CT200) must accompany the claim. If the surrendering company has already made a return under *TMA 1970, s 11* (see 54.2 RETURNS) for the period concerned, an amended return or returns (as the case may require) must accompany the notice to the inspector. Where the consent relates to more than one conditional claim for relief (see above), it must specify an order of priority. The surrendering company may consent to claims by more than one claimant in respect of an accounting period [*ICTA 1988, s 402(5)*], but see 29.25 below.

See 54.2 RETURNS as regards joint returns relating to group relief claims.

Assessments (or amendments) to give effect to the above are not out of time if made up to one year after an assessment for the period to which the claim relates becomes final and conclusive, or, in the case of withdrawal of a claim, within one year from the date of the withdrawal.

See 29.18 above as regards amounts available for relief.

Where the claimant company's accounting period ends after 30 September 1993 but the corresponding accounting period of the surrendering company does not, the above rules apply to the claimant company, but not to the surrendering company. (Revenue Tax Bulletin August 1993 p 84).

See Simon's Direct Tax Service D2.649.

Anti-avoidance. *FA 1973, ss 28, 29* introduced anti-avoidance legislation (now in *ICTA 1988, s 410*) aimed at preventing artificial group relief schemes, although it should be noted that the provisions are of wide scope and may impinge upon normal commercial transactions. Relief is denied where two companies are members of a group and 'arrangements' are in existence by virtue of which one company could leave the group and join another group, or any person could gain control of one company but not the other, or a third company could succeed to the trade of one of the companies. Similar restrictions apply to consortium relief (and see Revenue Tax Bulletin December 1996 pp 372, 373 for application of the decision in *Steele v EVC International NV* (see 16.6 CONNECTED PERSONS) in relation to consortium 'arrangements', the effect of which was subsequently reversed by legislation). [*ICTA 1988, s 410*; *FA 1997, s 68*]. '*Arrangements*' for this purpose are those in existence during the relevant period irrespective of when they came into existence (*Pilkington Bros Ltd v CIR HL 1982, 55 TC 705*) and without regard to the extent of their implementation (*Irving v Tesco Stores (Holdings) Ltd Ch D 1982, 58 TC 1*). Arrangements which could not legally be carried out without variation of the underlying agreement were ineffective for these purposes (*Scottish and Universal Newspapers Ltd v Fisher (Sp C 87), [1996] SSCD 311*). The restriction of relief applies only to accounting periods or parts thereof during which the arrangements subsisted (*Shepherd v Law Land plc Ch D 1990, 63 TC 692*).

If the inspector 'has reason to believe' that 'arrangements' may exist or may have existed at any time material to the claim, he may require either company, in writing, to supply, within 30 days or such longer period as he may allow, a written declaration that such arrangements did not exist at any material time, and/or such information as he may reasonably require to satisfy himself whether such arrangements existed at any material time. [*FA 1973, s 32(1)(3)*].

'Arrangements' (and 'option arrangements', see 29.17 above) are the subject of Revenue practice and concession (see Revenue Pamphlet IR 131, SP 3/93, 13 January 1993, and Revenue Pamphlet IR 1, C10). Under these, the special rules relating to 'arrangements' are not applied to the following.

(I) Certain types of agreement regulating the affairs of companies which hold shares or securities in a commercial joint venture company, under which those shares or securities could be transferred following certain triggering events, until such a triggering event occurs. Such agreements will be of a kind under which remaining members are allowed or required to acquire the holding of a departing company, or a departing company is allowed or required to transfer its holding to remaining members. For detailed guidance on the manner in which shares will be transferred under such an agreement, and of the triggering events which may apply, see Revenue Pamphlet IR 1, C10.

(II) The use of shares or securities as security for a loan, e.g. a mortgage. The mortgage etc. will not constitute 'arrangements' until an event occurs which allows the mortgagee to exercise his rights against the mortgagor, provided that, prior to the occurrence of such an event, the mortgagee possesses only such control over the shares etc. as is required to protect his interest. If a default is remedied before the mortgagee exercises his rights, the default will not be regarded as having brought 'arrangements' into existence.

(III) Straightforward negotiations for the disposal of shares or securities in a company, before the point at which an offer is accepted subject to contract or on a similar conditional basis.

(IV) An offer to the public at large of shares in a business, unless there are exceptional features.

(V) Operations leading towards the disposal of shares or securities in a company, until any necessary approval by shareholders has been given, or the company's directors become aware that it will be given.

(VI) Where, following negotiations with a number of potential purchasers, the vendor concentrates on one, unless there were an understanding between them in the character of an option, e.g. if the offer, whether or not formally made, were allowed to remain open for an appreciable period, allowing the potential purchaser to choose the moment to create a bargain.

(VII) Company reconstructions requiring the approval of shareholders, until the necessary approval is given or the directors are aware that it will be given.

(I) and (II) above do not apply where the person standing to acquire shares, securities or control could (alone or with CONNECTED PERSONS (16)) dictate the terms or timing of the acquisition in advance of the triggering event. Membership of the joint venture company will not of itself result in members being 'connected'.

'Arrangements' (but not 'option arrangements') may exist even though not enforceable. If an agreement provides for the creation of specified option rights exerciseable at some future time, 'option arrangements' come into existence when the agreement is entered into.

(Revenue Pamphlet IR 131, SP 3/93, 13 January 1993 and Revenue Pamphlet IR 1, C10). (SP 3/93 supersedes SP 5/80, published on 26 March 1980, but states that, although some features of SP 5/80 are omitted or revised, 'this does not indicate a more restrictive approach on the part of the Inland Revenue'.)

The power of a Minister to direct a statutory body as to the disposal of its (or any subsidiary's) assets is not an arrangement for this purpose. [*ICTA 1988, s 410(7)*].

Simon's Direct Tax Service. See D2.646B.

29.24 **Payment for group relief.** If, in pursuance of an agreement between them, the claimant company reimburses the surrendering company by paying it an amount equal to, or less than, the relief surrendered by it as above, that payment is ignored in the corporation tax computations of both payer and payee and is not treated as a distribution or a charge on income. [*ICTA 1988, s 402(6)*].

29.25 **Other limitations on relief.** Relief may not be given more than once in respect of the same amount. [*ICTA 1988, s 411(1)*].

For accounting periods ending *before 1 July 1999* (see below), if the inspector discovers that too much relief has been given, he may make an assessment to corporation tax under Schedule D, Case VI in the amount which ought in his opinion to be charged. (This is without prejudice to any other powers of adjustment which the inspector may have.) [*ICTA 1988, s 412(3)(4)*]. Where an assessment is made under *section 412(3)* to recover excess group relief, the provisions of *TMA 1970, s 43A*, which allow additional claims to relief outside normal time limits, apply as they do where a discovery assessment is made under *TMA 1970, s 29* (see Tolley's Income Tax under Claims).

For accounting periods ending *on or after 1 July 1999* (to which self-assessment applies), see 29.23 above.

See also 29.18, 29.22 above.

29.26 **Relationship to other reliefs.** Group relief is deducted from the claimant company's total profits (see 29.18 above) before reduction by any 'relief derived from a subsequent accounting period', but as reduced by any other relief from tax (including relief in respect of charges on income under *ICTA 1988, s 338(1)* or in respect of non-trading deficits on loan relationships (see 43.3 LOAN RELATIONSHIPS). Total profits for this purpose are calculated on the assumption that that company makes all relevant claims to set trading losses and capital allowances against total profits under *ICTA 1988, s 393A(1)* and *CAA 1990, s 145(3)* respectively. See 44.2 LOSSES and 8.2 CAPITAL ALLOWANCES.

'*Relief derived from a subsequent accounting period*' means trading losses carried back under *ICTA 1988, s 393A(1)(b)*, capital allowances carried back under *CAA 1990, s 145(3)*, and, for accounting periods ending after 31 March 1996, non-trading deficits carried back under *FA 1996, s 83(2)* (see 43.3 LOAN RELATIONSHIPS). For earlier accounting periods, it also included certain 'relievable amounts' in respect of exchange losses carried back under *FA 1993, s 131(7)* (see 23.31 EXCHANGE GAINS AND LOSSES). [*ICTA 1988, s 407; FA 1993, Sch 18 para 4; FA 1996, Sch 14 para 22*].

Example

A Ltd (a group member) has the following, for the accounting periods shown.

	To 31 December 2000	To 31 December 2001
Case I (loss) brought forward	(£500)	—
Case I income/(loss)	£1,000	(£1,000)
Case III income	£500	£500
Charges paid	(£200)	(£200)

Group relief available to A Ltd will be subject to the following options and restrictions.

(*a*) *For the accounting period ended 31 December 2000*

(i) The loss brought forward and the charges paid must be relieved in priority to group relief. The maximum amount of group relief claimable will accordingly be the amount of profits on which corporation tax would otherwise be borne, i.e. £800.

(ii) If relief for this period is claimed under *section 393A(1)* for so much of the trading loss of the following period as cannot be relieved in that period, i.e. £500, such relief would be displaced by a group relief claim, and would then be available for carrying forward.

(*b*) *For the accounting period ending 31 December 2001*

Whether or not the company claims relief under *section 393A(1)*, no group relief is obtainable.

Simon's Direct Tax Service. See **D2.644.**

29.27 **Consortia.** Group relief is available where either the surrendering company or the claimant company is a member of a consortium and the other company is

(*a*) a 'trading company' which is 'owned by the consortium' and which is not a 75% subsidiary (see 29.15 above) of any company, or

(*b*) a trading company which

(i) is a '90% subsidiary' of a 'holding company' which is owned by the consortium, and

(ii) is not a 75% subsidiary of any other company, or

(*c*) a holding company which is owned by the consortium and which is not a 75% subsidiary of any company.

[*ICTA 1988, s 402(3)*].

No claim may be made where the shares in the other company (or its holding company) are held by the member of the consortium as trading stock. [*ICTA 1988, s 402(4)*]. Before 1 April 2000, the claimant company, the surrendering company and each member of the consortium must be UK-resident [*ICTA 1988, s 413(5) as originally enacted*] or resident elsewhere in the European Union or European Economic Area (following the ECJ decision in *ICI plc v Colmer*, see below). For accounting periods or parts falling after 31 March 2000, the residence of the companies is not relevant in determining whether the consortium relationship requirement is satisfied (and see further below), although the claimant and surrendering companies must each either be resident in the UK or carry on a UK trade through a branch or agency. [*ICTA 1988, s 402(3A)(3B); FA 2000, Sch 27 paras 1, 2, 6(1)*].

Relief is restricted, where the claimant company is the consortium member, to the proportion of the surrendering company's losses, etc. corresponding to the consortium member's share in the consortium; and where the surrendering company is the consortium member, to the relief of the proportion of the claimant company's profits corresponding to the consortium member's share in the consortium. This provision ceases, however, to have effect following the introduction of the provisions described at 29.20 above. [*ICTA 1988, s 403(9); F(No 2)A 1997, Sch 7 para 3*].

Relief may also be restricted by reference to the surrendering company's losses, and the claimant company's profits, of the corresponding accounting period (see 29.19 above).

A '*holding company*' is a company the business of which consists wholly or mainly in the holding of shares or securities in trading companies which are its 90% subsidiaries. [*ICTA 1988, s 413(3)*]. A single subsidiary will constitute its parent a holding company. (ICAEW Technical Release TAX 15/92, 23 October 1992, para 3). The House of Lords held in *ICI plc v Colmer HL, [1996] STC 352* that the UK legislation clearly required the subsidiaries to be considered to be UK-resident for this purpose, but on a reference to the European Court of Justice (*[1998] STC 874*) it was held that, in relation to EU subsidiaries, this requirement was incompatible with Community law. Following the ECJ decision, the House of Lords reconsidered and affirmed its decision in relation to companies resident outside the EU and EEA (*[1999] STC 1089*). Open cases where the existence of a group or consortium is established by reference to a company or group of companies resident in the EU or EEA may be settled on the basis that a group or consortium relationship does exist for tax purposes. (Revenue Press Release 26 February 1999). See now above as regards the removal of the residence requirement from 1 April 2000.

A '*trading company*' is a company the business of which consists wholly or mainly of the carrying on of a trade or trades. [*ICTA 1988, s 413(3)*].

A company is '*owned by a consortium*' if at least 75% of its 'ordinary share capital' is directly and beneficially owned amongst them by companies each owning at least one-twentieth, which are the 'members of the consortium'. [*ICTA 1988, s 413(6)*]. For this purpose, '*ordinary share capital*' means all the issued share capital of a company other than shares carrying a fixed rate of dividend with no further right to participate in profits. 'Issued share capital' does not include founder members' deposits in a company limited by guarantee (*South Shore Mutual Insurance Co Ltd v Blair (Sp C 215), 1999 STI 1681*).

A company is the '*90% subsidiary*' of another if not less than 90% of its ordinary share capital is **directly** owned by that other. [*ICTA 1988, s 838*]. The definition of 'ordinary share capital' given above applies. The parent company must also be beneficially entitled to at least 90% of profits available for distribution to the equity holders as such of the subsidiary and of assets similarly available in a winding-up. [*ICTA 1988, s 413(7)*]. See 29.16–29.17 above, and note that a holder of 'ordinary share capital' of a company may not qualify as an 'equity holder', for which a different definition of 'ordinary shares' applies. [*ICTA 1988, s 832(1), Sch 18*].

For the definition of a 75% subsidiary, see 29.15 above.

A claim for group relief requires the consent of all other members of the consortium. [*ICTA 1988, Sch 17A para 10(2); FA 1990, Sch 15; FA 1998, Sch 18 para 70(2)*].

The provisions outlined in 29.22 above are specifically applied to consortia by *ICTA 1988, s 409(4)*, apart from those relating to two or more claimant or surrendering companies joining or leaving a group. Those in 29.18, 29.19, 29.20 and 29.23–29.25 also apply. See also 29.29 below.

Simon's Direct Tax Service. See D2.642A.

29.28 *Examples*

(A) *Loss by company owned by consortium*

On 1 April 2000 the share capital of E Ltd was owned as follows.

	%
A Ltd	40
B Ltd	40
C Ltd	20
	100

All the companies were UK resident for tax purposes.

During the year ended 31 March 2001 the following events took place.

On 1.7.00 D Ltd bought 20% from A Ltd

On 1.10.00 C Ltd bought 10% from B Ltd

The companies had the following results for the year ended 31 March 2001.

		£
A Ltd	Profit	40,000
B Ltd	Profit	33,000
C Ltd	Profit	10,000
D Ltd	Profit	70,000
E Ltd	Loss	(100,000)

Consortium relief for the loss sustained by E Ltd would be available as follows.

	A Ltd	B Ltd	C Ltd	D Ltd
	£	£	£	£
Profits for the year ended 31.3.01	40,000	33,000	10,000	70,000
Deduct Loss surrendered by E Ltd	(25,000)	(33,000)	(10,000)	(15,000)
Chargeable profits	£15,000	—	—	£55,000

E Ltd

	£	Losses £
Loss for the year ended 31.3.01		100,000
Deduct Loss surrendered to A Ltd	(25,000)	
B Ltd	(33,000)	
C Ltd	(10,000)	
D Ltd	(15,000)	(83,000)
Not available for consortium relief		£17,000

Notes

(*a*) Loss relief for each member of the consortium is the lower of its share of the loss and its own profit for the overlapping period.

(*b*) The share of losses of E Ltd appropriate to each member is

		%	£
A Ltd	$40\% \times \frac{3}{12} + 20\% \times \frac{9}{12}$	25	25,000
B Ltd	$40\% \times \frac{6}{12} + 30\% \times \frac{6}{12}$	35	35,000
C Ltd	$20\% \times \frac{6}{12} + 30\% \times \frac{6}{12}$	25	25,000
D Ltd	$20\% \times \frac{9}{12}$	15	15,000
		100	£100,000

(B) *Loss by consortium member*

A Ltd, B Ltd, C Ltd and D Ltd have for many years held 40%, 30%, 20% and 10% respectively of the ordinary share capital of E Ltd. All five companies are UK resident and have always previously had taxable profits. However, for the year ended 30 June 2000 D Ltd has a tax loss of £100,000, followed by taxable profits of £40,000 for the subsequent year. E Ltd's taxable profits are £80,000 and £140,000 for the two years ending 31 December 1999 and 31 December 2000 respectively.

With the consent of A Ltd, B Ltd and C Ltd, D Ltd can (if it wishes) surrender the following part of its loss of £100,000 to E Ltd.

	£
Common period 1.7.99 to 31.12.99	
E Ltd's profit $\frac{6}{12}$ × £80,000 × $\frac{1}{10}$	4,000
D Ltd's loss $\frac{6}{12}$ × £100,000	(50,000)
Common period 1.1.00 to 30.6.00	
E Ltd's profit $\frac{6}{12}$ × £140,000 × $\frac{1}{10}$	7,000
D Ltd's loss $\frac{6}{12}$ × £100,000	(50,000)

The lower common figures for the two periods are £4,000 and £7,000.

Therefore, E Ltd can claim £4,000 of D Ltd's loss against its own profits for the year ended 31.12.99 and £7,000 against its profits for the year ending 31.12.00.

29.29 **Group/consortium relief interaction.** Special provisions apply where both consortium group relief ('consortium relief') (see 29.27 above) and other group relief ('group relief') (see 29.14 *et seq.* above) may be claimed in respect of the same losses, etc., i.e. where either the member of a consortium or a company owned by a consortium is a member of a group, or both are members of separate groups. Restrictions apply to the consortium relief available as follows.

Company owned by consortium also a member of a group.

(i) Consortium relief is available to members of the consortium in respect of losses, etc. of the company owned by the consortium only after deduction of all possible group relief claims thereon (but taking into account any claims made by group companies in respect of other losses within the group).

(ii) The profits of the company owned by the consortium against which (or against a fraction of which) relief for losses, etc. of members of the consortium may be claimed are first reduced by any group relief claims it could make in respect of losses, etc. of other companies in the group (but taking into account any claims made by other group companies in respect of such losses).

Member of consortium also a member of a group (referred to as the 'link company').

(*a*) Any consortium relief claim the link company could make (disregarding any deficiency of profits) may be made by any other company in the group (provided that it is not itself a member of the consortium). The provisions at 29.20 above (which limit relief by reference to overlapping periods of the claimant and surrendering companies) apply as if any period during which the claimant company was not a group member were not comprised in the overlapping period and were a part of the claimant company's accounting period which did not coincide with any part of the surrendering company's accounting period. (Prior to enactment of those provisions (broadly for accounting periods ending after 1 July 1997), the requirement was that the claimant company be a member of the group throughout the accounting period(s) which would be the consortium member's corresponding accounting period(s) under 29.19 above if it were itself making the claim.) The total consortium relief of the link company and other companies in the same group may not exceed that claimable by the link company (but disregarding any deficiency of profits in the link company).

(*b*) Consortium relief may be claimed by a company owned by the consortium in respect of losses, etc. of members of the same group as the link company, which are not themselves members of the consortium, as if the surrendering company were a member of the consortium at all times at which the link company is a member. The fraction of the profits against which the losses, etc. may be claimed is determined by reference to the consortium member's share in the claimant company in the surrendering company's overlapping period of loss, etc.. The provisions at 29.20 above (which limit relief by reference to overlapping periods of the claimant and surrendering companies) apply as if any period during which the surrendering company was not a group member were not comprised in the overlapping period and were a part of the claimant company's accounting period which did not coincide with any part of the surrendering company's accounting period. (Prior to enactment of those provisions (broadly for accounting periods ending after 1 July 1997), the requirement was that the surrendering company be a member of the group throughout the period.) The total relief which may be claimed by the company owned by the consortium in an accounting period from the link company and other members of the same group may not exceed what it could have claimed from the link company if the link company's accounting period was the same as that of the company owned by the consortium.

Where a *company owned by a consortium* has trading losses and other profits against which the losses could be set under *ICTA 1988, s 393(2)* or *s 393A(1)* (see 44.2 LOSSES), the losses, etc. available for consortium relief are reduced by the amount of any such set-off which could be claimed. This operates in priority to (i) above where applicable.

Companies joining or leaving a consortium. These provisions are **repealed** by *F(No 2)A 1997, Sch 8 Pt II(14)* following the introduction of the wider anti-avoidance provisions in *ICTA 1988, ss 403A–403C* by *F(No 2)A 1997, Sch 7* (for which see 29.20 above). Prior to repeal, consortium relief is restricted where a claim is made and either

(A) the losses, etc. of a company owned by the consortium are surrendered to a member of the consortium (or, under (*a*) above, to another member of the same group as the consortium member), or

(B) the losses, etc. of a member of the consortium (or, under (*b*) above, of another member of the same group as the consortium member) are surrendered to a company owned by the consortium,

and the member of the consortium joined or left the consortium during the accounting period of the surrendering company in which the losses, etc. arose (the 'principal accounting period'). The claim (the 'original claim') will be disallowed, and any necessary adjustments made, if another claim (the 'subsequent claim') is made, on the same date or later, which meets the following conditions. These rules in relation to consortium relief replaced those applying generally to group relief (see 29.22 above) where two or more claimant companies join or leave a group, and are in turn replaced by the general provisions in 29.20 above.

Where (A) above applies, the conditions are that the subsequent claim must be made by the original claimant (or, where (*a*) above applies to either the original or the subsequent claim, by any other group member); it must be for losses, etc. of a company owned by the consortium other than the company in respect of whose losses the original claim was made; and it must relate to losses, etc. of an accounting period falling in whole or part within the principal accounting period.

Where (B) above applies, the conditions are that the subsequent claim must be made by a company, other than the original claimant, owned by the consortium or a fellow group member; it must be for losses, etc. of a member of the consortium which is either the company in respect of whose losses the original claim was made or a company which is in the same group but is not itself a member of the consortium; and it must relate to losses, etc. of an accounting period falling in whole or part within the principal accounting period.

[*ICTA 1988, s 403(10)(11) as originally enacted, s 403ZA(3)(4), s 405, s 406, s 409(5)–(8), s 411(9); F(No 2)A 1997, Sch 7 paras 4, 5, 6; FA 1998, Sch 5 para 29; FA 2000, s 100(2)(5)*].

Simon's Direct Tax Service. See D2.644.

29.30 *Example*

A Ltd owns 100% of the share capital of B Ltd

B Ltd owns 40% of the share capital of D Ltd

C Ltd owns 60% of the share capital of D Ltd

D Ltd owns 100% of the share capital of E Ltd

D Ltd owns 100% of the share capital of F Ltd

This can be shown as follows.

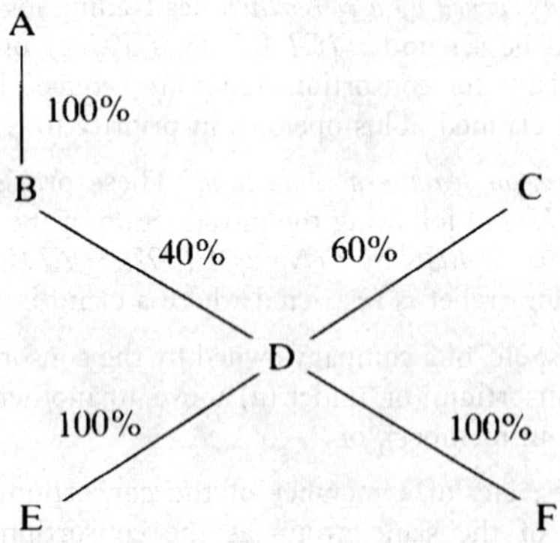

There are two groups, A and B, and D, E and F. D is owned by a consortium of B and C. This relationship has existed for a number of years with all companies having the same accounting periods. None of the companies has any losses brought forward.

The companies have the following results for year ended 31 July 2000.

A Ltd	£100,000	profit
B Ltd	£(30,000)	loss
C Ltd	£Nil	
D Ltd	£(20,000)	loss
E Ltd	£10,000	profit
F Ltd	£(3,000)	loss

E Ltd claims group relief as follows.

		£	£
Profit			10,000
Deduct Group relief: loss surrendered by F Ltd	note (*a*)	3,000	
Group relief: loss surrendered by D Ltd	note (*a*)	7,000	(10,000)
			—

A Ltd can claim group relief and consortium relief as follows.

		£	£
Profit			100,000
Deduct Group relief: loss surrendered by B Ltd	note (*b*)	30,000	
Consortium relief: loss surrendered by D Ltd	note (*c*)	5,200	(35,200)
Chargeable profit			£64,800

Notes

(*a*) Where a loss of a company owned by a consortium or of a company within its group may be used both as group relief and consortium relief, group relief claims take priority. In determining the consortium relief available, it is assumed that the maximum possible group relief is claimed after taking account of any other actual group relief claims within the consortium-owned company's group. As F Ltd has surrendered losses of £3,000 to E Ltd, D Ltd can only surrender £7,000 to E Ltd. Consortium relief is restricted to the balance of D Ltd's loss, i.e. £13,000. If E Ltd had not claimed £3,000 group relief for F Ltd's loss, D Ltd could have surrendered £10,000 to E Ltd by way of group relief and this would have reduced D Ltd's loss for consortium relief purposes to £10,000.

(*b*) Group relief available to A Ltd is the lower of £100,000 and £30,000.

(*c*) Consortium relief available to A Ltd is the lower of £70,000 (its profit as reduced by group relief) and £5,200 (40% of £13,000, see note (*a*) above). The relief available to A Ltd is the same as that which B Ltd could have claimed if it had had sufficient profits. A Ltd could also have claimed consortium relief in respect of F Ltd's loss if that had exceeded the £10,000 necessary to cover E Ltd's profit.

29.31 **Dual resident investing companies.** Group relief is not available for a loss, etc. of the company which would otherwise have been the surrendering company, if that company is a 'dual resident investing company'.

A UK resident company is a '*dual resident company*' if it is within the charge to tax under the laws of a territory outside the UK, whether it derives its company status under those laws, or because its place of management is in that territory, or because it is for any other reason regarded as resident in that territory, for the purposes of that charge. A dual resident company is a '*dual resident investing company*' in an accounting period if either:

(*a*) throughout that period it is not a '*trading company*', i.e. a company whose business consists wholly or mainly of the carrying on of a trade or trades; or

(*b*) although it is a trading company in that period, either:

(i) it carries on in that period a trade of which a main function is

(A) acquiring and holding, directly or indirectly, investments of any kind, including interests in companies which are CONNECTED PERSONS (16) within *ICTA 1988, s 839*; or

(B) paying charges on income, or

(C) making payments similar to charges but which are deductible in computing its profits, or

(D) making payments in relation to which debits fall to be brought into account under the LOAN RELATIONSHIPS (43) provisions as regards loan relationships, or

(E) obtaining funds in connection with any activity within (A)–(D) above; or

(ii) although not within (i) above, it carries on any of the activities within (i)(A)–(E) above

(A) to an extent which does not appear justified by any trade which it does carry on, or

(B) for a purpose which does not appear to be appropriate to any such trade; or

(iii) (before 1 April 1998)

(A) loan relationship debits and charges on income paid in the period exceed profits of the period determined as for group relief purposes, and

(B) those charges, etc. include a discount on a bill of exchange treated as a charge or (for accounting periods ending before 1 April 1996) a deep discount security income element (see 50.9, 50.7 PROFIT COMPUTATIONS), and

(C) the paying of those charges, etc. is a main activity of the company.

[*ICTA 1988, s 404; FA 1996, Sch 14 para 21, Sch 41 Pt V(3); FA 1998, Sch 5 para 37*].

Certain capital allowance restrictions apply to transactions between CONNECTED PERSONS (16) one of which is a dual resident investing company, as above. See also 8.3 CAPITAL ALLOWANCES, 9.19, 9.44 CAPITAL GAINS, and 44.10 LOSSES.

Simon's Direct Tax Service. See **D4.109**.

29.32 ARRANGEMENTS FOR PAYMENT OF TAX [*FA 1998, s 36*]

The Board may enter into arrangements with some or all of the members of a group of companies for one of those members to discharge the liabilities of each of those members to pay corporation tax for the accounting period(s) to which the arrangements relate. The arrangements may also cover interest and penalties and certain amounts treated as corporation tax liabilities. They do not affect the liability of any company to which the arrangements relate. A 'group' for this purpose is a company and all its 51% subsidiaries (i.e. companies more than 50% of whose ordinary share capital it beneficially owns, either directly or indirectly), together with 51% subsidiaries of those subsidiaries and so on.

See 48.1 PAYMENT OF TAX for the detailed arrangements.

Simon's Direct Tax Service. See **D2.843**.

29.33 **SURRENDER OF TAX REFUND, ETC. WITHIN GROUP** [*FA 1989, s 102; FA 1993, Sch 14 para 11; FA 1995, Sch 24 para 12(3); FA 1999, s 89(2)(3), Sch 11 para 3*]

Where two companies within a group jointly give notice to the inspector, a 'tax refund relating to an accounting period' which falls to be made to one of them may be surrendered in whole or part to the other. The surrendering company is then treated as having received on the 'relevant date' a payment equal to the refund (or part), and the recipient company as having paid on that date corporation tax equal to the amount of the refund (or part) (except that in relation to tax-based penalties under *TMA 1970, s 94(6)* or *FA 1998, Sch 18 para 18* for excessive delay in rendering corporation tax returns (see 49.2 PENALTIES, 55.3 SELF-ASSESSMENT) the corporation tax is treated as having been paid on the date of the notice referred to above). If the refund is of corporation tax and interest relating to that tax has been paid by the surrendering company, it is treated as having been paid by the recipient company. The notice referred to above must be given before the refund is made to the surrendering company.

Where the repayment to the surrendering company would have arisen from the carry-back of surplus ACT or losses or exchange losses, so that interest on tax repaid to the surrendering company would have been restricted (see 38.1 INTEREST ON OVERPAID TAX), a corresponding restriction applies in relation to the deemed payment by the claimant company.

The surrendering company accounting period to which the refund relates (the '*relevant accounting period*') must also be an accounting period of the recipient company. Both companies must be members of the group from the beginning of the relevant accounting period until the date of the notice referred to above.

A '*tax refund relating to an accounting period*' for these purposes means a repayment of corporation tax for the period, a repayment of income tax in respect of a payment received in the period, or a payment of the tax credit comprised in franked investment income received in the period. It also includes repayments of instalment payments (see 48.1 PAYMENT OF TAX).

The '*relevant date*' is the date on which corporation tax for the relevant accounting period became due and payable or, if later and if the refund is of corporation tax, the date on which the corporation tax was paid.

Any agreed payment by the recipient company to the surrendering company for a surrender as above (not exceeding the amount of the refund) is disregarded for tax purposes.

Simon's Direct Tax Service. See D2.706A.

29.34 *Example*

V Ltd has had, for some years, a 75% subsidiary, W Ltd, and both prepare accounts to 30 April. On 1 February 2000 (the due date), both companies make payments on account of their CT liabilities for the year ended 30 April 1999. V Ltd pays £250,000 and W Ltd pays £150,000. In January 2001, the liabilities are eventually agreed at £200,000 and £180,000 respectively. Before any tax repayment is made to V Ltd, the two companies jointly give notice that £30,000 of the £50,000 tax repayment due to V Ltd is to be surrendered to W Ltd. W Ltd makes a payment of £20,000 to V Ltd in consideration for the tax refund surrendered.

It is assumed for illustrative purposes that the rates of interest on overdue tax and overpaid tax are, respectively, 6.75% and 3.5% throughout.

If no surrender had been made, and all outstanding tax payments/repayments made on, say, 1 February 2001, the interest position would have been as follows.

		£
V Ltd		
Interest on CT repayment of £50,000 for the period 1.2.00 to 1.2.2001	£50,000 × 3.5% =	1,750
W Ltd		
Interest on late paid CT of £30,000 for the period 1.2.00 to 1.2.2001	£30,000 × 6.75% =	2,025
Net interest payable by the group		£275

The surrender has the following consequences.

(i) Only £20,000 of the repayment (the unsurrendered amount) is actually made, and is made to V Ltd together with interest of £700 (at 3.5% for one year).

(ii) V Ltd, the surrendering company, is treated as having received a CT repayment of £30,000 (the surrendered amount) on the 'relevant date' which in this case is the normal due date of 1.2.00, V Ltd having made its CT payment on time. V Ltd is thus not entitled to any interest on this amount.

(iii) W Ltd, the recipient company, is deemed to have paid CT of £30,000 on the 'relevant date', 1.2.00 as above. It thus incurs no interest charge.

(iv) The group has turned a net interest charge of £275 into a net interest receipt of £700, a saving of £975. This arises from the differential in the rates of interest charged on unpaid and overpaid tax. (The surrendered amount £30,000 × 3.25% (6.75 – 3.5) × 1 year = £975.)

(v) The payment of £20,000 by W Ltd to V Ltd, not being a payment in excess of the surrendered refund, has no tax effect on either company.

V Ltd could have given notice to surrender its full refund of £50,000 to W Ltd, instead of just £30,000. There would, in fact, have been no point in doing so, but if W Ltd had made its original CT payment later than the due date, so as to incur an interest charge on the £150,000 originally paid, a full surrender would have produced a saving as the amount surrendered would be treated as having been paid on the due date.

29.35 **DEMERGERS** [*ICTA 1988, ss 213–218*]

These provisions are intended to facilitate the breaking-up of large companies and groups of companies by exempting certain distributions of assets from the normal tax treatment (see 20 DISTRIBUTIONS). Enquiries concerning the demerger legislation should be addressed to Business Tax Division (Demergers), New Wing, Somerset House, London WC2R 1LB.

Simon's Direct Tax Service. See D1.5.

29.36 **Exempt distributions.** Subject to 29.50 below, the following are exempt distributions provided that they would otherwise have been distributions under the *Corporation Tax Acts* (see 20 DISTRIBUTIONS). (Revenue Pamphlet IR 131, SP 13/80, 14 October 1980).

(*a*) The transfer to all or any of its 'members' by a company ('the distributing company') of 'shares' in a '75% subsidiary' which

(i) are irredeemable, and

(ii) constitute the whole or 'substantially the whole' of the distributing company's holding of the subsidiary's 'ordinary share capital', and

(iii) confer the whole or 'substantially the whole' of the distributing company's voting rights in the subsidiary.

(*b*) The transfer by the distributing company to another company or companies of

(i) a 'trade' or trades (provided that no, or only a minor, interest in any such trade is retained), or

(ii) shares in one or more of its 75% subsidiaries. (In this case, the shares may be redeemable, but must otherwise meet the requirements set out in (*a*) above.)

To qualify for exemption, the transfer must be coupled with the issue by the transferee company (or companies) to all or any of the members of the distributing company of shares which

(A) are irredeemable, and

(B) constitute the whole or 'substantially the whole' of the transferee company's issued ordinary share capital, and

(C) confer the whole or 'substantially the whole' of the voting rights in that company.

The carrying on of the transferred trade or trades or the holding of the transferred shares must constitute the only or main activity of each and every transferee company after the distribution. This is not construed as meaning 'for ever after', but an intention that the conditions should cease to be satisfied at some later time would require consideration under the anti-avoidance provisions (see below). (Revenue Pamphlet IR 131, SP 13/80, 14 October 1980).

The distribution must be made wholly or mainly for the purpose of benefiting some or all of the 'trading activities' which before the distribution are carried on by a single company or 'group' and after the distribution will be carried on by two or more companies or groups. A distribution cannot be exempt if it forms part of a scheme or arrangements the main purpose or one of the main purposes of which is

(1) the avoidance of tax (including stamp duty), or

(2) the making of a 'chargeable payment' (see 29.50 below) (or what would be a chargeable payment if any of the companies were an unquoted company), or

(3) the acquisition (other than by members of the distributing company) of 'control' of that or of any other 'relevant company' or of any company in the same group as a relevant company, or

(4) the cessation of a trade, or

(5) the sale of a trade after the distribution.

[*ICTA 1988, s 213(1)–(11), s 218(1)*].

The Revenue's interpretation of several of these requirements is contained in Revenue Pamphlet IR 131, SP 13/80, 14 October 1980. In brief:

(i) the question of whether what is transferred constitutes a trade is considered from the transferee's point of view, and without regard to minor assets linked with trading assets. Whether only a part of the transferor's trade, or merely some of his assets, are transferred is not conclusive;

(ii) a 'minor interest in a trade' means around 10% or less, and does not include indirect involvement conferring no measure of control;

(iii) 'substantially the whole' means 90% or more;

(iv) the concurrent transfer of ordinary share capital to ordinary shareholders for consideration, or to preference shareholders, or of other shares or securities to ordinary shareholders, does not prevent relief being given under these provisions;

(v) 'after' in (5) means 'at any time after'.

For the treatment for income and capital gains tax purposes of trustees and beneficiaries where the trustees hold shares in a company which carries out an exempt distribution, see Revenue Tax Bulletin October 1994 pp 162–165 and Revenue Capital Gains Tax Manual, CG 33900 *et seq.*.

Simon's Direct Tax Service. See **D1.502**.

29.37 The 'distributing company' must at the time of the distribution be a 'trading company' or a 'member of a trading group' and resident in the UK. After the distribution (again not meaning 'for ever after' — see 29.36 above), it must continue to be a trading company or the 'holding company' of a trading group except where the distributing company is itself the 75% subsidiary of another, when the following conditions must be satisfied instead.

(*a*) The group (or, if more than one, the largest group) to which it belongs at the time of the distribution must be a trading group.

(*b*) The distribution must be followed by other exempt distributions within 29.36(*a*) or (*b*)(ii) above, as a result of which members of the holding company of the 'group' (or the largest group) to which the distributing company belonged at the time of the distribution become members of

(i) each and every transferee company to which a trade was transferred by the distributing company, or

(ii) each and every subsidiary shares in which were transferred by the distributing company, or

(iii) a company (other than that holding company) of which a company falling within (i) or (ii) above is a 75% subsidiary.

[*ICTA 1988, s 213(6)(b)(8)(e)(12)*].

See also 29.54 below.

29.38 A '*member*' of a company means a holder of ordinary share capital of that company. [*ICTA 1988, s 218(1)*].

29.39 '*Shares*' includes stock. [*ICTA 1988, s 218(1)*].

29.40 '*75% subsidiary*'. In determining whether a company the shares in which are transferred by the distributing company is a 75% subsidiary of that company, shares therein owned indirectly by the distributing company are to be disregarded. The subsidiary must, at the time of transfer, be either a trading company or the holding company of a trading group.

For all the purposes of these provisions, the parent company is to be treated as not owning shares held as trading stock either directly, or indirectly through another body corporate. [*ICTA 1988, ss 213(5), 218(2)(3)*].

29.41 '*Ordinary share capital*' is all the issued share capital of the company except that carrying a fixed dividend only. [*ICTA 1988, s 832(1)*]. 'Issued share capital' does not include founder members' deposits in a company limited by guarantee (*South Shore Mutual Insurance Co Ltd v Blair (Sp C 215), [1999] SSCD 296*).

29.42 '*Trade*' does not include dealing in shares, securities, land, trades or commodity futures, and '*trading activities*' are to be construed accordingly. [*ICTA 1988, s 218(1)*].

29.43 A '*group*', except for the purposes of 29.36(3) above, means a company and its 75% subsidiaries.

In 29.36(3) above, the term means a company and its 51% subsidiaries.

[*ICTA 1988, ss 213(11), 218(1)*].

See also 29.47 below.

29.44 '*Unquoted company*'. A company is unquoted if no class of shares or securities therein (disregarding debenture or loan stock or preferred shares) is listed in the Stock Exchange Official List and dealt in on the Stock Exchange. A company under the sole control of one or more companies which are not unquoted is outside this definition. [*ICTA 1988, s 218(1)*].

29.45 '*Control*' is as defined in *ICTA 1988, s 416(2)–(6)*, see 13.2 CLOSE COMPANIES.

29.46 '*Relevant company*' comprises, in relation to any distribution, the distributing company, any 75% subsidiary the shares in which are transferred and, in relation to a distribution within 29.36(*b*) above, any transferee company. Each company must be resident in the UK at the time of the distribution. [*ICTA 1988, s 213(3)(4)*].

29.47 A '*trading company*' is one the business of which consists wholly or mainly in the carrying on of a trade or trades, and a '*trading group*' is a group the business of the members of which (taken together) consists wholly or mainly in the carrying on of a trade or trades. [*ICTA 1988, s 218(1)*].

29.48 A '*holding company*' means a company the business of which (disregarding any trade that it carries on) consists wholly or mainly in the holding of shares or securities of one or more companies which are its 75% subsidiaries. [*ICTA 1988, s 218(1)*].

29.49 **Relief from tax on capital gains.** Any exempt distribution within 29.36(*a*) above is not a capital distribution for the purposes of *TCGA 1992, s 122*, and will not, therefore, give rise to a deemed disposal. The distribution is treated as if it were a reorganisation of the distributing company's share capital for the purposes of *TCGA 1992, ss 126–130*. [*TCGA 1992, s 192(2)*]. See Tolley's Capital Gains Tax under Shares and Securities.

An exempt distribution within 29.36(*b*)(ii) above is regarded as a scheme of reconstruction for the purpose of relief under *TCGA 1992, s 139* (see 9.6 CAPITAL GAINS), so that the transfer of assets to the transferee company is, in relation to corporation tax on capital gains, treated as giving rise to neither gain nor loss. (Revenue Pamphlet IR 131, SP 5/85, 21 May 1985).

Where a company ceases to be a member of a group solely because of an exempt distribution (within 29.36(*a*) or (*b*) above), no charge arises under *TCGA 1992, s 179* (see 9.47 CAPITAL GAINS). This relief is withdrawn if a chargeable payment (see 29.51 below) is made within five years after the exempt distribution; the time limit for making assessments is extended (where necessary) to three years after the making of the chargeable payment. [*TCGA 1992, s 192(3)(4); FA 2000, Sch 29 para 29, Sch 40 Pt II(12)*].

For the treatment of trustees and beneficiaries where the trustees hold shares in a company which carries out an exempt distribution, see Revenue Tax Bulletin October 1994 pp 162–165.

29.50 **Anti-avoidance.** If within five years after an exempt distribution there is a 'chargeable payment', that payment is treated as

(*a*) income chargeable under Schedule D, Case VI, and

(*b*) an annual sum payable otherwise than out of profits or gains chargeable to income tax for the purposes of *ICTA 1988, ss 349(1), 350* (requiring the payer to deduct and account for income tax at the basic rate) unless it is a transfer of *money's worth*, and

(*c*) a distribution for the purposes of *ICTA 1988, s 337(2)* and *s 338(2)* (distributions may not be deducted as charges on income or in computing income).

In no case is the payment to be treated as a repayment of capital for the purposes of *ICTA 1988, s 210* or *s 211* (see 20.10, 20.11 DISTRIBUTIONS). [*ICTA 1988, s 214(1); FA 1989, Sch 12 para 10*].

See also 29.49 above.

Simon's Direct Tax Service. See D1.503.

29.51 A '*chargeable payment*' is any 'payment' made by a 'company concerned in an exempt distribution'

(*a*) directly or indirectly to a member of that company or of any other such company; and

(*b*) in connection with, or with any transaction affecting, the shares of that or any other such company; and

(*c*) which is neither a distribution nor an exempt distribution nor made to a member of the same group as the paying company; and

(*d*) which is not made for *bona fide* commercial reasons or forms part of a scheme or arrangements a main purpose of which is the avoidance of tax (including stamp duty).

Where a company concerned in an exempt distribution is an 'unquoted company' (see 29.44 above), (*a*) above is extended to payments made by or to any other person in pursuance of a scheme or arrangements made with the unquoted company. If the unquoted company is

(i) under the control of five or fewer persons, and

(ii) not under the sole control of a company not within (i) above,

payments made in pursuance of a scheme or arrangements made with any of the persons referred to in (i) above are chargeable payments.

[*ICTA 1988, s 214(2)–(6), s 218(1)*].

29.52 '*Payment*' includes a transfer of money's worth including the assumption of a liability. [*ICTA 1988, s 214(6)*].

29.53 A '*company concerned in an exempt distribution*' includes every relevant company and any company connected with a relevant company (or with any other company which is so connected) at any time between the exempt distribution and the chargeable payment. In establishing connection, *ICTA 1988, s 839* (see 16 CONNECTED PERSONS) applies. [*ICTA 1988, ss 214(4), 218(1)*].

29.54 **Winding-up etc..** The requirement for a distribution company to be a trading company or the holding company of a trading group after the distribution (see 29.37 above) is removed in the following circumstances.

(*a*) **Distributions within 29.36(*a*) above**

Where the transfer relates to two or more 75% subsidiaries of the distributing company which is then dissolved without there having been, after the exempt distribution, net assets of the company available for distribution in a winding-up or otherwise. A company will, concessionally, not be regarded as failing to meet these conditions merely because it retains, after the distribution, sufficient funds to meet the cost of liquidation and to repay a negligible amount (i.e. £5,000 or less) of share capital remaining. (Revenue Pamphlet IR 1, C 11).

(*b*) **Distributions within 29.36(*b*) above**

Where there are two or more transferee companies, each of which receives a trade or shares in a separate 75% subsidiary of the distributing company, and the distributing company is dissolved without there having been, after the exempt distribution, net assets of the company available for distribution in a winding-up or otherwise.

[*ICTA 1988, s 213(7)(9)*].

29.55 **Returns.** Within 30 days after an exempt distribution, the distributing company must make a return to the inspector giving particulars of the distribution and the reasons why it is exempt. Where a clearance (see 29.57 below) has been given in respect of the distribution, the return need only refer to the clearance notification and confirm that the distribution is precisely that for which clearance application was made. (Revenue Pamphlet IR 131, SP 13/80, 14 October 1980).

If a chargeable payment is made consisting of the transfer of money's worth, the payer must, within 30 days of the payment, make a return to the inspector giving particulars of

(*a*) the transaction effecting the transfer, and

(*b*) the name and address of each and every recipient and the value of what is transferred to him, and

(*c*) any chargeable payment in money which accompanied the transfer.

In the case of a payment which is not a chargeable payment solely because it is made for *bona fide* commercial reasons and otherwise than for tax avoidance purposes (see 29.51 above), a return must be made within 30 days of the payment giving particulars of

(i) in the case of a transfer of money's worth, the transaction by which it is effected, and

(ii) the name and address of each and every recipient and the value of the payment made to him, and

(iii) the circumstances by reason of which the payment is not a chargeable payment.

[*ICTA 1988, s 216*].

See, however, 29.57 below.

29.56 **Power to obtain information.** If the inspector has reason to believe that a distribution which is otherwise exempt may form part of a scheme or arrangements within *ICTA 1988, s 213(11)* (see 29.36(1)–(5) above) he may give written notice to any relevant company or any person controlling such a company to supply the following information within such time as may be specified in the notice (but not less than 30 days).

(*a*) A written declaration stating whether or not, according to information which the company or that person has or can reasonably obtain, any relevant scheme or arrangements exist or have existed.

(*b*) Such other information as the inspector may reasonably require for the purposes of *ICTA 1988, s 213(11)* and the company or that person has or can reasonably obtain.

Similar powers exist, *mutatis mutandis*, if the inspector has reason to believe that a payment which is not otherwise a chargeable payment has been made in pursuance of such a scheme or arrangements as are outlined in 29.51 above. In addition, the inspector may require from any recipient of such payment the name and address of anyone on whose behalf it was received. [*ICTA 1988, s 217*].

If the inspector has reason to believe that a person has not delivered an account or made a return in accordance with the provisions outlined above, he may give written notice to that person to supply such information as the inspector may reasonably require for the purposes of *ICTA 1988, s 214(1)(b)* or *s 216(2)–(4)*. [*ICTA 1988, s 217(2)*].

29.57 **Clearance.** Application may be made for advance determination that a distribution is exempt or that a payment is not chargeable. Such application must normally be in writing and should be addressed to Inland Revenue, Room 100, New Wing, Somerset House, Strand, London WC2R 1LB. Where application for clearance is made in a single letter under *ICTA 1988, s 215* and one or both of *TCGA 1992, ss 138, 139* (see 9.6 CAPITAL GAINS) and *ICTA 1988, s 703* (see Tolley's Income Tax under Anti-Avoidance), the letter, with the requisite number of copies, may be sent to the address appropriate to any one of the clearances sought.

The application must fully and accurately disclose all facts and circumstances material for the decision of the Board, failing which any clearance granted is void. In general, it should include the following:

(i) The name of each relevant company (see 29.46 above), its tax district and reference, residence status, whether it is a distributing, subsidiary or transferee company (see 29.36 above) in relation to the proposed transactions, and whether it is a trading company or holding company (see 29.47, 29.48 above) under the demerger provisions definitions, or some other type of company.

(ii) Details of the group structure where appropriate.

(iii) A statement of the reasons for the demerger, the trading activities to be divided, the anticipated trading benefits and any other benefits expected to accrue.

(iv) A detailed description of all the proposed transactions, including any prior transactions or rearrangements in preparation for the demerger, making it clear why it is considered that all the relevant conditions are satisfied.

(v) Confirmation, together with all relevant information, that the distribution is not excluded from relief as part of a scheme (see 29.36 above), and a statement of the circumstances (if any) in which it is envisaged that control of a relevant company might be acquired by someone other than a member of the distributing company, or that a trade carried on by one of those companies before or after the demerger might cease or be sold.

(vi) The latest available balance sheets and profit and loss accounts of the existing companies (as listed at (i) above), and, where appropriate, a consolidated group balance sheet and profit and loss account, with a note of any material relevant changes between balance sheet date and the proposed demerger.

Where, exceptionally, it is not possible to explain the purpose of a demerger adequately in writing, the Revenue will invite the applicants to an interview.

(Revenue Pamphlet IR 131, SP 13/80, 14 October 1980).

The Board may call for further particulars within 30 days of the receipt of the application, or of particulars previously requested, and if these are not supplied within a further 30 days (or such longer period as the Board may allow) the Board need not proceed further on the application. Subject to this, the Board must notify its decision to the applicant within 30 days of the receipt of the application or of the particulars last requested. If the decision is unfavourable, or not communicated to him within the time limit, the applicant may, within 30 days after the receipt of the decision or after the expiry of the time limit, require the Board to place the matter before the Special Commissioners. The decision of the Special Commissioners is then treated as that of the Board.

Where a clearance has been given in respect of a payment which would otherwise be a chargeable payment, there is no obligation to make a return under these provisions (see 29.55 above).

[*ICTA 1988, ss 215, 216(4)*].

A company which becomes or ceases to be connected (see 16 CONNECTED PERSONS and 29.53 above) with another company may seek clearance for any payment which may be made at any time after it became, or ceased to be, so connected (whether or not there is any present intention to make any payment). No payment to which a clearance relates is to be treated as chargeable merely by reason of the company's being, or having been, connected with the other company. [*ICTA 1988, s 215*].

29.58 **Consequences of demerger.** The types of demerger detailed at 29.36(*a*) and (*b*)(ii) above result in a change of ownership of the subsidiary company demerged. If this is accompanied by a major change in the nature or conduct of the trade (which may result from those management changes the legislation is designed to bring about), the provisions of *ICTA 1988, ss 768, 768A* (see 44.13 LOSSES), *s 768D* (see 50.27 PROFIT COMPUTATIONS) and (for changes of ownership before 6 April 1999) *ICTA 1988, s 245* (see 3.10 ADVANCE CORPORATION TAX) may be triggered. Briefly, these act to prohibit the carry-forward of losses or surplus ACT arising before the change of ownership to be used in periods after the change of ownership. Since such restrictions contradict the intention of the demerger legislation, the Revenue will consider sympathetically the application of *ICTA 1988, s 768, s 768A, s 768D* and *s 245* where they apply as a result of an exempt distribution, and the underlying ownership of the trade is unchanged.

30 Housing Associations Etc.

Simon's Direct Tax Service D4.638 *et seq.*.

30.1 EXEMPTIONS FOR APPROVED ASSOCIATIONS [*ICTA 1988, s 488*]

Housing associations within the meaning of *Housing Associations Act 1985* (or the corresponding NI enactment) which are approved by the Secretary of State for the Environment, the Secretary of State for Scotland or Wales, or the Head of the Department of the Environment for NI (or under delegated authority) may claim that rent to which they are entitled from their members be disregarded for tax purposes. For (generally) 1999/2000 and earlier years, they may also claim that any yearly interest payable by them on let properties be treated as payable by the members individually, each member being deemed, for the purposes of *ICTA 1988, s 354* (relief for interest paid on loans for the acquisition or improvement of land), to be owner of the association's estate or interest in the property which he occupies. The total yearly interest paid by an association is apportioned in the ratio that rents bear to the total rent roll, and for this purpose a notional rent is attributed to each unlet property at the rate payable when it was last let by the association. Following the abolition of mortgage interest relief with effect, generally, for payments made after 5 April 2000 (see Tolley's Income Tax under Interest Payable), interest payable by a housing association is disregarded (in relation to the association). [*ICTA 1988, s 488(1)(2)(6)(7A); FA 1988, ss 43(3), 44(6); Housing Act 1996, Sch 3 para 8; FA 1999, Sch 4 paras 15, 18*].

Example

A housing association pays yearly interest of £2,000 in 2000/01. It has three properties, two of which are occupied and one vacant. The last rent charged for this latter property was £200 p.a.

Rents		£
Property A		200
Property B		400
Property C (notional)		200
Total rents		£800
Interest attributable		
Tenant of property A	$\frac{200}{800} \times £2,000$	£500
Tenant of property B	$\frac{400}{800} \times £2,000$	£1,000
Total interest attributed to tenants		£1,500

The balance of £500 interest paid by the association is treated as so paid for tax purposes.

Before 1 April 1998, where a claim is in force, no deduction for expenses within *ICTA 1988, s 25(3)–(7)* (repairs, maintenance, services etc.) may be made from the association's rental income. [*ICTA 1988, s 488(3); FA 1998, Sch 27 Pt III(4)*]. See now 50.27 PROFIT

COMPUTATIONS (and note that the mutual business provisions of *ICTA 1988, s 21C* do not affect the operation of *ICTA 1988, s 488*). [*ICTA 1988, s 21C(5); FA 1998, Sch 5 para 5*].

The Treasury may, by statutory instrument, make provision for the deduction of tax from certain interest payments by housing associations. See 31.5 INCOME TAX IN RELATION TO A COMPANY and Tolley's Income Tax under Deduction of Tax at Source.

30.2 APPROVED ASSOCIATIONS

A housing association may only be approved as in 30.1 above if certain conditions are satisfied.

(*a*) The association must be (or be deemed to be) duly registered under *Industrial and Provident Societies Act 1965* or its NI equivalent.

(*b*) Membership must be restricted to tenants or prospective tenants, and the grant or assignment of tenancies must be restricted to members.

(*c*) The association must satisfy such other requirements as may be laid down by the approving authority (under *ICTA 1988, s 488(8)*).

[*ICTA 1988, s 488(6)*].

30.3 CLAIMS

A claim must be made to the inspector within two years of the end of the accounting period to which it relates, in such form and containing such particulars as may be prescribed by the Board, but it is understood that there is no prescribed standard form for such a claim. An authority may be required from the association's members in relation to claims for 1999/2000 and earlier years for certain information in claims or returns to be used by the Board in relation to the claim. [*ICTA 1988, s 488(9)(12); FA 1996, Sch 20 para 28; FA 1998, Sch 19 para 48(3); FA 1999, Sch 4 paras 15, 18*].

For a claim to be effective, the following requirements must substantially be complied with for the period to which the claim relates:

(*a*) none of its property was let otherwise than to a member;

(*b*) none of its property was occupied other than by a member (or, for a maximum period of six months after a member's death, by his personal representatives); and

(*c*) all covenants required to be included in grants of tenancies by the approving authority (under *section 488(8)*) have been observed.

If the Board subsequently discover that these conditions (and those outlined in 30.1, 30.2 above) have not been fulfilled during the period to which the claim relates, acceptance of the claim may be withdrawn and the tax liability of all persons concerned adjusted accordingly. Similar adjustments are to be made, where necessary, on the acceptance of a claim. For accounting periods ending on or after 1 July 1999 (for which company self-assessment applies), such adjustments are made where, following an enquiry, the association's claim or company tax return is amended. [*ICTA 1988, s 488(4)(10)(11)(11A); FA 1996, Sch 20 para 28; FA 1998, Sch 19 para 48(2)*].

30.4 RELIEF BY GRANT

Housing associations as defined in *Housing Associations Act 1985*, which are not approved under *section 488* and do not trade for profit, may claim relief from corporation tax, by means of a grant. See *Haywards Heath Housing Society v Hewison Ch D 1966, 43 TC 321.* The claim must be made to the Secretary of State for the Environment or the Secretary of State for Scotland or Wales and the association must show that, throughout the period for which the claim is made, the association carried out the provision or maintenance of houses for letting or of hostels, and activities incidental thereto. The form of the claim and its supporting evidence are as may be required by the Minister, and the Board are authorised to disclose information to him. The terms and conditions of the grant are within the Minister's discretion, save that no relief is available for tax attributable to activities other than those specified above. These provisions do not extend to NI. A housing association must be registered to be eligible for relief. [*Housing Act 1988, s 54*].

30.5 **CHARGEABLE GAINS**

An approved housing association within *section 488* may claim exemption from corporation tax on chargeable gains accruing on the sale of any property which is or has been occupied by a tenant of the association. [*ICTA 1988, s 488(5)*]. A claim is made as under 30.3 above. [*ICTA 1988, s 488(9)–(11)*]. Disposals of land and other assets by a housing association (as defined in *Housing Associations Act 1985*) to the Housing Corporation, Housing for Wales (or the Secretary of State) or Scottish Homes under a scheme within *Housing Act 1964, s 5* or *Housing Associations Act 1985, Sch 7 para 5*, and subsequent disposals of those assets by the Corporation, etc. to a single housing association, are treated as taking place on a no gain, no loss basis. The same applies to

(*a*) transfers of land between the Housing Corporation, Housing for Wales (or the Secretary of State) or Scottish Homes and *registered* housing associations,

(*b*) transfers of land between such associations, and

(*c*) transfers under a direction from the Corporation, etc. of property other than land between such associations.

Similar relief applies to NI housing associations from 6 April 1984.

[*TCGA 1992, ss 218–220; Housing Act 1988, Sch 17 para 93; Government of Wales Act 1998, Sch 16 paras 77–80*].

A disposal to a registered housing association of an estate or interest in land otherwise than at arm's length may, on a joint claim, be treated as at a 'no gain, no loss' consideration, the transferor's acquisition being treated as that of the association on a subsequent disposal. [*TCGA 1992, s 259*].

30.6 **APPROVED SELF-BUILD SOCIETIES**

A self-build society (within the meaning of *Housing Associations Act 1985*) which is registered (or deemed to be registered) under *Industrial and Provident Societies Act 1965* and which is approved by the Secretary of State (or under delegated authority) may claim relief from corporation tax on rent receivable from its members and on chargeable gains arising on the disposal of any land to a member, provided that none of its land is occupied by a non-member. The relief applies, with appropriate modification, to NI self-build societies. [*ICTA 1988, s 489; FA 1996, Sch 20 para 29; Housing Act 1996, Sch 3 para 8; FA 1998, Sch 19 para 49*]. Claims are made as outlined in 30.3 above.

Disposals of land by unregistered self-build societies to the Housing Corporation, Housing for Wales (or the Secretary of State) or Scottish Homes are treated as being for such consideration that no chargeable gain or allowable loss arises. [*TCGA 1992, s 219; Housing Act 1988, Sch 17 para 93; Government of Wales Act 1998, Sch 16 para 79*].

31 Income Tax in relation to a Company

Cross-reference. See 29.2 *et seq.* GROUPS OF COMPANIES.

31.1 The corporation tax liability of a company is computed by reference to income tax principles, except as otherwise provided. [*ICTA 1988, s 9*]. See 50 PROFIT COMPUTATIONS.

31.2 *Income tax* is not charged on the income (other than income received in a fiduciary or representative capacity) of a company resident in the UK or, if the company is resident abroad, on any income which is chargeable to corporation tax (regarding which see 53 RESIDENCE). [*ICTA 1988, s 6(2)*].

31.3 **PAYMENTS BY A COMPANY ETC**

(*a*) **Annual payments.** Income tax at the basic rate is deductible from annuities, annual payments and certain royalties (and this applies whether the payments are made by a company or any other person). But certain annual payments made for non-taxable consideration do not have tax deducted and are not a charge for corporation tax purposes. [*ICTA 1988, s 125*]. See further details in Tolley's Income Tax (under Anti-Avoidance).

(*b*) **Interest.** Income tax at the lower rate (before 1996/97, the basic rate) is deductible from yearly interest of money chargeable to tax under Schedule D, Case III (as it applies for income tax purposes, regarding which see Tolley's Income Tax, under that heading) if such interest is paid

(i) *by* a company or local authority (otherwise than in a fiduciary or representative capacity), or

(ii) *by* or for a partnership of which a company is a member, or

(iii) *to* a person whose usual place of abode is outside the UK. [*ICTA 1988, s 349(2); FA 1996, Sch 14 para 18*].

Interest under the *Late Payment of Commercial Debts (Interest) Act 1998* (or under a contractual right but for which that *Act* would have applied) is *not* 'yearly interest'. (Revenue Tax Bulletin August 1999 pp 686, 687).

For advances made on or after 29 April 1996, interest payable on an advance from a bank (within *ICTA 1988, s 840A*, see 6.1 BANKS) is excluded where the person beneficially entitled to the interest is within the charge to corporation tax in respect of it, as is interest paid by such a bank in the ordinary course of its business. See 6.2 BANKS for earlier provisions and generally. See also 6.9 BANKS as regards certain payments of interest by banks and certain other borrowers. Interest paid to BUILDING SOCIETIES (7) is payable gross. [*ICTA 1988, s 349(3)(3A), s 476(9), s 477A(7); FA 1993, s 59; FA 1996, Sch 37 Pt II*]. See further details in Tolley's Income Tax (under Deduction of Tax at Source).

'*UK public revenue dividends*' (i.e. any income from securities which is paid out of the UK or NI public revenue, but excluding interest on local authority stock (see (i) above)) are, from 1 April 2001, payable under deduction of tax, subject to any provision to the contrary in the *Taxes Acts* (and see in particular 31.7 below as regards gilt-edged securities). The Board has wide powers to make regulations governing the accounting arrangements and modifying *ICTA 1988, ss 349, 350* in their application to UK public revenue dividends. [*ICTA 1988, ss 349(3C)(4),*

350A; FA 2000, s 112(2)–(5)]. For the deduction of tax from UK public revenue dividends by paying agents before 1 April 2001, see *ICTA 1988, ss 118A–118K* and regulations thereunder.

Interest paid on '*quoted Eurobonds*' (i.e. listed securities issued by a company and carrying a right to interest) is excluded from the above provisions for deduction of tax from interest from 1 April 2001. For payments made before that date, the exclusion applies only where the security is in bearer form and

(A) the payment is made by or through a person who is not in the UK; or

(B) where (A) above does not apply, either

 (i) the bond is held in a 'recognised clearing system' (as designated by the Board), or

 (ii) the beneficial owner of the bond is non-UK resident and is beneficially entitled to the interest.

The Board has regulatory powers to disapply (B) above unless certain declarations confirming eligibility are received by the payer or the Board has issued the appropriate notice. See *SI 1996 No 1779*. Before 29 April 1996, different requirements applied in relation to (B) above. [*ICTA 1988, ss 124, 841A; FA 1996, Sch 7 para 26, Sch 29 para 4, Sch 38 para 6, Sch 41 Pt V(19); FA 2000, s 111(2)(6), Sch 40 Pt II(17)*].

See *FA 1989, s 116* (repealed by *FA 1996, Sch 41 Pt V(3)*) as regards certain payments to Netherlands Antilles subsidiaries which were treated as being within *section 124*.

Broadly, designation by the Board as a 'recognised clearing system' requires that the applicant for designation is a substantial and reputable organisation which is internationally accepted in the Eurobond market as a clearing system for holding and trading in internationally traded Eurobonds for the institutions which participate in that market. The Cedel and Euro-clear clearing systems, the First Chicago Clearing Centre, the Bank of England European Settlements Office, the London Clearing House and the Depository Trust Company in New York have been so designated.

(*c*) **Copyright and design royalties and public lending rights.** Income tax must be deducted at the basic rate from such payments to an owner whose usual place of abode is outside the UK as if they were annual payments. A paying agent must deduct his commission (if any) before the tax is computed. [*ICTA 1988, ss 536, 537, 537B*].

But see 29 GROUPS OF COMPANIES for elections to pay intra-group and intra-consortium dividends without accounting for ACT and to pay charges without deducting income tax.

Simon's Direct Tax Service. See **A3.402** *et seq.*.

31.4 INCOME TAX DEDUCTIONS FROM PAYMENTS

A company must make a return to the Collector of Taxes of

(i) payments from which it was liable to deduct income tax and the income tax for which it is accountable, and

(ii) credits that it claims for income tax deducted from payments received.

[*ICTA 1988, s 350(4), Sch 16 paras 3, 5*].

Returns must be made for 'return periods' which end on 31 March, 30 June, 30 September, 31 December and at the end of an accounting period of the company. Such returns must be made within 14 days of the end of the return period. [*ICTA 1988, Sch 16 para 2*]. If a relevant payment is made outside an accounting period, a return must be made within 14 days of the payment. [*ICTA 1988, Sch 16 para 9*].

For return periods ending on or after 1 July 1999, the day appointed for the commencement of self-assessment for companies (see Revenue Press Release 25 November 1997), there is an additional requirement for amended returns where a company becomes aware of an error. [*ICTA 1988, Sch 16 para 7A; FA 1996, Sch 23 para 12*].

Credit can be claimed in a return for income tax deducted from payments received in the accounting period in which the return period falls. [*ICTA 1988, Sch 16 para 5*]. Certain payments made between 'related' companies, which, for accounting periods ending before 1 April 1996, are treated for corporation tax purposes as received on the date of payment (see 4.6 ANTI-AVOIDANCE), are also treated for this purpose as received on the date of payment, unless that date falls within the same accounting period as the actual date of receipt. [*ICTA 1988, s 341(4)(5); FA 1996, Sch 14 para 17*].

The company is liable to pay to the Revenue the income tax it deducted (or was liable to deduct) from payments (against which it may claim credit for income tax deducted from payments received) at the time by which the return is to be made, i.e. 14 days after the end of the return period (or 14 days after a payment which is not made in an accounting period). An officer of the Board has power to assess the company if he considers that a return is incorrect, or believes that a payment has not been returned. [*ICTA 1988, Sch 16 paras 4, 5; FA 1996, Sch 23 para 11*].

See 6.9 BANKS as regards returns of tax deducted from bank interest payments and 7.4 BUILDING SOCIETIES as regards building society interest.

See 39.6 INTEREST ON UNPAID TAX for the position if such income tax is not paid by the due date. The raising of an assessment on the company does not affect the due date of payment of the tax for interest purposes. [*ICTA 1988, Sch 16 para 4(2)*].

Return form CT61 is used for making returns required as above. Before the abolition of ACT (after 5 April 1999), it was also used for making ACT returns under *ICTA 1988, Sch 13* (see 3.4 ADVANCE CORPORATION TAX).

For the information which must be provided by the payer in relation to a distribution, see 20.18 DISTRIBUTIONS.

Simon's Direct Tax Service. See **D1.615** *et seq.*.

31.5 INCOME TAX SUFFERED BY A COMPANY

See 31.3 above which also indicates the extent to which income tax will be deducted from payments received by a company. Income tax is also deducted from certain 'relevant loan interest' payments by individuals to banks, building societies, insurance companies or local authorities. Such interest generally relates to loans for house purchase or improvement (for which relief ceases to be available after 5 April 2000) or for the purchase of a life annuity. See Tolley's Income Tax under Deduction of Tax at Source.

See 31.4 above for the relief that a company may obtain by setting off such income tax against its accountability to the Revenue for income tax deducted from payments by it in the same accounting period. For tax deducted from 'relevant loan interest', however, the company may claim repayment of the tax directly.

To the extent that relief is not obtained as above by a UK resident company (e.g. where income tax suffered on receipts exceeds income tax deducted from payments), such excess income tax suffered on receipts is set off against the corporation tax assessable on the company for the accounting period. If it exceeds the corporation tax payable, the company may claim a repayment. See 54.2 RETURNS, 55.5 SELF-ASSESSMENT. [*ICTA 1988, s 7(2); FA 1990, s 98*].

No payment received *from* another company resident in the UK is to be treated as made out of profits or gains brought into charge to income tax, and the obligation to deduct income tax is not affected by the fact that the recipient company is not chargeable to income tax. [*ICTA 1988, s 7(4)*].

31.6 *Example*

S Ltd, a company with two associated companies, prepares accounts each year to 31 October. During the two years ending 31 October 2000 it makes several annual payments from which basic rate income tax is deducted and receives several sums under deduction of basic rate income tax.

The following items are shown net.

	Receipts	Payments
	£	£
21.12.98		7,700
4.1.99	3,850	
9.8.99	7,700	
24.10.99	11,550	
25.3.00		7,700
14.8.00		9,360

The adjusted profits (*before* taking account of the gross equivalents of the above amounts) were as follows.

	£
Year ended 31.10.99	630,000
Year ended 31.10.00	860,000

S Ltd will use the following figures in connection with the CT61 returns rendered to the Collector of Taxes and will also be able to set off against its corporation tax liability the income tax suffered as shown.

Return period	Payments	Receipts	Cumulative payments less receipts	Income tax paid/ (repaid) with return
	£	£	£	£
Year ended 31.10.99				
1.11.98 to 31.12.98	7,700		7,700	2,300
1.1.99 to 31.3.99		3,850	3,850	(1,150)
1.4.99 to 30.6.99 (No return)			3,850	
1.7.99 to 30.9.99		7,700	(3,850)	(1,150)
1.10.99 to 31.10.99		11,550	(15,400)	
				—

Return period	Payments	Receipts	Cumulative payments less receipts	Income tax paid/ (repaid) with return
	£	£	£	£
Year ended 31.10.00				
1.11.99 to 31.12.99 (No return)				
1.1.00 to 31.3.00	7,700		7,700	2,300
1.4.00 to 30.6.00 (No return)			7,700	
1.7.00 to 30.9.00	9,360		17,060	2,640
1.10.00 to 31.10.00 (No return)			17,060	
				£4,940

Taxable profits

	Year ended 31.10.99	Year ended 31.10.00
	£	£
Adjusted profits as stated	630,000	860,000
Add Cumulative receipts £15,400 + net tax £4,600	20,000	
Deduct Cumulative payments £17,060 + tax of £4,940		22,000
Taxable profits	£650,000	£838,000

Tax payable

	Year ended 31.10.99	Year ended 31.10.00
	£	£
CT @ 31%/30% on profits	197,708	251,400
Deduct Income tax suffered	4,600	
Net liability	£193,108	£251,400

31.7 GILT-EDGED SECURITIES

See Tolley's Income Tax under Government Stocks for provisions of general application, and in particular for the general availability of gross payment of interest on gilt-edged securities from 6 April 1998. The following provisions apply to corporate bodies, and in particular to the gilt 'repos' (i.e. sale and repurchase) market introduced from 2 January 1996. For the general corporation tax treatment of gilts, see 43 LOAN RELATIONSHIPS.

Gross payment of interest. Where 'gilt-edged securities' of an 'eligible person' are held under arrangements in relation to which certain requirements are met (see below), they are deemed to have been issued on terms that interest on them is payable without deduction of income tax. This applies to interest paid on or after 2 January 1996 and falling due before 6 April 1998.

'*Gilt-edged securities*' are those specified in *TCGA 1992, Sch 9 Pt II*, and certain other sterling-denominated stocks and bonds so specified by Treasury order. See further Tolley's Capital Gains Tax under Government Securities. They are securities of an '*eligible person*' so long as:

(*a*) they are in the beneficial ownership of a company, local authority or local authority association or health service body (see 24.10 EXEMPT ORGANISATIONS), or of some other description of person prescribed for the purpose by Treasury regulations, which is beneficially entitled to the interest on them; or

(*b*) they are held so that the interest on them is exempt, either

(i) by charitable bodies (disregarding *ICTA 1988, s 505(3)*, see 11.9 CHARITIES), or

(ii) by exempt approved pension schemes or superannuation funds, or certain other such schemes, or by funds held for personal pension schemes or retirement annuity contracts; or

(*c*) they are assets of a Lloyd's member's premiums trust fund; or

(*d*) they are held so that the income is treated as arising to, or to the government of, a sovereign power or to an international organisation (as defined).

The requirements which must be met (as above) are that any conditions imposed by Treasury regulations are satisfied, and a declaration with respect to the satisfaction of those conditions made in accordance with such regulations by such person as may be determined under the regulations.

The Treasury has broad regulation-making powers both in relation to the conditions to be met (as above) and procedural requirements, and to impose obligations as regards the provision of information and documentation. There is provision for penalties not exceeding £25,000 for failure to comply with requirements under such regulations, or for fraudulent or negligent compliance.

[*ICTA 1988, s 51A; FA 1995, s 77; FA 1996, Sch 7 para 11; F(No 2)A 1997, s 37(5)(8)*].

Periodic accounting for tax. For payments of interest falling due **before 1 April 1999**, where the above arrangements apply for the gross payment of interest (and the general gross payment provisions of *ICTA 1988, s 50* (see Tolley's Income Tax under Government Stocks) do not), the Treasury may make regulations requiring periodic returns of the amounts of such payments and of the basic or lower rate tax thereon for (except in the case of certain payments of 'manufactured interest' within *ICTA 1988, Sch 23A* (see Tolley's Income Tax under Anti-Avoidance)) the year of assessment in which the payment is made, and providing for that tax to become due at the same time, and from the same person, as the return.

The Treasury has broad regulation-making powers to implement such accounting requirements, including provision for payments on account and for the set-off of payments treated as representative of interest on certain transfers of securities (see below).

Of the regulations made under these powers, *SI 1995 No 3224* (as amended) provides for periodic accounting for tax on interest paid gross under these arrangements (broadly within 14 days after the end of quarterly return periods) and for set-off against tax payable in returns under *ICTA 1988, Sch 16* (see 31.4 above) in certain circumstances. *SI 1995 Nos 3223, 3225, SI 1996 No 21* (as amended) and *SI 1999 Nos 623, 624* make further such provision in relation to insurance companies, Lloyd's underwriters and friendly societies.

Following the repeal of *section 51A* by *F(No 2)A 1997, Sch 8 Pt II(13)* with effect from 6 April 1998, periodic accounting continues to apply to gilt-edged securities issued on or after that date where the Treasury so directs (and has not subsequently directed to the contrary), and to be excluded from applying to gilt-edged securities issued before that date within the general gross payment provisions of *section 50*.

These provisions **cease to apply** to payments of interest falling due **on or after 1 April 1999**.

[*ICTA 1988, s 51B; FA 1995, s 78; FA 1996, Sch 6 para 4; F(No 2)A 1997, s 37(6)(8); FA 1998, s 37; SI 1999 No 619*].

Quarterly accounting for gilt interest is to be abolished from 1 April 1999 with the commencement of general quarterly accounting for corporation tax for large and medium-sized companies (see 48.1 PAYMENT OF TAX). (Revenue Press Release 25 November 1997).

To receive gilt interest gross as above, the securities have to be placed in a STAR account at the Central Gilts Office ('CGO') of the Bank of England through a CGO member. For an article setting out the procedures and the ways in which companies and other taxpayers are affected, see Revenue Tax Bulletin October 1995 pp 250–252.

The existing arrangements under which non-resident holders of certain gilt-edged securities may receive interest gross, and under which interest may be paid gross on National Savings Stock Register holdings, and other similar arrangements, are not affected by the above provisions, although it is open to holders covered by such arrangements to move to the STAR account system if eligible to do so. It should be noted that interest on strippable gilt-edged securities is payable gross to all holders and should be excluded from quarterly accounting returns (see Revenue Tax Bulletin June 1997 pp 436, 437). See also above as regards general gross payment of interest on gilt-edged securities from 6 April 1998.

For the changes, consequential upon the above provisions, to the anti-avoidance provisions relating to manufactured dividends and other payments and to the stock lending provisions, see Tolley's Income Tax under Anti-Avoidance and Schedule D, Cases I and II respectively. For the treatment of any price differential on the sale and repurchase of securities (including securities other than gilt-edged securities) as interest, see Tolley's Income Tax under Anti-Avoidance. These provisions were introduced by *FA 1995, s 80, ss 82–84*. See Revenue Press Release 27 March 1995 for a description of the operation of the proposed 'gilt repos' market and for the intended scope of the regulations under the legislation.

See generally Revenue Company Taxation Manual, CT 2370–2392.

Simon's Direct Tax Service. See A7.11.

31.8 LOCAL AUTHORITY SECURITIES

A local authority (as defined in *ICTA 1988, s 842A*) must (except as below) deduct income tax from payments of yearly interest at the lower rate (before 1996/97, the basic rate) for the year in which the payment is made. [*ICTA 1988, s 349(2)*].

Local authority securities issued in foreign currency. Interest on such securities issued after 5 April 1982 is, if the Treasury so directs, paid without deduction of income tax and exempt from income tax (but not corporation tax) in the hands of a non-resident beneficial owner. Where for repayment of the principal amount due under a security there is an option between sterling and one or more foreign currencies, these provisions apply only if that option is exercisable solely by the holder of the security. Income from such securities is not exempt merely because it is deemed to be income of a non-resident. [*ICTA 1988, s 581(1)–(3)*]. For securities issued before 6 April 1982, similar provisions apply where the securities were issued in the currency of a country outside the scheduled territories at the time of issue. [*ICTA 1988, s 581(6)*].

32 Industrial and Provident Societies

Cross-references. 30 HOUSING ASSOCIATIONS; 45.1 MUTUAL COMPANIES.

Simon's Direct Tax Service D4.625 *et seq.*.

32.1 The legislation outlined below applies to industrial and provident societies registered or deemed to be registered under *Industrial and Provident Societies Act 1965* or its NI equivalent. [*ICTA 1988, s 486(12)*]. See 32.4 below.

32.2 **SHARE OR LOAN INTEREST PAID**

Share or loan interest paid by a society is not a distribution (see 20 DISTRIBUTIONS). [*ICTA 1988, s 486(1)*]. Such interest payable by a society is treated as interest under a loan relationship (see 43.2 LOAN RELATIONSHIPS), provided that the society makes a return to the inspector, within three months of the end of the relevant accounting period, showing the name and place of residence of every recipient of more than £15 and the amount paid to him. For accounting periods ending before 1 April 1996, relief was by deduction from trading profits or, if the society did not trade, as a charge on income. [*ICTA 1988, s 486(1)(6)(7); FA 1996, Sch 14 para 30*]. See also 32.4 below.

Such interest is paid by a society without deduction of income tax (unless paid to a person whose usual place of abode is abroad, when income tax is deductible under *ICTA 1988, s 349*). [*ICTA 1988, s 486(2)(3)*]. It is chargeable on the recipient under Schedule D, Case III. [*ICTA 1988, s 486(4)*].

32.3 **AMALGAMATIONS AND TRANSFERS OF ENGAGEMENTS**

Assets disposed of by one society to another on a union, amalgamation or transfer of engagements are treated as disposed of, for the purpose of capital gains computations, at such a consideration as would secure that no gain or loss accrues on the disposal. [*ICTA 1988, s 486(8)*]. See also 32.4 below.

32.4 **CO-OPERATIVE ASSOCIATIONS**

The provisions outlined in 32.2, 32.3 above apply to co-operative associations established and resident in the UK with the primary objective of assisting their members in the carrying on of agricultural or horticultural businesses on land occupied by them in the UK or of fishery businesses. A 'co-operative association' is a body of persons with a written constitution from which the Minister of Agriculture, Fisheries and Food (or the Secretary of State for Scotland, or the Minister of Agriculture for NI, as the case may be) is satisfied that the body is 'in substance' a co-operative association. [*ICTA 1988, s 486(9)(12)*]. See also Revenue Pamphlet IR 1, C12, C13.

32.5 **TRADING LOSSES**

Trading losses brought forward under *ICTA 1988, s 393(1)* (see 44.2 LOSSES) may, concessionally, be set off against

(*a*) interest under Schedule D, Case III,

(*b*) annual interest received under deduction of tax, and

(*c*) amounts assessable under Schedule D, Case V.

(Revenue Pamphlet IR 1, C5).

33 Inland Revenue: Administration

33.1 The levying and collection of Corporation Tax on income and capital gains is administered by the **Commissioners of Inland Revenue** (normally referred to as 'the Board') Somerset House, London WC2R 1LB. [*TMA 1970, s 1(1)*].

Under them are local **Inspectors of Taxes,** permanent civil servants, with an expert knowledge of tax law, who are responsible for making most assessments, and dealing with claims and allowances, and *to whom all enquiries should be addressed.* The inspector responsible for dealing with the company's affairs will normally be the one for the District within which the company's registered office is situated.

The Inland Revenue maintains an Internet site (the address of which is http://www.inlandrevenue.gov.uk/home.htm) which provides access to detailed information on many aspects of the Revenue's activities, including publications, press releases and contact points.

33.2 **Collectors of Taxes** are also permanent civil servants and their duties for the most part relate only to the collection of tax. [*TMA 1970, ss 60–70*].

33.3 **Commissioners.** Except as otherwise provided, assessments (other than self-assessments) are made by inspectors but appeals against such assessments are heard by

(*a*) the General Commissioners (local persons appointed on a voluntary basis by the Lord Chancellor or, in Scotland, by the Secretary of State) [*TMA 1970, s 2; FA 1975, s 57; FA 1988, s 134(1)(4)*], or

(*b*) the Special Commissioners (full-time civil servants, being barristers, advocates or solicitors of at least ten years' standing, appointed for this purpose) [*TMA 1970, s 4; FA 1984, s 127, Sch 22 para 1*].

The Lord Chancellor has powers to provide for the General and Special Commissioners to hold office, and to be referred to, by a different name [*F(No 2)A 1992, s 75*], and to make regulations governing their jurisdiction and the conduct of appeals before them (and see now *SI 1994 Nos 1811–1813* and Tolley's Income Tax under Appeals). [*F(No 2)A 1992, Sch 16 paras 3, 4*].

33.4 **Amnesties and extra-statutory concessions, etc..** For the validity of amnesties by the Board, see *R v CIR (ex parte National Federation of Self-employed and Small Businesses Ltd) HL 1981, 55 TC 133.* INLAND REVENUE EXTRA-STATUTORY CONCESSIONS (35) have been the subject of frequent judicial criticism (see Lord Edmund-Davies' opinion in *Vestey v CIR (No 1) HL 1979, 54 TC 503* for a review of this), but their validity has never directly been challenged in the Courts. In *R v HMIT (ex p Fulford-Dobson) QB 1987, 60 TC 168*, a claim that the Revenue had acted unfairly in refusing a concession where tax avoidance was involved was rejected, but the taxpayer's right to seek judicial review of a Revenue decision to refuse the benefit of a concession was confirmed in *R v HMIT (ex p Brumfield and Others) QB 1988, 61 TC 589.* A decision by the Revenue to revoke its authorisation to pay a dividend gross was upheld in *R v CIR (ex p Camacq Corporation) CA 1989, 62 TC 651.* For a general discussion of the Board's care and management powers, and an example of a ruling by the Court that the Board had exercised a discretionary power reasonably, see *R v CIR (ex p Preston) HL 1985, 59 TC 1.* Where a discretionary power is given to the Revenue, it is an error in law to proceed on the footing that the power is mandatory (*R v HMIT and Others (ex p Lansing Bagnall Ltd) CA 1986, 61 TC 112*). See also *R v CIR (ex p J Rothschild Holdings plc) CA 1987, 61 TC 178*, where the Revenue were required to produce internal documents of a general character relating to their practice in applying a statutory provision.

The Revenue policy of selective prosecution for criminal offences in connection with tax evasion does not render a decision in a particular case unlawful or *ultra vires*, provided that the case is considered on its merits fairly and dispassionately to see whether the criteria for prosecution were satisfied, and that the decision to prosecute is then taken in good faith for the purpose of collecting taxes and not for some ulterior, extraneous or improper purpose (*R v CIR (ex p Mead and Cook) QB 1992, 65 TC 1*).

33.5 **Inland Revenue rulings.** For the extent to which taxpayers may rely on guidance given by the Revenue, see the letter from the Deputy Chairman to the various professional bodies following the decision in *R v CIR (ex p Matrix-Securities Ltd) HL 1994, 66 TC 587*. A code of practice in this area is to be published.

Following responses to consultation, plans for a system of pre-transaction rulings are not to be proceeded with for the time being, although the possibility of a selective scheme for product rulings is to be explored. These would relate to arrangements where the characteristics of participating taxpayers would not affect the ruling, such as financial instruments or savings plans marketed by insurance companies. There would be a charge for such rulings. A system of post-transaction rulings (without charge), to be given after the transaction has occurred but before the taxpayer makes his tax return, was introduced during 1997. See Code of Practice 10 (as revised April 1998) for the procedures in obtaining such a ruling.

33.6 **Taxpayer's Charter.** The Board of Inland Revenue and HM Customs and Excise have jointly produced a Taxpayer's Charter setting out the principles they try to meet in their dealings with taxpayers, the standards they believe the taxpayer has a right to expect, and what people can do if they wish to appeal or complain. Copies are available from local tax or collection offices and from local VAT offices.

A series of codes of practice, setting out the standards of service people can expect in relation to specific aspects of the Revenue's work, is to be published to support the Taxpayers' Charter. Each code will state the standards which the Revenue sets itself and the rights of taxpayers in particular situations. The first three, covering mistakes by the Revenue (see 33.7 below), the conduct of tax investigations and the conduct of inspections of employers' PAYE records were first published in February 1993, and are also available from local tax offices. Codes 4 and 5, relating to financial intermediaries and charities (see 11.1 CHARITIES) respectively, were first published in July 1993, copies being sent to the institutions concerned, and are available from FICO, St John's House, Merton Road, Bootle, Merseyside L69 9BB. Codes 6 and 7, on collection of tax generally and collection from employers and construction industry contractors, were first published in November 1994 and are available from local tax offices. Codes 8 and 9, on Special Compliance Office Investigations in cases other than suspected serious fraud and cases of such fraud respectively, were first published in January 1995 and are available from the Special Compliance Office, Angel Court, 199 Borough High Street, London SE1 1HZ. Code 10, on the provision by the Revenue of information and advice, was first published in June 1995 and is available from local tax offices. Code 11, dealing with enquiries into self-assessment income tax returns by local tax offices, was first published in July 1996, superseding Code 2 as regards such returns. It will be issued at the start of every such enquiry (except that in certain simple cases a short, single-page version will be issued). Code 14 (there currently being no Codes 12 or 13), dealing with enquiries into self-assessment company tax returns, was first published in July 1999, superseding Code 2 as regards such returns. It will be given to the company concerned at the start of every enquiry (except that where a simple enquiry is expected to be settled by a brief exchange of correspondence and not to involve penalties, a single-page version of the Code will be issued instead).

33.7 **Revenue error.** Code of Practice 1 (see 33.6 above), 'Mistakes by the Inland Revenue' (revised March 1996), gives general advice on the circumstances in which compensation may be claimed from the Revenue as a consequence of Revenue error. (The code also refers to waivers of tax under Extra-statutory Concession A19, see Tolley's Income Tax under Payment of Tax.) These fall into three categories.

(*a*) *Delays in replying to letters or other enquiries*, where, without good reason, there is a delay totalling six months or more (over and above the 28 days within which replies should normally be given).

(*b*) *Serious error*, e.g. the adoption of a wholly unreasonable view of the law, or the pursuit of enquiries into obviously trivial matters, or a simple or trivial mistake which the Revenue should have known could lead to far more serious consequences.

(*c*) *Persistent error*, even though not serious, e.g. where a mistake is continued after it has been pointed out, or the same type of mistake keeps being made, or there are a lot of unconnected mistakes within a year or in connection with a period of assessment.

In cases within (*a*), interest on overdue tax will be waived, and repayment supplement paid, for the period of the delay, and reasonable costs resulting from the delay reimbursed. Where (*b*) or (*c*) applies, the Revenue will reimburse reasonable loss or expense incurred directly because of the error, including professional and personal expenses and lost earnings, and incidental expenses such as postal and telephone charges. In exceptional circumstances, consolatory payments may also be made.

Repayment claims resulting from mistakes by the Revenue or any other Government department will be accepted up to 20 years after the year affected by the mistake.

33.8 **Revenue Adjudicator.** A taxpayer who is not satisfied with the Revenue response to a complaint has the option of putting the case to an independent Adjudicator for the Inland Revenue. The adjudicator's office opened on 1 May 1993, and considers complaints about the Revenue's handling of a taxpayer's affairs, e.g. excessive delays, errors, discourtesy or the exercise of Revenue discretion, where the events complained of occurred after 5 April 1993. Matters subject to existing rights of appeal are excluded.

Complaints normally go to the adjudicator only after they have been considered by the Controller of the relevant Revenue office, and where the taxpayer is still not satisfied with the response received. The alternatives of pursuing the complaint to the Revenue's Head Office, to an MP, or (through an MP) to the Ombudsman continue to be available. The adjudicator reviews all the facts, considers whether the complaint is justified, and, if so, makes recommendations as to what should be done. The Revenue will normally accept the recommendations 'unless there are very exceptional circumstances'.

From 1 April 1995, the adjudicator will also investigate complaints about Customs and Excise.

The adjudicator may be contacted at the Adjudicator's Office for the Inland Revenue and Customs and Excise, 3rd Floor, Haymarket House, 28 Haymarket, London SW1Y 4SP (tel. 0207–930 2292). A leaflet 'How to complain about the Inland Revenue' is obtainable from that office in a number of different languages.

The adjudicator publishes an annual report to the Board.

(Revenue Press Release 17 February 1993).

Leave to apply for judicial review of the rejection by the Adjudicator of a complaint concerning the use of information from unidentified informants was refused in *R v Revenue Adjudicator's Office (ex p Drummond) QB 1996, 70 TC 235.*

33.9 **Open Government.** Under the Government's 'Code of Practice on Access to Government Information', the Revenue (in common with other Government departments) is to make information about its policies and decisions more widely available. Revenue Pamphlet IR 141 ('Open Government') sets out the information to be made available, and how it may be obtained, and the basis on which a fee may be charged in certain circumstances to offset the cost of providing the information. Copies of the Code of Practice may be obtained by writing to Open Government, Room 417b, Office of Public Service and Science, 70 Whitehall, London SW1A 2AS (tel. 0345 223242). The Revenue has also published its own Code of Practice on the provision of information and advice (see 33.6 above).

As part of the Revenue's response to this process, most internal Revenue guidance manuals are now available for purchase (subject to the withholding of certain material under the exemptions in the Code of Practice).

33.10 **Employers' helpline.** A joint employers' telephone helpline has been set up on 0345 143 143 by the Inland Revenue, Contributions Agency and Customs & Excise for general enquiries about PAYE, national insurance and value added tax registration. The service is available from 0830 to 1700 on working days. Calls will be charged at local rates. See also 17.7 CONSTRUCTION INDUSTRY TAX SCHEME.

There is also a helpline for **new employers** on 0845 607 0143 (0800 to 2000 weekdays, 1000 to 1600 weekends), where the employer may register for PAYE, order an information pack on the operation of payroll tax and national insurance, and obtain help and information on payroll queries. Arrangements may also be made for access to business support teams and workshops providing further assistance.

33.11 **Use of electronic communications.** The Commissioners of Inland Revenue (and of Customs and Excise) have broad powers to make regulations, by statutory instrument, to facilitate two-way electronic communication in the delivery of information, e.g. tax returns (and see 54.13 RETURNS for earlier legislation to be replaced by such regulations), and the making of tax payments. The regulations may allow or require the use of intermediaries such as Internet service providers. They will have effect notwithstanding any existing legislation requiring delivery or payment in a manner which would preclude the use of electronic communications or intermediaries. [*FA 1999, ss 132, 133, Sch 20 Pt VII*]. The intention is to develop a range of electronic services which taxpayers can use as an alternative to paper if they so wish.

See *The Income Tax (Electronic Communications) Regulations 2000* (*SI 2000 No 945*), which make provision for electronic communications in relation to delivery of returns and other information under *TMA 1970, ss 8, 9* or *9A* (see Tolley's Income Tax under Self-Assessment) and payments or repayments in connection with the operation of those *sections.*

Incentives for electronic communications. Regulations may be made by statutory instrument by the Commissioners of Inland Revenue in relation to matters under their care and management (and by the Commissioners of Customs and Excise in relation to theirs) for the provision of incentives to use electronic communications. These may include discounts (or payments or repayments), or additional time for compliance or payment, or more convenient intervals for the delivery of information or the making of payments. Anything received by way of incentive is not regarded as income for tax purposes. The regulations may make provision as to the conditions of entitlement to incentives and for their withdrawal (which may be authorised to be made by direction), and may provide for penalties up to £1,000 for failure to comply with any specified provision. They may make different provision for different cases, and may make such incidental, supplemental, consequential or transitional provision as the Commissioners think fit. [*FA 2000, s 143, Sch 38*].

See 54.13 RETURNS for initial proposed incentives for making certain returns over the internet.

33.12 INTERNATIONAL EXCHANGES OF INFORMATION

ICTA 1988, s 815C (introduced by *FA 2000, s 146*) enables agreements with other governments for the exchange of information necessary for the purposes of income tax, corporation tax and capital gains tax (and corresponding taxes in the territory of the counterparty) to have effect. The Revenue may not, however, disclose information under any such arrangements unless they are satisfied that the counterparty is bound by, or has undertaken to observe, rules of confidentiality at least as strict as those applying in the UK. The power under *TMA 1970, s 20(1)–(8)(8C)–(9)* (see Tolley's Income Tax under Back Duty) to call for information relevant to income tax, corporation tax or capital gains tax liabilities is accordingly extended to liabilities to the corresponding taxes in a counterparty territory.

Similar provisions in relation to inheritance tax apply under *IHTA 1984, s 220A* introduced by *FA 2000, s 147.*

33.13 **Confidentiality.** For the confidential treatment of information supplied to the Revenue see Tolley's Income Tax under Inland Revenue: Confidentiality of Information.

34 Inland Revenue Explanatory Pamphlets

Simon's Direct Tax Service H5.

The Board publish explanatory pamphlets (with supplements from time to time) on Inland Revenue taxes, a catalogue of which is available. Those of particular relevance to companies are listed below, with the date of the latest edition in brackets, and are obtainable free of charge from any office of HM Inspector of Taxes, unless otherwise stated. Many of them (including those for which a charge is made) are available on the Inland Revenue's Internet site (see 33.1 INLAND REVENUE: ADMINISTRATION). As regards Inland Revenue internal guidance manuals, see 33.9 INLAND REVENUE: ADMINISTRATION.

IR 1	Extra-Statutory Concessions as at 31 August 1999 (January 2000).
IR 6	Double Taxation Relief for Companies (March 1994).
IR 12	Practice notes on the approval of occupational pension schemes. (Loose-leaf publication available only by subscription to the Pension Schemes Office mailing list (fee for year ended 31 March 1999 £20) through S R Communications Plc, Unit 9, Deptford Trading Estate, Blackhorse Road, London SE99 7TR (0207 463-8167)).
IR 14/15(CIS)	Construction Industry Tax Deduction Scheme (December 1998).
IR 20	Residents and Non-residents — Liability to Tax in the United Kingdom (December 1999).
IR 40(CIS)	Construction Industry: Conditions for getting a Sub-contractor's Tax Certificate (December 1998).
IR 46	Income Tax and Corporation Tax: Clubs, Societies and Voluntary Associations (January 2000).
IR 64	Giving to Charity: How Businesses can get Tax Relief (November 1993).
IR 68	Accrued Income Scheme (December 1990).
IR 69	Expenses: Form P11D — How to Save Yourself Work (April 1999).
IR 72	Inland Revenue Investigations: The Examination of Business Accounts (May 1995).
IR 73	Inland Revenue Investigations: How Settlements are Negotiated (January 1994).
IR 109	Employer Compliance Reviews and Negotiations (March 2000).
IR 116(CIS)	Guide for Subcontractors with Tax Certificates (April 1999).
IR 117(CIS)	A Subcontractor's Guide to the Tax Deduction Scheme (April 1999).
IR 119	Tax Relief for Vocational Training (September 1999).
IR 126	Corporation Tax Pay and File: A General Guide (July 1995).
IR 131	Statements of Practice as at 31 August 1999 (January 2000).
IR 136	Income Tax and Company Vans: A Guide for Employees and Employers (March 1994).
IR 137	The Enterprise Investment Scheme (July 1999).
IR 140	Non-resident landlords, their agents and tenants (April 1999).

IR 141	Open Government (March 2000).
IR 148	Construction Industry: Are your Workers Employed or Self-employed? (April 1999).
IR 150	Taxation of Rents: A Guide to Property Income (March 2000).
IR 155	PAYE Settlement Agreements (April 2000).
IR 160	Inland Revenue Enquiries under Self Assessment (April 1999).
IR 163	Millennium Gift Aid (September 1998).
IR 166	The Euro (December 1998).
IR 169	Venture Capital Trusts (February 2000).
IR 172	Income Tax and Company Cars (February 2000)
IR 173	Tax Credits — A Summary for Employers (Working Families' Tax Credit and Disabled Person's Tax Credit)(December 1999).
CGT 1	Capital Gains Tax: An Introduction (April 1999).
480	Expenses and Benefits — A Tax Guide (January 2000).
490	Employee Travel — A Tax and NICs Guide for Employers (January 1998).
CIS FACT 5	The New Construction Industry Scheme — A Handy Guide (October 1998).
CWG 1	Employer's Quick Guide to PAYE and NICs (January 2000).
CWG 2	Employer's Further Guide to PAYE and NICs (January 2000).
AO 1	How to Complain about the Inland Revenue (February 2000). (Also available in a range of languages, code RAO).
CB (1)	Setting up a Charity in Scotland (February 1993). (Obtainable from FICO (Scotland), Trinity Park House, South Trinity Road, Edinburgh EH5 3SD (tel. 0131–551 8127). Also obtainable in Gaelic (December 1995).)
CS 2	Trading by Charities — Guidelines on the Tax Treatment of Trades Carried on by Charities (April 1998). (Obtainable from FICO, St John's House, Merton Road, Bootle, Merseyside L69 9BB (tel. 0151-472 6106).)
Inst 1	A Modern System for Corporation Tax Payments — A Guide to Quarterly Instalment Payments (November 1998).
SVD 1	Shares Valuation Division — An Introduction (May 1999).
—	A Guide to Corporation Tax Self-Assessment (April 1999). (Obtainable from Inland Revenue Library, Room 28, New Wing, Somerset House, London WC2R 1LB.) Price £15.
—	The euro — Tax and national insurance options for UK businesses from 1 January 1999 (January 1999).
—	Guidance notes on the provisions of *ICTA 1988, Pt XVII, Ch IV* (Controlled Foreign Companies). (Obtainable from Inland Revenue Reference Library, Room 28, New Wing, Somerset House, Strand, London WC2R 1LB). Price £10.00.

— Guidelines on the tax treatment of disaster funds, giving guidelines on the organisation of disaster appeal funds. (Obtainable from Customer Services Manager, FICO, St John's House, Merton Road, Bootle, Merseyside L69 9BB (tel. 0151–472 6106)). Free.

— Fund-raising for charity, giving guidance on the operation of Extra-statutory Concession C4 (see 11.6 CHARITIES). (Obtainable from Customer Services Manager, FICO, St John's House, Merton Road, Bootle, Merseyside L69 9BB (tel. 0151–472 6106)). Free.

— Codes of Practice. See 33.6 INLAND REVENUE: ADMINISTRATION.

— Explanatory Statement on Exchange Gains and Losses and Financial Instruments. (Obtainable from Reference Library, New Wing, Somerset House, London WC2R 1LB). Price £4.00.

'Appeals and Other Proceedings before the Special Commissioners' (October 1994) dealing with procedural and other points is available free of charge from the Clerk to the Special Commissioners, 15/29 Bedford Avenue, London WC1B 3AS (tel. 0207–631 4242).

The Board also issue Concessions, Press Releases and Statements of Practice, summaries of, and references to, which are included in the following three chapters and elsewhere under the appropriate chapter heading. A Revenue Tax Bulletin is also published bi-monthly (annual subscription £22), relevant items from which are referred to in the appropriate chapter.

35 Inland Revenue Extra-Statutory Concessions

Simon's Direct Tax Service H4.

The following is a summary of the concessions applicable to companies published in Revenue Pamphlet IR 1 (2000) or subsequently announced. It should be borne in mind that in a particular case there may be special circumstances which will require to be taken into account in considering the application of a concession. A concession will not be given in any case where an attempt is made to use it for tax avoidance.

See also 33.4 INLAND REVENUE: ADMINISTRATION.

B1 **Machinery and plant: changes from 'renewals' to the capital allowances basis.** Capital allowances may be claimed on expenditure which has been the subject of a renewals allowance, provided that all items of the same class are changed to the new basis. See Tolley's Income Tax under Capital Allowances.

B3 **Industrial buildings allowance: private roads on industrial trading estates.** Allowances are given to the owner of an industrial trading estate for the cost of providing private roads if (although he does not carry on a qualifying trade) the lessees of the estate are carrying on qualifying trades. Now superseded by *CAA 1990, s 18(8)*. See Tolley's Income Tax under Capital Allowances.

B4 **Maintenance and repairs of property obviated by alterations etc.: Schedule A assessments.** The estimated cost is allowed, provided that the alterations do not amount to reconstruction, and that there is no change of use rendering such maintenance and repairs unnecessary. See 50.26 PROFIT COMPUTATIONS.

B5 **Maintenance expenses of owner-occupied farms not carried on on a commercial basis.** Where a loss claim against general income is precluded under *ICTA 1988, s 393A(3)* or *ICTA 1988, s 397* (see 44.9, 44.14 LOSSES), relief for the cost of maintenance, repairs and insurance of agricultural land and buildings is granted as under *ICTA 1988, s 33*. See 50.26 PROFIT COMPUTATIONS. One third of the relevant expenditure on a farmhouse is regarded as agricultural and the rest as domestic.

B7 **Benevolent gifts by traders** may be allowable trading expenses. See 50.6 PROFIT COMPUTATIONS.

B8 **Double taxation relief: income consisting of royalties and know-how payments.** Payments made by an overseas resident to a UK trader for the use of copyright etc. are treated as arising outside the UK except insofar as they represent consideration for services (other than merely incidental services) rendered in the UK by the recipient to the payer. See Tolley's Income Tax under Double Tax Relief.

B9 **Bank interest received, and profits on discounting transactions, etc.** by charities are exempt, as is overseas income not otherwise relieved. Superseded by *FA 1996, s 146*. See 11.3, 11.4, 11.6 CHARITIES.

B10 **Income of contemplative religious communities, or of their members,** which is paid into the common fund of such communities which are not charities, is regarded as income of each member up to £2,730 each for 1993/94 (£2,669 for 1992/93, £2,619 for 1991/92, £2,518 for 1990/91, £2,327 for 1989/90, £2,142 for 1988/89 and £1,986 for 1987/88). For 1995/96 and subsequent years, the allowable figure is set at the basic personal allowance for the year. Where the aggregate of 'allowable figures' exceeds income of the community, the excess may be set against chargeable gains of that or (in the case of an excess arising in a year up to and including 1994/95) a subsequent year.

35 Inland Revenue Extra-Statutory Concessions

B11 **Compensation for the compulsory slaughter of farm animals.** Provided that no election for the Herd Basis (see Tolley's Income Tax) is in force in respect of the animals, the profit attributable to the compensation (calculated as required in the Concession) may be spread over the three years following that in which the slaughter took place.

B13 **Untaxed interest paid to non-residents.** The income tax liability in respect of such interest is not sought to be recovered except by way of set-off in a claim to relief in respect of tax income from UK sources, provided that it is not chargeable in the name of a trustee or of a branch or agency having the management and control of the interest. This concession *does not apply* to corporation tax chargeable on the income of the UK branch or agency of a non-resident company or to income tax chargeable on the profits of a UK trade. It does, however, apply equally to discounts, to disposals of certificates of deposit, to building society dividends paid gross, to interest on quoted Eurobonds, to the 'income elements' chargeable in respect of a deep discount security, to 'deep gains' within *FA 1989, Sch 11* and to amounts representing interest on general client accounts. See Tolley's Income Tax under Overseas Matters.

B15 **Borrowing and lending of securities** with repayment in other securities of the same description is not a disposal for either Schedule D, Case I or capital gains purposes where it is standard practice designed to preserve a fluid market in securities. Extended to overseas securities lent in overseas market provided specific prior approval obtained from Revenue. Now superseded by *ICTA 1988, s 129*. See Tolley's Income Tax under Schedule D, Cases I and II.

B16 **Fire safety: capital expenditure incurred on certain trade premises (a) in Northern Ireland and (b) by lessors**

(*a*) Notwithstanding that *Fire Precautions Act 1971* (and, consequently, *CAA 1990, s 69(1)*) does not apply to NI, relief is generally given on the same basis as in Great Britain.

Where the expenditure qualifies for relief under *CAA 1990, s 7* (hotel buildings allowance), it may nevertheless be treated as above, provided that the claimant renounces his relief under *s 7*.

(*b*) Relief is allowed where the lessor incurs the expenditure himself, if similar expenditure by the tenant or licensee would have qualified for relief.

See Tolley's Income Tax under Capital Allowances.

B17 **Capital allowances: sale of invented patent to an associate.** Where an inventor sells the patent rights in his invention to a company which he controls at an undervalue, an assessment on the seller is restricted to the actual sale price provided that the purchaser undertakes to restrict its capital allowances claim to that amount. Applies to capital gains also with purchasing company's agreement. See Tolley's Income Tax under Capital Allowances.

B18 **Payments out of discretionary trusts.** Certain allowances and reliefs to which a beneficiary would have been entitled, had the beneficiary received directly the income out of which the payment was made, may be claimed as if that income had been so received. See Tolley's Income Tax under Settlements.

B19 **Capital allowances for buildings: balancing charge after cessation of trade.** Trading losses unused prior to the cessation of a trade may be set against any balancing charge arising after the cessation in respect of an industrial building, qualifying hotel or commercial building in an enterprise zone. Now superseded by *CAA 1990, s 15A*, introduced by *FA 1996, Sch 39 para 1(2)(4)*. See 44.4 LOSSES and Tolley's Income Tax under Capital Allowances.

B20 **Capital allowances for buildings: sales by property developers of buildings which have been let.** Where an industrial building, qualifying hotel or commercial building in an enterprise zone is sold by a person whose trade consists of the construction for sale of buildings, and has in the meanwhile been occupied by a tenant, writing-down allowances are concessionally made to the purchaser on the amount of the purchase price (or the construction cost if less) as if the vendor's expenditure were on capital rather than revenue account. Now superseded by *CAA 1990, s 10(4)(5)*. See Tolley's Income Tax under Capital Allowances.

B25 **Schedule D, Case V losses.** Deficiencies of income from lettings of overseas property, including caravans and houseboats, may be carried forward against future income from the same property. (Obsolete for 1998/99 onwards.) See Tolley's Income Tax under Schedule D, Cases IV and V.

B27 **Approved employee share schemes: jointly owned companies.** A scheme operated by a jointly owned company may nevertheless be granted approval. See Tolley's Income Tax under Share Incentives and Options.

B28 **Leased cars costing over £12,000: rebate of hire charges** will be treated as non-taxable in the same proportion as the hire charges themselves were disallowed under *CAA 1990, s 35(2)*. Now superseded by *section 35(2A)*, introduced by *FA 1996, Sch 39 para 1(3)(4)*. See Tolley's Income Tax under Capital Allowances.

B29 **Treatment of income from caravan sites where there is both trading and associated letting income.** In such circumstances, letting income from caravans and caravan pitch sites may be treated as income of the trade. See 50.26 PROFIT COMPUTATIONS.

B30 **Income from property in Scotland: property managed as one estate.** The tax treatment will continue to be by reference to 1978 gross rateable values where appropriate. See 50.26 PROFIT COMPUTATIONS.

B31 **Capital allowances: plant or machinery which is a fixture in a business building within an enterprise zone** may attract 100% initial allowances. Now superseded by *FA 1989, Sch 13 para 28*. See Tolley's Income Tax under Capital Allowances.

B35 **Borrowing and lending of securities: gilt lending to redemption.** Certain transactions are treated as being within *ICTA 1988, s 129*. Obsolete. See Tolley's Income Tax under Schedule D, Cases I and II.

B36 **Borrowing and lending of securities: replacement loans.** Certain transactions are treated as being within *ICTA 1988, s 129*. Obsolete. See Tolley's Income Tax under Schedule D, Cases I and II.

B37 **The herd basis: shares in animals.** The herd basis may be applied to a share in an animal. See Tolley's Income Tax under Herd Basis.

B38 **Tax concessions on overseas debts.** Relief may be available where they form part of profits assessable under Schedule D, Case I or Case II. See 6.3 BANKS.

B39 **Contributions to overseas pension schemes.** Employer contributions otherwise denied relief are allowed in certain circumstances. Now superseded by *FA 1996, Sch 39 para 2*. See Tolley's Income Tax under Retirement Schemes.

B40 **UK investment managers acting for non-resident clients.** The exemptions of *TMA 1970, ss 78(2), 82* are extended in certain cases. See Tolley's Income Tax under Overseas Matters.

B41 **Claims to repayment of tax.** Where an over-payment of tax has arisen because of official error, and there is no doubt or dispute as to the facts, claims to repayment of tax are accepted outside the statutory time limit (generally six years from the end of the year concerned). See Tolley's Income Tax under Claims.

B42 **'Free gifts' and insurance contracts.** Certain incentive gifts offered in connection with the issue of insurance policies are disregarded. See Tolley's Income Tax under Life Assurance Policies.

B43 **Alterations to old pension funds.** Certain minor rule amendments may be made without loss of exemption. See 24.14 EXEMPT ORGANISATIONS.

B44 **Profit-related pay: extraordinary items.** Existing treatment of certain items in the statutory profit and loss account is preserved following the replacement of SSAP6 by FRS3. See Tolley's Income Tax under Schedule E.

B45 **Automatic penalties for late company and employers' and contractors' end-of-year returns.** A temporary short period of grace is allowed for submission of annual returns following the introduction of automatic penalties. Obsolete. See 49.2 PENALTIES and Tolley's Income Tax under Penalties.

B46 **Automatic penalties for late company and employers' and contractors' end-of-year returns.** A short period of grace is allowed for submission of annual returns. See 49.2 PENALTIES, 55.3 SELF-ASSESSMENT and Tolley's Income Tax under Penalties.

B47 **Furnished lettings of dwelling houses — wear and tear of furniture.** As an alternative to the renewals basis, an allowance of 10% of rent may be claimed. (Revised November 1998.) See Tolley's Income Tax under Schedule A.

B48 **A deduction for an employer's national insurance Class 1A contributions when computing profits for tax purposes.** Such a deduction may be given in the same way as for secondary Class 1 contributions. Now superseded by *FA 1997, s 65*. See Tolley's Income Tax under Schedule D, Cases I and II.

B49 **CAA 1990, s 153 — repaid grants.** Capital allowances will be given for repayments of grants which were deducted from expenditure qualifying for capital allowances. See Tolley's Income Tax under Capital Allowances.

B50 **Capital allowances for caravans on holiday caravan sites.** An extended definition of 'caravan' applies for this purpose. See Tolley's Income Tax under Capital Allowances.

B52 **Subcontractors in the construction industry: the multiple turnover tests.** Until 1 August 2001, the number of partners or directors taken into account in determining the three-year turnover threshold may be taken as the maximum number at any time in the last six months of the three-year period, rather than at any time in the whole period, where this is more favourable. See 17.5 CONSTRUCTION INDUSTRY TAX SCHEME.

The following concession awaits publication in IR 1.

B53 **Non-UK resident individuals and companies and chargeable event gains on life policies, life annuities and capital redemption policies.** (i) The treatment, in the case of non-residents, of life assurance gains is brought more into line with that of other forms of income. (ii) The reporting requirements in relation to non-resident policy holders are relaxed. (iii) The transitional reliefs for holders of personal portfolio bonds issued before 17 March 1998 are extended. (Revenue Press Release 23 November 1999). See Tolley's Income Tax under Life Assurance Policies.

C1 **Credit for underlying tax: dividends from trade investments in overseas companies.** Credit is given along a chain of shareholdings in certain circumstances. See 21.3 DOUBLE TAX RELIEF.

C2 **Loan and money societies,** in computing corporation tax liability, may deduct the grossed up amounts of certain payments to members. Withdrawn from April 2001. See 14.3 CLUBS AND SOCIETIES.

C3 **Holiday clubs and thrift funds** are, for certain purposes, regarded as being outside the scope of corporation tax. Withdrawn from April 2001. See 14.4 CLUBS AND SOCIETIES.

C4 **Trading activities for charitable purposes** are exempt subject to certain conditions. (Revised by Revenue Press Release 31 March 2000.) See 11.6(ii) CHARITIES.

C5 **Industrial and provident societies** carrying on trades may treat certain income as trading income for the purposes of loss relief under *ICTA 1988, s 393(8)* (see 44.4 LOSSES). See 32.5 INDUSTRIAL AND PROVIDENT SOCIETIES.

C8 **Close companies: loan creditors.** Certain money brokers are excluded from 'loan creditors' in establishing close company control. See 13.3 CLOSE COMPANIES.

C9 **Associated close and small companies.** The rights and powers of a person's relatives (other than spouse and children) are not attributed to him in certain circumstances, and various other concessions made as regards associated status. See 56.7 SMALL COMPANIES—REDUCED RATES.

C10 **Groups of companies: arrangements.** Certain agreements etc. will not constitute 'arrangements' for the various purposes of the legislation relating to groups of companies. See 29.23 GROUPS OF COMPANIES.

C11 **Demerger: ICTA 1988, s 213(7).** The conditions imposed following a distribution are relaxed. See 29.54 GROUPS OF COMPANIES.

C12 A **retail co-operative society** which prepares half-yearly or quarterly accounts can be treated as having yearly accounting periods ending on an agreed date. See generally 2.4 ACCOUNTING PERIODS.

C13 **'Second and third tier' agricultural co-operative associations** are treated as if members of the basic level associations were members of them. See generally 32.4 INDUSTRIAL AND PROVIDENT SOCIETIES.

C15 **Dissolution of unincorporated associations: distributions to members.** Small distributions by social or recreational associations which have not carried on a trade or business are not treated as distributions under *ICTA 1988, s 209*. See 20.16(*b*) DISTRIBUTIONS.

C16 **Dissolution of companies under Companies Act 1985, ss 652, 652A: distributions to shareholders.** Distributions of assets to members on such a dissolution will in most circumstances not be treated as distributions under *ICTA 1988, s 209*. See 20.16(*a*) DISTRIBUTIONS.

C17 **Interest and currency swaps.** Annual swap fees may be treated as annual payments. Obsolete. See 50.28 PROFIT COMPUTATIONS.

C18 **Payments of interest to non-resident companies.** Certain interest paid by banks is excluded from treatment as a distribution under *ICTA 1988, s 209(2)(e)(iv)*. Obsolete. See 20.7 DISTRIBUTIONS.

C20 **Claims to group relief** may, from 1 September 1992, generally be signed by any person authorised to do so by the claimant company. Obsolete. See 29.23 GROUPS OF COMPANIES.

C21 **Life insurance companies: levies under the LAUTRO (Compensation Schemes) Rules** may be relievable as management expenses. Obsolete. See 41.2 LIFE INSURANCE COMPANIES.

C24 **General insurance business: claims and elections.** Non-life insurance companies using non-annual accounting will be allowed extensions of the time limits for certain claims. See generally 41 LIFE INSURANCE COMPANIES.

C25 **Long term insurance business: claims and elections.** Companies and friendly societies carrying on long term insurance business which have periodic actuarial investigations carried out at intervals greater than twelve months will have two year time limits for claims and elections extended in certain cases. Obsolete for accounting periods ending after 30 June 1999. See generally 28 FRIENDLY SOCIETIES, 41 LIFE INSURANCE COMPANIES.

C26 **Interest payable outside the UK.** Certain interest payable by a UK bank or discount house or a member of the Stock Exchange is treated as payable in the UK even where it is required under the loan agreement to be paid outside the UK. See 6.2 BANKS, 50.2 PROFIT COMPUTATIONS.

C27 **Life assurance business: calculation of investment return and profits.** The relief under *FA 1995, Sch 8 para 53(2)* is extended for an additional year. See 41.3 LIFE INSURANCE COMPANIES.

C28 **Loan relationships.** Certain connections between creditor and debtor companies will be disregarded for the purposes of granting bad debt reliefs. See 43.5 LOAN RELATIONSHIPS.

C29 **Transfers of long-term business: transitional relief for losses incurred in general annuity business.** Certain losses may be carried forward to the transferee for relief. See 41.16 LIFE INSURANCE COMPANIES.

C30 **Authorised unit trusts and open-ended investment companies – waivers of distributions.** Distribution treatment is disapplied in the case of certain *de minimis* waivers of distributions (or accumulations). See 40.6 INVESTMENT COMPANIES, 60.1 UNIT AND INVESTMENT TRUSTS.

C31 **Scientific research associations.** Tax exemptions will temporarily continue under the previous practice following a change in the DTI guidance on the qualification requirements. See 24.12 EXEMPT ORGANISATIONS.

D1 **Insurance recoveries: short leases.** Where property is held on a lease with 50 years or less to run, insurance payments received by the lessee in respect of the property are not treated as chargeable gains insofar as they are applied by the lessee in discharging an obligation to make good any damage to the property. Now superseded by *FA 1996, Sch 39 para 3.* See Tolley's Capital Gains Tax under Disposals.

D2 **Residence in the UK: year of commencement or cessation of residence.** Where a company's UK residence commences or ceases during a year of assessment, capital gains tax is not generally charged on gains arising during the part of that year during which it was non-resident. The concession is withdrawn (for companies) from 6 April 1998. See 53.4 RESIDENCE.

D10 **Unquoted shares acquired before 6 April 1965: disposal following reorganisation of share capital.** Where, in consequence of a reorganisation of share capital before 6 April 1965, a valuation at that date is required, or time apportionment is limited, under *TCGA 1992, Sch 2 para 19*, the gain chargeable to corporation tax on a disposal of the entire holding (whether in a single transaction or in separate transactions in the same accounting period) is limited to the actual gain realised. See Tolley's Capital Gains Tax.

D15 **Relief for the replacement of business assets: unincorporated associations.** Relief is available in respect of assets owned by companies whose shares are wholly (or apart from a very small proportion) held by or on behalf of such an association or its members. See Tolley's Capital Gains Tax under Rollover Relief.

D16 **Relief for the replacement of business assets: repurchase of same asset** will give rise to relief where for purely commercial reasons. See Tolley's Capital Gains Tax under Rollover Relief.

D17 **Unit trusts for exempt unitholders: TCGA 1992, s 100(2).** Exemption is not lost through intermittent holding of units by the managers under ordinary arrangements. See 60.3 UNIT AND INVESTMENT TRUSTS.

D18 **Default on mortgage granted by vendor.** In such circumstances and where the vendor regains beneficial ownership of the asset and so elects, the chargeable gain is limited to the net proceeds obtained from the transactions and the loan treated as never having existed. See Tolley's Capital Gains Tax under Disposal.

D19 **Replacement of buildings destroyed.** If a building is destroyed or irreparably damaged, and compensation is used for the construction or purchase of a replacement, the old and new buildings can (unless the land is a wasting asset) be treated for the purposes of *TCGA 1992, s 23(4)(5)* as assets separate from the land. Now superseded by *FA 1996, Sch 39 para 3*. See Tolley's Capital Gains Tax under Disposal.

D22 **Relief for the replacement of business assets: expenditure on improvements to existing assets** may attract relief provided that the existing assets are used only for trade purposes, or are so used on completion of the improvements. See Tolley's Capital Gains Tax under Rollover Relief.

D23 **Relief for the replacement of business assets: partition of land on the dissolution of a partnership.** Partitioned assets are treated as new assets provided that the partnership is immediately dissolved. See Tolley's Capital Gains Tax under Rollover Relief.

D24 **Relief for the replacement of business assets: asset not brought immediately into trading use** may attract relief provided that:

(*a*) it is proposed to incur expenditure on work for the purpose of enhancing its value;

(*b*) the work begins as soon as possible after acquisition, and is completed within a reasonable time;

(*c*) on completion of the work, the asset is taken into use for trade purposes only; and

(*d*) the asset is not let or used for non-trade purposes between acquisition and being taken into use for trade purposes.

See Tolley's Capital Gains Tax under Rollover Relief.

D25 **Relief for the replacement of business assets: expenditure on acquisition of an interest in an asset already used for the purposes of a trade** will attract relief as if the further interest acquired was a new asset taken into use for trade purposes. See Tolley's Capital Gains Tax under Rollover Relief.

D26 **Relief for exchange of joint interests** in land will apply to exchanges after 19 December 1984, on the lines of that available on compulsory purchase. After 29 October 1987, the relief is further extended to exchanges of joint interests in milk or potato quota in parallel with such exchanges of land. See Tolley's Capital Gains Tax under Rollover Relief.

D27 **Earn-outs.** *TCGA 1992, s 135* may be applied to a takeover which includes an 'earn-out' element. (Superseded by *FA 1997, s 89*.) See Tolley's Capital Gains Tax under Shares and Securities.

D28 **Asset of negligible value: time limits for claims.** Now superseded by *FA 1996, Sch 39 para 4*. See Tolley's Capital Gains Tax under Losses.

D30 **Relief for the replacement of business assets.** Relief is available in respect of certain assets held by non-trading companies within a group. Superseded by *TCGA 1992, s 175(2B)*, introduced by *FA 1995, s 48(1)*. See 9.44 CAPITAL GAINS.

D33 **Capital gains tax on compensation and damages.** Damages derived from underlying assets will be treated as exempt where the asset is exempt, and where there is no underlying asset damages will be exempt. See Tolley's Capital Gains Tax under Disposals.

D34 **Rebasing and indexation: shares held at 31 March 1982.** A single holding treatment will apply even if the shares were acquired before 7 April 1965. See Tolley's Capital Gains Tax under Assets held on 31 March 1982.

D36 **Relief for irrecoverable loans to traders: time limits for claims.** Revenue Statement of Practice SP 3/83 is revised and reclassified as a concession, and extended to cover loans evidenced by qualifying corporate bonds. Now superseded by *FA 1996, Sch 39 paras 8, 9*. See Tolley's Capital Gains Tax under Losses.

D38 **Capital gains tax: qualifying corporate bonds.** A further relief may apply to certain bonds which became qualifying corporate bonds through a change in definition, although not evidenced by a qualifying loan. See Tolley's Capital Gains Tax under Losses.

D39 **Extensions of leases.** Relief is given where a lessee surrenders an existing lease and is granted a new, longer lease at arm's length on the same property at a different rent, but otherwise on the same terms. See Tolley's Capital Gains Tax under Land.

D42 **Mergers of leases.** Indexation allowance may be given on the costs of acquisition of a lease by reference to the date on which it was acquired, even though it ceased to exist on the acquisition of a superior interest in the property, such as the freehold reversion. This replaces an earlier practice for disposals after 28 June 1992. See Tolley's Capital Gains Tax under Land.

D44 **Rebasing and indexation: shares derived from larger holdings held at 31 March 1982.** A more favourable basis of valuation at 31 March 1982 for rebasing and indexation purposes may be available in relation to shares and securities acquired intra-group. See Tolley's Capital Gains Tax under Assets held on 31 March 1982.

D46 **Relief against income for capital losses on the disposal of unquoted shares in a trading company.** Relief will be allowed in certain cases where a company without assets is dissolved and either no distribution is made during winding-up, or no final distribution is made. See 44.19 LOSSES.

D47 **Temporary loss of charitable status due to reverter of school and other sites.** Liabilities which may arise in the period before charitable status is re-established will be discharged or repaid. See 11.1 CHARITIES.

D50 **Capital gains tax treatment of compensation.** Gains arising on compensation from foreign governments may in certain circumstances be exempt. See Tolley's Capital Gains Tax under Disposal.

D51 **Transfer from a close company at undervalue.** *TCGA 1992, s 125* is not applied in certain cases where the transfer gives rise to a charge under other provisions. See 9.17 CAPITAL GAINS.

D52 **Share exchanges, company reconstructions and amalgamations — incidental costs of acquisition and disposal and warranty payments** may be treated as consideration given for the new holding. See Tolley's Capital Gains Tax under Shares and Securities.

I 1 **Gas and oil allowance.** Gas may be excluded from oil won and saved for certain PRT and APRT oil allowances.

I 3 **OTA 1975, Sch 3 para 9.** Certain time limits are extended.

I 4 **OTA 1983, s 9(5): tariff receipts allowance in respect of foreign 'user' fields** may be backdated to the date on which tariffs were first received or receivable.

I 5 **PRT instalments** may be withheld where production ceases following catastrophic loss or damage.

The following concessions applicable to individuals are also relevant to companies.

A37 **Tax treatment of directors' fees received by other companies.** Where a company has the right to appoint a director to the board of another company and the director is required to hand over to the first company any fees or emoluments received from the second company (and does so), and the first company agrees to accept liability to corporation tax on the fees, the director is not charged to tax on those fees. Where the first company is not chargeable to corporation tax but to income tax (e.g. a non-resident company not trading through a branch or agency in the UK) and agrees to accept liability, tax is deducted at the basic rate from the fees. This practice is extended to the case where the first company has no formal right to appoint the director to the board but the director is required to, and does, hand over his fees, provided the first company is (*a*) chargeable to corporation tax on its income and (*b*) not a company over which the director has 'control'. '*Control*' for this purpose means the power of a person by shareholding or voting power (whether directly or through another company), or under Articles of Association, to secure that the company's affairs are conducted according to his wishes. [*ICTA 1988, s 840*]. For this purpose, the rights and powers of his spouse, his children and their spouses, and his parents are taken into account.

A69 **Composite rate tax: non-resident depositors.** Certain declarations made to a building society are treated as having been made to the successor company following conversion to company status. See 6.9 BANKS, 7.6 BUILDING SOCIETIES.

36 Inland Revenue Press Releases

The following is a summary, in date order, of Press Releases referred to in this chapter other than those containing Statements of Practice, as to which see 37 INLAND REVENUE STATEMENTS OF PRACTICE below.

Copies of any individual Press Release may be obtained from Inland Revenue Information Centre, SW Wing, Bush House, Strand, London WC2B 4RD (tel. 0207–438 6420/6425/7772). A charge (currently £100) is made for Press Releases (including Extra-Statutory Concessions and Statements of Practice) mailed weekly throughout a calendar year. To receive Press Releases, application can be made to Tolley, 2 Addiscombe Road, Croydon, Surrey CR9 5AF (tel. 0208–686 9141). A separate application is needed to subscribe to the Revenue's Tax Bulletin for an annual charge of £22, which should be made to Inland Revenue, Finance Division, Barrington Rd., Worthing, West Sussex BN12 4XH.

1.8.77 **Investigation of incorrect business accounts and returns.** The Revenue practice in such investigations is explained. See 49.9 PENALTIES.

15.4.81 **Friendly societies registered after 3 May 1966: life assurance contracts.** In relation to exemption where only certain contracts may be entered into, 'widow' includes 'widower'. See 28.5 FRIENDLY SOCIETIES.

25.6.82 **Deep discounted and indexed stock.** Revenue practice as regards such corporate issues. See 50.7, 50.14 PROFIT COMPUTATIONS.

23.2.84 **Building societies: taxation of gains on realisation of gilts.** See 7.3(*d*) BUILDING SOCIETIES.

17.5.84 **Furnished holiday lettings and caravans.** The application of *ICTA 1988, s 503* to caravan lettings is clarified. See 50.26 PROFIT COMPUTATIONS.

23.7.85 **Extra-statutory concession: benefits in kind: the tax treatment of accommodation provided for employees.** Annual value is in practice taken as gross rateable value. See 50.26 PROFIT COMPUTATIONS.

9.8.89 **Transfer of Head Office work from London to Solihull.** The addresses for various clearance applications are set out. See 9.6 CAPITAL GAINS, 51.6 PURCHASE BY A COMPANY OF ITS OWN SHARES.

10.11.89 **Abolition of domestic rates and introduction of community charge.** The tax consequences are outlined. See 50.26 PROFIT COMPUTATIONS.

27.7.90 **Insurance companies and friendly societies: transfers of long term business: clearance applications.** See 41.16 LIFE INSURANCE COMPANIES.

31.1.91 **Double taxation: Ghana.** The 1977 Convention was never formally ratified in Ghana, and has therefore never had effect in place of the 1947 Arrangement. See 21.10 DOUBLE TAX RELIEF.

7.5.92 **Charitable giving.** The requirements for repayment claims relating to deeds of covenant are revised. See 11.5(*b*) CHARITIES.

31.7.92 **Claims to group relief.** From 1 September 1992, the form of group relief claims is specified, and claims may generally be signed by any authorised person. See 29.23 GROUPS OF COMPANIES.

13.8.92 **Tax on savings — getting it right.** The Revenue attitude to interest and penalties in cases of incorrect registration for gross payment of bank and building society interest is outlined. See 6.9 BANKS.

23.11.92 **Late claims for group relief.** The Revenue criteria for accepting such claims are explained. See 29.23 GROUPS OF COMPANIES.

16.3.93 **Council tax: income tax and corporation tax implications.** See 50.26 PROFIT COMPUTATIONS.

23.7.93 **Tax repayments to EC resident companies.** Claims to repayment supplement may be made following the *Commerzbank* decision. See 38.3 INTEREST ON OVERPAID TAX.

15.9.93 **Unitary taxation.** Implementation of the retaliatory provisions of *ICTA 1988, ss 812–815* is indefinitely deferred following the passage of modifying legislation in California. See 21.9 DOUBLE TAX RELIEF.

5.10.93 **Controlled foreign companies — excluded countries list.** See 18.11 CONTROLLED FOREIGN COMPANIES.

11.7.94 **Charities: tax treatment of lotteries.** Following the enactment of *FA 1995, s 138*, relief for earlier periods continues to be granted on a concessional basis. See 11.6(iii) CHARITIES.

9.11.94 **Clearance procedure for non-trading CFCs.** See 18.11 CONTROLLED FOREIGN COMPANIES.

17.2.95 **1995 Finance Bill, clause 114, Sch 23 — investment managers.** The effect of certain anti-avoidance provisions is explained. See 53.5 RESIDENCE.

20.2.95 **The Stock Exchange alternative investment market (AIM) — tax reliefs for investment in companies joining AIM.** Securities on the AIM are treated as unquoted for such tax purposes. See 44.19 LOSSES, 51.3 PURCHASE BY A COMPANY OF ITS OWN SHARES, 62.3 VENTURE CAPITAL TRUSTS.

27.3.95 **Gilt repo market — provisions concerning sales and repurchases of securities.** The *FA 1995* provisions relating to the proposed introduction from 2 January 1996 of an open market in gilt repos are explained. See 31.7 INCOME TAX IN RELATION TO A COMPANY.

14.9.95 **Venture capital trusts.** Inadvertent breaches of the 70% 'qualifying holdings' limit will not generally result in withdrawal of approval. See 62.2 VENTURE CAPITAL TRUSTS.

13.11.95 **Life assurance business: calculation of investment return and profits.** By concession, the relief under *FA 1995, Sch 8 para 53(2)* is extended for an additional year. See 41.3 LIFE INSURANCE COMPANIES.

1.4.96 **Interest and repayment interest — effective date of payment of tax and NICs.** See 39.5 INTEREST ON UNPAID TAX.

12.7.96 **Tax avoidance through authorised unit trusts using derivatives.** Legislation (effective 12 July 1996) was proposed countering the use of derivatives to convert interest into capital growth for tax purposes. See now, however, Press Release 3 January 1997 below. See 60.1 UNIT AND INVESTMENT TRUSTS.

3.1.97 **Tax avoidance through authorised unit trusts using derivatives.** The proposed legislation (see Press Release 12 July 1996 above) is not to be proceeded with. See 60.1 UNIT AND INVESTMENT TRUSTS.

25.11.97 **A modern system for corporation tax payments.** A system of quarterly accounting for corporation tax is to be phased in for large companies from 1999, and the special arrangements for quarterly accounting for gilt interest abolished from 1 April 1999. See 31.7 INCOME TAX IN RELATION TO A COMPANY, 48.1 PAYMENT OF TAX.

9.7.98 **Controlled foreign companies: excluded countries.** The excluded countries list is updated. See 18.11 CONTROLLED FOREIGN COMPANIES.

31.7.98 **Eighty countries eligible for millennium Gift Aid announced.** See 11.8 CHARITIES.

36 Inland Revenue Press Releases

1.9.98 **The construction industry scheme trading electronically.** An outline is given of how electronic data interchange will be used. See 17.7 CONSTRUCTION INDUSTRY TAX SCHEME.

23.10.98 **Construction industry tax scheme: type of certificate issued to limited companies.** Guidance is given on the conditions for issue of the CIS5 (previously 714C) rather than the CIS6 (previously 714P) certificate under the new scheme. See generally 17.4 CONSTRUCTION INDUSTRY TAX SCHEME.

26.2.99 **ICI v Colmer: handling of open cases** following the ECJ decision. See 29.27 GROUPS OF COMPANIES.

9.3.99 **New choice for taxpayers — returns via the Internet.** The planned extension of the use of electronic communication is outlined. (Joint Press Release with Customs and Excise.) See 33.11 INLAND REVENUE: ADMINISTRATION.

11.3.99 **Interest factor tables** for repayment supplement and overdue tax in relation to accounting periods ending before 1 October 1993 are published. See 38.3 INTEREST ON OVERPAID TAX, 39.3 INTEREST ON UNPAID TAX.

8.6.99 **A modern system for corporation tax payments: guidance on use of information and penalty powers in instalment payments regulations.** See 48.1 PAYMENT OF TAX.

7.7.99 **Construction industry tax scheme.** Special arrangements are made for the first few weeks of the new scheme. See 17.1 CONSTRUCTION INDUSTRY TAX SCHEME.

15.7.99 **Construction industry tax scheme — transitional arrangements.** Further arrangements are made for the period to 5 November 1999. See 17.1 CONSTRUCTION INDUSTRY TAX SCHEME.

6.10.99 **Controlled foreign companies (CFCs) — designer rate and similar regimes.** Companies subject to certain regimes designed to avoid CFC status are in effect to be deemed to fail the 'lower level of taxation' test. See 18.4 CONTROLLED FOREIGN COMPANIES.

10.1.00 **Corporation tax self-assessment — pre-return valuation checks for capital gains purposes.** The Revenue will, on request, check asset valuations. See 55.3 SELF-ASSESSMENT.

16.2.00 **Discounts to boost use of the internet.** Tax discounts for submitting returns via the internet and paying the tax due electronically are introduced for one year. See 54.13 RETURNS.

3.3.00 **New Revenue Pamphlet IR 1 published.** Concessions C2 and C3 are withdrawn from April 2001. See 14.3, 14.4 CLUBS AND SOCIETIES.

21.3.00 (BN1D) **Extra discount for employers paying tax credits.** Following Press Release 16 February 2000 above, a further £50 discount will be available where employers pay working families' or disabled person's tax credits. See 54.13 RETURNS.

31.3.00 **More charity fund-raising events exempted from tax—revised concession C4.** The exemption for certain trading activities is extended. See 11.6(ii) CHARITIES.

11.4.00 **Electronic commerce — tax status of websites and servers.** The Revenue take the view that a website, or a server on which e-commerce is conducted through a website, is not of itself a permanent establishment. See 21.3 DOUBLE TAX RELIEF.

37 Inland Revenue Statements of Practice

Simon's Direct Tax Service H3.

The following is a summary of those Statements of Practice published in Revenue Pamphlet IR 131 (2000), or subsequently announced, which are referred to in this book.

Statements are divided into those originally published before 18 July 1978 (which are given a reference letter (according to the subject matter) and consecutive number, e.g. A34) and later Statements (which are numbered consecutively in each year, e.g. SP 6/94).

Certain Statements marked in IR 131 as obsolete continue to be referred to in the text (having been relevant within the last six years), and the original source is quoted in such cases, as it is where the Statement awaits inclusion in IR 131.

Copies of individual SP-denominated Statements are available free of charge from Inland Revenue Information Centre, SW Wing, Bush House, Strand, London WC2B 4RD (tel. 0207–438 6420/6425/7772) (large SAE to accompany postal applications).

As regards Inland Revenue internal guidance manuals, see 33.9 INLAND REVENUE: ADMINISTRATION.

A4 **Partnerships: change in membership.** Where a continuation election is made, it may be revoked within the original time limit for making the election. Obsolete. See 59.23 TIME LIMITS.

B1 **Treatment of VAT.** Guidance on the general principles applied in dealing with VAT in the computation of corporation tax liabilities. See 61 VALUE ADDED TAX.

C1 **Lotteries and football pools.** Where part of the cost of a ticket is to be donated to a club, etc., that part is, in certain circumstances, not treated as a trading receipt. See 14.6 CLUBS AND SOCIETIES.

C2 **Group relief: ICTA 1988, s 412(1)(c).** Provisional claims for relief will be accepted where the surrendering company's loss has not been agreed before the expiry of the time limit. (ICAEW September 1968; British Tax Review 1968 p 433). See 29.23 GROUPS OF COMPANIES.

C4 **Close companies.** Brings together the various Statements relating to the taxation of close companies in the light of the introduction of corporation tax on 6 April 1973. (Revenue Press Release 26 February 1973; British Tax Review 1973 pp 421–5; Taxation Vol 90 p 375). See 13 CLOSE COMPANIES.

C5 **Interest paid to a bank in the UK on a loan made in foreign currency** is treated as payable gross in the UK even though the loan agreement may provide for payment to be made abroad. (Revenue Press Release 7 March 1973; British Tax Review 1973 pp 461–2; Taxation Vol 90 p 395). (Now superseded by SP 1/95 below.) See 6.2 BANKS, 50.2 PROFIT COMPUTATIONS.

C6 **Group relief: consortium: ICTA 1988, s 413(8).** Concerning the determination of the average percentage of a member's interest in a consortium. See 29.20 GROUPS OF COMPANIES.

C10 **Valuation fees.** Costs related to *Companies Act 1985* compliance are regarded as allowable expenses. See 50.32 PROFIT COMPUTATIONS.

D14 **Division of a company on a share for share basis.** Conditions for *TCGA 1992, s 139* relief. (Revenue Press Release 16 October 1975; British Tax Review 1975 pp 405–6; Taxation Vol 96 p 81). See 9.6 CAPITAL GAINS TAX. (Now encompassed in SP 5/85 below.)

D21 **Capital gains tax: 6 April 1965 valuation time limit: company leaving group: TCGA 1992, ss 178, 179.** The Revenue will exercise discretion to extend the time limit as appropriate. See 9.47 CAPITAL GAINS TAX.

37 Inland Revenue Statements of Practice

SP 8/79 **Compensation for acquisition of property under compulsory powers.** Guidance as to the treatment of compensation for temporary loss of profits and expenses. See 15.2 COMPENSATION, DAMAGES, ETC.

SP 5/80 **Group relief: ICTA 1988, s 410.** Guidance is given on the application of this section. (Revenue Press Release 26 March 1980). (Superseded by SP 3/93 below.) See 29.23 GROUPS OF COMPANIES.

SP 13/80 **Demergers: ICTA 1988, ss 213–218.** Guidance on the application of the provisions and on clearance procedures. See 29.36 *et seq.* GROUPS OF COMPANIES.

SP 18/80 **Unlisted Securities Market: securities** dealt in thereon are not treated as 'listed' or 'quoted'. (Now obsolete.) See 51.3 PURCHASE BY A COMPANY OF ITS OWN SHARES.

SP 8/81 **Replacement of business assets: groups of companies.** Conditions for relief explained where assets are disposed of or acquired by group companies after cessation or before commencement of trading. See 9.44 CAPITAL GAINS.

SP 11/81 **Additional redundancy payments: ICTA 1988, s 90.** The provisions for allowance as a deduction of such payments extended to partial discontinuances. See 50.24 PROFIT COMPUTATIONS.

SP 12/81 **Construction industry tax scheme: carpet fitting** is considered to be outside the scope of the scheme. See 17.2 CONSTRUCTION INDUSTRY TAX SCHEME.

SP 2/82 **Company purchasing own shares: ICTA 1988, ss 219–229.** The conditions for relief are clarified. See 51.4(2), 51.6 PURCHASE BY A COMPANY OF ITS OWN SHARES.

SP 6/83 **Company residence.** The Revenue's interpretation of the application of the case law on company residence is explained. (Revenue Press Release 27 July 1983). Superseded by SP 1/90 (below). See 53.2 RESIDENCE.

SP 1/84 **Trade unions: provident benefits: legal and administrative expenses.** See 24.15 EXEMPT ORGANISATIONS.

SP 6/84 **Non-resident lessors: FA 1973, s 38.** The factors governing liability to tax on profits or gains of such lessors of mobile drilling rigs etc. are outlined. See 53.9 RESIDENCE.

SP 4/85 **Income tax: relief for interest on loans used to buy land occupied for business purposes by company.** The practice regarding interest paid by companies on directors' loans used to purchase land occupied by the company for business purposes is clarified. See 50.15 PROFIT COMPUTATIONS.

SP 5/85 **Capital gains; division of a company on a share for share basis.** It is made clear that the existing practice (see D14 above) extends to demergers within *ICTA 1988, ss 213–218*. See 9.6 CAPITAL GAINS, 29.49 GROUPS OF COMPANIES.

SP 1/87 **Exchange rate fluctuations.** The Revenue practice following the *Marine Midland* decision is explained. See 23.3 EXCHANGE GAINS AND LOSSES.

SP 3/87 **Repayment of tax to charities on covenanted and other income.** See 11.5 CHARITIES.

SP 2/88 **Civil tax penalties and criminal prosecution cases.** The circumstances in which civil penalties will be sought are revised. See 49.12 PENALTIES.

SP 3/88 **Delay in rendering tax returns: interest on overdue tax.** The circumstances in which interest will be sought are clarified. (Revenue Press Release 10 May 1988). See 39.3 INTEREST ON UNPAID TAX. See also SP 6/89 below.

SP 6/88 **Double taxation relief: capital gains tax.** The conditions under which relief is available are clarified. See 21.5 DOUBLE TAX RELIEF.

SP 3/89 **Unit trust and investment trust monthly savings schemes.** A simplified method of calculating the chargeable gain arising on a disposal may be used. (Superseded by SP 2/97 below.) See 40.6 INVESTMENT COMPANIES, 60.1 UNIT AND INVESTMENT TRUSTS.

SP 6/89 **Delay in rendering tax returns: interest on overdue tax: TMA 1970, s 88.** SP 3/88 above is revised to remove the 'reasonable excuse' exemption. See 39.3 INTEREST ON UNPAID TAX.

SP 7/89 **Surrender of advance corporation tax.** ACT already allowed in a final assessment may nevertheless be surrendered. See 29.8 GROUPS OF COMPANIES.

SP 1/90 **Company residence.** SP 6/83 (above) is revised and updated. See 53.1, 53.2 RESIDENCE.

SP 2/90 **Guidance notes for migrating companies: notice and arrangements for payment of tax.** See 53.7 RESIDENCE.

SP 4/90 **Charitable covenants.** Revised practices in relation to retrospective validation and escape clauses are explained. See 11.5(*d*) CHARITIES.

SP 1/91 **Small companies' rate of corporation tax and corporation tax starting rate.** The claims procedure is explained. (Revised on re-publication in January 2000.) See 56.1, 56.4 SMALL COMPANIES—REDUCED RATES.

SP 3/91 **Finance lease rental payments.** See 50.17 PROFIT COMPUTATIONS.

SP 4/91 **Tax returns.** The principles followed by the Revenue in designing tax returns and determining the information required in them are explained, including returns in relation to European Economic Interest Groupings. Obsolete. See 50.12 PROFIT COMPUTATIONS.

SP 7/91 **Double taxation: business profits: unilateral relief.** Revenue practice as regards admission of foreign taxes for relief is revised. See 21.2 DOUBLE TAX RELIEF.

SP 10/91 **Corporation tax: a major change in the nature or conduct of a trade.** The Revenue interpretation of that expression is explained. See 9.31 CAPITAL GAINS, 44.13 LOSSES.

SP 12/91 **Income tax: 'in the ordinary course' of banking business.** The Revenue interpretation of this expression is explained. (Superseded by SP 4/96 below.) See 6.2 BANKS.

SP 14/91 **Tax treatment of transactions in financial futures and options.** See 60.4 UNIT AND INVESTMENT TRUSTS.

SP 2/92 **Transactions within ICTA 1988, s 765A: movements of capital between residents of EC Member States.** Guidance as to when the relevant provisions apply and on procedural matters. See 4.3 ANTI-AVOIDANCE.

SP 4/92 **Capital gains re-basing elections.** Certain disposals are ignored in relation to the time limit for such elections. See 9.45 CAPITAL GAINS. Replaces SP 2/89.

SP 3/93 **Groups of companies: arrangements.** Guidance on the Revenue interpretation of 'arrangements' for the various purposes of the group legislation. See 29.3, 29.9, 29.17, 29.23 , 29.27 GROUPS OF COMPANIES.

SP 5/93 **UK/Czechoslovakia double taxation Convention.** The Convention is regarded as applying to the Czech and Slovak Republics. See 21.10 DOUBLE TAX RELIEF.

SP 7/93 **Insurance companies: transfers of long-term business.** The Board's interpretation of the operation of the deferral under *TCGA 1992, s 211* in relation to mixed fund assets is explained. See 41.16 LIFE INSURANCE COMPANIES.

SP 9/93 **Pay and File — corporation tax returns.** The requirements for the form of returns are explained. See 54.2 RETURNS

37 Inland Revenue Statements of Practice

SP 10/93 **Pay and File — special arrangement for groups of companies.** The requirements for joint group relief returns are explained. See 54.2 RETURNS.

SP 11/93 **Pay and File — claims to capital allowances and group relief made outside the normal time limit.** The requirements for the acceptance of late claims are explained. See 8.2 CAPITAL ALLOWANCES, 29.23 GROUPS OF COMPANIES, 55.4 SELF-ASSESSMENT.

SP 12/93 **Double taxation — dividend income — tax credit relief** for dividends paid under a 'company tax deducted' arrangement may be restricted. See 21.6 DOUBLE TAX RELIEF.

SP 15/93 **Business tax computations rounded to nearest £1,000** will be accepted in certain cases. See 54.4 RETURNS.

SP 2/94 **Enterprise investment scheme and venture capital trust scheme — location of activity.** The requirement that trade(s) be carried on 'wholly or mainly in the UK' is clarified. (Superseded by SP 7/98 below.) See 62.3(*b*) VENTURE CAPITAL TRUSTS.

SP 5/94 **Associated companies for small companies' relief and corporation tax starting rate — holding companies.** The circumstances in which a holding company is disregarded in calculating profits limits are explained. (Revised on re-publication in January 2000.) See 56.7 SMALL COMPANIES—REDUCED RATES.

SP 7/94 **Investment trusts investing in authorised unit trusts.** The conditions under which such investments may be made are clarified. (Superseded by SP 3/97 below.) See 40.6 INVESTMENT COMPANIES, 60.4 UNIT AND INVESTMENT TRUSTS.

SP 9/94 **Application of foreign exchange and financial instruments legislation to partnerships which include companies.** (Superseded by SP 4/98 below.) See 23.30 EXCHANGE GAINS AND LOSSES, 25.19 FINANCIAL INSTRUMENTS.

SP 1/95 **Interest payable in the UK.** Interest payable to banks and certain other persons is treated as payable in the UK, even if it may be paid either within or outside the UK. See 6.2 BANKS, 50.2 PROFIT COMPUTATIONS.

SP 2/95 **Payment of tax credits to non-resident companies.** The Revenue consider that a claim for repayment of tax credits under *ICTA 1988, s 242* may not be made by a non-resident company notwithstanding the existence of a non-discrimination clause in the relevant double tax treaty. See 21.3 DOUBLE TAX RELIEF, 27.3 FRANKED INVESTMENT INCOME.

SP 3/95 **Financial instruments: definition of financial trader for purposes of FA 1994, s 177(1).** The guidelines used by the Revenue in deciding whether a company should be approved as a financial trader are explained. See 25.18 FINANCIAL INSTRUMENTS.

SP 4/95 **Long term insurance business — computations of profit for tax purposes.** The approach the Revenue adopt to the measurement of trading profit from life assurance and other types of long term business when accounts are drawn up in accordance with the Insurance Accounts Directive (91/674/EEC) is outlined. See generally 41.1, 41.4, 41.5, 41.6 LIFE INSURANCE COMPANIES.

SP 7/95 **Venture capital trusts — value of gross assets.** The Revenue's general approach to the valuation of gross assets in determining whether a holding is a 'qualifying holding' is explained. (Superseded by SP 5/98 below.) See 62.3(*e*) VENTURE CAPITAL TRUSTS.

SP 8/95 **Venture capital trusts — default terms in loan agreements.** Certain event of default clauses will not disqualify a loan from being a security for the purposes of approval. See 62.2 VENTURE CAPITAL TRUSTS.

SP 4/96 **Income tax — interest paid in the ordinary course of a bank's business.** The Revenue interpretation of this requirement is explained. See 6.2 BANKS.

SP 1/97 **The electronic lodgement service.** The Revenue operation and detailed requirements of the scheme are explained. See 54.13 RETURNS.

SP 2/97 **Authorised unit trusts, approved investment trusts, and open-ended investment companies — monthly savings schemes.** A simplified method of calculating the chargeable gain arising on a disposal may be used. (Replaced SP 3/89 above and superseded by SP 2/99 below.) See 40.6 INVESTMENT COMPANIES, 60.1 UNIT AND INVESTMENT TRUSTS.

SP 3/97 **Investment trusts investing in authorised unit trusts or open-ended investment companies.** The conditions under which such investments may be made are clarified. (Replaces SP 7/94 above.) See 40.6 INVESTMENT COMPANIES, 60.4 UNIT AND INVESTMENT TRUSTS.

SP 4/98 **Partnerships including companies: application of loan relationships, foreign exchange and financial instruments legislation.** See 23.30 EXCHANGE GAINS AND LOSSES, 25.19 FINANCIAL INSTRUMENTS, 43.9 LOAN RELATIONSHIPS.

SP 5/98 **Venture capital trusts and the enterprise investment scheme — value of 'gross assets'.** The Revenue's general approach to the valuation of gross assets is explained. (Replaces SP 7/95 above.) See 62.3(*e*) VENTURE CAPITAL TRUSTS.

SP 7/98 **Enterprise investment scheme, venture capital trusts and capital gains tax reinvestment relief — location of activity.** The requirement that trade(s) be carried on 'wholly or mainly in the UK' is clarified. (Replaces SP 2/94 above.) See 62.3(*b*) VENTURE CAPITAL TRUSTS.

SP 2/99 **Authorised unit trusts, approved investment trusts, and open-ended investment companies — monthly savings schemes.** The application of the simplified method of calculating the chargeable gain arising on a disposal, which ceases to be available for disposals after 5 April 1999, is explained. (Replaces SP 2/97 above.) See 40.6 INVESTMENT COMPANIES, 60.1 UNIT AND INVESTMENT TRUSTS.

SP 3/99 **Advance pricing agreements (APAs).** The detailed administration of the scheme of APAs relating to transfer pricing issues is explained. See 4.4 ANTI-AVOIDANCE.

38 Interest on Overpaid Tax

38.1 **ACCOUNTING PERIODS ENDING AFTER 30 SEPTEMBER 1993** [*ICTA 1988, ss 826, 826A; FA 1991, Sch 15 para 23; FA 1993, Sch 14 para 10, Sch 18 para 5; FA 1994, Sch 16 para 20; FA 1995, Sch 24 paras 11, 12; FA 1996, s 173(5)(6), Sch 14 para 48; F(No 2)A 1997, Sch 8 Pt II(4); FA 1998, s 34, Sch 3 para 38, Sch 4 paras 1–3, 5; FA 1999, s 90; FA 2000, Sch 21 para 1, Sch 30 para 29*]

Accounting periods ending beforel July 1999. Where a repayment falls to be made to a company for an accounting period ending after 30 September 1993 and before 1 July 1999, either of corporation tax for the period or of income tax in respect of a payment received in the period or (under the FOREIGN INCOME DIVIDENDS (26) scheme) of surplus ACT paid in respect of distributions made in the period, or a tax credit comprised in any franked investment income received in such a period falls to be wholly or partly paid to the company, the repayment or payment carries interest from the 'material date' until the payment order is issued. The rate of interest is adjusted automatically by reference to the average of base lending rates of certain clearing banks, the formula being the rounded-down average base rate less 1%, the subtotal being reduced by the full rate of corporation tax and rounded down. [*FA 1989, ss 178, 179; SI 1989 No 1297; SI 1993 No 2212*]. Changes are announced in Revenue Press Releases. Current and earlier rates are as follows.

3.25% p.a. from 1 October 1993 to 5 January 1994
2.50% p.a. from 6 January 1994 to 5 October 1994
3.25% p.a. from 6 October 1994 to 5 March 1995
4.00% p.a. from 6 March 1995 to 5 February 1996
3.25% p.a. from 6 February 1996 to 5 August 1997
4.00% p.a. from 6 August 1997 to 5 January 1999
3.25% p.a. from 6 January 1999 to 5 March 1999
2.75% p.a. from 6 March 1999 to 5 February 2000
3.50% p.a. from 6 February 2000 to

[*SI 1993 No 2212*].

It is understood that a denominator of 365 is used in calculations of repayment interest regardless of whether or not a leap year is involved.

The '*material date*' is:

(*a*) for corporation tax, the later of the date the corporation tax was paid and the date on which it became (or would have become) due and payable, i.e. nine months after the end of the accounting period (see 48.1 PAYMENT OF TAX);

(*b*) for income tax repayments and payments of tax credit, the due and payable date for corporation tax for the accounting period in which the payment was received by the company, i.e. nine months after the end of that accounting period;

(*c*) (in relation to accounting periods beginning before 6 April 1999) for repayments of surplus ACT, the date on which corporation tax for the period became (or would have become) due and payable, i.e. nine months after the end of the accounting period;

(*d*) in the case of a tax repayment in respect of repayment, release or writing off of a close company loan under *ICTA 1988, s 419(4)*, the later of the date the entitlement to the tax repayment accrued (i.e. the date nine months after the end of the accounting period in which the loan etc. was made or, if the loan had not been repaid, released or written off at that date, the date nine months after the end of the accounting period in which it was repaid, released or written off) and the actual date of payment of the tax to be repaid. (For a loan made in an accounting period ending before 31 March 1996, it is the later of the date the loan (or part) was repaid and the actual date of payment of the tax.)

In relation to repayments within (*d*) above, the repayment is treated as if it were a repayment of corporation tax for the accounting period in which the loan (or part) was repaid, released or written off.

Repayment supplement is not paid in respect of out of date claims, since the amount repaid is regarded as an *ex gratia* payment made without acceptance of any legal liability. (Revenue Claims Manual, RM 5104).

To the extent that a repayment of corporation tax, or of income tax in respect of a payment received, arises from surplus ACT carried back from a subsequent accounting period beginning before 6 April 1999 (see 3.8 ADVANCE CORPORATION TAX), interest as above is only payable from nine months after the end of the accounting period in which the surplus ACT arose.

Interest is similarly restricted where losses of an accounting period are carried back under *ICTA 1988, s 393A(1)* (see 44.6 LOSSES) to an accounting period not falling wholly within the twelve months preceding the period in which the loss was incurred. Interest on any repayment of corporation tax paid for the earlier period, or on any payment of income tax or tax credit in respect of payments received in that period, is only payable from nine months after the end of the accounting period in which the loss arose. Where, as a result of the loss being carried back, surplus ACT arises in the earlier period (beginning before 6 April 1999) which is itself carried back, the provisions described above in relation to interest in relation to the period in which the surplus ACT is applied are amended to prevent such interest being payable for any time before nine months after the end of the accounting period in which the loss arose (rather than the period in which the surplus ACT arose). (These provisions do not apply where the period to which the loss or surplus ACT is carried back ended before 1 October 1993, but the provisions of *ICTA 1988, s 825* (see 38.3 below) have similar effect.) See also 21.6 DOUBLE TAX RELIEF as regards similar provisions relating to relief for excess unrelieved foreign tax.

Similar restrictions also apply for accounting periods ending after 31 March 1996 where a non-trading deficit on a company's loan relationships is carried back on a claim under *FA 1996, s 83(2)* (see 43.3 LOAN RELATIONSHIPS). Previously the restrictions applied where a 'relievable amount' in respect of an exchange loss is carried back and set against exchange profits under *FA 1993, s 131* (see 23.14, 23.31 EXCHANGE GAINS AND LOSSES).

See Revenue Tax Bulletin May 1993 p 65 for an explanation of the operation of these restrictions, and April 1996 pp 304, 305 for an example illustrating the point that *ICTA 1988, s 826* only applies to repayments of tax paid for accounting periods ending after 30 September 1993, regardless of whether a repayment for an earlier period may arise from surplus ACT carried back from such a period.

Interest under these provisions is paid without deduction of tax. Corporation tax repayments are as far as possible treated as repayments of tax paid on a later rather than an earlier date.

Insurance companies. As regards ACT repaid to such companies, see 41.4 LIFE INSURANCE COMPANIES.

Accounting periods ending on or after 1 July 1999. For such accounting periods, to which self-assessment applies, the provisions described above in relation to earlier accounting periods continue to apply, but with a number of changes, as described below.

(i) Where interest is payable under these provisions to a company within the charge to corporation tax, it is brought into account in computing profits or income.

(ii) For corporation tax repayments, a special rate of interest applies, as follows, changes being announced in Revenue Press Releases.

5.00% p.a. from 7 January 1999 to 5 March 1999

4.00% from 6 March 1999 to 5 February 2000

5.00% p.a. from 6 February 2000 to

The rates listed above in relation to earlier accounting periods continue to apply in relation to other interest payments.

(iii) In the case of certain 'large' companies, which are required to make instalment payments in respect of their corporation tax liabilities, a special rate of interest (which is generally from 0.25% to 1.25% higher than that referred to in (ii) above) applies to any excess instalment payments until nine months after the end of the accounting period concerned. See 48.1 PAYMENT OF TAX.

(iv) Where corporation tax payments are made by a company which is *not* a large company (see (iii) above) before the day following the expiry of nine months after the end of an accounting period, interest is payable from the date of payment until that day, at the special rate referred to in (iii) above, although not for periods before the first instalment date which would apply under those provisions if the company were a large company.

(v) The material date for income tax repayments and payments of tax credit is brought forward nine months to the day after the end of the accounting period concerned.

(vi) Where, solely as a result of a change in a company's corporation tax liability, it appears to the Board that any interest paid under these provisions ought not to have been paid, it is recoverable without assessment as if it were INTEREST ON OVERPAID TAX (39).

(vii) The provisions are also applied to payments of 'R & D tax credit' (see 50.25 PROFIT COMPUTATIONS), for which the 'material date' is the filing date (see 55.3 SELF-ASSESSMENT) for the company tax return for the accounting period for which the credit is claimed (or if later the date of receipt by the Revenue of the return (or amended return) containing the claim).

[*SI 1989 No 1297, regs 3BA, 3BB; SI 1998 No 3175, reg 8; SI 1998 No 3176, regs 4, 7, 8*].

Simon's Direct Tax Service. See **D2.708.**

38.2 *Examples*

(A) *Pre-self-assessment*

W Ltd prepares accounts to 30 June. It makes a payment of £85,000 on 22 March 1999 on account of its CT liability for the year ended 30 June 1998. On 30 June 1999, it pays a further £2,235, having computed its total liability to be £87,235. In arriving at this amount, the company took a pessimistic view of the possibility of the Inspector allowing a particular deduction claimed in arriving at trading profits. However, after correspondence, the deduction is allowed and an assessment raised showing the company's total CT liability for the year to 30 June 1998 to be £83,750. A CT repayment of £3,485 is made to the company on 3 October 1999.

W Ltd will be entitled to interest on overpaid tax, calculated as follows.

		£
30.6.99 to 3.10.99	£2,235 × 2.75% × $\frac{95}{365}$ =	16.00
1.4.99 to 3.10.99	£1,250 × 2.75% × $\frac{185}{365}$ =	17.42
Total interest		£33.42

An interest charge would initially be raised by the Revenue on £2,235 from 1.4.99 to 30.6.99 but the interest would be refunded in full once the final liability had been agreed and the amount of £2,235 ascertained as having never been due.

(B) *Self-assessment*

X Ltd prepares accounts to 31 December. On 15 June 2001 it submits its tax return for the year ended 31 December 2000 showing a corporation tax liability for the period of £14,000, and accompanied by a payment of £7,000. On 1 October 2001 it makes a further payment of £7,000. It subsequently submits an amended return showing a reduced liability of £12,500, and £1,500 is repaid to the company on 1 December 2001.

It is assumed that interest rates remain unchanged after 21 February 2000.

X Ltd will be entitled to interest on overpaid tax, calculated as follows.

		£
15.6.01 to 13.7.01		—
14.7.01 to 30.9.01	£7,000 × 5.75% × $\frac{79}{365}$ =	87.12
1.10.01 to 30.11.01	£1,500 × 5% × $\frac{61}{365}$ =	12.53
Total interest		£99.65

(C) *Instalment payment*

Z Ltd has no associated companies and had taxable profits in excess of £1,500,000 for the year ended 30 September 1998. For the year ended 30 September 1999, Z Ltd pays £97,500 for the first instalment on 31 March 1999, this being equivalent to a quarter of 60% of its estimated corporation tax liability of £650,000 as calculated under the phasing-in provisions. The same amount is paid on the due dates for the second and third instalments and on 4 January 2000 for the fourth instalment. The balance of the estimated tax liability, £260,000, is paid on 25 June 2000. On 3 March 2001, the tax liability is agreed at £584,800 and £65,200 is repaid to the company on 22 March 2001.

The rates of interest are assumed for the purposes of this example to remain unchanged after 21 February 2000.

The interest on tax overpaid is calculated as follows.

Instalments due: on quarter dates £584,800 × 60% × $\frac{1}{4}$ = £87,720
on normal due date £584,800 × 40% = £233,920

	£
14 April 1999 to 18 April 1999	
97,500 – 87,720 = £9,780 @ 5.25% × $\frac{5}{365}$ =	7.03
19 April 1999 to 20 June 1999	
97,500 – 87,720 = £9,780 @ 5% × $\frac{63}{365}$ =	84.40
21 June 1999 to 13 July 1999	
97,500 – 87,720 = £9,780 @ 4.75% × $\frac{23}{365}$ =	29.27
14 July 1999 to 19 September 1999	
195,000 – 175,440 = £19,560 @ 4.75% × $\frac{68}{365}$ =	173.09
20 September 1999 to 13 October 1999	
195,000 – 175,440 = £19,560 @ 5% × $\frac{24}{365}$ =	64.31
14 October 1999 to 14 November 1999	
292,500 – 263,160 = £29,340 @ 5% × $\frac{32}{365}$ =	128.61
15 November 1999 to 3 January 2000	
292,500 – 263,160 = £29,340 @ 5.25% × $\frac{50}{365}$ =	211.01
4 January 2000 to 13 January 2000	
390,000 – 263,160 = £126,840 @ 5.25% × $\frac{10}{365}$ =	182.44
14 January 2000 to 23 January 2000	
390,000 – 350,880 = £39,120 @ 5.25% × $\frac{10}{365}$ =	56.27
24 January 2000 to 20 February 2000	
390,000 – 350,880 = £39,120 @ 5.5% × $\frac{27}{365}$ =	159.16
21 February 2000 to 24 June 2000	
390,000 – 350,880 = £39,120 @ 5.75% × $\frac{126}{365}$ =	776.51
25 June 2000 to 30 June 2000	
650,000 – 350,880 = £299,120 @ 5.75% × $\frac{6}{365}$ =	282.73
1 July 2000 to 21 March 2001	
650,000 – 584,800 = £65,200 @ 5% × $\frac{264}{365}$ =	2,357.92
Interest on overpaid tax	£4,512.75

38.3 **ACCOUNTING PERIODS ENDING ON OR BEFORE 30 SEPTEMBER 1993** [*ICTA 1988, s 825; FA 1989, ss 158(2), 178, 179; SI 1989 No 1297; FA 1991, Sch 15 para 22; SI 1993 No 753; FA 1993, Sch 14 para 10(6); FA 1995, Sch 24 para 12(5); SI 1996 No 3187*]

Where a repayment falls to be made to a company for an accounting period ending on or before 30 September 1993, of either corporation tax (including ACT), income tax or the tax credit attached to franked investment income, and the repayment is made more than twelve months after the 'material date', the repayment carries interest (a '*repayment supplement*').

The rates of interest are as under 39.3 INTEREST ON UNPAID TAX, except that the rates before 6 August 1986 are as follows.

6.00% p.a. before 6 April 1974
9.00% p.a. from 6 April 1974 to 5 January 1980
12.00% p.a. from 6 January 1980 to 5 December 1982
8.00% p.a. from 6 December 1982 to 5 May 1985
11.00% p.a. from 6 May 1985 to 5 August 1986

[*SI 1974 No 966; SI 1979 No 1687; SI 1982 No 1587; SI 1985 No 563; SI 1986 No 1181*].

Interest factor tables for use as ready reckoners in calculating interest on overpaid tax are published by the Revenue and updated as rates change (although not after 5 April 1999). (Revenue Press Release 11 March 1999).

Interest is disregarded for all tax purposes. In relation to repayments before 6 April 1993, the tax concerned had to amount to £100 or more for interest to be payable.

The interest runs to the end of the tax month (i.e. the month from the sixth day of one calendar month to the fifth day of the next) in which the order for repayment is issued, and commences on the date determined as follows.

	Interest commences
(a) Corporation tax originally paid on or after the first anniversary of the 'material date'.	At the beginning of the tax month following the next anniversary of the 'material date' after the tax was paid.
(b) In any other case (i.e. corporation tax paid before the first anniversary of the 'material date', income tax and tax credits relating to the relevant accounting period).	At the beginning of the tax month following the first anniversary of the 'material date'.

'*Material date*' means the earliest due date for payment of corporation tax for the accounting period in question (i.e. the date specified at 48.2 PAYMENT OF TAX).

Repayment supplement is not paid in respect of out of date claims, since the amount repaid is regarded as an *ex gratia* payment made without acceptance of any legal liability. (Revenue Claims Manual, RM 5104).

Corporation tax repayments are as far as possible treated as repayments of tax paid on a later rather than an earlier date.

Example

The earliest due date for payment of corporation tax by X Ltd is 9 months after the end of each accounting period. An estimated assessment for the accounting period 1 April 1992–31 March 1993 is raised on 23 April 1994, charging tax of £21,000. This is paid on 7 May 1994 and an appeal made against the assessment. The appeal is determined on 28 August 1995, following which the assessment is increased to charge a further £2,790.46. This further amount is paid on 1 October 1995. Subsequently, relief is claimed for part of a trading loss of the next following accounting period, and a corporation tax repayment of £6,726.64 is made on 15 November 1996.

The 'material date' is 9 months after the end of the accounting period, i.e. 1 January 1994.

Repayment supplement is calculated as follows.

(i) The tax of £2,790.46 falls within (*a*) above, and interest accordingly runs from the beginning of the income tax month following the first anniversary of the material date after the date of payment, i.e.

Date of payment	1 October 1995
Anniversary of material date	1 January 1996
Interest runs from	6 January 1996

Interest runs to the end of the income tax month in which the repayment is made (i.e. to 5 December 1996), a total of 11 months. For calculations, see below.

(ii) The balance of the repayment (£3,936.18) is attributable to the tax paid on 7 May 1994. This tax falls within (*b*) above, and interest accordingly runs *from* the beginning of the income tax month following 1 January 1995 (i.e. 6 January 1995). Interest runs *to* 5 December 1996, a total of 23 months.

Calculations

(i)	£2,790.46 @ 7.00% × $\frac{1}{12}$ =	16.28
	£2,790.46 @ 6.25% × $\frac{10}{12}$ =	145.34
(ii)	£3,936.18 @ 6.25% × $\frac{2}{12}$ =	41.00
	£3,936.18 @ 7.00% × $\frac{11}{12}$ =	252.57
	£3,936.18 @ 6.25% × $\frac{10}{12}$ =	205.00
Total supplement		£660.19

Using the interest factor tables published by the Revenue, the factors for the relevant months are

January 1995	3.1532
January 1996	3.2219
December 1996	3.2799

The interest due is then calculated as

£2,790.46 × (3.2799 – 3.2219) =	£161.85
+ £3,936.18 × (3.2799 – 3.1532) =	£498.71
Total supplement	£660.56

In order to qualify for the repayment supplement, the company must have been resident in the UK for the accounting period in connection with which the repayment of tax is made. Interest is paid for each **complete** tax month only.

In *R v CIR (ex p. Commerzbank AG) QB 1991, 68 TC 252*, repayment supplement was held not to fall within the scope of double tax agreements, but on a reference to the European Court of Justice (see *68 TC 264*), the Court upheld the view that, in the case of EC Member States, such discrimination against non-UK resident companies was prevented by the relevant Articles of the Treaty of Rome. The Revenue has invited claims to repayment supplement by companies resident within the EC for an accounting period for which a repayment was made without supplement, where the repayment was made more than twelve months after the end of the accounting period and in the six years before the date of the ECJ decision (13 July 1993). Claims should be sent to FICO (International) at either FitzRoy House, P.O. Box 46, Nottingham NG2 1BD or St John's House, Merton Road, Bootle, Merseyside L69 9BB.

Repayments relating to surplus ACT carried back to an earlier period claimed under *ICTA 1988, s 239(3)* (see 3.8 ADVANCE CORPORATION TAX) and tax on repayment of loans to participators etc. claimed under *ICTA 1988, s 419(4)* (see 13.9–13.13 CLOSE COMPANIES) are treated as repayments of tax for the accounting period in which the surplus ACT arose or the loan repayment was made. Similarly, a repayment relating to the carry back of a loss to an earlier period under *ICTA 1988, s 393A(1)* is treated as a repayment of tax paid for the period in which the loss was incurred, unless the earlier period falls wholly within the twelve months preceding the accounting period of the loss. This applies also to the repayment of a tax credit arising from a claim under *ICTA 1988, s 242* (see 27.3 FRANKED INVESTMENT INCOME) relating to the relief of losses under *ICTA 1988, s 393A(1)*, and to the carry-back of relievable amounts in respect of exchange losses (see 23.14 EXCHANGE GAINS AND LOSSES). These provisions continue to apply where the accounting period in which the loss or surplus ACT etc. arose ended after 30 September 1993, provided that the period for which the tax was repaid ended on or before that date.

For a case in which a repayment for earlier years (by means of a revised postponement application) was sought and made in advance of formal determination of surplus ACT available, but was held to have resulted from a claim to carry back ACT, see *Savacentre Ltd v CIR CA 1995, 67 TC 381*.

The above provisions do not apply to amounts paid by order of a court having power to allow interest.

Simon's Direct Tax Service. See **A3.617.**

38.4 REVENUE ERROR

The Revenue have published a Code of Practice (No 1, available from local tax offices) setting out the circumstances in which they will consider paying a repayment supplement on money owed to the taxpayer for any period during which there has been undue delay on the part of the Revenue. See 33.7 INLAND REVENUE: ADMINISTRATION.

38.5 UNAUTHORISED DEMANDS FOR TAX

There is a general right to interest under *Supreme Court Act 1981, s 35A* in a case where a taxpayer submits to such an unauthorised demand, provided that the payment was not made voluntarily to close a transaction. (*Woolwich Equitable Building Society v CIR HL 1992, 65 TC 265*).

38.6 VALUE ADDED TAX

Value added tax repayment supplements under *VATA 1994, s 79* are disregarded for corporation tax purposes. [*ICTA 1988, s 827(2)*].

38.7 OVER-REPAYMENTS

See 48.8 PAYMENT OF TAX, 55.13 SELF-ASSESSMENT as regards assessment of overpaid interest under these provisions.

39 Interest on Unpaid Tax

Cross-reference. See also 61.5 VALUE ADDED TAX.

39.1 ACCOUNTING PERIODS ENDING AFTER 30 SEPTEMBER 1993

Accounting periods ending before 1 July 1999. In relation to accounting periods ending after 30 September 1993 and before 1 July 1999, corporation tax carries interest from the due and payable date (see 48.1 PAYMENT OF TAX), even if it is a non-business day, until payment. [*TMA 1970, s 87A(1) (2); F(No 2)A 1987, s 85*]. See 39.6 below as regards ACT for accounting periods beginning before 6 April 1999. Where corporation tax assessed on a company may be assessed on other persons in certain circumstances, the due and payable date is that which refers to the company's liability. An assessment to recover excessive tax credit and interest thereon (see 3.6 ADVANCE CORPORATION TAX) carries interest from the date of payment of the tax credit. [*TMA 1970, s 87A(3)(5); F(No 2)A 1987, s 85; FA 1999, s 92(5)*]. The rate of interest is adjusted automatically by reference to the rounded down average of base lending rates of certain clearing banks, the formula being such average base rate plus 2.5%, the subtotal being reduced by the small companies rate of corporation tax (see 56 SMALL COMPANIES—REDUCED RATES) and rounded-down. [*FA 1989, ss 178, 179; SI 1989 No 1297; SI 1993 No 2212*]. Changes are announced in Revenue Press Releases. Current and earlier rates are as follows.

6.25% p.a. from 1 October 1993 to 5 January 1994
5.50% p.a. from 6 January 1994 to 5 October 1994
6.25% p.a. from 6 October 1994 to 5 March 1995
7.00% p.a. from 6 March 1995 to 5 February 1996
6.25% p.a. from 6 February 1996 to 5 August 1997
7.50% p.a. from 6 August 1997 to 5 January 1999
6.50% p.a. from 6 January 1999 to 5 March 1999
5.75% p.a. from 6 March 1999 to 5 February 2000
6.75% p.a. from 6 February 2000 to

It is understood that a denominator of 366 is used in calculations of such interest regardless of whether or not a leap year is involved.

Under the Pay and File system, interest has been charged on tax paid late, but before filing of the return for the period, without waiting for the final liability to be established. (Revenue Tax Bulletin February 1993 p 51). However, when the self-assessment computer system comes on line (which is scheduled to be 10 November 1999), interest for both pre- and post-self-assessment periods will not be calculated until a return is made or some other charge to tax arises. (Revenue Pamphlet 'A Guide to Corporation Tax Self Assessment' para 5.4.4).

Interest under these provisions is paid without deduction of tax and is not deductible in computing income, profits or losses. [*TMA 1970, s 90*]. Interest on tax subsequently discharged is adjusted or repaid so as to secure that the total is as it would have been had the tax discharged never been charged, except that where the discharge arises from the set-off (prior to its abolition) of surplus ACT of a later accounting period, calculation of any interest payable takes account of that set-off only from nine months after the end of the accounting period in which the surplus ACT arose. [*TMA 1970, s 87A(4), s 91(1A)(1B); F(No 2)A 1987, ss 85, 86(5); FA 1993, Sch 14 para 5; FA 1995, Sch 24 para 10; FA 1998, Sch 3 para 4, Sch 4 para 4*]. Similarly, where losses of an accounting period are carried back under *ICTA 1988, s 393A(1)* (see 44.6 LOSSES) to an accounting period not falling wholly within the twelve months preceding the period in which the loss was incurred, and if the carry-back had not been claimed interest would have arisen on unpaid corporation tax for that earlier period, then such interest may only be relieved by virtue of the carried-back losses from nine months after the end of the accounting period in which the loss was incurred. A claim for carry-back of any surplus ACT for the earlier period resulting from the loss relief claim is also disregarded for this purpose, but the provisions described above in relation to interest for the period to which the surplus ACT is carried back are then amended so that interest continues to run until nine months after the end of the accounting period in which the loss was incurred (rather than that in which the surplus ACT arose). [*TMA 1970, s 87A(6)(7); F(No 2)A 1987, s 85; FA 1991, Sch 15 para 2; FA 1993, Sch 14 para 4; FA 1998, Sch 3 para 4, Sch 4 para 4*]. Similar restrictions also apply for accounting periods ending after 31 March 1996 where a non-trading deficit on a company's loan relationships is carried back on a claim under *FA 1996, s 83(2)* (see 43.3 LOAN RELATIONSHIPS). Previously the restrictions applied where a 'relievable amount' in respect of an exchange loss was carried back and set against exchange profits under *FA 1993, s 131* (see 23.14, 23.31 EXCHANGE GAINS AND LOSSES). [*TMA 1970, s 87A(4A)(4B); FA 1993, Sch 18 para 1; FA 1995, Sch 24 paras 8, 9; FA 1996, Sch 14 para 1; FA 1998, Sch 3 para 4, Sch 4 para 4*]. Where relief is given by repayment, the amount repaid is, as far as possible, treated as if it were a discharge of the corporation tax charged for that period. [*TMA 1970, s 91(2A); F(No 2)A 1987, s 86(6)*]. Interest on tax charged on certain loans by close companies (see 13.9–13.13 CLOSE COMPANIES) is not, however, refunded when tax is repaid following repayment, release or writing off of the loan, and any relief from tax under *ICTA 1988, s 419* is, for the purposes of refund of interest under *TMA 1970, s 91*, set only against tax assessed under *section 419*. [*TMA 1970, s 109(4)(5)*]. Interest ceases to run, however, from the date of the repayment, etc. [*TMA 1970, s 109(3A); F(No 2)A 1987, s 91*], and for this purpose any tax unpaid at that time is assumed, as far as possible, to be tax under *section 419*. (Revenue Pamphlet 'A Guide to Corporation Tax Self Assessment', para 5.4.2).

See Revenue Tax Bulletin May 1993 p 65 for an explanation of the operation of these restrictions.

Accounting periods ending on or after 1 July 1999. For liabilities in relation to such accounting periods, to which self-assessment applies, the provisions described above in relation to earlier accounting periods continue to apply, but with a number of changes, as follows.

(i) Interest payable under these provisions is deductible in computing income, profits or losses. In the case of interest on tax assessable under *ICTA 1988, Sch 13* or *Sch 16*, this applies in relation to return periods in a self-assessment accounting period.

(ii) The rate of interest is accordingly revised as follows, changes being announced in Revenue Press Releases. The rates listed above continue to apply in relation to earlier accounting periods.

8.50% p.a. from 7 January 1999 to 5 March 1999
7.50% p.a. from 6 March 1999 to 5 February 2000
8.50% p.a. from 6 February 2000 to

(iii) In the case of certain 'large' companies, which are required to make instalment payments in respect of their corporation tax liabilities, a special rate of interest (which is generally from 1 to 1.75% lower than that referred to in (ii) above from 20 April 2000 onwards) applies to any unpaid instalments until nine months after the end of the accounting period. See 48.1 PAYMENT OF TAX.

[*TMA 1970, ss 87A, 90; FA 1998, s 33; SI 1989 No 1297, regs 3ZA, 3ZB; SI 1998 No 3175, reg 7; SI 1998 No 3176, regs 4–6*].

Simon's Direct Tax Service. See D2.708.

39.2 *Examples*

(A) *General*

S Ltd prepares accounts to 31 December. On 31 October 1999, it makes a payment of £120,000 on account of its corporation tax liability for the year to 31 December 1998, the due date being 1 October 1999. On completing its corporation tax return, the company ascertains its total CT liability for that year to be £142,500 and makes a further payment of £22,500 on 18 December 1999. Following the Inspector's examination of the accounts and tax computations, various adjustments are made and the final CT liability is agreed at £145,500. The company pays a further £3,000 on 11 May 2000.

Interest on overdue tax will be payable as follows.

		£
1.10.99 to 31.10.99	£120,000 × 5.75% × $\frac{30}{366}$ =	565.57
1.10.99 to 18.12.99	£22,500 × 5.75% × $\frac{78}{366}$ =	275.72
1.10.99 to 5.2.00	£3,000 × 5.75% × $\frac{128}{366}$ =	60.33
6.2.00 to 11.5.00	£3,000 × 6.75% × $\frac{95}{366}$ =	52.56
Total interest charge		£954.18

For its next accounting period to 31 December 1999, S Ltd makes a payment on 31 October 2000 of £80,000 on account of its corporation tax liability for the year, the due date being 1 October 2000. On completing its corporation tax return, the company ascertains its total CT liability for that year to be £105,000 and makes a further payment of £25,000 on 18 December 2000. The final CT liability is agreed at £107,500 on 27 April 2001. The company pays a further £2,500 on 11 May 2001.

It is assumed that the rate of interest remains at 8.5% p.a. throughout.

Interest on overdue tax will be payable as follows.

		£
1.10.00 to 31.10.00	£80,000 × 8.5% × $\frac{30}{366}$ =	557.38
1.10.00 to 18.12.00	£25,000 × 8.5% × $\frac{78}{366}$ =	452.87
1.10.00 to 11.5.01	£2,500 × 8.5% × $\frac{222}{366}$ =	128.89
Total interest charge		£1,139.14

(B) *Refund of interest charged*

On 1 November 1998, T Ltd pays CT of £100,000 for its year ended 31 December 1997. The due date for payment was 1 October 1998. The liability is finally agreed at £80,000 and a repayment of £20,000 is made to T Ltd on 1 May 1999.

The interest position will be as follows.

(i) T Ltd will be charged interest on £100,000 for the period 1.10.98 to 1.11.98 (31 days). The charge will be raised following payment of the £100,000 on 1.11.98.

£100,000 × 7.5% × $\frac{31}{366}$ = £635.25

(ii) The company will be entitled to interest on overpaid tax of £20,000 for the period 1.11.98 (date of payment) to 1.5.99 (date of repayment) (181 days).

	£
£20,000 × 4% × $\frac{66}{365}$ =	144.66
£20,000 × 3.25% × $\frac{59}{365}$ =	105.07
£20,000 × 2.75% × $\frac{56}{365}$ =	84.38
	£334.11

(iii) T Ltd will also receive a refund of interest charged on £20,000 for the period 1.10.98 to 1.11.98.

£20,000 × 7.5% × $\frac{31}{366}$ =	£127.05

(C) *Instalment payment*

R Ltd has no associated companies and had taxable profits in excess of £1,500,000 for the year ended 30 September 1998. For the year ended 30 September 1999, R Ltd makes instalment payments of £75,000 (this being equivalent to a quarter of 60% of its estimated corporation tax liability of £500,000 as calculated under the phasing-in provisions) on the first three due dates. The last instalment is not paid until 24 January 2000 and the balance of the estimated liability, £200,000, is paid on 14 July 2000. On 3 March 2001, the tax liability is finally agreed at £584,800. R Ltd pays the balance due of £84,800 on 10 March 2001.

The rates of interest are assumed for the purposes of this example to remain unchanged after 20 April 2000.

The interest on tax unpaid is calculated as follows.

Instalments due: on quarter dates £584,800 × 60% × $\frac{1}{4}$ = £87,720
on normal due date £584,800 × 40% = £233,920

	£
14 April 1999 to 18 April 1999	
87,720 – 75,000 = £12,720 @ 7.5% × $\frac{5}{366}$ =	13.03
19 April 1999 to 20 June 1999	
87,720 – 75,000 = £12,720 @ 7.25% × $\frac{63}{366}$ =	158.74
21 June 1999 to 13 July 1999	
87,720 – 75,000 = £12,720 @ 7% × $\frac{23}{366}$ =	55.95
14 July 1999 to 19 September 1999	
175,440 – 150,000 = £25,440 @ 7% × $\frac{68}{366}$ =	330.86
20 September 1999 to 13 October 1999	
175,440 – 150,000 = £25,440 @ 7.25% × $\frac{24}{366}$ =	120.94
14 October 1999 to 14 November 1999	
263,160 – 225,000 = £38,160 @ 7.25% × $\frac{32}{366}$ =	241.89
15 November 1999 to 13 January 2000	
263,160 – 225,000 = £38,160 @ 7.5% × $\frac{60}{366}$ =	469.18
14 January 2000 to 23 January 2000	
350,880 – 225,000 = £125,880 @ 7.5% ×$\frac{10}{366}$ =	257.95

	£
24 January 2000 to 20 February 2000	
350,880 – 300,000 = £50,880 @ 7.75% × $\frac{28}{366}$ =	301.67
21 February 2000 to 19 April 2000	
350,880 – 300,000 = £50,880 @ 8% × $\frac{59}{366}$ =	656.16
20 April 2000 to 30 June 2000	
350,880 – 300,000 = £50,880 @ 7% × $\frac{72}{366}$ =	700.64
1 July 2000 to 13 July 2000	
584,800 – 300,000 = £284,800 @ 8.5% × $\frac{13}{366}$ =	859.85
14 July 2000 to 9 March 2001	
584,800 – 500,000 = £84,800 @ 8.5% × $\frac{239}{366}$ =	4,706.86
Interest on unpaid tax	£8,873.72

39.3 **ACCOUNTING PERIODS ENDING ON OR BEFORE 30 SEPTEMBER 1993**

In relation to accounting periods ending on or before 30 September 1993, corporation tax carries interest from a 'reckonable date' (even if it is a non-business day) until payment. Interest of £30 or less arising in respect of any assessment may be remitted where the notice of assessment is issued before 19 April 1993. [*TMA 1970, s 86 as substituted by F(No 2)A 1975, s 46(1) and amended by FA 1989, ss 156(1), 158; SI 1993 No 753*]. See also 39.6 below as regards ACT. The rate of interest is adjusted automatically by reference to the average of base lending rates of certain clearing banks, the formula being such average base rate plus 2.5%, the subtotal being reduced by the basic rate of income tax. [*FA 1989, ss 178, 179; SI 1989 No 1297*]. Changes are announced in Revenue Press Releases. Current and earlier rates are as follows.

6.00% p.a. from 19 April 1969 to 30 June 1974
9.00% p.a. from 1 July 1974 to 31 December 1979
12.00% p.a. from 1 January 1980 to 30 November 1982
8.00% p.a. from 1 December 1982 to 30 April 1985
11.00% p.a. from 1 May 1985 to 5 August 1986
8.50% p.a. from 6 August 1986 to 5 November 1986
9.50% p.a. from 6 November 1986 to 5 April 1987
9.00% p.a. from 6 April 1987 to 5 June 1987
8.25% p.a. from 6 June 1987 to 5 September 1987
9.00% p.a. from 6 September 1987 to 5 December 1987
8.25% p.a. from 6 December 1987 to 5 May 1988
7.75% p.a. from 6 May 1988 to 5 August 1988
9.75% p.a. from 6 August 1988 to 5 October 1988
10.75% p.a. from 6 October 1988 to 5 January 1989
11.50% p.a. from 6 January 1989 to 5 July 1989
12.25% p.a. from 6 July 1989 to 5 November 1989
13.00% p.a. from 6 November 1989 to 5 November 1990
12.25% p.a. from 6 November 1990 to 5 March 1991
11.50% p.a. from 6 March 1991 to 5 May 1991
10.75% p.a. from 6 May 1991 to 5 July 1991
10.00% p.a. from 6 July 1991 to 5 October 1991
9.25% p.a. from 6 October 1991 to 5 November 1992

7.75% p.a. from 6 November 1992 to 5 December 1992
7.00% p.a. from 6 December 1992 to 5 March 1993
6.25% p.a. from 6 March 1993 to 5 January 1994
5.50% p.a. from 6 January 1994 to 5 October 1994
6.25% p.a. from 6 October 1994 to 5 March 1995
7.00% p.a. from 6 March 1995 to 5 February 1996
6.25% p.a. from 6 February 1996 to 5 August 1997
7.25% p.a. from 6 August 1997 to 5 January 1999
6.50% p.a. from 6 January 1999 to 5 March 1999
5.75% p.a. from 6 March 1999 to 5 February 2000
6.50% p.a. from 6 February 2000 to

[*TMA 1970, s 89; FA 1989, ss 178, 179; SI 1974 No 966; SI 1979 No 1687; SI 1982 No 1587; SI 1985 No 563; SI 1986 Nos 1181, 1832; SI 1987 Nos 513, 898, 1492, 1898; SI 1988 Nos 756, 1278, 1621, 2185; SI 1989 Nos 1000, 1297*].

Interest factor tables for use as ready reckoners in calculating interest on overdue tax are published by the Revenue and updated as rates change (although not after 5 April 1999). (Revenue Press Release 11 March 1999).

Interest is payable gross and is not deductible from profits or income. [*TMA 1970, s 90*]. Interest on tax subsequently discharged is adjusted or repaid so as to secure that the total is as it would have been had the tax discharged never been charged, except that where a trading loss of an accounting period ending after 31 March 1991 is carried back and set against profits of an accounting period starting more than twelve months before the start of the period in which the loss arose (see 44.6 LOSSES), interest which would otherwise have arisen in respect of corporation tax unpaid for the earlier period will continue to run until the due and payable date for corporation tax for the accounting period in which the loss arose. Tax repaid is as far as possible treated as if it were a discharge of tax charged for the period, but not of tax charged by assessments made after the repayment and not so as partially to relieve tax charged by more than one assessment. [*TMA 1970, s 91; FA 1991, Sch 15 para 1*]. Interest on tax charged on certain loans by close companies (see 13.9–13.13 CLOSE COMPANIES) is not refunded when tax is repaid following repayment of the loan, and any relief from tax under *ICTA 1988, s 419* is, for the purposes of refund of interest under *TMA 1970, s 91*, set only against tax assessed under *section 419*. [*TMA 1970, s 109(4)(5)*].

The '*reckonable date*' is normally the due and payable date (see 48.2 PAYMENT OF TAX). Where there is an appeal and postponement application, so that special rules apply for determining the due and payable date of non-postponed, postponed and additional tax (see 48.3 PAYMENT OF TAX), it is the due and payable date *unless* that date is later than the date given by the Table in *TMA 1970, s 86*. In that case, the reckonable date is the later of the date given by the Table and the date on which tax under the assessment would have been due and payable had there been no appeal against it (see 48.2 PAYMENT OF TAX).

In transitional cases, where a notice requiring a return of profits for an accounting period ended before 1 October 1993 is served after 31 December 1993, and the tax assessed for that accounting period does not become due and payable until after the date falling nine months after the end of the period, the reckonable date will be that date. The Board are given power to mitigate any resulting interest, and have stated that interest will not be charged if an assessment is made bringing sufficient tax into charge by the normal due date (in line with the normal practice on charging interest under *TMA 1970, s 88* for delay in making a return which applied before the introduction of Pay and File, see below). Where such an assessment is not made, the interest charge will be reduced to ensure, as far as possible, that it does not exceed what it would have been under the pre-Pay and File provisions (see above). Also, where the accounting period in question runs to the normal company accounting date (or, if it is the first accounting period, to a date notified to the inspector within eight months of its ending), and either the company has notified its chargeability or a notice has been issued requiring a return and the return is made within the Pay and File time limit (see 54.2 RETURNS), interest will be charged only from the later of 60 days after issue of the notice and the normal due date. (Revenue Tax Bulletin August 1993 p 84).

The Table date referred to above is generally six months after the normal due and payable date in relation to an accounting period (i.e. in most cases 15 months after the end of the accounting period). In the case of tax charged on certain loans by close companies (see 13.9–13.13 CLOSE COMPANIES), however, it is the last day of the three months after the end of the financial year in which the loan was made. [*TMA 1970, s 86 as substituted by F(No 2)A 1975, s 46(1) and amended by FA 1989, s 156(1) and FA 1993, Sch 14 para 3; TMA 1970, s 109(2)*].

Tax lost through fault of taxpayer. Where an assessment for an accounting period ending on or before 30 September 1993 is raised to make good tax lost due to the taxpayer's fault, the tax is chargeable with interest under *TMA 1970, ss 88, 88A* (as amended and inserted by *FA 1989, ss 159–161*) and not under *TMA 1970, s 86*, from the date on which the tax ought originally to have been paid. The rates of interest are as 39.1 above, except that it was chargeable at 3% prior to 19 April 1967, and at 6% from 19 April 1967 to 18 April 1969. This provision does not, however, apply in relation to ACT or income tax deducted from payments made by the company. [*TMA 1970, s 88(2)*]. For the extent to which regard should be had to events after the making of an assessment in determining whether *section 88* applies, see *Billingham v Myers CA 1996, 68 TC 512*. See also Tolley's Income Tax under Back Duty.

In the case of tax charged on certain loans by close companies (see 13.9–13.13 CLOSE COMPANIES), the date on which the tax ought to have been paid is, for the purposes of *section 88*, taken as the first day of the financial year following that in which the loan was made. [*TMA 1970, s 109(3)*].

Interest will not generally be charged as above where the late assessment results from delay in submission of a return unless that delay is 'substantial', i.e. if the relevant return has not been made by the later of 30 days after the date of issue of the return and 31 October following the end of the tax year in which the income or chargeable gain arose. It will similarly not be charged where it is not possible to lodge the return but, within that time limit, information sufficient for the raising of an adequate estimated assessment is provided. (Revenue Pamphlet IR 131, SP 3/88, 10 May 1988 and SP 6/89, 31 July 1989). These Statements of Practice refer mainly to individual taxpayers, but, by analogy, a company which has not submitted accounts and computations within seven months after the end of an accounting period should, if no estimated assessment has been received (or if an inadequate estimated assessment has not been appealed against), provide the inspector with the necessary information to raise an adequate estimated assessment, in order to avoid an interest charge under *TMA 1970, s 88*. The 'reasonable excuse' provisions of *TMA 1970, s 118(2)* (see 49.6 PENALTIES) do not apply as regards *section 88* interest in relation to failures occurring after 26 July 1989. [*FA 1989, s 159(3)*].

Simon's Direct Tax Service. See A3.1320 *et seq*..

39.4 *Example*

A CT assessment was issued to R Ltd for its accounting year ended 31 August 1993. The relevant facts are as follows.

Corporation tax charged	£60,000	
Assessment issued		25.4.94
Company appealed and claimed to postpone £20,000 of the tax charged		20.5.94
Commissioners determined that only £15,000 of the tax charged could be postponed		27.6.94
Appeal determined, total tax payable £73,000		15.11.94
Amended assessment raised by Inspector		21.11.94
Normal due date		1.6.94
Table date		1.12.94
Tax payments made £40,000		10.8.94
£33,000		19.12.94

Interest on unpaid tax is calculated over the following periods.

£40,000	27.7.94 to 10.8.94
£5,000	27.7.94 to 19.12.94
£15,000	1.12.94 to 19.12.94
£13,000	1.12.94 to 19.12.94

Note

It is assumed that the notice requiring a return of profits was served before 1 January 1994.

39.5 DATE OF PAYMENT OF TAX

Effective dates of payment. With effect generally from 6 April 1996, these are taken to be as follows.

(*a*) *Cheques, cash, and postal orders* handed in at the Revenue office or received by post — the day of receipt by the Revenue *unless* received by post following a day on which the office was closed, in which case it is the day (or the first day) on which the office was closed.

(*b*) *Electronic funds transfer* — one working day immediately before the date the value is received.

(*c*) *Bank giro or Girobank* — three working days prior to the date of processing by the Revenue.

(Revenue Press Release 1 April 1996).

Previously, effective dates were considered to be as follows.

(i) In-date cheques tendered by post — the third working day before the day on which the Collector receives the cheque.

(ii) Cash and in-date cheques (other than those returned to the drawer) tendered personally — the date of tender.

(iii) Post-dated cheques — the date of the cheque.

(iv) Bank giro credit — the date stamped on the payslip by the bank's cashier.

(v) National Giro bank in-payment — the date stamped on the payslip by the Post Office counter clerk.

(vi) National Giro bank transfer — the date of the Inland Revenue's National Giro bank statement on which the item appears.

(See also Tolley's Practical Tax 1981 p 42).

(vii) Where a payment of tax was made by electronic funds transfer, an effective date of payment one working day immediately before the date value was received by the Revenue was allowed. (Revenue Press Release 1 April 1993).

39.6 ADVANCE CORPORATION TAX AND INCOME TAX DEDUCTED FROM PAYMENTS BY A COMPANY

As regards (i) (for accounting periods beginning before 6 April 1999) ACT and (ii) income tax payable by companies that they have deducted from yearly interest and other payments, interest arises if payment is made after the due date. As regards assessments relating to accounting periods beginning before 19 April 1993, interest is not charged unless the amount of the interest is over £30.

The due dates are 14 days after the expiry of the return periods (ending 31 March, 30 June, 30 September, 31 December and with the ending of an accounting period) in which the relevant dividends or other payments were made and interest will run from these dates even if they are non-business days. [*TMA 1970, s 87; ICTA 1988, Schs 13, 16; FA 1989, s 158; FA 1998, Sch 3 paras 3, 41; SI 1993 No 753*]. Where ACT is assessed on a qualifying distribution which is not a payment, or on a payment of an uncertain nature (see 3.4 ADVANCE CORPORATION TAX), the due date is 14 days after the issue of the notice of assessment. [*ICTA 1988, Sch 13 para 10(2); FA 1998, Sch 3 para 41*].

If a payment is made by a company on a date not falling within an accounting period of the company, tax is due 14 days after the payment. [*ICTA 1988, Sch 13 para 9, Sch 16 para 9; FA 1998, Sch 3 para 41*].

Where ACT or income tax paid is repaid or discharged following the receipt in a later return period of FII or income suffering tax by deduction, interest will nevertheless be chargeable where the original payment was late. It will, however, cease to run 14 days after the end of the later return period, or, if the return for that period was made within those 14 days, from the date of the return. [*TMA 1970, s 87(2)(3); FA 1998, Sch 3 para 3*].

See 3.4, 3.6 ADVANCE CORPORATION TAX and 31.4 INCOME TAX IN RELATION TO A COMPANY.

Simon's Direct Tax Service. See A3.1324.

39.7 EXCHANGE RESTRICTIONS

Where corporation tax is payable in respect of income or chargeable gains arising abroad which cannot be remitted to the UK due to action of the foreign government, the Board may allow the tax to remain uncollected. If so, interest ceases to run from the date on which the Board were in possession of the information necessary to make their decision. No interest is payable if that date is within three months of the due and payable date.

Where a demand for payment is subsequently made by the Collector, interest begins to run again unless the tax is paid within three months. [*TMA 1970, s 92*]. See 53.3 RESIDENCE.

39.8 REVENUE ERROR

The Revenue have published a Code of Practice (No 1, available from local tax offices) setting out the circumstances in which they will consider waiving a charge to interest on unpaid tax where there has been undue delay on the part of the Revenue. See 33.7 INLAND REVENUE: ADMINISTRATION.

40 Investment Companies

Cross-references. See 13.18 CLOSE COMPANIES as regards close investment-holding companies.

Simon's Direct Tax Service D4.401 *et seq.*.

40.1 **An investment company** is defined as 'any company whose business consists wholly or mainly in the making of investments and the principal part of whose income is derived therefrom'. [*ICTA 1988, s 130*]. It accordingly will include UNIT AND INVESTMENT TRUSTS (60). '*The making of investments*' does not require turning them over (*Tyre Investment Trust Ltd KB 1924, 12 TC 646*). For treatment of income from land as investment income, see *Webb v Conelee Properties Ltd Ch D 1982, 56 TC 149.*

It appears that a company's status as an 'investment company' is to be based on its activities over a representative period, see *FPH Finance Trust Ltd v CIR HL 1944, 26 TC 1311.*

A company formed to run a family estate was held not to be an investment company (under similar Irish legislation) in *Casey v Monteagle Estate Co HC(I) 1960, [1962] IR 106.* A similar decision was reached by the Special Commissioner in *Tintern Close Residents Society Ltd v Winter (Sp C 7), [1995] SSCD 57*, in which a company formed to 'acquire, hold, manage and deal with' common land and buildings on a residential estate was held not to be an investment company. See Revenue Tax Bulletin October 1995 pp 253, 254 for an appreciation of this decision and for the Revenue's view of the scope of *section 130*, for which see also Revenue Company Taxation Manual, CT 810, 811. In *Cook v Medway Housing Society Ltd Ch D 1996, 69 TC 319*, however, the business of a society formed to acquire and manage local authority housing stock was held to consist in the making of investments.

Savings banks (other than trustee savings banks or successor companies) are investment companies. [*ICTA 1988, s 130*].

40.2 **MANAGEMENT EXPENSES**

Management expenses of a UK resident investment company are deductible in computing total profits for corporation tax purposes. They include commissions, but exclude expenses otherwise deductible in computing profits or in relation to which a debit falls to be brought into account in respect of a loan relationship (see 43.2 LOAN RELATIONSHIPS). But such expenses must be reduced by any income derived from sources not charged to tax (other than FRANKED INVESTMENT INCOME (27), FOREIGN INCOME DIVIDENDS (26) (until their abolition after 5 April 1999) and (before 6 April 1999) group income, for which see 29.2 GROUPS OF COMPANIES) such as share register amendment fees received. [*ICTA 1988, s 75(1)(1A)(2); FA 1996, Sch 14 para 8; F(No 2)A 1997, Sch 6 para 2; FA 1998, Sch 3 para 9*]. Any unrelieved excess in an accounting period may be carried forward and treated as management expenses of the next succeeding accounting period (together with unused capital allowances plus charges on income paid in the accounting period wholly and exclusively for the purposes of the company's business), and may continue to be so carried forward until relieved. [*ICTA 1988, s 75(3)–(5)*]. Where, after 31 March 1998, an investment company ceases to carry on a Schedule A business (see 50.27 PROFIT COMPUTATIONS), any unrelieved losses from that business may be carried forward and treated as management expenses of the following accounting period. [*ICTA 1988, s 392A(3); FA 1998, Sch 5 para 28*].

Certain provisions are specifically extended to include management expenses. Thus secondary Class 1, from 26 November 1996 Class 1A, and from 6 April 1999 Class 1B national insurance contributions [*ICTA 1988, s 617(3)(4); FA 1997, s 65; FA 1999, s 61*], statutory redundancy payments [*ICTA 1988, s 579(3)*], payments in relation to certain employee trusts [*ICTA 1988, s 85A; FA 1989, s 67; FA 1991, s 43*] (see 50.10 PROFIT COMPUTATIONS), costs of establishing certain profit sharing and share option schemes [*ICTA 1988, s 84A; FA 1991, s 42*], payments to certain approved pension schemes [*ICTA 1988, s 592(4); FA 1993, s 112*] (but not to non-approved schemes [*FA 1989, s 76*]), incidental costs of obtaining loan finance for accounting periods ending before 1 April 1996 (see 50.19 PROFIT COMPUTATIONS) [*ICTA 1988, s 77; FA 1996, Sch 14 para 9*], additional payments to redundant employees (see 50.24 PROFIT COMPUTATIONS) [*ICTA 1988, s 90*], discounts on bills of exchange and associated costs (see 50.9 PROFIT COMPUTATIONS) [*ICTA 1988, s 78, repealed by FA 1996, Sch 14 para 10, Sch 41 Pt V(3)*], and certain training costs [*ICTA 1988, s 588*] are allowable management expenses. Conversely, *ICTA 1988, s 577* applies to restrict allowance of entertainment expenditure, and *ICTA 1988, s 577A* to prohibit a deduction for certain illegal payments. The provisions of *ICTA 1988, s 781* (taxation as income of certain capital sums received by persons to whom tax relief is allowable in respect of payments under a lease of an asset other than land) similarly apply to investment companies. See also 50.7 PROFIT COMPUTATIONS regarding certain issues of securities at a deep discount.

Management expenses do not include an exchange loss on the payment of interest (*Bennet v Underground Electric Railways Co of London Ltd KB 1923, 8 TC 475*); or brokerage and stamp duty on investment changes (*Capital and National Trust Ltd v Golder CA 1949, 31 TC 265*); or payments to the guarantor of loan stock capital by the investment company issuing the stock (*Hoechst Finance Ltd v Gumbrell CA 1983, 56 TC 594*, but see now *section 77* as above). In *Holdings Ltd v CIR (Sp C 117), [1997] SSCD 144*, a Special Commissioner held that fees for professional advice concerning an investment company's potential liabilities under letters of assurance given to the bankers of a trading subsidiary were allowable. In *L G Berry Investments Ltd v Attwooll Ch D 1964, 41 TC 547*, the Special Commissioners' finding that part of the directors' remuneration was not allowable was upheld. For the interaction of management expenses and double tax relief, see *Jones v Shell Petroleum Co Ltd HL 1971, 47 TC 194*.

Contributions made to an approved profit sharing scheme within *ICTA 1988, s 186* (including, for example, sums paid to meet trustees' capital gains tax liability) are allowable as management expenses. (CCAB Memorandum TR 308, June 1978).

Where an investment company provides relocation packages for its employees who are obliged to relocate, reasonable costs may be allowed as management expenses. However, where the company acquires the beneficial interest in the employee's property, the purchase and subsequent sale of the property will normally fall to be dealt with under the CAPITAL GAINS (9) provisions. (Revenue Tax Bulletin May 1994 p 124).

Other items which generally qualify as management expenses include accounts, share register and annual general meeting costs; registered office expenses; stock exchange quotation cost; valuation costs; and Export Credit Guarantee Department payments. See generally Revenue Company Taxation Manual, CT 830 *et seq.*.

CAPITAL ALLOWANCES (8) on machinery and plant apply to investment companies as they apply in relation to machinery and plant for use in a trade. Such allowances are granted by deducting them from income of the business, any balance being treated as management expenses. Balancing charges are treated as income of the business. [*CAA 1990, s 28; FA 1995, Sch 8 para 24*]. Certain emoluments for accounting periods ending after 5 April 1989 which are not paid within nine months of the end of the period of account which includes or coincides with the accounting period to which they relate are not allowed as a deduction until the accounting period in which they are paid. [*FA 1989, s 44*].

See also 41.2 LIFE INSURANCE COMPANIES.

Appeals on management expense matters are to the Special Commissioners. [*ICTA 1988, s 75(5)*].

Claims may be made to set off unrelieved management expenses of an accounting period against surplus FRANKED INVESTMENT INCOME (27.3) under *ICTA 1988, s 242(2)* (prior to its repeal), or for GROUP RELIEF (29.18) under *ICTA 1988, s 403* of such expenses. Management expenses brought forward from an earlier accounting period may be relieved under *section 242(2)* (where applicable) but not under *ICTA 1988, s 403*.

Simon's Direct Tax Service. See D4.403 *et seq.*.

40.3 *Example*

XYZ Ltd, an investment company, makes up accounts to 31 March.

The following details are relevant.

	31.3.00	31.3.01
	£	£
Rents received	38,000	107,000
Interest receivable accrued (gross)	10,000	5,000
Chargeable gains	18,000	48,000
Management expenses		
attributable to property	20,000	25,000
attributable to management	50,000	40,000
Capital allowances		
attributable to property	1,000	500
attributable to management	2,000	1,000
Business charges on income	30,000	30,000
Charitable charges on income	5,000	5,000

The corporation tax computations are as follows.

Year ended 31.3.00

	£	£
Schedule A		
Rents		38,000
Deduct Capital allowances	1,000	
Management expenses	20,000	(21,000)
		17,000
Schedule D, Case III		10,000
Chargeable gains		18,000
		45,000
Deduct Management expenses	50,000	
Capital allowances	2,000	(52,000)
		(7,000)
Deduct Business charges	30,000	
Charitable charges	5,000	(35,000)
Unrelieved balance carried forward		£(42,000)

Year ended 31.3.01

	£	£
Schedule A		
Rents		107,000
Deduct Capital allowances	500	
Management expenses	25,000	(25,500)
		81,500
Schedule D, Case III		5,000
Chargeable gains		48,000
		134,500
Deduct Management expenses	40,000	
Capital allowances	1,000	
Unrelieved balance from previous accounting period	42,000	(83,000)
		51,500
Deduct Business charges	30,000	
Charitable charges	5,000	(35,000)
Profit chargeable to CT		£16,500

40.4 **LOSSES ON UNQUOTED SHARES**

As regards relief for losses on unquoted shares subscribed for in certain trading companies, see 44.19 LOSSES.

40.5 **CHANGE IN OWNERSHIP OF INVESTMENT COMPANY**

Deductions. Restrictions apply on the use of management expenses and charges brought forward where there is a change in the ownership of an investment company **on or after 29 November 1994** (other than in pursuance of a contract entered into before that date) and either:

(*a*) after the change there is a 'significant increase' in the company's capital; or

(*b*) within the period from three years before to three years after the change there is a major change in the nature or conduct of the company's business. This includes a change in the nature of the company's investments, even if it is the result of a gradual process which began before that period; or

(*c*) the change occurs after the scale of business activities carried on by the investment company has become small or negligible and before any considerable revival.

There is a '*significant increase*' in the company's capital if 'amount B' is more than twice 'amount A' or exceeds it by at least £1 million, where

'amount A' is the lower of (I) the amount of its capital immediately before the change and (II) the highest amount below which its capital did not fall during a 60 day period in the year immediately preceding the change, and

'amount B' is the highest amount below which its capital did not fall during a 60 day period in the three years beginning with the change.

For this purpose, the amount of the company's capital (expressed in sterling and rounded up to the nearest pound) is the aggregate of (I) its paid up share capital (including any share premium account), (II) any outstanding debts (including interest due) incurred by the company for any money borrowed or capital assets acquired by the company, for any right to receive income created in favour of the company, or for consideration the value of which to the company (at the time the debt was incurred) was substantially less than the amount of the debt (including any premium thereon), and (III) any outstanding redeemable loan capital.

As regards (II) above, loan capital or debt issued or incurred for money lent to the company in the ordinary course of a banking business is excluded. (ICAEW Technical Release TAX 22/95, 17 August 1995, para 172).

Where these provisions apply:

(i) the accounting period in which the change occurs is treated as two separate accounting periods, up to and after the change, the 'amounts in issue' being apportioned as specified below between those parts;

(ii) in computing the total profits of the company for an accounting period ending after the change, no deduction is made under *ICTA 1988, s 75* (see 40.2 above) by reference to sums disbursed or allowances falling to be made for an accounting period beginning before the change, or for charges paid in such an accounting period;

(iii) for accounting periods ending before 1 April 1996, to the extent that a payment of interest made in an accounting period ending after the change represents 'excess overdue interest', the payment is not deductible as a charge (see 50.3 PROFIT COMPUTATIONS) in the accounting period in which it is paid; and

(iv) for accounting periods ending after 31 March 1996, the debits to be brought into account in respect of the company's loan relationships (see 43.3 LOAN RELATIONSHIPS) are restricted by *ICTA 1988, Sch 28A, Pt IV* (see below).

Where deductions have been restricted as above, in applying the provisions of *CAA 1990* relating to balancing charges by reference to any event after the change, any allowance or deduction falling to be made for any period before the change is disregarded insofar as the profits or gains of that and any subsequent chargeable period before the change are insufficient to give effect to it (assuming that it is relieved in priority to any loss not attributable to such an allowance or deduction).

The '*amounts in issue*' within (i) above are:

(A) any management expenses (including commissions) disbursed for the accounting period being divided, but excluding any which (apart from these provisions) would be deductible otherwise than under *ICTA 1988, s 75*;

(B) any charges paid in that period wholly and exclusively for the purposes of the company's business;

(C) any management expenses or charges brought forward to that period;

(D) any capital allowances which would (apart from these provisions) be added to the management expenses of that period;

(E) for accounting periods ending after 31 March 1996,

  (i) the Schedule D, Case III profits and gains arising from the company's loan relationships, or non-trading deficit (if any) on those relationships, for that period, disregarding amounts within (ii)–(iv) below,

  (ii) any non-trading debit (not within (iv) below) falling to be brought into account for that period in respect of any debtor relationship,

  (iii) any non-trading debit carried forward to that period under *FA 1996, s 83(3)*, and

(iv) any non-trading debit for that period under the transitional provisions of *FA 1996, Sch 15 para 13* in respect of any debtor relationship

(see 43.2, 43.3, 43.11 LOAN RELATIONSHIPS); and

(F) any other amounts by reference to which the profits or losses of that period would (apart from these provisions) be calculated.

Amounts within (A) and (B) above are apportioned by reference to the time payment is due (interest being assumed to become due on a day to day basis as it arises); those within (C) and (E)(iii) above are apportioned to the pre-change part of the period in full; those within (D), (E)(i) and (F) above are apportioned on a time basis; those within (E)(ii) above (where an accruals basis applies, and except in the case of certain late interest payments, where the debit is apportioned to the pre-change part of the period in full) are apportioned by reference to the time of accrual of the amount to which the debit relates; and those within (E)(iv) above are apportioned to the pre-change part of the period in full. If in any case such apportionment would work unreasonably or unjustly, a just and reasonable method of apportionment may be substituted.

A payment or part payment of interest represents '*excess overdue interest*' within (iii) above to the extent that it discharges a liability to pay 'overdue interest' (i.e. interest due but not paid before the change in ownership) (and it is assumed to do so before it discharges any liability to pay interest which is not overdue interest), but limited to the amount (if any) by which all overdue interest exceeds the profits (after all deductions and reliefs) of the accounting period ending with the change in ownership. Interest is for these purposes assumed to become due on a day to day basis as it arises. A similar restriction applies under (iv) above by reference to non-trading debits to be brought into account on an accruals basis under the LOAN RELATIONSHIPS (43) provisions (see *ICTA 1988, Sch 28A Pt IV* as amended).

Assessment. Where these provisions are triggered by circumstances or events at any time in the three years after the change, an assessment to give effect to them may be made within six years of that time (or the latest such time).

Information. For the purposes of these provisions the inspector may, by notice in writing, require any person who is the registered owner of shares, stock or securities of a company to state whether he is the beneficial owner thereof and, if not, to supply the name and address of the person(s) on whose behalf he holds them.

[*ICTA 1988, s 768B, Sch 28A paras 1–12; FA 1995, s 135, Sch 26; FA 1996, Sch 14 para 54(4); FA 1998, s 82(3)(4)*].

See 44.13 LOSSES as regards what constitutes a 'major change' in the nature or conduct of a trade or business, which may be relevant to (*b*) above.

Asset transferred within group. Where there is a change in ownership of an investment company **on or after 29 November 1994** (other than in pursuance of a contract entered into before that date) and none of (*a*)–(*c*) above applies, restrictions similarly apply where

(1) after the change the company acquires an asset from another company in the same group so that *TCGA 1992, s 171* applies (transaction treated as giving rise to neither gain nor loss, see 9.19 CAPITAL GAINS), and

(2) a chargeable gain (the 'relevant gain') arises to the company on disposal of the asset (or of an asset deriving its value wholly or partly from that asset — in particular where the original asset was a leasehold, the lessee has acquired the reversion and the freehold is disposed of) within three years of the change.

The accounting period of the change is split as in (i) above, and if the total profits of the company for the accounting period in which the relevant gain accrues include, in accordance with *TCGA 1992, s 8(1)* and *Sch 7A* (see 9.3, 9.23 CAPITAL GAINS), an amount in respect of chargeable gains, the deductions as in (ii) and (iii) or (iv) above may not be set against profits equal to the lesser of that amount and the amount of the relevant gain.

The '*amounts in issue*', in addition to those detailed in (A)–(F) above, include

(G) the chargeable gains included, in accordance with *TCGA 1992, s 8(1)* and *Sch 7A*, in the total profits for the period being divided (as above).

The same basis of apportionment applies as is referred to in relation to (A)–(F) above, with the amount within (G) above being apportioned, insofar as it exceeds the relevant gain, to the pre-change part of the divided period, an amount equivalent to the relevant gain (or, if less, the amount within (G) above) being apportioned to the post-change part of the divided period.

The assessment and information powers under *section 768B* (see above) apply equally under these provisions.

[*ICTA 1988, s 768C, Sch 28A paras 13–17; FA 1995, s 135, Sch 26; FA 1996, Sch 14 paras 39, 40, 54; FA 1998, s 82(3)(4)*].

Schedule A losses. Where, in relation to an investment company carrying on a Schedule A business or an overseas property business (see 50.27 PROFIT COMPUTATIONS), either

(I) (*a*), (*b*) or (*c*) above applies (so that the provisions of *section 768B* apply, or would apply, in relation to management expenses and charges), or

(II) *Section 768C* (see above) applies in relation to an asset transferred within a group,

similar restrictions apply to prevent Schedule A losses (see 50.27 PROFIT COMPUTATIONS) incurred before the change being set against profits arising after the change. [*ICTA 1988, s 768D; FA 1998, Sch 5 para 31*].

General. The provisions of *ICTA 1988, s 769* (rules for ascertaining change in ownership, see 44.13 LOSSES) apply with appropriate modification in relation to these provisions as they apply to *ICTA 1988, ss 768, 768A*.

Simon's Direct Tax Service. See **D4.409A** *et seq.*.

40.6 OPEN-ENDED INVESTMENT COMPANIES [*FA 1995, s 152*]

Open-ended investment companies ('OEICs') are investment companies in which shares are continuously created or redeemed, according to investor demand. Regulations provide for the taxation of OEICs and their shareholders to be on a similar basis to that applicable to authorised unit trusts. The main such regulations, which came into force on 28 April 1997, are the *Open-ended Investment Companies (Tax) Regulations 1997* (*SI 1997 No 1154*) (as amended by *SI 1997 No 1715*), by virtue of which:

(*a*) OEICs are exempt from tax on capital gains realised for the benefit of investors;

(*b*) their income is subject to corporation tax at 20% (25% where they are invested primarily in interest-bearing assets);

(*c*) shareholders are taxed on the full net income earned for them, whether distributed or accumulated, this income to be treated, at the OEIC's option, as a dividend, a FOREIGN INCOME DIVIDEND (26), a dividend paired with a foreign income dividend, or a payment taxable as interest (subject to the abolition of foreign income dividends after 5 April 1999);

(*d*) OEICs are able to distribute income to non-resident shareholders (or to accumulate it) without deduction of UK tax if the OEIC invests in appropriate assets and the shareholders comply with the necessary formalities; and (*e*) there is generally continuity of tax treatment for an authorised unit trust converting into or merging with an OEIC.

Additionally, the *Personal Equity Plan (Amendment No 2) Regulations 1997* (*SI 1997 No 1716*) enable investments in OEICs to be held in personal equity plans (see Tolley's Income Tax under Exempt Income) on the same basis as those in authorised unit trusts.

Various other aspects of OEIC taxation are assimilated to those for authorised unit trusts by the reissue of Revenue Statements of Practice SP 3/89 and SP 7/94 (dealing with monthly savings schemes and investment trust holdings) as SP 2/97 and SP 3/97 respectively, SP 2/97 being subsequently superseded by SP 2/99. The concession in Revenue Pamphlet IR 1, C30 (concerning waivers of distributions) also applies equally to OEICs and authorised unit trusts. See generally UNIT AND INVESTMENT TRUSTS (60).

Regulations also deal with VAT (*Value Added Tax (Finance) Order 1997* (*SI 1997 No 510*)) and stamp duty and stamp duty reserve tax (*Stamp Duty and Stamp Duty Reserve Tax (Open-ended Investment Companies) Regulations 1997* (*SI 1997 No 1156*), *(Amendment) Regulations 1999* (*SI 1999 No 1467*) and *(Amendment No 2) Regulations 1999* (*SI 1999 No 3261*)) in relation to OEICs.

Simon's Direct Tax Service. See **D4.401, D4.402.**

41 Life Insurance Companies

Cross-reference. See 18.18 CONTROLLED FOREIGN COMPANIES, 23.31 EXCHANGE GAINS AND LOSSES, 25.21(*c*) FINANCIAL INSTRUMENTS, 43.10 LOAN RELATIONSHIPS, 50.17 PROFIT COMPUTATIONS.

Simon's Direct Tax Service D4.5.

Other sources. See Revenue Life Assurance Manual.

The headings in this chapter are as follows.

41.1 Introduction
41.2 Management expenses
41.3 Apportionment of income and gains between different types of business
41.4 Life assurance business — Schedule D, Case I
41.5 Other life assurance business (including general annuity business)
41.6 Pension business
41.7 Policy holders' fraction of profits etc.
41.8 Reinsurance business
41.9 Pre-1965 policies
41.10 Policies carrying rights not in money
41.11 Transfer of assets to non-resident company
41.12 Overseas life insurance companies
41.13 Cessation of residence
41.14 Overseas life assurance business
41.15 Transfers of assets, etc.
41.16 Transfers of long term business
41.17 Holdings of unit trusts etc.
41.18 Capital redemption business
41.19 Deduction of tax from premiums

41.1 INTRODUCTION

The following provisions apply to any company carrying on life assurance business, which includes the business of granting annuities on human life ('annuity business'). Life assurance business is to be treated as a separate business from any other category of business, and if (for accounting periods beginning before 1 January 1996) it comprises both industrial assurance and ordinary life assurance business, these are to be treated as separate. [*ICTA 1988, ss 76(8), 431(2), 432; FA 1996, s 167(1)*]. An '*insurance company*' is a company to which *Insurance Companies Act 1982, Pt II* applies or, for accounting periods ending after 30 June 1994, an 'EC company' carrying on 'insurance business' (within the meaning of that *Act*) through a branch or agency in the UK. [*ICTA 1988, s 431(2); FA 1995, s 52(1)(5)*].

The taxation of life insurance companies was substantially amended with effect from 1 January 1990. Provisions to alter the detailed rules for taxing pension and general annuity business profits, to spread relief for the expenses of acquiring new life assurance business, and to abolish life assurance policy duty, were included in *FA 1989*. Further provisions, contained in *FA 1990*, laid down new rules for the allocation of income and realised gains to different types of business; altered the rules for the taxation of overseas branch and agency business; introduced a revised approach to the allocation of investment income, capital gains and profits between shareholders and policy holders; altered the tax treatment of reinsurance commissions received; introduced a new basis of charge on life office holdings in exempt investment media; and provided continuity where life assurance business is transferred between companies. There were further amendments in *FA 1991* to abolish the distinction for tax purposes between general annuity business and basic life assurance business from 1 January 1992.

F(No 2)A 1992, s 65 was introduced with full retrospective effect to confirm the long-standing basis of taxation of proprietary life assurance companies. Neither the making of certain loss claims, nor the application of any commercial or accounting principle or practice in computing losses, nor the application of 'relevant provisions' (see *section 65(2)*) prevents the application of the so-called 'I minus E' basis in respect of a company's life assurance business or affects the calculation of income or gains in applying that basis.

FA 1993, ss 97–103, Schs 9–11 introduced substantial revisions to the taxation regime for overseas life insurance companies operating through UK branches or agencies, with effect for accounting periods beginning after 31 December 1992. These are summarised at 41.12 below.

FA 1995, ss 51–53, Schs 8, 9 make further changes, relating in particular to business written directly with certain non-residents by UK companies or branches of non-UK companies. There are also changes in the allocation of income and gains to different categories of business, in the taxation of reinsurance business, clarifying the availability of capital allowances, and dealing with minor anomalies.

FA 1996, s 99, Sch 11 contain special provisions for insurance companies relating to the taxation of LOAN RELATIONSHIPS (43), for which see also *FA 1996, Sch 9 para 12* re certain transfers of business and *FA 1996, Sch 15 para 1(3)* re reference of debits and credits under those provisions to different categories of business. *FA 1996, s 163, Sch 31* contain provisions for life assurance business losses.

F(No 2)A 1997, ss 23, 34, Sch 3, Sch 4 Pt II contain provisions applying, in the case of insurance companies, the abolition of tax credit payments and (from 6 April 1999) the reduction in the rate of tax credit. These apply to distributions after 1 July 1997 in relation to insured pension business and set-off against management expenses or trading losses, otherwise from 6 April 1999.

FA 1998, s 77 introduces a new *ICTA 1988, s 333B*, which gives the Treasury regulation-making powers to provide exemption from tax for income and gains of so much of an insurance company's long term business fund as is referable to individual savings account business. The regulations may modify the effect of the prohibition on tax credit payments for distributions made before 6 April 2004, may include special provision in relation to non-UK resident insurance companies, and may provide the Revenue with information powers. Corresponding provisions may also be made in relation to friendly societies. The principal regulations under these provisions (*Individual Savings Account (Insurance Companies) Regulations 1998* (*SI 1998 No 1871*)) come into force on 6 April 1999.

FA 1999, s 81 makes statutory provision for the bringing into charge of profits arising from certain intra-group transfers of investments following the withdrawal of extra-statutory arrangements into which groups have previously been able to enter with the Revenue. Under these, profits and losses from non-life business of insurance companies within the group have been computed and assessed to tax as if the group were a single company. *Section 81* gives statutory effect to the undertaking given by groups on entering into such arrangements. For details of extra-statutory group assessment, see chapter 11 of the Revenue General Insurance Manual.

FA 2000, s 107 introduces a charge where technical provisions by a general insurer give rise to an allowance in computing profits in a period of account beginning on or after 1 January 2000, and it becomes apparent in a later period beginning on or after 1 January 2001 that the amount allowed was excessive or insufficient. An amount representing interest on the excess or deficiency is treated as a receipt or expense for tax purposes in the later period. An election is available for any part of the technical provisions not to be taken into account for tax purposes in the period in which the provision is made, with a corresponding later adjustment. The Board has wide and flexible regulation-making powers to give effect to the adjustment. There are also detailed provisions in *FA 2000, Sch 30* relating to double tax relief for insurance companies.

See Revenue Pamphlet IR 131, SP 4/95, 22 March 1995, for the approach the Revenue adopt to the measurement of trading profit from life assurance and other types of long term business when accounts are drawn up in accordance with the Insurance Accounts Directive (91/674/EEC).

41.2 **MANAGEMENT EXPENSES**

'Management expenses' are deductible in computing total profits for corporation tax purposes, as in the case of INVESTMENT COMPANIES (40), by a company which is not charged to tax under Schedule D, Case I in respect of its life assurance business. The amount of management expenses available for relief for an accounting period is restricted, any relief so withheld being carried forward.

For accounting periods beginning **after 31 December 1995**, the management expenses otherwise available are reduced by the excess of profits calculated as under Schedule D, Case I (adjusted for certain unused Case I losses) over the amount found by deducting the following from the 'relevant income':

(A) management expenses not restricted under this provision;

(B) any non-trading deficit on loan relationships apportioned to that business under *FA 1996, Sch 11 para 2* (in relation to LOAN RELATIONSHIPS (43));

(C) any amount carried back on a claim to reduce profits of the period under *FA 1996, Sch 11 para 4(3)(5)*; and

(D) (for accounting periods beginning before 6 March 1997) any charges on income consisting of annuities or other annual payments referable to that business (and, if not annuities, payable wholly or partly in satisfaction of policy claims) (and see now 41.5 below).

'*Relevant income*' for this purpose is the sum of the company's life assurance business income and gains and either

(1) in relation to distributions made on or after 2 July 1997, franked investment income of, and foreign income dividends arising to, the company which are referable to its 'basic life assurance and general annuity business' (see below), or

(2) in relation to distributions made before 2 July 1997, franked investment income not already included in such income and gains which arises from assets held for the purposes of the life assurance business (but excluding any in respect of which the tax credits may be claimed under *ICTA 1988, s 438(4)* (pension business exemption, see 41.6 below) or *s 441A(7)* (distribution of assets of overseas life assurance fund, see 41.14 below)).

Management expenses taken into account in computing an allowable loss under Schedule D, Case I cannot also be deducted as management expenses in a computation on the 'I minus E' basis (*Johnson v The Prudential Assurance Co Ltd CA 1998, 70 TC 445*).

For earlier accounting periods, relief is withheld insofar as (added to the other reliefs (excluding ACT set off) to which the life assurance company is entitled) it would otherwise reduce the corporation tax liability (including tax credits not repaid (see *Utopia Assurance Co Ltd v Chaloner (Sp C 72), [1996] SSCD 204*)) below that which would have been paid if the life assurance business had been taxable under Schedule D, Case I; and any relief so withheld may be carried forward to the next accounting period. Where the company carries on business other than life assurance business (or carries on both ordinary and industrial life assurance business), ACT set off is apportioned among those businesses in proportion to the profits thereof charged to corporation tax for the accounting period.

[*ICTA 1988, s 76; FA 1989, s 44; FA 1996, s 164; FA 1997, s 67(4)(7); F(No 2)A 1997, Sch 3 para 1*].

'*Management expenses*' for this purpose include all sums paid by the life assurance company under a long-term business levy imposed by the *Policyholders Protection Act 1975*, or under a levy imposed in relation to an investor protection scheme, either under *Financial Services Act 1986, s 54* or by a self-regulating organisation where Treasury regulations so prescribe. [*ICTA 1988, s 76(7); FA 1991, s 47*]. Relief is extended by *SI 1992 No 2744* to levies made under the LAUTRO Indemnity Scheme, and also, by concession (see Revenue Pamphlet IR 1, C21), to levies imposed under the terms of the LAUTRO (Compensation Schemes) (No 2) Rules 1991 made on 17 December 1991 or the 1993 Rules made on 27 April 1993 and extended on 26 April 1994 (to meet liabilities attributable to members of FIMBRA). All fines, fees or profits arising from reversions are to be deducted from management expenses, as are certain life assurance business losses, but no deduction is made for income not chargeable to tax (cf. 40.2 INVESTMENT COMPANIES). [*ICTA 1988, s 76(1)(aa)(a); FA 1996, Sch 31 para 1; FA 2000, Sch 27 para 7*]. Discounts on certain premiums were held not to be a management expense in *North British & Mercantile Insurance Co v Easson CS 1919, 7 TC 463*, as were brokerage and stamp duties on changes of investments in *Sun Life Assurance Society v Davidson HL 1957, 37 TC 330.*

For capital allowances for accounting periods beginning after 31 December 1994, see 41.4 below. Previously, they were granted under similar provisions as apply to investment companies, see 40.2 INVESTMENT COMPANIES. [*CAA 1990, s 28; FA 1995, Sch 8 para 24*].

Exclusions. Expenses referable to pension business or overseas life assurance business or, for accounting periods beginning after 31 December 1994, life reinsurance business (or for accounting periods beginning before 1 January 1992, general annuity business) are not to be included as management expenses, and the amount of profits from which allowable management expenses may be deducted may not exceed the income and gains (after deduction of reliefs and exemptions other than management expenses) referable to 'basic life assurance and general annuity business'. Repayments or refunds of sums disbursed as acquisition expenses are deducted from allowable management expenses, as are reinsurance commissions referable to 'basic life assurance and general annuity business'. [*ICTA 1988, s 76(1)(c)–(e); FA 1989, s 87(1)–(5); FA 1990, ss 42, 44(3), Sch 7 para 1; FA 1991, Sch 7 para 1; FA 1995, Sch 8 para 7*].

Spreading of relief for acquisition expenses. Relief for expenses attributable to the acquisition of 'basic life assurance and general annuity business', previously allowable in full when incurred, is spread over a period which will ultimately comprise seven years. The immediately allowable fraction will reduce from five-sevenths for acquisition expenses of an accounting period (or part) falling within 1990 to one-seventh where it falls within 1994, with the balance being allowed in subsequent accounting periods at an annual rate of one-seventh. '*Acquisition expenses*' for this purpose are:

(*a*) commissions (however described) in respect of insurances made or varied after 13 March 1989 and annuity contracts made or varied in accounting periods beginning after 31 December 1991,

(*b*) any other management expenses disbursed solely for the purpose of the acquisition of business, and

(*c*) a proper proportion of other management expenses partly so disbursed;

less:

(i) any amounts repaid or refunded, as to which see above,

(ii) any reinsurance commission, referable to 'basic life assurance business' (or 'basic life assurance and general annuity business', as appropriate), in respect (in the case of basic life assurance business) of liabilities assumed after 13 March 1989 or subject to policy variation after that date, and

(iii) (for accounting periods ending after 31 December 1995), a specified proportion of any deduction from management expenses (as above) in respect of life assurance business losses.

Commissions for premiums collected from house to house (for accounting periods beginning before 1 January 1996, commissions in respect of industrial life assurance business) are acquisition expenses only if within (*b*) or (*c*) above.

[*FA 1989, s 86; FA 1990, s 44(2)(5); FA 1991, Sch 7 para 13; FA 1995, Sch 8 para 23(3); FA 1996, s 167(3)*].

'*Basic life assurance and general annuity business*' means life assurance business other than pension business and overseas life assurance business (and including, for accounting periods beginning after 31 December 1994, reinsurance business other than life reinsurance business, see 41.8 below). [*ICTA 1988, ss 431(2), 431F; FA 1991, Sch 7 para 2; FA 1995, Sch 8 para 2, Sch 29 Pt VIII(5)*].

Simon's Direct Tax Service. See D4.504.

41.3 **APPORTIONMENT OF INCOME AND GAINS BETWEEN DIFFERENT TYPES OF BUSINESS**

Detailed provisions apply for the apportionment of income and gains where an insurance company carries on in any period both ordinary long term business and industrial assurance business, or life assurance business and other long term business, or more than one class of life assurance business (for accounting periods beginning after 31 December 1994, where it carries on more than one of specified categories of business). Income arising from, and gains and losses on the disposal of, assets linked to any one category of business are treated as referable to that category. Any income, gains or losses not directly referable to any category are to be apportioned, with the 'relevant fraction' (as defined) being referred to each category. Only income, etc. from assets of the overseas life assurance fund is, however, referable to overseas life assurance business. [*ICTA 1988, ss 432ZA, 432A, Sch 5AA para 9; FA 1990, s 41, Sch 6 para 4; FA 1991, Sch 7 para 3; FA 1993, s 91(2); FA 1995, Sch 8 paras 11, 13; FA 1996, s 167(2); FA 1997, s 80, Sch 11 para 9; FA 2000, s 109*]. For the separate treatment of Schedule A business and overseas property business (see 50.27 PROFIT COMPUTATIONS), see *ICTA 1988, ss 432AA, 432AB* introduced by *FA 1998, Sch 5 para 39*.

Where it is necessary, in accordance with *FA 1989, s 83* (see 41.4 below), to apportion items brought into account in the revenue account(s) prepared for the purposes of the *Insurance Companies Act 1982*, there are separate provisions for cases where the relevant business relates exclusively to policies or contracts under which the policy holders or annuitants are not eligible to participate in any surplus ('non-participating funds'), and for cases where there is any such eligibility ('participating funds').

For non-participating funds, any income or change in the value of assets attributable to a particular category of business is related to that category, income etc. attributable to assets of the overseas life assurance fund (or, for accounting periods beginning after 31 October 1994, to UK land linked to overseas life assurance business) being referable to overseas life assurance business. Any income, etc. not directly referable to any category is to be apportioned, with the 'relevant fraction' (as defined) being referred to each category (except that income is not so apportioned to overseas life assurance business).

For participating funds, there are detailed provisions stipulating the way in which the amounts to be brought into account under *FA 1989, s 83* are to be referable to a particular category of business. Two amounts are determined: the first is that resulting from an apportionment which would produce the result that the ratio of the unallocated surplus of the business concerned to the overall unallocated surplus is equal to the ratio of the surplus of the business concerned allocated to persons entitled to benefits to the surplus of the overall business so allocated; the second is the aggregate of a specified percentage of the mean of the opening and closing liabilities concerned (reduced by the mean of opening and closing values of assets linked to that business) and the part of the net amount to be brought into account under *section 83* attributable to assets linked to that business. Where, for any accounting period ending after 31 December 1993, the first amount exceeds the second, the excess is carried forward cumulatively until an accounting period in which the second amount exceeds the first. The amount brought forward is then used to reduce the second amount for that period (but not to less than the first amount for that period), any unused part of the amount brought forward being carried forward for such use in later periods. For the first accounting period ending after 31 December 1993 in which the second amount exceeds the first, the first amount is treated as increased by any excesses of the first amount over the second for earlier accounting periods beginning after 31 December 1989, but not so as to increase the first amount to more than the second amount for that period. By concession, where such an earlier excess is not thereby exhausted, the balance may be carried forward to increase the first amount in the next period in which the second amount exceeds the first, but no further carry forward is permitted. (Revenue Pamphlet IR 1, C27). (In the case of mutual business, the first amount is instead that resulting from an apportionment which would produce the result that the allocated surplus of the business concerned is equal to the overall surplus of that business.)

The greater of the two amounts determined as above is to be treated as the amount referable to the category of business concerned. However, where some such amounts are determined under the first method outlined above, and other such amounts are determined under the second method, any amounts determined under the first method are themselves reduced by an appropriate fraction.

[*ICTA 1988, ss 432B–432F; FA 1990, s 41, Sch 6 para 4; FA 1991, Sch 7 para 3; FA 1995, Sch 8 paras 3, 12, 14–17; F(No 2)A 1997, Sch 3 para 2; FA 2000, s 109; SI 1990 Nos 1541, 2546; SI 1995 No 1211;SI 1998 No 2920*].

Simon's Direct Tax Service. See **D4.526**.

41.4 LIFE ASSURANCE BUSINESS — SCHEDULE D, CASE I

See Revenue Pamphlet IR 131, SP 4/95, 22 March 1995, for the approach the Revenue adopt to the measurement of trading profit from life assurance and other types of long term business when accounts are drawn up in accordance with the Insurance Accounts Directive (91/674/EEC).

Distributions made on or after 2 July 1997 are included in Schedule D, Case I life assurance profits, but exclusive of any tax credit (except, until 5 April 1999, in the case of certain overseas life assurance business, see 41.14 below). In relation to earlier distributions, FRANKED INVESTMENT INCOME (27) of, and FOREIGN INCOME DIVIDENDS (26) arising to, a life assurance company are taken into account as part of its trading profits. [*ICTA 1988, s 434(1)(1A)(1B); FA 1994, Sch 16 para 5(2); FA 1995, Sch 8 para 19(2); F(No 2)A 1997, Sch 3 para 3, Sch 4 para 27, Sch 6 para 6*]. See also *ICTA 1988, s 440B*.

For accounting periods beginning after 31 December 1994, new *ICTA 1988, ss 434A, 434B, 434D, 434E* are introduced dealing with life assurance business losses, interest and annuities and capital allowances. Broadly, these are as follows.

(*a*) *Losses.* Profits from investments (which include franked investment income and (before 6 April 1999) foreign income dividends of a UK resident company) are treated as profits in determining life assurance business losses. For accounting periods beginning after 31 December 1995, Schedule D, Case I losses are reduced (or eliminated) by non-Case I charges (see (*b*) below), (where the accounting period ends after 31 March 1996) certain non-trading deficits on loan relationships, and (where the accounting period ends after 31 March 2000) losses under *ICTA 1988, s 441* (overseas business, see 41.14 below). If all or part of losses so reduced is set off under *ICTA 1988, s 393A* (see 44.2, 44.6 LOSSES) or *s 403(1)* (group relief, see 29.18 GROUPS OF COMPANIES), any losses from pensions business or reinsurance business or (for accounting periods ending before 1 April 2000) overseas business are correspondingly reduced or eliminated. (For earlier accounting periods, Case I losses were reduced (or eliminated) by losses from pensions business, overseas business or reinsurance business and by certain interest and annuities treated as non-Case I charges, see (*b*) below.) No loss or group relief, or relief in respect of non-trading loan relationship deficits not referable to life assurance business, is allowable against the policy holders' share of relevant profits (see 41.7 below). (For accounting periods ending before 1 April 1996, the prohibition on relief for non-trading loan relationship deficits is replaced by a prohibition on relief for certain financial instrument non-trading losses (see 25.10 FINANCIAL INSTRUMENTS).) [*ICTA 1988, s 434A; FA 1995, Sch 8 para 20; FA 1996, Sch 14 para 23, Sch 31 para 2; F(No 2)A 1997, Sch 3 para 4; FA 2000, Sch 27 para 8*].

(*b*) *Interest and annuities.* For accounting periods beginning after 31 December 1995, any annuity payable by a company, and any other annual payment wholly or partly in satisfaction of a policy claim, is deductible in computing Schedule D, Case I profits or losses (and relief as a charge on income correspondingly denied). For earlier accounting periods, interest and annuities payable under long term business liabilities are deductible in computing life assurance business Schedule D, Case I profits or losses. (The treatment of interest is subsumed into the LOAN RELATIONSHIPS (43) provisions from 1 April 1996, and the previous treatment of interest is preserved until those provisions apply, i.e. for accounting periods ending before 1 April 1996.) In either case, in computing non-Case I profits or losses from basic life assurance and general annuity business, such payments may nonetheless be treated as charges on income (but this ceases to apply for accounting periods beginning after 5 March 1997 — see now 41.5 below for treatment of annuity payments as management expenses). A corresponding adjustment is made to the policyholders' share of relevant profits for corporation tax purposes (see 41.7 below). [*ICTA 1988, s 434B; FA 1995, Sch 8 para 21; FA 1996, s 165, Sch 14 para 24; FA 1997, s 67(4)(7)*].

(*c*) *Capital allowances* for plant and machinery provided for use or used for the management of life assurance business are generally apportioned between the different classes of life assurance business (although assets outside the UK used for overseas life assurance business are dealt with separately), allowances (or charges) being made accordingly. [*ICTA 1988, s 434D; FA 1995, Sch 8 para 23*]. Allowances for assets held for purposes other than management of the business and (after 31 March 1998) not let in the course of a Schedule A or overseas property business (see 50.27 PROFIT COMPUTATIONS) are referable to the category of business to which income arising from the asset is or would be referable. [*ICTA 1988, s 434E; FA 1995, Sch 8 para 23; FA 1997, Sch 15 para 8; FA 1998, Sch 5 para 40*]. See *ICTA 1988, ss 434D, 434E* generally and *CAA 1990, s 28* as amended by *FA 1995, Sch 8 para 24* as regards such allowances.

For accounting periods beginning before 1 January 1995, profits derived from the investments of a company's life assurance fund (including franked investment income and foreign income dividends) are treated as profits of its life assurance business for the purposes of *ICTA 1988, s 393* and *s 394* or *s 393A(1)*. See 44 LOSSES. Capital allowances for such periods were dealt with under *CAA 1990, s 28* (see 8.2 CAPITAL ALLOWANCES). [*ICTA 1988, s 434(2); FA 1994, Sch 16 para 5(3); FA 1995, Sch 29 Pt VIII(5)*].

Calculation of profits. In computing Schedule D, Case I profits, expenses include any amounts allocated to, and any amounts of tax or foreign tax expended on behalf of, policy holders or annuitants. An amount is so allocated only if bonus payments are made to policy holders and annuitants, or reversionary bonuses declared in their favour or a reduction made in their premiums, and the amount allocated is the amount of the bonus payments or the amount of the further liabilities assumed by the company. Any part of an unappropriated surplus on valuation (for *Insurance Companies Act 1982* purposes) at the end of the period may be included in the closing liabilities to the extent that it is required to meet the reasonable expectations of policy holders or annuitants with regard to bonuses and other discretionary additions to benefits, but the amount which may be so included is reduced (or extinguished) by any amounts which were excluded by *ICTA 1988, s 433* for periods of account ending before 14 March 1989 as being reserved for policy holders or annuitants and which have not before that date been expended on their behalf or treated as profits on ceasing to be so reserved.

[*FA 1989, s 82, Sch 8 para 2; FA 1990, s 43*].

Receipts to be brought into account. The investment income from the assets of the company's long-term business, and any increase in value of those assets (whether realised or not), so far as referable to the life assurance business and brought into account for *Insurance Companies Act 1982* revenue account purposes, are treated as receipts (and any decrease in value of those assets as an expense) in the Schedule D, Case I computation relating to that business.

For accounting periods beginning after 31 December 1994, any amount transferred from other assets, or otherwise added, to the long term business fund is taken into account as an increase in value of the assets of that fund in ascertaining whether, or to what extent, a loss has been incurred in respect of that business, except insofar as it would otherwise fall to be taken into account as a receipt, or is already taken into account under these provisions, or is specifically exempted from tax. For periods of account beginning **after 31 December 1996**, this applies only to amounts transferred or added to the long term business fund as part of, or in connection with, a 'transfer of business' (as defined) to the company or a 'demutualisation' (as defined) of the company not involving such a transfer. For application of any excess of such amounts over the loss which would otherwise have arisen, see *FA 1989, ss 83AA, 83AB* introduced by *FA 1996, Sch 31 para 5* (subject to transitional provisions in *FA 1996, Sch 31 para 9*).

[*FA 1989, ss 83, 83A; FA 1995, Sch 8 para 16; FA 1996, Sch 31 paras 4, 6*].

For the treatment of 'reverse premiums' (i.e. inducements to take a lease made by landlords to potential tenants), see *FA 1999, Sch 6 para 4(2)*.

For excessive or insufficient general reserves, see *FA 2000, s 107*.

See 41.3 above as regards apportionments for these purposes of items brought into account. See 50.17 PROFIT COMPUTATIONS as regards effect of these provisions in relation to certain finance leasing arrangements.

Equalisation reserves. For accounting periods ending after 22 December 1996, insurance companies are required, under regulations under *Insurance Companies Act 1982, s 34A*, to set aside a proportion of premiums from specified types of business into an equalisation reserve. *ICTA 1988, ss 444BA–444BD*, introduced by *FA 1996, s 166, Sch 32*, and *SI 1996 No 2991* (as amended by *SI 1999 No 1408*) provide for the tax treatment of such reserves, broadly allowing a deduction for transfers in and taxing transfers out.

Interest on ACT overpaid. Where ACT paid by a company carrying on life assurance business, in respect of a distribution made before 6 April 1999, is repaid, the repayment carries INTEREST ON OVERPAID TAX (38) under *ICTA 1988, s 826* from nine months after the end of that period. [*ICTA 1988, s 434C; FA 1995, Sch 8 para 22; FA 1998, Sch 3 para 26*].

Simon's Direct Tax Service. See D4.511, D4.513.

41.5 **OTHER LIFE ASSURANCE BUSINESS (INCLUDING GENERAL ANNUITY BUSINESS)**

See Revenue Pamphlet IR 131, SP 4/95, 22 March 1995, for the approach the Revenue adopt to the measurement of trading profit from life assurance and other types of long term business when accounts are drawn up in accordance with the Insurance Accounts Directive (91/674/EEC).

Where profits from life assurance business are not chargeable under Schedule D, Case I, any receipts of the company's 'basic life assurance and general annuity business' (see 41.2 above) which would be brought into account if the profits were computed on a Case I basis (disregarding the provisions of *FA 1989, s 83*, see 41.4 above), and which are not otherwise chargeable to tax, are chargeable under Schedule D, Case VI. Excluded are

(*a*) any premium; or

(*b*) any sum received by virtue of a claim under an insurance (or reinsurance) contract; or

(*c*) any repayment or refund (in whole or part) of a sum disbursed as acquisition expenses (see 41.2 above); or

(*d*) any reinsurance commission; or

(*e*) any fines, fees, etc. treated as a deduction from management expenses (see 41.2 above); or

(*f*) any sum not within the charge to tax (except under Case I) because of an exemption.

[*FA 1989, s 85; FA 1990, s 44*].

As regards the basic life assurance and general annuity business, annuities paid in an accounting period which are referable to that business and paid under contracts made in accounting periods beginning after 31 December 1991 ('*new annuities*') are regarded as charges on income only to the extent that they do not exceed an '*income limit*'. This is the total amount of the new annuities paid in the period less the capital elements therein. See below, however, as regards accounting periods ending after 4 March 1997. Annuities under 'group annuity contracts' made in an accounting period beginning before 1 January 1992 are included where they first become payable in an accounting period beginning on or after that date. A '*group annuity contract*' is a contract under which annuities may become payable to or in respect of persons subsequently specified or otherwise ascertained. Similar provisions apply as regards reinsurers' liabilities in respect of annuities.

A non-resident company carrying on general annuity business through a branch or agency cannot treat as paid out of profits or gains brought into charge to income tax (see 1.2 INTRODUCTION AND RATES OF TAX) any part of an annuity referable to that business.

There are transitional provisions for old general annuity contracts in *FA 1991, Sch 7 para 16*.

For accounting periods ending on or after 5 March 1997 (but not with effect for annuity payments made before that date), the income limit in the case of 'steep-reduction annuities' as defined in *ICTA 1988, s 437A* (broadly annuities under which the bulk of the payments are concentrated in a short period at the start of the term) is computed under *ICTA 1988, s 437(1CA)–(1CD)* (introduced by *FA 1997, s 67(2)*) rather than by reference to the capital element in the annuities. Also, for accounting periods beginning after that date, relief for annuities is as management expenses of an amount equal to the income limit rather than as charges on income as above. The broad effect of these anti-avoidance provisions is to limit the deductible income element to the amount which would arise if the annuity was actually for the short period over which the bulk of the payments are made, and to prevent excess annuities being set against other non-life assurance profits or being surrendered to another company in the same group.

[*ICTA 1988, ss 437, 437A; FA 1991, Sch 7 paras 4(4), 5, 12, 16; FA 1997, s 67*].

For accounting periods beginning after 31 December 1994, there are special provisions dealing with the taxation of investment return on policies or contracts attributable to basic life assurance and general annuity business the risk on which is reinsured. Regulations provide for an annual charge, and for a sweep-up charge or relief for the accounting period in which the policy, etc. ends. These provisions do not, however, apply where the policy etc. was made, and the reinsurance effected, before 29 November 1994. [*ICTA 1988, s 442A; FA 1995, Sch 8 paras 34, 57(2); SI 1995 No 1730; SI 1996 No 1621*].

For the treatment of 'reverse premiums' (i.e. inducements to take a lease made by landlords to potential tenants), see *FA 1999, Sch 6 para 4(3)*.

Simon's Direct Tax Service. See **D4.515** *et seq.*.

41.6 **PENSION BUSINESS**

See Revenue Pamphlet IR 131, SP 4/95, 22 March 1995, for the approach the Revenue adopt to the measurement of trading profit from life assurance and other types of long term business when accounts are drawn up in accordance with the Insurance Accounts Directive (91/674/EEC).

In the case of companies which are not charged under Schedule D, Case I in respect of their ordinary life assurance business, profits from pension business are charged to corporation tax under Schedule D, Case VI. They are computed in accordance with the provisions applicable to Schedule D, Case I, modified broadly as described at 41.4 above. No deduction is allowed for management expenses (see 41.2 above). Losses brought forward may be set against such profits, but *ICTA 1988, s 396* (Case VI losses — see 44.24 LOSSES) does not apply. [*ICTA 1988, s 436; FA 1989, Sch 8 para 6; FA 1991, Sch 7 para 4; F(No 2)A 1997, Sch 3 para 5*]. See also below.

A number of changes in relation to distributions made after 1 July 1997, which are contained in *F(No 2)A 1997, Sch 3*, are designed to remove entitlement to payment of tax credits relating to pension business and to include all dividends and other distributions in calculating life assurance business profit or loss. See further below and 41.4 above.

Pension business. Income from, and chargeable gains in respect of, investments and deposits of so much of the company's life assurance fund and separate annuity fund (if any) (for accounting periods beginning after 31 December 1994, its long term business fund) as is referable to pension business are exempt from corporation tax, though they may be taken into account in computing profits or losses. [*ICTA 1988, s 438(1)(2); FA 1995, Sch 8 para 4*]. In relation to distributions made before 2 July 1997, this includes a right to payment of tax credits included in exempt income (and see further below as regards payments on account). Also in relation to such distributions, profits for the purposes of *ICTA 1988, s 436* (see above) or, exceptionally, under Case I of Schedule D where they are so chargeable (and see in particular 41.8 below as regards reinsurance business) specifically include franked investment income and foreign income dividends (but see below), but after deducting group income (so far as referable to pension business) from the profits to be taken into account. See now *ICTA 1988, s 434(1)–(1B)* and 41.4 above). For accounting periods beginning before 1 January 1995, annuities referable to pension business are deductible in computing profits and therefore cannot be treated as paid out of profits or gains brought into charge to income tax (and see now 41.4 above). [*ICTA 1988, s 436(3)(d), s 438(3)(3AA)(4); FA 1990, Sch 6 para 5; FA 1994, Sch 16 para 6(2); FA 1995, Sch 29 Pt VIII(5); F(No 2)A 1997, Sch 3 paras 5, 6*].

For accounting periods beginning before 2 July 1997, the company may elect (by notice in writing to the inspector within two years of the end of the relevant accounting period or within such longer period as the Board may allow) that a specified amount of its 'relevant' franked investment income and 'relevant' foreign income dividends be excluded from the computation of profits under *ICTA 1988, s 436* (or, as the case may be, under Case I of Schedule D). The election is only available if a profit would otherwise have been shown. For this purpose, '*relevant*' franked investment income is the shareholders' share of franked investment income (disregarding distributions made after 1 July 1997), the 'shareholders' share' being as defined in *FA 1989, ss 89* (see 41.7 below), and '*relevant*' foreign income dividends are similarly defined. [*ICTA 1988, s 438(6)–(6C)(7), s 440B; FA 1990, s 45(9); FA 1994, Sch 16 para 6(4)(5); F(No 2)A 1997, Sch 3 para 6*]. See further *ICTA 1988, s 438(6D)(6E)* (introduced by *FA 1994, Sch 16 para 6(4)*) as regards restrictions on such elections. Only insofar as the franked investment income is covered by this election can it be used to frank the company's distributions. [*ICTA 1988, s 438(5); F(No 2)A 1997, Sch 3 para 6*].

'*Pension business*' means life assurance business referable to contracts as at (i)–(vi) below, or to the reinsurance of liabilities under such contracts.

(i) Certain retirement annuity contracts or any substituted contract.

(ii) Any contract with the managers of exempt approved schemes such that the company's liability under the contract corresponds with liabilities against which the contract is intended to insure the scheme.

(iii) Any contract under approved personal pension arrangements within *ICTA 1988, Pt XIV, Ch I*.

(iv) An annuity contract to secure 'relevant benefits' for an *ICTA 1988, Pt XIV, Ch I* scheme, a relevant statutory scheme or an *ICTA 1988, s 608* fund.

(v) A contract substituted for one within (iv) above and similarly securing relevant benefits.

(vi) Any contract with the managers of a retirement annuity fund, or a fund approved under *ICTA 1970, s 208* (subject to certain restrictions), solely for the purposes of that fund, and under which the liabilities of the company correspond as under (ii) above.

'*Relevant benefits*', in relation to a scheme within (iv) or (v) above, are such benefits within *ICTA 1988, s 612(1)* as correspond to benefits which could be provided under a hypothetical scheme of the same description.

[*ICTA 1988, s 431B; FA 1995, Sch 8 para 2*].

For accounting periods beginning before 1 January 1995, a similar definition applied, but without the reference to reinsurance business. [*ICTA 1988, s 431(3)–(6), s 431AA; FA 1994, s 143*].

Payments on account of tax credits and deducted tax. In relation to accounting periods beginning on or after 2 October 1992, a new *ICTA 1988, s 438A, Sch 19AB* are introduced which allow provisional repayments of deducted tax and (in relation to distributions made before 2 July 1997) tax credits (or a proportion thereof) in respect of pension business income to be made within the accounting period in which the income is received. They are amended for accounting periods ending **on or after 1 July 1999** to ensure their proper working under self-assessment. There are transitional provisions for accounting periods ending after 2 October 1992 and before 1 January 1998, during which repayments are reduced by 7.5% (10% for accounting periods ending before 1 January 1996 and after 31 December 1994, 12.5% for accounting periods ending before 1 January 1995 and after 31 December 1993, 7.5% for accounting periods ending before 1 January 1994). [*ICTA 1988, Sch 19AB; FA 1991, s 49, Sch 8; FA 1993, s 78(6); FA 1996, s 169, Sch 34 Pt I; F(No 2)A 1997, Sch 3 paras 10, 11; FA 1998, ss 37, 91, Sch 19 para 51; SI 1992 Nos 1746, 2326; SI 1993 No 3109; SI 1994 No 3036; SI 1995 No 3134; SI 1996 No 1; SI 1997 No 2865; SI 1998 No 3173*].

Restricted government securities are government securities issued on the condition that, except in such circumstances as may be specified in the conditions of issue, they are to be held by insurance companies against, and applied solely towards, meeting pension business liabilities. However holdings of Index-linked Treasury Stock 2% 1996, 2% 2006 or $2\frac{1}{2}$% 2011 are not restricted government securities unless, on 27 March 1982, they were held by an insurance company against, and applied solely towards, meeting the liabilities of the company's business. Restricted government securities are to be treated as linked solely to pension business, and all income, gains or losses of a company which relate to restricted government securities are to be referred to its pension business. If a company with other business has income which has to be apportioned in the ratio of pension business liabilities to total liabilities, the liabilities are first reduced by reference to the market value of the restricted Government securities.

Any stocks ceasing to be restricted Government securities (except through disposal or redemption) are treated as being disposed of and reacquired at market value. [*ICTA 1988, s 439; FA 1990, s 41, Sch 6 para 7*].

Simon's Direct Tax Service. See **D4.520** *et seq.*.

41.7 POLICY HOLDERS' FRACTION OF PROFITS ETC.

The 'policy holders' share' of the 'relevant profits' or, where the business is mutual business, the whole of those profits, (except in both cases for those chargeable under Schedule D, Case I and as below) of a company carrying on life assurance business are chargeable to corporation tax at a rate equal to the basic rate of income tax for the year of assessment beginning in the financial year concerned. The 'policy holders' share' of 'relevant profits' (the whole of those profits where the business is mutual business) is left out of account for small companies rate purposes (see 56 SMALL COMPANIES—REDUCED RATES). For 1996 and subsequent financial years, except where profits are charged under Schedule D, Case I, the rate of corporation tax applicable to basic life assurance and general annuity business net profits, to the extent that they represent 'lower rate income' for the periods, is the lower rate of income tax for the year of assessment beginning in the financial year. '*Lower rate income*' is broadly income taxable at the lower rate of income tax in the hands of an individual, but also includes certain gains on interest-bearing securities and authorised unit trust distributions. Profits '*represent*' such income to the extent that the company's total income and gains from basic life and general annuity business consist of lower rate income.

The '*relevant profits*' are the income and gains of the company's life assurance business less management expenses (see 41.2 above) and charges on income (and, for accounting periods ending after 31 March 1996, any amounts in respect of a non-trading deficit on the company's loan relationships under *FA 1996, Sch 11 para 4*) referable to that business. For accounting periods beginning before 1 January 1995, they were the total profits of the life assurance business less management expenses, but before loss or group reliefs (and see *Prudential Assurance Co Ltd v Bibby Ch D, [1999] STC 952*).

The '*policy holders' share*' of the relevant profits is the amount arrived at by deducting from those profits the Case I profits of the company for the period in respect of the life assurance business, but reducing the Case I profits so deducted

(i) (in relation to distributions made on or after 2 July 1997) by the 'shareholders' share' of any franked investment income, and (before 6 April 1999) of any foreign income dividends, arising in the period and referable to the company's basic life assurance and general annuity business, or

(ii) (in relation to distributions made before that date) by any unrelieved franked investment income for which the company has made an election under *ICTA 1988, s 438(6)* (see 41.6 above), and by the 'shareholders' share' of any other unrelieved franked investment income, and of any foreign income dividends, arising in the period from investments held in connection with the life assurance business.

The '*shareholders' share*' is an amount equal to the company's Case I profits in respect of its life assurance business, divided by an amount equal to the excess of the company's relevant non-premium income and relevant gains over its relevant expenses and relevant interest for the period. Where the company's relevant non-premium income and relevant gains do not exceed its relevant expenses and relevant interest, or where the Case I profits are greater than any excess, the whole of the income is the 'shareholders' share'. Where the company's relevant non-premium income and relevant gains exceed its relevant expenses and relevant interest, and there are no Case I profits, none of the income is the 'shareholders' share'.

The 'relevant non-premium income', 'relevant gains', 'relevant expenses' and 'relevant interest' are further defined. Franked investment income is '*unrelieved*' if it has not been excluded from a charge to tax, no tax credit comprised in it has been paid, and no relief has been allowed against it, either by deduction or by set-off.

[*FA 1989, ss 88, 88A, 89; FA 1990, s 45; FA 1993, s 78(3)(6)(7); FA 1994, Sch 16 para 9; FA 1995, Sch 8 para 21; FA 1996, Sch 6 para 26, Sch 14 para 56; F(No 2)A 1997, Sch 3 para 14, Sch 6 paras 18, 19*].

Loss and group reliefs and certain other amounts are not available against the policy holders' share of the relevant profits. [*ICTA 1988, s 434A; FA 1989, Sch 8 para 4; FA 1990, s 45(8); FA 1994, s 176(1); FA 1996, Sch 14 para 23, Sch 31 para 2*].

ICTA 1988, s 434(3)–(8) is correspondingly amended in relation to the restriction on set-off of franked investment income and to refer also to foreign income dividends, and, for accounting periods beginning after 31 December 1994, to clarify claims for relief under *ICTA 1988, s 242* (prior to its repeal, see 27.3 FRANKED INVESTMENT INCOME). [*FA 1989, Sch 8 para 3; FA 1990, s 45(4); FA 1994, Sch 16 para 5(4)(5); FA 1995, Sch 8 para 19(3); FA 1998, Sch 3 para 25*].

Simon's Direct Tax Service. See D4.514.

41.8 REINSURANCE BUSINESS

'*Life reinsurance business*' is reinsurance of life assurance business other than pension business or other business excluded by regulations by the Board. [*ICTA 1988, s 431C; FA 1995, Sch 8 para 2; SI 1995 No 1730, reg 11; SI 1996 No 1621*]. For accounting periods beginning after 31 December 1994, special provisions (as below) apply in relation to life assurance companies carrying on such business.

If the only life assurance business a company carries on is reinsurance business, and none of the reinsurance business is excluded from these provisions by regulations made by the Board, the profits of the business are charged to tax only under Schedule D, Case I. [*ICTA 1988, s 439A; FA 1995, Sch 8 para 26; SI 1995 No 1730, reg 12*].

Where profits from life reinsurance business are not charged to tax under Schedule D, Case I, then except insofar as the business is excluded by regulations made by the Board, they are treated separately and charged to tax as income under Schedule D, Case VI, but computed as under Case I. *FA 1989, ss 82, 83* (see 41.4 above) apply with appropriate modification for this purpose, and there is provision for carry-forward of losses from life reinsurance business (to which *ICTA 1988, s 396* (see 44.24 LOSSES) does not apply). In computing such losses, franked investment income and foreign income dividends in relation to distributions made before 2 July 1997 are specifically taken into account as profits. *ICTA 1988, ss 128, 399(1)* (dealing with commodity and financial futures, see Tolley's Income Tax under Schedule D, Cases I and II and Anti-Avoidance respectively) do not affect the charge under these provisions. Gains referable to life reinsurance business are not chargeable gains. [*ICTA 1988, s 439B; FA 1995, Sch 8 para 27; F(No 2)A 1997, Sch 3 para 7*].

Simon's Direct Tax Service. See **D4.525A**.

41.9 PRE-1965 POLICIES

Where policies issued before 5 August 1965 provide for benefits consisting of specified investments (or of sums determined by reference thereto) and the company, on becoming liable under such a policy, makes a chargeable gain on the specified investments in meeting that liability, tax thereon may be deducted by the company notwithstanding that the policy does not provide for such deduction. This provision applies only if that part of the life assurance fund referable to those policies consists wholly or mainly of the specified investments. [*ICTA 1988, s 444*].

41.10 POLICIES CARRYING RIGHTS NOT IN MONEY

Where investments or other assets are transferred to the holder of a policy issued in the course of life assurance business in accordance with that policy, the transfer is deemed to have been made at market value for the purposes of corporation tax on chargeable gains and of computing income under Schedule D, Case I or VI. [*ICTA 1988, s 443; TCGA 1992, s 204(3)*].

41.11 TRANSFER OF ASSETS TO NON-RESIDENT COMPANY

Where an *insurance company* resident in the UK transfers its foreign branch or agency business and assets to a non-resident company in exchange wholly or partly for shares in that company in circumstances similar to those set out in 9.6 CAPITAL GAINS, any profit or loss on the assets transferred which would otherwise be included in the computation of profits or losses under Schedule D, Case I will be disregarded for that purpose and treated as a chargeable gain or an allowable loss. [*ICTA 1988, s 442(1)–(3)*].

Note that this provision is not restricted to *life* assurance companies.

See also 9.6 CAPITAL GAINS as regards concessional treatment of certain transfers of long term business.

41.12 OVERSEAS LIFE INSURANCE COMPANIES

See Tolley's Income Tax under Life Assurance Policies for special treatment of policies issued after 17 November 1983 by non-UK resident companies outside the scope of UK tax. For the requirement for most overseas insurers (as widely defined) to nominate a UK tax representative responsible for providing information relating to life assurance policy gains, see *ICTA 1988, ss 552A, 552B* (introduced by *FA 1998, s 87* with effect from 6 April 1999) and regulations thereunder.

'*Overseas life insurance company*' means an insurance company not resident in the UK but carrying on life assurance business through a branch or agency in the UK. None of the life assurance business of such a company is treated as 'overseas life assurance business', as referred to elsewhere in this chapter. [*ICTA 1988, s 431(2); FA 1993, Sch 9 para 6(3)*].

Management expenses. The relief under 41.2 above is limited to expenses attributable to the life assurance or capital redemption business carried on by the company at or through a UK branch or agency. [*ICTA 1988, s 76(6); FA 1996, Sch 33 para 1(2)*].

Accounting periods beginning after 31 December 1992. *FA 1993, ss 97–103, Schs 9–11* introduce major changes to the taxation of overseas life insurance companies operating through UK branches or agencies (which are contained mostly in *ICTA 1988, Sch 19AC, FA 1989, Sch 8A* and *TCGA 1992, Sch 7B*). These are intended to bring the tax liabilities of such companies onto a comparable basis to that applying to UK insurance companies. They operate by repeal of most of the previous provisions applicable specifically to overseas life insurance companies, and by detailed amendment to the existing general provisions in their application to such companies. The main differences brought about by the changes are summarised below.

Investment income. The formula for apportioning income of the life assurance fund (excluding the pension and general annuity fund, if any) as between taxable and non-taxable elements is replaced by a factual determination of branch income, as applies in respect of gains and expenses.

Assets backing policies. When the assets held by a UK branch are less than would be required by a UK company to administer the same policies, income from and gains on assets held outside the branch in connection with the UK branch activities will be taken into account (on an arm's length basis). If this still provides insufficient support for the UK business, a proportion of the worldwide income and gains of the overseas company will be brought into charge.

UK company distributions from shareholdings held as part of branch activities will be treated as profits chargeable to corporation tax, against which management expenses etc. may be set, and will carry a tax credit entitlement.

Double tax relief will be available for foreign tax paid on the UK branch income, and gains on disposal, of the company's long-term business fund assets.

The provisions relating to *transfers of long term business* (see 41.16 below) are assimilated to apply to such transfers, sanctioned or authorised after 30 June 1994 by their home state regulatory authority, by certain EU and other companies operating in the UK (see *FA 1995, Sch 9*).

ICTA 1988, Sch 19AC and *FA 1989, Sch 8A* are further amended by *FA 1995, Sch 8 paras 35–49* to take account of changes made for UK insurance companies by *FA 1995*, in particular, with effect for accounting periods beginning after 31 December 1994, to deal with the extension of 'overseas life assurance business' to include business written directly from the UK with certain European residents (see 41.14 below). Minor amendments relating to tax-free securities, to provisional repayments relating to pension business, to additions to the long term business fund and to loan relationships are made by *FA 1996, Sch 14 para 51, Sch 28 para 5, Sch 31 para 8, Sch 34 Pt II*. Further amendments are made by *F(No 2)A 1997, Sch 3 para 13, Sch 4 para 29* relating to the restriction of tax credit payments in relation to distributions made on or after 2 July 1997 and their abolition for distributions made after 5 April 1999, and by *FA 2000, s 75(4)* in relation to certain transfers of machinery or plant.

Transfers of long term business. See 41.16 below.

Simon's Direct Tax Service. See **D4.536, D4.537**.

41.13 CESSATION OF RESIDENCE

These provisions apply where a company resident in the UK, which carries on insurance business wholly abroad and the whole or part of the ordinary share capital of which is beneficially owned by one or more companies resident in the UK, ceases to be so resident. Its profits or losses in respect of that business for the accounting period ending with the cessation are computed without regard to the profit or loss (or a corresponding part thereof) in respect of any asset which would otherwise be calculated under *ICTA 1988, s 100(1)* (valuation of stock on discontinuance) (see Tolley's Income Tax under Schedule D, Cases I and II). [*ICTA 1988, s 442(4)*].

41.14 OVERSEAS LIFE ASSURANCE BUSINESS

Profits arising from overseas life insurance business carried on by companies resident (or, for accounting periods beginning after 31 October 1994, carrying on business through a branch or agency) in the UK are – except where the company is charged to corporation tax under Schedule D, Case I on the profits of its life assurance business – treated separately, computed under the rules applicable to Schedule D, Case I, and charged to tax under Schedule D, Case VI. Losses arising from overseas life assurance business in any previous accounting period beginning after 31 December 1989 may be set against such profits.

ICTA 1988, s 396 (Case VI losses — see 44.24 LOSSES) is not to apply to a loss incurred by a company on overseas life assurance business.

For accounting periods beginning before 1 January 1995, interest payable under a liability of the company's long-term business and annuities payable, so far as referable to overseas life assurance business, are specifically deductible in computing the profits of the overseas life assurance business. See now 41.4 above.

Gains accruing on the disposal by a company of assets of its overseas life assurance fund are not chargeable gains.

[*ICTA 1988, s 441; FA 1990, s 42, Sch 7 para 3; FA 1995, Sch 8 para 30, Sch 29 Pt VIII(5)*].

'*Overseas life assurance business*' is defined, for accounting periods beginning after 31 October 1994, in *ICTA 1988, s 431D*, introduced by *FA 1995, Sch 8 para 2* and amended by *FA 2000, s 108*. Regulations giving effect to *section 431D* (made under *section 431E*) are contained in *SI 1995 Nos 3237, 3238* (as amended). Previously it was defined in *ICTA 1988, s 431(2)*, broadly as business with non-UK residents effected outside the UK, and the current definition *inter alia* takes account of the ability of UK companies (and UK branches of non-UK resident companies) to write certain European business direct with non-residents.

Distributions. For distributions made before 2 July 1997, *ICTA 1988, s 208* (see 20.17 DISTRIBUTIONS) does not apply to distributions in respect of a company's overseas life assurance fund. (See now *ICTA 1988, s 434(1)–(1B)*, 41.4 above.) There is no entitlement to tax credits under *ICTA 1988, s 231* (see 27.2 FRANKED INVESTMENT INCOME) in respect of distributions, except to the extent provided in regulations made by the Board (see *SI 1995 No 3238*). (For accounting periods beginning before 1 November 1994, a credit is available if an individual, resident in the territory in which the relevant branch or agency is situated, would have been entitled to a credit under *ICTA 1988, s 788* (see 21.3 DOUBLE TAX RELIEF). There are detailed provisions defining the 'relevant branch or agency' for this purpose, and where the overseas life assurance business carried on by or through a branch or agency included reinsurance business in respect of overseas liabilities, or retrocession business, the credit due is restricted accordingly.)

Where a tax credit is paid to a company under these provisions, none of the franked investment income to which the credit relates may be used to frank the company's distributions.

These provisions cease to have effect in relation to distributions made after 5 April 1999.

[*ICTA 1988, s 441A; FA 1990, s 42, Sch 7 para 3; FA 1993, s 78(6)(7); FA 1995, Sch 8 para 31; F(No 2)A 1997, Sch 3 para 9, Sch 4 para 28*].

For accounting periods beginning after 31 October 1994, there are special provisions for the treatment of UK land held as an asset linked to overseas life assurance business, or in respect of policies or contracts held by non-residents (see *ICTA 1988, s 441B* introduced by *FA 1995, Sch 8 para 32*).

Restriction of credit for overseas tax. For accounting periods beginning before 1 April 2000, there are restrictions on credit for overseas tax against corporation tax charged on the profits of a company's overseas life assurance business, except where the tax in question is computed wholly by reference to profits arising in the relevant territory. The amount of the credit is not to exceed the greater of the amount of tax chargeable by reference to profits arising in that territory, and the 'shareholders' share' of the tax so payable. The 'shareholders' share' is specifically defined for this purpose. Where credit for overseas tax is restricted under these provisions, the balance of the overseas tax in respect of which credit is not available may be taken into account in computing the profits of the overseas life assurance business. [*ICTA 1988, s 804A; FA 1990, s 42, Sch 7 para 5; FA 1996, Sch 41 Pt V(3); FA 2000, Sch 30 para 16*]. For accounting periods beginning on or after 1 April 2000, following the general double taxation relief changes introduced by *FA 2000, section 804A* is amended, and new *ICTA 1988, ss 804B–804F* introduced, to ensure that the new regime works as intended for insurance companies, and in particular life insurance companies. [*FA 2000, Sch 30 paras 16–19*].

Overseas life assurance fund. There are detailed provisions regulating which of a company's assets are to be treated as the assets of its overseas life assurance fund. [*ICTA 1988, Sch 19AA; FA 1990, s 42, Sch 7 para 6; FA 1995, Sch 8 paras 8, 33; FA 1996, Sch 28 para 4; SI 1994 No 3278*].

Capital allowances. For accounting periods beginning before 1 January 1995, where a life insurance company is charged to tax under *ICTA 1988, s 441* in respect of the profits of its overseas life assurance business, any capital allowance in respect of machinery or plant for use in the management of the overseas life assurance business is treated as a business expense, and any balancing charge in respect of such expenditure is treated as a business receipt. *CAA 1990, ss 73, 144 and 145* and *ICTA 1988, s 75(4)* do not apply in such cases. [*CAA 1990, s 28(2A); FA 1990, s 42, Sch 7 para 9*]. For capital allowances for accounting periods beginning after 31 December 1994, see 41.4 above.

Simon's Direct Tax Service. See **D4.524.**

41.15 TRANSFERS OF ASSETS ETC.

If at any time an asset (or a part of an asset) held by an insurance company ceases to be within a particular defined category of business and comes within another such category, there is a deemed disposal and re-acquisition of the asset at market value. There is also a deemed disposal and re-acquisition at market value where an asset is acquired by a company as part of the transfer to it of the whole or part of the business of an insurance company in accordance with a scheme sanctioned under *Insurance Companies Act 1982, Sch 2C Pt I* and is within a different category after the acquisition from that it was in before the acquisition. *TCGA 1992, ss 171, 173* do not apply on the acquisition or disposal of an asset which, immediately after the acquisition or before the disposal, falls within one of the defined categories.

Where an insurance company's assets include securities which would normally be treated as a single holding, any such securities which are identified in the company's records as relating to a particular specific category of business are to be treated as a separate holding. This is subject to further detailed provisions.

There are also further modifications where the profits from life assurance business are taxed under Schedule D, Case I.

[*ICTA 1988, ss 440, 440A, 440B; FA 1990, s 41, Sch 6 paras 8, 12; FA 1991, Sch 7 para 6; FA 1995, Sch 8 paras 5, 6, 28; FA 1996, Sch 14 para 25; F(No 2)A 1997, Sch 3 para 8*].

Note. These provisions are not restricted to *life* insurance companies.

Simon's Direct Tax Service. See **D4.532**.

41.16 **TRANSFERS OF LONG TERM BUSINESS** [*FA 1990, s 48, Sch 9*]

The detailed provisions described below apply to transfers of the whole or part of the long term business of an insurance company in accordance with schemes sanctioned under *Insurance Companies Act 1982, Sch 2C Pt I.*

Capital gains. *TCGA 1992, s 139* (see 9.6 CAPITAL GAINS) may still apply to assets transferred under such a scheme notwithstanding that the transfer is not part of a scheme of reconstruction or amalgamation, that the asset is trading stock of either the transferor or transferee, or (for disposals before 1 April 2000) that either or both of the companies is not resident in the UK at the time of the transfer. For disposals before 1 April 2000, this relaxation will only apply where any gain accruing to the transferor, and to the transferee if it transferred the asset immediately after acquisition, would be a chargeable gain forming part of the company's profits for corporation tax purposes, and from that date this continues to apply in relation to either of the companies (or both) if it is non-UK resident. [*TCGA 1992, s 211; FA 1993, s 90; FA 1994, s 251(11); FA 2000, Sch 29 para 30*].

Mixed fund assets. The fact that an asset is held by either transferor or transferee as partly backing taxable basic life assurance and general annuity business and partly backing exempt pension business will not of itself mean that a gain on its disposal would not be a chargeable gain, so that gains on such assets will not be denied the above deferral for that reason alone. Both transferor and transferee company will, however, be required to give an undertaking that this practice will be applied in the computations for the period of the transfer and, in the case of the transferee, for subsequent accounting periods. (Revenue Pamphlet IR 131, SP 7/93, 11 June 1993).

TCGA 1992, s 25(3) (which provides for a deemed disposal and reacquisition where a person ceases to carry on a trade in the UK through a branch or agency) is not to apply to such transfers in cases where *TCGA 1992, s 139* applies by virtue of the above provisions to disposals before 1 April 2000. [*TCGA 1992, s 25(4); FA 2000, Sch 29 para 6*].

Accounting periods. Where there is such a transfer, the day of the transfer is to be the end of an accounting period of the transferor company. [*ICTA 1988, s 12(7A); FA 1990, Sch 9 para 3*].

Expenses of management and losses. Where there is such a transfer, any management expenses which would have been deductible by the transferor company under *ICTA 1988, ss 75, 76* (see 40.2 INVESTMENT COMPANIES, 41.2 above) in a subsequent accounting period are to be treated as management expenses of the transferee.

Where acquisition expenses are treated as management expenses of the transferee by virtue of this provision, the amount deductible for the transferee's first accounting period ending after the transfer takes place is to be calculated as if that accounting period began with the day after the transfer. Any loss which would have been available under *ICTA 1988, s 436(3)(c), s 439B(3)(b)* or *s 441(4)(b)* (see 41.6, 41.8, 41.14 above) for set-off against subsequent profits of the transferor may instead be treated as a loss of the transferee, and available for set-off against subsequent profits of the same class of business as that in which it arose. An excess which would have been available for carry forward by the transferor under *ICTA 1988, s 432F(2)* (see 41.3 above) is similarly treated as available to the transferor in relation to its revenue account dealing with or including the business transferred.

Where the transfer is of part only of the transferor's long-term business, these provisions apply only to such amount as is 'appropriate'. Any question concerning what is 'appropriate' may be determined by the Special Commissioners.

These provisions only apply where the transfer is made for *bona fide* commercial reasons and does not form part of a scheme or arrangement of which the main purpose, or one of the main purposes, is avoidance of liability to corporation tax. There is a clearance procedure whereby the transferee may apply to the Board for notification that this restriction will not be applied. *TCGA 1992, s 138(2)–(5)* applies to such clearance applications. [*ICTA 1988, s 444A; FA 1990, Sch 9 para 4; FA 1995, Sch 8 para 17(4)(5), para 53(3), Sch 9 para 1(3)*].

Concessional relief applies to unused losses from general annuity business which, had the transferor continued to carry on the business, would have been available for set-off under *FA 1991, Sch 7 para 17* (relating to losses of accounting periods beginning before 1 January 1992, see 41.6 above). Such losses may be treated as losses of the transferee, provided that all the general annuity contracts made in accounting periods beginning before 1 January 1992 are transferred. Where not all such contracts are transferred, the transferor and transferee may jointly elect for the concession to apply to a specified part of the unrelieved losses. (Revenue Pamphlet IR 1, C29).

Capital allowances. Where such a transfer takes place, any capital allowances and balancing charges which would have been made to or on the transferor shall be made to or on the transferee instead. However, the transfer itself is not to be regarded as giving rise to any such allowance or charge. [*CAA 1990, s 152A; FA 1990, Sch 9 para 5*].

Friendly society. Where there is such a transfer to a friendly society, any life or endowment business relating to contracts included in the transfer will not be tax exempt life or endowment business (see 28.2 *et seq.* FRIENDLY SOCIETIES). [*ICTA 1988, s 460(10A); FA 1990, Sch 9 para 6*].

Clearance applications in relation to the above provisions should be made by the company or society to which the business is transferred, and should be sent to Inland Revenue, Financial Institutions Division, Rooms S15, S16, Somerset House, Strand, London WC2R 1LB. Appeal is to the Special Commissioners if clearance is refused or if the Board fails to make a decision within 30 days of receipt of the application (or of the supply of any further information requested in response to the application). (Revenue Press Release 27 July 1990).

Simon's Direct Tax Service. See **D4.528**.

41.17 HOLDINGS OF UNIT TRUSTS ETC.

Where, at the end of an accounting period, the assets of an insurance company's long term business fund include rights under an authorised unit trust, or relevant interests in an offshore fund, the company is deemed to have disposed of, and immediately re-acquired, the assets concerned at market value. However this provision does not apply to assets linked solely to pension business (or, for accounting periods beginning after 31 December 1994, to life reinsurance business), or to assets of the overseas life assurance fund, or, for accounting periods ending after 31 March 1996, to holdings treated as rights under a creditor relationship under *FA 1996, Sch 10 para 4* (see 43.9 LOAN RELATIONSHIPS). An interest is deemed to be a '*relevant interest in an offshore fund*' if it is a material interest in an offshore fund for the purposes of *ICTA 1988, Part XVII, Chapter V* (see Tolley's Income Tax under Overseas Matters), or if it would be such an interest if the shares and interests excluded by *ICTA 1988, s 759(6)(8)* were limited to shares or interests in trading companies or if the companies, etc. listed in *ICTA 1988, s 759(1)(a)–(c)* were not limited to those which were collective investment schemes.

In certain circumstances, an insurance company which exchanges old assets for new assets which are to be held as part of the long-term business fund may claim to be treated as if the exchange had not involved a disposal of the old assets or an acquisition of the new assets, but as if the old and the new assets were the same assets. Any claim for this provision to apply must be made within two years of the end of the accounting period in which the exchange occurs.

Where there is a transfer of the whole of the long-term business of an insurance company to another company in accordance with a scheme under *Insurance Companies Act 1982, Sch 2C Pt I*, the above provisions apply to the transferee as if the transferee had carried on the business at all material times. Where there is such a transfer of part only of the transferor's business, the provisions apply 'to such extent as is appropriate'. Any question concerning this provision may be determined by the Special Commissioners.

[*TCGA 1992, ss 212, 214; FA 1993, s 91; FA 1995, s 134(5)–(7)(10), Sch 8 para 9(2); FA 1996, Sch 14 para 63; SI 1991 No 2860*].

Spreading of gains and losses under TCGA 1992, s 212. The aggregate of any chargeable gains and allowable losses accruing at the end of an accounting period on deemed disposals under *section 212* is to be apportioned equally between the accounting period in question and the six succeeding accounting periods, provided that the gains and losses are referable to basic life assurance and general annuity business, or would otherwise be taken into account in computing the profits of any business treated as a separate business under *ICTA 1988, s 458* (see 41.18 below). Where any such accounting period is less than twelve months, the apportionment is adjusted accordingly. There is a balancing adjustment if the company ceases to carry on long-term business before the end of the last accounting period concerned. However, where the company's long-term business is transferred to another company under *Insurance Companies Act 1982, Sch 2C Pt I*, any chargeable gain or allowable loss which would have accrued to the transferor is deemed instead to accrue to the transferee. Where the transfer is of part only of the transferor's business, this provision applies to such extent 'as is appropriate'. Any question concerning this may be determined by the Special Commissioners.

Where there is a net gain as above in an accounting period and a net loss in any of the next six accounting periods (provided that there is no net loss or gain in any intervening accounting period), the company may claim to have both the net gain and the net loss reduced by an amount not exceeding the amount of the net loss. Such a claim must be made within two years of the end of the later accounting period. This provision is, however, disapplied where there is an intervening period ending after 16 March 1998 during which the company joined a group of companies (for which see 9.37 CAPITAL GAINS). Similarly, for gains arising in accounting periods ending after 16 March 1998, where the company joined a group of companies in the later period (i.e. that in which there was a net loss), a claim can only be made to the extent that (if gains accrued to the company immediately after the beginning of that period) the loss would be treated as a qualifying loss under *TCGA 1992, Sch 7AA para 4* (see 9.37, 9.39 CAPITAL GAINS).

[*TCGA 1992, s 213; FA 1993, s 91(4); FA 1998, s 137*].

An insurance company may claim, within two years after the end of an accounting period (the '*relevant period*') which is one of the company's first eight accounting periods beginning on or after 1 January 1993, for transitional provisions to apply in relation to the relevant period. Where such a claim is made, the above 'spreading' provisions are to have effect as if the amount of the chargeable gains which would otherwise be treated as accruing on disposals deemed by virtue of *TCGA 1992, s 212* to have been made at the end of the relevant period were reduced by a 'protected proportion', determined by a specified formula; and as if an amount equal to the 'appropriate part' of that reduction were a chargeable gain accruing at the end of each of the accounting periods in which the reduction is to be taken into account. Any such reduction made in respect of a company is to be taken into account in every succeeding accounting period of that company which is one of the company's first nine accounting periods beginning on or after 1 January 1993. The '*appropriate part*' of the reduction is the amount of the reduction divided by the number of the accounting periods after that in which the reduction is made in which the reduction falls to be taken into account (or would so fall apart from any cessation of the company's business). If the reduction only falls to be taken into account in one accounting period, the appropriate part is the whole of the reduction. Where a company ceases to carry on long-term business before the end of the first nine accounting periods after the end of 1992, the appropriate part of any reduction in relation to the accounting period ending with the cessation is to be such as to secure that the whole of the reduction has been taken into account as a chargeable gain.

Where there is a transfer of the whole or part of the long-term business of an insurance company in accordance with a scheme sanctioned by a court under *Insurance Companies Act 1982, Sch 2C Pt I*, these provisions are to have effect with a modification to the definition of the 'protected proportion' referred to above, and so that any reduction which, on the assumption that the transferor had continued to carry on the business, would have fallen to be made as above is to be taken into account as a chargeable gain in relation to the transferee. In relation to any such transfer, the only accounting periods to be included in any calculation of the number of accounting periods beginning on or after 1 January 1993, and the only periods in relation to which such a reduction may be taken into account, are the transferor's accounting periods ending on or before the day of the transfer (including any taken into account under an earlier application of these provisions), and the transferee's accounting periods ending after the transfer. These provisions are to have effect in relation to such a reduction as if the transferee's first accounting period to end after the day of the transfer began on the day after the transfer. Where the transfer is of part only of the transferor's long-term business, the above provisions are to apply only to that part. Any question arising as to the apportionment is to be determined by the Special Commissioners. Both the transferor and the transferee are entitled to appear and to be heard or to make written representations.

[*TCGA 1992, s 214A; FA 1993, s 91(5); FA 1995, Sch 8 para 9(3)*].

Simon's Direct Tax Service. See D4.527.

41.18 **CAPITAL REDEMPTION BUSINESS** [*ICTA 1988, ss 458, 458A; FA 1993, s 78(6); FA 1994, Sch 16 para 7; FA 1996, s 168, Sch 33; F(No 2)A 1997, Sch 6 para 7*]

Capital redemption business is treated as separate from any other business, and, in computing losses of that business for the purposes of *ICTA 1988, s 380* or *s 393* and *s 393A(1)*, profits from that business include those from investments held in connection with that business (including franked investment income of, and (until 5 April 1999) foreign income dividends arising to, a company resident in the UK). For accounting periods ending on or after 1 July 1999, the day appointed for the introduction of self-assessment for companies (see 55 SELF-ASSESSMENT), the relief for management expenses is assimilated to that for life assurance business by *FA 1996, Sch 33*. Previously, similar rules apply by concession and practice. The Treasury has regulation-making powers to apply life assurance provisions generally to capital redemption business (and see *SI 1999 No 498*).

'*Capital redemption business*' means effecting and carrying out contracts of insurance whereby, in return for one or more premiums paid to the insurer, a sum or series of sums is to become payable to the insured. It does not include life assurance or (for accounting periods beginning before 1 January 1996) industrial assurance business. For accounting periods ending on or after the day appointed for the introduction of self-assessment for companies, it is redefined as any insurance business, other than life assurance business, consisting of effecting on an actuarial basis, and carrying out, contracts under which a specified sum or sums become payable at a future time or over a period in return for one or more fixed payments.

Simon's Direct Tax Service. See **D4.530**.

41.19 **DEDUCTION OF TAX FROM PREMIUMS**

Premiums paid by UK residents to UK life insurance companies (and UK branches of overseas companies) for life insurance or deferred annuities are calculated after deducting tax relief at $12\frac{1}{2}$% for policies issued in respect of insurances made before 14 March 1984. Relief is generally abolished for new policies and for increases made on or after that date.

The companies recover any deficiency arising from the deductions from the Board, who make regulations for the administration of the system. [*ICTA 1988, s 266(1)(2)(3)(c)(4)(5)(8); FA 1988, s 29*].

42 Liquidation etc.

Cross-reference. See 53.2 RESIDENCE.

Simon's Direct Tax Service D2.515.

42.1 The passing of a resolution, or the making of an order, or any other act, for the winding-up of a company does not mean that a company (or any of its 75% subsidiaries) ceases to be a member of a group for the purpose of the capital gains provisions in *TCGA 1992, ss 171–181*, regarding which see 9.18 CAPITAL GAINS. [*TCGA 1992, s 170(11)*]. For other group purposes, e.g. group relief, such acts bring about the end of the group relationship, although the making of an administration order would not of itself bring about such a change. (ICAEW Guidance Note TR 799, June 1990).

42.2 For debts released as part of a voluntary arrangement under *Insolvency Act 1986* or a compromise or arrangement under *Companies Act 1985, s 425* (or NI equivalent), the release does not give rise to a taxable receipt in the debtor company. [*ICTA 1988, s 94; FA 1994, s 144(3)(7)*]. The creditor will obtain relief for a debt so released, provided that it is released wholly and exclusively for trade purposes. [*ICTA 1988, s 74(1)(j); FA 1994, s 144(1)(2)(6)*].

42.3 The vesting of a company's assets in a liquidator is disregarded for capital gains purposes and all acts of the liquidator in relation to those assets are treated as acts of the company. [*TCGA 1992, s 8(6)*].

All expenses properly incurred in a voluntary winding-up, including the remuneration of the liquidator, are payable out of the company's assets in priority to all other claims. [*Insolvency Act 1986, s 115*]. *Insolvency Rules 1986, Rule 4.218(1)* provides that expenses of a liquidation are to be paid out of the assets in the order of priority therein specified, subject to a discretionary power of the court under *Insolvency Act 1986, s 156* to vary the order where assets are insufficient to satisfy liabilities. [*SI 1986 No 1925, Rules 4.218(1), 4.220*]. Included in the normal order of priority is the amount of any corporation tax on chargeable gains accruing on the realisation of any asset of the company. [*Rule 4.218(1)(p)*]. Notwithstanding the specific inclusion of corporation tax on chargeable gains, corporation tax chargeable on a company's post-liquidation profits is to be treated as a 'necessary disbursement' of the liquidator (within *Insolvency Rules 1986, Rule 4.218(1)(m)*), and thus as an expense requiring priority as above (*Re Toshoku Finance UK plc, Kahn and another v CIR CA, [2000] STC 301*).

42.4 A company is chargeable to corporation tax on the profits arising in the winding-up of the company. [*ICTA 1988, s 8(2)*].

42.5 **CHARGE TO CORPORATION TAX IN FINAL AND PENULTIMATE YEARS**

Corporation tax is charged on the profits of a company arising in the winding-up in the financial year (i.e. a year to 31 March — see 1 INTRODUCTION AND RATES OF TAX) in which the affairs of the company are completely wound up (the final year) at the rate of corporation tax fixed or proposed for the previous financial year (the penultimate year), except that if, before the affairs of the company are completely wound up, the rate of corporation tax for the final year has been fixed or 'proposed', then that rate shall apply. Where the winding-up commenced before the company's final year, the company's profits arising in the penultimate year are charged at the rates applicable to that year. [*ICTA 1988, s 342(1)–(3)(8)*].

For the above purposes, the rate of corporation tax means the rate applicable (i.e. full rate, small companies rate or special rate) and chargeable gains are reduced by the appropriate fraction where this applies. '*Proposed*' means by a Budget resolution. [*ICTA 1988, s 342(7)*].

An assessment on a company's profits for an accounting period falling after the commencement of the winding-up is not invalid because made before the end of the accounting period. The liquidator may determine beforehand an assumed date when the winding-up will be completed for the purpose of making an assessment for a period intended to end with the completion of the winding-up. A date so assumed will not alter the company's final and penultimate year, and if it falls short of the actual completion date, a new accounting period will commence from the assumed date and *ICTA 1988, s 12(7)* (length of accounting period after commencement of winding-up, see 42.6 below) will apply as if that new accounting period began with the commencement of the winding-up. Where the winding-up was completed before 1 July 1999, the day appointed for the commencement of self-assessment for companies, the inspector and the liquidator had to agree the date to be so assumed. [*ICTA 1988, s 342(4)–(6); FA 1996, Sch 24 para 12; SI 1998 No 3173*].

Where the accounting period ending with the completion of winding-up ends on or after 1 July 1999, INTEREST ON OVERPAID TAX (38) is excluded from charge provided that it does not exceed £2,000. [*ICTA 1988, s 342(3A); FA 1998, Sch 4 para 6; SI 1998 No 3173*].

Crown priority was abolished with effect from 29 December 1986, except for sums due at the 'relevant date'

(*a*) on account of net tax deductions the company was liable to make under PAYE from emoluments paid during the twelve months before that date, and

(*b*) in respect of deductions required to be made in the twelve months before that date under the CONSTRUCTION INDUSTRY TAX SCHEME (17).

The '*relevant date*' is:

(i) if the company is being wound up by the court, then

  (*a*) if the winding-up order immediately follows the discharge of an administration order, the date of the administration order, or

  (*b*) if (*a*) does not apply, and the company had not commenced voluntarily to be wound up before the making of the winding-up order, the date of first appointment of a provisional liquidator or, if no such appointment has been made, the date of the winding-up order;

(ii) if (i) does not apply, the date of passage of the winding-up resolution.

[*Insolvency Act 1986, s 175, Sch 6*].

Corporation tax on chargeable gains is a 'necessary expense' of a winding-up within the meaning of *Companies Act 1985, s 560* (*Re Mesco Properties Ltd CA 1979, 54 TC 238*).

The Crown may set off a debt due **from** one Government Department to the company against a debt due **to** another Department (or other Departments) under *Bankruptcy Act 1914, s 312*. See *Re Cushla Ltd Ch D, [1979] STC 615* which involved a VAT repayment and liabilities to the Revenue and the DSS.

Simon's Direct Tax Service. See **D2.516.**

42.6 **ACCOUNTING PERIODS**

On the commencement of a winding-up (being the passing by the company of a resolution for winding-up, the presentation of a successful petition for winding-up etc.), an accounting period ends and a new one commences. Thereafter an accounting period only ends on the expiration of twelve months from its beginning or by completion of the winding-up (but see 42.5 above). [*ICTA 1988, s 12(7)*]. Neither the filing of an administration order petition nor the making of an administration order would bring about the end of an accounting period. (ICAEW Guidance Note TR 799, June 1990).

42.7 CANCELLATION OF TAX ADVANTAGES

See *ICTA 1988, ss 703–709*, described in Tolley's Income Tax (under Anti-Avoidance).

43 Loan Relationships

Cross-reference. See 31.7 INCOME TAX IN RELATION TO A COMPANY.

Simon's Direct Tax Service B3.19.

Other sources. See Tolley's Taxation of Corporate Debt and Financial Instruments. See also Revenue Company Taxation Manual, Vol V.

The headings in this chapter are as follows.

43.1	Introduction	43.7	Application of accounting methods
43.2	Taxation of loan relationships	43.8	Deduction of tax
43.3	— charge to, and relief from, tax	43.9	Special cases
43.4	— examples	43.10	Miscellaneous provisions
43.5	Computation of debits and credits	43.11	Transitional provisions
43.6	Authorised accounting methods	43.12	Associated repeals and amendments

43.1 INTRODUCTION

With effect **from 1 April 1996**, new rules for the taxation of corporate and government debt are introduced by *FA 1996, ss 80–105, Schs 8–15*. Broadly, these treat all profits and losses made by companies on loans, whether as borrowers or as lenders, as income. Thus interest payments and discounts and premiums are generally taxed or relieved as income on an accruals basis or, in the case of capital movements for lenders, on a mark-to-market basis. Subject to certain prohibitions, the rules are designed to align with how companies draw up their statutory accounts. Revenue Press Release 28 November 1995 (REV 21) contains a useful summary of the changes.

Trading items continue to be dealt with under Schedule D, Case I, and non-trading items are brought within Schedule D, Case III.

The rules which previously applied to both corporate borrowers and lenders and individual investors continue (subject to substantial modification and simplification) to apply to individual investors. For the most important of the provisions which previously applied, see 50.7, 50.16, 50.23 PROFIT COMPUTATIONS, Tolley's Income Tax under Interest Receivable and Schedule D, Case VI (accrued income scheme) and Tolley's Capital Gains Tax under Government Securities and Qualifying Corporate Bonds. For the modified income tax rules on discounts from 6 April 1996, see Tolley's Income Tax under Schedule D, Case III. For the transitional provisions at 1 April 1996, see 43.11 below.

See also 25 FINANCIAL INSTRUMENTS, over which the current provisions generally take priority.

43.2 TAXATION OF LOAN RELATIONSHIPS

All profits or gains arising to a company from 'loan relationships' are chargeable to corporation tax as income. To the extent that the company is a party to the relationship for trade purposes, the income is trading income. Otherwise, it is brought into account under Schedule D, Case III. See 43.3 below. Where interest is charged to tax as a trading receipt, this does not affect the requirement for deduction of tax by the payer (see 31.3(*b*) INCOME TAX IN RELATION TO A COMPANY). See Revenue Tax Bulletin August 1999 pp 685, 686.

For the treatment of deficits on 'loan relationships', see 43.3 below.

Unless otherwise specified, a charge or relief under these provisions precludes any other charge to or relief from corporation tax in respect of the same matter.

[*FA 1996, s 80*].

A company has a '*loan relationship*' wherever it is a creditor or debtor as respects any 'money debt' which arises from a transaction for the lending of money, i.e. any debt which is, under general law, a loan. For this purpose a debt is not taken to arise from such a transaction to the extent that it arises from rights conferred by shares in a company under which an entitlement to receive distributions may arise, and the same applies as regards permanent interest bearing shares ('PIBS') issued by building societies (although only in respect of gains (and losses), which are therefore brought within the charge to corporation tax on chargeable gains, interest on PIBS being within the loan relationship rules (see 43.10 below)). Subject to this, a debt is taken to arise from such a transaction where an instrument is issued by any person for the purpose of representing security for, or the rights of a creditor in respect of, the debt. 'Loan relationship' thus includes gilt-edged securities, corporate bonds, overdrafts and other corporate debt, but not trade debts (although see 43.10 below as regards interest on such debts, and also as regards other specific exclusions). Certain types of interest or imputed interest which do not arise from a loan relationship are treated as if they did so as regards interest credits and debits (see 43.10 below). For the circumstances in which a capital grant may be considered a loan relationship, see Revenue Company Taxation Manual, CT 12121.

A '*money debt*' is a debt falling to be settled by payment of money, or by the transfer of a right to settlement under a debt falling to be so settled.

[*FA 1996, s 81(1)–(4)*].

For these purposes, any payment or interest in pursuance of any of the rights or liabilities under a loan relationship, or under the agreement(s) by virtue of which the relationship exists (including a security representing the relationship), are treated as made or payable under that relationship. 'Money' is not restricted to sterling. [*FA 1996, s 81(5)(6)*].

Simon's Direct Tax Service. See B3.1902–B3.1904.

43.3 **Charge to, and relief from, tax.** The credits or debits for an accounting period in respect of any loan relationship (computed as described at 43.5 *et seq.* below) are brought into account as follows.

(*a*) Where the loan relationship is for trading purposes, they are treated as receipts or expenses of the trade for that period (in the case of expenses, notwithstanding *ICTA 1988, s 74* (allowable deductions)). (This does not affect the requirement for deduction of tax by the payer (see 31.3(*b*) INCOME TAX IN RELATION TO A COMPANY), see Revenue Tax Bulletin August 1999 pp 685, 686.)

(*b*) Where there are credits and/or debits in respect of a non-trading relationship, they are aggregated, and the net amount is chargeable under Schedule D, Case III or relievable as a non-trading deficit (see below) as the case may be.

[*FA 1996, s 82*].

For a creditor company, a loan relationship is taken to be for trade purposes only if it is a party to the relationship in the course of activities forming an integral part of that trade. Relief for all or part of a non-trading deficit of an accounting period (the '*deficit period*') may be claimed either:

(i) by set-off against profits of the same period; or

(ii) by group relief (see 29.14 *et seq.* GROUPS OF COMPANIES); or

(iii) by carry-back and set-off against profits of earlier accounting periods arising from non-trading loan relationships; or

(iv) by carry-forward and set-off against non-trading profits (i.e. profits exclusive of trading income) for the next accounting period.

Claims must be made within two years of the end of the deficit period (or, in the case of a claim under (iv) above, the next following accounting period), or within such further period as the Board may allow.

See below for the detailed rules on such claims. Different claims may be made as respects different parts of a non-trading deficit, but not so as to give relief more than once.

Any part for which relief is not so claimed is carried forward and treated as a deficit of the next accounting period, in respect of which, however, relief may only be claimed for that period under (iv) above (and the deficit brought forward is disregarded for the purposes of any claim under (iv) above relating to a deficit arising in that next accounting period).

Where, however, the company is established for *charitable purposes* only, no relief may be claimed for a non-trading deficit under (i)–(iv) above.

Claims. A claim under (i) above is given effect after relief for brought forward trading losses, but before relief under *ICTA 1988, s 392A(1)* or *s 393A(1)* (losses relieved against profits of current or earlier accounting periods, see 44.2, 44.6 LOSSES, 50.27 PROFIT COMPUTATIONS) or under (iii) above. Relief against oil companies' ring-fenced profits is prohibited.

Before 1 April 1998, a claim under (ii) above is given effect by treating the amount for which relief is claimed as a trading loss not excluded from relief by 29.18(*a*)(i)–(iii). Thereafter group relief is given by *ICTA 1988, s 403ZC*. See 29.18 GROUPS OF COMPANIES.

A claim under (iii) above must exclude any amounts claimed under (i) or (ii) above. Only profits for accounting periods (or parts) falling within a specified period immediately preceding the deficit period (disregarding any part of the specified period falling before 1 April 1996) may be relieved, and relief is given for later accounting periods before earlier ones. Profits of an accounting period straddling the start of the specified period are apportioned for this purpose. The specified period is twelve months for deficit periods ending after 1 July 1997 (except as below), three years (but not before 1 April 1996) for earlier periods. For deficit periods straddling 1 July 1997, the extension of the specified period back to 1 April 1996 is retained for the part of the deficit attributable to the part of the accounting period falling before 2 July 1997. Apportionment of the deficit for this purpose is made on a time basis unless this would produce an unjust or unreasonable result, in which case it is made on a just and reasonable basis. Relief is given after any relief under (i) or (ii) above and after any relief for losses or deficits of accounting periods before the deficit period, for trade charges, for trading losses of the same or subsequent periods, or, for INVESTMENT COMPANIES (40), for plant and machinery capital allowances, management expenses or business charges.

[*FA 1996, ss 83, 103(2), Sch 8; F(No 2)A 1997, s 40; FA 1998, s 82, Sch 5 para 64*].

Simon's Direct Tax Service. See **B3.1915, B3.1931**.

43.4 *Examples*

(A) *Loan relationship for trading purpose*

A Ltd requires additional trade finance, and on 1 January 2000 enters into an agreement with Bank plc to borrow £100,000 for three years. Interest at 10% p.a. is payable at six-month intervals commencing 1 July 2000. Legal fees and other professional costs in relation to the loan amount to £2,800, paid in December 1999. The company's accounting reference date is 31 March, and it adopts an authorised accruals basis of accounting for all its loan relationships.

A Ltd's accounts for the year ended 31 March 2000 show the following:

	£	£
Turnover		1,400,000
Purchases and expenses (all allowable for tax purposes)	900,000	
Finance charges		
Bank plc interest to 31 March 2000	2,500	
Legal fees etc.	2,800	
Depreciation*	120,000	1,025,300
Net profit per accounts		£374,700

* Capital allowances for the year are £95,000.

A Ltd's corporation tax computation for the same period is as follows.

	£
Net profit per accounts	374,700
Add: Depreciation	120,000
Less: Capital allowances	(95,000)
Corporation tax adjusted profit	£399,700

The accrued interest on the bank loan taken for trading purposes will be treated for corporation tax purposes as a trade expense.

The profit and loss charge for each relevant accounting period will be as follows.

Year ended	31.3.00	31.3.01	31.3.02	31.3.03
	£	£	£	£
Expenses	2,800	—	—	—
Interest payable	2,500	10,000	10,000	7,500

This conforms to the authorised accruals basis of accounting, as interest will be allocated to the period to which it relates.

(B) *Loan relationship for non-trading purpose*

T Ltd, a trading company, bought £10,000 nominal of gilt-edged securities at £94 per £100 nominal stock as a speculative venture on 1 January 2000. The securities will be redeemed on 1 January 2003 at par. Interest at 5% is payable annually on 31 December. The company uses the authorised accruals basis of accounting for all its loan relationships.

As the purchase does not relate to the company's trade, the income will be assessed under Schedule D, Case III. In addition to the interest, the company will be taxable on the discount, spread over three years.

Year ended	31.3.00	31.3.01	31.3.02	31.3.03
	£	£	£	£
Interest received	125	500	500	375
Discount	50	200	200	150
Schedule D, Case III	175	700	700	525

(C) *Non-trading deficit on a loan relationship*

C Ltd, which is not a member of a group, made a loan to X Ltd, outside its normal trading activities. X Ltd defaults on the loan on 1 October 2000, leaving a balance of £8,500 due to C Ltd.

C Ltd's computations for relevant years are as follows.

Year ended	31.3.99	31.3.00	31.3.01	31.3.02
	£	£	£	£
Schedule D, Case I	10,000	11,000	800	12,000
Schedule D, Case III (non-trading loan relationships)	2,000	2,000	100	400

The £8,500 deficit may be relieved in whole or in part in three different ways (group relief not being available), as follows.

	£
	8,500
(1) Set against total profits for year ended 31 March 2001	(900)
(2) Carry back against Schedule D, Case III profits from non-trading loan relationships of the preceding accounting period	(2,000)
(3) Carry forward and set against non-trading profits for year ended 31 March 2002	(400)
Net deficit to carry forward against subsequent non-trading profits	£5,200

43.5 **COMPUTATION OF DEBITS AND CREDITS**

The credits and debits to be brought into account by a company in respect of its loan relationships are sums which, in accordance with an authorised accounting method, and when taken together, fairly represent, for the accounting period in question,

(*a*) all profits, gains and losses (capital or otherwise) which (disregarding interest and any charges or expenses) arise to the company from its loan relationships and 'related transactions', and

(*b*) all interest under its loan relationships and all charges and expenses incurred under, or for the purposes of, those relationships and transactions.

Subject to *FA 1996, Sch 9 para 15* (see below), a '*related transaction*' is any disposal or acquisition (in whole or part) of rights or liabilities under a relationship. This includes the transfer or extinguishment of any such rights or liabilities by any sale, gift, exchange, surrender, redemption or release. Profits, gains and losses for this purpose exclude amounts required to be transferred to share premium account, but include those which, in accordance with normal accountancy practice, are carried to or sustained by any other reserve maintained by the company. Charges and expenses within (*b*) above include only those incurred directly

(i) in bringing any of the loan relationships into existence,

(ii) in entering into or giving effect to any of the related transactions,

(iii) in making payments under any of the relationships or in pursuance of any of the related transactions, or

(iv) in taking steps for ensuring the receipt of payments under any of the relationships or in pursuance of any of the related transactions.

They do, however, include charges and expenses connected with entering into, or giving effect to any obligation under, a prospective loan relationship or related transaction into which the company has not entered at the time they are incurred.

[*FA 1996, s 84*].

Costs directly incurred in varying the terms of a loan relationship may be brought into account as a debit under *FA 1996, s 84*. Guarantee fees are excluded unless the loan would not have been advanced without the provision of a guarantee, but may be allowable as trading deductions where incurred wholly and exclusively for trade purposes and not in respect of capital. (Revenue Tax Bulletin October 1996 p 357, December 1996 p 373).

See Simon's Direct Tax Service B3.1915–B3.1917.

Distributions. Credits and debits relating to any amounts treated as DISTRIBUTIONS (20) are excluded. [*FA 1996, Sch 9 para 1*].

Late interest. Where an authorised accruals basis of accounting is used as respects a debtor loan relationship under *FA 1996, s 87* (parties to relationship having connection, see 43.6 below), then if

(*a*) interest payable under the relationship is not paid within twelve months of the end of the accounting period in which it would otherwise be treated as accruing, and

(*b*) credits representing the full amount of the interest are not brought into account for any accounting period in respect of the corresponding creditor relationship,

debits relating to interest payable under the relationship are not brought into account until the interest is paid. [*FA 1996, Sch 9 para 2*].

Options etc.. Where the accruals basis of accounting applies for an accounting period, and the question of an amount becoming due under a loan relationship after the end of the period (or of its amount or timing) depends on the exercise of an option by a party to the relationship, it is assumed that the option will be exercised in the manner which, as at the end of the period, appears most advantageous to that party (disregarding taxation). This applies equally where the option is exerciseable by an associate of a party to the relationship (within *ICTA 1988, s 417(3)(4)*, see 13.5 CLOSE COMPANIES), and where a similar power is exerciseable other than under an option. [*FA 1996, Sch 9 para 3*].

Foreign exchange gains and losses. Without prejudice to the special EXCHANGE GAINS AND LOSSES (23) provisions, any accounting requirement for currency translation or conversion, under which sums reflecting currency gains or losses are included in credits or debits, is disregarded. [*FA 1996, Sch 9 para 4*].

Bad debts etc.. Except as detailed below, a departure is allowed from the normal accruals basis assumption that all amounts due under a creditor relationship will be paid on time for bad debts, for doubtful debts estimated to be bad and for debts released. The accounting arrangements allowing the departure must also require adjustment by way of credit for any debt ceasing to fulfil the conditions for relief.

Where a debt is released in an accounting period for which the debtor company uses the accruals basis as respects the relationship in question, no credit is required to be brought in in respect of the release if it is part of a relevant arrangement or compromise (see 42.2 LIQUIDATION ETC.), or if the relationship is such that *FA 1996, s 87* imposes an authorised accruals basis (for which see further below).

Where *FA 1996, s 87* (parties to relationship having connection, see 43.6 below) requires an authorised accruals basis to be applied for an accounting period as regards a creditor relationship of a company, a departure (as above) from the assumption that every amount due under the relationship will be paid in full is allowed only where the company treats the liability as discharged in consideration of shares (or an entitlement to shares) forming part of the ordinary share capital of the debtor company, and *section 87* would not have applied before the shares (or entitlement) were acquired. For an accounting period in which the company ceases to be a party to the relationship, the debits in respect of the relationship for that period shall be no more, and the credits no less, than they would have been had the relationship not ceased (disregarding any amounts which would have accrued after the relationship ceased). See, however, below for concessional disregard of a connection within *section 87* in certain cases for these purposes.

No credit is required to be brought into account in respect of the release of a liability by which a government investment is written off (for which see generally 44.21 LOSSES).

There are special provisions restricting relief in respect of sovereign debt, i.e. debt owed or guaranteed by an overseas State authority or estimated to be bad because of restrictions imposed by an overseas State or State authority. These replace the earlier provisions of *ICTA 1988, ss 88A–88C* (see 6.3 BANKS).

[*FA 1996, Sch 9 paras 5–9*].

See Simon's Direct Tax Service B3.1923.

Concessional bad debt relief. By concession, where a connection within *FA 1996, s 87* would otherwise prevent a creditor company obtaining bad debt relief (as described above), the company may (for this purpose only) choose (in respect of all its loan relationships potentially falling within the concession) that (i)–(iii) below apply in determining whether there is a connection within *section 87*. The company must notify the office dealing with its tax affairs that it wishes to take advantage of the concession, and must then within twelve months of the end of any accounting period notify that office of the relief it wishes to claim under the concession for the period.

(i) The rights and powers of 'associates' to be attributed to a person in applying *ICTA 1988, s 416* (definition of 'control') exclude those attributed to a participator by virtue only of the holder being a partner of the participator. This will, for example, prevent a company which is a general partner in a venture capital partnership automatically being treated as connected with a company in which the partnership is investing.

(ii) Rights attributable to a company as loan creditor in respect of a loan made in the ordinary course of its business of providing finance are disregarded in determining whether it has control (within *ICTA 1988, s 416*) of the debtor company by virtue of entitlement to the greater part of its assets available for distribution among the participators on a winding-up, etc.. This mirrors the statutory provision which already applies in the case of loans made by banks (see 43.6 below).

(iii) A company's possession, or entitlement to possession, of fixed rate preference shares (within *ICTA 1988, s 95*) which do not carry voting rights is disregarded in determining control within *ICTA 1988, s 416*, provided that:

(*a*) the creditor company is not a close company within *ICTA 1988, s 414* (see 13.1 CLOSE COMPANIES);

(*b*) the creditor company entered into the loan relationship in the ordinary course of its business of providing finance, and it (or any other company in the same group) similarly subscribed for the preference shares in the ordinary course of such a business;

(*c*) where the creditor company (or a member of the same group) acquired the preference shares through the exchange of loan for shares, it did so in the ordinary course of its business of providing finance, and the face value of the debt was significantly more than the market value of the shares for which it was exchanged; and

(*d*) the debtor company is within the charge to corporation tax in respect of any loan relationship exchanged for shares and any continuing loan relationship with the creditor company.

Where a company takes advantage of the concession, it must also accept any subsequent charges arising in respect of recoveries, decreases in provisions or profits on disposals of debts for which relief has been given under the concession. Where a loan relationship previously within the concession subsequently falls outside its terms, the connection will be treated as having started at that time. Relief previously given will not be withdrawn (except where there is a recovery, etc.). Relief is allowed under the concession in certain circumstances for loans in existence at 1 April 1996 where the creditor and debtor are connected as a result of an earlier exchange of shares.

The concession also deals with certain other ancillary matters, in particular its application to debt equity swaps and the effects of subsequent connection outside the concession.

(Revenue Pamphlet IR 1, C28).

See Simon's Direct Tax Service B3.1936.

Imported losses etc.. Special rules apply for an accounting period (the '*loss period*') of a company (the '*chargeable company*') for which an authorised accruals basis is used as respects a loan relationship where:

(A) under that basis, there is an amount of debit or credit which would otherwise fall to be brought into account in respect of that relationship;

(B) as a result of that amount being brought into account, a loss in connection with that relationship would be treated as arising under the current provisions; and

(C) that loss is wholly or partly referable to a time when the chargeable company (or any predecessor in the same position as respects the relationship at that time) would not have been liable to UK tax on any profits or gains arising from the relationship.

In those circumstances, the amounts brought into account in that period in respect of that relationship are adjusted to ensure that no part of the loss referable to such a time is treated for the purposes of the current provisions as arising in any accounting period of the chargeable company.

[*FA 1996, Sch 9 para 10*].

Transactions not at arm's length. Where debits or credits falling to be brought into account in respect of a loan relationship relate to amounts arising from a non-arm's length 'related transaction' (as above) (or are incurred for the purposes of such a transaction), they are determined on the assumption that the transaction was entered into on the same terms it would have been if at arm's length between independent persons. This does not, however, apply to debits arising from the acquisition of rights under a loan relationship for less than market value; or to any related transaction between two members of a group of companies (see 9.18 CAPITAL GAINS); or to any of a series of transactions by a member of a group which together have the same effect as a related transaction between members of a group. The changes to the residence requirements for groups of companies introduced by *FA 2000* (see 9.18 CAPITAL GAINS) apply for these purposes in relation to transactions entered into (or a series of transactions begun) on or after 1 April 2000, and for such transactions the exclusion applies only if both group members are within the charge to corporation tax in respect of the transaction. [*FA 1996, Sch 9 para 11; FA 2000, Sch 29 para 44(2)(3)(5)*]. See Simon's Direct Tax Service B3.1942.

Continuity of treatment: groups etc.. An adjustment is required where, as a result of a related transaction (as above) between two members of a group, one of those companies directly or indirectly replaces the other as a party to a loan relationship. An adjustment is similarly required where a series of transactions, having the same effect as a related transaction between two companies each of which has been a member of the same group at some time in the course of those transactions, results in such a replacement. The credits and debits to be brought into account for the two companies are (except for the purpose of identifying the company for which any other debit or credit is to be brought into account) determined disregarding the transaction(s) and treating the two companies as the same company.

The changes to the residence requirements for groups of companies introduced by *FA 2000* (see 9.18 CAPITAL GAINS) apply for these purposes in relation to transactions entered into (or a series of transactions begun) on or after 1 April 2000, and for such transactions the provisions apply only to a transaction in respect of which both group members are within the charge to corporation tax.

The provisions apply equally where one company becomes a party to a loan relationship with rights equivalent to those of the other company under a loan relationship to which the other company previously ceased to be a party. Rights are 'equivalent' for this purpose if they give entitlement to the same rights against the same persons as to capital, interest and dividends and to the same enforcement remedies, notwithstanding differences in nominal value, in the form held or in the manner of transfer.

Similar provisions apply to certain transfers between insurance companies which result in one replacing the other as a party to a loan relationship (and the above provisions are correspondingly disapplied to certain such transfers).

[*FA 1996, Sch 9 para 12; FA 2000, Sch 29 para 44(4)(5)*].

See Simon's Direct Tax Service B3.1937.

Loan relationships for unallowable purposes. Any debits which, on a just and reasonable apportionment, are attributable to an 'unallowable purpose' of a loan relationship in an accounting period are not to be brought into account for that period. A purpose for which the company, at times during an accounting period, either is a party to a loan relationship or enters into a related transaction (as above) is an '*unallowable purpose*' if it is not amongst the business or other commercial purposes of the company (which do not include the purposes of any part of its activities which are outside the charge to corporation tax). In this respect a purpose which consists in the securing of a tax advantage (within *ICTA 1988, ss 703–709*, see Tolley's Income Tax under Anti-Avoidance) for any person is a business or other commercial purpose only where it is not a main purpose for which the company is a party to the relationship or entered into the transaction. [*FA 1996, Sch 9 para 13*]. See Simon's Direct Tax Service B3.1942.

Interest etc. relating to capital expenditure. Debits or credits given by an authorised accounting method in respect of a loan relationship which, under normal accountancy practice, are allowed to be treated as amounts brought into account in determining the value of a fixed capital asset or project are to be brought into account as if they were treated as profit and loss items. [*FA 1996, Sch 9 para 14*]. See Simon's Direct Tax Service B3.1924.

Repo transactions and stock lending. Without prejudice to *ICTA 1988, s 730A(2)(6)* (deemed payments of loan interest in the case of the sale and repurchase of securities, see Tolley's Income Tax under Anti-Avoidance), a '*related transaction*' (as above) does not include a disposal or acquisition of rights or liabilities under a loan relationship made in pursuance of any 'repo or stock lending arrangements'. '*Repo or stock lending arrangements*' are arrangements consisting in or involving an agreement or series of agreements under which provision is made

(1) for the transfer of any rights under that relationship, and

(2) for the transferor (or a connected person within *ICTA 1988, s 839*, see 16 CONNECTED PERSONS) subsequently to be entitled, or to become entitled, or to be required, to have the same or equivalent (as above in relation to *FA 1996, Sch 9 para 12*) rights transferred to him, or to have rights in respect of benefits accruing in respect of that relationship on redemption.

The exclusion does not apply to any redemption or discharge of rights or liabilities under a loan relationship to which any repo or stock lending arrangements relate.

See also *SI 1998 No 3177, reg 19* as regards certain rights accruing on the conversion of a loan relationship from the currency of a State which has adopted the euro into euros.

[*FA 1996, Sch 9 para 15*].

See Simon's Direct Tax Service B3.1939.

Imputed interest. Where, under *ICTA 1988, ss 770–772* or, as the case may be, *ICTA 1988, Sch 28AA* (transfer pricing, see 4.4 ANTI-AVOIDANCE), any amount falls to be treated as interest payable under a loan relationship of a company, those provisions have effect so as to require credits or debits relating to the deemed interest to be brought into account to the same extent as if they were actual interest. This over-rides any provisions of an authorised accounting method. [*FA 1996, Sch 9 para 16; FA 1998, s 108(4)(5)*].

Discounted securities where companies have a connection and where issued by a close company. These provisions deal with the situation where, for any accounting period (the 'relevant period'), a debtor relationship is represented by a 'relevant discounted security' issued by a company, the benefit of which is at any time in that period available to another company which was 'connected' with the issuing company for that period. They do not apply where credits representing the full amount of the discount referable to that period are brought into account for any accounting period in respect of the corresponding creditor relationship. The benefit of a security is so available where the security, or any entitlement to rights attached to it, is beneficially owned by the company, or the company is indirectly entitled, by reference to a series of loan transactions, to the benefit of any rights attached to the security. Where these provisions apply, the debits to be brought into account in respect of the relationship are adjusted so that every debit which relates to the amount of the discount and which is referable to the relevant period is brought into account instead for the accounting period of redemption. The amount of the discount referable to the relevant period for this purpose is the amount which would otherwise be brought into account for the relevant period relating to the difference between the issue price and the amount payable on redemption. That difference is determined on the basis that 'redemption' does not include any redemption which may be made before maturity otherwise than at the option of the holder, and refers to the earliest occasion on which the holder may require redemption, and that the amount payable on redemption excludes any interest.

Companies are '*connected*' for these purposes for the relevant period if, at any time in that period or in the two years before the beginning of that period, one controls the other (within *ICTA 1988, s 416(2)–(6)*, see 13.2 CLOSE COMPANIES) or both are under the control of the same person (other than the Crown, a Minister of the Crown, a government or NI department, a foreign sovereign power or an organisation of which two or more sovereign powers, or their governments, are members).

FA 1996, s 88 (see 43.6 below) applies *mutatis mutandis* to exempt certain cases from this provision as it would apply to exempt the corresponding creditor relationship.

A '*relevant discounted security*' is as defined for the purposes of the income tax rules under *FA 1996, Sch 13 para 3 as amended* (and see Tolley's Income Tax under Schedule D, Case III for the full definition). It means any security which is such that, as at the time of issue, the amount payable on certain occasions on which redemption may occur is or might be an amount involving a 'deep gain'.

Exclusions *inter alia* are:

(I) gilt-edged securities which are not strips;

(II) excluded indexed securities (broadly, where the amount payable on redemption is linked to the value of capital gains tax chargeable assets); and

(III) certain securities issued under the same prospectus as other securities issued previously and not themselves 'relevant discounted securities'.

An amount payable on redemption represents a '*deep gain*' if (on the same basis as is referred to above) it exceeds the issue price by more than one twenty-fourth of one per cent of the amount payable on redemption (excluding interest) for each month (or part month) of the term of the security (or by more than 15% if the term exceeds thirty years).

Close companies. A similar restriction applies where a debtor relationship of a close company is represented by a relevant discounted security issued by the company, and at any time in or before the accounting period in question the security was beneficially owned by a person who at that time was either

(*aa*) a 'participator' (within *ICTA 1988, s 417*, see 13.3 CLOSE COMPANIES), or

(*bb*) an 'associate' (within *ICTA 1988, s 417(3)(4)*, see 13.5 CLOSE COMPANIES) of a participator, or

(*cc*) a company 'controlled' by a participator (within *ICTA 1988, s 416(2)–(6)*, see 13.2 CLOSE COMPANIES).

'Participator' excludes a person who is such only by virtue of his holding a relevant discounted security issued by the company, and in the case of a banking business securities acquired in the ordinary course of the business are disregarded.

[*FA 1996, Sch 9 paras 17, 18*].

43.6 AUTHORISED ACCOUNTING METHODS

Except as below, the alternative accounting methods authorised for the purposes of the current provisions are an accruals basis and a mark to market basis under which a fair value (on the basis of a transfer at arm's length) is brought into account in each accounting period for each loan relationship to which it applies. Whichever method is used must

(*a*) conform (subject to (*b*) and (*c*) below) to normal accountancy practice,

(*b*) contain proper provision for allocating payments under a loan relationship to accounting periods, and

(*c*) in the case of an accruals basis, not contain any provision (other than authorised bad debt arrangements, for which see 43.5 above) giving debits by reference to the valuation at different times of any asset representing a loan relationship.

As regards (*b*), a mark to market basis must allocate payments to the accounting period in which they become due and payable.

Also as regards (*b*), an accruals basis must:

(i) allocate payments to the period to which they relate, without regard to payment or receipt or their becoming due and payable;

(ii) apportion payments relating to two or more periods to those periods on a just and reasonable basis;

(iii) assume (subject to authorised bad debt arrangements, see 43.5 above), in relation to a creditor company, that every amount payable under the relationship will be paid in full when due;

(iv) secure the making of the adjustments required by authorised bad debt arrangements; and

(v) provide (subject to authorised arrangements for bad debt and for writing off government investments, see 43.5 above), in respect of debts released, for the appropriate amount to be credited to the debtor in the accounting period of the release.

Where a purchased loan is repayable on demand, (i) above does not always require that the loan is brought in on acquisition at full value (thus producing an immediate credit of the difference between that value and acquisition cost). If normal accountancy practice would not recognise the discount in the accounting period of the acquisition (whether or not the debt was doubtful), immediate recognition of the profit for tax purposes may also be inappropriate. However, in the case of a loan relationship between connected parties (see below), the assumption must still be made that all amounts will be paid in full without relief for bad or doubtful debts (see 43.5 above), so that the discount must be recognised on a time-scale which would be realistic for a loan repayable on demand and neither bad nor doubtful. (Revenue Tax Bulletin June 1997 pp 441, 442).

[*FA 1996, s 85*].

Parties to relationship with connection. In the case of a loan relationship of a company where there is a 'connection' between the company and the other party to the relationship (including any person standing indirectly in that position by reference to a series of loan relationships), the only authorised accounting method is an authorised accruals basis. For this purpose there is a '*connection*' between a company and another person for an accounting period if at any time in the period (subject to *FA 1996, s 88*, see below), or in the two years before the beginning of the period:

(A) where the other person is a company, one company controls the other (within *ICTA 1988, s 416*, see 13.2 CLOSE COMPANIES) or both are under the control of the same person (other than the Crown, a Minister of the Crown, a government or NI department, a foreign sovereign power or an organisation of which two or more sovereign powers, or their governments, are members); or

(B) in any case, the other person is a participator (or an 'associate' (within *ICTA 1988, s 417*, see 13.5 CLOSE COMPANIES) of a participator) in the company, it being a close company. 'Participator' is as under *ICTA 1988, s 417* (see 13.3 CLOSE COMPANIES) but disregarding loan creditors as such.

[*FA 1996, s 87*].

Where the *only* link between two parties is the loan relationship in question, the two parties will not be connected, even where the size of the loan would entitle the loan creditor to the greatest part of the assets in a winding up. The exclusion of loan creditors applies only in determining whether a particular loan creditor is connected with the debtor company — the rights of all loan creditors will be taken into account in applying the control tests to other parties. (Revenue Tax Bulletin December 1997 p 488).

As regards (B), connection through participation is not mutual, i.e. 'connection' has to be considered separately in relation to the debtor in a loan relationship and the creditor in the relationship. (Revenue Company Taxation Manual, CT 12455).

Exemption. Where a company is party to a creditor relationship in an accounting period in 'exempt circumstances', any 'connection' otherwise within *FA 1996, s 87* (see above) with a person who (directly or indirectly) stands in the position of the debtor is disregarded for the purposes of that *section*. Where the debtor is also a company, this does not apply in relation to that company. A company is party to a relationship in an accounting period in '*exempt circumstances*' if:

(*a*) in the course of carrying on activities forming an integral part of a trade carried on in that period it disposes of or acquires assets representing creditor relationships;

(*b*) for that period the company uses an authorised mark to market basis of accounting as respects all creditor relationships represented by assets acquired in the course of those activities;

(*c*) the asset representing the creditor relationship in question was acquired in the course of those activities and is either listed on a recognised stock exchange at the end of that period or a security which must be redeemed within twelve months of issue;

(*d*) at some time in that period assets of the same kind as the asset representing the creditor relationship in question are in the beneficial ownership of persons other than the company; and

(*e*) in not more than three months (in aggregate) in that period is the equivalent of 30% or more of the assets of that kind in the beneficial ownership of connected persons (and a connected person is taken as having beneficial ownership of an asset wherever there is (apart from the current exemption) a connection within *FA 1996, s 87* between the person having beneficial ownership of the asset and a person who (directly or indirectly) stands in the position of debtor as respects the debt by reference to which any loan relationship represented by that asset subsists).

As regards (*d*) above, assets are taken to be of the same kind where they are so treated by the practice of any recognised stock exchange (or would be if dealt with on such an exchange).

The definition of 'exempt circumstances' is modified in the case of an insurance company carrying on basic life and general annuity business.

[*FA 1996, s 88*].

Simon's Direct Tax Service. See **B3.1920, B3.1921, B3.1935.**

43.7 APPLICATION OF ACCOUNTING METHODS

Different authorised accounting methods may be used as respects different loan relationships, and for different accounting periods (or parts) as respects the same relationship. If an accounting basis which is, or which 'equates' with, an authorised accounting method is used as respects any loan relationship in a company's 'statutory accounts' (see *FA 1996, s 86(8)(9)*), it, or the authorised method with which it equates, must similarly be used for periods covered by those accounts. Where the method to be used is not thereby determined, an authorised accruals basis must be used.

A basis of accounting '*equates*':

(*a*) with an authorised accruals basis, if (not being within (*b*)) it purports to allocate payments under a loan relationship to accounting periods according to when they are taken to accrue;

(*b*) with an authorised mark to market basis if, otherwise being within (*a*), it purports to bring the loan relationship into account in each accounting period at a value representing an arm's length valuation on the basis that interest already accrued under the relationship was to be disregarded, and the resulting credits and debits correspond, for all practical purposes, to those under an authorised mark to market basis; and

(*c*) with an authorised mark to market basis, if (not being within (*a*)) it purports, in respect of a loan relationship, to produce credits or debits which relate to payments under the relationship according to when they become due and payable, and which are computed by reference to the determination, as at different times in an accounting period, of a fair value (on the basis of a transfer at arm's length).

[*FA 1996, s 86*].

Inconsistent application. Where there is any inconsistency or other material difference between the way in which an authorised accounting method is applied as respects the same loan relationship in successive accounting periods, a balancing debit or credit must be brought into account in the later of those periods (the '*second period*'). The amount to be debited or credited (as appropriate) is the aggregate (treating debits or net debits as negative) of:

(i) a debit (or, if the result is negative, a credit) equal to the amount by which the aggregate credits actually brought into account for all previous periods (i.e. periods before the second period) in which the accounting method was used exceeds the aggregate which would have been brought in had the method been applied in those periods in the same way as it was in the second period; and

(ii) a credit (or, if the result is negative, a debit) equal to the amount by which the aggregate debits actually brought into account for all previous periods in which the accounting method was used exceeds the aggregate which would have been brought in had the method been applied in those periods in the same way as it was in the second period.

[*FA 1996, s 89*].

Changes of accounting method. Where, as respects the same loan relationship, the use of one authorised accounting method is superseded by another during an accounting period, it is to be assumed that:

(1) the party ceased to be a party to the relationship immediately before the change, and again became a party to it immediately after the change;

(2) the relationship before the change is separate and distinct from the relationship after the change;

(3) the amount payable under each of the transactions comprised in the assumptions in (1) above was equal to the fair value (on the basis of a transfer at arm's length) of the relationship;

(4) so far as relevant, the amount in (3) above is deemed to have become due at the time of the change.

Each method is then applied on those assumptions as respects the part of the period for which it is used, the associated debits and credits being taken into account for the period. Where the change takes place at the beginning of an accounting period, the aggregate net credit or debit which would have arisen by the application of the methods actually used for that period and for the previous period without the making of those assumptions is subtracted from the aggregate which would have arisen on those assumptions, and the resulting net credit or debit is brought into account for the period as from the beginning of which the change takes effect.

Where a mark to market basis is superseded by an accruals basis of accounting after 13 November 1996, the relationship in question is one to which the company is still a party at the end of the accounting period (or part) for which the accruals basis is used, and the amount which would have accrued in that period (or part) falls to be determined in accordance with the above assumptions, that amount is computed using the closing value at the end of that period (or part) *without* making those assumptions. Previously, this provision applied whether or not the company was still a party to the loan relationship in question at the end of the period (or part) for which the accruals basis was used, and the amount falling to be determined as above was taken to be (B – A), where

A is the amount which on those assumptions is given as an opening value for the period (or part), and

B is whatever, in a computation in accordance with an authorised accruals basis of accounting of the amount accruing in that period (or part), would have been taken to be the closing value applicable as at the end of that period (or part) if such an accounting basis had always been used.

[*FA 1996, s 90; FA 1997, s 83*].

See 43.11 below as regards transitional provisions.

Simon's Direct Tax Service. See **B3.1920, B3.1922**.

43.8 DEDUCTION OF TAX

This provision deals with the situation where a company receives a payment under deduction of income tax, and a credit relating to that interest has been brought into account on the company under the current provisions for an accounting period ending more than two years before receipt of the payment. On a claim, the income tax deducted may be set against the corporation tax liability for the accounting period in which the payment is received.

In determining for which accounting period a credit was brought in in respect of a subsequent interest payment, interest payments are identified with the earliest possible outstanding liability for interest under the relationship in question, according to the accounting method most recently used. Thus where an accruals basis is used, the earliest outstanding liability is determined by reference to the time the interest accrued, whilst if a mark to market basis is used, it is determined by reference to the time the interest became due and payable.

A claim must be made to an officer of the Board by the end of two years after the accounting period in which the payment is received or, if later, by the end of six years after the accounting period in which the credit in respect of the interest was brought into account. Where a claim would be out of time in respect of a payment of interest, no claim may be made under *ICTA 1988, Sch 16 para 5* (see 31.4 INCOME TAX IN RELATION TO A COMPANY) for set-off of that payment.

[*FA 1996, s 91*].

43.9 SPECIAL CASES

Convertible securities etc.. This provision applies to an asset if:

(*a*) it represents a creditor relationship of a company;

(*b*) the rights attached to it include provision by virtue of which the company is, or may become, entitled to acquire any shares;

(*c*) the extent to which shares may be acquired under (*b*) is not determined using a cash value specified in the provision or ascertainable by reference to its terms;

(*d*) it is not a 'relevant discounted security' (see 43.5 above);

(*e*) when it came into existence, there was more than a negligible likelihood that the right to acquire shares (as in (*b*) above) would in due course be exercised to a significant extent; and

(*f*) its disposal by the company would not be treated as in the course of activities forming an integral part of a trade carried on by the company.

In those circumstances, the amounts falling to be brought into account under the current provisions in respect of the creditor relationship are confined to those relating to interest, and must be ascertained using an authorised accruals basis of accounting. The normal chargeable gains provisions apply to the asset as if it did not represent a loan relationship, with the appropriate adjustment for interest accrued but not received.

As regards (*d*) above, for accounting periods ending after 14 February 1999 (but not so as to affect disposals (or part disposals) completed on or before that date), the definition of 'relevant discounted security' is widened to take further account of potential redemptions before maturity (for which see Tolley's Income Tax under Schedule D, Case III). If an asset continuing to represent a creditor relationship ceases after that date to be a convertible security within these provisions (which would be the case if it becomes a relevant discounted security), there is deemed to be a disposal and reacquisition by the company at current value (adjusted for accrued interest) under the appropriate accounting method, with the resulting gain or loss deferred under the provisions concerning share reorganisations etc. involving the issue of a qualifying corporate bond (see Tolley's Capital Gains Tax under Qualifying Corporate Bonds).

[*FA 1996, s 92; FA 1999, s 65(7)(9)*].

See Simon's Direct Tax Service B3.1938.

Relationships linked to the value of chargeable assets. Where a loan relationship is 'linked' to the value of chargeable assets, the amounts falling to be brought into account under the current provisions in respect of the relationship are confined to those relating to interest, and must be ascertained using an authorised accruals basis of accounting. The normal chargeable gains provisions apply to the asset representing the relationship as if it did not represent a loan relationship, with the appropriate adjustment for interest accrued but not received. This provision does not, however, apply to a loan relationship the disposal of which would fall to be treated as in the course of activities forming an integral part of a trade carried on by the company.

A loan relationship is '*linked*' to the value of chargeable assets if, in pursuance of any provision having effect for the purposes of the relationship, the discharge payment is determined by applying to the amount of the original loan a percentage change over the 'relevant period' in the value of chargeable assets of any particular description (or in an index of the value of such assets — neither the retail prices index nor any similar foreign general prices index is such an index). If, however, there is such a provision which is made subject to any other provision applying to the determination of the amount of the discharge payment, whose only effect is to place a lower limit on the discharge payment of a specified percentage (which must not be more than 10%) of the original loan, then that other provision is disregarded for this purpose. An asset is for these purposes a chargeable asset if any disposal gain would (after 31 March 1996) be a chargeable gain (assuming the asset to belong to the company and not to be one the disposal of which would fall to be treated as in the course of activities forming an integral part of a trade carried on by the company, and disregarding gains rolled over into the asset on a capital reorganisation, etc.).

The '*relevant period*' is the period between the time of the original loan and the discharge of the debt, or any other period in which almost all of that period is comprised and which differs from it exclusively for valuation purposes.

[*FA 1996, s 93*].

See Simon's Direct Tax Service B3.1938.

Indexed gilt-edged securities. Where a loan relationship is represented by an index-linked gilt, an adjustment may be required to any non-trading debits and credits (see 43.3 above) to be brought into account in respect of the relationship. Wherever the authorised accounting method gives credits or debits by reference to the value of the gilt at two different times, and there is a change in the retail prices index (RPI) between the months in which those times fall, the value at the earlier time is adjusted for the RPI change. The Treasury may by order disapply this provision, or specify a different basis of adjustment, in relation to any description of index-linked gilt (but not with retrospective effect). [*FA 1996, s 94*]. See generally Revenue Company Taxation Manual, CT 12785–12788.

Gilt strips. Where a gilt is exchanged for strips of the same security, it is treated as redeemed at market value and the strips as acquired at that value in total, apportioned by reference to their own market values. Similarly where strips are consolidated into a gilt, each strip is treated as redeemed at market value and the gilt as acquired at the sum of those values. The Treasury may make regulations for determining market value for these purposes. [*FA 1996, s 95*]. See Simon's Direct Tax Service B3.1939.

Special rules for 3.5% Funding Stock 1999/2004 and 5.5% Treasury Stock 2008/2012. Where a loan relationship represented by these gilts is held otherwise than in the course of activities forming an integral part of a trade carried on by the company, debits and credits falling to be brought into account under the current provisions in respect of the relationship are confined to those relating to interest, and must be ascertained using an authorised accruals basis of accounting. [*FA 1996, s 96*].

Manufactured interest. This provision applies where an amount is payable under any contract or arrangements relating to the transfer of an asset representing a loan relationship, and that amount ('*manufactured interest*') is, or falls to be treated as, representative of interest ('*the real interest*') under the relationship. For the purposes of the current provisions, the manufactured interest is treated as interest under a loan relationship, and as regards the company to whom the manufactured interest is payable, as if that relationship were the one under which the real interest is payable. The trading or non-trading nature of the associated debits and credits (see 43.3 above) is determined by reference to the purposes for which the manufactured interest is paid.

The above applies equally to deemed manufactured interest payments under *ICTA 1988, s 737A(5)*. It does not, however, apply where manufactured interest is treated as not being income of the recipient under *ICTA 1988, Sch 23A para 5(2)(c)* or *para 5(4)(c)* (manufactured interest passing through the market, now repealed).

For the manufactured interest provisions generally, see Tolley's Income Tax under Anti-Avoidance.

[*FA 1996, s 97; FA 1997, Sch 18 Pt VI(10)*].

See Simon's Direct Tax Service B3.1939.

Collective investment schemes. *FA 1996, s 98, Sch 10* make special provision in relation to such schemes. Broadly, these are as follows.

Investment trusts and venture capital trusts. The Treasury may by order require the adoption of a modified accounting method for creditor relationships of investment trusts and venture capital trusts. [*FA 1996, Sch 10 para 1*]. See generally 60.4 UNIT AND INVESTMENT TRUSTS and 62 VENTURE CAPITAL TRUSTS.

Authorised unit trusts. The current provisions are disapplied from creditor relationships of authorised unit trusts. The income tax provisions applicable to unauthorised unit trusts are substituted. [*FA 1996, Sch 10 para 2*]. See generally 60 UNIT AND INVESTMENT TRUSTS.

Distributing offshore funds. In determining the UK equivalent profits of an offshore fund, *FA 1996, Sch 10 para 2* (see above) applies to the fund in determining total profits as it applies to authorised unit trusts. [*FA 1996, Sch 10 para 3*]. See generally Tolley's Income Tax under Offshore Funds.

Corporate holdings in unit trusts and offshore funds. Certain such holdings are treated for the purposes of the current provisions as rights under creditor relationships, in relation to which an authorised mark to market basis of accounting must be used. Credits relating to certain authorised unit trust distributions are excluded. There are special rules dealing with cases where a holding comes within, or ceases to be within, these provisions. The holdings concerned are rights under a unit trust scheme, or 'relevant interests in an offshore fund', which, at any time in an accounting period, fail to satisfy a 'non-qualifying investments test'. This test requires that not more than 60% of the market value of scheme or fund investments is represented by 'qualifying investments', i.e. broadly money placed at interest, securities, building society shares, holdings in unit trusts and offshore funds which would themselves fail to satisfy the test, or (from 25 February 1997) open-ended investment companies (see 40.6 INVESTMENT COMPANIES) subject to similar qualification. A '*relevant interest in an offshore fund*' is an interest which is a 'material interest in an offshore fund' within *ICTA 1988, s 759*, or would be but for the requirement that unit trust schemes and other arrangements constitute collective investment schemes. [*FA 1996, Sch 10 paras 4–8; SI 1997 No 213*].

See Simon's Direct Tax Service B3.1942.

Insurance companies. There are special provisions dealing with the application of the current provisions to loan relationships of insurers. In particular, the provisions do not apply to premiums trust fund assets and liabilities of corporate members of Lloyd's. [*FA 1996, s 99, Sch 11; F(No 2)A 1997 s 40(3)–(7); FA 2000, s 109(8); SI 1998 No 1200; SI 1999 No 1643*]. See Simon's Direct Tax Service B3.1943.

Partnerships which include companies within the loan relationship provisions. Revenue Pamphlet IR 131, SP 4/98, 16 November 1998 deals with the application of the loan relationships, EXCHANGE GAINS AND LOSSES (23) and FINANCIAL INSTRUMENTS (25) legislation to partnerships which include companies within those provisions. Where the current provisions are in point in relation to an accounting period of such a partnership, the approach of *FA 1994, s 172* as regards financial instruments (see 25.19 FINANCIAL INSTRUMENTS) will be adopted. Thus where the partnership consists wholly of companies within the current provisions, they will be treated as applying to the partnership.

For partnerships with one or more members which are not companies within the current provisions, the general rules, which require profits and losses to be computed as if the partnership were a company, ensure that corporation tax is applied to corporate members and income tax to individual members (see 47.2 PARTNERSHIPS). In such cases, partnership profits and losses will be computed both on the basis that the partnership is within the current provisions and on the basis that it is not, the appropriate computation being employed in relation to partners which are within the provisions and those which are not (including in the latter case a separate corporation tax computation in the unusual case of a corporate partner which is not within the provisions).

For these purposes, the partnership will be treated as itself a party to the loan relationship(s) in question.

The main elements of the Statement of Practice are as follows.

The *authorised accounting method* used should be that used in the partnership accounts (assuming it uses an authorised accounting method).

Continuity of treatment: groups etc.. The provisions of *FA 1996, Sch 9 para 12* (see 43.5 above) concerning continuity of treatment in intra-group transfers will not apply where a loan relationship is transferred to or by a partnership.

A change in *partnership profit-sharing ratios*, including a case where a company joins or leaves a partnership, does not of itself give rise to a related transaction in a loan relationship to which the partnership is a party.

Capital gains tax. TCGA 1992, s 59 (disposal of partnership assets) will continue to apply to the disposal of shares in partnership assets to which members who are not subject to corporation tax are entitled, regardless of the operation of the current (or the exchange gains and losses or financial instruments) provisions.

Connected persons and FA 1996, s 87. A partnership treated as a company (as above) is *not* so treated for the purposes of the connected persons rules in *FA 1996, s 87* (see 43.6 above).

Interest paid or received under deduction of tax. Yearly interest paid by or on behalf of the partnership should be paid under deduction of tax. Tax deducted from interest received by the partnership will be apportioned amongst the company partners in the same proportion as the interest under the loan relationship is apportioned.

Losses. A qualifying company's share of partnership trading loan relationship deficits (or exchange or financial instrument losses) will be relievable in the normal way. Its share of net partnership non-trading loan relationship credits or debits (and net non-trading exchange or financial instrument gains or losses) will in practice be merged with any other non-trading loan relationship credits or debits (or non-trading exchange or financial instrument gains or losses) accruing to it in its own right, for charge or relief in the normal way.

Differing accounting periods. Where partnership and company accounting periods differ, profits and losses will be allocated between the relevant company accounting periods, usually on a time basis.

Anti-avoidance provisions under the current provisions apply to the partnership (including any individual members) as if it were a qualifying company.

43.10 MISCELLANEOUS PROVISIONS

Interest on judgments, imputed interest etc.. Interest payable by or to a company on a money debt owed by or to the company, but not arising from a loan relationship (e.g. on a compensation award or trade debt), is assumed to be payable under a loan relationship to which the company is a party. However, the only debits or credits to be brought into account under the current provisions in respect of that relationship are those relating to the interest. This applies also to payments which fall under *ICTA 1988, ss 770–772* or, as the case may be, *ICTA 1988, Sch 28AA* (transfer pricing, see 4.4 ANTI-AVOIDANCE) to be treated as interest on a money debt or an amount treated as a money debt, and is subject to the provisions of *FA 1996, Schs 9, 11* (see 43.5, 43.9 above). It also applies to permanent interest bearing shares issued by building societies (see *ICTA 1988, s 477A(3)*).

The trading or non-trading nature of the associated debits and credits (see 43.3 above) is determined by reference to the purposes for which the interest is paid or the nature of the activities in the course of which it is received (or is deemed to be paid or received). However, any debits or credits which relate to INTEREST ON OVERPAID TAX (38) or INTEREST ON UNPAID TAX (39) for accounting periods ending on or after 1 July 1999 are treated as non-trading debits or credits.

[*FA 1996, s 100; FA 1998, s 108(4)(5), Sch 4 para 7; SI 1998 No 3173*].

Financial instruments. *FA 1994, Pt IV, Ch II* (financial instruments) does not apply to any profit or loss accruing to a company on a 'qualifying contract' (see 25.5 FINANCIAL INSTRUMENTS), by virtue of which the company is a party to a loan relationship, for any accounting period for which an amount representing that profit or loss, or the profit or loss accruing on that contract, is brought into account under the current provisions. [*FA 1996, s 101(1)*]. See also 25.5 FINANCIAL INSTRUMENTS as regards extension of those provisions to include debt contracts and options from 1 April 1996.

43.11 TRANSITIONAL PROVISIONS

The current provisions generally apply to accounting periods ending after 31 March 1996 (or, for income tax purposes, to 1996/97 and subsequent years of assessment). [*FA 1996, s 105(1)*]. Subject to special rules (see below) for interest paid after a loan relationship ceases, the amounts to be brought into account in respect of loan relationships terminated before 1 April 1996 are computed as for an accounting period ending on 31 March 1996, i.e. the current provisions do not apply. [*FA 1996, Sch 15 para 2*].

The following transitional provisions have effect, except as otherwise indicated, for transitional accounting periods (i.e. accounting periods straddling 1 April 1996) in relation to continuing loan relationships (i.e. loan relationships to which the company was a party both immediately before and on 1 April 1996).

See generally Simon's Direct Tax Service B3.1950 *et seq.*.

Basic rules. Amounts accruing or becoming due and payable before 1 April 1996 are brought into account under the current provisions only if they do so as interest. Where, however, a non-interest amount which accrued or became due and payable before 1 April 1996 would, apart from the current provisions, have been brought into account in the accounting period in which it accrued or became due and payable, it is brought into account for that period as if the current provisions did not apply, and is not otherwise brought into account under the current provisions.

Any opening valuation for the purposes of application of a mark to market basis is made as at 1 April 1996 rather than at any earlier time, unless an earlier valuation would have been required in the application of a mark to market basis apart from the current provisions. An opening valuation accordingly made at 1 April 1996, and any closing valuation for the same purposes at the end of the transitional period, is made disregarding any interest accrued in respect of any part of that period. For transitional accounting periods ending after 13 November 1996, where in the next following accounting period the loan relationship is still accounted for on a mark to market basis, the opening value for that next period is taken to be the same as the closing value determined (as above) for the transitional period.

[*FA 1996, Sch 15 para 3; FA 1997, Sch 12 paras 2, 7*].

Adjustment of opening value on change of accounting basis as at 1 April 1996. This applies where, in respect of a continuing loan relationship, amounts are brought into account for an accounting period beginning on 1 April 1996 and ending after 13 November 1996 on a mark to market basis, and for the immediately preceding accounting period they were (or would have been) brought in on a different basis. Where an opening valuation falls to be made for the accounting period next following that which began on 1 April 1996, for the purpose of bringing amounts into account on a mark to market basis, it is to be made without regard to any interest which accrued in the accounting period beginning 1 April 1996 or earlier. [*FA 1996, Sch 15 para 3A; FA 1997, Sch 12 paras 3, 7*]. See 43.7 above as regards changes of accounting basis generally.

Pre-commencement application of accruals basis. Where an authorised accruals basis is used, the same basis is applied first to determine what amounts had accrued before 1 April 1996. [*FA 1996, Sch 15 para 4*].

Pre-commencement trading relationships. Adjustments are required for any amounts which would have been brought into account as respects a loan relationship in computing profits or losses for trade purposes if the company had ceased to be a party to the relationship on 31 March 1996 and an accounting period had ended on that date. Any difference between the 'notional closing value' and the 'adjusted closing value' of the relationship as at 31 March 1996 is brought into account (see below).

The '*notional closing value*' at 31 March 1996 is the amount which at that date fell to be brought into account in computing trading profits or losses, as representing the value of the company's rights or liabilities under the relationship, or which would have fallen to be so brought into account had an accounting period ended on that date. If no amount is given by this definition, the notional closing value is the amount which would have been deductible for trade purposes as representing the cost of becoming a party to the relationship had the company ceased to be a party to it on 31 March 1996. In the case of creditor relationships continuing after 13 November 1996 (and certain replacement relationships), the cost of acquiring any right to accrued interest is excluded (except in certain cases where interest accruing before the company became a party to the relationship but paid to the company after it became a party to the relationship has been brought into account for corporation tax purposes). The '*adjusted closing value*' at 31 March 1996 is the opening value as at 1 April 1996 under the current provisions of the rights and liabilities under the relationship (and see further below as regards 'opening value' in certain cases). In the case of both the notional and the adjusted closing value, a different value is taken where the asset or liabilities representing a loan relationship is or are a 'relevant qualifying asset' or 'relevant liabilities'. The notional closing value is then the value given by *FA 1996, Sch 15 para 12* (see below under 'Other chargeable asset etc. adjustments') as at 31 March 1996 of that asset or those liabilities, and the adjusted closing value is the opening value of the asset or liabilities as at 1 April 1996 under the current provisions (and see further below as regards 'opening value' in certain cases). A '*relevant qualifying asset*' is a 'qualifying asset' within *FA 1993, Pt II, Ch II* the value of which has been determined as at the company's 'commencement day' for the purpose of calculating any attributed amount (see 23.8, 23.32 EXCHANGE GAINS AND LOSSES). A '*relevant liability*' is a liability the value of which has been so determined as at that day.

Where an accruals basis of accounting is used as respects a loan relationship for the first accounting period ending after 31 March 1996, the opening value as at 1 April 1996 of the rights and liabilities under the relationship is the value (disregarding interest) treated under *FA 1996, Sch 15 para 4* (see above under 'Pre-commencement application of accruals basis') as having accrued before that date.

Any adjustment required as above is made by bringing the difference between the notional and adjusted closing values into account in the accounting period in which the company ceases to be a party to the relationship. If the notional exceeds the adjusted closing value, and the relationship is a debtor relationship, the difference is brought in as a credit. Similarly if the adjusted exceeds the notional closing value and the relationship is a creditor relationship, the difference is brought in as a credit. Otherwise, it is brought in as a debit.

The company may alternatively elect for one-sixth of the debits or credits calculated as above to be brought into account in each of the six years beginning at the start of its first accounting period to end after 31 March 1996. Where necessary, debits or credits are time-apportioned to accounting periods within that six years. In calculating the debits or credits, the assumption is made that the company ceased on 1 April 1996 to be a party to the relevant relationship(s). If the company ceases to be within the charge to corporation tax at any time during the six year period, any balance is brought into account for the accounting period ending at that time.

An election as above must be made in writing to an officer of the Board before 1 October 1996. A debit or credit to be brought into account for any accounting period is a trading debit or credit (see 43.3 above) so long as the company continues to carry on the trade in question at some time during the accounting period. Otherwise, it is a non-trading debit or credit.

[*FA 1996, Sch 15 paras 5, 6; FA 1997, Sch 13 paras 4, 7*].

Chargeable gains general savings. As regards changes to the capital gains tax legislation, these do not apply to any disposal made, or deemed to be made, before 1 April 1996, or where a loan has become irrecoverable or its value negligible before that date. [*FA 1996, Sch 15 para 7*].

Chargeable assets continuing to be held after commencement. This provision applies where, on 31 March 1996, a company held any asset representing (in whole or part) a loan relationship to which it was a party, and the company did not dispose of that asset on that date, and is not otherwise deemed to have done so. It does not apply where the asset is:

(*a*) an asset to which *FA 1996, s 92* (convertible securities etc., see 43.9 above) or *FA 1996, Sch 15 para 15* (see below under 'Unit trusts etc.') applies; or

(*b*) an asset representing a loan relationship to which *FA 1996, s 93* (relationships linked to the value of chargeable assets, see 43.9 above) applies; or

(*c*) a 'relevant qualifying asset' (see above under 'Pre-commencement trading relationships').

Where a 'relevant event' occurs in relation to such an asset, any chargeable gain or allowable loss which would have accrued to the company if the asset had been disposed of on 31 March 1996 for a market value consideration is (subject to the election referred to below) brought into account in the accounting period in which the relevant event occurs. The gain or loss is reduced by any amount already brought into account on an accruals or mark to market basis in relation to the asset as respects times before 1 April 1996. A '*relevant event*' occurs on the first occasion after 31 March 1996 when any company falls to be treated as making a disposal (other than a no gain, no loss disposal) of the asset or of any asset falling to be treated as the same as that asset. Where the disposal is by a company other than the one holding the asset on 31 March 1996, the chargeable gain or allowable loss is brought into account on that company. Special rules apply to ensure that a gain or loss deemed to accrue under *TCGA 1992, s 116(10)(b)* (crystallisation of gain or loss on shares exchanged for qualifying corporate bonds on reorganisation, etc., see Tolley's Capital Gains Tax under Qualifying Corporate Bonds) which is included in the deemed gain or loss under these provisions does not give rise to further charge or allowance. Where the relevant event had not occurred before 14 November 1996, the deemed gain or loss under these provisions is computed without reference to *TCGA 1992, s 119(6)(7)* (transfer of securities with or without accrued interest, see Tolley's Capital Gains Tax under Shares and Securities).

Where the company was non-UK resident at any time before 1 April 1996 when it held the asset other than through a UK branch or agency, the company is treated for these purposes as having acquired the asset at market value on the first day on which a gain on the asset could have been included in the company's profits chargeable to corporation tax. This applies through any chain of no gain, no loss disposals.

For these purposes, a company ceasing to be within the charge to corporation tax at any time is treated as disposing of all its assets at market value immediately before that time.

Where this provision results in an amount being brought into account for an accounting period as an allowable loss, the company may instead elect for that amount to be treated as a debit under the current provisions for that period. The debit is a trading or non-trading debit (see 43.3 above) according to the treatment which would apply to any other debits as respects the same loan relationship for that period. The election must be made within two years after the relevant event. An election may not be made in respect of a loss on an asset which, as at 1 April 1996, fell under *TCGA 1992, s 127* or *214(9)* to be treated as the same as an asset not representing a loan relationship, or would have done so but for *TCGA 1992, s 116(5)*.

[*FA 1996, Sch 15 paras 8, 9; FA 1997, Sch 13 para 5; FA 2000, Sch 29 para 45*].

Adjustments of opening value for mark to market accounting for chargeable assets. Where a mark to market basis of accounting is used as respects any loan relationship for a company's first accounting period ending after 31 March 1996, and an opening valuation of a chargeable asset (as defined, and generally excluding qualifying corporate bonds) which represents that relationship, and which was held by the company on that date, falls to be made as at 1 April 1996, the opening value of the asset at that date is whatever its market value would have been for capital gains tax purposes on a disposal on 31 March 1996. [*FA 1996, Sch 15 para 10*].

Other chargeable asset etc. adjustments (interaction with EXCHANGE GAINS AND LOSSES (23) provisions). An adjustment may be required where an authorised accruals basis of accounting is applied for the first accounting period ending after 31 March 1996 to a loan relationship represented by a 'relevant asset' or under which any liability is a 'relevant liability'. Where, had the company ceased to be a party to the relationship on 31 March 1996, no amount would have fallen to be brought into account in computing trading profits or losses for any accounting period ending on or after that date, the accounting method is taken to require a 'notional closing value' as at 31 March 1996 to be given to that asset or liability.

In the case of loan relationships continuing after 13 November 1996 (and certain replacement relationships), an adjustment is required where there is a difference between (*a*) the 'notional closing value' at 31 March 1996 and (*b*) the amount which, in a computation on an authorised accruals basis and assuming such a basis had always been used as respects the relationship, would be taken as representing the accrued value of the relationship on 1 April 1996. That difference is brought into account under the current provisions for the accounting period in which the company ceases to be a party to the relationship, as a credit where (*b*) exceeds (*a*), otherwise as a debit. For loan relationships which ceased before 14 November 1996 (and were not replaced), an adjustment is required where, for the first accounting period ending after 31 March 1996, there is a difference between

(i) the amount which would have been brought into account as accruing in that period if the company had become a party to the loan relationship on 1 April 1996, the opening value at that date for the purposes of an authorised accruals basis of accounting had been the notional closing value on 31 March 1996, and the closing value at the end of the period for such purposes were the same as the closing value when applying such a basis for computing the amount in (ii) below, and

(ii) the amount which is in fact treated as accruing in that period (see above under 'Pre-commencement application of accruals basis').

That difference is brought into account under the current provisions for the accounting period in which the company ceases to be a party to the relationship. Where the amounts in (i) and (ii) above are credits, the amount brought in is a credit where the amount in (i) exceeds that in (ii), a debit where that in (ii) exceeds that in (i). Similarly where the amounts in (i) and (ii) above are debits, the amount brought in is a debit where the amount in (i) exceeds that in (ii), a credit where that in (ii) exceeds that in (i).

In all cases, the debit or credit is a non-trading debit or credit (see 43.3 above).

Where the company ceases to be within the charge to corporation tax at any time, it is treated for these purposes as ceasing to be a party to the relationship immediately before that time.

A '*relevant asset*' is a chargeable asset (as defined, and generally excluding qualifying corporate bonds) or a 'relevant qualifying asset'. For the meaning of 'relevant qualifying asset' and 'relevant liability', see above under 'Pre-commencement trading relationships'.

The '*notional closing value*' of an asset or liability as at 31 March 1996 is its market value or, if it is a relevant qualifying asset or a relevant liability, the value given to it as at the company's 'commencement day' for the purpose of computing any attributed amount (see 23.32 EXCHANGE GAINS AND LOSSES). An election may, however, be made in relation to all the company's relevant qualifying assets to which a notional closing value would otherwise be given as above and which would be chargeable assets but for the EXCHANGE GAINS AND LOSSES (23) provisions. The effect of the election is that the notional closing value as at 31 March 1996 is the market value as at 1 April 1996. The election must be made in writing to an officer of the Board before 1 October 1996.

[*FA 1996, Sch 15 paras 11, 12; FA 1997, Sch 13 paras 6, 7*].

Interest under loan relationships. The following transitional provisions apply to interest under loan relationships, including amounts brought into account under *ICTA 1988, s 477A(3)* (see 7.4 BUILDING SOCIETIES).

(*a*) Where an amount of interest accruing or becoming due and payable under a loan relationship in an accounting period ending after 31 March 1996 has already been brought into account for corporation tax purposes for an earlier accounting period, no credit or debit relating to that amount is brought into account under the current provisions.

(*b*) Where interest accrued or became due and payable in, but was not brought into account for, an accounting period ending before 1 April 1996, but is paid in an accounting period ending on or after that date, debits or credits (as appropriate) are brought into account under the current provisions (if they would not otherwise be brought in) as if the interest accrued, and became due and payable, when paid, provided that:

- (i) in the case of a debtor relationship, relief would have been allowable apart from the current provisions; or
- (ii) in the case of a creditor relationship, the interest is not 'unrealised interest' under *ICTA 1988, s 716* (accrued income scheme, see Tolley's Income Tax under Schedule D, Case VI) in relation to a transfer before 1 April 1996.

(*c*) Where interest under a debtor relationship was paid during an accounting period ending before 1 April 1996 but at a time on or after 20 December 1995, and not under any contractual obligation entered into before that date requiring payment at or before that time, then provided that the interest would not, on an authorised accruals basis of accounting, fall to be brought into account in an accounting period ending before 1 April 1996, it is not brought into account for corporation tax purposes in any such accounting period.

(*d*) Where, on 1 April 1996, interest under a loan relationship remained to be paid to or by a company which ceased to be a party to the relationship before that date, the loan relationship is treated under the current (including transitional) provisions as a continuing relationship, as regards interest under the relationship.

(*e*) Except as below, where any debits or credits relating to interest under a loan relationship are brought into account for an accounting period which, under the current provisions, is determined by reference to the time when, by virtue of (*a*)–(*d*) above, the interest is deemed to accrue or become due and payable, as appropriate, they are brought in as non-trading debits or credits (see 43.3 above), as appropriate. However, where

- (i) at the time the interest in fact accrued or became due and payable (as appropriate), the company was a party to the relationship for trade purposes, and
- (ii) the company carried on that trade for the whole or any part of the accounting period for which credits or debits relating to the interest fall to be brought into account,

those debits or credits are brought in as trade expenses or receipts (see 43.3 above).

[*FA 1996, Sch 15 para 13*].

Incidental expenses already allowed. Charges or expenses within *FA 1996, s 84(3)* (see 43.5 above) in respect of which a corporation tax deduction has been made in an accounting period ending before 1 April 1996 are not included in those in relation to which debits may be brought into account under the current provisions. [*FA 1996, Sch 15 para 14*].

Holdings of unit trusts etc.. Special provisions apply to certain assets held by insurance companies, requiring a deemed disposal at 31 March 1996. [*FA 1996, Sch 15 para 15*].

Bad debt relieved before commencement. Where an amount becomes, or is to become, due and payable under a creditor relationship in an accounting period ending after 31 March 1996, but under *ICTA 1988, s 74(1)(j)(i)–(iii)* (exceptions to prohibition on Schedule D, Case I deduction for debts) a deduction was allowed for any amount representing that amount (or part thereof) for an accounting period ending on or before that date, it does not have to be assumed for the purposes of the current provisions that any part of the amount to which the deduction relates will be paid in full as it becomes due. Where, however, the deduction relates to an amount proved or estimated to be bad, but the whole or any part of the liability to pay that amount is discharged by payment in an accounting period ending after 31 March 1996, a credit equal to the amount of that payment is brought into account for that period (unless a credit is brought into account in relation to the payment under *FA 1996, Sch 15 para 13(4)* (see (*b*) under *Interest under loan relationships* above)). [*FA 1996, Sch 15 para 16*].

Overseas sovereign debt etc.. Special provisions replace the usual valuation provisions as at 31 March 1996 in the case of sovereign debt previously dealt with under *ICTA 1988, ss 88A–88C* (see 43.5 above). [*FA 1996, Sch 15 para 17*].

Accrued income scheme. Where a company would, apart from the current provisions, be treated under *ICTA 1988, s 714(2)* or *(4)* (accrued income scheme, see Tolley's Income Tax under Schedule D, Case VI) as receiving any amount at the end of a period straddling 1 April 1996, or as entitled to an allowance of any amount for such a period, that amount is instead brought into account under the current provisions as a non-trading credit or debit respectively for the first accounting period ending after 31 March 1996. A debit in respect of an allowance relating to a security will not, however, be brought into account where the security was transferred to the company with accrued interest in an accounting period straddling 1 April 1996, and an authorised accruals basis of accounting is used for that period as respects the creditor relationship represented by the security. Credit for foreign tax under *ICTA 1988, s 807* may continue to be given in relation to such amounts, and *FA 1993, s 63* (which deals with debts between associated companies etc.) continues to apply up to 31 March 1996, which is for this purpose treated as the last day of an accounting period.

A special relief applies to certain excess reliefs brought forward by overseas life insurance companies.

[*FA 1996, Sch 15 para 18*].

Deep discount securities. The charge to tax after acquisition of deep discount securities under *ICTA 1988, Sch 4 para 3* continues to apply to income periods ending before 1 April 1996, as does the charge under *para 4* on disposals before that date. The relief for income elements under *para 5* also continues to apply for income periods ending on or before 31 March 1996, and for this purpose every income period current on that day is deemed to end on that day. The special deep discount security provisions relating to interest payable between associated companies, etc. under *FA 1993, s 64* (see 50.16 PROFIT COMPUTATIONS) also continue to apply to events before 1 April 1996 (and for this purpose 31 March 1996 is deemed to be the last day of an accounting period, where not actually so). Any income accordingly treated as arising after 14 February 1999 is treated as a non-trading credit (see

43.3 above). The position as regards income so treated as arising before that date is unclear.

Where a company issued a deep discount security before 1 April 1996 which was not redeemed before that date, and there is a difference between the 'adjusted issue price' as at 31 March 1996 and the 'adjusted closing value' as at that date, the difference is brought into account for the accounting period in which the security is redeemed as a non-trading credit or debit (see 43.3 above), according to whether the adjusted issue price is greater or less than the adjusted closing value. The '*adjusted issue price*' of a security as at 31 March 1996 is what it would have been for the purposes of the deep discount security provisions in *ICTA 1988, Sch 4* for an income period beginning 1 April 1996. The '*adjusted closing value*' of a security as at 31 March 1996 is the opening value as at 1 April 1996 under the current provisions of the company's rights and liabilities under the loan relationship represented by the security (adjusted, where appropriate, under *FA 1996, Sch 15 para 5*, see above).

Where a company held a deep discount security on 31 March 1996 (and did not dispose of it on that date), and *FA 1993, s 64* (see above) does not apply by reference to any event on that date, any amount which would have been chargeable under *ICTA 1988, Sch 4 para 4* on a disposal on that date is brought into account under the current provisions as a non-trading credit (see 43.3 above). The accounting period for which it is brought in is that in which falls the earliest of

(*a*) the earliest possible day after 31 March 1996 on which the holder can require redemption,

(*b*) the actual redemption day, and

(*c*) the day on which the company disposes of the security.

Where a company held a deep discount security on 31 March 1996 (and did not dispose of it on that date), and (where the earliest of the days in (*a*)–(*c*) above falls before 15 February 1999) *FA 1993, s 64* (see above) does not apply by reference to any event on that date, then if the security is not a relevant asset within *FA 1996, Sch 15 para 11* (see above), any difference between the adjusted issue price and the adjusted closing value (see above) as at 31 March 1996 is brought into account as a non-trading debit or credit (see 43.3 above), according to whether the adjusted issue price is greater or less than the adjusted closing value. The accounting period for which it is brought in is that in which falls the earliest of the times referred to in (*a*), (*b*) and (*c*) above.

[*FA 1996, Sch 15 para 19; FA 1999, s 67(1)(3)(6)(7)*].

See 50.7 PROFIT COMPUTATIONS for the treatment of deep discount securities generally prior to 1 April 1996.

Deep gain securities. The charge under *FA 1989, Sch 11* on the holder of a deep gain security continues to apply on any transfer or redemption before 1 April 1996. The special deep gain security provisions relating to interest payable between associated companies, etc. under *FA 1993, s 65* (see 50.16 PROFIT COMPUTATIONS) also continue to apply to events before 1 April 1996 (and for this purpose 31 March 1996 is deemed to be the last day of an accounting period, where not actually so). Any income accordingly treated as arising after 14 February 1999 is treated as a non-trading credit (see 43.3 above). The position as regards income so treated as arising before that date is unclear.

Where a company held a deep gain security on 31 March 1996 (and did not transfer or redeem it on that date), and *FA 1993, s 65* (see above) does not apply by reference to any event on that date, any amount which would have been chargeable under *FA 1989, Sch 11 para 5* on a sale on that date for its 'adjusted closing value' is brought into account under the current provisions as a non-trading credit (see 43.3 above). The accounting period for which it is brought in is that in which falls the earliest of (*a*) the earliest possible day after 31 March 1996 on which the holder can require redemption,

(*b*) the actual redemption day, and

(*c*) the day on which the company disposes of the security.

The '*adjusted closing value*' of a security held on 31 March 1996 is the opening value as at 1 April 1996 under the current provisions of the company's rights and liabilities under the loan relationship represented by the security (adjusted, where appropriate, under *FA 1996, Sch 15 para 5*, see above).

[*FA 1996, Sch 15 para 20; FA 1999, s 67(2)(6)*].

See Tolley's Income Tax under Interest Receivable for the treatment of deep gain securities generally prior to 1 April 1996.

Convertible securities. The charge under *FA 1990, Sch 10 para 12* on the transfer or redemption of a qualifying convertible security continues to apply on any transfer or redemption before 1 April 1996, as does the relief under *FA 1990, Sch 10 para 25* (see 50.23 PROFIT COMPUTATIONS) on any redemption before that date.

Where a company held a qualifying convertible security on 31 March 1996 (and did not transfer or redeem it on that date), any amount which would have been chargeable under *FA 1990, Sch 10 para 12* on a transfer on that date is brought into account under the current provisions as a non-trading credit (see 43.3 above). The accounting period for which it is brought in is that in which falls the earliest of

(*a*) the earliest possible day after 31 March 1996 on which the holder can require redemption,

(*b*) the actual redemption day, and

(*c*) the day on which the company disposes of the security.

Where a qualifying convertible security in respect of which an amount has been brought into account as above is redeemed, a like amount is brought into account on the issuing company as a non-trading debit (see 43.3 above) for the accounting period of redemption.

[*FA 1996, Sch 15 para 21*].

See also Tolley's Income Tax under Interest Receivable for the treatment of qualifying convertible securities generally prior to 1 April 1996.

Exchange gains and losses. *Accrual on variable debt. FA 1993, s 127(1A)* (deemed variation of debt in respect of amounts accruing in respect of discounts and premiums, see 23.10 EXCHANGE GAINS AND LOSSES) has effect in relation to the debt by reference to which the continuing loan relationship at any time subsists as if the company became subject or entitled to the debt on 1 April 1996, so that the nominal amount of the debt outstanding is only required to be treated as varied where the time of the deemed variation is after 31 March 1996. *Section 127* then has effect as if the nominal amount of the debt outstanding on that date were what it would have been if that provision did not apply and *section 127(1A)* had always had effect.

Qualifying liabilities. FA 1993, s 153(6), which excluded from being a qualifying liability a debt on a security (other than a deep gain security) which did not represent a normal commercial loan when created (see 23.8(ii) EXCHANGE GAINS AND LOSSES), continues to apply as respects times before 1 April 1996. A company subject, both immediately before and on 1 April 1996, to a liability which is a qualifying liability because of the repeal of *section 153(6)* is treated as having become subject to that liability on that date.

Transitional provisions. FA 1993, Sch 17 paras 4–6 (see 23.29 EXCHANGE GAINS AND LOSSES) continue to apply to disposals before 1 April 1996.

Non-trading losses carried back against exchange profits etc.. In setting any amount against exchange profits for an accounting period beginning before 1 April 1996, a claim may be made under *FA 1993, s 131(5)* or *(6)* in relation to any relievable amount for an accounting period ending after 31 March 1996 (see 23.14 EXCHANGE GAINS AND LOSSES). As regards a relievable amount for an accounting period ending after 1 July 1997, the 'permitted period' under *FA 1993, s 131(7)(10)(b)* is reduced from three years to twelve months (except in relation to the part of the relievable amount of an accounting period straddling 1 July 1997 which arose before 2 July 1997, generally determined by time apportionment). *FA 1993, ss 129–133* (including those provisions as applied by *FA 1994, Pt IV, Ch 2*, see 25.10 FINANCIAL INSTRUMENTS) have effect for the purposes of such a claim as they applied for accounting periods ending before 1 April 1996. If such a claim is made, the amount claimed is brought into account under the current provisions as a non-trading credit (see 43.3 above) for the accounting period.

Exchange losses etc. carried forward from before 1 April 1996. Where, apart from the current provisions, an amount would fall under *FA 1993, s 131(12)* (see 23.14 EXCHANGE GAINS AND LOSSES) to be carried forward to an accounting period ending after 31 March 1996, it is treated, in relation to that period, as an amount brought forward under *FA 1996, s 83(3)* (see 43.3 above).

[*FA 1996, Sch 15 paras 22–24; F(No 2)A 1997, s 40(9)*].

Financial instruments. *Debt contracts and options.* The *FA 1994* FINANCIAL INSTRUMENTS (25) provisions have effect in relation to certain debt contracts and options as if references therein to 1 April 1996 were to the beginning of the first accounting period ending after 31 March 1996. For that accounting period, *FA 1994, s 158(2)–(5)* (see 25.9 FINANCIAL INSTRUMENTS) have effect in relation to the debt contract or option with appropriate modification. This applies to any debt contract or option held both immediately before and on 1 April 1996 if, on a disposal on 31 March 1996, apart from the current provisions, either:

(*a*) the gain accruing on disposal would have been treated as a chargeable gain; or

(*b*) amounts with respect to the disposal would have been brought into account for an accounting period beginning before 1 April 1996 in computing trading profits or gains.

[*FA 1996, Sch 15 para 25*].

Simon's Direct Tax Service. See **B3.1950** *et seq.*.

43.12 ASSOCIATED REPEALS AND AMENDMENTS

In relation to the introduction of the provisions described at 43.1–43.11 above, there are a very large number of associated repeals and amendments, contained in *FA 1996, Sch 14, Sch 41 Pt V(3)*. These are mainly aimed either at removing or modifying provisions whose substantive effect is subsumed into the new provisions or at adapting existing provisions for the relief or charge of interest to the new regime. There are also widespread related (but separate) changes to income tax provisions relating to deep discounts and gains and to taxation of accrued income (for which see Tolley's Income Tax). The capital gains tax treatment (and definition) of qualifying corporate bonds are also correspondingly amended (see Tolley's Capital Gains Tax).

For the fundamental changes in the treatment of interest, see in particular 50.2, 50.3 PROFIT COMPUTATIONS.

The most significant of the repeals and amendments are as follows:

(*a*) *ICTA 1988, s 57, Sch 4* (deep discount securities), *FA 1989, s 94, Sch 11* (deep gain securities), *FA 1990, s 56, Sch 10* (convertible securities) and *FA 1993, ss 61–66* (interest payments between associated companies, etc.) are repealed. See 50.7, 50.16, 50.23 PROFIT COMPUTATIONS.

(*b*) Also repealed are *ICTA 1988, ss 88A–88C* (country risk debt, see 6.3 BANKS), *ICTA 1988, ss 126, 126A* (Treasury securities, etc., see 9.11 CAPITAL GAINS), *ICTA 1988, ss 484, 485* (savings banks, see 6.6 BANKS).

(*c*) The following are repealed subject to special transitional provisions: *ICTA 1988, ss 56, 56A* (transactions in deposits (see 23.31 EXCHANGE GAINS AND LOSSES)) and *ICTA 1988, s 78* (discounted bills of exchange, see 50.9 PROFIT COMPUTATIONS).

(*d*) The following are disapplied for corporation tax purposes only: *ICTA 1988, s 77* (incidental costs of loan finance, see 40.2 INVESTMENT COMPANIES, 50.19 PROFIT COMPUTATIONS) and *ICTA 1988, ss 711–728* (accrued income scheme).

(*e*) The EXCHANGE GAINS AND LOSSES (23) and FINANCIAL INSTRUMENTS (25) provisions are amended to deal with the interaction with the new provisions. In particular, the treatment of non-trading items is amalgamated with their treatment under the current provisions. The exclusion of charitable companies also ceases.

(*f*) DOUBLE TAX RELIEF (21) is subject to a number of changes to facilitate reliefs for tax on interest, etc..

(*g*) The Schedule D, Case III charge is redefined for corporation tax purposes to take account of the current provisions, including the subsuming of the income tax Schedule D charges under Case IV and (so far as relevant) Case V. See 50.2 PROFIT COMPUTATIONS.

44 Losses

Cross-references. See 27.3 FRANKED INVESTMENT INCOME; 29.14–29.26 GROUPS OF COMPANIES.

Simon's Direct Tax Service D2.4.

44.1 See 9.3 CAPITAL GAINS for the treatment of capital losses and 46 OIL COMPANIES for losses of such companies.

The headings in this chapter are as follows.

44.2	Set-off of trading losses	44.14	Farming and market gardening
44.3	— example	44.15	Leasing
44.4	Carry-forward of trading losses	44.16	Companies in partnership
44.5	— example	44.17	Oil companies
44.6	Carry-back of trading losses	44.18	Dealings in commodity futures
44.7	— examples	44.19	Losses on unlisted shares
44.8	Carry-back of terminal losses	44.20	— example
44.9	Losses eligible for relief	44.21	Write-off of government investment
44.10	Company reconstructions	44.22	Schedule A
44.11	— example	44.23	Schedule D, Case V
44.12	Privatisation	44.24	Schedule D, Case VI
44.13	Change in ownership of a company	44.25	Double taxation

44.2 **SET-OFF OF TRADING LOSSES**

A company which 'carries on a trade' within Schedule D, Case I may claim that losses incurred in that trade be set off against other profits (including chargeable gains) of the same accounting period. [*ICTA 1988, s 393(2) (repealed); ICTA 1988, s 393A(1)(a); FA 1991, s 73(1)*]. Claims must be made within two years of the end of the accounting period in which the loss is made or within such further period as the Revenue may allow. [*ICTA 1988, ss 393(11), 393A(10); FA 1991, s 73(1), Sch 15 para 8(b)*]. For the acceptance of late claims, see Revenue Company Taxation Manual, CT 452.

A trading loss is computed in the same way as trading income. [*ICTA 1988, s 393(7), s 393A(9)(a)(b); FA 1991, s 73(1)*]. A claim may require that unrelieved capital allowances which fall to be given by discharge or repayment of tax for an accounting period (i.e. they are not deducted as trading expenses) shall augment or create a loss for that period. Allowances brought forward from an earlier period may not be included in such a claim. [*CAA 1990, s 145(3); ICTA 1988, s 393A(5)(6); FA 1991, s 73(1)*].

A company '*carries on a trade*' if it is within the charge to corporation tax in respect of that trade. [*ICTA 1988, s 393(10), s 393A(9)(c); FA 1991, s 73(1)*].

Note that *capital losses* cannot generally be set off against trading profits (but see 44.19 below regarding certain losses of investment companies on unquoted shares).

See 23.14 EXCHANGE GAINS AND LOSSES as regards relief of certain 'relievable amounts' in respect of exchange losses.

See also 44.9, 44.15, 44.18–44.21 below.

Simon's Direct Tax Service. See D2.404.

44.3 *Example*

The results of A Ltd for the year ended 31 March 2001 show:

	£
Trading loss	(10,000)
Schedule A	3,000
Schedule D, Case III	4,000
Chargeable gains	7,200
Trade charges	(2,000)
Non-trade charges	(1,000)

The loss may be relieved as follows.

	£
Schedule A	3,000
Schedule D, Case III	4,000
Chargeable gains	7,200
	14,200
Deduct Trading loss	(10,000)
	4,200
Deduct Trade charges	(2,000)
Non-trade charges	(1,000)
Profits chargeable to CT	£1,200
CT payable at 20%	£240

44.4 CARRY-FORWARD OF TRADING LOSSES

Where a company which carries on a trade (see 44.2 above) suffers losses in that trade in an accounting period, those losses may be carried forward and set off against any 'trading income' from 'the same trade' in succeeding accounting periods. So long as the company carries on that trade, its trading income therefrom is treated as reduced by the losses so carried forward (or the balance of such losses not relieved in an earlier accounting period). [*ICTA 1988, s 393(1); FA 1990, s 99*].

See also *CAA 1990, s 15A* (introduced by *FA 1996, Sch 39 para 1(2)(4)*) regarding the relief of losses against post-cessation balancing charges on industrial buildings.

For the purpose of computing losses under these provisions, the excess of charges on income over the profits against which they are deductible is treated as a trading expense insofar as they were incurred wholly and exclusively for the purposes of the trade. [*ICTA 1988, s 393(9)*]. See Tolley's Income Tax under Schedule D, Cases I and II as regards the meaning of 'wholly and exclusively' and, for a case on the application of *section 393(9)*, *Commercial Union Assurance Co plc v Shaw CA, [1999] STC 109.* Otherwise a loss is computed in the same way as trading income. [*ICTA 1988, s 393(7)*]. See 44.9 below as regards determination of losses, and 29.18 GROUPS OF COMPANIES for group relief interaction.

'*Trading income*' means the income which is, or would be, included in respect of a particular trade in the total profits of the company. But where a loss incurred under Schedule D, Case I or V is carried forward to a later accounting period the trading income for which is insufficient to absorb it, interest and dividends which would be trading receipts but for having been otherwise subjected to tax (as in the case of banks, share dealers, and other companies carrying on financial business) are to be included in trading income. [*ICTA 1988, s 393(8)*]. In *Bank Line Ltd v CIR CS 1974, 49 TC 307*, it was held that, to constitute trading receipts for this purpose, the interest etc. must arise from capital actively employed in the trade and in a real and practical sense at risk in the ordinary course of current trading. Interest etc. received on reserve funds was thus excluded. Similarly in *Nuclear Electric plc v Bradley HL 1996, 68 TC 670*, the crucial test was considered to be whether the investments were employed in the business (of producing and selling electricity) in the year in question. The Court of Appeal, whose judgment was approved, considered decisive the facts that the liabilities against which the investments were provided were liabilities to third parties rather than customers, and that, in view of the long-term nature of the liabilities, the business could be carried on for a long period without maintaining a fund of investments at all. The Revenue have confirmed that current account and trade interest normally qualify, as does interest from the temporary lodgement of part of current working capital in a bank deposit account provided that (i) it is a short-term investment, (ii) the investment is an integral feature of the trading activities, and (iii) the funds can be regarded as continuing to form part of the current working capital. (Revenue Inspector's Manual, IM 500a).

As to what constitutes '*the same trade*' for these purposes, see *Morning Post Ltd v George KB 1940, 23 TC 514* and *Robroyston Brickworks Ltd v CIR CS 1976, 51 TC 230* (change of ownership of trade — but see now 44.10 below); *Gordon & Blair Ltd v CIR CS 1962, 40 TC 358* (cessation of manufacturing, retention of retailing); *Seaman v Tucketts Ltd Ch D 1963, 41 TC 422* (cessation of manufacturing and retailing, commencement of intra-group servicing); *Bispham v Eardiston Farming Co [1919] Ltd Ch D 1962, 40 TC 322* (transfer of trade from one farm to another); *Rolls-Royce Motors Ltd v Bamford Ch D 1976, 51 TC 319* (transfer of part of existing trade). See also 44.9–44.17, 44.21 below.

Simon's Direct Tax Service. See D2.406.

44.5 *Example*

B Ltd has carried on the same trade for many years. The results for the years ended 30 September 1999, 2000 and 2001 are shown below.

	1999	2000	2001
	£	£	£
Trading profit/(loss)	(20,000)	10,000	5,000
Schedule A	3,000	1,000	2,000
Schedule D, Case III	2,000	2,000	3,000
Chargeable gains	5,600	4,700	4,000
Trade charges	(3,000)	(9,000)	(5,000)

B Ltd may claim to set off the trading loss against other profits of the same accounting period. Assuming the claim is made (and that no claim is made to carry back the balance of the loss), the loss will be set off as follows.

	£	Loss memorandum £
Year ended 30 September 1999		
Trading loss		(20,000)
Schedule A	3,000	
Schedule D, Case III	2,000	
Chargeable gains	5,600	
	10,600	
Deduct Trading loss	(10,600)	10,600
	—	(9,400)
Trade charges	—	(3,000)
Profits chargeable to CT	—	
		(12,400)
Year ended 30 September 2000		
Schedule D, Case I	10,000	
Deduct Loss brought forward	(10,000)	10,000
	—	(2,400)
Schedule A	1,000	
Schedule D, Case III	2,000	
Chargeable gains	4,700	
	7,700	
Deduct Trade charges (restricted)	(7,700)	
Balance of trade charges carried forward		(1,300)
Profits chargeable to CT	—	
		(3,700)
Year ended 30 September 2001		
Schedule D, Case I	5,000	
Deduct Loss brought forward	(3,700)	3,700
	1,300	
Schedule A	2,000	
Schedule D, Case III	3,000	
Chargeable gains	4,000	
	10,300	
Deduct Trade charges	(5,000)	
Profits chargeable to CT	£5,300	

44.6 **CARRY-BACK OF TRADING LOSSES**

Where a company incurs a trading loss in an accounting period and makes a claim to set the loss against other profits of that accounting period (see 44.2 above), it may additionally claim that the balance of the loss not so relieved be carried back. It may then be set against the profits (including chargeable gains) of preceding accounting periods (at some time during which it was carrying on the same trade) falling wholly or partly within a 'specified period'. Profits of an accounting period beginning before, and ending within, that period are apportioned on a time basis. No relief is available for accounting periods ending earlier. The profits of each accounting period are treated as reduced by losses so carried back (or the balance of such losses not relieved in a later accounting period). Partial relief claims are not allowed, i.e. if carry-back of a loss is claimed, any part of the loss not relieved in the immediately preceding accounting period must be carried back to the period before that and so on, and losses of earlier accounting periods are relieved in priority to those of later periods.

For losses incurred in an accounting period ending after 1 July 1997 (subject to the transitional provisions described below), the '*specified period*' is the period of twelve months immediately preceding the accounting period in which the loss is incurred. For earlier accounting periods it is the period of three years immediately preceding that accounting period. The three year carry-back period continues to apply to terminal losses (see 44.8 below) and to certain losses arising from the special allowances for North Sea oil and gas installation decommissioning costs. Otherwise, where a loss is incurred in an accounting period straddling 1 July 1997, the three year carry-back period is retained for the part of the loss attributable to the part of the accounting period falling before 2 July 1997. Apportionment of the loss for this purpose is made on a time basis unless this would produce an unjust or unreasonable result, in which case it is made on a just and reasonable basis. In *Camcrown Ltd v McDonald (Sp C 208), [1999] SSCD 255*, it was held that where a significant proportion of the loss of a straddling period was referable to capital allowances on purchases during the period, the part of the loss so referable should be allocated to the part of that period during which the expenditure was incurred.

[*ICTA 1988, s 393A(1)(b)(2)–(2C); FA 1991, s 73(1); F(No 2)A 1997, s 39*].

A trading loss is computed in the same way as trading income. [*ICTA 1988, s 393(7), s 393A(9)(a)(b); FA 1991, s 73(1)*]. A claim may require that unrelieved capital allowances which fall to be given by discharge or repayment of tax for an accounting period (i.e. they are not deducted as trading expenses) shall augment or create a loss for that period. Allowances brought forward from an earlier period may not be included in such a claim. [*CAA 1990, s 145(3)(4); ICTA 1988, s 393A(5)(6); FA 1991, s 73(1)*].

Excess charges are excluded from losses available to be carried back (see 50.3 PROFIT COMPUTATIONS). Losses may not be carried back so as to interfere with relief given in earlier periods for trade charges. [*ICTA 1988, s 393A(8)*].

Claims must be made within two years of the end of the accounting period in which the loss is made or within such further period as the Revenue may allow. [*ICTA 1988, ss 393(11), 393A(10); FA 1991, s 73(1)*]. Late claims will in general only be admitted where, for reasons beyond the company's control, a timeous claim could not have been made. (Revenue Tax Bulletin November 1991 p 3).

See also 44.9 and 44.14 below.

Simon's Direct Tax Service. See D2.405.

44.7 *Example*

(A) *General*

X Ltd has the following results for the three years ending 31 December 1995, 1996 and 1997.

	1995	1996	1997
	£	£	£
Trading profit/(loss)	30,000	4,500	(30,000)
Schedule A	1,000	1,000	3,000
Schedule D, Case III	500	500	4,000
Chargeable gains	—	1,500	2,250
Trade charges	(4,000)	(4,000)	(2,000)
Non-trade charges	—	(1,000)	—

The loss can be relieved as follows.

	£	£	Loss memorandum £
Year ended 31 December 1997			
Trading loss			(30,000)
Schedule A		3,000	
Schedule D, Case III		4,000	
Chargeable gains		2,250	
		9,250	
Deduct Trading loss		(9,250)	9,250
Profits chargeable to CT		—	
			(20,750)
Unrelieved trade charges c/f	(2,000)		
Year ended 31 December 1996			
Schedule D, Case I		4,500	
Schedule A		1,000	
Schedule D, Case III		500	
Chargeable gains		1,500	
		7,500	
Deduct Trade charges		(4,000)	
		3,500	
Deduct Loss carried back		(3,500)	3,500
Profits chargeable to CT		—	
Unrelieved non-trade charges	(1,000)		
			(17,250)
Year ended 31 December 1995			
Schedule D, Case I		30,000	
Schedule A		1,000	
Schedule D, Case III		500	
		31,500	
Deduct Trade charges		(4,000)	
		27,500	
Deduct Loss carried back (see note below)		(14,959)	14,959
Profits chargeable to CT		£12,541	
Loss carried forward			£2,291

Note. The trading loss for the year to 31 December 1997 has to be apportioned between that part of the period falling before 2 July 1997 and the remainder. The loss apportioned to the latter part may only be carried back to periods falling within the period of one year immediately preceding the period of loss, whilst that apportioned to the earlier part may still be carried back up to three years. In this case, the pre-2 July 1997 period is 182 days, so that the part of the loss which may be carried back more than one year is

$$\frac{182}{365} \times 30{,}000 = £14{,}959$$

The loss carry-back to the year ended 31 December 1995 is correspondingly restricted.

For the years ending 31 December 1999 and 31 December 2000, X Ltd has the following results.

	1999	2000
	£	£
Trading profit/(loss)	6,000	(20,000)
Schedule A	3,000	3,000
Schedule D, Case III	2,000	1,000
Chargeable gains	1,500	4,500
Trade charges	(4,000)	(2,000)
Non-trade charges	(1,000)	—

The loss can be relieved as follows.

	£	£	Loss memorandum £
Year ended 31 December 2000			
Trading loss			(20,000)
Schedule A		3,000	
Schedule D, Case III		1,000	
Chargeable gains		4,500	
		8,500	
Deduct Trading loss		(8,500)	8,500
Profits chargeable to CT		—	
			(11,500)
Unrelieved trade charges c/f	(2,000)		
Year ended 31 December 1999			
Schedule D, Case I		6,000	
Schedule A		3,000	
Schedule D, Case III		2,000	
Chargeable gains		1,500	
		12,500	
Deduct Trade charges		(4,000)	
		8,500	
Deduct Loss carried back		(8,500)	8,500
Profits chargeable to CT		—	
Unrelieved non-trade charges	(1,000)		
Loss carried forward			£3,000

(B) *Accounting periods of different lengths*

Y Ltd, which previously made up accounts to 31 March, changed its accounting date to 31 December. Its results for the five accounting periods up to 31 December 1997 were as follows

	12 months 31.3.94	12 months 31.3.95	12 months 31.3.96	9 months 31.12.96	12 months 31.12.97
	£	£	£	£	£
Trading profit/(loss)	18,000	20,000	5,500	(9,000)	(66,000)
Schedule D, Case III	3,000	2,500	2,500	3,000	—
Chargeable gains	7,000	1,500	—	—	2,000

Y Ltd makes all available loss relief claims so as to obtain relief against the earliest possible profits.

The computations are summarised as follows.

	12 months 31.3.94	12 months 31.3.95	12 months 31.3.96	9 months 31.12.96	12 months 31.12.97
	£	£	£	£	£
Schedule D, Case I	18,000	20,000	5,500	—	—
Schedule D, Case III	3,000	2,500	2,500	3,000	—
Chargeable gains	7,000	1,500	—	—	2,000
	28,000	24,000	8,000	3,000	2,000
Loss relief					
Section 393A(1)(a)				(3,000)	(2,000)
Section 393A(1)(b)	(7,000)	(24,000)	(8,000)		
Profits chargeable to CT	£21,000	—	—	—	—

Loss memoranda

	9 months 31.12.96	12 months 31.12.97	Total
	£	£	£
Trading loss	9,000	66,000	75,000
Relieved against current year profits	(3,000)	(2,000)	(5,000)
Relieved by carry-back:			
To y/e 31.3.96	(6,000)	(2,000)	(8,000)
To y/e 31.3.95	—	(24,000)	(24,000)
To y/e 31.3.94	—	(7,000)	(7,000)
Carried forward	Nil	£31,000	£31,000

Note. See the note to the Example at 44.5 above as regards restriction on carry-back of the loss of the year ending 31 December 1997. In this case losses of £32,910 (£66,000 × $\frac{182}{365}$) may be carried back up to three years, and since the losses used outside the immediately preceding year amount to £32,500 (three-quarters of the £2,000 used in year ended 31 March 1996 (£1,500) + the whole of the £24,000 used in the year ended 31 March 1995 (£24,000) + the £7,000 restricted relief used in the year ended 31 March 1994), no further restriction applies.

Y Ltd again changes its accounting date after the year ended 31 December 1999, the next accounts being drawn up to 30 September 2000. Its results for the accounting periods to 31 December 1999, 30 September 2000 and 30 September 2001 are as follows.

	12 months 31.12.99	9 months 30.9.00	12 months 30.9.01
	£	£	£
Trading profit/(loss)	25,500	(9,000)	(42,000)
Schedule D, Case III	2,500	3,000	—
Chargeable gains	4,000	—	2,000

Y Ltd makes all available loss relief claims so as to obtain relief against the earliest possible profits.

The computations are summarised as follows.

	12 months 31.12.99	9 months 30.9.00	12 months 30.9.01
	£	£	£
Schedule D, Case I	25,500	—	—
Schedule D, Case III	2,500	3,000	—
Chargeable gains	4,000	—	2,000
	32,000	3,000	2,000
Loss relief			
ICTA 1988, s 393A(1)(a)		(3,000)	(2,000)
ICTA 1988, s 393A(1)(b)	(14,000)		
Profits chargeable to CT	£18,000	—	—

Loss memoranda

	9 months 30.9.00	12 months 30.9.01	Total
	£	£	£
Trading loss	9,000	42,000	51,000
Relieved against current year profits	(3,000)	(2,000)	(5,000)
Relieved by carry-back to y/e 31.12.99	(6,000)	(8,000)	(14,000)
Carried forward	Nil	£32,000	£32,000

Note. The 'specified period' for carry-back of the loss of the year ended 30 September 2001 is the twelve months from 1 October 1999 to 30 September 2000. Thus only one-quarter (£8,000) of the profits of the year ended 31 December 1999 are available for offset against the loss of the year ended 30 September 2001.

44.8 **CARRY-BACK OF TERMINAL LOSSES**

The relief described at 44.6 above (which permits the carry back of trading losses) also applies where a loss is incurred in the accounting period in which the trade ceases, except that:

(*a*) the general reduction in the carry-back period from three years to twelve months for losses incurred after 1 July 1997 does not apply (i.e. three year carry-back continues to be available); and (*b*) (for losses incurred in accounting periods ending on or after 2 July 1997) losses incurred in the twelve months prior to cessation (rather than, as previously, in the accounting period in which the trade ceases) may be carried back three years (with losses of any accounting period falling partly within and partly outside that twelve-month period being apportioned on a time basis).

In determining terminal losses for relief as above, charges on income paid wholly and exclusively for trade purposes are treated as trading expenses to the extent that total charges exceed any profits from which they may be deducted. The part of a loss as in (*b*) above which is apportioned to the part of the accounting period falling outside the twelve-month period is reduced by a similarly apportioned part of the charges treated as trading expenses (with no corresponding increase in the loss apportioned to the part of the accounting period falling within the twelve-month period).

Claims to relief must be made within two years of the end of the accounting period in which the loss is incurred, or within such further period as the Revenue may allow.

[*ICTA 1988, s 393A; FA 1991, s 73(1); F(No 2)A 1997, s 39*].

For the circumstances in which an inspector may allow a claim for carry-back of losses from the final period of account of a company which has collapsed despite no formal accounts having been prepared for the period, see Revenue Company Taxation Manual, CT 450a.

Simon's Direct Tax Service. See **D2.405.**

44.9 LOSSES ELIGIBLE FOR RELIEF

A loss is not available for relief under 44.2 or 44.6 above unless

(*a*) the trade is carried on in the exercise of functions conferred by or under any enactment, or

(*b*) for the accounting period in question, the trade was carried on **on a commercial basis and with a view to the realisation of gain** either in the trade itself or in any larger undertaking of which it formed part.

A trade carried on so as to afford a 'reasonable expectation of gain' is treated as carried on with a view to the realisation of gain, but if there is a change in the manner of carrying on the trade in an accounting period, it is treated as having throughout that period been carried on in the same manner as at the end of that period. [*ICTA 1988, s 393(5)(6) (repealed); ICTA 1988, s 393A(3)(4); FA 1991, s 73(1); FA 1996, Sch 20 para 26*].

These provisions are without prejudice to those in 44.14 below.

It should be noted that relief for a trading loss of a period under 44.2 to 44.8 above may be given regardless of an estimated assessment having become final for the period before the accounts were submitted. (Revenue Company Taxation Manual, CT 404a).

Determination of amount of losses. For accounting periods ending **before 1 July 1999** (see below), special provisions govern the determination of the amount of trading losses under *ICTA 1988, s 393* and of other amounts available for surrender by way of group relief under *ICTA 1988, s 403* (see 29.18 GROUPS OF COMPANIES), in relation to which the relevant information is required to be given in the return under *TMA 1970, s 11* (see 54.2 RETURNS). If the inspector is satisfied that the relevant information in that return is correct and complete, he must determine such amounts accordingly. If he is not satisfied, or if the return has not been delivered within the time specified for its delivery (see 54.2 RETURNS), he may determine them to the best of his judgement. The determination (which may be that the amount in question is nil) takes effect when the inspector gives written notice of it to the company. The normal right of appeal applies as if the determination were an assessment (see 5.2 ASSESSMENTS AND APPEALS), but otherwise the determination is conclusive for tax purposes except

(*a*) *TMA 1970, s 36(3)* (further claims for reliefs or allowances in fraudulent or negligent conduct assessments),

(*b*) *TMA 1970, s 43A* (further claims, etc. in relation to further assessments), and

(*c*) *TMA 1970, s 41B* (see below). [*TMA 1970, s 41A; FA 1990, s 95; FA 1998, Sch 5 para 33, Sch 19 para 19*].

An excessive amount determined as above may be reduced (including to nil) by direction by the inspector. The direction is treated as issued when written notice of it is given to the company, and the normal appeal rights apply as if it were an assessment (see 5.2 ASSESSMENTS AND APPEALS). When the direction becomes final, the determination to which it relates takes effect as if reduced by the amount specified in the direction. Pending the direction's becoming final, the determination to which it relates is not treated as conclusive. Successive directions may be issued in respect of the same determination. [*TMA 1970, s 41B; FA 1990, s 95; FA 1998, Sch 19 para 19*].

The time limit for issue of both determinations and directions is normally six years after the end of the accounting period to which the determination relates. A direction may, however, be issued up to 20 years after the end of that accounting period if the excessive amount in question arose from fraudulent or negligent conduct of the company or on its behalf. [*TMA 1970, s 41C; FA 1990, s 95; FA 1998, Sch 19 para 19*].

For accounting periods ending **on or after 1 July 1999**, self-assessment applies (see 55.5 SELF-ASSESSMENT).

Simon's Direct Tax Service. See D2.408, D2.720.

44.10 COMPANY RECONSTRUCTIONS

The following provisions apply where, on a company ('the predecessor') ceasing to carry on a trade, another company ('the successor') begins to carry it on, and

(*a*) on, or within two years after, the cessation, the trade is 'owned' as to at least three-quarters by the same persons as owned a similar interest within a year before the cessation, and

(*b*) throughout the periods referred to above, the trade is carried on by a company which is within the charge to tax in respect of it.

References to 'the trade' include any other trade comprising the activities of the original trade.

[*ICTA 1988, s 343(1)*].

'*Ownership*'. A trade carried on by two or more persons is treated as owned by them in the shares in which they are entitled to the profits thereof.

A trade or an interest therein belonging to trustees (other than for charitable or public purposes) is treated as owned by the persons entitled to the trust's income for the time being.

A trade or an interest therein belonging to a company shall (if necessary to bring the provisions of *section 343* into effect) be treated as owned by

(i) the beneficial owners of the 'ordinary share capital' of the company in proportion to their holdings; or

(ii) the company's 'parent company'; or

(iii) the beneficial owners of the 'ordinary share capital' of the parent company in proportion to their holdings; or

(iv) the person or body of persons controlling a corporate shareholder within (i)–(iii) above.

'*Ordinary share capital*' is as defined in *ICTA 1988, s 832(1)*. See 29.3 GROUPS OF COMPANIES.

A '*parent company*' is one owning, directly or indirectly, three-quarters of the ordinary share capital of the company (determined in accordance with *ICTA 1988, s 838(5)–(10)*) and which is not also a subsidiary of a third company.

In determining for the purposes of (*a*) and (*b*) above to what extent a trade belongs to the same persons, persons who are 'relatives' and the persons from time to time entitled to the income under a trust are respectively treated as a single person.

'*Relative*' means spouse, ancestor, lineal descendant, brother or sister.

[*ICTA 1988, s 344*].

Terminal losses. For accounting periods ending after 1 July 1997, the special reliefs for terminal losses (see 44.8 above) are not available to the predecessor. [*ICTA 1988, s 343(4A); F(No 2)A 1997, s 39(7)(8)*].

Trading losses may be carried forward (see 44.4 above) against income arising from the same trade to the successor, as if there had been no succession.

Where the amount of the 'relevant liabilities' immediately before a transfer exceeds the open market value of 'relevant assets' at that time, the losses which may be carried forward are reduced or extinguished by the amount of that excess. Where there are repeated successions (see below), the restriction applies only to transfers after 18 March 1986, and does not affect any earlier transfers on or before that date.

'*Relevant assets*' are assets which were vested in the predecessor immediately before the transfer, and which were not transferred to the successor, together with consideration given to the predecessor by the successor in respect of the change of company carrying on the trade (but the assumption by the successor of any liabilities of the predecessor is not treated as consideration for this purpose).

'*Relevant liabilities*' are liabilities outstanding and vested in the predecessor immediately before the transfer, and not transferred to the successor, but excluding any liability representing share capital, share premium account, reserves or 'relevant loan stock' of the predecessor unless such liability arose on a conversion of a liability not representing any such item within one year before the transfer. Where a liability was transferred to the successor, but the creditor agreed to accept part payment in settlement of the whole, the balance of the liability is treated as not having been transferred to the successor.

Any assets or liabilities apportioned to a successor on a previous application of these provisions (see below) are excluded.

'*Relevant loan stock*' is any loan stock or similar security, secured or unsecured, but excluding any in respect of which, at the time the liability giving rise to it was incurred, the creditor was carrying on a trade of lending money. The amount of a liability representing relevant loan stock which is not a relevant liability, but which is secured on a relevant asset, is deducted from the value of the asset for the purposes of this provision.

[*ICTA 1988, s 343(3)(4), s 344(5)–(12); FA 1993, Sch 14 para 8(2)*].

Capital allowances are given to, and balancing charges made on, the successor as if there had been no succession (and losses are calculated accordingly, see *ICTA 1988, s 393A(5)*), unless the successor is a 'dual resident investing company' (see 29.31 GROUPS OF

COMPANIES) and begins to carry on the trade after 31 March 1987. [*ICTA 1988, s 343(2)*]. Where the trade is transferred during the currency of accounting periods of the companies concerned,

(i) writing-down allowances are calculated on the 'pool' at the end of the transferee's accounting period, and apportioned on a time basis between the periods in which each company carried on the trade,

(ii) first-year allowances are given to the company incurring the expenditure, and

(iii) balancing adjustments are made on the company carrying on the trade at the relevant time.

(CCAB Guidance Notes TR 500, 10 March 1983).

Securities within ICTA 1988, s 731 held as trading stock are treated as having been sold by the predecessor and acquired by the successor at market value at the time of the succession. See Tolley's Income Tax under Anti-Avoidance. [*ICTA 1988, s 343(5)*].

Repeated successions are each treated in accordance with the above provisions, provided that the conditions in (*a*) and (*b*) above are satisfied on each occasion.

Where the successor takes over **part only** of the predecessor's trade, or where the activities to which it succeeds are carried on as part only of the successor's existing trade, the transferred activities are treated as a separate trade and receipts, expenses, etc. are apportioned as may be just. See *Falmer Jeans Ltd v Rodin Ch D, 1990, 63 TC 55* for a case in which this provision was held to apply. If more than one company's liability is affected, the matter is determined by

(A) the General Commissioners having jurisdiction over both companies (if any), or

(B) in default of (A), such body of General Commissioners, having jurisdiction over one of the companies, as the Board may direct, or

(C) if the companies agree, or in any other case, the Special Commissioners.

Each company is entitled to appear before, and be heard by, the Commissioners, or to make written representations. [*ICTA 1988, s 343(8)–(10)*].

See also 44.12 and 44.13 below.

Simon's Direct Tax Service. See D2.501.

44.11 *Example*

A Ltd and B Ltd are two wholly-owned subsidiaries of X Ltd. All are within the charge to corporation tax, although A Ltd has accumulated trading losses brought forward and unrelieved of £200,000 and has not paid tax for several years. As part of a group reorganisation, A Ltd's trade is transferred to B Ltd on 31 October 2000.

A Ltd's balance sheet immediately before the transfer is as follows.

	£		£
Share capital	100,000	Property	90,000
Debenture secured on property	50,000	Plant	20,000
		Stock	130,000
Group loan	10,000	Trade debtors	120,000
Trade creditors	300,000		
Bank overdraft	60,000		
	520,000		
Deficit on reserves	(160,000)		
	£360,000		£360,000

Book values represent the approximate open market values of assets. B Ltd takes over the stock and plant to continue the trade, paying £150,000 to A Ltd and taking over £15,000 of trade creditors relating to stock. A Ltd is to collect outstanding debts and pay remaining creditors.

A Ltd's 'relevant assets' are:

	£
Freehold property (£90,000 – £50,000)	40,000
Trade debtors	120,000
Consideration from B Ltd	150,000
	£310,000

A Ltd's 'relevant liabilities' are:

	£
Bank overdraft	60,000
Group loan	10,000
Trade creditors (£300,000 – £15,000)	285,000
	£355,000

Tax losses transferable with trade:
£200,000 – £(355,000 – 310,000) = £155,000

44.12 PRIVATISATION

British Telecommunications plc ('British Telecom') is treated for all purposes of corporation tax as being the same person as British Telecommunications, to whose business it succeeded on privatisation, except that it is not regarded by virtue of the above provision alone as a nationalised undertaking within *TCGA 1992, s 170(12)*. Additionally, there is a bar on the carry forward to the successor company of losses arising in the Post Office non-telecommunications business prior to their separation. [*British Telecommunications Act 1981, s 82; Telecommunications Act 1984, s 72*]. Similar provisions apply in relation to the successor companies to the British Airways Board and the National Freight Corporation [*ICTA 1988, s 513*], the British Airports Authority [*British Airports Act 1986, s 77*], the British Gas Corporation [*Gas Act 1986, s 60*], the British Steel Corporation [*British Steel Act 1988, s 11*], the General Practice Finance Corporation [*Health and Medicines Act 1988, s 6*], statutory port undertakings [*Ports Act 1991, s 35*], the National Research Development Council and National Enterprise Board [*British Technology Group Act 1991, s 12*], milk marketing boards [*Agriculture Act 1993, Sch 2 Pt I; FA 1996, s 203*], Northern Ireland Airports Ltd [*FA 1994, s 253, Sch 25*] and the Atomic Energy Authority [*Atomic Energy Authority Act 1995, Sch 3*]. See also *Water Act 1989, s 95*, *Electricity Act 1989, s 90, Sch 11*, *Environmental Protection Act 1990, ss 6–9*, *Coal Industry Act 1994, Sch 4* and *Broadcasting Act 1996, Sch 7*, and, as regards the *Railways Act 1993*, *FA 1994, s 252, Sch 24*.

Surplus ACT arising to the successor company on privatisation may not be carried back to a period before the transfer (*CIR v Aberdeen Milk Co Ltd CS, [1999] STC 787*).

44.13 CHANGE IN OWNERSHIP OF A COMPANY

For changes in ownership of investment companies, see 40.5 INVESTMENT COMPANIES.

The provisions outlined below apply if

(*a*) within any period of three years there is a 'change in the ownership of a company' preceded or followed by, or coinciding with, a 'major change in the nature or conduct of a trade' carried on by the company, or

(*b*) at any time after the scale of activities in a trade carried on by a company has become small or negligible, and before any considerable revival in the trade, there is a change in the ownership of the company.

[*ICTA 1988, s 768(1)*].

There is a '*change in the ownership of a company*' if

(i) a single person acquires as beneficial owner more than half the ordinary share capital (see *ICTA 1988, s 832(1)* or 29.3 GROUPS OF COMPANIES) of the company, or

(ii) two or more persons each acquire as beneficial owner a holding of at least 5% (or an addition to the holding sufficient to raise it to 5%) of the company's ordinary share capital, and the combined holdings exceed half that capital. Acquisitions by, and holdings of, CONNECTED PERSONS (16) are treated as a single acquisition or holding.

See, however, 29.58 GROUPS OF COMPANIES for the interaction of these provisions and the demerger provisions of *ICTA 1988, ss 213–218*.

In comparing a person's holdings at any two dates, he is to be treated at the later date as having acquired whatever he did not hold at the earlier date, irrespective of intervening acquisitions and disposals. Comparisons are made in percentage terms throughout.

Acquisitions of shares on death are left out of account as is any gift which was unsolicited and made without regard to these provisions.

The date of any acquisition corresponds with the date of the contract of sale, or with the assignment of the benefit of that contract, or with the acquisition of the option to acquire, as the case may be.

Where the existence of extraordinary rights or powers renders ownership of the ordinary share capital an inappropriate test of change of ownership, holdings of all kinds, or of any particular kind, of share capital, voting power or any other special kind of power may be taken into account instead.

A change in the direct ownership of a company is ignored if, before and after the change, it continues to be a '75% subsidiary' of the same company. Where there is a change in the ownership of a company under *ICTA 1988, s 769*, then the person(s) whose holding(s) is (are) taken into account under (i) or (ii) above is (are) deemed to acquire at the time of the change the 'appropriate proportion' of the ordinary share capital (or other rights or powers, see above) of any other company owned by the company whose ownership has changed. The '*appropriate proportion*' is the whole where only one person's holding is taken into account, in any other case the proportion of the aggregate holdings taken into account acquired by each person whose holding is taken into account.

'*75% subsidiary*' is defined by reference to direct or indirect ownership of at least 75% of ordinary share capital, with an additional requirement that the parent company would be beneficially entitled to at least 75% of any profits available for distribution to equity holders and of any assets so available on a winding-up (see 29.17 GROUPS OF COMPANIES).

No event or situation preceding a change of ownership to which these provisions have applied is to be taken into account in ascertaining whether a subsequent change has taken place.

[*ICTA 1988, s 769; FA 1989, s 100; FA 1998, Sch 5 para 32*].

'*Major change in the nature or conduct of a trade*' includes a major change in the type of property dealt in, or the services or facilities provided, in the trade, or in customers, outlets or markets, even if that change is the result of a gradual process which began outside the three-year period. A '*change*' for these purposes is to be decided by a qualitative test but in determining whether a change is '*major*' the change should not be viewed in isolation but a quantitative test of fact and degree should be applied (*Willis v Peeters Picture Frames Ltd CA (NI) 1982, 56 TC 436*). [*ICTA 1988, s 768(4)*]. The cessation of a trade is unlikely to be regarded as a major change in the nature or conduct of the trade, although the events leading up to it may be so; the interposition of a holding company between a company and its shareholders usually represents a change in ownership, but does not represent a major change in the nature or conduct of a trade carried on by the company. (ICAEW Technical Memorandum TR 854, 2 December 1991).

Revenue Pamphlet IR 131, SP 10/91, 7 August 1991 sets out other factors to which the Revenue will have regard in considering whether there has been a major change in the nature or conduct of a trade or business, for the purposes of both *ICTA 1988, ss 768, 768A* and (for changes of ownership before 6 April 1999) *ICTA 1988, ss 245, 245A* (see 3.10 ADVANCE CORPORATION TAX). These would include changes in factors such as location of the business premises, identity of suppliers, management or staff, methods of manufacture, or pricing or purchasing policies, insofar as they are indicative of a major change. It will not be regarded as a major change in the nature or conduct of a trade where all that has happened is that changes have been made to increase efficiency, or to keep pace with developing technology in the industry concerned or with developing management techniques, or to rationalise the product range by withdrawing unprofitable items and, possibly, replacing them with new items of a related kind. Although it is acknowledged that every case rests on its own facts, examples are cited where a change would *not* be regarded as major. These include removal from several obsolescent factories to one new factory without a change of product, the replacement of mechanical manufacturing components by electronic ones, and a switch by a dealership of brands dealt in where the same market is satisfied before and after the switch. Examples cited where a major change *would* be regarded as occurring include a saloon car dealership switching to tractors, a switch from owning a public house to operating a discotheque from the same (converted) premises, and a switch from fattening pigs for their owners to buying pigs for fattening and resale. Other examples relevant to changes in ownership of investment companies (see 40.5 INVESTMENT COMPANIES) are also given.

Where these provisions have to be considered in relation to the transfer of part of a trade which is to be treated as the transfer of a separate trade under *ICTA 1988, s 343(8)* (see 44.10 above), SP 10/91 indicates that the transfer of the part-trade will not of itself be regarded as a major change in the nature or conduct of either the part-trade transferred or that retained. Instead, each of the trades (or the relevant part of a combined trade) after the transfer will be compared with the equivalent part of the combined trade before the transfer. In cases where the transfer occurs *after* the relevant change of ownership, however, it may be necessary to consider whether it involves a major change in the nature or conduct of the undivided trade as it subsisted at the date of the change in ownership, and in such cases it may be appropriate to regard the transfer as constituting a major change, depending on the surrounding circumstances. The Revenue will not, however, take this point if there was no other major change in either the original trade, or the parts into which it was divided, in the relevant period.

Where these provisions apply, no relief may be claimed under *ICTA 1988, s 393* against the income or other profits of an accounting period ending after the change of ownership for losses incurred in an accounting period beginning before the change. Relief may similarly not be claimed under *ICTA 1988, s 393A(1)* for a loss incurred in an accounting period ending after the change to be set against profits of an accounting period beginning before the change. For these purposes only, the accounting period in which the change takes place is treated as two separate accounting periods, ending with the date of the change and beginning with the following date respectively. The profits or losses of the whole period are apportioned to each on a time basis, or by such other method as is just and reasonable. [*ICTA 1988, s 768(1)–(3), s 768A; FA 1991, Sch 15 para 20*].

If the carry-forward of loss relief is restricted as above, in applying the provisions of *CAA 1990* relating to balancing charges arising by reference to any event after the change of ownership, any allowance or deduction falling to be made in taxing the company's trade for any chargeable period before the change is to be disregarded insofar as the profits or gains of that and any subsequent chargeable period before the change are insufficient to give effect to it (assuming such effect to be given before any loss relief not attributable to any such allowance or deduction). [*ICTA 1988, s 768(6)(7)*].

Company reconstructions. Where the change in ownership takes place after a company reconstruction under *ICTA 1988, s 343* (see 44.10 above), for the purposes of the restriction on carry-forward of relief under *ICTA 1988, s 768*, references to the trade at (*a*) and (*b*) above *include* the trade as carried on by the predecessor, and relief for losses incurred before the company reconstruction are restricted in the same way as losses incurred after the company reconstruction. [*ICTA 1988, s 768(5)*].

Assessment. An assessment may be made within six years after the circumstances or events (after the change but within the three-year period) which bring these provisions into operation, in order to give effect to these provisions. [*ICTA 1988, s 768(8)*].

Powers to obtain information. The inspector may, by notice in writing, require any person who is the registered owner of shares, stock or securities of a company, to state whether he is the beneficial owner thereof, and, if not, to supply the name and address of the person or persons on whose behalf he holds them. [*ICTA 1988, s 768(9)*].

Schedule A losses. Where either (*a*) or (*b*) above applies in relation to a company carrying on a Schedule A business or an overseas property business (see 50.27 PROFIT COMPUTATIONS), so that the provisions described apply, or would apply, in relation to trading losses, a similar restriction applies to prevent Schedule A losses (see 50.27 PROFIT COMPUTATIONS) incurred before the change being set against profits arising after the change. [*ICTA 1988, ss 768D, 769; FA 1998, Sch 5 paras 31, 32*].

General. These provisions are intended to prevent the purchase of companies with accumulated trading or property losses, in order to claim relief against the purchaser's trading profits and vice versa.

See also 3.10 ADVANCE CORPORATION TAX, 40.5 INVESTMENT COMPANIES and 48.4 PAYMENT OF TAX.

Simon's Direct Tax Service. See **D2.410.**

44.14 FARMING AND MARKET GARDENING [*ICTA 1988, s 397*]

A loss incurred in any accounting period in carrying on a trade of farming or market gardening cannot be relieved against other income or gains or carried back if a loss, ignoring capital allowances, has been incurred in that period and in each of the five years up to the beginning of that accounting period.

ICTA 1988, s 397 does not deny relief where

(i) the farming, etc. is part of, and ancillary to, a larger trading undertaking, or

(ii) the farming, etc. activities in the year are carried on in a way which might reasonably be expected to produce profits in the future and the activities in the preceding five years could not reasonably have been expected to become profitable until after the year under review. [*ICTA 1988, s 397(3)(4); FA 1996, Sch 20 para 27*].

Simon's Direct Tax Service. See **B3.531.**

44.15 **LEASING**

Where a company incurs capital expenditure on machinery or plant which it lets to another person under a leasing contract, and that company would otherwise be entitled to relief under *ICTA 1988, s 393(1)(2)* or *s 393A(1)* (see 44.2–44.6 above) for losses *incurred on that contract*, the relief is denied if, in the accounting period for which a 'first-year allowance' (where available) in respect of the expenditure is made, arrangements exist for a 'successor company' to take over all or part of the first company's obligations under the leasing contract. [*ICTA 1988, s 395(1); FA 1993, Sch 14 para 8(3)*].

'*Losses incurred on a leasing contract*' (and profits arising) are computed, and are treated for relief purposes, as if the leasing contract constituted a separate trade, begun at the time of the letting. [*ICTA 1988, s 395(3)(4)*]. Loss relief is thus restricted to future profits on the leasing contract.

'*First-year allowance*' is as defined in *CAA 1990, Pt II*. [*ICTA 1988, s 395(1)*]. See Tolley's Income Tax under Capital Allowances.

'*Successor company*' is as defined in *section 343* (see 44.10 above) **or** a company connected with the first company. [*ICTA 1988, s 395(2)*]. See 16 CONNECTED PERSONS.

Leasing partnerships. For restrictions on the set-off against an individual's total income of certain losses arising from first-year allowances incurred by the individual in partnership with a company, see Tolley's Income Tax under Losses.

Simon's Direct Tax Service. See D2.409.

44.16 **COMPANIES IN PARTNERSHIP**

There is a restriction on loss relief where a company ('the partner company') is a member of a trading partnership and arrangements exist whereby another partner (or a person connected with him, see 16 CONNECTED PERSONS) receives any payment or enjoys any benefit in money's worth in respect of the partner company's 'share in the profits or losses' of the partnership or whereby the partner company (or a person connected with it) receives any payment or enjoys any such benefit in respect of its share of losses (other than by way of a payment for group relief, see 29.14–29.26 GROUPS OF COMPANIES).

If the above conditions are satisfied for any accounting period, the company's share of partnership losses and charges on income (see *ICTA 1988, s 338*) may be set off only against its share of profits from the partnership's trade, and no other loss incurred by the company in that period may be set against such profits. Furthermore, for accounting periods beginning before 6 April 1999, no ACT may be set against the company's corporation tax liability on those profits.

[*ICTA 1988, s 116; FA 1998, Sch 3 para 10*].

The company's '*share in the profits or losses*' of the partnership is determined under *ICTA 1988, s 114(2)* (see 47 PARTNERSHIPS), but with appropriate deductions and additions for capital allowances and balancing charges.

See also 44.15 above and 44.21 below and 47.7 PARTNERSHIPS.

44.17 **OIL COMPANIES**

See 46.6 OIL COMPANIES.

44.18 **DEALINGS IN COMMODITY FUTURES** [*ICTA 1988, s 399(2)–(5)*]

If a company carries on the trade of dealing in commodity futures in partnership, and a scheme has been effected or arrangements have been made whereby the sole or main benefit that might be expected to accrue to the company from its partnership interest is the making of a loss to be set off against general income under *ICTA 1988, s 393(2)* or *s 393A(1)* (see 44.2 and 44.6 above), such relief is denied. Any relief already given is recouped by an assessment under Schedule D, Case VI.

44.19 LOSSES ON UNLISTED SHARES [*ICTA 1988, s 573*]

Investment companies (as defined by *ICTA 1988, s 130* – see 40.1 INVESTMENT COMPANIES – but excluding the holding company of a 'trading group') may claim relief against income for losses arising on the disposal of unlisted shares for which it subscribed and which are ordinary share capital of 'qualifying trading companies'. The vendor must have been an investment company throughout the six years prior to the sale (or for a shorter such period before which it had not been a 'trading company' or an 'excluded company') and must not have been 'associated' with, or a member of the same group as, the qualifying trading company during its ownership of the shares. [*ICTA 1988, s 573(1)*].

The shares must have been issued in consideration of money (or money's worth). [*ICTA 1988, s 573(6)*].

A claim is available only if the disposal is at arm's length for full consideration, or by way of a distribution in a winding-up, or if the value of the shares has become negligible and a claim to that effect made under *TCGA 1992, s 24(2)*. [*ICTA 1988, s 575(1)*]. For disposals on or after 1 April 2000, relief is extended to disposals within *TCGA 1992, s 24(1)* (consisting of the entire loss, destruction, dissipation or extinction of an asset). [*ICTA 1988, s 575(1)(ba); FA 2000, Sch 16 para 3(3)*]. For earlier disposals, a more limited extension of the relief is available by concession, provided that all the other conditions are fulfilled, where the company had no assets and was dissolved, the shareholder had not received a distribution in the course of dissolving or winding up the company (or an anticipated final distribution had not been made), and the shareholder had not made a deemed disposal of the shares under *TCGA 1992, s 24(2)*. (Revenue Pamphlet IR 1, D46).

The allowable loss is as calculated for the purposes of corporation tax on chargeable gains. [*ICTA 1988, s 573(1)*]. The normal rules for the substitution of market value for consideration apply [*TCGA 1992, s 17*], so that the allowable loss may not exceed the actual loss incurred.

Companies are '*associated*' where one controls the other or both are under common control, control being as defined in *ICTA 1988, s 416* (see 13.2 CLOSE COMPANIES). [*ICTA 1988, s 573(5)*].

As regards shares issued **after 5 April 1998**, a '*qualifying trading company*' is a company which at all times in the period beginning with the incorporation of the company (or, if later, one year before the date on which the shares were issued) and ending with the disposal of the shares (the '*relevant period*') has been an 'unquoted' company and which

(*a*) either (i) is an 'eligible trading company' on the date of disposal, or (ii) has ceased to be an 'eligible trading company' within three years before that date and has not since that cessation been an 'excluded company', an 'investment company' or a 'non-eligible trading company', and

(*b*) either (i) has been an 'eligible trading company' for a continuous period of at least six years prior to the disposal (or prior to the cessation in (*a*)(ii) above, as the case may be), or (ii) has been an 'eligible trading company' for a shorter continuous period ending with the disposal or cessation and has not previously been an 'excluded company', an 'investment company' or a 'non-eligible trading company', and

(*c*) has carried on its business wholly or mainly in the UK throughout the relevant period (as above).

A company is '*unquoted*' for this purpose if none of its shares etc. are listed on a recognised stock exchange or on a designated foreign exchange, or dealt in outside the UK by such means as may be designated for the purpose. *ICTA 1988,* surities on the Alternative Investment Market are treated as unquoted for these purposes (see Revenue Press Release 20 February 1995). If it is unquoted at the time of the share issue, it does not cease to be unquoted in relation to those shares because any shares etc. of the company subsequently become so listed, or start to be dealt in by any means designated by an order made after the date of the share issue.

A '*trading company*' is a company, other than an 'excluded company', whose business consists wholly or mainly of the carrying on of trade(s), or which is the holding company of a 'trading group'. A '*trading group*' is a group (i.e. a company and all its '51% subsidiaries', see 29.3 GROUPS OR COMPANIES) the business of whose members, taken together, consists wholly or mainly of the carrying on of trade(s) (ignoring trades carried on by 'excluded' companies). An '*eligible trading company*' is a company which is, or could be, a qualifying company for the purposes of the enterprise investment scheme (see Tolley's Income Tax under Enterprise Investment Scheme), with appropriate minor modifications (see *ICTA 1988, s 576(4A)(4B)*), e.g. in the definition of 'relevant period', and a '*non-eligible trading company*' is a trading company which is not an eligible trading company.

An '*excluded company*' is a company whose trade consists mainly of dealing in land, in commodities or futures, or in shares, securities or other financial instruments, or is not carried on on a commercial basis with a reasonable expectation of profit; or which is the holding company of a non-trading group; or which is a building society (see 7.2 BUILDING SOCIETIES) or a registered industrial and provident society (see 32.1 INDUSTRIAL AND PROVIDENT SOCIETIES).

An '*investment company*' is a company within *ICTA 1988, s 130* (see 40.1 INVESTMENT COMPANIES), except that it does not include the holding company of a trading group.

As regards shares issued **on or before 5 April 1998**, a '*qualifying trading company*' is a company none of whose shares have, at any time in the period beginning with the incorporation of the company (or, if later, one year before the date on which the shares were issued) and ending with the disposal of the shares, been listed on a recognised stock exchange, and which

(A) either (i) is a 'trading company' (as above, except that the trades of non-resident members of a trading group are disregarded for this purpose) on the date of disposal or (ii) has ceased to be a trading company within the previous three years and has not since that time been an 'investment company' (as above) or an 'excluded company' (as above, except that the dealing restriction related to dealing in shares, securities, land, trades or commodity futures); and

(B) either (i) has been a trading company for a continuous period of six years ending on the date of disposal of the shares or at the time it ceased to be a trading company, or (ii) has been a trading company for a shorter continuous period ending on that date or at that time and had not, before the beginning of that period, been an investment company or an excluded company; and

(C) has been UK resident from incorporation to the date of disposal.

Alternative Investment Market securities are again treated as unquoted for this purpose.

[*ICTA 1988, s 576(4)(4A)(4B)(5); FA 1989, Sch 12 para 14; FA 1996, Sch 38 para 6; FA 1998, s 80*].

Claims. Relief must be claimed within two years of the end of the accounting period in which the loss was incurred. [*ICTA 1988, s 573(2)*].

Relief is given against income of the accounting period in which the loss was incurred and, if the company was then an investment company and the claim so requires, any balance of loss may be set against the proportion of income of preceding accounting periods arising in the twelve months before the start of the accounting period in which the loss was incurred. It must be claimed before any deduction for charges on income, management expenses or other expenditure available against profits generally. An earlier loss is relieved in priority to a later one. [*ICTA 1988, s 573(2)(3)(4); FA 2000, Sch 16 para 3(2)*]. Where relief for a loss on disposal of shares is claimed under *FA 2000, Sch 15 Pt VII* (see 19.20 CORPORATE VENTURING SCHEME), it must be claimed in priority to relief under *ICTA 1988, s 573*. [*ICTA 1988, s 573(4A); FA 2000, Sch 15 para 70, Sch 16 para 3(2)(b)*].

Identification. Where a company holds shares of the same class, only some of which qualify for the above relief because they were subscribed for, then disposals are identified with acquisitions on a 'last in, first out' basis, and relief is limited to the cost of the qualifying shares.

For disposals after 5 April 1998, there is an exception to the above rule where the holding includes any of the following:

(i) shares in respect of which business expansion scheme relief has been given and not withdrawn;

(ii) shares to which enterprise investment scheme income tax relief is attributable; or

(iii) shares to which enterprise investment scheme capital gains deferral relief is attributable.

See Tolley's Income Tax and Tolley's Capital Gains Tax under Enterprise Investment Scheme. In such cases, disposals are identified in accordance with the identification rules generally applicable to such shares (broadly, a 'first in, first out' basis).

For disposals after 31 March 2000, a similar exception applies where the holding includes shares to which corporate venturing scheme investment relief is attributable, and which were held continuously from issue to disposal (see 19.2, 19.20(a) CORPORATE VENTURING SCHEME). The identification rules under that scheme (see 19.17 CORPORATE VENTURING SCHEME) apply instead.

Loss relief under these provisions on the disposal of qualifying shares which form part of a share pool (see Tolley's Capital Gains Tax under Shares and Securities — Identification Rules) is restricted to the sums which would be allowed as deductions in computing the loss if the qualifying shares had been acquired and disposed of as a separate holding.

[*ICTA 1988, s 576(1)–(1C); FA 1998, s 80(1)(2); FA 2000, Sch 16 para 3(4)*].

Anti-avoidance. Any claim to relief will bring in the provisions of *TCGA 1992, s 30* (value-shifting to give a tax-free benefit) so that the relief may be adjusted for any benefit conferred whether tax-free or not. [*ICTA 1988, s 576(2)*].

Company reconstructions. Where, following a reorganisation or reduction of share capital, the shares disposed of represent a new holding identifiable under *TCGA 1992, s 127* with 'old shares', relief is not available unless it could have been given, on the disposal of the old shares for full consideration, at the reorganisation, etc. had this legislation then been in force and had the reorganisation, etc. been a chargeable occasion producing a loss. Where these conditions are not fulfilled, but 'new consideration' was given for the new holding, relief is limited to the allowable part of the new consideration. Where, under *TCGA 1992, s 137*, shares are deemed to have been disposed of on a reorganisation, etc., no relief is available under the above provisions. [*ICTA 1988, s 575(2)(3)*].

'*New consideration*' is money or money's worth excluding any surrender or alteration to the original shares (or rights attached thereto), and excluding the application of assets of the company or of distributions declared but not made out of those assets. [*ICTA 1988, s 576(5)*].

Where relief is claimed under these provisions, no relief may be claimed against chargeable gains in respect of the loss so relieved, and all necessary adjustments to corporation tax in respect of chargeable gains may be made. [*ICTA 1988, ss 573(4), 576(3); FA 2000, Sch 16 para 3(2)*].

Simon's Direct Tax Service. See D2.416.

44.20 *Example*

Z Ltd has been an investment company since its incorporation in 1970. It is not part of a trading group and has no associated companies. It makes up accounts to 31 December. On 6 February 2000, Z Ltd disposed of part of its holding of shares in T Ltd for full market value. Z Ltd makes no global re-basing election under *TCGA 1992, s 35(5)*.

Details of disposal

Contract date	6.2.00
Shares sold	2,000 Ord
Proceeds (after expenses)	£4,500

Z acquired its shares in T Ltd as follows

			£
6.4.78 subscribed for	1,000 shares	cost (with expenses)	5,000
6.4.88 acquired	1,500 shares	cost (with expenses)	4,000
	2,500		£9,000

T Ltd shares were valued at £3 per share at 31 March 1982. T Ltd has been a UK resident trading company since 1978. Its shares are not quoted on a recognised stock exchange.

Z Ltd may claim that part of the loss incurred be set off against its income as follows.

Identification on last in, first out basis.

(i) Shares acquired 6.4.88 (not subscribed for)

	£
Proceeds of 1,500 shares $\frac{1,500}{2,000} \times £4,500$	3,375
Cost of 1,500 shares	(4,000)
Capital loss *not* available for set-off against income	£(625)

(ii) Shares acquired 6.4.78 (subscribed for)

	Cost basis £	31.3.82 value basis £
Proceeds of 500 shares $\frac{500}{2,000} \times £4,500$	1,125	1,125
Cost of 500 shares	(2,500)	
31.3.82 value		(1,500)
	£(1,375)	£(375)
Capital loss available for set-off against income		£(375)

The loss of £375 is available primarily against income of the year ended 31 December 2000, with any balance being available against, broadly speaking, income of the 12 months ended 31 December 1999 (see 44.19 above).

44.21 WRITE-OFF OF GOVERNMENT INVESTMENT [*ICTA 1988, s 400*]

Where any amount of Government investment in a company is written-off, an equal amount is set against the company's 'tax losses' as at the end of the accounting period before that in which the investment was written-off, and against such losses of subsequent accounting periods until the amount written-off is extinguished. [*ICTA 1988, s 400(1)*].

'*Tax losses*' at the end of an accounting period are any trading losses, losses from a Schedule A or overseas property business, management expenses, capital allowances or allowable capital losses available for carry-forward at the end of the period, and any unused charges on income of the period. [*ICTA 1988, s 400(2); FA 1993, Sch 14 para 8(5); FA 1998, Sch 5 para 36*]. The set-off is made against allowable capital losses of a period only after all other tax losses of the period have been exhausted. [*ICTA 1988, s 400(3)*].

In determining the tax losses at the end of the accounting period before that of the write-off, valid claims for group relief, or for relief of trading losses or capital allowances against profits generally and/or of earlier accounting periods, are effective provided that they are made before the write-off date. Such claims made on or after that date are ineffective until the amount written-off has been set off in full. [*ICTA 1988, s 400(4)*].

Where the company concerned is a member of a group (see 29.3 GROUPS OF COMPANIES), the set-off for an accounting period may be made against tax losses of any other company which is a group member at the end of the accounting period, any allocation between group companies being on a 'reasonable and just' basis. [*ICTA 1988, s 400(5)*].

An amount of Government investment in a company is treated as written off if

(*a*) its liability to repay money lent out of public funds by a Minister of the Crown or Northern Ireland department is extinguished, or

(*b*) any of its shares subscribed for out of public funds by a Minister etc. are cancelled, or

(*c*) any 'commencing capital debt' (i.e. any debt to a Minister etc. assumed as such under an enactment) is reduced otherwise than by being paid off, or

(*d*) any 'public dividend capital' (i.e. any amount paid by a Minister etc. under an enactment which so describes it or which corresponds with enactments relating to similar payments so described) is reduced otherwise than by being repaid.

The amount and date of the write-off are determined accordingly. No restriction is, however, made under these provisions if, and to the extent that, the amount written-off is replaced in some other form by money provided out of public funds by a Minister etc. [*ICTA 1988, s 400(7)–(10)*].

Where a government investment is written off by the extinguishment, in whole or part, of a liability under a loan relationship, these provisions apply notwithstanding *FA 1996, s 80(5)* (matters to be brought into account in the case of loan relationships only under *FA 1996, Pt IV, Ch II*, see 43.2 LOAN RELATIONSHIPS). [*ICTA 1988, s 400(9A); FA 1996, Sch 14 para 19*].

Simon's Direct Tax Service. See D2.411.

44.22 **SCHEDULE A**

From 1 April 1998, losses arising from a Schedule A business in an accounting period are set against total profits of that period. Any balance of unrelieved loss may be carried forward and treated as a Schedule A loss of the following and succeeding accounting periods, for so long as the company continues to carry on the Schedule A business. Relief is, however, denied for non-commercial losses in the same circumstances as apply in the case of trading losses under *ICTA 1988, s 393A(3)(4)* (see 44.9 above). [*ICTA 1988, s 392A; FA 1998, Sch 5 para 28*]. See generally 50.27 PROFIT COMPUTATIONS.

For losses from overseas property businesses, see 44.23 below.

See also 40.5 INVESTMENT COMPANIES for the conversion of Schedule A losses to management expenses where an investment company ceases to carry on a Schedule A business.

See 50.26 PROFIT COMPUTATIONS as regards the restrictions on relief of deficiencies on property income before 1 April 1998.

44.23 **SCHEDULE D, CASE V**

Losses from overseas trades and, from 1 April 1998, from overseas property businesses (see 50.27 PROFIT COMPUTATIONS), both of which are within Schedule D, Case V, are available for carry forward against future profits from the same trade or business (subject, in the case of overseas property businesses, to the same commerciality test as applies to Schedule A business losses, see 44.22 above). [*ICTA 1988, ss 392B, 393; FA 1998, Sch 5 para 28*]. Otherwise, there is no statutory relief for Schedule D, Case V losses.

Before 1 April 1998, losses from overseas property lettings were by concession available for carry forward against future income from the same property (see Revenue Pamphlet IR 1 B25).

See generally Tolley's Income Tax under Schedule D, Case V and Overseas Matters.

44.24 **SCHEDULE D, CASE VI**

Losses on transactions in respect of which a company is within the charge to corporation tax under this Case may be set off against income from such transactions in the same or any subsequent accounting period. Such income is then treated as reduced by so much of the loss as has not been relieved in an earlier accounting period. [*ICTA 1988, s 396; FA 1990, s 99*].

These provisions do not apply to losses within *ICTA 1988, ss 34–36* (premiums, leases at an undervalue, etc.) (see Tolley's Income Tax under Schedule A), nor to certain amounts in respect of exchange losses (see 23.14 EXCHANGE GAINS AND LOSSES).

Companies in partnership (see 44.6 above). Where tax in respect of any of the profits of a partnership of which a company is a member (and to which arrangements as outlined in 44.16 above apply) is chargeable under Schedule D, Case VI, so much of such profits or losses as forms the company's share is treated (for the purposes of *ICTA 1988, s 116*) as arising from a trade carried on by the partnership and any allowance under *CAA 1990, s 61(1)* as made in taxing that trade. [*ICTA 1988, s 116*].

44.25 **DOUBLE TAXATION** [*ICTA 1988, s 808; FA 1994, s 140*]

Interest, dividends or royalties accruing to a non-resident company carrying on a business in the UK which have been treated as tax-exempt under double taxation arrangements are not to be excluded from trading income or profits of the business so as to give rise to losses to be set off against income or profits.

45 Mutual Companies

Cross-references. See 7 BUILDING SOCIETIES; 14 CLUBS AND SOCIETIES; 50.27(2) PROFIT COMPUTATIONS.

Simon's Direct Tax Service B3.237 *et seq.*.

45.1 A person cannot derive a taxable profit from trading with himself except in certain cases of self-supply by a trader of trading stock, see *Sharkey v Wernher HL 1955, 36 TC 275*. This principle is extended to a group of persons engaged in mutual activities of a trading nature, if there is an identifiable 'fund' for the common purpose with complete identity between contributors to, and participators in, the fund (the 'mutuality principle'). A body not liable as regards transactions with members may nevertheless be liable under Schedule D, Case I on transactions with non-members and is liable in the ordinary way on any investment etc. income. Whether the mutuality principle applies depends on the facts. For mutual insurance see *Styles v New York Life Insce Co HL 1889, 2 TC 460* (an early leading case on the mutuality principle but there are now special provisions for life insurance companies — see 41 LIFE INSURANCE COMPANIES). See also *Liverpool Corn Trade Association Ltd v Monks KB 1926, 10 TC 442* (trade association providing corn exchange etc. held to be trading and not 'mutual' — but see Tolley's Income Tax under Schedule D, Cases I and II for special arrangements available for trade associations); *English & Scottish Joint CWS Ltd v Assam Agricultural IT Commr PC 1948, 27 ATC 332* (wholesale co-operative with two members held to be trading and not mutual — there was no 'common fund'). A members' club does not trade and is not liable on its surplus from the provision of facilities for members (*Eccentric Club Ltd CA 1923, 12 TC 657*), but it is liable on the surplus attributable to non-members (*Carlisle & Silloth Golf Club v Smith CA 1913, 6 TC 48*). For further cases, see Tolley's Income Tax under Mutual Trading.

45.2 PAYMENTS ON LIQUIDATION ETC.

If at any time a payment made to a body corporate for the purpose of its mutual business has been allowed as a deduction in computing the profits of a trade for tax purposes, any money or money's worth received in respect of the liquidation or dissolution of that body not representing loan or other capital subscribed or income charged to tax in its hands is

(*a*) chargeable as a trading receipt of that trade if the recipient is a person, or one of the persons, carrying it on (notional discontinuances under *ICTA 1988, s 113* or *s 337(1)* being ignored), or

(*b*) chargeable on the recipient under Schedule D, Case VI for the year of assessment in which it is received if, though he is not then carrying on the trade, he was the person or one of the persons carrying it on at the time the original payment was made.

In the latter case, the amount chargeable is treated as earned income if the profits of the trade were so treated, while if the trade has been permanently discontinued before the sum is received deduction is made therefrom of expenses or losses (other than those arising from the discontinuance) which would have been allowed to the person carrying on the trade if it had not ceased, and any unused balance of his CAPITAL ALLOWANCES (8) down to the date of discontinuance. These provisions do not apply where the original payment was made to a registered industrial and provident society. [*ICTA 1988, s 491*].

These provisions apply only to *companies* and *incorporated societies* carrying on a trade. Professional societies, trade protection societies etc. do not usually engage in trading and so will normally be exempt on surpluses from members.

45.3 CREDIT UNIONS

In making loans to its members or placing its surplus funds on deposit, a credit union (within *Industrial and Provident Societies Act 1965* or *Credit Unions (Northern Ireland) Order 1985*) is not regarded as trading and interest received on the former is not chargeable to tax. Other income is liable to corporation tax. Share or loan interest etc. paid by a credit union is disregarded for corporation tax purposes. For accounting periods ending after 31 March 1996, references to interest received or paid are replaced by references to credits or debits brought into account in respect of loan relationships, to similar effect. [*ICTA 1988, s 487; FA 1996, Sch 14 para 31*].

45.4 MUTUAL LIFE ASSURANCE COMPANIES

Payments made to persons participating in the mutual activities of a company carrying on mutual life assurance business are not treated as DISTRIBUTIONS (20). [*ICTA 1988, s 490(2)*]. See 41 LIFE INSURANCE COMPANIES.

46 Oil Companies

Simon's Direct Tax Service D4.10.

46.1 The general provisions of the Taxes Acts apply to oil companies with modifications by the *Oil Taxation Acts 1975* and *1983*; *Petroleum Revenue Tax Act 1980*; *Advance Petroleum Revenue Tax Act 1986*; and annual *Finance Acts.*

46.2 PETROLEUM REVENUE TAX

This tax (PRT) is imposed on profits (based on total receipts (subject to seasonal supply adjustments) less specified deductions) from winning oil (including gas sold to British Gas) in the UK, the territorial seas and the continental shelf (see 53.9 RESIDENCE).

The tax is charged on the computed profits of half-yearly periods ending 30 June and 31 December and commencing with the first of those periods in which specified initial production is attained. Tax is payable six months after the end of each period, or 30 days after the issue of the notice of assessment, if later. For timing of assessments to PRT, see *Amoco (UK) Exploration Co v CIR Ch D 1983, 57 TC 147.* A payment on account of tax is due without assessment at the time for submission of a return, two months after the end of the period. Certain reliefs apply to help marginal fields.

The rate of tax for chargeable periods ending after 30 June 1993 is 50% (previously 75%). [*OTA 1975, s 1(2); FA 1982, s 132; FA 1993, s 186(1)*].

Transfer of a share of oil won out of an oil field from one 'participator' oil company to another will generally be disregarded where the obligations connected with the oil field, as regards that share, remain with the transferor company. Companies involved in certain agreements with the British National Oil Corporation will thus be liable to PRT on their profits from oil passed to BNOC. [*OTA 1975, Pt I; FA 1980, s 106, Sch 17; FA 1995, s 148*].

PRT is abolished for oil and gas fields given development consent after 15 March 1993. [*FA 1993, s 185*].

46.3 SPECIAL CORPORATION TAX PROVISIONS

Provisions apply to treat the activities of each 'field' as a separate trade and a 'ring fence' excludes the set-off of external losses, etc. except the net final loss of another field. [*ICTA 1988, s 492*]. Special provisions impose market valuation of oil disposed of or appropriated in certain circumstances. [*ICTA 1988, s 493*]. Losses from the oil activities may, however, be carried forward and set against trading income of subsequent accounting periods from activities which, apart from the 'ring fence' provisions, would form part of the same trade. [*ICTA 1988, s 492(4)*]. Similarly, where a company's non-oil activities give rise to an excess of charges on income over profits, the charges available for surrender by group relief may be calculated ignoring the oil activities. If, however, there is an excess of charges over profits for the oil activities, the normal rules apply to allow the overall excess of charges to be surrendered. The gross profits of the surrendering company against which charges (and certain other items) must first be set do not include certain ring fence profits. Non-ring fence loan relationship debits are treated as non-trading debits (see 43.3 LOAN RELATIONSHIPS). [*ICTA 1988, ss 494, 494A; FA 1996, Sch 14 para 32; FA 1998, Sch 5 para 30, Sch 27 Pt III(4)*]. There are also provisions restricting the set-off of lease payments under sale and leaseback transactions where the sale takes place after 8 March 1999. The finance charge element of such payments can be set against ring fence profits only to the extent that the finance raised is used for oil extraction activities or in purchasing certain oil rights. [*ICTA 1988, s 494AA; FA 1999, s 100*]. The aggregate gains and losses on certain disposals are also brought within the ring fence, as is any charge under *TCGA 1992, s 178(3)* in respect of an asset acquired on such a disposal. An aggregate loss on such disposals may, however, on election be treated as a non-ring fence loss. [*ICTA 1988, ss 492, 494, 497, 502(1)*]. The ring fence rules also apply to prevent rollover of gains on certain disposals other than into assets used only for the ring fence trade (which assets are conclusively presumed to be depreciating assets for this purpose). [*TCGA 1992, s 198*].

There are special provisions relating to disposals of oil licences relating to undeveloped areas [*TCGA 1992, ss 194–196; FA 1996, s 181*] and preventing double allowances being given for research and development expenditure in relation to disposals of oil licences. [*CAA 1990, ss 138A, 138B; FA 1996, s 180*].

Intangible costs of drilling the second and subsequent production wells in an area are not allowable where they were incurred after 25 November 1996 (unless incurred before 26 November 1997 under a contract entered into before 26 November 1996 and not varied on or after that date to increase such costs). Such costs will attract mineral extraction capital allowances ('MEAs', see Tolley's Income Tax under Capital Allowances (Mines, Oil Wells)). Similarly, in relation to claims made after 25 November 1996, MEAs are denied in cases where oil licences are transferred, and the purchaser would otherwise obtain allowances for expenditure which had already been allowed in full to the seller. [*ICTA 1988, s 91C; CAA 1990, s 115(2A); FA 1997, s 66*].

For ownership for capital allowance purposes of certain assets transferred under oil production sharing contracts to the government or representative of the production territory, see *CAA 1990, s 64A* (introduced by *FA 2000, s 81*).

A provision by a company for anticipated future expenditure on the completion of North Sea exploitation, in dismantling installations used and (as required under its licence) in 'cleaning up' the sea bed, was disallowed as capital when incurred in *RTZ Oil & Gas Ltd v Elliss Ch D 1987, 61 TC 132*. Companies may, however, elect for 100% capital allowances in respect of net expenditure incurred on demolition of offshore machinery and plant as part of the closing down of a field under an abandonment programme within *Petroleum Act 1987, Pt I*. Such expenditure incurred after cessation of the ring fence trade but within three years may be allowed in the final accounting period of that trade. Where a charge to corporation tax arises as a result of a PRT repayment attributable to the carry-back of losses, the repayment will be treated as chargeable for the accounting period in which ends the PRT period in which the loss accrued, rather than (as previously) for the accounting period for which the deduction was originally given. There is, however, a cap on the PRT repayment interest which may arise where losses are carried back to earlier periods. [*FA 1990, ss 60, 62, 121*].

Relief for expenditure on abandonment guarantees, and for certain other abandonment expenditure, is allowed as a deduction in computing ring fence income. [*FA 1991, ss 62–65*].

PRT is deductible in computing profits for corporation tax purposes. [*ICTA 1988, s 500*]. An agreed amount is repayable whether or not the relevant corporation tax assessment has been made (or loss agreed) (*Elliss v ICI Petroleum Ltd Ch D 1983, 57 TC 176*). For accounting periods beginning before 6 April 1999, there is a limited right to carry back surrendered ACT where the subsidiary to which it is surrendered itself carries on oil activities. [*ICTA 1988, s 498; FA 1998, Sch 3 para 30*]. ACT may also (prior to its abolition) in certain circumstances be surrendered to (but not carried back by) a company carrying on oil activities and owned by a two member consortium (with equal shares) as if it were a subsidiary of each of those companies. [*ICTA 1988, s 499; FA 1998, Sch 3 para 31*].

Certain restrictions apply on the availability of indexation allowance on disposal of oil-related assets. [*TCGA 1992, s 200, Sch 3 para 7*]. *TCGA 1992, s 200* ceases to have effect for disposals on or after 30 November 1993. [*FA 1994, s 93(7)*].

See 23.40 EXCHANGE GAINS AND LOSSES for special provisions applicable to petroleum extraction activities.

46.4 **Advance corporation tax ('ACT').** For accounting periods beginning before 6 April 1999, ACT paid on distributions to an associated company (as defined) or under certain substitution arrangements is restricted in its application, as is advance corporation tax on certain redeemable preference shares. [*ICTA 1988, ss 497, 502(4); FA 1991, s 66; FA 1998, Sch 3 para 29*]. ACT is abolished after 5 April 1999 (see 3.1 ADVANCE CORPORATION TAX).

46.5 **Anti-avoidance.** The provisions of *ICTA 1988, s 770* (trading transactions at other than market price) are modified in regard to 'transfer-pricing'. [*ICTA 1988, s 771*].

46.6 **Losses.** Special provisions apply to losses incurred before 31 December 1972. In general, such losses

(*a*) **may not** be carried forward against income from the activities treated as a separate trade under *ICTA 1988, s 492* unless they were incurred in such activities,

(*b*) **may** be carried forward against income of the same trade (other than a trade falling within (*a*) above) to the extent of

(i) such trading income arising between 1 January 1973 and 11 July 1974 and

(ii) £50 million,

whichever is the greater.

[*F(No 2)A 1975, s 43*].

47 Partnerships

Cross-reference. See also 23.30 EXCHANGE GAINS AND LOSSES, 25.19 FINANCIAL INSTRUMENTS, 43.9 LOAN RELATIONSHIPS, 44.16, 44.24 LOSSES.

Simon's Direct Tax Service D4.8.

47.1 A partnership cannot be a company (see *ICTA 1988, s 832(1)*), but a company can be a member of a partnership, in which case the tax effects are as set out below.

47.2 ASSESSMENTS

Where one of the persons carrying on a trade, profession or business in partnership is a company, the partnership profits excluding chargeable gains are computed as for corporation tax purposes and by reference to ACCOUNTING PERIODS (2), but ignoring distributions, charges on income, capital allowances, balancing charges, losses brought forward or carried back and pre-trading expenditure. The *company* is chargeable to corporation tax as if its apportioned share of profits, and of each of the items specified above, arose from a trade, etc. it carried on alone in the accounting period or periods comprising the partnership accounting period (with any necessary apportionment between such periods). All computations are to be made without regard to any change in the partners. For 1996/97 and earlier years as regards partnership trades, etc. commenced before 6 April 1994, the profits (computed as above) apportionable to *individual* partners are assessed to income tax as if they were those of a normal partnership of individuals, capital allowances and charges on income for the accounting period being treated as for the years of assessment in which that period falls, with apportionment where necessary. But, regardless of any difference between the partners' interests in the year of assessment and those in the accounting period of the partnership on the profits of which the income tax computation for that year is based, the total assessed on the *individual* partners for any year of assessment for which those profits form the basis cannot be less than the amount of the total profits of the basis period, reduced by the company's share, as above. For 1994/95 and subsequent years as regards partnership trades, etc. commenced (or treated as commenced) after 5 April 1994, and for 1997/98 and subsequent years as regards those commenced on or before that date, individual partners are charged to tax in respect of their profit shares and given relief for losses in the same way as if all the partners were individuals. [*ICTA 1988, ss 111, 114, 115; FA 1994, s 215(2)–(5); FA 1995, s 117(2), Sch 29 Pt VIII(15)*].

Where the control and management of the partnership business is situated abroad, any UK resident company partner is assessable as if the partnership were resident in the UK. [*ICTA 1988, ss 114(1), 115(4); FA 1995, s 125*].

For accounting periods ending **on or after 1 July 1999**, a system of corporation tax self-assessment is introduced (see 55 SELF-ASSESSMENT), operating alongside the income tax self-assessment system applicable to partnerships. The company tax return of a company in a partnership will accordingly be required to include details from the partnership return (for which see Tolley's Income Tax).

Simon's Direct Tax Service. See **D4.802** *et seq.*.

47.3 *Example*

X Ltd and Mr Brown have been in partnership for many years and share profits in the ratio 2:1. The partnership's trading results for the six years ended 30 September 1999 are as follows.

47.3 Partnerships

	Trading profits	Capital allowances
	£	£
1994	42,000	3,000
1995	33,000	9,000
1996	36,000	6,000
1997	39,000	12,000
1998	51,000	15,000
1999	45,000	18,000

X Ltd's chargeable profits in respect of the partnership are as follows.

Year ended 30.9.96

	£
Trading profits	24,000
Deduct Capital allowances	4,000
Schedule D, Case I	£20,000

Year ended 30.9.97

	£
Trading profits	26,000
Deduct Capital allowances	8,000
Schedule D, Case I	£18,000

Year ended 30.9.98

	£
Trading profits	34,000
Deduct Capital allowances	10,000
Schedule D, Case I	£24,000

Year ended 30.9.99

	£
Trading profits	30,000
Deduct Capital allowances	12,000
Schedule D, Case I	£18,000

Mr Brown will have the following assessments and allowances based on the above results.

	Basis of assessment	Profit	Capital allowances
		£	£
1995/96 Profits	y/e 30.9.94	14,000	
Capital allowances $\frac{6}{12} \times$ £3,000 + $\frac{6}{12} \times$ £2,000	actual		2,500
1996/97 Profits	$\frac{1}{2} \times$ (y/e 30.9.95 + y/e 30.9.96)	11,500	
Capital allowances $\frac{6}{12} \times$ £2,000 + $\frac{6}{12} \times$ £4,000	actual		3,000
1997/98 Profits (Transitional overlap relief $\frac{6}{12} \times$ £9,000 = £4,500)	y/e 30.9.97	9,000	

	Basis of assessment	Profit	Capital allowances
		£	£
1998/99 Profits	y/e 30.9.98	12,000	
1999/2000 Profits	y/e 30.9.99	9,000	

Notes

(*a*) Mr Brown's profits for 1996/97 are calculated under the transitional rules on the introduction of the current year basis of assessment.

(*b*) For 1997/98 onwards, capital allowances are a deduction in arriving at profits for both income and corporation taxes.

(*c*) Transitional overlap relief for 1997/98 is computed by reference to profit *after* capital allowances. This applies only where the individual is in partnership with a company and compensates for the fact that a proportion of capital allowances is doubly relieved (in 1996/97 and 1997/98).

47.4 INTEREST PAID

Yearly interest of money chargeable to tax under Schedule D, Case III (as it applies for income tax purposes) and paid by a partnership of which a company is a member must be paid under deduction of income tax at the lower rate (before 1996/97, the basic rate) in force for the year in which the payment is made. [*ICTA 1988, s 349(2); FA 1996, Sch 14 para 18*].

47.5 CHANGES IN PARTNERSHIP

On a partnership change, the cessation and commencement provisions under *ICTA 1988, s 113(1)* apply only if an *individual* begins or ceases to be a partner (and in such a case an election for the continuation basis may be made only if there is at least one continuing individual, notice under *section 113(2)* requiring signature by the *individual* partners before and after the change). For 1994/95 and subsequent years as regards partnership trades, etc. commenced (or treated as commenced) after 5 April 1994, and for 1997/98 and subsequent years as regards those commenced on or before that date, a partnership trade, etc. is *not* treated as discontinued and recommenced on a change of partner (where there is at least one continuing partner). [*ICTA 1988, ss 113, 114; FA 1994, s 215(2)–(5), s 216(1)(2)*].

The trade is treated as transferred from a company ceasing to be a partner to a company then becoming a partner. [*ICTA 1988, s 114(1)(c)*].

47.6 PARTNERSHIP LIABILITIES

Partnership liabilities include the whole of the income tax liability of the individual partners, notwithstanding that a company partner's profit share is liable only to corporation tax. Furthermore, individual partners are not obliged to give credit for personal allowances etc., provided that the Revenue issues the partnership assessment on that basis. (*Barber v Eppell, QB 24 February 1981.*)

47.7 LIMITED PARTNERSHIPS [*ICTA 1988, ss 117, 118; FA 1998, Sch 5 para 35*]

Where a company which is a 'limited partner' in a partnership sustains a loss or incurs capital expenditure in the partnership trade, or pays a charge in connection with it, relief may be restricted.

A '*limited partner*' is a partner carrying on a trade

(*a*) as a limited partner in a limited partnership registered under the *Limited Partnerships Act 1907*, or

(*b*) as a general partner in a partnership, but who is not entitled to take part in the management of the trade, and who is entitled to have his liabilities for debts or obligations incurred for the trade discharged or reimbursed by some other person, in whole or beyond a certain limit, or

(*c*) who, under the law of any territory outside the UK, is not entitled to take part in the management of the trade, and is not liable beyond a certain limit for debts or obligations incurred for the trade.

The restriction applies to any excess of the loss, etc. in respect of the trade during an accounting period of the partner company over the company's 'contribution' to the trade at the end of that accounting period (or at the time the company ceased to carry on the trade if it did so during that accounting period). That excess may not be relieved under

(i) *ICTA 1988, s 393(2)* or *s 393A(1)* (see 44.2 LOSSES),

(ii) *CAA 1990, s 145* (see 8.2 CAPITAL ALLOWANCES),

(iii) *ICTA 1988, s 338* (see 50.3 PROFIT COMPUTATIONS), or

(iv) *ICTA 1988, s 403* (see 29.18 GROUPS OF COMPANIES),

other than against profits arising from the trade.

A further restriction applies where relief has previously been given under any of the provisions at (i)–(iv) above to the company (or to any other company) for a loss, etc. of the partner company in the partnership trade in any accounting period at any time during which the partner company carried on the trade as a limited company. Relief for the loss, etc. for the accounting period in question is restricted by the excess of the sum of the loss, etc. for that accounting period and the earlier amounts so relieved, over the 'contribution'.

The company's '*contribution*' to the trade at any time is the aggregate of

(A) capital contributed and not directly or indirectly withdrawn (excluding any the company is or may be entitled to withdraw at any time it carries on the trade as a limited partner, or which it is or may be entitled to require another person to reimburse to it), and

(B) any profits of the trade to which the company is entitled but which it has not received in money or money's worth.

48 Payment of Tax

Cross-references. See 3 ADVANCE CORPORATION TAX; 31 INCOME TAX IN RELATION TO A COMPANY; 39 INTEREST ON UNPAID TAX; 46 OIL COMPANIES; 53.4 RESIDENCE.

48.1 ACCOUNTING PERIODS ENDING AFTER 30 SEPTEMBER 1993

Pre-self-assessment. For accounting periods ending **before 1 July 1999**, corporation tax is due and payable without assessment on the day following the expiry of nine months from the end of the period. The amount shown in the return for the period under *TMA 1970, s 11* (see 54.2 RETURNS) as the corporation tax due for the period is treated for collection purposes as tax charged and due and payable under an assessment on the company.

If the company subsequently has grounds for believing that a change in circumstances has rendered that payment excessive, it may, by notice to the inspector stating the grounds and the amount it considers should be repaid, claim repayment of the excess. Such notice may not be given before the date on which the tax became (or would have become) due and payable, as above, or after an assessment for the period has become final (although in practice the Revenue will not resist a claim made before the due date, see Revenue Tax Bulletin February 1993 p 52). If the company wishes to claim repayment at a time when an assessment for the period is under appeal, the company must apply to the Appeal Commissioners for a determination of the amount to be repaid pending determination of the appeal. Such an application may be combined with an application for postponement under *TMA 1970, s 55* (see 48.3 below). [*ICTA 1988, s 10; FA 1990, s 106*].

The liability to pay corporation tax does not depend on any prior action by the Revenue. Nevertheless, payslips are issued to all companies believed to be potentially liable to corporation tax (other than companies known or believed to be dormant) about three months after the end of the accounting period, with the notice requiring a return to be made, and, where appropriate, with reminders about a month before the due date and again about a month after that date. Interest is charged on tax paid after the due date without waiting for the final liability to be established. (Revenue Tax Bulletin February 1993 p 51).

Self-assessment. For accounting periods ending **on or after 1 July 1999** [*SI 1998 No 3173*], and subject to the instalment provisions described below, *section 10* is repealed and replaced by a new *TMA 1970, s 59D*. Corporation tax continues to be due and payable on the day following the expiry of nine months from the end of the accounting period, on the basis of the amount computed in the company tax return for the period (see 55.5 SELF-ASSESSMENT). Any excess over the tax payable of 'relevant amounts' stated in the company tax return is repaid. '*Relevant amounts*' are corporation tax paid and not repaid, corporation tax refunds surrendered to the company intra-group (see 29.33 GROUPS OF COMPANIES), certain income tax suffered and CONSTRUCTION INDUSTRY TAX SCHEME (17) deductions. [*TMA 1970, s 59D; FA 1994, Sch 26 Pt V(23); FA 1998, Sch 19 para 29*]. A company may claim repayment of corporation tax paid for an accounting period where the company's circumstances change so that it has grounds for believing that the amount paid exceeds its probable (although not yet finally established) liability. No claim may be made before the 'material date' in relation to the tax (see 38.1 INTEREST ON OVERPAID TAX). If the tax is the subject of an outstanding appeal, the company may apply to the Commissioners for a determination of the amount to be repaid (and the application may be combined with a postponement application under *TMA 1970, s 55*, see 48.3 below). If the company tax return (see 55.3 SELF-ASSESSMENT) has not been made, CONSTRUCTION INDUSTRY TAX SCHEME (17) deductions are ignored for these purposes. [*TMA 1970, s 59DA; FA 1998, Sch 19 para 29(2)*]. 'Large' companies to which instalment payments apply are precluded from making a claim under *section 59DA* where a claim for repayment of instalment payments is made (see below). [*SI 1998 No 3175, reg 6(8)*].

Instalment payments. For accounting periods ending **on or after 1 July 1999** [*SI 1998 No 3173*], a system of quarterly accounting for corporation tax is phased in for 'large companies'. [*TMA 1970, s 59E; SI 1998 No 3175*]. Corporation tax for this purpose includes any liability under *ICTA 1988, s 419* (loans to participators, see 13.9 CLOSE COMPANIES) or *s 747(4)(a)* (amounts apportioned in respect of controlled foreign companies, see 18.7 CONTROLLED FOREIGN COMPANIES).

The self-assessment company tax return (see 55.3 SELF-ASSESSMENT) requires the company to state whether it is liable to make instalment payments on account of its corporation tax liabilities. Although the Revenue will at some stage check the position, initial payment applications, interest calculations, etc. will be based on the company's statement of its position. (Revenue Booklet 'A Guide to Corporation Tax Self Assessment', para 12.10.6).

Large companies. A '*large company*', subject to the exclusions described below, is a company whose profits in any accounting period exceed the small companies rate upper relief limit (the 'upper relevant maximum amount') in force at the end of the accounting period (see 56.2 SMALL COMPANIES—REDUCED RATES). This is currently £1,500,000 divided by one plus the number of 'associated companies' (if any) at any time in the period (see 56.7 SMALL COMPANIES—REDUCED RATES), proportionately reduced for periods of less than twelve months. Certain adjustments made in the case of insurance companies (see 41.7 LIFE INSURANCE COMPANIES) are, however, disregarded. A company is *not* large as respects an accounting period for which:

(*a*) its total corporation tax liability, reduced by any deductions under the CONSTRUCTION INDUSTRY TAX SCHEME (17) from payments in the period, does not exceed £10,000 (£5,000 in relation to accounting periods ending before 1 July 2000), proportionately reduced for accounting periods of less than twelve months; or

(*b*) its profits do not exceed £10,000,000, provided that it was not a large company (disregarding the £10,000,000 exclusion) in the twelve months preceding the period.

As regards (*b*) above, the £10,000,000 limit is reduced in the same proportion as the upper relevant maximum amount for short accounting periods or where there are associated companies (see 56.2, 56.7 SMALL COMPANIES—REDUCED RATES), except that the number of associated companies required to be taken into account is determined as at the end of the immediately preceding accounting period, or at the commencement of the accounting period concerned if there was no immediately preceding accounting period or there was a gap between the two accounting periods. Also as regards (*b*) above, a company is treated as not having been large in the twelve months preceding the period in question where either

(i) during any part of the twelve months it did not exist or did not have an accounting period, or

(ii) an accounting period during which it was not a large company (other than by virtue of (*b*) above) either falls within or ends in the twelve months.

'Profits' of an accounting period for these purposes are the assessable profits on which corporation tax finally falls to be charged for the period plus FRANKED INVESTMENT INCOME (27) ('FII') of the period other than any FII received from fellow group members (and distributions are treated as coming from within the group if, but only if, dividends so received are group income or would be if the companies so elected (see 29.2–29.7 GROUPS OF COMPANIES)).

[*SI 1998 No 3175, regs 2(2)(3), 3; SI 2000 No 892*].

Instalments. Subject to the transitional provisions described below, amounts in respect of a large company's total corporation tax liability for an accounting period (as reduced by any deductions under the CONSTRUCTION INDUSTRY TAX SCHEME (17) from payments in the period) become due and payable in up to four instalments as follows.

(1) The first instalment is due six months and thirteen days from the start of the accounting period, and the last instalment is due three months and fourteen days from the end of the accounting period, except that if the latter date precedes the former (i.e. where the accounting period is less than three months), a single instalment equal to the total corporation tax liability is due and payable on the latter date.

(2) Where there is a gap of more than three months between the two dates referred to in (1) above (i.e. where the accounting period is longer than six months), a second instalment is due and payable three months after the first, and if the gap exceeds six months, a third instalment is due and payable three months after the second. Thus for the year ending 31 December 2002, instalments will be due on 14 July 2002, 14 October 2002, 14 January 2003 and 14 April 2003.

(3) The amount of the first instalment (other than in the case of the single instalment referred to in (1) above) is the total corporation tax liability divided by the number of months in the accounting period (including a decimal equivalent to two places of any days in excess of a whole number of months) and multiplied by three.

(4) The amount of any second or third instalment (other than the final instalment) is the smaller of the amount calculated as in (3) above and the balance remaining of the total corporation tax liability. (The latter can apply only where the estimated amount of that liability has been substantially reduced (see below) since the previous instalment.)

(5) The amount of the final instalment is the balance remaining of the total corporation tax liability.

Thus in the case of the year ending 31 December 2002 instanced at (2) above, the four instalments are each of one-quarter of the final corporation tax liability. For an accounting period of eight months ending 31 August 2002, instalments are due on 14 July 2002, 14 October 2002 and 14 December 2002, the first two being of three-eighths of the total corporation tax liability and the final one of the balance of one-quarter.

Where the company's estimate of the amount of its total corporation tax liability for the period is revised, subsequent instalment payments are recalculated accordingly, and top-up payments may be made at any time. The due and payable amount of each instalment for the purposes of interest on over- or under-payments (see below) is that based on the total corporation tax liability as returned by the company (or as determined by the inspector where the normal due date has passed).

[*SI 1998 No 3175, reg 5*].

Although the Revenue will send a reminder and payslip (Form CT608) to those companies which it appears likely will be required to make instalment payments, it is in any event the company's responsibility to make such payments if they are due. (Revenue Tax Bulletin April 1999 p 646).

A *repayment* may be claimed where the company has grounds for believing that changed circumstances since an instalment or instalments were paid has rendered its earlier calculation of its total corporation tax liability excessive, so that the aggregate amount of the instalments paid exceeds what would have been payable by the date of the claim based on the new figure for that liability. Repayment of that excess may be claimed, and the claim must state the amount to be repaid and the grounds for the company's belief that its earlier calculation was excessive. If an appeal against an assessment, or an amendment of a self-assessment, in respect of the total liability for the accounting period concerned is outstanding, the company may apply to the Commissioners for a determination of the amount to be repaid pending determination of the appeal. Such claims and applications are treated in the same way as appeals, and an application for determination of a repayment may be combined with an application for postponement of payment of tax under *TMA 1970, s 55* (see 48.3 below).

Alternatively, the provisions of *FA 1989, s 102* (surrender of tax refund within group, see 29.33 GROUPS OF COMPANIES) are applied to allow the surrender of excess instalment payments intra-group.

[*SI 1998 No 3175, regs 6, 9; SI 1999 No 1929*].

Transitional provisions. For accounting periods ending before 1 July 2002, only a proportion of the total corporation tax liability is subject to instalment payment as above, the balance being payable on the normal due date nine months and one day after the end of the accounting period. The proportion subject to instalment payment is as follows.

(A) For accounting periods ending after 30 June 1999 and before 1 July 2000, 60%.

(B) For accounting periods ending after 30 June 2000 and before 1 July 2001, 72%.

(C) For accounting periods ending after 30 June 2001 and before 1 July 2002, 88%.

[*SI 1998 No 3175, reg 4*].

Interest on unpaid instalments. Unpaid instalment payments carry interest at a special rate from the due date to the date of payment during the period until nine months after the end of the accounting period concerned (whereafter the normal interest rate provisions apply). The special rate was set initially at 8.25% p.a., whereas the rate applicable under self-assessment from the normal corporation tax due date was initially set at 8.5% (and the differential will generally vary between 1 and 1.75% from 20 April 2000). See 39.1 INTEREST ON UNPAID TAX. The special rate changes more frequently than the normal rate, and changes are announced in Revenue Press Releases. Details are as follows.

8.25% p.a. from 7 January 1999 to 17 January 1999

8.00% p.a. from 18 January 1999 to 14 February 1999

7.50% p.a. from 15 February 1999 to 18 April 1999

7.25% p.a. from 19 April 1999 to 20 June 1999

7.00% p.a. from 21 June 1999 to 19 September 1999

7.25% p.a. from 20 September 1999 to 14 November 1999

7.50% p.a. from 15 November 1999 to 23 January 2000

7.75% p.a. from 24 January 2000 to 20 February 2000

8.00% p.a. from 21 February 2000 to 19 April 2000

7.00% p.a. from 20 April 2000 to

[*TMA 1970, s 87A; SI 1989 No 1297, regs 3ZA, 3ZB; SI 1998 No 3175, reg 7; SI 1998 No 3176, regs 4–6; SI 2000 No 893*].

See example at 39.2 INTEREST ON UNPAID TAX.

Interest (and penalties) will only be calculated after the company has filed its return (or the Revenue have determined the liability in the absence of a return) *and* the normal due date (nine months and one day after the end of the accounting period) has passed. (Revenue Tax Bulletin April 1999 p 647).

Interest on overpaid instalments. Excess payments in respect of instalments carry interest at a special rate (which also applies to early payments by companies not liable to pay by instalments) from the date the excess arises (but not earlier than the due date of the first instalment) until it is extinguished (but not later than nine months after the end of the accounting period concerned, from when the normal interest rate provisions apply). The special rate was initially set at 6% p.a., whereas the rate applicable under self-assessment from the normal corporation tax due date was initially set at 5% p.a. (and the differential will vary between 0.25% and 1.25%). See 38.1 INTEREST ON OVERPAID TAX. The special rate changes more frequently than the normal rate, and changes are announced in Revenue Press Releases. Details are as follows.

6.00% p.a. from 7 January 1999 to 17 January 1999

5.75% p.a. from 18 January 1999 to 14 February 1999

5.25% p.a. from 15 February 1999 to 18 April 1999

5.00% p.a. from 19 April 1999 to 20 June 1999

4.75% p.a. from 21 June 1999 to 19 September 1999

5.00% p.a. from 20 September 1999 to 14 November 1999

5.25% p.a. from 15 November 1999 to 23 January 2000

5.50% p.a. from 24 January 2000 to 20 February 2000

5.75% p.a. from 21 February 2000 to

[*ICTA 1988, s 826; SI 1989 No 1297, regs 3BA, 3BB; SI 1998 No 3175, reg 8; SI 1998 No 3176, regs 4, 7, 8; SI 1999 No 1928*].

See example at 38.2 INTEREST ON OVERPAID TAX.

Information, etc. powers. The Revenue have powers to require the production of a wide range of information and records relating to instalment payments once the filing date for the return for the accounting period (normally twelve months after the end of the period, see 54.2 RETURNS) has passed. [*SI 1998 No 3175, regs 10–12; SI 1999 No 1929*]. The Revenue will seek to make use of these powers only where there are indications that a company may have deliberately or recklessly failed to comply with its instalment payment obligations, or fraudulently or negligently made a repayment claim (see guidance notes annexed to Revenue Press Release 8 June 1999).

Penalties. Where interest is charged on unpaid instalments as above, and the company, or a person acting on its behalf, either

(I) deliberately or recklessly failed to make an instalment payment, or

(II) fraudulently or negligently made a claim for repayment of an excess amount of instalment payments,

the company is liable to a penalty of up to twice the amount of the interest. [*SI 1998 No 3175, reg 13*]. The Revenue will seek a penalty under these provisions only in the most serious cases involving flagrant abuse of the regulations (see guidance notes annexed to Revenue Press Release 8 June 1999, also reproduced in Revenue Tax Bulletin August 1999 pp 683, 684).

Generally, penalties under *TMA 1970, s 98* apply for any failure to provide information, produce documents, etc. as required under these provisions. [*FA 1999, s 89(1)(3)*].

Anti-avoidance. A special anti-avoidance provision may apply where, in the period from 25 November 1997 to 29 June 2002, a company either

(*aa*) changes the dates of any of its accounting periods which would otherwise have been consecutive and of twelve months duration and have ended in that period, and/or (*bb*) enters into arrangements or transactions which have the effect of transferring taxable profits intra-group.

If the result is that, on various assumptions about what would have happened if the company had not done so, corporation tax on profits of any accounting period beginning after 1 July 1998 and ending before 1 July 2002 becomes payable on a later date (whether under the instalment arrangements or under the normal corporation tax payment arrangements), then an amount corresponding to interest by reference to the overall deferral of payments may become chargeable on the company. There are various exclusions depending on the timing and circumstances of the decision by the company to take the action in question.

For an example of the application of this provision, see Revenue Booklet 'A Guide to Corporation Tax Self Assessment', para 12.14.2.

[*SI 1998 No 3175, reg 14*].

Group payment arrangements. Any group of companies with instalment payment liabilities which wishes to do so may make arrangements with the Revenue to account for corporation tax relating to accounting periods ending on or after 31 December 1999 on a group basis rather than company by company (see 29.32 GROUPS OF COMPANIES). This will enable profit forecasts to be made at group level and mitigate the interest differential on over- and under-paid tax. Groups wishing to take part in such arrangements should contact the Group Payment Team at the appropriate Accounts Office (Shipley tel. 01274 539561 or Cumbernauld tel. 01236 783488). Broadly, a nominated company may contract with the Revenue to make instalment payments on behalf of group companies covered by the arrangements ('participating companies') on the due dates on the basis of the most recent forecast of group profits. Once all the participating companies have either filed their returns or had their corporation tax liabilities determined by the Revenue (the 'closing date', which cannot be earlier than the normal due date nine months after the end of the accounting period), the nominated company will be issued with a notice showing what it has paid and the liability at the closing date. It will then be invited to make good any shortfall, or allocate it to any company whose liability it has reason to believe will decrease after the closing date, and to apportion payments to the participating companies. It may allocate any surplus to participating companies or require its repayment. The arrangements need not apply to all group members, and separate arrangements may be entered into for different sub-sets within a group. Not all companies covered by the arrangements need be UK-resident, although the nominated company must be. All companies must have filed returns and paid the due tax in respect of their last but one accounting period. They must have a common accounting period (subject to special arrangements for companies joining the group and aligning their accounting date). There is provision for either the nominated company or the Revenue to remove a company from the arrangements in specified circumstances where the rules regarding eligibility to enter the arrangements would no longer be met. Any group wishing to take part in the arrangements must normally deliver its signed contract to the appropriate Accounts Office (as above) at least two months prior to the first instalment payment due date. All payments must be made by electronic funds transfer. For detailed requirements, see the relevant part of the article in Revenue Tax Bulletin April 1999, at pp 647–650, which is slightly expanded in chapter 13 of Revenue Booklet 'A Guide to Corporation Tax Self-Assessment'. The group payment arrangements document and guidance notes are available on the Revenue Internet site (see 33.1 INLAND REVENUE: ADMINISTRATION).

Insurance companies and friendly societies. Special provision is made for the interest consequences of the set-off of a provisional repayment under *ICTA 1988, Sch 19AB* (see 41.6 LIFE INSURANCE COMPANIES, 28.2 FRIENDLY SOCIETIES) against an instalment payment under the current provisions. [*SI 1998 No 3175, reg 15*].

Revenue guidance. See also Revenue Tax Bulletin April 1999 pp 645–650, February 2000 pp 723–726 and Revenue Booklets Inst 1 'A Modern System for Corporation Tax Payments — A Guide to Quarterly Instalment Payments' and 'A Guide to Corporation Tax Self Assessment'.

Example

A Ltd has the following corporation tax liabilities.

Year ended 31 December	1999	2000	2001	2002
	£'000	£'000	£'000	£'000
	2,565	2,250	1,280	1,575

The due dates and corporation tax payable are as follows.

	£
y/e 31 December 1999	
14 July 1999, 14 October 1999, 14 January 2000 and 14 April 2000	384,750
1 October 2000	1,026,000
y/e 31 December 2000	
14 July 2000, 14 October 2000, 14 January 2001 and 14 April 2001	405,000
1 October 2001	630,000
y/e 31 December 2001	
14 July 2001, 14 October 2001, 14 January 2002 and 14 April 2002	281,600
1 October 2002	153,600
y/e 31 December 2002	
14 July 2002, 14 October 2002, 14 January 2003 and 14 April 2003	393,750

Simon's Direct Tax Service. See **D2.705** *et seq.*.

48.2 ACCOUNTING PERIODS ENDING ON OR BEFORE 30 SEPTEMBER 1993

Corporation tax assessed for an accounting period ending on or before 30 September 1993 is due and payable within nine months from the end of the period or, if later, within 30 days from the date of issue of the notice of assessment. [*ICTA 1988, s 10(1)(b)*].

48.3 PAYMENT OF TAX PENDING APPEAL

Where there is an appeal against an assessment to corporation tax or income tax (but excluding ACT and income tax accountable by quarterly etc. returns, see 39.6 INTEREST ON UNPAID TAX), the full amount charged will be due and payable unless the appellant applies for payment of part of the tax assessed to be postponed. The application must in the first instance be made in writing to the inspector within 30 days after the date of the issue of the notice of assessment, stating the amount of tax believed to be overcharged (and payment of which is to be postponed), and the grounds for that belief. Application may be made outside the normal 30 day time limit if there is a change in circumstances giving grounds for belief that the appellant is overcharged. In the Revenue view, this condition requires a change in the circumstances in which the original decision not to apply for postponement was made, not just a change of mind, e.g. further accounts work indicating a substantially excessive assessment, or further reliefs becoming due. (Notes of CCAB meeting with Revenue on the

1982 Finance Bill TR 477, 22 June 1982). The appellant and an inspector may agree the amount of tax to be postponed and written confirmation of such agreement shall be treated as if the Commissioners had determined it. Failing such agreement the appeal Commissioners determine the amount, in the same way as an appeal. Any tax which is the subject of such an application and which is not postponed by agreement or by the Commissioners shall be due and payable as if charged by an assessment issued on the date of the Commissioners' determination (or of written confirmation of the agreement with the inspector) and against which no appeal is pending. If circumstances change, a further application may be made by either the appellant or the inspector giving notice to the other to vary the amount postponed. On determination of the appeal, any tax overpaid is repaid and any postponed tax then becoming collectable or not previously charged becomes due and payable as if charged under an assessment issued when the inspector issues to the appellant notice of the total amount payable. [*TMA 1970, s 55; F(No 2)A 1975, s 45; FA 1982, s 68; FA 1989, s 156(2); FA 1990, s 104(2)*]. For accounting periods ending **on or after 1 July 1999**, *section 55* is amended so as to apply equally to appeals against amendments to self-assessments (see 55.5 SELF-ASSESSMENT). [*FA 1994, Sch 19 para 18; FA 1998, Sch 19 para 28; SI 1998 No 3173*].

Simon's Direct Tax Service. See A3.1308.

48.4 **RECOVERY OF TAX FROM THIRD PARTIES**

Change in ownership of company. Where it appears to the Board that

(*a*) there has been a change in ownership of a company,

(*b*) any corporation tax assessed on the company for an accounting period beginning before the date of the change remains unpaid at any time after the '*relevant date*' (i.e. the date six months after the date of the corporation tax assessment), and

(*c*) any of the three conditions referred to below is fulfilled,

any of the following persons may be assessed and charged in the name of the company to an amount of corporation tax as below:

(i) any person who at any time during the '*relevant period*' (i.e. the period of three years before the change in ownership, but not so as to include any period before a previous change in ownership) had 'control' of the company; and

(ii) any company of which a person within (i) has at any time in the three years before the change in ownership had 'control'.

'*Control*' is as under *ICTA 1988, s 416* (see 13.2 CLOSE COMPANIES), except that 50% only (rather than 'the greater part') of the share capital, issued share capital or voting power is sufficient to give control, and where two or more persons together satisfy any of the conditions for control, control will only be imputed to each of them where they have acted together to put themselves in a position where they will in fact satisfy the condition in question.

The three alternative conditions referred to at (*c*) above are as follows.

(A) At any time during the three years before the change in ownership the activities of a trade or business of the company cease or the scale of those activities become small or negligible, and there is no significant revival of those activities before the change occurs.

(B) At any time after the change in ownership, but under arrangements made before that change, the activities of a trade or business of the company cease or the scale of those activities become small or negligible.

(C) (*a*) At any time during the six years beginning three years before the change in ownership, there is a major change in the nature or conduct of a trade or business of the company (including any change within *ICTA 1988, s 245(4)(a)–(d)* (see 3.10 ADVANCE CORPORATION TAX), and also any such change achieved gradually as the result of a series of transfers — see 44.13 LOSSES generally);

(*b*) assets of the company are transferred (including any disposal, letting or hiring of an asset, and any grant or transfer of any right, interest or licence in or over it, or the giving of any business facilities with respect to it) to a person within (i) above (or to a person connected with such a person within *ICTA 1988, s 839*), or under arrangements which enable any of those assets (or assets representing those assets) to be transferred to such a person, during the three years before the change in ownership (or after the change but under arrangements made before the change); and

(*c*) the major change in the nature or conduct of the trade or business of the company is attributable to the transfer(s) of the company's assets.

The tax charged in an assessment under these provisions must not exceed the amount of the tax which, at the time of the assessment, remains unpaid by the company, and the assessment is not out of time if made within three years of the final determination of the liability of the company for the accounting period concerned. *TMA 1970, s 87A* (see 39.1 INTEREST ON UNPAID TAX) apply in relation to tax so assessed by reference to the company's due and payable (or reckonable) date. The tax paid is not an allowable deduction for any tax purposes, but the payer is entitled to recover an amount equal to the tax (and any interest thereon under *TMA 1970, s 87A*) from the company. An amount so recovered (or received under an indemnity in this respect) is not chargeable to tax on the recipient. (Revenue Tax Bulletin April 1995 p 208).

Power to obtain information. The inspector may, by notice in writing, require any person who is the registered owner of shares, stock or securities of a company to state whether he is the beneficial owner thereof and, if not, to supply the name and address of the person(s) on whose behalf he holds them.

Rules for ascertaining change in ownership. The provisions of *ICTA 1988, s 769* (see 44.13 LOSSES) apply with appropriate modification (see *FA 1994, s 135(2)–(5)*) in relation to these provisions as they apply to *ICTA 1988, ss 768, 768A*.

[*ICTA 1988, ss 767A, 767B; FA 1994, s 135*].

For the circumstances and the manner in which the above provisions will in practice be used by the Revenue, see Revenue Tax Bulletin October 1994 pp 168, 169.

See also 9.5, 9.6, 9.46, 9.47 CAPITAL GAINS and 53.6 RESIDENCE.

Postponed corporation tax. Provisions supplementing the above deal with cases where a corporation tax liability has been postponed to a period commencing after a change in ownership. They apply to changes occurring **on or after 2 July 1997**, unless in pursuance of a contract entered into before that date. *ICTA 1988, s 769* (see 44.13 LOSSES), modified as for *ICTA 1988, s 767A* (see above), applies for determining whether there is a change in ownership of a company.

Where it appears to the Board that there has been a change in the ownership of a company (the 'transferred company'), and that any corporation tax relating to an accounting period ending on or after the change which has been assessed on that company or an 'associated' company remains unpaid at any time more than six months after it was assessed, then (subject to the further condition referred to below) any one of the persons listed below may be assessed and charged (in the name of the company in default) to an amount of corporation tax not exceeding the amount remaining unpaid. Such an assessment is not out of time if made within three years of the date of final determination of the liability of the company in default for the accounting period for which the tax was assessed. INTEREST ON UNPAID TAX (39) then runs by reference to the date of the original liability of the transferred (or 'associated') company.

A company is '*associated*' with another for these purposes if, at the time of the assessment (or at an earlier time before the change in ownership), it has control of or is controlled by the other or they are under common control. 'Control' is defined as for *ICTA 1988, s 767A* (above).

The further condition referred to above is that it would be reasonable (apart from these provisions) to infer, from either or both of the terms of any transactions entered into in connection with the change (for which see below) and the other circumstances of the change and of any such transactions, that at least one of those transactions was entered into by one or more of the parties to it on the assumption that a 'potential tax liability' would be unlikely to be met, or met in full, were it to arise.

A '*potential tax liability*' is a corporation tax liability which, in circumstances reasonably foreseeable at the time of change in ownership (or in circumstances the occurrence of which is something of which there was at that time a reasonably foreseeable risk), would or might arise from an assessment made, after the change in ownership, on the transferred company or an associated company (see above), whether or not a particular associated company.

A transaction is for these purposes entered into in connection with a change in ownership if the change is effected by the transaction (with or without other transactions) or by other transactions forming part of the same series of transactions or scheme (by whomsoever entered into). A 'scheme' is any scheme, arrangements or understanding, whether or not legally enforceable, involving one or more transactions, and the cases in which transactions form part of a scheme or series include cases in which it would be reasonable to assume that one or more of them would not have been entered into independently of the other(s), or that if entered into independently it would not have taken the same form or been on the same terms.

The persons who may be assessed and charged are any person who at any time during the 'relevant period' had control of the transferred company, and any company of which such a person has at any time had control within the period of three years before the change in ownership. The '*relevant period*' is the period of three years before the change in ownership, or if, during that three years, there was an earlier change in ownership of the transferred company, the period between those changes.

Tax paid under these provisions is not an allowable deduction for tax purposes, but the payer is entitled to recover an amount equal to the tax (and any interest thereon) from the transferred (or associated) company.

The Board has wide powers to require any person (subject to certain exclusions) to supply (within not less than 30 days) specified documents and other particulars relating to liabilities which may arise under these provisions (but excluding documents etc. relating to the conduct of any pending tax appeal).

[*ICTA 1988, ss 767AA, 767B, 767C; FA 1998, ss 114–116*].

See Simon's Direct Tax Service D2.517.

Recovery of tax payable by non-resident company. For an accounting period ending on or after 1 April 2000, where corporation tax assessed on a non-UK resident company (i.e. in respect of UK branch profits) remains in whole or part unpaid six months after the due date, the following companies may be served notice by the Revenue requiring them to pay the tax.

(1) Any company which was, at any time in the 'relevant period', a 51% subsidiary (by reference to ordinary share capital) of the non-resident company, or of which the

non-resident company was a 51% subsidiary, or where both were 51% subsidiaries of a third company.

(2) Any company which was, at any time during the 'relevant period', a member of a consortium which owned (see 29.27 GROUPS OF COMPANIES) the non-resident company at that time.

(3) Any company which was, at any time during the 'relevant period', a member of the same group (as for group relief purposes, see 29.15 GROUPS OF COMPANIES) as a company which was at that time a member of a consortium which owned (see 29.27 GROUPS OF COMPANIES) the non-resident company.

The '*relevant period*' is the period beginning twelve months before the start of the accounting period in question (or on 1 April 2000 if later) and ending when the unpaid tax first became payable.

The notice may require payment, within 30 days of service, of the unpaid tax or (in the case of a company within either or both of (2) and (3) above but not within (1) above) of an appropriate proportion thereof (see *FA 2000, Sch 28 para 5*). A payment made in pursuance of a notice is not an allowable deduction in computing profits, but the paying company may recover the amount from the non-resident company. The notice must state the amount of the unpaid tax, the date it first became payable and the amount required to be paid by the recipient. For recovery and appeals purposes, it has effect as if it were a notice of assessment of an amount of tax due from the recipient. INTEREST ON UNPAID TAX (39) runs from the original due date.

The Revenue have three years from the date on which the liability of the non-resident company is finally determined (including a determination under *FA 1998, Sch 18 para 36* or *37* in the absence of a full return, see 55.10 SELF-ASSESSMENT) in which to serve notice under these provisions. In the case of a self-assessed liability, including one superseding a determination, the date of determination of the liability is taken as the last date on which notice of an enquiry into the return may be given (see 55.7 SELF-ASSESSMENT), or, if such notice is given, 30 days after the action which concludes the enquiry process. In the case of a discovery assessment (see 55.8 SELF-ASSESSMENT), it is the due and payable date or (if there is an appeal against the assessment) the date the appeal is finally determined.

[*FA 2000, s 98, Sch 28*].

48.5 RECOVERY OF TAX FROM OFFICERS

Tax which has fallen due may be recovered from the treasurer or acting treasurer (the 'proper officer') of a company which is not a body corporate or not incorporated under a UK enactment or by charter. That officer then has a right of reimbursement out of moneys coming into his hands on behalf of that company, and to be indemnified by the company for any balance. [*TMA 1970, s 108(2)(3)*].

48.6 PARTNERSHIP LIABILITIES

See 47.6 PARTNERSHIPS.

48.7 DATE OF PAYMENT

As to the date on which tax is treated as having been paid, see 39.5 INTEREST ON UNPAID TAX.

48.8 **OVER-REPAYMENTS**

Tax over-repaid and not assessable under *TMA 1970, s 29* or *FA 1998, Sch 18 para 41* may be assessed under Schedule D, Case VI as if it were unpaid tax. Any associated excess INTEREST ON OVERPAID TAX (38) may be included in the assessment. The time limit for such assessments is extended to the end of the accounting period following that of the repayment if it would otherwise be out of time, subject to the usual fraudulent or negligent conduct provisions.

Similar provisions apply to enable excess set-offs of ACT (prior to its abolition) and excess set-offs or payments of tax credit to be recovered, including any INTEREST ON OVERPAID TAX (38) in respect of tax credits. See also 3.6 ADVANCE CORPORATION TAX.

Where the assessment is to recover a repayment of tax paid for an accounting period, or a repayment of tax on a payment received in an accounting period, the assessment is treated as being for that accounting period, and the sum assessed carries interest under *TMA 1970, s 87A* (see 39.1 INTEREST ON UNPAID TAX) from the date the repayment being recovered was made until payment.

For accounting periods ending **on or after 1 July 1999**, these provisions are amended to apply the discovery assessment rules of *FA 1998, Sch 18 paras 41–48* to recovery assessments, and to extend the period during which assessments may be made to the completion of enquiries in certain cases. See 55.13 SELF-ASSESSMENT.

[*TMA 1970, s 30; ICTA 1988, s 252; FA 1982, s 149; F(No 2)A 1987, s 88; FA 1989, s 149(3)(a); FA 1990, s 105; FA 1994, Sch 19 para 4; FA 1998, Sch 3 para 21, Sch 18 paras 52, 53, Sch 19 para 13; SI 1998 No 3173*].

Simon's Direct Tax Service. See D2.708.

49 Penalties

Cross-reference. See also 53.6 RESIDENCE and 61.5 VALUE ADDED TAX.

Simon's Direct Tax Service A3.8.

49.1 NOTIFICATION OF CHARGEABILITY

A company chargeable to corporation tax which has not already made a company tax return for an accounting period, and has not received a notice requiring such a return (see 54.2 RETURNS, 55.3 SELF-ASSESSMENT), must give notice of its chargeability to the inspector within twelve months from the end of the period.

Failure to do so in respect of an accounting period ending **on or after 1 July 1999** (i.e. under SELF-ASSESSMENT (55)) renders the company liable to a penalty not exceeding so much of the tax payable for the period as remains unpaid twelve months after the end of the period, any relief deferred under *ICTA 1988, s 419(4A)* in respect of the repayment, etc. of a loan to a participator (see 13.12 CLOSE COMPANIES) being disregarded. For accounting periods ending before 1 July 1999, the maximum penalty is the amount by which so much of the corporation tax chargeable on its profits for the period as remains unpaid twelve months after the end of the period exceeds any income tax which, under *ICTA 1988, s 7(2)* (see 31.5 INCOME TAX IN RELATION TO A COMPANY) or *ICTA 1988, s 11(3)* (see 53.4 RESIDENCE), is to be set off against the corporation tax so chargeable. For accounting periods beginning before 6 April 1999, the amount of corporation tax outstanding is determined disregarding the discharge of any liability for that tax attributable to surplus ACT carried back under *ICTA 1988, s 239(3)* (see 3.8 ADVANCE CORPORATION TAX). [*TMA 1970, s 10; FA 1988, s 121; FA 1993, Sch 14 para 1; FA 1998, Sch 3 para 2, Sch 18 para 2, Sch 19 para 1*].

See 49.6 below as regards reasonable excuse for failure.

Simon's Direct Tax Service. See A3.803.

49.2 FAILURE TO RENDER RETURN

A company which fails to make a return for any period, when required to do so by notice (see 54.2 RETURNS, 55.3 SELF-ASSESSMENT), is liable to a penalty of £200 (£100 if the return is delivered within three months of the final day for delivery). If the return period is one for which accounts are required under *Companies Act 1985* (or NI equivalent), penalties do not apply provided that the return is delivered by the last day for delivery of those accounts. The penalties are increased to £1,000 and £500 respectively for failure in relation to a return for an accounting period where a penalty under these provisions was incurred for each of the two immediately preceding accounting periods, and the company was within the charge to corporation tax for the whole of the three accounting periods. An additional penalty is imposed, where the return is still outstanding at the later of the end of the final day for delivery of the return and 18 months after the end of the return period. The additional penalty is 10% of the tax unpaid at the time the penalty arises if the return is delivered within two years after the end of the return period, otherwise 20%. The tax taken into account for this purpose, for accounting periods ending **on or after 1 July 1999** (i.e. under SELF-ASSESSMENT (55)) is the tax payable for the return period, disregarding any relief deferred under *ICTA 1988, s 419(4A)* in respect of the repayment, etc. of a loan to a participator, see 13.12 CLOSE COMPANIES. For earlier accounting periods, it is the unpaid corporation tax for the return period less any income tax which, under *ICTA 1988, s 7(2)* (see 31.5 INCOME TAX IN RELATION TO A COMPANY) or *ICTA 1988, s 11(3)* (see 53.4 RESIDENCE), is to be set off against the corporation tax so chargeable, disregarding any discharge of liability by set-off of surplus ACT (see 3.8 ADVANCE CORPORATION TAX) arising (prior to its abolition) in an accounting period ending more than two years after the end of the return period. [*TMA 1970, s 94; F(No 2) A 1987, s 83; FA 1993, Sch 14 para 6; FA 1998, Sch 3 para 5, Sch 18 paras 17, 18, 19, Sch 19 para 33, Sch 27 Pt III(28)*]. By concession, for returns with a statutory filing date no later than 30 September 1995, automatic penalties are not charged provided that the return was received within 14 days from the filing date. (Revenue Pamphlet IR 1, B45). For subsequent returns, this will apply provided that the return is received on or before the last business day within seven days following the filing date. (Revenue Pamphlet IR 1, B46).

If, exceptionally, the company is unable to produce final figures for the return by the due date, it should make estimates to the best of its ability and alert the inspector to the basis on which the estimates are made. When the company can replace the estimates with accurate figures, or becomes aware that an estimate is no longer the best estimate, the inspector should be so informed without unreasonable delay. Provided these guidelines are followed, no late filing penalty (see above) or incorrect return penalty (see 49.3 below) should be imposed, provided in the latter case that neither fraud nor negligence was involved. The inclusion in a return of unreasonable estimates, while not invalidating the return, may render the company liable to incorrect return penalties. Any extension of the time limit for making a return under *TMA 1970, s 118(2)* (see 49.6 below) must be agreed with the inspector in advance. (ICAEW Technical Release TAX 12/92, 25 June 1992).

See 49.6 below as regards reasonable excuse for failure.

Simon's Direct Tax Service. See A3.804A.

49.3 NEGLIGENCE OR FRAUD

The maximum penalty for negligently or fraudulently delivering, making, or submitting an incorrect return or claim for allowance or relief etc., or incorrect accounts, in addition to any tax actually chargeable, is the amount of tax underpaid, by reason of the incorrectness, for the accounting period(s) to which the return etc. relates.

See also 55.7 SELF-ASSESSMENT.

Accounts are deemed to have been submitted on behalf of a company unless it is shown that they were submitted without the company's consent or connivance.

[*TMA 1970, ss 95, 96, 97; FA 1989, s 163; FA 1998, Sch 18 paras 20, 89, Sch 19 paras 34, 35*].

Simon's Direct Tax Service. See A3.805.

49.4 For the position if an agent is negligent or fraudulent, see *Mankowitz v Special Commrs Ch D 1971, 46 TC 707* and cf. *Clixby v Pountney Ch D 1967, 44 TC 515*. Assisting in, or inducing, the preparation or delivery of any information, return, accounts or other document known to be incorrect and to be, or to be likely to be, used for any tax purpose carries a maximum penalty of £3,000. [*TMA 1970, s 99; FA 1989, s 166*]. See also 49.11 below.

49.5 OTHER RETURNS ETC.

Failure to render any return, certificate, statement or other document required under the provisions listed in the Table in *TMA 1970, s 98* carries a maximum penalty of £300, plus £60 for each day the failure continues after that penalty is imposed (but not for any day for which such a daily penalty has already been imposed).

The maximum penalty for fraudulently or negligently making an incorrect return, etc. under any of these provisions is £3,000.

Penalties for failure to render information etc. required by notice cannot be imposed after the failure is rectified, and daily penalties can similarly not be imposed where the information etc. was required other than by notice. [*TMA 1970, s 98; FA 1989, s 164*].

Special penalties are imposed by regulation in relation to failure to make a return in accordance with provisions under the PAYE and CONSTRUCTION INDUSTRY TAX SCHEME (17) regulations. [*TMA 1970, s 98A; FA 1989, s 165*].

See 50.12 PROFIT COMPUTATIONS as regards penalties under *TMA 1970, s 98B* in relation to European Economic Interest Groupings.

Failure to allow access to computer records renders a person liable to a £500 penalty. [*FA 1988, s 127*].

For unlawfully possessing or disposing of an exemption certificate relating to a sub-contractor in the construction industry, or making false statements relating thereto, the maximum penalty is £3,000 (a maximum fine of £5,000 applying before 1 August 1999). [*ICTA 1988, s 561(10)(11); FA 1995, Sch 27 para 3*].

See 49.6 below as regards reasonable excuse for failure.

For accounting periods ending **on or after 1 July 1999** (see *SI 1998 No 3173*), penalties apply:

(*a*) of up to £3,000 under *FA 1998, Sch 18 para 23* for failure to keep records as required under *FA 1998, Sch 18 para 21* (see 55.6 SELF-ASSESSMENT); and

(*b*) of £50, plus a daily fine of up to £150 for continuing failure, under *FA 1998, Sch 18 para 29* for failure to provide documents as required under *FA 1998, Sch 18 para 27* (see 55.7 SELF-ASSESSMENT).

49.6 REASONABLE EXCUSE FOR FAILURE

It is generally provided that a person is deemed not to have failed to do anything required to be done where there was a reasonable excuse for the failure and, if the reasonable excuse ceased, provided that the failure was remedied without unreasonable delay after the excuse had ceased. Similarly, a person is deemed not to have failed to do anything required to be done within a limited time if he did it within such further time as the Board, or the Commissioners or officer concerned, may have allowed. [*TMA 1970, s 118(2); F(No 2)A 1987, s 94*]. In *Creedplan Ltd v Winter (Sp C 54), [1995] SSCD 352*, the Special Commissioner, in confirming a penalty under *TMA 1970, s 94(1)(a)* (see 49.2 above), considered that 'there is no reasonable excuse . . . for sending in a return which was less than was required' (but cf. *Akarimsons Ltd v Chapman (Sp C 116), [1997] SSCD 140* in which a penalty under *section 94(1)(b)* was quashed). See also *Steeden v Carver (Sp C 212), [1999] SSCD 283*, in which reliance on the Revenue's advice as to the practical extension of a deadline, unequivocally given, was held to be 'as reasonable an excuse as could be found'.

See Revenue Company Taxation Manual, CT 10412 for the Revenue approach to 'reasonable excuse'.

49.7 COMMISSIONERS' PRECEPTS

Summary penalties in accordance with *TMA 1970, s 98* (see 49.5 above) may be determined by Commissioners against an appellant who fails to comply with a precept, order for inspection, or other request for evidence. [*TMA 1970, ss 51, 53; FA 1989, s 168(3)*]. If a person refuses or neglects to obey a witness summons; appears but refuses to be sworn; or refuses to answer any lawful question concerning the matters under consideration, the maximum penalty is £50 (with no provision for a continuing penalty). A person who is confidentially employed in the taxpayer's affairs (e.g. his servant or agent) has the right to refuse to be sworn or to answer any question to which he objects. [*TMA 1970, s 52*]. For appeals against summary penalties, see *QT Discount Foodstores Ltd v Warley Commrs Ch D 1981, 57 TC 268.*

49.8 **PROCEDURE**

Except in the case of

(*a*) penalty proceedings instituted before the courts in cases of suspected fraud (see below),

(*b*) penalties imposed for failure to comply with Commissioners' precepts (see 49.7 above),

(*c*) penalties under

- (i) *TMA 1970, s 93(1)(a)*,
- (ii) *TMA 1970, s 94(1)* before the substitution by *F(No 2)A 1987, s 83* (see 49.2 above),
- (iii) *TMA 1970, s 98(1)(i)* (see 49.5 above),
- (iv) *TMA 1970, s 98A(2)(a)(i)* (see 49.5 above), or
- (v) *TMA 1970, s 98B(2)(a)* (see 49.5 above),

(for which see further below),

an authorised officer of the Board may make a determination imposing a penalty of an amount which he considers correct or appropriate.

The notice of determination must state the date of issue and the time within which an appeal can be made. It cannot be altered unless

(i) there is an appeal (see below), or

(ii) an authorised officer discovers that the penalty is or has become insufficient (in which case he may make a further determination), or

(iii) the penalty arises under *TMA 1970, s 94(6)* or *FA 1998, Sch 18 para 18(2)* (see 49.2 above), and an authorised officer subsequently discovers that the amount of tax is or has become excessive (in which case it is to be revised accordingly).

A penalty under these provisions is due 30 days after the date of issue of the notice of determination, and is treated as tax charged under an assessment and due and payable. [*TMA 1970, ss 100, 100A; FA 1989, s 167; FA 1998, Sch 19 para 38*].

Appeals. The general appeals provisions (see ASSESSMENTS AND APPEALS (5)) apply to an appeal against a determination as if it were an appeal against an assessment to tax, and the Commissioners are given broad specific powers to confirm, set aside or amend determinations.

Without prejudice to the general procedural rules in *TMA 1970, s 56*, an appeal against a determination lies to the High Court (in Scotland, the Court of Session). [*TMA 1970, s 100B; FA 1989, s 167*].

Proceedings before Commissioners. For a penalty within (*c*)(i)–(v) above, an authorised officer may commence proceedings before the General or Special Commissioners. The proceedings are by way of information in writing to the Commissioners, and upon summons issued by them to the defendant (or defender), and are heard and decided in a summary way. An appeal lies to the High Court (or Court of Session) on a question of law or, by the defendant (defender), against the amount. The court can confirm, set aside or vary the determination as seems appropriate. The penalty is treated as tax charged in an assessment and due and payable. [*TMA 1970, s 100C; FA 1989, s 167*].

Proceedings before court. If the Board consider that liability arises from fraud by any person, proceedings can be brought in the High Court (or Court of Session). If the Court does not find fraud proved, it can nevertheless impose a penalty to which it considers the person liable. [*TMA 1970, s 100D; FA 1989, s 167*].

General matters. Non-receipt of notice of the hearing at which the Commissioners awarded penalties is not a ground of appeal to the courts. A mere denial of liability to penalties implies an intention by the taxpayer to set up a case in refutation, and details must be supplied.

Statements made or documents produced by or on behalf of a company are admissible evidence in proceedings against it, notwithstanding that reliance on the Board's practice in cases of full disclosure may have induced it to make or produce them. [*TMA 1970, s 105; FA 1989, s 168(5)*].

For relevant cases, see Tolley's Income Tax and/or Tolley's Tax Cases.

Simon's Direct Tax Service. See **A3.807** *et seq.*.

49.9 MITIGATION OR LIMITATION OF PENALTIES

The Board may mitigate penalties before or after judgment [*TMA 1970, s 102; FA 1989, s 168(4)*], and in doing so they will give credit for co-operation by the company. (Revenue Press Release 1 August 1977). See Tolley's Tax Cases generally.

Where two or more tax-geared penalties relate to the same liability, the aggregate amount of the penalties is limited to the greater or greatest penalty applicable. [*TMA 1970, s 97A; FA 1988, s 129; FA 1998, Sch 18 para 90, Sch 19 para 37*]. For an example of this under self-assessment, see Revenue Booklet 'A Guide to Corporation Tax Self Assessment', para 10.8.1.

Negotiated settlements. In the case of tax-based penalties where a maximum penalty of 100% is in strict law exigible, the inspector will start with the figure of 100% and then take the following factors into account in arriving at the penalty element which he will expect to be included in any offer in settlement of liabilities.

(*a*) Disclosure. A reduction of up to 20% (or 30% where there has been full voluntary disclosure), depending on how much information was provided, how soon, and how that contributed to settling the investigation.

(*b*) Co-operation. A reduction of up to 40%, depending upon a comparison of the extent of co-operation given in the investigation with the co-operation which the inspector believes would have been possible.

(*c*) Gravity. A reduction of up to 40%, depending upon the nature of the offence, how long it continued and the amounts involved.

(Revenue Pamphlet IR 73).

Simon's Direct Tax Service. See **A3.813.**

49.10 **TIME LIMITS**

The time within which a penalty can be determined, or proceedings commenced, depends on the penalty, as follows.

(*a*) If the penalty is ascertainable by reference to tax payable, the time is the later of six years after the penalty was incurred and three years after the determination of the amount of the tax.

(*b*) If the penalty arises under *TMA 1970, s 99* (see 49.4 above), the time is 20 years after the date when it was incurred.

(*c*) In any other case, the time is six years from the time when the penalty was, or began to be, incurred.

[*TMA 1970, s 103; FA 1989, s 169*].

Final determination of tax. Provisional agreement of the amount due subject to the inspector's being satisfied with statements of assets, etc. is not final determination for these purposes (*Carco Accessories Ltd v CIR CS 1985, 59 TC 45*).

Simon's Direct Tax Service. See **A3.810.**

49.11 **FAILURE TO STATE TAX CREDIT ETC.**

Failure to provide the required written statement of the amount of dividend or interest paid and the amount of the related tax credit etc. (see 20.18 DISTRIBUTIONS) carries a penalty of £60 for each offence with a maximum of £600 in respect of any one distribution etc.. [*ICTA 1988, ss 234(4), 234A(9); FA 1989, s 170(2); F(No 2)A 1992, s 32(1)*].

49.12 **LIABILITY UNDER CRIMINAL LAW**

'False statements to the prejudice of the Crown and public revenue' are criminal offences. (*R v Hudson CCA 1956, 36 TC 561*).

Apart from the above, false statements in income tax returns, or for obtaining any allowance, reduction or repayment may involve liability to imprisonment for up to two years, under the *Perjury Act 1911, s 5*, for 'knowingly and wilfully' making materially false statements or returns for tax purposes. Also, in Scotland, summary proceedings may be taken under *TMA 1970, s 107*.

The Revenue practice as regards the seeking of civil penalties where a criminal prosecution has been brought for fraud are set out in Revenue Pamphlet IR 131, SP 2/88, 10 May 1988.

The Crown Prosecution Service ('CPS') is not precluded from instituting criminal proceedings in circumstances where the Revenue has accepted a monetary settlement. (*R v W and another CA, [1998] STC 550*). The Attorney-General made it clear, however, in a Parliamentary Written Answer, that proceedings brought by the CPS will ordinarily encompass charges relating to tax evasion only in circumstances where that is incidental to allegations of non-fiscal criminal conduct. A 'Convention between Prosecuting Authorities to provide arrangements for ensuring effective co-ordination of decision making and handling in related cases which are the responsibility of different authorities' was established on 11 February 1998 (for which see the Attorney General's Press Release of that date). See Hansard Vol 310, No 155 at Cols 230, 231 and Revenue Tax Bulletin June 1998 pp 544, 545.

See generally Revenue Pamphlet IR 73 as regards negotiation of settlements.

49.13 The penalties referred to at 49.1–49.12 above may also, where appropriate, apply to individuals. See Tolley's Income Tax (under Penalties) for these and also for procedure and other relevant cases.

50 Profit Computations

Simon's Direct Tax Service D2.2.

The headings in this chapter are as follows.

50.1	Profits to be included	50.6–50.32	Particular computational matters (see sub-index)
50.2	Corporation tax computations	50.33	Corporation tax return
50.3	Allowance for 'charges on income'	50.34–50.37	Examples
50.4	— example		
50.5	— charged to capital		

50.1 PROFITS TO BE INCLUDED

See 1.2 INTRODUCTION AND RATES OF TAX. As regards non-resident companies, see 53.3 RESIDENCE, and see 18 CONTROLLED FOREIGN COMPANIES for treatment of interests in such companies. For the calculation of chargeable gains to be included in profits, see 9 CAPITAL GAINS and Tolley's Income Tax. See also 31 INCOME TAX IN RELATION TO A COMPANY.

'Profits' are defined as 'income and chargeable gains' [*ICTA 1988, s 6(4)(a)*] and include

(*a*) overseas profits of a UK resident company, whether remitted to the UK or not [*ICTA 1988, s 70(1)*],

(*b*) profits arising in the winding-up of a company [*ICTA 1988, s 8(2)*] (see 42 LIQUIDATION ETC.),

(*c*) profits accruing to the company's benefit under any trust, or arising from a PARTNERSHIP (47), which would be chargeable if they accrued to the company directly [*ICTA 1988, s 8(2)*], and

(*d*) dividends or interest from BUILDING SOCIETIES (7).

Profits do not include dividends and any other DISTRIBUTIONS (20) from UK resident companies [*ICTA 1988, s 208*], nor profits accruing to the company in a fiduciary or representative capacity and in which it has no beneficial interest. [*ICTA 1988, s 8(2)*].

Save as otherwise provided, any income tax provision conferring an exemption from income tax also applies to corporation tax. [*ICTA 1988, s 9(4)*].

As regards certain directors' fees paid to other companies, see Revenue Pamphlet IR1, A 37.

For treatment of profits arising from underwriting business of a corporate member of Lloyd's, see *FA 1994, ss 219–230, Sch 21* and, in relation to general insurance reserves, *FA 2000, s 107*.

50.2 CORPORATION TAX COMPUTATIONS

Profits are computed *separately for each source* within the charge to corporation tax (see 1.2 INTRODUCTION and 53.3 RESIDENCE) under the income tax Schedules and Cases applicable to income from that source as if the accounting period were a year of assessment, and in accordance with income tax law and practice (excluding provisions applicable solely to individuals, and subject to any special corporation tax provision, see below and 50.6 *et seq.* below) for the year of assessment in which the accounting period ends, but on the basis *of the actual income arising in the accounting period*. [*ICTA 1988, s 9*]. See Tolley's Income Tax for general principles.

The revision and simplification for income tax purposes of Schedule A (and the incorporation therein of furnished lettings previously within Schedule D, Case VI) from 6 April 1995 does not apply for corporation tax, for the purposes of which the previous rules continued to apply (see 50.26 below) until the revised corporation tax rules were introduced, broadly from 1 April 1998 (see 50.27 below). [*FA 1995, s 39(1)(4)(b); FA 1998, Sch 27 Pt III(4)*]. See also 50.3(D) below as regards related interest relief.

For accounting periods ending after 31 March 1996, Schedule D, Case III as it applies for corporation tax purposes is amended to encompass tax in respect of non-trading profits or gains from loan relationships (see 43.3 LOAN RELATIONSHIPS), tax in respect of any annuity or other annual payment (not chargeable under Schedule A) payable in respect of anything other than a loan relationship (wherever, and at whatever intervals, payable), and any discount arising otherwise than in respect of a loan relationship. Schedule D, Case IV, and Case V insofar as it applies to profits or gains from loan relationships now within Case III, are accordingly disapplied for corporation tax purposes. [*ICTA 1988, s 18(3A); FA 1996, Sch 14 para 5*].

Income of a trade assessable under Schedule D, Case V is to be computed in accordance with the rules of Schedule D, Case I. [*ICTA 1988, s 70(2)*]. Income from an overseas property business assessable under Schedule D, Case V (see 50.27 below) is to be computed in accordance with the rules of Schedule A. [*ICTA 1988, s 70A; FA 1998, Sch 5 para 25*].

See 23.35 *et seq.* EXCHANGE GAINS AND LOSSES as regards use of currencies other than sterling.

Subject to any express authorising provision, no deduction may be made in computing income from any source in respect of any dividend or other DISTRIBUTION (20). [*ICTA 1988, s 337(2)(a)*]. Nor may any such deduction be made in respect of

(*a*) any annuity,

(*b*) any other annual payment (not being interest),

(*c*) any royalty or other sum in respect of the user of a patent, or

(*d*) any rent, royalty or other payment which under *ICTA 1988, s 119* (mining, quarries and similar concerns, before 1 May 1995 only) or *s 120* (electric line wayleaves, before 6 April 1997 only) is subject to deduction of income tax as if it were within (*c*) above,

unless such sums are, or but for an exemption would be, assessable on the recipient under Schedule A. [*ICTA 1988, s 337(2)(b); FA 1996, Sch 14 para 14, Sch 41 Pt V(3)*].

For accounting periods ending after 31 March 1996, there is also a prohibition on any corporation tax deduction in respect of interest except under the LOAN RELATIONSHIPS (43) provisions introduced by *FA 1996, Pt IV, Ch II*. [*ICTA 1988, s 337A; FA 1996, Sch 14 para 15*]. For earlier accounting periods (prior to the introduction of those provisions), there is a prohibition, additional to (*a*)–(*d*) above, of any deduction in respect of any yearly interest, except that such interest payable in the UK to a bank carrying on a *bona fide* UK banking business may be deducted in computing income from a trade. [*ICTA 1988, s 337(2)(b)(3) as originally enacted*]. For this purpose, interest which is a trading receipt of the bank's UK business is treated as payable in the UK, even if the loan agreement permits payment to be made both within and outside the UK. (Revenue Pamphlet IR 131 (October 1995 Supplement), SP 1/95, 30 January 1995). (This Statement of Practice replaces an earlier Statement (C5), and where a taxpayer has taken advantage of the original Statement, it will continue to apply to existing transactions as at the date of the new Statement, where this is to the taxpayer's benefit.) By concession, where a UK bank enters into such a loan agreement after 29 January 1995, the interest is treated as payable in the UK even where it is required under the loan agreement to be paid outside the UK. (Revenue Pamphlet IR 1, C26). In practice, the Revenue do not regard *section 337(2)(b)* as preventing a bank from deducting yearly interest as a trading expense. See 6.2 BANKS.

See, however, 50.3–50.5 below regarding allowance of 'charges on income'. See also 50.6 *et seq.* below as regards special corporation tax computational provisions.

Total profits for the accounting period are arrived at by aggregating the amounts shown by these separate computations.

See also 8 CAPITAL ALLOWANCES as to the means of making such allowances, and generally 50.34 *et seq.* below.

See 54.4 RETURNS as regards rounding of tax computations.

Simon's Direct Tax Service. See **D2.202** *et seq.*.

50.3 ALLOWANCE FOR 'CHARGES ON INCOME'

Charges on income. *Accounting periods ending after 31 March 1996.* The items listed at 50.2 (*a*)–(*d*) above, so far as they are not dividends or other distributions and are not deductible in computing income, are classed as 'charges on income'. A sum is deductible in computing income when it is so deductible under the ordinary principles of commercial trading, whether or not it is actually so deducted (*Wilcock v Frigate Investments Ltd Ch D 1981, 55 TC 530*). Specifically excluded is:

(i) any payment to a non-resident *unless* the paying company is UK resident, and either the company deducts, and accounts under *ICTA 1988, Sch 16* (see 31.3 INCOME TAX IN RELATION TO A COMPANY) for, income tax under *ICTA 1988, s 349*, or the payment is payable out of income chargeable under Schedule D, Case IV or V; and

(ii) any payment which is charged to capital (see 50.5 below), or is not ultimately borne by the company; and

(iii) any payment not made under liability incurred for valuable and sufficient consideration (in relation to which an expected business advantage is not sufficient, see *Ball v National and Grindlays Bank Ltd CA 1971, 47 TC 287*); and

(iv) any annual payment for non-taxable consideration within *ICTA 1988, s 125* (see Tolley's Income Tax under Anti-Avoidance).

As regards (i) above, a company is regarded as having deducted the full amount of income tax in cases where it deducts at a reduced rate, or makes no deduction, in accordance with a direction from FICO (International) (see *SI 1970 No 488, reg 6*). As regards (iii) above, in the case of a non-resident company, to escape the exclusion the liability must in addition be for the purposes of a trade carried on (or to be carried on) by its UK branch or agency. A covenanted donation to charity made before 1 April 2000 (see 11.11(*a*) CHARITIES) is not excluded from being a charge by (iii) above.

For a case in which relief for interest paid under a circular arrangement was allowed, see *Macniven v Westmoreland Investments Ltd CA, [1998] STC 1131*.

A qualifying donation to charity (see 11.10 CHARITIES) is a charge on income if so claimed, as are certain gifts of shares and securities to charities (see 11.13 CHARITIES).

[*ICTA 1988, s 338(2)–(7); FA 1996, Sch 14 para 16; FA 2000, s 43(2)*].

Accounting periods ending before 1 April 1996. The above provisions applied for earlier periods subject to the following additions and exceptions. Also treated as charges on income (again subject to their not being dividends or other distributions and not being deductible in computing income) are:

(*a*) any yearly interest (whether charged to revenue or capital); and

(*b*) any other interest (whether charged to revenue or capital) payable in the UK on an advance from a bank carrying on *bona fide* banking business in the UK (see *Hafton Properties Ltd v McHugh Ch D 1986, 59 TC 420*), or from a member of a UK stock exchange *bona fide* carrying on business as such, or from a person *bona fide* carrying on the business of a discount house in the UK.

[*ICTA 1988, s 338(3) as originally enacted*].

All interest payments must, however, satisfy one of the following conditions:

(A) the company must exist wholly or mainly for the purposes of carrying on a trade; or

(B) the payment must be wholly and exclusively for the purposes of a trade carried on by the company (see *Olin Energy Systems Ltd v Scorer Ch D 1982, 58 TC 592*); or

(C) the company must be an investment company (see 40 INVESTMENT COMPANIES) or an authorised unit trust (see 60 UNIT AND INVESTMENT TRUSTS); or

(D) the payment would be eligible for relief under *ICTA 1988, s 353* (relief for interest paid on land), provided that the land was occupied by the company otherwise than as a residence (or an individual occupied the land, in right of the company, as his only or main residence) or was commercially let. The £30,000 limit only applies in the case of occupation as an individual's only or main residence. [*ICTA 1988, s 338(6); FA 1995, Sch 7 para 1*].

As regards (D) above, *FA 1995, s 42* abolished the special income tax provisions for interest relief for commercially let property from 6 April 1995. The relevant parts of those provisions are re-enacted for accounting periods ending after 31 March 1995, for the purposes of corporation tax relief for such interest as a charge on income. [*ICTA 1988, s 338A; FA 1995, s 42(6), Sch 7*].

Interest payments are also not charges on income if at any time a scheme has been effected or arrangements made whereby the sole or main benefit which might be expected to accrue to the payer was a reduction in tax liability. Where relief for interest is claimed by way of group relief (see 29.14–29.27 GROUPS OF COMPANIES), both claimant and surrendering companies are to be considered in determining the expected benefit. [*ICTA 1988, s 787; FA 1998, Sch 5 para 44*].

The exclusion of payments to non-residents does not apply to interest other than yearly interest, and in the case of yearly interest there are two further exceptions where the paying company is UK resident:

(1) if the company is carrying on a trade and

  (*a*) under the contract the interest is or may be required to be paid outside the UK,

  (*b*) it is in fact paid outside the UK, and

  (*c*) the liability was incurred wholly or mainly for the purposes of the company's trade outside the UK *or* the interest is payable in a currency other than sterling for the purposes of a trade wherever carried on (although the latter alternative condition does not apply if the payee company controls the payer (or *vice versa*) or the same person controls both); or

(2) if the payment is of interest on quoted Eurobonds from which tax is not deducted (see 31.3(*b*) INCOME TAX IN RELATION TO A COMPANY).

As regards (1)(*c*) above, 'control' is as defined in *ICTA 1988, s 840*, i.e., in relation to a company, the power by shareholding or voting (directly or through another company), or under Articles of Association, to secure that the company's affairs are conducted in accordance with one's wishes, and in relation to a partnership, the right to more than a one-half share in income or assets. The payer is treated as carrying on the trades of its UK resident '75% subsidiaries' (within *ICTA 1988, s 838*, see 29.15 GROUPS OF COMPANIES, but disregarding shares held directly or indirectly by the payer as trading stock or in non-resident bodies corporate).

[*ICTA 1988, s 338(4) as originally enacted, s 340*].

The exclusion of payments charged to capital or not ultimately borne by the company does not apply to interest. [*ICTA 1988, s 338(5)(a) as originally enacted*].

Relief. Charges on income are deductible in the accounting period in which they are paid (except in the case of certain charitable donations made before 1 April 2000, see 11.11(*e*) CHARITIES) from company profits as reduced by all other reliefs except group relief (see 29.14 GROUPS OF COMPANIES). [*ICTA 1988, s 338(1)*]. Interest (including yearly interest, see *Macarthur v Greycoat Estates Mayfair Ltd Ch D 1995, 67 TC 598*) is for these purposes treated as paid when debited in the books of the person to whom it is payable. [*ICTA 1988, s 338(3) proviso as originally enacted*].

Annuities to former partners. Where a partnership business is incorporated, or a company takes over a partnership, and the agreement in either case refers to the company assuming responsibility for payment of an annuity to a former partner, then provided that the annuity is commercial in amount, the payment will not be prevented by (iii) above from being a charge on income. *ICTA 1988, s 125* (annual payments for non-taxable consideration, see 31.3(*a*) INCOME TAX IN RELATION TO A COMPANY) is not in practice considered to apply to such payments in respect of a *bona fide* commercial transaction. (Revenue Tax Bulletin August 1994 p 151).

Excess charges. Charges on income (provided that they are incurred wholly and exclusively for the purposes of a trade) are taken into account in computing losses to be carried forward and terminal losses, but not losses to be carried back. See 44.4–44.8 LOSSES. They may be set against surplus FRANKED INVESTMENT INCOME (27.3(*a*)) whether or not so incurred.

Simon's Direct Tax Service. See **D2.209** *et seq.*.

50.4 *Example*

X Ltd, a UK resident company, made a Schedule D, Case I profit of £12,000 in the year to 31 October 2000. It paid the following charges (shown gross).

	Situation (i)	Situation (ii)
	£	£
For business purposes	10,000	1,000
For non–business purposes	4,000	13,000

The corporation tax position is as follows.

	£	£
Schedule D, Case I	12,000	12,000
Charges on income		
£14,000, restricted to	12,000	12,000
Chargeable profits	Nil	Nil
Excess charges carried forward	£2,000	£1,000

50.5 **Charged to capital.** In a number of pre-corporation tax cases it was established that if in its commercial accounts a company elects to capitalise interest, e.g. interest on money borrowed to finance a capital scheme, thereby increasing the fund available for distribution to its shareholders, that interest cannot be said to have been paid out of its profits charged to income tax, with the consequence that it must account for the income tax deducted from the interest (under legislation similar to *section 349*). The leading case here is *Chancery Lane Safe Deposit & Offices Co Ltd v CIR HL 1965, 43 TC 83*, in which interest on moneys used to finance the reconstruction of the company's premises was capitalised. This decision was followed in *Fitzleet Estates Ltd v Cherry HL 1977, 51 TC 708*. See also *Central London Railway Co v CIR HL 1936, 20 TC 102* and *B W Nobes & Co Ltd v CIR HL 1965, 43 TC 133*.

Interest is not prevented from being a charge on income for accounting periods ending before 1 April 1996 by its being charged to capital. [*ICTA 1988, s 338(3)(a)(5); FA 1996, Sch 14 para 16*].

PARTICULAR COMPUTATIONAL MATTERS

The following paragraphs refer to matters relating specifically to corporation tax, or of especial relevance to companies. Headings are in alphabetical order.

50.6 Charitable donations and other small gifts
50.7 Deep discount securities
50.8 Directors' remuneration
50.9 Discounts on bills of exchange
50.10 Employee share schemes
50.11 Euroconversion of shares
50.12 European Economic Interest Groupings
50.13 Gilt-edged securities and bonds
50.14 Index linked corporate stock
50.15 Interest on director's property loan
50.16 Interest payable between associated companies or to associates of banks
50.17 Lease rental payments
50.18 Life policies etc. held by companies
50.19 Loan costs
50.20 Losses on unlisted shares
50.21 Pre-trading expenditure
50.22 Profit sharing and share option schemes
50.23 Qualifying convertible securities
50.24 Redundancy — additional payments to employees
50.25 Research and development expenditure
50.26 Schedule A — income from property (to 31 March 1998)
50.27 Schedule A — income from property (from 1 April 1998)
50.28 Swap fees
50.29 Telecommunications licences
50.30 Tonnage tax
50.31 Transfer fees
50.32 Valuation fees

50.6 CHARITABLE DONATIONS AND OTHER SMALL GIFTS

Expenditure incurred in making a gift to a CHARITY (11) is not subject to the restrictions on business entertainment expenditure (see Tolley's Income Tax under Schedule D, Cases I and II) but must be 'wholly and exclusively' incurred for the purposes of the trade if it is to be deductible against profits. [*ICTA 1988, s 577(8)(9)*]. Costs incurred in respect of an employee temporarily seconded to a charity or educational establishment continue to be deductible either from the trading profits under Case I or as a management expense, as appropriate, as if wholly and exclusively incurred for business purposes. [*ICTA 1988, s 86; FA 1999, s 58*].

Other gifts, reasonably small in relation to the donor's trade, and made wholly and exclusively for trade purposes, are allowable by concession, provided that they are made for the benefit of a body, established for educational, cultural, religious, recreational or benevolent purposes, which is (*a*) local in relation to the donor's business activities, and

(*b*) not restricted to persons connected with the donor (see 16 CONNECTED PERSONS).

The payment of an ordinary annual subscription to a local trade association by a non-member is similarly allowable if made wholly and exclusively for trade purposes.

(Revenue Pamphlet IR 1, B7).

Gifts in kind to charities. See 11.12 CHARITIES for relief for gifts in kind (i.e. of trading stock or machinery or plant used in the trade) to charities and certain other bodies on or after 27 July 1999, and 11.14 CHARITIES for the earlier, more limited relief for gifts for third world health or education. Where such reliefs do not apply, donations of trading stock to charities are dealt with on normal Schedule D, Case I principles. See Revenue Tax Bulletin June 1996 p 319 for the Revenue's view of the application of those principles.

See also 11.10 CHARITIES.

50.7 **DEEP DISCOUNT SECURITIES** [*ICTA 1988, s 57, Sch 4; FA 1989, Sch 10; FA 1990, s 59, Sch 10 para 26; FA 1996, Sch 14 para 50, Sch 41 Pt V(3)*]

For accounting periods ending **before 1 April 1996**, relief may be obtained by companies issuing 'deep discount securities' after 13 March 1984 in respect of the discount to redemption at issue.

A '*deep discount security*' is a redeemable security issued at a discount exceeding either 15% of the amount payable on redemption overall or $\frac{1}{2}$% per annum to the earliest possible redemption date. Shares, index-linked securities and securities within *ICTA 1988, s 209(2)(c)* (see 20.4 DISTRIBUTIONS) are excluded. The amount payable on redemption excludes any amount payable by way of interest. Where securities issued before 14 March 1984 are exchanged, on or after that date, for new securities which would otherwise be deep discount securities, the new securities are *not* deep discount securities if

(1) the original securities would not have been deep discount securities if issued after 13 March 1984;

(2) the earliest redemption date of the new securities is not later than that for the original securities; and

(3) the amount payable on redemption of the new securities does not exceed that on the original securities.

A security is not a deep discount security if it was issued after 31 July 1990 and, under the terms of issue, either

(*a*) it can be converted into share capital in any company, or

(*b*) there is more than one date on which the holder is entitled to require redemption by the issuer,

and a security which is a 'qualifying convertible security' (see 50.23 below) at the time of issue and would otherwise be a deep discount security at that time is treated as not at any time being a deep discount security.

Certain other securities issued by public bodies known as 'deep gain securities', are treated similarly to deep discount securities, but the relief described below is inapplicable to such securities.

The **relief allowed** for an accounting period is the 'income element' for any 'income period' ending in or with the accounting period.

'*Income element*' for an 'income period' is the amount obtained by the formula

$$\frac{A \times B}{100} - C$$

where

A is the issue price plus 'income elements' of all previous 'income periods'.

B is the annual percentage appreciation rate (compounded at the end of each 'income period') required for the issue price to grow to the redemption value at the earliest possible redemption date, after allowing for any interest payments.

C is the interest (if any) attributable to the 'income period'.

'*Income period*' is the period to which any interest is attributable, or, if no interest is payable, any year ending with the anniversary of issue of the security, or shorter period ending with the earliest redemption date.

Relief is given against total profits as reduced by any other reliefs other than group relief, and is generally treated as a charge on income (see 50.3 above), provided that:

(i) the cost of the income element is ultimately borne by the company;

(ii) it would not otherwise be deductible for corporation tax purposes;

(iii) either

(*a*) the issuing company exists wholly or mainly for the purpose of carrying on a trade, or

(*b*) it is an investment company within *ICTA 1988, s 130* (see 40.1 INVESTMENT COMPANIES), or

(*c*) the security is issued wholly and exclusively for the purposes of a trade carried on by the issuing company; and

(iv) no part of the amount payable on redemption is a distribution within *ICTA 1988, s 209(2)(d)(e)* (see 20.7 DISTRIBUTIONS).

There are also **anti-avoidance provisions**

(A) prohibiting relief where there is any scheme or arrangement under which the sole or main benefit expected from issue of the security is a reduction in tax liability through relief under these provisions, and

(B) deferring relief until redemption where the securities are owned by associated companies (within *ICTA 1988, s 416*, see 56.7 SMALL COMPANIES—REDUCED RATES) or fellow members of GROUPS OF COMPANIES (29) (groups being defined by reference to 51% subsidiary status), or where the issuing company is a close company and the securities are owned by a participator (or associate) or by a company of which a participator has control (see 13 CLOSE COMPANIES and *ICTA 1988, Sch 4 para 6* as regards these terms).

On **early redemption** or **winding-up** the relief allowable for the accounting period in which the security is redeemed (or a payment made in respect of it in the winding-up) is the amount paid on redemption (or winding-up) (excluding any amount payable by way of interest) *less* the sum of the issue price and the accrued income elements up to and including the preceding accounting period. Relief previously deferred under the anti-avoidance provisions (see above) is similarly granted.

Where the amount paid on the redemption or winding-up is less than the sum of the issue price and the accrued income elements, the excess (limited to the accrued income elements) is charged to corporation tax under Schedule D, Case VI for the accounting period in which the security is redeemed, or in which the payment is made in the case of a winding-up.

For the **charge on the holder of the security**, see Tolley's Income Tax under Interest Receivable. Broadly, liability arises under Schedule D, Case III or Case IV, on disposal of the securities or on redemption, on the income elements (as above) accrued since the previous disposal (or since issue) of the securities in question. The chargeable gain on the disposal is adjusted accordingly. On early redemption or winding-up, the final holder's liability is adjusted to take account of the amount actually received on the redemption or winding-up. There are special provisions charging each income element in the income period to which it relates to prevent a device known as 'coupon-stripping'. These apply to certain securities issued after 18 March 1985. [*ICTA 1988, Sch 4*]. 'Deep gain securities', which are subject to a similar charge, do not give rise to a relief as above. See Tolley's Income Tax for detailed coverage.

Miscellaneous points

(1) The issuing company is required to state on the bond certificate the amount of the income element for each income period in the security's life.

(2) Tax is not deducted from the accrued income elements included in the amount payable on redemption.

(3) Incidental costs in issuing the security are allowed as a deduction subject to the same conditions as apply for qualifying loans, etc. under *ICTA 1988, s 77* (see 50.19 below).

(4) A security comprised in any letter of allotment or similar instrument is treated as issued unless the right to the security is provisional and has still to be accepted.

(5) There are exemptions from charge applicable to CHARITIES (11), retirement benefits schemes and stock lending transactions.

(6) Identification of securities disposed of follows the capital gains tax rules in *TCGA 1992, s 108* (see Tolley's Capital Gains Tax).

(7) Where these specific provisions do not apply to a stock issued at a price well below par and with a low interest rate, the discount element paid on redemption is regarded as chargeable to tax as rolled-up interest in the lender's hands and as allowable against the borrower's profits, regardless of any transactions during the life of the stock. (Revenue Press Release 25 June 1982).

(8) In certain cases where additional tranches of securities are issued at a price which includes an element in respect of accrued interest on the existing securities to the date of issue of the new securities, the 'issue price' of the new securities is reduced for the purposes of the deep discount securities legislation by that additional element. [*ICTA 1988, Sch 4 para 11B; FA 1991, Sch 12 para 3*]. See generally Tolley's Income Tax under Schedule D, Case VI.

See also 50.16 below.

These provisions are **abolished** for accounting periods ending **after 31 March 1996**. See now 43 LOAN RELATIONSHIPS.

Simon's Direct Tax Service. See **B5.410–B5.414.**

50.8 **DIRECTORS' REMUNERATION**

Remuneration paid to directors is only deductible in computing profits if it is paid wholly and exclusively for the purposes of the trade. See *Copeman v William Flood & Sons Ltd KB 1940, 24 TC 53.*

Directors' remuneration for a period of account is deductible only if it is paid within nine months of the end of the period. Remuneration paid at a later date is deductible for the period of account in which it is paid. The time at which the remuneration is treated as paid is the earliest of the following:

(*a*) when payment is actually made of, or on account of, such remuneration;

(*b*) when a director becomes entitled to such payment;

(*c*) when sums on account of such remuneration are credited in the company's accounts or records, regardless of any restrictions on the director's right to draw those sums;

(*d*) when a period of account ends and the amount of remuneration for that period has already been determined;

(*e*) when the amount of emoluments for a period of account is determined and that period has already ended.

Computations prepared before the end of the nine-month period in question must be prepared on the basis that any unpaid remuneration will not be paid before the expiry of that period and is not therefore deductible for that period of account. If such remuneration is paid within the said nine-month period, the computation can be adjusted accordingly on a claim being made to the inspector within two years of the end of the period of account concerned.

[*FA 1989, s 43*].

Similar provisions apply in relation to investment and insurance companies. [*FA 1989, s 44*].

See generally ICAEW Technical Release TAX 11/93 (25 June 1993) 'Tax implications of certain payments to directors'.

See also Tolley's Income Tax under Schedule D, Cases I and II. For the receipts basis generally, see Tolley's Income Tax under Schedule E.

Simon's Direct Tax Service. See B3.1425.

50.9 DISCOUNTS ON BILLS OF EXCHANGE

For bills of exchange drawn before 1 April 1996 (and subject to transitional provisions for bills so drawn but paid on or after that date), discounts on bills drawn by a company are normally allowable as a trading expense if the company is a trading company. Where they are not otherwise deductible from profits, discounts on bills, accepted by a UK bank and discounted by that (or any other) UK bank or by a UK discount house, are so deductible for corporation tax purposes after all other deductions except group relief, provided that they are ultimately suffered by the company, and either

(i) the company exists wholly or mainly for the purpose of carrying on a trade, or

(ii) the funds obtained are expended wholly and exclusively for trade purposes, or

(iii) the company is an INVESTMENT COMPANY (40).

Discounts so allowed are treated as charges on income (except for the purposes of relief under *ICTA 1988, s 338(1)* — see 50.3 above). Fees, commission and other expenditure wholly and exclusively incurred in securing acceptance of a bill on which a discount is so allowed are deductible in computing profits or gains or as a management expense (see 40.2 INVESTMENT COMPANIES). [*ICTA 1988, s 78; FA 1996, Sch 14 para 10*].

Simon's Direct Tax Service. See B3.1321.

50.10 **EMPLOYEE SHARE SCHEMES**

Employee share ownership plan ('ESOP') trusts. A UK resident company may obtain relief under Schedule D as a trading expense (or as a management expense, see 40.2 INVESTMENT COMPANIES) in respect of contributions to the trustees of a trust which is a 'qualifying ESOP trust', provided that at least some of the company's employees (or those of a company it controls (within *ICTA 1988, s 840*)) are eligible to benefit from the trust. The relief must be claimed within two years of the end of the period of account, and is given only if the payment is used by the trustees, within nine months of the end of the period of account (or such longer time as the Board may allow), for any of the following purposes:

(*a*) the acquisition of shares in the company;

(*b*) the repayment of borrowings;

(*c*) the payment of interest on borrowings;

(*d*) payments to beneficiaries; or

(*e*) payments of expenses (including income or capital gains tax, see Revenue Inspector's Manual, IM 680e).

The trustees are treated as using payments on a first in/first out basis, regardless of the number of companies contributing to the trust. Contributions received are deemed to be used first to meet expenditure for qualifying purposes, expenditure for non-qualifying purposes being treated as far as possible as met out of other income (e.g. dividends or interest). (Revenue Inspector's Manual, IM 680f). In certain circumstances, a charge may arise on the trustees which, if not paid within six months of becoming final and conclusive, may be recovered from a company which established or contributed to the trust. [*FA 1989, ss 67, 68*].

Relief may similarly be obtained for expenditure incurred in establishing a 'qualifying ESOP trust'. If the deed establishing the trust is executed more than nine months after the end of the period of account in which the expenditure is incurred, it is treated as incurred in the period in which the deed is executed. [*ICTA 1988, s 85A; FA 1991, s 43*].

See Tolley's Income Tax under Share Incentives and Options for the definition of 'qualifying ESOP trust' (in *FA 1989, Sch 5*), for the charge on trustees and for certain information requirements relating to trustees. See Tolley's Capital Gains Tax under Shares and Securities for details of a limited rollover relief on sale of shares to the trustees of such a trust in *TCGA 1992, ss 227–235*.

See Simon's Direct Tax Service D2.221 *et seq.*.

Employee share ownership plans. Where, under an approved share ownership plan within *FA 2000, s 47, Sch 8* (see Tolley's Income Tax under Share Incentives and Share Options), shares are awarded to employees as free or matching shares by reason of their employment with a company, a deduction is allowed to the company, in computing its trading profits for the period of account in which the shares are awarded to the employees, of an amount equal to the market value of the shares at the time they were acquired by the scheme trustees. No other deduction is permissible by that or any other company in respect of the provision of the shares (but see further below as regards plan setting up and running costs). If the plan is a group-wide plan, the market value of the shares awarded to the employees of the company concerned is the corresponding proportion of the total market value of the shares awarded. In determining market value for these purposes, it is assumed that shares acquired earlier by the trustees are awarded before those acquired later. Where partnership shares (for which the employee makes a contribution) are so awarded, and their market value when acquired by the trustees exceeds the employee contribution, a deduction is similarly allowed to the company for the excess. No deduction is, however, allowed in relation to any such award where:

(*a*) the employee to whom the shares are awarded is not, at the time of the award, chargeable under Schedule E on emoluments from the employment, and would not be so chargeable were such emoluments remitted to the UK;

(*b*) the shares are liable to depreciate substantially in value for reasons not generally applicable to the company's shares;

(*c*) any deduction in computing trading profits has previously been made on any basis by the company (or an associated company, see *FA 2000, Sch 8 para 126*) in respect of the provision of the same shares for this or any other trust, whatever its nature or purpose. For this purpose it is again assumed that shares acquired earlier by the trustees are awarded before those acquired later; or

(*d*) the shares have previously been forfeited by a participant in the plan.

If plan approval is withdrawn, the Revenue may direct that any deduction allowed as above in relation to the plan is also withdrawn, with the result that the an amount equal to the aggregate of such deductions is treated as a trading receipt for the period of account in which notice of withdrawal of approval is given.

Amounts which would otherwise be treated as deductions from trading profits under the above provisions are, in the case of INVESTMENT COMPANIES (40) and insurance companies to which *ICTA 1988, s 75* (management expenses) applies by virtue of *ICTA 1988, s 76* (see 41.2 LIFE INSURANCE COMPANIES), treated instead as management expenses. Trading profits are similarly in these circumstances treated instead as Schedule D, Case VI income.

Setting-up costs. A trading deduction is allowed for the costs of establishing the plan, unless any employee acquires plan rights, or trustees acquire plan shares, before Revenue approval is given. If such approval is given more than nine months after the end of the period of account in which the expenses are incurred, they are treated as incurred in the period in which approval is given. Where such a deduction is allowed, no other trading deduction is allowed in respect of the expenses.

Running costs. A trading deduction is allowed, subject to the normal Schedule D, Case I rules, for contributions by the company to the trustees' expenses in operating the plan, including interest paid by the trustees on money borrowed by them to operate the plan, but excluding share acquisition costs other than fees, commission, stamp duty and similar incidental costs of acquisition.

Dividend shares. Subject to the deduction for running costs (as above), no deduction is allowed for expenses incurred in providing dividend shares under a plan (i.e. shares acquired by the trustees on behalf of participants out of the proceeds of cash dividends on shares held under the plan).

[*FA 2000, Sch 8 paras 105–114*].

Profit sharing and share option schemes. See 50.22 below.

50.11 EUROCONVERSION OF SHARES [*SI 1998 No 3177, Pt II*]

Costs incurred in respect of the conversion of a trading company's shares or other securities from the currency of a State which has adopted the euro into euros (a 'euroconversion', see *SI 1998 No 3177, reg 3*) which is effected solely by the issue of replacement shares and other securities are allowable as a Schedule D, Case I deduction.

In the case of an investment company (or, subject to special provisions, a company carrying on life assurance business), such costs are treated as management expenses (see 40.2 INVESTMENT COMPANIES).

50.12 **EUROPEAN ECONOMIC INTEREST GROUPINGS** [*FA 1990, s 69, Sch 11*]

A European Economic Interest Grouping ('EEIG') within *Directive No. 2137/85/EEC* (which, from 1 January 1994, applies to all EEIGs established within the European Economic Area), wherever it is registered, is regarded as acting as the agent of its members. Its activities are regarded as those of its members acting jointly, each member being regarded as having a share of EEIG property, rights and liabilities, and a person is regarded as acquiring or disposing of a share of the EEIG assets not only where there is an acquisition or disposal by the EEIG while he is a member but also where he becomes or ceases to be a member or there is a change in his share of EEIG property.

A member's share in EEIG property, rights or liabilities is that determined under the contract establishing the EEIG or, if there is no provision determining such shares, it will correspond to the profit share to which he is entitled under the provisions of the contract. If the contract makes no such provision, members are regarded as having equal shares.

Where the EEIG carries on a trade or profession, the members are regarded for the purposes of tax on income and gains as carrying on that trade or profession in partnership. The amount on which members are chargeable to income tax in respect of the trade or profession is computed (but not assessed) jointly, and the provisions of *ICTA 1988, s 112* concerning partnerships controlled abroad are correspondingly amended in the case of EEIGs. [*ICTA 1988, s 510A; FA 1990, Sch 11 paras 1, 5; FA 1995, Sch 29 Pt VIII(16)*].

Contributions to an EEIG from its members are not assessable on the EEIG, and the members are not assessable on distributions from the EEIG (which is equally not obliged to account for ACT thereon). (Revenue EEIGs Manual, EEIG 34).

For the purposes of making assessments to income tax, corporation tax or capital gains tax on members of EEIGs (or of securing that members are so assessed), an inspector may, in the case of an EEIG which is registered, or has an establishment registered, in Great Britain or Northern Ireland, by notice require the EEIG to make a return containing such information as the notice may require, accompanied by such accounts and statements as the notice may require, within a specified time. In any other case, he may issue a similar notice to any UK resident member(s) of the EEIG (or if none is so resident, to any member(s)). Notices may differ from one period to another and by reference to the person on whom they are served or the description of EEIG to which they refer. Where a notice is given to an EEIG registered in Great Britain or Northern Ireland (or having an establishment registered there), the EEIG must act through a manager, except that if there is no manager who is an individual, the EEIG must act through an individual designated as a representative of the manager under the *Directive.* The return must in all cases include a declaration that, to the best of the maker's knowledge, it is correct and complete, and where the contract establishing the EEIG requires two or more managers to act jointly for the EEIG to be validly bound, the declaration must be given by the appropriate number of managers. [*TMA 1970, s 12A; FA 1990, Sch 11 para 2; FA 1994, Sch 19 para 2*]. See Revenue Pamphlet IR 131, SP 4/91, 1 May 1990 for the form and content of returns.

A penalty not exceeding £300 (and £60 per day for continued failure) may be imposed in the case of failure to comply with a notice under the above provisions. No penalty may be imposed after the failure has been remedied, and if it is proved that there was no income or chargeable gain to be included in the return, the maximum penalty is £100. Fraudulent or negligent delivery of an incorrect return, etc. or of an incorrect declaration may result in a penalty not exceeding £3,000 for each member of the EEIG at the time of delivery, and the act or omission giving rise to the penalty is treated as the act or omission of each member of the EEIG for the purposes of fraud or negligence assessments and consequential claims. For accounting periods ending **on or after 1 July 1999** the £300 and £60 per day maximum penalties are multiplied by the number of members of the EEIG at the time of the failure or at the end of the day for which a continuing penalty is imposed. [*TMA 1970, ss 36(4), 98B; FA 1990, Sch 11 paras 3, 4; FA 1994, Sch 19 para 30; FA 1998, Sch 18 para 91, Sch 19 para 18; SI 1998 No 3173*].

Simon's Direct Tax Service. See **D4.901–D4.903.**

50.13 GILT-EDGED SECURITIES AND BONDS

A new taxation regime is introduced in *FA 1996* with effect from 1 April 1996 for corporate investors and borrowers in gilt-edged securities and bonds. See 43 LOAN RELATIONSHIPS.

50.14 INDEX LINKED CORPORATE STOCK

The issue of such stock by a company was considered by the Revenue to give rise to the following consequences.

(i) If the indexation constituted a capital uplift of the principal on redemption to take account of no more than the fall in real value because of inflation, the borrowing company was not allowed any deduction against its profits, and the lender was generally liable to capital gains tax on the uplift.

(ii) If the indexation applied to the interest element and additional sums of interest were rolled up to be paid with the capital on redemption, the indexed uplift and the rolled up interest, when paid, were treated as interest for both borrower and lender.

(Revenue Press Release 25 June 1982).

See now 43 LOAN RELATIONSHIPS and 50.7 above, 50.23 below.

50.15 INTEREST ON DIRECTOR'S PROPERTY LOAN

Before the 1995 Finance Act changes to the taxation of income from property (for which see Tolley's Income Tax under Schedule A), there was doubt concerning the correct treatment of interest paid by a company on a loan (other than an overdraft) taken out by a director to purchase land (including buildings etc.) occupied rent-free by the company and used for business purposes. In practice, if the interest was treated as emoluments of the director, relief as an allowable expense was generally available to the company. Where the company instead paid rent, this was an allowable expense to the company, and the director could set his interest payments against the rent received under *ICTA 1988, s 355(1)(b)*. Where the company paid neither rent nor interest, no deduction would be allowed to the company for the interest paid by the director. (Revenue Pamphlet IR 131, SP 4/85, 5 February 1985).

Following the 1995 Finance Act changes, SP 4/85 is considered obsolete. It is considered that relief as a trading expense for interest payable by the company on the director's behalf would be available in the normal way, and that the payments would not normally constitute either emoluments or a benefit of the director. The director's Schedule A business computation would include the interest payments made by the company on the director's behalf, but these would be offset by a deduction for the interest payable by the director (which would be allowable regardless of the interest payments having been met by the company). The Schedule A business profit would therefore generally be nil. (Revenue Tax Bulletin June 1997 pp 437, 438).

50.16 **INTEREST PAYABLE BETWEEN ASSOCIATED COMPANIES OR TO ASSOCIATES OF BANKS** [*FA 1993, ss 61–66; FA 1995, ss 88, 89; FA 1996, Sch 41 Pt V(3); FA 1999, s 67(4)(5)(8)*]

For accounting periods ending **before 1 April 1996**, special provisions apply to bring into charge to UK tax on an accruals basis interest accruing after 31 March 1993 on certain debts between associated companies, where the company liable for the debt is non-UK resident. They are extended for interest accruing after 28 November 1994 (or in certain cases 31 March 1996) to interest payable by any company to an associate of a banking company. For these purposes, an '*accrued income security*' is a security within the accrued income scheme provisions of *ICTA 1988, ss 710–728* (for details of which see Tolley's Income Tax under Schedule D, Case VI), a '*deep discount security*' is a security within the deep discount provisions of *ICTA 1988, Sch 4*, and a '*deep gain security*' is a security within the deep gain provisions of *FA 1989, Sch 11* (for details of both of which see Tolley's Income Tax under Interest Receivable). In applying *FA 1989, Sch 11* for these purposes, however, the exclusion of 'qualifying indexed securities' from those provisions is omitted (but not so as to bring into charge under these provisions any income accruing before 1 April 1993 in respect of the debt on such securities).

Where a debt on an accrued income or deep gain security

(i) was a 'qualifying debt' at the end of the day before the 'commencement day', or

(ii) becomes such a debt on any day after that day, or

(iii) ceases to be such a debt on any day after that day, or

(iv) is such a debt at the end of the last day of an accounting period ending after that day of the company entitled to the debt,

the security is treated for the purposes of the accrued income scheme or the deep gain provisions (as appropriate) as transferred with accrued interest by the company entitled to the debt on the 'relevant day' or, in the case of (ii), and provided that the company held the security on the day before the 'relevant day', on that preceding day. Similarly, where a debt on an accrued income or deep gain security

(I) was a 'qualifying debt' at the beginning of the 'commencement day', or

(II) becomes such a debt on any day after that day, or

(III) ceases to be such a debt on any day after that day, or

(IV) is such a debt at the beginning of the first day of an accounting period beginning after that day of the company entitled to the debt,

the security is treated for the purposes of the accrued income scheme or the deep gain provisions (as appropriate) as transferred with accrued interest to the company entitled to the debt on the 'relevant day' or, in the case of (III), and provided that the company held the security on the day following the 'relevant day', on that following day.

The '*relevant day*' is the day mentioned in (i)–(iv) or (I)–(IV) above, as appropriate.

The above applies equally to a debt on a deep discount security, but by reference to times falling within such relevant days.

Special provisions for accrued income scheme securities. The settlement day for these purposes is the day of the deemed transfer. Also, in a case within (iii) above where the security is not a 'variable interest rate security' (within *ICTA 1988, s 717*), it will cease to be treated as such after the relevant day. Where a security is treated as transferred by virtue of (iii) or (iv) above, any period which, under *ICTA 1988, s 711(3)(4)*, would otherwise, in relation to the security, be an interest period beginning on or before and ending after the day of the deemed transfer is not itself an interest period but is split into two interest periods, the first ending on the day of the deemed transfer and the second beginning on the following day.

Transitional relief. Income which would otherwise be treated as arising under the above provisions by virtue of (i) or (ii) above is treated as not arising until the earliest of

(1) the earliest date on which the company entitled to the debt can, under the terms of issue, require redemption of the security,

(2) the day on which the security is redeemed, and

(3) the day on which the company makes a disposal of it for the purposes of *TCGA 1992* (before 15 February 1999, the day on which it is transferred by the company).

See 43.11 LOAN RELATIONSHIPS for the application of those provisions to a charge so deferred until after 31 March 1996.

Deemed debts on securities. Where the terms of a debt which is not a debt on a security are such that, if it were, it would be an accrued income, deep gain or deep discount security (as appropriate), then, at any time when the debt is a 'qualifying debt', an accrued income, deep gain or deep discount security (as appropriate) incorporating the terms of the debt is deemed to be held by the company entitled to the debt, and the debt is deemed to be a debt on that security.

Qualifying debt. A debt is a '*qualifying debt*' at any time at which:

(*a*) the person entitled to the debt is a UK resident company (the '*resident company*');

(*b*) the person liable for the debt is either a 'qualifying company' or a 'qualifying third party'; and

(*c*) the debt is not an 'exempted debt'.

The '*commencement day*' in relation to such debts is 1 April 1993.

A debt is also a '*qualifying debt*' at any time at which the person entitled to the debt is a UK resident company associated (within *ICTA 1988, s 416*) with a company carrying on a banking business in the UK, unless either the debt is held at that time for the purposes of long term insurance business (within *Insurance Companies Act 1982, Sch 1*) or three further conditions are fulfilled at that time, and have been and are likely to continue to be fulfilled throughout the period of the debt. The first condition is that any interest under the terms of the debt is at either a constant fixed rate, or a rate fixed by a constant relationship to the retail prices index (or foreign equivalent). The second condition is that any such interest is payable as it accrues at intervals of twelve months or less. The third condition is that the terms of the debt are not such that it is (or would if it were a debt on a security be) a deep discount or deep gain security (as above). The '*commencement day*' in relation to such debts is generally 29 November 1994, but commencement is deferred until 1 April 1996 where any of certain higher education institutions or housing associations is liable for the debt (and was so at the end of 28 November 1994).

A company is a '*qualifying company*' at any time at which it is an 'associated company' of the resident company, and is resident outside the UK. Before 30 November 1993, it was specially provided for this purpose that any company which, though UK-resident, was regarded as resident elsewhere under any double taxation agreement was to be treated as resident outside the UK, but this was superseded by the general provision of *FA 1994, s 249* (see 53.1 RESIDENCE) to similar effect. A company is an '*associated company*' of another company at any time if, at that time or within the previous year, one controls the other or both are under common control ('control' being within *ICTA 1988, s 416*, see 13.2 CLOSE COMPANIES).

A third party (which is not an associated company of the resident company) is a '*qualifying third party*' at any time at which it satisfies both the following conditions.

(1) The third party has, under any arrangements made with him, been put in funds (directly or indirectly) at any earlier time *either* by the resident company or a company which was at that earlier time an associated company of the resident company, *or* by a person from whom the resident company has (directly or indirectly) acquired the debt or a company which was at that earlier time an associated company of that person.

(2) A company which is a qualifying company has under the arrangements in (1) above been put in funds (directly or indirectly) at any earlier time by the third party or by a company which was at that earlier time an associated company of that party.

A debt is an '*exempted debt*' at any time at which:

(A) each of the first, second and third conditions mentioned below is fulfilled at that time, has been fulfilled throughout so much of the period of the debt as falls before that time, and is likely to be fulfilled in the remainder of the period of the debt; or

(B) the inspector (or, on appeal, the Commissioners) is (are) satisfied that the fourth condition mentioned below is fulfilled, and either

  (i) he is (or they are) satisfied that the fifth condition is also fulfilled, or

  (ii) the sixth condition is also fulfilled; or

(C) the inspector (or, on appeal, the Commissioners) is (are) satisfied that the seventh condition mentioned below is fulfilled.

The first condition is that the debt terms provide that any interest carried by the debt is at a rate which falls into one, and only one, of the following categories: a fixed rate unchanged throughout the period of the debt; a rate which bears the same fixed relationship to a standard published rate throughout the period; and a rate which bears the same fixed relationship to a published index of prices (broadly, any retail or general index of prices published by an overseas government). The second condition is that those terms provide for any such interest to be payable as it accrues at intervals of twelve months or less. The third condition is that either the debt terms are such that the amount payable (excluding interest) on the debt's redemption cannot exceed the consideration given for it, or the debt must be redeemed within twelve months of its creation.

The fourth condition is that the possibility of returns on the debt being chargeable as they arise rather than as they accrue was not the main reason, or one of the main reasons, why the UK resident company created the debt on terms that would preclude it being an exempted debt under (A) above, acquired the debt on those terms or (as the case may be) agreed to the subsequent inclusion of those terms. The fifth condition is that, even if the person liable for the debt were neither a 'qualifying company', nor a 'qualifying third party', nor a person who would be such a company or party if a qualifying company could include a company resident in the UK, the UK resident company would still have created the debt on terms that would preclude it being an exempted debt under (A) above, acquired the debt on those terms or (as the case may be) agreed to the subsequent inclusion of those terms. The fact that it is not the resident company's business to make loans generally is ignored for this last condition. The sixth condition is that the terms of the debt either are such that it must be redeemed before the end of the 'relevant period', or provide for any interest accruing during that period to be payable no later than immediately after the end of that period and for any interest subsequently accruing to be payable as it accrues at intervals of twelve months or less. The '*relevant period*' for this purpose is the period of 24 months beginning with the date on which the UK resident company created the debt on terms that would preclude it being an exempted debt under (A) above, acquired the debt on those terms or (as the case may be) agreed to the subsequent inclusion of those terms.

The seventh condition is that, at that time, by reason of its inability to pay its debts, the qualifying company liable for the debt or, as the case may be, the qualifying company mentioned in (2) above,

(*a*) has been, is in the course of being or is likely to be wound up, or

(*b*) has been or is likely to be dissolved (which includes its otherwise having ceased or being likely to cease to exist) under the laws of the territory in which it is or was incorporated.

Avoidance of double charge. There are provisions to prevent a double charge arising where a security is by virtue of the above treated as transferred under both the accrued income scheme provisions and the deep gain provisions.

These provisions are **abolished** for accounting periods ending **after 31 March 1996**. See now 43 LOAN RELATIONSHIPS, and in particular the transitional provisions described at 43.11.

Simon's Direct Tax Service. See **D2.240** *et seq.*.

50.17 LEASE RENTAL PAYMENTS

FA 1997, Sch 12 introduces anti-avoidance and other provisions effective from 26 November 1996 in relation to the taxation of receipts under finance leasing arrangements. *Part I* applies in relation to asset leasing arrangements which, in the case of UK-incorporated companies, are dealt with by normal accountancy practice as finance leases or loans, and whose effect is that some or all of the investment return is or may be in non-rental form and would not, apart from these provisions, be wholly taxed as lease rental. The principal purposes of the provisions are to charge any person entitled to the lessor's interest to tax by reference to the income return for accounting purposes (taking into account the substance of the matter as a whole, e.g. as regards connected persons or groups of companies); and to recover reliefs, etc. for capital and other expenditure as appropriate by reference to sums received which fall within the provisions.

Part II applies to arrangements, not within *Part I*, which involve the lease of an asset and are of a kind which, in the accounts of a UK-incorporated company, would be treated under normal accountancy practice as finance leases or loans. The main purpose of the provisions is to charge tax on amounts equal to the income return on investment under normal accountancy practice (taking into account the substance of the matter as a whole, e.g. as regards connected persons or groups of companies).

Part III deals with company lessors carrying on life insurance business. Broadly the provisions of *Parts I* and *II* are disapplied where the leased asset is an asset of the long term business fund and any life assurance business profits are computed under Schedule D, Case I rules, and in determining whether they otherwise apply, sums are not regarded as brought into account as rent or a return on investment for certain purposes by reason only of their being taken into account under *FA 1989, s 83(2)* (see 41.4 LIFE INSURANCE COMPANIES).

For all these purposes, a period of account straddling 26 November 1996 is treated as two separate periods of account, ending immediately before and beginning with that date.

From 1 April 1998, those provisions of *Schedule 12* which require the application of Schedule D, Case I principles to Schedule A receipts cease to have effect, following the general application of such principles to Schedule A businesses (see 50.27 below).

[*FA 1997, s 82, Sch 12; FA 1998, Sch 5 para 74, Sch 27 Pt III(4)*].

See Tolley's Income Tax under Schedule D, Cases I and II (Lease Rental Payments) for the detailed provisions, and also for Revenue Statement of Practice SP 3/91 dealing with rental payments by lessees under finance leases. For the Revenue's views on various points of interpretation regarding these provisions, see Revenue Tax Bulletin April 1997 pp 414–417.

50.18 **LIFE POLICIES ETC. HELD BY COMPANIES**

A gain arising under a policy, etc. held by or for a company is generally brought into charge under Schedule D, Case VI (with, from 6 April 1998, a right of recovery against trustees where the policy, etc. was held in trust), but policies, etc. issued before 14 March 1989 are excluded. [*ICTA 1988, s 547(1)(b)(8), s 551A; FA 1989, Sch 9 paras 5, 8; FA 1991, Sch 7 para 9; FA 1998, Sch 14 para 3*]. Certain events which are excluded from the charge on individual policy holders are treated as chargeable events where, immediately before the event, the rights conferred by the policy were in the beneficial ownership of a company, or were held on trusts created, or as security for debt owed, by a company. [*ICTA 1988, s 540(5A); FA 1989, Sch 9 para 3*]. *ICTA 1988, s 548* (which treats certain loans as giving rise to a partial surrender of rights under a policy) is also applied to policies issued after that date and held by or for companies. [*ICTA 1988, s 548(1)(3); FA 1989, Sch 9 para 6*]. Special provisions apply in relation to chargeable events in respect of 'qualifying endowment policies' (within *ICTA 1988, Sch 15 para 2*) held as security for a debt owed by the company. [*ICTA 1988, s 541(4A)–(5); FA 1989, Sch 9 para 4*].

For these purposes, a policy made before 14 March 1989 is to be treated as made on or after that date if it is varied on or after that date so as to increase the benefits secured or to extend the term of the policy, and any exercise of rights conferred by the policy is to be regarded for this purpose as a variation. [*ICTA 1988, s 539(9); FA 1989, Sch 9 para 2*].

50.19 **LOAN COSTS** [*ICTA 1988, s 77; FA 1996, Sch 14 para 9*]

For accounting periods ending **before 1 April 1996**, 'incidental costs' of obtaining 'qualifying loans' (or of issuing 'qualifying loan stock') are deductible in computing trading profits (and are treated as management expenses for investment companies, etc.).

'*Incidental costs*' means expenditure on fees, commissions, advertising, printing and 'other incidental matters', provided that the expenditure is wholly and exclusively incurred for the purposes of obtaining the loan finance (whether or not it is in fact obtained), of providing security therefor, or of repaying it. Stamp duties, sums paid in connection with currency fluctuations, and repayments related to premiums or discounts are excluded. Costs of a flotation the proceeds of which were used to repay loan finance were held not allowable as the motive of the company in arranging for the flotation was not wholly and exclusively to repay the debt (*Focus Dynamics plc v Turner (Sp C 182), [1999] SSCD 71*).

'*Qualifying loans*' and '*qualifying loan stock*' must carry interest which is deductible in computing the profits of the company by which the incidental costs are incurred, or allowable as a charge against its total profits (see 50.3 above). A loan or loan stock carrying a right of conversion into, or acquisition of, shares or other securities within three years of the date when it was obtained or issued is excluded unless the right is not wholly exercised within the three years. Proportionate costs are allowed where the loan is partially converted within the three years. All costs incurred in the three year period (or before) are treated as incurred immediately after its end.

See 7.7 BUILDING SOCIETIES for similar relief for incidental costs of issue of certain building society shares.

These provisions **cease** to apply for corporation tax purposes for accounting periods ending **after 31 March 1996**. See now 43.5 LOAN RELATIONSHIPS.

Simon's Direct Tax Service. See B3.1321.

50.20 LOSSES ON UNLISTED SHARES

As regards relief available to investment companies for losses on shares subscribed for in certain unlisted trading companies, see 44.19 LOSSES.

50.21 PRE-TRADING EXPENDITURE [*ICTA 1988, s 401; FA 1993, s 109; FA 1995, s 120; FA 1996, Sch 14 para 20; FA 1998, Sch 27 Pt III(4)*]

Expenditure incurred for the purposes of a trade not more than seven years before the commencement of that trade, which would be allowable in computing the profits of that trade if incurred after such commencement, is treated as having been incurred on the first day of trading. The expenditure must have been incurred by the person who carries on the trade on commencement.

The relief is extended to include charges on income paid for trade purposes before the commencement of trading and not otherwise deducted from any profits. For accounting periods ending after 31 March 1996, this is replaced by a special relief for non-trading debits arising under the provisions introduced in *FA 1996* (see 43.3 LOAN RELATIONSHIPS). The provisions for relief of allowable pre-trading expenditure do not apply to expenditure in relation to which such debits arise. The company may, however, elect for a non-trading debit not to be brought into account in the period in which it arises, within two years of the end of that period. If the company then begins to carry on a trade within seven years after the end of that period, and the debit would have been a trading debit if it had been given in the accounting period in which the trade commenced, it is brought into account as a trading debit in that period.

From 1 April 1998, the above provisions apply equally to a Schedule A business carried on by a company (see 50.27 below).

Simon's Direct Tax Service. See B3.1204.

50.22 PROFIT SHARING AND SHARE OPTION SCHEMES

Expenditure incurred on establishing an approved profit sharing or share option scheme under *ICTA 1988, Sch 9* (see Tolley's Income Tax under Share Incentives and Share Options) is deductible under Schedule D as a trading expense (or as a management expense, see 40.2 INVESTMENT COMPANIES), provided that:

(*a*) in the case of a profit sharing scheme, the trustees acquire no shares under the scheme before it is approved; or

(*b*) in the case of a share option scheme, no employee or director obtains rights under the scheme before it is approved.

If the scheme is approved more than nine months after the end of the period of account in which the expenditure is incurred, it is for these purposes treated as incurred in the period in which the approval is given. [*ICTA 1988, s 84A; FA 1991, s 42*]. It should be noted that approved profit sharing schemes are phased out after 5 April 2001.

In the case of an approved profit sharing scheme, a similar deduction is available for payments made to the scheme trustees which are either necessary to meet their reasonable administration expenses or applied by them, within nine months after the end of the period of account in which the expenditure is incurred (or such longer time as the Revenue may allow), in acquiring shares for appropriation to participators. This provision is to be phased out in line with the phasing out of reliefs under profit sharing schemes. Payments to meet administration expenses of the trustees may not be deducted where they paid to the trustees more than three years after the last appropriation of shares made before 6 April 2002 under the scheme. Payments to the trustees after 20 March 2000 and before 6 April 2002 which are applied by the trustees in acquiring shares for appropriation may not be deducted unless the shares are appropriated before 6 April 2002 *and* within nine months after the end of the period of account in which the payment was made to the trustees (such payments after 5 April 2002 attracting no deduction in any event). [*ICTA 1988, s 85; FA 2000, s 50*].

Simon's Direct Tax Service. See D2.220.

50.23 **QUALIFYING CONVERTIBLE SECURITIES** [*FA 1990, s 56, Sch 10; FA 1996, Sch 41 Pt V(3)*]

For accounting periods ending **before 1 April 1996**, where a company issues a 'qualifying convertible security' and, on the redemption thereof, a charge arises on the holder under *FA 1990, Sch 10 para 12*, the excess of the amount paid on redemption (excluding any interest) over the issue price is treated as a charge on income (see 50.3 above) for the accounting period in which the redemption occurs. [*FA 1990, Sch 10 para 25*].

A '*qualifying convertible security*' is a security issued after 8 June 1989 which, at the time of its issue, meets each of the following conditions.

(*a*) It is not a share, is redeemable, and its issue does not fall, wholly or partly, to be treated as, or as part of, a distribution by virtue of *ICTA 1988, s 209(2)(c)* (see 20.4 DISTRIBUTIONS).

(*b*) It is quoted on a recognised stock exchange or is so quoted within one month after the issue date.

(*c*) Under the terms of issue:

  (i) the security can be converted into ordinary share capital (i.e. any share capital other than that carrying a right to a fixed-rate dividend and no other right to share in profits) in the issuing company;

  (ii) it carries either no right to interest or a right to interest at a fixed (not variable) rate determined at the time of issue; and

  (iii) any amount payable, either on redemption (at any time) or by way of interest, is payable in the currency in which the issue price is denominated.

(*d*) At the time of issue, the security is subject to one, and only one, 'qualifying provision for redemption'.

(*e*) The 'yield to redemption' (as defined by *FA 1990, Sch 10 para 9*) for the 'relevant redemption period' represents no more than a reasonable commercial return. The '*relevant redemption period*' is the 'redemption period' which ends with the day on which the occasion for redemption under the 'qualifying provision for redemption' falls.

(*f*) The security is either a 'deep discount security' or a 'deep gain security' (see 50.7 above), but only because of the 'qualifying provision for redemption'. *ICTA 1988, Sch 4 para 21* and *FA 1989, Sch 11 para 22B(1)* (which prevent a qualifying convertible security from being a deep discount or deep gain security) are disregarded for this purpose.

(*g*) The obtaining of a tax advantage within *ICTA 1988, s 709(1)* (see Tolley's Income Tax under Anti-Avoidance) by any person is not the main benefit, or one of the main benefits, which might be expected to accrue from the issue of the security.

(*h*) Where the security carries a right to interest, the first (or only) interest payment day must fall either one year or six months after the day of issue, and subsequent interest payment days (if any) must continue to fall at yearly or six-monthly intervals respectively.

Having satisfied the above conditions at the time of issue, a security continues to be a qualifying convertible security unless at any time

(i) it becomes subject to a new 'qualifying provision for redemption' and the conditions in *FA 1990, Sch 10 para 4(3)* are not satisfied, or

(ii) any of the prohibited events listed below occurs in relation to the security,

in which case the security ceases to be a qualifying convertible security at the time in question. Any of the following is a prohibited event.

(A) The security ceases to be quoted on a recognised stock exchange.

(B) It becomes subject to a provision under which either of the conditions at (*c*)(ii) or (iii) above will no longer be satisfied.

(C) It becomes subject to a condition which would be a 'qualifying provision for redemption' but for the fact that the conditions at (II) and (III) below are not fully satisfied.

(D) There is a time when more than 10% of the securities issued, under the prospectus under which the security concerned was issued, are held by companies which are at that time 'linked companies' (as defined).

[*FA 1990, Sch 10 paras 2–5, 9, 11*].

A '*qualifying provision for redemption*', in relation to a security, is a provision which

(I) provides for redemption before maturity only at the option of the person holding the security for the time being,

(II) provides for such redemption on one occasion only, which must occur on the last day of an 'income period', and

(III) is such that the amount payable on the exercise of the option is fixed (not variable), is determined at the time the security becomes subject to the provision and constitutes a 'deep gain'.

[*FA 1990, Sch 10 para 1*].

The amount payable on redemption on exercise of the option under a provision for redemption constitutes a '*deep gain*' if the issue price is less than that amount (excluding any amount payable by way of interest) by more than 15% of that amount (excluding interest) or one-half per cent per annum of that amount (excluding interest) for each complete year between day of issue and the occasion for redemption under the provision concerned. Where, however, the security became subject to one or more qualifying provisions for redemption before becoming subject to the provision concerned, the above applies with the substitution of 'base amount' for 'issue price' and of 'base day' for 'day of issue'. The '*base amount*' is the amount payable on redemption on exercise of the option provided for by the previous qualifying provision for redemption or, if there was more than one, the one to which the security last became subject. The '*base day*' is the day on which the occasion for redemption falls under that previous, or last, qualifying provision for redemption. [*FA 1990, Sch 10 paras 6, 11(2)*].

An '*income period*' is the inclusive period from day of issue to the first (or only) interest payment day or any period from one interest payment day to the next. Where the security carries no right to interest, an income period is any period of one year ending with an anniversary of the day of issue. [*FA 1990, Sch 10 para 7*].

A '*redemption period*' is the inclusive period from the day of issue to the day on which falls the first (or only) occasion for redemption under a qualifying provision for redemption, or any period beginning with a day after that on which one such occasion falls and ending with the day on which the next such occasion falls. [*FA 1990, Sch 10 para 8*].

A **chargeable event** occurs, subject to various exemptions, where there is either a transfer, or a redemption in exercise of an option under a qualifying provision for redemption, of a qualifying convertible security. [*FA 1990, Sch 10 para 12*]. See Tolley's Income Tax under Interest Receivable for details of this charge.

These provisions are **abolished** for accounting periods ending **after 31 March 1996**. See now 43 LOAN RELATIONSHIPS.

Simon's Direct Tax Service. See B5.425–B5.429.

50.24 **REDUNDANCY — ADDITIONAL PAYMENTS TO EMPLOYEES** [*ICTA 1988, s 90*]

Payments additional to a redundancy payment (or to the corresponding amount of any other employer's payment) within *ICTA 1988, s 579* which would be allowable as a deduction in computing trading profits or as management expenses but for the permanent discontinuance of the trade are to be allowable notwithstanding the discontinuance and, if made thereafter, are treated as having been made on the last day of trading. This treatment applies to such payments insofar as they do not exceed three times the amount of the redundancy payment, etc. '*Discontinuance*' includes deemed discontinuance under *ICTA 1988, s 113(1)* or *s 337(1)*. It also includes a partial discontinuance. (Revenue Pamphlet IR 131, SP 11/81, 6 November 1981).

Simon's Direct Tax Service. See B3.1477.

50.25 **RESEARCH AND DEVELOPMENT EXPENDITURE**

This relief applies to expenditure of a revenue nature incurred **on or after 1 April 2000** on 'research and development'. [*FA 2000, Sch 20 para 26(1)*]. For reliefs for research and development expenditure of a capital nature (previously 'scientific research allowances'), see Tolley's Income Tax under Capital Allowances.

'*Research and development*' ('*R & D*') means activities treated as such under normal UK company accounting practice, subject to any Treasury regulations excluding any activities from, or adding them to, the definition. It does not include oil and gas exploration and appraisal (within *ICTA 1988, s 837B*). Any dispute as to what constitutes research and development is subject to the normal appeal procedures. [*ICTA 1988, s 837A; FA 2000, Sch 19 para 1, Sch 20 para 25(1)*].

Conditions for relief. A company is entitled to 'R & D tax relief' as described below for an accounting period in which it is a 'small or medium-sized enterprise' with 'qualifying R & D expenditure' of not less than £25,000 (proportionately reduced for accounting periods of less than 12 months) which is allowable as a trade deduction for that period (disregarding the pre-trading expenditure provisions of *ICTA 1988, s 401*, see 50.21 above) or which would be so allowable if, at the time of the expenditure, the company had been carrying on a trade consisting of the activities in respect of which it was incurred. The relief does not apply to expenditure incurred before 1 April 2000, again disregarding *ICTA 1988, s 401*. For accounting periods straddling 1 April 2000, only so much of the period as falls on or after that date is considered for this purpose.

A '*small or medium-sized enterprise*' is as defined in *Commission Recommendation 96/280/EC* of 3 April 1996 (although the Treasury may substitute another definition by order). This requires that the company, together with any other company in which it holds more than 25% of the capital or voting rights, has less than 250 employees and either or both of annual turnover not exceeding 40 million euros and annual balance sheet total not exceeding 27 million euros. A company the capital or voting rights in which are owned as to more than 25% by enterprises not themselves small or medium-sized enterprises is excluded *unless* either those enterprises are public investment corporations, venture capital companies or institutional investors not exercising individual or joint control over the company in question, or the company's capital is spread in such a way that it is not possible to determine by whom it is held, and the company declares that it can legitimately presume that it is not owned as to 25% or more by an enterprise or enterprises which are not small or medium-sized. A company is not a small or medium-sized enterprise until it has satisfied these criteria over two consecutive financial years, and similarly does not cease to be one until it has ceased to fulfil the criteria over two financial years.

'*Qualifying R & D expenditure*' is expenditure (other than capital expenditure) meeting the following conditions.

(1) It must be attributable to R & D, undertaken directly by the company or on its behalf, which is either related to a trade carried on by the company or from which it is intended that such a trade will be derived. This includes R & D which may lead to or facilitate an extension of that trade, or which is of a medical nature and has a special relation to the welfare of workers employed in that trade.

(2) It must be incurred on staffing costs or consumable stores or be qualifying expenditure on sub-contracted R & D.

Staffing costs include all emoluments (other than benefits in kind), employer NICs and pension contributions, and such costs are within (1) if paid to, or in respect of, directors or employees directly and actively engaged in R & D within (1). If between 20% and 80% of a director's or employee's time is spent directly and actively so engaged, an appropriate proportion of staffing costs related to him qualify. If less than 20% is so spent, none qualify, and if more than 80% the whole of the costs qualify. Staff providing support services (e.g. secretarial or administrative services) are not thereby treated as engaged in the activities they support, although ancillary staff employed in a dedicated R & D facility (e.g. technicians, maintenance, clerical and security staff) may qualify.

Expenditure is incurred on consumable stores if so treated in accordance with normal UK company accounting practice, and it falls within (1) if the stores are directly employed in R & D.

A company incurs expenditure on sub-contracted R & D if it makes a payment to a sub-contractor in respect of R & D within (1) contracted out by the company to that person. Except where the company and the sub-contractor are, or elect to be treated as if they were, connected persons (as to which see further below), 65% of such payments qualify.

(3) Any intellectual property created as a result of the R & D is or will be vested in the company (either alone or with others). 'Intellectual property' for this purpose means:

(*a*) any industrial information or techniques likely to assist in the manufacture or processing of goods or materials, the working of, or winning access to, mines, oil wells or other mineral deposits, or the carrying out of any agricultural, forestry or fishing operations; and

(*b*) any patent, trade mark, registered design, copyright, design right or plant breeders' right, and any corresponding or similar rights under the law of a country outside the UK.

(4) The expenditure must not have been incurred in carrying on activities contracted out to the company by any other person.

(5) The expenditure must not be subsidised. This excludes expenditure in respect of all or part of which State aid notified to and approved by the European Commission is or has been obtained (or where such aid is or has been obtained for any other expenditure attributable to the same R & D project). To the extent that some other grant or subsidy is obtained in respect of expenditure, or it is otherwise met directly or indirectly by any person other than the company, it is similarly excluded. Aid, grants, etc. not allocated to particular expenditure are for this purpose allocated in a just and reasonable manner. Reliefs under the current provisions are not State aid for this purpose.

As regards (2) above insofar as it relates to sub-contractor payments, special provision is made where the company and the sub-contractor are connected persons within *ICTA 1988, s 839*. Provided that, in accordance with normal UK company accounting practice, the whole of the sub-contractor payment and all of the sub-contractor's 'relevant expenditure' has been brought into account in determining the sub-contractor's profit or loss for a 'relevant period', the whole of the sub-contractor payment (up to the amount of the sub-contractor's 'relevant expenditure') qualifies. '*Relevant expenditure*' is expenditure on staffing costs or consumable stores (as under (2) above), not of a capital nature, which is incurred by the sub-contractor in carrying on, on behalf of the company, the activities to which the sub-contractor payment relates, and which satisfies (5) above. A '*relevant period*' is a period of account ending not more than twelve months after the end of the period of account of the company in which, in accordance with normal UK company accounting practice, the sub-contractor payment is brought into account in determining the company's profit or loss. Any necessary apportionment of expenditure for these purposes is made on a just and reasonable basis. The company and the sub-contractor may in any case jointly and irrevocably elect to be treated as connected for these purposes in relation to all sub-contractor payments paid under the same contract or other arrangement, such election to be made by written notice to the Revenue within two years after the end of the company accounting period in which the contract or arrangement is entered into.

[*FA 2000, Sch 20 paras 1–12, 26*].

The reliefs. The following reliefs are available where a company is entitled to R & D tax relief (as above) for an accounting period.

(*a*) If, in that period, it is carrying on a trade in computing the profits of which a deduction may be claimed for qualifying R & D expenditure (as above), the company may claim relief for an additional 50% of that expenditure, i.e. for **150%** of that expenditure in total.

(*b*) If, in that period, it has incurred qualifying R & D expenditure which is *not* allowable as under (*a*), but which would have been so allowable had it then been carrying on a trade consisting of the activities in respect of which the expenditure was incurred (i.e. pre-trading expenditure), the company may elect to be treated as having incurred a trading loss in the accounting period equal to **150%** of the amount of the expenditure, for which relief may be claimed in the usual ways (see 44 LOSSES). The pre-trading expenditure rules (see 50.21 above) do not then apply to treat the expenditure as incurred on the first day of trading. Such an election must be made in writing to the Revenue, specifying the accounting period to which it relates, within two years after the end of that period.

The trading loss may not be carried back to an earlier accounting period under *ICTA 1988, s 393A(1)(b)* (see 44.6 LOSSES) unless the company is entitled to R & D tax relief for the earlier period. If and when the company begins, in the same or any subsequent accounting period, to carry on a trade derived from the R & D in relation to which the relief was obtained, the loss (to the extent not otherwise relieved or surrendered) is treated as if it were a trading loss brought forward to that period under *ICTA 1988, s 393* (see 44.4 LOSSES).

(*c*) For an accounting period in which the company has a 'surrenderable loss', the company may instead claim an 'R & D tax credit' equal to the lesser of

 (i) 16% of the amount of the 'surrenderable loss', and

 (ii) the company's total PAYE and Class 1 NICs liability for payment periods (i.e. periods ending on the fifth day of each month for which liability to account for PAYE and NICs arises) ending in the accounting period.

The 16% figure is subject to revision by the Treasury by order. PAYE and Class 1 NICs liabilities are determined for this purpose disregarding any deduction in respect of working families' tax credits or disabled person's tax credits, and for Class 1 NICs, deductions in respect of statutory sick pay and statutory maternity pay are also disregarded.

A '*surrenderable loss*' arises for an accounting period where either (*a*) above applies and the company incurs a trading loss in the accounting period in the trade concerned, or (*b*) above applies and the company is thereby treated as incurring a trading loss. The amount of the surrenderable loss is so much of that trading loss as is 'unrelieved' or, if less, 150% of the related qualifying R & D expenditure. A trading loss is '*unrelieved*' for this purpose to the extent that the loss has not and could not have been relieved by a claim under *ICTA 1988, s 393A(1)(a)* (against profits of the same period, see 44.2 LOSSES), and has not otherwise been relieved (including under *ICTA 1988, s 393A(1)(b)* against profits of earlier periods, see 44.6 LOSSES), and has not been surrendered under *ICTA 1988, s 403(1)* (group or consortium relief, see 29.14 *et seq.* GROUPS OF COMPANIES). Losses carried back or brought forward to the accounting period in question are disregarded for this purpose.

See below as regards claims for R & D tax credits. On such a claim, the Revenue will pay to the company the amount of the tax credit, and the amount of the company's trading losses available to be carried forward from the period is accordingly reduced by the surrenderable loss for the period (or by a corresponding proportion thereof where the amount of the credit was less than 16% of the surrenderable loss). The payment is not treated as income for any tax purposes, and (together with any interest paid with it, see below) may be applied to any corporation tax liability of the company. Where there is an enquiry into the company's tax return for the period (see 55.7 SELF-ASSESSMENT), payment need not be made until the enquiry is completed (although the Revenue has discretion to make a payment on a provisional basis if they think fit). Similarly payment need not be made until all the relevant PAYE and NICs payments (as above) have been made.

[*FA 2000, Sch 20 paras 13–20, 23*].

Claims and overpayments. As regards (*c*) above, a claim for payment of an R & D tax credit must be made in a company tax return (or amended return) (see 55.3 SELF-ASSESSMENT) for the accounting period for which the credit is claimed, within one year of the filing date for that return (see 55.3 SELF-ASSESSMENT) or by such later time as the Revenue may allow. It can similarly only be amended or withdrawn by amendment of the company tax return within the same time limit. It must specify the quantum of the amount claimed. Penalties not exceeding the excess credit claimed apply for fraudulent or negligent claims, and for failure to remedy other incorrect claims without unreasonable delay. [*FA 1998, Sch 18 paras 10(2), 83A–83F; FA 2000, Sch 21 paras 2, 4*]. For recovery of overpayments of R & D tax credit, see 55.13 SELF-ASSESSMENT.

Anti-avoidance. Any transaction attributable to arrangements (including any scheme, agreement or understanding, whether or not legally enforceable) whose sole or main object is to enable a company to obtain a relief or payment under (*a*), (*b*) or (*c*) above to which it would not otherwise be entitled, or a greater relief or payment than that to which it would otherwise be entitled, is disregarded in determining the amount of any such relief or payment. [*FA 2000, Sch 20 para 21*].

Consortium relief. Where a company claims relief under (*a*) or (*b*) above for an accounting period at any time during which it is owned by a consortium whose members include at least one company which is *not* a small or medium-sized enterprise (as above), no amount may be surrendered (see 29.27 GROUPS OF COMPANIES) in respect of that period to any member which is not a small or medium-sized enterprise. [*FA 2000, Sch 20 para 22*].

A company not within the charge to corporation tax which incurs qualifying R & D expenditure is treated as having accounting periods as if it were carrying on a trade consisting of the activities in respect of which that expenditure is incurred which commenced when it started to carry on the R & D. [*FA 2000, Sch 20 para 25(3)*].

INTEREST ON OVERPAID TAX (38) applies to R & D tax credit payments from the filing date (see 55.3 SELF-ASSESSMENT) for the company tax return for the accounting period for which the credit is claimed (or if later the date of receipt by the Revenue of the return (or amended return) containing the claim) until payment. Such interest is recovered (as if it were INTEREST ON UNPAID TAX (39)) where there is a change in the tax credit payable resulting in an assessment (or amendment) to recover an amount of the credit (unless the change in the available credit results in a change in the company's corporation tax liability – see 38.1(vi) INTEREST ON OVERPAID TAX – or is in whole or part to correct a Revenue error). [*ICTA 1988, s 826(1)(d)(3A)(8A)(8BA); FA 2000, Sch 21 para 1*].

50.26 SCHEDULE A — INCOME FROM PROPERTY (TO 31 MARCH 1998)

The following provisions, which applied for income tax purposes for 1994/95 and earlier years, continue to apply for corporation tax purposes until 31 March 1998 (and see 50.27 below for the position after that date and for transitional provisions).

Rents etc. [*ICTA 1988, s 15*]. Schedule A applies to profits or gains arising in respect of

(*a*) rents (including sums treated as such in respect of premiums, see Tolley's Income Tax under Schedule A) under leases (including any tenancy) of land (including buildings) in UK,

(*b*) rent-charges, ground annuals, feu duties and other annual payments reserved in respect of, or charged on or issuing out of, such land,

(*c*) any other receipts from an estate or interest in, or right over, such land or any incorporeal hereditament or incorporeal heritable subject in the UK,

generally on the basis of rents or receipts arising in the chargeable period, less allowable deductions as below. Receipts from sales of turf are within (*c*) although they may alternatively be taxed as trading receipts within Schedule D, Case I (*Lowe v J W Ashmore Ltd Ch D 1970, 46 TC 597*): but from sale of colliery dross bings held to be capital (*Roberts v Lord Belhaven's Executors CS 1925, 9 TC 501*). Sums received for licence to tip soil on land held capital (*McClure v Petre Ch D 1988, 61 TC 226*).

Schedule A does not, however, include the following.

(I) *Rents etc. from furnished lettings.* These are assessed under Schedule D, Case VI unless the landlord elects for Schedule A in respect of payments for use of the premises within two years of the end of the chargeable period. [*ICTA 1988, s 15(1)(2); F(No 2)A 1992, s 58*]. The rent for the furnishings, etc. then remains under Case VI. See, however, Tolley's Income Tax under Schedule A as to holiday lettings. Income from letting caravan pitches, i.e. site rents, is assessable under Schedule A to the extent that it arises from exploitation of land, but, by concession, where the site proprietor carries on associated activities (e.g. shops) which constitute trading and account for a substantial part of the income, the letting income may be included as receipts of the trade under Schedule D, Case I. (Revenue Press Release 17 May 1984 and see Revenue Pamphlet IR 1, B29).

(II) *Woodlands.* Profits or gains arising from occupation of woodlands under commercial management with a view to profit.

(III) *Yearly interest.*

(IV) *Mineral rents, royalties etc.* charged to tax under Schedule D by virtue of *ICTA 1988, s 55, s 119* or *s 120* (see Tolley's Income Tax under Deduction of Tax at Source). However, from 6 April 1997, wayleave payments within *section 120* are charged under Schedule A (instead of Schedule D) where for the same period some or all of the land to which the easement relates is included in land by reference to which a Schedule A charge arises on the same person. [*ICTA 1988, s 15(1); FA 1988, Sch 6 para 6; FA 1997, s 60*].

Rents etc. from connected persons. Special provisions apply where the payer and recipient are 'connected' and the rents etc. accrue in a chargeable period of the recipient before that in which they are payable. If the payer is entitled to a deduction for the rents etc. in computing profits or gains for tax purposes, the recipient is regarded as becoming entitled to the rents etc. in the chargeable period in which they accrue (rather than that in which they become payable). For these purposes, rents etc. are treated as accruing at the same times and in the same amounts as they are so treated for the purposes of calculating the deduction to which the payer is entitled in respect of them, and the payer and recipient are 'connected' if they are CONNECTED PERSONS (16) within *ICTA 1988, s 839* either when the rents etc. accrue or at any earlier time after 9 March 1992 and after the making of the lease or agreement under which they accrue.

Similar provisions apply where the recipient of rents etc. in relation to land is connected with a person, other than the payer, who is entitled to a deduction for other rents etc. payable after they accrue under a lease or agreement relating to all or part of the same land, and those other rents etc. accrued before the rents etc. in question became payable. In such a case the rents etc. are treated as accruing, and hence chargeable, at the times and in the amounts they would be so treated if paid by rather than to the recipient and relieved as a trading deduction. [*ICTA 1988, ss 33A, 33B; F(No 2)A 1992, s 57*].

Expenses deductible — specific items. [*ICTA 1988, ss 25, 33*]. From *rent* (including sums treated as such in respect of premiums) to which the landlord becomes entitled in any chargeable period in respect of leased premises or land there may be deducted the aggregate of payments (but not interest [*ICTA 1988, s 25(2)*] nor items recoverable under insurance or from some other person) made by him for

(A) maintenance or repairs (arising from dilapidation during the currency of the lease and while he was landlord [*ICTA 1988, s 25(3)(b)*]), insurance or management (see below),

(B) other services the landlord was obliged, without separate consideration, to provide,

(C) rates or other charges on the occupier which the landlord was obliged to defray, and

(D) any rent (including allowances in respect of premiums, see Tolley's Income Tax under Schedule A), rent-charge, ground annual, feu duty or other periodical payment made by him in respect of the leased premises,

in that chargeable or any previous period, within the currency of the lease, during which he was the landlord.

In practice, relief under (B) above will be given for landlord's expenditure on services, amenities, etc. for tenants, even if not under an express lease covenant, but only if as under an arm's length agreement.

As regards (C), a deduction will normally be available for council tax (introduced on 1 April 1993) paid on let property (or for that part of any council tax paid which is attributable to the letting). (Revenue Press Release 16 March 1993). As regards the community charge, which was replaced by the council tax, a deduction is available for the standard community charge (payable in respect of premises which were not the sole or main residence of the occupier) where the property concerned was let. Similarly a deduction against rent is available for any amount of the collective community charge (payable by landlords in respect of certain houses in multiple occupation) which was not met by contributions from residents. (Revenue Press Release 10 November 1989). The deduction of business rates is unaffected by these changes.

Allowance for maintenance and repairs is limited to expenditure incurred by the taxpayer concerned in respect of current dilapidation [*ICTA 1988, s 25(3)*], and there is thus no allowance for remedying deterioration which occurred before the landlord purchased the property. As regards pre-purchase dilapidation see *Law Shipping Co Ltd v CIR CS 1923, 12 TC 621* and *Odeon Associated Theatres Ltd v Jones CA 1971, 48 TC 257* (but *Odeon* does not displace *section 25(3)* for Schedule A purposes).

Expenditure on improvements, additions or alterations is not allowed, nor is any outlay which has been allowed otherwise in computing income, e.g. under Schedule D, Case I [*ICTA 1988, s 31(6)*], nor expenditure balanced by the receipt of insurance moneys or recovered from, or borne by, any person other than the taxpayer (except where the receipt itself is income chargeable under Schedule A). [*ICTA 1988, s 31(5)*].

But, concessionally, the estimated cost of any maintenance and repairs obviated by alterations, etc., is allowed provided the alterations are not so extensive as to amount to reconstruction, and there has been no such change in the use of the property as would have rendered the repairs, etc., unnecessary. (Revenue Pamphlet IR 1, B4).

The following are types of expenditure normally allowable in respect of the property which is let.

(i) Current repairs and redecorations, inside and out.

(ii) Where falling under (B) above, upkeep of gardens of flats, and remuneration of porters, cleaners, etc..

(iii) Expenditure, so far as incurred for the benefit of tenants, on keeping up private roads, drains, ditches, embankments, etc., on an estate containing property let by the landlord (but not road works payments by frontager, *Davidson v Deeks Ch D 1956, 37 TC 32*).

(iv) Maintenance of common parts of blocks of offices, etc.

(v) Capital allowances under *CAA 1990, Pt II* are given (if the taxpayer so elects in writing) on machinery or plant provided for use, or used, by a person entitled to rents or receipts falling under Schedule A, for maintenance, repair, etc., of the properties concerned. Such an election has effect for the year of claim and all subsequent years, and may relate to all such machinery or, conditionally, to a specified class thereof only. Allowances or balancing charges are added to, or deducted from, total admissible outlay for the year; if a charge cannot be so dealt with it is assessed under Schedule D, Case VI. For accounting periods ending after 31 March 1997, these rules are revised so that machinery and plant allowances and charges are calculated as if all the activities of the company which would constitute the Schedule A business of an individual, and which are not chargeable under Schedule D, Case VI, were a separate trade for which the machinery or plant was provided (subject to further separation where there are furnished holiday lettings). Expenditure is thus pooled in the normal way. Allowances or charges are given or made by discharge or repayment, allowances being given primarily against Schedule A income (including any charge(s) under these provisions). Machinery or plant provided for use in a dwelling-house is excluded (with a just and reasonable apportionment of expenditure where such use is partial). [*ICTA 1988, s 32; CAA 1990, ss 28A, 73(1A); FA 1997, Sch 15 paras 1, 3, 6, 9*]. As an alternative to the above, renewals basis may be claimed.

(vi) Insurance premiums against damage to the fabric of the property by fire, food or tempest etc..

(vii) Valuation fees for purposes of insurance (but not for sale, probate, etc.).

(viii) Cost of rent collection. (But not rents embezzled by agent, *Pyne v Stallard-Penoyre Ch D 1964, 42 TC 183*. See also *Clapham's Trustees v Belton Ch D 1956, 37 TC 26*.)

(ix) Upkeep of estate offices.

(x) Salaries and wages of employees engaged full-time on estate management.

(xi) Pensions (not under covenant) customarily paid to retired employees or their widows so far as attributable to former services which were an allowable expense for Schedule A purposes.

(xii) Legal costs relating to the drawing up of a lease or tenancy agreement, although strictly capital, are in practice allowed, provided that:

(*a*) in the case of a first letting, the letting is for a period which does not exceed 21 years;

(*b*) on a re-letting, the re-letting is for a period which does not (and could not at the lessee's option) exceed 50 years.

(xiii) Legal and accountancy costs for preparing accounts, tax computations, etc. for the property.

(xiv) As regards agricultural property, costs of arbitration to determine rent, obtaining certificate of bad farming, or making a record of the holding. (Costs and compensation under claims for disturbance, unexhausted manures, etc., are not allowed.)

(xv) Ordinary annual subscriptions to The Country Landowners' Association, The Scottish Landowners' Federation and The National Association of Property Owners.

See generally Revenue Property Income Manual, PIM 5100–5120.

Expenses and deficiencies deductible — general provisions.

(1) Expenditure on property the rent from which is assessable under Schedule A is deductible, normally on the basis of actual payments made in the chargeable period. If the income for that period is insufficient to permit of full deduction, expenditure may be allowed for the period in which the payment became due. Any unrelieved

excess may be carried forward during the currency of the lease and set against rents of the next subsequent period, and so on [*ICTA 1988, ss 25, 31, 37(9)*].

In the case of expenditure on maintenance, repair, insurance and management of agricultural property, any unrelieved excess may be set against other income of the same year. [*ICTA 1988, s 33(1)*]. Where a loss claim against general income by an owner-occupier of a farm is precluded by *ICTA 1988, s 393A(3)* (non-commercial basis, see 44.9 LOSSES), relief for maintenance expenses of land, houses, etc. may be claimed under *ICTA 1988, s 33*. (Revenue Pamphlet IR 1, B5).

In the case of a property dealer, expenditure unrelieved under Schedule A in the current year may be allowed against Schedule D, Case I income. (Revenue Pamphlet IR 27, para 114, now withdrawn).

There is also a limited right of offset against income from other properties in the same ownership, see below.

(2) Where a lease is at a '*full rent*' (i.e. sufficient, on average, to cover the landlord's obligations, maintenance, repairs, insurance, etc.) deductions as above include unrelieved outlay incurred during (i) the period of any previous full-rent lease of the premises by the same landlord, or (ii) any 'void period' which either immediately follows the end of such a lease, or which commences with the acquisition of the property by the present landlord. However expenditure in these earlier periods may not be deducted if there is a period which does not fall into either (i) or (ii) between the earlier period and the period in which the deduction is claimed. A '*void period*' is a period during which the owner is entitled to possession of the premises but during which he is not in occupation. [*ICTA 1988, s 25(2)(5)(6)*].

(3) There is further relief for excess expenditure as under (1) or (2) above on properties let at a full rent (or in void periods following such lettings). Any such excess may be set against rents receivable by the same landlord from other properties, provided that those other properties are let at full rents and *not* on 'tenant's repairing leases'. Thus in effect all rents and expenses of properties let at full rents and not on 'tenant's repairing leases' are pooled, and against any aggregate balance of receipts may be set:

(i) excess expenditure of past years as under (2) above on properties in the pool; and

(ii) excess expenditure of the same year and of past years as under (2) above on other properties of the same landlord let at full rents on tenant's repairing leases.

[*ICTA 1988, s 25(7)*].

A '*tenant's repairing lease*' is one under which the lessee is obliged to maintain and repair the whole, or substantially the whole, of the premises. [*ICTA 1988, s 24(6)(c)*]. A lease under which all repair and maintenance work falls on the tenant apart from one structural item, such as maintenance of the foundations, is usually regarded as a tenant's repairing lease.

Deficiencies on leases not at full rent cannot be offset against any other source of income. They can only be carried forward for relief against income from the same property under the same lease while in the same ownership. [*ICTA 1988, s 25(3)(4)*].

(4) For applying the above provisions to land which, at 5 April 1963, was in one ownership and managed as one estate, the owner may elect to be treated as receiving, for any part of the estate not let (other than premises he occupies for estate management or trade), rent at a rate equivalent to its 'annual value', and, for any part

let at less than a full rent, rent at a rate at least equal to its annual value. He may then claim deduction of expenditure, as above, in respect of each of the properties in the estate. Any excess expenditure on such a property may not be set against rents from properties outside the estate, but excess expenditure on properties outside the estate let at full rent may be set against estate property rent, subject to the usual conditions at (3) above. [*ICTA 1988, s 26*]. The election, which applies to all subsequent years in which the estate is in the same ownership, must be made within one year (extendible by the Board) after the end of the first tax year for which it could have been made, and then (except in the case of the first possible election) is valid only if the previous owner had made a similar election. Property acquired after 5 April 1963 does not form part of the estate.

'*Annual value*' (as under *ICTA 1988, s 837*) is the rent reasonably to be expected from a letting on terms of the tenant paying tenant's rates etc. and the landlord bearing repairs, insurance and expenses necessary to maintain the property so as to command that rent. In practice, a property's gross rateable value is taken as its annual value. (Revenue Press Release 23 July 1985). In the case of Scottish estates, 1978 gross rateable values will continue to be used for this purpose, despite the 1985 rating revaluation, 'for the time being'. (Revenue Pamphlet IR 1, B30).

(5) From a receipt other than rent (rent charges, feu duties and other non-rental income) deductions may be made for payments as under (A) or (D) above, and any other non-capital expenses, constituting expenses of the transaction under which the sum arose, or which could be, but have not been, deducted from sums arising from other similar transactions in the year of assessment or any previous year. [*ICTA 1988, s 28*]. For treatment of sporting rights, and allowances for expenditure on making sea walls, see *ICTA 1988, ss 29, 30* and *Hesketh v Bray CA 1888, 2 TC 380.*

(6) *ICTA 1988, s 577* (business entertaining) and *s 577A* (expenditure involving crime) both apply to prohibit deductions.

Lost rents etc.. Where any rent or receipt to which the landlord was entitled is not in fact received (by default of the payer, despite reasonable steps for enforcement, or by waiver reasonably made, without consideration, to avoid hardship) a claim may be made to leave that sum out of account. But if any sum so ignored is subsequently recovered the Revenue must be notified (under penalty) within six months thereafter and the relevant liabilities are then readjusted. [*ICTA 1988, s 41*].

Collection from lessee or agent. For accounting periods ending before 31 March 1995, if liability to Schedule A tax falls on a person who is not in occupation of the property concerned, any lessee of the property whose interest derives from him may be required to pay the tax, to the extent of any rent falling due. The lessee then has a right of recoupment when paying his rent. A person receiving rents, etc., on behalf of another may, in default of payment by the latter, be required, under penalty, to pay them to the Revenue in settlement. [*ICTA 1988, s 23; FA 1995, s 39(4), Sch 6 para 3*].

Interest. As regards interest relief for loans to purchase commercially let property, see 50.3 above.

Simon's Direct Tax Service. See **A4.101** *et seq.*.

50.27 SCHEDULE A — INCOME FROM PROPERTY (FROM 1 APRIL 1998)

A new regime incorporating the concept of a 'Schedule A business' (including furnished lettings previously within Schedule D, Case VI) was introduced by *FA 1995* for income tax purposes only and applied from 1995/96 onwards. The old provisions which applied to income tax for 1994/95 and earlier years, continued to apply for corporation tax purposes until 30 March 1998 (see 50.26 above). With effect from 1 April 1998, the *Finance Act 1998* has brought the computation of Schedule A income for corporation tax purposes into line with the new treatment applying for income tax purposes, whilst retaining the flexibility of current reliefs for corporate interest and management expenses. The new provisions for corporation tax purposes, and the transitional provisions from the old to the new regime, are dealt with below.

Schedule A charge [*ICTA 1988, s 15; FA 1998, Sch 5 paras 1, 2*]. Schedule A applies to the annual profits arising from a business carried on for the exploitation, as a source of rents or other receipts, of any estate, interest or rights in or over land in the United Kingdom. This includes:

(*a*) payments in respect of a licence to occupy, or otherwise to use, land, or the exercise of any other right over land; and

(*b*) rent-charges, ground annuals, feu duties and other annual payments reserved in respect of, or charged on or issuing out of, the land.

It includes receipts from furnished lettings, which were previously within Schedule D, Case VI in most cases, unless the lettings fall within Schedule D, Case I; amounts paid for the use of furniture in connection with furnished lettings (with a corresponding allowance of expenses in connection with its provision), again unless the profits are within Schedule D, Case I; casual lettings; and lettings from caravans and house boats which are at a fixed location. See (III) below as regards furnished holiday lettings.

The following items are excluded from the computation for corporation tax purposes:

(*a*) interest payable, and other amounts falling within the loan relationships legislation in *FA 1996, Pt IV, Ch II* (see 43 LOAN RELATIONSHIPS);

(*b*) foreign exchange gains and losses falling within the legislation in *FA 1993, Pt II, Ch II* (see 23 EXCHANGE GAINS AND LOSSES); and

(*c*) profits and losses on financial instruments falling within the legislation in *FA 1994, Pt IV, Ch II* (see 25 FINANCIAL INSTRUMENTS).

Profits from occupying land (e.g. from woodlands) are excluded, as are profits chargeable under Schedule D, Case I from farming and market gardening [*ICTA 1988, s 53(1)*] or mining, quarrying and other such concerns [*ICTA 1988, s 55*], trading receipts and expenses from tied premises [*ICTA 1988, s 98*], and rent charged to tax under Schedule D in connection with mines, quarries, etc. [*ICTA 1988, s 119*] or electric line wayleaves. [*ICTA 1988, s 120(1)*].

The letting of all property in the UK by the same person is to be treated as a single business, except in the case of the following. (See (1) below for rental income from land outside the UK.)

(I) *Companies not resident in the UK.* In the case of a non-resident company trading in the UK through a branch or agency, a Schedule A business within the charge to corporation tax is treated as a separate business from any Schedule A business chargeable to income tax. [*ICTA 1988, s 15(1A)*]. See 53.4 RESIDENCE.

(II) *Insurance companies.* There are special rules dealing with the profits of Schedule A businesses and overseas property businesses in the case of insurance companies. [*ICTA 1988, ss 432AA, 432AB, 434E, 441B; FA 1998, Sch 5 paras 39–41*]. The single business concept does not apply to insurance companies as the computation of profits is based on the component business parts, which have different tax treatments. See generally 41 LIFE INSURANCE COMPANIES.

(III) *Furnished holiday lettings.* Income from the commercial letting of furnished holiday accommodation which does not amount to the carrying on of a trade has been brought within Schedule A, having previously generally been within Schedule D, Case VI. For various purposes it is treated as income from a separate trade and all such lettings are treated as one trade, separate from any other trade or the trade forming the remainder of the company's Schedule A business. [*ICTA 1988, s 503; FA 1998, Sch 5 para 42*]. See Tolley's Income Tax under Schedule A.

Flat management companies. Residential service charges received by an occupier-controlled flat management company are normally received as capital by the landlord in his capacity as trustee. See Revenue Tax Bulletin October 1998 pp 598, 599.

Computation of amount chargeable [*ICTA 1988, ss 21A, 21B; FA 1998, Sch 5 para 4*]. Schedule A profits are to be computed in accordance with the principles applicable to the computation of trading profits for the purposes of Schedule D, Case I (for which see Tolley's Income Tax under Schedule D, Cases I and II). In particular, profits are calculated on an accruals basis rather than a cash basis [*FA 1998, ss 42, 46(1)(2)*] and the following rules apply:

(*a*) the rules of apportionment [*ICTA 1988, s 72*];

(*b*) business entertaining expenses [*ICTA 1988, s 577*];

(*c*) expenditure involving crime [*ICTA 1988, s 577A*];

(*d*) redundancy payments [*ICTA 1988, ss 579 and 580*];

(*e*) training courses and counselling for employees [*ICTA 1988, ss 588–589B*];

(*f*) consideration for restrictive undertakings [*FA 1988, s 73(2)*];

(*g*) deductions in respect of certain emoluments [*FA 1989, s 43*];

(*h*) expenses relating to non-approved retirement benefit schemes [*FA 1989, s 76*]; and

(*j*) expenditure in connection with the provision of security assets or services [*FA 1989, ss 112, 113*].

The computational provisions relating to the Schedule D charge within *ICTA 1988, Pt IV, Ch V (ICTA 1988, ss 74–99)* apply generally to the computation of Schedule A profits (including the provisions relating to post-cessation receipts and expenses, etc.) as if the Schedule A business were a trade, except for the following:

(*a*) the restriction in *ICTA 1988, s 82* on the deductibility of interest paid to non-UK residents;

(*b*) the relief in *ICTA 1988, s 96* for fluctuating profits for farming and market gardening; and

(*c*) the treatment of receipts and expenses relating to tied premises as those of a trade under *ICTA 1988, s 98*.

The provisions for the treatment of a company commencing or ceasing to carry on a trade [*ICTA 1988, s 337(1)*] and for relief of pre-trading expenditure [*ICTA 1988, s 401(1)*] also apply to the computation of the profits of a Schedule A business. *ICTA 1988, ss 34 et seq.* continue to provide for the treatment of premiums on the grant of leases or subleases of less than 50 years.

Treatment of losses. *Schedule A losses.* A Schedule A loss may be set off against the company's total profits for the same accounting period. Any unrelieved part of the loss may be treated as a Schedule A loss of succeeding periods, for set-off against total profits of such periods, provided that the company continues to carry on the Schedule A business in the period concerned. Where the company is an investment company (see 40.1 INVESTMENT

COMPANIES), and the Schedule A business ceases, unrelieved losses can be treated as excess management expenses, provided that the company continues to be an investment company. These reliefs are available only where the Schedule A business is carried on on a commercial basis or in the exercise of statutory functions (see 44.9 LOSSES). [*ICTA 1988, s 392A; FA 1998, Sch 5 para 28*]. Where a claim is made to set off a non-trade loan relationship deficit against the gross profits for the deficit period, that deficit is set off before relief for Schedule A losses. [*FA 1996, Sch 8 para 1; FA 1998, Sch 5 para 64*]. See 43.3 LOAN RELATIONSHIPS.

Group relief. ICTA 1988, s 403 has been extensively amended to incorporate the tax treatment of Schedule A losses (and at the same time, the general rules have been drafted in a clearer, simpler language). [*ICTA 1988, s 403; FA 1998, Sch 5 para 29*]. See 29.18 GROUPS OF COMPANIES.

Change of ownership of company. The carry forward of Schedule A losses is restricted on the change of ownership of a company in a similar manner as applies to trading losses and excess management expenses. [*ICTA 1988, ss 768D, 769; FA 1998, Sch 5 paras 31, 32*]. See 40.5 INVESTMENT COMPANIES, 44.13 LOSSES.

Rent factoring. For the following purposes a transaction entered into **after 20 March 2000** is a '*finance agreement*' if, in accordance with normal UK company accounting practice, the accounts of a company receiving money under the transaction would record a financial obligation in relation thereto, and any amount so received is a '*finance amount*'. In the case of a member of a group of companies (within *Companies Act 1985, s 262(1)*), this applies also to the consolidated group accounts (within *Companies Act 1985, s 227*). A company is treated for this purpose as receiving any money which falls to be taken into account as a receipt in calculating the company's corporation tax liability (or would do so were the company UK-resident).

If a finance agreement transfers a right to receive rent (including any sum chargeable under Schedule A) in respect of UK land (other than by means of the grant of a lease of UK land), any person receiving a finance amount is treated as receiving it as rent in the chargeable period in which the agreement is made in the course of a Schedule A business, and the finance amount is taken into account in computing profits of that business for that period. 'Transfer of a right to receive rent' includes any arrangement under which rent ceases to form part of the receipts taken into account in computing a company's liability to income tax or corporation tax.

This provision does *not* apply where either:

(*a*) the term over which the financial obligation is to be reduced exceeds 15 years (no account being taken of any period beginning after the financial obligation has been substantially reduced and during which the arrangements for reduction differ from the arrangements applicable in a previous period otherwise than as the result of a provision for periodic review, on commercial terms, of rent under a lease); or

(*b*) the arrangements for reduction of the financial obligation substantially depend on the entitlement to a capital allowance of a person not connected (within *ICTA 1988, s 839*) with the person from whom the right to receive rent was transferred; or

(*c*) *ICTA 1988, s 36(1)* (sale with right to reconveyance) applies (disregarding its extension under *section 36(3)* to cases where land is leased back to the vendor within one month after the sale), or would apply if the price at which an estate or interest is sold were to exceed the price at which it is to be reconveyed; or

(*d*) *ICTA 1988, s 780* (sale and leaseback) applies; or

(*e*) the finance amount is brought into account in computing Schedule D, Case I profits other than by virtue of *FA 1989, s 83* (life assurance receipts, see 41.4 LIFE INSURANCE COMPANIES).

Where the provision *does* apply, *ICTA 1988, s 36(1)* does *not* apply if it would do so only by virtue of *section 36(3)*.

Interposed leases. Where, under a finance agreement, a lease under which a premium is payable is granted in respect of UK land, and it is in respect of the receipt of the premium that the financial obligation would be recorded (i.e. the premium is effectively a loan in return for the right to receive future rental income), the person to whom the premium is payable is treated as receiving it as rent in the chargeable period in which the agreement is made in the course of a Schedule A business, and the premium is taken into account in computing profits of that business for that period. This provision does *not* apply if:

(1) the term over which the financial obligation is to be reduced exceeds 15 years (and see the qualification under (*a*) above); or

(2) the length of the lease (calculated as under *ICTA 1988, s 38*) either does not exceed 15 years or is not significantly different from the term over which the financial obligation is to be reduced; or

(3) the arrangements for reduction of the financial obligation substantially depend on the entitlement to a capital allowance of a person not connected (within *ICTA 1988, s 839*) with the person who granted the lease in respect of which the premium is payable; or

(4) all or part of the premium is brought into account in computing Schedule D, Case I profits other than by virtue of *FA 1989, s 83* (life assurance receipts, see 41.4 LIFE INSURANCE COMPANIES).

Where the provision *does* apply, *ICTA 1988, s 34* (treatment of premiums as rent) does *not* apply.

Insurance business. As regards companies carrying on insurance business, the above provisions do not require any amount to be brought in in any life assurance business profits computation made on Schedule D, Case I principles. *ICTA 1988, s 432A* (apportionment of income and gains between different classes of business, see 41.3 LIFE INSURANCE COMPANIES) has effect in relation to any sum which is or would be treated as received by virtue of the above provisions. The accounts by reference to which the existence or otherwise of a finance agreement is determined do not include those required to be prepared under *Insurance Companies Act 1982, Pt II*.

Definitions. A 'lease' for the above purposes includes an underlease, sublease, tenancy or licence and an agreement for any of those things, but does not include a mortgage or heritable security. 'Premium' includes any like sum, whether payable to the immediate or a superior landlord or to a person connected (within *ICTA 1988, s 839*) with either (and in Scotland it includes a grassum payable to any landlord or intermediate landlord on the creation of a sub-lease), and also certain payments deemed to be premiums under *ICTA 1988, s 34(4)(5)*.

[*ICTA 1988, ss 43A–43G; FA 2000, s 110*].

Capital gains [*TGCA 1992, s 241; FA 1998, Sch 5 para 62*]. Any Schedule A business is treated as a trade for the purposes of replacement of business assets relief, relief for loans to traders and retirement relief. See Tolley's Capital Gains Tax under Furnished Holiday Accommodation, Losses and Rollover Relief.

General provisions

The corporation tax provisions are assimilated, with effect from 1 April 1998, to those which apply for income tax from 1995/96 onwards, for which see generally Tolley's Income Tax under Schedule A. *Finance Act 1998* introduces a number of changes for both income tax and corporation tax, from 6 April 1998 and 1 April 1998 respectively. The main areas of change from those dates are as follows.

(1) *Overseas property business.* Rental income from land situated outside the UK continues to be chargeable under Schedule D Case V. The letting is treated as a separate business and the same computational rules (including the lease premium rules) apply in determining the receipts and expenses to be included in the Schedule A computation as if the property were situated in the UK. [*ICTA 1988, s 70A; FA 1998, Sch 5 para 25*]. (This mirrors the rules applying for income tax purposes under *ICTA 1988, s 65A*, introduced by *FA 1998, Sch 5 para 24*.) The special rules governing the tax treatment of furnished holiday lettings do not apply to an overseas property business. [*ICTA 1988, s 70A(6); FA 1998, Sch 5 para 25*]. Case V losses may be carried forward and set off against Case V profits from the same business in subsequent accounting periods, provided that the business is carried on on a commercial basis or in the exercise of statutory functions. [*ICTA 1988, s 392B; FA 1998, Sch 5 para 28*].

(2) *Mutual business.* In the case of a mutual business (see 45 MUTUAL COMPANIES) rental profits are computed as if the parties concerned were not connected by any relationship of mutuality. Any surplus is chargeable on the person to whom the profits arise or who is entitled to the profits. [*ICTA 1988, s 21C; FA 1998, Sch 5 para 5*]. The treatment of cooperative housing associations remains unchanged (see 30 HOUSING ASSOCIATIONS).

(3) *Land managed as one estate.* The election relating to land in one ownership and managed as one estate under *ICTA 1988, s 26* (whereby the cost of maintenance can be set against a notional Schedule A rental income called the 'annual value') is abolished for accounting periods beginning on or after 1 April 2001. [*FA 1998, s 39*].

(4) *Lease premiums.* The part of a lease premium which is treated as rent is brought into the Schedule A computation for the chargeable period in which the payment is received. Hardship need no longer be proved to the satisfaction of the Board for payment of tax by instalments where the premium is payable by instalments. Also, in relation to assignments of leases granted at an undervalue, the chargeable excess premium on a subsequent assignment is brought into the Schedule A computation in the period in which the payment is due. [*ICTA 1988, s 34(7A)(8), s 35(2A); FA 1998, Sch 5 paras 15, 16*].

(5) *Sale with right of reconveyance.* Where land is sold subject to a right to reconveyance and the sale price is greater than the repurchase price, *ICTA 1988, s 36(4A)(4B)* now clarify that amounts deemed to have been received are brought into Schedule A profits in the period in which the estate or interest is sold, and that the date of sale is the date of the unconditional contract or the date on which a conditional contract becomes unconditional. [*ICTA 1988, s 36(4A)(4B); FA 1998, Sch 5 para 17*].

Transitional provisions

FA 1998, Sch 5 paras 65–76 make provision as follows for the computation of Schedule A profits during the transition to the new rules which apply (as above) from 1 April 1998.

(*a*) Receipt and expenses taken into account before 1 April 1998 (i.e. on the arising basis) are not taken into account again on or after that date (i.e. on the accruals basis). This applies notwithstanding the provisions of *FA 1989, s 43* relating to the deferred deduction for emoluments not paid within nine months after the end of the accounting period to which they relate.

(*b*) To the extent that receipts or expenses would, under the new rules, have been brought into account before 1 April 1998, but were not in fact brought into account before that date, they are brought into account on that date.

(*c*) Expenses incurred, but not taken into account, before 1 April 1998 may not be carried back for relief before that date under *ICTA 1988, s 25(3)* or *s 31(3)*.

(*d*) Where any estate, interest or rights in or over land is or are transferred from one person to another, (*a*)–(*c*) above apply to receipts or expenses taken into account in relation to either party.

(*e*) Where relief under *ICTA 1988, s 41* for rent, etc. not paid was given before 1 April 1998, any receipt on or after that date is taken into account under the new rules. Any writing off on or after that date is taken into account under the new rules, regardless of when the receipt was brought into account.

(*f*) For the above purposes an amount is 'taken into account' when it is brought into account for tax purposes, or would have been if the person concerned were chargeable to tax.

(*g*) Where a pre-1 April 1998 furnished lettings loss would have been carried forward as a Schedule D, Case VI loss but for the transfer of such lettings to Schedule A or Schedule D, Case V (see above), it is treated as a loss brought forward and available for set-off under the new rules.

(*h*) Where, in an accounting period straddling 1 April 1998, a source ceases to be within the charge to tax under Schedule A or Schedule D, Case V or VI, the new rules do not apply to that source *provided that* the company acquired the source more than twelve months before the start of the straddling period.

Simon's Direct Tax Service. See A4.101 *et seq.*.

50.28 SWAP FEES

By concession, where annual fees relating to interest and currency swaps (i.e. financial instruments enabling firms to diversify their interest and currency exposures) are not deductible in the computation of trading income under strict law, the net fees paid will be treated as if they were annual payments for the purpose of computing corporation tax profits. Where fees are paid by or to a recognised bank (as for *ICTA 1988, s 349*) or swaps dealer (for which see the text of the concession) in the ordinary course of its trade, deduction of the fees as a charge will not be conditional on tax having been deducted and accounted for. (Revenue Pamphlet IR 1, C17).

Swaps otherwise within this concession fall within the FINANCIAL INSTRUMENTS (25) provisions of *FA 1994, ss 147–177, Sch 18*, and the concession will therefore apply only to existing interest swaps on the 'commencement day' under those provisions (provided it does not fall after 22 March 1996, and provided that no election is made to bring them within the provisions) and in any event only for six years from the commencement day (see 25.5 FINANCIAL INSTRUMENTS). See sections 6.2 and 6.3 of the Explanatory Statement on Financial Instruments referred to at 25.1 FINANCIAL INSTRUMENTS.

50.29 TELECOMMUNICATIONS LICENCES

Special rules apply in relation to licences granted under *Wireless Telegraphy Act 1949, s 1* as a result of bidding for such licences under *Wireless Telegraphy Act 1998, s 3* regulations, and to rights derived directly or indirectly therefrom. They also apply to indefeasible rights to use a telecommunications cable system ('IRUs') acquired after 20 March 2000, unless they were acquired from an 'associate' (within *ICTA 1988, s 417(3)(4)*, see 13.5 CLOSE COMPANIES) or an 'associated company' (within *ICTA 1988, s 416(1)* (see 13.11 CLOSE COMPANIES) or, in relation to an individual, being a company of which that individual has control under *ICTA 1988, s 416(2)–(6)* (see 13.2 CLOSE COMPANIES)) which acquired them on or before that date, and to derived rights.

Acquisition costs and disposal proceeds in respect of such rights which, in accordance with normal UK company accounting practice, may be taken into account in determining accounting profit or loss, and which are so taken into account in any relevant statutory accounts required under *Companies Act 1985, s 226* (or NI or foreign equivalent), are treated as being of a revenue nature in computing profits chargeable to income tax or corporation tax. This applies equally to costs of extension of attached rights or of cancellation or restriction of rights attached to derivative rights, and to receipts from cancellation or restriction of attached rights or from granting derivative rights or extensions of rights attached to derivative rights.

Similar treatment applies to amounts in respect of the revaluation of such rights provided that, in accordance with normal UK company accounting practice, they fall to be taken into account for accounting purposes, whether or not they may be so taken into account in determining profit or loss or are so taken into account in any relevant statutory accounts. The period of account for which such an amount is taken into account for tax purposes is that in which it is recognised for accounting purposes in accordance with normal UK company accounting practice.

Where the taxpayer company is a member of a group of companies (within *Companies Act 1985, s 262(1)* or NI or foreign equivalent) which is required to produce consolidated group accounts (within *Companies Act 1985, s 227* or NI or foreign equivalent), the company's accounting policies, and method of applying those policies, in respect of rights within these provisions must not be more cautious than that adopted in the group accounts. This applies in relation to each group of which the company is a member, if there is more than one.

[*FA 2000, s 87, Sch 23*].

50.30 TONNAGE TAX

A new corporation tax regime is introduced in the *Finance Act 2000* enabling shipping companies which are 'qualifying companies', or groups of companies of which at least one member is a 'qualifying company', to elect for their corporation tax profits from the activities of 'qualifying ships' to be calculated by reference to the net tonnage of each of those ships, and for losses to be left out of account for corporation tax purposes. All 'qualifying companies' within a group must be taxed on the same basis.

A '*qualifying company*' is a company within the charge to corporation tax which operates 'qualifying ships' which are strategically and commercially managed in the UK. Certain temporary cessations from operating any 'qualifying ships' may be disregarded. '*Qualifying ships*' are broadly ships carrying on certain activities which are of at least 100 tons gross tonnage, but excluding fishing and factory support vessels, pleasure craft, harbour and river ferries, fixed and floating oil rigs and platforms, floating production, storage and offtake vessels, existing dedicated shuttle tankers subject to the petroleum revenue tax regime, dredgers, and any vessel whose main purpose is the provision of goods or services normally provided on land. Other types of vessel may be added to or removed from the excluded categories by Treasury order. The activities in which they must be engaged are transportation by sea, the provision of marine assistance or the provision of transport for services necessarily provided at sea. They may also, to a limited extent, include certain secondary and incidental activities.

Foreign dividends from non-UK resident shipping companies are (subject to conditions) also included in the profits covered by an election, as is any loan relationship credit (see 43.5 LOAN RELATIONSHIPS), exchange gain (see 23.7 EXCHANGE GAINS AND LOSSES) or profit on an interest rate or currency contract (see 25.5 FINANCIAL INSTRUMENTS) which would otherwise be treated as trading income. Otherwise, investment income is excluded.

Profits within the tonnage tax regime are 'ring-fenced', with appropriate anti-avoidance measures to prevent exploitation of the regime, and there are similarly capital allowance 'ring-fencing' provisions. No chargeable gains will arise during the currency of the election in relation to assets used for the qualifying activities, and balancing charges (on the disposal of assets for which capital allowances had previously been given) will be phased out using a sliding scale.

Capital allowances to lessors leasing to companies within the tonnage tax regime are similarly 'ring-fenced' and restricted.

Special provisions apply to the chartering in of qualifying ships and joint charters and to the chartering out of short-term over-capacity. There are also special rules for offshore activities in the UK sector of the continental shelf, and for group mergers and demergers.

Companies participating in the tonnage tax regime must also meet a minimum training obligation.

For existing qualifying companies, the *election* must be made within twelve months from 28 July 2000. If the company is not a qualifying company on that date, it may be made up to twelve months after its first becoming a qualifying company. In the case of a group no member of which was a qualifying company on 28 July 2000, it may be made within twelve months of a group company first becoming a qualifying company, provided that the group is not substantially the same as a group which at any earlier time had a member which was a qualifying company. The Treasury may provide further opportunities for elections by statutory instrument. Special provisions apply in relation to mergers and demergers. An election generally has effect from the beginning of the accounting period in which it is made (or, where that accounting period began before 1 January 2000, from the beginning of the following accounting period), subject to earlier or later effect in certain cases with Revenue agreement. It normally remains in effect for ten years for so long as the company (or group) qualifies and is not excluded, and (subject to the training requirements having been met) may at any time be renewed (such renewal being treated in effect as a valid new election). There is provision for exit charges on a company leaving the tonnage tax regime, and a bar on re-entry to the regime within ten years.

The Treasury may make provision by regulations for the application of the above provisions to activities carried on by a company in partnership.

[*FA 2000, s 82, Sch 22*].

Draft regulations under the new provisions were published on 17 May 2000. These set out the rules for determining written-down value of machinery and plant on exit from the tonnage tax regime or where machinery and plant is moved to offshore activities, and provide the definition of, and limits on, those secondary activities in which a qualifying ship may be engaged. A very lengthy and detailed draft Statement of Practice was published on the same day, covering all practical aspects of operation of the regime. Both are available on the Revenue's website (see 33.1 INLAND REVENUE: ADMINISTRATION).

50.31 TRANSFER FEES [*FA 1999, s 63*]

The accounting treatment of transfer fees paid by football or other sports clubs may be affected by either FRS 10 issued by the Accounting Standards Board on 4 September 1997 or the FRS for Smaller Entities issued by the Board on 10 December 1998. Where a transfer fee is paid under a contract entered into before the beginning of the first accounting period for which either of those standards has effect, then unless the club elects to the contrary (within two years after the end of that accounting period), the tax treatment of the payment is not affected by anything in the standard. Any necessary adjustments to give effect to this provision may be made, notwithstanding any relevant time limits.

50.32 **VALUATION FEES**

Property valuation fees incurred in order to comply with *Companies Act 1985, Sch 7 para 1* are allowable as trading or management expenses. (Revenue Pamphlet IR 131, C10). It is understood that regular property valuation fees (other than in connection with property acquisitions or sales) are similarly allowable.

50.33 **CORPORATION TAX RETURN**

See 54.14 RETURNS for the return form (Form CT200) required under 'Pay and File' prior to the introduction of self-assessment for accounting periods ending **on or after 1 July 1999**, and 55.14 SELF-ASSESSMENT for the self-assessment return form (Form CT600).

50.34 **EXAMPLES**

The following examples illustrate various aspects of corporation tax computations, including computational profit adjustments, loss relief and group considerations.

50.35 A Ltd, incorporated on 1 June 1995, commences business on 1 January 2000. The accounts for the year ended 31 December 2000 show the following

	£		£
Wages and salaries	178,400	Gross trading profit	2,288,760
Directors' remuneration	82,200	Income from property	8,000
Rent, rates and insurance	49,200	Government securities	340
Motor expenses	38,000	UK company dividends	1,500
Bad debts	8,200	Profit on sale of shares	64,000
Patent royalties payable (gross)	14,000		
General expenses	148,000		
Legal and professional costs	16,000		
Overdraft interest	6,000		
Debenture finance charges	3,500		
Audit and accountancy	16,000		
Depreciation of fixed assets	82,000		
Loss on sale of fixed assets	6,000		
Net profit	1,715,100		
	£2,362,600		£2,362,600

The following further information is available.

(*a*) Capital allowances for the year are:

	£
Plant and machinery (including advertising sign)	48,000
Industrial buildings allowance (re premises let)	24,000
Scientific research	24,000

(*b*) Bad debts consist of:

Trade debts written off	6,100
Reserve created — general	1,800
— specific	300
	£8,200

(*c*) General expenses include:

Advertising — erection of permanent sign (see (*a*) above)	1,050
Defalcations by junior staff	1,280
Entertaining — small promotional gifts	1,400
— UK customers	3,300
— overseas customers	800
— staff Christmas party	450
Gifts, donations — wines, etc. on exhibition stand	800
— trade protection society	250
— Oxfam (within *ICTA 1988, s 339*)	500
— political party	500
Inducement to planning official	750
Interest on unpaid tax	500
New premises — rehabilitation costs	3,000
Share sale — commission and fees	1,500
VAT — penalty for late return	400

(*d*) Patent royalties are paid under deduction of basic rate income tax. Of £14,000 royalties payable, £12,500 were paid in the year.

(*e*) Legal and professional costs consist of:

Company secretarial services	6,150
Debenture issue (see (*f*) below)	1,800
Debt collection	2,100
Industrial tribunal representation	750
Lease variation	1,000
Patent infringement claim work	3,400
Preparation of staff service agreements	800
	£16,000

(*f*) Debenture finance charges relate to £50,000 nominal stock issued on 1 January 2000 for trade finance at £96 per £100, carrying interest at 6.6% payable annually in arrears, for redemption 31 December 2009. The charge to profit and loss comprises interest of £3,300 and redemption reserve costs of £200 on a straight line basis. As these are arrived at under an authorised accruals basis of accounting, the charges are allowable for tax purposes. The issue costs included in legal and professional costs (see (*e*) above) are also allowable.

The overdraft interest charge is similarly on an authorised accruals basis and allowable.

The £340 Government securities credit relates to £4,000 nominal stock acquired in May 1999 at £4,040 with two years to redemption. It represents gross interest £360 less £20 premium amortisation charge on a straight line basis. It is thus properly chargeable under Schedule D, Case III as a non-trade credit. The interest was received under deduction of lower rate income tax on 31 March and 30 September.

(*g*) Chargeable gain on share sale 30 September 2000 £51,100.

(*h*) 26 year lease on new premises, at annual rent £22,500, purchased on 1 January 1996 at a premium of £200,000.

Cost of rehabilitation of premises to make suitable for trade use, between 1 January 1999 and 31 March 2000, £18,000.

Rates, etc. incurred before 1 January 2000, £20,000.

The computation for *year ended 31 December 2000* is as follows.

	£	£
Net profit		1,715,100
Add: Bad debts — general reserve	1,800	
Patent royalties	14,000	
Advertising — sign erection	1,050	
Entertaining	4,100	
Gifts, donations — wines, etc.	800	
— Oxfam	500	
— political party	500	
Inducement	750	
Interest on unpaid tax	500	
New premises — rehabilitation costs	3,000	
Share sale commission and fees	1,500	
VAT penalty	400	
Lease variation expenses	1,000	
Depreciation	82,000	
Loss on sale of fixed assets	6,000	117,900
		1,833,000
Less: Income from property	8,000	
Government securities	340	
Dividends received	1,500	
Profit on share sale	64,000	73,840
		1,759,160
Less: Plant and machinery allowances	48,000	
Scientific research allowances	24,000	
Lease premium allowance		
200,000 $(1 - \frac{25}{50}) \div 26$	3,846	
Pre-trading expenditure in seven years before 1 January 2000 (rent and rates)	110,000	185,846
		£1,573,314

	£	£
Schedule D, Case I trading profit		1,573,314
Schedule D, Case III		340
Income from property	8,000	
Less: Industrial buildings allowance	8,000	—
Chargeable gain		51,100
Total profits		1,624,754
Less: Industrial buildings allowance in excess of property income (claimed under *CAA 1990, s 145(3)*)		16,000
		1,608,754
Less: Charges paid — patent royalties	12,500	
— qualifying donation	500	13,000
Profits chargeable to corporation tax		£1,595,754
Tax chargeable:		
FY 1999 @ 30% on $\frac{1}{4} \times$ 1,595,754 = 398,938		119,681.40
FY 2000 @ 30% on $\frac{3}{4} \times$ 1,595,754 = 1,196,816		359,044.80
		478,726.20
Less: Income tax borne on interest on Government securities (assuming no claim made to set income tax suffered by deduction against liability to account for income tax deducted from charges paid)		
£180 @ 23%	41.40	
£180 @ 22%	39.60	81.00
		£478,645.20

50.36 B Ltd's profits chargeable to corporation tax have been as follows:

Year ended 30 June 1994	£8,000
Year ended 30 June 1995	£6,000
Year ended 30 June 1996	£6,000
Nine months to 31 March 1997	£4,000

For the year ended 31 March 1998, the accounts show the following:

	£
Trading income (after adjustment for corporation tax purposes, but before capital allowances)	10,000
Capital allowances (machinery and plant allowances)	57,000
Income from property	4,850
Chargeable gain on disposal	9,000
Patent royalties paid (for trade purposes)	8,000
Annuity paid (*not* for trade purposes)	3,000

The computation for *year ended 31 March 1998* is as follows.

Trading income	10,000
Less: Capital allowances	57,000
Trading loss	£47,000
Income from property	4,850
Chargeable gain	9,000
Total profits	13,850
Less: Trading loss claimed against total profits [*under ICTA 1988, s 393A(1)*]	13,850
Profits chargeable to corporation tax	—

Balance of trading loss (£47,000 – £13,850 = £33,150) is claimed against profits of earlier accounting periods under *ICTA 1988, s 393A(1)*.

Revised computation for *nine months to 31 March 1997*

	£
Profits (as previously determined)	4,000
Less: Trading loss of year ended 31 March 1998 (part)	4,000
Revised profits chargeable to corporation tax	—

Revised computation for *year ended 30 June 1996*

	£
Profits (as previously determined)	6,000
Less: Trading loss of year ended 31 March 1998 (part)	6,000
Revised profits chargeable to corporation tax	—

Revised computation for *year ended 30 June 1995*

	£
Profits (as previously determined)	6,000
Less: Trading loss of year ended 31 March 1998 (part)	6,000
Revised profits chargeable to corporation tax	—

Revised computation for *year ended 30 June 1994*

	£
Profits (as previously determined)	8,000
Less: Trading loss of year ended 31 March 1998 (part) (relief restricted, see note below)	1,347
Revised profits chargeable to corporation tax	£6,653

Balance of trading loss of year ended 31 March 1998 available for carry-forward and set-off against future trading income [*ICTA 1988, s 393(1)*] consists of:

Trading loss unrelieved (£33,150 – £17,347)	15,803
Trade charges [*ICTA 1988, s 393(9)*]	8,000
	£23,803

The non-trade charges (£3,000) cannot be utilised.

Note. The trading loss for the year to 31 March 1998 has to be apportioned between that part of the period falling before 2 July 1997 and the remainder. The loss apportioned to the latter part may only be carried back to periods falling within the period of one year immediately preceding the period of loss, whilst that apportioned to the earlier part may still be carried back up to three years. In this case, the pre-2 July 1997 period is 92 days, so that the part of the loss which may be carried back more than one year is

$$\frac{92}{365} \times 47{,}000 = £11{,}847$$

The losses used outside the year immediately preceding the year of loss are thus three-quarters of the £6,000 used in the year ended 30 June 1996 (£4,500) and the whole of the £6,000 used in the year ended 30 June 1995 (£6,000), the balance of £1,347 being available for use in the year ended 30 June 1994. Since this is less than the proportion of the profits of that year arising in the period 1 April to 30 June 1994 (i.e. within the period of three years immediately preceding the year of loss), relief for that year is restricted to £1,347.

50.37 D Ltd and E Ltd are wholly-owned subsidiaries of C Ltd, no other company being associated with any of them. Results for each for the year ended 31 December 1999 are as follows.

	£
C Ltd	
Trading profit (after capital allowances)	452,000
Chargeable gain on disposal	65,000
D Ltd	
Trading loss (after capital allowances)	84,000
Income chargeable Schedule D, Case III	2,000
Charges paid	3,000
E Ltd	
Trading profit (after capital allowances)	118,000
Income from property	2,000

On 5 April 1999, C Ltd paid a dividend of £140,000 (ACT accounted for £35,000), and surrenders any surplus ACT to E Ltd.

Ignoring group relief, the computation for each company is as follows.

C Ltd	
Total profits	£517,000

The upper limit for profits to be taxable at the small companies rate is £300,000 *divided by* 1 + the number of associated companies, i.e. £100,000. The limits for marginal relief are similarly reduced to profits between £100,000 and £500,000. C Ltd's profits are thus taxable in full at 31%/30%.

Corporation tax liability:	
FY 1998 @ 31% on $\frac{1}{4} \times 517{,}000 = 129{,}250$	40,067
FY 1999 @ 30% on $\frac{3}{4} \times 517{,}000 = 387{,}750$	116,325
	156,392
Less: ACT (maximum 20% × 517,000 × $\frac{95}{365}$ (see note below))	26,912
Corporation tax payable	£129,480

D Ltd	
Total profits	2,000
Less: Trading loss set against profits [*ICTA 1988, s 393A(1)*]	2,000
Corporation tax liability	—
Trading loss unrelieved	82,000
Charges paid	3,000
Loss available for group relief	£85,000

E Ltd	
Total profits	£120,000

Since this is between the upper and lower limits for marginal small companies relief (see under C Ltd above), such relief is available.

Corporation tax liability:	
FY 1998 @ 31% on $\frac{1}{4}$ × 120,000 = 30,000	9,300
FY 1999 @ 30% on $\frac{3}{4}$ × 120,000 = 90,000	27,000
	36,300
Less: $\frac{1}{40}$ × (500,000 – 120,000) =	9,500
Corporation tax liability	26,800
Less: ACT surrendered by C Ltd (maximum 20% × 120,000 × $\frac{95}{365}$ (see note below))	6,247
Corporation tax payable	£20,553

If D Ltd surrenders its losses by group relief, £65,000 to C Ltd, £20,000 to E Ltd, the computations are as follows.

C Ltd	
Total profits	517,000
Less: Group relief	65,000
Profits chargeable to corporation tax	£452,000

Corporation tax liability:	
FY 1998 @ 31% on $\frac{1}{4}$ × 452,000 = 113,000	35,030
FY 1999 @ 30% on $\frac{3}{4}$ × 452,000 = 339,000	101,700
	136,730
Less: $\frac{1}{40}$ × (500,000 – 452,000) =	1,200
Corporation tax liability	135,530
Less: ACT (maximum 20% × 452,000 × $\frac{95}{365}$ (see note below))	23,529
Corporation tax payable	£112,001

D Ltd	
Losses available for group relief	85,000
Less: Losses surrendered	85,000

E Ltd	
Total profits	120,000
Less: Group relief	20,000
Profits chargeable to corporation tax	£100,000
Corporation tax liability:	
FY 1998 @ 21% on $\frac{1}{4} \times 100{,}000 = 25{,}000$	5,250
FY 1999 @ 20% on $\frac{3}{4} \times 100{,}000 = 75{,}000$	15,000
	20,250
Less: ACT (maximum 20% $\times$ 100,000 $\times \frac{95}{365}$ (see note below))	5,205
Corporation tax payable	£15,045

This gives the optimum group tax position, as any switch of group relief from C Ltd to E Ltd saves tax on E Ltd at 20.25%, whereas C Ltd's marginal tax rate is 32.75%. A switch of relief from E Ltd to C Ltd has no effect on the overall liability, as E Ltd would also be taxable at a marginal rate of 32.75% on its additional profits coming into charge.

Note. The trading profit against which ACT can be offset has been apportioned to that period falling before 6 April 1999. If C Ltd is unable to carry back the surplus ACT (£1,841 when ignoring group relief and £6,266 when losses are surrendered by group relief) it will be carried forward and dealt with under the provisions for shadow ACT (see 3.8 ADVANCE CORPORATION TAX).

51 Purchase by a Company of its Own Shares

[*ICTA 1988, ss 95, 219–229*]

Simon's Direct Tax Service D1.110, D2.506 *et seq.*.

51.1 *Companies Act 1985, s 162 et seq.* permit a company to purchase its own shares, subject to various conditions. Such a purchase would normally be classified for tax purposes as a DISTRIBUTION (20), but in order to increase the attractions to entrepreneurs and investors of equity capital, *FA 1982* introduced a measure of relief for certain companies, generally small and family ones.

51.2 Treatment as a DISTRIBUTION (20) does not apply to certain payments (and other items normally treated as distributions) made by a company for the purchase, redemption or repayment of its own shares. The company does not have to account for ADVANCE CORPORATION TAX (3) on such payments etc., which, in the hands of the vendor, are brought into account for capital gains purposes only (but see 51.7 below as regards dealers in securities).

See, however, 20.10 DISTRIBUTIONS as regards certain subsequent bonus issues.

Where the purchase, etc. *is* treated as a distribution, see also 20.17 DISTRIBUTIONS as regards capital gains consequences and, for payments on or after 8 October 1996, 4.7 ANTI-AVOIDANCE for the treatment of the distribution as a FOREIGN INCOME DIVIDEND (26).

See also 29.8 GROUPS OF COMPANIES regarding ACT which a company accounts for in respect of *any* distribution made on the purchase etc. of its own shares.

The conditions for non-distribution treatment of such payments are set out at 51.3, 51.4 below. Revenue Tax Bulletin February 1996 pp 280–282 contains a short article dealing with various matters which in the Revenue's experience are sometimes overlooked or misunderstood, although these are all covered in this chapter.

Simon's Direct Tax Service. See **D1.110.**

51.3 **CONDITIONS TO BE SATISFIED BY COMPANY**

(i) The company must be an 'unquoted company', i.e. neither the company, nor any company of which it is a '*51% subsidiary*', must have any class of shares listed in the official list of a stock exchange. (Shares dealt in on the Stock Exchange Unlisted Securities Market were not treated as quoted, see Revenue Pamphlet IR 131, SP 18/80, 23 December 1980.)

Securities on the Alternative Investment Market ('AIM') are similarly treated as unquoted for these purposes. (Revenue Press Release 20 February 1995).

A company is a '*51% subsidiary*' of another if more than 50% of its ordinary share capital is beneficially owned directly or indirectly by the other company. [*ICTA 1988, s 838*].

(ii) The company must be either a 'trading company' or the 'holding company of a trading group' (for definitions, see 29.43, 29.47, 29.48 GROUPS OF COMPANIES). For this purpose, 'trade' does not include dealing in shares, securities, land or futures.

[*ICTA 1988, ss 219(1), 229(1)*].

Simon's Direct Tax Service. See **D2.507.**

51.4 CONDITIONS TO BE SATISFIED IN RESPECT OF PURCHASE ETC.

There are two different sets of conditions, one of which must be met to enable the payment etc. to qualify for the treatment as in 51.2 above. In addition, as a general condition, the consideration must be in money and must be paid immediately, i.e. instalment payment is not possible. (Revenue Tax Bulletin February 1996 p 281).

(1) Substantially the whole of the payment etc. (apart from any sum applied in paying capital gains tax on the disposal) must be used to **meet the payee's inheritance tax liability** on a death, within two years of that death, being a liability he could not have met without undue hardship other than through the purchase etc. of the shares or the purchase etc. of its own shares by another company within 51.3 above. [*ICTA 1988, s 219(1)(b)*].

(2) The purchase etc. of the shares must be made wholly or mainly to **benefit a trade carried on by the company** or by any '75% subsidiary'; it must **not form part of a scheme** or arrangement the main, or one such, purpose of which is either the obtaining by the vendor of a share in the company's profits without receiving a dividend, or the avoidance of tax; and the further conditions (i) to (viii) below must be satisfied in relation to the vendor. [*ICTA 1988, s 219(1)(a)*]. As regards whether a purchase etc. is for the benefit of the trade, the Revenue have given their interpretation in Revenue Pamphlet IR 131, SP 2/82, 3 August 1982. This emphasises that the purpose must be the benefit of a trade and not, for example, the benefit of the vending shareholder (although he will usually also benefit), or of some wider commercial purpose to which the payment etc. may be put, or of a non-trading activity of the trading company. Generally, the condition will be satisfied where (after taking into account any associate's interests) the vending shareholder is genuinely giving up his entire interest of all kinds in the company. Four examples are cited.

(*a*) The withdrawal of his investment by an outside shareholder providing equity finance.

(*b*) The retirement of the proprietor of a company to make way for new management.

(*c*) The death of a shareholder, on which his personal representatives or the beneficiaries do not wish to keep the shares.

(*d*) A disagreement over the management of the company.

In the last example, however, the condition would only be satisfied if the disagreement would, as will usually be the case, have an adverse effect on the running of the trade. It would not be satisfied if the disagreement were, for example, over whether the company should discontinue trading and become an investment company, and the vending shareholder advocated the continuance of trading.

In the case of an employee holding shares under e.g. a share option scheme, the Revenue do not regard the test as satisfied unless the employee leaves the company. (Tolley's Practical Tax 1984 p 206).

It may happen that the company wants, but cannot afford, to buy out a shareholder completely. In these circumstances, it is acceptable for the repurchase to proceed and for the shareholder to lend part of the consideration back to the company immediately after the purchase. Where the shares are of high market value and the issued capital is relatively small, this could result in the shareholder continuing to be 'connected with' the company (see condition (vii) below). To prevent this, it is acceptable for the company to make a bonus issue to increase its issued capital before the repurchase. (Revenue Tax Bulletin February 1996 p 281).

Where a shareholder is only 'substantially reducing' his interest (see (iii) below), the only situations in which the Revenue envisage the condition being satisfied are where a complete disinvestment is to be achieved in a number of transactions, or where a small shareholding (not exceeding 5% of issued share capital) is retained for sentimental reasons.

A company is a '*75% subsidiary*' of another if not less than 75% of its ordinary share capital is beneficially owned directly or indirectly by the other company. [*ICTA 1988, s 838*].

The further conditions which must be satisfied (as above) are as follows.

(i) The vendor (and any nominee holder) must be **resident** and (except for companies) **ordinarily resident** in the UK in the year of assessment of the purchase etc. The residence and ordinary residence of trustees is determined as under *TCGA 1992, s 69* (see Tolley's Capital Gains Tax under Settlements), and that of personal representatives follows that of the deceased immediately before his death.

(ii) The vendor must have held the shares for the **five years** before the purchase etc. If he acquired them under a will or intestacy, or as a personal representative, ownership by the deceased person (and, in the former case, by his personal representative) counts as ownership by the vendor, and the qualifying period is reduced to three years. Similarly, where the shares were transferred to the vendor by his spouse living with him at the time of transfer, the spouse's ownership counts as ownership by the vendor *provided that* the transferor either is still his spouse living with him or is deceased at the time of the purchase etc. Where identification of different holdings of shares of the same class is necessary, earlier acquisitions are taken into account before later ones, and previous disposals identified with later acquisitions before earlier ones, for this purpose.

Except in the case of certain shares allotted as stock dividends and falling within *ICTA 1988, s 249* (see Tolley's Income Tax under Stock Dividends), the time of acquisition of shares acquired through a reorganisation of share capital or conversion of securities etc. is that determined under *TCGA 1992, Pt IV, Ch II* (i.e. generally the date of acquisition of the original shares) (see Tolley's Capital Gains Tax under Shares and Securities).

(iii) The vendor's shareholding must be **substantially reduced** or eliminated by the purchase etc.

A shareholding is '*substantially reduced*' if and only if the proportion of the company's issued share capital held by him immediately after the purchase etc. does not exceed 75% of that immediately before the purchase. It is **not** regarded as so reduced if the share of profits to which the vendor would be entitled (beneficially except in the case of trustees or personal representatives) on a *distribution of available profits* by the company immediately after the purchase etc. exceeds 75% of the corresponding share immediately before the purchase etc.

Profits available for distribution by a company are as defined in *Companies Act 1985, s 263* (broadly, accumulated realised profits not distributed or capitalised *less* accumulated realised losses not written off) *plus* £100 *plus*, where any person is entitled to periodic distributions calculated by reference to fixed rates or amounts, the amount required to make the maximum distribution to which he would be entitled for a year. The division of profits available for distribution also assumes that the full amount of any such fixed entitlement for a year is attributed to the person entitled to it. Where the total of the payments etc. made at one time for the purchase etc. of the company's own shares exceeds the profits available for distribution, those profits are increased by the amount of the excess for the purposes of these provisions.

(iv) **Associated persons.** If, immediately after the purchase etc., any shares in the company are owned by an *associate* of the vendor, the combined interests of the vendor and his associate(s) must satisfy (iii) above.

Associate includes spouse and minor children, and a broad range of relationships whereby an individual or company may be able to influence the actions of another, or to benefit from the co-ordination of their actions. See *ICTA 1988, s 227* as regards trustees and certain employees.

(v) If the company making the purchase etc. is, immediately before that purchase etc., a member of a 'group of companies', and, immediately after the purchase etc., either

(*a*) the vendor owns shares in other group member(s), or

(*b*) he still owns shares in the company making the purchase etc. *and* had immediately before the purchase etc. owned shares in other group member(s),

then (iii) above must be satisfied in relation to his interest in the group as a whole, taken as the average of his proportionate holdings of the issued share capital of the company purchasing (etc.) the shares and of all other group members in which he holds shares immediately before or after the purchase etc. (including, for averaging purposes, companies in which he held shares immediately before or after the purchase etc. but in which he holds no shares when the average is to be determined).

A '*group of companies*' for this purpose is a company (not a 51% subsidiary (see 51.3(i) above) of any other company) and its 51% subsidiaries, *except that* a company which ceased to be a 51% subsidiary of another before the time of purchase etc. of the shares is treated as continuing to be such a subsidiary if at that time there were arrangements in existence under which it could again become such a subsidiary. Also, where the whole or a significant part of the business first carried on within three years before the purchase etc. by an unquoted company (see 51.3(i) above), the 'successor company', was previously carried on by the company purchasing (etc.) the shares (or by a member of the same group), the successor company and any company of which it is a 51% subsidiary are treated as being members of the same group as the company purchasing (etc.) the shares.

(vi) Where an associate (see (iv) above) of the vendor owns shares in any company in the same group (see (v) above) as the company purchasing (etc.) the shares immediately before the purchase etc., the combined interests of vendor and associate(s) must satisfy (v) above.

(vii) The vendor must not, immediately after the purchase etc., be 'connected with' the company purchasing (etc.) the shares or any company in the same group (see (v) above).

He is so '*connected with*' a company if, together with his associates (see (iv) above), he directly or indirectly possesses or is (or will be) entitled to acquire

(*a*) more than 30% of its voting power, its issued ordinary share capital, or its issued share capital and loan capital (i.e. any debt incurred by the company for money borrowed (including, it is understood, a bank overdraft used to finance the business operations, see Tolley's Practical Tax 1986 p 14), for capital assets acquired, for any right to income created in its favour or for insufficient consideration), or

(*b*) rights enabling him to more than 30% of its assets *available for distribution to the company's equity holders* (see 29.16, 29.17 GROUPS OF COMPANIES)

or if he has 'control' of it. '*Control*' for this purpose means the power of a person by shareholding or voting power (whether directly or through another company), or under Articles of Association, to secure that the company's affairs are conducted according to his wishes. [*ICTA 1988, s 840*]. An interest in loan capital acquired in the normal course of a money-lending business is disregarded provided the lender takes no part in the management or conduct of the company.

(viii) The purchase etc. must not be part of a scheme or arrangement the likely result of which is the acquiring by the vendor of rights such that, had he had them immediately after the purchase etc., any of (iii) to (vii) above could not have been satisfied. Any transaction within one year of the purchase etc. is deemed to be part of a scheme of which the purchase etc. is also a part.

Where any of (iii) to (viii) above are not satisfied, they will nevertheless be treated as satisfied where the vendor proposed or agreed to the purchase etc. in order that the conditions in (iv) or (vi) above regarding the substantial reduction of combined interests of a vendor and his associate(s) could be satisfied in respect of a purchase etc. of shares owned by such an associate, to the extent that that result is produced by virtue of the purchase etc.

[*ICTA 1988, s 219(1)(a), ss 220–229*].

Simon's Direct Tax Service. See D2.508–D2.510.

51.5 REVENUE INFORMATION POWERS

Within 60 days of making a payment etc. treated by the company as not being a distribution under the provisions at 51.2 to 51.4 above, the company must notify the inspector of the particulars of the payment etc., and why it is regarded as falling within those provisions. If within 51.4(2) above, any person connected with the company (see 51.4(2)(vii) above) who knows of any scheme or arrangement within 51.4(2)(viii) above must give details thereof to the inspector within 60 days of his coming to know of both the payment etc. and the scheme etc.

If the inspector has reason to believe that a payment etc. treated by the company as being within the above provisions may form part of a scheme etc. within 51.4(2) or 51.4(2)(viii) above, he may require the company or any person connected with it (see 51.4(2)(vii) above) to furnish him, within not less than 60 days, with a written declaration as to whether, according to information reasonably obtainable, any such scheme, etc. exists or has existed, and with such other information reasonably required by him as the company or person can reasonably obtain.

Any person receiving a payment etc. treated as falling within the above provisions, or on whose behalf such a payment etc. is received, may be required to notify the inspector as to whether he received the payment etc. on his own or another's behalf and, in the latter case, to supply the other person's name and address.

The penalty provisions of *TMA 1970, s 98* (see Tolley's Income Tax under Penalties) apply to returns required as above.

[*ICTA 1988, s 226*].

51.6 **CLEARANCE PROCEDURE**

A company may apply in writing for clearance from the Board of Inland Revenue that a proposed transaction falls or, as the case may be, does not fall within the provisions at 51.2 to 51.4 above. The Board must notify its decision within 30 days of receiving the application or, if further particulars are requested, within 30 days of the furnishing of the last such particulars. Such particulars must be requested within 30 days of the application (or of the furnishing of particulars previously requested), and must be supplied by the company within 30 days (or such longer period as the Board may allow). Failure to supply full and accurate information voids any clearance.

[*ICTA 1988, s 225*].

Applications for clearance should be sent to Inland Revenue, Central Correspondence Unit, New Wing, Somerset House, Strand, London WC2R 1LB. Where clearance is also being sought under *ICTA 1988, s 707*, a single application may be made to that address with an extra copy of the application and enclosures. If capital gains tax clearances are also sought, a copy should be sent to the appropriate address in Solihull (see 9.6 CAPITAL GAINS). (Revenue Press Release 9 August 1989).

The application should state whether the purchase, etc. is regarded as falling within *ICTA 1988, s 219(1)(a)* or *s 219(1)(b)* (see 51.4(2) or (1) above respectively), and give details of any earlier clearance applications (by the company or by a fellow group member). If the purchase etc. is regarded as within *ICTA 1988, s 219(1)(a)*, the application should include

(i) the name, tax district and reference number, and status (e.g. whether a trading company, etc.) of the purchasing (etc.) company, and confirmation that it is unquoted,

(ii) full details of any group of which it is a member, and of company and (if appropriate) group shareholdings,

(iii) details of the proposed share purchase and of any other transactions between the company and vendor at or about the same time, and confirmation that the purchase is permitted by the company's Articles,

(iv) full details of any prior transactions and of the reasons for, and the benefits expected from, the purchase, etc.,

(v) confirmation, with any necessary calculations, etc., that the other conditions outlined in 51.4(2) above are satisfied, and

(vi) the company's latest available balance sheet and profit and loss account (and, in the case of a member of a group, those of any fellow group members and, if appropriate, of the group as a whole) together with a note of any later relevant and material changes.

If the purchase, etc. is regarded as within *ICTA 1988, s 219(1)(b)*, the application should include the information as at (i) to (iv) and (vi) above, together with full details of the inheritance tax liability concerned and of the circumstances in which 'undue hardship' would arise.

An application for clearance that a proposed purchase, etc. does **not** fall within the provisions at 51.2 to 51.4 above should give full details of the purchasing (etc.) company and of the proposed purchase, etc., and be accompanied by a statement of the grounds on which clearance is sought.

(Revenue Pamphlet IR 131, SP 2/82, 3 August 1982).

Simon's Direct Tax Service. See **D2.511.**

51.7 **DEALERS IN SECURITIES**

From 1 July 1997, the following special provisions are subsumed into the revised *ICTA 1988, s 95*, which requires all distributions by UK-resident companies (and payments representative thereof) received by a dealer in securities, and any payment representative of such a distribution (or payment) made by such a dealer, to be taken into account in the dealer's Schedule D, Case I or II computation. For the details of the wider provisions, see Tolley's Income Tax under Schedule D, Cases I and II.

For earlier distributions made **after 25 November 1996**, all actual or deemed qualifying distributions to which *FA 1997, Sch 7* applies (which includes payments made on the redemption, etc. of own shares, see 4.7 ANTI-AVOIDANCE) received by a dealer are taken into account in computing the dealer's Schedule D, Case I or II profits. Accordingly:

(*a*) income tax under Schedule F is not chargeable;

(*b*) the distribution is not treated as received as a foreign income dividend;

(*c*) the normal exemption from corporation tax of UK company distributions (see 20.17 DISTRIBUTIONS) does not apply.

Where, as a result of any transaction, a qualifying distribution to which *FA 1997, Sch 7* applies is receivable by a dealer, the distribution is not, in relation to that transaction, treated as interest in determining whether *ICTA 1988, s 732* applies by virtue of *section 731* (purchase and sale of securities, see Tolley's Income Tax under Anti-Avoidance).

A person is for these purposes a dealer in relation to a qualifying distribution if, on a sale of the shares in respect of which the distribution is made, the price would be taken into account in computing Schedule D, Case I or II profits (assuming that it would not fall to be treated as a qualifying distribution).

Schedule D, Case I or II treatment also applies to payments by dealers which are representative of qualifying distributions within *FA 1997, Sch 7* (see 4.7 ANTI-AVOIDANCE). The prohibition on the deduction of manufactured dividends by non-UK resident companies from a day appointed for the purpose (see Tolley's Income Tax under Anti-Avoidance) does not apply to such payments.

The above provisions do not, however, apply to the redemption of fixed-rate preference shares (as defined), or of other preference shares issued before 6 April 1982 and redeemed on terms substantially settled before that date, if the shares were issued to and continuously held by the person from whom they are redeemed.

For distributions made **before 26 November 1996**, the above provisions applied only in relation to payments by a company for the redemption, etc. of its own shares, the definition of 'dealer' being correspondingly revised. (*b*) above had no application, but no tax credit was available in respect of any distribution element. The disapplication of interest treatment under *ICTA 1988, s 732* did not apply.

[*ICTA 1988, s 95; FA 1997, Sch 7 para 8(1)(3); F(No 2)A 1997, s 24, Sch 8 Pt II(8)*].

The requirement for certain profits from insurance business to be calculated on Schedule D, Case I principles does not bring them within *section 95* (see *Oakes v The Equitable Life Assurance Society; Bibby v The Prudential Assurance Co Ltd Ch D, [2000] STC 459*).

52 Regional Development Grants

Simon's Direct Tax Service B3.929.

52.1 Regional development grants, under *Industry Act 1972, Part I*, were payable on expenditure on certain buildings and certain new plant, machinery and mining works in special development areas, development areas, intermediate areas and derelict land clearance areas (which altogether covered a large part of UK except S.E. England). The amount of a grant does **not** operate to reduce capital expenditure on which CAPITAL ALLOWANCES (8) are claimable, except where the grant results in a reduction in the expenditure allowable for PRT purposes (see 46 OIL COMPANIES). [*CAA 1990, s 153(1); FA 1982, ss 137, 138*]. The same provisions apply to corresponding grants in NI.

Any such grant paid to a trader under *Industry Act 1972, s 7* or *8* or the corresponding NI legislation (and certain other NI payments) and not designated as paid for specified capital expenditure or as compensation for the loss of capital assets is treated as a trading receipt (or, in the case of INVESTMENT COMPANIES (40), as a Case VI receipt) insofar as it would not otherwise be so treated. [*ICTA 1988, s 93*]. An 'interest relief grant' under that *section* was held to be a trading receipt in *Burman v Thorn Domestic Appliances (Electrical) Ltd Ch D 1981, 55 TC 493*, as was an indeterminate grant under that *section* in *Ryan v Crabtree Denims Ltd Ch D 1987, 60 TC 183*. Grants under *Industrial Development Act 1982, Part II* to traders, etc. or to investment companies are exempt from corporation tax. [*ICTA 1988, s 92*].

See also 58 TEMPORARY EMPLOYMENT SUBSIDY.

53 Residence

Cross-references. See 2.3 ACCOUNTING PERIODS; 4.3, 4.4 ANTI-AVOIDANCE; 6.5 BANKS; 9.7, 9.53 CAPITAL GAINS; 18 CONTROLLED FOREIGN COMPANIES; 20.6, 20.7(v)(vi) DISTRIBUTIONS; 21 DOUBLE TAX RELIEF; 23 EXCHANGE GAINS AND LOSSES; 29.31 GROUPS OF COMPANIES; 31.2 INCOME TAX IN RELATION TO A COMPANY; 41.11–41.13 LIFE INSURANCE COMPANIES. For special rules concerning disposals of certain interests in offshore funds, see Tolley's Income Tax under Overseas Matters.

Simon's Direct Tax Service D4.1.

53.1 RESIDENCE

After 14 March 1988, a company incorporated in the UK is regarded for the purposes of the *Taxes Acts* as resident there, irrespective of any rule of law giving a different place of residence.

This 'incorporation test' does not, however, apply in the following circumstances.

(*a*) Where, immediately before 15 March 1988, a company was carrying on business and was not UK resident, having ceased to be so resident in pursuance of a Treasury consent given under *ICTA 1988, s 765* (or any predecessor legislation), and, where the consent was a general consent, the company was liable, by reason of domicile, residence or place of management, to tax on income in a territory outside the UK. If, after 14 March 1988, the company ceases to carry on business or, where the consent was a general consent, ceases to be taxable in a territory outside the UK, the incorporation test applies after that time (or after 14 March 1993 if later).

(*b*) Where a company which carried on business at any time before 15 March 1988 ceases to be UK resident after 14 March 1988 in pursuance of a Treasury consent, and immediately thereafter carries on business. If, after ceasing to be UK resident, the company at any time ceases to carry on business, the incorporation test applies after that time (or after 14 March 1993 if later).

(*c*) Where a company not within (*a*) above carried on business at any time before 15 March 1988, and was not UK resident immediately before that date, the incorporation test applies only after 14 March 1993.

(*d*) Where a company not within (*b*) above carried on business at any time before 15 March 1988, and ceases to be UK resident on or after that date in pursuance of a Treasury consent, the incorporation test applies only after 14 March 1993.

If a company within (*a*)–(*d*) above becomes UK resident at a time after 14 March 1988, the incorporation test applies to it after that time.

Residence for the purposes of (*a*)–(*d*) above is determined without reference to the incorporation test.

A company which is no longer carrying on any business, or is being wound up outside the UK, is treated as continuing to be resident in the UK if it was regarded as so resident immediately before it ceased business or any of its activities came under the control of the liquidator (or foreign equivalent). [*FA 1988, s 66*].

Revenue Pamphlet IR 131, SP 1/90, 9 January 1990, clarifies the Revenue's interpretation of three points in relation to the above rule.

(i) As regards whether a company is 'carrying on business' at a particular time, 'business' has a wider meaning than 'trade', and can include, for instance, the purchase of stock prior to trading, or the holding of investments (which could include the holding of shares in a subsidiary company, or a holding consisting of a single non-income producing investment). A company (e.g. a 'shelf' company) whose transactions have been limited to those formalities necessary to maintain its registration is not regarded as having carried on business. Where, in terms of the application of general case law to the question of residence (see 53.2 below), a company can demonstrate that it is or was resident outside the UK by reference to the place 'where its real business is carried on', it will have carried on business for the above purposes.

(ii) As regards the requirement under (*a*) that a company be taxable in a territory outside the UK, the liability must be to tax on income, so that liability to a flat rate fee or lump sum duty does not fulfil the test. It is, however, satisfied where the company is within the charge to tax, even though it may pay no tax because, for example, it makes losses or claims double taxation relief.

(iii) The exceptions granted to companies who have ceased to be resident in pursuance of a Treasury consent do not apply to companies who ceased to be resident without Treasury consent but who were subsequently informed by letter that no action would be taken against them.

Companies becoming resident under the above provisions (e.g. on 15 March 1993) are under an obligation to notify chargeability (see 49.1 PENALTIES) where appropriate, whether or not notice has been served requiring a return (see 54.2 RETURNS). A helpline has been set up to help companies becoming newly resident on 15 March 1993, in particular to assist in deciding whether they are entitled to indefinite or limited exemption from the incorporation rule of residence, and in ascertaining the appropriate tax district for correspondence. It may be contacted by telephone on 0207–438 7551 or by writing to Janet Holdsworth, Inland Revenue International Division, Melbourne House, Aldwych, London WC2B 4LL. See also Revenue Tax Bulletin May 1993 p 67 for common questions and responses.

With effect from 30 November 1993, a company which would otherwise be regarded as UK-resident (whether under *FA 1988, s 66(1)* or by virtue of some other rule of law), and which is regarded for the purposes of any double taxation arrangements under *ICTA 1988, s 788* as resident in a territory outside the UK and as not UK-resident, is treated as resident outside the UK and as not UK-resident. (See Revenue Tax Bulletin December 1994 p 179 for a list of double tax agreements to which this is applicable.) It is assumed for this purpose that the company has made a claim for relief under the arrangements, in consequence of which a decision falls to be made as to its residence status thereunder. Where a company became non-UK resident on 30 November 1993 as a result of these provisions:

(*a*) *FA 1988, s 130(1)–(6), s 131(1)–(5)* (see 53.7 below) do not apply;

(*b*) *TCGA 1992, s 179* (see 9.47 CAPITAL GAINS) is similarly disapplied where the company or another company thereby ceases to be a member of a group; and

(*c*) if, by virtue of *TCGA 1992, s 185(2)* (see 53.6 below), the company is deemed to have disposed of assets immediately before ceasing to be UK-resident, the tax is due and payable on the earlier of the day it actually disposes of the assets and 30 November 1999 (but not before the day on which the tax would otherwise have been payable under *TCGA 1992, s 185(2)*), and this is also the due and payable date for the purposes of INTEREST ON UNPAID TAX (39). Tax and interest are apportioned in the case of part disposals.

[*FA 1994, ss 249, 250*].

See generally Revenue Tax Bulletin December 1994 pp 179–181 for the application in practice of *FA 1994, ss 249, 250*.

Note. See also the *Note* at the end of 53.2 below.

Simon's Direct Tax Service. See **D4.101** *et seq.*.

53.2 There is no general statutory definition of residence, and before the enactment of the deeming provisions described in 53.1 above the courts had determined that a company resides where its real business is carried on, i.e. *where its central management and control actually abide*. This criterion continues to apply for companies incorporated outside the UK and for companies covered by the transitional provisions. In the following cases, the company was held to be managed and controlled from, and hence resident in, the UK: *Calcutta Jute Mills Co Ltd v Nicholson Ex D 1876, 1 TC 83* (UK company operating abroad but directors and shareholders meeting in UK); *De Beers Consolidated Mines Ltd v Howe HL 1906, 5 TC 198* (South African company operating there but important affairs controlled from UK where majority of directors resided); *New Zealand Shipping Co Ltd v Thew HL 1922, 8 TC 208* (New Zealand company with New Zealand directors, but overall control lay with separate London board); *American Thread Co v Joyce HL 1913, 6 TC 163* (UK company operating in USA with US directors in charge of current business, but overall control in London); *John Hood & Co Ltd v Magee KB (I) 1918, 7 TC 327* (company registered in both UK and USA, with the only director resident in USA, but general meetings and material trading activities in UK). But in *A-G v Alexander Ex D, (1874) LR 10 Ex 20*, a foreign state bank with a UK branch was held resident abroad, notwithstanding that shareholders' meetings were held in London.

See also *Untelrab Ltd v McGregor; Unigate Guernsey Ltd v McGregor (Sp C 55), [1996] SSCD 1*, in which subsidiaries of a UK-resident parent were held to be resident where their boards met and their business was transacted, as they did 'function in giving effect to [the] parent's wishes', notwithstanding that they were 'complaisant to do [the parent company's] will'. The Special Commissioners also held that the burden of proving residence on an appeal lies on the Crown.

The Revenue's approach to applying the basic test is firstly to ascertain whether the directors in fact themselves exercise central management and control; if so, to determine where that central management and control is exercised (not necessarily where they meet); if not, to establish where and by whom it is exercised. The concept of the place of central management and control is directed at the highest level of control of the company's business, rather than the place where the main business operations are to be found. This must always be a question of fact in any particular case, but the place of directors' meetings will usually be of significance if they are the medium through which central management and control is exercised. If, however, central management and control is in reality exercised by, for example, a single individual, the company's residence will be where that individual exercises his powers. With regard to the particular problem of residence of a subsidiary, the Revenue would not normally seek to impute to the subsidiary the residence of its parent unless the parent in effect usurps the functions of the Board of the subsidiary. Matters taken into account would include the extent to which the directors of the subsidiary take decisions on their own authority as to investment, production, marketing and procurement without reference to the parent (and see below).

In all cases, the Revenue will seek to determine whether a major objective of the existence of any particular factors bearing on residence is the obtaining of tax benefits from residence or non-residence, and to establish the reality of the central management and control. (Revenue Pamphlet IR 131, SP 1/90, 9 January 1990, replacing SP 6/83, 27 July 1983).

See 53.1 above as regards deemed residence of companies incorporated in the UK. However, under the general law, incorporation in the UK and compliance with the requirements of the *Companies Acts* do not in themselves render a company resident here. See *Todd v Egyptian Delta Land and Investment Co Ltd HL 1928, 14 TC 119* and cf. *Eccott v Aramayo Francke Mines Ltd HL 1925, 9 TC 445*. A company may be resident in more than one country. See *Swedish Central Railway Co Ltd v Thompson HL 1925, 9 TC 342*, and for an authoritative discussion of dual residence, *Union Corporation Ltd v CIR HL 1953, 34 TC 207*.

As regards companies in liquidation, the appointment of a UK liquidator of a non-UK resident company may result in the company's becoming UK resident. The exercise of central management and control remains, however, a question of fact, and if it is exercised overseas by the liquidator, or if the liquidator acts in accordance with the wishes of non-resident shareholders so that it is not in fact exercised in the UK, the company will not become UK resident. (ICAEW Guidance Note TR 799, June 1990).

A company may have a domicile (see *Gasque v CIR KB 1940, 23 TC 210*), but it would seem from the *Union Corporation* case above that, for a company, ordinary residence and residence are synonymous. See Tolley's Income Tax under Overseas Matters. Similar rules apply for ascertaining the residence of PARTNERSHIPS (47).

Note. For DOUBLE TAX RELIEF (21) purposes, the definition of residence will often be affected by the terms of the relevant agreement.

See 29.31 GROUPS OF COMPANIES as regards certain 'dual resident investing companies'.

53.3 OVERSEAS INCOME AND CHARGEABLE GAINS

A UK resident company is chargeable to corporation tax on its overseas profits, and income, whether remitted to the UK or not. [*ICTA 1988, s 70(1)*].

Where control of a UK resident company's trade rests abroad, the trade is a foreign possession, income from which is within Case V of Schedule D (*Egyptian Hotels Ltd v Mitchell HL 1915, 6 TC 152, 542*).

Where overseas income cannot, despite reasonable endeavour, be remitted to the UK, by reason of the laws or executive action of, or the impossibility of obtaining foreign currency in, the territory concerned, and where the income has not been realised outside that territory for sterling or an unblocked currency, then that income may be disregarded if the company so claims before any assessment by reference to that income becomes final. For accounting periods ending on or after 1 July 1999 (to which company self-assessment applies, see 55 SELF-ASSESSMENT), the claim must be made within two years of the end of the accounting period in which the income arises.

When the above conditions are no longer satisfied, the income becomes chargeable (on its value at that date taking into account foreign taxes chargeable on it in the territory concerned). Disputes are to be settled by the Special Commissioners.

[*ICTA 1988, s 584; FA 1996, Sch 20 para 33*].

Where tax on overseas income or chargeable gains has been assessed, the Board may allow that tax to remain uncollected, without payment of interest, if they are satisfied that the income etc. cannot be remitted due to government action in the country of origin and that it is otherwise reasonable to do so. Interest then ceases to run from the date on which the Board were first in possession of information necessary to enable them to agree to deferment. If that date is three months or less from the due and payable date, no interest is payable. But where a demand is later made for payment of the deferred tax, interest is exigible if the tax is not paid within three months of that demand. [*TMA 1970, s 92*]. The Board may defer collection indefinitely.

53.4 NON-RESIDENT COMPANIES

See 18 CONTROLLED FOREIGN COMPANIES as regards special rules applying to those with an interest in such companies.

53.4 Residence

A company not resident in the UK but carrying on a trade in the UK through a branch or agency is liable to corporation tax on

(*a*) trading income arising through or from the branch or agency, and

(*b*) income from property or rights used by, or held by or for, the branch or agency (excluding DISTRIBUTIONS (20) from UK resident companies), and

(*c*) chargeable gains from assets used for the branch or agency (see Tolley's Capital Gains Tax under Overseas Matters).

[*ICTA 1988, ss 6, 11; TCGA 1992, s 10(3)*].

Such companies are assessable under the appropriate Case of Schedule D on income chargeable as in (*a*) and (*b*) above which would be assessed under those cases if the company were resident in the UK (but excluding income specifically exempt in the hands of non-residents). [*ICTA 1988, s 70(3); FA 1996, Sch 14 para 7*]. In general, SMALL COMPANIES—REDUCED RATES (56) will be available (governed by world-wide company profits) as if the overseas company were UK resident, provided that there is a non-discrimination clause in the relevant double tax treaty. Associated companies are taken into account wherever resident. (CCAB Guidance Notes TR 500, 10 March 1983).

See Revenue Tax Bulletin August 1995 pp 237–239 as regards application of the arm's length principle in measuring the profits chargeable on a non-resident in respect of UK trading.

Income tax borne by a non-resident company on income on which it is liable to corporation tax is set off against the corporation tax chargeable. If income tax suffered on such income exceeds the corporation tax liability for the relevant accounting period, repayment of the excess may be claimed. [*ICTA 1988, ss 7(5), 11; FA 1990, s 98; FA 1998, Sch 18 para 10, Sch 27 Pt III(28)*].

A non-resident company is not liable to UK income tax on its UK income chargeable to corporation tax as above. [*ICTA 1988, s 6(2)(b)*]. It is liable to UK income tax on income from other sources in the UK (excluding income specifically exempt in the hands of a non-resident).

Where a non-resident company is within the charge to corporation tax in respect of one source and is assessable to income tax on that from another source, capital allowances related to each source are given against income from that source according to the rules of the tax involved. [*CAA 1990, s 149; FA 1990, Sch 13 para 4*].

Where a company becomes UK resident during a year of assessment, it is strictly liable to capital gains tax on gains arising in the year prior to its becoming resident. Similarly, on a company's ceasing to be UK resident during a year of assessment, it is strictly liable to capital gains tax on gains arising in the year after it ceases to be resident. By concession, such liabilities are generally waived for disposals before 6 April 1998. The concession is withdrawn from that date. (See Revenue Pamphlet IR 1, D2 and Revenue Capital Gains Manual, CG 42370, CG 42410.)

Non-payment of tax. There are special arrangements for collection of corporation tax unpaid within six months of the due date where any part of the tax relates to a chargeable gain accruing to the company on a disposal **before 1 April 2000**. The Board may seek to recover that tax (or part) within three years of its determination from any person who is, or in the twelve months before the disposal was, a controlling director of the company (or of a company controlling it) or a member of the same 51% group. [*TCGA 1992, s 191; FA 2000, Sch 29 para 9(1)(3)*]. See now 9.46 CAPITAL GAINS.

See 29.31 GROUPS OF COMPANIES as regards certain 'dual resident investing companies'. See also 27.3 FRANKED INVESTMENT INCOME.

Simon's Direct Tax Service. See **D4.122** *et seq.*.

53.5 **Charge to tax of non-resident companies.** For accounting periods beginning after 31 March 1996, obligations and liabilities in relation to income tax or corporation tax which are imposed on non-resident companies are also imposed on a branch or agency which is the company's 'UK representative' in relation to the amounts giving rise to the tax. This applies to the assessment, collection and recovery of tax, or of interest on tax. Either the company itself or its 'UK representative' may satisfy such obligations and liabilities, and the company is bound by the acts or omissions of its 'UK representative'. A person is, however, guilty of a criminal offence in relation to any of the above only where he committed the offence himself or consented to, or connived in, its commission. Formal notices, etc., where relevant, must be notified to the 'UK representative' for these provisions to apply. The 'UK representative' is treated as a person separate and distinct from the company for these purposes.

The branch or agency through which a non-resident company carries on a trade, profession or vocation in the UK is the company's '*UK representative*' in relation to income and gains referable to the branch or agency, even after cessation of the branch or agency. Where the trade, etc. is carried on in partnership, the partnership is the '*UK representative*'. The following are, however, excluded.

(*a*) An agent acting other than in the course of carrying on a regular agency for the company.

(*b*) A broker.

(*c*) An investment manager acting in an independent capacity through whom certain investment transactions (see *FA 1995, s 127(3)–(12)*) are carried out.

(*d*) A Lloyd's member's agent or syndicate managing agent for the company.

As regards (*b*) and (*c*) above, the transactions must be carried out in the ordinary course of a broking or investment management business, which may be part of a larger business, and for the customary consideration, but the broker or investment manager must not otherwise be the '*UK representative*' of the company. As regards (*c*), a person is not regarded as acting in an independent capacity on behalf of the non-resident unless their relationship is on an arm's length basis as between independent businesses (and see Revenue Press Release 17 February 1995).

Independent agents. An '*independent agent*' is a person who is a non-resident company's UK representative in respect of any agency in which he acts on the company's behalf in an independent capacity, i.e. their relationship is at arm's length between independent businesses. Such an agent is entitled to be indemnified in respect of any of the company's liabilities discharged by him, and to retain out of sums received on behalf of, or due to, the company amounts sufficient to meet any such liabilities. Information requirements imposed on an independent agent only require that, so far as practicable, he acts to the best of his knowledge and belief after taking all reasonable steps to obtain the necessary information. This does not, however, relieve the company itself from its obligations in this respect, nor bind the company by any error or mistake (unless resulting from the company's own acts or omissions, or from acts or omissions to which it consented or in which it connived). Similarly, such an agent is not liable to any civil penalty or surcharge resulting from the acts or omissions of others (to or in which he neither consented nor connived), provided that he can show that he is unable to recover the amount thereof out of moneys retained (as above).

[*FA 1995, ss 126, 127, Sch 23*].

For earlier accounting periods, the income tax and capital gains tax provisions of *TMA 1970, ss 78–84* were assimilated for corporation tax purposes by *TMA 1970, s 85* (see

Tolley's Income Tax under Overseas Matters). *TMA 1970, ss 78–85* are repealed by *FA 1995, Sch 29 Pt VIII(16)*.

Limits on income chargeable. For 1996/97 onwards and for accounting periods beginning after 31 March 1996, limits are imposed on the amount of income tax or corporation tax chargeable on a non-resident company, broadly to the sum of the tax otherwise chargeable, disregarding certain excluded income, and any tax deducted at source from the excluded income. (These limits apply also, with appropriate modification, to 1995/96 and to any accounting period beginning before 1 April 1996 and ending after 5 April 1995.) [*FA 1995, ss 128, 129; FA 1996, Sch 7 para 31*].

Simon's Direct Tax Service. See B3.125.

53.6 **COMPANY BECOMING NON-RESIDENT**

If, at any time (the '*relevant time*') after 14 March 1988, a company ceases to be resident in the UK, except with Treasury consent under *ICTA 1970, s 482(1)(a)* or *ICTA 1988, s 765(1)(a)* (see 4.3 ANTI-AVOIDANCE), and does not cease to exist, then

(*a*) it is deemed to dispose of, and immediately re-acquire, all its assets at their market value at that time, and

(*b*) rollover relief under *TCGA 1992, s 152* is not subsequently available by reference to disposals of old assets made before that time.

If at any later time the company carries on a trade in the UK through a branch or agency, (*a*) above does not apply to any assets which, immediately after the relevant time, are situated in the UK and are used in or for a trade, or are used or held for the branch or agency. Similarly (*b*) above does not apply to new assets acquired after the relevant time which are so situated and used or held. For this purpose assets situated in the UK include various assets and rights relating to exploration or exploitation activities in the UK or designated areas of the sea within *TCGA 1992, s 276*.

Similarly, where at any time after 14 March 1988 and before 30 November 1993 a company, while continuing to be UK resident, commences to be regarded, for the purposes of any double taxation relief arrangements (see 21.3 DOUBLE TAX RELIEF), as resident in a territory outside the UK, and as not liable to UK tax on gains on disposals of assets specified in those arrangements, (*a*) and (*b*) above apply to those assets. See now 53.1 above as regards the general provisions of *FA 1994, s 249*.

[*TCGA 1992, ss 185, 186; FA 1994, s 251(9)*].

See also 4.3 ANTI-AVOIDANCE.

If the deemed disposal in (*a*) above includes any '*foreign assets*' (i.e. assets situated, and used in or for a trade carried on, outside the UK), postponement of tax will be available, as described below, if

(i) immediately after the relevant time the company was a 75% subsidiary of a company (the '*principal company*') which was resident in the UK (i.e. not less than 75% of its ordinary share capital was owned directly by the principal company), and

(ii) both companies so elect in writing within two years after that time.

Any excess of gains over losses arising on the foreign assets included in the deemed disposal is treated as a single chargeable gain not accruing to the company on that disposal. An equal amount (the '*postponed gain*') is instead treated as follows.

If, within six years after the relevant time, the company disposes of any assets (the '*relevant assets*') chargeable gains on which were taken into account in arriving at the postponed gain, a chargeable gain equal to the whole, or the 'appropriate proportion', of the postponed gain, so far as this has not already been treated as a chargeable gain under these provisions, is deemed to accrue to the principal company. The '*appropriate proportion*' is the proportion which the chargeable gain taken into account in arriving at the postponed gain in respect of the part of the relevant assets disposed of bears to the aggregate of the chargeable gains so taken into account in respect of the relevant assets held immediately before the time of the disposal.

If at any time

(*a*) the company ceases to be a 75% subsidiary of the principal company on a disposal by the principal company of ordinary shares in it, or

(*b*) after the company otherwise ceases to be a 75% subsidiary, the principal company disposes of ordinary shares in it, or

(*c*) the principal company ceases to be resident in the UK,

a chargeable gain equal to so much of the postponed gain as has not previously been charged under these provisions is deemed to arise to the principal company.

If any part of the postponed gain becomes chargeable on the principal company, and the subsidiary has unrelieved capital losses, the companies may jointly elect, in writing within two years, for part or all of the losses to be set against the amount so chargeable.

[*TCGA 1992, s 187*].

Simon's Direct Tax Service. See D4.108.

53.7 After 14 March 1988, a company must, before ceasing to be resident in the UK otherwise than with Treasury consent under *ICTA 1970, s 482(1)(a)* or *ICTA 1988, s 765(1)(a)*, give to the Board

(*a*) notice of its intention to cease to be UK resident, specifying the time when it intends so to cease,

(*b*) a statement of the amount of tax which it considers payable for periods beginning before that time, and

(*c*) particulars of the arrangements which it proposes to make to secure payment of that tax.

It must also make arrangements to secure the payment of that tax, and the arrangements must be approved by the Board. Guidance notes regarding the giving of notice and the making of arrangements have been published by the Revenue. (Revenue Pamphlet IR 131, SP 2/90, 9 January 1990). In particular, notice under (*a*) above should be sent to Inland Revenue, International Division (Company Migrations) (at Room 311, Melbourne House, Aldwych, London WC2B 4LL) to whom an initial enquiry may be made via the Inland Revenue Information Centre (0207–438 6420/6425/7772).

Any reference to tax payable includes the following (and tax under corresponding earlier legislation).

(i) Tax under PAYE regulations.

(ii) Income tax payable under *ICTA 1988, s 350(4)(a)* (company payments which are not distributions, see 31.3 INCOME TAX IN RELATION TO A COMPANY).

(iii) Income tax payable under *ICTA 1988, s 555* (entertainers and sportsmen) or regulations under *ICTA 1988, s 476(1)* (see 7.3 BUILDING SOCIETIES).

(iv) Any amount payable under *ICTA 1988, s 559(4)* (see 17.2 CONSTRUCTION INDUSTRY TAX SCHEME).

(v) Any amount payable under *FA 1973, Sch 15 para 4* (territorial extension of charge to tax, see 53.9 below).

(vi) Interest on tax within (i)–(v) (whether or not the tax is paid).

Any question as to the amount of tax payable is to be determined by the Special Commissioners. If any information provided by the company does not fully and accurately disclose all the material facts and considerations, any resulting approval is void. [*FA 1988, s 130*].

See 53.1 above for the disapplication of these provisions in certain cases where a company was treated as becoming non-resident on 30 November 1993.

A person who is, or who is deemed to be, involved in a failure to comply with the foregoing provisions is liable to a penalty not exceeding the amount of unpaid tax for periods beginning before the failure occurred. [*FA 1988, s 131*].

Any tax not paid within six months of becoming payable can, within the three years following determination of the amount, be recovered from a person who is, or who was so in the year before residence ceased (or, if shorter, in the period beginning on 15 March 1988 and ending with the cessation of residence), a member of the same group or a controlling director. The changes to the definition of a group following *FA 2000* (see 9.18 CAPITAL GAINS) apply for this purpose where residence ceases on or after 1 April 2000, and also in the twelve-month period before residence so ceases. [*FA 1988, s 132; FA 2000, Sch 29 para 15*].

Simon's Direct Tax Service. See **D4.113.**

53.8 BANKS, INSURANCE COMPANIES AND DEALERS IN SECURITIES

Banks, insurance companies and dealers in securities which are non-resident but carrying on business in the UK are not exempt on income from overseas securities, stocks and shares by reason of non-residence. Income previously covered by *ICTA 1988, s 48* (foreign state securities) or *ICTA 1988, s 123(4)* (foreign dividends and interest on quoted Eurobonds) had, notwithstanding the exemption otherwise conferred by those provisions, to be included in computing profits and losses. [*ICTA 1988, s 474(1); FA 1996, Sch 7 para 18*]. See *Owen v Sassoon Ch D 1950, 32 TC 101* in which funds deposited against default by a Lloyd's underwriter were held to be within *ICTA 1988, s 474*.

For accounting periods ending before 1 April 1996, expenses, profits and losses attributable to the acquisition or holding of, or to any transaction in, securities issued by the Treasury, the interest whereon is, by a condition of the issue thereof, exempt from tax, are to be excluded from the computation of profits. [*ICTA 1988, s 474(2)*]. This does not cover interest on borrowed money, which is deductible in computing profits (or as a charge on income) only insofar as it exceeds a year's interest at the average rate paid in the accounting period on the smaller of

(i) all money borrowed for the purposes of the business which *is outstanding in the accounting or basis period*. It appears that successive loans will be aggregated for this purpose, notwithstanding that they were not both outstanding at the same time, and

(ii) the total cost of such tax-free Treasury securities as are held at any time in that period.

For accounting periods of less than twelve months, the amount of interest used in the calculation is proportionately reduced. Borrowings are excluded from (i) if they carry interest which is otherwise ineligible for relief. [*ICTA 1988, s 475; FA 1995, Sch 8 para 25*].

For accounting periods ending after 31 March 1996, these provisions are repealed, being displaced by the general provisions relating to FOTRA securities contained in *FA 1996, s 154*, except that *ICTA 1988, s 475* is retained in modified form and applied only to 3.5% War Loan 1952 or after. [*FA 1996, Sch 14 para 27, Sch 28 paras 2, 3*].

In the case of insurance companies, the above provisions apply to insurance business of any category. For accounting periods beginning before 1 November 1994, they applied equally to the calculation of profits or losses from pension business under *ICTA 1988, s 436*. [*ICTA 1988, s 474(1)(b); FA 1991, Sch 7 para 8; FA 1995, Sch 8 para 25*]. See 41.6 LIFE INSURANCE COMPANIES.

See Tolley's Income Tax under Life Assurance Policies for special treatment of policies issued by non-UK resident companies outside the scope of UK tax.

Simon's Direct Tax Service. See **A6.203** *et seq.*, **D4.536.**

53.9 UNITED KINGDOM

The United Kingdom for tax purposes comprises England, Scotland, Wales and Northern Ireland. The Channel Islands (Jersey, Guernsey, Alderney, Sark, Herm and Jethou) and the Isle of Man are not included. Great Britain comprises England, Scotland and Wales only.

Territorial extension of tax area. The territorial sea of the UK is regarded as part of the UK for tax purposes. Emoluments, profits and gains from exploration or exploitation activities in a designated area (under *Continental Shelf Act 1964, s 1(7)*) (and unlisted shares deriving most of their value from assets used for such activities) are treated as arising in the UK. Transfers of exploration or exploitation rights by a company not resident in the UK to a company which is so resident or which is resident in the same territory, are brought within the provisions relating to intra-group transfers. See 9.18–9.47 CAPITAL GAINS. A resident licence-holder under *Petroleum (Production) Act 1934* may be held accountable for the liability of a non-resident and may be required by the inspector to provide information concerning transactions with other persons and emoluments or other payments made. [*ICTA 1988, s 830; FA 1973, s 38, Sch 15; TCGA 1992, s 276; FA 1996, Sch 38 paras 1, 10; FA 2000, Sch 29 para 35*]. For the liability of a non-resident company engaged in exploration and exploitation activities to apply PAYE to its employees subject to tax under Schedule E, see *Clark v Oceanic Contractors Incorporated HL 1982, 56 TC 183.* For the liability to tax on profits or gains of non-resident lessors of mobile drilling rigs, vessels or equipment used in connection with exploration or exploitation activities, see Revenue Pamphlet IR 131, SP 6/84, 31 July 1984.

Simon's Direct Tax Service. See **A1.153.**

54 Returns

Simon's Direct Tax Service A3.110, D2.7.

The headings in this chapter are as follows.

54.1 Returns of profits etc. — 'Pay and File'
54.2 — accounting periods ending after 30 September 1993
54.3 — accounting periods ending on or before 30 September 1993
54.4 — rounding of tax computations
54.5 — examples
54.6 Returns for the purpose of advance corporation tax
54.7 Returns of income tax deducted from payments made by a company
54.8 Returns of non-qualifying distributions
54.9 Returns of stock dividends issued
54.10 Returns of interest by bankers etc.
54.11 Returns of income from UK securities
54.12 Other returns
54.13 Electronic lodgement of tax returns etc.
54.14 Corporation tax return

54.1 RETURNS OF PROFITS ETC.

'Pay and File' is the system under which companies are required to make returns and pay corporation tax. The underlying legislation was introduced by *F(No 2)A 1987, ss 82–91, 95, Sch 6*, *FA 1989, s 102*, *FA 1990, ss 91, 95–103, 106, Schs 15–17* and *FA 1991, Sch 15*, and applies to accounting periods ending after 30 September 1993 (*SI 1992 No 3066*). The provisions were in effect consolidated in *FA 1998, Sch 18* prior to the commencement of self-assessment for companies (see 55 SELF-ASSESSMENT). The following is a brief summary of the Pay and File provisions as a whole prior to the commencement of self-assessment. Reference as appropriate is made to the detailed coverage elsewhere in this work.

Under Pay and File, a company pays its own estimate of its corporation tax liability by the normal due date, nine months after the end of its accounting period, and further payments may be made (or repayments claimed) where appropriate until the liabilities are agreed. The completed return, accounts and computations must be submitted within twelve months of the end of the accounting period, with substantial penalties for late delivery. Amended returns may be made after the main return is submitted. See 48.1 PAYMENT OF TAX, 49.2 PENALTIES, 54.2 below.

See, however, 48.1 PAYMENT OF TAX as regards the introduction from 1999 of quarterly accounting in advance for corporation tax liabilities for large companies.

When liabilities are agreed, an assessment is made (or, exceptionally, an estimated assessment amended), and interest runs (either way, although at different rates) from the normal due date. See 38.1 INTEREST ON OVERPAID TAX, 39.1 INTEREST ON UNPAID TAX, 48.1 PAYMENT OF TAX. Special arrangements apply for groups of companies, see 29.33 GROUPS OF COMPANIES.

Revised procedures apply in relation to determination of claims for losses (see 44.4, 44.9 LOSSES), capital allowances (see 8.2 CAPITAL ALLOWANCES) and group relief (see 29.18, 29.23 GROUPS OF COMPANIES, 44.9 LOSSES), and to withdrawal or revision of such claims, which are made in the main or amended return (see 54.2 below).

There are also special provisions relating to the charge on loans to participators under *ICTA 1988, s 419* (see 13.9, 13.13 CLOSE COMPANIES), to the carry-back of surplus ACT (see 3.8 ADVANCE CORPORATION TAX) and to chargeable gains on a company leaving a group (see 9.47 CAPITAL GAINS).

See 54.13 below as regards electronic lodgement of returns.

Simon's Direct Tax Service. See **D2.7.**

54.2 **Accounting periods ending after 30 September 1993.** For accounting periods ending **before 1 July 1999**, if so required by notice (Form CT203) by an inspector, a company must make a 'company tax return' on a prescribed form (or an approved substitute) of such information, relevant to its corporation tax liabilities, as is required under the notice. Supporting accounts, statements and reports may also be required, although the accounts required of companies resident in the UK throughout the return period, and required to prepare accounts under *Companies Act 1985* for a period consisting of or including the return period, are only those it is so required to prepare. Details of assets acquired on which chargeable gains or allowable losses may arise may also be required.

The form prescribed by the Board under *TMA 1970, s 113(1)* for these purposes is Form CT200, which, with the accompanying guidance notes, also explains the requirements as to accompanying accounts, statements and reports. (Revenue Pamphlet IR 131, SP 9/93, 8 October 1993). See 54.14 below as regards layout of the return.

The return must include a declaration to the effect that, to the best of the knowledge of the person making it, it is correct and complete, and must be delivered by the later of

(*a*) twelve months after the end of the period to which it relates,

(*b*) twelve months after the end of the period of account in which falls the last day of the accounting period to which it relates (except that periods of account in excess of 18 months are treated as ending after 18 months for this purpose), and

(*c*) three months after service of the notice requiring the return.

A return is not 'delivered' to the inspector until it is received in the inspector's office. As regards (*c*) above, the date of service of the notice is the fourth working day after the date of posting unless the company proves otherwise. (Revenue Corporation Tax Pay and File Manual, CT 10307, 10315).

See 49.2 PENALTIES as regards late delivery of returns.

If the period specified by the notice is not an accounting period of the company, but the company is within the charge to corporation tax for some part of the specified period, the notice is to be taken as referring to all company accounting period(s) ending in or at the end of the specified period. If there is no such accounting period, but there is a part of the specified period which does not fall within an accounting period, the notice is to be treated as requiring a return for that part of the period. Otherwise, the notice is of no effect, and the company is not required to make any return pursuant to it.

Amendments to returns must be in such form, and accompanied by such information, etc., as the Board may require. Form CT201 is prescribed for this purpose, but amendments may be made using an unofficial form or by letter, as long as it gives clear and sufficient information concerning the change to be reported, shows the amount of tax (if any) payable or repayable as a result of the change, and includes a declaration signed by a person authorised by the company (or the liquidator of a company in liquidation) that the information is to the best of his or her knowledge correct and complete. (Revenue Pamphlet IR 131, SP 9/93, 8 October 1993).

[*TMA 1970, s 11; F(No 2)A 1987, s 82; FA 1990, s 91; FA 1998, Sch 19 paras 1, 2*].

The company tax return (or amended return) includes claims (or revisions or withdrawals of claims) for group relief (see 29.23 GROUPS OF COMPANIES) and capital allowances (see 8.2 CAPITAL ALLOWANCES), and also claims for payment of tax credit (where still available, see

27.2 FRANKED INVESTMENT INCOME) other than in the case of companies entitled to certain corporation tax exemptions, and for repayment of income tax deducted from payments received (see 31.5 INCOME TAX IN RELATION TO A COMPANY, 53.4 RESIDENCE). For claims under self-assessment, see 12.1 CLAIMS. [*ICTA 1988, s 7(6), Sch 17A para 6; TMA 1970, s 42; CAA 1990, Sch A1 para 7; FA 1990, ss 97(3), 98(3), Schs 15, 16 ; FA 1995, s 107; F(No 2)A 1997, Sch 4 paras 2, 3; FA 1998, Sch 18 paras 9, 10, 67, 79, Sch 19 para 20, Sch 27 Pt III(28)*]. An amended return will also be required if the assessment has not been made and the company wishes to revise the figure of corporation tax chargeable (which otherwise remains due and can be collected without assessment). Adjustments to figures other than those specified above do not require an amended return (although the company may make such a return if it wishes), and an amended return is similarly not required if there is an agreed reduction of a previously returned amount of capital allowances or group relief (which would reflect a disallowance of relief rather than a reduced claim). (Revenue Pamphlet IR 131, SP 9/93, 8 October 1993). In relation to group relief claims and surrenders, special arrangements may be entered into, with the agreement of the inspector, by groups of companies (or by some of the members of such groups) all having the same accounting date and dealt with mainly in one tax district. The effect of the arrangements is that the group may make joint amended returns covering all the companies within the arrangements, and may dispense with formal notices of consent for group relief surrenders amongst those companies. (Revenue Pamphlet IR 131, SP 10/93, 8 October 1993).

Self-assessment. For accounting periods ending **on or after 1 July 1999** (see *SI 1998 No 3173*), the company tax return must include a self-assessment by the company of its corporation tax liability on the basis of the information contained in the return, and taking account of reliefs or allowances claimed in the return. See 55.3 *et seq.* SELF-ASSESSMENT.

Simon's Direct Tax Service. See **D2.710** *et seq.*.

54.3 **Accounting periods ending on or before 30 September 1993.** *Transitional cases.* Exceptionally, the notice requiring a return for an accounting period ending before 1 October 1993 will be made after 31 December 1993, so that the Pay and File provisions (see above) will apply to the return (although not to any corporation tax liability for the period). In such cases, the Revenue will not impose late filing penalties or higher rates of such penalties (see 49.2 PENALTIES) before the time when a penalty (or higher penalty) would have been incurred had the accounting period ended on 1 October 1993, so that

(*a*) where the statutory filing date falls before 1 October 1994, the £100 penalty will not apply if the return is delivered before that date, and the £200 penalty will be reduced to £100 if it is filed before 1 January 1995,

(*b*) where the date for incurring a tax-geared penalty falls before 1 April 1995, it will not apply if the return is filed by that date, and

(*c*) where the date for incurring a 20% penalty falls before 1 October 1995, a 10% penalty will apply if the return is filed between 1 April and 1 October 1995.

See also 39.3 INTEREST ON UNPAID TAX. (Revenue Tax Bulletin August 1993 p 83).

Simon's Direct Tax Service. See **A3.110.**

54.4 **Rounding of tax computations.** To reduce the compliance burden on large companies whose statutory accounts are produced in round thousands, the Revenue are generally prepared to accept profit computations for tax purposes in figures rounded to the nearest £1,000 from single companies with an annual turnover of at least £5 million (including investment and estate income) in the accounts in question or in the preceding year, where rounding at least to that extent has been used in preparing the accounts. (Turnover of groups of companies is not aggregated for this purpose.) Such computations must be accompanied by a certificate by the person preparing the computations stating the basis of rounding, and confirming that it is unbiased, has been applied consistently and produces a fair result for tax purposes (and stating the program or software used where relevant), or, if there have been no changes from the previous year in these respects, confirming the unchanged basis. The rounding may not extend to the tax payable or other relevant figures of tax. Rounding is not acceptable where it would impede the application of the legislation, or where recourse to the underlying records would normally be necessary to do the computation. Thus it is not acceptable e.g. in computations of chargeable gains (except in relation to the incidental costs of acquisition and disposal), in accrued income scheme computations, in computations of tax credit relief, in relation to the CFC exemption limit (see 18.11(iv) CONTROLLED FOREIGN COMPANIES) or in certain capital allowance computations. The inspector may exceptionally insist that roundings are not used in other circumstances, and any existing arrangements falling outside the above arrangements must cease for periods ending after 31 May 1995. (Revenue Pamphlet IR 131, SP 15/93, 18 May 1993).

54.5 *Examples of return periods*

(A)

Aquarius Ltd has always prepared its accounts to 31 October. In 2000, it changes its accounting date, preparing accounts for the nine months to 31 July 2000. On 31 January 2000, the Inspector issues a notice specifying a return period of 1 November 1998 to 31 October 1999. On 31 January 2001, he issues a notice specifying a return period of 1 November 1999 to 31 October 2000.

In respect of the first-mentioned notice, Aquarius Ltd is required to make a return for the period 1.11.98 to 31.10.99 accompanied by accounts and tax computations for that period.

In respect of the second of the above-mentioned notices, the company is required to make a return for the period 1.11.99 to 31.7.00 accompanied by accounts and tax computations for that period.

(B)

Pisces Ltd has always prepared its accounts to 31 December. In 2000, it changes its accounting date, preparing accounts for the nine months to 30 September 2000. On 15 December 2000, the Inspector issues a notice specifying a return period of 1 October 1999 to 30 September 2000.

Pisces Ltd is required to make returns both for the period 1.1.99 to 31.12.99 and for the period 1.1.00 to 30.9.00, each return being accompanied by accounts and tax computations for the period covered by it.

(C)

Aries Ltd has always prepared accounts to 31 October. After 1999, it changes its accounting date, preparing accounts for the fifteen months to 31 January 2001. On 21 August 2000, the Inspector issues a notice specifying a return period of 1 November 1998 to 31 October 1999. On 31 January 2001, he issues a notice specifying a return period of 1 November 1999 to 31 October 2000.

In respect of the first-mentioned notice, Aries Ltd is required to make a return for the period 1.11.98 to 31.10.99 accompanied by accounts and tax computations for that period.

In respect of the second of the above-mentioned notices, the company is required to make a return for the accounting period 1.11.99 to 31.10.00, accompanied by accounts and tax computations for the period of account 1.11.99 to 31.1.01.

(D)

Taurus Ltd has always prepared accounts to 31 October. After 1999, it changes its accounting date, preparing accounts for the fifteen months to 31 January 2001. On 31 January 2000, the Inspector issues a notice specifying a return period of 1 November 1998 to 31 October 1999. On 1 April 2000, the Inspector issues a notice specifying a return period of 1 November 1999 to 31 January 2000.

In respect of the first-mentioned notice, the position is as in (C) above.

In respect of the second of the above-mentioned notices, Taurus Ltd is not required to make a return, but should notify the Inspector of the correct accounting dates and periods.

(E)

Gemini Ltd was incorporated on 1 July 1997 but remains dormant until 1 April 1999 when it begins to trade. The first trading accounts are prepared for the year to 31 March 2000 and the company retains that accounting date. On 1 May 2001, the Inspector issues notices specifying return periods of 1 July 1997 to 30 June 1998, 1 July 1998 to 30 June 1999, 1 July 1999 to 30 June 2000 and 1 July 2000 to 31 March 2001.

In respect of the notice for the period 1.7.97 to 30.6.98, Gemini Ltd is required to make a return for that period.

In respect of the notice for the period 1.7.98 to 30.6.99, the company is required to make a return for the period 1.7.98 to 31.3.99.

In respect of the notice for the period 1.7.99 to 30.6.00, the company is required to make a return for the period 1.4.99 to 31.3.00 accompanied by accounts and tax computations for that period.

In respect of the notice for the period 1.7.00 to 31.3.01, the company is required to make a return for the period 1.4.00 to 31.3.01 accompanied by accounts and tax computations for that period.

(F)

The final dates for the filing with the Revenue of the returns in (A)–(E) above, and for the payment of corporation tax (assuming none of the companies concerned fall within the definition of a 'large company', see 48.1 PAYMENT OF TAX), are as follows.

Return period	Filing date	Payment date
(A) above		
1.11.98 – 31.10.99	31.10.00	1.8.00
1.11.99 – 31.7.00	31.7.01	1.5.01
(B) above		
1.1.99 – 31.12.99	15.3.01	1.10.00
1.1.00 – 30.9.00	30.9.01	1.7.01
(C) above		
1.11.98 – 31.10.99	21.11.00	1.8.00
1.11.99 – 31.10.00	31.1.02	1.8.01
(D) above		
1.11.98 – 31.10.99	31.10.00	1.8.00

Return period	Filing date	Payment date
(E) above		
1.7.97 – 30.6.98	1.8.01	1.4.99
1.7.98 – 31.3.99	1.8.01	1.1.00
1.4.99 – 31.3.00	1.8.01	1.1.01
1.4.00 – 31.3.01	31.3.02	1.1.02

Notes

(*a*) The time allowed for filing returns is effectively extended to the time allowed under the *Companies Act 1985* if this would give a later filing date. This will not be so in the majority of cases.

(*b*) The Inspector may grant an extension, on an application by the company, if he is satisfied that the company has a 'reasonable excuse' (see 49.6 PENALTIES) for not being able to meet the filing date as above.

54.6 RETURNS FOR THE PURPOSE OF ADVANCE CORPORATION TAX (ACT) [*ICTA 1988, Sch 13; FA 1998, Sch 3 para 41*]

For distributions **before 6 April 1999**, returns of franked payments (i.e. dividends and other qualifying distributions made by a company, plus ACT attributable thereto) and FRANKED INVESTMENT INCOME (27) received by a company must be made within 14 days of the end of a 'return period'. [*ICTA 1988, Sch 13 paras 1, 2; FA 1998, Sch 3 para 41*]. If the return includes FII received, it will be treated as a claim for relief. [*ICTA 1988, Sch 13 para 5; FA 1998, Sch 3 para 41*].

A '*return period*' ends on 31 March, 30 June, 30 September and 31 December and at the end of a company's accounting period. [*ICTA 1988, Sch 13 para 1; FA 1998, Sch 3 para 41*].

See 3.4 ADVANCE CORPORATION TAX, 26.11 FOREIGN INCOME DIVIDENDS.

ACT is abolished for distributions made after 5 April 1999 (see 3.1 ADVANCE CORPORATION TAX).

Simon's Direct Tax Service. See **D1.605.**

54.7 RETURNS OF INCOME TAX DEDUCTED FROM PAYMENTS MADE BY A COMPANY [*ICTA 1988, Sch 16*]

Returns must be made by reference to 'return periods', as at 54.6 above. For details, see 31.4 INCOME TAX IN RELATION TO A COMPANY.

54.8 RETURNS OF NON-QUALIFYING DISTRIBUTIONS [*ICTA 1988, s 234(5)–(9); FA 1989, Sch 12 para 11*]

Where a company makes a *non-qualifying distribution* (see 20.18 DISTRIBUTIONS) it must make a return to the inspector (*a*) within 14 days of the end of the accounting period in which the distribution is made or (*b*) if the distribution is not made in any accounting period, within 14 days of when it is made. The return must show particulars of the transaction, the name and address of the person(s) receiving the distribution and the amount or value received by each.

Simon's Direct Tax Service. See **D1.608.**

54.9 **RETURNS OF STOCK DIVIDENDS ISSUED** [*ICTA 1988, s 250*]

Where a company issues stock dividends (see 20.16(*h*) DISTRIBUTIONS), it must make a return to the inspector within 30 days of the end of the return period as specified in 54.6 above. The return must show the first date on which the company was required to issue the shares, particulars of terms of issue and the appropriate amount in cash. See Tolley's Income Tax under Stock Dividends.

Simon's Direct Tax Service. See **D1.610.**

54.10 **RETURNS OF INTEREST BY BANKERS ETC.**

On receipt of notice from an inspector, any person (including the National Savings Bank and a building society) paying or crediting interest, on money received or retained in the UK in the ordinary course of his business, must make a return for any specified year of assessment (ending not more than three years before the date of service of the notice). The return must show the name and address of the recipient, the gross amount of interest paid or credited and the amount (if any) of tax deducted. The payer may exclude from that return interest paid to a person who has so requested and has given written notice that the person beneficially entitled to the interest is a non-UK resident company. Similarly, where a declaration of non-ordinary residence has been given to the payer to enable interest to be paid gross (see 6.9 BANKS, 7.4 BUILDING SOCIETIES), and the person who made that declaration has so requested, the payer is not required to include interest paid, credited or received before 6 April 2001 in the return under this provision. Notices may be issued concerning different parts or branches of a business. The Board have powers by statutory instrument to make regulations requiring further prescribed information with the return, or providing that prescribed information is *not* required, or requiring information and returns to be in prescribed form, or providing for inspection of books, documents, records, etc.. [*TMA 1970, s 17; FA 1988, s 123; FA 1990, s 92; F(No 2)A 1992, s 29; FA 1996, Sch 37 para 11; FA 2000, s 145; SI 1990 No 2231; SI 1992 No 2915*]. The Inland Revenue Financial Intermediaries and Claims Office may be contacted for technical advice in relation to *section 17* returns on 0151 472 6156.

Returns may similarly be required from any other person paying interest or receiving it on behalf of others. [*TMA 1970, s 18; FA 1988, s 123(3); FA 1990, s 92; FA 1996, Sch 37 para 11; FA 2000, s 145*].

Simon's Direct Tax Service. See **A3.120.**

54.11 **RETURNS OF INCOME FROM UK SECURITIES**

A person receiving income on behalf of, or by or through whom income is paid to, another person resident in the UK must, within 28 days (or such longer time as may be specified in the necessary notice) make a return giving details similar to those in 54.10 above. [*TMA 1970, s 24; FA 1996, Sch 37 para 11*].

54.12 **OTHER RETURNS**

For returns by employers, hoteliers, stockbrokers, partnerships etc. and in respect of fees, commissions and copyrights, see Tolley's Income Tax under Returns. For returns by companies purchasing own shares, see 51.3 PURCHASE BY A COMPANY OF ITS OWN SHARES. For returns of Eurobond interest payments, see 31.3(*b*) INCOME TAX IN RELATION TO A COMPANY.

54.13 ELECTRONIC LODGEMENT OF TAX RETURNS ETC.

There are currently no facilities for electronic submission of company self-assessment tax returns for accounting periods ending on or after 1 July 1999.

Certain other returns required to be made to the Board or to an officer of the Board may, subject to the conditions detailed below, be lodged electronically. The provision under which the return is required must be specified for this purpose by Treasury order, which will also appoint a commencement day. Any supporting documentation (including accounts, statements or reports) required to be delivered with a return may similarly be lodged electronically if the return is so lodged (or may instead be delivered by the last day for submission of the return).

The normal powers and rights applicable in relation to returns, etc. delivered by post are applied to information transmitted electronically. A properly made and authenticated hard copy (see (*c*) below) is treated in any proceedings as if it were the return or other document in question, but if no such copy is shown to have been made, a hard copy certified by an officer of the Board to be a true copy of the information transmitted is so treated instead.

There are four conditions for electronic lodgement.

(*a*) The transmission must be made by a person approved for the purpose by the Board. A person seeking approval must be given notice of the grant or refusal of approval, which may be granted for the transmission of information on the person's own behalf or on behalf of another person or persons. Approval may be withdrawn by notice from a given date, and any notice refusing or withdrawing approval must state the grounds. An appeal against refusal or withdrawal must be made within 30 days of such notice having been given, and lies to the Special Commissioners, who may grant approval from a specified date if they consider the refusal or withdrawal to have been unreasonable in all the circumstances.

(*b*) The transmission must comply with any requirements notified by the Board to the person making it, including in particular any relating to the hardware or software to be used.

(*c*) The transmission must signify, in an approved manner, that a hard copy was made under arrangements designed to ensure that the information contained in it is the information in fact transmitted.

(*d*) The information transmitted must be accepted under a procedure selected by the Board for this purpose, which may in particular consist of or include the use of specifically designed software.

As regards (*c*) above, the hard copy must have been authenticated by the person required to make the return:

(i) in the case of a return required by notice, by endorsement with a declaration that it is to the best of his knowledge correct and complete; or

(ii) otherwise by signature.

[*TMA 1970, s 115A, Sch 3A; FA 1995, s 153, Sch 28; FA 1998, Sch 19 para 43*].

Agents may pre-register for the electronic lodgement service. Copies of an information pack and registration form are available from the Agent Educator in all local tax offices. Revenue Statement of Practice SP 1/97, 16 January 1997, describes how the Revenue will operate electronic lodgement and the detailed requirements.

The above provisions are to be repealed from a date (or dates) to be appointed. They will be replaced by rules of more general application, with appropriate modification, to be introduced by regulations (see 33.11 INLAND REVENUE: ADMINISTRATION). [*FA 1999, s 133(3)(4), Sch 20 Pt VII*].

See Simon's Direct Tax Service A3.111A.

Incentives for electronic communications. Regulations may be made by statutory instrument by the Commissioners of Inland Revenue in relation to matters under their care and management (and by the Commissioners of Customs and Excise in relation to theirs) for the provision of incentives to use electronic communications. These may include discounts (or payments or repayments), or additional time for compliance or payment, or more convenient intervals for the delivery of information or the making of payments. Anything received by way of incentive is not regarded as income for tax purposes. The regulations may make provision as to the conditions of entitlement to incentives and for their withdrawal (which may be authorised to be made by direction), and may provide for penalties up to £1,000 for failure to comply with any specified provision. They may make different provision for different cases, and may make such incidental, supplemental, consequential or transitional provision as the Commissioners think fit. [*FA 2000, s 143, Sch 38*].

Internet filing discount. The Revenue has announced a number of incentives for which regulations as above will make provision. From April 2001, small businesses filing their VAT returns and/or their PAYE end-of-year returns via the internet and paying any tax due electronically will receive a discount of £50, or £100 for both VAT and PAYE filing, and a further £50 will be available where there are one or more working families' or disabled person's tax credit cases. The discounts will be available for one year for each service. (Revenue Press Releases 16 February 2000, 21 March 2000(BN1D)).

54.14 CORPORATION TAX RETURN

Pre-self-assessment. For accounting periods prior to the introduction of self-assessment (i.e. those ending **before 1 July 1999**) the standard form of return adopted for 'Pay and File' was Form CT200, which (or an approved substitute version for which) must be used by all companies required to do so by a Notice to Deliver a Corporation Tax Return (Form CT203). Form CT200 Notes provides guidance on the completion of Form CT200.

Form CT200 consists of ten sections.

1. Summary and declaration.
2. Short return.
3. Detailed return.
4. Capital allowances and balancing charges.
5. ACT.
6. Group relief — amounts claimed.
7. Group relief — amounts surrendered.
8. Overpayments and repayment claims.
9. Amounts brought forward and carried forward.
10. Directors' remuneration.

Apart from section 1, only those sections relevant to any particular case need to be completed. Sections 9 and 10 are entirely optional.

See 54.2 above for statutory requirements in relation to 'Pay and File' returns.

Self-assessment. See 55.14 SELF-ASSESSMENT for self-assessment return form (Form CT600) for accounting periods ending **on or after 1 July 1999**.

55 Self-Assessment

55.1 **Accounting periods ending on or after 1 July 1999.** Following the introduction of 'Pay and File' (see 54.1 RETURNS) for accounting periods ending after 30 September 1993, corporation tax moved to a full self-assessment regime for accounting periods ending **on or after 1 July 1999**. [*FA 1994, s 199(2)(b); SI 1998 No 3173*]. Corporation tax for this purpose includes amounts chargeable under *ICTA 1988, s 419* (loans to participators, see 13.9 *et seq.* CLOSE COMPANIES) and *ICTA 1988, s 747* (CONTROLLED FOREIGN COMPANIES (18)). [*FA 1998, Sch 18 para 1*]. The return and self-assessment provisions are brought together in *FA 1998, Sch 18.*

For the revisions to the controlled foreign company and transfer pricing régimes to bring them within self-assessment, see 18.1 CONTROLLED FOREIGN COMPANIES and 4.4 ANTI-AVOIDANCE respectively.

The essence of the self-assessment system is that returns are processed on receipt, by transfer to the Revenue's computer system, without checking (save insofar as amendments are required to enable the return to be processed, e.g. to correct arithmetical errors), with any enquiries being carried out later (within the statutory time limits, see 55.7 below).

The Revenue have published a detailed 'Guide to Corporation Tax Self Assessment', a free copy of which was sent to tax agents in May 1999. Further copies (price £15) may be ordered from Inland Revenue Library, Room 28, New Wing, Somerset House, London WC2R 1LB or obtained by personal callers to the Inland Revenue Information Centre, Ground Floor, SW Wing, Bush House, Strand, London WC2B 4RD. It is also available on the Revenue's website (see 33.1 INLAND REVENUE: ADMINISTRATION). References in this chapter to the 'Revenue Guide' are to that publication.

Simon's Direct Tax Service. See **D2.8.**

55.2 **Notification of chargeability.** A company chargeable to corporation tax which has not already made a company tax return for an accounting period, and has not received a notice requiring such a return (see 55.3 below), must give notice of its chargeability to the inspector within twelve months from the end of the period. Failure to do so renders the company liable to a penalty not exceeding so much of the corporation tax chargeable on its profits for the period as remains unpaid twelve months after the end of the period (disregarding any relief deferred under *ICTA 1988, s 419(4A)* in respect of the repayment, etc. of a loan to a participator, see 13.12 CLOSE COMPANIES). [*FA 1998, Sch 18 para 2*]. See 49.6 PENALTIES as regards 'reasonable excuse' for failure.

55.3 **RETURNS**

If so required by notice (Form CT603), a company must make a 'company tax return' on a prescribed form (or an approved substitute) of such information, relevant to its corporation tax liabilities, as is reasonably required under the notice. Supporting accounts, statements and reports may similarly be required. A completed return form unaccompanied by the related accounts and computations does not satisfy the filing obligation (see Revenue Guide para 3.2.1). Details of assets acquired on which chargeable gains or allowable losses may arise may also be required.

Most company tax returns will be by companies resident in the UK throughout the return period, and required to prepare accounts under *Companies Act 1985* (or NI equivalent) for a period consisting of or including the return period, and in such cases the accounts required are only those it is required to prepare under the *Companies Acts*, and any attachments required under the *Companies Acts* must also accompany the company tax return. In the case of a non-resident company trading through a UK branch or agency, the accounts required are (English language) trading and profit and loss accounts of both the company and the UK branch or agency together with the balance sheet of the company and (if prepared) of the UK branch or agency. Other companies are required to deliver the accounts they are required to prepare by law or under their constitution. (Revenue Guide paras 3.4).

Forms CT603 are usually issued to all active companies between three and seven weeks after the end of the period specified in them, which is usually a period thought to be an accounting period of the company. In a continuing case this will be based on the company's history. In the case of a new, or newly active, company, it will be based on information provided by the company in Form CT41G, which is issued to all such companies. If the company does not reply to such enquiries, it is assumed that the first accounting period runs for twelve months from the date of incorporation. (Revenue Guide paras 2.2, 2.3.1). As regards dormant companies, Forms CT204 are sent at intervals of not more than five years to check whether the company has traded or carried on any other activity, received any income or disposed of any assets in the review period, and to enquire about its future intentions. (Revenue Guide para 2.4). See below as regards discretionary treatment as dormant of certain members' clubs etc..

The company tax return form prescribed by the Board under *TMA 1970, s 113(1)* is Form CT600, which, with the accompanying guidance notes, also explains the requirements as to accompanying accounts, statements and reports. See 55.14 below as regards layout of the return. Guidance on the Revenue's main requirements for substitute forms is available from Business and Management Services Division, Forms Unit, Room 9/3A, NW Wing, Bush House, London WC2B 4PP. Form CT600 and guidance notes are normally issued with the notice requiring a return, except where an agent acts for the company or the company is recorded as using an approved substitute version of the return form (see Revenue Guide para 3.9.2). There are no facilities for electronic filing of company tax returns.

The return must include a declaration to the effect that, to the best of the knowledge of the person making it, it is correct and complete, and must be delivered (together with all the supplementary information, etc. required) by the 'filing date', i.e. the later of

(*a*) twelve months after the end of the period to which it relates,

(*b*) twelve months after the end of the period of account in which falls the last day of the accounting period to which it relates (except that periods of account in excess of 18 months are treated as ending after 18 months for this purpose), and

(*c*) three months after service of the notice requiring the return.

[*FA 1998, Sch 18 paras 3, 4, 11, 13, 14*].

Before making their returns, companies may ask their Tax Office (on Form CG34) to check their valuations used for capital gains purposes in completing their returns. (Revenue Press Release 10 January 2000).

A return is not 'delivered' to the inspector until it is received in the inspector's office. As regards (*c*) above, the date of service of the notice is the fourth working day after the date of posting unless the company proves otherwise. (Revenue Corporation Tax Pay and File Manual, CT 10307, 10315). The Revenue propose to issue an acknowledgement of receipt of every company tax return. (Revenue Guide para 4.10.2).

The notice requiring the return specifies the period to which it relates. A return is required for any accounting period which ends during or at the end of that period (separate returns being required if there is more than one such accounting period). If no accounting period ends during or at the end of the specified period, but there is an accounting period which commences during that period, then a return is required for the part of the specified period which falls before the start of that accounting period. If the company was outside the corporation tax charge throughout the specified period a return is required for the whole of the period. If none of the above applies, no return is required in response to the notice. [*FA 1998, Sch 18 para 5*].

Where the company carries on a trade, profession or business in partnership, the return must include its share of any income, loss, consideration, tax, credit or charge stated in the partnership return under *TMA 1970, s 12AB* for any period including, or including any part of, the company tax return period. [*FA 1998, Sch 18 para 12*].

Concessional exemption from requirement to deliver return. Members' clubs and similar organisations that exist primarily for recreational and other non-commercial purposes may, at the inspector's discretion, be treated as dormant even though they receive small amounts of investment income. The inspector will write to the company proposing this treatment, and if a company has not had such a letter the treatment does not apply. If a concern to which the concessional treatment applies is sent a notice to file, it will still have to make a return, and it will be expected to give notice of chargeability (see 55.2 above) if there are changes to the types and level of its income, to its rules or constitution, or to the way its financial affairs are controlled, or if chargeable assets are likely to be disposed of.

The concessional treatment is not extended to

(i) a club run by its members as a commercial enterprise for personal profit,

(ii) a housing association or registered social landlord (under *Housing Associations Act 1986*),

(iii) any organisation that carries on, or intends to carry on, a trade,

(iv) a trade association,

(v) a collective savings or investment arrangement,

(vi) a mutual insurance arrangement,

(vii) a company that is a subsidiary of, or wholly owned by, a charity, or

(viii) a company that has one or more associated companies.

The concessional treatment may be extended to non-profit-making flat management companies which pay no dividends and make no other distributions of profit, *which nevertheless remain liable to income tax* if they receive investment income on sinking funds, etc. held in designated accounts.

(Revenue Guide para 2.6).

Estimates. Where, despite the company's best efforts, a figure cannot be finalised by the filing date, the company may make its best estimate of the figure, tell the inspector that the figure is estimated and say when a final figure is expected. Provided that the company has taken all reasonable steps, a return so completed is not incomplete. If the company subsequently becomes aware that the estimate is no longer a 'best estimate', or that it can be replaced by an accurate figure, this information should be sent to the inspector without unreasonable delay. If estimates are submitted which prove not to be reasonable, the return is not thereby rendered incomplete, although penalties may arise if the return was completed fraudulently or negligently (see 55.7 below). (Revenue Guide para 3.8).

Failure to render return. A company which fails to make a return for any period, when required to do so, is liable to a penalty of £200 (£100 if the return is delivered within three months of the final day for delivery). If the return period is one for which accounts are required under *Companies Act 1985* or NI equivalent (see above), penalties do not apply provided that the return is delivered by the last day for delivery of those accounts. Extensions granted by the Secretary of State for the delivery of *Companies Act* accounts are taken into account in this context, and in practice the disapplication of penalties also applies where the return period overlaps the *Companies Act* accounts period (see Revenue Guide paras 10.4.1, 10.4.2). The penalties are increased to £1,000 and £500 respectively for failure in relation to a return for an accounting period where a penalty under these (or preceding) provisions was incurred for each of the two immediately preceding accounting periods, and the company was within the charge to corporation tax for the whole of the three accounting periods. An additional penalty is imposed where the return is still outstanding at the later of the end of the filing date and 18 months after the end of the return period. The additional penalty is 10% of the tax unpaid at the time the penalty arises if the return is delivered within two years after the end of the return period, otherwise 20%. The tax taken into account for this purpose is the unpaid tax for the return period (disregarding any relief deferred under *ICTA 1988, s 419(4A)* in respect of the repayment, etc. of a loan to a participator, see 13.12 CLOSE COMPANIES). [*FA 1998, Sch 18 paras 17, 18, 19*]. By concession, automatic penalties are not charged provided that the return is received on or before the last business day within seven days following the filing date. (Revenue Pamphlet IR 1, B46).

Amendments to returns. The company may, by notice to the Revenue within twelve months of the filing date (see above), amend its own return. A return made for the wrong period must be amended within twelve months of what would have been the final date for delivery of a return for the period if it had been an accounting period. The Revenue may, by notice to the company, amend the return to correct obvious errors or mistakes (including arithmetical errors and errors of principle, but *not* where any judgement as to the accuracy of figures in the return is involved) up to nine months after the date of delivery of the return (or after the date of the amendment if the correction relates to a company amendment). A Revenue correction is, however, of no effect if the company amends the return so as to reject the correction or, if the time limit for an amendment has passed, gives written notice rejecting it to the officer of the Board by whom the notice of correction was issued within three months of the date of issue. [*FA 1998, Sch 18 paras 15(1)(4), 16*].

Amendments to returns must be in such form, and accompanied by such information, etc., as the Board may require. [*FA 1998, Sch 18 para 15(2)(3)*]. No official form is prescribed for this purpose, and amendments may be made using an unofficial form or by correspondence. (Revenue Guide para 4.8.2).

Simon's Direct Tax Service. See **D2.805** *et seq.*, **D2.821**.

55.4 **Claims and elections.** All claims must be expressed in figures at the time the claim is made, and (subject to any provision prescribing a different time limit) must be made within six years from the end of the accounting period to which they relate. Claims and elections may be amended by the making of a supplementary claim or election within the time allowed for the original claim or election. [*FA 1998, Sch 18 paras 54–56*].

Subject to any express provision to the contrary:

(*a*) claims and elections affecting only one accounting period, and which are made after notice has been given requiring the delivery of a company tax return for that period, must be made in the return, or by amendment of the return, if they can be so made. A claim, etc. made after the return has been delivered is treated as an amendment of the return (as under 55.3 above). Group relief and capital allowance claims (see further below) and claims to 'R & D tax credit' (see 50.25 PROFIT COMPUTATIONS) can *only* be made by inclusion in a tax return;

(*b*) claims, etc. which affect an accounting period or periods other than that in which the event or occasion giving rise to the claim, etc. occurs are treated as amending the return for that period (or for the period affected), as under 55.3 above, where that return has already been delivered and can be so amended;

(*c*) otherwise, *TMA 1970, Sch 1A* (as amended by *FA 1998, Sch 19 para 42*) provides the procedure for claims etc. (see 55.11 below).

(*a*)–(*c*) above do not, however, affect the time limit or any other condition for making a claim or election.

A joint claim or election may be made in a return. The written claim etc. signed by the appropriate person(s) need be delivered with only one of the returns to which it applies, the return(s) of the other party or parties being required to reveal its existence and be prepared in accordance with it. (Revenue Guide para 7.6.6).

[*FA 1998, Sch 18 paras 10(2), 57–60; FA 2000, Sch 21 para 2*].

Certain claims not required to be made in a company tax return may not be made before the return for the period to which the claim relates is delivered. This applies to claims for payment of tax credits, where still available (see 27.2 FRANKED INVESTMENT INCOME), excluding claims by companies entitled to certain corporation tax exemptions unless *ICTA 1988, Sch 19AB* applies (see 41.6 LIFE INSURANCE COMPANIES), to certain claims for income tax repayments, and to claims for relief under *FA 2000, Sch 15 Pt V* (CORPORATE VENTURING SCHEME (19)). [*FA 1998, Sch 18 para 9; FA 2000, Sch 16 para 5(3)*].

Consequential claims. For consequential claims, elections etc. arising out of Revenue assessments or amendments to self-assessments, see 55.9 below.

Group relief. A claim to group relief must be included in the company tax return (or amended return) for the accounting period for which the claim is made. It must specify the quantum of the amount claimed and the surrendering company. For accounting periods ending on or after 1 April 2000, it must also state whether any of the following:

(1) the claimant company;

(2) the surrendering company; or

(3) any other company by reference to which either those companies are members of the same group or the conditions for consortium relief are satisfied,

was not UK resident in either or both of the surrendering company's accounting period to which the surrender relates or the corresponding accounting period of the claimant company.

The claim must be made (and may be withdrawn) at any time up to the latest of

(i) the first anniversary of the filing date for the company tax return,

(ii) 30 days after closure of any enquiry into that return (unless the enquiry, being otherwise out of time, was limited, as referred to in 55.7 below, to matters to which a previous amendment making or withdrawing a group relief claim relates, or which are affected by the amendment),

(iii) 30 days after notice of any amendment of that return by the Revenue following such an enquiry, and

(iv) 30 days after determination of any appeal against an amendment within (iii),

or at a later time if the Revenue allow it. See 29.23 GROUPS OF COMPANIES (in relation to earlier accounting periods ending after 30 September 1993) for Revenue Statement of Practice SP 11/93 setting out the Revenue approach to the admission of late claims. SP 11/93 is, however, to be replaced by a new Statement of Practice before the earliest date on which a group relief claim under self-assessment can be late.

These time limits override the normal time limits for amendment of a company tax return. Withdrawals of claims must be made by amending the return, and a claim can only be amended by withdrawal and replacement by another claim.

A claim may be made after the surrendering company has left the group (*A W Chapman Ltd v Hennessey Ch D 1981, 55 TC 516*).

A claim may be made for less than the full amount available for surrender at the time of the claim, but is ineffective if it is for more than that amount. The amount available for surrender at any time is the total amount available under *ICTA 1988, s 403* (see 29.18 GROUPS OF COMPANIES) on the basis of the surrendering company's tax return, disregarding any amendment whose effect is deferred pending completion of an enquiry (see 55.7 below), *less* all amounts for which notices of consent (see below) have been given and not withdrawn. Withdrawals are given effect before any claims made on the same day. Where claims are made on the same day for an aggregate amount in excess of the amount available for surrender, the Revenue determines which of the claims is to be ineffective to prevent an excess arising. In practice, they will treat as ineffective the claim(s) in the lowest amount(s) consistent with achieving this objective (see Revenue Guide para 8.4.5).

Claims may be made by more than one company in respect of the same surrendering company accounting period.

A claim requires the written consent of the surrendering company (and a consortium claim also that of each member of the consortium), which must be given to the officer of the Board to whom the company makes its tax returns at or before the time the claim is made, and a copy of which must accompany the claim. The consent notice must give the names and tax district references of the surrendering company and the company to which relief is being surrendered, the amount of the relief, and the surrendering company accounting period to which the surrender relates. It may not be amended, but may be withdrawn (by notice to the officer to whom the consent was notified) and replaced within the normal time limits (as above). Notice of withdrawal must be accompanied by the written consent of the claimant company, unless the withdrawal is the result of a reduction in the amount available for surrender (for which see below), and the claimant company must, so far as it may do so, amend its return accordingly.

See, however, below as regards simplified claim and surrender procedures.

Where the surrendering company has already made its return for the period to which the surrender relates, it must, at the same time as giving its consent, amend its return to reflect that consent. Where the consent relates to a trading loss for which relief has already been obtained by carry-forward, the surrendering company must (notwithstanding any time limits otherwise applicable) amend its return(s) for the subsequent period(s) in which relief was given for the loss to reflect the consent (relief for such periods being treated as given for carry-forward losses of earlier accounting periods before later ones).

Where there is a reduction in the total amount available for surrender (as above) below the amount for which consent to surrender has already been given, the company must, within 30 days, withdraw its consent (and may issue new notices of consent) so as bring the total of amounts for which consent is given within the total amount available. Copies of the withdrawal notices and any new consents must be sent to the companies affected and to the Revenue. If the company fails to take such corrective action, the Revenue may by written notice to the company give directions as to which consents are to be treated as reduced or eliminated to the extent necessary to achieve that objective (subject to appeal in writing by the company within 30 days of the notice to the officer by whom it was given), and must copy the notice to any claimant company affected by those directions. A claimant company notified of any withdrawal or new consent or Revenue direction must, so far as it may do so, amend its return for the period in question accordingly.

Where a claimant company becomes liable to tax in consequence of receiving a notice of withdrawal or new consent or Revenue direction (as above), and any of the tax is unpaid six months after the company's 'time limit for claims' (see below), the Revenue may, up to two years after that time limit, make an assessment in the name of the claimant company on any other company which has obtained group relief as a result of the surrender. The amount of the assessment is limited to the lesser of the amount of the unpaid tax and the amount of tax the other company saves by virtue of the surrender. The other company may recover the tax (and any interest thereon) from the claimant company. The company's 'time limit for claims' for this purpose is the latest of the dates in (i)–(iv) above on which the company could make or withdraw a group relief claim for the accounting period for which the claim in question was made.

An assessment may be made to recover group relief which in the opinion of the Revenue is or has become excessive. This is without prejudice to the making of a discovery assessment (see 55.8 below) or to the making of adjustments by way of discharge or repayment of tax. As regards notices of assessment, time limits and appeals, the same conditions apply as in relation to discovery assessments. Where a claimant company fails, or is unable, to amend its return following receipt of a notice of withdrawal or new consent or Revenue direction (as above), an assessment may be made (if otherwise out of time) up to one year after the date of the notice (the date of the new notice if a new notice of consent follows a withdrawal notice).

Simplified group relief procedures. Under *The Corporation Tax (Simplified Arrangements for Group Relief) Regulations 1999* (*SI 1999 No 2975*), a group of companies all, or substantially all, of whose tax returns are made to the same tax office, may enter into special arrangements enabling an authorised company within the group to act for the group in relation to group relief claims. The authorised company may then, in a form provided or authorised by the Board, provide a written statement containing the information necessary for the amendment of company tax returns of the companies covered by the arrangements for the purpose of making or withdrawing group relief claims and surrenders. Group companies remain liable for any incorrect claim or return arising from the authorised company's statement. Consortium companies which can claim or surrender group relief may be included in the arrangements (and the authorised company may be a consortium company). For the detailed requirements as to the making of an application by an authorised company, and the consequences of entering into such arrangements, see *SI 1999 No 2975*. These arrangements replace and extend those available for pre-self-assessment accounting periods under Revenue Statement of Practice SP 10/93, 8 October 1993 (see 54.2 RETURNS). In particular, it is no longer necessary for all the companies included in the arrangements to have identical accounting periods.

[*ICTA 1988, s 402(5); FA 1998, Sch 18 paras 10(2), 66–77; FA 1999, s 92; FA 2000, Sch 27 para 11*].

Capital allowances. A capital allowance claim under self-assessment must be included in the company tax return (or amended return) for the accounting period for which the claim is made. It must specify the quantum of the amount claimed. It must be made (and may be amended or withdrawn) at any time up to the latest of

(A) the first anniversary of the filing date for the company tax return,

(B) 30 days after closure of any enquiry into that return (unless the enquiry, being otherwise out of time, was limited, as referred to in 55.7 below, to matters to which a previous amendment making or withdrawing a capital allowance claim relates, or which are affected by the amendment),

(C) 30 days after notice of any amendment of that return by the Revenue following such an enquiry, and

(D) 30 days after determination of any appeal against an amendment within (iii),

or at a later time if the Revenue allow it. See 8.2 CAPITAL ALLOWANCES (in relation to earlier accounting periods ending after 30 September 1993) for Revenue Statement of Practice SP

11/93 setting out the Revenue approach to the admission of late claims. SP 11/93 is, however, to be amended or replaced for claims under self-assessment.

These time limits override the normal time limits for amendment of a company tax return. Amendments or withdrawals of claims must be made by amending the return.

If the effect of a claim is to reduce the available capital allowances for another accounting period for which a return has already been made, the company has 30 days to make the necessary amendments of that return. If it fails to do so, the Revenue may, by written notice and subject to a right of appeal within 30 days of the issue of the notice, amend the return to correct the position (notwithstanding any time limit otherwise applicable).

[*FA 1998, Sch 18 paras 10(2), 78–83*].

For claims to 'R & D tax credits', see 50.25 PROFIT COMPUTATIONS.

Simon's Direct Tax Service. See D2.831 *et seq.*.

55.5 **Assessment and payment of tax.** The company tax return must include a self-assessment by the company of its corporation tax liability on the basis of the information contained in the return, and taking account of reliefs or allowances claimed in the return. For this purpose a return is regarded as a return for an accounting period if the period is so treated in the return and is not longer than twelve months, whether or not it is in fact an accounting period. The self-assessment is required even if no tax is payable or a repayment due.

The calculation proceeds in four steps.

Step 1 The corporation tax chargeable on the company's profits (including its share(s) of any partnership profits) is calculated by applying the applicable rate or rates of corporation tax to those profits.

Step 2 Effect is given to any available set-offs or reliefs under *ICTA 1988, s 13(2)* or *s 13AA(2)* (marginal small companies' reliefs, see 56.2, 56.5 SMALL COMPANIES—REDUCED RATES), *FA 2000, Sch 15 Pt V* (CORPORATE VENTURING SCHEME (19)), *ICTA 1988, s 788* or *s 790* (double taxation relief, see 21.2, 21.3 DOUBLE TAX RELIEF) or *ICTA 1988, s 239* or *SI 1999 No 358* (ACT or shadow ACT, see 3.6, 3.8 ADVANCE CORPORATION TAX).

Step 3 Amounts assessable or chargeable as if they were corporation tax under *ICTA 1988, s 419(1)* (loans to close company participators, see 13.9 CLOSE COMPANIES) or *ICTA 1988, s 747(4)(a)* (see 18.7 CONTROLLED FOREIGN COMPANIES) are added, as reduced by any reliefs specific to those amounts.

Step 4 Amounts to be set off against the overall corporation tax liability under *ICTA 1988, s 7(2)* or *s 11(3)* (income tax borne by deduction, see 31.5 INCOME TAX IN RELATION TO A COMPANY, 53.4 RESIDENCE) or *ICTA 1988, s 246N* or *s 246Q* (ACT set-off in respect of foreign income dividends, see 26.6 FOREIGN INCOME DIVIDENDS) are deducted.

[*FA 1998, Sch 18 paras 7, 8; FA 1999, s 28(5); FA 2000, Sch 16 para 5(2)*].

Subject to the instalment provisions applicable to 'large' companies (see below and 48.1 PAYMENT OF TAX), corporation tax is due and payable on the day following the expiry of nine months from the end of the accounting period, on the basis of the amount computed (as above) in the company tax return for the period. Any excess over the tax payable of 'relevant amounts' stated in the company tax return is repaid. '*Relevant amounts*' are corporation tax paid and not repaid, corporation tax refunds surrendered to the company intra-group (see 29.33 GROUPS OF COMPANIES), income tax as described in *Step 4* above (so far as not set off under that calculation) and CONSTRUCTION INDUSTRY TAX SCHEME (17) deductions. [*TMA 1970, s 59D; FA 1998, Sch 19 para 29*]. Payment applications and reconciliations by the Revenue relate to a single accounting period (without the issue of 'taxpayer statements' covering more than one chargeable period as under income tax self-assessment). (Revenue Guide para 5.1.3). A company may claim repayment of corporation tax paid for an accounting period where the company's circumstances change so that it has grounds for believing that the amount paid exceeds its probable (although not yet finally established) liability. The claim must state the amount the company considers has been overpaid and the grounds for believing the payment to have become excessive. No claim may be made before the 'material date' in relation to the tax (see 38.1 INTEREST ON OVERPAID TAX). If the tax is the subject of an outstanding appeal, the company may apply to the Commissioners for a determination of the amount to be repaid (and the application may be combined with a postponement application under *TMA 1970, s 55*, see 48.3 PAYMENT OF TAX). If the company tax return has not been made, CONSTRUCTION INDUSTRY TAX SCHEME (17) deductions are ignored for these purposes. [*TMA 1970, s 59DA; FA 1998, Sch 19 para 29(2)*]. 'Large' companies to which instalment payments apply are precluded from making a claim under *section 59DA* where a claim for repayment of instalment payments is made (see 48.1 PAYMENT OF TAX). [*SI 1998 No 3175, reg 6(8)*].

See generally 38.1 INTEREST ON OVERPAID TAX, 39.1 INTEREST ON UNPAID TAX.

The company tax return requires the company to state whether it is liable to make instalment payments on account of its corporation tax liabilities (see 48.1 PAYMENT OF TAX). Although the Revenue will at some stage check the position, initial payment applications, interest calculations, etc. will be based on the company's statement of its position. (Revenue Guide para 12.10.6).

Losses, etc.. It should be noted that losses and other negative amounts also have to be included in the return and become final in the same way as the assessment itself, and are similarly subject to enquiry, although this would not apply to e.g. a loss in a self-assessment return brought forward from a pre-self-assessment period. The same figure must be used for a negative amount which becomes final in any other return affected by it. (Revenue Guide para 4.3.2). The use of the figure in another return does not give the Revenue an opportunity to enquire into the figure by means of an enquiry into that return (although this does not prevent an enquiry into the use of the negative amount in that return). (Revenue Guide para 6.4.1).

Simon's Direct Tax Service. See D2.808, D2.841 *et seq.*.

55.6 **Preservation of records.** A company which may be required to deliver a company tax return (see 55.3 above) for any period must preserve for at least six years after the end of that period the records required to enable it to make a complete and correct return for the period. This includes records and supporting documents (e.g. accounts, books, deeds, contracts, vouchers and receipts) of all receipts and expenses, and the matters in respect of which they arise, and, in the case of a trade involving dealing in goods, of all trade sales and purchases. If the company is required by notice to deliver a return for the period, the records must be preserved until the later of the end of the six years and either

(*a*) the date on which any enquiry into the return is completed (see 55.7 below), or

(*b*) if there is no enquiry, the date on which the Revenue no longer have power to enquire into the return (see 55.7 below).

If the notice requiring the return is given after the expiry of the six years, the records which must be preserved are any which the company still has in its possession at the time the notice is given.

The duty to preserve records may generally be satisfied by the preservation of the information contained in them (e.g. in electronic form), and a copy of any document forming part of the records is admissible in evidence before the Commissioners to the same extent as the records themselves. This does not, however, apply to vouchers, certificates etc. which show tax credits or deductions at source of UK or foreign tax, e.g. dividend vouchers, interest vouchers (including those issued by banks and building societies), or to evidence of tax deducted from payments to sub-contractors under the CONSTRUCTION INDUSTRY TAX SCHEME (17), which must be preserved in their original form.

The maximum penalty for failure to preserve records as above is £3,000 in relation to any one accounting period. No penalty is incurred where the records not preserved are such as might have been needed only for the purposes of claims, elections or notices not included in the return, or where they are vouchers, certificates, etc. showing UK tax credits or deductions at source (e.g. dividend vouchers and interest certificates) and the Revenue are satisfied that other documentary evidence supplied to them proves any facts they reasonably require to be proved and which the voucher, etc. would have proved. In practice the Revenue will seek such penalties only in the more serious cases where, for example, records have been destroyed deliberately to obstruct an enquiry or there has been a history of serious record-keeping failures (see Revenue Guide para 4.13.6).

[*FA 1998, Sch 18 paras 21–23*].

See Revenue Tax Bulletin October 1998, at pp 587–589 for an article on the general application in practice of the record-keeping requirement, and at pp 579, 580 on its application to transfer pricing matters. Both these extracts are reproduced in Appendix 2 to the Revenue Guide.

55.7 **Enquiry into return.** The Revenue may enquire into a company tax return if they give notice of their intention to do so within twelve months after the filing date (see 55.3 above) or, if the return was delivered after that date, by the quarter day (31 January, 30 April, 31 July or 31 October) next following the first anniversary of the day on which the return was delivered. The Revenue consider that notice is 'given' when the notice is issued, which, in the case of notice by post, means the date of posting (see Revenue Guide para 6.3.5), but in a Special Commissioner's decision on the similar provisions for individual self-assessment, it was held that service of the notice is treated as effected at the time at which the letter would be delivered in the ordinary course of post, i.e. on the second working day after posting for first class mail or on the fourth working day after posting for second class mail (*Wing Hung Lai v Bale (Sp C 203) [1999] SSCD 238*). An enquiry following an amendment to a return must be notified by the quarter day next following the first anniversary of the making of the amendment, and if it is given at a time when notice of an enquiry could no longer have been given had the return not been amended, is limited to matters to which the amendment relates or which are affected by it. (In practice, except where an amendment relates to or affects matters fundamental to the whole return, Revenue enquiries will normally be limited to the area of the return that was amended, regardless of whether a full enquiry would still be in time (see Revenue Guide para 6.6.11)). Only one notice of enquiry may be given in respect of a return, except one given in consequence of an amendment (or further amendment(s)) by the company of the return.

The Revenue does not have to justify an enquiry, by stating dissatisfaction with the return or identifying particular aspects giving cause for concern, and will not give reasons (although they may identify particular areas on which the enquiry will focus). Enquiries will range from questioning simple errors not identified during initial processing of the return through to full in-depth reviews of companies' affairs, including the underlying records. Business documents and records will commonly be requested. Although random selection will play a part, most enquiry cases will continue to be selected on the basis of a judgement, informed by all the information in the Revenue's possession, of the risk of tax loss. (Revenue Guide paras 6.1.12–6.1.16, 6.6).

A Code of Practice (No 14) was published in July 1999 covering all aspects of enquiries under self-assessment. It will be given to the company concerned at the start of every enquiry (except that where a simple enquiry is expected to be settled by a brief exchange of correspondence and not to involve penalties, a single-page version of the Code will be issued instead).

When the time limit for enquiry into a return has passed, the Revenue can still ask questions about the return, but further action can only be taken in cases of fraudulent or negligent conduct or failure to disclose all relevant information (see 55.8 below). (Revenue Guide para 6.2.4).

Subject to the limitation referred to above in the case of enquiries into amendments to returns, an enquiry extends to anything contained (or required to be contained) in the return, including any claim or election and any amount that affects or may affect the tax liability of another accounting period or another company. If it appears to the Revenue that the return is or may be for the wrong period, or has become for the wrong period as a result of a Revenue direction under *ICTA 1988, s 12(5A)* (see 2.4 ACCOUNTING PERIODS), the enquiry may extend to the period for which the return should have been made. A return is for this purpose made for the wrong period if either it is made for a period treated as, but not in fact, an accounting period, or it is made on the basis that there is no accounting period ending in or at the end of the period specified in the notice requiring the return but there is in fact such an accounting period. The time limits for notice of enquiry into a return for the wrong period are by reference to the date by which the return would have been required to be delivered had the period for which the return was made not been the wrong period.

These provisions are amended to provide for extended time limits in the cases of non-annual accounting of general insurance business and of insurance companies and friendly societies with non-annual actuarial investigations.

[*FA 1998, Sch 18 paras 24–26, 85–87*].

Production of documents, etc.. After (or at the same time as) giving notice of an enquiry, the Revenue may by notice require the company to produce such documents in the company's possession or power, and such information in such form, as they may reasonably require for the purposes of the enquiry. The notice is not restricted to documents, etc. the company is obliged to keep (see 55.6 above), but may require other information such as a profit and loss account, a balance sheet or a detailed factual account of how an entry in a return is made up, so long as they are relevant to the purposes of the enquiry and are in the company's possession or power. (Revenue Guide paras 6.7.4, 6.8.2). The notice must specify a period of not less than 30 days (from the date of receipt of the notice — see *Self-assessed v Inspector of Taxes (Sp C 207), [1999] SSCD 253*) within which the documents, etc. are to be produced, although if the company has genuine difficulty in meeting the deadline, the Revenue may be prepared to agree a revised time scale (Revenue Guide para 6.7.7). Documents, etc. relating to the conduct of any pending appeal by the company (i.e. those brought into existence as part of the preparation for presentation of the appeal, see Revenue Guide para 6.7.11) are excluded. For a case on the scope of such a notice, see *Mother v Inspector of Taxes (Sp C 211), [1999] SSCD 279* (concerning the similar powers in *TMA 1970, s 19A* relating to individual self-assessment enquiries).

Photographic or other facsimile copies of documents may be produced, but the Revenue may by notice require production for inspection of the originals within a specified time of not less than 30 days. The Revenue may take copies of, or make extracts from, any document produced to them.

The company may appeal in writing against any such notice within 30 days of the notice being given. The appeal is heard and determined in the same way as an appeal against an assessment, and the Appeal Commissioners are required to confirm the notice only insofar as the documents or information appear to them to be reasonably required for the purposes of the enquiry, and to set it aside insofar as that condition is not met, their decision being final and conclusive. To the extent that a notice is confirmed on appeal, it must be complied with within 30 days after determination of the appeal.

The penalty for failure to comply with a notice is £50 and, for each day on which the failure continues after imposition of such a penalty, a further penalty not exceeding £30 if the penalty is determined by an officer of the Board under *TMA 1970, s 100* or £150 if it is determined by the Commissioners under *TMA 1970, s 100C* (see 49.8 PENALTIES), subject to the normal right of appeal. No penalty may be imposed after the failure has been remedied.

No penalty can be imposed where it is genuinely impossible to comply with a notice, e.g. where the documents concerned do not exist. If such documents were required to be kept, a penalty as under 55.6 above may arise, but no penalty for failure to produce can arise. (Revenue Guide paras 6.10.7, 6.10.8).

[*FA 1998, Sch 18 paras 27–29*].

For powers to obtain information from third parties under *TMA 1970, s 20 et seq.*, see Tolley's Income Tax under Back Duty.

Amendments during enquiry. If during the course of an enquiry the Revenue form the opinion that the company's self-assessed tax is insufficient and that unless the assessment is immediately amended there is likely to be a loss of tax, they may by notice to the company amend its self-assessment to make good the deficiency. An appeal in writing may be made against such an amendment within 30 days of the notice, but will not be heard and determined before completion of the enquiry (although application for postponement may be made under *TMA 1970, s 55*, see 48.3 PAYMENT OF TAX). If the enquiry is limited to matters arising from an earlier amendment by the company of its self-assessment (as above), the notice may only apply to a deficiency attributable to that amendment. In practice, the Revenue will normally ask the company to make an additional payment on account to cover any deficiency identified during an enquiry, and only make an amendment as above where the company refuses to make such a payment and they believe that tax is at risk, e.g. where the company might dispose of its assets or go into liquidation (see Revenue Guide paras 6.11.7, 6.11.8).

If a company amends its return during an enquiry, the amendment does not restrict the scope of the enquiry, but may be taken into account in the enquiry. So far as the amendment affects the self-assessed tax, or any amount that affects or may affect the tax payable for another accounting period or by another company, it does not take effect until after the enquiry is completed (without prejudice to any claim for repayment of tax under *TMA 1970, s 59DA*, see 55.5 above). On completion of the enquiry, if the conclusions in the closure notice (see below) state either that the amendment was not taken into account or that no amendment is required arising from the enquiry, the deferred amendment takes effect immediately. Otherwise, it is taken into account by the company in amending its return in accordance with the closure notice.

In practice, if the closure notice states that no amendment of the return is required, the Revenue will give effect to the company amendment, and if it states that the return should be amended in consequence of the enquiry, the suggested amendments will normally take account of the company amendment. Where it says that the amendment has not been taken into account, the company may, if it so wishes, include its own amendment with those it makes in accordance with the closure notice, although this gives the Revenue the opportunity (as above) to make further enquiries into matters relating to or affected by that amendment. (Revenue Guide para 6.12.6).

[*FA 1998, Sch 18 paras 30, 31*].

Completion of enquiry. An enquiry into a return is completed when a closure notice is issued by the Revenue to the company stating their conclusions. If the return was for the wrong period, the notice must designate the accounting period for which a return should have been made. If there is more than one accounting period ending in or at the end of the period specified in the notice requiring a return, the closure notice may only designate the first of those accounting periods for which no return has been delivered. If there is then another period for which a return should have been made under the original notice, and which no other return by the company can be amended to refer to, the original notice is taken to require the company to deliver a return in respect of the outstanding period. The filing date for the return for that period is the later of the original filing date and the thirtieth day after it is finally determined that the outstanding return is required.

The company may apply to the Commissioners for a direction that the Revenue give a closure notice within a specified period. Any such application is heard and determined as if it were an appeal. The Commissioners must give a direction unless they are satisfied that the Revenue have reasonable grounds for not giving a closure notice within a specified period. Such a direction does not require the Revenue to confirm that the company's return and self-assessment are correct, and the closure notice will include the Revenue's conclusions based on the information available at the time of completion and representing what they believe to be the correct amounts to be included in the return on the basis of that information (see Revenue Guide para 6.14.6).

[*FA 1998, Sch 18 paras 32, 33, 35*].

Amendment of return following completion of enquiry. The company has 30 days following completion of an enquiry into a return to amend the return in accordance with the conclusions in the closure notice and, if the return was for the wrong period, to make it a return for the period designated in the notice, and to make such amendments of its other returns as may be required to give effect to those conclusions. Any time limit constraints are lifted for this purpose. If after the 30 days has elapsed the Revenue are not satisfied that the return is correct and complete and for the appropriate period, and that amendments required to other returns have been made, they have a further 30 days to make such amendments as they consider necessary. An appeal may be made in writing within 30 days of notification to the company of any such amendment(s). [*FA 1998, Sch 18 para 34*].

Penalties. The maximum penalty for

(*a*) negligently or fraudulently delivering, or failing within a reasonable time to remedy, an incorrect return, or

(*b*) making any incorrect return, statement or declaration in connection with a claim for any allowance, deduction or relief, or

(*c*) submitting incorrect accounts,

in addition to any tax actually chargeable, is the amount of tax underpaid, by reason of the incorrectness, for the accounting period(s) to which the return etc. relates (disregarding any relief deferred under *ICTA 1988, s 419(4A)* in respect of the repayment, etc. of a loan to a participator, see 13.12 CLOSE COMPANIES). Accounts are deemed to have been submitted on behalf of a company unless it is shown that they were submitted without the company's consent or connivance.

Where more than one tax-geared penalty is incurred in relation to an accounting period, each penalty after the first is reduced so that the total penalties in relation to any particular part of the tax do not exceed the amount of the greatest penalty imposed in relation thereto. For an example, see Revenue Guide para 10.8.1.

[*FA 1998, Sch 18 paras 20, 89, 90*].

Contract settlements (see Tolley's Income Tax under Back Duty) for all outstanding liabilities will continue to be available in appropriate cases, in particular where penalties are involved. (Revenue Guide para 6.15.9).

Simon's Direct Tax Service. See D2.815 *et seq.*.

55.8 DISCOVERY ASSESSMENTS OR DETERMINATIONS

If the Revenue 'discover' (see Tolley's Income Tax under Assessments) that an amount which ought to have been assessed to tax has not been assessed, or that an assessment has become insufficient, or that relief has been given which is or has become excessive, they may make a 'discovery assessment' in the amount (or further amount) which, in their opinion, should be charged in order to make good the loss of tax. Similarly if they discover that a return for an accounting period incorrectly states an amount that affects, or may affect, the tax payable for another accounting period or by another company, they may make a 'discovery determination' of the amount which, in their opinion, ought to have been stated in the return. Notice of a discovery assessment or determination must be served on the company, stating the date of issue and the time limit for any appeal, and the assessment or determination may be altered after the notice has been served only under express provisions.

A discovery assessment will thus be appropriate where, for example, a discovery leads to an additional tax liability on the company for the period. A discovery determination would be appropriate where there is a discovery that losses carried forward or surrendered as group relief have been overstated. If such a determination reduces losses, etc. available for another period or to another company, and the time allowed for the required amendment has expired, a discovery assessment would be appropriate. (Revenue Guide paras 6.17.6, 6.17.7).

In practice, where a return has been filed and the time limit for opening an enquiry has not expired (nor an enquiry already been closed), the Revenue will normally deal with matters by opening an enquiry rather than by issuing a discovery assessment or determination. (Revenue Guide para 6.17.5).

Except where a discovery assessment or determination gives effect to a discovery determination duly made in relation to another company's return, a discovery assessment for an accounting period for which the company has delivered a return, or a discovery determination, may only be made in the following circumstances:

(*a*) where the discovery arose from a situation attributable to 'fraudulent or negligent conduct' (see Tolley's Income Tax under Back Duty) on the part of the company, a person acting on behalf of the company, or a partner of the company at the relevant time; or

(*b*) where, at the time the Revenue ceased to be entitled to give notice of enquiry into the return (see 55.7 above) or completed their enquiries into the return, they could not reasonably have been expected, on the basis of the information made available to them before that time, to be aware of the situation giving rise to the discovery. Information is for this purpose regarded as made available to the Revenue if it is contained

(i) in the company's returns (or accompanying documentation) for the period or the two immediately preceding accounting periods, or

(ii) in a claim (or accompanying documentation) made by the company as regards the period, or

(iii) in any documents, accounts or information produced to or provided for the Revenue for the purposes of an enquiry into a return (as in (i)) or claim (as in (ii)),

or if it is information the existence and relevance of which are notified in writing to the Revenue by the company (or a person acting on its behalf) or could reasonably be expected to be inferred by the Revenue from information falling within (i)–(iii) above.

As regards (*b*) above, there is an onus on the company to draw attention to any important information relevant to a tax liability, particularly if there is some doubt as to the interpretation which could be placed on that information. Information made available by the company's agent on its behalf is made available by the company, but where information is made available by, or on behalf of, someone other than the company, e.g. in the return of another group company, a discovery assessment or determination on the company is not precluded. (Revenue Guide paras 6.18.8, 6.18.9).

A discovery assessment or determination may in any event not be made if the discovery arose from a situation attributable to a mistake in the return as to the basis on which the company's liability ought to have been computed, and the return was in fact made on the basis of or in accordance with the practice generally prevailing at the time the return was made.

Any objection to a discovery assessment or determination on the grounds that the above conditions have not been complied with can only be made on an appeal against the assessment or determination.

Time limit. Subject to any specific provision allowing a longer period, assessments and discovery determinations must be made within six years after the end of the accounting period to which they relate, increased to 21 years where fraud or negligence is involved. Any objection to an assessment or determination as out of time can only be made on an appeal against the assessment or determination.

Appeals. An appeal may be brought against any discovery assessment or determination by written notice to the Revenue within 30 days after issue of the notice of the assessment or determination.

[*FA 1998, Sch 18 paras 41–49*].

See also 55.13 below as regards recovery of over-repayments, etc..

Simon's Direct Tax Service. See D2.823, D2.824.

55.9 CONSEQUENTIAL CLAIMS ARISING FOLLOWING CERTAIN REVENUE AMENDMENTS OR ASSESSMENTS

Where

(*a*) a company tax return is amended by the Revenue under *FA 1998, Sch 18 para 34(2)(b)* (i.e. an amendment, following closure of an enquiry, to a return other than the return which was the subject of the enquiry) so that the tax payable is increased (see 55.7 above), or

(*b*) a discovery assessment (see 55.8 above) is made, or

(*c*) an assessment to recover excessive group relief (see 55.4 above) is made,

the following provisions apply to allow certain claims, elections, applications and notices to be made or given, or revoked or varied. Where an assessment is made in a case involving fraudulent or negligent conduct (see 55.8 above), the more restricted relief described below applies instead.

A claim, etc. relating to the accounting period in respect of which the amendment or assessment was made, or made or given by reference to an event occurring in that period, and the making etc. of which has or could have the effect of reducing a 'relevant liability' of the company, may be made or given at any time within one year from the end of the '*relevant accounting period*', i.e. that in which the closure notice was issued or the assessment made. Similarly if previously made or given, it may be varied or (unless irrevocable) revoked in the same manner as it was made or given, and by or with the consent of the same person(s) who made it, gave it or consented to it (or their personal representatives). A '*relevant liability*' is the increased liability arising from the amendment or assessment, or any other liability of the company for the accounting period to which the amendment or assessment relates or any subsequent accounting period ending not later than one year after the end of the relevant accounting period.

If the effect of a consequential claim, etc. as above would be to alter the tax liability of another person, the written consent of that person (or their personal representative) to the claim, etc. is required. If the effect is to increase that person's liability, neither the above provisions nor *TMA 1970, s 43A* (the corresponding income and capital gains tax provisions) apply in relation to any amendment or assessment made because of the increased liability.

Where one or more claims etc. as above are made in consequence of an amendment or assessment, the combined tax liability of the company and any other persons affected cannot be reduced by an amount which exceeds the additional tax liability resulting from that amendment or assessment. Where this limitation involves more than one period or more than one person, the limited amount available is apportioned between the periods or persons concerned. The manner in which the apportionment is to be made is specified by the Revenue by written notice to the person(s) concerned, who may, however, within 30 days from the date of the notice (where more than one person is concerned, the last notice), give (or jointly give) written notice substituting a different manner of apportionment.

The claims appeals provisions are appropriately modified in relation to revocations or variations of claims under the above provisions.

Where an assessment is made in a case involving *fraudulent or negligent conduct*, the above provisions for consequential claims are disapplied. Instead, if the company so requires, effect is given, in determining the tax charged by the assessment, to any relief or allowance to which the company would have been entitled for the accounting period on a claim or application made within the normal time limits. The claims or applications must be made either before the assessment is made or within the time provided for an appeal against the assessment (see Revenue Guide para 7.15.1).

[*FA 1998, Sch 18 paras 61–65*].

Simon's Direct Tax Service. See D2.834.

55.10 REVENUE DETERMINATIONS

If no return is delivered, in response to a notice requiring one, on or before the filing date for the return required by the notice (see 55.3 above) (or, if no such date can be ascertained, by the later of 18 months from the end of the period specified in the notice and three months from the date of service of the notice (which is assumed to be four working days after its issue, see Revenue Guide para 9.3.3)), the Revenue have power to determine, to the best of their information and belief, the tax payable by the company for the accounting period or periods ending in or at the end of the period specified in the notice. They may also determine what those accounting periods are if they have insufficient information to identify the company's accounting periods. Notice of a determination under these provisions must be served on the company, stating the date of issue, but no determination may be made more than five years after the first day on which the power of determination could have been exercised. The determination is of no effect if the company shows that it has no accounting period ending in or at the end of the period specified in the notice requiring the return, or that it has delivered the return(s) for that accounting period or each of those accounting periods, or that no return is yet due for any such period. An effective determination is superseded where, before the expiry of five years from the day on which the power of determination first became exercisable (or, if later, the expiry of twelve months from the date of the determination), the company delivers a return for an accounting period ending in or at the end of the period specified in the notice requiring a return. If there is more than one determination in relation to the notice concerned, the determination superseded is that for the period which is, or most closely approximates to, the period for which the return is made.

In practice the Revenue normally review cases for determination 18 months after the end of what is assumed or believed to be the company's accounting period. If the filing date is believed to be later than that, they will wait until after the presumed filing date before making a determination. Where, for example, they believe there would be a risk of loss of tax if no immediate action was taken, or the absence of a return prevents a proper review of other companies in the same group, an earlier review may be made of the need for a determination. (Revenue Guide para 9.2.1).

If a return is delivered, in response to a notice requiring one, for an accounting period ending in or at the end of the period specified in the notice, but it appears to the Revenue that there is another ('outstanding') period so ending which is or may be an accounting period, they have power to determine, to the best of their information and belief, the corporation tax payable by the company for the outstanding period. The power becomes exercisable once the filing date for the outstanding period has passed without a return being delivered, or, if no such filing date can be ascertained, once the later of 30 months from the end of the period specified in the notice and three months from the date of service of the notice has passed without a return for the outstanding period being delivered. Notice of a determination under these provisions must be served on the company, stating the date of issue, but no determination may be made more than five years after the first day on which the power of determination could have been exercised. The determination is of no effect if the company shows that the outstanding period is not an accounting period or that it has delivered a return for that period. An effective determination is superseded where, before the expiry of five years from the day on which the power of determination first became exercisable (or, if later, the expiry of twelve months from the date of the determination), the company delivers a further return for an accounting period ending in or at the end of the period specified in the notice requiring a return.

The power to make a determination in the circumstances described above includes power to determine any of the constituent amounts required to calculate the amount of tax payable. The notice of determination may be accompanied by a notice of any determination by the Revenue of the due and payable dates under *TMA 1970, s 59D* or *s 59E* (see 48.1 PAYMENT OF TAX). For enforcement purposes (i.e. payment, collection and recovery, interest, penalties, etc.) the determination has effect as if it were a self-assessment, and is treated as made for an accounting period where the Revenue had insufficient information to determine whether a period was an accounting period (see above). Where the Revenue have begun any proceedings for the recovery of tax charged by a determination, and before the proceedings are concluded the determination is superseded (as above), the proceedings may be continued as if they were for the recovery of so much of the tax charged by the self-assessment as is due and payable but unpaid.

[*FA 1998, Sch 18 paras 36–40*].

Simon's Direct Tax Service. See **D2.821, D2.822**.

55.11 CLAIMS ETC. NOT INCLUDED IN RETURNS

Subject to any specific provision requiring a claim or election to be made to the Board, a claim or election made otherwise than in a return must be made to an officer of the Board. The claim etc. must include a declaration by the claimant that all particulars are correctly stated to the best of his information or belief. No claim requiring a tax repayment can be made unless the claimant has documentary proof that the tax has been paid or deducted. The claim must be made in a form determined by the Board and may require, *inter alia*, a statement of the amount of tax to be discharged or repaid and (except as below) supporting information and documentation. In practice, the Board do not generally determine the particular form in which a claim must be made. In the case of a claim by or on behalf of a person who is not resident in the UK, the Revenue may require a statement or declaration in support of the claim to be made by affidavit.

A person who may wish to make a claim must keep all such records as may be requisite for the purpose and must preserve them until such time as the Revenue may no longer enquire into the claim or such enquiries are treated as completed. There is a maximum penalty of £3,000 for non-compliance in relation to any claim *actually made*. Similar provisions and exceptions apply as in 55.6 above as to the preservation of the information contained in documents instead of originals and the exception from penalty for non-compliance in relation to dividend vouchers, interest certificates etc..

A claimant may, at any time within twelve months of making a claim, amend the claim by notice to an officer of the Board. An officer of the Board may similarly, at any time within nine months of the claim being made, amend the claim to correct any obvious errors or mistakes (including errors of principle and arithmetical mistakes). No such amendments may, however, be made while the claim is under enquiry (see below). The Revenue have powers to enquire into a claim etc. (or amendment thereof) similar to those relating to company tax returns (see 55.7 above). Notice of intention to enquire must be given by the first anniversary of the end of the accounting period to which the claim relates or, if later, by the quarter day (meaning 31 January, 30 April etc.) next following the first anniversary of the date of claim etc.. In the event of such an enquiry, they have powers to call for documents similar to those relating to enquiries into company tax returns (see 55.7 above). Where an enquiry is in progress, an officer of the Board may give provisional effect to the claim etc. (or amendment thereof) to such extent as he thinks fit. Provisions similar to those relating to enquiries into company tax returns (see 55.7 above) apply as regards amendments of claims upon completion of an enquiry. The Revenue must give effect to such an amendment, by assessment if necessary, within 30 days after it is made. An appeal may be made against a Revenue amendment to a claim following an enquiry, written notice of appeal to be given normally within 30 days after the amendment is made (extended to three months where questions of residence are involved). If an amendment is varied on appeal, the Revenue have a further 30 days to give effect to the variation. Where a claim etc. does not give rise to a discharge or repayment of tax (for example, a claim to carry forward trading losses), there are provisions as to disallowance of such claims on completion of the enquiry, with appeal procedures similar to those above.

Appeals against amendments to claims are normally made to the General Commissioners. Where the claim was made to the Board or under certain specified provisions, appeal is to the Special Commissioners. In other cases, there are special rules enabling the taxpayer to elect to bring the appeal before the Special Commissioners, but this election may be disregarded in certain circumstances. If the taxpayer also has an appeal pending concerning an assessment and the appeals relate to the same income, both appeals must be to the same body of Commissioners.

Where these provisions apply to a claim, etc. which results in an increase in the tax payable, all necessary adjustments, by way of assessment or otherwise, may be made so as to give effect to it.

[*TMA 1970, s 42(11), Sch 1A; FA 1998, Sch 18 para 60(3), Sch 19 para 42*].

Simon's Direct Tax Service. See **D2.832.**

55.12 APPEALS

Appeals must specify the grounds of appeal, although on the hearing of the appeal the Commissioners may consider new grounds if they are satisfied that their omission was not wilful or unreasonable. An appeal against

(*a*) a Revenue amendment of a self-assessment during an enquiry to prevent a loss of tax (see 55.7 above), or of a company tax return on completion of the enquiry where the company fails to amend the return within 30 days (see 55.7 above), or

(*b*) a Revenue discovery determination (see 55.8 above), or

(*c*) an assessment other than a self-assessment

is to the Special Commissioners. Otherwise, subject to *TMA 1970, ss 44–59*, an appeal is to the General Commissioners unless the company elects for it to be heard by the Special Commissioners. The Revenue may, however, refer any such election to the General Commissioners, who must direct that the election be disregarded unless satisfied that the company has arguments to present or evidence to adduce on the merits of the appeal.

[*FA 1998, Sch 18 paras 92–94; FA 1999, Sch 11 para 9*].

As regards claims etc. to which *TMA 1970, Sch 1A* applies, see 55.11 above.

Simon's Direct Tax Service. See **D2.837.**

55.13 MISCELLANEOUS

Crown option. There are provisions concerning enquiries into a return which includes amounts which may be taxed on more than one basis, i.e. under Case I or Case III or V of Schedule D, or (in relation to life assurance business) under Case I of Schedule D or on the 'I minus E' basis (see 41.1 LIFE INSURANCE COMPANIES). The Revenue have the right to determine (finally and conclusively) which method is to be used (the 'Crown option'). The powers to require production of documents, etc. under *FA 1998, Sch 18 paras 27–29* (see 55.7 above) apply equally for this purpose. [*FA 1998, Sch 18 para 84*].

Effect of return on other periods or companies. Where an amount required to be included in a company tax return may affect tax payable for another accounting period or by another company, and that amount can no longer be altered (for which see *FA 1998, Sch 18 para 88(3)–(5)*), it is taken as conclusively determined in relation to the other period or company (without affecting the Revenue's power to make assessments). [*FA 1998, Sch 18 para 88*].

Double assessment. If the Revenue are satisfied, on a written claim by a company, that it has been assessed (including self-assessment) more than once for the same cause and for the same accounting period, they must take the necessary steps to eliminate the double charge. An appeal against their decision on a claim may be brought before the Commissioners having jurisdiction to hear an appeal relating to the assessment (or the later of the assessments) to which the claim relates. [*FA 1998, Sch 18 para 50*].

Error or mistake relief. Where a company believes it has paid too much tax under an assessment (or self-assessment) by reason of some error or mistake in a return, it may claim relief by written notice to the Revenue not more than six years after the end of the accounting period to which the return relates. After enquiring into the matter, and having regard to all the relevant circumstances, the Revenue will then give by repayment such relief as is just and reasonable. In determining the claim they will, in particular, consider whether the granting of relief would result in amounts being excluded from the charge to tax, taking into consideration accounting periods of the company other than that to which the claim relates. No relief may, however, be given in respect of a mistake as to the basis on which the liability ought to have been computed where the return was made on the basis, or in accordance with the practice, generally prevailing at the time. Nor may relief be given where the mistake was in a claim or election included in the return. An appeal against a decision of the Revenue on a claim lies to the Special Commissioners, who determine the claim in accordance with the same principles as apply to the Revenue's decision. An appeal to the High Court against a decision of the Special Commissioners can only be made on a point of law in connection with the computation of profits (including amounts chargeable under *ICTA 1988, s 419* (loans to participators, see 13.9 et seq. CLOSE COMPANIES) and *ICTA 1988, s 747* (CONTROLLED FOREIGN COMPANIES (18)). [*FA 1998, Sch 18 para 51*].

Over-repayments. The discovery assessment provisions (see 55.8 above) apply also to an amount paid to a company by way of repayment of tax (or payment of tax credit), INTEREST ON OVERPAID TAX (38) or 'R & D tax credit' (see 50.25 PROFIT COMPUTATIONS), to the extent that it ought not to have been paid, unless it is recoverable under *ICTA 1988, s 826(8A)* (interest recoverable as if it were INTEREST ON UNPAID TAX (39)). Any such assessment is under Schedule D, Case VI, and INTEREST ON UNPAID TAX (39) runs from the date when the payment being recovered was made. For these purposes amounts allowed by way of set-off are treated as paid, and an intended repayment which exceeds the tax paid is nonetheless treated as a repayment. In the case of an assessment to recover tax repaid in respect of an accounting period (or interest thereon), income tax repaid in respect of a payment received in an accounting period (or interest thereon), or R & D tax credit paid for an accounting period, the assessment is treated as being for that accounting period. Except in cases of fraud or negligence (for which see 55.8 above), the time limit for a discovery assessment by virtue of these provisions is (where relevant) extended to the later of the end of the accounting period following that in which the amount assessed was paid and the expiry of three months from the day on which the Revenue complete an enquiry into a relevant company tax return (see 55.7 above). [*FA 1998, Sch 18 paras 52, 53; FA 2000, Sch 21 para 3*].

European Economic Interest Groupings ('EEIGs'). See 50.12 PROFIT COMPUTATIONS.

55.14 COMPANY TAX RETURN FORM CT600 (1999)

The form of company tax return (see 55.3 above) specified by the Board of Inland Revenue is Form CT600 (1999), which will be issued (together with the CT600 Guide) with Form CT603, the notice requiring a return. Additional or replacement copies may be obtained from the Inland Revenue Orderline (tel. 0845–300 6555, fax. 0845–300 6777). The following supplementary pages will also be supplied on request to the Orderline.

CT600A *Loans to participators by close companies.* This must be completed if the company is a close company and made loans to an individual participator, or associate of a participator, that remained outstanding at the end of the period. See 13.9 *et seq.* CLOSE COMPANIES.

CT600B *Controlled Foreign Companies.* This must be completed if the company had an interest of 25% or more in the period in a foreign company which was controlled from the UK. See 18 CONTROLLED FOREIGN COMPANIES. See also section 2.1 of the Revenue Guidance Notes referred to at 18.1 as regards completion of these supplementary pages.

CT600C *Group and consortium companies.* This must be completed if the company is claiming or surrendering any amounts under the group or consortium relief provisions for the period. See 29.14 *et seq.* GROUPS OF COMPANIES.

CT600D *Insurance companies and friendly societies.* This must be completed if, in the period, the company either made claims under *ICTA 1988, Sch 19AB* to provisional payments (including notional repayments in respect of tax on gilt interest)(see 41.6 LIFE INSURANCE COMPANIES), or entered into business which it treats as overseas life assurance business (see 41.14 LIFE INSURANCE COMPANIES).

CT600E *Charities.* This must be completed if the company is, in the period, a charity claiming exemption or partial exemption from tax. See 11 CHARITIES.

Form CT 600 (1999) consists of opening pages requiring company information, a summary of the return information and a declaration by the signatory, and giving information on completion of the return, and eight sections as follows.

Section 1 *Which Supplementary Pages must be completed?* See above.

Section 2 *Turnover of the company.* This must be completed by all trading companies.

Section 3 *Short calculation.* All companies must complete either this section or section 4.

Section 4 *Detailed calculation.* See section 3.

Section 5 *Claims for capital allowances and details of balancing charges arising.* This must be completed to claim capital allowances and to show balancing charges included in the section 3 or 4 calculation.

Section 6 *Losses, deficits and excess amounts.* This must be completed if relevant. Group companies must show the maximum amounts available for surrender by group or consortium relief.

Section 7 *Overpayments and repayment claims.* This must be completed if a repayment claim is made.

Section 8 *Directors' remuneration.* Completion of this section is optional.

56 Small Companies—Reduced Rates

Cross-reference. See 13.18 CLOSE COMPANIES, 53.4 RESIDENCE, 60.4 UNIT AND INVESTMENT TRUSTS.

Simon's Direct Tax Service D2.109.

56.1 REDUCED RATE IF PROFITS ARE £300,000 (OR EARLIER LIMIT) OR LESS

As mentioned in 1.3 INTRODUCTION AND RATES OF TAX, a special reduced rate of corporation tax, known as the 'small companies rate', applies to the 'basic profits' of a UK resident company the 'profits' of which do not exceed £300,000 (£250,000 for financial years 1991, 1992 and 1993, lower for earlier financial years) (the 'lower limit') for a 12-month accounting period, with marginal relief as in 56.2 below (but in both cases see 56.7 below where there are associated companies). See, however, 13.18 CLOSE COMPANIES as regards close investment-holding companies to which the reduced rate does not apply. See also 56.4 below as regards the lower 'starting rate' introduced from financial year 2000.

The rate for the financial years 1999 and 2000 is 20%; that for financial years 1997 and 1998 is 21%; that for financial year 1996 is 24%; and that for financial years 1988 to 1995 inclusive is 25%. [*ICTA 1988, s 13; F(No 2)A 1987, s 74(4); FA 1988, s 27(1); FA 1989, s 35; FA 1990, s 20; FA 1991, s 25; F(No 2)A 1992, s 22; FA 1993, s 54; FA 1994, s 86; FA 1995, s 38; FA 1996, s 78; F(No 2)A 1997, s 18(2); FA 1998, ss 28, 29; FA 2000, s 36*]. Where a company's accounting period straddles the end of a financial year (31 March), and the lower limits for the two financial years contained in the accounting period differ, then the periods before 1 April and after 31 March are treated as separate accounting periods for this purpose. [*FA 1989, s 35(3); FA 1990, s 20(3); FA 1991, s 25(3); FA 1994, s 86(3)*].

'*Profits*' (but not the 'basic profits') are the profits on which corporation tax falls finally to be borne plus FRANKED INVESTMENT INCOME (27) and (until their abolition after 5 April 1999) FOREIGN INCOME DIVIDENDS (26) arising to the company. There is, however, an exclusion for franked investment income received:

(*a*) (in relation to distributions made on or after 6 April 1999) from a UK-resident '51% subsidiary' (see 29.3 GROUPS OF COMPANIES) or from a fellow 51% subsidiary of a UK-resident parent company, or from a consortium-owned company within 29.3(*b*) GROUPS OF COMPANIES;

(*b*) (in relation to distributions before that date) from companies within the same group (for which purpose distributions are treated as coming from within the group if dividends so received are group income or would be if the companies so elected, see 29.2-29.7 GROUPS OF COMPANIES).

(*a*) above applies equally to franked investment income received by another person on behalf of or in trust for the company, but not to any received by the company on behalf of or in trust for another person. [*ICTA 1988, s 13(7); FA 1994, Sch 16 para 11; F(No 2)A 1997, Sch 6 para 1; FA 1998, Sch 3 para 7*].

'*Basic profits*' are the profits on which corporation tax falls finally to be borne. [*ICTA 1988, s 13(8)*]. See 60.4 UNIT AND INVESTMENT TRUSTS for the exclusion from basic profits *for small companies rate purposes only* of certain housing investment profits.

Claims. The small companies rate (or marginal relief, see 56.2 below) must be claimed. In practice, a clear indication in the company's return, computation or accompanying correspondence that profits of the accounting period should be charged at the small companies rate (or attract marginal relief) is accepted as a valid claim. The claim should, however, except in the case of an unincorporated association or other members' club or society, include a statement of the number (or absence) of associated companies in the period (see 56.7 below). (Revenue Pamphlet IR 131, SP 1/91, 6 March 1991).

For an accounting period of less than twelve months, or one overlapping the end of a financial year, see 56.2 below.

56.2 **Marginal relief.** Where the 'profits' of a UK resident company for a 12-month accounting period exceed a lower limit (the 'lower relevant maximum amount') but do not exceed an upper limit (the 'upper relevant maximum amount'), the corporation tax otherwise chargeable on the 'basic profits' is reduced by the following amount (unless there are associated companies, see 56.7 below).

$$\text{Small companies rate marginal fraction} \times (\text{Upper relevant maximum amount} - \text{Profits}) \times \frac{\text{Basic profits}}{\text{Profits}}$$

'*Profits*' and '*basic profits*' are as defined in 56.1 above.

The small companies rate marginal fraction for the financial years 1997, 1998, 1999 and 2000 is $\frac{1}{40}$, that for financial year 1996 is $\frac{9}{400}$, that for financial years 1994 and 1995 is $\frac{1}{50}$, and the upper and lower limits for those years are set at £1,500,000 and £300,000 respectively. Where the profits consist of basic profits only, the effective marginal rate is 32.5% for financial years 1999 and 2000, 33.5% for financial years 1997 and 1998, 35.25% for financial year 1996, 35% for financial years 1994 and 1995.

Marginal relief for earlier years is granted by reference to the following fractions and figures.

	Upper limit	Lower limit	Relief fraction	Marginal rate
1991–1993	£1,250,000	£250,000	$\frac{1}{50}$	35%
1990	£1,000,000	£200,000	$\frac{9}{400}$	36.25%
1989	£750,000	£150,000	$\frac{1}{40}$	37.5%
1988	£500,000	£100,000	$\frac{1}{40}$	37.5%

[*ICTA 1988, s 13(2)(3); F(No 2)A 1987, s 74(4); FA 1988, s 27(2); FA 1989, s 35; FA 1990, s 20; FA 1991, ss 23(2), 25; F(No 2)A 1992, s 22; FA 1993, s 54; FA 1994, s 86; FA 1995, s 38; FA 1996, s 78; FA 1997, s 59(b); FA 1998, ss 28, 29; FA 2000, s 36(b)*].

Where a company's accounting period straddles the end of a financial year (31 March), and the upper or lower limits for the two financial years contained in the accounting period differ, then the periods before 1 April and after 31 March are treated as separate accounting periods for the purposes of small companies relief. [*FA 1989, s 35(3); FA 1990, s 20(3); FA 1991, s 25(3); FA 1994, s 86(3)*].

Where an accounting period is less than twelve months, the upper and lower limits are proportionately reduced. [*ICTA 1988, s 13(6)*].

The chargeable profits of an accounting period which overlaps the end of a financial year are, if necessary, apportioned between the two years. [*ICTA 1988, s 8(3)*].

See 56.1 above as regards claims for relief.

56.3 *Examples*

(A)

In its accounting period 1 April 2000 to 31 March 2001, X Ltd, a trading company, has chargeable profits of £300,000, including chargeable gains of £40,000, and also has franked investment income of £75,000 (representing net distributions received of £67,500). X Ltd has no associated companies.

Corporation tax payable is calculated as follows.

	£
Corporation tax at full rate of 30% on £300,000	90,000
$\frac{1}{40} \times$ £(1,500,000 – 375,000) $\times \dfrac{300,000}{375,000}$	22,500
Corporation tax payable	£67,500

(B)

In its accounting period 1 April 2000 to 31 March 2001, Y Ltd, a trading company, has chargeable profits of £375,000 including chargeable gains of £40,000, but has no franked investment income. Y Ltd has no associated companies.

Corporation tax payable is calculated as follows.

	£
Corporation tax at full rate of 30% on £375,000	112,500
$\frac{1}{40} \times$ £(1,500,000 – 375,000)	28,125
Corporation tax payable	£84,375

An alternative method of calculation, where there is no franked investment income, is to apply small companies rate up to the small companies rate limit and marginal rate (32.5% for FY 2000) to the balance of profits. Thus:

		£
£300,000	at 20%	60,000
75,000	at 32.5%	24,375
£375,000		£84,375

(C)

In its accounting period 1 January 1997 to 31 December 1997, Z Ltd had chargeable profits of £540,000 and franked investment income of £60,000. Z Ltd had no associated companies during that period.

Corporation tax payable is calculated as follows.

Part of the accounting period falling in financial year 1996

		£	£
Profits $\frac{3}{12} \times$ £600,000	= £150,000		
Basic profits $\frac{3}{12} \times$ £540,000	= £135,000		
Lower relevant maximum	= £75,000		
Corporation tax at full rate			
£135,000 at 33%		44,550	
Less marginal relief			
$\frac{9}{400} \times$ £(375,000 – 150,000) $\times \dfrac{135,000}{150,000}$		4,556	c/f 39,994

Part of the accounting period falling in financial year 1997

		£	£
			b/f 39,994
Profits $\frac{9}{12} \times$ £600,000	= £450,000		
Basic profits $\frac{9}{12} \times$ £540,000	= £405,000		
Lower relevant maximum	= £225,000		
Corporation tax at full rate			
£405,000 at 31%		125,550	
Less marginal relief			
$\frac{1}{40} \times £(1{,}125{,}000 - 450{,}000) \times \frac{405{,}000}{450{,}000}$		15,188	110,362
Corporation tax payable			£150,356

56.4 **STARTING RATE IF PROFITS ARE £10,000 OR LESS**

As mentioned in 1.3 INTRODUCTION AND RATES OF TAX, for financial year 2000 and subsequent years a special 'corporation tax starting rate' applies to the 'basic profits' of a UK resident company the 'profits' of which do not exceed a specified amount (the '*first relevant amount*'), with marginal relief as in 56.5 below (but in both cases see 56.7 below where there are associated companies). The starting rate does not, however, apply to close investment-holding companies (see 13.18 CLOSE COMPANIES) or to investment trusts in receipt of eligible rental income (see 60.4 UNIT AND INVESTMENT TRUSTS). '*Basic profits*' and '*profits*' are defined as for small companies rate purposes (see 56.1 above).

For the financial year 2000 the starting rate is **10%**, and the first relevant amount is **£10,000** for a twelve-month accounting period, being proportionately reduced for shorter accounting periods. An accounting period straddling 31 March 2000 is for these purpose treated as two separate accounting periods ending on and beginning immediately after that date.

[*ICTA 1988, s 13AA(1)(4)(6)–(8); FA 1999, ss 28(1)(7), 29*].

The chargeable profits of an accounting period which overlaps the end of a financial year are, if necessary, apportioned between the two years. [*ICTA 1988, s 8(3)*].

Claims. The starting rate (or marginal relief, see 56.5 below) must be claimed. In practice, a clear indication in the company's return, computation or accompanying correspondence that profits of the accounting period should be charged at the starting rate (or attract marginal relief) is accepted as a valid claim. The claim should, however, except in the case of an unincorporated association or other members' club or society, include a statement of the number (or absence) of associated companies in the period (see 56.7 below). (Revenue Pamphlet IR 131, SP 1/91, 6 March 1991 as revised).

56.5 **Marginal relief.** Where the profits for a twelve-month accounting period of a company otherwise entitled to claim application of the corporation tax starting rate exceed the first relevant amount but do not exceed an upper limit (the '*second relevant amount*'), the company may claim that the corporation tax chargeable on its basic profits be calculated as if the rate of corporation tax were the small companies rate (see 56.1 above) and then reduced by the following amount (unless there are associated companies, see 56.7 below).

$$\text{Starting rate marginal fraction} \times (\text{Second relevant amount} - \text{Profis}) \times \frac{\text{Basic profits}}{\text{Profits}}$$

'*Profits*' and '*basic profits*' are as defined in 56.1 above.

The first and second relevant amounts for the financial year 2000 are £10,000 and £50,000 respectively. The starting rate marginal fraction for that year is $\frac{1}{40}$.

Where a company's accounting period is less than twelve months, the first and second relevant amounts are proportionately reduced.

An accounting period straddling 31 March 2000 is for these purpose treated as two separate accounting periods ending on and beginning immediately after that date.

[*ICTA 1988, s 13AA(2)–(7); FA 1999, ss 28(1)(7), 29*].

The chargeable profits of an accounting period which overlaps the end of a financial year are, if necessary, apportioned between the two years. [*ICTA 1988, s 8(3)*].

See 56.4 above as regards claims for relief.

56.6 *Examples*

(A)

In its accounting period 1 April 2000 to 31 March 2001, X Ltd, a trading company, has chargeable profits of £10,000, including chargeable gains of £400, and also has franked investment income of £2,500 (representing net distributions received of £2,250). X Ltd has no associated companies.

Corporation tax payable is calculated as follows.

	£
Corporation tax at small companies rate of 20% on £10,000	2,000
$\frac{1}{40} \times £(50{,}000 - 12{,}500) \times \frac{10{,}000}{12{,}500}$	750
Corporation tax payable	£1,250

(B)

In its accounting period 1 April 2000 to 31 March 2001, Y Ltd, a trading company, has chargeable profits of £12,500 including chargeable gains of £400, but has no franked investment income. Y Ltd has no associated companies.

Corporation tax payable is calculated as follows.

	£
Corporation tax at small companies rate of 20% on £12,500	2,500
$\frac{1}{40} \times £(50{,}000 - 12{,}500)$	938
Corporation tax payable	£1,562

An alternative method of calculation, where there is no franked investment income, is to apply the starting rate up to the starting rate limit and the marginal rate (22.5% for FY 2000) to the balance of profits. Thus:

		£
£10,000	at 10%	1,000
2,500	at 22.5%	562
£12,000		£1,562

56.7 A COMPANY WITH AN ASSOCIATED COMPANY OR COMPANIES

The upper and lower relevant maximum amounts mentioned in 56.1 and 56.2 above, and from financial year 2000 the first and second relevant amounts mentioned in 56.4 and 56.5 above, in each case as reduced where an accounting period is less than twelve months, are divided by one plus the number of 'associated companies' which the company has in the accounting period. [*ICTA 1988, s 13(3)b), s 13AA(4)(b); FA 1999, s 28(1)*].

A company is an '*associated company*' of another for this purpose if one of the two has 'control' of the other or both are under the control of the same person or persons. This may include non-UK resident companies. '*Control*' is as defined in *ICTA 1988, s 416*, see 13.2 CLOSE COMPANIES. In applying the definition, however, the Revenue will not seek to attribute to any person the rights and powers of relatives, other than those of his or her spouse and minor children, except where there is substantial commercial interdependence between the companies. (Prior to 20 June 1994, the concession referred to substantial trading interdependence, and where companies with substantial commercial interdependence but no substantial trading interdependence are concerned, the revision to the concession applies only for accounting periods commencing on or after that date.) Similarly, two companies will not be treated as associated where they may be treated as under common control, or one may be treated as controlled by the other, only by taking into account fixed rate preference shares held as a business investment by a non-close company taking no part in management etc., or where that control is by an otherwise unconnected commercial loan creditor (not being a close company) or trustee. (Revenue Pamphlet IR 1, C9). The Revenue is also understood to consider that for two companies to be under the control of the same persons, an irreducible group of persons having control of one must be identical with an irreducible group of persons having control of the other (i.e. in neither case could any definition of control be satisfied if any one of them were excluded) (see Taxation 2 September 1993 p 537).

An associated company is counted even if it was associated for part of the accounting period only and two or more are counted even if they were associated for different parts of the accounting period. However, an associated company which has not carried on any trade or business at any time in that accounting period (or the part thereof when it was associated) is disregarded.

[*ICTA 1988, s 13(4)(5), s 13AA(5); FA 1999, s 28(1)*].

For a case in which a company whose sole activity was the receipt of bank deposit interest was held not to be carrying on any business, see *Jowett v O'Neill and Brennan Construction Ltd Ch D 1998, 70 TC 566*. Similarly a company set up for the sole purpose of owning a holiday home used exclusively by its sole shareholder and his family was held not to be carrying on any business (*John M Harris (Design Partnership) Ltd v Lee (Sp C 130), [1997] SSCD 240*). The Revenue in practice disregard a non-trading holding company if it has no assets (other than shares in its subsidiaries), no income or gains (other than dividends distributed in full to its shareholders and which either are (or could be) group income under *ICTA 1988, s 247(1)* (see 29.2 GROUPS OF COMPANIES) or are FOREIGN INCOME DIVIDENDS (26)), and no entitlement to a deduction, as charges or management expenses, in respect of any outgoing. (Revenue Pamphlet IR 131, SP 5/94, 20 July 1994).

Where a company's accounting period straddles the end of a financial year (31 March), and the marginal relief limits for the two financial years contained in the accounting period differ, then the periods before 1 April and after 31 March are treated as separate accounting periods for these purposes. [*FA 1989, s 35(3); FA 1990, s 20(3); FA 1991, s 25(3); FA 1994, s 86(3)*].

Examples

(A)

Y Ltd has profits, consisting wholly of income, of £320,000 for the 12-month accounting period ended 31 December 1994. It had no associated company until 1 November 1994, when its shares were acquired by a company with three wholly-owned subsidiaries, of which one was dormant throughout the 12-month period.

Y Ltd is to be treated as having no associated company in the notional accounting period from 1 January to 31 March 1994, but as having three associated companies (i.e. its new parent and that company's existing active subsidiaries) throughout the notional accounting period from 1 April to 31 December 1994. (This difference arises because of the change of marginal relief limits from 1 April 1994 — see above.)

Y Ltd's profits for the notional accounting period (see 56.2 above) from 1 January to 31 March 1994 are

$$£320{,}000 \times \frac{3}{12} = £80{,}000$$

The upper limit of profit for marginal relief for that notional period is

$$£1{,}250{,}000 \times \frac{3}{12} = £312{,}500$$

The relief for the notional accounting period is thus

$$\frac{1}{50} \times (312{,}5000 - 80{,}000) = £4{,}650$$

Y Ltd's profits for the notional accounting period from 1 April to 31 December 1994 are

$$£320{,}000 \times \frac{9}{12} = £240{,}000$$

The upper limit of profit for marginal relief for that notional period is

$$\left(£1{,}500{,}000 \times \frac{9}{12}\right) \div 4 = £281{,}250$$

The relief for the notional accounting period is thus

$$\frac{1}{50} \times (281{,}250 - 240{,}000) = £825$$

and (subject to any loss or group relief being available) the corporation tax charge for the accounting period on Y Ltd will be

Financial year 1993	£80,000 @ 33%	26,400
Financial year 1994	£240,000 @ 33%	79,200
		105,600
Less marginal small companies' relief (4,650 + 825)		5,475
		£100,125

(B)

The figures and other information are exactly as in (A) above for the year ended 31 December 1997. Y Ltd is, however, treated as having three associated companies throughout the accounting period. There is no change in the marginal relief limits and hence no split into two notional accounting periods. (The change in the corporation tax rate and in the marginal relief fraction require only that the profits be apportioned to the relevant financial years, see 1.2 INTRODUCTION AND RATES OF TAX.)

Y Ltd's corporation tax liability for the year ended 31 December 1997 is therefore calculated as follows.

FY 1996

	£
£80,000 at 33%	26,400
Less $\frac{9}{400}$ × (93,750 – 80,000) =	309
	26,091

FY 1997

	£
£240,000 at 31%	74,400
Less $\frac{1}{40}$ × (281,250 – 240,000) =	1,031
	73,369

	£
Total liability: FY 1996	26,091
FY 1997	73,369
	£99,460

(C)

The figures and other information are exactly as in (B) above but for the year ended 31 December 1999. There is no change in the marginal relief limits nor in the marginal relief fraction. Hence the change in the corporation tax rate only requires the profits to be apportioned to the relevant financial years (see 1.2 INTRODUCTION AND RATES OF TAX).

Y Ltd's corporation tax liability for the year ended 31 December 1999 is therefore calculated as follows

		£
Financial year 1998	£80,000 @ 31%	24,800
Financial year 1999	£240,000 @ 30%	72,000
		96,800
Less $\frac{1}{40}$ × (375,000 – 320,000) =		1,375
Corporation tax liability		£95,425

57 Statutory Bodies

57.1 **Marketing Boards.** Agricultural marketing boards etc. which are obliged to pay any trading surplus into a reserve fund (with restricted rights of repayment etc.) may deduct such payments from the profits of the trade carried on by them. Any withdrawal from the fund which is not required to be passed on to a Minister or government department, producers, or persons paying levies or duties, is treated as a trading receipt. [*ICTA 1988, s 509*].

57.2 The **Atomic Energy Authority** and the **National Radiological Protection Board** are exempt from corporation tax under Schedules A, B (and, prior to its abolition, Schedule C), under Schedule D in respect of yearly interest and annual payments received and, following the abolition of Schedule C, public revenue dividends received, under Schedule F in respect of distributions received, and on chargeable gains.

Income and chargeable gains from investments or deposits held for the purposes of a pension scheme operated by the former are also exempt. [*ICTA 1988, s 512; TCGA 1992, s 271(7); FA 1996, Sch 7 para 20*].

57.3 **Harbour reorganisation schemes.** Where, under such a scheme, the trade of a body corporate (other than a limited liability company) is transferred to a harbour authority, the trade is not treated as discontinued; loss relief is given and capital allowances and corporation tax on chargeable gains apply as if there had been no change. If only part of the body corporate's trade is transferred, it is treated as a separate trade. [*ICTA 1988, s 518*].

57.4 Local authorities, local authority associations and health service bodies are exempt from tax. [*ICTA 1988, ss 519, 519A, 842A; FA 1990, s 127, Sch 18; TCGA 1992, ss 271(3), 288(1)*]. See 24.10 EXEMPT ORGANISATIONS.

57.5 Subject to the special provisions above and, where appropriate, to the Crown exemption (see 24.5 EXEMPT ORGANISATIONS), statutory bodies are liable in the ordinary way to corporation tax on their income and capital gains. Whether their activities amount to trading depends on the facts. See *Mersey Docks and Harbour Board v Lucas HL 1883, 2 TC 25* (trading surplus held chargeable notwithstanding that it had to be applied in reducing debt), *Port of London Authority v CIR CA 1920, 12 TC 122*, and *Forth Conservancy Board* cases, *HL 1928, 14 TC 709*, and *HL 1931, 16 TC 103* (liable under Case VI on surplus from shipping dues) and *British Broadcasting Corporation v Johns CA 1964, 41 TC 471* (liable under Case I on profits from publications etc. but not on rest of surplus; not entitled to Crown exemption). For further cases, see Tolley's Tax Cases.

57.6 **Statutory corporation borrowing in foreign currency.** Interest on securities issued after 5 April 1982 by, or on a loan to, a statutory corporation (as defined) in a currency other than sterling shall, if the Treasury directs, be paid without deduction of income tax and be exempt from income tax (but not corporation tax) in the hands of a non-resident beneficial owner of such securities or, in the case of a loan, in the hands of the person for the time being entitled to repayment or eventual repayment of the loan. Securities issued before 6 April 1982 in the currency of a country outside the scheduled territories at the time of issue were similarly treated. [*ICTA 1988, s 581(4)*].

58 Temporary Employment Subsidy

58.1 Temporary employment subsidy was paid under *Employment and Training Act 1973, s 5* (as amended by *Employment Protection Act 1975, Sch 14 para 2* and continued by *Employment Subsidies Act 1978, ss 1, 3*) as a flat-rate weekly payment or (in the textile, clothing and footwear industries) by way of reimbursement of payments made to workers on short time.

Such payments were held to be taxable as trading receipts in *Poulter v Gayjon Processes Ltd Ch D 1985, 58 TC 350*, distinguishing grants made by the Unemployment Grants Committee which were held **not** to be taxable receipts in *Seaham Harbour Dock Co v Crook HL 1931, 16 TC 333. Gayjon Processes Ltd* was followed in *Ryan v Crabtree Denims Ltd Ch D 1987, 60 TC 183*, concerning an 'interest relief grant' under *Industry Act 1972, s 7.*

See also 52 REGIONAL DEVELOPMENT GRANTS.

59 Time Limits

Except where other time limits are prescribed, claims, elections etc. must be made within six years of the end of the accounting period to which they relate. [*TMA 1970, s 43(1); FA 1998, Sch 18 para 55*]. See also Tolley's Income Tax.

It should be noted that a number of time limits (particularly in relation to procedural matters) are revised following the introduction of self-assessment for accounting periods ending **on or after 1 July 1999**.

Simon's Direct Tax Service A3.620, D2.711.

59.1 **ADVANCE CORPORATION TAX**

(*a*) Claims for surplus ACT to be carried back must be made within **two years** of the end of the accounting period in which the surplus arose. See 3.8 ADVANCE CORPORATION TAX.

(*b*) Claims for ACT to be surrendered must be made within **six years** of the end of the accounting period to which it relates. See 29.8 GROUPS OF COMPANIES.

ACT is **abolished** after 5 April 1999 (see 3.1 ADVANCE CORPORATION TAX).

59.2 **APPEALS**

(*a*) Formal notice of appeal against corporation tax assessments must be lodged within **30 days** after the date of issue of the notice of assessment. See 5.2 ASSESSMENTS AND APPEALS.

(*b*) Dissatisfaction with the decision of the Commissioners must be expressed **'immediately'** after that decision is given. It is understood that expression of dissatisfaction within **30 days** will be accepted. See Tolley's Income Tax under Appeals.

(*c*) A stated case must be requested within **30 days** of that decision if an appeal to the High Court is contemplated. See Tolley's Income Tax under Appeals.

(*d*) Appeals on a question of residence or domicile must be lodged within **three months** of receipt of written notice of the Board's decision. [*TMA 1970, s 42(3), Sch 1A para 9(2)*].

(*e*) Except as indicated above, appeals must be lodged within **30 days** after the date of a notice of assessment, or within **30 days** of the receipt of the decision on a claim or of an amendment of a claim by the inspector, as the case may be. [*TMA 1970, ss 31(1), 42(3), Sch 1A para 9; FA 1998, Sch 18 para 48*].

59.3 **CAPITAL ALLOWANCES**

(*a*) Claims for capital allowances to be set off against income other than that against which they are primarily given must be made within **two years** of the end of the accounting period for which the allowances are made. [*CAA 1990, s 145*].

(*b*) A notice that machinery or plant on which a first-year allowance has been given has ceased, during the 'requisite period', to be used for a 'qualifying purpose' must be given within **three months** of the end of the accounting period in which the non-qualifying use takes place, or within **30 days** of the cessation's coming to the notice of the lessor, whichever is the later. [*CAA 1990, ss 23(2), 49(2)*].

See generally 8 CAPITAL ALLOWANCES and Tolley's Income Tax under Capital Allowances.

59.4 **CAPITAL GAINS**

(*a*) **Assets held on 6 April 1965.** An election for such assets to be valued at 6 April 1965 must be made within **two years** after the end of the accounting period in which the relevant disposal was made. [*TCGA 1992, Sch 2 para 17; FA 1996, Sch 21 para 42(3)*]. For certain concessional treatment on a company's leaving a group see 9.47 CAPITAL GAINS.

(*b*) **Assets held on 31 March 1982.** An irrevocable election for assets to be valued at 31 March 1982 must be made by 6 April 1990 or within two years of the end of the accounting period in which the first relevant disposal occurs (or such longer time as the Board may allow).

(*c*) **Assets of negligible value.** A claim must be made within **two years** after the end of the accounting period in which the relevant date falls. (Revenue Pamphlet CGT 8 para 230).

(*d*) **Groups of companies.** A company leaving a group remains liable for unpaid corporation tax on chargeable gains arising from the disposal before 1 April 2000 of any asset formerly owned by that company while it was a member of the group where the disposal occurs within **two years** following its departure from the group. From 1 April 2000 any group member in the **twelve months** before the disposal may be liable for any unpaid tax. [*TCGA 1992, s 190; FA 2000, Sch 29 para 9*].

(*e*) **Know-how.** An election for so much of the consideration for the sale of a trade (or part of a trade) **not** to be treated as a payment for goodwill must be made within **two years** of the disposal. [*ICTA 1988, s 531(3)*].

(*f*) **Residence.** An election for any part of the 'postponed gain' on cessation of residence which becomes chargeable to be offset by capital losses of the subsidiary concerned must be made within **two years** of the cessation of residence. See 53.6 RESIDENCE.

(*g*) **Rollover relief** is only available if the acquisition of the new assets is made within **three years** after the disposal of the old or within **twelve months** before. See 9.44 CAPITAL GAINS.

For further details of the above and other time limits, see Tolley's Capital Gains Tax under the appropriate heading.

59.5 **CASE VI**

Prior to the inclusion of *furnished lettings* within Schedule A businesses from 1 April 1998 (see 50.27 PROFIT COMPUTATIONS), an election for the rent payable under a lease and included in income from such lettings to be assessed under Schedule A instead of under Case VI must be made within **two years** from the end of the relevant accounting period. [*ICTA 1988, s 15(1)(2); FA 1998, Sch 5 para 1, Sch 27 Pt III(4)*].

See Tolley's Income Tax under Schedule D, Case VI.

59.6 **CHARGEABILITY TO TAX**

A company chargeable to corporation tax for any accounting period which has not received notice requiring a return for that period must notify the inspector that it is so chargeable within **one year** of the end of that period. [*TMA 1970, s 10; FA 1988, s 121; FA 1998, Sch 18 para 2, Sch 19 para 1*].

59.7 **CONSTRUCTION INDUSTRY: TAX DEDUCTION SCHEME** [*SI 1993 No 743; SI 1998 No 2622*]

The requirements are equivalent to those in 59.25(*a*) and (*b*) below (except that the relevant form is SC 35).

59.8 **CONTROLLED FOREIGN COMPANIES** [*ICTA 1988, ss 747–756, Schs 24–26 ; FA 1998, Sch 17*]

(*a*) Prior to the commencement of self-assessment, appeals against notices under *ICTA 1988, s 747(1)* or amended notices under *section 751(5)* must be made within 60 days of the date of the notice. See 18.16 CONTROLLED FOREIGN COMPANIES.

(*b*) Claims under *ICTA 1988, Sch 24 para 9* for losses of certain periods to be taken into account in computing chargeable profits, are to be made within the time limit at (*a*) above for appeals against the notice for the period to which the claim relates for periods prior to the commencement of self-assessment, thereafter within 20 months after the end of the accounting period. The same applies to claims under *para 4* for certain deemed claims and elections to be disregarded in computing chargeable profits, except that, for pre-self-assessment ADP exempt periods, the time limit is 20 months after the end of the period. See 18.9 CONTROLLED FOREIGN COMPANIES.

(*c*) Prior to the commencement of self-assessment, where a charge is raised for an accounting period under *ICTA 1988, s 749(4)*, group relief claims for the period may be made up to the end of the following accounting period (if otherwise out of time). See 18.17 CONTROLLED FOREIGN COMPANIES.

59.9 **DIRECTORS' REMUNERATION**

A claim for the computation for a period of account to be adjusted for directors' remuneration paid after the computation has been made, but within nine months after the end of the period, must be made within two years of the end of the period of account. [*FA 1989, s 43(5)*]. See 50.8 PROFIT COMPUTATIONS.

59.10 **DOUBLE TAXATION**

Relief by way of credit for foreign tax in respect of any income must be claimed within **six years** after the end of the accounting period for which the income is chargeable or, if later, within one year after the end of the accounting period in which the foreign tax is paid. [*ICTA 1988, s 806(1)(b); FA 2000, Sch 30 para 20*]. A similar time limit applies to claims to utilise unrelieved foreign tax. [*ICTA 1988, ss 806G, 806M(7); FA 2000, Sch 30 paras 21, 23*].

See 21.5 DOUBLE TAX RELIEF.

59.11 **EMPLOYEE SHARE OWNERSHIP TRUSTS**

Claims for relief for contributions to qualifying trusts must be made within two years of the end of the period of account for which the sum is charged as an expense of the company. [*FA 1989, s 67(6)*]. See 50.10 PROFIT COMPUTATIONS.

59.12 ERROR OR MISTAKE

Relief for an error or mistake in the corporation tax return must be claimed within **six years** after the relevant accounting period. [*TMA 1970, s 33; FA 1998, Sch 18 para 51, Sch 19 para 15*]. See 12.4 CLAIMS, 55.13 SELF-ASSESSMENT.

59.13 EXCHANGE GAINS AND LOSSES

(*a*) A claim for deferral of unrealised gains on long-term capital assets or liabilities must be made within two years of the end of the accounting period for which the exchange gain accrued if an assessment for the period has become final and conclusive (otherwise six years or such longer period as the Board may determine). [*FA 1993, s 139(6)–(8)*]. See 23.18 EXCHANGE GAINS AND LOSSES.

(*b*) A claim for relief of non-exchange losses in respect of assets or liabilities in respect of which exchange gains have previously arisen must be made within two years of the end of the accounting period in which the non-exchange losses accrued. [*SI 1994 No 3229, reg 2(7)*]. See 23.23 EXCHANGE GAINS AND LOSSES.

(*c*) An election for the normal commencement provisions to apply in relation to certain fluctuating debts must be made within 92 days of the company's commencement day. [*SI 1994 No 3226, reg 3(5)*]. See 23.32 EXCHANGE GAINS AND LOSSES.

(*d*) In certain cases where an allowable loss would otherwise accrue in respect of an asset, or an allowable loss be reduced, an election for the loss to be set against exchange gains of the accounting period in which the asset is disposed of or subsequent accounting periods may be made within two years of the end of the accounting period in which the disposal occurs. [*SI 1994 No 3226, reg 14(5)*]. See 23.32 EXCHANGE GAINS AND LOSSES.

(*e*) An election to treat pre-commencement day gains and losses as accruing after the company's commencement day over a six-year period must be made within 92 days of the commencement day. [*SI 1994 No 3226, reg 15(1)*]. See 23.32 EXCHANGE GAINS AND LOSSES.

(*f*) An election to set certain pre-commencement day losses against exchange gains must be made within 92 days of the commencement day. [*SI 1994 No 3226, reg 16(1)*]. See 23.32 EXCHANGE GAINS AND LOSSES.

(*g*) Certain 'local currency elections' are required to be made within 92 days of the company's commencement day. [*SI 1994 No 3230, regs 5(7), 9(2)(3)*]. See 23.39, 23.40 EXCHANGE GAINS AND LOSSES.

59.14 FINANCIAL INSTRUMENTS

(*a*) An election for certain existing contracts to be treated as qualifying contracts must be made within three months of the company's 'commencement day'. See 25.5 FINANCIAL INSTRUMENTS.

(*b*) A claim for certain qualifying payments to be treated as having become irrecoverable in an accounting period must be made within two years of the end of the accounting period. See 25.13 FINANCIAL INSTRUMENTS.

59.15 FRANKED INVESTMENT INCOME

(*a*) A claim to set off management expenses and charges on income must be made within **six years** of the accounting period in which they were incurred. [*ICTA 1988, s 242(8)(b)*].

(*b*) A claim under *ICTA 1988, s 243* (losses carried forward and terminal losses) must be made within **six years** of the end of the accounting period for which the claim is made or in which the company ceased to trade. [*ICTA 1988, s 243(6)*].

Sections 242 and *243* are repealed for accounting periods beginning after 1 July 1997. [*F(No 2)A 1997, s 20*]. See 27 FRANKED INVESTMENT INCOME.

59.16 **GROUP RELIEF**

Prior to the commencement of corporate self-assessment, claims for group relief must generally be made within **two years** after the end of the surrendering company's accounting period to which the claim relates. See 29.23 GROUPS OF COMPANIES.

For the position under self-assessment, see 55.4 SELF-ASSESSMENT.

59.17 **HERD BASIS**

An election by a farming company for the herd basis must be made within **two years** of the end of the first accounting period during which a production herd of the class concerned was kept or in which compensation is received for compulsory slaughter. [*ICTA 1988, Sch 5 paras 2, 6*]. See Tolley's Income Tax under Herd Basis.

59.18 **HOUSING ASSOCIATIONS**

Exemption from corporation tax on rents and chargeable gains must be claimed within **two years** of the end of the relevant accounting period. The same applies to self-build societies. See 30 HOUSING ASSOCIATIONS ETC..

59.19 **INCOME TAX**

(*a*) Elections for charges on income to be paid within groups of companies without deduction of income tax become effective **three months** after they are made, or on the inspector's notifying his satisfaction therewith. See 29.2 GROUPS OF COMPANIES.

(*b*) Returns of income tax deducted from payments made by a company are due within **14 days** of the end of the return period. See 31 INCOME TAX IN RELATION TO A COMPANY.

59.20 **LOAN RELATIONSHIPS**

(*a*) *Relief for a non-trading deficit* of an accounting period may be claimed by set-off against other profits of the period, by group relief or by carry back within two years of the end of the accounting period (or within such longer time as the Board may allow). Carry-forward to the following period must be claimed within two years of the end of that period (or within such longer time as the Board may allow). [*FA 1996, s 83(6)(7)*]. See 43.3 LOAN RELATIONSHIPS.

(*b*) *Income tax deducted from certain payments giving rise to a loan relationship credit may be set against corporation tax liability* on a claim within two years of the end of the accounting period in which the payment from which tax was deducted was received or, if later, by the end of the period of six years after the end of the accounting period in which the loan relationship credit was brought into account. [*FA 1996, s 91(6)*]. See 43.8 LOAN RELATIONSHIPS.

59.21 **LOANS TO PARTICIPATORS**

The time limit for claiming repayment of tax paid on a loan by a close company to certain participators is **six years** after the end of the **financial year** in which the loan is repaid. See 13.12 CLOSE COMPANIES.

59.22 **OVER-REPAID TAX**

Assessments to recover tax over-repaid may, if otherwise out of time, be made up to the end of the accounting period following that of the repayment or, if later, within three months of the closure of a Revenue enquiry into a self-assessment return. [*TMA 1970, s 30; FA 1998, Sch 18 para 53, Sch 19 para 13*].

59.23 **PARTNERSHIPS**

An election for continuance under *ICTA 1988, s 113* when there is a change in the persons comprising the partnership must be made within **two years** after the change. See Tolley's Income Tax under Partnerships. Elections may be revoked within the same time limit. (See Revenue Pamphlet IR 131, A4).

59.24 **PATENTS** [*ICTA 1988, ss 524, 525; FA 1996, Sch 21 para 15*]

(*a*) Where a company resident in the UK sells patent rights wholly or partly for a capital sum, and does not wish that sum to be spread over six years, an election to have the entire sum charged to tax for the accounting period in which it was received must be made within **two years** of the end of that period.

(*b*) A non-resident company selling UK patent rights wholly or partly for a capital sum may claim to have that sum spread over six years (and not treated as a single lump sum) within **two years** of the end of the accounting period in which it was received.

See Tolley's Income Tax under Patents.

59.25 **PAYE**

(*a*) Remittances must be made to the Collector within **14 days** after the end of the tax month (ending on the fifth of the calendar month) or in certain cases the tax quarter (ending on 5 July etc.). [*SI 1993 No 744, regs 40, 41*].

(*b*) End-of-year returns, deduction cards and Form P35 are due within **44 days** after the end of the tax year. [*SI 1993 No 744, reg 43*].

(*c*) Supplementary end-of-year returns are due within **61 days** after the end of the tax year. [*SI 1993 No 744, reg 46*].

59.26 **PAYMENT OF TAX**

Corporation tax is generally payable **nine months** after the end of the accounting period (subject to any requirement for instalment payment). See 48 PAYMENT OF TAX.

59.27 **POST-CESSATION RECEIPTS**

An election for post-cessation receipts received within six years after the discontinuance of a trade to be treated as having been received on the date of discontinuance must be made within **two years** after the end of the year of assessment in which the payment was received. See Tolley's Income Tax under Post-Cessation Receipts. For 1996/97 and subsequent years, the claim must be made by 31 January next but one following the year of assessment. [*ICTA 1988, s 108; FA 1996, s 128(4)*].

59.28 PRE-TRADING EXPENDITURE

An election for a pre-trading debit on a loan relationship to be deferred to the period in which the trade commences must be made within two years of the end of the accounting period in which the debit arose. [*ICTA 1988, s 401(1AB); FA 1996, Sch 14 para 20*].

59.29 RENTS ETC.

Before 1 April 1998, rents under a lease under which payment is also made for the use of furniture may be charged under Schedule A, rather than under Schedule D, Case VI, if an election is made by the landlord within **two years** after the end of the relevant accounting period. See 50.26 PROFIT COMPUTATIONS. [*ICTA 1988, s 15(2); FA 1998, Sch 27 Pt III(4)*]. See now 50.27 PROFIT COMPUTATIONS.

59.30 RESEARCH AND DEVELOPMENT EXPENDITURE

(*a*) A claim for payment of an 'R & D tax credit' for an accounting period may be made, amended or withdrawn in the company tax return (or amended return) for the period up to one year after the filing date for that return (see 55.3 SELF-ASSESSMENT) or by such later time as the Revenue may allow. [*FA 1998, Sch 18 para 83E; FA 2000, Sch 21 para 4*].

(*b*) An election for 'connected persons treatment' to be applied to all sub-contractor payments made under the same contract or arrangement must be made within two years after the end of the accounting period in which the contract or arrangement is entered into. [*FA 2000, Sch 20 para 11*].

(*c*) An election for the alternative treatment of pre-trading expenditure in an accounting period must be made within two years after the end of the accounting period to which the election relates. [*FA 2000, Sch 20 para 14(6)*].

See 50.25 PROFIT COMPUTATIONS.

59.31 RETURNS

(*a*) Company tax returns must be made within one year of the end of the accounting period (or of the period of account in which falls the last day of the accounting period) or, if later, within three months of the date of the notice requiring the return. [*TMA 1970, s 11; FA 1998, Sch 18 para 14*]. See 54.2 RETURNS, 55.3 SELF-ASSESSMENT.

(*b*) *Non-qualifying distributions* must be returned within **14 days** of the end of the accounting period in which they were made or within **14 days** of their having been made (if they were not made in an accounting period).

(*c*) *Stock dividends* must be returned within **30 days** of the end of the return period.

See 54.6 *et seq.* RETURNS and 59.1 and 59.19 above.

59.32 **SCHEDULE A**

Prior to its abolition for accounting periods beginning on or after 1 April 2001, an election for alternative treatment in respect of land managed as one estate at 5 April 1963 must be made within **twelve months** after the end of the first chargeable period for which it is available. [*ICTA 1988, s 26; FA 1998, s 39*]. See 50.26, 50.27 PROFIT COMPUTATIONS. See also 59.5 above.

59.33 **SHARE DEALERS**

Where a share dealing company exchanges securities on or before 31 July 1998 in connection with conversion operations, nationalisation etc. by the Government, the company may elect for this to constitute a disposal of trading stock within **two years** of the end of the accounting period in which the exchange takes place. [*ICTA 1988, s 471; FA 1996, Sch 21 para 12; FA 1998, s 101(1)(3)*]. See 9.6 CAPITAL GAINS and Tolley's Income Tax under Schedule D, Cases I and II.

59.34 **TRADING LOSSES**

A claim for trading losses to be set off against profits of the same or an earlier accounting period must be made within **two years** of the end of the accounting period in which the losses were incurred, or within such further period as the Board may allow.

[*ICTA 1988, s 393A(10)*].

See 44 LOSSES.

59.35 **TRADING STOCK**

On the discontinuance of a profession or vocation, an election may be made for work in progress to be taken at cost within **twelve months** of the discontinuance. For accounting periods ending on or after 1 July 1999, to which self-assessment applies for companies (see 55 SELF-ASSESSMENT), the election may be made up to two years after the end of the accounting period in which the discontinuance occurs. [*ICTA 1988, s 101; FA 1996, Sch 21 para 3*]. See Tolley's Income Tax under Schedule D, Cases I and II.

59.36 **UNLISTED SHARES**

Claims for relief of losses on such shares by investment companies must be made within **two years** of the end of the accounting period in which the loss was incurred. [*ICTA 1988, s 573*]. See 44.19 LOSSES.

60 Unit and Investment Trusts

Cross–references. See 9.6, 9.19, 9.43, 9.55 CAPITAL GAINS, 40.6 INVESTMENT COMPANIES, 50.3 PROFIT COMPUTATIONS.

Simon's Direct Tax Service D4.413 *et seq.*.

60.1 AUTHORISED UNIT TRUSTS

An '*authorised unit trust*' is a 'unit trust scheme' which is the subject of an order under *Financial Services Act 1986, s 78* for the whole or part of an accounting period. A '*unit trust scheme*' is as defined under *Financial Services Act 1986*, but subject to certain exclusions by Treasury order (see *SI 1988 No 267, SI 1992 Nos 571, 3133, SI 1994 No 1479*). [*ICTA 1988, ss 468(6), 469(7); TCGA 1992, s 99(2)*]. See below as regards court common investment funds. The *Tax Acts* have effect as if the trustees were a company resident in the UK, and the rights of unit holders were shares in the company (but without prejudice to the making of 'interest distributions' (see below) for distribution periods beginning after 31 March 1994). Expenses of management (including managers' remuneration) are allowed as if the company were an investment company (see 40.2 INVESTMENT COMPANIES). [*ICTA 1988, s 468(1)(4); FA 1994, Sch 14 para 3*]. For capital gains purposes, any unit trust scheme is treated as if the scheme were a company and the rights of the unit holders shares in the company, and, in the case of an authorised unit trust, as if the company were UK resident and ordinarily resident. [*TCGA 1992, s 99(1)*]. For the capital gains tax treatment, for disposals before 6 April 1999, of individuals acquiring units through monthly savings schemes, see Revenue Pamphlet IR 131, SP 2/99, 31 March 1999 (replacing SP 2/97, which itself replaced SP 3/89) and Tolley's Capital Gains Tax under Unit and Investment Trusts. For company reorganisations involving authorised unit trusts, see 9.6 CAPITAL GAINS.

For special provisions for treatment of loan relationships, see 43.9 LOAN RELATIONSHIPS.

A special rate of corporation tax applies to the trustees of an authorised unit trust. For financial year 1996 and subsequent years, it is equal to the lower rate of income tax (currently 20%) for the year of assessment beginning in the financial year. For earlier financial years, it is equivalent to the basic rate of income tax for the year of assessment beginning in the financial year concerned, except that in certain cases (see below) it is the lower rate of income tax which applies, and for financial year 1993 only, the rate was set at 22.5%. Relief for interest as a charge on income is denied in respect of certain borrowings breaching duties imposed under *Financial Services Act 1986, s 81* (or such borrowings as may be specified in substitution by Treasury regulation). [*ICTA 1988, ss 468(1A), 468E; FA 1994, s 111; FA 1996, Sch 6 para 10; FA 1999, s 28(3)*].

For financial years 1994 and 1995, the corporation tax rate is equivalent to the lower rather than the basic rate of income tax (as above) where, on a claim for an accounting period all or part of which falls in the financial year concerned, the inspector is satisfied that, throughout the accounting period, no more than 60% of the market value of the investments subject to the trusts (disregarding cash awaiting investment) is represented by 'qualifying investments'. The claim must be made within twelve months of the end of the accounting period. '*Qualifying investments*' are defined as

(*a*) money placed at interest,

(*b*) building society shares,

(*c*) securities (other than company shares) of any Government, public or local authority or company, whether secured or unsecured, and including any loan stock or similar security, and (*d*) an entitlement to a share in the investments of another authorised unit trust unless, throughout the accounting period in question, no more than 60% of the market value of that other unit trust's investments is represented by investments falling within (*a*)–(*c*) above,

but the Treasury may, by order, extend or restrict the meaning of 'qualifying investments', including any necessary or expedient transitional provisions. [*ICTA 1988, s 468EE; FA 1994, s 111(2); FA 1996, Sch 6 para 10(3)*].

'*Umbrella schemes*' (i.e. schemes which provide separate pools of contributions between which participants may switch) which are authorised unit trusts may treat each of the separate pools as an authorised unit trust. This applies from 1 April 1994, subject to transitional arrangements for schemes which were umbrella schemes immediately before that date. [*ICTA 1988, s 468(7)–(9); FA 1994, s 113*].

Futures and options. Income derived from transactions relating to futures or options contracts is exempt from tax under Schedule D, Case I in the hands of the trustees. A contract is not excluded from this exemption by the fact that any party is, or may be, entitled to receive and/or liable to make only a payment of a sum (rather than a transfer of assets other than money) in full settlement of all obligations. [*ICTA 1988, s 468AA; FA 1990, s 81(1)*].

For **distribution periods beginning before 1 April 1994** (except in the case of an authorised unit trust which is an approved personal pension scheme), any income available for distribution or investment for a distribution period is treated as dividends on the deemed shares held by unit holders paid to them in proportion to their rights, the date of payment, in the case of income not paid to unit holders, being the latest (or only) date for distribution under the terms of the trust or, if there is no such date, the last day of the distribution period. [*ICTA 1988, s 468(2); FA 1994, Sch 14 para 3(3)*].

Where income of the trustees is, with respect to the accounting period in which the distribution period falls, treated (as above) as dividends paid by the trustees to unit holders (other than certain investment trusts) who are within the charge to corporation tax (and, in relation to payments made before 30 November 1993, not dual resident — see now 53.1 RESIDENCE), then, except as below, for the purposes of computing corporation tax chargeable in the case of the unit holder, the payment is deemed

(*a*) to be an annual payment and not a dividend or other distribution, and

(*b*) to have been received by the unit holder after deduction of tax at the basic (for 1993/94, the lower) rate of income tax for the year of assessment of the payment from a corresponding gross amount.

This treatment does not apply where the rights in respect of which the dividend is treated as paid are held either by the trustees of an authorised unit trust or by the manager of the scheme in the ordinary course of business. From 1 April 1993, it applies only to a proportion of the deemed payment corresponding to the proportion of the trustees' gross income brought into account in determining the payment which does *not* represent FRANKED INVESTMENT INCOME (27). [*ICTA 1988, ss 468F, 468G; FA 1990, s 51; FA 1993, Sch 6 paras 4, 5; FA 1994, s 251(2), Sch 14 para 4*].

For **distribution periods beginning after 31 March 1994**, the total amount available for distribution to unit holders is to be shown in the distribution accounts as available for distribution either as dividends which are not FOREIGN INCOME DIVIDENDS (26) (a 'dividend distribution'), or (where the distribution date (see below) for the period is after 30 June 1994 and before 6 April 1999) as foreign income dividends (a 'foreign income distribution'), or as yearly interest (which may not include any amount deriving from Schedule A income) (an 'interest distribution') or as divided between the first two categories (in which case no discrimination between unit holders is permitted). For distribution periods ending after

25 November 1996, amounts deriving from distributions made before 6 April 1999 to which *FA 1997, Sch 7* applies (see 4.7 ANTI-AVOIDANCE) must be shown as available for distribution as foreign income dividends, as must other amounts which would fall to be treated as distributions to which *FA 1997, Sch 7* applies if they were shown as available for distribution as dividends. These provisions do not apply to an authorised unit trust which is an approved personal pension scheme. [*ICTA 1988, ss 468H(6), 468I; FA 1994, Sch 14 paras 2, 7; FA 1997, Sch 7 para 11; F(No 2)A 1997, s 36(2)(3)*]. For distribution periods ending after 31 March 1996, no amount may be shown as an interest distribution unless the authorised unit trust satisfies a 'qualifying investments test' throughout the distribution period. This requires that, at all times in the period, at least 60% of the market value of the trust's investments (excluding cash awaiting investment), is represented by 'qualifying investments' (as above but (from 25 February 1997) including certain shares in open-ended investment companies (see 40.6 INVESTMENT COMPANIES) subject to similar qualification, and subject to further amendment by Treasury order). [*ICTA 1988, s 468L(8)–(14); FA 1996, Sch 6 para 11; SI 1997 No 212*].

For these purposes, the making of a distribution includes the investment of an amount on behalf of the unit holder in respect of his accumulation units. [*ICTA 1988, s 468H(2); FA 1994, Sch 14 para 2*]. See, however, Revenue Pamphlet IR 1, C30 as regards concessional relief from such treatment in the case of certain *de minimis* distribution (or accumulation) waivers.

As regards dividend distributions, they are treated as dividends on shares paid on the '*distribution date*' (i.e. the date specified under the trust or, if there is no such date, the last day of the distribution period), in respect of which (prior to the abolition of foreign income dividends from 6 April 1999) no foreign income dividend election may be made. [*ICTA 1988, s 468J; FA 1994, Sch 14 para 2; F(No 2)A 1997, Sch 6 para 8(3)*]. Where, on the distribution date, the unit holder is within the charge to corporation tax, then (unless the unit holder is the manager of the scheme holding the units in the ordinary course of business) for the purpose of computing the unit holder's corporation tax liability, the 'unfranked' part of a dividend distribution is deemed

(i) to be an annual payment and not a dividend, foreign income (where still applicable) or interest distribution, and

(ii) to have been received by the unit holder after deduction of tax at the lower rate of income tax for the year of assessment in which the distribution date falls from a corresponding gross amount.

For distribution periods beginning on or after 6 April 1999, where tax is deemed to have been deducted under (ii) above, repayment to the unit holder may not exceed the unit holder's portion (by reference to unit holders' rights in the trust in the distribution period in question) of the amount of the liability of the trustees to corporation tax in respect of that gross income, as reduced by any double tax relief, whether under an agreement or by way of credit under *ICTA 1988, s 790(1)* (see 21.2, 21.3 DOUBLE TAX RELIEF). The statement sent to the unit holder relating to the distribution must show that net liability of the trustees.

The '*unfranked*' part of the dividend distribution is found by the formula

$$\left((A + B) \times \frac{C}{D}\right) - B$$

A is the amount of the dividend distribution,

B is the amount of any foreign income distribution (where still applicable) made for the distribution period,

C is the gross income of the fund brought into account in determining the amount available for distribution for the period excluding any part deriving from franked investment income (and reduced, for distribution periods beginning on or after 6 April 1999, by the amount of the liability of the trustees to corporation tax in respect of that gross income less any double tax relief, whether under an agreement or by way of credit under *ICTA 1988, s 790(1)* (see 21.2, 21.3 DOUBLE TAX RELIEF)), and

D is the gross income of the fund as in C (and similarly reduced for distribution periods beginning on or after 6 April 1999), but including any part deriving from franked investment income.

[*ICTA 1988, s 468Q; FA 1994, Sch 14 para 2; F(No 2)A 1997, Sch 6 para 8(6); FA 1998, Sch 3 para 27*].

As regards foreign income distributions (prior to their abolition from 6 April 1999), they are treated as foreign income dividends on shares paid on the '*distribution date*' (as above) to which *ICTA 1988, ss 246A, 246B* (elections for foreign income dividend treatment, see 26.2 FOREIGN INCOME DIVIDENDS), *ss 246K–246M* (subsidiaries, see 26.5 FOREIGN INCOME DIVIDENDS) and *ss 246S–246W* (international headquarters companies, see 26.8, 26.9 FOREIGN INCOME DIVIDENDS) do not apply. Where, on the distribution date, the unit holder is within the charge to corporation tax, the provisions applicable to dividend distributions in such cases (see above) apply with appropriate modification, except that the formula for determining the unfranked part of the foreign income distribution is

$$\left((A + B) \times \frac{E}{D}\right) - A$$

where

A is the amount of any dividend distribution made for the distribution period,

B is the amount of the foreign income distribution,

E is the gross income of the fund brought into account in determining the amount available for distribution for the period excluding any part derived from foreign income dividends, and

D is the gross income of the fund as in E but including any part derived from foreign income dividends.

For distribution periods ending after 27 November 1995, no repayment may be made of any tax deemed to have been deducted under (ii) above as it applies in relation to a foreign income distribution.

[*ICTA 1988, ss 468K, 468R; FA 1994, Sch 14 para 2; FA 1996, Sch 27 para 6; F(No 2)A 1997, Sch 6 para 8(4)(7)*].

As regards interest distributions, they are treated as payments of yearly interest made on the '*distribution date*' (as above). No amount is brought into account in respect of them under *FA 1996, Pt IV, Ch II* other than by virtue of *FA 1996, Sch 10 para 4(4)* (see 43.3, 43.9 LOAN RELATIONSHIPS), but they are deductible from total profits for the accounting period in which the last day of the distribution period falls. (For accounting periods ending before 1 April 1996, they are not charges on income within *ICTA 1988, s 338(1)* (see 50.3 PROFIT COMPUTATIONS), but if paid under deduction of tax (see below) they are deductible from total profits.) (See *ICTA 1988, s 468L(5)–(7)* introduced by *FA 1994, Sch 14 para 2* and amended by *FA 1996, Sch 14 para 26*). Lower (before 1996/97, basic) rate tax is deductible under *ICTA 1988, s 349(2)* except in certain cases where the unit holder to whom the payment is made satisfies the residence condition of *ICTA 1988, ss 468O, 468P* (introduced by *FA 1994, Sch 14 para 2*) on the distribution date, broadly that a valid declaration is made in prescribed form that either he is non-UK ordinarily resident or, if he holds the units as personal representative of a deceased unit holder, at the time of his death the unit holder was non-UK ordinarily resident. In relation to company unit holders, the declaration must be that the company is not UK resident. In the case of distributions made to or received under a trust, under regulations effective from 27 September 1994 (see *SI 1994 No 2318*), the requirement is for a valid declaration from the trustees both that they are non-UK resident and that each beneficiary known to them satisfies the individual or company residence conditions as appropriate (except that where the whole of the distribution is, or is treated as, income of a person other than the trustees, the residence conditions apply only to that person). If the gross income in the distribution accounts derives entirely from 'eligible income', payments to unit holders satisfying the appropriate residence condition may be made without deduction of tax. There is a formula for determining the amount which may be paid without deduction of tax where the gross income does not derive entirely from 'eligible income' (see *ICTA 1988, s 468N(4)–(6)* introduced by *FA 1994, Sch 14 para 2*). *SI 1994 No 2318* also provides the Revenue with the appropriate powers to determine whether interest distributions have properly been paid gross. '*Eligible income*' is defined in *ICTA 1988, s 468M(4)(5)* (introduced by *FA 1994, Sch 14 para 2* and amended by *FA 1996, Sch 7 para 17, F(No 2)A 1997, Sch 6 para 8(5)* and *FA 2000, Sch 40 Pt II(17)*), and is broadly income which would not be subject to deduction if received directly by a non-resident. [*ICTA 1988, ss 468L, 468M, 468N; FA 1994, Sch 14 para 2; FA 1996, Sch 7 para 17, Sch 14 para 26; F(No 2)A 1997, Sch 6 para 8(5)*].

Court common investment funds (CCIFs) are a form of unit trust set up by the Lord Chancellor under *Administration of Justice Act 1982, s 42(1)*. They are available only for individuals whose money is under control of certain Courts, e.g. road accident victims and the mentally incapacitated. The Public Trustee as Accountant General of the Supreme Court holds all units in the fund on the investors' behalf. As regards any income arising to a CCIF after 5 April 1999 and any distribution made for a distribution period beginning after that date, CCIFs are treated for tax purposes as authorised unit trusts. The investment manager is treated as the trustee, and the persons whose interests entitle them, as against the Accountant General (or other authorised person), to share in the fund's investments are treated as the unit holders. Previously, CCIFs fell to be treated as unauthorised unit trusts (see 60.2 below). For these purposes, a distribution period of a CCIF in existence on 5 April 1999 is deemed to have ended on that date, and its first accounting period and distribution period under the authorised unit trust regime are deemed to begin on 6 April 1999. [*ICTA 1988, s 469A; FA 1999, s 68*].

Proposed action on use of derivatives. It was proposed to introduce legislation effective from 12 July 1996 to block the use of derivative instruments (such as swaps, options and futures) by unit trusts to deliver artificially tax-advantaged returns. After consultation with the industry, it was agreed that the Government's concerns could be met by appropriate amendment to the relevant Statement of Recommended Practice. Legislation is therefore no longer to be proceeded with. (Revenue Press Releases 12 July 1996, 3 January 1997). See Tolley's Income Tax under Anti-Avoidance for provisions on the use of derivatives other than by authorised unit trusts.

Simon's Direct Tax Service. See **D4.413–D4.418.**

60.2 UNIT TRUSTS NOT TREATED AS AUTHORISED UNIT TRUSTS

Special provisions apply to the income of a unit trust scheme not within 60.1 above unless the trustees are non-UK resident. Such a trust is outside the scope of *ICTA 1988, s 468* (see 60.1 above). Income arising to the trustees is treated as income of the trustees (rather than the unit holders), and is subject to basic rate tax. Capital allowances are available to the trustees (but, since the trustees are not treated as a company, there is no relief for management expenses). The unit holders are treated as receiving annual payments, under deduction of basic rate tax, equal to their respective entitlements to the grossed-up income available for distribution or investment. The date the payment is treated as having been made is the latest (or only) date for distribution under the terms of the trust or (if there is no such date or it is more than twelve months after the end of the distribution period) the last day of the distribution period. For the definition of 'distribution period', see *ICTA 1988, s 469(6)* as amended by *FA 1994, Sch 14 para 5*.

UK company qualifying distributions (see 20.8 DISTRIBUTIONS) made after 1 July 1997 but before 6 April 1999 which are income of the trustees are treated as FOREIGN INCOME DIVIDENDS (26) (if they would not otherwise be so treated). This does not, however, apply to common investment funds under *Administration of Justice Act 1982, s 42* (but see 60.1 above from 6 April 1999) or if, were it not treated as income of the trustees, the whole of a distribution would be income either of a charity (within *ICTA 1988, s 506(1)*, see 11.1 CHARITIES) or of a body treated as if it were a charity under *ICTA 1988, s 507* or *s 508* (see 24.3, 24.8, 24.11, 24.12, 24.17 EXEMPT ORGANISATIONS). With effect from 6 April 1999, no tax credit is attached to any qualifying distributions received by the trustees, who are not treated as having paid income tax thereon (and the latter applies also to non-qualifying distributions (see 20.8 DISTRIBUTIONS) received by the trustees).

The liability of the trustees to account for tax deducted from annual payments treated as made by them, so far as not covered by tax deducted from income received, is reduced where there is a cumulative uncredited surplus of income on which they are chargeable to tax over such annual payments. [*ICTA 1988, s 469; FA 1988, s 71; FA 1989, s 80; FA 1990, s 52(2)(3); FA 1994, Sch 14 para 5; FA 1996, Sch 6 para 12; FA 1997, s 80(5); F(No 2)A 1997, s 29, Sch 4 para 12*].

Pension fund pooling. Regulations which came into force on 11 July 1996 make special provision to ensure that certain international pooled pension funds (registered as 'pension fund pooling vehicles') are transparent for UK tax purposes, by disapplying the tax rules for unauthorised unit trusts (as above). Participants in such schemes must be approved by the Revenue, and are treated for income tax, capital allowances and capital gains tax purposes as though they themselves owned directly a share of each of the trust assets. There is also relief from stamp duty (or stamp duty reserve tax) on transfers of assets (other than land or buildings) by participants into the scheme. Participation in pension fund pooling vehicles is restricted to exempt approved pension schemes, UK-based superannuation funds used primarily by companies employing British expatriates working overseas, and pension funds established outside the UK broadly equivalent to UK exempt approved pension schemes. [*SI 1996 Nos 1583, 1584, 1585*]. The position in the country in which any overseas participator is based will of course be crucial to the operation of such schemes.

Simon's Direct Tax Service. See **D4.420.**

60.3 UNIT TRUSTS FOR EXEMPT UNIT HOLDERS

If, for any reason other than non-residence, none of the holders of units in a unit trust scheme would be liable to capital gains tax (or to corporation tax on chargeable gains) on a disposal of units, gains accruing to the trust itself are not chargeable gains. [*TCGA 1992, s 100(2)*]. This exemption applies whenever the gains accrued, but is of practical importance only in relation to unit trust schemes which have not been designated as in 60.1 above. It is not withdrawn by reason of units being temporarily held by the trust's managers under ordinary arrangements of the trust for the issue and redemption of units. (Revenue Pamphlet IR 1, D17).

60.4 **INVESTMENT TRUSTS**

An investment trust is a 'company' fulfilling the following conditions.

(*a*) It is not a close company.

(*b*) It is resident in the UK.

(*c*) It derives its income wholly or mainly (in practice, 70% or more) from 'shares' or securities or from certain investments in housing (see below).

(*d*) No 'holding' in any one company represents more than 15% of the value of its investments, unless that company is itself an investment trust or would be so but for being unquoted. This requirement is waived in respect of investments which, when acquired, represented no more than 15% of the value of the investments, and in respect of an investment held on 6 April 1965, provided that the holding represented not more than 25% of the overall value of the investments at that date. There is no waiver in either case where there has been an 'addition' to the holding.

(*e*) Its 'ordinary share capital' (and every class thereof, if there is more than one) is listed in the Official List of the Stock Exchange.

(*f*) Its Memorandum or Articles prohibit the distribution by way of dividend of gains arising from the sale of investments.

(*g*) It does not retain more than 15% of its income derived from shares and securities or from certain investments in housing (see below) in any accounting period.

(*h*) It is approved by the Board.

As regards (*c*) and (*g*) above, stock lending fees are not regarded as income from securities (see Revenue Capital Gains Manual, CG 41417). Also as regards (*c*) and (*g*) above, units in an authorised unit trust are treated as shares in a company, and where condition (*d*) above is then relevant, and in relation to open-ended investment companies ('OEICs', see 40.6 INVESTMENT COMPANIES), that condition is regarded as being satisfied *provided that*, during any accounting period in which units in the unit trust or shares in the OEIC were held by the investment trust, the unit trust or OEIC itself satisfied the condition at (*c*) above. This will always be considered to be the case where the unit trust is a securities fund under the *Financial Services Act 1986* regulations or the OEIC is a securities company under the corresponding OEIC regulations (and for certain similarly constituted sub-funds). (Revenue Statement of Practice SP 3/97, 18 July 1997, replacing SP 7/94). As regards (*g*), see also 25.21(*d*) FINANCIAL INSTRUMENTS concerning treatment of certain profits as income derived from shares or securities.

(*g*) above does not apply if the amount the company would be required to distribute to meet the 15% requirement for a period is less than £10,000 (proportionately reduced for periods of less than twelve months), or if the company is required by law to retain income in excess of the 15% limit for the period. The latter exclusion only applies, however, if the aggregate of the excess of retentions over those required by law and any distribution for the period is less than £10,000 (proportionately reduced for periods of less than twelve months). As regards the measure of income retained under (*g*) above, see Revenue Capital Gains Manual, CG 41437 *et seq.*.

'*Company*' includes any body corporate or unincorporated association, but not a partnership.

'*Shares*' includes stock.

'*Holding*' means the shares or securities of whatever class or classes held in any one company. Where, in connection with a scheme of reconstruction or amalgamation (see 9.6 CAPITAL GAINS), a company issues shares or securities to persons holding shares or securities in another in respect of, and in proportion to (or as nearly as may be in proportion to) such holdings, without the recipients' becoming liable for any consideration, the old and the new holdings are treated as the same. If the investing company is a member of a group (i.e. a company and its 51% subsidiaries, see 29.9 GROUPS OF COMPANIES), money owed to it by another group member is treated as a security and, as such, as part of its holding in that other group member. Holdings in companies which are members of a group (whether or not including the investing company) are treated as holdings in a single company.

An '*addition*' is made to a holding whenever the investing company acquires further shares or securities in any company in which it already has a holding, otherwise than by being allotted them without liability for consideration (e.g. a bonus issue). The holding is deemed to have been acquired at the date of the latest addition.

[*ICTA 1988, s 842; TCGA 1992, s 288(1); FA 1988, s 117; FA 1990, s 55; FA 1996, Sch 38 para 7*].

'*Ordinary share capital*' is as defined in *ICTA 1988, s 832(1)*. See 9.18 CAPITAL GAINS.

Investment trusts are exempt from tax on capital gains realised on disposals. [*TCGA 1992, s 100(1)*].

For the treatment of forward currency transactions as being of a capital or revenue nature, and their effect on the test in (*c*) above, see Revenue Pamphlet IR 131, SP 14/91, 21 November 1991 and Revenue Capital Gains Manual, CG 41445.

See generally Revenue Capital Gains Manual CG 41400 *et seq.*.

Investments in housing. For accounting periods beginning on or after 29 April 1996, investment in residential properties by investment trusts is permitted. A property must first have been acquired after 31 March 1996, have subsequently been let on an assured tenancy, and must satisfy certain other conditions. In particular:

(i) the trust's interest must be either freehold or under a long lease (i.e. with at least 21 years remaining) at low rent (i.e. not more than £250 p.a. (£1,000 p.a. in Greater London));

(ii) the cost of the property (including construction, renovation or conversion costs and certain costs of related interests) must not exceed £85,000 (£125,000 in Greater London) (both figures variable by Treasury order);

(iii) the property must have been let without a lease premium and without an option to purchase being granted to the tenant (or an associate); and

(iv) the interest acquired by the trust must not have been subject to any letting or statutory tenancy other than a shorthold tenancy, and the trust must not have made any arrangements for letting, at the time of acquisition of the interest. Prior arrangements by CONNECTED PERSONS (16) of the trust are similarly excluded, except for certain arrangements for continuation of a shorthold tenancy.

Where a connected person has previously acquired the interest in the property, or another interest which that person continues to hold when the trust acquires its interest, the time at which the interest was first acquired by the connected person is treated as being the time when the interest was first acquired by the company.

Rents and other receipts deriving from such properties are '*eligible rental income*'.

Provided that these conditions are met, in addition to the normal capital gains exemption, profits chargeable in respect of eligible rental income ('*housing investment profits*') are chargeable at the small companies rate and are excluded from 'basic profits' (see 56.1, 56.2 SMALL COMPANIES—REDUCED RATES).

The provisions apply *mutatis mutandis* to Scotland.

[*ICTA 1988, ss 508A, 508B, 842(1)(a)(1AA); FA 1996, s 160, Sch 30*].

For company reorganisations involving investment trusts, see 9.6 CAPITAL GAINS. For the transfer of assets within a group of companies to a company which subsequently becomes an investment trust, see 9.49 CAPITAL GAINS.

Simon's Direct Tax Service. See **D4.422, D4.423.**

61 Value Added Tax

61.1 NON-TAXABLE PERSONS

VAT which is related to expenditure deductible for corporation tax purposes is also deductible. Capital allowances on any such expenditure are based on the VAT-inclusive cost. See Revenue Pamphlet IR 131, B1.

61.2 TAXABLE PERSONS

Income and expenditure are taken into account *exclusive* of VAT, and capital allowances are determined accordingly. However, capital allowances on motor cars are computed on the VAT-inclusive cost and entertainment expenses *disallowed* for corporation tax purposes include VAT. The full amount of a bad debt (i.e. including irrecoverable VAT) is allowable as a trading expense. See Revenue Pamphlet IR 131, B1.

61.3 PARTLY-EXEMPT PERSONS

Entertainment expenses and expenditure on motor cars are treated as under 61.2 above. Input VAT on items of expenditure which constitute exempt output must be allocated to the categories of such expenditure, and will be treated for corporation tax purposes as part of that expenditure. Inspectors are prepared to consider any 'reasonable arrangements' for allocation.

VAT unreclaimed due to the excessive cost of keeping the necessary records may be treated as part of the expenditure to which it relates for corporation tax purposes. See Revenue Pamphlet IR 131, B1.

61.4 PRE-INCORPORATION EXPENDITURE

Regulations may be made to allow deduction as input tax of VAT paid on goods acquired before incorporation and for services supplied before that time for its benefit or in connection with its incorporation. [*VATA 1994, s 24 (6)(c)*].

61.5 INTEREST, PENALTIES, SURCHARGE AND REPAYMENT SUPPLEMENT

No deduction is allowed for corporation tax purposes in respect of any payment by way of VAT

(*a*) penalty under *VATA 1994, ss 60–70,*

(*b*) interest under *VATA 1994, s 74,* or

(*c*) surcharge under *VATA 1994, s 59.*

Similarly any VAT repayment supplement under *VATA 1994, s 79* is disregarded for corporation tax purposes. [*ICTA 1988, s 827*].

See 14.8 CLUBS AND SOCIETIES as regards certain repayments to sports clubs.

62 Venture Capital Trusts

Simon's Direct Tax Service E3.6.

62.1 From 6 April 1995, the venture capital trust scheme described at 62.2 *et seq.* below is introduced to encourage individuals to invest in unquoted trading companies through such trusts. The provisions dealing with the approval of companies as venture capital trusts, and with the reliefs for investors, are introduced in *FA 1995, ss 70–72, Schs 14–16* . The Treasury has wide powers to make regulations governing all aspects of the reliefs applicable to venture capital trust investments, and for the requirements as regards returns, records and provision of information by the trust. [*FA 1995, s 73; FA 1996, Sch 18 para 16, 17(1)(3)*]. See now *SI 1995 No 1979; SI 1999 No 819.*

For company reorganisations involving venture capital trusts, see 9.6 CAPITAL GAINS. For the transfer of assets within a group of companies to a company which subsequently becomes a venture capital trust, see 9.50 CAPITAL GAINS.

62.2 **CONDITIONS FOR APPROVAL** [*ICTA 1988, s 842AA; FA 1995, s 70; FA 1996, Sch 38 para 7; FA 1997, s 75; FA 1998, s 73(1)(6), Sch 27 Pt III(13); FA 1999, s 69(4)(5)*]

A '*venture capital trust*' ('VCT') is a company approved for this purpose by the Board. CLOSE COMPANIES (13) are excluded. The time from which an approval takes effect is specified in the approval, and may not be earlier than the time the application for approval was made or, for approvals given in 1995/96, 6 April 1995.

Except as detailed further below, approval may not be given unless the Board are satisfied that the following conditions are met.

(*a*) The company's income in its most recent complete accounting period has been derived wholly or mainly from shares or securities, and not more than 15% of its income from shares and securities has been retained.

(*b*) Throughout that period at least 70% by value of the company's investments has been represented by shares or securities in 'qualifying holdings' (see 62.3 below), at least 30% of which (by value) has been represented by holdings of '*eligible shares*', i.e. ordinary shares carrying no present or future preferential right to dividends or to assets on a winding up, and no present or future right (before 6 April 1998, no present or future preferential right) to redemption.

(*c*) The company's ordinary shares (or each class thereof) have been listed in the Official List of the Stock Exchange throughout that period.

(*d*) No holding in any company other than a VCT (or a company which could be a VCT but for (*c*) above) has at any time in that period represented more than 15% of the value of the company's investments.

'Securities' for these purposes are deemed to include liabilities in respect of certain loans not repayable within five years, and any stocks or securities relating to which are not re-purchasable or redeemable within five years of issue. Provided that the loan is made on normal commercial terms, the Revenue will not regard a standard event of default clause in the loan agreement as disqualifying a loan from being a security for this purpose. If, however, the clause entitled the lender (or a third party) to exercise any action which would cause the borrower to default, the clause would not be regarded as 'standard'. (Revenue Pamphlet IR 131, SP 8/95, 14 September 1995).

As regards the 15% limits in (*a*) and (*d*) above, the provisions which apply to the similar restrictions on investment trusts (see 60.4 UNIT AND INVESTMENT TRUSTS) apply with appropriate modification.

Where (*a*)–(*d*) above are met, the Board must also be satisfied that they will be met in the accounting period current at the time of application for approval. Where any of (*a*)–(*d*) above are not met, approval may nevertheless be given where the Board are satisfied that:

(i) in the case of (*a*), (*c*) or (*d*), the condition will be met in the accounting period current when the application for approval is made or in the following accounting period;

(ii) in the case of (*b*), the condition will be met in an accounting period beginning no more than three years after the earlier of the time approval is given and the time it takes effect; and

(iii) in any case, that the condition will continue to be fulfilled in accounting periods following that referred to in (i) or (ii).

On a second and subsequent issues by an approved VCT, the requirements of condition (*b*) above do not have to be met, in relation to the money raised by the further issue, in the accounting period of the further issue or any later accounting period ending no more than three years after the making of the further issue.

Where the 70% limit in (*b*) is breached inadvertently, and the position corrected without delay after discovery, approval will in practice not be withdrawn on this account. Full details of any such inadvertent breach should be disclosed to the Revenue as soon as it is discovered. (Revenue Press Release 14 September 1995).

The value of any investment for the purposes of (*b*) and (*d*) above is the value when the investment was acquired, except that where it is added to by a further holding of an investment of the same description, or a payment is made in discharge of any obligation attached to it which increases its value, it is the value immediately after the most recent such addition or payment.

Share exchanges and conversions. With effect from 16 June 1999, certain transactions in shares held by a VCT are in effect disregarded in considering the value of holdings for the purposes of the 70%, 30% and 15% tests in (*b*) and (*d*) above. The transactions concerned are as follows.

(i) Where, as part of a restructuring, shares or securities in a company are exchanged for corresponding shares and securities in a new holding company. Certain deemed securities (see above) which are not thus acquired by the new company may be disregarded where these provisions would otherwise be prevented from applying.

(ii) Where a VCT exercises conversion rights in respect of certain convertible shares and securities.

In these circumstances, and subject to detailed conditions (see *ICTA 1988, Sch 28B paras 10C, 10D* introduced by *FA 1999, s 69*), the value of the new shares is taken to be the same as the value of the old shares when they were last valued for these purposes.

Approval may be **withdrawn** where there are reasonable grounds for believing that either:

(A) the conditions for approval were not satisfied at the time the approval was given; or

(B) a condition that the Board were satisfied (as above) would be met has not been or will not be met; or

(C) where (ii) above applies, any other conditions prescribed by regulation in relation to the three-year period have not been met; or

(D) in either the most recent complete accounting period or the current one, one of conditions (*a*)–(*d*) above has failed or will fail to be met (unless the failure was allowed for under (i)–(iii) above); or

(E) where, in relation to a second or further issue by an approved VCT, (*b*) above does not have to be met in the period of issue or certain following accounting periods (see above), either

(i) one of conditions (*a*)–(*d*) above will fail to be met in the first period for which (*b*) above must be met, or

(ii) any other conditions prescribed by regulations have not been met in relation to, or to part of, an accounting period for which (*b*) above does not have to be met.

The withdrawal is effective from the time the company is notified of it, except that:

(1) where approval is given under (i)–(iii) above, and is withdrawn before all the conditions (*a*)–(*d*) above have been satisfied in relation to either a complete twelve-month accounting period or successive complete accounting periods constituting a continuous period of twelve months or more, the approval is deemed never to have been given; and

(2) for the purposes of relief for capital gains accruing to a VCT under *TCGA 1992, s 100* (see 62.5 below), withdrawal may be effective from an earlier date, but not before the start of the accounting period in which the failure occurred (or is expected to occur).

An assessment consequent on the withdrawal of approval may, where otherwise out of time, be made within three years from the time notice of the withdrawal was given.

For the detailed requirements as regards granting, refusal and withdrawal of approval, and appeals procedures, see *SI 1995 No 1979, Pt II*.

Applications for approval should be made to the Financial Intermediaries and Claims Office, St John's House, Merton Road, Bootle, Merseyside L69 9BB.

62.3 **QUALIFYING HOLDINGS** [*ICTA 1988, s 842AA(5AD)(5AE)(13), Sch 28B; FA 1995, Sch 14; FA 1996, s 161; FA 1997, Sch 9; F(No 2)A 1997, s 25(2)–(4); FA 1998, s 70(1)(3), s 72, s 73(2)–(6), Sch 12 paras 3, 4, 5(2)(3); FA 1999, s 69(2)(3)(5); FA 2000, Sch 18 paras 4–8*]

Shares or securities in a company are comprised in a VCT's '*qualifying holdings*' at any time if they were first issued to the VCT, and have been held by it ever since, and the following conditions are satisfied at that time.

(*a*) The company is an '*unquoted company*' (whether or not UK resident), i.e. none of its shares, stocks, debentures or other securities is

(i) listed on a recognised stock exchange, or a designated exchange outside the UK, or

(ii) dealt in on the Unlisted Securities Market, or outside the UK by such means as may be designated for the purpose by order.

Securities on the Alternative Investment Market ('AIM') are treated as unquoted for these purposes. (Revenue Press Release 20 February 1995).

If the company ceases to be an unquoted company at a time when its shares are comprised in the qualifying holdings of the VCT, this condition is treated as continuing to be met, in relation to shares or securities acquired before that time, for the following five years.

(*b*) Either

(i) the company must exist wholly for the purpose of carrying on one or more 'qualifying trades' (disregarding any purpose having no significant effect on the extent of its activities as a whole), or

(ii) (after 26 November 1996) it must be the 'parent company of a trading group' (previously, its business had to consist entirely in holding shares in or securities of, or making loans to, one or more 'qualifying subsidiaries' (see (*f*) below), with or without the carrying on of one or more 'qualifying trades').

In addition, the company, or a 'qualifying subsidiary' (from 6 April 1998, a 'relevant qualifying subsidiary'), must, when the shares were issued to the VCT and ever since, have been carrying on a 'qualifying trade' wholly or mainly in the UK, or preparing to carry on such a trade intended to be carried on wholly or mainly in the UK. In the latter case, there is a time limit of two years from the issue of the shares for the trade to be commenced as intended. A '*relevant qualifying subsidiary*' is a company which would be a 'qualifying subsidiary' (see (*f*) below) if the references to 75% in (*f*)(ii) below were instead to 90%.

After 20 March 2000, a company does not cease to satisfy the above conditions by reason of anything done as a consequence of its being in administration or receivership under an *Insolvency Act 1986* order (or NI or foreign equivalent), provided that anything so done (and the making of the order) is for *bona fide* commercial reasons and not part of a scheme or arrangement a main purpose of which is tax avoidance.

A trade is a '*qualifying trade*' if it does not, or not substantially, consist of any of the activities at (A)–(L) below. Research and development from which it is intended that there will be derived a qualifying trade carried on wholly or mainly in the UK is treated as the carrying on of a qualifying trade. For shares issued on or after 6 April 2000, 'research and development' is as defined in *ICTA 1988, s 837A* (see 50.25 PROFIT COMPUTATIONS). For shares issued before that date, it means any activity intended to result in a patentable invention or a computer program.

(A) Dealing in land, in commodities or futures or in shares, securities or other financial instruments.

(B) Dealing in goods otherwise than in an ordinary trade of wholesale or retail distribution.

(C) Banking, insurance, money-lending, debt-factoring, hire-purchase financing or other financial activities.

(D) Leasing (including letting ships on charter or other assets on hire) or receiving royalties or licence fees.

(E) Providing legal or accountancy services.

(F) Property development (as defined, see *ICTA 1988, Sch 28B paras 5, 7* as amended by *FA 1998, Sch 12 para 4*).

(G) Farming or market gardening.

(H) Holding, managing or occupying woodlands, any other forestry activities or timber production.

(J) Operating or managing hotels or comparable establishments (including guest houses, hostels and other establishments whose main purpose is to offer overnight accommodation with or without catering) or managing property used as such.

(K) Operating or managing nursing homes or residential care homes (both as defined, see *ICTA 1988, Sch 28B para 5(1)* as amended by *FA 1998, Sch 12 para 4*) or managing property used as such.

(L) Providing services or facilities for any trade, profession or vocation within (A)–(K) above and which is carried on by another person (other than a parent company), where one person has a 'controlling interest' in both trades.

(F)–(K) above (and the reference to them in (L)) apply in determining whether any shares or securities are, at any time after 16 March 1998, to be regarded as comprised in a qualifying holding. They do not, however, apply in relation to shares or securities acquired with money raised by the issue of VCT shares or securities before that date, or of money derived from the investment of money so raised. (J) and (K) apply only if the person carrying on the activity in question has an estate or interest (e.g. a lease) in the property concerned or occupies that property.

Adventures and concerns in the nature of trade, and trades not carried on commercially and with a view to the realisation of profits, are also excluded.

In relation to similar provisions under the Business Expansion Scheme, the Revenue are understood to have regarded as 'substantial' for the above purposes a part of a trade which gives rise to 20% or more of total turnover. (Tolley's Practical Tax 1987 p 162). Similarly, as regards (A) above, it is understood that it was not intended to exclude from relief what is mainly a building trade, despite the technical position that what the builder sells is the land with the buildings on it. (Tolley's Practical Tax 1984 p 206).

As regards (B) above, a trade of wholesale or retail distribution is a trade consisting of the offer of goods for sale either to persons for resale (or processing and resale) (which resale must be to members of the general public) by them ('*wholesale*') or to the general public ('*retail*'). A trade is not an 'ordinary' wholesale or retail trade if it consists to a substantial extent of dealing in goods collected or held as an investment (or of that and any other activity within (A)–(L) above), and a substantial proportion of such goods is held for a significantly longer period than might reasonably be expected for a vendor trying to dispose of them at market value. Whether such trades are 'ordinary' is to be judged having regard to the following features, those under (1) supporting the categorisation as 'ordinary', those under (2) being indicative to the contrary.

(1) (*a*) The breaking of bulk.

(*b*) The purchase and sale of goods in different markets.

(*c*) The employment of staff and incurring of trade expenses other than the cost of goods or the remuneration of persons connected (within *ICTA 1988, s 839*) with a company carrying on the trade.

(2) (*a*) The purchase or sale of goods from or to persons connected (within *ICTA 1988, s 839*) with the trader.

(*b*) The matching of purchases with sales.

(*c*) The holding of goods for longer than might normally be expected.

(*d*) The carrying on of the trade at a place not commonly used for wholesale or retail trading.

(*e*) The absence of physical possession of the goods by the trader.

As regards (D) above, for shares issued to the VCT after 5 April 2000, a trade is not excluded by reason only of the receiving of royalties or licence fees where they (or all but an insubstantial part of them by value) are attributable to the exploitation of 'relevant intangible assets'. A '*relevant intangible asset*' is an asset which is treated in accordance with normal UK company accounting practice as intangible and the whole or greater part of which (in terms of value) has been created by the company carrying on the trade, or by a company which at all times during the creation was its parent company or a qualifying subsidiary (see (*f*) below) of that parent company. For this purpose a parent company is a company with a 51% subsidiary (see 29.3 GROUPS OF COMPANIES) or subsidiaries but not itself a 51% subsidiary. If the asset is intellectual property, i.e. any patent, trade mark, registered design, copyright, design right, performer's right or plant breeder's right or any corresponding or similar right under the law of a country outside the UK, the right to exploit it must vest in the company (either alone or with others).

For shares issued before 6 April 2000, a more limited relief from exclusion under (D) above applies. The trade of a company engaged in the production of original master films, tapes or discs is not excluded by reason only of the receipt of royalties or licence fees, provided that all royalties and licence fees received by the company are in respect of films, etc. produced by it since the issue of the shares to the VCT or in respect of by-products arising therefrom. The company may also be engaged in the distribution of films produced by it since those shares were issued. Similarly the trade of a company engaged in research and development is not excluded by reason only of the receipt of royalties and licence fees attributable to that research and development.

Also as regards (D) above, a trade carried on by a company will not be excluded by reason only of its consisting of chartering ships, other than oil rigs or ships of a kind primarily used for sport or recreation, provided that

(I) the company beneficially owns all the ships it so lets,

(II) every ship beneficially owned by the company is UK-registered,

(III) the company is solely responsible for arranging the marketing of the services of its ships, and

(IV) in relation to every letting on charter, certain conditions as to length and terms of charter, and the arm's length character of the transaction, are met,

and if any of (I)–(IV) above is not met in relation to certain lettings, only those lettings (together with any other excluded activities) are taken into account in determining whether a substantial part of the trade consists of excluded activities.

Also in relation to (D) above, the Revenue has given its views on the scope of the exclusions in its Tax Bulletin. The leasing and letting exclusion covers all cases where (subject to reasonable conditions imposed by the trader) the customer is free to use the property as his own. Where this is not so (e.g. the hire of chauffeur-driven cars, or storage of articles by the trader in warehouses or safes) exclusion does not apply. Royalties and licence fees are received where property rights are exploited by the company granting permission to another to make use of the property. In the case of royalties, the exclusion applies regardless of whether the company itself brought that property into existence (although see above as regards film and research and development royalties and licence fees). In the case of licence fees, the grant of the right to use the property is often incidental to the supply of services, and the exclusion does not apply in such cases. Similarly where, although there is no direct provision of services, continuous work is required to keep the property in a fit state for use, the question to be considered is whether such work is or is not greater than the work involved in obtaining the fees. The Revenue thus consider that receipts from an actively supervised gymnasium, with trainers in attendance to advise on personal fitness programmes and the use of equipment, are not licence fees, whereas receipts from letting out tennis courts to the general public by the hour are licence fees. The description of what is in effect a season ticket for the use of property as a membership fee (e.g. in the case of some sports clubs) does not affect the status of the payments. (Revenue Tax Bulletin August 1995 pp 240, 241).

As regards (L) above, a person has a '*controlling interest*' in a trade carried on by a company if he 'controls' the company; or if the company is close (see 13.1 CLOSE COMPANIES) and he or an 'associate' (within *ICTA 1988, s 417*, see 13.5 CLOSE COMPANIES, but excluding a brother or sister) is a director of the company and the beneficial owner of, or able to control, more than 30% of its ordinary share capital; or if at least half of its ordinary share capital is directly or indirectly owned by him. In any other case, it is obtained by his being entitled to at least one-half of the assets used for, or income arising from, the trade. Rights and powers of 'associates' (as above) are taken into account for these purposes. '*Control*' of a company for these purposes is as under *ICTA 1988, s 416* (see 13.2 CLOSE COMPANIES), except that possession of, or entitlement to acquire, fixed-rate preference shares (as defined) of the company which do not, for the time being, carry voting rights is disregarded, as is possession of, or entitlement to acquire, rights as a loan creditor of the company.

In considering whether a trade is carried on 'wholly or mainly in the UK', the totality of the trade activities is taken into account. Regard will be had, for example, to where capital assets are held, where any purchasing, processing, manufacturing and selling is done, and to where the employees customarily carry out their duties. No one of these factors is itself likely to be decisive in any particular case. Accordingly a company may carry on some such activities outside the UK and yet satisfy the requirement, provided that the major part of them, that is over one-half of the aggregate of these activities, takes place within the UK. Thus relief is not excluded solely because a company's products or services are exported, or because its raw materials are imported, or because its raw materials or products are stored abroad, or because its marketing facilities are supplied from abroad. Similar principles apply in considering the trade(s) carried on by a company and its qualifying subsidiaries. In the particular case of a ship chartering trade, the test is satisfied if all charters are entered into in the UK and the provision of crews and management of the ships while under charter take place mainly in the UK. If these conditions are not met, the test may still be satisfied depending on all the relevant facts and circumstances. (Revenue Pamphlet IR 131, SP 7/98, 30 November 1998, replacing SP 2/94, 9 May 1994).

A company is the '*parent company of a trading group*' if it has one or more subsidiaries, each of which is a 'qualifying subsidiary' (see (*f*) below), and if, taking all the activities of the company and its subsidiaries as one business, neither that business nor a substantial part of it consists in either or both of:

(*aa*) activities within (A)–(L) above, other than those within (D) which, as noted above, do not result in a trade being excluded from being a qualifying trade (and those within (F)–(K) above (or (L) above insofar as it refers to (F)–(K)) applying only as they apply for the purposes of the definition of qualifying trade); and

(*bb*) non-trading activities.

Activities are for these purposes disregarded to the extent that they consist in:

(AA) holding shares in or securities of, or making loans to, one or more of the company's subsidiaries; or

(BB) holding and managing property used by the company or any of its subsidiaries for the purposes of either

(i) research and development (as defined — see above) from which it is intended that a qualifying trade to be carried on by the company or any of its subsidiaries will be derived, or

(ii) one or more qualifying trades so carried on.

Activities of a subsidiary are similarly disregarded to the extent that they consist in the making of loans to the company or, where the subsidiary exists wholly for the purpose of carrying on one or more qualifying trades (apart from '*insignificant purposes*', i.e. purposes capable of having no significant effect, other than in relation to incidental matters, on the extent of the subsidiary's activities), of activities carried on in pursuance of those insignificant purposes.

(*c*) The money raised by the issue of shares to the VCT must have been employed wholly for the purposes of, or of preparing for the carrying on of, the qualifying trade (disregarding insignificant amounts used for other purposes), or be intended to be so employed. In the latter case, the money must actually be so employed within twelve months of the later of the issue of the shares to the VCT and the date the qualifying trade was commenced.

After 26 November 1996, where the company is a 'parent company of a trading group' within (*b*)(ii) above, the '*trader company*' (i.e. the company carrying on (or preparing to carry on) the required qualifying trade) must either:

(i) satisfy the requirements in (*b*)(i) above; or

(ii) be a company in relation to which those requirements would be satisfied if activities within (*b*)(AA) or (*b*)(BB) above, or consisting of a subsidiary making loans to its parent, were disregarded; or

(iii) be a 'qualifying subsidiary' (see (*f*) below) (from 6 April 1998, a '*relevant qualifying subsidiary*', i.e. a company which would be a 'qualifying subsidiary' if the references to 75% in (*f*)(ii) below were instead to 90%) which either

(1) exists wholly for the purpose of carrying on activities within (*b*)(BB) above (disregarding purposes capable of having no significant effect (other than in relation to incidental matters) on the extent of its activities), or

(2) has no corporation tax profits and no part of its business consists in the making of investments.

Money whose retention can reasonably be regarded as necessary or advisable for financing current trade requirements is regarded as employed for trade purposes, but by the end of the twelve months funds should no longer be held which are clearly surplus to day-to-day needs. (Revenue Inspector's Manual, IM 7209).

(*d*) The aggregate of money raised from shares issued by the company to the VCT must not have exceeded the 'maximum qualifying investment' of £1 million in the period from six months before the issue in question (or, if earlier, the beginning of the year of assessment of the issue) to the time of the issue in question. Disposals are treated as far as possible as eliminating any such excess. The £1 million limit is proportionately reduced where, at the time of the issue, the qualifying trade is carried on, or to be carried on, in partnership or as a joint venture, and one or more of the other parties is a company.

(*e*) The value of the company's 'relevant assets' did not exceed £10 million immediately before the issue or £11 million immediately thereafter (raised to £15 million and £16 million respectively for holdings issued on or after 6 April 1998). '*Relevant assets*' are the gross assets of the company and, at any time when it has one or more 'qualifying subsidiaries' (see (*f*) below), of all such subsidiaries. In the latter case, assets consisting in rights against, or shares in or securities of, another member of the group consisting of the company and its qualifying subsidiaries are disregarded.

The general approach of the Revenue is that the value of a company's gross assets is the sum of the value of all the balance sheet assets. Where accounts are actually drawn up to a date immediately before or after the issue, the balance sheet values are taken provided that they reflect usual accounting standards and the company's normal accounting practice, consistently applied. Where accounts are not drawn up to such a date, such values will be taken from the most recent balance sheet, updated as precisely as practicable on the basis of all the relevant information available to the company. Values so arrived at may need to be reviewed in the light of information contained in the accounts for the period in which the issue was made, and, if they were not available at the time of the issue, those for the preceding period, when they become available. The company's assets immediately before the issue do not include any advance payment received in respect of the issue. Where shares are issued partly paid, the right to the balance is an asset, and, notwithstanding the above, will be taken into account in valuing the assets immediately after the issue regardless of whether it is stated in the balance sheet. (Revenue Pamphlet IR 131, SP 5/98, 30 November 1998, replacing SP 7/95, 14 September 1995).

(*f*) The company must not 'control' (with or without 'connected persons') any company other than a 'qualifying subsidiary', nor must another company (or another company and a person connected with it) control it. Neither must arrangements be in existence by virtue of which such control could arise. For these purposes, '*control*' is as under (*b*) above, and '*connected persons*' as under *ICTA 1988, s 839* (see 16 CONNECTED PERSONS) except that the definition of 'control' therein is similarly modified. For the application of the 'control' test to co-investors in a company, and in particular the question of whether co-investors are connected by virtue of their 'acting together to secure or exercise control' of the company, see Revenue Tax Bulletin October 1997 pp 471, 472.

A company is a '*qualifying subsidiary*' for these purposes provided that it (and any fellow subsidiary):

(i) either:

(A) satisfies the condition in (*b*)(i) above, or

(B) exists wholly for the purpose of holding and managing property used by the parent or a fellow subsidiary or subsidiaries for the purposes of a qualifying trade (disregarding any purpose having no significant effect on the extent of its activities as a whole), or for research and development from which it is intended that a qualifying trade will be derived, or

(C) has no corporation tax profits, and no part of its business consists in the making of investments;

(ii) the parent or a fellow subsidiary possesses at least 75% of both its issued share capital and its voting power, and would be beneficially entitled to at least 75%

of its assets available for distribution to equity holders on a winding-up, etc. and of any profits available for distribution to equity holders (see 29.17 GROUPS OF COMPANIES). (The references to 75% are to 90% before 6 April 1998.);

(iii) no person other than the parent or a fellow subsidiary has control of the company within *ICTA 1988, s 840* (see 51.4(vii) PURCHASE BY A COMPANY OF ITS OWN SHARES); and

(iv) no arrangements are in existence which could result in failure to fulfil (ii) or (iii).

(i) above ceases to apply after 26 November 1996 (but see now additional conditions at (*b*) and (*c*) above).

Where

(A) the subsidiary is being wound up, or

(B) arrangements are in existence for the disposal of all the parent company's (or fellow subsidiary's) interest in the subsidiary,

it is not regarded as failing to meet conditions (i)–(iv) above provided that the winding up or disposal is for *bona fide* commercial reasons and not part of a scheme or arrangement a main purpose of which is the avoidance of tax and, in the case of (A), that it would meet those conditions apart from the winding up.

(*g*) Where the company is being wound up, none of conditions (*a*)–(*f*) above are regarded on that account as not being satisfied provided that those conditions would be met apart from the winding up, and that the winding up is for *bona fide* commercial reasons and not part of a scheme or arrangement a main purpose of which is the avoidance of tax.

(*h*) The holding in question must not include any securities (as defined in 62.2 above) relating to a guaranteed loan. A security relates to a guaranteed loan if there are arrangements entitling the VCT to receive anything (directly or indirectly) from a 'third party' in the event of a failure by any person to comply with the terms of the security or the loan to which it relates. It is immaterial whether or not the arrangements apply in all such cases. '*Third party*' includes any person other than the investee company itself and, if it is a parent company of a trading group (see (*b*) above), its subsidiaries. This condition applies for accounting periods (of the VCT) ending after 1 July 1997, but does not apply in the case of shares or securities acquired by the VCT by means of investing money raised by the issue by it before 2 July 1997 of shares or securities (or money derived from the investment of any such money raised).

(*j*) At least 10% (by value) of the VCT's *total* holding of shares in or securities of the company must consist of 'eligible shares' (as defined in 62.2(*b*) above — broadly, ordinary, non-preferential, shares). For this purpose, the value of shares etc. at any time is taken to be their value immediately after the most recent of the events listed below, except that it cannot thereby be taken to be less than the amount of consideration given by the VCT for the shares etc.. The said events are as follows.

(i) The acquisition of the shares etc. by the VCT.

(ii) The acquisition by the VCT (other than by way of bonus issue for no consideration) of any other shares etc. in the same company which are of the same description as those already held.

(iii) The making of any payment in discharge (or part discharge) of any obligation attached to the shares etc. in a case where such discharge increases the value of the shares etc..

This condition applies for accounting periods (of the VCT) ending after 1 July 1997, but, if necessary in order to satisfy the condition, there may be disregarded shares and securities acquired by the VCT by means of investing money raised by the issue by it before 2 July 1997 of shares or securities (or money derived from the investment of any such money raised).

As regards (*c*) and (*d*) above, where either condition would be met as to only part of the money raised by the issue, and the holding is not otherwise capable of being treated as separate holdings, it is treated as two separate holdings, one from which that part of the money was raised, the other from which the rest was raised, with the value being apportioned accordingly to each holding. In the case of (*c*), this does not require an insignificant amount applied for non-trade purposes to be treated as a separate holding.

As regards (*c*) above, in relation to buy-outs (and in particular management buy-outs), the Revenue will usually accept that where a company is formed to acquire a trade, and the funds raised from the VCT are applied to that purchase, the requirement that the funds be employed for the purposes of the trade is satisfied. Where the company is formed to acquire another company and its trade, or a holding company and its trading subsidiaries, this represents an investment rather than employment for the purposes of the trade. However, the Revenue will usually accept that the requirement is satisfied if the trade of the company, or all the activities of the holding company and its subsidiaries, are hived up to the acquiring company as soon as possible after the acquisition. In the case of a holding company and its subsidiaries, to the extent that the trades are not hived up, the holding cannot be a qualifying holding. (Revenue Tax Bulletin August 1995 pp 243, 244).

As regards (*b*)–(*f*) and (*j*) above, with effect from 16 June 1999, certain transactions in shares held by a VCT are in effect disregarded in considering whether the relevant condition is satisfied. The transactions concerned are as follows.

(A) Where, as part of a restructuring, shares or securities in a company are exchanged for corresponding shares and securities in a new holding company. Certain deemed securities (see 62.2 above) which are not thus acquired by the new company may be disregarded where these provisions would otherwise be prevented from applying.

(B) Where a VCT exercises conversion rights in respect of certain convertible shares and securities.

In these circumstances, and subject to detailed conditions (see *ICTA 1988, Sch 28B paras 10C, 10D* introduced by *FA 1999, s 69*), to the extent that the condition was satisfied in relation to the old shares, it will generally be taken to be satisfied in relation to the new shares.

The Treasury has power by order to modify the requirements under (*b*) above as they consider expedient, and to alter the cash limits referred to in (*d*) and (*e*) above.

To deal with cases where shares or securities comprised in a qualifying holding are exchanged, after 20 March 2000, for shares, etc. which do not meet all the requirements to be part of a qualifying holding, and the exchange is made for *bona fide* commercial reasons and not as part of a scheme or arrangement a main purpose of which is tax avoidance, the Treasury also has power to make regulations under which the replacement shares, etc. are treated as meeting those requirements. The regulations may similarly deal with any other form of company reconstruction or other arrangement involving the holder of shares, etc. receiving other shares, etc., whether the original shares, etc. are transferred, retained or cancelled, and whether the new shares, etc. are in the same or another company. They may also provide for the value of the new holding and of any original shares retained to be of such amount as to continue to satisfy the requirements of 62.2(*b*) and (*d*) above. They must specify the cases to which they will apply and any conditions, and which requirements are to be treated as met (and for what period). They may be retrospective, may make different provision for different cases and may include administrative, supplementary, incidental and transitional provisions. They may also authorise the Revenue to require information by notice (and subject to penalty for non-compliance) to determine whether conditions imposed by the regulations are met.

62.4 INCOME TAX RELIEFS

Relief from income tax is granted for 1995/96 and subsequent years, in respect of both investments in VCT share issues (up to £100,000 in a year of assessment) and distributions from such trusts (in respect of shares acquired up to a 'permitted maximum' in any year of assessment). [*ICTA 1988, s 332A, Sch 15B; FA 1995, s 71, Sch 15; FA 1999, s 70; FA 2000, Sch 18 paras 1, 3*]. For the detailed conditions for both reliefs, and for the circumstances in which investment relief is withdrawn, see Tolley's Income Tax under Venture Capital Trusts.

62.5 CAPITAL GAINS TAX RELIEFS

From 6 April 1995, the capital gains of a VCT are not chargeable gains. [*TCGA 1992, s 100(1); FA 1995, s 72(2)*]. In addition, for 1995/96 and subsequent years, individual investors in VCTs are entitled to two reliefs:

(*a*) on disposal of VCT shares (up to a 'permitted maximum' acquired in any year of assessment); and

(*b*) by deferral of chargeable gains on re-investment in VCT share issues (up to the income tax relief limit, see 62.4 above).

[*TCGA 1992, ss 151A, 151B, Sch 5C; FA 1995, s 72, Sch 16; FA 2000, Sch 18 paras 2, 3*].

For the detailed conditions for these reliefs, and for relief on withdrawal of approval, see Tolley's Capital Gains Tax under Venture Capital Trusts.

63 Finance Act 2000 — Summary of Corporation Tax Provisions

(Royal Assent 28 July 2000)

s 35	**Charge and main rate for financial year 2001.** The full rate is set at 30%. See 1.3(*a*) INTRODUCTION AND RATES OF TAX.
s 36	**Small companies' rate for financial year 2000.** The small companies' rate is set at 20% and the marginal relief fraction accordingly remains at $\frac{1}{40}$. See 1.3(*a*) INTRODUCTION AND RATES OF TAX, 56.1, 56.2 SMALL COMPANIES—REDUCED RATES.
s 40	**Giving to charity: gift aid payments by companies.** The lower limit and certain other restrictions are removed, and other scheme conditions revised. See 11.10 CHARITIES.
s 41	**Giving to charity: covenanted payments to charities.** Amendments are made consequential on such payments being brought within the Gift Aid scheme. See 11.9, 11.11 CHARITIES.
s 43	**Giving to charity: gifts of shares and securities to charities etc..** A deduction is allowed for such gifts. See 11.13 CHARITIES.
s 46	**Giving to charity: exemption for small trades etc..** The existing concessionary reliefs are extended. See 11.6(i) CHARITIES.
s 63, Schs 15, 16	**Corporate venturing scheme.** New corporation tax reliefs are introduced for investments in certain small, higher-risk trading companies. See 19 CORPORATE VENTURING SCHEME.
s 65, Sch 18	**Venture capital trusts: amendments.** Certain relief restrictions are relaxed. See 62.3, 62.4 VENTURE CAPITAL TRUSTS.
s 68, Sch 19	**Meaning of "research and development".** A revised definition is adopted for both capital and revenue expenditure reliefs. See *section 69* below and 50.25 PROFIT COMPUTATIONS.
s 69, Schs 20, 21	**Tax relief for expenditure on research and development.** Enhanced reliefs are introduced for such expenditure by small and medium-sized companies. See 50.25 PROFIT COMPUTATIONS.
s 81	**Capital allowances: production sharing contracts.** The availability of capital allowances where oil production assets pass into foreign government ownership is clarified. See 46.3 OIL COMPANIES.
s 82 Sch 22	**Tonnage tax.** A new tonnage-based corporation tax regime is introduced for shipping companies. See 50.30 PROFIT COMPUTATIONS.
s 86	**Loan where return bears inverse relationship to results.** Subject to conditions, interest on such loans is not treated as a distribution. See 20.7 DISTRIBUTIONS, 29.16 GROUPS OF COMPANIES.
s 87, Sch 23	**Tax treatment of acquisition, disposal or revaluation of certain rights.** Relief is introduced for acquisition costs of certain telecommunications licences. See 50.29 PROFIT COMPUTATIONS.
s 88	**Contribution to local enterprise agencies, etc..** Relief for such contribution is made permanent. See Tolley's Income Tax under Schedule D, Cases I and II.
s 97, Sch 27	**Groups and group relief: group relief for non-resident companies etc..** The reliefs are extended to UK branches or agencies of non-resident companies. See 29 GROUPS OF COMPANIES for the principal changes, 18.9 CONTROLLED FOREIGN COMPANIES, 41.2, 41.4(*a*) LIFE INSURANCE COMPANIES, 55.5 SELF-ASSESSMENT.

s 98, Sch 28 **Groups and group relief: recovery of tax payable by non-resident company.** Provision is made for the recovery from third party companies of tax unpaid by non-resident companies. See 48.4 PAYMENT OF TAX.

s 99 **Groups and group relief: joint arrangements for claims.** Minor change to the authority required under the simplified arrangements for group claims. See generally 29.23 GROUPS OF COMPANIES.

s 100 **Groups and group relief: limit on amount of group relief in case of consortium claim.** A minor technical defect is corrected. See 29.20, 29.29 GROUPS OF COMPANIES.

s 101 **Groups and group relief: notional transfers within groups of companies.** Two group companies may elect that a disposal by one of them to a person outside the group be deemed to have been made by the other and to have been preceded by an intra-group transfer of the asset at no gain/no loss. See 9.20 CAPITAL GAINS.

s 102, Sch 29 **Groups and group relief: chargeable gains: non-resident companies and groups etc..** The condition that members of a CGT group of companies be UK-resident is removed. Various specific provisions instead now focus on whether assets are within the charge to UK corporation tax. There are numerous consequential changes. See 9 CAPITAL GAINS for the principal changes, 7.6 BUILDING SOCIETIES, 23.17, 23.29 EXCHANGE GAINS AND LOSSES, 29.49 GROUPS OF COMPANIES, 41.16 LIFE INSURANCE COMPANIES, 43.5, 43.11 LOAN RELATIONSHIPS, 53.4, 53.7, 53.9 RESIDENCE.

s 103, Sch 30 **Double taxation relief.** A number of significant changes are made to the scope of double tax reliefs. See 21 DOUBLE TAX RELIEF.

s 104, Sch 31 **Controlled foreign companies.** A number of new anti-avoidance measures are added to the controlled foreign companies provisions. See 18.2, 18.4, 18.14 CONTROLLED FOREIGN COMPANIES.

s 105 **Corporation tax: use of currencies other than sterling.** New rules are provided for the calculation of company profits in currencies other than sterling. See 23.33–23.37 EXCHANGE GAINS AND LOSSES.

s 106 **Foreign exchange gains and losses: use of local currency.** A number of changes are made to the exchange gains and losses rules, mainly in consequence of the changes introduced by *section 105*. See 23.11, 23.16–23.18, 23.24, 23.31 EXCHANGE GAINS AND LOSSES.

s 107 **General insurance reserves.** Provision is made for the clawback of excess provisions. See 41.1, 41.4 LIFE INSURANCE COMPANIES, 50.1 PROFIT COMPUTATIONS.

s 108 **Overseas life assurance business.** The definition of such business is made more flexible by the use of secondary legislation. See 41.14 LIFE INSURANCE COMPANIES.

s 109 **Insurance business: apportionment rules.** Changes are made to the rules for apportionment of income and gains between different classes of business. See 41.3 LIFE INSURANCE COMPANIES, 43.9 LOAN RELATIONSHIPS.

s 110 **Rent factoring.** Anti-avoidance provisions are introduced relating to sales of rights to future rental income by companies. See 50.27 PROFIT COMPUTATIONS.

s 143, Sch 38 **Power to provide incentives to use electronic communications.** The Revenue are given powers to offer incentives to taxpayers using electronic communications. See 33.11 INLAND REVENUE: ADMINISTRATION, 54.13 RETURNS.

s 145 **Information about interest etc. paid, credited or received.** Changes are made to third party information requirements. See 6.9 BANKS, 54.10 RETURNS and Tolley's Income Tax under Returns.

s 146 **International exchange of information: general.** Provision is made for international exchange of tax-related information. See 33.12 INLAND REVENUE: ADMINISTRATION. See also Tolley's Income Tax under Inland Revenue: Administration and Inland Revenue: Confidentiality of Information.

s 149, Sch 39 **Orders for the delivery of documents.** New powers are provided, subject to judicial approval. See Tolley's Income Tax under Back Duty.

s 150 **Search warrants: miscellaneous amendments.** See Tolley's Income Tax under Back Duty.

s 155 **Interpretation.**

s 156, Sch 40 **Repeals.**

s 157 **Short title.**

OTHER PROVISIONS

ss 1–29, Schs 1–5 **Customs and Excise.**

s 30, Schs 6, 7 **Climate change levy.**

s 31 **Charge and rates for 2000/01.** The starting, basic and higher rates of income tax for 2000/01 are 10%, 22% and 40% respectively. See Tolley's Income Tax under Allowances and Tax Rates.

s 33 **Deduction of income tax from foreign dividends.** The rate of deduction under the paying and collecting agents scheme is set retrospectively. See Tolley's Income Tax under Deduction of Tax at Source.

s 38 **Giving to charity: payroll deduction scheme.** The annual limit is removed, a temporary 10% supplement provided and a number of consequential amendments made. See Tolley's Income Tax under Charities.

s 39 **Giving to charity: gift aid payments by individuals.** The lower limit on donations is removed and the scope of the scheme extended. See Tolley's Income Tax under Charities.

s 42 **Giving to charity: millennium gift aid.** Minor amendments are made to the scheme following the extension of Gift Aid for individuals (see *section 39* above). See Tolley's Income Tax under Charities.

s 47, Sch 8 **Employee share ownership plans.** A new share scheme is introduced. See 50.10 PROFIT COMPUTATIONS and Tolley's Income Tax under Share Incentives and Options.

s 48, Sch 9 **Relief for transfers to employee share ownership plans.** Capital gains tax rollover relief is available for certain transfers of shares to the new plans (see *section 47* above). See Tolley's Income Tax under Share Incentives and Options.

s 49 **Phasing out of approved profit sharing schemes.** See Tolley's Income Tax under Share Incentives and Options.

s 50 **Phasing out of relief for payments to trustees of profit sharing schemes.** See 50.22 PROFIT COMPUTATIONS and Tolley's Income Tax under Share Incentives and Options.

s 51 **Approved profit sharing scheme: other awards of shares.** The obtaining of relief under both profit sharing schemes and the new employee share ownership plans (see *section 47* above) is prevented. See Tolley's Income Tax under Share Incentives and Options.

s 52 **Approved profit sharing schemes: restriction on type of shares.** An anti-avoidance measure is introduced preventing the use of shares in certain service companies. See Tolley's Income Tax under Share Incentives and Options.

s 53 **Approved profit sharing schemes: loan arrangements.** An anti-avoidance measure is introduced preventing the granting of certain employee loans under scheme arrangements. See Tolley's Income Tax under Share Incentives and Options.

s 54 **Employee share ownership trusts.** Capital gains tax rollover relief on transfers of shares to such trusts is withdrawn. See Tolley's Income Tax under Share Incentives and Options.

s 55 **Shares transferred from employee share ownership trust.** Provision is made for transfers of shares by the trustees of such trusts to employee share ownership plans (see *section 47* above). See Tolley's Income Tax under Share Incentives and Options.

s 56 **Further provisions about share options.** Employer national insurance contributions borne by an employee are deductible in computing the employee's share option gain for income tax purposes. Certain amendments are made to employer reporting requirements. See Tolley's Income Tax under Share Incentives and Options.

s 57, Sch 10 **Benefits in kind: deregulatory amendments.** A number of relaxations of conditions and of reporting requirements are introduced. See Tolley's Income Tax under Schedule E.

s 58 **Education and training.** Relief is introduced for employer contributions to education and training costs of employees with individual learning accounts. See Tolley's Income Tax under Schedule E.

s 59, Sch 11 **Cars available for private use.** A new company car scheme is introduced from 6 April 2002. See Tolley's Income Tax under Schedule E.

s 60, Sch 12 **Provision of services through intermediary.** Provisions are introduced aimed at removing the tax advantages of personal service companies and other intermediaries. See Tolley's Income Tax under Personal Service Companies Etc..

s 61, Sch 13 **Occupational and personal pension schemes.** Changes are made to facilitate the inclusion under the personal pension scheme provisions of stakeholder pension arrangements. See Tolley's Income Tax under Personal Pension Schemes (including Stakeholder Pensions).

s 62, Sch 14 **Enterprise management incentives.** A new share incentive scheme is introduced. See Tolley's Income Tax under Share Incentives and Options.

s 64, Sch 17 **Enterprise investment scheme: amendments.** Certain relief restrictions are relaxed. See Tolley's Income Tax under Enterprise Investment Scheme.

s 66 **Capital gains tax: taper relief: taper for business assets.** The maximum taper is to be achieved after holding the asset for four years rather than ten as before. The bonus year addition for assets held at 17 March 1998 is withdrawn for such disposals. See Tolley's Capital Gains Tax under Taper Relief.

s 67 **Capital gains tax: taper relief: assets qualifying as business assets.** The definition of a business asset is widened to include all shareholdings in unquoted companies, quoted shares in the taxpayer's employer company and quoted shares held by an outside investor able to exercise at least 5% of the voting rights. See Tolley's Capital Gains Tax under Taper Relief.

s 70 **Capital allowances: first year allowances for small or medium-sized enterprises.** The temporary 40% allowances are made permanent. See Tolley's Income Tax under Capital Allowances.

s 71 **Capital allowances: first year allowances for information and communications technology expenditure by small enterprises.** 100% allowances are introduced for such expenditure. See Tolley's Income Tax under Capital Allowances.

s 72 **Capital allowances: expenditure of a small enterprise.** 'Small enterprise' in *section 71* is defined. See Tolley's Income Tax under Capital Allowances.

s 73 **Capital allowances: repeal of notification requirements.** The requirement to notify expenditure on machinery and plant is removed. See Tolley's Income Tax under Capital Allowances.

s 74 **Capital allowances: pool for certain leased assets and inexpensive cars.** The separate pool is abolished. See 41.12 LIFE INSURANCE COMPANIES and Tolley's Income Tax under Capital Allowances.

s 75 **Capital allowances: machinery and plant allowances for non-residents etc..** The basis of relief for non-residents is clarified, and new rules relating to changes in use introduced. See Tolley's Income Tax under Capital Allowances.

s 76 **Capital allowances: production animals.** The herd basis rules are extended to shared animals (as previously applied by concession), and the exclusion of capital allowances for farm animals confirmed. See Tolley's Income Tax under Capital Allowances and Herd Basis.

s 77 **Capital allowances: sale and leaseback.** An anomalous result of the existing provisions is corrected. See 8.4 CAPITAL ALLOWANCES and Tolley's Income Tax under Capital Allowances.

s 78 **Capital allowances: meaning of "fixture".** The existing practice as regards space or water heating system equipment is made statutory. See Tolley's Income Tax under Capital Allowances.

s 79 **Capital allowances: leased assets under the Affordable Warmth Programme.** Allowances are granted on certain equipment installed under the programme. See Tolley's Income Tax under Capital Allowances.

s 80 **Capital allowances: fixtures and machinery and plant on hire-purchase etc..** It is confirmed that the special fixtures provisions take precedence over the hire-purchase provisions of *CAA 1990, s 60*. See Tolley's Income Tax under Capital Allowances.

s 89 **Waste disposal: entitlement of successor to allowances.** See Tolley's Income Tax under Schedule D, Cases I and II.

s 90 **Capital gains tax: restriction of gifts relief.** Business asset hold-over relief is no longer available on a transfer of shares or securities to a company. See Tolley's Capital Gains Tax under Hold-Over Reliefs.

s 111 **Payments under deduction of tax.** The paying and collecting agents scheme is abolished, and consequential changes made to the rules for deduction of tax in certain cases. See 6.9 BANKS, 7.4 BUILDING SOCIETIES, 31.3(*b*) INCOME TAX IN RELATION TO A COMPANY. See also Tolley's Income Tax under Deduction of Tax at Source and Government Stocks.

s 112 **UK public revenue dividends: deduction of tax.** A new tax deduction scheme is introduced. See Tolley's Income Tax under Deduction of Tax at Source and Government Stocks.

s 113 **Tax treatment of expenditure on production or acquisition of films.** Minor technical revisions and clarifications to the reliefs available. See Tolley's Income Tax under Schedule D, Cases I and II.

ss 114–134, Schs 32–34 **Stamp duty and stamp duty reserve tax.**

ss 135–137, Schs 35, 36	**Value added tax.**
s 138	**Inheritance tax.**
s 139	**Petroleum revenue tax.**
ss 140–142, Sch 37	**Landfill tax.**
s 144	**Offence of fraudulent evasion of income tax.**
s 147	**International exchange of information: inheritance tax.**
s 148	**Use of minimum wage information.** See Tolley's Income Tax under Inland Revenue: Confidentiality of Information.
ss 151–154	**Government borrowings etc..**

64 Table of Cases

Note: Citation where appropriate is of the Official Reports of Tax Cases, Simon's Tax Cases, one set of the official series (i.e. either the Law Reports or the Weekly Law Reports), and the All England Law Reports. Only in default of these are other series referred to. For abbreviations, see page ix.

Aberdeen Milk Co Ltd, CIR *v* — 3.8, 9.54, 44.12
CS 1999: [1999] STC 787.

Addies, Collins *v* — 13.13
CA 1992: 65 TC 190; [1992] STC 746.

Administrator of Hungarian Property, Bank voor Handel en Scheepvaart NV *v* — 24.5
HL 1954: 35 TC 311; [1945] AC 584; [1954] 1 All ER 969.

Akarimsons Ltd *v* Chapman — 49.6
Sp C 1997: [1997] SSCD 140.

Alexander, Attorney-General *v* — 53.2
Ex D 1874: (1874) LR 10 Ex 20.

American Thread Co *v* Joyce — 53.2
HL 1913: 6 TC 163.

Ametalco Ltd *v* CIR — 4.4
Sp C 1996: [1996] SSCD 399.

Ametalco UK *v* CIR — 4.4
Sp C 1996: [1996] SSCD 399.

Amoco (UK) Exploration Co *v* CIR — 46.2
Ch D 1983: 57 TC 147; [1983] STC 634.

Andrew Grant Services Ltd *v* Watton and cross-appeal — 13.10
Ch D 1999: 71 TC 333; [1999] STC 330.

Anglo-American Oil Co Ltd, Ward *v* — 23.2
KB 1934: 19 TC 94.

Anglo-French Exploration Co Ltd *v* Clayson — 15.4
CA 1956: 36 TC 545; [1956] 1 WLR 325; [1956] 1 All ER 762.

Anglo-Persian Oil Co Ltd *v* Dale — 15.8(*a*)
CA 1931: 16 TC 253.

Aproline Ltd *v* Littlejohn — 3.6, 3.8
Sp C 1995: [1995] SSCD 201.

Aramayo Francke Mines Ltd, Eccott *v* — 53.2
HL 1925: 9 TC 445; [1925] AC 634.

Armpledge Ltd, Carr *v* — 3.8
CA 2000: [2000] STC 410.

Arndale Properties Ltd, Coates *v* — 9.22
HL 1984: 59 TC 516; [1984] STC 637; [1984] 1 WLR 1328; [1985] 1 All ER 15.

Ashmore, Racal Group Services Ltd *v* — 11.5(*a*)
CA 1995: 68 TC 86; [1995] STC 1151.

Ashmore (JW) Ltd, Lowe *v* — 50.26
Ch D 1970: 46 TC 597; [1971] Ch 545; [1971] 1 All ER 1057.

Aspden *v* Hildesley — 16.1
Ch D 1981: 55 TC 609; [1982] STC 206; [1982] 1 WLR 264; [1982] 2 All ER 53.

Assam Agricultural Income Taxes Commissioner, English and Scottish Joint Co-operative Wholesale Society Ltd *v* — 45.1
PC 1948: [1948] AC 405; [1948] 2 All ER 395.

Attorney-General *v* Alexander — 53.2
Ex D 1874: (1874) LR 10 Ex 20.

Attwooll, Berry (L G) Investments Ltd *v* 40.2
Ch D 1964: 41 TC 547; [1964] 1 WLR 693; [1964] 2 All ER 126.
Attwooll, London & Thames Haven Oil Wharves Ltd *v* 15.6
CA 1966: 43 TC 491; [1967] Ch 772; [1967] 2 All ER 124.
Bains, Greenfield *v* 13.13
CA 1992: 65 TC 190; [1992] STC 746.
Bale, Wing Hung Lai *v* 55.7
Sp C 1999: [1999] SSCD 238.
Ball *v* National and Grindlays Bank Ltd 50.3
CA 1971: 47 TC 287; [1973] Ch 127; [1971] 3 All ER 485.
Bamford, Rolls-Royce Motors Ltd *v* 44.4
Ch D 1976: 51 TC 319; [1976] STC 162.
Banco da Brasil SA, CIR *v* 21.11
Ch D 1990: 63 TC 218; [1990] STC 285.
Bank Line Ltd *v* CIR 44.4
CS 1974; 49 TC 307; [1974] STC 342.
Bank voor Handel en Scheepvaart NV *v* Administrator of Hungarian Property 24.5
HL 1954: 35 TC 311; [1954] AC 584; [1954] 1 All ER 969.
Barber *v* Eppell 47.6
QB 24 February 1981.
Barnes *v* Hely-Hutchinson 21.3
HL 1939: 22 TC 655; [1940] AC 81; [1939] 3 All ER 803.
Barr, Crombie & Co Ltd *v* CIR 15.7
CS 1945: 26 TC 406.
Barrett, Homeowners Friendly Society Ltd *v* 28.2
Sp C 1995: [1995] SSCD 90.
Barrie (Hugh T) Ltd, CIR *v* 15.8(*d*)
CA (NI) 1928; 12 TC 1223.
Baylis *v* Gregory 4.1
HL 1988: 62 TC 1; [1988] STC 476; [1988] 3 WLR 423; [1988] 3 All ER 495.
Beauchamp *v* F W Woolworth Ltd 23.2
HL 1989: 61 TC 542; [1989] STC 510; [1989] 3 WLR 1.
Becker *v* Finanzamt Munster-Innenstadt 22.2
CJEC 1982: [1982] 1 CMLR 499.
Belhaven's (Lord) Executors, Roberts *v* 50.26
CS 1925: 9 TC 501.
Bellow Machine Co Ltd, Fleming *v* 15.4
Ch D 1965: 42 TC 308; [1965] 1 WLR 873; [1965] 2 All ER 513.
Belton, Clapham's Trustees *v* 50.26(viii)
Ch D 1956: 37 TC 26; [1956] TR 305.
Bennett *v* Underground Electric Railways Co of London Ltd 40.2
KB 1923: 8 TC 475; [1923] 2 KB 535.
Berry (L G) Investments Ltd *v* Attwooll 40.2
Ch D 1964: 41 TC 547; [1964] 1 WLR 693; [1964] 2 All ER 126.
Bibby, Prudential Assurance Co Ltd *v* 41.7
Ch D 1999: [1999] STC 952.
Bibby *v* Prudential Assurance Co Ltd (No 2) 51.7
Ch D 2000: [2000] STC 459.
Bibby (J) & Sons Ltd *v* CIR 13.5
HL 1945: 29 TC 167; [1945] 1 All ER 667.
Billingham *v* Myers 39.3
CA 1996: 68 TC 512; [1996] STC 593.
Bispham *v* Eardiston Farming Co (1919) Ltd 44.4
Ch D 1962: 40 TC 322; [1962] 1 WLR 616; [1962] 2 All ER 376.

Black, CIR *v* 11.11
Ch D 1940: 23 TC 715; [1940] 4 All ER 447.
Blackburn *v* Close Bros Ltd 15.4
Ch D 1960: 39 TC 164.
Blackpool Marton Rotary Club *v* Martin 1.2, 14.1
Ch D 1988: 62 TC 686; [1988] STC 823.
Blair, South Shore Mutual Insurance Co Ltd *v* 9.18, 29.3, 29.27, 29.41
Sp C 1999: [1999] SSCD 296.
Boarland *v* Madras Electric Supply Corporation Ltd 24.5
HL 1955: 35 TC 612; [1955] AC 667; [1955] 1 All ER 753.
Bolton, Marshall Hus & Partners Ltd *v* 2.4
Ch D 1980: 55 TC 539; [1981] STC 18.
Borax & Chemicals Ltd, Cattermole *v* 15.8(*c*)
KB 1949: 31 TC 202.
Bowater Paper Corporation Ltd *v* Murgatroyd 21.6
HL 1969: 46 TC 37; [1970] AC 266; [1969] 3 All ER 111.
Bowater Property Developments Ltd, CIR *v* 4.1
HL 1988: 62 TC 1; [1988] STC 476; [1988] 3 WLR 423; [1988] 3 All ER 495.
Bowen, Croydon Hotel & Leisure Co Ltd *v* 15.8(*a*)
Sp C 1996: [1996] SSCD 466.
Bracken Developments Ltd, Joint *v* 13.12
Ch D 1994: 66 TC 560; [1994] STC 300.
Bradbury *v* The United Glass Bottle Manufacturers Ltd 15.8(*b*)
CA 1959: 38 TC 369.
Bradley, Nuclear Electric plc *v* 44.4
HL 1996: 68 TC 670; [1996] STC 405; [1996] 1 WLR 529.
Brander & Cruickshank, CIR *v* 15.5
HL 1970: 46 TC 574; [1971] 1 WLR 212; [1971] 1 All ER 36.
Bray, Hesketh *v* 50.26
CA 1888: 2 TC 380; 21 QBD 444.
Brennan, The Deanby Investment Co Ltd *v* 13.9
Sp C 2000: [2000] SSCD 172.
Bricom Holdings Ltd *v* CIR 18.9
CA 1997: 70 TC 272; [1997] STC 1179.
British-Borneo Petroleum Syndicate Ltd *v* Cropper 15.7
Ch D 1968: 45 TC 201; [1968] 1 WLR 1701; [1969] 1 All ER 104.
British Broadcasting Corporation *v* Johns 57.5
CA 1964: 41 TC 471; [1964] 2 WLR 1071; [1964] 1 All ER 923.
British Legion *v* CIR 11.6
CS 1953: 35 TC 509.
Brooke Bond & Co Ltd *v* Butter 21.3
Ch D 1962: 40 TC 342.
Brown & Cousins, McGowan *v* 15.5
Ch D 1977: 52 TC 8; [1977] STC 342; [1977] 1 WLR 1403; [1977] 3 All ER 844.
Brumfield and Others, ex parte, R *v* HMIT 33.4
QB 1988: 61 TC 589; [1989] STC 151.
Burmah Oil Co Ltd, CIR *v* 4.1
HL 1981: 54 TC 200; [1982] STC 30.
Burmah Steam Ship Co Ltd *v* CIR 15.6
CS 1930: 16 TC 67.
Burman *v* Thorn Domestic Appliances (Electrical) Ltd 52.1
Ch D 1981: 55 TC 493; [1982] STC 179.
Burrell, Conservative and Unionist Central Office *v* 1.2
CA 1981: 55 TC 671; [1982] STC 317; [1982] 1 WLR 522; [1982] 2 All ER 1.

Bush, Beach & Gent Ltd *v* Road 15.3
KB 1939: 22 TC 519; [1939] 1 KB 524; [1939] 3 All ER 302.
Butter, Brooke Bond & Co Ltd *v* 21.3
Ch D 1962: 40 TC 342.
Cairns *v* MacDiarmid 4.1
CA 1983: 56 TC 556; [1983] STC 178.
Calcutta Jute Mills Co Ltd *v* Nicholson 53.2
Ex D 1876: 1 TC 83; 1 Ex D 428.
Camacq Corporation, ex parte, R *v* CIR 33.4
CA 1989: 62 TC 651; [1989] STC 785; [1990] 1 WLR 191; [1990] 1 All ER 173.
Camcrown Ltd *v* McDonald 44.6
Sp C 1999: [1999] SSCD 255.
Canadian Eagle Oil Co Ltd *v* R 21.3
HL 1945: 27 TC 205; [1946] AC 119; [1945] 2 All ER 499.
Capital & National Trust Ltd *v* Golder 40.2
CA 1949: 31 TC 265; [1949] 2 All ER 956.
Carco Accessories Ltd *v* CIR 49.10
CS 1985: 59 TC 45; [1985] STC 518.
Carlisle & Silloth Golf Club *v* Smith 45.1
CA 1913: 6 TC 48; [1913] 3 KB 75.
Carnaby, Harrower, Barham & Pykett, Walker *v* 15.5
Ch D 1969: 46 TC 561; [1970] 1 WLR 276; [1970] 1 All ER 502.
Carr *v* Armpledge Ltd 3.8
CA 2000: [2000] STC 410.
Carver, Steeden *v* 49.6
Sp C 1999: [1999] SSCD 283.
Casey *v* Monteagle Estate Company 40.1
HC (I) 1960: 3 ITC 313; [1962] IR 106.
Cattermole *v* Borax & Chemicals Ltd 15.8(*c*)
KB 1949: 31 TC 202.
Centaur Clothes Group Ltd, Walker *v* 2.3, 3.6, 3.8
HL 2000: [2000] STC 324.
Central London Railway Co *v* CIR 50.5
HL 1936: 20 TC 102; [1937] AC 77; [1936] 2 All ER 375.
Chaloner, Utopia Assurance Co Ltd *v* 41.2
Sp C 1996: [1996] SSCD 204.
Chancery Lane Safe Deposit & Offices Co Ltd *v* CIR 50.7
HL 1965: 43 TC 83; [1966] AC 85; [1966] 1 All ER 1.
Chapman, Akarimsons Ltd *v* 49.6
Sp C 1997: [1997] SSCD 140.
Chapman (AW) Ltd *v* Hennessey 29.23, 55.4
Ch D 1981: 55 TC 516; [1982] STC 214.
Cherry, Fitzleet Estates Ltd *v* 50.5
HL 1977: 51 TC 708; [1977] STC 397; [1977] 1 WLR 1345; [1977] 3 All ER 996.
Chibbett *v* Robinson (J) & Sons 15.5
KB 1924: 9 TC 48.
Clapham's Trustees *v* Belton 50.26(viii)
Ch D 1956: 37 TC 26; [1956] TR 305.
Clark *v* Oceanic Contractors Incorporated 53.9
HL 1982: 56 TC 183; [1983] STC 35; [1983] 2 WLR 94; [1983] 1 All ER 133.
Clark, Van den Berghs Ltd *v* 15.7
HL 1935: 19 TC 390; [1935] AC 431.
Clayson, Anglo-French Exploration Co Ltd *v* 15.4
CA 1956: 35 TC 545; [1956] 1 WLR 325; [1956] 1 All ER 762.

Clixby *v* Pountney 49.4
Ch D 1967: 44 TC 515; [1968] Ch 719; [1968] 1 All ER 802.
Close Bros Ltd, Blackburn *v* 15.4
Ch D 1960: 39 TC 164.
Coates *v* Arndale Properties Ltd 9.22
HL 1984: 59 TC 516; [1984] STC 637; [1984] 1 WLR 1328; [1985] 1 All ER 15.
Collins *v* Addies 13.13
CA 1992: 65 TC 190; [1992] STC 746.
Colmer, ICI plc *v* 29.27
HL 1996: 72 TC 1; [1996] STC 352; [1996] 1 WLR 469; [1996] 2 All ER 23; [1999] STC 1089.
Colmer (Case C–264/96), ICI plc *v* 29.15; 29.27
ECJ 1998: [1998] STC 874; [1999] 1 WLR 108.
Coman, Rotunda Hospital Dublin (Governors of) *v* 11.2
HL 1920: 7 TC 517.
Commercial Union Assurance Co plc *v* Shaw 21.7, 44.4
CA 1998: [1999] STC 109.
Commerzbank AG, CIR *v* 21.11
Ch D 1990: 63 TC 218; [1990] STC 285.
Commerzbank AG, ex parte, R *v* CIR 21.3, 38.3
QB 1991: 68 TC 252; [1991] STC 271.
Commerzbank AG, ex parte, R *v* CIR 21.3, 38.3
CJEC 1993: 68 TC 264; [1993] STC 605; [1994] 2 WLR 128; [1993] 4 All ER 37.
Commissioner of Taxes *v* Nchanga Consolidated Copper Mines Ltd 15.8(*a*)
PC 1964: [1964] AC 948; [1964] 1 All ER 208.
Conelee Properties Ltd, Webb *v* 40.1
Ch D 1982: 56 TC 149; [1982] STC 913.
Conservative and Unionist Central Office *v* Burrell 1.2
CA 1981: 55 TC 671; [1982] STC 317; [1982] 1 WLR 522; [1982] 2 All ER 1.
Cook *v* Medway Housing Society Ltd 40.1
Ch D 1996: 69 TC 319; [1997] STC 90.
Cooper, Greyhound Racing Association (Liverpool) Ltd *v* 15.3
KB 1936: 20 TC 373; [1936] 2 All ER 742.
Copeman *v* William Flood & Sons Ltd 50.8
KB 1940: 24 TC 53; [1941] 1 KB 202.
'Countess Warwick' Steamship Co Ltd *v* Ogg 15.8(*b*)
KB 1924: 8 TC 652; [1924] 2 KB 292.
Crabtree Denims Ltd, Ryan *v* 52.1, 58.1
Ch D 1987: 60 TC 183; [1987] STC 402.
Crawley, CIR *v* 11.11
Ch D 1986: 59 TC 728; [1987] STC 147.
Craven *v* White 4.1
HL 1988: 62 TC 1; [1988] STC 476; [1988] 3 WLR 423; [1988] 3 All ER 495.
Creed *v* H & M Levinson Ltd 15.3
Ch D 1981: 54 TC 477; [1981] STC 486.
Creedplan Ltd *v* Winter 49.6
Sp C 1995: [1995] SSCD 352.
Cricket plc *v* Inspector of Taxes 29.9
Sp C 1998: [1998] SSCD 101.
Crimmin, Tesco plc *v* 9.51
Ch D 1997: 69 TC 510; [1997] STC 981.
Crook, Seaham Harbour Dock Co *v* 58.1
HL 1931: 16 TC 333.

Cropper, British-Borneo Petroleum Syndicate Ltd *v* 15.7
Ch D 1968: 45 TC 201; [1968] 1 WLR 1701; [1969] 1 All ER 104.
Croydon Hotel & Leisure Co Ltd *v* Bowen 15.8(*a*)
Sp C 1996: [1996] SSCD 466.
Cullington, United Steel Companies Ltd *v*, (No 1) 15.8(*a*)(*b*)
CA 1939: 23 TC 71.
Cushla Ltd, Re 42.5
Ch D 1979: [1979] STC 615; [1979] 3 All ER 415.
Dale, Anglo-Persian Oil Co Ltd *v* 15.8(*a*)
CA 1931: 16 TC 253.
Davidson *v* Deeks 50.26
Ch D 1956: 37 TC 32; [1956] 1 WLR 1388; [1956] 3 All ER 612.
Davidson, Sun Life Assurance Society *v* 41.2
HL 1957: 37 TC 330; [1958] AC 184; [1957] 2 All ER 760.
Davies, The Shell Co of China Ltd *v* 23.2
CA 1951: 32 TC 133.
Davis, Floor *v* 16.6
HL 1979: 52 TC 609; [1979] STC 379; [1979] 2 WLR 830; [1979] 2 All ER 677.
Dawson, Furniss *v* 4.1
HL 1984: 55 TC 324; [1984] STC 153; [1984] 2 WLR 226; [1984] 1 All ER 530.
De Beers Consolidated Mines Ltd *v* Howe 53.2
HL 1906: 5 TC 198; [1906] AC 455.
Dean Leigh Temperance Canteen *v* CIR 11.6
Ch D 1958: 38 TC 315.
Deanby Investment Co Ltd, The, *v* Brennan 13.9
Sp C 2000: [2000] SSCD 172.
Deeks, Davidson *v* 50.26
Ch D 1956: 37 TC 32; [1956] 1 WLR 1388; [1956] 3 All ER 612.
Dingle *v* Turner 11.1
HL 1972: [1972] AC 601; [1972] 1 All ER 878.
Dreyfus (Camille & Henry) Foundation Inc *v* CIR 11.1
HL 1955: 38 TC 126; [1956] AC 39; [1955] 3 All ER 97.
Drummond, ex parte, R *v* Revenue Adjudicator's Office 33.8
QB 1996: 70 TC 235; [1996] STC 1312.
Duke of Westminster *v* CIR 4.1
HL 1935: 19 TC 490.
Dunlop International AG *v* Pardoe 9.47
CA 1999: 72 TC 71; [1999] STC 909.
Dura Manufacturing Co Ltd, Shove *v* 15.3
KB 1941: 23 TC 779.
Eardiston Farming Co (1919) Ltd, Bispham *v* 44.4
Ch D 1962: 40 TC 322; [1962] 1 WLR 616; [1962] 2 All ER 376.
Earlspring Properties Ltd *v* Guest 13.12
CA 1995: 67 TC 259; [1995] STC 479.
Easson, North British & Mercantile Insurance Co *v* 41.2
CS 1919: 7 TC 463.
Eccentric Club Ltd, CIR *v* 45.1
CA 1923: 12 TC 657; [1924] KB 390.
Eccott *v* Aramayo Francke Mines Ltd 53.2
HL 1925: 9 TC 445; [1925] AC 634.
Egyptian Delta Land & Investment Co Ltd, Todd *v* 53.2
HL 1928: 14 TC 119; [1929] AC 1.
Egyptian Hotels Ltd *v* Mitchell 53.3
HL 1915: 6 TC 152, 542; [1915] AC 1022.

Eilbeck *v* Rawling 4.1
HL 1981: 54 TC 101; [1981] STC 174; [1981] 2 WLR 449; [1981] 1 All ER 865.
Ellis *v* Lucas 15.4
Ch D 1966: 43 TC 276; [1967] Ch 858; [1966] 2 All ER 935.
Elliss *v* ICI Petroleum Ltd 46.3
Ch D 1983; 57 TC 176; [1983] STC 675.
Elliss, RTZ Oil and Gas Ltd *v* 46.3
Ch D 1987: 61 TC 132; [1987] STC 512.
English and Scottish Joint Co-operative Wholesale Society Ltd, Assam Agricultural Income Tax Commissioner *v* 45.1
PC 1948: [1948] AC 405; [1948] 2 All ER 395.
Ensign Shipping Co Ltd *v* CIR 15.7
CA 1928: 12 TC 1169.
Ensign Tankers (Leasing) Ltd *v* Stokes 4.1
HL 1992: 64 TC 617; [1992] STC 226; [1992] 2 WLR 469; [1992] 2 All ER 275.
Eppell, Barber *v* 47.6
QB 24 February 1981.
Equitable Life Assurance Society, Oakes *v* 51.7
Ch D 2000: [2000] STC 459.
European Vinyls Corp (Holdings) BV (now EVC International NV), Steele *v* 16.6, 21.9, 29.23
CA 1996: 69 TC 88; [1996] STC 785.
Evans, Firestone Tyre and Rubber Co Ltd *v* 23.2
Ch D 1976: 51 TC 615; [1977] STC 104.
EVC International NV (formerly European Vinyls Corp (Holdings) BV), Steele *v* 16.6, 21.9, 29.23
CA 1996: 69 TC 88; [1996] STC 785.
FPH Finance Trust Ltd *v* CIR 40.1
HL 1944: 26 TC 131; [1944] AC 285; [1944] 1 All ER 653.
Fairrie *v* Hall 15.8(*c*)
KB 1947: 28 TC 200; [1947] 2 All ER 141.
Falkirk Ice Rink Ltd, CIR *v* 15.5
CS 1975: 51 TC 42; [1975] STC 434.
Falmer Jeans Ltd *v* Rodin 44.10
Ch D 1990: 63 TC 55; [1990] STC 270.
Finanzamt Munster-Innenstadt, Becker *v* 22.2
CJEC 1982: [1982] 1 CMLR 499.
Firestone Tyre and Rubber Co Ltd *v* Evans 23.2
Ch D 1976: 51 TC 615; [1977] STC 104.
Fisher, Scottish and Universal Newspapers Ltd *v* 29.23
Sp C 1996: [1996] SSCD 311.
Fitzleet Estates Ltd *v* Cherry 50.5
HL 1977: 51 TC 708; [1977] STC 397; [1977] 1 WLR 1345; [1977] 3 All ER 996.
Fitzwilliam (Countess) *v* CIR 4.1
HL 1993: [1993] STC 502; [1993] 1 WLR 1189; [1993] 3 All ER 184.
Fleming *v* Bellow Machine Co Ltd 15.4
Ch D 1965: 42 TC 308; [1965] 1 WLR 873; [1965] 2 All ER 513.
Flood (Wm) & Sons Ltd, Copeman *v* 50.8
KB 1940: 24 TC 53; [1941] 1 KB 202.
Floor *v* Davis 16.6
HL 1979: 52 TC 609; [1979] STC 379; [1979] 2 WLR 830; [1979] 2 All ER 677.
Focus Dynamics plc *v* Turner 50.19
Sp C 1999: [1999] SSCD 71.
Forth Conservancy Board, CIR *v*, (No 1) 57.5
HL 1928: 14 TC 709; [1929] AC 213.

Forth Conservancy Board, CIR *v*, (No 2) 57.5
HL 1931: 16 TC 103; [1931] AC 540.
Freeman, Sommerfelds Ltd *v* 15.3
Ch D 1966: 44 TC 43; [1967] 1 WLR 489; [1967] 2 All ER 143.
Frigate Investments Ltd, Wilcock *v* 50.3
Ch D 1981: 55 TC 530; [1982] STC 198.
Fulford-Dobson, ex p, R *v* HMIT 33.4
QB 1987: 60 TC 168; [1987] STC 344; [1987] 3 WLR 277.
Furniss *v* Dawson 4.1
HL 1984: 55 TC 324; [1984] STC 153; [1984] 2 WLR 226; [1984] 1 All ER 530.
GCA International Ltd, Yates *v* 21.2
Ch D 1991: 64 TC 37; [1991] STC 157.
Gasque *v* CIR 53.2
KB 1940: 23 TC 210; [1940] 2 KB 80.
Gayjon Processes Ltd, Poulter *v* 58.1
Ch D 1985: 58 TC 350; [1985] STC 174.
George, Morning Post Ltd *v* 44.4
KB 1940: 23 TC 514.
Glasgow Musical Festival Association, CIR *v* 11.6
CS 1926: 11 TC 154.
Glasgow Ornithological Association, CIR *v* 24.1
CS 1938: 21 TC 445.
Glaxo Group Ltd and others *v* CIR 4.4
CA 1995: 68 TC 166; [1996] STC 191.
Gleig, T & C Hill (Haulage) *v* 17.4
Sp C 2000: [2000] SSCD 64.
Glenboig Union Fireclay Co Ltd *v* CIR 15.7
HL 1922: 12 TC 427.
Golder, Capital & National Trust Ltd *v* 40.2
CA 1949: 31 TC 265; [1949] 2 All ER 956.
Goodhews, Murray *v* 15.5
CA 1977: 52 TC 86; [1978] STC 207; [1978] 1 WLR 499; [1978] 2 All ER 40.
Gordon & Blair Ltd *v* CIR 44.4
CS 1962: 40 TC 358.
Gorge Fabrications Ltd *v* Wilson 17.4
Sp C 1999: [1999] SSCD 293.
Grant (Andrew) Services Ltd *v* Watton and cross-appeal 13.10
Ch D 1999: 71 TC 333; [1999] STC 330.
Greenfield *v* Bains 13.13
CA 1992: 65 TC 190; [1992] STC 746.
Gregory, Baylis *v* 4.1
HL 1988: 62 TC 1; [1988] STC 476; [1988] 3 WLR 423; [1988] 3 All ER 495.
Greycoat Estates Mayfair Ltd, Macarthur *v* 50.3
Ch D 1995: 67 TC 598; [1996] STC 1.
Greyhound Racing Association (Liverpool) Ltd *v* Cooper 15.3
KB 1936: 20 TC 373; [1936] 2 All ER 742.
Grinten, Océ van, NV *v* CIR 21.9
Sp C 2000: 2000 STI 251.
Grove *v* Young Men's Christian Association 11.2
KB 1903: 4 TC 613.
Guest, Earlspring Properties Ltd *v* 13.12
CA 1995; 67 TC 259; [1995] STC 479.

Guild and Others (as Trustees of the William Muir (Bond 9) Ltd Employees' Share Scheme) *v* CIR 11.1
CS 1993: 66 TC 1; [1993] STC 444.
Gumbrell, Hoechst Finance Ltd *v* 40.2
CA 1983: 56 TC 594; [1983] STC 150.
Hafton Properties Ltd *v* McHugh 6.2, 13.3, 50.3(*a*)
Ch D 1986: 59 TC 420; [1987] STC 16.
Hall, Fairrie *v* 15.8(*c*)
KB 1947: 28 TC 200; [1947] 2 All ER 141.
Harris (John M) (Design Partnership) Ltd *v* Lee 56.7
Sp C 1997: [1997] SSCD 240.
Harton Coal Co Ltd, CIR *v* 13.2
Ch D 1960: 39 TC 174; [1960] Ch 563; [1960] 3 All ER 48.
Hatton *v* CIR 4.1
Ch D 1992: [1992] STC 140.
Haywards Heath Housing Society Ltd *v* Hewison 30.4
Ch D 1966: 43 TC 341.
Hely-Hutchinson, Barnes *v* 21.3
HL 1939: 22 TC 655; [1940] AC 81; [1939] 3 All ER 803.
Hennessey, A W Chapman Ltd *v* 29.23, 55.4
Ch D 1981: 55 TC 516; [1982] STC 214.
Hesketh *v* Bray 50.26
CA 1888: 2 TC 380; 21 QBD 444.
Hewison, Haywards Heath Housing Society Ltd *v* 30.4
Ch D 1966: 43 TC 341.
Hildesley, Aspden *v* 16.1
Ch D 1981: 55 TC 609; [1982] STC 206; [1982] 1 WLR 264; [1982] 2 All ER 53.
Hill (T & C) (Haulage) *v* Gleig 17.4
Sp C 2000: [2000] SSCD 64.
Hoechst Finance Ltd *v* Gumbrell 40.2
CA 1983: 56 TC 594; [1983] STC 150.
Holdings Ltd *v* CIR 40.2
Sp C 1997: [1997] SSCD 144.
Homeowners Friendly Society Ltd *v* Barrett 28.2
Sp C 1995: [1995] SSCD 90.
Hood (John) & Co Ltd *v* Magee 53.2
KB(I) 1918: 7 TC 327.
Howe, De Beers Consolidated Mines Ltd *v* 53.2
HL 1906: 5 TC 198; [1906] AC 455.
Hudson, R *v* 49.12
CCA 1956: 36 TC 561; [1956] 2 QB 252; [1956] 1 All ER 814.
ICI plc *v* Colmer 29.27
HL 1996: 72 TC 1; [1996] STC 352; [1996] 1 WLR 469; [1996] 2 All ER 23; [1999] STC 1089.
ICI plc *v* Colmer (Case C–264/96) 29.15; 29.27
ECJ 1998: [1998] STC 874; [1999] 1 WLR 108.
ICI Petroleum Ltd, Elliss *v* 46.3
Ch D 1983: 57 TC 176; [1983] STC 675.
Imperial Tobacco Co Ltd *v* Kelly 23.2
CA 1943: 25 TC 292; [1943] 2 All ER 119.
Ingram *v* CIR 4.1
Ch D 1985: [1985] STC 835; [1986] 2 WLR 598.
Innocent *v* Whaddon Estates Ltd 9.19
Ch D 1981: 55 TC 476; [1982] STC 115.

Inspecteur der Belastingdienst/Ondernemingen Amsterdam 2 (Case C-28/95), Leur-Bloem *v* 22.3
ECJ 1997: [1997] STC 1205; [1998] 2 WLR 27.

Inspector of Taxes, Cricket plc *v* 29.9
Sp C 1998: [1998] SSCD 101.

Inspector of Taxes, Lion Ltd *v* 9.41
Sp C 1997: [1997] SSCD 133.

Inspector of Taxes, Mother *v* 55.7
Sp C 1999: [1999] SSCD 279.

Inspector of Taxes, Self-assessed *v* 55.7
Sp C 1999: [1999] SSCD 253.

Irving *v* Tesco Stores (Holdings) Ltd 29.23
Ch D 1982: 58 TC 1; [1982] STC 881.

Jenkins (HT) & Son Ltd, McKinlay *v* 23.2
KB 1926: 10 TC 372.

Johns, British Broadcasting Corporation *v* 57.5
CA 1964: 41 TC 471; [1964] 2 WLR 1071; [1964] 1 All ER 923.

Johnson *v* Prudential Assurance Co Ltd 41.2
CA 1998: 70 TC 445; [1998] STC 439.

Johnson *v* W S Try Ltd 15.6
Ch D 1946: 27 TC 167; [1946] 1 All ER 532.

Joint *v* Bracken Developments Ltd 13.12
Ch D 1994: 66 TC 560; [1994] STC 300.

Jones *v* Shell Petroleum Co Ltd 40.2
HL 1971: 47 TC 194; [1971] 1 WLR 786; [1971] 2 All ER 569.

Jones, Odeon Associated Theatres Ltd *v* 50.26
CA 1971: 48 TC 257; [1973] Ch 288; [1972] 1 All ER 681.

Jones, Simpson *v* 15.8(*d*)
Ch D 1968: 44 TC 599; [1968] 1 WLR 1066; [1968] 2 All ER 929.

Jowett *v* O'Neill and Brennan Construction Ltd 56.7
Ch D 1998: 70 TC 566; [1998] STC 482.

Joyce, American Thread Co *v* 53.2
HL 1913: 6 TC 163.

Kahn and another *v* CIR (Re Toshoku Finance UK plc) 42.3
CA 2000: [2000] STC 301.

Kelly, Imperial Tobacco Co Ltd *v* 23.2
CA 1943: 25 TC 292; [1943] 2 All ER 119.

Kelsall *v* Stipplechoice Ltd 2.4
CA 1995: 67 TC 349; [1995] STC 681.

Kelsall Parsons & Co *v* CIR 15.4
CS 1938: 21 TC 608.

Knight *v* Parry 15.8(*c*)
Ch D 1972: 48 TC 580; [1973] STC 56.

Ladkarn Ltd *v* McIntosh 17.7
CA 1982: 56 TC 616; [1983] STC 113.

Landes Bros *v* Simpson 23.2
KB 1934: 19 TC 62.

Lansing Bagnall Ltd, ex parte, R *v* HMIT 33.4
CA 1986: 61 TC 112; [1986] STC 453.

Law Land plc, Shepherd *v* 29.23
Ch D 1990: 63 TC 692; [1990] STC 795.

Law Shipping Co Ltd *v* CIR 50.26
CS 1923: 12 TC 621.

Lawrence *v* CIR 11.4
KB 1940: 23 TC 333.
Lee, John M Harris (Design Partnership) Ltd *v* 56.7
Sp C 1997: [1997] SSCD 240.
Leur-Bloem *v* Inspecteur der Belastingdienst/Ondernemingen Amsterdam 2 (Case C-28/95) 22.3
ECJ 1997: [1997] STC 1205; [1998] 2 WLR 27.
Levinson (H & M) Ltd, Creed *v* 15.3
Ch D 1981: 54 TC 477; [1981] STC 486.
Lithgows Ltd, CIR *v* 4.4
CS 1960: 39 TC 270.
Littlejohn, Aproline Ltd *v* 3.6, 3.8
Sp C 1995: [1995] SSCD 201.
Liverpool Corn Trade Association Ltd *v* Monks 45.1
KB 1926: 10 TC 442; [1926] 2 KB 110.
London & Thames Haven Oil Wharves Ltd *v* Attwooll 15.6
CA 1966: 43 TC 491; [1967] Ch 772; [1967] 2 All ER 124.
Lookers Ltd, Sabine *v* 15.7
CA 1958: 38 TC 120.
Lowe *v* J W Ashmore Ltd 50.26
Ch D 1970: 46 TC 597; [1971] Ch 545; [1971] 1 All ER 1057.
Lucas, Ellis *v* 15.4
Ch D 1966: 43 TC 276; [1967] Ch 858; [1966] 2 All ER 935.
Lucas, Mersey Docks & Harbour Board *v* 57.5
HL 1883: 2 TC 25; (1883) 8 App. Cas. 891.
Lyntress Ltd, Shepherd *v* 4.1
Ch D 1989: 62 TC 495; [1989] STC 617.
Macarthur *v* Greycoat Estates Mayfair Ltd 50.3
Ch D 1995: 67 TC 598; [1996] STC 1.
McClure *v* Petre 50.26
Ch D 1988: 61 TC 226; [1988] STC 749; [1988] 1 WLR 1386.
MacDiarmid, Cairns *v* 4.1
CA 1983: 56 TC 556; [1983] STC 178.
McDonald, Camcrown *v* 44.6
Sp C 1999: [1999] SSCD 255.
McGowan *v* Brown & Cousins 15.5
Ch D 1977: 52 TC 8; [1977] STC 342; [1977] 1 WLR 1403; [1977] 3 All ER 844.
McGregor, Unigate Guernsey Ltd *v* 53.2
Sp C 1995: [1996] SSCD 1.
McGregor, Untelrab Ltd *v* 53.2
Sp C 1995: [1996] SSCD 1.
McGuckian, CIR *v* 4.1
HL 1997: 69 TC 1; [1997] STC 908; [1997] 1 WLR 991; [1997] 3 All ER 817.
McHugh, Hafton Properties Ltd *v* 6.2, 13.3, 50.3(*a*)
Ch D 1986: 59 TC 420; [1987] STC 16.
McIntosh, Ladkarn Ltd *v* 17.7
CA 1982: 56 TC 616; [1983] STC 113.
McKinlay *v* H T Jenkins & Son Ltd 23.2
KB 1926: 10 TC 372.
Macniven *v* Westmoreland Investments Ltd 50.3
CA 1998: [1998] STC 1131.
Madras Electric Supply Corporation Ltd, Boarland *v* 24.5
HL 1955: 35 TC 612; [1955] AC 667; [1955] 1 All ER 753.

Magee, John Hood & Co Ltd *v* 53.2
KB(I) 1918: 7 TC 327.
Mallett *v* The Staveley Iron & Coal Co Ltd 15.8(*a*)
CA 1928: 13 TC 772; [1928] 2 KB 405.
Mankowitz *v* Special Commissioners of Income Tax 49.4
Ch D 1971: 46 TC 707.
Marine Midland Ltd, Pattison *v* 6.1, 23.2, 23.3
HL 1983: 57 TC 219; [1984] STC 10; [1984] 2 WLR 11.
Marshall Hus & Partners Ltd *v* Bolton 2.4
Ch D 1980: 55 TC 539; [1981] STC 18.
Martin, Blackpool Marton Rotary Club *v* 1.2, 14.1
Ch D 1988: 62 TC 686; [1988] STC 823.
Matrix-Securities Ltd, ex parte, R *v* CIR 33.5
HL 1994: 66 TC 587; [1994] STC 272; [1994] 1 WLR 334; [1994] 1 All ER 769.
Mead and Cook, ex parte, R *v* CIR 33.4
QB 1992: 65 TC 1; [1992] STC 482; [1993] 1 All ER 772.
Medway Housing Society Ltd, Cook *v* 40.1
Ch D 1996: 69 TC 319; [1997] STC 90.
Memec plc *v* CIR 21.2, 21.3
CA 1998: 71 TC 77; [1998] STC 754.
Mersey Docks & Harbour Board *v* Lucas 57.5
HL 1883: 2 TC 25; (1883) 8 App. Cas. 891.
Mesco Properties Ltd, Re 42.5
CA 1979: 54 TC 238; [1979] STC 788; [1980] 1 WLR 96; [1980] 1 All ER 117.
Mitchell *v* B W Noble Ltd 15.8(*a*)
CA 1927: 11 TC 372; [1927] 1 KB 719.
Mitchell, Egyptian Hotels Ltd *v* 53.3
HL 1915: 6 TC 152, 542; [1915] AC 1022.
Monks, Liverpool Corn Trade Association Ltd *v* 45.1
KB 1926: 10 TC 442; [1926] 2 KB 110.
Monteagle Estate Co, Casey *v* 40.1
HC (I) 1960: 3 ITC 313; [1962] IR 106.
Moodie *v* CIR and Sinnett 4.1
HL 1993: 65 TC 610; [1993] STC 188; [1993] 1 WLR 266; [1993] 2 All ER 49.
Morning Post Ltd *v* George 44.4
KB 1940: 23 TC 514.
Mother *v* Inspector of Taxes 55.7
Sp C 1999: [1999] SSCD 279.
Murgatroyd, Bowater Paper Corporation Ltd *v* 21.6
HL 1969: 46 TC 37; [1970] AC 266; [1969] 3 All ER 11.
Murray *v* Goodhews 15.5
CA 1977: 52 TC 86; [1978] STC 207; [1978] 1 WLR 499;
[1978] 2 All ER 40.
Myers, Billingham *v* 39.3
CA 1996: 68 TC 512; [1996] STC 593.
Nagel, Rolfe *v* 15.5
Ch D 1981: 55 TC 585; [1982] STC 53.
National & Grindlays Bank Ltd, Ball *v* 50.3
CA 1971: 47 TC 287; [1973] Ch 127; [1971] 3 All ER 485.
National Federation of Self-employed and Small Businesses Ltd, R *v* CIR
(ex parte) 33.4
HL 1981: 55 TC 133; [1981] STC 260; [1981] 2 WLR 722; [1981] 2 All ER 93.
Nchanga Consolidated Copper Mines Ltd, Commissioners of Taxes *v* 15.8(*a*)
PC 1964: [1964] AC 948; [1964] 1 All ER 208.

New York Life Insurance Co, Styles *v* 45.1
HL 1889: 2 TC 460; (1889) 14 App. Cas. 381.
New Zealand Shipping Co Ltd *v* Thew 53.2
HL 1922: 8 TC 208.
Newcastle Breweries Ltd, CIR *v* 15.6
HL 1927: 12 TC 927.
Newfields Developments Ltd, ex parte, R *v* CIR 13.2
CA 1999: [2000] STC 52.
Nicholson, Calcutta Jute Mills Co Ltd *v* 53.2
Ex D 1876: 1 TC 83; 1 Ex D 428.
Nobes (BW) & Co Ltd *v* CIR 50.5
HL 1965: 43 TC 133; [1966] 1 WLR 111; [1966] 1 All ER 30.
Noble (BW) Ltd, Mitchell *v* 15.8(*a*)
CA 1927: 11 TC 372; [1927] 1 KB 719.
North British & Mercantile Insurance Co *v* Easson 41.2
CS 1919: 7 TC 463.
Northfleet Coal & Ballast Co Ltd, CIR *v* 15.3
KB 1927: 12 TC 1102.
Nova Securities Ltd, Reed *v* 9.22
HL 1985: 59 TC 516; [1985] STC 124; [1985] 1 WLR 193; [1985] 1 All ER 686.
Nuclear Electric plc *v* Bradley 44.4
HL 1996: 68 TC 670; [1996] STC 405; [1996] 1 WLR 529.
Oakes *v* Equitable Life Assurance Society 51.7
Ch D 2000: [2000] STC 459.
Océ van Grinten *v* CIR 21.9
Sp C 2000: 2000 STI 251.
Oceanic Contractors Incorporated, Clark *v* 53.9
HL 1982: 56 TC 183; [1983] STC 35; [1983] 2 WLR 94; [1983] 1 All ER 133.
O'Connor, J Sainsbury plc *v* 9.18, 29.15, 29.17
CA 1991: 64 TC 208; [1991] STC 318; [1991] 1 WLR 963.
Odeon Associated Theatres Ltd *v* Jones 50.26
CA 1971: 48 TC 257; [1973] Ch 288; [1972] 1 All ER 681.
Ogg, 'Countess Warwick' Steamship Co Ltd *v* 15.8(*b*)
KB 1924: 8 TC 652; [1924] 2 KB 292.
O'Keeffe *v* Southport Printers Ltd 15.8(*a*)
Ch D 1984: 58 TC 88; [1984] STC 443.
Olin Energy Systems Ltd *v* Scorer 50.3
Ch D 1982: 58 TC 592; [1982] STC 800.
O'Neill and Brennan Construction Ltd, Jowett *v* 56.7
Ch D 1998: 70 TC 566; [1998] STC 482.
Oppenheim *v* Tobacco Securities Trust Co Ltd 11.1
HL 1951: [1951] AC 297; [1951] 1 All ER 31.
Overseas Containers (Finance) Ltd *v* Stoker 23.2
CA 1989: 61 TC 473; [1989] STC 364; [1989] 1 WLR 606.
Owen *v* Sassoon 53.8
Ch D 1950: 32 TC 101.
Owton Fens Properties Ltd *v* Redden 5.4
Ch D 1984: 58 TC 218; [1984] STC 618.
Pardoe, Dunlop International AG *v* 9.47
CA 1999: 72 TC 71; [1999] STC 909.
Parnell & Zeitlin Ltd, Vaughan *v* 15.6
KB 1940: 23 TC 505.
Parry, Knight *v* 15.8(*c*)
Ch D 1972: 48 TC 580; [1973] STC 56.

Pattison *v* Marine Midland Ltd 6.1, 23.2, 23.3
HL 1983: 57 TC 219; [1984] STC 10; [1984] 2 WLR 11.
Peeters Picture Frames Ltd, Willis *v* 44.13
CA (NI) 1982: 56 TC 436; [1983] STC 453.
Pemsel, Special Commissioners of Income Tax *v* 11.1
HL 1891: 3 TC 53; [1891] AC 531.
Peterborough Royal Foxhound Show Society *v* CIR 24.1
KB 1936: 20 TC 249; [1936] 2 KB 497; [1936] 1 All ER 813.
Petre, McClure *v* 50.26
Ch D 1988: 61 TC 226; [1988] STC 749; [1988] 1 WLR 1386.
Pigott *v* Staines Investment Co Ltd 3.8, 4.1
Ch D 1995: 68 TC 342; [1995] STC 114.
Pike, Watneys London Ltd *v* 15.8(*b*)
Ch D 1982: 57 TC 372; [1982] STC 733.
Pilkington Bros Ltd *v* CIR 29.23
HL 1982: 55 TC 705; [1982] STC 103; [1982] 1 WLR 136; [1982] 1 All ER 660.
Pittas Ltd, Stephens *v* 13.10
Ch D 1983: 56 TC 722; [1983] STC 576.
Port of London Authority *v* CIR 57.5
CA 1920: 12 TC 122; [1920] 2 KB 612.
Poulter *v* Gayjon Processes Ltd 58.1
Ch D 1985: 58 TC 350; [1985] STC 174.
Pountney, Clixby *v* 49.4
Ch D 1967: 47 TC 515; [1968] Ch 719; [1968] 1 All ER 802.
Preston, ex parte, R *v* CIR 33.4
HL 1985: 59 TC 1; [1985] STC 282; [1985] 2 WLR 836; [1985] 2 All ER 327.
Procter & Gamble Ltd *v* Taylerson 3.8
CA 1990: 63 TC 481; [1990] STC 624.
Prudential Assurance Co Ltd *v* Bibby 41.7
Ch D 1999: [1999] STC 952.
Prudential Assurance Co Ltd, Bibby *v* (No 2) 51.7
Ch D 2000: [2000] STC 459.
Prudential Assurance Co Ltd, Johnson *v* 41.2
CA 1998: 70 TC 445; [1998] STC 439.
Pyne *v* Stallard-Penoyre 50.26(viii)
Ch D 1964: 42 TC 183; [1965] Ch 705; [1965] 1 All ER 487.
QT Discount Foodstores Ltd *v* Warley Commrs and CIR 49.7
Ch D 1981: 57 TC 268; [1982] STC 40.
R, Canadian Eagle Oil Co Ltd *v* 21.3
HL 1945: 27 TC 205; [1946] AC 119; [1945] 2 All ER 499.
R *v* CIR (ex parte Camacq Corporation) 33.4
CA 1989: 62 TC 651; [1989] STC 785; [1990] 1 WLR 191; [1990] 1 All ER 173.
R *v* CIR (ex parte Commerzbank AG) 21.3, 38.3
QB 1991: 68 TC 252; [1991] STC 271.
R *v* CIR (ex parte Commerzbank AG) 21.3, 38.3
CJEC 1993: 68 TC 264; [1993] STC 605; [1994] 2 WLR 128; [1993] 4 All ER 37.
R *v* CIR (ex parte Matrix-Securities Ltd) 33.5
HL 1994: 66 TC 587; [1994] STC 272; [1994] 1 WLR 334; [1994] 1 All ER 769.
R *v* CIR (ex parte Mead and Cook) 33.4
QB 1992: 65 TC 1, [1992] STC 482; [1993] 1 All ER 772.
R *v* CIR (ex parte National Federation of Self-employed and Small Businesses Ltd) 33.4
HL 1981: 55 TC 133; [1981] STC 260; [1981] 1 WLR 722; [1981] 2 All ER 93.
R *v* CIR (ex parte Newfields Developments Ltd) 13.2
CA 1999: [2000] STC 52.

R *v* CIR (ex parte Preston) 33.4
HL 1985: 59 TC 1; [1985] STC 282; [1985] 2 WLR 836; [1985] 2 All ER 327.
R *v* CIR (ex parte Rothschild (J) Holdings plc) 33.4
CA 1987: 61 TC 178; [1987] STC 163.
R *v* HMIT (ex parte Brumfield and Others) 33.4
QB 1988: 61 TC 589; [1989] STC 151.
R *v* HMIT (ex parte Fulford-Dobson) 33.4
QB 1987: 60 TC 168; [1987] STC 344; [1987] 3 WLR 277.
R *v* HMIT (ex parte Lansing Bagnall Ltd) 33.4
CA 1986: 61 TC 112; [1986] STC 453.
R *v* Hudson 49.12
CCA 1956: 36 TC 561; [1956] 2 QB 252; [1956] 1 All ER 814.
R *v* Revenue Adjudicator's Office (ex parte Drummond) 33.8
QB 1996: 70 TC 235; [1996] STC 1312.
R *v* Special Commr (ex parte Stipplechoice Ltd) (No 3) 2.4
QB 1988: 61 TC 391; [1989] STC 93.
R *v* Special Commrs (ex parte Shaftesbury Homes) 11.4
CA 1922: 8 TC 367.
R *v* Ward 2.4
QB 1988: 61 TC 391; [1989] STC 93.
RTZ Oil and Gas Ltd *v* Elliss 46.3
Ch D 1987: 61 TC 132; [1987] STC 512.
Racal Group Services Ltd *v* Ashmore 11.11(*a*)
CA 1995: 68 TC 86; [1995] STC 1151.
Radio Pictures Ltd *v* CIR 23.2
CA 1938: 22 TC 106.
Ramsay (WT) Ltd *v* CIR 4.1
HL 1981; 54 TC 101; [1981] STC 174; [1981] 2 WLR 449; [1981] 1 All ER 865.
Rawling, Eilbeck *v* 4.1
HL 1981: 54 TC 101; [1981] STC 174; [1981] 2 WLR 449; [1981] 1 All ER 865.
Redden, Owton Fens Properties Ltd *v* 5.4
Ch D 1984: 58 TC 218; [1984] STC 618.
Reed *v* Nova Securities Ltd 9.22
HL 1985: 59 TC 516; [1985] STC 124; [1985] 1 WLR 193; [1985] 1 All ER 686.
Revenue Adjudicator's Office, R *v* (ex parte Drummond) 33.8
QB 1996: 70 TC 235; [1996] STC 1312.
Reynolds (John) (Insurances) Ltd, Simpson *v* 15.5
CA 1975: 49 TC 693; [1975] STC 271; [1975] 1 WLR 617; [1975] 2 All ER 88.
Road, Bush, Beach & Gent Ltd *v* 15.3
KB 1939: 22 TC 519; [1939] 1 KB 524; [1939] 3 All ER 302.
Roberts *v* Lord Belhaven's Executors 50.26
CS 1925: 9 TC 501.
Robinson (J) & Sons, Chibbett *v* 15.5
KB 1924: 9 TC 48.
Robinson (J) & Sons *v* CIR 15.3
KB 1929: 12 TC 1241.
Robroyston Brickworks Ltd *v* CIR 44.4
CS 1976: 51 TC 230; [1976] STC 229.
Rodin, Falmer Jeans Ltd *v* 44.10
Ch D 1990: 63 TC 55; [1990] STC 270.
Rolfe *v* Nagel 15.5
CA 1981: 55 TC 585; [1982] STC 53.
Rolfe, Wimpey (George) International Ltd *v* 21.5
Ch D 1989: 62 TC 597; [1989] STC 609.

Rolls-Royce Motors Ltd *v* Bamford 44.4
Ch D 1976: 51 TC 319; [1976] STC 162.
Rothschild (J) Holdings plc, ex parte, R *v* CIR 33.4
CA 1987: 61 TC 178; [1987] STC 163.
Rotunda Hospital Dublin (Governors of) *v* Coman 11.2
HL 1920: 7 TC 517.
Rowles, Scammel (G) & Nephew Ltd *v* 15.8(*a*)
CA 1939: 22 TC 479; [1939] 1 All ER 337.
Royal Choral Society *v* CIR 11.6
CA 1943: 25 TC 263; [1943] 2 All ER 101.
Ryan *v* Crabtree Denims Ltd 52.1, 58.1
Ch D 1987: 60 TC 183; [1987] STC 402.
Sabine *v* Lookers Ltd 15.7
CA 1958: 38 TC 120.
Sainsbury (J) plc *v* O'Connor 9.18, 29.15, 29.17
CA 1991: 64 TC 208; [1991] STC 318; [1991] 1 WLR 963.
St Luke's Hostel Trustees, CIR *v* 11.11
CA 1930: 15 TC 682.
Salmon Estate (Kingsbury) Ltd, Shadbolt *v* 15.3
KB 1943: 25 TC 52.
Sassoon, Owen *v* 53.8
Ch D 1950: 32 TC 101.
Savacentre Ltd *v* CIR 3.8, 38.3
CA 1995: 67 TC 381; [1995] STC 867.
Scammell (G) & Nephew Ltd *v* Rowles 15.8(*a*)
CA 1939: 22 TC 479; [1939] 1 All ER 337.
Scorer, Olin Energy Systems Ltd *v* 50.3
Ch D 1982: 58 TC 592; [1982] STC 800.
Scottish and Universal Newspapers Ltd *v* Fisher 29.23
Sp C 1996: [1996] SSCD 311.
Scottish Woollen Technical College *v* CIR 11.3
CS 1926: 11 TC 139.
Seaham Harbour Dock Co *v* Crook 58.1
HL 1931: 16 TC 333.
Seaman *v* Tucketts Ltd 44.4
Ch D 1963: 41 TC 422.
Self-assessed *v* Inspector of Taxes 55.7
Sp C 1999: [1999] SSCD 253.
Shadbolt *v* Salmon Estate (Kingsbury) Ltd 15.3
KB 1943: 25 TC 52.
Shaftesbury Homes, ex parte, R *v* Special Commrs 11.4
CA 1922: 8 TC 367.
Sharkey *v* Wernher 45.1
HL 1955: 36 TC 275; [1956] AC 58; [1955] 3 All ER 493.
Sharp (William) & Son, CIR *v* 15.8(*b*)
CS 1959: 38 TC 341.
Shaw, Commercial Union Assurance Co plc *v* 21.7, 44.4
CA 1998: [1999] STC 109.
Shell Co of China Ltd, The, Davies *v* 23.2
CA 1951: 32 TC 133.
Shell Petroleum Co Ltd, Jones *v* 40.2
HL 1971: 47 TC 194; [1971] 1 WLR 786; [1971] 2 All ER 569.
Shepherd *v* Law Land plc 29.23
Ch D 1990: 63 TC 692; [1990] STC 795.

Shepherd *v* Lyntress Ltd 4.1
Ch D 1989: 62 TC 495; [1989] STC 617.
Short Bros Ltd *v* CIR 15.3
CA 1927: 12 TC 955.
Shove *v* Dura Manufacturing Co Ltd 15.3
KB 1941: 23 TC 779.
Simpson *v* Jones 15.8(*d*)
Ch D 1968: 44 TC 599; [1968] 1 WLR 1066; [1968] 2 All ER 929.
Simpson, Landes Bros *v* 23.2
KB 1934: 19 TC 62.
Simpson *v* Reynolds (John) (Insurances) Ltd 15.5
CA 1975: 49 TC 693; [1975] STC 271; [1975] 1 WLR 617; [1975] 2 All ER 88.
Sinnett, CIR and, Moodie *v* 4.1
HL 1993: 65 TC 610; [1993] STC 188; [1993] 1 WLR 266; [1993] 2 All ER 49.
Smith, Carlisle & Silloth Golf Club *v* 45.1
CA 1913: 6 TC 48; [1913] 3 KB 75.
Sommerfelds Ltd *v* Freeman 15.3
Ch D 1966: 44 TC 43; [1967] 1 WLR 489; [1967] 2 All ER 143.
Southport Printers Ltd, O'Keeffe *v* 15.8(*a*)
Ch D 1984: 58 TC 88; [1984] STC 433.
South Shore Mutual Insurance Co Ltd *v* Blair 9.18, 29.3, 29.27, 29.41
Sp C 1999: [1999] SSCD 296.
Special Commissioners of Income Tax, Mankowitz *v* 49.4
Ch D 1971: 46 TC 707.
Special Commissioners of Income Tax *v* Pemsel 11.1
HL 1891: 3 TC 53; [1891] AC 531.
Staines Investment Co Ltd, Pigott *v* 3.8, 4.1
Ch D 1995: 68 TC 342; [1995] STC 114.
Stallard-Penoyre, Pyne *v* 50.26(viii)
Ch D 1964: 42 TC 183; [1965] Ch 705; [1965] 1 All ER 487.
Staveley Iron & Coal Co Ltd, The, Mallett *v* 15.8(*a*)
CA 1928: 13 TC 772; [1928] 2 KB 405.
Steeden *v* Carver 49.6
Sp C 1999: [1999] SSCD 283.
Steele *v* EVC International NV (formerly European Vinyls Corp (Holdings) BV) 16.6, 21.9, 29.23
CA 1996: 69 TC 88; [1996] STC 785.
Stephens *v* Pittas Ltd 13.10
Ch D 1983: 56 TC 722; [1983] STC 576.
Stipplechoice Ltd, Kelsall *v* 2.4
CA 1995: 67 TC 349; [1995] STC 681.
Stipplechoice Ltd (ex parte) (No 3), R *v* Special Commr 2.4
QB 1988: 61 TC 391; [1989] STC 93.
Stoke-on-Trent City Council *v* Wood Mitchell & Co Ltd 15.2
CA 1978: [1979] STC 197; [1980] 1 WLR 254; [1979] 2 All ER 65.
Stoker, Overseas Containers (Finance) Ltd *v* 23.2
CA 1989: 61 TC 473; [1989] STC 364; [1989] 1 WLR 606.
Stokes, Ensign Tankers (Leasing) Ltd *v* 4.1
HL 1992: 64 TC 617; [1992] STC 226; [1992] 2 WLR 469; [1992] 2 All ER 275.
Strong & Co of Romsey Ltd *v* Woodifield 15.8(*c*)
HL 1906: 5 TC 215; [1906] AC 448.
Styles *v* New York Life Assurance Co 45.1
HL 1889: 2 TC 460; (1889) 14 App. Cas. 381.
Sun Life Assurance Society *v* Davidson 40.2
HL 1957: 37 TC 330; [1958] AC 184; [1957] 2 All ER 760.

Swedish Central Railway Co Ltd *v* Thompson 53.2
HL 1925: 9 TC 342; [1925] AC 495.
Sweet, London County Freehold & Leasehold Properties Ltd *v* 40.2
KB 1942: 24 TC 612; [1942] 2 All ER 212.
Taylerson, Procter & Gamble Ltd *v* 3.8
CA 1990: 63 TC 481; [1990] STC 624.
Tesco plc *v* Crimmin 9.51
Ch D 1997: 69 TC 510; [1997] STC 981.
Tesco Stores (Holdings) Ltd, Irving *v* 29.23
Ch D 1982: 58 TC 1; [1982] STC 881.
Thew, New Zealand Shipping Co Ltd *v* 53.2
HL 1922: 8 TC 208.
Thompson, Swedish Central Railway Co Ltd *v* 53.2
HL 1925: 9 TC 342; [1925] AC 495.
Thorn Domestic Appliances (Electrical) Ltd, Burman *v* 52.1
Ch D 1981: 55 TC 493; [1982] STC 179.
Tintern Close Residents Society Ltd *v* Winter 40.1
Sp C 1995: [1995] SSCD 57.
Tobacco Securities Trust Co Ltd, Oppenheim *v* 11.1
HL 1951: [1951] AC 297; [1951] 1 All ER 31.
Todd *v* Egyptian Delta Land & Investment Co Ltd 53.2
HL 1928: 14 TC 119; [1929] AC 1.
Toshoku Finance UK plc, Re, Kahn and another *v* CIR 42.3
CA 2000: [2000] STC 301.
Try (W S) Ltd, Johnson *v* 15.6
CA 1946: 27 TC 167; [1946] 1 All ER 532.
Tucketts Ltd, Seaman *v* 44.4
Ch D 1963: 41 TC 422.
Turner, Dingle *v* 11.1
HL 1972: [1972] AC 601; [1972] 1 All ER 878.
Turner, Focus Dynamics plc *v* 50.19
Sp C 1999: [1999] SSCD 71.
Tyre Investment Trust Ltd, CIR *v* 40.1
KB 1924: 12 TC 646.
Underground Electric Railways Co of London Ltd, Bennet *v* 40.2
KB 1923: 8 TC 475; [1923] 2 KB 535.
Unigate Guernsey Ltd *v* McGregor 53.2
Sp C 1995: [1996] SSCD 1.
Uniholdings Ltd, Whittles *v* (No 3) 23.2
CA 1996: 68 TC 528; [1996] STC 914.
Union Corporation Ltd *v* CIR 53.2
HL 1953: 34 TC 207; [1953] AC 482; [1953] 1 All ER 729.
United Glass Bottle Manufacturers Ltd, Bradbury *v* 15.8(*b*)
CA 1959: 38 TC 369.
United Steel Companies Ltd *v* Cullington (No 1) 15.8(*a*)(*b*)
CA 1939: 23 TC 71.
Untelrab Ltd *v* McGregor 53.2
Sp C 1995: [1996] SSCD 1.
Utopia Assurance Co Ltd *v* Chaloner 41.2
Sp C 1996: [1996] SSCD 204.
Van den Berghs Ltd *v* Clark 15.7
HL 1935: 19 TC 390; [1935] AC 431.
Vaughan *v* Parnell & Zeitlin Ltd 15.6
KB 1940: 23 TC 505.

Vestey *v* CIR (No 1) 33.4
HL 1979: 54 TC 503; [1980] STC 10; [1979] 3 WLR 915; [1979] 3 All ER 976.

Vestey's Executors & Vestey *v* CIR 13.5, 13.11, 16.1
HL 1949: 31 TC 1; [1949] 1 All ER 1108.

Von Glehn (Alexander) & Co Ltd, CIR *v* 15.8(*c*)
CA 1920: 12 TC 232; [1920] 2 KB 553.

Walker *v* Carnaby, Harrower, Barham & Pykett 15.5
Ch D 1969: 46 TC 561; [1970] 1 WLR 276; [1970] 1 All ER 502.

Walker *v* Centaur Clothes Group Ltd 2.3, 3.6, 3.8
HL 2000: [2000] STC 324.

Ward *v* Anglo-American Oil Co Ltd 23.2
KB 1934: 19 TC 94.

Ward, R *v* 2.4
QB 1988: 61 TC 391; [1989] STC 93.

Warley Commrs and CIR, QT Discount Foodstores Ltd *v* 49.7
Ch D 1981: 57 TC 268; [1982] STC 40.

Waterloo Main Colliery Co Ltd *v* CIR (No 1) 15.7
KB 1947: 29 TC 235.

Watneys London Ltd *v* Pike 15.8(*b*)
Ch D 1982: 57 TC 372; [1982] STC 733.

Watton, Andrew Grant Services Ltd *v*, and cross-appeal 13.10
Ch D 1999: 71 TC 333; [1999] STC 330.

Webb *v* Conelee Properties Ltd 40.1
Ch D 1982: 56 TC 149; [1982] STC 913.

Wernher, Sharkey *v* 45.1
HL 1955: 36 TC 275; [1956] AC 58; [1955] 3 All ER 493.

West, CIR *v* 15.7
CS 1950: 31 TC 402.

Westminster (Duke of) *v* CIR 4.1
HL 1935: 19 TC 490.

Westmoreland Investments Ltd, Macniven *v* 50.3
CA 1998: [1998] STC 1131.

Whaddon Estates Ltd, Innocent *v* 9.19
Ch D 1981: 55 TC 476; [1982] STC 115.

White, Craven *v* 4.1
HL 1988: 62 TC 1; [1988] STC 476; [1988] 3 WLR 423; [1988] 3 All ER 495.

Whittles *v* Uniholdings Ltd (No 3) 23.2
CA 1996: 68 TC 528; [1996] STC 914.

Wilcock *v* Frigate Investments Ltd 50.3
Ch D 1981: 55 TC 530; [1982] STC 198.

William Flood & Sons Ltd, Copeman *v* 50.8
KB 1940: 24 TC 53; [1941] 1 KB 202.

Willis *v* Peeters Picture Frames Ltd 44.13
CA (NI) 1982: 56 TC 436; [1983] STC 453.

Wilson, Gorge Fabrications Ltd *v* 17.4
Sp C 1999: [1999] SSCD 293.

Wimpey (George) International Ltd *v* Rolfe 21.5
Ch D 1989: 62 TC 597; [1989] STC 609.

Wing Hung Lai *v* Bale 55.7
Sp C 1999: [1999] SSCD 238.

Winter, Creedplan Ltd *v* 49.6
Sp C 1995: [1995] SSCD 352.

Winter, Tintern Close Residents Society Ltd *v* 40.1
Sp C 1995: [1995] SSCD 57.

Wolfson, CIR *v* 11.11
HL 1949: 31 TC 141; [1949] 1 All ER 865.
Woolworth (FW) Ltd, Beauchamp *v* 23.2
HL 1989: 61 TC 542; [1989] STC 510; [1989] 3 WLR 1.
Wood Mitchell & Co Ltd, Stoke-on-Trent City Council *v* 15.2
CA 1978: [1979] STC 197; [1980] 1 WLR 254; [1979] 2 All ER 65.
Woodifield, Strong & Co of Romsey Ltd *v* 15.8(*c*)
HL 1906: 5 TC 215; [1906] AC 448.
Woolwich Equitable Building Society *v* CIR 38.5
HL 1992: 65 TC 265; [1992] STC 657; [1992] 3 WLR 366; [1992] 3 All ER 737.
Worthing Rugby Football Club Trustees, CIR *v* 14.1
CA 1987: 60 TC 482; [1987] STC 273; [1987] 1 WLR 1057.
Yates *v* GCA International Ltd 21.2
Ch D 1991: 64 TC 37; [1991] STC 157.
Young Men's Christian Association, Grove *v* 11.2
KB 1903: 4 TC 613.

65 Table of Statutes

1907 **Limited Partnerships Act** 47.7
1911 **Perjury Act**
s 5 49.12
1914 **Bankruptcy Act**
s 312 42.5
1923 **Industrial Insurance Act**
s 1 28.5
s 24 28.4(*c*)
1929 **Industrial Assurance and Friendly Societies Act**
s 3 28.4(*c*)
1945 **Bretton Woods Agreement Act** 24.6
1949 **Wireless Telegraphy Act**
s 1 50.29
1954 **Charitable Trusts (Validation) Act** 11.1
1955 **International Finance Corporation Act** 24.6
1958 **Recreational Charities Act**
s 1 11.1
1960 **Charities Act**
ss 22, 22A 11.9
1960 **International Development Association Act** 24.6
1964 **Continental Shelf Act**
s 1(7) 53.9
1964 **Housing Act**
s 5 30.5
1965 **Industrial and Provident Societies Act** 30.2; 30.6; 32.1; 45.3
1968 **International Organisations Act** 24.6
1970 **Income and Corporation Taxes Act**
s 208 24.14; 41.6
ss 333,335 28.5
s 482 53.6; 53.7
1970 **Taxes Management Act**
s 1(1) 33.1
ss 2,4 33.3
ss 8–9A 33.11
s 10 49.1; 59.6
s 11 8.2; 12.1; 12.3; 26.6; 29.23; 44.9; 47.2; 48.1; 54.2; 59.31(*a*)
s 12A 50.12
s 12AB 55.3
s 17 6.2; 54.10
s 18 54.10
s 20 33.12; 55.7
s 24 54.11
s 29 5.1; 29.25; 48.8
s 30 48.8; 59.22
s 31 5.2; 12.3
(1) 59.2(*e*)
(4) 5.3
s 33 12.4; 59.12
s 36(3) 44.9
(4) 50.12
s 41A 8.2; 29.18; 44.9
ss 41B, 41C 29.18; 44.9
s 42 12.1; 12.3; 54.2
(1),(2) 12.1
(3) 59.2(*d*)(*e*)
(8) 12.1
(11) 55.11
s 43 18.17(*a*)
(1) 12.2; 59
s 43A 29.25; 44.9; 55.9
s 44(1),(3) 5.3
s 46(1) 5.3
ss 46B–46D 12.3
ss 51–53 49.7
s 54 5.3
s 55 18.17; 48.1; 48.3; 55.5; 55.7
s 56 49.8
s 59D 48.1; 55.5; 55.10
s 59DA 48.1; 55.7
s 59E 48.1; 55.10
ss 60–70 33.2
ss 78–85 53.5
s 86 3.6; 39.3
s 87 39.6
s 87A 9.5; 9.6; 9.46; 9.47; 23.31; 29.18; 39.1; 48.1; 48.4; 48.8
s 88 13.12; 39.3
s 88A 39.3
s 89 39.3
ss 90,91 39.1; 39.3
s 92 39.7; 53.3
s 93(1) 49.8
s 94 49.2; 49.6; 49.8
(6) 29.33
s 95 49.3
s 96 49.3
s 97 49.3
s 97A 49.9
s 98 4.3; 19.10; 26.4; 48.1; 49.5; 49.7; 49.8; 51.5
s 98A 17.7; 49.5; 49.8
s 98B 49.8; 50.12
s 99 49.4; 49.10

65 Table of Statutes

1970 Taxes Management Act
s 99A 6.9
ss 100–100D 49.8; 55.7
s 102 49.9
s 103 49.10
s 105 49.8
s 107 49.12
s 108(1) 1.2
(2) 48.5
(3) 1.2; 48.5
s 109 13.12; 39.3
(3) 39.3
(3A) 39.1
(4) 39.1; 39.3
(5) 39.1; 39.3
s 113(1) 54.2; 55.3
s 115A 54.13
s 118(2) 39.3; 49.2; 49.6
Sch 1A 12.1; 12.3; 55.4; 55.11
para 9 59.2(*d*)(*e*)
Sch 2 5.3; 12.3
Sch 3 5.3
Sch 3A 54.13
1971 Finance Act
Sch 3 para 1 24.14
1972 European Communities Act 24.6
s 2 22.2
1972 Finance Act
s 84(1),(2) 1.3(*d*)
s 91(4) 29.5
s 93 1.3(*b*)
1972 Industry Act
s 7 52.1; 58.1
s 8 52.1
1973 Employment and Training Act
s 5 58.1
1973 Finance Act
ss 28,29 29.23
s 32 29.23
s 38 53.9
Sch 15 53.7; 53.9
1974 Finance Act
s 9 1.3(*a*)
s 10(1) 1.3(*b*)
(2) 1.3(*a*)
s 12 1.3(*d*)
1974 Friendly Societies Act
s 84 28.8
1975 Employment Protection Act
Sch 14 para 2 58.1
1975 Finance Act
s 57 33.3(*a*)
1975 Finance (No 2) Act
s 26 1.3(*a*)
s 27(2) 1.3(*a*)
s 28 1.3(*d*)
s 43 46.6
s 44(5) 5.1
s 45 48.3
s 46(1) 39.3
1975 Oil Taxation Act
Pt I 46.2
1975 Policyholders Protection Act 41.2
1976 Finance Act
s 25 1.3(*a*)
s 26 1.3(*d*)
s 27(2) 1.3(*a*)
1976 Lotteries and Amusements Act 14.6
ss 3, 5 11.6(iii)
1977 Finance Act
s 18 1.3(*a*)
s 19 1.3(*d*)
s 20 1.3(*a*)
1978 Employment Subsidies Act
ss 1, 3 58.1
1978 Finance Act
s 15 1.3(*a*)
s 16 1.3(*d*)
s 17(2) 1.3(*a*)
1978 Interpretation Act
s 17 29.5
1979 Banking Act
s 33 6.8
1979 Capital Gains Tax Act
s 26 9.13
1979 Finance Act
s 2 1.3(*a*)
1979 Finance (No 2) Act
s 5 1.3(*d*)
1980 Finance Act
s 19 1.3(*a*)
s 20 1.3(*d*)
s 21 1.3(*a*)
s 106 46.2
s 107 21.12
Sch 17 46.2
1980 Housing Act
s 56(4) 8.3
1980 Petroleum Revenue Tax Act 46.1
1981 British Telecommunications Act
s 82 44.12
1981 Finance Act
s 20 1.3(*a*)
s 21 1.3(*d*)
s 22 1.3(*a*)

1981 Supreme Court Act
s 35A 38.5
1982 Administration of Justice Act
s 42 60.1; 60.2
1982 Finance Act
s 21 1.3(*a*)
s 22 1.3(*d*)
s 23 1.3(*a*)
s 68 48.3
s 86(1) 9.1(iii)
s 132 46.2
ss 137, 138 52.1
s 149 48.8
1982 Industrial Development Act
Pt II 52.1
1982 Insurance Companies Act
s 34A 41.4
s 49 41.15–41.17
1983 Finance Act
s 11 1.3(*a*)
s 12 1.3(*d*)
s 13 1.3(*a*)
1983 Oil Taxation Act 46.1
1984 Finance Act
s 18 1.3(*a*)(*b*)
s 19 1.3(*d*)
s 20 1.3(*a*)
s 127 5.3; 33.3(*b*)
Sch 22 33.3(*b*)
paras 3, 5 5.3
1984 Friendly Societies Act
s 1 28.5
s 2 28.5
1984 Inheritance Tax Act
s 220A 33.12
1984 Telecommunications Act
s 72 9.54; 44.12
1985 Companies Act
s 117 19.15
s 135 9.51
s 162 51.1
s 226 50.29
s 227 50.27; 50.29
s 262(1) 50.27; 50.29
s 263 51.4(iii)
s 425 42.2
s 560 42.5
ss 652, 652A 20.16(*a*)
Sch 7 para 1 50.32
1985 Finance Act
s 35 1.3(*d*)
s 68 9.1
Sch 19 9.1
1985 Housing Associations Act
s 89 17.2
Sch 7 para 5 30.5
1986 Advance Petroleum Revenue Tax Act 46.1
1986 British Airports Act
s 77 9.54; 44.12
1986 Building Societies Act 7.7
s 97(6),(7) 7.6
s 100(2) 7.6
s 120 7.2
Sch 18 7.2
1986 Finance Act
s 17(1) 1.3(*d*)
s 18 1.3(*a*)
1986 Financial Services Act
s 54 41.2
ss 78, 81 60.1
s 142(6) 26.8
1986 Gas Act
s 60 9.54; 44.12
1986 Insolvency Act 42.2
s 115 42.3
s 156 42.3
s 175 42.5
Sch 6 42.5
1987 Finance Act
s 20(1) 1.3(*d*)
s 21 1.3(*a*)
s 22(1) 1.3(*a*)
1987 Finance (No 2) Act
s 74 1.3(*b*)
(4) 56.1; 56.2
s 82 54.1; 54.2
s 83 49.2; 54.1
s 84 54.1
s 85 39.1; 54.1
s 86 54.1
(5),(6) 39.1
s 87 54.1
s 88 48.8; 54.1
ss 89, 90 54.1
s 91 39.1; 54.1
s 94 49.6
s 95 54.1
Sch 5 paras 1, 2 1.3(*b*)
Sch 6 54.1
1988 British Steel Act
s 11 9.54; 44.12
1988 Copyright, Designs and Patent Act
Sch 7 para 36 18.14
1988 Health and Medicines Act
s 6 9.54; 44.12

65 Table of Statutes

1988 Income and Corporation Taxes Act

Provision	Reference
s 6	53.4
(1)	1.2
(2)	31.2
(3)	9.1
(4)	1.2; 50.1
s 7(2)	18.4(iii); 18.10(ii); 31.5; 49.1; 49.2; 55.5
(4)	31.5
(5)	53.4
(6)	54.2
s 8(1)	1.2
(2)	42.4; 50.1
(3)	1.2; 2.1; 9.2; 56.2; 56.5
s 8A	1.3(*c*)
s 9	31.1; 50.2
(1)	2.4
(4)	24; 50.1
s 10	48.1
(1)	48.2
s 11	1.2; 53.4
(3)	49.1; 49.2; 55.5
s 12	2.3; 2.4; 18.7; 41.16
(7)	42.5; 42.6
s 13	9.2; 56.1
(1)	13.18
(2)	55.5; 56.2
(3)	56.2; 56.7
(4),(5)	56.7
(6)	56.2
s 13A	13.18
s 13AA	9.2; 56.4; 56.5
(2)	55.5
(4)(5)	56.7
(8)	13.18
s 14(1)	3.1; 20.18
(3)	3.2
(4)	20.18
s 15	50.26; 50.27
(1)	59.5
(2)	59.5; 59.29
s 18	50.2
ss 21A, 21B	50.27
s 21C	30.1; 50.27
s 23	50.26
s 24(6)	50.26
s 25	30.1; 50.26
(3)	50.27
s 26	50.26; 50.27; 59.32
ss 28–30	50.26
s 31	50.26
(3)	50.27
s 32	50.26
ss 33–33B	50.26
s 34	44.24; 50.27
s 35	44.24
(2A)	50.27
s 36	44.24; 50.27
(4A)(4B)	50.27
s 37(9)	50.26
s 38	50.27
s 41	50.26; 50.27
ss 43A–43G	50.27
s 48	53.8
s 49(2)	53.5
s 50	31.7
ss 51A, 51B	31.7
s 53(1)	50.27
s 55	50.26; 50.27
s 56	11.9(G); 23.31; 43.12
s 56A	43.12
s 57	43.12; 50.7
ss 64, 65	2.4
s 65A	50.27
s 70(1)	50.1(*a*); 53.3
(2)	50.2
(3)	53.4
s 70A	50.2; 50.27
(5)	2.4
s 72	1.2; 2.4; 50.27
s 74	23.11; 25.10; 42.2; 43.3; 43.11
s 75	27.3; 40.2; 40.5; 41.16; 50.10
(3)	9.3
(4)	41.14
s 76	27.3; 41.2; 41.16; 50.10
(6)	41.12
(8)	41.1
s 76A	8.4
s 77	40.2; 43.12; 50.19
s 78	40.2; 43.12; 50.9
s 82	50.27
s 83A	11.12; 11.13
s 84A	40.2; 50.22
s 85	50.22
s 85A	40.2; 50.10
s 86	50.6
ss 88A–88C	6.3; 43.5; 43.11; 43.12
s 90	40.2; 50.24
s 91C	46.3
ss 92, 93	52.1
s 94	42.2
s 95	51.7
s 96	50.27
s 98	50.27
s 100	7.6
(1)	41.13
s 101	59.35

1988 Income and Corporation Taxes Act
s 108 59.27
s 111 47.2
s 112 50.12
s 113 45.2; 47.5; 59.23
(1) 50.24
s 114 47.2; 47.5
(2) 44.16
s 115 47.2
s 116 3.11; 44.16; 44.24
ss 117, 118 47.7
ss 118A–118K 31.3(*b*)
ss 119, 120 50.2; 50.26; 50.27
s 123(4) 53.8
s 124 7.4; 31.3(*b*)
s 125 4.1; 31.3(*a*); 50.3
s 126 43.12
s 126A 9.11; 43.12
s 128 41.8
s 130 6.6; 40.1
s 134 17.2
s 160(2) 13.13
s 168(8)(9) 9.46
(11) 13.11
s 186 40.2
s 188 15.4
s 208 18.12; 20.17; 27.2; 41.14; 50.1
s 209 13.13; 20.1
(1) 20.16(*a*)
(2) 9.17; 18.9(xiii); 18.12; 20.2–20.7; 20.18(*a*); 50.23
(3)(3A) 20.8
(4) 9.17; 11.10; 20.9
(5) 20.9
(6) 20.3; 20.9
(7) 20.9
(8) 20.4
(8A)–(8F) 20.6
(9)–(11) 20.7
s 210 20.1; 20.10; 20.18(*a*); 29.50
s 211 20.1; 20.11; 29.50
s 212 20.7
(4) 20.6
s 213(1),(2) 29.36
(3),(4) 29.36; 29.46
(5) 29.36; 29.40
(6) 29.36; 29.37
(7) 29.36; 29.54
(8) 29.36; 29.37
(9) 29.36; 29.54
(10) 29.36
(11) 29.36; 29.43; 29.56
(12) 29.37
s 214(1) 29.50; 29.56
s 214(2),(3) 29.51
(4) 29.51; 29.53
(5) 29.51
(6) 29.51; 29.52
s 215 29.57; 51.6
s 216 29.55; 29.56
(4) 29.57
s 217 29.56
s 218(1) 29.36; 29.38; 29.39; 29.42–29.44; 29.47; 29.48; 29.51; 29.53
(2),(3) 29.40
s 219 20.16(*k*); 20.17
(1) 51.3; 51.4; 51.6
ss 220–224 20.16(*k*); 20.17; 51.4
s 225 20.16(*k*); 20.17; 51.4; 51.6
s 226 20.16(*k*); 20.17; 51.4; 51.5
ss 227, 228 20.16(*k*); 20.17; 51.4
s 229 20.16(*k*); 20.17; 51.4
(1) 51.3
s 230 20.16(*h*)
s 231 41.14
(1) 3.3; 11.5; 26.3; 27.1
(2) 27.2
(3)–(3D) 13.18
s 231A(6) 21.3
s 233 26.3
s 234(4) 49.11
(5)–(9) 20.18; 54.8
s 234A 20.18; 26.4
(9) 49.11
s 235 4.1; 11.5; 29.2
s 236 4.1; 11.5
s 237 4.1; 11.5; 29.2
s 238(1) 3.3; 20.18; 27.1–27.3
(1A) 3.3; 27.3
(4) 23.18; 26.5; 26.6(iv)
s 239 9.2; 55.5
(1) 3.6
(2) 3.6; 21.7; 29.12
(3) 3.6; 3.8; 3.10; 26.6(*c*); 29.11; 38.3; 49.1
(4) 3.8
(6) 3.6
s 240 26.6(*d*); 29.8
(2)–(5) 29.11
(7) 29.10
(8) 20.16(*d*); 29.13
(10)–(13) 29.9
s 241(1),(2) 3.3
(3) 3.3; 27.3
s 242 8.2; 23.31; 27.3; 27.4; 38.3; 41.7; 59.15
(2) 40.2

1988 Income and Corporation Taxes Act
s 243 27.3; 59.15
s 244(2) 27.3
s 245 3.8; 3.10; 29.58; 44.13
(4) 48.4
s 245A 3.8; 3.10; 44.13
s 245B 3.8; 3.10
s 246(5) 3.3; 3.6
(6) 1.3(*d*); 3.2; 3.4
s 246A 4.7; 26.2; 26.7
(1) 26.1
(10) 29.2
s 246B 26.2
s 246C 26.3; 27.1
s 246D 26.1; 26.3
s 246E 26.4
s 246F 26.3; 26.4; 26.6(ii)
ss 246G, 246H 26.4
ss 246I–246M 26.5
ss 246N–246R 26.6; 55.5
s 246S 26.8
ss 246T–246W 26.9
s 246X 26.10
s 246Y 26.1
s 247 18.9(vi); 29.2; 29.7
(1) 29.3; 56.7
(1A) 29.3
(4) 29.3
(6),(7) 29.4
(8),(8A),(9) 29.3
s 248 29.2
s 250 54.9
s 252 3.6; 11.5; 26.6; 48.8
s 254(1) 20.12–20.14
(2) 20.7
(5)–(7) 20.12
(8) 20.15
(9) 20.3
(10) 20.4
(11) 20.14
(12) 20.15
s 255 3.12
s 266 41.19
s 312(1) 19.6
s 326 7.3(*a*); 7.6
s 332A 62.4
s 333B 41.1
s 337(1) 45.2; 50.24; 50.27
(2) 11.11; 29.50; 50.2
(3) 50.2
s 337A 50.2
s 338 11.11; 23.11; 23.13; 23.14; 27.3; 47.7; 50.3
(1) 2.4; 29.26; 50.9; 60.1
s 338(2) 29.50
(3),(5) 50.5
s 338A 50.3
s 339 11.10; 11.11
(6) 20.16(*c*)
(8) 20.16(*c*)
(9) 11.1; 24.8
s 340 50.3
s 341 4.6
(4),(5) 31.4
s 342 42.5
s 343 17.2; 18.9(viii); 44.10; 44.13
(2) 9.8
(8) 44.13
s 344 44.10
s 347A(7) 11.9
(8) 11.11
s 348 13.13; 26.3
s 349 6.9; 7.4; 29.2; 31.3(*b*); 32.2; 50.3
(1) 7.3(*a*); 13.13; 26.3; 29.50
(2) 6.9; 31.8; 47.4; 60.1
(3) 6.2; 6.9
(3A) 7.3
(3AA),(3AB) 6.2
s 350 29.2; 29.50; 31.3(*b*)
(4) 31.4; 53.7
s 350A 31.3(*b*)
s 354 30.1
s 355(1) 50.15
s 369 6.2
s 380 41.18
s 392A 44.22; 50.27
(1) 43.3
(3) 40.2
s 392B 44.23; 50.27
s 393 21.6; 29.18; 41.4; 41.18; 44.9; 44.13; 44.15; 44.23; 50.25
(1) 27.4; 32.5; 44.4; 44.15; 50.36
(2) 27.3; 29.29; 44.4; 44.15; 44.18; 47.7
(5) 44.9
(6) 44.9
(7) 44.2; 44.4; 44.6
(8) 44.4
(9) 44.4; 50.36
(10) 44.2
(11) 44.2; 44.6
s 393A 27.4(*c*); 41.4; 44.8

1988 Income and Corporation Taxes Act
s 393A(1) 23.14; 27.3; 27.4; 29.18; 29.26; 29.29; 38.1; 38.3; 39.1; 41.18; 43.3; 44.2; 44.6; 44.13; 44.15; 44.18; 47.7; 50.25; 50.36; 50.37
(2)–(2C) 44.6
(3) 44.9; 44.22; 50.26
(4) 44.9; 44.22
(5) 44.2; 44.6; 44.10
(6) 44.2; 44.6
(8) 44.6
(9) 44.2; 44.6
(10) 44.2; 44.6; 59.34
s 394 41.4
s 395 44.15
s 396 23.13; 41.6; 41.8; 41.14; 44.24
s 397 29.18; 44.14
s 399(1) 41.8
(2)–(5) 44.18
s 400 44.21
s 401 50.21; 50.25; 59.28
(1) 50.27
s 402(1),(2) 29.14
(3)–(3B) 29.14; 29.27
(4) 29.27
(5) 29.23; 55.4
(6) 20.16(*d*); 29.24
s 403 23.14; 29.18; 29.23; 40.2; 44.9; 47.7; 50.27; 55.4
(1) 41.4; 50.25
(9) 29.27
(10),(11) 29.29
s 403ZA 29.18; 29.29
s 403ZB 29.18
s 403ZC 29.18; 43.3
ss 403ZD, 403ZE 29.18
ss 403A, 403B 9.47; 29.19–29.22; 29.29
s 403C 29.19–29.22; 29.29
ss 403D, 403E 29.20
s 404 29.31
ss 405, 406 29.29
s 407 23.31; 29.26
s 408 29.19
s 409 9.47; 29.18; 29.22
(4) 29.27
(5)–(8) 29.29
s 410 13.13; 29.23
s 411 29.22
(1) 29.25
(9) 29.29
s 411A 29.18
s 412(3),(4) 29.25
s 413(2A) 29.19
(3) 29.15; 29.27
(4) 29.15
(5) 29.14; 29.15; 29.27
(6) 29.27
(7) 29.15; 29.27
s 414(1) 13.1; 13.6
(2)–(2D) 13.1
(4)–(6) 13.6
s 415 13.6
s 416 13.2; 13.6
(1) 13.11
s 417(1) 13.3
(3),(4) 13.5; 50.29
(5) 9.46; 13.4; 13.11
(6) 9.46; 13.4
(7),(8),(9) 13.3
s 418 20.19; 20.20
s 419 13.9–13.13; 39.1; 39.3; 48.1; 54.1; 55.1; 55.5; 55.13
(4) 38.1; 38.3
(4A) 49.1; 49.2; 55.2; 55.3; 55.7
s 420 13.9
(1) 13.10
(2) 13.11
s 421 13.13
s 422 13.10
s 423 13.1; 13.8
s 424–430 13.8
s 431(2) 41.1; 41.2; 41.12; 41.14
(3)–(6) 41.6
s 431AA 41.6
s 431B 41.6
s 431C 41.8
ss 431D,431E 41.14
s 431F 41.2
s 432 41.1
s 432ZA 41.3
s 432A 41.3; 50.27
ss 432AA, 432AB 41.3; 50.27
ss 432B–432E 41.3
s 432F 41.3; 41.16
s 433 41.4
s 434(1)–(1B) 41.4, 41.6, 41.14
(2) 41.4
(3)–(7) 41.7
(8) 41.7
s 434A 25.21(*g*); 41.4; 41.7
ss 434B–434D 41.4
s 434E 41.4; 50.27
s 436 41.6; 41.16; 53.8

1988 Income and Corporation Taxes Act

s 437	41.5
s 437A	41.5
s 438	41.6; 41.7
(4)	41.2
s 438A	41.6
s 439	41.6
(3)	41.16
s 439A	41.8
s 439B	41.8
(3)	41.16
ss 440–440A	41.15
s 440B	41.4; 41.6; 41.15
s 441	41.4(*a*); 41.14; 41.16
s 441A	41.14
(7)	41.2
s 441B	41.14; 50.27
s 442(1),(2)	41.11
(3)	9.9; 41.11
(4)	41.13
s 442A	41.5
s 443	41.10
s 444	41.9
s 444A	41.16
ss 444BA–444BD	41.4
s 458	41.17; 41.18
s 458A	41.18
s 459	28.1
s 460	24.7
(1)	28.2; 28.4
(2)	28.3; 28.4; 28.5
(3)–(6)	28.3
(7)–(10)	28.3; 28.5
(10A)	41.16
(11), (12)	28.3; 27.8
s 461	24.7; 28.6
(1)	28.2
(3)	20.23
(4)	28.8
s 461B	9.19(viii)
(1)	28.2; 28.6
(2),(3)	28.6
(5)–(7)	28.8
s 461C	24.7; 28.6
s 462	24.7
(1)	28.4
(2)	28.2
s 462A	24.7; 28.4
s 463	24.7; 28.7
(1)	28.2
ss 465, 466	28.4
s 467	24.15
s 468	60.1; 60.2
(1)	23.6; 25.4
s 468(6)	1.2
s 468AA	60.1
s 468E–468R	60.1
s 469	4.7; 26.3; 60.2
(7)	60.1
s 469A	60.1
s 471	9.6; 59.33
ss 474, 475	6.4; 53.8
s 476	7.1
(1)	53.7(iii)
(3)	3.3(*b*); 20.16(*g*); 27.1
(9)	31.3(*b*)
s 477	7.1
s 477A	7.1; 7.3; 7.4
(3)	3.3(*b*); 20.16(*g*); 27.1(ii); 43.10; 43.11
(7)	31.3(*b*)
s 477B	7.1; 7.7
s 478	7.1
ss 479–482A	6.9
s 484	43.12
(1)	6.6
s 485	43.12
s 486(1)	20.16(*e*); 32.2
(2)–(4),(6),(7)	32.2
(8)	20.16(*e*); 23.32; 32.3
(9)	20.16(*e*); 32.4
(10),(11)	20.16(*f*)
(12)	20.16(*f*); 32.1; 32.4
s 487	45.3
s 488	30.1; 30.4
(4)	30.3
(5)	30.5
(6)	30.2
(8)	30.2; 30.3
(9)–(12)	30.3; 30.5
s 489	30.6
s 490	20.22
(2)	45.4
s 491	45.2
s 492	46.3; 46.6
(1)	4.4
ss 493–494A	46.3
s 497	46.3; 46.4
ss 498–500	46.3
s 502(1)	46.3
(4)	46.4
s 503	50.27
s 505	11.9; 25.21(*b*)
(1)	11.2–11.4; 11.6
(3)	31.7
(6)	11.11
s 506	11.9; 11.12; 11.13
(1)	11.1; 60.2

1988 Income and Corporation Taxes Act
s 507 11.2; 11.5; 24.3; 60.2
(1) 11.12; 11.13; 24.8; 24.11; 24.17
s 508 11.2; 11.5; 11.10; 24.12; 61.2
ss 508A,508B 60.4
s 509 57.1
s 510 24.1
s 510A 50.12
s 512 57.2
s 513 9.54; 44.12
s 515 24.6
ss 516, 517 6.5; 24.2
s 518 57.3
ss 519, 519A 24.10; 57.4
s 520(4) 8.2
ss 524, 525 59.24
s 530(2) 8.2
s 531(3) 59.4(*e*)
s 536–537B 31.3(*c*)
ss 539–541 50.18
ss 547, 548 50.18
s 551A 50.18
ss 552A, 552B 41.12
s 555 53.7(iii)
s 559 17.2
(4) 17.7; 53.7(iv)
(4A)–(5A) 17.7
s 560 17.2
s 561 17.4
(1) 17.2
(6) 17.4
(8)(9) 17.7
(10)(11) 17.7; 49.5
s 562 17.4
s 564 17.4
(2A)–(2C) 17.5
s 565 17.4
(2A)–(2D) 17.5
s 566 17.7
(2A) 17.3; 17.5
(2B) 17.2; 17.5; 17.7
(2C)–(2F) 17.7
s 567 17.2
s 573 9.13; 19.20; 27.3; 44.19; 59.36
s 574 9.13
ss 575(1)–(3) 44.19
s 576 44.19
(2) 9.13
s 577 40.2; 50.26; 50.27
(8) 50.6
(9) 24.8; 50.6
s 577A 40.2; 50.26; 50.27
s 579 50.24; 50.27
s 579(3) 40.2
s 580 50.27
s 581 31.8
(4) 57.6
s 582A 24.6
s 584 23.15; 53.3
s 587B 11.13
s 588 40.2; 50.27
ss 589–589B 50.27
s 592 24.14
(4) 40.2
s 601 24.14
s 608 24.14
ss 613–615 24.14
s 617(3),(4) 40.2
s 620(6) 24.14
(9) 24.15
s 660 11.11
s 660A(9) 11.11
s 660G(1)(2) 16.7
s 677 13.13
s 681(4),(5) 16.7
s 682A(2) 16.7
s 686 4.7; 6.9; 26.3
s 703 4.1; 11.5; 29.57
s 704 4.1
s 704D 4.1; 20.10; 20.11
ss 705, 706 4.1
s 707 4.1
s 708 4.1
s 709 4.1; 50.23
ss 710–712 7.7; 43.12; 50.16
s 713 7.7; 23.8; 43.12; 50.16
ss 714–728 7.7; 43.11; 43.12; 50.16
ss 729, 730 4.1
s 730A 4.1; 43.5
ss 731–739 4.1; 51.7
s 732 4.2
s 736 4.2; 16.9
s 737A(5) 43.9
s 739 18.18
ss 741–746 4.1
s 747 18.9; 21.6; 55.1; 55.13
(1) 18.1; 18.2; 18.5; 59.8(*a*)
(1A) 18.14
(2) 18.1; 18.2
(3) 18.6
(4) 18.6; 18.7; 18.18; 48.1; 55.5
(5) 18.7
s 747A 18.9
s 748(1) 18.9; 18.11; 18.12; 18.14
(2) 18.12
(3) 18.11
(4),(5) 18.9

Provision	Paragraph
1988 Income and Corporation Taxes Act	
s 749	18.3
(4)	18.3; 59.8(*c*)
(4A)	18.2
(5)–(7)	18.6
s 749A	18.3
s 749B	18.6
s 750	18.4
(2),(3),(5)–(8)	18.9
s 750A	18.4
s 751	23.31
(1)–(3)	18.7
(4)	18.1; 18.7
(5)	18.7; 59.8(*a*)
(6)	18.10
ss 752–752C	18.7
s 753	18.16
s 754	18.17
(3)	18.16
s 754A	18.12
s 754AA	18.18
s 754B	18.6
ss 755–755C	18.18
s 755D	18.2
s 756(3)	18.2
s 759(1)	11.13; 41.17
(6),(8)	41.17
s 765	4.3; 53.1(*a*); 53.6; 53.7
ss 765A–767	4.3
ss 767A–767C	48.4
s 768	3.10; 9.31; 29.58; 40.5; 44.13; 48.4
s 768A	29.58; 40.5; 44.13; 48.4
ss 768B, 768C	40.5
s 768D	29.58; 40.5; 44.13; 50.27
s 769	3.10; 40.5; 44.13; 48.4; 50.27
s 770	4.4; 18.9; 18.12; 23.17; 43.5; 43.10; 46.5
s 770A	4.4
s 771	4.4; 43.5; 43.10; 46.5
s 772	4.4; 43.5; 43.10
s 773	4.4
s 774	4.5
ss 775–779	4.1
s 780	4.1; 50.27
s 781	4.1; 40.2
ss 782–786	4.1
s 787	50.3
s 788	18.17; 25.18(iii); 26.5; 41.14; 53.1; 55.5
(1)	21.5
(2),(3)	21.3
(5)	21.2
s 790	18.17; 21.2; 26.5; 55.5
s 790(1)	21.5; 60.1
(2),(3)	21.5
s 793	21.5
s 793A	21.2
s 794(2)	21.2; 21.11
s 795A	21.5
s 796	18.17
s 797	18.12; 18.17
(1)	21.5
(3)–(5)	21.7
s 797A	21.7
ss 798–798B	21.11
s 799	18.12; 21.3; 21.6
s 800	21.2
s 801	21.2; 21.3
s 801A	21.2; 21.3; 21.4; 21.6
s 801B	21.3
s 801C	21.6
s 802	21.2
s 803	21.6; 21.11
s 803A	21.3
s 803B(13)	59.10
ss 804A–804F	41.14
s 806	21.5; 59.10
ss 806A–806C	21.6
ss 806D–806F	21.5; 21.6
s 806G	21.5; 21.6; 59.10
ss 806H–806K	21.6
s 806L	21.5
s 806M	21.5
(7)	59.10
s 807	43.11
s 807A	21.2; 21.3
s 808	44.25
ss 808A, 808B	21.3
s 811	21.6
(1)	4.4
ss 812–815	21.9
s 815A	9.9
s 815AA	21.3
s 815B	4.4
s 815C	33.12
s 816(2A)	4.4
s 825	38.1; 38.3
s 826	23.31; 38.1; 41.4; 50.25
(7BB), (7BC)	21.6
(8A)	55.13
s 826A	38.1
s 827	61.5
(2)	38.6
s 829(1),(2)	24.5
s 830	53.9

1988 Income and Corporation Taxes Act
s 832(1) 1.2; 3.3; 7.2; 8.2; 9.18; 14.7; 29.3; 29.27; 29.41; 47.1
(2) 1.2
s 834(1) 1.2
(4) 2.4
s 837A 19.7, 50.25; 62.3
s 837B 50.25
s 838 9.18; 20.7; 29.3; 29.9; 29.15; 29.27; 51.3; 51.4
(1) 20.3
s 839 16
(1)–(4),(8) 4.4
s 840 4.3; 4.4; 19.6; 51.4(2)(vii)
s 840A 6.1; 6.2; 11.9; 20.18; 31.3(*b*)
s 841 13.6
s 841A 31.3(*b*)
s 842 9.49; 23.6; 25.4; 25.21(*d*); 60.4
s 842A 24.10; 31.8; 57.4
s 842AA 9.6; 9.50; 62.2; 62.3
Sch 4 43.11; 43.12; 50.7; 50.16; 50.23
Sch 5 para 2 59.17
para 6 59.17
Sch 5AA para 9 41.3
Sch 9 50.22
Sch 13 3.4; 3.5; 26.4; 26.11; 31.4; 39.1; 39.6; 54.6
Sch 13A 29.8
Sch 15 paras 3, 4 28.4
Sch 15B 62.4
Sch 16 6.9; 7.3(*a*); 11.10; 11.11; 31.4; 31.7; 39.1; 39.6; 50.3; 54.7
para 5 43.8
para 7A 31.4
Sch 17A 29.23; 29.27
para 6 54.2
Sch 18 9.18; 29.27
para 1 23.29; 29.16
paras 2–4 29.17
paras 5–5F 9.18; 29.17
paras 6, 7 29.17
Sch 19 13.8
Sch 19AA 41.14
Sch 19AB 28.2; 41.6; 48.1; 55.4; 55.14
Sch 19AC 41.12
Sch 20 11.9
Sch 22 24.14
Sch 23A 3.8; 4.7; 31.7; 43.9
Sch 24 18.4; 18.9; 18.10; 23.15
para 4 59.8(*b*)
para 9 59.8(*b*)
Sch 25 paras 1–4 18.12
paras 5–12 18.14
paras 13–15 18.15
paras 16–19 18.11
Sch 26 18.17
para 3 18.18
Sch 27 para 5 23.31; 25.21(*g*)
Sch 28A 40.5
Sch 28AA 4.4; 23.17; 43.5; 43.10
Sch 28B 26.2; 62.3
paras 10C, 10D 62.2

1988 Finance Act
s 23 1.3(*d*)
s 26 1.3(*a*)
s 27(1) 1.3(*a*); 56.1
(2) 56.2
s 29 41.19
s 43(3) 30.1
s 44(6) 30.1
s 66 53.1
s 71 60.2
s 73(2) 50.27
s 105(6) 4.3
s 117 60.4
s 121 49.1; 59.6
s 123 54.10
s 127 49.5
s 129 49.9
ss 130, 131 53.1; 53.7
s 132 53.7
s 133(1) 5.3
s 134(1)(4) 33.3
s 145 7.6
Sch 3 para 16 13.11
Sch 6 para 6 50.26
Sch 12 7.6

1988 Housing Act
s 54 30.4
Sch 17 para 93 30.5; 30.6

1989 Electricity Act
s 90 9.54; 44.12
Sch 11 9.54; 44.12

1989 Finance Act
s 30 1.3(*d*)
s 34 1.3(*a*)
s 35 1.3(*a*); 56.1; 56.2; 56.7
s 43 50.8; 50.27
(5) 59.9
s 44 40.2; 41.2; 50.8
s 59 11.11(*c*)

1989 Finance Act
s 60 24.3
(2) 11.10
s 67 40.2; 50.10
(6) 59.11
s 68 50.10
s 76 40.2; 50.27
s 80 60.2
s 82 41.4; 41.8
s 83 41.3; 41.4; 41.5; 41.8; 50.27
(2) 50.17
ss 83AA, 83AB, 83A 41.4
s 85 41.5
s 86 4.4; 41.2
s 87 41.2
ss 88, 88A 4.4; 41.7
s 89 41.6; 41.7
s 90 50.18
s 94 43.12
s 97 29.11
s 98 3.10
s 99 29.3
s 100 44.13
s 101 29.16
s 102 29.33; 48.1; 54.1
s 103 13.8
s 104 13.1; 13.18
(3) 13.6
s 105 13.18
ss 112, 113 50.27
s 115 21.9
s 116 31.3(*b*)
ss 135–137 9.13
s 149(3) 48.8
s 156(1) 39.3
(2) 48.3
s 157 3.6
s 158 39.3; 39.6
(2) 38.3
s 159 39.3
ss 160, 161 39.3
s 163 49.3
s 164 49.5
s 165 49.5
s 166 49.4
s 167 49.8
s 168(3) 49.7
(4) 49.9
(5) 49.8
s 169 49.10
s 170(2) 49.11
ss 178, 179 38.1; 38.3; 39.1; 39.3
s 182(5) 6.9
s 182A 4.4
Sch 5 50.10
Sch 8 para 2 41.4
paras 3, 4 41.7
para 6 41.6
Sch 8A 41.12
Sch 9 50.18
Sch 10 50.7
Sch 11 23.8; 23.31; 35.B13; 43.11; 43.12; 50.16; 50.23
Sch 12 Pt I 13.9; 13.18
para 8 13.11
para 10 29.50
para 11 54.8
para 14 44.19
Sch 17 Pt V 13.8

1989 Water Act
s 95 9.54; 44.12

1990 Capital Allowances Act
s 15A 44.4
s 23(2) 59.3(*b*)
s 24(2) 2.5; 8.2
s 26(3) 8.4
s 28 40.2; 41.2; 41.4; 41.14
s 28A 50.26
ss 34, 35 18.9(x)
s 49(2) 59.3(*b*)
s 61(1) 44.24
(5) 8.2
(7) 8.2; 29.18
s 64A 46.3
s 73 41.14
(1A) 50.26
ss 75, 76 8.4
s 76B 8.4
s 96 18.9(x)
s 98(6) 8.2
s 115(2A) 46.3
ss 138A,138B 46.3
s 144 8.2; 41.14
(2) 23.39; 23.40
s 145 8.2; 41.14; 47.7; 59.3(*a*)
(3) 27.3; 29.26; 44.2; 44.6; 50.35
(4) 44.6
s 149 53.4
s 152A 41.16
s 152B 9.8
s 153(1) 52.1
ss 157, 158 8.3
Sch A1 8.2
para 7 54.2

1990 Environmental Protection Act
ss 6–9 9.54; 44.12

1990 Finance Act
s 17 1.3(*d*)

1990 Finance Act
s 19 1.3(*a*)
s 20 1.3(*a*); 56.1; 56.2; 56.7
s 26 11.10
s 30 7.1
s 41 41.3; 41.6; 41.15
s 42 41.2; 41.14
s 43 41.4
s 44 41.2; 41.5
s 45 41.7
(9) 41.6
s 48 41.16
s 49 28.3
s 50 28.7
s 51 60.1
s 52 60.2
s 55 60.4
s 56 43.10; 50.23
s 59 50.7
ss 60, 62 46.3
s 67(1) 18.2
(2) 18.7
(3) 18.12
(4) 18.2; 18.12
s 68 4.3
s 69 50.12
s 74 6.3
s 81 24.14; 60.1
s 86 9.18
s 91 54.1; 54.2
s 92 6.2; 54.10
s 95 29.18; 44.9; 54.1
s 96 29.18; 54.1
s 97 12.1; 54.1
(3) 54.2
s 98 12.1; 31.5; 53.4; 54.1
(3) 54.2
s 99 12.1; 44.4; 44.24; 54.1
s 100 12.1; 54.1
s 101 12.1; 29.18; 54.1
s 102 8.2; 12.1; 54.1
s 103 12.1; 54.1
s 104(2) 48.3
s 105 48.8
s 106 48.1; 54.1
s 121 46.3
s 127 24.10; 57.4
Sch 5 7.1
para 2 7.3(*a*)
para 4 3.3(*b*); 7.3(*a*); 7.4
20.16(*g*); 27.1
paras 7–12 6.9
Sch 6 para 4 41.3
paras 5, 7 41.6
Sch 6 paras 8, 12 41.15
Sch 7 41.14
para 1 41.2
Sch 9 41.16
Sch 10 43.11; 43.12; 50.23
para 26 50.7
Sch 11 50.12
Sch 13 53.4
Sch 15 12.1; 29.23; 29.27; 54.1; 54.2
Sch 16 12.1; 54.1; 54.2
Sch 17 12.1; 54.1
Sch 18 57.4

1990 National Health Service and Community Care Act
s 61(1) 24.10

1991 British Technology Group Act
s 12 9.54; 44.12

1991 Finance Act
s 21 1.3(*d*)
s 23 1.3(*a*); 56.2
s 24 1.3(*a*)
s 25 1.3(*a*); 56.1; 56.2; 56.7
s 42 40.2; 50.22
s 43 40.2; 50.10
s 47 41.2
s 49 41.6
s 51 7.7
s 52 7.3; 7.4
ss 62–65 46.3
s 66 46.4
s 73 44.2; 44.6–44.9
s 74 24.15
s 75 6.9
s 77 29.16
s 118 24.6
Sch 7 paras 1, 2 41.2
para 3 41.3
para 4 41.5; 41.6
para 5 41.5
para 6 41.15
para 8 53.8
para 9 50.18
para 12 41.5
para 13 41.2
para 16 41.5
para 17 41.16
Sch 8 41.6
Sch 9 28.3; 28.4
Sch 10 7.7
Sch 11 7.3; 7.4
Sch 12 50.7
Sch 15 54.1
para 1 39.3
para 2 39.1

1991 Finance Act
Sch 15 paras 5, 6 27.3
para 8 44.2
para 20 44.13
para 22 38.3
para 23 38.1
1991 Ports Act
s 35 9.54; 44.12
1992 Charities Act
Sch 6 para 17 11.9
1992 Finance Act
s 10 1.3(*d*)
1992 Finance (No 2) Act
s 19(6) 13.13
s 21 1.3(*a*)
s 22 1.3(*a*); 56.1; 56.2
s 25 9.47
s 28 11.2
s 29 54.10
s 31 20.7
s 32 20.18; 49.11
s 44 9.8
s 45 9.9
s 46 9.7; 9.43
s 50 9.9
s 51 4.4
s 52 21.3
s 56 28
ss 57, 58 50.26
s 65 41.1
s 67 9.8
s 75 33.3
Sch 6 9.18; 29.17
Sch 8 6.9; 7.4
Sch 9 28
Sch 12 6.1
Sch 16 5.3; 33.3
1992 Friendly Societies Act
s 91 28.8
Sch 2 28.4
1992 Museums and Galleries Act
Sch 8 24.3
1992 Taxation of Chargeable Gains Act
s 8 1.3(*b*)
(1) 2.4; 9.3; 9.29; 40.5
(2) 9.3
(3)–(5) 9.1
(6) 9.4; 42.3
s 10 9.6; 9.12; 9.19; 9.46; 19.21
(3) 1.2; 9.1; 9.8; 9.21; 53.4
s 16 9.3
s 17 44.19
s 18(3) 9.14
s 24 19.11; 19.20; 44.19
(2) 9.51
s 25(3) 9.8; 9.21; 41.16
(4) 41.16
s 29 9.13
s 30 9.13–9.16; 9.47; 19.20; 44.19
s 31 9.13–9.15
s 31A 9.14–9.16
s 32 9.13; 9.14
s 33 9.13; 9.15
s 34 9.13; 9.16
s 35 9.43–9.45
(3) 9.35
s 38 9.10; 9.25; 9.27
s 40 9.10
s 41 9.43
s 42 9.27
s 43 9.24
s 54 9.25
s 55(1)(2)(5)(6) 9.47
(8) 9.25
s 56(2) 9.25
(3) 9.25
s 59 23.30; 25.19; 43.9
s 69 51.4(2)
s 76(1) 7.6
s 87 11.7
s 99 60.1
s 100 62.2
(1) 24.16; 60.4; 62.5
(2) 9.6; 60.3
s 101 9.6
s 101A 9.49
s 101B 9.6
s 101C 9.50
s 103(7) 23.29
s 105 9.12
s 106 9.12
s 108 50.7
(8) 9.12
s 110 9.25
s 116 9.30; 19.22; 23.15(D); 23.29
(5) 43.11
(10) 9.24; 9.25; 43.11
s 117 7.7; 23.8; 23.29
s 122 9.17; 29.49
s 125 9.17
s 126 19.22; 23.15(A); 29.49
s 127 9.19; 9.25; 9.40; 19.17; 19.22; 23.15(D); 23.29; 29.49; 43.11; 44.19
s 128 19.22; 23.29; 29.49
(3) 9.16
ss 129, 130 9.26; 19.22; 23.29; 29.49

1992 Taxation of Chargeable Gains Act
s 132 9.13; 23.28; 23.29
s 135 9.14; 9.19; 19.23; 19.24
s 136 9.16; 19.20; 19.23
s 137 4.1; 44.19
(1) 19.20
s 138 4.1; 9.6; 9.8; 9.9; 29.57; 41.16
s 139 9.6; 23.29; 23.32; 29.49; 29.57; 41.16
s 140 9.7; 9.9; 23.15(C)
s 140A 9.8; 9.43; 23.32
s 140B 9.8
s 140C 9.7; 9.9
s 140D 9.9
s 143 23.29
s 144 7.6
s 149 7.7
ss 151A, 151B 62.5
s 152 9.44; 53.6
ss 153–158 9.44
s 161 9.22
(3) 9.33
s 170 7.6; 9.15; 9.16; 9.18; 9.24; 9.45; 23.17; 25.5
(10) 9.14; 9.24; 9.32
(11) 42.1
(12) 9.54; 44.12
s 171 3.10; 9.7; 9.19; 9.20; 9.24; 9.25; 9.43; 9.49; 9.50; 23.29; 23.32; 40.5; 41.15; 42.1
(1) 9.13–9.15; 9.18
(6) 9.18
s 171A 9.20
s 172 9.21; 9.43; 23.29; 23.32; 42.1
s 173 9.22; 41.15; 42.1
s 174 9.43; 42.1
s 175 9.44; 42.1
s 176 9.51; 42.1
s 177 9.52; 16.9; 42.1
s 177A 9.23; 42.1
s 177B 9.37
s 178(3) 46.3
s 179 7.6; 9.13–9.15; 9.47; 29.20; 29.49; 42.1; 53.1
s 180 42.1
s 181 9.47; 42.1
s 185 53.6
(2) 53.1
ss 186, 187 53.6
s 189 9.5
s 190 9.46; 59.4(*d*)
s 191 53.4
s 192 29.49
ss 194–196 46.3
s 198 46.3
s 200 46.3
s 204(3) 41.10
s 211 41.16
s 212 9.24; 41.17
s 213 9.24; 41.17
(1) 9.37
s 214 41.17
(9) 43.11
s 214A 41.17
(2) 9.37
s 215 7.3(*c*); 23.32
s 216 7.6; 23.32
s 217 7.6
s 217A 23.32
s 218 30.5
s 219 30.5; 30.6
s 220 30.5
ss 227–235 50.10
s 239 9.17
s 241 50.27
s 247 9.44
s 251(6) 23.29
s 254 7.7; 23.29
s 256 11.7; 11.9
s 257 11.7
(2) 11.13
s 259 30.5
s 271(1) 24.14
(3) 24.10; 57.4
(5) 24.6
(6) 24.3; 24.12
(7) 24.8; 24.11; 57.2
(8) 6.5; 24.2
s 276 53.6; 53.9
ss 284A, 284B 9.1
s 286 16.8
s 288(1) 57.4; 60.4
Sch 2 para 17 59.4(*a*)
Sch 3 para 1 9.48
para 2 9.43
para 7 46.3
paras 8, 9 9.45
Sch 4 para 4 9.7
Sch 5C 62.5
Sch 7A 9.23–9.35; 9.39; 40.5
para 1 9.24–9.26; 9.30
para 2 9.25
para 3 9.26; 9.27
para 4 9.26–9.28
para 5 9.28
para 6 9.29

1992 Taxation of Chargeable Gains Act
Sch 7A para 7 9.30; 9.39
para 8 9.31
para 9 9.24; 9.32
para 10 9.33
para 11 9.34
para 12 9.35
Sch 7AA 9.37; 9.38
para 1 9.38; 9.39
paras 2, 3 9.39
para 4 9.39; 41.17
para 5 9.40
para 6 9.41
para 7 9.37
Sch 7B 41.12
Sch 9 31.7
Sch 10 para 14 9.11
Sch 11 para 12 9.3
1993 Agriculture Act
Sch 2 Pt I 9.54; 44.12
1993 Charities Act 11.1
ss 24, 25 11.9(B)
1993 Finance Act
s 53 1.3(*a*)
s 54 1.3(*a*); 56.1; 56.2
s 59 6.9; 31.3(*b*)
s 60 23.5; 23.33; 23.34
ss 61–66 43.11; 43.12; 50.16
s 67 11.10
s 77 13.13
s 78(1) 1.3(*d*); 3.2; 11.5
(2) 3.2
(3) 11.5; 41.7
(4) 3.3
(6) 41.7; 41.14; 41.18
(7) 41.7; 41.14
s 80 11.5
s 81 3.10
s 88 9.23
s 90 41.16
s 91 41.17
(2) 41.3
(5) 41.17
s 92 23.5; 23.35; 23.38
s 93 23.5; 23.11; 23.18; 23.24; 23.36; 23.39
s 94 23.5; 23.18; 23.37; 23.40
s 94A 23.5; 23.40
s 95 23.5; 23.39; 23.40
(5) 23.41
(6) 23.33
s 96 23.5
ss 97–103 41.1; 41.12
s 109 50.21
s 112 40.2
s 117 8.3
s 119 18.4
s 121 28.2
s 125 23.5; 23.7; 23.8; 23.10
s 126 23.5; 23.7; 23.9; 25.21(*h*)
s 127 23.5; 23.7; 23.10; 43.11
s 128 23.5; 23.11
s 129 23.5; 23.13; 25.10; 43.11
s 130 23.5; 23.14; 25.10; 25.21(*b*); 43.11
s 131 23.5; 23.14; 25.10; 25.21(*b*); 38.1; 39.1; 43.11
(4) 27.3
(7) 29.26
ss 132, 133 23.5; 23.14; 25.10; 43.11
s 134 23.5
s 135 23.5; 23.16; 23.17
s 135A 23.16; 23.17
s 136 4.4; 23.5; 23.17
(11) 23.15
s 136A 4.4; 23.5; 23.15; 23.17
ss 137, 138 23.5; 23.17
s 139 23.5; 23.18; 59.13(*a*)
s 140 23.5; 23.18
(3) 23.18
(9) 23.15
ss 141–143 23.5; 23.18
ss 144, 145 23.5; 23.20
s 146 23.5; 23.21
s 147 23.5; 23.22
s 148 23.5; 23.23
s 149 23.5; 23.24
s 150 23.5; 23.25; 23.32
s 151 23.5; 23.25
s 152 23.5; 23.6
s 153 23.5; 23.8; 43.11
s 154 23.5; 23.26
(14) 23.7
s 155 23.5; 23.27
(13) 23.7
s 156 23.5; 23.28
s 157 23.5; 23.9
s 158 23.5; 23.8
s 159 23.5; 23.8
(10)–(12) 23.10
ss 160, 161 23.5; 23.8
s 162 23.5; 23.10
s 163 23.5; 23.24
(1) 23.8
s 164 23.5
(5) 23.8
(9)–(11) 23.28
s 165 23.5; 23.32

1993 Finance Act
ss 166–168A 23.5; 23.31
s 169 23.5
s 170 23.5
ss 185, 186 46.2
s 206 1.3(*c*)
Sch 6 60.1
Sch 8 9.23
Sch 9 41.1; 41.12
Schs 10, 11 41.1; 41.12
Sch 14 para 1 49.1
para 3 39.3
paras 4, 5 39.1
para 6 49.2
para 7 1.2
para 8 44.10; 44.15; 44.21
para 10 38.1; 38.3
para 11 29.33
Sch 15 23.5; 23.15
Sch 16 23.5; 23.32
Sch 17 23.5; 23.29; 23.32; 43.11
Sch 18 23.5; 23.31; 27.3; 29.26; 38.1; 39.1
1993 Railways Act 9.54; 44.12
1994 Coal Industry Act
Sch 4 9.54; 44.12
1994 Finance Act
s 85 1.3(*a*)
s 86 1.3(*a*); 56.1; 56.2; 56.7
s 93 9.28
(4) 9.25
(5) 9.28
(7) 23.29; 46.3
(8) 9.25
(9) 9.27
s 94 9.23; 9.25; 9.32
s 111 60.1
s 113 60.1
s 114(1),(2) 23.26
(3) 23.27
s 115(1) 23.9
(2) 23.21
s 116(2),(3) 23.15
s 119 8.3
s 134 18.12
s 135 48.4
s 136 23.40
s 140 44.25
s 143 41.6
s 144 42.2
s 147 25.2; 25.5; 43.10; 43.11
(2) 25.9(*c*); 25.20
s 147A 25.2; 25.5
s 148 25.2; 25.5
(2),(3) 25.9(*c*)
s 149 25.2; 25.5; 25.21(*h*)
(2)–(4) 25.6(*a*)
s 150 25.2; 25.5; 25.21(*h*)
(2) 25.6(iii)
(3) 25.6(*b*)
(8) 25.8(*a*)
(9) 25.6(*b*)(*c*)
s 150A 25.2; 25.5; 25.21(*h*)
(5), (6) 25.6(*d*)
s 151 25.2; 25.5; 25.6; 25.21(*h*)
(2) 25.15
s 152 25.2; 25.3; 25.5; 25.21(*h*)
s 153 21.2; 25.2; 25.6; 25.21(*h*)
(4),(5) 25.20
s 154 25.2; 25.4
s 155 25.2; 25.3; 25.13
(4) 25.12
(5) 25.11
s 156 25.2; 25.7; 25.8
s 157 25.2; 25.8
s 158 25.2; 25.9; 43.11
(2),(4) 25.20
s 159 25.2; 25.10
s 160 23.13; 25.2; 25.10; 25.21(*b*)(*d*)
s 161 25.2; 25.11
s 162 23.11; 25.2; 25.12
s 163 25.2; 25.13
s 164 25.2; 25.14
s 165 25.2; 25.15; 25.16; 25.17
s 166 25.2; 25.16; 25.17
s 167 25.2; 25.17; 25.18; 25.21(*a*)
s 168 25.2; 25.18
s 169 25.2; 25.21(*c*)
s 170 25.2; 25.21(*d*)
s 171 25.2; 25.21(*b*)
s 172 23.30; 25.2; 25.19; 43.9
s 173 25.2; 25.21(*f*)
s 174 25.2; 25.21(*e*)
s 175 25.2; 25.20
s 176 25.2; 25.21(*g*)
(1) 41.7
s 177 25.2
(1) 25.5; 25.18
(2) 25.5
(3),(4) 25.21(*a*)
(6) 25.21(*h*)
s 199(2) 55.1
s 213(4)(8) 8.2
s 214(4)(6) 8.2
s 215(2)–(5) 47.2; 47.5
s 216(1)(2) 47.5

1994 Finance Act	
s 218(1A)	8.2
ss 219–230	50.1
s 249	9.21; 9.53; 18.2; 50.16; 53.1; 53.6
s 250	53.1
s 251(2)	60.1
(4)	18.2; 18.7
(7)	9.19; 9.21
(9)	53.6
(11)	41.16
ss 252, 253	9.54; 44.12
Sch 14	60.1; 60.2
Sch 16 para 1	26.1–26.10; 29.2
para 3	26.11
para 5	41.4; 41.7
para 6	41.6
para 7	41.18
para 9	41.7
para 10	26.4
para 11	56.1
para 13	29.2
para 14	20.22
para 20	38.1
Sch 18	25.2; 25.21(*c*)
Sch 19 para 2	50.12
para 3	49.5
para 4	48.8
para 7	5.2; 12.3
para 8	12.4
para 18	48.3
para 29	49.5
para 30	50.12
para 35	12.3
Sch 21	50.1
Schs 24, 25	9.54; 44.12
Sch 26 Pt V(23)	48.1
1994 Value Added Tax Act	
s 24(6)	61.4
ss 59–70	61.5
s 74	61.5
s 79	38.6; 61.5
1995 Atomic Energy Authority Act	
Sch 3	9.54; 44.12
1995 Finance Act	
s 37	1.3(*a*)
s 38	1.3(*a*); 56.1; 56.2
s 39	50.2
(4)	50.26
s 42	50.3
s 48	9.44
(1)	35.D30
s 49	9.47
s 51	41.1
s 52	41.1
(2)	23.31
s 53	41.1
s 70	62.1; 62.2
s 71	62.1; 62.4
s 72	62.1; 62.5
(2)	24.16
s 73	62.1
ss 77, 78	31.7
s 80	31.7
ss 82–84	31.7
s 86	6.9
s 87(1)	20.6
(2)	20.6; 20.7
(3)	20.6
(4)	20.6; 20.7
ss 88, 89	50.16
s 102	8.2
s 107	54.2
s 113	9.3
s 117(2)	47.2
s 120	50.21
s 121	2.4
s 125	47.2
ss 126–129	53.5
s 131	23.32
s 132	25.20
s 134(5)–(7),(10)	41.17
s 135	40.5
s 138	11.6(iii)
s 139	17.2
(1)	17.7
s 144	24.10
s 148	46.2
s 152	40.6
s 153	54.13
Sch 6 para 3	50.26
Sch 7	50.3
Sch 8	41.1
para 2	41.2; 41.6; 41.8; 41.14
para 3	41.3
para 4	41.6
paras 5, 6	41.15
para 7	41.2
para 8	41.14
para 9	41.17
paras 11–15	41.3
para 16	41.3; 41.4
para 17	41.3; 41.16
para 18	3.3; 27.3
para 19	41.4; 41.7
para 20	25.21(*g*); 41.4
para 21	41.4; 41.7
para 22	41.4

Provision	Paragraph
1995 Finance Act	
Sch 8 para 23	41.2; 41.4
para 24	40.2; 41.2; 41.4
para 25	53.8
para 26, 27	41.8
para 28	41.15
paras 30–33	41.14
para 34	41.5
para 35–49	41.12
para 53	41.16
para 57	41.5
Sch 9	41.1; 41.12
para 1	41.16
Sch 10 para 1	28.3
paras 3, 4	28.4
Sch 14	62.1; 62.3
Sch 15	62.1; 62.4
Sch 16	62.1; 62.5
Sch 17 para 1	11.11; 16.7
para 4	11.11
para 7	11.9
para 11	16.7
para 20	4.4; 16.7
Sch 23	53.5
Sch 24 para 2	23.11
para 3	23.13
para 4	23.8
para 5, 6	23.29
para 7	23.31
paras 8–10	23.31; 39.1
para 11	23.31; 38.1
para 12	23.31; 29.33; 38.1; 38.3
Sch 25 paras 2–6	18.9
para 7	23.31
Sch 26	40.5
Sch 27 paras 1, 2	17.2
para 3	17.4; 17.7; 49.5
para 4	17.4; 17.5
para 5	17.4
paras 6, 7	17.4; 17.5
para 9	17.7
Sch 28	54.13
Sch 29 Pt VIII(5)	41.2; 41.4; 41.6; 41.14
Pt VIII(15)	47.2
Pt VIII(16)	50.12; 53.5
1996 Broadcasting Act	
Sch 7	9.54; 44.12
1996 Finance Act	
s 77	1.3(*a*)
s 78	1.3(*a*); 56.1; 56.2
s 80	25.1; 43.1; 43.2
(5)	44.21
s 81	25.1; 43.1; 43.2
s 82	25.1; 43.1; 43.3
s 83	21.7; 25.1; 43.1; 43.3
(2)	29.26; 38.1; 39.1
(3)	40.5; 43.11
(6), (7)	59.21(*a*)
s 84	25.1; 43.1; 43.5
(3)	43.11
s 85	25.1; 43.1; 43.6
s 86	25.1; 43.1; 43.7
s 87	25.1; 43.1; 43.5; 43.6; 43.9
s 88	25.1; 43.1; 43.5; 43.6
ss 89, 90	25.1; 43.1; 43.7
s 91	25.1; 43.1; 43.8
(6)	59.21(*b*)
ss 92, 93	23.8; 25.1; 25.5; 43.1; 43.9; 43.11
ss 94–98	25.1; 43.1; 43.9
s 99	25.1; 41.1; 43.1; 43.9
s 100	25.1; 43.1; 43.10
s 101	25.1; 43.1
(1)	43.10
(2), (4)	25.5
(6)	25.6
s 102	25.1; 43.1
s 103	25.1; 43.1
(2)	43.3
s 104	25.1; 43.1
s 105	25.1; 43.1
(1)	43.11
s 122(5)	26.3
(6)	13.13
s 124	54.2
s 128(4)	59.27
s 140	9.6
s 146	11.4
(2)	11.3
(4)	11.6
(5)	11.3; 11.6
s 154	53.8
s 160	60.4
s 161	62.3
s 163	41.1
s 164	41.2
ss 165, 166	41.4
s 167(1)	41.1
(2)	41.3
(3)	41.2
s 168	41.18
s 169	41.6
s 171(1)	28.4
(5), (6)	28.7
s 173(2), (3)	13.12
(4)	13.9

1996 Finance Act
s 173(5) 38.1
(6) 13.9; 13.12; 38.1
s 178 17.3; 17.7
(1) 17.2
ss 180, 181 46.3
s 203 9.54; 44.12
Sch 6 para 4 31.7
para 9 13.13
paras 10, 11 60.1
para 12 60.2
para 26 41.7
Sch 7 para 11 31.7
para 17 60.1
para 18 53.8
para 19 11.4
para 20 57.2
para 21 6.5; 24.2
para 22 24.6
para 26 31.3(*b*)
para 31 53.5
Sch 8 25.1; 43.1; 43.3
para 1 50.27
Sch 9 25.1; 43.1; 43.5; 43.9; 43.10
para 12 41.1; 43.9
Sch 10 25.1; 43.1; 43.9
para 4 41.17; 60.1
Sch 11 25.1; 41.1; 43.1; 43.9; 43.10
para 2 41.2
para 4 41.2; 41.7
Sch 12 25.1; 25.5; 43.1
Sch 13 25.1; 43.1
Sch 14 25.1; 43.1; 43.12
para 1 23.31; 39.1
para 5 50.2
para 6 23.31
para 7 53.4
para 8 40.2
para 9 40.2; 50.18
para 10 40.2; 50.9
para 11 20.8
para 12 27.3
para 13 29.2
paras 14, 15 50.2
para 16 50.3; 50.5
para 17 4.6; 31.4
para 18 31.3(*b*); 47.4
para 19 44.21
para 20 50.21; 59.28
para 21 29.31
para 22 23.31; 29.26
para 23 25.21(*g*); 41.4; 41.7
para 24 41.4
para 25 41.15
Sch 14 para 26 60.1
para 27 53.8
para 28 7.3(*a*)
para 29 6.6
para 30 32.2
para 31 45.3
para 32 46.3
paras 39, 40 40.5
paras 42, 43 21.7
para 44 21.11
para 46 21.2
para 48 23.31; 38.1
para 50 50.7
para 51 41.12
para 54 40.5
para 56 41.7
para 63 41.17
para 67 23.10
para 68 23.13
para 69 23.14
para 70 23.8
para 71 23.26
para 72 23.27
para 73 23.8
para 74 23.31
para 75 23.13; 25.10
para 76 25.17
para 77 25.21(*f*)
para 78 25.5
Sch 15 25.1; 43.1; 43.11
para 1 41.1
para 13 40.5
para 25 25.5
Sch 19 para 6 5.2; 12.3
Sch 20 para 12 13.18
para 26 44.9
para 27 44.14
para 28 30.3
para 29 30.6
para 33 53.3
para 38 21.9
para 39 9.9
para 46 9.13
para 47 9.13; 9.14; 9.15
para 57 9.51
para 58 9.47
paras 68, 69 23.20
para 70 23.15
para 71 25.13
Sch 21 para 3 59.35
para 12 9.6; 59.33
para 15 59.24
para 23 21.5
para 35 9.45

1996 Finance Act
Sch 21 para 42 59.4(*a*)
Sch 22 para 4 5.2; 12.3
para 6 5.3
para 10 5.3
Sch 23 26.11
paras 11, 12 31.4
Sch 24 para 10 1.3(*c*)
para 11 2.4
para 12 42.5
Sch 25 29.8
Sch 27 para 1 26.1
para 2 26.3
para 3 26.5; 26.6
para 4 26.8
para 6 60.1
Sch 28 paras 2, 3 53.8
para 4 41.14
para 5 41.12
Sch 29 para 4 31.3(*b*)
Sch 30 60.4
Sch 31 41.1
para 1 41.2
para 2 41.4; 41.7
paras 4–6 41.4
para 8 41.12
para 9 41.4
Sch 32 41.4
Sch 33 41.18
para 1 41.12
Sch 34 41.6; 41.12
Sch 36 para 1 18.9
para 2 18.11
para 3 18.9
para 4 18.11; 18.12; 18.14
Sch 37 6.2; 31.3(*b*)
para 1 6.1
para 2 11.9; 20.18
para 5 11.9
para 7 20.18
para 10 11.9
para 11 54.10; 54.11
Sch 38 para 1 53.9
para 6 7.4; 11.9; 13.6; 18.15; 20.7; 20.14; 27.8; 29.16; 31.3(*b*); 44.19
para 7 20.10; 60.4; 62.2
para 10 53.9
Sch 39 para 1 44.4
Sch 41 Pt V(3) 6.3; 9.11; 23.6; 23.29; 23.31; 25.21(*b*); 29.31; 31.3(*b*); 40.2; 41.14; 43.12; 50.2; 50.7; 50.16; 50.23
Sch 41 Pt V(19) 31.3(*b*)

1996 Housing Act
Sch 3 para 8 30.1; 30.6

1997 Finance Act
s 59 56.2
s 60 50.26
s 64 11.10; 11.11(*e*)
s 65 40.2
s 66 46.3
s 67 41.5
(4), (7) 41.2; 41.4
s 68 29.23
s 69 4.7
s 71 27.3
s 72 26.3
s 75 62.2; 62.3
s 80 41.3; 60.2
s 82 50.17
s 83 43.7
s 90 21.3
s 91 21.2
Sch 7 4.7
para 2 26.2
para 8 51.7
para 10 29.2
para 11 60.1
Sch 9 62.3
Sch 10 para 10 26.4
Sch 11 para 9 41.3
Sch 12 50.17
Sch 13 43.11
Sch 15 50.26
para 8 41.4
Sch 18 Pt VI(10) 43.9

1997 Finance (No 2) Act
s 18 1.3(*a*); 56.1
s 19 13.18; 21.3; 24.14; 27.2
s 20 27.3; 59.15
s 23 27.2; 41.1
s 24 51.7
s 25 4.7; 26.2; 62.3
s 29 60.2
s 30 3.3; 11.5; 13.18; 21.3; 24.14; 27.1; 27.2
s 34 41.1
s 35 11.5
s 36 26.1; 60.1
s 37 31.7
s 39 27.4(*c*); 44.6; 44.8; 44.10
s 40 43.3; 43.9; 43.11
s 46 8.4
Sch 3 27.2; 41.1; 41.6
para 1 41.2
para 2 41.3

1997 Finance (No 2) Act
Sch 3 paras 3, 4 41.4
paras 5, 6 41.6
para 7 41.6; 41.8
para 8 41.5
para 9 41.14
paras 10, 11 41.6
para 12 28.2
para 13 41.12
para 14 41.7
Sch 4 paras 2, 3 54.2
para 8 27.2
para 11 13.13
para 12 60.2
para 23 3.4
para 26 41.1
para 27 41.1; 41.4
para 28 41.1; 41.14
para 29 41.1; 41.12
para 30 41.1
Sch 5 11.5
Sch 6 26.1
para 1 56.1
para 2 40.2
para 6 41.4
para 7 41.18
para 8 60.1
para 9 20.22
paras 18, 19 41.7
para 21 4.7
para 22 26.3; 26.4; 26.5
para 23 26.1
Sch 7 29.19–29.22; 29.29
para 3 29.27
para 8 9.47
Sch 8 Pt II(4) 38.1
(8) 51.7
(9) 13.18; 21.3; 24.14; 27.2
(11) 26.1
(13) 31.7
(14) 29.18; 29.19; 29.22; 29.29

1998 Finance Act
s 28 1.3(*a*); 56.1; 56.2
s 29 1.3(*a*); 56.1; 56.2
s 31 3.1; 3.3
s 32 3.8
s 33 39.1
s 34 38.1
s 36 29.32
s 37 31.7; 41.6
s 39 50.27; 59.32
s 42 50.27
s 46(1)(2) 50.27
s 47 11.14
s 55(2)(3) 17.2
s 70 62.3
s 72 62.3
s 73 62.2; 62.3
s 77 41.1
s 80 44.19
s 82 21.7; 40.5; 43.3
s 87 41.12
s 90 28.2
s 91 41.6
s 101 9.6; 59.33
ss 103–105 21.11
s 107 21.5
s 108 4.4; 23.17; 43.5; 43.10
s 109 23.16; 23.17; 25.17
s 110 4.4; 23.17; 25.17
s 111 4.4
s 112 18.14
s 113 18.1
ss 114–116 48.4
ss 121–124 9.1
s 133 9.47; 9.49
s 134 9.6
s 135 9.19; 9.47; 9.50
s 136 9.18; 9.19
s 137 9.37–9.41; 41.17
s 138 9.32
s 139 9.47
s 163 9.1
Sch 3 para 2 49.1
para 3 39.6
para 4 39.1
para 5 49.2
para 6 13.12
para 7 56.1
para 8 3.1; 3.2; 20.18
para 9 40.2
para 10 44.16
para 11 3.3; 20.18; 27.1; 27.2; 27.3
para 12 3.6; 3.8
para 13 20.16(*d*); 29.8–29.13
para 14 3.3; 27.3
paras 15–17 3.10
para 18 3.2–3.4; 3.6
para 19 29.2–29.4
para 20 29.2
para 21 3.6; 48.8
para 23 3.12
para 24 13.9; 13.12
para 25 41.7
para 26 41.4
para 27 60.1

1998 Finance Act
Sch 3 para 28 20.22
para 29 46.4
paras 30, 31 46.3
para 35 21.7
para 37 21.9
para 38 38.1
para 39 3.3; 27.1
para 41 3.4; 39.6; 54.6
para 42 29.8
para 43 18.9
para 44 18.17
Sch 4 paras 1–3 38.1
para 4 39.1
para 5 38.1
para 6 42.5
para 7 43.10
Sch 5 para 1 50.27; 59.5
para 2 50.27
para 4 50.27
para 5 30.1; 50.27
paras 15–17 50.27
para 24 50.27
para 25 2.4; 50.2; 50.27
para 28 40.2; 44.22; 44.23; 50.27
para 29 29.18; 29.29; 50.27
para 30 46.3
para 31 40.5; 44.13; 50.27
para 32 44.13; 50.27
para 33 44.9
para 35 47.7
para 36 44.21
para 37 29.31
para 39 41.3; 50.27
para 40 41.4; 50.27
paras 41, 42 50.27
para 44 50.3
para 46 18.17
para 55 29.18
para 62 50.27
para 64 43.3; 50.27
paras 65–73 50.27
para 74 50.17; 50.27
para 75 29.18; 50.27
para 76 50.27
Sch 8 para 2 17.2; 17.7
paras 3–5 17.5
para 6 17.7
Sch 12 62.3
Sch 14 para 3 50.18
Sch 16 4.4
Sch 17 18.1; 59.8
para 1 18.1; 18.6; 18.7
para 2 18.9
para 3 18.11; 18.12
para 4 18.3; 18.6
para 5 18.4
para 6 18.7; 18.10
para 7 18.7
para 8 18.16
para 9 18.17
Sch 17 para 10 18.12
para 11 18.6
paras 12–15 18.18
paras 17–24 18.9
paras 26–28 18.12
paras 29–33 18.14
para 34 18.17
para 35 18.18
para 36 18.17
para 37 18.1
Sch 18 54.1; 55.1
para 1 55.1
para 2 49.1; 55.2; 59.6
para 3 17.5; 23.36
paras 4, 5 17.5
paras 7, 8 55.5
para 9 54.2; 55.4
para 10 50.25; 53.4; 54.2; 55.4
paras 11–13 55.5
para 14 55.5; 59.31(*a*)
para 16 55.5; 62.1
para 17 49.2; 55.5; 62.1
para 18 29.33; 49.2; 49.8; 55.5
para 19 49.2; 55.5
para 20 49.3; 55.7
para 21 49.5; 55.6
para 22 55.6
para 23 49.5; 55.6
paras 24–26 55.7
para 27 49.5; 55.7; 55.13
para 28 55.7; 55.13
para 29 49.5; 55.7; 55.13
paras 30–33 55.7
para 34 55.7; 55.9
para 35 55.7
paras 36, 37 9.46; 48.4; 55.10
paras 38–40 55.10
paras 41–47 5.1; 48.8; 55.8
para 48 5.1; 48.8; 55.8; 59.2(*e*)
para 49 5.1; 55.8
para 50 55.13
para 51 12.4; 55.13; 59.12
para 52 48.8; 55.13
para 53 48.8; 55.13; 59.22

1998 Finance Act
Sch 18 para 54 — 55.4
para 55 — 12.2; 55.4; 59
para 56 — 55.4
paras 57–59 — 12.3; 55.4
para 60 — 55.4; 55.11
paras 61–65 — 55.9
para 66 — 29.23; 55.4
para 67 — 29.23; 54.2; 55.4
paras 68, 69 — 29.23; 55.4
para 70 — 29.23; 29.27; 55.4
paras 71–77 — 29.23; 55.4
para 78 — 8.2; 55.4
para 79 — 8.2; 54.2; 55.4
paras 80–83 — 8.2; 55.4
paras 83A–83D — 50.25
para 83E — 50.25; 59.30
para 83F — 50.25
para 84 — 55.13
paras 85–87 — 55.7
para 88 — 55.13
para 89 — 49.3; 55.7
para 90 — 49.9; 55.7
para 91 — 50.12
paras 92–94 — 5.3; 55.12
Sch 19 para 1 — 49.1; 54.2; 59.6
para 2 — 54.2
para 12 — 5.1
para 13 — 48.8; 59.22
para 15 — 12.4; 59.12
para 18 — 50.12
para 19 — 29.18; 44.9
para 20 — 54.2
para 21 — 12.2; 59
para 28 — 48.3
para 29 — 48.1; 55.5
para 33 — 49.2
paras 34, 35 — 49.3
para 37 — 49.9
para 38 — 49.8
para 42 — 12.1; 12.3; 55.4; 55.11
para 43 — 54.13
para 44 — 26.6
para 45 — 26.9
para 47 — 13.12
para 48 — 30.3
para 49 — 30.6
para 50 — 29.8
para 51 — 41.6
Sch 24 — 9.37–9.41
Sch 27 Pt III(4) — 30.1; 46.3; 50.2; 50.17; 50.21; 59.5; 59.29
(13) — 62.2
(28) — 49.2; 53.4; 54.2

1998 Government of Wales Act
Sch 16 — 17.2; 30.5; 30.6

1998 Late Payment of Commercial Debts (Interest) Act — 31.3

1998 Wireless Telegraphy Act
s 3 — 50.29

1999 Finance Act
s 27 — 1.3(*a*)
s 28 — 56.4; 56.5
(1) — 13.18; 56.7
(3) — 60.1
(5) — 55.5
s 29 — 1.3(*a*); 56.4; 56.5
s 53 — 17.5
s 55 — 11.12
(2),(3) — 11.14
s 58 — 50.6
s 59(7),(9) — 43.9
s 61 — 40.2
s 63 — 50.31
s 67 — 43.11; 50.16
s 68 — 60.1
s 69 — 62.2; 62.3
s 70 — 62.4
s 74 — 9.14–9.16
s 76 — 9.1
s 81 — 41.1
ss 85–87 — 4.4
s 88 — 18.12
s 89(1) — 48.1
(2) — 29.33
(3) — 29.33; 48.1
s 90 — 38.1
s 92 — 29.23; 55.4
(5) — 39.1
(6) — 29.18
s 100 — 46.3
s 132 — 33.11
s 133 — 33.11; 54.13
Sch 4 paras 15, 18 — 30.1; 30.3
Sch 6 para 4 — 41.4; 41.5
Sch 9 para 2 — 9.14
para 3 — 9.15
para 4 — 9.16
para 5 — 9.14–9.16
Sch 11 para 1 — 29.18
para 3 — 29.33
para 9 — 5.3; 55.12

1999 Finance Act
Sch 20 Pt VII 33.11; 54.13
2000 Finance Act
s 35 1.3(*a*)
s 36 1.3(*a*); 56.1; 56.2
s 40 11.10
s 41 11.11
(5)(9) 11.9
s 43 11.13
(2) 50.3
s 46 11.6(i)
s 47 50.10
s 50 50.22
s 63(1)(4) 19.1
s 75(4) 41.12
s 77 8.4
s 81 46.3
s 82 50.30
s 86(1) 20.7
(2) 29.16
s 87 50.29
s 98 48.4
s 100(1) 29.20
(2) 29.29
(5) 29.20; 29.29
s 101 9.20
s 102 9.18
s 105(1) 23.35–23.37
(2), (3) 23.37
(4), (5) 23.33
s 106(1)–(5) 23.24
(6) 23.11
(7) 23.16
(8)–(11) 23.18
(12), (13) 23.24
(15) 23.31
(16) 23.17
(17) 23.11; 23.16; 23.18; 23.24
s 107 41.1; 41.4; 50.1
s 108 41.14
s 109 41.3
(8) 43.9
s 110 50.27
s 111(2) 31.3(*b*)
(3) 6.9
(4) 7.4
(6) 6.9; 7.4; 31.3(*b*)
s 112 31.3(*b*)
s 143 33.11; 54.13
s 145 54.10
(10), (11) 6.9
ss 146, 147 33.12
Sch 8 paras 105–114 50.10
Sch 15 para 1 19.1
paras 2, 3 19.2
paras 4–14 19.5
paras 15–24 19.6
paras 25–33 19.7
paras 34–38 19.8
para 39 19.3
paras 40–44 19.4
para 45 19.3
para 46 19.11
paras 47, 48 19.12
paras 49, 50 19.13
paras 51–53 19.12
para 54, 55 19.14
paras 56–58 19.15
para 59 19.16
paras 60–66 19.10
paras 67–69 19.20
para 70 19.20; 44.19
paras 71, 72 19.20
paras 73–79 19.21
para 80 19.22; 19.24
para 81 19.22
para 82 19.23
paras 83–87 19.24
paras 89–92 19.9
para 93 19.17
para 94 19.19
para 96 19.11; 19.23
para 97 19.20
para 99 19.5; 19.6; 19.13
para 101 19.5; 19.6
para 102(1) 19.5–19.8; 19.12
(3) 19.5; 19.6; 19.14
(4) 19.4; 19.6
(5) 19.13; 19.14
Sch 16 para 1 19.10
para 3 44.19
para 5 55.4; 55.5
Sch 18 para 1 62.4
para 2 62.5
para 3 62.4; 62.5
paras 4–8 62.3
Sch 19 para 1 50.25
para 6 29.16
Sch 20 50.25
paras 11, 14 59.30
Sch 21 para 1 38.1; 50.25
para 2 50.25; 55.4
para 3 55.13
para 4 50.25; 59.30
Sch 22 50.30
Sch 23 50.29

2000 Finance Act
Sch 27 para 1 29.14; 29.27
para 2 29.14; 29.15; 29.27
paras 3, 4 29.20
para 5 29.17
para 6 29.14; 29.15; 29.20; 29.27
paras 7 41.2
para 8 41.4(*a*)
para 10 18.9
para 11 29.23; 55.4
Sch 28 48.4
Sch 29 para 1 9.18
para 2 9.18; 9.19
para 3 9.21
para 4 9.47
para 5 9.6
para 6 41.16
para 7 9.24
para 8 9.38
para 9 9.46; 53.4; 59.4(*d*)
para 10 9.44
para 11 9.22
paras 12, 13 9.43(*a*)
para 15 53.7
para 17 9.14
para 18 9.12
para 23 9.7
para 24 9.51
para 25 9.52
para 28 9.47
para 29 29.49
para 30 41.16
para 31 7.6
para 35 53.9
Sch 29 para 38 9.45
para 41 23.17
para 43 23.29
para 44 43.5
para 45 43.11
para 46 9.18
Sch 30 41.1
paras 2, 3 21.2
para 4 21.2; 21.3; 21.11
para 5 21.2
para 6 21.5
para 7 21.7(iii)
para 8 21.3
para 9 21.6
paras 11, 12 21.3
para 13 21.6
para 14 21.2
para 15 21.3
paras 16–19 21.2; 41.14
para 20 21.5; 59.10
para 21 21.5; 21.6; 59.10
para 22 21.6
para 23 21.5; 59.10
para 24 21.2
para 25 21.3
para 28 21.3
para 29 21.6
Sch 31 para 2 18.2
para 3 18.4
para 4 18.2
paras 5–9 18.14
Sch 38 33.11; 54.13
Sch 40 Pt II(1) 20.16(*c*)
(12) 7.6; 9.13; 9.14; 9.43; 29.49
(17) 31.3(*b*); 60.1

STATUTORY INSTRUMENTS

Note. The bulk of statutory instruments mentioned in this book relate to double tax relief (to be found in Chapter 20) or interest on overpaid or unpaid tax (in Chapters 38, 39).

Others are as follows:

1946 No 36	**Bretton Woods Agreement Order in Council SR&O 1946**	24.6
1955 No 1954	**International Finance Corporation Order 1955**	24.6
1960 No 1383	**International Development Association Order 1960**	24.6
1970 No 488	**DTR (Taxes on Income) (General) Regulations 1970**	50.3
1974 No 1261	**United Nations and International Court of Justice (Immunities and Privileges) Order 1974**	24.6
1985 No 1773	**European Communities (Immunities and Privileges of the North Atlantic Salmon Conservation Organisation) Order 1985**	24.6
1986 No 482	**Income Tax (Building Societies) Regulations 1986**	7.1
1987 No 352	**Pension Scheme Surpluses (Administration) Regulations 1987**	24.14
1988 No 267	**Income Tax (Definition of Unit Trust Scheme) Regulations 1988**	11.8; 60.1
No 1153	**Building Societies (Transfer of Business) Regulations 1988**	7.6
1989 No 473	**Finance Act 1988 (Commencement) Order 1989**	33.3
No 1297	**Taxes (Interest Rate) Regulations 1989**	48.1
1990 No 1541	**Life Assurance (Apportionment of Receipts of Participating Funds) (Applicable Percentage) Order 1990**	41.3
No 1671	**Movements of Capital (Required Information) Regulations 1990**	4.3
No 2231	**Income Tax (Building Societies) (Dividends and Interest) Regulations 1990**	7.1; 7.4; 54.10
No 2232	**Income Tax (Deposit-takers) (Interest Payments) Regulations 1990**	6.9
No 2529	**Debt of Overseas Governments (Determination of Relevant Percentage) Regulations 1990**	6.3
No 2546	**Life Assurance (Apportionment of Receipts of Participating Funds) (Applicable Percentage) (Amendment) Order 1990**	41.3
1991 No 512	**Income Tax (Building Societies) (Annual Payments) Regulations 1991**	7.3(*a*)
No 702	**Building Societies (Designated Capital Resources) (Permanent Interest Bearing Shares) Order 1991**	7.7
No 1694	**International Organisations (Miscellaneous Exemptions) Order 1991**	24.6
No 2860	**FA 1990, s 46 (Appointed Day) Order 1991**	41.17
1992 No 10	**Income Tax (Building Societies) (Audit Powers) Regulations 1992**	7.4

1992 No 11	Income Tax (Building Societies) (Dividends and Interest) (Amendment) Regulations 1992	7.4
No 12	Income Tax (Deposit-takers) (Audit Powers) Regulations 1992	6.9
No 13	Income Tax (Deposit-takers) (Interest Payments) (Amendment) Regulations 1992	6.9
No 14	Income Tax (Deposit-takers) (Non-residents) Regulations 1992	6.9
No 15	Income Tax (Interest Payments) (Information Powers) Regulations 1992	6.9
No 571	Income Tax (Definition of Unit Trust Scheme) (Amendment) Regulations 1992	60.1
No 1746	FA 1991, s 49 (Appointed Day) Order 1992	41.6
No 1900	Charities Act 1992 (Commencement No 1 and Transitional Provisions) Order 1992	11.9
No 2326	Insurance Companies (Pension Business) (Transitional Provisions) Regulations 1992	41.6
No 2383	United Kingdom Ecolabelling Board Regulations 1992	24.17
No 2744	Income Tax (Insurance Companies) (Expenses of Management) Regulations 1992	41.2
No 2915	Income Tax (Building Societies) (Dividends and Interest) (Amendment No 2) Regulations 1992	7.4; 54.10
No 3066	Corporation Tax Acts (Provisions for Payment of Tax and Returns) (Appointed Days) Order 1992	54.1
No 3133	Income Tax (Definition of Unit Trust Scheme) (Amendment No 2) Regulations 1992	60.1
No 3218	Banking Coordination (Second Council Directive) Regulations 1992	6.1; 6.9
No 3234	Income Tax (Prescribed Deposit-takers) Order 1992	6.9
1993 No 743	Income Tax (Sub-Contractors in the Construction Industry) Regulations 1993	17; 59.7
No 744	Income Tax (Employments) Regulations 1993	59.25
No 1623	Debts of Overseas Governments (Determination of Relevant Percentage) (Amendment) Regulations 1993	6.3
No 3109	Insurance Companies (Pension Business) (Transitional Provisions) (Amendment) Regulations 1993	41.6
No 3112	Friendly Societies (Provisional Repayments for Exempt Business) Regulations 1993	28.2
1994 No 295	Income Tax (Deposit-takers) (Interest Payments) (Amendment) Regulations 1994	6.9
No 687	VAT (Sport, Physical Education and Fund-Raising Events) Order 1994	14.8
No 1479	Income Tax (Definition of Unit Trust Scheme) (Amendment) Regulations 1994	11.8; 60.1

1994 No 1811	Special Commissioners (Jurisdiction and Procedure) Regulations 1994	5.3; 33.3
No 1812	General Commissioners (Jurisdiction and Procedure) Regulations 1994	5.3; 33.3
No 1813	General and Special Commissioners (Amendment of Enactments) Regulations 1994	5.3; 33.3
No 2318	Income Tax (Authorised Unit Trusts) (Interest Distributions) Regulations 1994	60.1
No 3036	Insurance Companies (Pension Business) (Transitional Provisions) (Amendment) Regulations 1994	41.6
No 3224	FA 1993, s 165 (Appointed Day) Order 1994	23.32; 23.33
No 3225	FA 1994, Pt IV, Ch 2 (Appointed Day) Order 1994	25.5
No 3226	Exchange Gains and Losses (Transitional Provisions) Regulations 1994	23.32; 59.13
No 3227	Exchange Gains and Losses (Alternative Method of Calculation of Gain or Loss) Regulations 1994	23.15
No 3228	Exchange Gains and Losses (Deferral of Gains and Losses) Regulations 1994	23.18
No 3229	Exchange Gains and Losses (Excess Gains and Losses) Regulations 1994	23.23; 59.13(*b*)
No 3230	Local Currency Elections Regulations 1994	23.39; 23.40; 59.13(*g*)
No 3231	Exchange Gains and Losses (Insurance Companies) Regulations 1994	23.31
No 3232	Exchange Gains and Losses (Debts of Varying Amounts) Regulations 1994	23.17
No 3233	Currency Contracts and Options (Amendment of Enactments) Order 1994	23.9; 25.5; 25.21(*h*)
No 3278	Overseas Life Assurance Fund (Amendment) Order 1994	41.14
1995 No 408	Exchange Gains and Losses (Transitional Provisions) (Amendment) Regulations 1995	23.32
No 1211	Life Assurance (Apportionment of Receipts of Participating Funds) (Applicable Percentage) (Amendment) Order 1995	41.3
No 1370	Deposit-takers (Interest Payments) (Discretionary or Accumulation Trusts) Regulations 1995	6.9
No 1730	Insurance Companies (Taxation of Reinsurance Business) Regulations 1995	41.5; 41.8
No 1979	Venture Capital Trust Regulations 1995	62.1; 62.2
No 2934	Income Tax (Gilt-edged Securities) (Gross Payments of Interest) Regulations 1995	31.7
No 3134	Insurance Companies (Pension Business) (Transitional Provisions) (Amendment) Regulations 1995	41.6

1995 No 3223	Insurance Companies (Gilt-edged Securities) (Periodic Accounting for Tax on Interest) Regulations 1995	31.7
No 3224	Gilt-edged Securities (Periodic Accounting for Tax on Interest) Regulations 1995	31.7
No 3225	Lloyd's Underwriters (Gilt-edged Securities) (Periodic Accounting for Tax on Interest) Regulations 1995	31.7
No 3237	Insurance Companies (Overseas Life Assurance Business) (Compliance) Regulations 1995	41.14
No 3238	Insurance Companies (Overseas Life Assurance Business) (Tax Credit) Regulations 1995	41.14
1996 No 1	Insurance Companies (Pension Business) (Transitional Provisions) (Amendment) Regulations 1996	41.6
No 21	Friendly Societies (Gilt-edged Securities) (Periodic Accounting for Tax on Interest) Regulations 1996	31.7
No 673	Exchange Gains and Losses (Insurance Companies) (Amendment) Regulations 1996	23.33
No 1179	European Investment Bank (Designated International Organisation) Order 1996	6.1
No 1347	Exchange Gains and Losses (Alternative Method of Calculation of Gain or Loss) (Amendment) Regulations 1996	23.15
No 1348	Exchange Gains and Losses (Deferral of Gains and Losses) (Amendment) Regulations 1996	23.18
No 1349	Exchange Gains and Losses (Transitional Provisions) (Amendment) Regulations 1996	23.32
No 1485	Exchange Gains and Losses (Insurance Companies) (Amendment No 2) Regulations 1996	23.31
No 1583	Capital Gains Tax (Pensions Funds Pooling Schemes) Regulations 1996	60.2
No 1584	Stamp Duty and Stamp Duty Reserve Tax (Pension Funds Pooling Schemes) Regulations 1996	60.2
No 1585	Income Tax (Pension Funds Pooling Schemes) Regulations 1996	60.2
No 1621	Insurance Companies (Taxation of Reinsurance Business) (Amendment) Regulations 1996	41.5; 41.8
No 1779	Income Tax (Interest on Quoted Eurobonds) Regulations 1996	31.3(*b*)
No 2991	Insurance Companies (Reserves) (Tax) Regulations 1996	41.4
1997 No 212	Authorised Unit Trusts (Interest Distributions) (Qualifying Investments) Order 1997	60.1
No 213	Unit Trust Schemes and Offshore Funds (Non-qualifying Investments Test) Order 1997	43.9
No 471	Friendly Societies (Modification of the Corporation Tax Acts) (Amendment) Regulations 1997	28.7
No 472	Friendly Societies (Taxation of Transfers of Business) (Amendment) Regulations 1997	28.7

1997 No 473	Friendly Societies (Modification of the Corporation Tax Acts) Regulations 1997	28.7
No 481	Insurance Companies (Overseas Life Assurance Business) (Compliance) (Amendment) Regulations 1997	28.7
No 510	Value Added Tax (Finance) Order 1997	40.6
No 1154	Open-ended Investment Companies (Tax) Regulations 1997	40.6
No 1155	Exchange Gains and Losses (Insurance Companies) (Amendment) Regulations 1997	23.31
No 1156	Stamp Duty and Stamp Duty Reserve Tax (Open-ended Investment Companies) Regulations 1997	40.6
No 1715	Open-ended Investment Companies (Tax) (Amendment) Regulations 1997	40.6
No 1716	Personal Equity Plan (Amendment No 2) Regulations 1997	40.6
No 2856	Insurance Companies (Pension Business) (Transitional Provisions) (Amendment) Regulations 1997	41.6
No 2877	Friendly Societies (Modification of the Corporation Tax Acts) (Amendment No 2) Regulations 1997	28.7
1998 No 1200	Insurance Companies (Loan Relationships) (Election for Accruals Basis) Order 1998	43.9
No 1868	Gifts for Relief in Poor Countries (Designation) Order 1998	11.14
No 1871	Individual Savings Account (Insurance Companies) Regulations 1998	28.7; 41.1
No 2620	FA 1995, s 139(3) (Appointed Day) Order 1998	17.2; 17.4; 17.8
No 2622	Income Tax (Sub-contractors in the Construction Industry) (Amendment) Regulations 1998	17; 59.7
No 2920	Life Assurance (Apportionment of Receipts of Participating Funds) (Applicable Percentage) (Amendment) Order 1998	41.3
No 3081	Controlled Foreign Companies (Excluded Countries) Regulations 1998	18.11
No 3173	FA 1994, s 199 (Appointed Day) Order 1998	4.4; 5.3; 9.6; 12.3; 18.1; 41.6; 42.5; 43.10; 47.2; 48.1; 48.3; 48.8; 49.5; 50.12; 54.2; 55.1
No 3175	Corporation Tax (Instalment Payments) Regulations 1998	48.1; 55.5
No 3176	Taxes (Interest Rate) (Amendment No 2) Regulations 1998	48.1
No 3177	European Single Currency (Taxes) Regulations 1998	9.1; 18.9; 23.9; 23.18; 23.39; 25.5; 43.5; 50.11
1999 No 358	Corporation Tax (Treatment of Unrelieved Surplus Advance Corporation Tax) Regulations 1999	3.8; 55.5
No 498	Insurance Companies (Capital Redemption Business) (Modification of the Corporation Acts) Regulations 1999	41.18
No 619	FA 1998, s 37 (Appointed Day) Order 1999	31.7
No 622	Friendly Societies (Provisional Repayments for Exempt Business) Regulations 1999	28.2

1999 No 623	Insurance Companies (Gilt-edged Securities) (Periodic Accounting for Tax on Interest) Regulations 1999	31.7
No 624	Friendly Societies (Gilt-edged Securities) (Periodic Accounting for Tax on Interest) Regulations 1999	31.7
No 819	Venture Capital Trust (Amendment) Regulations 1999	62.1
No 825	Income Tax (Sub-contractors in the Construction Industry) (Amendment) Regulations 1999	17.7
No 1408	Non-resident Companies (General Insurance Business) Regulations 1999	18.18; 41.4
No 1467	Stamp Duty and Stamp Duty Reserve Tax (Open-ended Investment Companies) (Amendment) Regulations 1999	40.6
No 1643	Insurance Companies (Loan Relationships) (Election for Acccruals Basis) Order 1999	43.9
No 1928	Taxes (Interest Rate) (Amendment No 2) Regulations 1999	48.1
No 1929	Corporation Tax (Instalment Payments) (Amendment) Regulations 1999	48.1
No 1953	Capital Gains Tax (Definition of Permanent Interest Bearing Share) Regulations 1999	7.7
No 2156	FA 1995, s 139(3) (Appointed Day) Order 1999	17.4
No 2159	Income Tax (Sub-contractors in the Construction Industry) (Amendment No 2) Regulations 1999	17.2; 17.5; 17.7
No 2636	Friendly Societies (Modification of the Corporation Tax Acts) (Amendment) Regulations 1999	28.7
No 2975	Corporation Tax (Simplified Arrangements for Group Relief) Regulations 1999	29.23; 55.4
No 3261	Stamp Duty and Stamp Duty Reserve Tax (Open-ended Investment Companies) (Amendment No 2) Regulations 1999	40.6
2000 No 892	Corporation Tax (Instalment Payments) (Amendment) Regulations 2000	48.1
No 893	Taxes (Interest Rate) (Amendment) Regulations 2000	48.1
No 921	ICTA 1988, s 559(4A) Order 2000	17.2
No 922	FA 1995, s 139(3) (Appointed Day) Order 2000	17.2
No 1151	Income Tax (Sub-contractors in the Construction Industry) (Amendment) Regulations 2000	17.7

66 Index

This index is referenced to the chapter and paragraph number.
The entries printed in bold capitals are main subject headings in the text.
For the meaning of words and phrases, see under Definitions.

A

Account,
period of,
—variable date, to, 2.4
ACCOUNTING PERIODS, 2
administration order, effect on, 42.6
assessments by reference to, 2.1
capital allowances given by reference to, 8.2
capital gains in, 9.1
change in ownership of company, 3.10, 44.13
commencement of, 2.3, 3.10, 44.13
corresponding, 29.19
end of, 2.3(*b*), 2.4
group relief, 29.17, 29.19–29.22
inspector, determined by, 2.4
liquidation, effect of, 42.5, 42.6
long, apportionments, 2.4
profits of, 1.2
qualifying distributions not within, 3.4
rate of ACT, change of, in, 3.3
short, apportionment of relief limits, 56.2
subsequent, relief derived from, 3.8, 29.26, 44.6
variable dates, to, 2.4
Accounts,
submission of, negligent, 49.3, 49.4
Accrued income scheme, 43.11
Addresses, Inland Revenue, etc., 33.1
Adjudicator, 33.8
Board of Inland Revenue, 33.1
Business Tax Division, 29.35
Capital Gains Clearance Section, 9.6
Central Correspondence Unit, 51.6
Central Registry, 51.6
Charity Commissioners, 11.1
City 4 District Inspector, 6.2
Commissioners of Inland Revenue, 33.1
Finance Division, 36
Financial Intermediaries and Claims Office, 11.1
—International, 21.6
—Scotland, 11.1
Information Centre, 36
International Division, 4.3, 4.4, 20.6, 21.3, 21.10, 53.7
Internet site, 33.1
Library, 18.1
Oil Taxation Office, 4.4
Pension Schemes Office, Controller, 34
Revenue Adjudicator, 33.8
Treasury, 4.3
ADVANCE CORPORATION TAX, 3
abolition of, 3.1, 3.8
carried back, 3.6, 3.8, 29.10, 29.11
carried forward, 3.8, 3.10, 29.11
change in ownership of company, 3.10
company purchasing own shares, 51.2
corporation tax, set against, 3.6, 3.8, 29.11
distributions to non-residents, 21.9
double tax relief, 21.7, 21.9
excessive, recovery of, 3.6
foreign income dividends, 26.4, 26.9, 26.11
—repayment or set off, 26.6
franked investment income set against, 3.3, 3.4, 27.2
—'shadow' ACT, 3.8(*e*)
groups of companies,
—distributions within, 29.2
—'shadow' ACT, 3.8(*j*)
—surrendered within, 3.10, 20.16(*d*), 29.8, 29.10, 29.11, 29.13
interest on, 3.6, 39.6
liability to, 1.1, 3.1
life insurance companies, on, 41.2
—interest on ACT overpaid, 41.4
mainstream corporation tax, set against, 3.6, 3.8
oil companies, 46.3, 46.4
overdue, interest on, 39.6
overpaid, interest on, 38.3, 41.4
partnerships, 44.16
payment of, 3.4
preference dividends, on, 3.12
qualifying distributions, on, 3.4, 20.18
rate of, 1.3(*d*), 3.2, 27.1
—change in, 1.3(*d*), 3.2, 3.3, 3.6
—wrong, payment at, 3.3

66 Index

Advance Corporation Tax
repayment of,
—interest on, 38.1, 38.3, 41.4
return periods, 3.4, 39.6
returns of, 3.4, 54.6
self-assessment, 29.8
set-off of, 1.1, 3.6, 29.11, 46.3
—excessive, 3.6
—maximum, 3.6
'shadow', 3.1, 3.8
surplus, 3.1, 3.6, 3.8, 26.6, 29.11
—carried back, 3.8, 29.10, 29.11
—carried forward, 3.8, 3.10, 29.10, 29.11
—change in ownership of company, 3.10
surrender of, 3.8, 3.10, 20.16(*d*), 29.8, 29.10, 29.11, 29.13
tax credit, 1.1, 3.3
—franked investment income, part of, 27.1
—life assurance companies, non-resident, 41.12
—repayment of, 27.2, 27.3
—warrant, stated in, 20.18, 49.11
time limits, 3.4, 3.8, 59.1
ultra vires dividends, 3.1
unpaid, interest on, 39.6
Advance pricing agreements, 4.4
Advances, *see* Loans
Agent,
abroad, trading through, 21.2, 21.3
charges on income related to, 50.3
commission deducted by, 31.3(*c*)
fraud by, 49.4
independent, 53.5
insurance company, for, 21.2, 21.3, 41.11, 41.12
negligence of, 49.4
paying, 31.3(*c*)
refusal to be sworn, right of, 49.7
return by, 49.4, 54.11
tax charged on, 35.B13
termination of agency, compensation for, 15.4
trade carried on through, 1.2, 6.2, 6.3, 6.5, 9.7, 21.11, 29.14, 29.15, 29.20, 41.6, 41.11, 41.12, 53.4
UK representative, 53.5
Agriculture,
agricultural buildings,
—maintenance etc. of, 35.B5
agricultural societies, exemption, 24.1
co-operatives, 32.4
horticultural societies, exemption, 24.1
insurance, 35.B5
land,
—maintenance etc. of, 35.B5
losses, 44.14
marketing boards, 57.1
uncommercial, 35.B5
Alternative investment market (AIM), 44.19, 51.3, 62.3
Amalgamations,
building societies, of, 7.3(*c*)
capital allowances on, 44.10
capital gains, on, 9.6
corporate venturing scheme, 19.23
friendly societies, of, 28.4, 28.5, 28.7
group of companies, 9.18, 9.47
industrial and provident societies, of, 32.3
losses on, 44.10
shares issued in connection with, 9.6, 60.4
Amnesties, 33.4
Annual payments,
Atomic Energy Authority, to, 57.2
chargeable payments treated as, 29.50
charges on income, 50.3
charities, to, 11.4, 11.10, 11.11
covenant, under, 11.11, 20.16(*c*)
income tax on, 31.3(*a*), 31.6
National Radiological Protection Board, to, 57.2
Annuities,
charges on income, 50.3
charities, paid to, 11.4
friendly societies, insured by, 28.3
income tax on, 31.3(*a*), 31.6
life insurance company, paid by, 41.4, 41.5, 41.6, 45.4
superannuation funds, paid by, 24.14
ANTI-AVOIDANCE, 4
amalgamations, on, 9.6
annuities, 41.5
capital allowances, 8.3
change in ownership of company, 3.10, 40.5, 44.13, 48.4
charges between related companies, 4.6
company migration, 4.3
company purchase schemes, 48.4
company purchasing own shares, 4.7
Courts' attitude to schemes, 4.1
date of receipt of charges, 4.6
dealers,
—commodity futures, in, 44.18
—land, in, 4.5
—shares, in, 4.2, 4.5
demergers, 29.36, 29.50
depreciatory transactions, 9.51, 9.52
dividend stripping, 4.2

Anti-Avoidance
dividends, special, 4.7, 29.2
double tax relief, 21.3
dual resident investing companies, 29.31
extra-statutory concessions, 9.1, 33.4, 35
financial instruments, 25.15–25.18
general principles, 4.1
groups of companies, 29.9, 29.23, 29.31, 29.36, 29.50, 40.5, 50.3
instalment payments, 48.1
interest, payment of, 4.6, 50.3
life insurance company annuities, 41.5
non-resident, becoming, 4.3
oil companies, 46.5
overvalue, transactions at, 4.4
own share purchase, 4.7
payment of tax,
—instalment, 48.1
—third party, recovery from, 48.4
reconstructions, on, 9.6
related companies, payments between, 4.6
rent factoring, 50.26
schemes, 4.1
shares,
—dealers in, 4.2, 4.5
—depreciatory transactions, 9.51, 9.52
—issued by non-resident, 4.3
—transferred to non-resident, 4.3
special dividends, 4.7
trading transactions not at market price, 4.4
transfer pricing, 4.4
value-shifting, 9.13–9.16

Appeals, 5
accounting period, determination of, 2.4
agreement, settled by, 5.3
assessments, against, 5.2, 5.3, 5.4, 33.3
claims, on, 12.3
Commissioners, hearing by, 5.3
construction industry tax scheme, 17.7
courts, to, 49.8
interest pending, 39.3
management expenses, in connection with, 40.2
payment of tax pending, 48.3
penalties, against, 49.8
Revenue determinations, against, 4.4, 5.3, 18.6, 18.17, 23.17, 25.17
self-assessment, 5.2, 5.3, 12.3, 55.12
settlement of, 5.3
time limits, 12.3, 48.3, 59.2
total profits, against, 5.4
transfer pricing, 4.4

Apportionments, 13.8

Assessments, 5, *see also* Self-assessment
accounting period, based on, 2.1
appeal against, 5.2, 5.3, 5.4, 33.3
change in ownership of a company, on, 44.13
charities' capital gains, on, 11.7
close company loans, on, 13.12
discovery, 55.8
double, 55.13
error or mistake relief, 12.4
foreign profits, on, 39.7, 53.3
group relief,
—excessive, to recoup, 29.25
income tax, to, 31.4
inspectors, made by, 33.3
liquidations, in, 42.5
notices of, 5.1
partnerships, on, 47.2
self, 55
total profits, on, 5.4

Associated companies,
defined, 4.4, 9.15, 9.47, 13.11, 44.19, 50.16, 56.7
distribution to, ACT, 46.4
groups of companies, leaving, 9.47
interest payable between, 50.16
loan creditors, controlled by, 56.7
loans to, 13.11
non-trading, 56.7
payments to, 4.5
rights against, 4.5
small companies, of, 56.7
value-shifting, 9.13–9.16

Associates, 13.5, 13.9
attribution of rights etc. of, 13.2, 13.4, 13.6
banks, of, interest payable to, 50.16
directors, of, 13.4(iii), 13.6(ii)
participators, of, 20.20
—loans to, 13.9
patents sold to, 35.B17
transfer pricing, 4.4

Atomic Energy Authority, 9.54, 44.12, 57.2

B

BANKS, 6
associates of, interest payable to, 50.16
business of, definition, 6.2
central, non-resident, 6.5, 24.2
compulsory liquidation of, 6.1
country-risk debts, 6.3

Banks
deduction of tax by, 6.9
Deposit Protection Fund, payments to, 6.8
double tax relief, 21.11, 44.25
exchange profits or losses, 6.1
exemptions for, 6.5, 24.2
franked investment income of, 27.3
interest,
—charities, paid to, 11.4
—paid by, 6.2, 6.6, 6.9, 11.4, 31.3(*b*), 50.2, 54.10
—paid to, 6.1, 6.2, 21.11, 31.3(*b*), 50.2, 50.3
—payable to associates of, 50.16
international loans, 6.3
loan creditors, as, 13.3, 29.16
National Savings Bank, return by, 54.10
non-resident, 6.2, 6.4, 6.5, 44.25, 53.8
—loans to, security for, 4.3
—parent, loans by, 6.2
ordinary course of business of,
—loans made in, 4.3, 6.2, 13.3, 29.16, 54.10
returns by, 54.10
savings, 6.6, 40.1
Beneficial ownership, 29.15
Bills of exchange, discounts on, 50.9
Board of Inland Revenue, 33.1
amnesty, powers of, 33.4
appeals to, 4.4
care and management, powers of, 33.4
claims to, 11.2, 12.1, 12.4
clearance by, 9.6, 9.8, 9.9, 18.11, 29.57, 41.16, 51.6
concessions, 33.4, 35
direction by, 4.4
explanatory pamphlets issued by, 34
information,
—disclosure of, by, 30.4
—power to require, 4.4
interest remitted by, 39.3
investment trusts approved by, 60.4
pamphlets published by, 34
penalties,
—proceedings for, by, 49.8
—reduction or mitigation of, by, 49.9
press releases, 36
special arrangements with, 7.1
statements of practice, 37
stock exchange, recognition of, by, 13.6
tax, power not to collect, 33.4, 39.8, 53.3
Taxpayers' Charter, 33.6
Bona fide commercial reasons,
amalgamations, reconstructions, etc., for, 9.6, 9.47
chargeable payments made for, 29.51(*d*)
long-term business, transfer of, 41.16
trade, transfer of, 9.7, 9.8
value-shifting, 9.14
venture capital trust holdings, 62.3
Branch or agency,
abroad, trading through, 21.2, 21.3
charges on income relating to, 50.3
insurance company, of, 21.2, 21.3, 41.6, 41.11, 41.12
trade carried on through, 1.2, 6.2, 6.3, 6.5, 9.7, 21.11, 29.14, 29.15, 29.20, 41.6, 41.11, 41.12, 53.4
transfer of, 9.8, 9.9, 9.21
UK representative, 53.5
British Airports Authority, 9.54, 44.12
British Airways, 9.54, 44.12
British Gas Corporation, 9.54, 44.12, 46.2
British Museum, 11.10, 11.11, 24.3
British National Oil Corporation, 46.2
British Steel, 9.54, 44.12
British Telecom, 9.54, 44.12
Buildings,
agricultural
—maintenance of, 35.B5
charity,
—owned by, 11.3
—used by, 11.4
fire safety, expenditure on, 35.B16
maintenance and repair of, 11.4, 35.B4, 34.B5
BUILDING SOCIETIES, 7
agencies, 15.4
amalgamation of, 7.3(*c*)
change of status, 7.6
close companies, not, 13.6(*c*)
company, becoming, 7.6
deduction of tax by, 7.3(*a*), 7.4
defined, 7.2
dividends paid by, 7.4, 20.16(*g*)
franked investment income, exclusions, 3.3(*b*), 27.1(ii)
gross payments by, 7.4
interest,
—paid by, 3.3(*b*), 7.3(*a*), 7.4, 20.16(*g*), 27.1(ii), 32.5, 50.1, 54.10
—paid to, 31.3(*b*)
liability of, 7.3
loan relationships, 7.3(*a*)
losses on shares in, 44.19
marketable securities, 7.3(*a*), 7.4, 7.7, 43.2

Building Societies
mergers, 7.3(*c*)
payment of tax by, 7.3
permanent interest bearing shares, 7.3(*a*)(*b*), 7.4, 7.7, 43.2, 43.10
special arrangements with Revenue, 7.1
transfer of business to company, 7.6

C

CAPITAL ALLOWANCES, 8
accounting periods, by reference to, 8.2
amalgamation, on, 44.10
anti-avoidance, 8.3
balancing charges on cessation of trade, 35.B19
building society change of status, on, 7.6
carried back, 8.2
carried forward, 8.2
cessation of trade, balancing charges on, 35.B19
change in ownership of company, on, 44.13
chargeable periods, 8.2
charitable gifts, 11.14
claims, 8.2, 55.4
'connected person' transactions, 8.3, 8.4
'control' and 'main benefit' transactions, 8.3
controlled foreign companies, 18.9(x)
deduction of, 8.2
disclaimer of, 8.2
dual resident investing companies, 8.3, 29.31
franked investment income, set against, 8.2, 27.3
gifts, charitable, 11.12, 11.14
group relief, 29.18
—relationship to, 29.26
harbour reorganisation schemes, 57.3
industrial buildings allowance, 8.2, 35.B3, 34.B19, 34.B20
insurance companies, 8.2, 41.2, 41.4, 41.14, 41.16
investment companies, 8.2, 40.2
—change of ownership, on, 40.5
lessor companies, 8.2
life assurance companies, 8.2, 41.2, 41.4, 41.14, 41.16
loss relief due to, 8.2, 44.6, 44.8, 44.10
—restriction of, 9.43(*a*)
machinery and plant,
—'connected persons' transactions, 8.4
—gifts of, 11.12, 11.14
—renewals basis, change from, 35.B1
'main benefit' and 'control' transactions, 8.3
motor cars, on, 61.2, 61.3
non-residents, 8.3, 53.4
non-trading activities, 8.2
oil companies, 46.3
partnerships, 44.16, 47.2
patents, on, 35.B17
production sharing contracts, 46.3
reconstructions, on, 44.10
regional development grants, effect on, 52
renewals basis, change from, 35.B1
returns of, 8.2, 54.1, 54.2
Schedule A, 50.26, 50.27
self-assessment, 8.2, 55.4
set-off of, 8.2, 59.3(*a*)
time limits, 59.3
trading expenses, treated as, 8.2
transfer of UK trade, 9.8
value-added tax, impact of, 61.1–61.3
writing-down, 8.2, 8.4
written-down value, election for, 8.3
Capital distributions, 20.2
groups of companies, 9.19, 29.49
recovery of tax from recipient, 9.5
CAPITAL GAINS, 9
accounting period, in, 9.1
acquisitions and disposals in short period, 9.12
amalgamations, on, 9.6, 9.18
asset valuations, 55.3
assets held at 6 April 1965, 9.43, 9.47
assets held at 31 March 1982, 9.43, 9.45
British Airports Authority, 9.54
British Airways, 9.54
British Gas Corporation, 9.54
British Telecom, 9.54
building society change of status, on, 7.6
building society shares, 7.7
business, transfer of, 9.6
capital distributions, on, 9.5, 9.19
capitalised interest, 9.10
charge to corporation tax, 1.3(*b*), 9.2
charges on income set against, 13.9(*e*)
charities, of, 11.7
clearances, 9.6, 9.8, 9.9
close companies' transfers at undervalue, 9.17
company migration, on, 53.6, 53.7
compensation, receipt of, 9.19, 15.7
connected persons, 16.8

Capital Gains
—recovery of tax from, 9.5
conversion of securities, 9.6
corporate venturing scheme, 19.18–19.21
corporation tax on, 1.3(*b*), 9.2
deferment of tax on, 9.7–9.9
depreciatory transactions, 9.51, 9.52
disposal, acquisition and, in short period, 9.12
disposal outside group, 9.20, 9.43
dual resident companies, 9.19, 9.21, 9.44, 9.53
EEC Directives, 9.8, 9.9
Euro, use of, 9.1
exchange of joint interests, 35.D26
exchange of securities, 9.6
extra-statutory concessions, 9.1
government securities, 9.6, 9.11, 43
groups of companies, 9.18 *et seq.*
—acquisitions by, 9.43
—assets held at 6 April 1965, 9.43, 9.47, 9.51
—assets held at 31 March 1982, 9.35, 9.43–9.45, 9.51
—assets transferred within, 9.19–9.43, 9.49–9.52
—associated company leaving, 9.47
—cessation of membership of, 9.47, 59.4(*d*)
—demergers, 29.49
—depreciatory transactions in, 9.51, 9.52
—disposals outside group, 9.20, 9.43
—indexation allowance, 9.55
—pre-entry gains, 9.37–9.41
—pre-entry losses, 9.23–9.36
—rollover relief, 9.44
—transfer of branch or agency, 9.21
harbour reorganisation schemes, 57.3
housing associations, 30.5
indexation allowance, 9.55
industrial and provident societies, 32.3
interest, capitalised, 9.10
investment clubs, of, 14.5
investment trust, 60.4
—acquisitions from, 9.43
—business transferred to, 9.6
—company becoming, 9.6, 9.48
—disposals to, 9.19, 9.43
know-how, 59.4(*e*)
land, compulsory acquisition of, 9.44
life insurance companies, of, 41.9–41.11, 41.14, 41.15, 41.16
liquidation, on, 9.4, 9.6, 42.3, 42.5
losses, 9.3, 9.23–9.43, 14.5, 44.2
management expenses set against, 40.2
migration of company, on, 53.6, 53.7
nationalisation, on, 9.6
negligible value, assets of, 9.51, 59.4(*c*)
non-resident companies, 9.2, 53.3
—assets transferred to, 9.7–9.9
overseas, 39.7
permanent interest bearing shares, 7.7
pre-entry gains, losses set against, 9.37–9.41
—assets acquired at different times, 9.41
—insurance companies, 9.37
—pooled assets, 9.40
pre-entry losses, restrictions on set-off, 9.23–9.36
—appropriations to stock in trade, 9.33
—change of company's nature, 9.31
—companies changing groups, 9.35
—continuity provisions, 9.34
—gains from which deductible, 9.30
—pooled assets, disposals of, 9.26
—pre-entry assets, definition, 9.24
—'relevant group', identification of, 9.32
privatisation, 9.54
rate of tax on, 1.3(*b*), 9.2
re-basing, 9.43, 9.45
reconstructions, on, 9.6
recovery of tax from third parties, 9.5, 9.6, 9.46, 9.47, 48.4
reduction of, for tax purposes, 1.3(*b*)
replacement of business assets, 35.D22–34.D25
residence, cessation of, on, 53.6, 53.7
returns of, 54.1–54.3
rollover relief, 9.44, 59.4(*g*)
Schedule A business, 50.27
shares,
—acquisition and disposal in short period, 9.12
—dealers in, 9.6, 9.11, 9.52
—depreciatory transactions, 9.51, 9.52
—group members, in, 9.47, 9.51
—value-shifting, 9.13–9.16
short-term losses, 9.3
single currency, use of, 9.1
stock, appropriations to and from, 9.11, 9.22, 9.33
time limits, 59.4
trade, transfer of,
—non-UK, 9.9
—UK, 9.8
trading losses set against, 9.3
transfer of trade, 9.8, 9.9
undervalue, transfers at, 9.17

Capital Gains
unit trusts, 60.1, 60.3
—business transferred to, 9.6
unremittable, 39.7
valuations, 55.3
value at 6.4.65, 9.43(*a*)
—election for, 59.4(*a*)
value at 31.3.82
—election for, 9.22, 9.43(*b*), 9.45, 59.4(*b*)
value-shifting, 9.13–9.16
venture capital trust, 62.2, 62.5
—business transferred to, 9.6
—company becoming, 9.6, 9.49
Capital gains tax,
principles applied to corporation tax, 9.1
Caravan sites, 35.B29
Certificates of deposit, 35.B13
banks, issued by, 6.9
building society, issued by, 7.4
paperless, 6.9, 7.4
Certificate of tax deducted, 11.11, 20.18
CERTIFICATES OF TAX DEPOSIT, 10
Cessation of trade, 2.4(*c*)
balancing charges on, 35.B19
demergers, 29.36(4)
franked investment income, effect on, 27.3
mutual companies, 45.2
partnerships, 47.5
post-cessation receipts, 59.27
terminal losses, 44.8, 44.10
Change in ownership of company,
ACT, effect on, 3.10
investment companies, 40.5
losses, 44.13
payment of tax, 48.4
Chargeable gains, *see* Capital Gains
Charges on income,
allowance for, 50.3
annuities as, 41.6, 50.3
carried forward, 40.2, 44.4
covenants for charity as, 11.11, 50.3
date of receipt, 4.6
defined, 50.3
donations to charity as, 11.10
double tax relief, 21.7
franked investment income, set against, 27.3
group relief, 29.18(*d*), 59.19(*a*)
—payment for, not, 29.24
groups of companies,
—paid within, 29.2
income tax on, 29.2
interest as, 50.3
interest charged to capital, 50.5
investment company, paid by, 40.2
—change of ownership, on, 40.5
partnerships, 47.2
related companies, between, 4.6
returns of, 54.1, 54.2
trading expenses, treated as, 44.4
CHARITIES, 11
assessment of, 11.7
assets donated to, 11.12–11.14, 50.6
British Museum, 11.10, 11.11, 24.3
buildings,
—owned by, 11.3
—used for, 11.4
capital gains of, 11.7
ceasing to be, 11.7
charitable purposes, defined, 11.1
claims by, 11.2, 11.11
Commissioners, jurisdiction of, 11.1
covenants for, 11.11, 20.16(*c*), 50.3
defined, 11.1
discounts to, exempt, 11.4
donations to, 11.10–11.14, 50.6
educational, overseas, 11.14
employee seconded to, 50.7
employee trusts not, 11.1
exemptions for, 11.2 *et seq.*
—denial of, 11.9
financial instruments, 25.21(*b*)
Gift Aid, 11.10
gifts to, 11.10–11.14, 50.6
Historic Buildings and Monuments Commission for England, 11.10, 11.11
income of, exempt, 11.2 *et seq.*
inspection of records of, 11.2
interest paid to, 11.4, 20.6
land,
—owned by, 11.3
lotteries, 11.6(iii)
medical, overseas, 11.14
National Heritage Memorial Fund, 11.10, 11.11, 24.10
non-qualifying expenditure, 11.9
overseas, 11.1
payroll giving, administrative costs of, 35.B32
poverty relief, 11.14
property ceasing to be subject to, 11.7
public benefit, for, 11.1
qualifying donations, 11.10
records of, 11.2
recreation, for, 11.1
registration of, 11.1
repayment of income tax to, 11.11

Charities
restrictions on relief, 11.9
Schedule F, 11.4, 11.5
scientific research associations treated as, 24.12
shares and securities, gifts of, 11.13
small trade exemption, 11.6(i)
temporary loss of charitable status, 11.1
trading, 11.6
trading stock, donation of, 11.12, 11.14, 50.6
underwriting commissions, 11.6(iv)
unit trust schemes, 11.8
Charity Commissioners, 11.1
CLAIMS, 12
ACT, for, 54.6
appeals, 12.3
Board, to, 11.2, 12.1, 12.4
capital allowances, 8.2, 55.4
capital losses, 9.3
charities, by, 11.2, 11.11
corporate venturing scheme, 19.4
error or mistake, 12.1, 12.4
false statements in, 49.12
foreign income dividends,
—ACT repayment or set off, 26.6
fraud in connection with, 49.3, 49.4
group relief, 29.23, 55.4
housing associations by, 30.1, 30.3, 30.4
inspector, to, 12.1
negligence in connection with, 49.3, 49.4
negligible value, for, 59.4(*c*)
pension funds, by, 12.3
repayment of tax, for, 11.11, 13.12
research and development tax credits, 50.25
residence, relating to, 12.3
returns, in, 54.1–54.6
self-assessment, 12.1, 55.4, 55.9, 55.11
self-build societies, by, 30.6
set-offs, 35.B13
small companies rate, 56.1
supplementary, 12.1
time limits, 11.2, 12.2, 12.4, 13.12, 30.3, 59
Clearance, by Revenue, 9.6, 9.8, 9.9, 18.11, 19.9, 29.57, 41.16, 51.6
advance rulings, 33.5
CLOSE COMPANIES, 13
apportionments, 13.8
assets transferred at undervalue, 9.17
associated company, *see also* Associated companies, 13.5, 13.11
associates, 13.5, 13.9
—attribution of rights of, 13.2, 13.4, 13.6
—benefits to, 20.20
benefits, 13.15
building societies not, 13.6(*c*)
close investment-holding company, 13.18
company controlled by, 13.10(*d*)(*e*)
connected persons, as, 16.4–16.6, 16.7, 16.9
control, 13.2
—Crown, by, 13.6(*d*)
—non-close company, by, 13.6(*e*)(*f*)
debt,
—assigned to, 13.10(*b*)
—due to, 13.10(*a*)
defined, 13.1
demergers, 29.51
director, 13.4
—associates of, 13.4(iii), 13.6(ii)
—companies controlled by, 13.6(iii)
—full-time working, 13.11
—loans to, 13.11
—public, not, 13.6(i)
distributions by, 13.3, 20.10, 20.11, 20.16(*h*)(*j*), 20.19
—benefits, 13.15
—interest, 13.15
donations to charity, 11.11
employee trusts, payments to, 20.16(*j*)
groups of, demergers, 29.51
income of, 13.6
interest on unpaid tax, 39.1, 39.3
interest paid by, 13.15
industrial and provident societies not, 13.6(*b*)
investment-holding companies, 13.18
listed companies, 13.6(*g*)
loan creditors of, 13.1, 13.3, 13.6(*f*)
loan relationships, 43.5
loans to participators, 13.9–13.14, 39.1, 39.3, 55.5, 59.21
—procedure, 13.12
—written off or released, 13.13
material interest in, 13.11
misappropriations from, 13.10
non-resident companies not, 13.6(*a*)
—loans to, 13.9
non-residents, controlled by, 13.6(*e*)(*f*)
participators, 13.3, 13.9
—benefits to, 13.15, 20.20, 39.1, 39.3
—debts due by or to, 13.10
—loans and advances to, 13.9–13.14, 39.1, 39.3, 55.5, 59.21
—recovery of tax due from, 13.8
payment of tax by, 13.12

Close Companies
pensions from, 20.20
principal member, 13.6
quoted companies, 13.6(*g*)
—companies controlled by, 13.6(iv)
reciprocal arrangements, 20.20
recovery of tax from, 13.8
repayment,
—share capital, of, 20.10
—tax, of, 13.12
settlement, connected with, 16.2, 16.7
undervalue, assets transferred at, 9.17
unquoted, 29.51
Close investment-holding company, 13.18
CLUBS AND SOCIETIES, 14
agricultural, 24.1
credit unions, 45.3
dissolution of, 14.7
football pool run by, 14.6
holiday clubs, 14.4
investment clubs, 14.5
loan societies, 14.3
lotteries run by, 14.6
members' sports clubs, 14.8
money societies, 14.3
mutual trading, 14.2
sporting clubs, 14.8
supporters' clubs, 14.6
thrift funds, 14.4
transfer fees, 50.31
Codes of practice, 33.6
Collective investment schemes, 60
loan relationships, 43.9
Collectors of Taxes, 33.2
ACT, excess, reclaimed from, 3.3
certificates of tax deposit from, 10.1
demand by, 39.7
—unauthorised, 38.5
group income, notification of, to, 29.2
returns to, 31.4, 54.1
Commissioners, 33.3
General, appeals to, 5.3, 12.3, 13.20, 33.3(*a*)
penalty proceedings before, 49.8
precepts by, 49.7
Special, appeals to, 4.4, 5.3, 9.6, 11.5, 12.3, 12.4, 18.16, 18.18, 29.57, 33.3(*b*), 40.2, 41.16, 41.17, 44.10, 53.3, 53.7, 54.13
Commodity futures,
losses on, 44.18
Company,
building society becoming, 7.6
change in ownership,
—ACT, effect on, 3.10
—investment, 40.5
—losses, 44.13
—payment of tax, 48.4
close, *see* Close companies
connected person, 16.4–16.7, 16.9
defined, 1.2, 9.18, 16.7, 60.4
demergers, 29.35 *et seq.*
dual resident, 9.53, 29.31
friendly society becoming, 28.2
groups, *see* Groups of companies
holding companies, 3.10, 18.11, 18.14, 29.3, 29.27, 29.37, 29.40, 29.48, 29.54, 44.19, 51.3, 56.7, 62.3
incorporation in UK, 53.1
international headquarters, 26.8, 26.9
investment, 40
investment trust, becoming, 9.6, 9.48
liquidation, 42
migration, 41.13, 53.6, 53.7
officer of, recovery of tax from, 48.5
purchase of own shares, 4.7, 51
relevant, 29.46
reorganisations, 9.6, 9.16, 19.22, 44.10
residence, 53.1, 53.2
tax return, 55.3
trading companies,
—change in ownership, 3.10, 9.31, 44.13
—charitable donations by, 11.10, 50.6
—consortium, owned by, 29.27
—demergers, 29.47
—gifts by, 11.10, 50.6
—group income elections, 29.3
—interest paid by, 50.3
—investment companies, becoming, 3.10(iii)
—losses of, 44
trading companies
—royalties paid to, 35.B8
—stock relief, 58
—unremittable receipts, 6.3
unlisted,
—demergers, in, 29.36(2), 29.44, 29.51
—investment in, 62.3
—losses on investments in, 44.19
—purchase of own shares, 51.3
—repayment of capital, 20.10
venture capital trust, becoming, 9.6, 9.49
Company purchasing own shares, *see* Purchase by a company of its own shares
Company tax return, 55.3

COMPENSATION, DAMAGES ETC., 15
agencies, termination of, for, 15.4
animals, slaughter of, for, 35.B11
capital assets, relating to, 9.19, 15.7
capital expenditure, 15.8(*b*)
capital gains, 9.19
compulsory acquisition, for, 15.2
contracts, variation etc. of, for, 15.3
date of payment, 15.8(*d*)
deductible, 15.8(*a*)
ex gratia payments, 15.5
groups, within, 9.19
income, assessable as, 15.6
interest, for, 15.2
leases, short, on, 35.D1
payment of, 15.8
profits, loss of, for, 15.2, 15.3
removal expenses, for, 15.2
statutory, 15.2, 15.6
trading agreements, cancellation etc. of, 15.3
trading stock, loss on, for, 15.2, 15.6
Competent authority, 21.3
Compulsory acquisition,
compensation for, 15.2
Computations, *see* Profit Computations
CONNECTED PERSONS, 16
capital allowances, and, 8.3, 8.4
capital gains, for, 16.8
companies, 16.4–16.7, 16.9, 29.53, 29.57
definitions, 16.7
individuals, 16.1
loan relationships, 43.5
partners, 16.3, 44.16
recovery of tax from, 9.5
transfer pricing, 4.4
trustees, 16.2
Consortia, 29.3, 29.27, 29.29
research and development expenditure, 50.25
shares owned by, 59.4(*g*)
CONSTRUCTION INDUSTRY TAX SCHEME, 17
administration, 17.7
construction operations, 17.2
contractor, 17.2
deduction of tax, 17.2, 17.7
old scheme, 17.8
penalties, 17.7, 49.5
registration cards, 17.3
sub-contractor, 17.2
sub-contractor's tax certificate, 17.4
—misuse of, 17.7, 49.5
—renewal of, 17.6
transitional arrangements, 17.1
turnover threshold, 17.5
Contract,
cancellation of, compensation for, 15.3
variation of, compensation for, 15.3
CONTROLLED FOREIGN COMPANIES, 18
acceptable distribution policy, 18.12, 21.6
accounting periods, 18.7
accounts, currency used in, 18.9
appeals, 18.16, 18.17
assessments in respect of, 18.17, 55.5
available profits, 18.12
basis of charge, 18.7
capital allowances, 18.9(x)
chargeable gains on shares in, 18.18
chargeable profits, 18.9
clearances, 18.1, 18.11
creditable tax, 18.10
companies chargeable in respect of, 18.6
control, 18.2
currency used by, 18.9
'designer rate' regimes, 18.4
dividends paid by, 18.17
—acceptable distribution policy, 18.12, 21.6
double tax relief, 21.6
euro, use of, 18.9
exceptions from charge, 18.11
exchange gains and losses, 18.9(xii), 23.15(B), 23.31
exempt activities, 18.14
foreign currency accounts, 18.9
guidance notes, 18.1
information regarding, 18.18
lower level of taxation, 18.4, 18.5
motive test, 18.11
notices, 18.16
public quotation, 18.15
residence of, 18.3
self-assessment, 18.1, 18.3, 18.6, 18.7, 18.9(xiii), 18.11(v), 18.12, 18.17, 18.18, 55.5
transfer pricing, 18.9(xiii)
Co-operatives, 32.4
interest paid by, 20.16(*e*)
Copyright royalties,
charges on income, as, 50.2
double tax relief, 35.B8
income tax on, 31.3(*a*)(*c*), 50.2
non-resident, paid to, 31.3(*c*)
CORPORATE VENTURING SCHEME, 19
advance clearance, 19.9

Corporate Venturing Scheme
allowable losses, 19.19–19.21
amalgamations, 19.23
chargeable gains, 19.19–19.21
claims, 19.4
clearance, 19.9
company reorganisations, 19.22–19.24
deferral relief, 19.21
disposals, 19.11
identification, 19.17
information requirements, 19.10
investment relief, 19.2
—reduction or withdrawal, 19.10–19.16
loss relief, 19.20, 44.19
options, 19.16
qualifying investing company, 19.5
qualifying issuing company, 19.6
qualifying trade, 19.7
value received, 19.12–19.15
withdrawal of relief, 19.10–19.16
Court common investment funds, 60.1, 60.2
Court of Session,
penalty proceedings before, 49.8
Covenants,
certificate of tax deducted, 11.11(*b*)
charges on income, 11.11, 50.3
charities, for, 11.11, 20.16(*c*), 50.3
small amounts, for, 11.11
Credit unions, 45.3
Crown, The,
companies controlled by, 13.6(*d*)
debts due to, 42.5
exemption for, 24.5
statements prejudicing, 49.12
Crown option, 55.13
Currency,
exchange gains and losses, 6.1, 21.6, 23
financial instruments, 25
hedging, 25
swap fees, 50.28

D

Dealers in securities,
anti-avoidance legislation, 4.2, 4.5
company purchasing own shares, 51.7
depreciatory transactions, 9.52
double tax relief, 44.25
exchange of securities by, 9.6, 59.33
franked investment income of, 27.3
groups of companies, members of, 29.2
non-resident, 53.8
shares held by, 4.2, 9.6, 9.11, 9.52, 20.9, 29.2, 29.3, 29.9, 29.15, 29.27, 29.40, 44.10, 50.3
stock, appropriations to and from, 9.11
trade, not carrying on, 29.42
Debt, 43
assignment of, 13.10(*b*)
assumption of, 29.52
bad, 43.5, 43.11, 61.2
close company, due to, 13.10(*a*)
composition, 42.2
contracts, 25.5
Crown, due to, 42.5
disposal of, 9.19, 13.10(*b*), 20.3
international, 6.3, 43.11
liquidation, in, 42.5
ordinary course of business, incurred in, 13.10(*a*)
overseas government, etc., of, 6.3, 43.11
repayment of, 9.19
sovereign, 6.3, 43.11
trade, 13.10(*a*)
voluntary arrangements, 42.2
Deep discount securities, 35.B13, 43.11, 50.7, 50.23
Deep gain securities, 43.11
Definitions,
acceptable distribution policy, 18.12
—exempt period, 18.9
accounting period, 2, 29.17
—corresponding, 29.19
—final, 3.8
accrual period, 23.8
acquisition expenses, 41.2
acquisitions, 9.12
actual amount of interest, 43.11
actual provision, 4.4
adjusted amount, 9.39
adjusted closing value, 43.11
adjusted issue price, 43.11
advantaged person, 4.4
affected persons, 4.4
alternative company turnover threshold, 17.5
alternative partnership turnover threshold, 17.5
amounts in issue, 40.5
annuity business, 41.1
—general, 41.6
annuity fund, 41.6
appropriate certificate, 9.9
appropriate part of surrendered amount, 29.11
appropriate person, 6.9

Definitions
appropriate proportion, 9.7, 9.14, 44.13, 53.6
arrangements, 29.23
—relevant, 29.23
asset, 41.15
—enhanced value, of, 9.14
asset-holding company, 9.14
assets available for distribution in winding-up, 29.17
associated companies, 4.4, 9.15, 9.47, 11.10, 13.11, 44.19, 50.16, 56.7
associates, 4.4, 13.5, 51.4, 62.3
authorised unit trusts, 60.1
available profits, 18.12
available shares, 9.12
avoidance scheme, 21.3
bank, 6.1
base amount, 50.23
base date, 41.15
base day, 50.23
basic life assurance business, 41.2
basic profits, 56.1
basic profits and losses, 23.39, 22.40
basic valuation, 23.8
body of persons, 8.3
building society, 7.2
capital redemption business, 41.18
carrying on a trade, 44.2
change in ownership of a company, 44.13
chargeable asset, 9.19
chargeable company, 9.14
chargeable payment, 29.51
chargeable periods, 8.2
chargeable profits, 9.14, 18.9
chargeable shares, 9.12
charges on income, 50.3
charitable purposes, 11.1
charity, 11.1, 11.10
close company, 13.1
close investment-holding company, 13.18
company, 1.2, 9.18, 16.7, 59.4
—concerned in exempt distribution, 29.53
—large, 48.1
connected persons, 16
connected with, 51.4
connection, 43.6
consortium, 29.3, 29.27
construction operations, 17.2
contractor, 17.2
contribution, 47.7
control, 4.3, 4.4, 9.47, 13.2, 18.2, 48.4, 51.4, 56.7
controlled foreign company, 18.2
controlling director, 9.46
controlling interest, 62.3
co-operative associations, 32.4
corresponding accounting period, 25.16, 29.19
corresponding UK tax, 18.4
creditable tax, 18.10
currency contract, 23.9, 25.5
currency option, 25.5
dealing company, 4.2
debt contract, 25.5
debt option, 25.5
deep discount security, 50.7
deep gain, 43.5, 50.23
deficit period, 43.3
depreciatory transactions, 9.51
deposit-taker, 6.9
designer rate tax provisions, 18.4
director, 13.4, 13.11
disadvantaged person, 4.4
disposal, 41.15
disposal group, 9.14
distributable,
—foreign profit, 26.5
—profits, 9.14
distributing company, 29.37
distributions, 20.1
—non-qualifying, 20.18
—qualifying, 20.18
dual resident company, 9.53
dual resident investing company, 29.31
effective 51% subsidiary, 9.18, 20.6
eligible income, 60.1
eligible profit, 26.5
eligible rental income, 60.4
eligible shares, 62.2
eligible trading company, 44.19
entry time, 9.40
equity holder, 29.16
equity note, 20.7
Eurobond, 31.3(*b*)
excepted pre-sale distribution, 4.7
excess overdue interest, 40.5
exchange difference, 23.8, 23.9
exchange gain, 23.11
exchange loss, 23.11
exchange profit, 23.14
excluded activities, 19.7
excluded company, 44.19
excluded dividend, 18.12
excluded period, 18.12
exempt activities, 18.14, 23.21
exempt circumstances, 23.15, 43.6

Definitions
exempt distributions, 29.36
exempt trading company, 18.14
exempted debt, 50.16
filing date, 55.3
final accounting period, 3.8
finance agreement, 50.26
financial trading stock, 7.6
financial year, 1.2
first relevant accounting period, 18.9
first relevant amount, 56.4
fixed-rate preference shares, 29.16
foreign held company, 26.8
foreign life assurance funds, 41.14
foreign source profit, 26.5
franked investment income, 1.1, 3.3, 27.1
—unrelieved, 41.7
—surplus, 3.3, 27.3
franked payments, 3.3, 27.2
friendly society, 28.4
full-time working director, 13.11
funds, 4.3
gain period, 9.39
general annuity business, 41.6
general client account deposit, 6.9
Great Britain, 53.9
group annuity contract, 41.5
group company, 19.5
group income, 29.2
groups of companies, 9.18, 9.51, 29.43, 51.4
—head of, 9.18
—members of, 29.15
holding, 60.4
—addition to, 60.4
holding company, 3.10, 18.14, 29.3, 29.27, 29.48
—superior, 18.14
housing investment profits, 60.4
in respect of, 20.15
incidental costs, 50.19
income element, 50.7
income period, 50.7, 50.23
incoming company, 9.45
independent agent, 53.5
independent individual, 19.6
individual, 13.10(*c*)
individual turnover threshold, 17.5
initial exchange gain, 23.8–23.10
initial exchange loss, 23.8–23.10
insignificant purposes, 62.3(*b*)
insurance company, 4.3, 41.1
interest
—actual amount of, 43.11
—manufactured, 43.9
—notional amount of, 43.11
—real, 43.9
interest rate contract, 25.5
interest rate option, 25.5
international headquarters company, 26.8
investment company, 3.10, 40.1
investment trust, 60.4
large company, 48.1
life assurance business
—overseas, 41.14
life or endowment business, 28.4
—tax-exempt, 28.3
life reinsurance business, 41.8
limited partner, 47.7
linked currency option, 25.8
loan creditor, 13.3, 29.16
loan relationship, 43.2
—linked, 43.9
local authority association, 43.1
local currency, 23.24
local currency equivalent, 23.8
local currency of a trade, 23.18
long term assets, 41.15
long term capital assets and liabilities, 23.18
loss period, 43.5
lower level of taxation, 18.4
lower rate income, 41.7
lower relevant maximum amount, 56.2
major change in ownership, 4.7
major change in the nature or conduct of a trade, 3.10, 9.31, 44.13
major participant, 4.4
majority assessable interest, 18.3
management expenses, 40.2, 41.2
manufactured interest, 43.9
matched foreign distributable profit, 26.6
matched foreign income dividend, 26.6
matched foreign source profit, 26.6
material date, 38.1, 38.3
material interest, 13.11
material time, 9.25
member, 29.38
member of a group, 29.15
—trading, 13.9
money debt, 43.2
multiple company turnover threshold, 17.5
multiple partnership turnover threshold, 17.5
net chargeable profits, 18.12
new annuities, 41.5
new consideration, 20.12, 44.19

Definitions
—not derived from ordinary shares, 20.10
nominal currency, 23.8
non-financial trade, 19.5
non-qualifying expenditure, 11.9
non-taxable sums, 11.9
non-trading exchange gain, 23.13
non-trading exchange loss, 23.13
normal commercial loan, 23.8, 29.16
notional amount of interest, 43.11
notional closing value, 43.11
notional foreign source ACT, 26.6
notional pre-entry loss, 9.40
option arrangements, 29.23
ordinary course of business, 6.2
ordinary share capital, 9.18, 19.5, 29.3, 29.16, 29.27, 29.41, 44.10
ordinary shares, 20.10, 29.16
outgoing company, 9.45
overlapping period, 29.20
overseas life assurance business, 41.14
overseas life insurance company, 41.12, 53.4
ownership, 44.10
parent company, 44.10
—trading group, of, 62.3(*b*)
participator, 13.3, 13.9, 20.20, 43.6
pension business, 41.6
period of restriction, 19.12
permitted period, 43.11
policy, 28.4
—term of, 28.4
policy holders' share, 41.7
post-entry securities, 9.40
postponed gain, 53.6
potential advantage, 4.4
potential participant, 4.4
potential tax liability, 48.4
pre-entry asset, 9.24
pre-entry gain, 9.39
pre-entry loss, 9.24
pre-entry securities, 9.40
preference shares, 20.10
—fixed-rate, 29.16
principal company, 9.18, 53.6
principal member, 13.6, 18.15
profits, 1.2, 3.6, 50.1, 56.1
—available for distribution, 29.17, 51.4
prohibited company, 19.21
proper officer, 48.5
proposed (rate of tax), 42.5
public, the, 13.6
public quotation, 18.15
qualification period, 19.2
qualifying asset, 23.8
qualifying certificate of deposit, 7.4
qualifying circumstances, 23.8
qualifying company, 9.8, 9.9, 23.6, 25.4, 50.16, 50.30
qualifying contract, 25.5
qualifying convertible security, 50.23
qualifying debt, 23.8, 50.16
qualifying deposit right, 6.9, 7.4
qualifying dividend, 18.14
qualifying donation, 11.10
qualifying exempt activity income, 18.14
qualifying expenditure, 11.9
qualifying foreign income dividend, 26.6
qualifying holding, 62.3
qualifying investing company, 19.5
qualifying investment, 11.9, 60.1
qualifying issuing company, 19.6
qualifying liability, 23.8
qualifying loan stock, 50.19
qualifying loans, 11.9, 50.19
qualifying losses, 9.39
qualifying payment, 19.13, 25.6
qualifying period, 17.4
qualifying policy, 28.4
qualifying provision for redemption, 50.23
qualifying receipt, 19.14
qualifying research and development expenditure, 50.25
qualifying share, 7.7
qualifying ships, 50.30
qualifying subsidiary, 19.6, 62.3
qualifying third party, 50.16
qualifying trade, 19.7, 62.3
qualifying trading company, 44.19
real interest, 43.9
reckonable date, 39.3
recognised clearing system, 31.3
recognised stock exchange, 13.6
redemption period, 50.23
related companies, 4.6, 19.5, 21.3
related person, 18.7
related transaction, 4.4, 43.5
relative, 13.5(i), 16.7, 44.10
relevant accounting period, 18.12, 25.17, 25.18
relevant ACT, 26.6
relevant amount, 48.1, 55.5
relevant amount of tax, 26.5
relevant assets, 7.6, 9.13, 43.11, 44.10, 53.6
relevant benefits, 41.6

Definitions
relevant company, 9.37, 29.46
relevant connection, 20.6
relevant deposit, 6.9
relevant discounted security, 43.5, 43.9
relevant entry time, 9.40
relevant event, 9.24, 43.11
relevant expenditure, 50.25
relevant fraction, 29.20
relevant franked investment income, 41.6
relevant income and gains, 11.9
relevant intangible asset, 62.3
relevant interest, 18.7
relevant interest in an offshore fund, 41.17, 43.9
relevant liabilities, 43.11, 44.10
relevant loan interest, 6.2
relevant loan stock, 44.10
relevant part, 4.7
relevant payment, 17.5, 25.5
relevant period, 23.25, 26.5, 26.6, 41.17, 43.5, 43.9, 48.4, 50.16, 50.25
relevant person, 17.5
relevant preference shares, 19.5
relevant profits, 18.12, 41.7
relevant proportion, 25.17
relevant qualifying asset, 43.11
relevant qualifying subsidiary, 62.3
relevant redemption period, 50.23
relevant reduction, 4.2
relevant shares, 19.2
relevant trade, 19.8
relevant transaction, 4.7, 25.15, 25.17
relief derived from subsequent accounting period, 29.26
relievable amount, 23.14
repayment of share capital, 20.11
repayment supplement, 38.3
repo or stock lending arrangements, 43.5
research and development, 50.25
residence, 18.3, 53
return period, 3.4, 31.4, 39.6, 54.6
ring fence trade, 4.4
second relevant amount, 56.5
securities, 9.51, 20.14
—connected with shares, 20.7
settlement, 16.7
—body corporate connected with, 16.7
—currency, 23.8
settlor, 16.7
shareholders' share, 41.7
shares, 20.13, 29.39, 60.4
—ordinary, 20.10, 29.16
—preference, 20.10, 29.16
significant increase, 40.5
single company, 19.5
small companies rate, 56.1
small or medium-sized enterprise, 50.25
specified matters, 4.7
specified period, 44.6
starting rate, 56.4
steep-reduction annuity, 41.5
sub-contractor, 17.2
subsidiary,
—50%, 21.2
—51%, 9.18, 20.3, 26.5, 29.3, 29.9, 51.3
—75%, 9.18, 20.7, 29.3, 29.15, 29.40, 44.13, 51.4
—90%, 29.3, 29.27
—100%, 26.8
substantially reduced, 51.4
superior holding company, 18.14
surplus ACT, 3.6
surrenderable loss, 50.25
surrendering company, 29.8
tax credit fraction, 3.3, 27.1
tax-free benefit, 9.13
tax losses, 44.21
tax month, 38.3
time limit for claims, 29.23, 55.4
trade, 29.42
trader company, 62.3(*c*)
trading activities, 29.42
trading company, 3.10, 29.3, 29.27, 29.31, 29.47, 44.19
trading group, 44.19
—member of, 29.47
trading income, 44.4
transaction, 4.4
translation time, 23.8
unapplied non-qualifying expenditure, 11.9
unallowable purpose, 43.5
unit trust scheme, 60.1
United Kingdom, 53.9
UK grouping, 20.6
UK public revenue dividends, 31.3(*b*)
UK representative, 53.5
unquoted company, 29.44, 44.19
unrealised exchange gains and losses, 23.18
unrelieved foreign tax, 21.5
upper relevant maximum amount, 56.2
venture capital trust, 62.2
voting power, 13.6
wife, 13.5, 13.11
yield to redemption, 50.23
Demergers, 29.35–29.58

Depreciatory transactions, 9.51, 9.52
Design royalties,
non-residents, paid to, 31.3(*c*)
Directors, 13.4
close company, of, 13.4
—associates of, 13.4(iii), 13.6(ii)
—companies controlled by, 13.6(iii)
—full-time working, 13.11
—loans to, 13.11
—public, not, 13.6(i)
fees of, 35.A37
full-time working, 13.11
knowledge imputed to, 4.3
loans to, interest on, 50.15
non-resident, appointed by, 35.A37
proceedings against, 4.3
remuneration of, 50.8, 59.9
qualifying shares, transfer of, 4.3
Discount, 43
bill of exchange, on, 50.9
deep, securities, 50.7
house, interest paid to, 50.3
securities issued at, 20.14
Discovery, 55.8
DISTRIBUTIONS, 20
ACT on, 3, 20.18
—'shadow', 3.8
anti-avoidance, 4.7
assets, transfer of, 20.3, 20.9
'associated companies', to, 46.4
benefits, 13.15
bonus issues, 20.4, 20.10, 20.18
bonuses, 20.16(*f*)
building society change of status, on, 7.6
capital, 9.5, 9.19, 20.2, 29.49
capitalised, 20.4
cash equivalent, 20.20
chargeable payments as, 29.50
charges on income, not, 50.3
charities, to, 11.4, 11.5, 20.6
close companies, by, 13.3, 13.10, 20.10, 20.11, 20.16(*h*)(*j*), 20.19
—associates, benefits to, 20.20
—directors, benefits to, 20.20
clubs, by, 14.3
company purchasing own shares, 4.7, 51.2
covenants for charity not, 11.11, 20.16(*c*)
dissolution, on, 20.16(*a*)
dividends, 20.2
—building societies, paid by, 7.4, 20.16(*g*)
—groups of companies, within, 29.2, 29.3, 29.8, 29.11
—industrial and provident societies, paid by, 20.16(*f*)
—mutual companies, paid by, 20.16(*f*)
—non-resident, paid by, 21.2, 21.3, 35.C1
—non-resident, paid to, 21.9, 53.4
—preference, 3.12
—stock, 20.16(*h*), 54.9, 59.31(*c*)
equity loans, 20.7
equity notes, 20.7
exempt, 29.36
franked investment income, 1.1, 3.3, 3.4, 27.1
franked payments, 3.3, 27.2
friendly societies, by, 20.23, 28.6
gilts and bonds, 43.5
group relief, payment for, 20.16(*d*), 29.24
information required with, 20.18
interest, 13.15, 20.5–20.7, 20.16(*e*)(*g*)(*i*), 32.2
liquidation, on, 14.7, 20.16(*a*)
—assets available for, 29.17
loan relationships, 43.5
mutual companies, by, 20.22
National Radiological Protection Board, to, 57.2
new consideration given for, 20.10, 20.12
non-qualifying,
—returns of, 20.18, 54.8, 59.31(*b*)
non-resident companies, 20.7, 21.2, 21.9, 41.12, 53.4
non-trading companies, by, 20.22
oil companies, by, 46.3, 46.4
profits available for, 29.17
profits, not, 50.1
public revenue dividends, 31.3(*b*)
qualifying, 20.12, 20.18
—life insurance companies, to, 41.12
—reciprocal arrangements, 20.15, 20.20
redeemable share capital, in respect of, 20.11
returns of, 20.18, 54.6–54.8
securities, in respect of, 20.5–20.7, 20.14, 20.16(*i*)
'shadow' ACT, 3.8
share capital, repayment of, 20.3, 20.4, 20.10, 20.12
shares, in respect of, 4.2, 20.3–20.7
societies, by, 14.3
special dividends, 4.7
stock dividends, 20.10, 54.9, 59.31(*c*)
tax credit restrictions, 21.3, 24.14, 27.2, 28.2, 41.1, 41.6, 41.12, 60.2
tax treatment, 20.17
terminal payments, 20.16, 20.20
trading income, treated as, 44.4

Distributions
ultra vires, 3.1
value-shifting, 9.13, 9.14
Dividend stripping, 4.2
Dividend warrants etc., 20.18
omissions from, 49.11
Dividends, *see* Distributions and Foreign Income Dividends
Documents, production of, 49.8
DOUBLE TAX RELIEF, 21
admissible taxes, 21.2
ACT, 21.7, 21.9
agreement, by, 21.3
agreements in force, 21.10
air transport, shipping and, on, 21.10
anti-avoidance, 21.3
arbitration convention, 4.4
banks, 44.25
carry back or forward, 21.5, 21.6
charges on income, allocation of, 21.7
competent authority, 21.3
credit, by way of, 21.5
currency realignment, 21.6
dealers in securities, accruing to, 44.25
discretionary trusts, payments out of, 35.B18
distributable profits, by reference to, 21.6
dividends, 21.3
—non-residents, paid to, 21.9
—onshore pooling, 21.6
double relief prevention, 21.2
dual residence, 53.1
EEC convention, 4.4
foreign entities, 21.2, 21.3
foreign income dividends, 26.5
information exchanges, 33.12
insurance companies, accruing to, 21.2(*c*), 21.3, 41.12, 44.25
interest, 21.3
—non-residents, paid to, 21.9
—overpaid tax, on, 38.3
know-how payments, on, 35.B8
loan relationships, 21.2, 21.7
losses, effect of, 44.25
management expenses, allocation of, 21.7
measure of, 21.6
mixer companies, 21.3, 21.6
non-resident banks, 44.25
non-residents,
—dividends, 21.9
—interest, 21.9
oil companies, 21.12
onshore pooling, 21.6
permanent establishment, 21.3
pooling, 21.6
portfolio shareholders, for, 21.3
provisional treaty relief, 21.9
rates of, 21.6
related companies, for, 21.3
royalties, on, 21.3, 35.B8
shipping and air transport, on, 21.10
spared tax, 21.2
special relationships, 21.3
tax credits, 21.3
time limits, 21.5, 59.10
transfer of non-UK trade, 9.9
trusts, discretionary, 35.B18
underlying tax, 21.3, 21.6
—avoidance, 21.3, 21.6
—calculating relief for, 21.6
—chain of shareholdings, on, 21.3, 21.6
—rates of, 21.6
unilateral, 21.2
unitary taxation, 21.9
unrelieved tax, 21.6
utilisation of relief, 21.5, 21.6
Dual resident companies, 9.53, 53.1
'investing', 8.3, 9.19, 9.21, 9.44, 29.31, 44.10

E

Elections,
continuation of trade, for, 47.5, 59.23
foreign income dividends, 26.2, 26.5
franked investment income, to exclude, 41.6
group dividends etc., in respect of, 29.2, 29.4, 29.5, 29.6, 29.7
—before 6 April 1973, 29.5
—companies, eligible, 29.3
—failure to make, 29.6
—form of, 29.7
—invalid, 29.4
—joint, 29.7
—revocation of, 29.2
herd basis, for, 59.17
know-how, in respect of, 59.4(*e*)
land to be treated as one estate, for, 59.29, 59.32
long term assets, in respect of, 41.15
nationalisation, on, 9.6, 59.4(*g*), 59.33
partnerships,
—continuation of, for, 47.5, 59.23
patents, disposal of, on, 59.24
qualifying contracts, 25.5
re-basing, 9.43, 9.45

Elections
rents, in respect of, 59.29
rollover relief on nationalisation, for, 9.6, 59.4(*g*)
Schedule D, Case VI, for, 59.5
self-assessment, 55.4, 55.9, 55.11
share dealers, by, 9.6, 59.33
value at 6 April 1965, for, 9.47, 59.4(*a*)
written-down value, for, 8.3
Electronic communications, 33.11, 54.13
Electronic lodgement of returns, 54.13
Employee share schemes, 40.2, 50.10, 50.22
Employee trusts,
charities, not, 11.1
close company, payments to, 20.16(*j*)
costs, 40.2
disposals to, 9.17
interests in, 13.5(iv)
public, not, 13.6(v)
share ownership, 50.10, 59.11
Employers' associations, 24.15
Enquiries, Revenue, 55.7
Enterprise zones, 8.2(iv), 35.B31
Entertaining expenses,
management expenses, as, 40.2
VAT on, 61.2, 61.3
Equity loans, 20.7
Equity notes, 20.7
Error or mistake relief, 12.4, 55.13
ESOPs, 40.2, 50.10
Euro,
conversion to, 23.9, 23.18, 25.5, 43.5, 50.11
use of, 9.1, 18.9, 23.39, 25.5
Eurobonds, 7.4, 31.3(*b*), 35.B13, 50.3, 53.8
EUROPEAN COMMUNITY LEGISLATION, 22
arbitration convention, 4.4
double taxation, 4.4, 9.9
mergers directive, 9.8, 9.9
movements of capital, 4.3(iv)
transfer pricing, 4.4
transfers of trades, 9.8, 9.9
European Economic Interest Groupings, 50.12
Evidence,
admissible, 49.9
request for, non-compliance, 49.7
Exchange controls, 39.7, 53.3
EXCHANGE GAINS AND LOSSES, 23
accrual of gains and losses, 23.7–23.10
—accrual on currency contracts, 23.9
—accrual on debts, 23.10
—accrual on qualifying assets and liabilities, 23.8
alternative method of calculation, 23.15
arm's length test, loss relief restriction, 23.17
chargeable gains, 23.29
commencement and transitional provisions, 23.32
controlled foreign companies, 18.9(xii), 23.15(B), 23.31
currency contracts, 23.7, 23.9, 23.15, 23.21, 23.22, 25.12
currency provisions, 23.33–23.41
early termination of currency contract, 23.21
entitlement to an asset, 23.26
euro,
—conversion to, 23.9, 23.18
—use of, 23.39
excess gains or losses, 23.23
exchange rate to be used, 23.25
explanatory statement, 23.5
general case law and practice, 23.2, 23.3
groups of companies, 23.4, 23.14, 23.17, 23.29
interest not deductible, 23.34
irrecoverable debts, 23.20
loan relationships, 23.8, 23.10, 23.27, 23.28, 43.5, 43.11
local currency, 23.24
main benefit test, loss relief restriction, 23.16
matching, 23.4, 23.15
non-sterling currency, use of, 23.16, 23.36, 23.39
non-trading gains and losses, 23.13
partnerships, 23.30
parts of trades, 23.40
qualifying companies, special provisions, 23.5–23.32
reciprocal currency contracts, 23.22
single currency, use of, 23.5
subjection to a liability, 23.27
time limits, 59.13
trading gains and losses, 23.11
unrealised gains, deferral of, 23.18
EXEMPT ORGANISATIONS, 24
agricultural societies, 24.1
Atomic Energy Authority, 57.2
banks, 6.5, 24.2
British Museum, 24.3
charities, 11
clubs and societies, 14, 24.1
Crown, The, 24.5

Exempt Organisations
employers' associations, 24.15
friendly societies, 28
Historic Buildings and Monuments Commission for England, 24.8
holiday clubs, 14.4
housing associations, 30
international organisations, 24.6
investment trusts, 24.16
issue departments of banks, 24.2
local authorities, 24.10
marketing boards, 57.1
mutual companies, 45
National Heritage Memorial Fund, 24.11
National Radiological Protection Board, 57.2
pension schemes, 24.14
Police Federations, 24.15
public authorities, 24.5
scientific research associations, 24.12
self-build societies, 30.6
statutory bodies, 57
superannuation funds, 24.14
supplementary benefit schemes, 24.14
thrift funds, 14.4
trade unions, 24.15
unit trusts, 24.16
venture capital trusts, 24.16
Exploration and exploitation activities, 53.9
Extra-statutory concessions, 33.4, 35

F

Farm animals,
herd basis, election for, 59.17
slaughter of, compensation for, 35.B11
Farming and market gardening,
agricultural societies, exemption, 24.1
buildings,
—maintenance etc. of, 35.B5
co-operatives, 32.4
horticultural societies, exemption, 24.1
insurance, 35.B5
land,
—maintenance etc. of, 35.B5
losses, 44.14
marketing boards, 57.1
uncommercial, 35.B5
FINANCE ACT 2000,
summary of provisions, 63
Finance lease rentals, 50.17
Financial futures, 24.14
FINANCIAL INSTRUMENTS, 25
accounting, basis of, 25.7, 25.8, 25.9
—accruals, 25.3
—mark to market, 25.3
anti-avoidance provisions,
—non-arm's length transactions, 25.17
—non-residents, contracts with, 25.18
—transfers of value, 25.15, 25.16
charities, 25.21(*b*)
currency contracts, 25.5
—exchange gains and losses, 25.12
currency options, 25.5
—linked, 25.8
debt contracts, 25.5
euro,
—conversion to, 25.5
—use of, 25.5
explanatory statement, 25.1
general provisions, 25.1
gilts and bonds, 43.10, 43.11
groups of companies, 25.5
insurance companies, 25.21(*c*)
interest rate contracts or options, 25.5
investment trusts, 25.21(*d*)
irrecoverable payments, 25.13
loan relationships, 25.5, 43.10, 43.11
mutual trading companies, 25.21(*c*)
partnerships, qualifying companies in, 25.19
profits and losses, 25.10
—accrual of, 25.3
—non-trading, 23.13
qualifying companies, 25.2, 25.4
—partnerships, in, 25.19
qualifying contracts, 25.5
—non-residents, with, 25.18
—termination of, 25.11
qualifying payments, 25.6
—released, 25.14
swap fees, 50.28
transfers of value,
—associated companies, to, 25.16
—qualifying companies, by, 25.15
transitional provisions, 25.20
unit trusts, use by, 60.1
Fire safety,
expenditure on, 35.B16
Foreign currency,
Euro, use of, 9.1, 23.5
exchange gains and losses, 6.1, 21.6, 23
interest paid in, 50.3
loans in, 6.2, 57.6
local authority securities in, 31.8, 41.14

Foreign currency
swap fees, 50.28
unobtainable, 53.3
use of, 23.16, 23.36, 23.39
—Euro, 9.1, 23.5
Foreign income,
dividends, *see* Foreign Income Dividends
life insurance companies, of, 41.14
relief for tax on, 21
unremittable, 39.7, 53.3
FOREIGN INCOME DIVIDENDS, 26
abolition of, 26.1
ACT, 26.4, 26.9
—collection of, 26.11
—repayment of, 26.6
—set off of, 26.6
claims, 26.6
company purchase of own shares, 4.7
distributable foreign profits, 26.5
double taxation relief, 26.5
election for, 26.2
foreign source profits, 26.5
franked investment income, not, 26.3
groups of companies, 26.2, 26.5
—group income, 29.2
information on, 26.4
international headquarters companies, 26.8, 26.9
matching, 26.5
own share purchase, 4.7
payment of, 26.4, 26.9
receipt of, 26.3
returns of, 26.11
special dividends, 4.7
subsidiary,
—matching election, 26.5
vouchers, 26.4
Foreign taxes, *see* Double tax relief
Forms,
CIS 4, 17.3
CIS 5, 17.4
CIS 6, 17.4
CIS 23, 17.4
CIS 24, 17.4
CIS 25, 17.2, 17.7
CIS 40, 17.7
CIS 41, 17.7
CIS 65, 17.1
CT 61Z, 3.4, 26.11, 29.2, 31.4
CT 200, 54.2, 54.14
CT 201, 54.2
CT 203, 54.2
CT 204, 55.3
CT 41G, 55.3
CT 600, 55.3, 55.14
CT 603, 55.3
P35, 59.25(*b*)
R68, 11.11(*b*)
R85 (1990), 6.9
R185(AP), 11.11(*b*)
R185 (Covenant), 11.11(*b*)
R240(SD), 11.10
SC35, 59.7
185–1, 14.5
FRANKED INVESTMENT INCOME, 27
ACT, set against, 3.3, 3.4, 27.2
banks, of, 27.3
building society interest etc. not, 3.3(*b*), 27.1
capital allowances set against, 8.2, 27.3
cessation of trade, effect of, 27.3
charges on income set against, 27.3, 50.3
defined, 1.1, 3.3, 27.1
distributions from, 20.22
election to exclude, 41.6
foreign income dividends not, 26.3
franked payments, set against, 27.2
group income not, 3.3(*a*), 27.1, 29.2
life insurance companies, of, 41.4, 41.6, 41.7, 41.12, 41.18
loss relief, use of, 27.3
management expenses set against, 27.3, 40.2
non-resident companies, 27.3
profits, treated as, 27.3, 56.1
returns of, 54.6
'shadow' ACT, set against, 3.8(*e*)
share dealers, of, 27.3
surplus, 3.3, 3.4, 27.3
tax credit fraction, 27.1, 27.2
time limits, 27.3, 59.15
trading receipt, treated as, 27.3
Franked payments, 3.3, 27.2
cessation of trade, effect of, 27.3
franked investment income set against, 27.2
groups of companies, 29.2
losses, treated as, 27.3
returns of, 54.6
Fraud etc.,
agent, of, 49.4
interest, 39.3
penalties for, 49.3, 49.12
FRIENDLY SOCIETIES, 28
amalgamation of, 28.4, 28.5, 28.7
annuities insured by, 28.3–28.5
distributions by, 20.23, 28.6

Friendly Societies
health insurance business, 28.4, 28.5
incorporated, 28.2
industrial assurance business, 28.5
instalment payments, 48.1
intra-group disposals, 9.19
life or endowment business, 28.4
policy issued by, 28.3–28.5
registered, 28.2
—after 31 March 1973, 28.6
—ceasing to be, 28.8
tax credits, 28.2
transfer of business, 28.7, 41.16
Treasury, powers of, 28.7
unregistered, 28.1
Furnished lettings, 50.26, 50.27

G

Gas production, 46.2
General Commissioners, 5.3, 12.3, 33.3(a)
General Practice Finance Corporation, 9.54, 44.12
Gift Aid, 11.10
Gifts in kind to charities, 11.12–11.14, 50.6
Gilt-edged securities, *see* Government securities and Loan relationships
Gilts and bonds, *see* Loan relationships
Goodwill,
group member, of, 9.51
know-how treated as, 59.4(*e*)
Government investment, written off, 44.21
Government securities, 31.7 *and see* Gilts and Bonds
capital gains on, 9.11
exchanged for nationalised shares, 9.6
restricted, 41.6
trading stock, as, 9.11
GROUPS OF COMPANIES, 29
accounting period, 29.17, 29.22
—corresponding, 29.19
acquisitions and disposals in short period, 9.12
advance corporation tax,
—company purchasing own shares, 51.2
—'shadow', 3.8(*j*)
—surrender of, 3.8, 3.10, 20.16(*d*), 29.8, 29.10, 29.11, 29.13
aircraft industry, in, 59.4(*g*)
amalgamation of, 9.18, 9.47
anti-avoidance provisions, 29.9, 29.23, 29.31, 29.36, 29.50, 40.5, 50.3
assets transferred within, 9.19–9.43, 9.49–9.52, 40.5
associated companies leaving, 9.47
capital allowances,
—group relief, 29.18(*b*)
—loss restricted by, 9.43
capital gains, 9.18–9.52, 29.49
charges on income, 29.2, 29.18(*d*)
close companies, of,
—transfers within, 9.17
consortia, 29.3, 29.27, 29.29
corresponding accounting period, 29.19
defined, 9.18, 9.51, 29.3, 29.43, 51.4
demergers, 29.35–29.58
depreciatory transactions, 9.51
directions by parent, 53.2
disposals outside, 9.20, 9.43
distributions, 26.2
—distributable profits, 9.14
—exempt, 29.36
—foreign income dividends, 29.2
—value-shifting, 9.13, 9.14
—within, 9.19
dividends paid within, 29.2, 29.3, 29.8, 29.11
double tax relief, 21.2
dual resident investing companies, 29.31
election by, 29.2–29.7
equity holder, 29.16
exchange gains and losses, 23.4, 23.14, 23.17, 23.29
exploration and exploitation rights within, 53.9
financial instruments, 25.5
foreign income dividends, 26.2, 26.5, 29.2
goodwill, appropriation of, within, 9.51
government securities transferred within, 9.11
group income, 29.2
—distributions from, 20.22
—franked investment income not, 3.3(*a*), 27.1
—investment company, of, 40.2
—life insurance company, of, 41.6
—profits, treated as, 56.1
group relief, 29.14–29.32
—accounting period for, 29.19–29.22
—amount available, 29.18, 44.9
—anti-avoidance provisions, 29.23, 29.31
—assessments to recover, 29.18, 29.25
—carry-forward relief, and, 29.18
—claims for, 29.23, 55.4

Groups of Companies
—consortia, 29.27, 29.29, 50.25
—dual resident investing companies, 29.31
—kinds of, 29.18
—limitation of, 29.20, 29.25, 29.31
—liquidation, in, 42.1
—loan relationships, 43.3
—overlapping periods, 29.20
—overseas losses, 29.20
—payment for, 20.16(*d*), 29.24
—recovery of, 29.18, 29.25
—relationship to other reliefs, 29.26
—relevant arrangements, 29.23
—residence requirement, 29.15
—self-assessment, 29.23, 55.4
—simplified procedures, 29.23, 55.4
—time limits, 29.23
head of, 9.18
investment companies, 29.18(*c*)
—change in ownership of, 40.5
investment trust in, 60.4
—disposals to, 9.19
life insurance companies, 29.18(*c*)
liquidation of member, 9.18, 9.47, 29.54, 42.1
loan relationships, 29.2, 43.3, 43.5
loss relief, 29.18(*a*)
—pre-entry gains, 9.37–9.41
—pre-entry losses, 9.23–9.36
management expenses, 29.18
members of, 29.15, 29.38
—becoming, 29.22
—ceasing to be, 9.47, 29.22, 29.49, 42.1, 59.4(*d*)
—goodwill of, appropriation of, 9.51
—recovery of tax from, 9.6(*b*), 9.46, 9.47, 29.4, 59.4(*d*)
—shares in, disposal of, 9.7
—single person, treated as, 9.44
—trades of, treated as one, 9.44
nationalisation of assets of, 59.4(*g*)
non-residents included in, 9.7, 9.51
overlapping periods, 29.20
parent company, 44.10
—directions by, 53.2
—sole subsidiary leaving group, 9.47
payment of tax, 29.32
—instalment, 48.1
pre-entry gains, 9.37–9.41
pre-entry losses, 9.23–9.36
profits available for distribution, 29.17
re-basing, 9.45
reconstructions in, 9.51
relief derived from subsequent accounting period, 29.26
reorganisations in, 9.16, 29.49
residence requirement, 9.18, 29.15
rollover relief, 9.44
'shadow' ACT, 3.8(*j*)
shares,
—acquisitions and disposals in short period, 9.12
—member, in, depreciatory transactions in, 9.51
shipbuilding industry, in, 59.4(*g*)
special dividends, 29.2
sub-subsidiaries, 29.9
subsidiaries,
—50%, 21.2
—51%, 9.18, 20.3, 26.5, 29.3, 29.9, 51.3
—75%, 9.18, 20.7, 29.3, 29.15, 29.40, 44.13, 51.4
—90%, 29.3, 29.27
surrender of ACT, 3.8, 3.10, 20.16(*d*), 29.8, 29.10, 29.11, 29.13
surrender of tax refund, 29.33
tax payment arrangements, 29.32
—instalment, 48.1
trading, member of, 29.47
trading losses, group relief, 29.18(*a*)
trading stock transferred within, 9.22
transfers within, 9.19–9.43, 9.49–9.52, 40.5
—depreciatory, 9.51
—shares reduced below market value, 9.51
valuation of assets at 6 April 1965, 9.43
—election for, 9.47
value-shifting, 9.13–9.16

H

Harbour reorganisation schemes, 57.3
Health service bodies, 24.10, 57.4
Hedging,
financial instruments, 25
High Court,
appeals to, 12.4, 49.8
penalty proceedings before, 49.8
Historic Buildings and Monuments Commission for England, 11.11, 24.8
Holding company, 3.10, 18.11, 18.14, 29.3, 29.27, 29.37, 29.40, 29.48, 29.54, 44.19, 51.3, 56.7, 62.3

Hospital,
land owned by, 11.3
HOUSING ASSOCIATIONS ETC., 30
approval of, 30.1, 30.2
capital gains, exemption for, 30.5
claims by, 30.1, 30.3, 59.18
exemption for, 30.1, 30.5
Housing Corporation, dealings with, 30.5, 30.6
interest paid to, 30.1
land transferred by, 30.5
registered, 30.2, 30.4, 30.5
rents paid to, 30.1
Housing Corporation,
land transferred to or from, 30.5, 30.6
Housing, investment in, 60.4
Housing society,
land transferred by, 30.6

I

Illegal payments, 40.2
Imputation system, 1.1
Income,
chargeable payment treated as, 29.50
compensation assessable as, 15.2–15.6
overseas, unremittable, 39.7
property, *see* Schedule A
—overseas, 44.23, 50.2, 50.27
religious communities, of, 35.B10
source of, acquired, 2.3(*a*)
Income tax,
annual payments, on, 31.3(*a*)
annuities, on, 31.3(*a*)
charges on income, on, 29.2
company, in relation to, 31
CT computations,
—included in, 31.4, 31.5
—relationship to, 31.1
covenants, on, 11.11
deduction of, 6.9, 7.4, 14.3, 17.2, 31.3(*b*), 31.4, 47.4, 55.5
foreign currency securities exempt from, 24.10, 41.14
industrial and provident societies, not deducted by, 32.2
interest, on, 31.3(*b*), 31.5, 31.7, 32.2
interest on overdue, 39.6
local authorities, deductible by, 31.3(*b*), 31.8
non-qualifying distributions, on, 20.18
non-resident,
—credit for, 53.4
—life insurance company, paid by, 41.12
—interest paid to, on, 31.3(*b*), 32.2, 50.3
overdue, interest on, 39.6
paid,
—CT, set against, 31.5, 55.5
—credit for, 31.4, 53.4
partnerships, deductible by, 47.4
payment of, 31.4
principles of, applicable to companies, 31.1, 50.1, 50.2
rate of, change in, 3.2
related companies, payments between, 31.4
repayment of, 38.1, 38.3
—charity, to, 11.11
—company, to, 31.5
returns of, 31.4, 54.7
royalties, on, 31.3(*a*)(*c*), 50.2
time limits, 31.4, 59.1(*a*), 59.19
unpaid, interest on, 39.6
INCOME TAX IN RELATION TO A COMPANY, 31
Incorporation of company, 53.1
Independent agents, 53.5
Indexation allowance, 9.55
Index-linked bonds, 50.14
Index-linked securities, 41.6, 43.9
India, Reserve Bank of, 6.5, 24.2
Individual savings accounts,
insurance companies, 41.1
INDUSTRIAL AND PROVIDENT SOCIETIES, 32
amalgamations of, 32.3
bonuses paid by, 20.16(*f*)
capital gains, 32.3
companies, treated as, 9.18
co-operative associations, 32.4
dividends paid by, 20.16 (*f*)
engagements, transfer of, by, 32.3
interest,
—paid by, 20.16(*e*), 32.2
—paid to, 32.5
losses on shares in, 44.19
mutual companies, payments received from, 45.2
registered, 32.1
returns by, 32.2
share capital of, 9.18, 29.15
trade carried on by, 32.5
trading losses of, 32.5
Inland Revenue addresses, 33.1
Adjudicator, 33.8
Board of Inland Revenue, 33.1
Business Tax Division, 29.35

Inland Revenue addresses
Capital Gains Clearance Section, 9.6
Central Correspondence Unit, 51.6
Central Registry, 51.6
City 4 District Inspector, 6.2
Commissioners of Inland Revenue, 33.1
Finance Division, 36
Financial Intermediaries and Claims Office, 11.1
—International, 21.6
—Scotland, 11.1
Information Centre, 36
International Division, 4.3, 4.4, 20.6, 21.3, 21.10, 53.7
Internet site, 33.1
Library, 18.1
Oil Taxation Office, 4.4
Pension Schemes Office, Controller, 34
Revenue Adjudicator, 33.8
Treasury, 4.3
INLAND REVENUE: ADMINISTRATION, 33
advance pricing agreements, 4.4
amnesty, powers of, 33.4
care and management, powers of, 33.4
codes of practice, 33.6
Collectors of Taxes, 33.2
Commissioners,
—General, 33.3
—Inland Revenue, of, 33.1
—Special, 33.3
competent authority, 21.3
construction industry tax scheme, 17.7
electronic communications, 33.11
employer's helpline, 33.10
extra-statutory concessions, 33.4, 35
Inspectors of Taxes, 33.1
internet site, 33.1
manuals, 33.10
open Government, 33.10
provisional treaty relief, 21.9
Revenue Adjudicator, 33.8
Revenue error, 33.7
rulings, 33.5
Taxpayer's Charter, 33.6
Inland Revenue determinations, 55.10
appeals, 5.3
controlled foreign companies, 18.6, 18.17
discovery, 55.8
exchange gains and losses, 23.17
financial instruments, 25.17
transfer pricing, 4.4
Inland Revenue enquiries, 55.7
INLAND REVENUE EXPLANATORY PAMPHLETS, 34
INLAND REVENUE EXTRA-STATUTORY CONCESSIONS, 33.4, 35
agricultural co-operatives, 35.C13
agricultural land and buildings, 35.B5, 50.26
associated companies, 35.C9, 56.7
authorised unit trusts, *see* unit trusts
borrowing and lending of securities, 35.B15, 35.B35, 35.B36
building societies,
—conversion to company status, 6.9(xii), 7.6, 35.A69
capital allowances,
—balancing charges, 35.B19
—caravans, 35.B50
—enterprise zone fixtures, 35.B31
—grants, repaid, 35.B49
—industrial buildings, 35.B3, 35.B20
—machinery and plant, 35.B1, 35.B31
—patents sold to associate, 35.B17
capital gains,
—assets of negligible value, 35.D28
—charitable status, temporary loss of, 11.1, 35.D47
—company reorganisations, 35.D52
—compensation and damages, 35.D33, 35.D50
—earn-outs, 35.D27
—indexation, rebasing and, 35.D34, 35.D44
—insurance recoveries, short leases, 35.D1
—irrecoverable loans, 35.D36
—land, exchange of joint interests, 35.D26
—leases, extension of, 35.D39
—leases, merger of, 35.D42
—loans, irrecoverable, 35.D36
—mortgage default, 35.D18
—qualifying corporate bonds, 35.D38
—rebasing and indexation, 35.D34, 35.D44
—replacement of buildings, 35.D19
—replacement of business assets, 9.44, 35.D15, 35.D16, 35.D22–35.D25, 35.D30
—residence, split year, 35.D2, 53.4
—share exchanges, etc., 35.D52
—share valuations, 35.D44
—undervalue, transfer at, 9.17, 35.D51
—unit trust exemption, 35.D17, 60.3

Inland Revenue Extra-Statutory Concessions
—unquoted shares, losses on, 35.D46, 44.19
—unquoted shares owned at 6.4.65, 35.D10
caravan sites, 35.B29, 50.26
cars, leased, 35.B28
cessation of trade, balancing charges on, 35.B19
charities,
—gifts to, 35.B7, 50.6
—interest etc. paid to, 11.6(ii), 35.B9
—temporary loss of charitable status, 11.1, 35.D47
—trading activities of, 11.3, 11.4, 11.6, 35.C4
close companies,
—loan creditors, 13.3, 35.C8
—transfer at undervalue, 9.17, 35.D51
company reorganisations, 35.D52
compensation for slaughter, 35.B11
construction industry tax deduction scheme,
—turnover tests, 17.5, 35.B52
co-operative associations, 32.4, 35.C13
co-operative societies, 32.4, 35.C12
currency swaps, interest and, 35.C17, 50.28
debts, overseas, 6.3, 35.B38
demergers, 29.54, 35.C11
directors' fees, 35.A37
discounts, 11.4, 35.B9
discretionary trusts, payments to beneficiaries, 35.B18
dissolution, 20.16, 35.C15, 35.C16
double tax relief,
—payments out of discretionary trust, 35.B18
—royalties etc., 35.B8
—underlying tax, 21.3, 35.C1
employee share schemes, 35.B27
enterprise zone, plant and machinery in, 35.B31
farm animals,
—compensation for, 35.B11
—herd basis, 35.B37
fire safety expenditure, 35.B16
furnished lettings, 35.B47
gifts to charities etc., 35.B7, 50.6
group relief, 29.23, 35.C10, 35.C20
herd basis,
—shares in animals, 35.B37
holiday clubs, 14.4, 35.C3
indexation, rebasing and, 35.D34
industrial and provident societies, 32.5, 35.C5
insurance companies,
—claims and elections, 35.C24, 35.C25
—LAUTRO levy, 35.C21, 41.2
—life assurance business investment returns, 35.C27, 41.3
—transfer of long term business, 35.C29, 41.16
insurance contracts, free gifts and, 35.B42
insurance recoveries, short leases, 35.D1
interest and currency swaps, 35.C17, 50.28
interest paid,
—charities, to, 11.4, 35.B9
—industrial and provident societies, to, 32.5, 35.C5
—non-residents, to, 20.7, 35.B13, 35.C18
—outside UK, 6.2, 35.C26, 50.2
investment managers, UK, 35.B40
land, exchange of joint interests, 35.D26
leased cars, 35.B28
leases, extension of, 35.D39
leases, merger of, 35.D42
life assurance business
—investment return and profits, 35.C27, 41.3
—non-resident policy holders, 35.B53
loan and money societies, 14.3, 35.C2
loan relationships,
—bad debts, 35.C28, 43.5
loans,
—irrecoverable, 35.D36
—securities, of, 35.B15, 35.B35, 35.B36
losses, Sch D, Case V, 35.B25
maintenance and repairs, expenditure on, 35.B4, 35.B5, 50.26
national insurance contributions, 35.B48
non-residents,
—composite rate tax, 6.9(xii), 7.6, 35.A69
—interest paid to, 20.7, 35.B13, 35.C18
—investment managers for, 35.B40
—life assurance, etc. policies, 35.B53
oil taxation, 35.I1–35.I5
open-ended investment companies,
—distribution waivers, 35.C30, 40.6, 60.1
overseas debts, 6.3, 35.B38
overseas pension schemes, 35.B39
penalties, automatic, 35.B45, 35.B46, 49.2
pension funds, alterations to, 24.14, 35.B43
pension scheme contributions, overseas, 35.B39

Inland Revenue Extra-Statutory Concessions
petroleum revenue tax, 35.I1–35.I5
profit-related pay,
—extraordinary items, 35.B44
property managed as one estate, 35.B30, 50.26
qualifying corporate bonds, 35.D38
rebasing and indexation, 35.D34, 35.D44
religious communities, income of, 35.B10
repayment claims, 35.B41
residence, split year, 35.D2, 53.4
returns, late, 35.B45, 35.B46, 49.2
royalties, 35.B8
scientific research associations, 24.12, 35.C31
Scotland, property income from, 35.B30, 50.26
securities, loans of, 35.B15, 35.B35, 35.B36
share schemes, 35.B27
share valuations, 35.D44
thrift funds, 14.4, 35.C3
trade associations, payments to, 35.B7, 50.6
trade receipts and debts, unremittable, 6.3, 35.B38
underlying tax, 21.3, 35.C1
unincorporated associations, 20.16(*b*), 35.C15
unit trusts, 35.D17, 60.3
—distribution waivers, 35.C30, 40.6, 60.1
unquoted shares, losses on, 35.D46, 44.19
unquoted shares owned on 6 April 1965, 35.D10
unremittable trade receipts, 6.3, 35.B38
Inland Revenue manuals, 33.9
INLAND REVENUE PRESS RELEASES, 36
accounts investigations (1.8.77), 49.9
administration of trusts and estates (1.4.99), 35
alternative investment market (20.2.95), 44.19, 51.3, 62.3
annual value (23.7.85), 50.26
chargeable gains,
—asset valuations (10.1.00), 55.3
building societies,
—taxation of gains (23.2.84), 7.3(*d*)
charitable fund-raising events (31.3.00), 11.6(ii)
charitable giving (7.5.92), 11.11(*b*)
charitable lotteries (11.7.94), 11.6(iii)
community charge (10.11.89), 50.26
construction industry tax scheme,
—company certificates (23.10.98), 17.4
—electronic trading (1.9.98), 17.7
—transitional arrangements (7.7.99, 15.7.99), 17.1
controlled foreign companies (5.10.93), 18.11
—clearance procedures (9.11.94), 18.11
—'designer rate' regimes (6.10.99), 18.4
—excluded countries (9.7.98), 18.11
council tax (16.3.93), 50.26
deep discounted stock (25.6.82), 50.7, 50.14
discounted securities (15.2.99), 43.11, 50.16
double taxation relief,
—arbitration convention (19.5.98), 4.4
—Ghana (31.1.91), 21.10
electronic commerce (11.4.00), 21.3
European Union,
—resident companies, repayments to (23.7.93), 38.3
friendly societies,
—transfers of long term business (27.7.90), 41.16
—widowers' contracts (15.4.81), 28.5
furnished holiday lettings,
—caravans (17.5.84), 50.26
gilt repo market (27.3.95), 31.7
group relief,
—claims (31.7.92, 23.11.92), 29.23
holiday clubs and thrift funds (3.3.00), 14.4
ICI plc v Colmer, open cases (26.2.99), 29.27
indexed stock (25.6.82), 50.7, 50.14
insurance companies,
—life assurance business (13.11.95), 41.3
—transfers of long term business (27.7.90), 41.16
interest factor tables (11.3.99), 38.3, 39.3
interest, gross payment of (13.8.92), 6.9
interest, unpaid tax, on (1.4.96), 39.5
internet, returns via (9.3.99), 33.11
—discounts for (16.2.00, 21.3.00), 54.13
investigation of accounts and returns (1.8.77), 49.9
investment managers (17.2.95), 53.5
loan and money societies (3.3.00), 14.3
millennium Gift Aid (31.7.98), 11.12
payment of tax,
—date of (1.4.96), 39.5

Inland Revenue Press Releases
—information and penalty powers (8.6.99), 48.1
—quarterly (25.11.97), 31.7, 48.1
property,
—annual value (23.7.85), 50.26
—community charge (10.11.89), 50.26
—council tax (16.3.93), 50.26
returns,
—asset valuations (10.1.00), 55.3
—incorrect (1.8.77), 49.9
—internet, via (9.3.99), 33.11
subcontractors, *see* construction industry tax scheme
transfer of Head Office work (9.8.89), 9.6, 29.57, 51.6
unitary taxation (15.9.93), 21.9
unit trusts,
—use of derivatives (12.7.96, 3.1.97), 60.1
valuations (10.1.00), 55.3
venture capital trusts (14.9.95), 62.2
widow, meaning of (15.4.81), 28.5
Inland Revenue rulings, 33.5
INLAND REVENUE STATEMENTS OF PRACTICE, 37
additional redundancy payments, 37.SP 11/81, 50.2
advance corporation tax, surrender of, 29.8, 37.SP 7/89
banks,
—foreign currency loans, 6.2, 37.C5, 50.2
—ordinary course of business, 6.2, 37.SP 12/91
capital allowance late claims, 8.2, 37.SP 11/93
capital gains tax,
—company leaving group, 9.47, 37.D21
—division of a company, 9.6, 29.49, 37.SP 5/85
—double taxation relief, 21.5, 37.SP 6/88
—intra-group transfers, 9.44, 37.SP 8/81
—re-basing election, 9.45, 37.SP 4/92
—*Sec 267* relief, 9.6, 37.D14
—value at 6.4.65, election for, 9.47, 37.D21
capital movements, 4.3, 37.SP 2/92
charities,
—covenants, 11.11(*d*), 37.SP 4/90
—repayments to, 11.11, 37.SP 3/87
close companies, 13, 37.C4
company migration, 37.SP 2/90, 53.7
company purchasing own shares, 20.17, 37.SP 2/82, 51
company residence, 37.SP 6/83, 37.SP 1/90, 53.1, 53.2
compulsory acquisitions, compensation for, 15.2, 37.SP 8/79
computations, rounding, 37.SP 15/93, 54.4
consortium relief, 29.27, 37.C6
construction industry tax scheme,
—carpet fitting, 17.2, 37.SP 12/81
demergers, 29.36 *et seq.*, 37.SP 13/80
double taxation relief,
—admissible taxes, 21.2, 37.SP 7/91
—capital gains tax, 21.5, 37.SP 6/88
—company tax deducted, 21.6, 37.SP 12/93
—UK/Czechoslovakia Convention, 21.10, 37.SP 5/93
enterprise investment scheme,
—location of activity, 37.SP 2/94, 62.3(*b*)
EEC, capital movements within, 4.3, 37.SP 2/92
exchange gains and losses,
—partnerships, 23.30, 37.SP 9/94
exchange rate fluctuations, 23.3, 37.SP 1/87
finance lease rentals, 37.SP 3/91, 50.17
financial futures and options, 37.SP 14/91, 60.4
financial instruments,
—financial traders, 25.18, 37.SP 3/95
—partnerships, 25.19, 37.SP 9/94
football pools, 14.6, 37.C1
group relief,
—'arrangements', 29.23, 37.SP 5/80, 37.SP 3/93
—consortia, 29.27, 37.C6
—late claims, 29.23, 37.SP 11/93
—provisional claims, 29.23, 37.C2
interest,
—directors' loans, 37.SP 4/85, 50.15
—foreign currency loans, 6.2, 37.C5, 50.2
—ordinary course of banking business, paid in, 6.2, 37.SP 4/96
—payable in UK, 6.2, 37.SP 1/95, 50.2
investment trusts,
—investments in authorised unit trusts and open-ended investment companies, 37.SP 7/94, 37.SP 3/97, 40.6, 60.4
—monthly savings schemes, 37.SP 3/89, 37.SP 2/97, 37.SP 2/99, 40.6, 60.1

Inland Revenue Statements of Practice
lease rental payments, 37.SP 3/91, 50.17
lessors, non-resident, 37.SP 6/84, 53.9
life assurance companies,
—long-term business, profits of, 37.SP 4/95, 41.1, 41.4, 41.5, 41.6
—transfers of long-term business, 37.SP 7/93, 41.16
losses,
—change in ownership of trade, 37.SP 10/91, 9.31, 44.13
lotteries, 14.6, 37.C1
non-resident companies, tax credits of, 21.3, 27.3, 37.SP 2/95
non-resident lessors, 37.SP 6/84, 53.9
open-ended investment companies,
—investment trust investments, 37.SP 3/97, 40.6, 60.4
—monthly savings schemes, 37.SP 3/89, 37.SP 2/97, 37.SP 2/99, 40.6, 60.1
partnerships,
—companies, including, 23.30, 25.19, 37.SP 4/98, 43.9
—continuation elections, 37.A4, 59.23
penalties, civil, 37.SP 2/88, 49.12
returns,
—delayed, 37.SP 3/88, 37.SP 6/89, 39.3
—electronic lodgement, 37.SP 1/97, 54.13
—form of, 37.SP 4/91, 37.SP 9/93, 50.11, 54.2
—group, 37.SP 10/93, 54.2
small companies rate, 37.SP 1/91, 56.1
—associated companies, 37.SP 5/94, 56.7
starting rate, 37.SP 1/91, 56.4
—associated companies, 37.SP 5/94, 56.7
subcontractors, *see* construction industry tax scheme
trade unions, provident benefits, 24.15, 37.SP 1/84
transfer pricing,
—advance pricing agreements, 4.4, 37.SP 3/99
unit trusts,
—investment trust investments, 37.SP 7/94, 37.SP 3/97, 40.6, 60.4
—monthly savings schemes, 37.SP 3/89, 37.SP 2/97, 37.SP 2/99, 40.6, 60.1
Unlisted Securities Market, 37.SP 18/80, 51.3
valuation fees, 37.C10, 50.32
VAT, 37.B1, 61
venture capital reliefs, 37.SP 5/98, 37.SP 7/98, 62.3(*b*)(*e*)
venture capital trusts,
—loan default terms, 37.SP 8/95, 62.2
—location of activity, 37.SP 2/94, 62.3(*b*)
—value of gross assets, 37.SP 7/95, 62.3(*e*)

Inspector of Taxes, 33.1
accounting period, power to revise, 2.4
claims to, 12.1
information, power to require, 4.4, 6.2, 29.23, 29.56, 44.13, 53.9
negotiation of settlements with, 49.9
pamphlets available from, 34
penalty proceedings by, 49.8
postponement of tax by, 48.3
return, power to require, 6.2, 54
transactions not at market value, powers of, 4.4, 9.51
value added tax, power to allocate, 61.3

Instalment payment, 48.1
interest on overpayments, 38.1
interest on unpaid tax, 39.1

Insurance,
agricultural land and buildings, of, 35.B5
recoveries, short leases, 35.D1

Insurance companies, *see also* Life insurance companies
agency, trading through, 21.2, 21.3, 41.11, 41.12
capital allowances, 8.2, 41.2, 41.4, 41.14, 41.16
defined, 4.3, 41.1
double tax relief, 21.2(*c*), 21.3, 41.12, 44.25
financial instruments, 25.21(*c*)
individual savings accounts, 41.1
instalment payments, 48.1
interest paid to, 44.25
loan relationships, 41.1, 41.2, 41.4, 43.9
Lloyd's underwriters, 50.1
non-resident, 21.2(*c*), 44.25, 53.8
ordinary course of business of, loans in, 4.3
pre-entry gains, 9.37
property income, 50.27
reserves, 41.1
Schedule A business, 50.27
security given to, 4.3

Interest, *see* Loan relationships
anti-avoidance legislation, 4.6, 50.3
associated companies, payable between, 50.16
associates of banks, payable to, 50.16
Atomic Energy Authority, paid to, 57.2
banks,
—associates of, payable to, 50.16

Interest
—paid by, 6.2, 6.6, 6.9, 11.4, 31.3(*b*), 50.2, 54.10
—paid to, 6.1, 6.2, 21.11, 31.3(*b*), 50.2, 50.3
bond, 43
building society,
—paid by, 3.3(*b*), 7.3, 7.6, 20.16(*g*), 27.1(ii), 32.5, 50.1, 54.10
—paid to, 31.3(*b*)
capitalised, 9.10, 50.5
certificates of tax deposit, on, 10.1
charge on income, as, 50.3
charged to capital, 9.10, 50.5
charities, paid to, 11.4, 20.6
close company, paid by, 13.15
compensation for, 15.2
co-operatives, paid by, 20.16(*e*)
court order, payable under, 38.3
credit unions, paid by or to, 45.3
date of receipt, 4.6
deduction of tax, under, 6.2, 6.9, 7.4, 7.5, 30.1, 31.4, 31.5
delayed tax repayments, on, 38
directors' loans, on, 50.15
discount house, paid to, 50.9
distribution, as, 13.15, 20.5–20.7, 20.16(*e*)(*g*)(*i*), 32.2
Eurobond, 31.3(*b*), 50.3, 52.8
financial instruments, 25
foreign currency, paid in, 50.3
gilt-edged securities, on, 43
hedging, 25
housing associations, paid to, 30.1
income tax on, 31.3(*b*), 31.5, 31.7, 32.2
index-linked bonds, 50.14
industrial and provident societies,
—paid by, 20.16(*e*), 32.2
—paid to, 32.5
investment companies, paid by, 50.3
—change of ownership, on, 40.5
life insurance companies, 44.25
local authorities, paid by, 31.3(*b*), 31.8
losses set against, 32.5, 44.4
National Radiological Protection Board, paid to, 57.2
non-residents, paid to, 20.7, 21.9, 31.3(*b*), 32.2, 35.B13, 41.14, 43.3, 44.25, 50.3, 53.4, 54.10, 57.6
overdraft, 43.2
overdue tax, on, 39
overpaid tax, on, 38
overseas, payable, 6.2, 50.2
partnership, paid by, 31.3(*b*), 47.4
payment of, 31.4
rates of, 38.1, 38.3, 39.1, 39.3
related companies, between, 4.6
'relevant loan', 6.2, 7.5, 30.1, 31.5
returns of, 54.10
securities, on, 20.5–20.7, 20.14, 20.16(*i*), 43
statutory bodies, paid by, 57.6
stockbroker, paid, to, 50.3
swap fees, 50.27
tax overdue, on, 39
tax repayments, delayed, on, 38
trading expense, as, 6.2
trading income, treated as, 27.3, 44.4
unit trusts, paid by, 50.3
unpaid tax, on, 39
untaxed, paid to non-residents, 35.B13
warrants, content of, 20.18

INTEREST ON OVERPAID TAX, 38
ACT, 41.4
assessability, 38.1
double tax relief, 21.3
life insurance companies, ACT, 41.4
over-repayments, 38.7
rates of, 38.1, 38.3
research and development tax credits, 50.25
Revenue error, 38.4
self-assessment, 38.1
unauthorised demands, 38.5
VAT, 61.5

INTEREST ON UNPAID TAX, 39
ACT, 3.6, 39.6
appeal, pending, 39.3
date of payment, 39.5
dates due, 39.1, 39.3, 39.6
deductible, 39.1
exchange restrictions, effect of, 39.7, 53.3
fraud, wilful default or neglect, 39.3
income tax, 39.6
late returns, consequent on, 54.2, 54.3
loans by close companies, 39.1, 39.3
postponed tax, on, 39.3
rates of, 39.1, 39.3
reckonable date, 39.3
remission of, 39.3
residence, cessation of, on, 53.7
Revenue error, 39.8
self-assessment, 39.1
unauthorised demands for tax, 38.5
VAT, 61.5

International headquarters companies, 26.8, 26.9

International loans, risks on, 6.3

International Organisations,
exemptions for, 24.6
Internet,
incentives for use, 33.11, 54.13
permanent establishment, 20.3
Revenue website, 33.1
INVESTMENT COMPANIES, 40
ACT, 3.10
capital allowances of, 8.2, 40.2
change in ownership, 40.5
charges on income of, 40.2, 50.3
close investment-holding company, 13.18
dual resident, 29.31
excess overdue interest, 40.5
interest paid by, 50.3
losses,
—Schedule A, 40.5
—unquoted shares, on 27.3(*e*), 40.4, 44.19
management expenses of, 29.18(*c*), 40.2
National Insurance contributions, 40.2
open-ended, 40.6
savings banks treated as, 6.6, 40.1
trading companies becoming, 3.10(iii)
unit trusts treated as, 40.1, 60.1
unquoted shares, losses on, 27.3(*e*), 40.4, 44.19
venture capital trusts, 62
Investment relief, *see* Corporate Venturing Scheme
Investment trusts, 60.4
acquisitions from, 9.43
business transferred to, 9.6
company becoming, 9.6, 9.48
disposals to, 9.19, 9.43
exemption for, 24.16
financial instruments, 25.21(*d*)
housing investment, 60.4
interest paid by, 50.3
investment companies, as, 40.1, 60.4
venture capital trusts, 62

K

Know-how,
goodwill, treated as, 59.4(*e*)
payments for, double tax relief, 35.B8

L

Land,
agricultural, maintenance, of, 35.B5
British Museum, owned by, 24.3
charities,
—owned by, 11.3
compulsory acquisition of, 9.44
dealers in, 4.5, 29.42, 44.19, 51.3, 62.3(A)
estate, single, treated as, 35.B30, 59.29, 59.32
housing association, owned by, 30.1, 30.5
Housing Corporation, owned by, 30.5
housing society, owned by, 30.5, 30.6
industrial estate, capital allowances, 35.B3
interest paid in respect of, 50.3
leases of, 35.B16, 34.D1
maintenance and repairs, 35.B4, 35.B5
Schedule A, 50.2, 50.26, 50.27
self-build societies, owned by, 30.6
trading estate, capital allowances, 35.B3
Leases,
cars, of, rebates, 35.B28
finance, 50.17
land, of,
—short, insurance recoveries on, 35.D1
—trade premises, of, 35.B16
machinery and plant, of, losses on, 44.15
rental payments, 50.17
LIFE INSURANCE COMPANIES, 41
ACT overpaid, interest on, 41.4
annuities paid by, 41.4, 41.5, 41.6, 45.4
annuity business, 41.1, 41.12
—general, 41.6, 41.12, 53.8
apportionment of income and gains, 41.3
assets,
—transfers of, 41.15
—transferred to non-resident, 41.11
capital allowances, of, 8.2, 41.2, 41.4, 41.14, 41.16
capital gains of, 41.9–41.11, 41.14–41.16
—foreign life assurance fund, on, 41.14
capital redemption business, 41.18
controlled foreign companies, 18.18
double tax relief, 21.2, 21.3, 41.12, 44.25
election by,
—franked investment income to exclude, 41.6
—long term assets, in respect of, 41.15
equalisation reserves, 41.4
exemptions for, 41.6, 41.14
franked investment income of, 41.4, 41.6, 41.7, 41.12, 41.18
friendly societies, 28.2–28.6
general annuity business, 41.5, 41.6, 41.12, 53.8
gilts and bonds, 41.1, 41.2, 41.4, 43.9
Government securities, restricted, 41.6

Life Insurance Companies
group income of, 41.6
health insurance, 28.4
income tax paid by, 41.12
index-linked Government securities, 41.6
individual savings accounts, 41.1
industrial life assurance business, 41.3, 41.18
—ACT apportioned to, 41.2
—separate, treated as, 41.1
interest on ACT overpaid, 41.4
interest paid by, 41.4, 53.8
investments, profits from, 41.4, 41.6, 41.9, 41.12, 41.14, 41.18
levies, 41.2
life assurance business, 41.4, 41.5
—ACT apportioned to, 41.2
life assurance business
—profits of, 41.7
—treated as separate, 41.1
life policies held by companies, 50.18
loan relationships, 41.1, 41.2, 41.4, 43.9
long term business, 9.24, 41.15
—transfers of, 41.16
losses of, 41.4, 41.6
management expenses of, 41.2, 41.6, 41.12, 41.16, 53.8
—overseas life assurance funds, 41.14
mutual, 20.22, 45.4
non-resident, 41.5, 41.6, 41.12, 53.8
—assets transferred to, 41.11
—becoming, 41.12
—trade transferred to, 41.11
non-residents, contracts with, 41.14
overseas life assurance business, 41.2, 41.12, 41.14
overseas tax, credit for, 41.14
pension business, 41.6, 41.12, 53.8
policies,
—issued before 5 August 1965, 41.9
—rights not in money, carrying, 41.10
policyholders' fraction of profits, 41.7
pre-entry gains, 9.37
premiums paid to, 41.19
property income, 50.27
provisional repayments of tax, 41.6
reinsurance business, 41.8
remittances by, 41.14
reserves, 41.1
restricted Government securities, 41.6
returns by, 41.12, 41.14
Schedule A business, 50.27
shares in, ownership of, 41.13
tax credit due to, 41.12
—provisional repayment, 41.6
—restrictions on, 21.3, 24.14, 27.2, 28.2, 41.1, 41.6, 41.12
trade transferred to non-resident, 41.11
transfer of long term business, 41.16
transfers of assets, etc., 41.15
unit trust holdings, 41.17
Limited partnership, 47.7
LIQUIDATION ETC., 42
accounting periods, 42.5, 42.6
administration orders, 42.7
assessments during, 42.5
assets available for distribution in, 29.17
banks, of, 6.1
capital gains, 9.4, 9.6, 42.3, 42.5
clubs, of, 14.7
compositions, 42.2
consortium member, of, 29.27
demergers, following, 29.54
distributions on, 14.7, 20.16(*a*)
expenses, 42.3
group members, of, 9.18, 9.47, 42.1
liquidator, assets vesting in, 42.3
mutual companies, of, 45.2
profits arising in, 42.4, 42.5, 50.1
—rate of tax on, 42.5
residence of company in, 53.2
set off of debts in, 42.5
voluntary arrangements, 42.2
Loan creditor, 13.3
companies controlled by, 56.7
group of companies, of, 29.16
non-close company as, 13.6(*f*)
LOAN RELATIONSHIPS, 43
accounting methods, authorised, 43.6, 43.7
arm's length, not at, 43.5
bad debts, 43.5, 43.11
building societies, 7.3(*a*)
—permanent interest-bearing shares, 43.2, 43.10
chargeable assets, linked to, 43.9
charges in respect of, 43.3
charges on income, 50.3
close companies, 43.5
collective investment schemes, 43.9
computation of debits and credits, 43.3, 43.5, 50.2, 50.3
connected companies, 43.5, 43.6
convertible securities, 43.9, 43.11
credits, 43.3
debits, 43.3
debt contracts, 25.6
deduction of tax, 43.8

Loan Relationships
deep discount securities, 43.11
deep gain securities, 43.11
deficits, 43.3
distributions, 43.5
double tax relief, 21.2, 21.7
dual resident investing companies, 29.31
euro, conversion to, 43.5
exchange gains and losses, 23.8, 23.10, 23.27, 23.28, 43.5, 43.11
financial instruments, 25.5, 43.10, 43.11
foreign exchange, 43.5
Funding Stock 3.5% 1999/2004, 43.9
gilt strips, 43.9
groups of companies, 43.5
—group income, 29.2
—group relief, 43.3
guarantee fees, 43.5
imported losses, etc., 43.5
indexed gilts, 43.9
insurance companies, 41.1, 41.2, 41.4, 43.9
interest,
—imputed, 43.5, 43.10
—judgments, on, 43.10
—late, 43.5
—overdraft, 43.2
—quarterly accounting, 31.7
investment company,
—change of ownership, 40.5
life insurance companies, 41.1, 41.2, 41.4, 43.9
management expenses, 41.2
manufactured interest, 43.9
non-arm's length, 43.5
non-trading, 43.3
options, 43.5
partnerships, 43.9
permanent interest bearing shares, 43.2, 43.10
related transactions, 43.5
relevant discounted securities, 43.5
reliefs in respect of, 27.3, 43.3
repo transactions, 43.5
Schedule D, Case III, 50.2
stock lending, 43.5
trading, 43.3
transitional provisions, 43.11
Treasury Stock 5.5% 2008/2012, 43.9
unallowable, 43.5

Loans, 43
associates, to, 13.9, 13.11
banks,
—by, 4.3(ii), 6.2, 6.3, 13.3, 50.3
building societies, to, 20.16(*g*)
close companies, by, 13.9–13.14, 39.1, 39.3, 55.5, 59.21
costs of obtaining, 7.7, 40.2, 50.19
credit unions, by, 45.3
directors, to, 13.11, 20.20
—interest on, 50.15
discount house, by, 50.9
discounts on, 43
double tax relief, 21.11
dwelling house, to purchase, 13.11
employees, to, 13.11
foreign currency, in, 6.2, 57.6
interest on, 43
international, risks on, 6.3, 43.11
misappropriations, 13.10
money brokers, by, 13.3
new consideration, of, 29.17
non-resident, to, 4.3, 6.2, 13.9, 21.11
normal commercial, 23.8, 29.16
ordinary course of business, in, 6.2, 13.3, 13.9, 13.10
participators, to, 13.9–13.14, 39.1, 39.3, 55.5, 59.21
repayment of, 13.12
securities, of, 35.B15
shares, secured on, 29.23
stockbroker, by, 50.3
stock-jobbing company, to, 13.3
unsecured, 20.14

Local Authorities, 24.10
foreign currency securities issued by, 31.8, 41.14
income tax deductible by, 31.3(*b*), 31.8
interest paid by, 31.3(*b*), 31.8
securities issued by, 31.8, 41.14

LOSSES, 44
amalgamations, on, 44.10
amounts available for relief, 44.9
capital, 9.3, 9.23–9.43, 14.5, 44.2
capital allowances, arising from, 8.2, 9.43(*a*), 44.6, 44.8, 44.10
capital gains, set against, 9.3
capital redemption business, in, 41.18
carried back, 38.1, 38.3, 39.1, 39.3, 44.6, 44.8
carried forward, 41.6, 44.4, 44.10, 46.6
change in ownership of company, effect of, 44.13
charges on income deductible in computing, 50.3
commodity futures, on, 44.18
compensation for, 15.2
computation of, 44.4, 44.15

Losses
conditions for relief, 44.9
denationalisation, 44.12
depreciatory transactions, on, 9.51, 9.52
determination of, 44.9
double taxation, 44.25
farming and market gardening, 44.14
franked investment income, set against, 27.3
franked payments treated as, 27.3
Government investment, write-off, on, 44.21
group relief, 29.14–29.32
harbour reorganisation schemes, 57.3
industrial and provident societies, of, 32.5
investment clubs, of, 14.5
leasing, on, 44.15
life insurance companies, of, 41.4, 41.6
limited partnerships, 47.7
market gardening, in, 44.14
mutual companies, 45.2
non-resident companies, 44.25
oil companies, of, 46.6
partnerships, of, 44.16, 44.18, 44.24, 47.7
privatisation, on, 44.12
profits, set against, 44.1
reconstructions, on, 44.10
same trade, in, 44.4, 44.6
Schedule A, 44.22, 50.26, 50.27
Schedule D,
—Case V, 44.23
—Case VI, 44.24, 59.5
self-assessment, 55.5
short-term, 9.3
terminal, 44.8, 44.10
—franked investment income set against, 27.3
time limits, 27.3, 44.2, 44.4, 44.6, 44.8, 44.24, 59.5, 59.15, 59.34
Treasury securities, on, 53.8
unlisted shares, on, 27.3(*e*), 44.19
write-off of Government investment, on, 44.21
Lotteries, charitable, 11.6(iii)

M

Machinery and plant,
'connected persons' transactions, 8.4
gifts of, 11.12, 11.14
leases of, losses on, 44.15
regional development grants, 52
renewals basis, change from, 35.B1
Mainstream corporation tax,
ACT set against, 3.6, 3.8, 29.11
Management expenses, 40.2, 41.2
appeals relating to, 40.2
brought forward, 29.18, 40.2
capital gains, set against, 40.2
double tax relief, 21.7
entertaining expenses, 40.2
franked investment income, set against, 27.3, 40.2
group relief, 29.18
investment companies, of, 29.18(*c*), 40.2
—change of ownership, on, 40.5
life insurance companies, of, 41.2, 41.6, 41.12, 41.14, 41.16
—non-resident, 53.8
loan finance, costs of obtaining, 40.2, 50.19
National Insurance contributions as, 40.2
profit sharing scheme, payments to, 40.2
redundancy payments, 40.2
relocation packages, 40.2
returns of, 54.3
training costs, 40.2
unit trusts, of, 60.1
valuation fees, 50.32
Market gardening,
co-operatives, 32.4
horticultural societies, exemption, 24.1
insurance, 35.B5
losses, 44.14
marketing boards, 57.1
uncommercial, 35.B5
Market value,
capital allowances,
—control and main benefit transactions, 8.3
capital gains,
—appropriations to trading stock, 9.22, 9.33
—asset transfers, 9.7, 9.17
—charities, of, 11.7
—company leaving group, 9.47
—company reconstructions, 9.6
—depreciatory transactions, 9.51
—dual resident companies, 9.51
—gilt-edged securities, 9.11
—pre-entry losses, 9.28
—qualifying corporate bonds, 9.11
—undervalue, assets transferred at, 9.17
—value shifting, 9.14
charities, gains of, 11.7
company migration, 53.6

Market value
controlled foreign companies, 18.9(x), 18.18
distributions, 20.9
loan relationships,
—chargeable assets, 43.11
—gilt strips, 43.9
life insurance companies,
—policies carrying non-monetary rights, 41.10
—restricted government securities, 41.6
—transfers of assets, 41.15
—unit trust holdings, 41.17
losses,
—terminal loss relief, 44.10
transfer pricing, 4.4
Members' clubs, 14.2, 14.8
Mergers,
building societies, of, 7.3(*c*)
capital allowances on, 44.10
capital gains, on, 9.6
friendly societies, of, 28.4, 28.5, 28.7
group of companies, 9.18, 9.47
industrial and provident societies, of, 32.3
losses on, 44.10
shares issued in connection with, 9.6, 60.4
Migration of companies, 41.13, 53.6, 53.7
Milk Marketing boards, 9.54, 44.12
Misappropriations, loans, as, 13.10
Money broker,
loan creditor, as, 13.3
MUTUAL COMPANIES, 45
bonuses paid by, 20.16(*f*)
clubs, 14.2
credit unions, 45.3
distributions by, 20.22
dividends paid by, 20.16(*f*)
financial instruments, 25.21(*c*)
industrial and provident societies, 45.2
life insurance, 20.22, 45.4
—friendly societies, 28.7
liquidation of, 45.2
property income, 50.27
Schedule A business, 50.27

N

National Enterprise Board, 9.54, 44.12
National Freight Corporation, 9.54, 44.12
National Heritage Memorial Fund, 11.11, 24.11
National Insurance contributions, 40.2
National Radiological Protection Board, 57.2
National Research Development Council, 9.54, 44.12
Nationalisation,
exchange of securities on, 9.6, 59.33
reversal of, 9.54, 44.12
Natural History Museum, 24.3
Negligence etc., 49.3
agent, of, 49.4
interest, 39.3
time limits, 49.10
Negligible value,
assets of, claim for, 9.51, 59.4(*c*)
Nominee,
attribution of rights and powers of, 4.4, 13.2, 13.6, 18.15
Non-resident,
assets transferred to, 4.3, 9.7
banks, 6.2, 6.4, 6.5, 44.25, 53.8
becoming, 4.3, 41.13, 53.6, 53.7
branch or agency, trading through, 1.2, 6.2, 6.3, 6.5, 9.7, 21.11, 29.14, 29.15, 29.20, 41.6, 41.11, 41.12, 53.4, 53.5
capital allowances, 8.3, 53.4
capital gains of, 53.3, 53.4(*c*)
charge to tax, 53.5
claims by, 12.3
close companies, 13.6(*a*)
—controlled by, 13.6(*e*)(*f*)
controlling UK company, 13.6(*e*)(*f*), 20.3, 20.7
dealers in securities, 53.8
directors appointed by, 35.A37
dividends,
—paid by, 21.2, 21.3
—paid to, 21.9, 27.3, 53.4
double tax relief, 21.2, 21.3, 21.9
exploration and exploitation rights transferred by, 53.9
foreign entities, 21.2, 21.3
franked investment income, 27.3
group member, treated as, 9.7, 9.51
income tax borne by, 53.4
insurance company, 21.2(*c*), 44.25, 53.8
interest paid to, 20.7, 21.9, 31.3(*b*), 32.2, 35.B13, 41.14, 43.3, 44.25, 50.3, 53.4, 54.10, 57.6
liability of, accountability for, 53.9
life insurance companies, 41.5, 41.6, 41.12, 53.8
loan creditor, 13.6(*f*)
loans to, 4.3, 6.2, 13.9, 21.11

Non-resident
partnerships, 4.3, 47.2, 53.5
patents sold by, 59.24(*b*)
payment of tax, 48.4
payments to, 50.3
property income, 50.27
recovery of tax, 48.4
royalties,
—paid by, 35.B8
—paid to, 31.3(*c*), 44.25
Schedule A business, 50.27
securities held by, 20.7
security given by, 4.3
shareholders, double tax relief for, 21.9
shares etc.,
—disposed of by, 9.7
—held by, 21.9
—in, 4.3, 20.9, 21.2, 21.3, 29.3, 29.9, 29.15
—issued by, 4.3, 9.7
split year, 53.4
tax credits, 21.3, 27.3
transfer of branch or agency, 9.21
transfer of securities to, 4.3
UK representative, 53.5
Non-trading companies,
associated, 56.4
distributions by, 20.22
Northern Ireland Airports Ltd, 9.54, 44.12

O

Offshore funds, 9.55
OIL COMPANIES, 46
abandonment expenditure, 46.3
ACT on, 46.3, 46.4
anti-avoidance legislation, 46.5
British Gas Corporation, sale to, 46.2
—assets transferred to subsidiaries, 9.54
British National Oil Corporation,
—agreements with, 46.2
—assets transferred to subsidiaries, 9.54
capital allowances, 46.3
double tax relief, 21.12
exchange gains and losses, 23.40
intangible costs, 46.3
losses of, 46.6
petroleum revenue tax, 46.2
petroleum royalties, payment of, 10.1
production sharing contracts, 46.3
sale and leaseback transactions, 46.3
Open-ended investment companies, 40.6
Open Government, 33.10
Options,
corporate venturing scheme, 19.16
financial instruments, 25
investments, 24.14
traded, 24.14
Ordinary course of business,
banks, loans by, in, 4.3, 6.2, 13.3, 29.16, 54.10
debts incurred in, 13.10
loans not in, 13.9, 13.10
Overpaid tax, interest on, 38
Over-repayments of tax, 38.7, 48.8, 55.13
Overseas governments, etc., debts of, 6.3, 43.11
Overseas property business, 50.2, 50.27
losses, 44.23

P

Pakistan, State Bank of, 6.5, 24.2
Participators, 13.3, 13.9
benefits to, 13.15, 20.20, 39.1, 39.3
debts due by or to, 13.10
loans and advances to, 13.9–13.14, 39.1, 39.3, 55.5, 59.21
Partners,
associates, as, 13.5(ii)
connected persons, 16.3
PARTNERSHIPS, 47
annuities, 50.3
assessments on, 47.2, 55.5
capital allowances, 44.16
changes in, 47.5
connected persons, 16.3, 44.16
control of, 4.4
election following cessation, 47.5, 59.23
exchange gains and losses, 23.30
financial instruments, 25.19
income tax deductible by, 31.3(*b*), 47.4
interest paid by, 31.3(*b*), 47.4
liabilities, 47.6
limited, 47.7
loan relationships, 43.9
losses of, 44.16, 44.18, 44.23, 47.7
non-resident, 4.3, 47.2
profits from, ACT set against, 44.16
retired partner, annual payments to, 50.3
Patents,
disposal of, 35.B17, 59.24
royalties from, 50.3

Pay and file, 54.1
quarterly accounting, 48.1
self-assessment, 5.1, 54.2, 55.5
—advance corporation tax, 3.4, 29.8
—partnerships, 47.2, 54.2
PAYE, 59.25
exploration etc., activities in connection with, 53.9
PAYMENT OF TAX, 48
ACT, 3.4
appeal, pending, 48.3
certificates of tax deposit, by, 10.1
change in ownership of company, 48.4
close companies, by, 13.12
company officers, recovery from, 48.5
date of, 39.5
gilt-edged securities,
—interest on, 31.7
group arrangements, 29.32
instalment payment, 48.1
—interest on overpayments, 38.1
—interest on unpaid tax, 39.1
non-resident company, 48.4
over-repayments, 38.7, 48.8
'pay and file' provisions, 54.1
petroleum revenue tax, of, 46.2
postponement of, 48.3
priority of, 42.5
quarterly, 31.7, 48.1
residence, cessation of, on, 53.6, 53.7
self-assessment, 5.1, 48.1, 54.2, 55.5
third party, by, 48.4
time limits, 29.4, 31.4
unauthorised demands, 38.5
Payroll giving, administrative costs of, 35.B32
PENALTIES, 49
anti-avoidance, 4.3
appeals against, 49.8
civil, 49.12
Commissioners' precepts, non-compliance with, 49.7
company migration, on, 4.3
criminal offences, for, 49.12
evidence, request for, non-compliance with, 49.7
exemption certificates, in respect of, 49.5
false statements, for, 49.12
fraud etc., for, 49.3, 49.4, 49.10, 55.7
imprisonment, 49.12
incorrect returns, 55.7
inspection, order for, non-compliance with, 49.7
instalment payment, 48.1
late returns, 49.2, 54.1, 54.2, 54.3, 55.3
limitation of, 49.9
mitigation of, 49.9
negligence etc., for, 49.3, 49.4, 49.10, 55.7
negotiation of settlements, 49.9, 55.7
non-resident, becoming, on, 4.3
notification of chargeability, not given, 49.1, 55.2
'pay and file' provisions, 49.2, 54.1
procedure, 4.3, 49.8
reasonable excuse, 49.6
records, failure to preserve, 55.6
returns not made, 49.1, 49.2, 49.5, 55.3
sub-contractor's tax certificate, in respect of, 17.7, 49.5
summary, 49.7, 49.12
tax credit, failure to state, 49.11
tax-geared, limitation of, 49.9
time limits, 49.10
VAT, 61.5
variation of, 49.8
witness summons, non-compliance with, 49.7
Pension funds,
Atomic Energy Authority, of, 57.2
exempt approved, 13.6(v), 41.6
friendly societies, insured by, 28.3
insured, 41.6
occupational, exemption for, 24.14
overseas employees, for, 12.3, 24.14
Parliamentary, exemption for, 24.14
personal, exemption for, 24.14
pooling, 60.2
restricted Government securities in, 41.6
surpluses, 24.14
tax credit restrictions, 21.3, 24.14, 27.2, 28.2, 41.1, 41.6, 41.12, 60.2
Period of account,
variable date, to, 2.4
Permanent interest bearing shares, 7.3(*a*)(*b*), 7.4, 7.7, 43.2, 43.10
Personal pension schemes, 24.14
Personal representatives,
housing association member, of, 30.3(*b*)
Petroleum revenue tax, 46.2
abandonment expenditure, 46.3
British Gas Corporation, sales to, 46.2
British National Oil Corporation, agreements with, 46.2
interaction with corporation tax, 46.3
payment of, 46.2
royalties, payment of, 10.1
Police Federations, 24.15

Pooled assets,
disposals of, 9.26
pension funds, 60.2
pre-entry losses on, 9.27
Port undertakings, 9.54, 44.12
Post-cessation receipts, 59.27
Postponement of tax, 48.3
Pre-entry assets, definition, 9.24
Pre-entry gains, 9.37–9.41
assets acquired at different times, 9.41
insurance companies, 9.37
pooled assets, 9.40
Pre-entry losses,
appropriations to stock in trade, 9.33
change of company's nature, 9.31
companies changing groups, 9.35
continuity provisions, 9.34
gains from which deductible, 9.30
'relevant group', identification of, 9.32
restrictions on set-off, 9.23–9.36
Pre-incorporation expenditure (VAT), 61.4
Pre-trading expenditure, 50.21
Preference dividends, 3.12, 46.4
Privatisation, 9.54, 44.12
surplus ACT on, 3.8
PROFIT COMPUTATIONS, 50
capitalised interest, 50.5
charges on income, allowance for, 50.3
charitable donations, 11.12, 50.6
compensation, deductible, 15.8
directors' remuneration, 50.8
employee seconded to charity, 50.6
employee share schemes, 40.2, 50.10, 50.22
euroconversion of shares, 50.11
European Economic Interest Groupings, 50.12
examples, 50.34–50.37
interest, 6.2, 43, 50.2, 50.3
—overpaid tax, on, 38.1
—unpaid tax, on, 39.1
interest paid in foreign currency, 50.3
interest payable between associated companies, 50.16
land, income from, 50.2, 50.26, 50.27
life policies, etc. held by companies, 50.18
loans, costs of obtaining, 50.19
losses on unquoted shares, 50.20
non-residents, payments to, 50.3
pre-trading expenditure, relief for, 50.21
profit sharing schemes, 40.2, 50.22
profits to be included, 50.1
property, income from, 50.2, 50.26, 50.27
qualifying convertible securities, 50.23
redundancy payments, relief for, 50.24
research and development expenditure, 50.25
return, 50.32
rounding of, 54.4
Schedule A, 50.2, 50.26, 50.27
share schemes, 40.2, 50.10, 50.22
supporters' clubs, of, 14.6
swap fees, 50.28
telecommunications licences, 50.29
tonnage tax, 50.30
transfer fees, 50.31
valuation fees, 50.32
Profit-related pay, 35.B44
Profit sharing schemes, 40.2, 50.22
Profits, 1.2, 50.1, 56.1
capital allowances deductible from, 8.2
capital losses not set against, 9.3
charities, of, 11.6
distribution, available for, 29.17
franked investment income treated as, 27.3, 56.1
life insurance companies, of, 41.4
limits, for small companies rates, 56
liquidation, arising on, 42.4, 42.5, 50.1
loss of, compensation for, 15.2
losses set against, 44.1
overseas, 50.1, 53.3
partnership, of, 44.16, 47.2, 50.1
petroleum revenue tax, deduction of, 46.2
realisation of, view to, 44.9
returns of, 54.1, 54.2
Schedule D, Case I, computed under, 50.2
Treasury securities, on, 53.8
trust, arising under, 50.1
unremitted, 50.1
Property income, ***see*** Schedule A
overseas property, 44.23, 50.2, 50.27
Public lending rights,
payments to non-residents, 31.3(*c*)
Public revenue dividends, 31.3(*b*)
Public school,
land owned by, 11.3
PURCHASE BY A COMPANY OF ITS OWN SHARES, 51
anti-avoidance, 4.7
associated persons, 51.4(2)(iv)
clearance procedure, 51.6
dealers in securities, 51.7
Revenue information powers, 51.5

Q

Qualifying convertible securities, 43.9, 43.11, 50.23
Qualifying corporate bonds, 9.11, 9.12
Quarterly accounting, 31.7, 48.1

R

Rates of corporation tax (see inside front cover), 1.3
ACT, 1.3(*d*), 3.2, 3.3, 3.6, 27.1
average rate, for clubs, 14.3
capital gains, 1.3(*b*), 9.2
close investment-holding companies, 13.18
fixing of, 1.3(*c*)(*d*), 3.2, 3.3, 42.5
liquidations, in, 42.5
small companies rate, 1.3(*a*), 56.1–56.3, 56.7
starting rate, 1.3(*a*), 56.4–56.7
Re-basing (capital gains), 9.43, 9.45
Recognised clearing system, 31.3(*b*)
Recognised stock exchange, 13.6
Reconstructions and amalgamations,
capital allowances, 44.10
capital gains, 9.6
corporate venturing scheme, 19.22–19.24
groups of companies, 29.23
losses, 44.10, 44.13
value-shifting, 9.16
Records, preservation of, 55.6
Recovery of tax,
company officers, from, 48.5
licence-holder, from, 53.9
third parties, from, 9.5, 9.6, 9.46, 9.47, 29.4, 48.4, 48.5, 53.9
Redundancy payments, 50.24
REGIONAL DEVELOPMENT GRANTS, 52
Registration cards, 17.3
Reinsurance business, 41.8
Relatives, 13.5(i), 16.7
attribution of powers of, 4.4, 13.5, 56.7
Remittances, 53.3
life insurance companies, by, 41.14
Remuneration,
directors, of, 50.8
Rent,
charge on income, as, 50.3
election in respect of, 59.29
factoring, 50.26
housing association, paid to, 30.1
self-build societies, paid to, 30.6
Repayment of tax,
charities, to, 11.11
construction industry tax scheme, 17.7
delayed, interest on, 38
income tax, 11.11, 31.5
instalment payments, 48.1
loans, on, 13.12, 59.21
non-resident, to, 53.4
repayment supplement, 21.3, 38.3, 61.5
'Repos', 31.7
Research and development expenditure, 50.25
time limits, 59.30
RESIDENCE, 53
appeals relating to, 12.3, 59.2(*d*)
ceasing, 2.4(*d*), 4.3, 41.11, 53.1, 53.6, 53.7
central management and control, 53.2
claims, 12.3
commencing, 2.3(*a*), 2.4(*d*)
domicile, 53.2
dual resident companies, 9.53, 29.31, 53.1
Great Britain, 53.9
groups of companies, 9.18, 29.15
incorporation in UK, 53.1, 53.2
liquidations, in, 53.2
non-residents, *see* Non-residents
ordinary residence, 53.2
overseas control, 53.3
split year, 53.4
United Kingdom, 53.9
Restricted Government securities, 41.6
Retirement benefit schemes,
close companies, 20.20
exemption for, 24.14
pension business constituting, 41.6
public, the, representing, 13.6(v)
surpluses, 24.14
RETURNS, 54
ACT, for, 3.4, 54.6
agent, by, 49.4, 54.11
asset valuations, 55.3
banks, by, 54.10
capital allowances, of, 8.2, 54.1, 54.2
claims, returns, in, 54.1–54.6, 55.4
Collector, to, 31.4, 54.1
computations, rounding of, 54.4
delivery of, 54.2, 55.3
demergers, in respect of, 29.55, 29.57
distributions, of, 20.18
electronic lodgement, 33.11, 54.13
enquiries into, 55.7
error or mistake in, 12.4, 55.13
failure to make, 49.1, 49.2, 49.5, 55.3

Returns
false statements in, 49.12, 55.7
foreign income dividends, of, 27.11
form of, 50.33, 54.14, 55.14
fraud in connection with, 49.3, 49.4, 55.7
income from UK securities, of, 54.11
income tax, of, 31.4, 54.7, 59.19
incomplete, 54.1, 54.2, 55.7
incorrect, 55.7
industrial and provident societies, by, 32.2
interest, of, 54.10
late, 49.2, 54.1, 54.2, 54.3, 55.3
life insurance company, by, 41.12, 41.14
National Savings Bank, by, 54.10
negligence in connection with, 49.3, 49.4, 55.7
non-qualifying distributions, of, 20.18, 54.8
'pay and file' provisions, 54.1
PAYE, 59.25
profits, of, 54.1–54.4, 55.3
reasonable excuse for failure, 49.6, 54.5
return period, 3.4, 31.4, 54.6, 54.7, 55.3
securities, income from, 54.11
self-assessment, 54.2, 55.3
—partnerships, 47.2
stock dividends, of, 54.9
time limits, 3.4, 29.55, 31.4, 32.2, 49.1, 49.2, 49.5, 54.1–54.11, 55.3, 59.19(*b*), 59.25(*b*)(*c*), 59.31
valuations, 55.3
Revenue Adjudicator, 33.8
Rounding of computations, 54.4
Royalties,
charges on income, as, 50.2
double tax relief, 35.B8
income tax on, 31.3(*a*)(*c*), 50.2
non-resident, paid to, 31.3(*c*), 44.25
petroleum, payment of, 10.1

S

Schedule A business, 50.2, 50.26, 50.27
losses, 44.22
—change in company ownership, 44.13
—group relief, 29.18(*e*)
—investment companies, 40.5
overseas property, 44.23, 50.2, 50.27
pre-trading expenditure, 50.21
rent factoring, 50.26
time limits, 59.5, 59.29, 59.32
Scientific research associations, 24.12
Secretary of State,
powers of, 6.9(v), 30.4, 55.1(*a*)
Securities, *see* Shares and Securities *and see also* Government Securities and Loan Relationships
SELF-ASSESSMENT, 55
advance corporation tax,
—surrender, 29.8
appeals, 5.3, 12.3, 18.6, 18.17, 48.3, 55.12
asset valuations, 55.3
capital allowances, 8.2, 55.4
capital losses, 9.3
chargeability, notification of, 55.2
claims, 12.1, 55.4
—consequential, 55.9
—group relief, 29.23
—returns, not included in, 55.11
—surrender of ACT, 29.8
company tax return, 54.2, 55.3
—enquiries into, 55.7
—error or mistake in, 55.13
controlled foreign companies, 18.1, 18.3, 18.6, 18.7, 18.9(xiii), 18.11(v), 18.12, 18.17, 18.18
Crown option, 55.13
determinations, *see* Inland Revenue determinations
discovery,
—assessments, 55.8
—determinations, 55.8
double assessment, 55.13
elections, 55.4
—consequential, 55.9
—returns, not included in, 55.11
enquiries, 55.7
error or mistake relief, 55.13
guidance notes, 55.1
Inland Revenue determinations, 55.10
—appeals, 5.3
—controlled foreign companies, 18.6, 18.17
—discovery, 55.8
—exchange gains and losses, 23.17
—financial instruments, 25.17
—transfer pricing, 4.4
group relief, 29.23, 55.4
insurance companies, 18.18
interest,
—overpaid tax, on, 38.1
—unpaid tax, on, 39.1
losses, 55.5
over-repayments, 55.13
payment of tax, 48.1, 48.3, 55.5

Self-Assessment
penalties, 49.1, 49.2, 55.2, 55.3, 55.6, 55.7
records, 55.6
returns, 54.2, 55.3
—enquiries into, 55.7
—error or mistake in, 55.13
—partnership, 47.2
Revenue determinations, *see* Inland Revenue determinations
time limits, 59
transfer pricing, 4.4
valuations, 55.3
Self-build societies, 30.6
Settlements, 16.7
associates under, 13.5
body corporate connected with, 4.4
connected persons, 16.2
demergers, shares received in, 29.36
discretionary, payments out of, 35.B18
employees, for, 13.5(iv)
Settlor, 16.7
associates of, 13.5(iii)
attribution of powers of, 4.4
connected person, 16.2
'Shadow ACT', 3.1, 3.8
Share incentive schemes, 40.2, 50.22
Share option schemes, 40.2, 50.22
Shares and securities,
acquisition and disposal in short period, 9.12
amalgamations, issued on, 9.6, 60.4
assets exchanged for, 9.7, 41.11
available, 9.12
bonus, issue, of, 20.4, 20.10, 20.18
borrowing and lending of, 35.B15
building society, 7.3(*a*)(*b*), 7.4, 7.7, 43.2, 43.10
cancellation of, 9.51, 20.4, 20.10, 20.12
charitable donation of, 11.13
connected persons, held by, 4.2
connected with other shares etc., 20.7
consideration derived from, 20.10, 20.12
conversion of, 9.6, 59.33, 62.2, 62.3
convertible, 20.7, 43.9, 43.11
dealers, held by, 4.2, 9.6, 9.11, 9.51, 20.9, 29.2, 29.3, 29.9, 29.15, 29.27, 29.40, 44.10, 50.3, 51.7
deep discount, 35.B13, 43.11, 50.7, 50.23
defined, 9.51, 20.13, 20.14, 29.39, 60.4
demergers by transfer of, 29.36
depreciatory transactions, 9.51, 9.52
discount, issued at, 20.14
disposal and acquisition in short period, 9.12
distributions in respect of, 20.3–20.7
dividend stripping, 4.2
double tax relief, 21.3, 21.9
employee share schemes, 40.2, 50.10, 50.22
euroconversion of, 23.9, 23.18, 25.5, 43.5, 50.11
exchange of, 9.6, 62.2, 62.3
—assets, for, 9.7, 41.11
—nationalisation etc., on, 9.6, 59.33
foreign currency, in, 31.8, 41.14, 57.6
gifts to charity of, 11.13
gilt-edged, 31.7 *and see* Loan relationships
group members, in, 9.51
held at 6.4.65, 35.D10
holders of, recovery of tax from, 9.5
identification of, 9.12
'in respect of', 20.15
income from, returns of, 54.11
industrial and provident society, of, 9.18, 29.15
interest paid on, 20.5–20.7, 20.16(*e*)(*i*)
investment trust, held by, 60.4
issued, paying up of, 20.4
joint holdings, 13.2
loans of, 35.B15
—security for, 29.23(II)
local authority, issued by, 31.8, 41.14
market value, reduced below, 9.51, 9.52
nationalisation of, 9.6, 59.33
negligible value, of, claims for, 9.51
new consideration received for, 20.3, 20.4, 20.10–20.12, 29.16, 29.17, 44.19
non-resident,
—disposed of by, 9.7
—held by, 21.9
—in, 20.9, 21.2, 21.3, 29.3, 29.9, 29.15
—issued by, 4.3, 9.7
—transfer to, 4.3
option schemes, 40.2, 50.22
options on, 24.14
ordinary share capital, 9.18, 29.3, 29.16, 29.27, 29.41, 44.10
ordinary shares, 20.10, 29.16
paying up of, 20.4
permanent interest bearing, 7.3(*a*)(*b*), 7.4, 7.7, 43.2, 43.10
portfolios of, double tax, 21.3
preference shares, 20.10
—fixed-rate, 29.16
premiums on, 20.4, 20.11

Shares and securities
profit sharing schemes, 40.2, 50.22
public offer of, 29.23(IV)
purchase or redemption by company, 51
redeemable,
—bonus, issue of, 20.4, 20.10, 20.18
—redemption of, 9.19
reduction in value of, 9.13–9.16
reorganisation of, 9.16, 29.49, 35.D10
repayment of, 9.19, 20.3, 20.4, 20.10, 20.11
'repos', 31.7
settled, 13.5
share capital, 20.12
stock dividends, 20.16(*h*), 54.9, 59.31(*c*)
trade exchanged for, 9.7, 41.11
trading stock,
—held as, 4.2, 9.6, 9.11, 9.52, 20.9, 29.2, 29.3, 29.9, 29.15, 29.27, 29.40, 44.10, 50.3
transfer to non-resident, 4.3
Treasury, issued by, 31.7, 41.14, 53.8
unquoted or unlisted, 20.10, 51.3
—demergers, in, 29.36(2), 29.44, 29.51
—investment in, 62.3
—losses on, 27.3(*e*), 44.19
value of, materially reduced, 4.2
value-shifting, 9.13–9.16
venture capital trusts, 62
voting power, 13.6
Shipping,
tonnage tax, 50.30
Single currency,
conversion to, 23.9, 23.18, 25.5, 43.5, 50.11
use of, 9.1, 18.9, 23.39, 25.5
SMALL COMPANIES—REDUCED RATES, 56
associated companies, 56.7
close investment-holding companies, 13.18
housing investment, 60.4
marginal relief, 56.2, 56.5
small companies rate, 56.1
starting rate, 56.4
Sovereign debt, 6.3, 43.11
Special Commissioners,
appeals to, 4.4, 5.3, 9.6, 11.5, 12.3, 12.4, 18.16, 18.18, 29.57, 33.3(*b*), 40.2, 41.16, 41.17, 44.10, 53.3, 53.7, 54.13
Special dividends, 4.7
Sports clubs, 14.8
Spouse, 16.1
associate, as, 13.5
attribution of powers of, 4.4, 13.5, 56.4
connected person, 16.1, 16.3
Stamp duty,
building society change of status, on, 7.6
not deductible, 50.19
Starting rate, 56.3
STATUTORY BODIES, 57
Atomic Energy Authority, 57.2
foreign currency, borrowing in, 57.6
harbour reorganisation schemes, 57.3
local authorities, 43, 57.3
marketing boards, 57.1
National Radiological Protection Board, 57.2
trading activities of, 57.5
Stock dividends, 20.16(h), 54.9, 59.31(c)
Stock exchange,
member of, loans by, 50.3
recognised, 13.6
—company quoted on, 13.6(*g*)
transactions through, 9.12
Unlisted Securities Market, 11.9(D), 29.16(C), 51.3, 62.3(*a*)
Stockbroker, loans by, 50.3
Stock-jobbing company, loans to, 13.3
Sub-contractors, construction, *see* Construction Industry Tax Scheme
Subsidiaries,
50%, 21.2
51%, 9.18, 20.3, 26.5, 29.3, 29.9, 51.3
75%, 9.18, 20.7, 29.15, 29.40, 44.13, 51.4
90%, 29.3, 29.27
100%, 26.8
Superannuation funds,
exemption for, 24.14
insurance of, 41.6(vi)
public, the, representing, 13.6(v)
surpluses, 24.14
Supplementary benefit schemes, 24.14
Swap fees, 50.28

T

Tax avoidance, 4
company migration, 4.3
Courts, approach of, 4.1
dividend-stripping, 4.2
general principles, 4.1
overvalue, transactions at, 4.4
undervalue, transactions at, 4.4
Tax credits, 1.1
failure to state, 49.11
foreign income dividends, 26.3

Tax credits
fraction, 3.3, 27.1, 27.2
franked investment income, part of, 27.1
friendly societies, 28.2
life insurance company, due to, 41.12
non-residents, 21.3, 27.3
related, 3.3
repayment of, 12.1, 21.3, 24.14, 27.2, 27.3, 28.2, 29.2, 41.1, 41.6, 41.12, 60.2
research and development, 50.25
Taxpayer's Charter, 33.6
open Government, 33.9
Telecommunications licences, 50.29
TEMPORARY EMPLOYMENT SUBSIDY, 58
Third parties,
recovery of tax from, 9.5, 9.6, 9.46, 9.47, 29.4, 48.4, 48.5, 53.9
TIME LIMITS, 59
ACT, 3.4, 3.8, 59.1
—surrender of, 29.8
appeals, 12.3, 48.3, 59.2
capital allowances, 59.3
capital gains, 59.4
chargeability, notification of, 49.1, 59.6
claims, 11.2, 12.2, 12.3, 12.4, 13.12, 29.23, 30.3
clearance applications, 9.6, 29.57, 41.16, 51.6
close companies, 13.11, 13.12, 59.21
construction industry: tax deduction scheme, 59.7
controlled foreign companies, 59.8
covenants, 11.11
directors' remuneration, 50.8, 59.9
distributions, 20.10, 20.11
double tax relief claim, 21.5, 41.12, 59.10
election for 6 April 1965 value, 9.47, 59.4(*a*)
election for 31 March 1982 value, 9.45, 59.4(*b*)
employee trusts, 59.11
error or mistake relief, 12.4, 59.12
exchange gains and losses, 59.13
financial instruments, 59.14
franked investment income, in respect of, 27.3, 59.15
gilts and bonds, 43.3, 43.8, 43.11, 59.20
groups of companies,
—election for group income, 29.2, 59.1(*b*)
—group relief, claim for, 29.23, 59.16
—liability of, 59.4(*d*)
herd basis, election for, 59.17
housing associations, relating to, 30.3, 59.18
income tax, 31.4, 59.19
industrial and provident societies, returns by, 32.2
interest on delayed tax repayments, 38
interest on overdue tax, payment of, 39, 53.3
life insurance company, election by, 41.6, 41.17
loan relationships, 43.3, 43.8, 43.11, 59.20
loans,
—participators, to, 13.12, 59.21
long-term assets, disposal of, 41.15
loss relief claims, 27.3, 44.2–44.8, 44.24, 59.5, 59.15, 59.34
management expenses claims, on, 27.3, 59.15
nationalisation, election on, 9.6
over-repaid tax, 59.22
partnerships, 59.23
patents, in respect of, 59.24
PAYE, 59.25
payment of tax, 3.4, 29.4, 31.4, 48, 59.26
penalties, 49.10
post-cessation receipts, 59.27
pre-trading expenditure, 59.28
reasonable excuse for failure to meet, 49.6, 54.5
remittances, for, 53.3
rents etc., in respect of, 59.29
repayment of tax, claim for, 11.11, 13.12, 59.22
research and development expenditure, 59.30
returns, 3.4, 29.55, 31.4, 32.2, 49.1, 49.2, 49.5, 54.1–54.11, 59.19(*b*), 59.25(*b*)(*c*), 59.31
rollover relief, 9.44, 59.4(*g*)
Schedule A, 59.5, 59.29, 59.32
Schedule D, Case VI, 59.5
self-build societies, 30.6, 59.18
share dealers, relating to, 9.6, 59.33
surrender of ACT, 29.8
trading stock, relevant to, 59.35
unlisted shares, losses on, 44.19, 59.36
Tonnage tax, 50.30
Trade,
association, payment to, 50.6
carrying on, 44.2
cessation of, 2.4(*c*)
—balancing charges on, 35.B19
—demergers, 29.36

Trade
—franked investment income, effect on, 27.3
—mutual companies, 45.2
—partnerships, 47.5
—post-cessation receipts, 59.27
—terminal losses, 44.8, 44.10
change in, 3.10, 9.31, 44.13
charity, of, 11.6
commencement of, 2.3(*b*), 2.4(*c*), 47.5
—expenditure incurred before, 50.21
commercial basis, on, 44.9
debts, 13.10(*a*)
demergers by transfer of, 29.36(*b*)
harbour authority, transferred to, 57.3
income of, 4.5, 44.4
industrial and provident society, of, 32.5
losses of, 44
more than one, 2.4, 4.5
negligible, 3.10, 9.31, 44.13
non-resident, of, 9.7, 53.4
overseas, 50.3
partnership, of, 47.5
profit computations, 50
research and development expenditure, 50.25
revival of, 3.10, 9.31, 44.13
sale of, 29.36(5)
Schedule D, Case V, charged under, 50.2
statutory, 57.5
transfer of, 9.7–9.9, 41.11, 57.3
unremittable receipts, 6.3
Trade unions, 24.15
Traded options, 24.14
Trading companies,
change in ownership, 3.10, 9.31, 44.13
charitable donations by, 11.10–11.14, 50.6
consortium, owned by, 29.27
demergers, 29.47
gifts by, 11.10–11.14, 50.6
group income elections, 29.3
interest paid by, 50.3
investment companies, becoming, 3.10(iii)
losses of, 44
royalties paid to, 35.B8
unquoted, losses on investments in, 27.3(*e*), 44.19
unremittable receipts, 6.3
Trading group,
demergers, 29.47
Trading losses,
carry-back, 44.6, 44.8
carry-forward, 44.4
commodity futures, dealings in, 44.18
farming and market gardening, 44.14
oil companies, 46.6
set-off, 44.2
terminal, 44.8
time limits, 59.34
Trading stock,
building society, of, 7.6
dividends paid on investments held as, 29.2
financial, 7.6
gifts of, 11.12, 11.14, 50.6
government securities as, 9.11
groups, transfers of, within, 9.22
loss on, compensation for, 15.2
shares and securities held as, 4.2, 9.6, 9.11, 9.52, 20.9, 29.2, 29.3, 29.9, 29.15, 29.27, 29.40, 44.10, 50.3
time limits in respect of, 59.35
Training costs, 40.2
Transfer fees, 50.31
Transfer pricing, 4.4
controlled foreign companies, 18.9(xiii)
Treasury,
address of, 4.3
consent of, required, 4.3
foreign currency securities, direction by, 31.8, 57.6
friendly societies, regulated by, 28.7
rates of interest fixed by, 10.1, 38.1, 38.3, 39.1, 39.3
securities issued by, 41.14, 53.8
Trustees,
assets transferred to, at undervalue, 9.17
associates, as, 13.5
charities, of, *see* Charities
connected persons, 16.2
demergers, shares received in, 29.36
discretionary, payments by, 35.B18
interest of, in trust shares, 13.5(iv)
interest payable to, 6.9(1)
powers imputed to, 4.4
special dividends, 4.7
trade owned by, 44.10

U

Underlying tax, 21.3
avoidance, 21.3
calculating relief for, 21.6
chain of shareholdings, on, 21.3
rates of, 21.6

UNIT AND INVESTMENT TRUSTS, 60
acquisitions from, 9.43
authorised, 60.1
—becoming, 9.6
business transferred to, 9.6
capital gains, 60.1, 60.3
certified, 60.1
charitable, 11.8
court common investment funds, 60.1, 60.2
derivatives, use by, 60.1
disposals to, 9.6, 9.19
distributions by, 60.1
exempt holders, for, 60.3
exemption for, 24.16
futures and options, 60.1
interest paid by, 50.3
investment companies, as, 40.1, 60.4
investment trusts, 60.4
—acquisitions from, 9.43
—conversion to, 9.6, 9.48
—disposals, to, 9.19, 9.43, 9.48
management expenses, 60.1
pension fund pooling, 60.2
rate of tax, 60.1
unit trust schemes, 60.1
unitholders not associates, 13.5
venture capital trusts, in, 62.3
Unitary taxation, 21.9
United Kingdom, 53.9
UK Ecolabelling Board, 24.17
UK public revenue dividends, 31.3(*b*)
UK representatives, 53.5
United Nations, 24.6
Unlisted shares, *see* Unquoted shares
Unlisted Securities Market, 11.9(D), 29.16(C), 51.3, 62.3(*a*)
Unpaid tax, interest on, 39
Unquoted shares,
demergers, in, 29.36(2), 29.44, 29.51
losses on, 27.3(*e*), 44.19
own share purchases, 51.3
repayment of, 20.10
Unremittable receipts, 6.3

V

Valuation,
6 April 1965, 9.43(*a*), 59.4(*a*)
31 March 1982, 9.22, 9.43(*b*), 9.45, 59.4(*b*)
fees, 50.32
returns, in, 55.3
VALUE ADDED TAX, 61
repayment supplement, 38.6
Value-shifting, 9.13–9.16
Venture capital, *see* Corporate Venturing Scheme and Venture Capital Trusts
VENTURE CAPITAL TRUSTS, 62
approval, 62.2
business transferred to, 9.6
capital gains tax reliefs, 62.5
company becoming, 9.6, 9.49
distributions by, 62.4
eligible shares, 62.2
income tax reliefs, 62.4
intra-group disposals, 9.19
investment in, 62.4
investments by, 62.2, 62.3
qualifying holdings, 62.3
qualifying trade, 62.3
qualifying subsidiary, 62.3
re-investment in (CGT), 62.5
share exchanges and conversions, 62.2, 62.3
unquoted companies, investment in, 62.3
withdrawal of approval, 62.2
Voluntary associations, 14

W

Wages,
issue of directions on, 53.2